# 100
# Natural Wonders
# of the World

Writers: Nishat Fatima, Pradipta Sarkar, Sankar Sridrar

Maps and text © Automobile Association Developments Limited 2007
Relief maps images supplied by Mountain High Maps® Copyright © 1993 Digital Wisdom Inc.
Reprinted 2008

Published by AA Publishing (a trading name of Automobile Association
Developments Limited, whose registered office is Fanum House, Basing View,
Basingstoke, Hampshire, RG21 4EA; registered office 1878835).

Design layouts for AA Publishing by IL&FS Education & Technology Services
Origination by Keene Group, Andover
Printed and bound by C&C Offset Printing Co., Limited

The contents of this book are believed correct at the time of printing.
Nevertheless, the publisher cannot be held responsible for any errors,
omissions or for changes in the details given in this book or for the
consequences of any reliance on the information provided by the same.
This does not affect your statutory rights.

ISBN-13: 978-0-7495-5544-3

A03754

# 100
# Natural Wonders
# of the World

# Contents

**Europe**

**Asia**

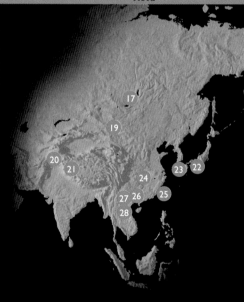

# Central & South America

# Australia & Oceania

# Introduction

## NATURAL WONDERS

**H**ow does one decide which natural feature or phenomenon is a "wonder" and which is "more (or less) awe-inspiring" than the other? For those who have seen Niagara Falls but not the Iguaçu Falls, Niagara would win hands down for its sheer beauty, even though it is dwarfed in both size and magnificence by its South American counterpart. Similarly, the Andes stretching for 4,500 miles (7,243km) may be the longest range in the world, but does that make it any more spectacular than the Rocky Mountains, the Alps, the Caucasus Mountains, or the Himalayas? And should one really be guided by the long and the short of it, or by any other relative measure?

Most of the the planet's natural features are undergoing constant changes, some natural and some caused by man's intrusion into the environment, or by irreversible occurrences such as climate change. The wonderful Great Barrier Reef—which boasts some of the most enchanting and colorful corals and equally mesmerizing marine life—is slowly dying due to global warming, with many of its corals turning into dead debris. North America's celebrated Arizona desert may soon turn into an oasis of green if the rainfall patterns do not change—as has happened to the Gir National Park in India, where the Indian lion struggles to adapt to a new environment in which savannah grasslands are turning into lush jungle.

It's a difficult choice to make as to which wonders to include, more so since we are not dealing with one to ten, but one to thousands of natural wonders that exist on our planet, each more magnificent and significant than the other. The selection of natural wonders in this book is, therefore, a slightly subjective one; one on which the editors have worked to balance the old with the new, so that you as the reader can get a broad picture of all those places that have kept us and continue to keep us linked to this wonderful planet, Earth..

## MAN AND NATURE

Man's affinity with nature is intrinsic to human evolution. From the pre-historic age to the present, we have always revered nature and celebrated its wonders. If animal life on land, sea, and air has made us conscious of our evolutionary link to the rest of the animal kingdom, the mighty expanse of oceans, mountain ranges, deserts and polar caps has made us aware of our own possibilities and limitations.

Most of what we know today is the result of human exploration that has sought to map the world we live in. While our adventurers and explorers have brought many amazing things to our notice, our scientists and naturalists have helped us to understand and explain their origin, evolution, and importance. The discovery and study of the Galapagos Islands, for example, has helped us to value this natural phenomenon more than we would a few crocodiles in a zoo. Reptiles may not be man's most-loved creatures, yet the probable extinction of "Lonely George"— the last survivor of the Galapagos Islands species of giant tortoise—is no less a loss. Caught gaping at the Blue Mountains in Australia, we have been made wiser by the information that the wonderful blue haze that envelops this craggy outcrop is caused by the oil exhaled into the atmosphere by the area's eucalyptus trees.

Many of our natural wonders have also survived because of the sacredness with which our ancestral tribes have regarded them. American Indians have warned tourists and administration against indiscriminate "recreational climbing" of Devils Tower, which has already caused considerable damage to this monument; in Australia, the Aboriginal tribes have come forward with a similar demand to protect Uluru (Ayers Rock), and in India and Nepal, hill people have traditionally regarded the Himalayas as the sacred abode of the gods and were aghast when man first decided to climb its highest peak, Mount Everest. Edmund Hillary's successful ascent of Mount Everest helped us to

appreciate human grit and Himalayan topography but nowadays it has also made us aware of the growing pile of non-bio-degradable garbage left behind by every climbing expedition that has sought to repeat the feat.

Fortunately, in most cases, our natural wonders have been protected by turning the surrounding areas into natural reserves, or simply by their relative inaccessibility, being situated in deep jungles, high mountain ranges, deserts, or icy landscapes. But today, we face a different enemy, a malaise born out of industrialization and our own thoughtless exploitation of natural resources and the environment—the phenomenon of climate change.

## CLIMATE CHANGE

Climate change is nothing new. Since the birth of the planet, the world has witnessed many cataclysmic climate changes that have altered the shape of continents and the flora and fauna that existed. However, while this change in the past was a result of natural causes, the current scenario has been largely caused by human behavior.

One of the most important causes of climate change in recent years has been the uncontrolled emission of greenhouse gases into the earth's atmosphere. The greenhouse effect relates to the gases that keep our planet warm; if they were to escape through the ozone, the temperature of our planet would drop to below freezing point. By trapping warm air, the greenhouse effect keeps the earth's surface temperature warm. Today, however, the additional greenhouse gases produced by humans—carbon dioxide, methane, and nitrous oxide—is overheating the stratosphere, causing temperatures to rise. This has led to a series of chain reactions that affect every living organism on earth.

Human beings are resilient. But, the animal world, and in particular plant life, cannot adapt as rapidly to the changes. Consequently, they face a bleak future. Less snow in winter, warmer temperatures in summer, and more winter rain have all had impact on our environment.

The effects of global warming in the Arctic and Antarctic regions—where ice is melting faster than Senator Al Gore's campaign to convince the world of the impending cataclysm—has already endangered the life of walruses, sea lions, penguins, and many sea birds. According to the 2007 report of the Intergovernmental Panel on Climate Change, the largest ice mass of the northern hemisphere is losing 12cu miles (5cu km) of ice per year, whereas in the Antarctic 1,160sq miles (3,000sq km) of the Larsen B ice shelf has already disintegrated. Lest we think these places and and their inhabitants are too remote to worry about, an exploration of our own backyards will reveal alarming facts. The traditionally warmer region of southern England is getting colder and already there are reasons to believe that its famous beech woodlands may not survive the change.

In Costa Rica, according to WWF, global warming has claimed its first victim, the Golden Toad, which is now believed to be extinct. In China, one of its mightiest rivers—the Yangtze—is facing shortages as glaciers that feed it are retreating. A similar fate awaits the Indian rivers that rise in the Himalayas. An increase in summer temperatures is causing frequent forest fires that could spell the end of the Valdivian rainforests of Chile and Argentina, not to speak of the rest of the Amazon—the lungs of the Earth—which, according to some estimates, may be half its size by 2050. Time, clearly, is running out—for us and many of the world's natural wonders.

1. Lake Myvatn
2. Vatnajökull Glacier
3. Jökulsárlón Glacial Lakes
4. The Great Geysir
5. The Great Fjords
6. The Giant's Causeway
7. The Cliffs of Moher
8. Ardennes
9. The Eisriesenwelt Caves
10. Skocjan caves
11. The Matterhorn
12. Mont Blanc
13. Plitvice Lakes
14. Transylvanian Alps
15. Mount Vesuvius
16. Cappadocia

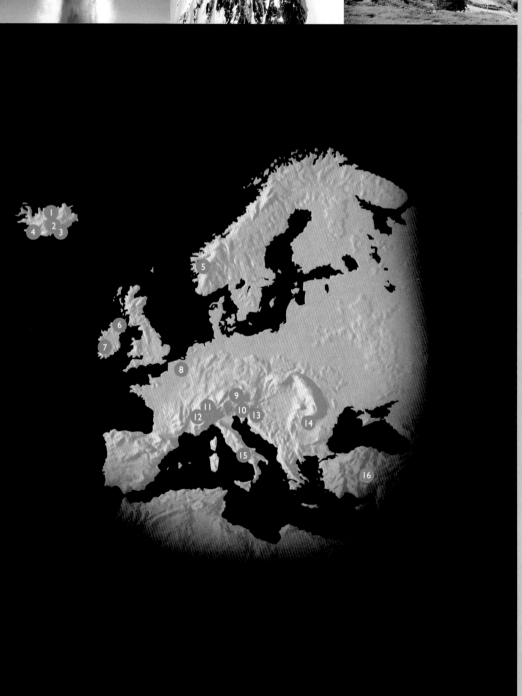

# Europe

The epic story of Europe's natural wonders began three billion years ago. From then until now, humans have come face to face with many incredible features that have left us both excited and perplexed. Covering an area of 3,930,520sq miles (10,180,000sq km) of the westernmost Eurasian peninsula, who would have thought that thousands of years ago dinosaurs walked Oxford, or that the area occupied by some of France's most famous vineyards was a tropical sea? Some of the region's most stunning wonders are situated in the harsh icy landscapes of the Nordic countries, while others lie nestled in the great leafy Alps or the Caucasian Mountains and forests of Central and Western Europe. Still more survive along the coastal regions that touch upon the Atlantic Ocean, the Arctic Ocean, the Baltic, Mediterranean, and Black seas, and the innumerable lakes and mountain ranges that dot the continent.

In this section of the book you will have the opportunity to take a closer look at some of these wonders. Like the Giant's Causeway—a natural volcanic pathway on the Antrim Plateau in Northern Ireland; the icy region of Iceland's Lake Myvatn—the ecosystem of a stunning series of lakes and islets; the largest glacier mass in Europe, the Vatnajökull Glacier, which covers seven active volcanoes with a blanket of ice; or the underground giant ice cave tunnels of the Austrian Alps where you can come across an ice cathedral. And if that's not enough, the Cliffs of Moher will bring you close to some of the most amazing birdlife off the west-coast of Ireland; the Slovenian Skocjan caves and tunnels will explain the origin of a beautiful black stone that has so captivated women; and the coniferous plateau of Ardennes, full of valleys, swamps, and marshes will enchant you to return time and again to those pages or even plan a visit there.

- The blue-green algae (*Cyanophyta*) found in the lake lend a greenish-brown tinge to the waters of Myvatn during the summer months.
- Myvatn (midge) lake is named after the swarms of midges that thrive in its waters, forming an integral part of the food chain as they are consumed by fish as well birds.

**Lake Myvatn,** Iceland

# Lake Myvatn

The beautiful and serene Lake Myvatn lies in northern Iceland, 30 miles (48km) east of the town of Akureyri and is drained by the Laxa river which flows northward into the Greenland Sea. The fourth largest lake in Iceland, Myvatn is one of the most popular tourist attractions of the country.

Lake Myvatn is approximately 6 miles (9.5km) long with a width of about 4 miles (6.5km); the total surface area of the lake is roughly 14sq miles (37sq km). Despite this, Myvatn is a very shallow lake with an average depth of 8ft (2.5m)—the maximum depth of the lake is only about 13ft (4m).

The surface of Lake Myvatn is dotted with around 50 volcanic islands and islets, and numerous small bays and inlets indent its shores. Surrounded by countless hot springs and craters, the Myvatn area is famous for its volcanic topography. A variety of lava formations are found in the area. These extraordinary features and the geological peculiarities can be attributed to the heavy volcanic activity that the region has experienced over thousands of years. The

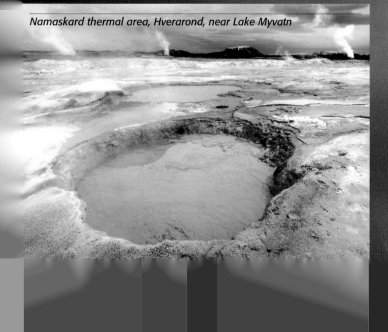

*Namaskard thermal area, Hverarond, near Lake Myvatn*

## MYVATN'S BIRDS

The Myvatn and Laxa area is reputed to house one of the largest concentrations of ducks in the world. All species of water birds in Iceland, including the Tufted duck, Harlequin duck, Red-breasted merganser, Red-Necked phalarope, Whooper swan, and Greylag geese, nest here. The most characteristic bird of the area is the Barrow's Goldeneye; a non-migratory bird, it nests in holes and crevices in the lava fields, and spends winter in holes in the ice. The Slavonian grebe is also found in the area, and nests in vegetation at the banks of the lake.

## CONSERVATION EFFORTS

The area of Lake Myvatn and the River Laxa has been demarcated a protected region according to laws of the Environment and Food Agency of Iceland since June 2004. The aim of the law is to ensure the protection of the biodiversity and geological formations and landscape, as well as active conservation of the area because of its sociological, scientific, and esthetic importance. Lake Myvatn and River Laxa are also listed as internationally important wetlands according to the Ramsar Convention.

*River Laxa flowing from Lake Myvatn*

area is situated on the boundary of two tectonic plates—the North American and the Eurasian. These plates drift apart by about 0.8in (2cm) every year; lava then forces its way up through the earth's crust and fills the widening rift. It is this phenomenon that is responsible for the intense geothermal activity of the region.

On the eastern edge of the lake is the Dimmu Borgir (meaning "dark castle") badlands, marked by magnificent dark lava pillars, some as tall as 213ft (65m). To the north of the lake is the vast Hverfjall crater—a smooth volcanic cone that is about 0.62 miles (1km) in diameter and 459ft (140m) deep. This stadium-shaped crater was formed by eruptions 2,500 years ago. The boiling mud pits of Hverarond form another one of the Myvatn area's strange but fascinating spectacles. The explosion crater of Viti showcases natural hot springs—people can bathe in the waters which are comfortably warm at 72°F (22°C). The most staggering of Myvatn's sights, however, is perhaps the absolutely barren lava field of Eldhraun (fire lava), where the Apollo 11 crew was trained in the 1960s for their impending moonwalk.

Created when a lava field blocked the course of a river, Myvatn is fed primarily by spring waters. Rainfall is quickly absorbed by the bedrock and surfaces as springs on the banks of the lake. This water is rich in minerals and is primarily responsible for the lake's flourishing ecosystem despite its altitude of 912ft (278m) above sea level. Salmon, trout, and the Arctic char abound in the waters of Myvatn and the Laxa river, and bird life is varied and abundant.

• The Vatnajökull Glacier is estimated to hold almost 960cu miles (4,000cu km) of ice.

• Vatnajökull National Park is scheduled to open in the summer of 2008. It will cover one-eighth of Iceland's surface and will include the current Skaftafell and Jokulsargljufur national parks.

**Vatnajökull Glacier,** Iceland

# Vatnajökull Glacier

Aptly referred to as the "Land of Fire and Ice," Iceland is a land like no other. It continues to be built by nature—constantly being pulled apart because it happens to lie across the vast undersea split known as the mid-Atlantic ridge. The land is constantly being stretched and is subject to sudden upheavals. Such eruptions, due to the mid-Atlantic ridge, have included Eldgja (1896) and Laki (1783).

Vatnajökull, located in the southeast of Iceland, is the largest ice cap in Europe, covering several geothermal sources. The glacier covers an area of roughly 3,200sq miles (8,400sq km), about 8 percent of Iceland's total area. The sub-glacial landscape consists of an undulating plateau dissected by valleys and gorges, and lies up to 5,000ft (1,524m) above sea level. This frost-bound area is home to hundreds of rivers, some of the largest being the Skjálfandafljót, Jökulsá á Fjöllum, Thjórsá, and Lagarfljót. Of the numerous geothermal areas and active volcanoes that are scattered throughout the ice field, the noteworthy ones are Kverkfjöll, towering at 6,298ft (1,920m), which—along with its two calderas—is a potent, partly glaciated geothermal area that dominates the northern

## EXPLORING VATNAJÖKULL

The first man to cross the Vatnajökull was the Englishman W.L. Watts in 1875. Later, Bárðarbunga, the highest dome on the ice cap, was scaled by an Austrian-Italian expedition in 1935. Researchers, mountaineers, and travelers today crisscross the expanse of this slow moving ocean of ice. With the use of radio-echo depth soundings efforts are being made to formulate a complete picture of the land underlying Vatnajökull. Other scientific research being conducted in the region includes studies on mass balance, and movement and chemical research.

## THE 1996 JÖKULHLAUP

An eruption beneath the center of Vatnajökull on September 30, 1996, generated prodigious amounts of heat and rapidly melted the ice. Even though the eruption had effectively ceased by October 14, the melt water accumulating beneath the ice had raised the level of Grimsvötn's sub-glacial lake by 308ft (94m). In November,1996, this trapped water finally broke out onto the surface, devastating the Skeidarasandur region before ultimately draining into the Atlantic Ocean.

*Four-wheel vehicles atop the largest glacier in Europe*

margin of Vatnajökull; the Bárðarbunga Volcano, on the other hand, lies under the central portion of the ice cap, at an elevation of 6,560ft (2,000m), and has an ice-filled caldera.

The Grimsvötn, at a height of 5,638ft (1,719m), is the largest volcano under the Vatnajökull Glacier. This volcano contains a unique lake within the ice cap, of which the surface is usually frozen solid. Located in an expanse of high geothermal activity, Grimsvötn's periodic eruptions cause the surrounding ice to melt and the level of the lake rises until it breaks through the ice walls and partly empties itself in the form of a glacier flood called jökulhlaup, or "glacier run."

Nunataks, or the exposed summits of ridges, such as Grendill and Goðahnúkar in the east and Pálsfjall in the west, are the only structures that break up the immense white expanse of Vatnajökull. Esjufjöll and Mávabyggðir are two large massifs that rise high above the rest of the ice field, like islands emerging from a frozen sea. About 23 outlet glaciers which flow out from the accumulation area of Vatnajökull have been identified. Most of the outlet glaciers in the north and the west are either of the surging kind or flat, broad ice slopes.

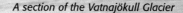

*A section of the Vatnajökull Glacier*

**Jökulsárlón,** Iceland

# Jökulsárlón

Placed at the foot of Vatnajökull, the largest glacier in Europe, the Jökulsárlón lake forms one of the most spectacular sights in Iceland. Huge chunks of ice of innumerable shapes and assorted shades of blue dot the surface of this magnificent body of water. Jökulsárlón, the largest and most famous pro-glacial lake in Iceland, is situated at the southern margin of Vatnajökull, between Höfn and the Skaftafell National Park.

The retreat of the Vatnajökull ice cap from the southern coast of Iceland is responsible for the creation and growth of Jökulsárlón. Since the formation of the lake in 1934, it has been continuously growing in size. Occupying an area of 3sq miles (8sq km) in 1975, it is now more than twice its original size. The lake's dramatic growth can be attributed to the large volume of melt water from the Breidamerkurjökull, the outlet glacier of Vatnajökull that drains into Jökulsárlón.

Prior to 1950, the glacial river Jökulsá flowed directly into the sea from underneath. However, since then the tongue of the glacier has been retreating, leaving in its wake a vast and still-growing lagoon, further deepened by the scouring effect of Jökulsá on the basin. It is due to this that the size of the Jökulsárlón—which translates as "glacier lagoon"—has been constantly increasing. Clustered with ice floes, Jökulsárlón nestles today between the Breidamerkurjökull glacier and a ridge of glacial till, with only the narrow river Jökulsa as a channel of outflow.

Most of the pro-glacial lakes at the edges of Vatnajökull are freshwater lakes. However, increasing penetration of sea water into Jökulsárlón is responsible for the distinctive

*Sight-seeing boat sailing among icebergs, alongside a glacier*

## THREAT POSED BY THE SEA

The bridge over the Jökulsá river in Breidamerkursandur, which was built in 1967 and forms a part of the Iceland Ring Road, is close to being torn down by the constant erosion of the sea. The sea, it is believed, will continue to shorten Jökulsá and encroach inward, and convert the Jökulsárlón lagoon into a deep bay; and as the snout of the glacier retreats further, into an inlet of the sea. The road authorities launched a project in 2003 to prevent further erosion—attempts are being made to raise the level of the lagoon and construct sturdy boulder dykes to stall the erosion.

*Icebergs and coastline*

## THE GREAT SKUA

The sand and gravel dunes around Jökulsárlón form the primary breeding ground of a large seabird called the great skua. The birds usually nest around the lake and are often spotted during the summer months; they migrate to warmer climes during winter. These birds are predators, and often prey on smaller birds like puffins; fish and carrion are aslo part of their diet.

lagoon-like character of the lake. Ongoing erosion by the sea has caused the shoreline of the Breidamerkursandur area to recede, reducing the length of the river Jökulsá. Jökulsá was about 0.93 miles (1,500m) long in 1950; in 1998 a distance of only about 1,640ft (500m) separated Jökulsárlón from the sea.

Approaching 656ft (200m) in depth, Jokulsarlon is probably the second deepest lake in Iceland today. The lake is visually stunning, as the edge of the snout of the glacier floats on the surface of the water and large chunks of ice—over 1,000 years old with shades of blue and gray rather than white—break off and land in the water with a spectacular crash—and then slowly the icebergs float toward the sea. Boat rides allow visitors to experience this breathtaking waterscape from close quarters.

Over the years the steady infilitration of sea water, particularly after the end of the summer melting season when the volume of water discharged by Jökulsá decreases, has led to several species of fish such as herring, salmon, and capelin entering the lake, followed by harbor seals. A variety of birdlife, including the eider duck, Arctic tern, and great skua, can also be found around the lake.

- Encrusted with colorful minerals, the vent of the Great Geysir in Iceland is about 60ft (12m) wide.
- The Great Geysir has been known to spurt streams as high as 200ft (61m) at the peak of its activity.

**The Great Geysir,** Iceland

# The Great Geysir

O ne of Iceland's greatest natural attractions, the Great Geysir is a spouting hot spring situated in the Haukadalur Valley in southwest Iceland. The word "geyser"—the general term for erupting hot water fountains—has been in use since 1647 and is derived from the Icelandic word *geysir*, which means "to gush." Majestic columns of hot water shooting out from the mouth of the Great Geysir make it a spectacular geothermal phenomena.

The Great Geysir is the world's oldest known geyser. Though the exact date of its formation is not known, the first written record of the Geysir's activity dates from 1294, when the thermal areas of southwestern Iceland were modified to a great extent by earthquakes. As strong

periodic tremors increased activity in the Geysir area, it gained fame and popularity since erupting geysers were unheard of in the rest of Europe.

For centuries, the outbursts of the Geysir were considered to be supernatural, with no concrete explanation for their occurrence. It was the German chemist Robert Bunsen who first came up with a scientific explanation for the Geysir's eruptions after visiting Iceland in 1846. He summarized the cause to be overheating of water below the surface in high temperature geothermal areas—areas of volcanic and seismic activity—where the subsurface temperature is greater than 392°F (200°C) at a depth less than 0.62 miles (1km).

Geysers are formed where subsurface hot water ascends to the surface through narrow channels in the

## THE GREAT GEYSIR AREA

Occupying roughly 1.2sq miles (3sq km) at the surface, the Great Geysir area is a thermal park atop a vast bubbling cauldron of geothermal activity. Hot and cold springs, hissing fumaroles, and sulphurous mud pots of unusual colors dot the surface. Beautiful and delicate silica sinters decorate the area around the hot springs. Other remarkable geysers in the area include the less majestic but very active Strokkur (Churn) and Litli Geysir (Little Geysir). Primitive plants are also found in the area. The small Laugarfjall mountain situated a short distance away offers a panoramic view of the Geysir area.

*Geothermal hot springs*

*A geyser erupting, Strokkur*

## OWNING THE GREAT GEYSIR

Until 1894, the Great Geysir was part of the local farm, Laug. The owners sold the area to James Craig, who later became the prime minister of Northern Ireland. Craig fenced the land and collected entry fees from visitors for a year, and then gifted it to a friend who dropped the entry fee. The site was eventually purchased by the filmmaker Sigurdur Jonasson, who presented it as a gift to the people of Iceland.

earth's crust. When water at considerable depth in the geyser pipe boils, it gets converted to steam, and expands to occupy greater volume within the pipe, forcing the water above to spurt out of the mouth of the geyser. The consequent decrease in pressure within the pipe allows more water to boil and form steam, and a chain reaction is set up.

The Geysir's activity has been interspersed with periods of dormancy. It lay silent for almost 40 years before being jolted out of its slumber by an earthquake in 1630. A long period of inactivity also preceded its reawakening in 1896 following a series of earthquakes. A period of extensive activity followed, leading to eruptions at a frenetic pace; the Great Geysir would erupt once every 30 minutes in 1910. However, it became almost dormant yet again in 1916. Artificial channels dug in order to lower the water table and clear out Geysir's silica-clogged channel failed to have much effect in reviving activity. Tourists tried to stimulate eruptions by throwing rocks into the vent, a practice which is strictly prohibited now. The earthquake of 2000, however, led to another awakening, and today the Geysir erupts every day, though not with the same force as before.

The Geysir has been drawing travelers, explorers, and naturalists from around the world for centuries. Despite its declining activity, no visitor to Iceland gives this majestic and powerful geyser a miss even to this day. Commemorative coins and stamps issued by the government have immortalized the Great Geysir.

**The Great Fjords,** Norway

# The Great Fjords

**F**jords, one of the most exquisite natural formations to be found in the world, are long, narrow inlets of sea that cut into land. Formed during the process of glaciation, they usually have high-walled sides with steep slopes. *Fjord* is a Norwegian word meaning "arm of the sea." Norway, the country to which the Vikings sailed and then settled in, is as rich in fjords as it is in myths and tales of Nordic gods. Its many fjords have earned for Norway the epithet, 'Land of Fjords.'

The Scandinavian fjords, formed as a result of heavy glacial erosion during the Ice Age, span most of Norway's 17,452-mile (28,148-km) coastline. Though geologists believe that glacial action was not entirely responsible for the creation of the fjords—some of the deepest fjords are too far below sea level to have been affected by the dredging masses of ice—they agree that these rivers of ice carved out most of the bays and inlets, and did the majority of the work in carving the U-shaped valleys as they gouged out mountains on their way to the sea. Patterned scars on the sheer cliffs that hem in the channels of water bear testimony to the ravages of the glaciers. Today, however, not much remains of these massive glaciers and ice caps apart from a few places places such as Jostedalsbreen, an isolated patch of ice to the north of Sognefjorden.

Thanks to the many fjords that cut into it, the actual Norwegian coastline, if stretched out straight, is more than half circumference of the earth. These so-called arms of the sea extend all the way from Stavanger in the south

## FJORD ROYAL

The well-known fjord Sognefjorden is known by two names—King of the Fjords and the Fjord of Kings. The first refers its size; it is Norway's longest and deepest fjord, stretching 112 miles (180km) and is more than 4,000ft (1,220m) deep. The second name is a reference to the fjord's royal connection; it is Norway's King Harald's favorite place for fishing.

*Elevated view, Aurlandsfjord*

## How Green is the Valley

Previous inhabitants of the fjords would seek out grassy patches near the floor of the valley and set up a pulley system at the top the mountain, similar to the ones used to draw water from wells. Instead of water, however, they would use the buckets to lower goats to the valley floor to graze, and adolescent children who would shepherd them. This system was followed in areas that could not be reached by shimmying down the almost-vertical rock faces. The risk involved and the meager pasture, however, forced an end to this practice.

*Red church on Lofoten islands, Nordland*

to the Russian border. The vast number of fjords make communicating by land in Norway a difficult task. For instance, villages sequestered in the curves of fjords which are only a few hours apart by boat would take far longer to reach if you were to travel by land.

The fjords also offer toursits a host of trekking trails. Four counties—Møre and Romsdal, Sogn and Fjordane, Hordaland, and Rogaland—make up the Fjord Norway area. Bergen is considered the gateway to this land of scoured rocks and sheer cliffs. About 150,000 off-shore isles dot the fjords, many of them inhabited by small pockets of population.

The very deep Geirangerfjord is considered by Norwegians to be the country's most beautiful fjord. With its many waterfalls—among them, the famous Seven Sisters—it is the second busiest destination in Norway for cruise ships, with more than 100 ships visiting in the summer. The *Hurtigruten* is one of the vessels that makes regular trips from Bergen to Kirkenes, a return voyage that takes 12 days. This vessel is also the only form of communication and source of supplies for some of the remotest islands.

The Seven Sisters is a single waterfall with seven separate streams—the tallest among them has a free fall of over 820ft (250m). According to folklore, the sisters dance naked as they gleefully splash down the mountain, while the Courtier—another waterfall on the mountain opposite the Seven Sisters—flirts playfully from across the fjord.

- Columns similar to the Giant's Causeway—though not as grand in scale, and formed in different ways—can be found in Armenia, California, Mexico, New Zealand, Russia, and Sicily.

- Though most of the columns in the Giant's Causeway are hexagonal, there are several which have five, seven, or even eight sides. The tallest columns measure about 39ft (12m).

**The Giant's Causeway,** Northern Ireland

# The Giant's Causeway

*Basalt rock formations, The Giant's Causeway*

Approximately 40,000 columns of basalt emerging from the base of the Antrim plateau makes up the magnificent Giant's Causeway in Northern Ireland. The colonnade stretches for about 300 yards (273m) across the coast from the cliffside and extends more than 448ft (146m) into the sea. It was declared a UNESCO World Heritage Site in 1986, and designated a National Nature Reserve by the Department of Environment of Northern Ireland the year after. The area is home to a host of birds, including the fulmar, petrel, cormorant, shag, guillemot, and razorbill. Exotic and endangered plant species such as sea spleenwort, hare's foot trefoil, vernal squill, sea fescue, and frog orchid grow here as well.

This natural pathway was born of a volcanic eruption some 50–60 million years ago, when the boiling basalt erupted through fissures in the chalk beds, and solidified to form a plateau. As the lava cooled, it contracted. Though the vertical contractions reduced the thickness without causing fractures, the horizontal contractions created hexagonal cracks throughout the lava layers. It was these cracks that were responsible for producing the incredible columns that we see today.

Sir Richard Bulkeley, a scholar at Trinity College, Dublin, announced the discovery of the Giant's Causeway in a paper presented to the Royal Society in 1693. It had, however, already been discovered by the Bishop of Derry a year earlier. The site garnered international acclaim only when Susanna Drury, an artist from Dublin, exhibited a series of watercolors depicting the landform in 1739.

According to legend, the Giant's Causeway finds its origin in a feud between two giants—Finn MacCool of Ireland and Benandonner of Scotland. Myth has it that Finn MacCool built a path so that he could walk to Scotland

to fight his rival. Upon finishing his task, Finn MacCool fell asleep. Meanwhile Benandonner, who was much larger than Finn, walked over to challenge him. Fearing for his life, Finn's wife, Oonagh placed a blanket over Finn, pretending that he was her son. The trick succeeded in fooling Benandonner, who assumed that the father of such a big baby would be an unbeatable adversary. He ran back to Scotland in terror, tearing up the rocks on his way so that Finn would not be able to cross the sea. The myth about the giants, it is believed, was propagated in the 18th century with the specific intention of attracting visitors to the area. Today, the Giant's Causeway is the most popular tourist attraction in Northern Ireland, drawing more than 750,000 visitors annually.

## OLDEST DISTILLERY

Before the construction of the famous coast road, visitors had to travel a long way on horseback to see the Giant's Causeway. The town of Bushmills, home to the world's oldest (licenced) distillery, was the last stop before the end of the journey. It had been a tradition for travelers to revive themselves with magnums of the King's whiskey. The Bushmills Distillery is still in business today.

## FINGAL'S CAVE

Columnar basalts are not confined to Northern Ireland alone. Another of the best known examples of this phenomenon is to be found off Scotland's west coast, in the Inner Hebrides. These columns are well developed over a large part of the island of Staffa, and a huge cave, where the sea has eroded the columns, is known as Fingal's Cave, after a mythical giant. The Cave has featured in many novels and poems over the centuries, and a rather rough boat trip to the island by the composer Felix Mendelssohn in 1829 inspired his famous orchestral overture *The Hebrides*.

**The Cliffs of Moher,** Ireland

# The Cliffs of Moher

**S**heer cliffs ascending majestically out of the Atlantic Ocean form the dramatic landscape of the Cliffs of Moher. Located on the west coast of Ireland, at the southwestern edge of the Burren area near Doolin, they extend for about 5 miles (8km)—from Luogh Point in the north to Cancregga in the south.

The rocks of Moher are a result of sediments deposited roughly 320 million years ago on an ancient sea bed. The sea shore then lay further north, and the rivers that flowed into it formed a series of deltas, depositing the silt that they carried onto the bed. With the passage of time and the intervention of geological processes, these sediments were converted into layers of Namurian shale, sandstone, and siltstone that lay on top of each other. As the level of the sea dropped, these rocks emerged out of the ocean as towering vertical walls.

The different rock strata are clearly defined in the face of the cliffs. The tier of rocks are partially inclined toward the southwest, and layers that are at the bottom of the cliff toward the south appear at the top edges a few kilometers to the north. Since sandstone is more resistant than the other rocks, they jut further out of the cliff-face than the intervening layers of shale and siltstone. The edges of the cliffs are naturally eroding areas, and many sections along the expanse of the Cliffs of Moher are severely undercut; chunks of the stone ledges thus often break off and drop into the ocean.

In 1835, local landlord Sir Cornelius O'Brien, a descendant of Ireland's High King Brian Boru, built an observation tower roughly at the mid-point of the Cliffs of Moher. It served as a viewing point for visitors who flocked to the cliffs to marvel at their grandeur. To this day, the tower stands proudly and the view from it extends beyond

## CREATURES OF MOHER

The Cliffs of Moher are famous for their abundant avifauna. Thirty thousand birds belonging to 29 varied species have been identified in the area. Nine species of nesting seabirds, including the guillemot, razorbill, puffin, kittiwake, and fulmar are present here. Most remarkable of these are the razorbill and the famous Atlantic Puffin, whose numbers are increasing in Moher in direct contrast to the decline in their population throughout the rest of Europe. The Atlantic Puffin nests in large colonies on the cliffs and the nearby islet called Goat Island. The edges of the cliffs are grassy and green, and rare lichens are found here.

Galway Bay to the Twelve Pins (or Twelve Bens) and Maum Turk Mountains in Connemara in the north, Loop Head at the southern tip of Clare, as well as the Kerry Mountains further south. The three Aran Islands to the west can also be seen unless visibility is exceptionally poor owing to bad weather.

Just below O'Brien's Tower is An Bhreannán Mór, a spectacular rock pillar or stack rising to a height of 230ft (70m), which provides a close view of the numerous birds that nest in the area. The cliffs at Hag's Head rise to a height of 394ft (120m) above the sea; a square stone ruin called Moher Tower, believed to be the remnant of a Napoleonic watch tower, is located here. The cliffs reach their maximum height of 702ft (214m) near O'Brien's Tower. A walking trail, mostly unenclosed, running along the top edge of the entire length of the cliffs—often perilously close to the sheer drop off the edge—provides a magnificent and impressive view of the whole area.

*A view of Doonagore Castle and O'Brien's Tower*

## CONSERVATION OF THE CLIFFS

Home to one of the major colonies of nesting seabirds in Ireland, the Cliffs of Moher were designated as a Refuge for Fauna in 1988 and declared a Special Protection Area for Birds (SPA) under the EU Birds Directive in 1989. The demarcated area covers 0.77sq miles (2sq km) and includes the cliffs, the fragile habitat formed by the cliff-top maritime grassland and heath, and a 656ft (200m) zone of open water in front of the cliffs in order to safeguard the feeding area of the birds. In 2006, the Clare County Council and the Burren and Cliffs of Moher Geopark Committee submitted an application to UNESCO to recognize the Burren and Cliffs of Moher Geopark as part of the European Geoparks Network. An interpretive visitor center called Atlantic Edge has also been established.

- The healing properties of mineral springs led to the opening of the world-famous health resort, Espa, which contributed the word "spa" to the English language.

- The Ardennes département of France has a nuclear power station in Chooz, and a plant that generates hydroelectric power from the Meuse river at Revin.

**Ardennes,** France/Belgium/Luxembourg

# Ardennes

The ancient wooded plateau of Ardennes comprises the western extension of the Middle Rhine Highlands and is spread across part of the Grand Duchy of Luxembourg, the Belgian provinces of Luxembourg, Namur, and Liège, and the Département of Ardennes in France. The product of a complex geological history, the plateau occupies an area of more than 3,860sq miles (10,000sq km), and encompasses the Forest of Ardennes consisting of an impressive 585sq miles (1,500sq km) of oak, beech, and ash.

A patchwork of diverse environments including barren lands, sparse heaths, dense woods, and rich meadows, the Ardennes has some of the most diverse and astonishingly beautiful landscapes in the world. Argonne in the east is a land of exquisite forests in which one can wander for calm and solitude. Bubbling streams run through pastures, and orchards neatly tucked away behind hills and farms bounded by copse hedges mark out the areas of human habitation. The Ardennes Hills are stumps of mountains, overgrown with forests of oak, ash, and birch, and with a thriving undergrowth of mosses and ferns; foxglove decorates the clearings. Orchids, the sundew, and the cotton grass are also found in abundance. Wildlife includes species such as roe deer, foxes, beavers, and the nightjar. The picturesque cliffs of Ardennes provide spectacular views of the surrounding lands.

Today, the name Ardennes is usually used to indicate the southern part of the area, where elevations vary between 1,150ft and 1,640ft (350m and 500m); the plateau reaches its greatest height of 2,277ft (694m) at Botrange, south of Liège. Made up of sandstone, quartzite, slate, and limestone, the rounded summits of the Ardennes are interspersed with shallow depressions

## CASTLES, FORTS, AND CHURCHES

Fortified castles, fortresses, and bastions have been built in the Ardennes since the early Middle Ages because of its location on a traditional invasion route. A majority were destroyed during the Hundred Years War, though some ruins still survive. Though most were built in semi-medieval styles, some excellent examples of brick and stone architecture from the Louis XIII period can still be seen. Residential chateaux started appearing in the 18th century. A fortified castle at Sedan, built in the 15th century, remains the largest in Europe. Churches—Romanesque, baroque or fortified like the castles— are found in every village. Remarkable among these are the Church of Asfeld, the abbey church of Mouzon, and Saint-Juvin en Argonne.

*Church of Asfeld, France*

containing peat bogs and narrow winding valleys carved out by the rivers that rise from them. The desolate uplands are characterized by heavy rainfall, low clouds, fog, and frost. Though forests cover half of the area, the thin acidic soil is mostly waterlogged, and can sustain only heath. The relatively lower northern portion of the Ardennes—measuring between 655ft and 985ft (200m–300m)—is, in contrast, covered by green pastures and cultivated farmlands. The high Ardennes forms a watershed between rivers which flow toward the Meuse and the Moselle rivers.

The Ardennes was formed as a result of intense tectonic activity involving folding, faulting, uplifts, and denudations, with older strata of rocks being thrust over newer layers. Part of the Hercynian orogenic belt that extends from western Ireland to Germany, the Ardennes region was formed approximately 300 to 400 million years ago, during the second half of the Paleozoic era. The plateau is cut extensively by the Meuse river and its tributaries, and has poor drainage in the higher areas, which are more conducive to the growth of swamps, bogs, and mossy patches than crops and trees. A large depression, which is known east of the Meuse as the Famenne and west of it as the Fagne, marks out the geological and topographical separation of Ardennes from the northern foothills.

*The lush green Ardennes forests*

## BATTLES AT ARDENNES

The Ardennes region—despite its difficult terrain—has been the scene of many battles since the French Revolution. Remarkable encounters include the campaign of 1794 and the Franco-German War, when Napoleon III surrendered at Sedan in 1870. Ardennes was also affected by the World Wars—the Battle of the Ardennes took place during World War I, and a bitter US-German encounter broke out in Argonne in 1918. The German breakthrough occurred near Sedan in 1940, marking the Battle of France. Ardennes was also the site for the final offensive action by the Germans in France during World War II, in December 1944— the famous encounter known as The Battle of the Bulge.

The Eisriesenwelt Caves are not lit by electric lights. Visitors have to wear carbide lamps, and the most spectacular sights are illuminated with magnesium ribbon strips.

• The Eisriesenwelt Caves represent the largest accessible ice caves in the world today

**Eisriesenwelt Caves,** Austria

*Tourists entering the Eisriesenwelt ice cave*

## SKIING AT TENNENGEBIRGE

The Tennengebirge range can be scaled at any time vof the year but the best months are September and October. Summer months are known for thunderstorms and in June many of the higher peaks are covered with snow. During this time the snow bridges over vertical caves get so thin that it is dangerous to ski. Skiers come here between February and April, although world climatic changes are forcing many to follow weather reports rather than traditional winter timings. It needs to be kept in mind that to enable skiing or snowboarding, karstic areas require far more snow than other mountains.

# The Eisriesenwelt Caves

The "Giant Ice Caves"–the Eisriesenwelt Höhle–were first discovered in 1879 when a natural scientist from Salzburg, Anton Posselt, stumbled into a giant cave on the Tennengebirge plateau and came face to face with the incredible wonderland of ice chambers and natural ice sculptures. It was not until the 1920s, when the speleologist Alexander von Mörk pursued the matter, that the uniqueness of the Eisriesenwelt ice caves was recognized and the first scientific expeditions and climbing routes established. Situated 25 miles (40km) south of Mozart's birthplace (Salzburg), the Tennengebirge range dominates the Salzach Valley to the west and offers one of the most stunning views of the Austrian Alps in the Hohe Tauern region.

The Eisriesenwelt Höhle, of which 26 miles (42 km) has been explored, and roughly only half a mile (0.8km) is open to visitors, are constantly being shaped and reshaped by the circulation of air and water precipitation caused by innumerable crevices, tunnels, and cave openings in the Tennengebirge range. The average temperature inside the freezing caverns is largely dependent on the outside temperature. In winter, the air inside the mountain is warmer whereas in spring, it is cooler. Located on the 7,976-ft (2,432-m) high triangular Tennengebirge plateau, the caves are part of the impressive set of cave ruins (partly collapsed and eroded caves) known as the Giant Caves Niveau. The plateau itself is devoid of any vegetation and is criss-crossed with tectonic faults and large ditches that are treacherous to cross during summer when the snow melts. In winter, however, it is possible to trek the area from east to west in a single day.

Geologically younger and found at higher elevations—4,920ft to 5,904ft (1,500m to 1,800m)—than the older Eiskogel Eishöhle, the Eisreisenwelt caves are part of the Austrian Alps formed during the Pleistocene Epoch. Its unique cave system is the work of the Central Alp rivers, which tore through the limestone and karst deposits to carve out one of the most astounding labyrinth's of natural wonders in the world.

When Posselt first stepped into the Eisriesenwelt entrance cave, a huge ice wall blocked the entry beyond the first chamber; today visitors can explore an entire series of caves connected with gangplanks, stairs, and handrails. Mörk, who likened his expeditions to that of Thor's journey to the Ice Giants, named the caves' chambers after characters from Norse mythology. These include the magnificent Hall of Hymir, Frigga's Veil, the Odin Room, the Ice Palace, and the 120-ft (36-m) high Alexander von Mörk Cathedral. In acknowledgment of his work and wishes, an urn containing his remains was placed here after he died during World War I.

*Hikers on the Tennengebirge mountain range, Salzburg*

## EXPLORING THE LIMESTONE MOUNTAIN RANGE

An interesting fact about Tennengebirge is that it is not a single mountain but a huge limestone karst range. It has steep slopes and a vast plateau that covers approximately 18sq miles (45sq km). The total mountain range extends over 94sq mile (240sq km). The highest peaks in this range are located at the western and southern rim of the Tennengebirge plateau. To get here one can follow the marked paths that often lead to huts located on the margins of the mountain range. Though the range is only 7,872ft (2,400m) high, the vertical distance between the surrounding valleys and the peaks exceeds 5,904ft (1,800m). The Tennengebirge is squeezed between the valleys of the River Salzach in the west, River Lammer in the north, and River Fritzbach in the south. Although it is one of the wettest places in Austria, its plateau resembles a desert during summer. This is due to karstification during which all water immediately disappears into the open joints, shafts, and caves of the limestone massif.

- The 49ft (15m) tall Orjak stalagmite, in the Velika Dvorana Hall, is the largest of its kind found in the Skocjan Caves.

- The Martel Chamber—479ft (146m) high, 394ft (120m) wide, and 1,010ft (308m) long—is the largest underground chamber in Europe.

**Skocjan Caves**, Slovenia

# Skocjan Caves

The Skocjan Caves is an extraordinary system of vast limestone caverns that lie in a region called Kras, or Karst, in southwestern Slovenia. It is from this karst plateau that the geological phenomenon derives its name. Comprising one of the largest underground canyons in the world, caves that are more than 66ft (200m) deep, underground passages extending for 3 miles (5km), dramatic collapsed dolines or sinkholes, and numerous picturesque waterfalls, the Skocjan Caves are a world-renowned site for the study and research of karst limestone phenomena.

The Skocjan Caves Regional Park, or Regijski Park Skocjanske jame, is situated 8 miles (13km) east of Trieste. Occupying an area of 1.6sq miles (4.13sq km), the park stretches from the area in the east where the River Reka first makes its appearance in a shallow canyon to a highway to Italy in the west. It encompasses the lower portion of the River Susica, the Skocjan Caves, and the area above the caves. First protected as a 0.3sq mile (0.8sq km) natural monument in 1980, the area was inscribed as a UNESCO World Heritage Site in 1986. It was expanded to its present size in 1990 and established as a

*Woman standing on a bridge in cave Zelske Jame in Rakov Skocjan*

## FLORA AND FAUNA

Though the surface of the caves consists primarily of dry grasslands, a variety of natural habitats are found within the caves. The disintegrated galleries and shallow chasms of the river valley experience microclimatic conditions, and thus different vegetations such as Mediterranean, sub-Mediterranean, Dinaric, and Illyrian thrive next to each other. Endemic species include the giant dead nettle. The speleofauna consists of creatures such as the snow vole, and a number of species of bats. Rare and endemic invertebrates, crustaceans, and cave beetles also abound; the cave salamander is one of the more remarkable and endemic vertebrates found in the Skocjan Caves.

*Stalagmites and stalactites in the Skocjan caves*

## CULTURAL HERITAGE

Excavations in the area of the Skocjan Caves demonstrate that the region has been occupied for more than 10,000 years. About 30 archeological sites are situated within the Skocjan Caves Regional Park, and 18 more such sites exist in the neighboring areas. According to the findings from the sites, the area was continuously inhabited from the middle Stone Age to the Iron Age; a fort was erected where Skocjan stands today during this latter period. The same place also saw the construction of another fort during the period of Roman settlement, and a fortified rural settlement was established during the Middle Ages. The written records of the Skocjan Caves date back two millennia, when Pozidonius of Apamea (135-50BC) wrote of them.

regional park in 1996. The Ramsar Convention established it as a Wetland of International Importance in 1999.

The underground passages carved out by the River Reka are among the most fantastic examples of large-scale karst drainage and topography. Entering the Skocjan grotto through a 1,148-ft (350-m) long subterranean passage, the Reka reappears at the bottom of two chasms which are 492ft (150m) deep and 98ft (300m) long. The river then disappears into one of the largest underground canyons in the world

The network of underground passages of Skocjan extends right up to Timavo on the Gulf of Trieste in Italy. The collapse of the gallery surfaces on various levels has produced many magnificent deep chasms, including the Sokolak in the south, Globocak in the west, and Sapen dol and Lisicina. The cave system also includes the Mahorcic grotto with its many underground lakes

and five extraordinary cascades. Other striking features within the subterranean network include a narrow canal and five side galleries, including a 1,64-0ft (500-m) long gallery that leads to the surface. Breathtaking stalactites and stalagmites adorn these underground grottos, which reach a maximum depth of around 754ft (230m).

This impressive karst network also contains 25 waterfalls; among them is a magnificent cascade that is 535ft (163m) high. The most exceptional dripstone formations have many limestone pools and natural bridges that span the river at various points. The karstic terminology for a flat-floored depression with steep sides—doline or dolina—owes its origin to the two famous sinkholes of Mala dolina and Velika dolina. A number of species considered endangered the world over are preserved within the safety of the ecosystems of the dolinas and grottos of the Skocjan Caves.

**e Matterhorn,** Switzerland

- Kraft Foods in Switzerland, the makers of Toblerone, say that the triangular shape of their chocolate bar has been inspired by the Matterhorn.

- The Matterhorn Museum has on display the original rope used by the first successful expedition to the summit of the Horn in 1865. Of the seven-member climbing team, four lost their lives when the rope tore during the descent.

# ne Matterhorn

The Matterhorn is a classic rock pyramid, with steep narrow ridges that jut out of the surrounding glaciers. The distinctive shape of this dramatic peak makes it a favorite with photographers and tourists around the world. Straddling the border between Switzerland and Italy, the mountain towers over the Swiss village of Zermatt and the Italian village of Breuil-Cervinia. Soaring to a height of 14,692ft (4,478m), it is the most famous mountain of the European Alps. While it is known as Mont Cervin in France and Monte Cervino in Italy, the residents of Zermatt call it Horu. The name Matterhorn is believed to be a combination of the German words Matt, meaning 'valley' or 'meadow,' and Horn, meaning 'peak.'

The peak that we see today was formed as a result of the dual action of tectonic movements and glacial activity. The process of formation began about 180 million years ago with the collision of the African and European plates. It reached a climax about 40 million years ago when the African plate convulsed, as it slid under the European plate, and mountains emerged out of the earth's crust—among them, the framework for today's Matterhorn. Around 2 million years ago, glacial activity took over, chiseling

## ALPINE PEAKS

The Alps have fascinated generations of visitors for their beauty and for the challenge they present. The highest mountain is Mont Blanc in France, which is 15,771ft (4,807m) high. The Jungfrau is considered one of the most spectacular of the snow-capped mountains.

The Eiger has achieved a place of importance because of the difficulty of its climbs: the almost sheer north face, 1 mile (1.8km) high, was not mastered until 1938. In Austria, the towering Zugspitze is the tallest of the Bavarian Alps and is popular with skiers and climbers. In the valley below, Garmisch-Partenkirchen—site of the 1936 Winter Olympics—has tramways to the crest of the mountain.

the mountain—made up of granite, mica schist, gneiss, sandstone, and other rocks—and shaping it to form four tapering faces, converging at the peak. The steepness of the gradient keeps snow and ice from clinging tightly to the mountain, and any excess is regularly shed in the form of avalanches.

Although it is not the highest peak in the Alps, the shape of the Matterhorn has been a deterrent for mountaineers. The first serious attempts to scale the mountain from the Italian side were made in as late as 1857. The weather and the extremely challenging climb forced all parties back. The peak was finally conquered on July 14, 1865 by a team of seven men led by the British explorer Edward Whymper. They attempted the ascent from the Swiss side and began their climb along the now famous Hornli Ridge. Though the team managed to reach the peak, four of its members lost their lives during the descent. Three days after Whymper's team reached the peak, on July 17, 1865, four men led by the Italian guide Giovanni Carrel reached the summit via a ridge on the Italian side. After more successful summit attempts over the next few years, Lucy Walker became the first woman to ascend the mountain in 1871, and a few weeks later, Meta Brevoort followed suit.

Today, all the ridges and faces of the Matterhorn have been scaled, and in all seasons. Yet, it would be unwise to underestimate the perils inherent in attempting to conquer this peak. The difficult conditions and bad weather often lead to many climbers losing their lives to the mountain every year.

## SCALING THE MATTERHORN

The Matterhorn is one of the world's most frequently climbed mountains. Every part of it has been tackled, and the most popular routes have fixed ropes, ladders and huts. However, this should not fool anyone into thinking of it as an easy climb: the Matterhorn also has one of the highest death rates.

Local guides now take most climbers along the easiest and first ascent, Hornli Ridge and Lion Ridge, which have sections of fixed climbing aids. More experienced climbers go to the Zmutt and Furggen ridges, and the North Face presents the greatest challenge of all. Inexperienced climbers are advised to leave this mountain to the experts.

*A climber tackles the Matterhorn*

- Formed by the union of the Leschaux and the Geant glaciers, the Mer de Glace is one of the longest glaciers in the Alps, and extends for 3.5 miles (5.6km) on the northern side of Mont Blanc.

- Conifers and grasslands cover the Mont Blanc Massif, which is also home to many animals including the Alpine ibex, chamois, mountain pheasant, royal eagle, and the white Alpine partridge.

**Mont Blanc,** France/Italy

# Mont Blanc

The highest peak in the French Alps, and also the highest point in Europe, Mont Blanc stands tall at 15,771ft (4,807m). Part of the Savoy Alps, and variously referred to as The Roof of Europe, Mecca of Alpinism, and The Royal Summit, Mont Blanc straddles the Aosta Valley in Italy and Haute-Savoie in France. Though it is called Monte Bianco in Italy, the mountain is better known to the rest of the world by its French name, Mont Blanc. Both names translate as "white mountain," and are derived from the 40sq miles (100sq km) of the massif that is covered by glaciers.

Chamonix, a French town located at the foot of Mont Blanc, shot to worldwide fame when it was chosen as the venue for the first Winter Olympic Games in 1924. The area, however, had been well-known in scientific circles since the early 18th century, when glaciers such as Mer de Glace (sea of ice) and the Argentiere Glacier—which is the second largest in France—on the Mont Blanc Massif became a subject of research undertaken to understand the process of mountain formation. Glaciers spread across more than 66sq miles (170sq km) around Mont Blanc form a natural museum of dazzling beauty. There is great diversity in the glacial structures as well, ranging from glaciers such as the

*Climbers descending Mont Blanc, Rhône-Alpes, Haute-Savoie*

## HEIGHT OF MONT BLANC

A thick blanket of ice and snow covering the Mont Blanc is the cause of the instability of the summit height of the mountain. The peak has been under constant observation since the 1980s, and though the official height has been kept at 15,771ft (4,807m), according to GPS and satellite measurements, the height actually fluctuates between 15,771ft (4,807m) and 15,781ft (4,811m). In 2001, the height was recorded as 15,748.6ft (4,810.4m); following heat waves in Europe, the height was recorded as 15,770ft (4,808m) in 2005. Not only does its height vary, the snowy peak is also known to shift position very slightly. The rock summit of the mountain, under the layer of ice and snow, measures 15,718ft (4,792m), and is situated about 131ft (40m) away from the snow summit.

## MONT BLANC TUNNEL

The Mont Blanc Tunnel passes through the mountain and links Haute-Savoie in France and the Aosta Valley in Italy. This tunnel is a lifeline for Italy, which depends on it for the transportation of around 33 percent of its freight to northern Europe. Built at a height of 4091ft (1,247m) on the French side and 4,530ft (1,381m) on the Italian side, the construction of this 7.3-mile (11.7-km) long tunnel began in 1957, and it was finally opened to traffic in 1965. Subsequent plans of expansion of the tunnel have, however, been shelved because of protests about the detrimental effect of heavy vehicular traffic. The tunnel was closed for three years after a disastrous fire broke out inside in March 1999, but was reopened in March 2002.

*A view of Rhône-Alpes, Haute-Savoie*

Le Tour, which terminates in a stunning hanging glacier, to the Les Bossons, which exhibits a magnificent vertical drop of 11,152ft (3,400m) from the top of Mont Blanc to the valley at its base.

The evolution of Mont Blanc is divided into three phases, with the first dating back almost 500 million years. This period of evolution spans the Jurassic and Tertiary Ages, and tracks of dinosaurs found in the region now known as Emosson, give credence to the theory. Scientists believe that a massive body of water—Tetide—appeared at the site of the Alps during the Second Phase, between 250 and 60 million years ago; the Alps lay buried under a sea bed several hundred meters thick, formed from marine sedimentation. During the Third Phase, the African and European plates collided with each other, causing the Alps to rise from the ocean bed approximately 30 million years ago; the Mont Blanc Massif emerged about 28 million years ago.

Mountaineers, too, were drawn to Mont Blanc from the early 18th century. However, climbing as a sport grew in stature only when Horace Bénédict de Saussure, a scientist from Geneva, took it upon himself in 1760 to declare a reward for anyone who could climb the peak. The money was finally claimed more than two decades later, on August 8,1786, by Chamonix doctor Michel-Gabriel Paccard and his porter Jacques Balmat. In 1808, Marie Paradis became the first woman to reach the summit. Today, more than 20,000 people climb the mountain annually.

- Though temperatures at the Lakes Prosce and Kozjak climb up to 75°F (24°C) in summer, the entire Plitvice is snow-covered from November to March, and the lakes freeze December–January, creating a pristine and magical landscape.

- The "Milka Trnina Waterfalls" have been named in recognition of the famous Croatian opera singer's contribution to the Society for Protection and Embellishment of the Plitvice Lakes in 1897.

**Plitvice Lakes,** Croatia

# Plitvice Lakes

An unbroken chain of beautiful lakes, caves, and cascades make up the beautiful Plitvice Lakes (or Plitvicka Jezera in Serbo-Croatian) in western Croatia. Divided into the Upper Lakes (Gornja jezera) and Lower Lakes (Donja jezera), the lakes are mostly fed by the waters of the Black River and the White River which form a confluence near Plitvicki Ljeskovac, and then run together to the first of the lakes as the Matica River. The 16 lakes of Plitvice form a chain that is 5 miles (8km) long.

The Upper Lakes comprises 12 picturesque lakes, starting with Proscansko (Lake Prosce). Situated 2,096ft (639m) above sea level, this is the highest of them, and is linked to the other lakes by numerous waterfalls. Kozjak, the very last in the Upper Lakes section, is also the largest of the Plitvicka Jezera. Measuring nearly 150ft (46m), these are also the deepest water bodies in the area. The Upper and Lower Lakes have different geological origins. While the former occupies a wide, gently sloping dolomite basin in the Korana Valley, the smaller and shallower Lower Lakes

*Waterfall, Plitvice Lakes National Park*

## HERITAGE OF PLITVICE

Also called the Land of the Falling Lakes, the Plitvice Lakes area was the cradle of the prehistoric Illarian tribe of Yopuds, from around 1,000BC Roman settlements followed the Yopudic society, and the area has been continuously occupied by the Slavs since the 8th century. Tools dating back to the Bronze Age, as well as ceramics and remnants of fortifications, have been found in the area.

## PLITVICE NATIONAL PARK

Though the Plitvice Lakes were accorded the status of a national park as early as 1928, the region's boundaries were only finalized and properly designated and developed in 1949. The Croatian Parliament expanded the area of the park further by 39sq miles (100sq km) in 1997, leading to its present size of 114sq miles (295sq km). The Plitvice National Park was inscribed as a UNESCO Natural World Heritage Site in 1979. The Balkan War in the 1990s led to the park being placed on a list of World Heritage sites in danger in 1992, but it was removed in 1996.

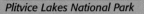

*Plitvice Lakes National Park*

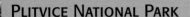

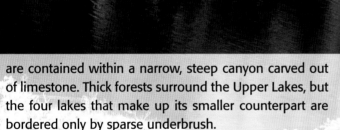

are contained within a narrow, steep canyon carved out of limestone. Thick forests surround the Upper Lakes, but the four lakes that make up its smaller counterpart are bordered only by sparse underbrush.

Waterfalls at the Plitvice Lakes range from "splashers", which are only a few feet high, to huge "tumblers" that drop from heights of over 82ft (25m). The Novakovica Brod, separated from another lake by a travertine barrier only 6.5ft (2m) high and at an elevation of 1,650ft (503m), is the last and the lowest of the Plitvice Lakes. Waters from this lake form numerous waterfalls that tumble over the edge to a wide stone depression called Sastavci. The waters then continue to the Plitvice Brook, where a vertical fall—measuring 249ft (76m)—into a rocky scar marks the beginning of the flow of the Korana River.

The formation of this exquisite landscape is largely attributed to the deposition of phytogenetic travertine, (calcareous tufa), over the last 4,000 years. These deposits grew thickly in places, creating barriers behind which the water was barricaded, and thus the lakes were formed. A number of caves and vaults are scattered over the lake area. Fourteen limestone caves and six travertine caves have been discovered in the cliffs that surround the lakes and border the Korana River. The most remarkable among these is the Supljara Cave, situated just above Kaluderovac Lake in the Lower Lakes region. A dark tunnel that leads into the mountainside, this cavern was formed by the dissolution of porous limestone by the water that seeped in, and showcases ancient fossil clams that once lived in the shallow sea that covered this area millions of years ago.

This isolated corner of Croatia was once called Lika, or "Land of the Wolf", by its native inhabitants; even today gray wolves roam the forests of beech, fir, maple, elm, and spruce that surround the lakes. Brown bears, lynx, olms, the European pond turtle, the black stork, and Ural owls also inhabit the area.

- The Transylvanian Alps are known as *Carpatii Meridionali* in Romanian.

- First established in 1935, the Retezat National Park today covers 218sq miles (559sq km) of the mountainside and provides refuge to many creatures including the chamois.

**Transylvanian Alps,** Romania

# Transylvanian Alps

Scattered villages beneath a soaring mountain range make up the almost medieval landscape of the Transylvanian Alps. Arching across the country of Romania, the wild and rugged Carpathian Mountains are Eastern Europe's backbone. The southernmost section of this sprawling mountain system, from the Prahova River valley in the east to the valley of the Cerna and Timis rivers in the west, forms the picturesque Transylvanian Alps in south central Romania.

Formed during the Tertiary Age, the Carpathians are a part of the Alpine-Himalayan system and the eastern segment of the European Alpine fold chain. Composed primarily of dense crystalline and volcanic rocks, the Southern Carpathians have a rather looming character that distinguishes them from the other sections of the Carpathians. One of the final bastions of untamed nature in Europe, the Transylvanian Alps have a total length of about 155 miles (250km). The average elevation of the mountain range is between 4,920ft and 5,740ft (1,500m and 1,750m). Higher and more continuous than the other sections of the Carpathians, the Transylvanian Alps are also more impassable and bridged by only four passes. Brezoi, Hateg, and Petrosani form the notable lowland depressions in the area.

## TRANSYLVANIAN WEATHER

Winter in the mountains lasts from November or December through May or June, and temperatures often dip below freezing point. The Transylvanian Alps remain covered by snow and ice, and the area is the sole preserve of well-equipped veterans of Alpine mountaineering. Skiing in the mountains, however, is restricted to the eastern slopes of Bucegi. The summer months herald the return of hikers and walkers, even though the weather can often be unpredictable, and mist and rainfall is common.

*Winter view of a village and steepled church, Bukkloka-Fagetel, Transylvania*

The Fagaras, Bucegi, Parang, and Retezat-Godeanu massifs form the major subdivisions of the Transylvanian Alps. Ease of access makes Bucegi the favored destination of holidaymakers since the main road from Brasov to Bucharest passes through the Prahova Valley, which forms the eastern boundary of this massif. While three main routes through thick forests allow walkers and trekkers to explore the mountains, other tourists can use the two cable cars that serve the area. The mountain paths pass along rocky precipices carved out by the wind and through Alpine meadows, finally leading to Mount Omu, which at 8,216ft (2,505m) is the tallest peak in the mountain chain.

Squeezed between Bucegi in the east and Fagaras in the west is the ridge of the Piatra Craiului. One of the most beautiful sights in the Transylvanian Alps, this closely arranged sliver of white limestone peaks is only 11 miles (18km long). Walking trails begin from the north and then follow a precarious path along the tapering spine of the ridge, before descending southwards into an area of remarkable karst topography, with deep gorges, pitted slopes, and a series of caves carved into the mountainside.

Overlooking the Fagaras depression through which the Olt River gently flows south to the Carpathian foothills, the steep northern face of the Fagaras massif rises 8,000ft (2,450m) above sea level. This range—the highest in the Transylvanian Alps—runs for about 30 miles (48km), and is heavily glaciated, with scalloped peaks and moraine deposits. A relatively inaccessible and isolated section of the Transylvanian Alps, this massif also contains the two of the highest points in Romania: at 8,346ft (2,544m), Mount Moldoveanu is the tallest of the Southern Carpathian peaks, followed closely by Mount Negoiu, which measures 8,317ft (2,535m).

Covered with lush and abundant vegetation, the Transylvanian Alps also provide sanctuary to a rich and varied wildlife, including wolves and bears.

## COMMUNICATION AND POWER

Though the high passes of Bran, Novaci-Sugag, and Valcan allow communication at elevations reaching up to 7,400ft (2,256m), the main roads and railways that connect the Transylvanian Alps are located in the scenic river valleys of Olt, Jiu, and Danube. A joint Romanian-Yugoslav navigation and power project has harnessed the fast-flowing waters of the Danube at the Iron Gate (Portile de Fier) gorge. This power station has greatly improved navigation facilities in the area and is capable of generating a few million kilowatts of power. Deposits of iron, coal, and lignite have also been discovered in the southern Carpathians.

*Bran Castle (Vlad the Impaler's alleged castle), Bran, Transylvanian Alps*

- The wine produced on the slopes of Mount Vesuvius is known as "Lacrima Christi." In ancient Pompeii, wine containers would often be labeled with the name Vesuvinum.

- The sudden explosive bursts that have come to characterize Vesuvius's eruptions are called "Plinian" because of the description of the AD79 explosion by Pliny the Younger.

**Mount Vesuvius,** Italy

## FLIRTING WITH FIRE

The Osservatorio Vesuviano was founded in 1841 by Ferdinand II of Bourbon. It was housed in the side of an old building called Eremo, a resting spot for travelers who intended to climb the mountain. Situated on the southern border of the Somma caldera, it was sandwiched between two deep valleys. The aim was to observe the manner in which the mountain evolved and to understand it better. The observatory has weathered eruptions since the 1850s without any significant damage.

# Mount Vesuvius

Located in the Campania region of Italy, Mount Vesuvius looms large in the background of the beautiful landscape of the Bay of Naples. Part of the larger Campanian volcanic arc, it is the only volcano on the European mainland to have erupted in the last century.

Though it shows no signs of life today, Vesuvius is considered one of the world's most dangerous volcanoes for the threat it poses to the dense population of the surrounding area. More than 200,000 people crowd around this volcano, drawn by the fertile soils which are perfect for growing a variety of crops.

Mount Vesuvius rose as a result of the collision between the African and Eurasian tectonic plates, which caused the earth to buckle and fold, and finally rise as the African plate slid under the other. The friction in turn caused the crust to melt, forming magma that found its way to the earth's surface and resulted in the formation of the volcano we see today.

Vesuvius was considered sacred by the Greeks and the Romans because of its association with the god Hercules; the town of Herculaneum was constructed at its base. The volcano's most famous eruption in AD79 resulted in Herculaneum as well as Pompeii being buried under molten lava, ash, and dust several feet deep. An estimated 20,000 people were killed.

Over 50 eruptions have been recorded since the catastrophe of AD79, though none can match the severity of the devastation caused during that cataclysmic explosion. The height of the eruption column is estimated to have risen a staggering 20 miles (32km). The impact of the 1906 eruption blew away the top of the mountain itself, leading to the death of several hundred people. The 1944 eruption resulted in the height of the mountain being raised by approximately 492ft (150m), and the size of the crater increased threefold. Today, at its highest point, Vesuvius reaches 4,200ft (1280m).

The vineyards and orchards that cover the slopes of Vesuvius make way for groves of oak and chestnut further up along the gradient. The forests extend to the peak on the northern side, and higher up on the western side undulating plateaus are covered with broom. Inside the caldera the slopes are almost barren except for clusters of meadow plants. During the long period of dormancy before the violent eruption in 1631, the crater once held forests and lakes. Volcanic gases given off during periods of eruption, however, destroy all vegetation on the slopes.

*A view over Pompeii toward Mount Vesuvius*

## PRESERVING POMPEII

Parco Nationale Vesuvio, or the Vesuvius National Park, is the smallest park in Italy. Occupying only 34.7sq miles (84.8sq km), it encompasses the areas surrounding the mountain and the Somma caldera. It was set up in June 5,1995 with the aim of preserving the flora and fauna of the area, and the many geological irregularities and paleontological formations that have been uncovered by archeologists over the years. Regulated tourism has also been promoted in the area to ensure that the local residents can earn a living and to increase awareness regarding the need for preservation of the ruins.

*Restored buildings in the Roman town buried in AD79 by ash flows from Mount Vesuvius*

- The name Cappadocia derives from the Persian word *Katpatuka*, which means "Land of Beautiful Horses."

- Today, many visitors choose to view Cappadocia from hot air balloons; floating gently over this incredible vista can be a unique experience.

**Cappadocia,** Turkey

*Church site cut into the rocks in the Göreme Valley; ropes are used to climb the ancient steps*

## CAPPADOCIA'S CHURCHES

The Apple Church and the Church of the Buckle (Tokali Kilise) are among the well-known churches in Cappadocia. The largest church in Göreme, Tokali Kilise, was restored to some of its early glory in the 1960s. The ninth-century frescos contained in the main nave make this church a remarkable one; also showcased are 11th-century frescos painted in the metropolitan style. These include depictions of the 12 apostles, the saints, and scenes from the life of Jesus.

# Cappadocia

**M**yriad shapes and contours carved out by the elements over millennia have earned Cappadocia in Anatolia (ancient Asia Minor) the name "Lunar Land." Situated in modern-day Turkey, there is something alien and lunar about the bizarre stone towers and cones, and the mysterious crags that dot the landscape of this ancient land.

The formation of Cappadocia began millions of years ago, as volcanic eruptions shook the earth. A long chain of lava-spewing eruptions during the Cenozoic era (between 30 and 60 million years ago to the present) are believed to have been responsible for the creation of Cappadocia. The lava from the upheavals were converted over eons to form a malleable stone called "tuff"—a mix of volcanic ash, lava, and mud. Elements eroded and molded this stony land, creating deep valleys bordered by steep undulating cliffs and giving rise to the structures that are seen today—formations that resemble palaces, steeples, towers, and sometimes even giant-headed mushrooms. Wind and water worked on these structures, smoothening and polishing them until they evolved into the present day visual wonders that they are. These magnificent stone façades are multi-hued, their colors ranging from bone white to blue to tan, orange, and pink.

The most unusual and famous of Cappadocia's natural formations, however, are the "fairy chimneys."

A photographer's delight, the fairy chimneys are scattered all over the Cappadocia landscape. These amazing structures are nothing but cones of tuff and volcanic ash covered with protective slabs of hard basalt at the top, which resemble cut columns with hats. Spectacular from all angles, these stone columns look particularly beautiful at dusk, burnished by the glow of the setting sun.

When man first arrived in the area, he dug, dredged, and carved the stone, leaving behind a sculpted record of life dating back to the Hittites of the late Bronze Age. Cappadocia hosts treasures below the ground too—subterranean cities more than 10 stories deep have been discovered here. Built as a defense against attacks, the cities boast mazes and labyrinthine tunnels—which often lead to inescapable pitfalls—constructed to bewilder and dispose of particularly persistent enemies. The cities of Kaymakli and Derinkuyu have today been opened up to visitors; however, because of the many treacherous passages they are strongly advised to follow directions and signs. The discovery of both Hittite artifacts and a Roman tomb at Derinkuyu suggest that these cities were expanded and occupied by Christians fleeing Arab persecution. They were used as recently as 1839, when the Turks, facing an Egyptian invasion, sought refuge in them.

Above ground, Cappadocia's rocks were converted into churches, monasteries, and sanctuaries adorned with Byzantine art. This ranged from the primitive icons of the seventh century to geometric designs derived from the cross during the Iconoclastic period (726–843) and 13th-century art (when a Mongol invasion and Islam severed Cappadocia's connection with Byzantium).

Thus, Cappadocia, with its magnificent lunar landscape and its hidden subterranean cities, remains one of the world's most fascinating natural as well as historical attractions.

## GÖREME

Situated in the "fairy chimneys" region of Cappadocia, Göreme has been inhabited constantly for at least 16 centuries. The presence of spectacular rock formations, evidence of Byzantine art, dwellings, troglodyte villages, and underground towns led to the Göreme Valley being declared a historical national park in 1986. Göreme National Park and the Rock Sites of Cappadocia were inscribed on the UNESCO World Heritage List in 1986

*View of Göreme with houses carved in conical rock formations (troglodyte dwellings)*

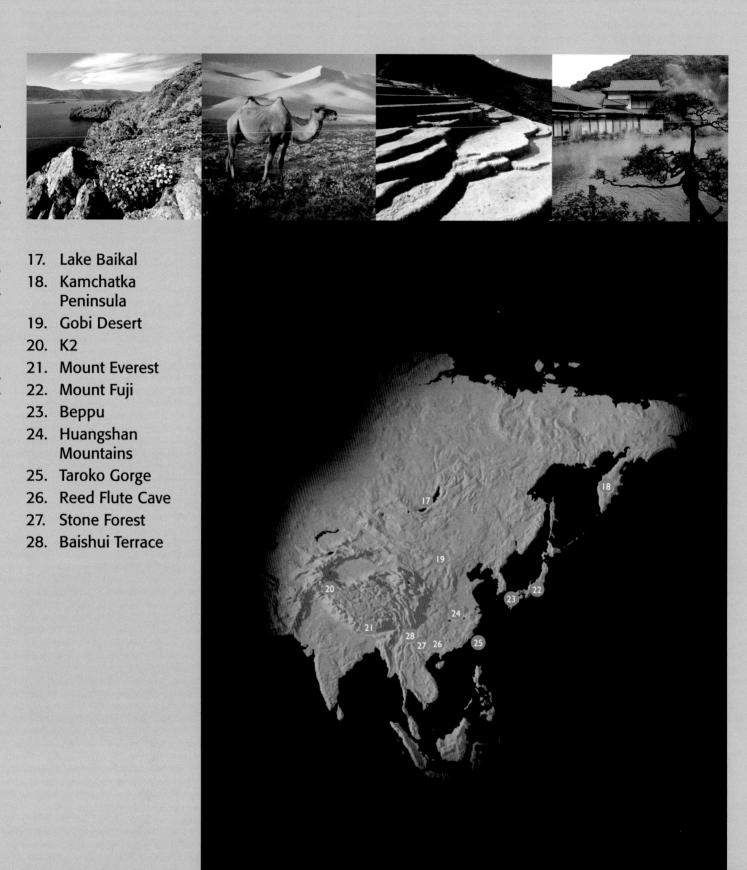

# Asia

Occupying four-fifths of the great Eurasian landmass, Asia is the world's largest and most diverse continent. Bound by the Arctic Ocean to the north, the Bering Strait and the Pacific Ocean to the east, the Indian Ocean to the south, and the Mediterranean and Red Sea in the southwest, it encompasses mighty civilizations and wildlife kingdoms in a vast area of 4.7 million sq ft (439,100 sq miles).

The highest point on earth, Mount Everest is to be found here, as is the most active volcanic site, the Kamchatka Peninsula in Siberia where 29 active volcanoes stage one of the most spectacular shows witnessed by humankind. In the continent's waters south and southeast of the mainland lies an entire realm of water-bound countries—archipelagos and islands—that extend to the Oceanic and Australian realms—Sri Lanka, Java, Sumatra, Borneo, Indonesia, the list is long.

The latest studies conducted by the American Museum for Natural History in 2006, and published in the acclaimed journal Nature, point to some startling discoveries in the region. Not only is this landmass home to some of the most ancient civilizations, it could also be the planet's original laboratory of mammals!

Like other parts of the globe, Asia is home to some magnificent splendors of nature. The "blue eye" of Siberia, Lake Baikal, one of world's deepest lakes, has as many as 330 rivers flowing into it; the chain of isles off the Indian east coast, the Andaman and Nicobar Islands, is home to one of the nomadic tribes that is close to extinction; the only three rivers to run parallel to each other—the Yangtze, the Mekong, and the Salween—cut through Yunnan Province in China and form one of the richest regions in the world in terms of biodiversity; and in Japan, the Beppu Hot Springs set the trend for "onsen culture" (thermal spring saunas in manicured Japanese gardens) that's as old as people can remember. Charlie Chaplin tried it, as did Mother Teresa, and the hordes of tourist that make their way to the springs every year.

**Lake Baikal,** Russia

- It would take approximately one year for all the major rivers—Volga, Don, Dnieper and Yenisei, Ural and Ob, Ganges and Orinoko, Amazon and Thames, Seine and Oder—to fill up the basin of Lake Baikal.

- Age and isolation are responsible for the unique freshwater fauna of Lake Baikal, which has earned it the name the "Galapagos of Russia." Eighty percent of the species that inhabit this lake are endemic.

# Lake Baikal

F lanked by mountains that rise higher than 6,600ft (2,000m) above the surface of the sea, Lake Baikal is situated in a depression in southeastern Siberia, within the Republic of Buryatia and the Irkutsk province of Russia. Created approximately 25 million years ago, Baikal is the oldest existing freshwater lake in the world. With a maximum depth of 5,315ft (1,620m), it is the deepest continental body of water.

The largest freshwater lake in the world in terms of volume—approximately 5,500cu miles (23,000cu km)— it holds about 20 percent of all the freshwater on the earth's surface. The lake measures 395 miles (636km) in length and has an average width of 30 miles (48km).

## NATURE RESERVES

The Barguzinsky Nature Reserve on the northeastern shore of the lake and the Baikalsky Nature Reserve on the southern shore were established in 1916 and 1969 respectively, in order to protect and conserve the lake and its environs. Between the two of them, the reserves protect over 1,000sq miles (2,564sq km) of territory, and help maintain the Baikal ecosystem in an undisturbed condition. Apart from protecting the area's vegetation and wildlife, these reserves also carry out research in the area of natural sciences. Since their creation, another nature reserve, two wildlife reserves, and two national parks have also been created in the area.

*Baikal Seal resting on a rock, Zabaikalsky National Park, Lake Baikal*

## BAIKAL'S HERITAGE

Around 1,200 archeological sites have been discovered around Lake Baikal, including rock drawings, stone walls, and remnants of ancient settlements; 1,000 of these monuments are legally protected. Mentioned in ancient Chinese, Muslim, and Russian writings, the Lake Baikal Basin has been inhabited in the past by tribes such as the Huns, ancient Turks, Uighurs, Kidanhs, and the Kaganates of Zhouzhanhs. The area also has a rich heritage of Mongolian culture, and the 13th-century Mongolian leader Genghis Khan is believed to have been born on Ol'khan Island. Today, the area is inhabited primarily by the Sayat and the Buryat people, many of whom lead very traditional lifestyles.

*About 50 species of edible fish live in Lake Baikal's icy waters, and are fished by locals*

The basin of Lake Baikal has been formed by a complex of grabens—that is, portions of the land dropping considerably lower than their surroundings along fault lines in the earth's crust. Faults are common in the area, and account for the presence of many hot mineral springs. The region is also prone to occasional but severe earthquakes, such as the one in 1862 that flooded a very large area in the northern Selenga delta, and created the new Proval Bay in Baikal.

The basin of this vast lake is asymmetrical—the steep western slopes provide a dramatic foil to the gently sloping eastern shore. The shoreline meanders for almost 1,300 miles (2,100km), and indents at the bays and inlets. The lake is fed by 336 rivers and streams, including the large Selenga, Barguzin, Upper Angara, Chikoy, and Uda rivers; however, only one river, the Angara, flows out of it again. About 45 islands and islets dot the surface of the almost crystal-clear water of the lake; Olkhon, occupying 270sq miles (700sq km), is the largest among them. Though Baikal's climate is milder than that of its surrounding territory, the surface of the lake freezes in January, and thaws only in May or June. In the deeper areas of the lake, waves can rise as high as 15ft (4.6m).

The great depths of Lake Baikal are a treasure house of an incredible variety of flora and fauna. While hundreds of plant species, most of which are endemic to Baikal, survive on or near the surface, between 1,500 and 1,800 animal species roam its depths. As many as 50 species of fish—with 25 species of gobies forming the majority—swim the lake. The golomyanka, a species of fish that is extraordinary for giving birth to live young, is endemic to Lake Baikal; so is the Baikal seal, or nerpa, the only mammal to live in the lake. More than 320 bird species have been discovered around the lake.

Covering an area of 33,980sq miles (88,000sq km), the lake and its surroundings, were declared a UNESCO World Heritage Site in 1996.

- The first official expedition to the Kamchatka Peninsula was commissioned by Tsar Peter I of Russia in 1725.

- The rivers of Kamchatka are said to contain the world's greatest diversity of salmonid fish, 11 species of which are known to co-exist peacefully in a single river.

## FLYING HIGH

In 1994 the eruption of the Klyuchevskoy Volcano in north Kamchatka, blasted a 49,000-ft (14,935-m) ash column into the sky. Winds of 150mph (240km/h) blew the ash cloud more than 620 miles (1,000km) southeast over the Pacific Ocean at altitudes of 31,000ft to 38,000ft (9,500m to 11,500m), sweeping across vital air routes in both Russian and US air space.

# Kamchatka Peninsula

The sight of bears dashing across the steaming thermal terrain is unforgettable, as are the fuming volcanoes, geysers, and hot springs of Russia's Kamchatka Peninsula. The geological uniqueness of Kamchatka is that it lies at the junction of major tectonic plates in an area of active volcanic activity where contemporary processes and the history of our planet cannot be separated from each other.

Jutting into the North Pacific Ocean and located in the northeast corner of Siberia, with Alaska to its northwest, Kamchatka—a 4,920-mile (1,500-km) long peninsula, roughly the size of Germany, Austria, and Switzerland put together—currently has 29 active volcanoes, plus 300 hibernating giants, looming over a wilderness of more than 150 thermal and mineral springs, geysers, and grizzlies. The region is also home to some unique species of animals, amphibians, birds and fish, such as salmon fish, sea otters, brown bears (the Kamchatka subspecies is one of the largest bears in the world), white-tailed eagles, gyr falcons, and Stellar's sea eagle. Out of the 1,168 plant species, 10 percent are not found anywhere else.

The remoteness and ruggedness of Kamchatka has prevented many from exploiting the land and defiling this beautiful landscape. Though it was first discovered by the Cossacks, it escaped attention until a Soviet strategic military base was set up here during the Cold War. It was only after the collapse of the Soviet Union that the area was opened to the public. The region today includes three federal reserves—the Kronotsky, Koryaksky, and Komandorsky, and four natural parks, Bystrinsky,

Yuzhno-Kamchatsky, Klyuchevskoy, and Nalychevo—and has been included in the UNESCO World Heritage site list since 1996. The nature reserve's greatest draws are the Uzon Caldera and the Valley of Geysers.

The Kamchatka is exceptionally beautiful—with large symmetrical volcanoes interspersed with lakes, wild rivers, and a spectacular coastline. It also boasts the unique phenomena of salmon-spawning areas and major concentrations of sea bird colonies along the coastal zone of the Bering Sea. The interior areas, such as Uzon Caldera, formed 40,000 years ago by a volcano that is now extinct, present a living on-site geological museum—containing hot springs, cold rivers, poisonous mud cauldrons, as well as pristine lakes full of fish, a berry tundra and birch forest, mountains, bogs, animals, and birds

Though untouched so far, the Kamchatka Peninsula is today facing increasing environmental degradation caused by gold mining, unregulated tourism, forest logging, and oil extraction.

*A brown bear mother and her cubs in a river at the foot of a volcanic mountain, Kamchatka Peninsula*

## VALLEY OF GEYSERS TRAGEDY

On June 3, 2007 the Valley of Geysers was seriously damaged by a massive slide of boulders, gravel, snow, and ice. Fortunately, the main geyser field Vitrazh (Stained Glass) and the largest geyser Velikan (The Giant) escaped the devastation. At the same time, however, the famous entrance to the valley and some of the most beautiful geysers including Pervenets (The Firstborn), Sakharny (Sugar), Sosed (The Neighbor), and Troynoy (The Triplets), were lost forever. It was the largest landslide ever to have taken place on the peninsula.

*The world-famous Geyser Valley in the Kronotsky Nature Reserve. The valley is one of the few places in the world where geysers jab holes through the earth's surface to spew boiling hot water into the air.*

- It was during the expeditions to the Gobi Desert—which took place between 1922 and 1925—that the first fossil dinosaur eggs were discovered.

- The American explorer Roy Chapman Andrews and his adventures in the Gobi are believed to have been the inspiration for the fictional character, Indiana Jones, the intrepid archeologist and adventurer.

**Gobi Desert,** Mongolia

*A camel in the Gobi Desert National Park, Khongoryn Els Dunes*

# Gobi Desert

Not unlike the waves that rise and fall in a vast ocean, the sand dunes of the great Gobi ripple and sing smoothly, belying its reputation of being one of the harshest and coldest deserts in the world. It is from this land, spread across 500,000sq miles (1,295,000sq km), dotted with flat hills, dry lakebeds, and arid grasslands that Genghis Khan and his fierce armies rode out to conquer new worlds.

In the 13th century Marco Polo crossed the Gobi Desert on his legendary travels to Asia and China; the renowned Venetian traveler went on to spend several years in the service of the Great Khan, Kublai Khan. Centuries later, between 1922 and 1930, explorer Roy Chapman Andrews staved off thirst and dehydration, thanks to leather pouches filled with water his party was carrying, and fought off brigands with his pistol as he scoured the dunes for the bones and nests of dinosaurs. Today, friendly Mongolian nomads, with their herds of sheep and camel, roam Gobi, the planet's northernmost desert.

Stretching more than 1,000 miles (1,613km) wide across northern Asia, the Gobi, meaning "waterless place," straddles the border of Mongolia and the area of northern China that makes up Inner Mongolia. Legend has it that this desert was created by a spell cast by a Mongolian chief accomplished in the art of necromancy. Forced to flee his village, with the Chinese army in hot pursuit, the Mongolian chieftain, unable to shake off his foes, employed black magic to shrink and shrivel the land behind him. Trapped in this harsh land devoid of water and vegetation, his Chinese adversaries died a slow and painful death.

The Gobi holds a special place in the hearts of prehistorians. It is one of the richest sites in the world for discovering dinosaur bones and eggs, with some of them being found mere inches below the surface. Gobi's hidden treasures include among others the well-preserved remains of the Oviraptor, a flying dinosaur, brooding over its eggs. It was the discovery of this skeleton that led paleontologists to consider for the first time that dinosaurs did actually protect their offspring, providing precious insight into the social behavior of the creatures.

Though it appears barren of any life forms to the ordinary eye, the Gobi does have its residents. Khulan (wild asses), Saiga antelopes, takhi horses, the endangered snow leopard, and the Gobi bear—the only kind of bear known to live in any desert—call Gobi their home. It also has a large population of ibex. The Gobi Desert is also home to poisonous reptiles—in his autobiography, *Under A Lucky Star*, Chapman describes killing 47 vipers in a single night! Hardy creatures that they are, these animals have to withstand temperatures that soar to more than 104°F (40°C) in summer and drop to well below freezing in winter.

## EKHIINGOL

An abandoned oasis encompassed within the southern end of the arid Gobi Desert, Ekhiingol was once a significant agricultural research station during the communist regime. Today, the township is inhabited by less than 20 families. Basic vegetables and fruits that are grown here are sold locally. Also, the absence of air transport facilities make trade with the outside world an impossible task; even the provincial capital is roughly 248 miles (400km) away, with no easily accessible routes.

## GOBI GURVANSAIKHAN NATIONAL PARK

Established in 1993, the Gobi Gurvansaikhan is the largest national park in Mongolia. Covering an area of around 10,530sq miles (27,000sq km), it is situated at the northern edge of the Gobi Desert. The name Gurvansaikhan meaning "Three Beauties," refers to the three sub-ranges of the desert—the east, middle, and west. A host of rare plants and animals are found in this park, including wild herds of gazelles and Bactrian camels. The world's most endangered big cat, the snow leopard, and the Siberian ibex are found in this park as well. The Gobi Gurvansaikhan National Park also encompasses the Yolyn Am, a deep and narrow gorge containing an ice field. The famous Khongoryn Els, or the "Singing Sands," is an area of sand dunes surrounded by stunningly beautiful colored sandstone formations.

*Gurvansaikhan National Park, Gobi Desert*

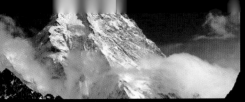

Austen Glacier.

**K2,** China/Pakistan

# K2

Rising up from the heart of the Karakoram Range, the magnificent K2 stands tall at a height of 28,251ft (8,611m). The second largest peak in the world after Mount Everest, K2 stands at the head of the Godwin Austen Glacier, a branch of the famous Baltoro Glacier.

Situated partly in China and partly in Pakistan, this gigantic pyramid-like mountain is currently under the jurisdiction of Pakistan. K2 was discovered and measured by Colonel T. G. Montgomerie of the Survey of India in 1856. While surveying the mountains of Kashmir, Montgomerie first noticed a high and prominent mountain in the direction of the Karakorams, and assigned it the symbol K1 (K standing for Karakoram); consequently, this mountain turned out to be the Masherbrum in the Hushe Valley. Behind it, Montgomerie noticed another impressive summit, and christened it K2. Known as Chogori by the locals, K2 is also called Mount Godwin Austen, after the 19th century geographer Colonel H. H. Godwin Austen, the first surveyor of the peak.

A majority of the mountain ranges of Asia—the Hindu Kush, the Pamir, the Karakoram, and the Himalayas—are a result of the collision of the Indian and Asian tectonic plates. Karakoram and its surrounding ranges were created in the Eocene Epoch, approximately 40 million years ago, by the upliftment of the earth's crust. The series of Ice Ages that occurred during the Pleistocene Epoch (over the past one million years) and the erosion processes of the Holocene Epoch (in the last 12,000 years) covered the peaks with snow and gave the mountain range its current shape and topography.

The K2 area comprises some of the most astounding peaks in the world. Trekking on the Baltoro Glacier is distinctly rewarding, as it provides amazing views of the Masherbrum at 25,420ft (7,750m), the Uli Biaho Tower at 20,042ft (6,109m), and Grand Cathedral at 17,148ft (5,228m). From Concordia—the point where Baltoro is met by its tributary glacier Godwin Austen Glacier—a spectacular view of K2 is possible, as well as of Broad Peak, Gasherbrum Group, Golden Throne, and Chogolisa.

## K2'S WALLS

The towering north face of K2 is one of the biggest rock walls in the world; the right side of this wall is occupied by the enormous north pillar. The incredible east wall rises high over the Godwin Austen Glacier and houses the gigantic terrace of ice called "K2's Arm." The west wall of the mountain is divided into two parts by the west pillar—one section rises over the Negrotto Glacier, while the main part rises over the Savoia Glacier. A huge rocky section called the "Barrel" can be found here. The south face of the mountain comprises two spurs; while the right one extends to the Abruzzi Spur, the left spur combines with the southwest pillar over the hanging glacier de Filippi.

*Broad Peak above Godwin Austen Glacier, Karakoram mountains, Pakistan*

## KARAKORAM'S IMPORTANCE

The Karakoram Range is of immense significance to geologists and scientists for many reasons. Located at the boundary of two colliding continental landmasses, it is one of the most geologically active areas in the world, thus forming a valuable source of information and observation in the understanding of tectonic plate movements. It is also of importance to studies that concentrate on uplift and thrust processes of a smaller scale. Continuing research of the mountain range are predicated on some very compelling assumptions, including one that holds such young and swiftly eroding mountains responsible for alterations in the global climate since their formation. Precious gemstones and fossils have also been discovered in some areas of the Karakoram Range.

*A section of the formidable Karakoram Range*

The first attempt to scale K2 was made in 1902 by an Anglo-Swiss expedition which ascended to a height of 18,600ft (5,670m) on the northeastern crest of the peak. Other remarkable but unsuccessful summit attempts include the Italian one of 1909. Led by Luigi Amadeo Giuseppe (Duke of Abruzzi), the party attempted the summit along the southeast ridge, which is today known as the Abruzzi Ridge. It was in 1954 that the summit was finally conquered along the Abruzzi by an Italian expedition—Achille Compagnoni and Lino Lacedelli reached the summit on July 31, 1954. The first woman to climb the peak was Wanda Rutkiewicz of Poland in 1986.

- The air at the top of Mount Everest is so thin that the human heart beats more than 170 times every minute to supply enough oxygen to keep the body functioning. At sea level the heart normally beats at around 70 times per minute.

- In 1852, Radhanath Sikdar, an Indian mathematician and surveyor, became the first person to classify Everest as the world's highest peak. Everest was then known by the name Peak XV.

**Mount Everest,** Nepal/China (Tibet)

# Mount Everest

Towering over the border of Nepal and Tibet, Mount Everest is the highest peak in the world at 29,035ft (8,850m). The peak is called Chomolungma, meaning "Mother Goddess of the Universe" in Tibetan, and Sagarmatha, meaning "Ocean Mother" in Sanskrit. The Everest massif is also the site for the fourth, fifth, and sixth highest mountains in the world—Lhotse at 27,939ft (8,516m), Makalu at 27,765ft (8,462m), and Cho Oyu at 26,906ft (8,201m). This cluster of peaks, joined by ridges that branch out from Everest, lies within the 56-mile (90-km) long subrange called Mahalangur Himal.

Everest was named in 1865 by the British Surveyor-General Andrew Scott Waugh after his predecessor George Everest. He said of his decision: "I was taught… by George Everest to assign to every geographical object its true or native appellation. But here is a mountain, most probably the highest in the world, without any local name… In the meantime the privilege… devolves on me to assign… a name whereby it may be known among civilized nations."

## THE WORST YEAR

In 1996, 12 people died because of unexpected bad weather while trying to reach the summit. The disaster gained wide publicity when John Krakauer, a journalist, wrote the bestselling book *Into Thin Air*. Later, it was made into a movie of the same name.

*Hiker on Mount Everest*

Ever since the peak gained popularity, conquering it has become a global obsession. Numerous summit expeditions were mounted, with the British spearheading with two unsuccessful attempts in the 1920s. George Leigh Mallory, a member of both the 1921 and 1922 British expeditions, along with Andrew Irvine, made an ill-fated summit attempt on June 8, 1924—the duo disappeared on the North Col route, never to return. His passion for peaks is perhaps best summed up in his famous retort to a journalist who asked him why he returned time and again to Everest: "Because it is there," he said.

In 1953, a successful assault on the summit was led by John Hunt, the leader of the ninth British expedition. Hunt selected two climbing pairs. The first pair, consisting of Tom Bourdillon and Charles Evans, turned back after coming close to the summit because of sheer exhaustion. On the following day, the expedition made its final attempt with its second climbing pair, Edmund Hillary and Tenzing Norgay, who approahed it via the South Col Route. They successfully scaled the peak on May 29.

By 1996, more than 15 routes had been charted to the peak, and by the year 2000, more than 1,600 people had achieved the precious feat of setting foot on top of the world's highest peak. The peak, however, has paid a heavy price for its popularity. Due to the increase in refuse, the area surrounding the base camp, as well as the peak itself, has earned the dubious credit of being referred to as the world's highest garbage dump.

## SAGARMATHA NATIONAL PARK

An area of 443 sq miles (1,148sq km) around the base of Everest on the Nepalese side was first declared a protected area in 1976, and given the name Sagarmatha National Park. It was designated a UNESCO Heritage Site in 1979 to protect it from increasing tourist incursions. The park is home to the Himalayan tahr, the Himalayan black bear, and the rare endangered snow leopard. The park also contains a variety of fauna, including the juniper and rhododendron, and more than 26 species of butterfly have been identified here. With its lowest point at 9,343ft (2,848m), the reserve is one of the highest in the world.

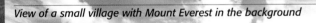
*View of a small village with Mount Everest in the background*

• Mount Fuji has been the inspiration for many artists and writers. One of the most celebrated artworks representing the mountain is the print series by artist Hokusai, depicting 36 views of the volcano.

• Owing to its religious associations, Mount Fuji is a popular site for pilgrimages. The devout not fit enough to undertake the climb up the mountain take lava soil from the base and fashion miniatures of it to worship in their houses.

**Mount Fuji,** Japan

# Mount Fuji

Situated within the Circum-Pacific volcanic chain, or the Ring of Fire, Japan has had a fairly dramatic history of volcanic activity. Long-dead lava fields, hot springs, and volcanoes—many of them still active—stand witness to this. Many of the country's volcanoes exhibit the classical cone shape, the most famous among them being Mount Fuji.

Fuji-san, better known as Mount Fuji, rises to an intimidating height of 12,388ft (3,776m). Situated on the island of Honshu, on the border of the Yamanashi and Shizuoka prefectures, Fuji is Japan's highest mountain, and also considered its holiest. The explosion crater Hoei-zan, halfway up the southern flank of the mountain, was formed during its last eruption in 1707. The eruption lasted 16 days, producing a 6-mile (10-km) wide cloud of smoke and ash that blocked the sunlight for days. The mountain's summit is actually its central crater, measuring around 1,600ft (500m) in diameter and 820ft (250m) in depth.

On the northern slope of the mountain lie the Fuji Five Lakes formed by the effects of lava flows—Lake Yamanaka, Lake Kawaguchi, Lake Sai, Lake Shoji, and Lake Motosu.

Mount Fuji's composition has been divided by scientists into four distinct phases of volcanic activity. The first, known as Sen-komitake, is composed of andesite—an igneous volcanic rock—that lies deep within the mountain. The second, a basalt layer, is called Komitake Fuji. Old Fuji, the next layer, was probably formed almost 100,000 years ago, over Komitake Fuji. What we see today is called New Fuji, believed to have been formed only about 10,000 years ago.

The geological history of the peak—the formation of a composite volcano by the deposition of successive layers of lava and ash—appears to almost mirror the peak's sacred past, shaped and affected by successive sects, religions, and beliefs. Shintoism, established around the sixth century, spawned the belief that natural features such as trees,

## WAITING TO EXHALE

In 2002, Japan issued a report hinting at a possible eruption of Mount Fuji, with projected damages of around $21 billion. Following the report, seismologists and volcano experts have been conducting tests and carrying out research, hoping to predict the route that the flowing lava might take and thus preparing evacuation plans on the basis accordingly.

*Mount Fuji from a distance*

lakes, and mountains were the dwelling places of the Kami, spirits which could be invoked through prayer and ritual. The Buddhists considered Fuji a symbol of meditation, and named its summit *zenjo*—a term that describes the perfect meditative state. The Shugendo religious sect, which gained prominence in the ninth century, cemented the beliefs of those who wanted to commune with deities on mountain summits and gain supernatural powers. Historically, the Shugendo were also the first people to establish a climbing route all the way to the mountain's summit in the 14th century.

Mount Fuji's perfectly conical summit and the peak's startling beauty have inspired many works of art and literature, and attract millions of pilgrims every year. Apart from its religious heritage, Mount Fuji also has a rich warrior tradition. In ancient times, the Samurai would use the base of the mountain as a training area. The Japan Self-Defence Forces and the US armed forces have operated bases nearby since 2006.

*Lake in front of mountain*

## VOLCANIC SOURCES

The younger rocks of Japan are largely volcanic in origin. However, the country is not unique in this respect—all the lands and islands of the Circum-Pacific region experience some form of volcanic activity.
The Pacific Rim is called the "Ring of Fire" by geologists. The expansion of the ocean floor is the reason for the creation of such a ring. When the ocean floor expands in one area, it needs to be accommodated elsewhere; this usually happens around the margins of the ocean, as the oceanic crust slides under the adjacent continental crust.
But with the descent of the oceanic crust into the earth's mantle, it becomes heated due to friction between the two plates, causing melting and expansion. The resulting increase in pressure is reduced by volcanic activity, and the accompanying tension in the rocks is relieved by earthquakes.

The hot springs and geysers of Beppu emit over 2 million cu ft (56,600cu m) of water every day.
- There are about 3,500 fumaroles (vents which allow gases to escape), hot springs and geysers in the Beppu area.

**Beppu,** Japan

*A thermal spa pool in Beppu*

## HOT HOUSE

Agricultural research facilities such as the Oita Research Station for Agricultural Utilization of Hot Springs also make use of geothermal water. The mineral-rich water is used to irrigate and heat the greenhouses all year round, and experimental crops of fruits and vegetables such as tomatoes, cucumbers, mangos, and bananas are harvested regularly. The breeding of species such as azaleas, rhododendrons, carnations, and so on is also being researched extensively at the facility.

# Beppu

Situated at the base of a steep slope of volcanic detritus flung out by one of the several volcanoes in its immediate neighborhood, the city of Beppu has been one of Japan's most famous tourist destinations since the end of the 19th century. Huge quantities of water are emitted every day by its hot springs and geysers. Visitors flock in from all over the world, eager to immerse their bodies in the hot sand baths and the healing, mineral-laden waters that Beppu offers.

Part of the Beppu-Shimabara graben, in Kyushu, Beppu is situated at its eastern end. One of the largest thermal areas in the world, Beppu, exhibits the typical volcanic features that are associated with the formation of a graben—an elongated and lowered portion of the earth's crust that lies between two fault lines.

The Beppu district has eight distinct areas of hot water springs: Beppu Onsen, Kannawa Onsen, Shibaseki Onsen, Myoban Onsen, Kamegawa Onsen, Kankaiji Onsen, Hotta Onsen, and Hamawaki Onsen. Apart from its spas, Beppu is also famous worldwide for its distinctive boiling ponds, or *jigokus*. Expelling mud high into the air, these steaming geysers are the most extraordinary of Beppu's natural attractions. The word *jigoku* means "burning hell", and the name is derived from ancient Buddhist scriptures.

Beppu's nine jigokus exhibit a fantastic range of colors and sizes. Boiling gray viscous mud that bubbles

## VOLCANOES AND THERMAL SPRINGS

Japan has been described as sitting on "Mother Earth's Cradle," and with more than 500 volcanoes on the main island, the description is apt. Many volcanoes are extinct but some remain active, including Fuji, Asama, and Aso. In addition to volcanoes there are hundreds of areas of thermal activity, the best known being Noboribetsu, Beppu, and Kusatsu.

Noboribetsu, on Hokkaido, Japan's largest island, is home to the Jigokudani Hot Springs. Geysers, boiling springs, and bubbling mud, as well as vents that give off a rather unpleasant sulphurous gas, occupy a volcanic crater 1.25 miles (2km) across.

*Area of thermal activity*

continuously with a sinister sound characterizes the Bozu jigoku. The large Umi jigoku (sea hell) is deep blue and reflects the color of the sky. Jets of water that often reach a height of 82ft (20m) are forcefully ejected by the Tatsumaki jigoku (water-spout hell) at intervals of 20–30min. The most spectacular, however, is the vermilion-hued Chinoike jigoku (blood-pond hell)—the waters of this jigoku are colored red because of oxidized precipitates. This jigoku is a hydrothermal eruption crater, and nine eruptions have been recorded between 1875 and 1927.

Beppu's onsens cater to a diverse clientele, ranging from sophisticated vacationers to local workers. Since central heating is limited in Japan, Beppu's baths serve as a refuge for many people during the bitterly long cold winters. However, the baths are primarily meant for soaking and relaxation; nobody enters a bath unclean or without being freshly washed. Very often, Beppu's waters need to be diluted and cooled since they are often too hot for the human skin.

Human beings are not the only creatures that benefit from the hot springs of Beppu. In winter, small monkeys often seek comfort from the volcanically heated waters of the area. The animals head to Beppu's thermal pools, and sit submerged up to the neck in the warm water, while snow settles on their heads. Often, these clever creatures formulate a rota system—one or two delegates are sent to gather food while the others soak in the warm waters.

- The most famous Buddhist monasteries in the Huangshan Mountains—Xiangfu, Ciguang, Cuiwei, and Zhibo—are together referred to as the Four Big Monasteries.
- Mao Feng, meaning Fur Peak, named because of the downy tips of its leaves, is a world-renowned green tea from the Huangshan area.

Huangshan Mountains, China

# Huangshan Mountains

*Pagoda on Mount Huangshan*

The magnificent Huangshan Mountains, nestled in the southern reaches of the Anhui province in eastern China, were born of tectonic upheavals almost 100 million years ago. The movements of the earth's crust resulted in granite being thrust vertically upwards from the sea bed. Later, glacial erosion worked into the rock to carve out and shape the peaks and valleys that we see today. The scenic reserve spans an area of 60sq miles (154sq km) and encompasses numerous peaks, 77 of which are more than 3,280ft (1,000m) in height. The tallest peaks are Lian Hua Feng, or Lotus Flower Peak, at 6,114ft (1,864m); Guang Ming Ding, or Bright Summit Peak, at 6,035ft (1,840m); and Tian Du Feng, or Celestial Peak, at 6,000ft (1,829m).

## BUDDHA'S LIGHT

A frequent occurrence in Huangshan, Buddha's Light is better known as a "glory" or an anthelion. An optical phenomenon, it occurs when a combination of diffraction, reflection, and refraction scatters light back to its source. The Buddha's Light displays all the colors of the spectrum, and occurs only when mountains reach higher than the level of the lowest clouds. Seen in the direction opposite the sun, it sometimes forms a circle around the shadow, resembling a halo. According to legends, a person whose shadow is so encircled by Buddha's Light is led to the path of enlightenment. On average, Buddha's Light appears once or twice a month in the Huangshan.

## GUEST-GREETING PINE

The most photographed of the famous pine trees in the Huangshan Mountains is the Guest-Greeting Pine, which stands at the entrance of the Jade Screen Pavilion. The branches of the tree are like arms outstretched to embrace visitors in a gesture of welcome. This popular pine has become a symbol of hospitality and warmth of the Chinese people.

*The* Ying Ke Song *or*
*Welcoming Guest Pine*

The unusual terrain of these mountains is responsible for a vertical change in its climate. Thus, the slopes of the mountains exhibit a distinctive vertical distribution of vegetation—the summit, the middle zones, and the foot of the mountains have plants that belong in the frigid, temperate, and subtropical climes respectively. Declared a World Heritage Site by UNESCO in 1990, this mountain chain nurtures more than 1,450 different plant species. The Huangshan also provides a natural habitat for a considerable variety of fauna. Monkeys, goats, deer, and many rare and exotic birds are among those who call these mountains their home.

These beautiful mountains have spawned countless legends over the centuries. The shapes given to the mountains by the actions of natural elements are often reflected in the exotic names of the peaks. Extraordinarily shaped natural formations such as the Immortal Showing the Way, Rooster Crowing at Dawn, Squirrel Jumping into Heavenly Capital, and Monkey Watching the Sea are shrouded in rich and colorful fables, and are also the reason why the Huangshan Mountains are considered a museum of natural sculptures.

This mountain range had been known as the Yishan since the reign of the Qin Dynasty (c. 221–207BC). The name Huangshan, which translates to Yellow Mountains, is credited to the famous Tang poet Li Bai, and it has been known as the Huangshan since AD747. The mountains have inspired artists and poets from time immemorial. The famous traveler and geographer of the Ming Dynasty (1368–1644), Xu Xiake, described Huangshan as the best of all mountains in China, unequaled by any other. Huangshan's stunning beauty and its fascinating and surreal atmosphere are estimated to have inspired more than 100 works of prose and almost 20,000 poems. The famous Four Wonders of the Huangshan—the peculiarly shaped pines, the rock figurines, the sea of clouds that swathes the peaks, and the clusters of hot springs—have been praised by many.

- More than half the area of the Taroko National Park is covered by mountains over 6,560ft (2,000m) tall; the most famous of these are Mount Nanhu, the Hehuan Snow Cap, and the Cilai Peaks.
- The name Taroko comes from the Aboriginal language *Truku*, which means "magnificent and splendid."

**Taroko Gorge,** Taiwan

# Taroko Gorge

Sheer marble cliffs and twisting tunnels make up the rugged landscape of the Taroko Gorge in Taiwan. Located in Hualien County on the eastern coast of the country, it is characterized by steep slopes and craggy ravines, through which the Liwu River flows.

The origin of this spectacular network of gorges can be traced back 230 million years to the formation of coral reefs in tropical shallows where Taiwan stands today. Over time, a process called lithification occurred and the coral reefs were transformed into limestone. Subsequently, the intense pressure and subterranean heat caused the limestone to metamorphose into marble. Approximately 70 million years ago, collisions between tectonic plates forced the sea bed to fracture and the Taiwan Mountain Range rose out of the ocean, along with the stratum of marble. The action of streams and rainwater over millions of years has since then eroded this layer of marble to carve out the breathtaking Taroko Gorge.

Much of Taroko's beauty is attributed to the Liwu river that rushes enthusiastically through the middle of the gorge. The erosive action of the river, coupled with the phenomenon of uplifting, has sculpted the layers of marble and forged through the 12-mile (19-km) long ravine resulting in incredible formations of sheer cliffs, dark tunnels, steep chasms, deep valleys, columns of marble, cascading waterfalls, and churning white water rapids. Together, these features combine to form the most spectacular natural landscape found in Taiwan.

## Eternal Spring Shrine

The Changchun or "Eternal Spring Shrine" is a Zen monastery that straddles a waterfall near the entrance to Taroko Gorge. This shrine was constructed in memory of the workers who lost their lives during the construction of the Cross-Island Highway that runs along the bottom of the gorge, commanding magnificent views of the Pacific Ocean and the mountains on either side. Behind the monastery are stone steps called the "Heavenly Stairs," which lead to the Guanyin Cave.

*The location of the Eternal Spring Shrine affords visitors a breathtaking panorama of mountains*

## ANCIENT HERITAGE

Seven prehistoric sites, which testify to human habitation of the area for 3,000 years, have been discovered within Taroko National Park. The most famous of these is the Taroko Site, which comprises 85 neatly-arranged monoliths. The artifacts found in this region indicate a blend of several ancient cultures such as the Pei-Nan, Chi-Lin, and Shih San Hang. Other relics found in the park include fragments of pottery, stone axes, stone spinning wheels, and coffins.

The Taroko National Park was set up in 1937 as the Tsugitaka Taroko National Park while Taiwan was still a colony of the Empire of Japan, and abolished after Japan's defeat in World War II. It was subsequently re-established on November 28, 1986. Running 22 miles (36km) from north to south and 26 miles (42km) from east to west, the park exhibits a great range of altitude—while the mouth of the Liwu River is close to sea level, the highest point is the peak of the majestic Mount Nanhu which rises to a height of 12,273ft (3,742m).

Numerous trails that traverse the park provide visitors with the opportunity to experience its astounding ecosystem and topography. Most famous of these is the Tunnel of Nine Turns Trail, which takes visitors through an area of cliff, canyon, tunnel, and waterfall, and provides a small but comprehensive taste of the park's scenic beauty. The Pai Yang, Yin Tai, Chang Chun, and Lu Shui are the most dramatic and exquisite of the park's waterfalls.

The natural habitats in the Taroko National Park remain generally undisturbed, and thus it is home to a great variety of wildlife. The different climactic zones of the park mean that its vegetation is very diverse, the variety of plants ranging from the alpine juniper to the dwarf bamboo. More than 1,200 native species of plants, 132 of which are endangered, have been discovered within the park boundaries. The park is also home to 144 species of birds and scores of other animals. On top of this, researchers have identified 251 types of butterfly.

**Reed Flute Cave,** China

- The Reed Flute Cave gets its name *Ludi Yan* in Chinese from the lush and verdant growth of *Ludi cao* (a reed grass—used for making flutes) that is found at its entrance.
- Large enough to accommodate a thousand people at a time, the Reed Flute Cave was used as an air-raid shelter during World War II.

# Reed Flute Cave

A dazzling array of stalactites and stalagmites in countless hues make up the extraordinarily mesmerizing Reed Flute Cave in Guilin. Located in the Guangxi Zhuang Autonomous Region of China, on the shores of the beautiful Lijiang River, Guilin is an ancient city surrounded by majestic mountains, sparkling waters, and exquisite limestone topography that adds to the natural beauty of the city. The Reed Flute Cave is situated on the southern shoulder of the Guangming Hill, to the northwest of the city, a short distance away from it.

The formation of the Reed Flute Cave (Ludi Yan) can be traced back millions of years. The area that is now Guilin was once occupied by a vast sea until about 190 million years ago, when movements of the tectonic plates thrust the sea bed up. The uplifted bedrock made of limestone has since then been weathered and eroded by water to form the fantastic karst features, underground streams, and caves that are characteristic of Guilin's topography.

## THE STRUCTURES OF LUDI YAN

Often called "A Palace of Natural Art," the formations within the cave resemble gemstones such as jade, agate, and amber in the colored light. Some of the more remarkable decoration (speleothems) of this cave include a huge stalagmite and a rather small conical stalactite—the peculiar combined shape of the two earns it the epithet "Fish Tail Peak." One of the grottos within the cave—an area that looks somewhat like a miniature Guilin—is called the Crystal Palace of the Dragon King. The cave also contains several drapery formations and exquisite reflecting pools.

*Stalactites and stalagmites, Reed Flute Cave, Guilin'*

The largest of the caves in the Guilin area, the Reed Flute Cave was carved out by an underground stream which left carbonate deposits that are responsible for creating the enthralling assortment of stalactites, stone pillars, and intriguingly shaped rocks that inhabit the cave. This dripstone cave is approximately 790ft (240m) long. Zigzagging paths have been laid down through the serried columns of stone so that visitors are able to get a closer look at every remarkable formation in the cave. The U-shaped sightseeing route enables tourists to enter the cave from one side and, after taking in the sights and sounds of the extraordinary structures and significnant areas, to exit from another cavern very close to the point of entry. A tour through the cave usually takes up to an hour.

The names given to the various features within the cave bear witness to the Chinese penchant for storytelling. Bearing picturesque and evocative names such as Virgin Forest, Flower and Fruit Mountain, Dragon Pagoda, Crystal Palace, and so on, several features within the caves are not unsurprisingly swathed in myth and fable. Imagination is required to associate the structures with plants, animals, and other creatures, and the stories associated with these features abound, further adding to the magic and romance of the stone formations.

The formations within the cave are artificially illuminated to create a mystical aura and enhance their attributes; many kinds of lights are employed in the different sections of the cave. Photography within the cave is usually not permitted because the light is not sufficient; however, certain spots such as the Crystal Palace and Flower and Fruit Mountain have arrangements for special illumination, and visitors are allowed to take photographs for a fee.

The Reed Flute Cave has been a popular destination for tourists for the last 13 centuries. Seventy inscriptions, believed to be travelogues and poems, dating back to the rule of the Tang Dynasty (AD618–907) have been discovered on its walls.

## GUILIN

Guilin has been the socio-political and cultural center of the Guangxi area for more than two millennia. Located in the northeastern part of the province, Guilin's claim to fame since long ago has been its astounding scenic beauty. While the city is a wonderful place to visit at any time of the year because of its mild subtropical climate, it is particularly attractive in autumn, when the fragrance of the sweet osmanthus in bloom pervades the air throughout the city; the name Guilin, in fact, translates as "forest of sweet osmanthus." Apart from the mountains, the Banyan and Fire Tree lakes, the Reed Flute, and the Seven Star Caves are the most outstanding and sought after tourist destinations around the city.

**Stone Forest,** China

- The Sani is the largest tribe of the Yi ethnic group that has inhabited Yunnan for centuries. Other tribes of the group include the Axi, Heiyi, Baiyi, Yiqing, and Ayizi.
- The Lunan Stone Forest Scenic Zone has been on the tentative list at UNESCO, to be considered as a World Heritage Site, since 1996.

# Stone Forest

Fantastic peaks, pillars, stalagmites, depressions, underground rivers, caves, and spectacular stone pinnacles make up Shilin, or the Lunan Stone Forest, in the Yunnan Province of China. Located in the Lunan Yi Nationality Autonomous County, 78 miles (126km) southeast of Kunming city, the area derives its name from the magnificent natural formations crowding together like a dense jungle of stone.

A popular tourist destination, this region of magnificent karst topography attracted attention as early as the 12th century. Its popularity can be traced back to the days of the Ming Dynasty (which flourished between 1368 and 1644). It was during this period that the Stone Forest was termed the "First Wonder of the World," a moniker that is often used even today. Steeped in myth and legend, this stony wilderness occupies about 156sq miles (400sq km),

and is roughly divided into three sections—the Greater Stone Forest, Lesser Stone Forest, and Outer Stone Forest.

The area of densest karst formations is known as the Greater Stone Forest. Resembling a strange fairyland carved out of stone, this area is covered with bizarre formations that look like castles, trees, ancient fortresses, birds, and animals. Adjoining the Greater Stone Forest, an area of odd shapes interspersed with lush lawns and clusters of trees and bamboos, make up the Lesser Stone Forest. Surrounding these sections is the Outer Stone Forest, an area across which various stone peaks of myriad shapes—such as the Lion Hill, which resembles a lion squatting—are scattered. Many of the stone structures found in the area bear fantastic names, such as "Cluster of Pinnacles Propping Up the Sky" and "Stone Singing Praises of Plum," and have marvelous legends attached to their formation.

## SHILIN'S CAVES

The Zhiyun and Strange Wind caves are two of the most remarkable karst caves in the Stone Forest Area. Zhiyun encompasses several caverns and grottos, many of which have astounding acoustic effects. It also showcases the wonders of underground lava topography at its best, with columns and pillars of strange and unique shapes. The Strange Wind Cave is remarkable for the short gusts of air that blow intermittently out of the cave during the months of August through to November every year. A peculiar conjunction and positioning at different levels of an underground river and a siphon spring are responsible for this odd phenomenon.

*Limestone pinnacles, Shilin*

Geologist have attributed the formation of the Stone Forest to uplift and erosion. About 270 million years ago, during the carboniferous period of the Paleozoic era, the Shilin area was a shallow sea overlying a bed of sandstone and limestone. The sea retreated due to tectonic upheavals and triggered movements of the lithosphere, which in turn caused it to crumple and rise. Over eons, these clusters of hunkering rock were subjected to erosion by the elements, resulting in the formation of the incredible structures that we see today.

The Lunan Stone Forest region also houses several ponds, reservoirs, waterfalls, and five underground rivers. The most striking of these include the Long Lake, Moon Lake, Feilong Waterfall, Da Dieshui Falls, and the Dadie Waterfall.

The picturesque Stone Forest area has been inhabited by the Sani people of the Yi ethnic group for thousands of years. The lifestyle of these warm and kind people is closely interlinked with the environment, and they live in perfect harmony with nature. With their many festivals of song and dance, the Sani people themselves have become a major attraction for tourists visiting the area.

*The Stone Forest, Yunnan Province*

## THE LEGEND OF ASHIMA

According to a popular legend that surrounds the Stone Forest, Ashima, a young Sani girl defied the will of a tyrannical landlord who wanted to marry her. While trying to flee her tormentor, Ashima was turned into a stone peak at Shilin. The subject of a folk poem, the story of Ashima has gained such popularity that it has to date been translated into more than 20 languages, including English, Russian, and Japanese, and has even been adapted as a movie. The word *Ashima* translates into "girl as beautiful as gold," and is today considered a symbol of the virtues that the people of the area try imitate

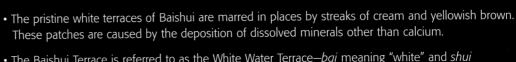

- The pristine white terraces of Baishui are marred in places by streaks of cream and yellowish brown. These patches are caused by the deposition of dissolved minerals other than calcium.

- The Baishui Terrace is referred to as the White Water Terrace—*bai* meaning "white" and *shui* meaning "water."

**Baishui Terrace,** China

## BAISHUI AND THE DONGBA CULTURE

The Baishui Terrace is of immense religious significance to the Naxi people of the Dongba culture, and is considered a sacred site by the locals. Three traditional pieces of Dongba literature were discovered in the Baishui Terrace area—*Chongbangtong* (an account of the world's creation), *Dong'aishu'ai* (an epic about Naxi heroes), and *Lubanlurao* (a description of the ancient Naxis' quest for their current home).

# Baishui Terrace

A magnificent karst terrain composed of calcite minerals, the Baishui Terrace is ranked among the most beautiful scenic spots in China. Located near the Baidi Village at Sanba, 63 miles (101km) south of the county seat of Zhongdian, the Baishui Terrace is one of the most spectacular examples of its kind.

Geologists believe that the formation of the Baishui Terrace dates back 200,000 to 300,000 years. This dazzling sinter was formed by the deposition of calcium bicarbonate by flowing spring water rich in minerals over hundreds of thousands of years. The subsequent piling up of calcite sediments after the decomposition of the calcium bicarbonate led to the creation of this impressive landform.

The sparkling white Baishui Terrace is situated on a slope at the foot of the Haba Snow Mountain at a height of 7,806ft (2,380m) above sea level. Occupying a total area of 1.2sq miles (3sq km), it is actually made up of a series of short terraces. These individual levels taken together make Baishui one of the largest terraces in China and the world. Stretching for about 525ft (160m) at its widest point, the Baishui Terrace runs 459ft (140m) down the slope of the mountain.

Spring water flows down from the top of the mountain into a semi-circular pool at the top of the terrace, and then trickles slowly over the rim of one row of the terrace to another, right to the bottom, leaving behind patterned tracks of exquisite beauty. The terrace, with its gleaming wet, marble-white walls, and the sparkling water that fills the shallow basins behind the terrace walls, looks like a silver waterfall arrested and frozen in time and place.

Baishui Terrace is believed to be the place where the founding father of the Dongba culture settled on his way back from Tibet and first started preaching his beliefs. Every year, on the eighth day of the second month of the lunar calendar, the Naxi people gather together at

*Series of limestone terraces, Baishui Terrace, China*

the terrace to commemorate the foundation of the Dongba culture. People from all over the country assemble around Baishui Terrace and the festival is celebrated with song and dance. Visitors in the area, too, are encouraged to participate in the festival.

The Baishui Terrace forms a part of the greater Three Parallel Rivers scenic area in the northwestern Yunnan Province. Deriving its name from the Nu, Jinsha, and Lancang rivers, the Three Parallel Rivers area is spread over 13,260sq miles (34,000sq km) and encompasses a wide range of geological features and biological environments, including the mesmeric and mystical Shangri-la. With its high mountain glacier lakes, karst topography, waterfalls, grassy marshlands, and other such stunning natural formations, the area was inscribed as a World Heritage Site by UNESCO in 2003.

## PAMUKKALE

The pristine white Pamukkale in Turkey is the only other outstanding example of a limestone terrace in the world. Formed in much the same way as Baishui, the Pamukkale is also characterized by mineral springs, to which tourists were granted free access until recently. Ill-managed tourist activity in the area has led to the discoloration of the white stone basins and choked the natural drainage. Visitors are now allowed to walk only along carefully demarcated pathways.

*Pools in eroded limestone terraces, Pamukkale, Turkey*

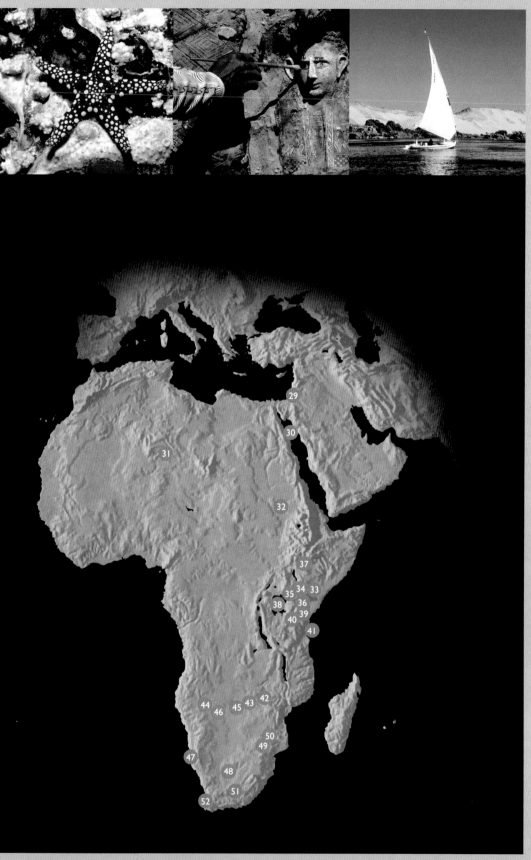

# Africa & Middle East

The Dead Sea, North Sea, Mediterranean Sea, the indomitable Kalahari and Namib deserts, the mighty rivers Nile, Tigris, Euphrates, Lakes Victoria, and Nakuru, Mount Kenya and Mount Kilimanjaro are just a few of this region's wonders. There are many, many more natural monuments and national parks located in what is often described as the "cradle of civilization"—Africa, and the area known as the Middle East. Africa boasts the largest combinations of natural diversity and wildlife density in a single continent. With the help of exciting safaris in the region one can explore its hot deserts, sweeping savannahs and wet rainforests, and meet its illustrious, but often endangered, residents, such as the elephant, giraffe, zebra, lion, black rhino, cheetah and gazelle.

And this vast region is still on the move—the Great Rift Valley in east Africa is growing wider by the year, tearing a chunk of land from the African continent in a tectonic process that has been going on for 20 million years. It is predicted that one day, not in our lifetimes, the country of Somalia will be set adrift from the rest of the African mainland. Meanwhile, archeologists continue to find the remains of our earliest ancestors, revealed by this constant upheaval.

From the southern and eastern shores of the Mediterranean Sea extending from Morocco to the Arabian Peninsula and Iran, fed by the Nile and the Euphrates rivers, the Middle East is not short of spectacular attractions. In its Elburz Mountains, in central Iran, lies one of the most intriguing deserts—the Great Salt Desert, made entirely of salt. Meanwhile, in Oman's Wadi Dawkah, UNESCO has come forward to protect the only known group of frankincense trees that supplied exotic smells to the world in ancient and medieval times. And who can ignore the wonders of the Dead Sea—the only place where the crust of Earth actually sinks 1,364ft (416m) below sea level!

- Seven million tons of water evaporate daily from the Dead Sea; figures for the sea's salinity vary from 26 to 35 percent.

- Since the 1960s, the flow from the Jordan River has reduced by 90 percent, reducing the surface level of the Dead Sea by 82ft (25m).

**Dead Sea,** Israel/Jordan

# Dead Sea

The lowest body of water on the earth's surface, as well as the most saline and buoyant, the Dead Sea is a salt lake of which the minerals have served as a natural spa for thousands of years. Forming part of the Israel–Jordan border, it is 50 miles (80km) in length and 11 miles (18km) wide, and at 1,371ft (418m) below sea level, the lowest point on the planet. A dramatically beautiful landscape formed of the blue sea and otherworldly salt deposits on the shore and rocks, the Dead Sea is flanked by majestic desert mountains and rolling hills rising to the east and west, which are believed to have been home to the Biblical cities of Sodom and Gomorrah. Subtropical oases outline the sea, and mineral-rich springs, primarily sulphur, rise from deep down into little ponds along the Dead Sea shores.

The name Dead Sea aptly describes this body of water; no plant or animal life can survive in its waters, though a negligible measure of bacteria and microbial fungi manage to withstand the hypersalinity. Humans can float effortlessly on the surface of the sea; in fact, it is so buoyant that most swimmers can't put their feet down. It is, however, dangerous to swallow the water. The shores of the Dead Sea are an ideal place to sunbathe because the more harmful ultraviolet rays get filtered out, and the surrounding atmosphere is high in oxygen due to the high barometric pressure.

## HARVESTING THE DEAD SEA

The salts and minerals of the Dead Sea caught the eye of chemists in the early part of the 20th century and it became an economically important source of potash, bromine, gypsum, salt, and other chemical products, which could be extracted inexpensively. Today, potash is the most valuable of the minerals extracted, used in the manufacture of fertilizers. The Dead Sea Works Ltd. harvests the valuable minerals in Israel, while the Arab Potash Works does the same in Jordan.

*Eastern shore of the Dead Sea, with a salt concentration of more than 30 percent*

A landlocked body of water, fed primarily by the river Jordan, it owes its existence to the 22,960ft (7,000m) fault line that links Asia and Africa's Great Rift Valley. As the water has no outlet and can only evaporate, what is left behind is saturated with salts and minerals. As a result, salt precipitates and piles up at the bottom of the sea. So the mysterious depths of the sea serve up a cocktail of chloride salts—magnesium, sodium, potassium, and others.

Its surface being least saline, the sea turns saltier as its depth increases. At 130ft (40m) below the surface, each liter of water contains about 12oz (300g) of salt, making it ten times more saline than a regular ocean. Below 300ft (91m), however, the salt content for similiar quantities of water increases to 13.2oz (332g) of salt per liter. The Dead Sea does not restrict itself to supplying salts, and regularly spits out black pebbles of asphalt. Little wonder then that the ancient Greeks referred to it as "Lake Asphaltites."

Though the lake itself is devoid of life, its surrounding mountain areas are home to a number of animals, including the Nubian ibex, the caracal, jackals, foxes, and the Arabian leopard, as well as hundreds of bird species. Both Jordan and Israel have established nature reserves around the Dead Sea—the Mujib Nature Reserve located in the Wadi Mujib gorge in Jordan and the Ein Gedi Nature Reserve in Israel.

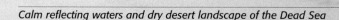
*Calm reflecting waters and dry desert landscape of the Dead Sea*

## DEAD SEA SCROLLS

On the northern shores of the Dead Sea, in the Judaean Desert (now the Qumran National Park), lie the ancient caves and settlement where, in 1947, a young Bedouin shepherd went searching for a stray goat. He instead stumbled upon a long-forgotten cave, and in it, jars filled with ancient scrolls, the oldest Biblical documents ever found. The search by the Bedouins yielded seven scrolls, but a decade of intensive search later thousands of scroll fragments were discovered from 11 caves. These scrolls outdate any other surviving Biblical manuscript by almost one thousand years. Named the *Dead Sea Scrolls*, they were well preserved because of the low atmospheric humidity. Many of the original *Dead Sea Scrolls* are displayed in the Shrine of the Book at the Israel Museum, Jerusalem.

- The Red Sea was formed because of continental rift that took place millions of years ago. However, in 2006, after another unusually large rift in Ethiopia, scientists have reason to believe that the Red Sea is widening and in future will extend further southward.

- It is not just the waters at Ras Mohammed that are rich in coral; the peninsula is also made up of a fossil coral reef, which is thought to have emerged from the waters some 75,000 years ago.

**n Red Sea,** Egypt/Israel/Jordan

# Northern Red Sea

*Hawksbill turtle, Red Sea, Egypt*

The Northern Red Sea follows the coastline of Egypt and extends its arms into the Gulf of Suez and the Gulf of Aqaba, where it touches Israel and Jordan. Its vast surrounding expanses of sand make it difficult to imagine that some of the planet's richest and most magnificent coral reefs rise from the floor of its northern reaches, especially at the confluence of the two gulfs. Here lies an underwater paradise, with dramatically lit caves and caverns, populated by an amazing diversity and richness of species, not just of coral but also of fish, from the deadly stone fish and butterfly fish to triggerfish and parrotfish, as well as dolphins, sea turtles, and sharks. Add shipwrecks, clear visibility, insignificant wave action, and warm temperatures all year long, and it is not surprisingly considered to make for some of the world's finest diving.

The many marine splendors of the Northern Red Sea are showcased in Egypt's Ras Mohammed National Park, home to some of the world's finest coral reefs. Such is their scale, and abundance, that they almost constitute a coral plateau. The intense sunlight of the region pierces the sea, causing an explosion of color on the reefs' swaying soft corals, which shine in a sunburst of shades from yellow to orange, purple to green. It is not just the corals that add color to the blue depths; sea anemones glow a bright orange and schools of shimmering tropical fish swim by in all hues, shapes, and sizes.

## CORAL EXAMINATION

The Northern Red Sea boasts a thriving coral reef ecosystem. Reasons for this wealth of corals include the lack of sedimentation, which would have otherwise hindered coral growth; benevolent undersea currents that disperse larva and the coral fragments necessary for reproduction; intense sunlight that provides abundant solar energy for the photo-synthesizing zooxanthellae that live within the corals, and the fact that the area is relatively sheltered from powerful storms. Interestingly, coral growth is restricted by salinity, yet it thrives in the Red Sea, which is an extremely saline body of water.

A starfish feeding on coral in the Northern Red Sea

## LIFE AQUATIC

Thirty million years ago, the northern end of the Red Sea flowed into the Mediterranean Sea, but was closed at its southern end. Thus, hundreds of species of marine life from the Atlantic entered the sea to breed. Ten million years later, shifts in the earth's tectonic plates barricaded the Red Sea's northern end and opened its southern end to the Indian Ocean, letting in Indo-Pacific species of fish, which are now found in these waters. This explains the abundant marine life and the richness of species in its depths.

The reefs at Ras Mohammed are made up of hundreds of varieties of coral, from the tiny soft ones to the harder reef-building kind that form the backbone of these undersea wonders. More than 200 species of hard and 100 species of soft coral have been recorded in these waters. The corals that are exposed are dominated by the Acropora species, the sheltered ones by the Porites, and the semi-sheltered corals by the Millepora species. Even more astonishing is the amount of coral cover found around the islands near Ras Mohammed, which averages 70 percent.

It is not only the scale of the reefs that makes the Northern Red Sea so unique, it is also the way they have transformed the waterscape, forming everything from plunging columns that reach the ocean floor thousands of feet below and spreading gardens and lagoons, to oases of caves and plateaus. These reefs are made up of both fossil and live corals, whose age is mind-boggling—some of them are around two million years old!

- The Sahara is the largest desert in the world, which covers an area of 3,579,000sq miles (9,269,594sq km).
- Dunes in parts of the Sahara roll forward at the rate of 36ft (11m) per year.

**Sahara Desert,** North Africa

# Sahara Desert

Occupying approximately 10 percent of the African continent, the Sahara stretches from Egypt and the Sudan to the west coasts of Mauritania and Spanish Sahara, to the Red Sea, and down to the highlands of Ethiopia.

The mere mention of its name summons images of vast, baking-hot sand dunes, interrupted all too infrequently by jewel-like oases of green. The immense area of the Sahara contains just about every kind of desert terrain, including sand seas and dunes (known as ergs); stony plateaus, gravel plains (serirs or regs), and dry valleys (wadis); salt flats and deeply dissected mountain massifs; and parched scrub land and underground aquifers that occasionally rise to the surface as oases. On a single swathe of land you will find Mount Koussi, towering over the desert at 11,204ft (3,415m) as well as the Qattara Depression in Egypt, which is 436ft (133m) below sea level. Over 25 percent of the Sahara's surface is monotonously covered with sand sheets and dunes.

The bulk of the desert is far inland, and the prevailing winds absorb any moisture from the air before it can reach the interior. Mountain ranges between the desert and the sea cause clouds to drop their rain long before they reach the interior. With scanty clouds in the sky, daytime in the desert is ferociously hot. Cloudless skies also allow the heat to escape into the atmosphere once the sun has set, and temperatures can drop to below freezing. One of the hottest places on the planet, at its worst temperatures during the day can soar above 122°F (50°C). Dust-laden gales and whirlwinds also disperse and destroy the precious fauna and flora of the desert.

Archeologists have discovered proof that just a few thousand years ago the Sahara actually possessed abundant resources of water, and was densely populated. Fossils, rock art, stone artifacts, bone harpoons, and shells as well as the remains of animals and even aquatic

## DESERT ART

The barren wastes of the Sahara are home to the earliest known African rock art. This treasure trove in the desert consists of more than 30,000 engravings and paintings on rocks. Carved around 7,000 years ago, many of these artworks represent the region's flora and fauna; at that time the Sahara was open savannah, which sustained animals no longer found in the desert but which were instead captured for posterity in art.

*An archeologist brushes away dirt from the figure of a child*

creatures have been found in areas which today are considered too hot and dry to inhabit.

Present day Sahara, however, is so harsh that it has one of the lowest population densities in the world. Most of this inhospitable land's inhabitants are nomads, largely the Tuareg, Tibbu, and Moors who survive by nomadic pastoralism, hunting, and trading. It is not just the human population that is scarce in the area, plant and animal life is negligible too, though the latter far outstrips the former. Some of its notable residents include the desert owls with wingspans of four feet, the well-camouflaged Houbara bustards, the iridescent scarab beetles, dama gazelles, and the scimitar-horned oryxes. Antelopes known as addaxes—with large, flat hooves that allow them to walk over the sand without sinking, high levels of tolerance for dehydration and high temperatures, and the ability to find shelter in depressions that they dig in the sand—are another species that have adapted extremely well to harsh desert life.

*A desert tribesman*

## DISCOVERY OF LAKE CHAD

Before the 19th century Europeans had very little knowledge of the interior of the Sahara. Their first accurate information came from attempts to solve the mysteries surrounding the source of the River Niger. The first significant exploration involved three British explorers—Dixon Denham, Hugh Clapperton, and Walter Oudney.

The small party left Tripoli in 1822, spent 68 days journeying through the uncharted desert and on February 4, 1823, they became the first Europeans to see Lake Chad. Denham went on to explore the area to the south, while Clapperton and Oudney turned west toward the Niger. Not long afterwards Oudney died but Clapperton reached the great towns of Kano and Sokoto, both of which are in Nigeria.

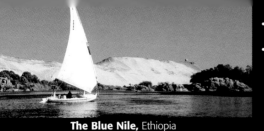

- Egyptians honored the Nile god Hapi during floods, for bringing fertility to the land.
- The Blue Nile derives its name from the color of its water, which is a clear blue in all seasons except the monsoons, when the river turns a muddy brown because of the sediment it carries.

**The Blue Nile,** Ethiopia

# The
# Blue Nile

**M**eandering through thousands of miles of desert, plains, and swamps—sometimes gently, sometimes as rapids and cataracts—the Blue Nile forms the headstream of the Nile river, and is the source of more than half its water. The river originates from Lake Tana in the Ethiopian highlands. Though many small streams feed the lake, the sacred source of the Blue Nile is believed to be the Abay Wenz (meaning "Great River"), which starts off as a small spring at an altitude of approximately 6,000ft (1,800m) at Gishe Abbai. The river flows out of Lake Tana, over the lava barrier near Bahir Dar in the southeast, and plunges down 138ft (42m) to form the breathtaking Blue Nile, or Tisisat (which translates as "Water That Smokes"), Falls.

The river then cuts a 400-mile (644-km) long arc through the Ethiopian plateau. As it runs through Ethiopia, the Blue Nile also carves out a gigantic gorge through

## THE NILE CROCODILE

The ancient Egyptions revered the Nile crocodile. The god Sebek had the head of a crocodile, and the crocodiles were kept in temples and given gold bracelets to wear. Even a city, Crocodilopolis, was named after the creature. Archeologists have discovered thousands of crocodile graves, where the animals were buried with great care and sometimes expensive jewels.

The Nile crocodile no longer abounds on the shores of the Egyptian Nile and is in fact quite rare in Africa today. There are some conservation programs and small populations are being monitored and protected in places such as Lake Turkana in northern Kenya.

the middle of the plateau, reaching a depth of 1 mile (1.6km) and a width of 15 miles (24km) in some places. The river then drops down to the hot plains of Sudan and joins the White Nile at Khartoum to converge and form the Nile; it eventually flows out into the vastness of the Mediterranean Sea.

The volume of the Blue Nile peaks during the rainy season between June and September, when it contributes to almost two-thirds of the flow of the Nile. Together with the Atbara River, which also flows out of the Ethiopian highlands, the Blue Nile was responsible for the annual Nile floods that led to the fertility of the Nile Valley and the consequent flourishing of the great Egyptian civilization. The Aswan High Dam, which was completed in 1970, regulates the flooding of the river today. The Blue Nile is also a vital source of power and irrigation in Sudan, thanks to the two dams of Sannar and Roseires, completed in 1925 and 1966. respectively

The first European to have sighted the Blue Nile appears to have been a Spanish Jesuit priest, Father Pedro Páez, in 1618. However, better known is the Scottish explorer James Bruce, the first person to navigate the Blue Nile from Lake Tana to the Nile delta, in 1770. Bruce's comment regarding the Tisisat Falls is truly evocative: "It was a most magnificent sight, that ages, added to the greatest length

of human life, would not deface or eradicate from my memory." The course of the river, however, remained a vague dotted line on maps until the late 1920s. This changed when the British Consul Major R. Cheesman surveyed the river by walking along its banks and charting its course through the highlands. In 1968, a team led by the British explorer Col. John Blashford-Snell traveled the length of the river in Ethiopia.

The waters of the Blue Nile, people believe, have the power to cure a thousand ailments, break evil spirits, and bless the land upon which it is sprinkled with a good harvest.

### SEARCH FOR THE SOURCE

While the source of the Blue Nile is undisputedly Lake Tana, the search for the source of the White Nile was not so straight forward. It had become the world's greatest geographical challenge by the middle of the 19th century. In 1858 John Hanning Speke, on a diversionary journey from an expedition led by Richard Francis Burton, was the first European to reach Lake Victoria, which he proclaimed as the White Nile's source. Burton, meanwhile, insisted that Lake Tanganyika was the source. A number of explorers, including Scottish missionary David Livingstone attempted to resolve the question.

In the 1870s, Henry Morton Stanley circumnavigated Lake Victoria, proving that it did not have a major river running into it and that it had only one major outlet, Ripon Falls, where the Nile actually starts. Speke had been right all along.

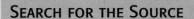

*The Blue Nile Falls*

- The Meru National Park is part of a group of protected areas along the Tana River, the others being the Bisanadi and Mwingi National Reserves, Kora National Park, and Rahole National Reserve.

- The phrase "Big Five" was coined by game hunters to refer to the five large animals that were most sought after in Africa—the lion, the African elephant, the African buffalo, the leopard, and the black rhino. All of the Big Five can be found in the Meru National Park.

**Meru National Park,** Kenya

# Meru National Park

Lush grasslands and thick wild forests, crisscrossed by permanent streams and a diverse range of habitat and wildlife, make the Meru National Park a naturalist's paradise. Straddling the Equator, Meru lies in the northeastern lowlands below the Nyambene Hills in Kenya, 216 miles (348km) from Nairobi. Designated a national park in 1966, it occupies an area of 339sq miles (870sq km).

In addition to the countless streams that water the reserve, Meru National Park is bound by three massive rivers—the Tana to the south, the Ura to the southwest, and the Rojeweru to the east. The hilly northwestern section of the park is wetter with rich volcanic soils. Alluvial soils are found towards the flatter east side. River irrigation and adequate rainfall are responsible for the untamed wilderness that makes Meru so attractive.

Thirty years ago, the park boasted a diverse range of wildlife, housing more than 3,000 elephants, the black and white species of rhino, reticulated giraffes, Grevy's zebras, antelopes, elands, lesser kudus, gerenuks, leopards, cheetahs, and lions. Over 300 varieties of birds—rare species such as Peter's Finfoot and Pel's Fishing Owl—could be found here. Up until the early 1970s, the park managed to attract in excess of 40,000 tourists every year.

The fortunes of the park, however, took a tumble with a sharp rise in poaching activity. Meru supplied happy hunting grounds to poachers for whom the dense swamps and the riverine forests populated by fig trees, tamarinds, and doum plants provided an ideal cover.

Inadequate security resulted in rampant poaching that lasted more than a decade and decimated the park's

## ELEPHANT RELOCATION

The translocation of elephants from private ranches in Laikipia to Meru has been touted as the biggest relocation of its kind in all of eastern and central Africa. To help them adjust to the new surroundings and so that their social bonds were not the disturbed, the animals were moved in family groups. Sixty-six animals have been relocated to the Meru National Park. The successful translocation of the elephants was followed by the relocation of four rhinos. The efforts to replenish Meru's stock continue, with 20 rare Grevy's zebras having been brought in, and several species of antelope to follow.

## BLACK OR WHITE

The name "white" rhinos is misleading because its color is very similar to that of the black rhino. The name is said to have originated from the Afrikaans word "wyd," which in turn is derived from the Dutch word "wijd," meaning wide. The reference to the square lip of the animal— specially adapted for chomping on grass—was misinterpreted by English settlers who called the rhino "white" instead of "wyd." A more appropriate name for the animal, would be the square-lipped rhino.

animal population, depleting stocks of the larger beasts in particular. In the incident that was to eventually spur the government into action, poachers wiped out the five white rhinos in the park for their horns, and killed seven park rangers during their escape.

Today, the park has succeeded in reclaiming much of its former glory largely because of the efforts of African wildlife conversationists George and Joy Adamson. Through the touching story of Elsa, the orphaned lioness they hand-raised after her mother was shot dead in 1956 and later released into the park, the couple managed to make the park famous. Their book—and later, movie— *Born Free* has won them millions of admirers across the world. The couple later separated and in 1980 Joy Adamson was found murdered in the Shaba Game Reserve. Her husband paid the price for his unyielding stance against poaching when nine years later he was killed at the isolated Kora National Reserve.

With security arrangements now in place to protect its animals, Meru has launched an aggressive campaign to attract tourists. In order to replenish the stock in Meru, elephants and rhinos from nearby reserves have been translocated and brought in.

*Ostriches walking along the road, Meru National Park*

- Mount Kenya's summit was first scaled in 1899 by British geographer Halford John Mackinder, along with Swiss guides César Ollier and Joseph Brocherel.

- The Kikuyu people of Africa consider the mountain as the home of their god *Ngai*. They call it *Kirinyaga*, which translates as "mountain of whiteness."

**Mount Kenya National Park,** Kenya

# Mount Kenya National Park

Straddling the equator, a single mountain soars into the sky, its snow-covered summit thrown into sharp relief by the bare rock and glaciers below and the dense forests and high moorland on its lower reaches. This is Mount Kenya, an ancient extinct volcano, and the second highest mountain in Africa. The mountain was inscribed as a UNESCO World Heritage Site in 1997 and as an international Biosphere Reserve in 1978.

Mount Kenya National Park encompasses this mountain and its unique ecosystem, covering all ground above 10,500ft (3,200m) and sprawling across 279sq miles (715sq km). The park offers a uniquely dramatic landscape, one that has been crafted by its combination of hot and cold, volcanic and glaciated, and equatorial and alpine. Erosion too has played a major part in the formation of this awe-inspiring mountain scenery: from the enormous steep-sided valleys and fantastically rugged rock formations to the fields filled with huge rocks. There are waterfalls, streams, and tarns (small lakes); grasslands and bamboo forests; and flowing down its surface, the waters of the melting snow and glaciers form the country's most important river, the Tana. Last but not least is the giant Afro-Alpine vegetation.

The Afro-Alpine vegetation is a memorable, almost otherworldly sight that unfolds on moorlands where plants must adapt to the mountain's unique climate and conditions; they do so by breaking all known botanical rules. These plants—heather, senecios, and lobelias—tower over humans and can reach heights of up to 30ft (9m). There are 13 species of endemic plant found in the park,

## PEAK PERFORMANCE

Mount Kenya's summit is made up of a number of steeply jagged peaks, the most important—and the tallest—being Batian at 17,058ft (5,199m), Nelion at 17,022ft (5,188m), and Point Lenana at 16,355ft (4,985m). While it is possible for trekkers to reach Point Lenana without difficulty, Batian and Nelion can only be scaled by professional mountaineers. All the peaks were originally part of the "plug" that filled the volcano and are made of an igneous rock called nepheline-syenite. More evidence of the mountain's volcanic origins is found on the lower slopes, where lava has been largely responsible for fashioning the rock.

*Sunrise on Batian, the highest peak on Mount Kenya*

## WHERE PARK MEETS PEOPLE

Mount Kenya National Park is spread over the districts of Meru, Nyeri, Kirnyaga, and Embu in the Eastern and Central Provinces. Electrified fences, to ensure that there is no damage to either farmlands or inhabitants from the wildlife, and also to protect the animals from poachers, surround a small portion of the Park.

*Rock climbing 17,000ft (2,134m) up the top pitch of Mount Kenya*

which include the giant thistle and giant groundsels. The Afro-Alpine vegetation is unique to East Africa and is found only on the region's highest peaks—Mount Kilimanjaro, Mount Elgon, and the Aberdares.

Game to be spotted at the park range from hyraxes, rhinos, and the black and white colobus monkeys to waterbuck, genets, giant forest hogs, hyenas, and zebras. There are also a number of endangered species of fauna in the park. These include animals such as the albino zebra, sunni buck, bongos (a number of which are being reintroduced to the area from zoos in America), Mount Kenya mole shrew, skinks (lizard), as well as birds like the Abyssinian long-eared owl, the scarce swift, and the green ibis. The park is enclosed within the Mount Kenya National Reserve.

**Lake Nakuru,** Kenya

• Archeological evidence suggests that the earliest settlers on the banks of the lake appeared about 30,000 years ago—a small hunter-gatherer tribe called the Eburran. Later residents of the area were the Masai, who live in areas of the basin even now.

• Among the seasonal rivers that flow into Lake Nakuru, the most important ones are the Njoro, Makalia, Nderit, and Lamudhiak.

# Lake Nakuru

Situated in the Rift Valley in west-central Kenya, Lake Nakuru is the site of one of the most impressive ornithological spectacles in the world. This hypersaline lake is located at an altitude of 5,768ft (1,758m), within the national park of the same name which was established in 1961. It plays host to as many as 2 million flamingos—of the greater and lesser variety—which flock to the lake in order to feed on the abundant algae that thrives in its warm waters.

In the Masai language, Nakuru means "dusty place"—a name that can be explained by the nature of the lake itself. The lake, which does not have a major outflow, is fed only by rain and a handful of small seasonal rivers. The waters of the lake are used by the locals for various purposes, and levels of evaporation are also fairly high. Because of this, Lake Nakuru's water levels tend to fluctuate drastically.

Between 1951 and 1953, the lake dried up completely and it came close to drying up in 1990. The size of the lake can thus vary from a mere 2sq miles (5sq km) to 12sq miles (30sq km); the mean depth is 8ft (2.5m). The lake receives around 38.6in (98cm) of rain annually.

Lake Nakuru is bordered by the Menengai crater to the north, the Bahati hills to the northeast, the Lion Hill ranges to the east, Eburu crater to the south, and the Mau escarpment in the west. The lake and catchment area of the basin are composed primarily of volcanic rock dating from the tertiary age. The soil is composed of volcanic ash, making it very fertile, but highly porous. Thus it fractures easily during and after rains, causing immense erosion.

The salinity of the waters of Lake Nakuru is a result of the high levels of carbonates and bicarbonates present. This has ensured that only the most adaptable and

### LIFE CYCLES

Scientists believe that the flamingo population at Nakuru consumes about 550,000lbs (250,000kg) of algae per 2.5 acres (1 hectare) of surface area every year. The beta-carotenes in the plankton are responsible for the birds' brilliant plumage. The plankton, on the other hand, survives on the droppings of the flamingos.

*Lesser flamingos washing and eating in a freshwater stream*

resilient aquatic species can survive here. Six species of phytoplankton, five species of zooplankton, four species of water boatmen, two varieties of midge larvae, and a calanoid copepod have been identified here. The phytoplankton forms the lowest rung of the food chain—among them, the blue-green alga *Spirulina platensis* is so prolific that it turns the water dark green, thickening it like a broth.

However, the limited variety in water species is more than compensated for by the explosion of bright color that the flamingos of the lake showcase. These graceful birds, which the lake provides feeding and nesting grounds to, are siphon feeders, using their upturned bills to sieve plankton from the water. Apart from the lesser and greater flamingo, more than 400 species of birds have been identified in the lake area, including pelicans, smaller species such as little grebes, white-winged black terns, stilts, avocets, and many species of duck. And each winter, migratory birds seek refuge here too. The lake has been designated a Ramsar (Wetland of International Importance) site.

The Nakuru National Park is also home to several large animals including lions, leopards, hyenas, hippos, and otters. Only a single species of fish, introduced to control the mosquito population in the 1960s, live in the lake. The diminutive *Tilapia grahami*, with its high salinity tolerance, has thus thrived in the lake and is the only source of food for the pelicans.

## MORE THAN A LAKE

The park was declared a rhino sanctuary in 1983. Under the ensuing rhino stocking program, white rhinos from South Africa were introduced to the park. Currently, the sanctuary has approximately 45 of the black and 31 of the white variety—the highest combined population of rhinos in Africa. The park is also a sanctuary for the Rothschild's giraffe translocated from South Africa. The borders of the park are fenced in order to prevent the animals from wandering and falling prey to the bullets of poachers.

*Black rhinoceros* (Diceros bicornis)

- The Mount Kilimanjaro National Park was created in 1973 with the aim of protecting the mountain and its forest corridors. The park was designated a UNESCO World Heritage Site in 1987.

- Ernest Hemingway's classic 1936 short story, *The Snows of Kilimanjaro*, is set against the backdrop of Mount Kilimanjaro.

**Mount Kilimanjaro,** Tanzania

# Mount Kilimanjaro

**T**he spectacular snow-capped peak of Mount Kilimanjaro, Africa's tallest mountain, towers over the semi-desert of northern Tanzania. Rising to 19,350ft (5,899m) above sea level at its highest point—the Uhuru Peak on the Kibo volcano—Kilimanjaro rises just east of the Rift Valley on the border of Tanzania and Kenya, and is one of the largest volcanic massifs in the world.

Relatively young in geological terms, the formation of Kilimanjaro began approximately 750,000 years ago due to tectonic activity. The mountain has three summits—each of them a volcano—joined together by a complex history of eruptions. Shira, the oldest of them, rises to a height of about 12,500ft (3,810m). Believed to have been taller in the past, geologists are of the opinion that the mountain collapsed as a result of an eruption, leaving behind a much shorter, flattened plateau. The second oldest volcano is Mawenzi at a height of 17,500ft (5,334m). Kibo, the youngest, was formed during a series of eruptions and is topped by a caldera about 1.2 mile (2km) wide. Subsequent eruptions created a second volcanic cone inside the caldera, within which another cinder cone was formed during further eruptions.

The caldera of Kibo is what forms the distinctive elongated and flattened summit of the mountain. Though the older peaks have undergone heavy erosion and retain only their jagged peaks, Kibo, in all its permanently snow-clad glory, continues to captivate visitors. However, only a small fraction of the mountain's glacial cover remains today, an event that can be attributed primarily to global warming. It is believed that at the current rate of glacial recession, the

*View of Mount Kilimanjaro*

## AGRICULTURE

The Kilimanjaro region happens to be one of the leading producers in Tanzania of mild coffee, barley, wheat, and sugar. Other crops produced in the area include sisal, maize, beans, bananas, cotton, pyrethrum, and potatoes. The Chaga, Pare, Kahe, and Mbugu peoples are the native inhabitants of the area. Located at the southern foot of Kilimanjaro, the town of Moshi is the chief trading center for the area, and also the base for ascent.

mountain top will be brown and bare by the year 2200. Some scientists also believe that the warming up of the volcano itself is aggravating the problem.

Kilimanjaro displays a whole range of vegetation zones—the semi-arid scrub of the surrounding plateau, the cultivated irrigated southern slopes, dense cloud forest, open moorland, alpine desert, and moss and lichen communities. The giant lobelia and the giant groundsel are two notable species of plants that grow in the moorlands. The forests of Kilimanjaro's southern slopes are also home to elephants, buffalo, eland, many species of monkey and duiker, among other creatures. A whole host of bird species, including the rare Abbot's starling, are also to be found here.

The first serious attempts to scale the Kilimanjaro were made in 1848 by the German missionaries Johannes Rebmann and Johann Ludwig Krapf. However, reports of the presence of a snow-capped mountain so close to the equator were scoffed at by Europeans until at least a decade later. Rumor of a quartz, limestone, and crystal laden peak ran rife for 40 years before the German geographer Hans Meyer and the Austrian mountaineer Ludwig Purtscheller scaled the Kibo summit for the first time in 1889. Since the Kibo summit can be ascended without the aid of any mountaineering equipment, every year, thousands of ambitious visitors attempt the climb.

## MICROCLIMATE

The sheer size of Kilimanjaro is responsible for it being able to influence and create its own weather pattern. The summit is mostly crowned with clouds brought by the moisture-laden winds from the Indian Ocean—they rise up against the flank of the mountain and sprinkle its crest with water or snow. Though the average rainfall is only about 8in (20cm) a year, it is sufficient to enrich the soil on the slopes and support Kilimanjaro's varied botanical systems.

*Kibo peak bathed in clouds*

- The Great Rift Valley is home to spectacular highs and lows: the Danakil Depression in Ethiopia is one of the lowest points on the planet while Mount Kilimanjaro is Africa's highest peak.

- Water bodies in the rift include Lake Tanganyika, the Sea of Galilee (Lake Tiberias), the Jordan River, the Red Sea, the Gulf of Aqaba, and the Gulf of Aden.

**The Great Rift Valley,** Africa/Middle East

# The Great Rift Valley

It has been called the "cradle of civilization," and the "backbone of Africa" but neither adequately describes the Great Rift Valley, one of the most amazing geological features on the planet. The Great Rift Valley is a vast split in the earth's crust, one that stretches almost 4,000 miles (6,400km) from its northern tip in Jordan down through eastern Africa before finally exiting at its southern end into the Zambezi River in Mozambique. The result of tectonic activity, the rift was created around 20 million years ago when Africa and the Arabian Peninsula tore apart. In fact, Africa is still undergoing the process, and it has been predicted that Somalia will someday be separated from the rest of the continent.

The Great Rift Valley was named by the British explorer John Walter Gregory, although it was the German meteorologist Alfred Wegener who developed the theory of continental drift. He noticed that the opposing shores of the Red Sea formed a perfect match, and that the sea could be closed by sliding Africa against Arabia—except that Yemen would then overlap the Afar Triangle. Geologists now recognize that the volcanic rocks in both these areas are younger than the Red Sea, and so could not have existed before the Red Sea opened; thus the match would have been perfect. Active rifts are characterized by earthquakes and volcanic activity, and in the African rift, the Afar Triangle is currently the most active part.

## THE CRADLE OF HUMAN CIVILIZATION

There is evidence to support the claim that the Great Rift Valley is the place where evolution began, some three million years ago. In the Olduvai Gorge in Tanzania, in 1959, archeologists discovered a 1.75 million-year-old hominid skeleton. Further archeological discoveries have been made throughout the valley, including those at Awash River in Ethiopia.

*Olduvai Gorge, Tanzania*

Lake Natron and Ol Doinyo Lengai active volcano, The Great Rift Valley

The Valley is actually divided into two forks, the eastern rift and the western rift. The eastern arm starts to the east of Lake Victoria and continues northward for about 1,600 miles (2,574km). It goes from Tanzania through Kenya and into Ethiopia and the Afar Triangle. Here the rift divides, with one part continuing north toward the Red Sea, while the other strikes eastward into the Gulf of Aden. The western arm of the rift extends for about 1,900 miles (3,057km) from Lake Malawi in the south, close to the Mozambique coast, then northward along the line of the great African lakes to the west of Lake Victoria. This arm is not only surrounded by some of the continent's deepest lakes, such as Lake Tanganyika, but also by some of its highest mountains, including Mount Kilimanjaro, the highest peak in Africa.

For most of its length, the Rift Valley has a width of about 35 miles (60km), and in many places— from Kenya, for example—it is possible to look down and across its spectacular expanse. One of the few ecosystems to remain unchanged for centuries, the valley abounds with wildlife and is home to numerous national parks, including those in Kenya, Tanzania and Congo (Ngorongoro Crater Conservation Area being the most famous)—the definitive safari destinations in the world, where you can spot not only the Big Five, but also watch the annual Serengeti migration. Also interesting are the shallow soda lakes littering the valley floor that owe their existence to poor drainage. These are home to clouds of pink flamingos as well as dozens of other migratory birds that like to feed off the sulphuric algae and crustaceans.

## FRACTURED EARTH

A rift valley is formed by the tension in the earth's crust where the opposite sides of the valley are slowly moving apart. As the valley widens, the floor of the valley drops between two roughly parallel escarpments.

The fault systems along the valley margin are complex but generally result in wedge-shaped slices that slip downward to jam the widening gap.

Over millions of years, the valley gradually widens and deepens, but continued erosion blurs the sharp lines of escarpments and sediments accumulate on the valley floor. When the crust grows too thin, a new crust is formed by magma erupting from the underlying mantle.

- The greatest length of Lake Victoria measured from north to south is 210 miles (337km); while the width from east to west is 150 miles (240km).

- Of the 200 or so species of fish found in Lake Victoria, the Tilapia is the most important economically.

**Lake Victoria,** Tanzania/Uganda/Kenya

# Lake Victoria

The largest lake in the continent, and the second largest freshwater lake in the world, exceeded in size only by the North American Lake Superior, Lake Victoria occupies an area of 26,828sq miles (69,484sq km). The heavily indented coastline of this enormous lake runs for more than 2,000 miles (3,220km) through central Africa. Its waters are shared between three countries—Tanzania, Uganda, and Kenya. Also called Victoria Nyanza, it forms the chief reservoir of the Victoria Nile, or the White Nile; it is this river that converges with the Blue Nile to form the longest river in the world.

Shaped like an irregular quadrilateral, Lake Victoria occupies a shallow depression in the middle of a great plateau that is bordered on its two sides by the Eastern and Western Rift Valleys. The surface of the lake is situated 3,720ft (1,134m) above sea level; however, it is considered shallow for its remarkable size and the maximum depth has been recorded as being around 270ft (82m). Numerous archipelagos dot the surface of the lake, and several reefs are visible just below. The most noteworthy river that enters the lake is the Kagera; the largest of the rivers that feed Lake Victoria, it enters from the western side of the lake, just north of latitude 1° south. Flowing out from the northern coast of the lake is its only outlet, the Victoria Nile.

The shores of Lake Victoria showcase many kinds of natural features. While the southwestern coast consists of 300-ft (90-m) high towering cliffs and precipices, the western coast is characterized by swamps of ambatch and papyrus that mark the Kagera River delta. The northern coast is deeply indented, but flat and bare, with only a narrow channel that leads into the Kavirondo Gulf. The Emin Pasha and Speke gulfs are situated at the southwestern and southeastern corners respectively. The densely populated Ukerewe, situated north of the Speke Gulf, is the largest of the lake islands; wooded hills on

## THE OWEN FALLS

The Owen Falls is located just below the Victoria Nile's outlet from the lake at Jinja in Uganda. This waterfall serves as the site for the Owen Falls Dam, which utilizes a hydroelectric station to harness the water, and provides hydroelectric power to western Kenya and the industries of Uganda. Using Lake Victoria as a reservoir, the dam was completed in 1954. The dramatic Ripon Falls was submerged by the dam. The water channelling of the lake through this waterfall accounts for only 20 percent of the total outflow of the lake; the rest of the water is lost by evaporation.

*Owen Falls Dam*

## DISCOVERING VICTORIA

Even though the early charts of Ptolemy delineated Lake Victoria as a vague patch of water, it was not until 1858 that it was first sighted by a European. The British explorer John Hanning Speke discovered the lake on his quest for the source of the Nile, and in 1862 located the exit point of the river and named it Ripon Falls. The vast lake was first circumnavigated by Sir Henry Morton Stanley in 1875, and later explored by him and others. Sir William Garstin, in 1901, conducted a detailed survey of the lake. Previously known as the Ukerewe, the lake was renamed by Speke in honor of Queen Victoria.

*Chimpanzees on Ngamba Island, Lake Victoria*

the island rise to a height of 650ft (200m) above the surface of the lake. The northwestern corner of the lake houses the 62 islands of the strikingly beautiful Sese archipelago. The northern coast of Lake Victoria is the site for the Ugandan cities of Kampala and Entebbe.

One of the most densely populated areas in Africa, the Lake Victoria region is inhabited by approximately 30 million people, most of whom depend on the lake for subsistence—shipping and the catching, preparation, and sale of the cichlids (fish) in the lake form the most important industries. Local steamer services around the lake serve as the mode of transportation and communication. Most of the native inhabitants are Bantu-speaking; many of them, particularly the Ganda and Tutsi tribes, have developed the decorative arts to levels of great distinction.

**Serengeti,** Tanzania

- The Serengeti region encompasses the Serengeti National Park, the Ngorongoro Conservation Area, Maswa Game Reserve, the Loliondo, Grumeti, and Ikorongo Controlled Areas, and the Masai Mara National Reserve in Kenya.

- Considered a jewel in the crown of Tanzania's protected areas, the Serengeti altogether accounts for approximately 14 percent of the country's land area, an unmatched conservation record.

## SALT OF THE EARTH

A few million years ago, during the Pleistocene Epoch, rock and ash from the volcanoes of the Ngorongoro area covered the present day Serengeti plains. The volcanic ash contains salts, such as potassium, sodium, and calcium that are washed down into the soil during the seasonal rains where they precipitate. In the Serengeti plains, the salts are deposited less than a foot below the surface, and form a hard layer called a hardpan, which prevents tree roots from going further into the soil. However, the hardpan is perfect for grasses—because it traps rainwater close to the surface and makes it available for grasses that grow thick and dense—as well as for animals.

*A lioness and her cub drinking water*

# Serengeti

Serengeti—a word that conjures up images of every kind of wildlife, of vast plains, and the great migration—is one of the oldest ecosystems in the world. The Serengeti's essential features, climate, and vegetation have remained almost unchanged for a million years. The Serengeti is not one place but many, all interlinked to each other in the ecosystem. To the north lies Kenya's Masai Mara; to the west Lake Victoria; to the east the soda lakes of the Great Rift Valley; and to the south the extraordinary Ngorongoro Crater and the highlands of Tanzania. Perhaps that's why the Masai called it *Siringitu*, "the place where the land moves on forever." Occupying an area of 11,600sq miles (30,000sq km), it encompasses two World Heritage sites and two biosphere reserves.

The Serengeti is home to one of the greatest and most diverse variety of wildlife on earth as well as one of the last great migratory systems known to mankind. It is home to over three million large mammals, including more than 35 different species of land animals, more than 500 species of birds, as well as the most fierce and intimidating predators: lions, leopards, cheetahs, crocodiles, hyenas, rhinos, and hippos. A savannah made up of grasslands

and woodlands, plains, kopjes, marshes, and riverine forests, the Serengeti is a kaleidoscope of colors, particularly at the end of February when the plains near Olduvai Gorge and Ngorongoro Crater are green with fresh grass and teaming with wildflowers.

The single most arresting sight in the Serengeti is the migration of more than a million wildebeest, about 200,000 zebras, and other grazing ungulates. The greatest spectacle in the animal kingdom is driven by rain, responsible for grass and grazing. The wildebeest spend the rainy season from December to May in the open volcanic plains below the Ngorongoro Crater. With the end of the monsoons in May or June, the plains dry out, prompting the wildebeest to move west toward Lake Victoria in search of food. Still following the rains, the migration moves north, into the Masai Mara, where the rift wall catches the last rains even in the middle of the dry season.

Once the Masai Mara's grass has been devoured and Tanzania has been bestowed with fresh rain, the vast herds travel back across hundreds of miles to their breeding grounds in the Serengeti and Ngorongoro plains. There, the young are born in time to grow sufficiently strong to undertake the long march north six months later. But migration is not devoid of danger, as predators, from lions and tigers to hyenas and crocodiles, are on the look out for easy game. Thousands of the migrating animals meet their end en route, many in the jaws of crocodiles while crossing the Grumeti and Mara rivers. This is survival of the fittest, yet so strong is the ancient instinct to move that no drought, gorge, or crocodile-infested river succeeds in holding them back.

## RIVERINE FORESTS

Riverine Forests are a unique habitat within the Serengeti. Large rivers, which remain dry for most of the year, flood during the wet season. Higher water levels give rise to a dense forest of evergreen trees, transforming the environment below it and making it a special habitat for a variety of plants, insects, birds, and animals. On the forest floor live an amazing variety of frogs, lizards, and snakes. Plant-eaters such as dikdik, duiker, and bushbuck are common, while the rivers are home to crocodiles and hippos.

*A rhino in a field of tall grass in the Serengeti*

- The total elevation of the rim of the Ngorongoro Crater is 7,500ft (2,286m) above sea level.
- Ol Doinyo Lengai (Mountain of God) is an active volcano situated within the Ngorongoro Conservation Area; it is said to have last erupted in 1983.

**Ngorongoro Crater,** Tanzania

# Ngorongoro Crater

The spectacular bowl of the Ngorongoro Crater forms the largest intact caldera in the world. Located 75 miles (120km) west of the town of Arusha in northern Tanzania, this extinct volcanic caldera lies in the Eastern Rift Valley. The rim of the crater is shrouded in dense forests, and rises to a height of 2,000ft (610m) above the floor of the caldera. Estimated to have been formed about 2.5 million years ago, the Ngorongoro Crater is the result of the major eruption of a large active volcano, whose cone is believed to have collapsed inward with the subsidence of the molten lava.

Measuring between 10 and 12 miles (16 and 19km) across, the Ngorongoro Crater has an area of approximately 102sq miles (264sq km). This vast unbroken caldera houses a great variety of ecological environments. The floor of the crater comprises primarily open grasslands; swamps and forests also proliferate. Lake Makat, the soda lake situated in the middle of the caldera, is fed by the waters of the Munge River. Owning to its exceptional geographical characteristics, the Ngorongoro Crater and its surroundings, encompassing about 3,200sq miles (8,300sq km) of area around the crater, were designated a national conservation area.

Situated to the southeast of the Serengeti National Park in the Arusha region, the Ngorongoro Conservation Area was originally included as a section of the national park in 1951. However, it was demarcated as a separate and independent conservation area in 1959. Today, this remarkable conservation area provides refuge to a diverse array of animals, and serves as a stalking ground for up to 20,000 to 30,000 wild beasts at a time.

*Giraffes the in Ngorongoro Conservation Area*

## OLDUVAI GORGE

Located in the eastern Serengeti, within the Ngotongoro Conservation, Olduvai Gorge is the mystical place where the Leakeys uncovered the hominoid remains of a 1.75-million-year-old skeleton of Australopithecus boisei, an important link in the human evolutionary chain. In a small canyon just north of the crater, the Leakeys along with international archeologists unearthed the remains of at least three recognized hominoid species, and also chanced upon a series of hominid footprints estimated to be over 3.7 million years old. Its claim of being one of the oldest sites of hominid habitation in the world is well substantiated by the excavated fossils that have been discovered here.

The marvelous landscape of this conservation area is sprinkled with exotic forests, savannah woodlands, swamps and marshes, grassy plains, mountains, volcanic craters, rivers, and lakes. The wildlife that has made this extraordinary assortment of habitats their home includes leopards, cheetahs, spotted hyenas, elephants, buffalo, zebras, black rhinos, warthogs, wildebeests, and Grant's and Thomson's gazelles. The Ngorongoro Conservation Area is home to the densest population of lions in the world. Four hundred species of birds abound in the area including the uncommon silvery-cheeked hornbill, the superb starling, and bronze and tacazze sunbirds.

Apart from the Ngorongoro Crater, the other chief volcanic attractions within the conservation area are the Olmoti and Empakaai volcanoes, which were formed between 2 and 20 million years ago. The oldest volcanoes in the area—including the ones mentioned earlier, along with the Lemagrut, Sadiman, Oldeani, Sirua, and Lolmalasin—developed along the Eyasi Rift, which today forms sweeping cliffs at Lake Eyasi. Other striking features in the area include a remarkably deep soda lake that covers nearly half of the floor of Empakaai's caldera. A shallow soda lake called Magadi, surrounded by many extinct volcanoes, is famous as a habitat for large flocks of pink flamingos.

The Ngorongoro Conservation Area was inscribed as a UNESCO World Heritage Site in 1979. Even though cultivation is prohibited within the limits of the conservation area, the local Masai people are allowed to graze their livestock in the grasslands within the Crater.

## MASAI

The word Masai or Maasai is used to refer to the nomadic pastoralist tribes who inhabit East Africa. Essentially a linguistic term, the word encompasses all the peoples who speak this eastern Sudanic language. Also called Maa, this tongue belongs to the Chari-Nile branch of the Nilo-Saharan family. The general term "Masai" indicates, among others, the pastoral Masai of the Great Rift Valley, the Samburu of Kenya, and the semi-pastoral Arusha and Baraguyu (or Kwafi) of Tanzania. Fully nomadic, the pastoral Masai travel throughout the year without any permanent settlement, and subsist entirely on the meat and produce of their herds.

*Masai tribesmen in face paint*

• Misali Island, just west of Pemba, has been singled out for having some of the highest recorded coral cover, and a high diversity of species, with 40 types of coral and 350 fish species.

• Fringing reefs, of the type found in Zanzibar, are relatively young and border land masses of islands and shorelines. They are found in shallow waters, not very far out to sea.

**Zanzibar Coral Reefs,** Indian Ocean

# Zanzibar Coral Reefs

**A**lso referred to as "Spice Island," Zanzibar is an alluring paradise with palm-fringed beaches and idyllic coves, fascinating dhows (sailing boats), and ancient Islamic ruins. An archipelago made up of three main islands—Unguja (also known as Zanzibar Island), and Pemba and Mafia islands—as well as many smaller islands and islets, Zanzibar boasts some of the world's finest coral reefs. With warm temperatures around the year and plenty of sunshine, the waters of the West Indian Ocean have the perfect conditions for coral formation, as seen by the extensive and luxurious fringing reefs off the islands.

In the clear blue and turquoise depths of the waters around Zanzibar is an ecosystem whose beauty defies description. Over millions of years, corals have formed gardens and caves, walls and gaps, mountains and overhangs, and even the backbone of many of the islands in the archipelago. Illuminated by sunlight, the corals paint the waters in vivid hues with reefs of green, gardens of rose, and caves of blue. Soft corals undulate in the waters while schools of fish swim around and through them. The reefs are made up of everything from columna and cabbage corals to honeycombs, gorgonian fans, and brain and plate corals. The waters guarantee sightings of barracuda, manta rays, moray eels, octopus, tuna, parrotfish, and pufferfish.

Two islands within the archipelago, Chumbe and Pemba, have already achieved world renown. Chumbe, an island created by fossilized corals (it even has a petrified coral forest), is home to the Chumbe Island Coral Park. Comprising 200 species of hard

*The beautifully filigreed gorgonian sea fans found among the Zanzibar Coral Reefs*

reef-building corals, 400 species of fish, and visited by turtles, dolphins, and humpback whales, its reefs are considered to be the healthiest on the coast. Not surprisingly, it has been named the world's finest marine park by a host of authorities. In comparison, Pemba is unknown, yet the completely unspoilt coral reefs around it stretch far out to sea, where they can be found at a depth of 210ft (64m). The reefs around Pemba are considered unmatched in their beauty and variety. The numerous challenging dive spots they offer include such evocative names as Emerald Reef, Misali Coral Garden, and the Gauntlet.

Other islands in the Zanzibar archipelago whose coral reefs are worth a visit are Mafia Island and archipelago, home to the Mafia Island Marine Park, which protects the extensive coral reefs that surround it, as well the hundreds fish species that live in the waters. Mnemba Island, located off the northeastern tip of Zanzibar Island, is also rich in coral reef.

## HERITAGE CITY

In addition to its coral reefs, Zanzibar is famous for one of its towns, which is also a World Heritage Site. Stone Town is a coastal trading township whose architecture and culture is a testament to the many peoples that shaped Zanzibar—Arab, African, European, and Indian.

*Red starfish marooned after a spring tide on Zanzibar island*

## WRONG DIRECTIONS

The amount of coral cover found in the Zanzibar archipelago varies dramatically depending on the direction of the shore. Cover on eastern shores is much lower than on the western ones, and rarely reaches above 15 percent. This has been attributed to the vigorous and high-impact movement of the waves hitting the shore; coral thrives best in waters that are largely undisturbed.

Victoria Falls is known among the Kalolo-Lozi people as Mosi-oa-Tunya, meaning "the smoke that thunders."

The Scottish missionary and explorer David Livingstone, the first European to sight the towering falls in 1855, named it Victoria Falls after the British Queen, Victoria.

**Victoria Falls,** Zambia/Zimbabwe

# Victoria Falls

A thunderous roar and a veil of mist shrouds the waters of Zambezi as they tumble over the edge of a sheer cliff to form the magnificent Victoria Falls. Situated almost halfway down the river's course, on the border between Zambia in the north and Zimbabwe in the south, Victoria Falls plummets into a narrow chasm formed by the precipice and a barrier wall. Tiny islands, promontories, and depressions split the lip of the precipice into many sections, some of which remain dry during periods of low water flow of the river.

Victoria Falls is believed to have been created because of the diversion of the waters of the Zambezi caused by tectonic movements during an earlier geological period. This alteration led the waters over a massive bed of basalt and resulted in the formation of the waterfall; the heavy volume of water swiftly and easily eroded the soft rock with its many cracks and fissures.

Boasting a maximum drop of 350ft (107m) and spanning the complete breadth of the Zambezi at one of its widest points—more than 5,500ft (1,700m)—Victoria Falls forms the world's largest single curtain of falling water. Foggy columns of spray are visible from miles away as approximately 33,000cu ft (935cu m) of water plunges over the edge of this formidable waterfall every second. The spray from the falls has been known to rise upto a staggering height of 1,000ft (305m).

Today, Victoria Falls, with its awe-inspiring magnitude and its astonishing beauty, is one of Africa's greatest natural attractions, and a prime focus for conservation. The lands surrounding the waterfall have also been demarcated as protected areas. While the Victoria Falls National Park girds the waterfall on its Zimbabwean side, it is bounded on the Zambian side by the Mosi-oa-Tunya National Park, which was established in 1972. Together, the two national parks host an astounding variety of wild animals and vegetation.

*The mighty Victoria Falls*

## DEVIL'S CATARACT

Constant erosion of the soft material within the basalt in the Victoria Falls area has resulted in the creation of many fault lines along which the water is often diverted as it falls over the precipice. The Devil's Cataract, on the Zimbabwe side, is one instance of the sheer force of water cutting backwards along such a line of weakness. Approximately 69ft to121ft (21m to 37m) lower than the rest of the present waterfall, the cataract is probably a sign that another new line of flow for Victoria Falls will be established in the future because of the erosive action of water.

*A view of water rushing over Victoria Falls*

Dense forests with trees such as fig, ebony, teak, ivory palm, and acacia throng the region. There is also a considerable growth of ferns and mopane. More than 400 species of bird make up the area's rich avifauna; significant among them are the Taita and peregrine falcons, the black stork, the augur buzzard, and eagles. Elephants, lions, wildebeest, zebra, giraffes, and other creatures roam the grasslands and the rainforests. Antelopes and hippos are usually found close to the waterfall. Victoria Falls also marks a geological barrier between the distinct upper and middle river fish varieties of the Zambezi. Together with Victoria Falls, the two adjoining national parks were inscribed as a UNESCO World Heritage Site in 1989.

With its rich combination of a diverse animal population, a vast range of flora, and the breathtaking waterfall, the Victoria Falls region forms an amazing focal point of the African landscape. Thousands of tourists flock to the waterfall every year for a glimpse of one of nature's most spectacular creations.

## THE VICTORIA FALLS BRIDGE

The narrow gorge through which the waters of Victoria Falls cascades down is spanned by the Victoria Falls (Zambezi) Bridge. Commissioned by Cecil John Rhodes in 1900, the bridge is a part of Rhodes' dream of building a railway line from the Cape in South Africa to Cairo in Egypt. Though Rhodes died before the construction began, the bridge is today fully functional and people are transported between Zambia and Zimbabwe across it by rail, automobile, or on foot.

- Chobe has the highest concentration of elephants in the world. However, the elephants here have smaller and more brittle tusks than those in other parts of Africa.

- As a national park, Chobe encompasses the most diverse landscape in Africa—from flood plains to savannah, from lush green stretches to arid desert.

**Chobe National Park,** Botswana

# Chobe National Park

Home to more than 450 species of birds and a host of predators including lions, leopards, cheetahs, wild dogs, and crocodiles, Chobe National Park, the second largest game reserve in Botswana, boasts the greatest concentration of animals in the entire continent. This 4,121sq mile (10,566sq km) park in northwest Botswana provides sanctuary to possibly the largest continuous population of elephants in the world—the migratory herds are estimated to be around 120,000. This record has earned it the nickname Elephant Capital. The park is also considered the best place to spot four of Africa's Big Five—the lion, the leopard, the elephant, and the buffalo.

The first human inhabitants to arrive here were the hunter-gatherer Bushmen (Basarwa), also called San, which means "person." Though not much is known about their way of life, rock paintings discovered throughout the park give us glimpses of their lives. The San later shared space with other tribes such as the Basubiya, and later the Batawana, who moved to the area sometime in the early 20th century. The park can be divided into four distinct ecosystems: Serondela in the northeast, with its lush plains and dense forests through which the Chobe River flows, is a favorite watering hole for elephants and buffaloes during the dry season. Lion prides roam the marshlands of Savuti in the west. The Linyanti wetlands in the northwest have

### ELEPHANTS OF CHOBE NATIONAL PARK

Though listed as a threatened species, the elephants of the park are faring well enough to make park authorities fear that they might strip the park bare and irrevocably alter its landscape. The authorities had considered culling in order to control the population and reduce pressure on the parkland. Large-scale protests against the proposed plan of action, however, have kept them from executing it, and the elephants continue to thrive.

*African Elephant, Chobe National Park*

## The Cape Buffalo

Often considered more dangerous than the lion by park rangers, the Cape buffalo is the biggest of the buffalos. It can weigh as much as 1,984lb (900kg), has horns that can reach 3.28ft (1m) in length, and stands 5ft (1.5m) at the shoulder. It is known to turn on its aggressor and hold its ground or charge at hunters even after being shot. Living in herds of sometimes more than several hundred, the Cape buffalo has no natural enemies and has been documented attacking—and on occasion, even killing—lions.

a similar landscape. In between Savuti and Linyanti lies a hot dry hinterland.

The idea of cordoning off the land as a protected reserve was first raised in 1931. A year later, 9,360sq miles (24,000sq km) around the Chobe district was set aside as a no-hunting zone. An additional 2,730sq miles (7,000sq km) was added to this in 1933 in order to make space for the growing number of animals. The initiative suffered a huge setback about a decade later, when a deadly tsetse fly attack resulted in the decimation of the animal population. The future of the park remained uncertain for the next 10 years after which the animal numbers soon began to stabilize. The project of creating a national park to protect animals and boost tourism was revived in earnest. However, the reserve was not formally designated a national park until 1967.

Since many industrial settlements dealing in timber dotted the landscape of the selected area, it cost the government a great deal of time and effort to enforce restrictions that a protected reserve park demanded. The last of human settlers were finally moved out of the park in 1975, and plans for spreading out continued. The last expansion took place in 1987. The remnants of the abandoned industrial sites can still be seen at Serondela.

- The Etosha National Park harbours the largest and only protected-area population of the extremely rare and endangered black-faced impala.

- Etosha is one of the few reserves in Africa that has been able to provide sanctuary to the black rhino, which had been hunted to the point of extinction for its horns. Fortunately, thanks to the tough anti-poaching measures that the park authorities have adopted, the population of the animal in the park is now on the rise.

# Etosha National Park

The Etosha National Park in Namibia, home to myriad exotic creatures, covers an area of more than 8,500sq miles (22,000sq km). Designated a national park in 1907, this game reserve is inhabited by 114 species of mammals, 340 species of birds, 110 reptile species, and 16 of amphibians. Lions, elephants, leopards, cheetahs, and the endangered black rhino are among the larger animals that populate this reserve. The elephants at Etosha are believed to be the largest of all species of pachyderms found on earth, with some males measuring more than 13ft (4m) at the shoulder, which is 3ft (0.9m) more than the normal size.

Etosha translates literally as Great White Place; it is also known as the Place of Dry Water or the Great Void. The massive silvery white mineral pan that covers a quarter of the reserve—around 1,930sq miles (5,000sq km)—is probably responsible for the park being referred to by that name. Part of the Kalahari Basin, the pan is estimated to have been formed about 1,000 million years ago. The pan was once a perennial body of water, thanks to the Kunene River that flowed into it. But today, all that remains of the lake is a dusty, salt-crusted depression. The process of drying began thousands of years ago when tectonic movements forced the river

to change its course, which in turn cut off the source of water for the depression.

Folklore, however, offers a less mundane theory for the lake's creation. The formation of the pan is attributed to a tribal woman who lost her husband and children during a raid in which everyone, save the women of the village, were killed by the assailants. So grief-struck was she that she cried inconsolably for days on end. Her tears drenched the soil until the earth was saturated, and slowly the lake was formed. The tale does not tell of what happened to the woman afterwards; it only says that when the tears finally dried up, this pan of caked earth was all that was left.

The dryness of the saline pan, however, does not mean there is an absence of wildlife. During the monsoon months, the mineral-rich waters of this lake lure hundreds of species of wading birds, including the flamingo—one of the greatest tourist attractions. The area also attracts other magnificent animals such as elephants, lions, herds of wildebeest, and the black-faced impala—Etosha's most prized resident. In the summer months, the dry mineral deposits found on the lake's bed are scattered by the winds and serve to fertilize the lands surrounding the park.

Decades before this area was set aside as a protected reserve for animals, American trader G. McKeirnan visited it in 1876 and was captivated by the stunning range of wildlife to be found in this flatland. "All the menageries in the world turned loose would not compare to the sight I saw that day," wrote a fascinated McKeiran.

## THE HAUNTED FOREST

The peculiarly shaped Moringa trees that cluster around the saline pan are a great tourist draw. The trunks of these trees are thick and swollen, with branches that are bare except for a few leaves at the tips—they look as if they have been planted upside down, with the roots reaching for the sky. Owing to this eerie appearance, this part of the reserve is called The Haunted Forest.

## CUTTING DOWN

When the idea of protecting animals for conservation and tourism was first discussed and implemented, the Etosha game reserve was spread over an unbelievable 38,600sq miles (100,000sq km), making it the largest reserve on the planet. Political pressures in the 1960s, however, forced a reduction of the area, bringing it to down to less than a quarter of its original size.

*White rhinos at Ongava Camp, Etosha National Park*

103

- The Scottish missionary David Livingstone is believed to have been the first European to reach the swampy delta of the Okavango in 1849.

- The *mokoro*, a dugout canoe, forms the primary mode of transportation in the Okavango Delta.

**Okavango Delta,** Botswana

# Okavango Delta

The fourth longest river in southern Africa, the Okavango runs for about 1,000 miles (1,600km); rising as the Kubango in the highlands of central Angola, it flows southeastwards to the Kalahari in Botswana, and then disappears into the dry, arid sands of the desert before it has a chance to meet the sea. The slow-moving waters of the Okavango River pass through an intricate network of channels as it terminates in this enormous inland delta—the largest of its kind in the world.

Taking its name from the Kavango people of northern Namibia, the Okavango forms a triangular-shaped delta that covers a core area of around 6,000sq miles (15,540sq km), which during periods of floods can increase to 8,500sq miles (22,015sq km). More than 95 percent of the water of the Okavango Delta is lost by evaporation. The remaining waters travel either southward via the Boteti River to the Makgadikgadi Pans or to Lake Ngami in the southwest.

## CHANGE AND MANAGEMENT

The delta's grassy plains are inhabited by cattle-herding tribes. In the past their livestock was confined to the margins of the delta because of attacks by tsetse flies, carriers of sleeping sickness. Aerial spraying has all but eradicated the fly, allowing cattle and herdsmen to enter the swamps. The unfortunate side effect of this success has been to reduce the range available to the antelope, by disturbing its habitats and making it compete with cattle for grazing. The numbers of antelope are thus in decline and the fragile integrity of this wilderness is threatened. This risk has been recognized by the local people, and the Moremi Wildlife Reserve, covering 1,500sq miles (3,885sq km), is the first wildlife sanctuary in southern Africa to be created and managed by the local people.

*Lechwe sprinting at Okavango Delta*

*Zebra herd at a waterhole*

The unique character granted to the Okavango Delta by the curious juxtaposition of the prolific wetlands and arid wastelands makes it an extraordinary chunk of the African wilderness. The delta provides sanctuary and sustenance to a wide variety of flora and fauna. An extensive growth of dense reeds, predominantly papyrus, covers the upper reaches of the delta. Interspersed with the beds of reed are areas of permanent water. Large masses of water lilies sprout in these standing waters; they are a great favorite of the pygmy goose, who feeds almost exclusively on the lily fruit.

The wetland habitat offered by the Okavango Delta is ideally suited to the needs of hippos, crocodile, and several species of antelope. The sitatunga is the most remarkable of these species; related to the bushbuck and kudu and having specifically adapted to an aquatic lifestyle, this creature remains largely confined to the impenetrable reaches of the delta, and occupies other similar areas in Africa. The kobs, including the waterbuck and the lechwe, are species of antelope that have adapted to water and can be found only in southern Africa. The delta serves as the last refuge of the largest remaining number of the red lechwe antelope; at least 20,000 of these animals thrive in the grasslands.

A great number of birds, among them some of Africa's rarest species, also call the reed swamps and open waters of the Okavango Delta their home. The spectacular African fish eagle, with its distinctive piercing cry, hunts here. Many other species such as the little bee-eater, malacite kingfisher, varieties of heron and egret, and the African fishing owl feed and nest in the delta.

Reeds make way for scrublands of acacia thorn and grassy flood plains in the lower reaches of the delta. Many migrating herds of plains animals, including creatures such as the elephant, buffalo, and zebra, thus make their way to these areas, and predators such as the hyena, wild dog, leopard, and lion also follow them in pursuit.

## LAKE NGAMI

Situated at the southwestern corner of the Okavango Swamp, Ngami is a shallow lake fed by the Okavango River after it has lost most of its water due to evaporation in the marshes of the delta. Situated at an elevation of 3,057ft (932m) above sea level, the lake was first sighted by the explorer David Livingstone in 1849. The circumference of the lake was then estimated to be more than 170 miles (275km); however, by 1950, the lake had been transformed almost entirely into a sea of grass. During a particularly severe drought in1965–66, the lake dried up completely. The village of Maun, the traditional capital of the Tswana people of Botswana, and the centre of the safari industry, lies to the northeast of the lake.

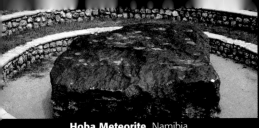

- Believed to be between 200 and 400 million years old, the Hoba Meteorite is estimated to have landed on earth approximately 80,000 years ago.

- The curator of the American Museum of Natural History in New York made a fruitless attempt to purchase the Hoba Meteorite in 1954; problems of transporting this mammoth object were largely responsible for the failure of the venture.

**Hoba Meteorite,** Namibia

# Hoba Meteorite

Discovered only in the early 20th century, the famous Hoba Meteorite has been sitting unmoved at the Hoba Farm near Grootfontein in northern Namibia for thousands of years. Though there are rumors of the presence of a larger meteorite in Mauritiana, the Hoba Meteorite has the distinction of being the largest known meteorite in the world.

According to legend, J. Brits, the erstwhile owner of Farm Hoba West, chanced upon the meteorite in 1920 while he was ploughing his field. The ox-driven plough apparently ground to a halt with a grating metallic sound when it came across an obstruction; digging around the area the farmer uncovered a huge boulder of iron. Assuming a roughly quadratic shape, this slab of iron measures approximately 9.76ft (2.95m) in length, and 9.64ft (2.94m) in breadth; the average vertical thickness of the slab is 3.28ft (1m), with a maximum thickness of 4ft (1.22m) and a minimum of 2.5ft (0.75m). This giant block, which gleams with a metallic luster, is estimated to be roughly 66 tons—it is because of this immense weight that no one has seriously attempted to move the meteorite from its original site.

The composition of the meteorite is believed to be 82.4 percent iron, 16.4 percent nickel, and 0.76 percent cobalt, with faint traces of other metals; the surface of the slab is sometimes covered with iron hydroxides because of the formation of a thin oxidation layer. Despite its large size, the Hoba Meteorite belongs to a rare category of

## THE LARGEST METEORITES

Due to the greater stability of iron meteorites over stony or stony-iron meteorites, the largest meteorites in the world usually belong to the former category. The latter two types of meteorites fracture upon entering the earth's atmosphere, and are responsible for the creation of the spectacular meteor showers that we often see. However, they also suffer greater ablation and disintegrate almost entirely upon impact. The iron meteorites, on the other hand, are less susceptible to ablation, have greater resistance to the effects of terrestrial erosion, and can thus be preserved almost intact for thousands of years.

*A view of the single largest meteorite known to mankind sitting in its enclosure*

## GROOTFONTEIN

The Hoba Farm situated 12 miles (19km) west of Grootfontein, acts as the railway terminus for northeastern Namibia. Situated at an elevation of 4,793ft (1,461m), the Grootfontein area is well-known for its nearby copper and lead deposits. The area also has excellent grazing potential and is populated by several beautiful trees. The name Grootfontein (Great Spring) was given to it by Boer trekkers.

meteorites, and is scientifically classified as a nickel-rich ataxite. Composed of a dense packing of the mineral taenite (a combination of nickel and iron), ataxites do not exhibit the Widmannstätten patterns typical of other meteorites.

The absence of an impact crater is one of the peculiarities of the Hoba Meteorite. Excavations around it have shown a marked absence of the typical temperature and pressure induced features that are associated with the crashing impact of a meteorite. Although no definitive explanation exists, scientists speculate that the meteorite probably entered the earth's atmosphere at a very low trajectory, was considerably slowed down by atmospheric drag, and then rolled or bounced to its current location after impacting somewhere several miles away.

Today, the Hoba Meteorite is one of Namibia's major tourist attractions, and draws thousands of visitors every year. Unrestricted access to the meteorite since its discovery, however, resulted in vandalism of the metallic structure. Apart from samples that were taken for scientific research, the meteorite also lost bits and chunks to tourists eager to return with souveniers; saw-marks on the meteorite bear witness to this damage. Though it was protected as a national monument in 1955, the vandalism only came to an end in 1985 after the Rössing Uranium Ltd. Foundation took over the restoration and preservation of this extraterrestrial object. Since then, the entire meteorite has been excavated, and all the exposed surfaces of the iron block can be studied in detail.

• The human inhabitants of this barren land are limited to the Damara and Himba people, who wear simple goatskin clothing with leather, metal, and shell ornaments.

• Dune 45 and Big Daddy are the two most famous dunes in the Namib. Big Daddy is the largest, towering at 1,000ft. (305m). Below it lies the Dead Vlei, a dry lake bed.

**Namib Desert,** Namibia

## Fairy Rings

A curious feature of the Namib Desert are the circles found on the desert floor, known as "fairy rings," which are clearly visible from the air. They occur near the eastern border of the desert, and while their presence has generated much interest over the centuries, their origin was only recently attributed to termites.

*A view of fairy rings in the Namib Desert*

# Namib Desert

The oldest, driest, and perhaps the richest, the Namib, with its towering sand dunes is one of the most spectacular deserts on Earth. Arid for the past 55 million years, the Namib stretches for 1,200 miles (2,000km) along the southwestern coast of Namibia, averaging a width of only 70 miles (113km). It is bordered by the Atlantic Ocean whose cold Benguela current is instrumental for the desert receiving negligible amounts of rain, between 0.08in to 3in annually (0.2cm to 7.6cm). Coastal fog, however, sometimes rolls inland and is the only form of moisture that parts of the desert receive over the years. The Namib is so intensely dry that, though sloping downhill, no watercourse meets the ocean.

The word Namib comes from the Hottentot word, meaning desert or "place of no people." Due to its inaccessibility, the desert remains largely unpopulated. It occupies an area of around 31,000 miles (50,000km) and

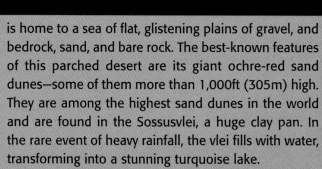

is home to a sea of flat, glistening plains of gravel, and bedrock, sand, and bare rock. The best-known features of this parched desert are its giant ochre-red sand dunes—some of them more than 1,000ft (305m) high. They are among the highest sand dunes in the world and are found in the Sossusvlei, a huge clay pan. In the rare event of heavy rainfall, the vlei fills with water, transforming into a stunning turquoise lake.

The dunes of the Namib have been crafted by the elements over millions of years. They are thought to have been formed of sand that was dumped into the Atlantic Ocean by the Orange river, which in turn was moved northward by the Benguela current and cast back on to the land by the surf. Wind blew the sand inland, and created the dunes. Even now, it continues to reshape them, forcing grains of sand to fly upward to the crest of the dune, where they drop, resulting in the characteristically steep leeward slope.

Stability of its climate over time has ensured that the Namib contains a number of species of ancient origins, as well as those that have accustomed themselves specifically to the arid conditions. One of the most remarkable is the *Welwitschia mirabilis*, a two leaf plant with the longest-lived leaves of any species in the plant kingdom; some plants are about 2,500 years old. Also found here are 70 reptile species, including the wedge-snouted sand lizard, the small-scaled sand lizard, and the barking and day geckos. There are also rodents like the gerbil and the eyeless Grant's golden mole, which can swim through the loose sand of the dunes. Hartmann's zebras, gemsbok, and oryx (Namibia's national animal), are among the biggest animals found in the desert, while cheetahs, brown and spotted hyenas, and the cape and bat-eared foxes are the main predators. Six birds are endemic to this desert: the dune lark, Benguela long-billed lark, Gray's lark, bank cormorant, tractrac chat, and Rüppell's korhaan.

## BEETLE MANIA

Several varieties of beetles are found in the Namib Desert, especially those belonging to the *Tenebrionidae* family. These beetles have acclimatized to the aridity of the desert by evolving methods to use the condensing fog as their source of moisture. An example is the head-standing beetle, which finds its way to the crest of a dune at the site of fog. Positioning itself to face the wind, it stretches its back legs so that its body tilts forward with its head down. As the fog precipitates all over its body, it flows into its mouth, and quenches the beetle's thirst.

*Fog-Basking Beetle, or Darkling Beetle, sucking moisture from a drop of water in the Namib Desert*

**Kalahari Desert,** southern Africa

- The second largest desert in Africa after the Sahara, the Kalahari derives its name from the word *Kgalagadi*, which in Tswana means "the great thirst" or "a waterless place."

- After the independence of Botswana, large diamond deposits were discovered in the country. The inauguration of the diamond mine at Orapa in 1971 marked the beginning of mining activity throughout the Kalahari.

*Quivertrees in the Quivertrees forest near Keetmanshoop*

## KGALAGADI TRANSFRONTIER PARK

The Kgalagadi Transfrontier Park comprises two adjoining parks—the Kalahari Gemsbok National Park in South Africa and the Gemsbok National Park in Botswana. A historic bilateral agreement was signed by South Africa and Botswana in 1999 whereby both countries agreed to undertake the management of these two parks as a single ecological unit; they agreed to jointly promote and cooperate in tourism in the region, and share profits and duties equally. Thus the Kgalagadi Transfrontier Park was born, and formally launched as southern Africa's first peace park in 2000. Together, these parks provide a safe haven for diverse and valuable wildlife.

# Kalahari Desert

The Kalahari, with its open woodlands and an evergreen and deciduous forest in the northeast, doesn't resemble most people's idea of a desert. Though the southwestern section of the desert receives less than 10in (25cm) of rainfall and is sparsely dotted with a few drought-resistant shrubs, the relatively high precipitation and density of vegetation found in the rest of the plain makes it more of a savannah than a desert in the true sense of the word.

Sprawling across an area of roughly 360,000sq miles (930,000sq km) that covers almost all of Botswana, the eastern third of Namibia and the northernmost part of South Africa's Northern Cape province, the Kalahari has an average elevation of 3,000ft (900m) above sea level. It runs for approximately 1,000 miles (1,600km) from north to south, and measures 600 miles (970km) at its widest east–west stretch, and merges with the Namib desert in the southwest.

The Kalahari is a gently undulating sanded plain made up of sand sheets and longitudinal dunes. While the sand sheets—formed by wind and rare flood action during the Pleistocene Epoch 1.6 million to 10,000 years ago, and usually deeper than 200ft (61m)—occupy the eastern part of the Kalahari, the western part of the plain is dominated by dunes that are at least 1 mile long, several hundred feet wide and 20ft (6m) to 200ft (21m) high. In places, kopjes, or low vertical-walled hills, rise up conspicuously, exposing the underlying rock. The most remarkable of the Kalahari features, however, are the scattered vleis (pans) or "dry lakes" formed due to ephemeral streams draining their waters into the depressions. Because of its loose and frequently thick sand covering, the Kalahari surface has no standing water. The reddish soil, too, is dry, and often calcareous or saline to the point of toxicity in the pans.

The desert encompasses three of the world's most remote game reserves—the Central Kalahari Game Reserve, the Khutse Game Reserve, and the Kgalagadi Transfrontier Park. The wildlife includes the famous Kalahari black-maned lion, leopards, cheetahs, brown hyenas, elephants, ostriches, and a host of antelopes including the gemsbok. The desert also provides sanctuary to a host of other creatures such as wild hunting dogs, foxes, jackals, hyenas, warthogs, baboons, badgers, porcupines, and numerous small rodents. There are also several types of snakes and lizards, and a wealth of birdlife too. As with the plant life, the fauna that is supported by the northern Kalahari is more varied and abundant.

The Kalahari today is inhabited by the Khoisan-speaking San and the Bantu-speaking Africans, along with a few Europeans. Due to its sparse population, the network of roads connecting various parts of the Kalahari is poor. Most of the infrequently used roads and tracks are negotiable only by trucks and four-wheel drives. However, administrative centers, major habitations, and mining areas are connected by proper roads; eastern Botswana, the Okavango Swamp, and mining areas in the south too, are linked by a regular network of roads.

*San bushmen hunting*

## VLEIS

One of the Kalahari's most striking and fascinating features are its pans. Formed from streams that drained their water into the sands of the Kalahari itself, the pans are made up of fine silt particles deposited by the streams, and soluble calcium salts and minerals precipitated when the water evaporates. Hardened by the cementing action of the minerals, these pans gleam white when they are dry. From time to time, the pans may be covered by a shallow sheet of water. Only in areas where the salt content is low do the pans display a cover of grass just after the rains.

- The Taita Falcon, one of the rarest birds in the world, was discovered in the Blyde River Canyon as recently as the 1990s.
- Blyde River Canyon is the point where the supercontinent Gondwanaland broke apart some 200 million years ago, separating Madagascar and Antarctica from Africa.

**Blyde River Canyon,** South Africa

# the Blyde River Canyon

Carved out of red sandstone and set against the greater Drakensberg escarpment, the Blyde River Canyon showcases some of the most spectacular and dramatic landscapes in Africa. Erosion by wind and water through millennia has contributed in making this sprawling canyon one of the most stunning natural formations in the world. The third deepest canyon in the world—after the Grand Canyon in the USA and Namibia's Fish Eagle Canyon—the magnificent panoramic views offered by craggy cliffs that rise up to 2,624ft (800m) from the river bed defy description.

The Blyde River Canyon slices through the Drakensberg Mountains in South Africa. One of the seven major mountain systems in the continent, it was formed as a result of volcanic eruptions. Previously known as uKhahlamba (Barrier of Spears) by the local Zulu people, this massive stretch of mountain and gorge was recently rechristened Motlatse.

The Blyde River Canyon is a treasure house of astounding structures fashioned by nature. The Three Rondavels—three huge dolomite rocks that rise out of the canyon walls and then taper off to resemble the roofs of traditional African huts (called *rondavels*)—are considered sacred by the indigenous of the area. At the convergence of the Blyde and the Treur rivers, erosion of water has given rise to phenomenal spirals of rock—the Bourke's Luck Potholes, named after a pioneering gold prospector, Tom Bourke. Thousands of years of work on the rocks by the whirling waters has carved out incredible cylindrical rock sculptures embellished with streaks of white and yellow lichen. Scientists contend that these shapes were carved out when the churning waters of the rivers, laden with sand, silt, and debris, crashed through the rocks. In between these rock formations nestle smooth, dark pools of water.

## PILGRIM'S REST

Pilgrim's Rest was a gold mining town established in the early 20th century when gold was found along certain stretches of the Blyde River Canyon. Though the mines were exhausted by the mid 1970s, Pilgrim's Rest did not fall into disrepair. The provincial authorities developed it into a tourist attraction, and it remains a hugely popular destination for visitors even today.

*Blyde River Canyon, Mpumalanga Province*

Other remarkable features of the canyon include the Pinnacle, a startling single column of quartzite that rises out of the woods. The occasional rainbow stretching across the top of the rock bestows it with a rather mesmeric quality. The God's Window Escarpment, another popular vantage point where cliffs plunge more than 2,296ft (700m) to the Lowveld, opens out onto a vista of extraordinary beauty—the Wonder View is yet another spectacular viewpoint. Masses of waterfalls are also found along the canyon.

The extreme climate, the range of altitudes, and the varying soil conditions of the canyon ensure a rich variety of flora. The Blyde Canyon Nature Reserve houses plants such as orchids, lilies, tree ferns, and cycads. The diverse plant life of the Blyde River Canyon also supports varied fauna. The gorge provides a safe haven for creatures such as hippos, crocodiles, impala, kudu, blue wildebeest, waterbuck, and zebra, along with several species of primate and many birds.

## BIO DIVERSITY

The Blyde River Canyon Nature Reserve is one of the few areas in Mpumalanga where montane grass still grows. More than 1,000 species of flora are found in this reserve. Many of these are endemic to the escarpment, and not found anywhere else in the world. The reserve provides shelter to nearly 20 rare or endangered species, many of them being cycads.

- A "gold rush" explosion in the area of the Kruger National Park in 1869 decimated the animal population due to a rise in hunting and trading of animal horns and skins.
- The Great Limpopo Transfrontier Park—Africa's largest game reserve—was opened to the public in early 2003.

# Kruger National Park

Low ranges of hills dot the otherwise flat terrain of the Kruger National Park in South Africa. Previousy South Africa's largest national park, Kruger is now part of the Great Limpopo Transfrontier Park. Comprising the Limpopo Park in Mozambique, Gonarezhou Park in Zimbabwe, and the Kruger National Park, this peace park was set up in 2002. About 200 miles (320km) long and between 25 and 50 miles (40 and 80 km) wide, Kruger individually occupies an area of about 7,523sq miles (19,485 square km)

Despite the fact that it is fed by six perennial rivers, drought is not unknown in the park. Vegetation in the park ranges from open veld to dense bush, including marula, acacia, mopane, and baobab trees. Wild beasts such as elephants, lions, leopards, cheetahs, buffalo, rhinoceros, zebra, wildebeest, and impala that roam the wilderness are among the 147 animal species, 114 species of reptile, and 507 varieties of birds that populate this untamed ecosystem. More than 1,986 types of plants can also be found in the park.

*Giraffes, Kruger National Park*

## MAN ON A MISSION

The Scottish born James Stevenson-Hamilton took charge as the first ranger of the reserve in 1902. His means of working—summary and often ruthless eviction of settlers to make more room for the animals in the reserve—earned him the nickname *Skukuza*, meaning "he who sweeps clean" or "he who turns everything upside down." The name of the main rest camp in the park was changed to Skukuza in his honor in 1936.

_Young hippos play in a river_

By the early 1800s, the region had turned into a fighting ground for the Difaqane tribal wars and inspite of the repeated introduction of hunting laws, the slaughter continued well into the late 1800s. It was Paul Kruger who started the uphill battle for conservation in 1884, demanding that the region be declared a protected area. Finally in 1898 he managed to convince the government to set aside a 1,794sq miles (4,600sq km) swathe between the Sabie and Crocodile Rivers as a game reserve. Prohibition on hunting did not succeed in deterring poachers who continued to skulk in the area. The final blow came in 1899—with the eruption of the three-year long Boer War, the animal population plummeted further because of indiscriminate killings. After the war, however, the park staged a comeback under the aegis of James Stevenson-Hamilton, who was appointed as game warden.

Stevenson-Hamilton and his team of rangers and scouts cleared the area of human habitation and brought an end to poaching. Because of their efforts, the Shingwedzi Game Reserve, between the Letaba and Luvuvhu rivers, was formed in 1903, and within two years the area of the park went up to 6,630sq miles (17,000sq km). It was on his insistence that the reserve came to be declared a national park in 1926 and was consequently named, in order to honor Paul Kruger's contribution to the cause of conservation. In the same year the park was further expanded and has thus reached its current size.

## SUCCESS OF TOURISM

Kruger's popularity skyrocketed soon after it was declared a national park in 1926. Compared to 1927, when three vehicles roamed the park, 900 vehicles loaded with tourists were scouring the park by 1930, and more than 310 miles (500m) of road had been laid. Today, millions of tourists visit the park each year, and nearly 5,000 miles (8,065km) of paved and gravel roads traverse the area.

- The Cango Caves were the first to be protected by environmental legislation and also the first natural wonder with a full-time tourist guide.

- Dripstone caverns, similar to the Cango Caves, are found in several places around the world; another example would be the Damlatas Dripstone Cavern in Alanya, Turkey, which was discovered in 1948.

**Cango Caves,** South Africa

*The entrance and ticket office at the Cango Caves*

# Cango Caves

O ver time, water, limestone, and carbon dioxide have toiled to create one of the planet's most spectacular sights. The Cango Caves, situated near Oudtshoorn in South Africa's Western Cape, in a limestone ridge parallel to the Swartberg Mountains, are an underground marvel featuring some of the world's finest dripstone caverns. Ancient tools have been uncovered here which suggest that humans have inhabited these caves for at least 80,000 years. Not surprisingly, they are also South Africa's oldest tourist attraction.

Inside the Cango Caves are vast halls with towering formations of stalactites, stalagmites, helicites (columns sprouting in several directions), and stalagnates (various trajectories formed when stalactites and stalagmites join), that have been growing for the past one-and-a-half million years. The bizarrely shaped helicites are composed mainly

## CAVE PROTECTION

When the caves were opened to the public in the 19th century, vandalism was rife as people carried away parts of the delicate stalactites and stalagmites as souvenirs or defaced the cave walls. To put an end to this destruction, the governor of the Cape Colony, Lord Charles Somerset, published the first Caves Regulation in 1820, which became the first law in South Africa designed to protect an environmental resource.

of calcium carbonate that condenses as lime water drips from the stones and evaporates.

The caves were believed to have been first explored by a colonial farmer, Jacobus van Zyl, in the late 18th century, though no proof exits to substantiate this claim or the fact that somebody by that name even lived in the area in the 1770s. Nonetheless, the myth has lived on—the first chamber in the caves is called Van Zyl's Hall, a massive space measuring 321ft (98m) in length, 160ft (49m) in width, and 49ft (15m) in height. It is not clear just how much of the space he explored, but over the years a vast sequence of chambers—with imaginative names like Lumbago Alley, the Crystal Palace, Tunnel of Love, the Coffin, the Post Box, and the Devil's Chimney—were discovered and christened Cango One, and subsequently opened to the public. It ran 2,499ft (762m) from the entrance and then came to an abrupt halt, though draughts of fresh air convinced explorers that there were still more chambers to be discovered.

Cango Two, an 886-ft (270-m) extension of the existing cave sequence was discovered in 1972. In 1975, another extension of about 5,248ft (1600m) was revealed and named Cango Three. The natural colors, crystalline beauty, and formations inside the two caves combined are several times more magnificent than those of Cango One. However, in order to preserve the beauty of the limestone formations inside, neither Cango Two or Three are open to the public.

Some of the notable dripstone formations inside the caves are Cleopatra's Needle—a 29-ft (9-m) high and at least 150,000-year-old stalagmite—and Completed Column, which rises 410ft (125m) from the floor to the ceiling in the center of Cango One's second chamber. A remarkable feature of Van Zyl's Hall is its beautiful dark gray roof that has been smoothly sculpted into hollows and pendants—a dramatic contrast to the softer limestone walls that are a mellow yellow.

The Cango Caves are maintained at a constant temperature of 64.4°F (18°C) and are perfectly illuminated, making them the biggest showcave operation in Africa. Thousands of tourists are drawn to these natural wonders annually. In 1938, the caves were declared a national monument.

## ENGRAVED IN STONE

A fine example of cave art survives in the Cango Caves. It is an engraving of an elephant superimposed on an eland. Depending on the viewing angle, only one of these two creatures can be seen at a time. Puzzlingly, this piece of art was created in a completely dark area.

*Cleopatra's Needle, a stalagmite in Van Zyl's Hall*

- Maclear's Beacon—a stone cairn on the highest point on Table Mountain—was constructed by Sir Thomas Maclear in 1865 for the purpose of a trigonometrical survey.
- Table Mountain is one of the few places in the world with extensive sandstone caves, with the Wynberg Caves being the largest among them.

**le Mountain,** South Africa

# Table Mountain

The imposing figure of the Table Mountain looms over the hustle and bustle of Cape Town in South Africa, often obscured from view by white clouds. Draped in mist, when viewed from the bay the mountain appears to be a monolith—with a perfectly flat summit and steep cliffs which rise abruptly—that shimmers gently in the heat. Table Mountain was referred to as *Hoerikwaggo*, meaning "sea mountain" or "mountain in the sea," by the original inhabitants of the Cape, the Khoekhoen and San tribes.

One of the oldest mountains in the world, Table Mountain rises to a height of 3,560ft (1,085m). Millennia of erosion of almost horizontal layers of sandstone by strong winds and water have given the mountain its unusual tabular shape. While the 2-mile (3.2-km) long northern face of the mountain is desolate and scarred, the summit plateau is crisscrossed with small streams and valleys.

Table Mountain forms the northern extremity of a mountain range that lies between Cape Town and the Cape of Good Hope. Flanked in the northeast by the Devil's Peak, which rises to 3,200ft (975m), and in the northwest by the Lion's Head, which descends from a height of 2,100ft (640m) to the 1,100-ft (335-m) high Signal Hill (Lion's Rump), Table Mountain is made up of layers of sandstone and granite resting on shale and an older granite base. The jagged escarpment of the mountain, as it stretches out against the sky, is popularly referred to as the Twelve Apostles.

Table Mountain has its very own cloud cover, responsible for the lush vegetation found on the plateau. Formed by winds blowing in from the southeast, the spectacular "tablecloth" is a thin layer of clouds that settles neatly on top of the flat summit. The clouds formed during this extraordinary phenomenon, however, do not reach the lower slopes of the mountain. Rainfall brought in winter by the northwesterly winds is also greater at the summit, and caught by five mountain reservoirs.

## STAR ATTRACTION

The French astronomer Abbé Nicolas Louis de Lacaille conducted important observations of the southern sky from the Table Mountain. When he introduced a new constellation in 1763, he named it *Mons Mensae*, which translates from Latin as "table mountain." Though the constellation lacks bright stars—its brightest star, the *Alpha Mensae*, is barely visible at a magnitude of 5.09—it contains a portion of the Large Magellanic Cloud. Known as Mensa (the Table) today, the star cluster bestows Table Mountain the unique distinction of being a natural feature after which a constellation has been named.

*Aerial view of Robben Island and Table Mountain*

*Table Mountain*

## BIODIVERSITY HOTSPOT

Owing to its incredibly rich biodiversity, the Table Mountain area has been declared a national park. Formed as the Cape Peninsula National Park in the 1990s and renamed Table Mountain National Park in 1998, the park stretches for 37 miles (60km) from Signal Hill in the north to Cape Point in the south. With its beautiful valleys, bays, beaches, cliffs, and sandy flats, in addition to its remarkable flora and fauna, the park has immense natural, historical, and scenic significance. With more than 1,500 plant species, Table Mountain forms the heart of the Cape Floral Kingdom. One of the six floral kingdoms in the world, the Cape Floral Kingdom is a Natural World Heritage Site.

The gullies and gorges of the Table Mountain provide shelter to indigenous Afromontane forests; fynbos (fine bush), disa orchids, silver trees, and 250 species of daisies also form part of the abundant vegetation. The ecosystem of the mountain also supports a large number of animals, including antelopes such as klipspringer and grysbok, Himalayan tahr, reptiles such as the venomous Cape Cobra, and endangered amphibians like the Table Mountain Ghost Frog.

The plateau is also popular among hikers, with most choosing the easiest route to the top via the Platteklip, or "flat stone," Gorge. Formed by the erosion of rock by heavy rains, this is the deepest ravine that splits the cliff face. This was the route used by the Portuguese explorer Admiral Antonio de Saldanha for the first recorded climb of the mountain in 1503. Today, there are more than 350 routes that lead to the summit. Less adventurous visitors can take the Table Mountain Aerial Cableway (built in 1929) to the top.

119

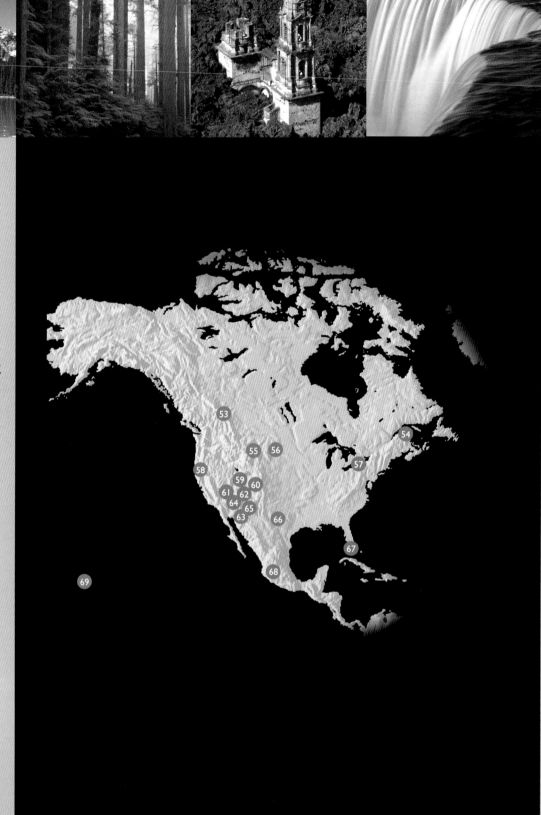

# North America

**T**he sweeping North American territories of Canada, British Columbia, Greenland, United States of America, and Hawaii are part of the Earth's western hemisphere that also includes Central America, the West Indies and South America. Surrounded by the Atlantic Ocean to the west and the Pacific Ocean, to the east, the North American continent also includes the Hudson and Baffin bays, the Gulf of Alaska, California and Mexico, and the Labrador Sea.

Canada and British Columbia and the water world stretching into the Atlantic Ocean has the highest peaks in North America, the largest ice fields outside the polar caps, and some of the most ecologically interesting islands. Some 370 years ago, for example, the coast of Gaspe Peninsula facing Baie des Chaleurs was a tropical estuary—the craggy peaks of the Appalachians lined the horizon and trees covered the land, providing a home to giant spiders and scorpions, while its waters were home to a variety of armored and lobe-finned fish. Off Vancouver, the SGang Gwaay Island, part of the Queen Charlotte Islands known today for its birds, species of moss and ferns, migrating whales and sea lions, was until the 19th century home to the 300 member strong Haida community who subsisted on hunting until wiped out by disease.

In the United States of America, the Great American Desert, stretching from Oregon to central Mexico, encompassing the Mojave, Sonoran, Great Basin and Chihuahuan, is the depository of 2 billion years of geological history. Its Yosemite Valley in the Sierra Nevada is a glacially carved valley and its Great Lakes create the largest expanse of freshwater in the world. Further south, the Hawaiian waters—stretching 360sq miles (932sq km) in the southeastern portion of Big Island—are home to yet another spectacular feature, sea volcanoes. Two of which—Mauna Loa and the Kilauea—awe the world with annual eruptions. Mauna Volcano, considered to be the highest in the world—measured from the seabed—at 56,000 ft (17,169m), is twice the height of Everest.

- The explorer Tom Wilson was the first non-native to see the now-famous Lake Louise in 1882. He gave it the name Emerald Lake, which was later changed to honor Queen Victoria's daughter Princess Louise.

- Mount Robson, the highest peak in the Canadian Rockies, can be seen clearly only for about 14 days a year. The bad weather close to its summit makes it a very challenging climb for mountaineers.

**Canadian Rockies,** Canada

## CHINAMAN'S PEAK

Ha Ling Peak in the Kananaskis Provincial Park in the Canadian Rockies was named after a Chinese cook who in 1886 won a bet with his co-workers by climbing the peak, planting a flag and descending in five and a half hours. The peak was named Chinaman's Peak to honor his feat, and then renamed Ha Ling after the man himself in 1997.

# Canadian Rockies

Bordered by undulating prairies to the east and the innumerable subsidiary ranges of the Columbia Mountains to the west, the Canadian Rockies extend from the forests of central Mexico through to the US–Canada border, forming a natural boundary of sorts between the provinces of British Columbia and Alberta.

About 75 million years ago, the collision of tectonic plates forced the bed of what was probably an inland sea to buckle and rise until it formed the framework of the mountains that we see today. The process of glaciation began with the onset of the Ice Age about 35,000 years ago when massive glaciers covered the entire Rockies. These rivers of ice scrubbed the mountains clean of vegetation and molded its valleys and gorges, polishing the rocks and sculpting them into various extraordinarily shaped formations. As the earth grew warmer and the glaciers melted, the debris frozen in the ice was deposited on the rocks to form lateral moraines. Lakes were formed where the deposits were large enough to choke the natural drainage. In time, the flood of water ate through the debris and rocks, forming deep gorges and channels.

The only remnants of the Ice Age today are the glacial fields scattered across the continental divide, the most impressive of those being the Columbia Icefield, spread over 126sq miles (325sq km). Lake Louise is the most famous of the moraine lakes of the Canadian Rockies, while the credit for being the tallest peak goes to Mount Robson, with a towering height of 12,970ft (3,954m).

The Canadian Rockies come in various shapes and sizes. "Castellate" mountains, comprising horizontal layers of rocks, are so named because they often have vertical towers that resemble castle turrets—Banff's Castle Mountains, for example. "Dogtooth" mountains, such as Mount Louis, were formed by severe erosion that left behind hard base rock layers which jut out into the sky in sharp points. A ridge of near-vertical rock layers similar to the dogtooth variety and resembling a saw blade is called a "sawtooth" mountian. Mount Assiniboine, often compared to the famous Matterhorn in Europe, was formed when glaciers scoured four sides of the summit to create a square-topped peak instead of a pinnacle.

Rocks thrusting upwards at angles of 50 or 60 degrees create peaks—Mount Rundle, for instance—which have one smooth sweeping face and one sharp steep face with dipping layers. Anticlinal and synclinal peaks are also common—the former is created when rocks are compressed to form smooth domes without cracking; the latter are formed in the troughs of depressions. The oddest peaks are the "complex" mountains. With their complicated combinations of up-folds and down-folds, these mountains result in structures that defy classification.

*Mount Robson above Yellowhead Highway*

## PEAKS OF THE CANADIAN ROCKIES

The wilderness of the Canadian Rockies houses five national parks—the Waterton, Banff, Jasper, Kootenay, and the Yoho. These, excluding the Waterton which lies along the international boundary further south, interlock and were together declared the Canadian Rocky Mountain Parks World Heritage Site by UNESCO in 1984. The site also includes three adjoining British Columbia provincial parks. All these parks have been established with the intention of protecting and preserving the diverse wildlife of the region and their natural habitat. One of the pioneers in the push for preservation measures was J. B. Harkin, the first Commissioner of Dominion Parks in 1930.

*Mount Assiniboine at dawn*

## one

- The name Gaspé is said to be derived from a Micmac Indian word which means "land's end."
- The Percé Rock contains 150 species of fossils including brachiopods, trilobites, Percé dalminites, marine worms, and corals.

, Canada

# Percé Rock and Gaspé Peninsula

A rugged extension of the Appalachian mountain chain, the Gaspé Peninsula is situated in the eastern Quebec province of Canada. It runs from the east towards the northeast for 150 miles (240km), from the Matapédia River into the Gulf of St. Lawrence. The St. Lawrence River forms the northern boundary for the peninsula, and it is bounded in the south by Chaleur Bay and New Brunswick. One of the most picturesque areas of Canada, the peninsula encompasses a diverse and majestic landscape of mountains, valleys, rivers, bays, and coastlines.

Elevations in the northern parts of the Gaspé Peninsula are higher than in the southern coast, with Mont Jacques-Cartier rising to a height of 4,198ft (1,280m) amid the forest-covered Monts Chic-Choc (Shickshock Mountains) in the north central area. The peninsula is drained by a number of spectacular rivers including the Cascapédia, Saint-Jean, York, Grande, and du Grand Pabos. The forests, beaches, cliffs, and meadows of Gaspé provide sanctuary to an immense variety of flora and fauna.

Percé Rock (or Rocher-Percé) is a sheer, gigantic monolith that rises out of the Gulf of St. Lawrence just off the outer tip of the Gaspé Peninsula, 465 miles (750km) east of Quebec City. Attached to the shoreline at one time, this peninsular rock island is connected to the mainland by a sand and gravel bar, which is visible only at low tide. This spectacular block of ochre-colored limestone is believed to be 375 million years old.

The Percé Rock is 1,437ft (438m) long, 295ft (90m) wide, and touches 290ft (88m) at its highest point. The name Rocher-Percé translates as "pierced rock" and has

## CONSERVATION IN THE GASPÉ PENINSULA

Large sections of the Gaspé Peninsula are within conservation areas. Major protected areas on the peninsula include the Gaspésian Provincial Park which occupies 313sq miles (802sq km), and the Forillon National Park, which encompasses 93sq miles (240sq km) at the northeastern tip of the peninsula. The Bonaventure Island and Percé Island National Park form the largest gannet seabird colony in North America. The Miguasha Provincial Park was inscribed as a UNESCO World Heritage Site in 1999.

## EROSION OF PERCÉ ROCK

The mammoth Percé Rock is said to weigh in at a staggering 551 million tons. However, because of erosion by the sea, it loses about 330 tons of rock every year, and is likely to disappear completely in 16,000 years at the present rate of erosion. The massive rock had earlier had another hole carved into it by the sea; but constant erosion coupled with a lightning strike in 1845 severed the arch and left behind an isolated column of rock a little way from the main body. This obelisk measures 148ft (45m) in height.

*Hikers at low-tide crossing to the Pierced Rock (Rocher-Percé). Percé Rock is a major tourist attraction in Quebec, with picturesque views of the rock from both Percé and nearby Bonaventure Island*

its origin in the huge hole that has been carved into the rock by the waters of the sea. This 33ft (10m) wide and 60ft (18m) high gap that pierces the calcite veined mass of rock makes it one of the largest natural arches in the world.

Although the Frenchman Jacques Cartier first landed in Gaspé Bay in 1534 and claimed the land for the king of France, the original inhabitants of the Gaspé Peninsula were native people who spoke the language. Only a few of the foreigners ended up settling permanently in the area. The peninsula was inhabited by the Micmac people at the beginning of the 17th century, when Samuel de Champlain sailed along the coasts of Gaspé. Converted to Christianity by the French missionaries, the Micmacs have continued to live in the area since then.

Today, most of the population of Percé Rock and the Gaspé Peninsula resides along the coast, within a few miles of the Gulf of St. Lawrence, with the exception of the copper-mining town of Murdochville. The principal areas of settlement are Matane, Gaspé, Percé, Chandler, and New Carlisle. The peninsula—with its forests and fish-filled clear streams—is excellent for hunting and fishing and thus beneficial for both the local and sporting interests of its community. Other economic activities in the area are lumbering, production of pulp for papermaking, and some mining of lead, copper, and zinc.

- Established by the US Congress on March 1, 1872, Yellowstone National Park is the oldest national park in the world.
- The park holds more than 200 geysers; some erupting to heights greater than 100ft (30m).

# Yellowstone National Park

The oldest and most popular national park in the United States, Yellowstone National Park contains the greatest concentration of geothermal features in the world. Designated a UNESCO World Heritage Site in 1978, the park encompasses 3,472sq miles (8,987sq km) of rugged mountains, spectacular deep valleys, and broad volcanic plateaus.

Several noteworthy geologic features are scattered across the surface of Yellowstone Park. The most striking among these are a black obsidian (volcanic-glass) mountain, eroded basaltic lava flows, fossil forests, and occasional odd structures carved out by the erosive action of wind and water. The most famous and popular of Yellowstone's attractions, however, remain the 10,000 or so hot springs and geysers that bubble underground and burst onto the surface in the form of geysers, mud cauldrons, hot pools of myriad hues, steam vents, fumaroles, and hot rivers.

Yellowstone's extraordinary geothermal activity can be attributed to the unusual thinness of the earth's crust in the area. This, combined with the intrusions of magma at depths of 4 to 10 miles (6.5 to 16km) and a very steep subsurface temperature gradient serves to heat the precipitation water—that percolates through cracks and fissures on the surface—to very high temperatures, until it boils and expands. This superheated water is thrust out under pressure through the hard and strong rhyolite, silica-bearing rock at the surface.

## OLD FAITHFUL

Though not the highest, Old Faithful is the most famous geyser in North America. Located at the head of the Upper Geyser Basin, this 200 to 300-year-old geyser was so named by the Washburn-Langford-Doane Expedition in 1870 because of its apparently "faithful" eruptions every 63 to 70 minutes. On closer observation, however, the interval has been recorded as varying between 33 and 120 minutes. The geyser's eruptions are accompanied by billowing hot steam, and on clear and windless days, its fountain-like eruption column has been known to reach 170ft (52m). The average height of the eruptions, however, is approximately 130ft (40m), and the column stands for about 4 minutes.

*A group of American bison rest near the Old Faithful geyser*

*A bighorn lamb on the alpine slope of Mount Washburn, Yellowstone National Park'*

## CONNECTING YELLOWSTONE

Lieutenant William Clark, who sailed down the Yellowstone River in 1806, was the first person to explore the area. The first trading post on Yellowstone was established by a native American trader called Manuel Lisa, accompanied by a trapper called John Colter, at the mouth of the Bighorn River in 1807. Today, more than 500 miles (800km) of roads and 1,000 miles (1,600km) of trails spread throughout the entire park. Established in 1972, the 80-mile (130-km) scenic John D. Rockefeller Jr. Memorial Parkway today connects Yellowstone to the Grand Teton National Park in the south.

Yellowstone National Park is headquartered at the Old Faithful and Mammoth Hot Springs, and several of the most famous geysers and hot springs are located between the two.

Included among these is the Giantess, which is situated close to the Old Faithful and erupts at intervals of every six to eight months. There is also the Fountain Paint Pot—located in the Lower Geyser Basin, it consists of fumaroles, pink plopping mud geysers, and a blue hot spring pool. The Minerva—located at Mammoth Hot Springs—is a multi-colored terrace with hot water cascades.

Yellowstone is also famous for its many lakes and rivers. The huge Yellowstone Lake, the largest mountain lake in North America, occupies a caldera formed by an eruption 600,000 years ago. Fishing and boating are among the most popular sports. The Yellowstone River traverses a magnificent, brilliantly colored gorge and has two majestic waterfalls along its course.

Forests cover most of the park. Though the lodgepole pine accounts for the majority of the trees found in the area, other species of conifers, cottonwoods, and aspens also abound. The warm months see a profusion of wildflower blossoms.

The wildlife prowling the jungles of Yellowstone is typical of the Rocky Mountains, and consists of elk, bighorn sheep, deer, moose, bison (buffalo), coyotes, and black and grizzly bears. Reintroduced into the park in 1995, 13 packs of wolves now make Yellowstone their home. Bird species in the park number hundreds; several of these species are waterfowl, including the rare trumpeter swan. The fish-filled lakes and streams of Yellowstone draw many anglers, with the trout being the most popular catch.

- The name Devils Tower is derived from the American-Indian term "The Bad God's Tower." It was called this for the first time by Colonel Richard Irving Dodge in his 1879 book, *The Black Hills*.

- The idea of preserving the tower as a national or state park was first brought up in 1892, but it was not until 14 years later, on September 24, 1906, that it was declared a National Monument by President Theodore Roosevelt.

# Devils Tower

**L**ong before explorers wandered into the West, the Indian tribes of the northern plains, looked at the Devils Tower rising above the surrounding grassland and the ponderosa pine forest with awe. They called it "Grizzly Bear's Lodge" and believed its existence was holy. To this date, various Native American plains tribes including the Sioux, Cheyenne, and Kiowa, worship regularly at the Tower.

Rising 867ft (264m) from its base, 1,267ft (386m) above the Belle Fourche River, and 5,117ft (1,560m) above sea level, Devils Tower is a prominent landmark in northeastern Wyoming. Geological estimates put its age at approximately 50 million years, though erosion probably uncovered the rock formations only one or two million years ago. Its slightly dome-shaped summit is roughly 200ft by 400ft (61m by 122m). Chipmunks, mice, rats, and occasionally snakes are found on top. The area in which the tower stands was once home to prairie dogs, gray wolf,

*A prairie dog eats grass at Devils Tower National Monument*

## NATIVE AMERICAN TRIBES

According to the National Park Service, over 20 tribes have cultural affiliation with the Devils Tower. They include the Arapaho, Lakota (Sioux), Blackfeet, Crow, Cheyenne, Kiowa, Eastern and Southern Shoshone, and Oglala Lakota to name a few. These tribes have been known to have offered prayers and to hold vision quests and funerals here. The Arapaho called Devils Tower by the name "Bear's Tipi," the Cheyenne know it as "Bear's Lodge" and "Bear's Peak," and the Kiowa refer to it as "Tree Rock." The Sioux traditionally held their sacred Sun Dance at Devils Tower (around summer solstice) and used to refer to the Belle Fourche River as the Sun Dance River.

black bear, and the grizzly bear. This might well be the reason why the American Indians identified the Tower with bears and their lairs. A favorite with climbers, the Devils Tower every year observes a voluntary closure in June, to allow Indians to worship at the site. Various tribes have over the years objected to the recreational climbing at Devils Tower and this voluntary closure is the administration's attempt to encourage and respect the American Indian culture.

The exact process of how this rock was formed is unknown, though a majority of geologists contend that is was once part of a shallow sandstone seabed during the Triassic period (195 to 225 million years ago). This red sandstone and maroon siltstone can still be seen along the edges of the Belle Fourche River flowing by the tower. It was shaped by a molten rock forced upward from deep within the earth. Debate continues, however, as to whether molten rock tore through the earth's crust or cooled underground. The distinctive furrowed columns are a result of contractions that occurred during the cooling of the rock. The Tower slowly emerged after years of water and wind erosion exposed it. While most of its outer sandstone layer and shales wore off, its harder ingenious core survived.

Today, as rain pounds its furrows, cracks, and surviving sedimentary surface, more and more of the tower will become exposed and eventually erode completely. Pieces of it continue to break off and fall from its steep walls, as do occasionally entire columns, which can be seen lying in a pile of rubble at its base. As this process of weathering continues, Devils Tower will eventually collapse completely—but it is likely to be around for a good million years yet.

## SCALING THE TOWER

The first major non-American Indian event held here was on July 4, 1893 and it included the successful scaling of the mountain by William Rogers, a local rancher. According to a handbill circulated for the occasion, people were invited to witness the first climb and were promised, "plenty to eat and drink on the grounds" with "lots of hay and grain for horses" and "dancing day and night." Rogers climbed the Rock with the help of a 350-ft (107-m) wooden ladder that was held in place with oak, ash, and willow pegs driven into the vertical crack found between the two columns on the southeast side of the giant formation. It is estimated that some 1,000 people, who arrived here by horseback, wagon, and buckboard, witnessed the event.

*Silhouette of man hiking up one of the steep paths at Devils Tower*

- The name Niagara is said to have been derived from the Iroquois Indian word *Onguiaahra* meaning "the strait."

- The flow over the American section of the Niagara Falls was halted for several months in 1969 in order to remove rubble and rocks from the riverbed in an attempt to improve its appearance. The plan was eventually shelved due to unforseen expenses.

**Niagara Falls,** Canada/USA

# Niagara Falls

The air is enveloped in a blanket of mist and spray where the dark green waters of Niagara Falls thunder into the frothing cauldron at its base. The second largest waterfall in the world after Victoria Falls, Niagara is the collective name given to three waterfalls—Horseshoe or Canadian Falls, American Falls, and the much smaller Bridal Veil Falls. Estimated to have been formed only around 10,000 years ago during the last Ice Age, the falls are relatively young in geological terms. Since then, however, they have shifted about 7 miles (11km) from their spot of origin. This shift was caused by the swiftly flowing waters of the Niagara River, eroding the soft shale and sandstone and causing them to cave in. As a result the river gradually retreated, leaving in its wake a deep gorge.

Approximately 500 years ago, the river encountered an obstacle that caused it to split into two channels, forming an island between them, now called Goat Island. Thus, American Falls lies on the east, while Horseshoe Falls is to its west on the Canadian side of the border. Of the two waterfalls, Horseshoe—named so because of its 2,600ft (792m) long horseshoe-shaped arc—is the more overwhelming. It is 185ft (56m) high, and more than 600,000 gallons (2.27 million liters) of water pour over the edge every second. The almost straight brink of American Falls, on the other hand, is 1,000ft (305m)

*An aerial view of Niagara Falls*

## CANADA'S THUNDERING WATERFALLS

Canada is home to many other spectacular waterfalls. At Virginia Falls, in the Northwest Territories, the South Nahanni River thunders over a precipice almost twice the height of Niagara. This little-known river descends 3,000ft (915m) over a distance of 370 miles (595km) in a series of tumbling rapids and deep gorges. Hunlen Falls and Helmcken Falls are both in British Columbia. At Helmcken Falls, the Murtle River cascades over a cliff to a spray-filled basin 450ft (137m) below. Hunlen Falls are seven times the height of the Niagara and drop in a curtain of spray 1,200ft (366m) to the rocks below.

*The Maid of the Mist carrying tourists into the Niagara Falls spray*

## OVER THE FALLS

Some people have taken the sheer power and size of Niagara Falls as an irresistible personal challenge. Several adventurers have gone over the falls, in a variety of different vessels, including barrels, boats, and sealed capsules.

One of the most famous death-defying escapades took place on June 30, 1859, when Jean Francois Gravelet, better known as Charles Blondin, crossed the falls on a tightrope. The rope was 1,100ft (335m) long, and suspended 160ft (49m) above the falls. Evidently Blondin found the whole experience a bit too tame: a year later he made the crossing again, but this time with his agent on his back!

long, and the fall height is 190ft (58m)—but the actual fall is only 70ft (21m) because of rock piled up at the base—and about 150,000 gallons (568,000 liters) of water pass over the brink of the escarpment every second. Today, about 50 percent of the Niagara waters is diverted and harnessed to generate electricity.

The Belgian Franciscan friar, Father Louis Hennepin, is credited as being the first European to discover Niagara Falls; his description of 1678 was instrumental in bringing the falls to the world's attention. Today, the falls attract more than 12 million visitors annually. Bridges and parks on either side of the river provide great vantage points for viewing the stunning falls. Rainbow Bridge, named because of the rainbows perennially shimmering in the spray, offers visitors a glorious view. The oldest and most famous tourist attraction at Niagara Falls is the Maid of the Mist boat cruise. The cruise, named after a mythical Onguiaahra character, has been operating since 1846 and has been carrying passengers to the whirlpools at the foot of the falls. Cruise boats operate from both the United States and Canadian sides of the stunning falls.

Niagara Falls have also featured in Hollywood movies, most notably in the 1953 movie Niagara starring Marilyn Monroe, Superman II in 1980, and Teenage Mutant Ninja Turtles shot in 1987. The falls have also been the subject of an IMAX movie.

- The survival of the mighty coast redwood is largely dependent on fog, which is responsible for one-fourth of the precipitation in the area.

- The giant sequoia (*Sequoiadendron giganteum*) found in the Redwood National Park is generally considered to be the largest living organism in the world.

**Redwood National Park,** USA

# Redwood National Park

Occupying the northwestern corner of California, the Redwood National Park contains magnificent forests of sequoia redwood trees that cover the coastal mountain region bordering the Pacific Ocean north of San Francisco. Formerly established in 1968, the boundaries of the park were redefined in 1978, and it was inscribed as a UNESCO World Heritage Site in 1980. Home to some of the tallest and most impressive trees in the world, the 172sq mile (445sq km) Redwood National Park showcases 40 miles (64km) of the picturesque Pacific coastline. The park also encompasses land belonging to the Jedediah Smith Redwoods, the Del Norte Coast Redwoods, and the Prairie Creek Redwoods state parks.

## THE SEQUOIA SEMPERVIRENS

The fast-growing coast redwood is among the longest-lived species in the world. Individual trees have an average lifespan of about 600 years and are also the tallest trees in the world. A redwood called "Tall Tree" was identified in the Tall Trees Grove near Redwood Creek in 1963. Measuring 367.8ft (112.1m) in height, when the top broke off later, its diameter was calculated at 14ft (4m). Though commercial logging has largely reduced the population of these magnificent trees, protected from fire by their thick sapless bark they can live to more than 2,000 years.

*Couple standing on a giant sequoia stump in the Redwood National Park*

*Rhododendrons in the Redwood National Park*

## EXPLOITING THE FOREST GIANTS

The redwood and giant sequoia produce high-quality timber, prized as a multi-purpose wood suitable for a range of uses including house-building, furniture-making, and rail sleepers. They are straight-growing, with few knots and a fine grain, making them light but strong. A combination of natural oils and resins makes them almost rot-proof and resistant to termite attacks.

In the latter half of the 19th century these trees were heavily exploited, and were nearly wiped out. Though felling of these trees continues, the US National Parks Service has stepped up its efforts to annex remaining tracts of forest to the existing protected areas.

More than one-third of the national park's area is covered with old growth or virgin groves of ancient redwoods. The two species that dominate the old growth redwood groves are the coast redwood (*Sequoia sempervirens*) and Douglas-fir (*Pseudotsuga menziesii*). Ideal growing conditions for the coast redwood are found in the sheltered valleys and alluvial flats alongside creeks and streams in the Redwood National Park. As a result, many of these trees reach heights greater than 300ft (92m). The trees are protected from the injurious salty spray and bitter salt-laden winds from the coast by a natural buffer formed by the dunes and communities of scrub plants that grow on the beach. The growth of these trees, however, is stunted by water stress on drier and windier slopes and ridges, and their height is often restricted to 200ft (61m) or less.

Further inland and at a greater altitude, the growth of redwoods is hampered by hot and dry climatic conditions, with the redwood forests making way for mixed evergreen forests of Douglas firs. Other trees that populate the area include hardwoods such as tanoak, madrone, big-leaf maple, California bay or laurel, and red alder. The most common plants that make up the undergrowth of the redwood forests are the redwood sorrel and the sword fern, accompanied by rhododendron, azalea, salal, huckleberry, and other shrubs.

The Redwood National Park is watered by three large river systems—the Smith River, the Klamath River, and the Redwood Creek. Renowned for their sheer beauty and the opportunity that they provide for fishing salmon and steelhead, the rivers have carved out deep gorges in the forest and mountainous terrain of the park. Beginning in the Siskiyou Mountains, the Smith River—named after the explorer Jedediah Smith, who crossed this area in 1828—flows through the northern section of the park and is one of the longest free-flowing river systems in California. The Redwood Creek flows through the southern section of the park and travels northwest along the Grogan Fault, while the Klamath River traversing the middle of the park is the largest river of the North Coast.

The rivers of Redwood National Park provide substantial natural habitats along their banks and estuaries. A wide range of animals, including moose, elk, black bear, beaver, white-tailed deer, and mule deer, thrive and abound in the park's forests.

- Carved out by the Virgin River, the Zion Canyon is only about 15 miles (24km) long, and yet reaches depths of 2,500ft (762m) in places.

- Located deep within the Zion National Park, the Kolob Arch is one of the largest free-standing arches in the world.

**Zion National Park,** USA

# Zion National Park

S licing through the rocks of the Washington, Iron, and Kane counties of southwestern Utah, the Zion Canyon is the chief attraction of the Zion National Park. Situated at the edge of the Colorado Plateau, the park encompasses a picturesque region of distinctly colored canyons.

Largely a flat basin close to sea level, Zion evolved approximately 240 million years ago. A small stream headed southward meandered its way across the soft young rocks of a plateau. As the land rose, the stream began to cut itself a path, scouring the underlying rock with particles of grit and sand that eroded further upstream. The result of this was Zion Canyon, a winding gorge slicing through the Navajo sandstone to the older, underlying Kaibab limestone.

The idea of a sanctuary was first discussed in 1909, with the creation of the Mukuntuweap National Monument. More of the wilderness surrounding the canyon was included in the protected zone in 1919 and the Zion National Park was thus established, occupying an area of 148sq miles (383sq km). The park was expanded in 1956, to include 229sq miles (593sq km) of land.

The Great White Throne

## ZION'S SETTLERS

The earliest inhabitants of Zion were hunter-gatherers who arrived approximately 12,000 years ago, when mammoths and giant sloths roamed the area. After these species became extinct, the hunters turned their attention to smaller animals, and eventually took up farming as a means of subsistence around 2,600 years ago. The tribe, now known as the Anasazi, abandoned the area about 800 years ago after which the Paiute people settled there. Mormons arrived at the canyon in 1858 and gave the park its present name, Zion, meaning "refuge" in Hebrew. In some of the larger caves of the canyon, archeologists have also discovered artifacts from the Pueblo people.

Spectacular rock formations—including towering cliffs, forbidding domes, and deep chasms—make up the landscape of the Zion National Park, ranging in color from deep glowing red to a delicate rose-pink. The Weeping Rock, where water from springs seeps out of the rock surface and drops like tears from the overhang, is among the park's many famous features. While the great sandstone slab of Checkerboard Mesa looms over the road, its surface intricately carved into squares by wind and water, the flat-topped Great White Throne is an imposing monolith rising 2,394ft (730m) above the canyon floor. A natural arch spans two cliff faces in Verkin Canyon. The West Temple, which rises to a height of 3,800ft (1,158m) from the base of the canyon, marks the highest point in the park. A group of jagged sandstone peaks, ranging along the west wall of the canyon, is collectively dubbed the Towers of the Virgin. The Grand Staircase, the Hanging Garden, the Emerald Pool, and the natural amphitheater of the Temple of Sinawava are the other striking features of the Zion.

The topography of the Zion National Park includes forested highlands and lowland deserts, and it includes over 900 varieties of plants. The park provides sanctuary to 75 species of mammals, 291 species of birds, and 44 types of reptiles and amphibians, including a species of desert tortoise. Eight species of fish are found in waters of the Virgin River which flows through the park. The Virgin Spinedace, the Peregrine falcon, and the Zion snail are among the rarest and most remarkable creatures that inhabit this park.

## AMERICA'S NATURAL BEAUTY

An area of about 120,300sq miles (310,000sq km), which includes around 320 different sites, falls under the care of the US National Park Service, which covers historical sites as well as sites of unrivaled natural wonder. These include battlefields (such as Saratoga and Gettysburg), early trading posts and archeological sites where evidence of Indian settlements have been discovered.

The first national park, founded in 1872—and which remains one of the most popular in America—is the Yellowstone National Park. Since then many other sites have been recognized for their fundamental reflection of America's rich historical and geological heritage, and their protection has been guaranteed by their designation as national parks or national monuments.

*The Emerald Pools*

- Monument Valley earned worldwide fame from its inclusion in western movie classics such as *Stagecoach*, *She Wore A Yellow Ribbon*, and *Cheyenne Autumn*.

- The climate of this region has changed negligibly in the last 700 years. Periods of heavy rain continue to alternate with those of drought.

**Monument Valley,** USA

## FORAYS INTO MONUMENT VALLEY

After early attempts by Spanish and Mexican explorers to control the area, the Navajos fled to the Navajo Mountain. In the early 1860s, however, they were rounded up by the legendary Kit Carson and relocated to a reservation. They returned to the area in 1868, only to find themselves competing against prospectors of silver. President Chester Arthur added this area to the Navajo Reservation in 1884, but the search for silver did not stop. In the year 1906, a trading post was established at Oljeto by John Wetherill and Clyde Colville. Established as a trading post by Harry Goulding in the 1920s, the small town of Goulding provides a comprehensive range of facilities for visitors today.

*White Mesa Arch, Arizona*

# Monument Valley

**M**yriad mesas, sandstone buttes, spires, and monoliths projecting from the land make up the dramatic landscape of Monument Valley in the Colorado Plateau. Straddling the border of southeastern Utah and northeastern Arizona, Monument Valley is a Navajo Nation Tribal Park that contains some of the most striking geological formations in the southwestern United States. Contrary to what the latter half of its name suggests, Monument Valley is a wide and flat land from which crumbling formations—the remains of layers of sandstone that once covered the entire region—raise their heads high into the air.

Seated atop the crest of the wide anticline of Monument Upwarp, Monument Valley is composed of beautiful layers of sandstone, siltstone, and shale of various hues.

Large quantities of rocky sediments were deposited in the region when it was a vast lowland basin millions of years ago, during the Eocene epoch of the Cenozoic era. Several millennia later, this area too, underwent the processes of uplifting and folding along with the rest of the Colorado plateau; it twisted and broke to reveal the soft rocks that had been buried beneath the surface.

The erosive action of wind and water over the last 50 million years has created the magnificent spires and buttes of sandstone that we see today. While iron oxide gives the sands and rocks of Monument Valley a reddish tinge, black streaks of desert varnish are caused by the presence of manganese dioxide. Though Monument Valley is home to the famous purple sage of western lore, few trees, except for a rare juniper at the edges of

## THE NAVAJO PEOPLE

Of all the Native American groups that live in the United States, the Navajo is among the largest in terms of population. Believed to have migrated to the United States from Canada between 900 and 1200, the Navajo, are found mostly in northwestern New Mexico, southeastern Utah, and Arizona. Toward the end of the 20th century their population was approximately 170,000. The Navajo speak an Apachean language which belongs to the Athabascan family. Since the supposed period of migration, however, the resemblance between these two groups has been lessened because of the subsequent influence of the Pueblo Indians on the Navajos.

*Elderly Navajo woman weaving carpets, Monument Valley, Utah*

the valley, grow on these soils because of the extreme dryness and lack of moisture. Cliffrose, rabbitbrush, and snakewood can be seen in the rare moist patches of the valley. The scarcity of adequate habitats coupled with the presence of Navajo residents account for the absence of an abundant wildlife.

Today the Navajo Nation Tribal Park spreads across 115sq miles (298sq km), and has been the site of human habitation for thousands of years. The area was occupied by Ice Age Paleo-Indian hunters between 12,000 and 6,000BC. Between then and the Christian era, archaic hunter-gatherers populated the area, followed by the ancient Anasazi people who arrived at the beginning of the Christian era, and then disappeared around AD1300; they left behind beautiful petroglyphs and pictographs that have been well preserved. The area was then frequented by the Paiute, who ascribed many legends and supernatural tales to it and called the valley "The Treeless Area Amid the Rocks."

The Navajo people who make their home within the park have been preserving their heritage, language, art forms, and traditional way of life for centuries, maintaining a careful relationship of harmony and respect with the land. Guided tours through the tribal park provide a complete experience to visitors, who are told stories and legends associated with this stunning land as it unfolds in front of them. The stark and desolate beauty of Monument Valley is thus complemented by the warm, rich heritage of the Navajo people.

- Fed mostly by snowmelt, peak flow for the Yosemite Falls usually occurs in late May, and by August it often becomes dry. It begins flowing again a few months later, after the winter snows arrive.

- The Half Dome at the head of the Yosemite Valley has a broad sculpted base and rises almost 5,000ft (1,525m) above the valley floor.

**Yosemite National Park,** USA

# Yosemite National Park

ew places in the world can have as many spectacular features concentrated in one small area as Yosemite Valley, a 7.5-mile (12-km) long natural masterpiece of staggering beauty and diversity nestling in the heart of the Sierra Nevada mountain range of California. Yosemite was first designated a state park in 1864; the boundaries were redefined and additional land incorporated in 1890 to make it a national park. Comprising 1,189sq miles (3,080sq km) it includes groves of giant sequoias, some of them thousands of years old, the meandering Merced River, the stunning Yosemite Valley, and the Yosemite Falls, as well as sheer rock walls, giant buttresses, and imposing peaks. The Yosemite National Park is home to some of the most picturesque and breathtaking scenic landscapes in the United States and became a UNESCO World Heritage Site in 1984.

## JOHN MUIR AND YOSEMITE'S CONSERVATION

The renowned naturalist John Muir is credited with the task which eventually resulted in the establishment of national parks such as the Yosemite and Sequoia. His first visit to the Yosemite Valley was in 1868, after which his interest in glaciers and forests led him to states such as Alaska, Nevada, and Washington. Eight years after his first visit to the Yosemite Valley, Muir advocated a forest conservation policy which led to the establishment of Yosemite as a national park; the conservation efforts initiated by President Theodore Roosevelt were greatly influenced by him. Muir's most significant contribution was the formulation of the idea of Yosemite's glacial origin—a theory that has now found universal acceptance.

*Bank of the Merced River*

The astounding valley landscape of Yosemite was created as a result of glaciation. The granite bedrock of the area was gouged and molded into steep cliffs, bare summits, rounded domes, and gigantic monoliths during the last Ice Age. The flat floor of the Yosemite Valley has evolved from the slow sedimentation of a large lake fed by melt water from ancient glaciers. The process of geological evolution still continues, and the lakes of the valley continue to silt up. The Yosemite Valley floor lies at an elevation of about 4,000ft (1,220m) above sea level.

Today, the Yosemite Valley is filled with blossoming meadows and surrounded by spectacular waterfalls. The most dramatic of these waterfalls is the Yosemite Falls, which is formed by creeks tumbling into the valley from the overhanging edges of tributary valleys. While the Upper Yosemite Falls has a drop height of 1,430ft (436m), the Lower Falls drop down 320ft (98m). Together, the falls have a combined height of 2,425ft (739m) from the crest of the Upper Falls to the base of the Lower, and form one of the tallest and most exquisite cataracts in the world. Other remarkable waterfalls located within the Yosemite National Park include the Bridalveil and Ribbon falls on the western slopes of the Sierra Nevada.

Rock formations within the Yosemite National Park are simply magnificent. El Capitan, a granite buttress that rises about 3,604ft (1,098m) from the floor of the valley, is the most popular site in the park. Other impressive rocks in the park include the Three Brothers, North Dome, Glacier Point, Sentinel Dome, and Cloud's Rest—all of them ranging from 2,800 to 6,000ft (610 to 1,829m) in height.

While the lower reaches of the park are characterized by scattered deciduous and coniferous trees, the higher elevations have a denser growth of conifers, mountain hemlock, and lodgepole pine. However, the Yosemite National Park's most enduring and attractive trees are the magnificent giant sequoias. Mule deer, black bear, chipmunks, squirrels, and various other creatures make up the animal life within the park.

## ROCK CLIMBING IN YOSEMITE

Yosemite Valley offers all types of climbing surfaces: crack, chimneys, faces, overhangs, artificial aid, high angle, low angle—whatever a climber could desire, including Sentinel Rock, Royal Arches, and El Capitan, one of the largest granite faces in the world. Yosemite became the focus for rock-climbing in the US in the 1950s and 1960s, when Royal Robbins, Yvon Chouinard, and Warren Harding first made ascents on climbs that had previously been thought impossible. Robbins, Jerry Galwas, and Mike Sherrick were the first climbers to conquer the sheer 2000-ft (610-m), northwest face of Half Dome in 1957; and Harding, Wayne Merry, and George Whitwore made the first ascent of the Nose Route of El Capitan the following year.

*Loose rope walking above the Yosemite*

- Lava Falls, one of the largest rapids in the Grand Canyon with a 37-ft (11-m) drop, is also the fastest stretch of navigable water in North America.

- The Grand Canyon Skywalk is a horseshoe-shape glass bridge that enables tourists to look down at the Colorado River 4,000ft (1,220m) below.

**The Grand Canyon,** USA

# The
# Grand Canyon

A spectacular complex of waterfalls, caverns, towers, ledges, and ravines, the Grand Canyon landscape appears to change constantly with the play of sunlight—the shadows shift through the day and the rocks lighten to pale pink and blue-grey, then darken to purple-brown and black as the rays of the sun peek through clouds and slant across the massive gorge.

The word "grand" does little to convey the raw beauty of the Grand Canyon. The canyon is 277 miles (446km) long and 10 miles (16km) across; it extends 18 miles (29km) at its widest point, and dips down to 6,000ft (1,829m) at its deepest. Statistics, however, are inadequate for conveying the majesty and grandeur of this dramatic landscape, which has been fashioned by

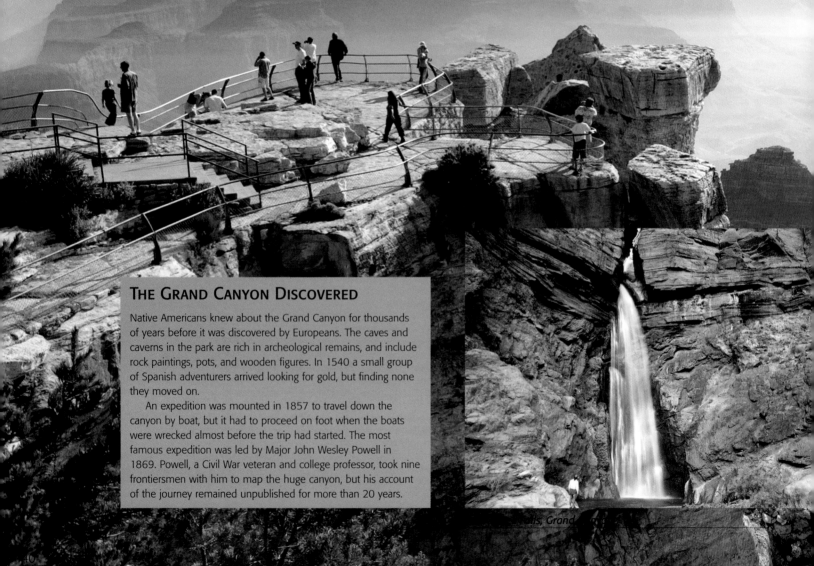

## THE GRAND CANYON DISCOVERED

Native Americans knew about the Grand Canyon for thousands of years before it was discovered by Europeans. The caves and caverns in the park are rich in archeological remains, and include rock paintings, pots, and wooden figures. In 1540 a small group of Spanish adventurers arrived looking for gold, but finding none they moved on.

An expedition was mounted in 1857 to travel down the canyon by boat, but it had to proceed on foot when the boats were wrecked almost before the trip had started. The most famous expedition was led by Major John Wesley Powell in 1869. Powell, a Civil War veteran and college professor, took nine frontiersmen with him to map the huge canyon, but his account of the journey remained unpublished for more than 20 years.

## ROOSEVELT VISITS THE GRAND CANYON

One of the early visitors to the Grand Canyon was President Theodore Roosevelt, who first came in 1903, and made it a national monument in 1908.

Roosevelt was influenced by the writings of the conservation campaigner John Muir, and pursued policies aimed at protecting vast areas of American wilderness and maintaining the balance of their delicate ecology. Even at the turn of the 20th century, Roosevelt was aware of the delicate ecology of the area. He commented that the wisest course was for Americans to "leave it as it is. You cannot improve on it. The ages have been at work on it and man can only mar it."

*Point Sublime after sunset, North Rim, Grand Canyon National Park*

continuous carving for over 6 million years. At that time, what is now the canyon was simply a huge plain through which the Colorado River meandered. Then movements in the earth's surface caused the land to rise and the river began to cut a channel through the rocks. Today, the Grand Canyon bears the imprint of almost 2 billion years of North America's geological history.

The red terrain appears almost Martian at first glance—dusty depths walled with limestone and studded with fossils and ferrous mudflats. Though it might seem desolate and inhospitable now, before its designation as a national park in 1919, this land was home to various civilizations for at least 10,000 years. From around AD700 until AD1150 the Anasazi people lived here, farming and hunting for a living. Though they were driven out by drought, the pottery and the rundown granaries that they left behind have weathered the ravages of time and tell tales of the ancient culture. Painted pictographs by other tribes and split-twig figurines have been found throughout the canyon, too. Even before

that, Paleo-American hunters roamed these gorges, tracking animals such as the giant ground sloth.

Before it was finally christened the Grand Canyon, the site was known by various names given by the Native American tribes residing in the area. To the Hopi tribe, it was *Ongtukpa*, their ancestral home; the Southern Paiute considered it their holy land, *Puaxant Tuvip*; for the Western Apache tribes it was simply *Ge da'cho* or "edge of the big cliff."

Today, as one of the most visited natural wonders of the world, the Grand Canyon attracts about 5 million visitors every year. But tourists tend to visit only the better-known areas of the canyon and it is possible to find many secluded nooks and valleys, undisturbed by the hordes of visitors. The Grand Canyon is also home to surprisingly lush areas of flora—the Fern Glen Canyon, with its extraordinary microclimate, is one such spot where flowers and plants flourish in the middle of the desert. Calm green pools of water can be found at the base of the walls of the North Canyon Walsh.

- Other famous rock formations around Sedona include Bell Rock, Courthouse Butte, Snoopy, and Coffeepot Rock
- One of the best views of Cathedral Rock can be had from Oak Creek in the canyon of the same name. The road winding through this breathtaking canyon is Arizona's first officially designated scenic highway.

**Cathedral Rock,** Arizona

# Cathedral Rock

Cathedral Rock in Red Rock State Park, near Sedona, Arizona, is one of the world's most famous red rock formations. Glowing ochre, orange, red, gold, and gray with the play of the light, it rises high among the famed stratified red rock cliffs of Arizona, created by sedimentation and erosion over a period of 350 million years, from what was once a wetland area. Some parts of the red rock range are an extension of the Mogollon Rim, the southern edge of the Colorado Plateau, which is home to the world-renowned Grand Canyon.

Towering 900ft (274m) over Oak Creek, Cathedral Rock—a monolithic masterpiece sculpted in sandstone—takes its name from the startling similarity of its appearance to a cathedral. Topped by twin spires with a saddle in between, it offers spectacular vistas of the endless formations of red rock country: the buttes, bluffs, mesas, pinnacles, spires, canyons, and creeks are spread out on all sides. Some of the better-known formations you can spot from the saddle include Courthouse Rock, The Nuns, Lee Mountain, and Twin Buttes.

There is a legend attached to the stone fingers of Cathedral Rock, involving a constantly bickering man and wife who disregard the Great Spirit's decree to live in harmony and therefore end up being etched in stone for eternity as a lesson to the rest of humanity. Legends apart, the red cliffs around Cathedral Rock were home to Native Americans who considered certain spots sacred and magical. Hundreds of years later, New Age followers believe that the region has many vortex centers emanating electromagnetic energy; one of these vortices is Cathedral Rock, which is thought to be a "feminine energy" site.

## BLAST FROM THE PAST

Sedona, Oak Tree Canyon, and Cathedral Rock are part of the Verde Valley, located in north central Arizona. Millions of years ago, in Precambrian times, this area was a submarine volcanic environment. Plate action led to a fault in the region, which in turn showed up in volcanic activity and caused the formation of hot springs. These hot springs threw up deposits of gold, silver, and copper, and were responsible not only for the mineral deposits in the area, but also for the famously colored mountains.

*A section of Sedona's famous red rocks*

## MOVIE MAGIC

The beauty of the red rock range around Sedona was first seen on the big screen in an adaptation of Zane Grey's book, *The Call of the Canyon* in 1923. For the next 30 years, dozens of westerns were shot in these stunning locales, including *The Rounders*, *Apache*, *Leave her to Heaven*, and *Johnny Guitar*.

These prehistoric rocks shelter within their environs, a variety of animals, everything from the dangerous cougar, bobcat, rattlesnake, mountain bear, and coyote, to the harmless deer, elk, badger, chipmunk, and squirrel. More than 200 species of bird can be found in the neighboring canyons, including hawks and bald eagles that can be seen circling the skies above. The plant life is correspondingly rich and beautiful; when it rains, the ground is transformed into a carpet of wildflowers, while throughout the year, trees like sycamore, ash, walnut, cottonwood, scrub oak, and mountain mahogany jostle for space.

The climbing route to Cathedral Rock is nationally feted, though the top 300ft (91m) are considered too dangerous for any but experienced climbers, as the sandstone here is brittle and crumbles easily. However, this has hardly been a deterrent to the five million tourists who visit Sedona and Cathedral Rock annually.

- The area of Death Valley 282ft (86m) below sea level and about 4.75 miles (7.64 km) west of Badwater, forms the single lowest point in the western hemisphere.
- Death Valley was declared a national monument in 1933. and established as a national park only in 1994.

**Death Valley,** USA

# Death Valley

The lowest, hottest, and driest fraction of the North American continent makes up the bleak landscape of Death Valley. This structural depression in Inyo County, southeastern California is bounded by the Panamint Range to the west and the mountains of the Amargosa Range to the east. The valley is inclined roughly north to south and runs for approximately 140 miles (225km); its width ranges from 5 to 16 miles (8 to 26km). Though it is geologically a part of the southwestern part of the Great Basin, Death Valley actually lies near the undefined boundary between the Great Basin and the Mojave deserts.

Death Valley closely resembles other structural basins in the region, but its uniqueness is defined by its great depth. Part of the valley floor is made up of salt pans, sections of which constitute the lowest land areas in the Americas. About 550sq miles (1,425sq km) of the floor of Death Valley is situated below sea level.

## BALLARAT

Named after an Australian gold camp and located at the base of the Panamint Mountain Range to the west of Death Valley proper, Ballarat came into being in 1897. The town's gold mines produced 16,535 tons of gold ore till 1903. One of the town's early residents, an Australian immigrant, George Riggins, named the town. Within a year of its establishment, the town had approximately 400 residents who lived in settlements made of adobe bricks. However, once the Radcliffe Mines ceased operations after 1903, the town lost much of its attraction. Apart from the gold mine, the town was also made famous by legendary figures such as Frank "Shorty" Harris and "Seldom" Seen Slim. Privately owned today, the ghost town of Ballarat offers tourists the chance to view the ruins of old adobe buildings.

*Beavertail cactus in full bloom in the Goler Wash*

The geological history of the creation of Death Valley involves various kinds of fault activity at different periods of time. Crustal sinking and volcanic activity have also played a role in the formation of this vast desolate land. Essentially, the rift valley was formed by the sinking of a huge expanse of rock along parallel fault lines in between the mountain ranges to its east and west. This sinking started approximately 30 million years ago, during the middle Tertiary period. As the valley sank, it was filled continuously by eroded sediments from the surrounding mountain ranges. Today, at the centre of the valley—the bedrock is believed to be buried under 9,000ft (2,745m) of sediments—tilting and sinking of the valley floor continues.

The floor of Death Valley is legendary for its arid conditions and extreme temperatures. Ground temperatures as high as 190°F (88°C) have been recorded in the area, and summer temperatures often exceed 120°F (49°C). Most of the rainfall is blocked by the mountains in the west, and the heat combines with the low humidity to make the area very dry and inhospitable. The salt pan that covers much of the valley floor is the remains of a shallow lake that existed in the area a few thousand years ago. Most of the surface water in Death Valley today is contained in the saline ponds and marshes that surround the pan.

Despite the dry and desert-like conditions, there is no dearth of life in the Death Valley. Hardy and salt-tolerant species of picklewood and saltgrass are found around the springs and at the edges of the salt pan. Creosote bushes, desert holly, cacti, desert wildflowers, and mesquite are also found in some areas. Animal life is varied as well, with rabbits, many species of rodents, coyotes, bobcats, wild burros, and the bighorn sheep making Death Valley their home.

## AMARGOSA RANGE

The Amargosa Range consists of a group of mountains that occupy the stretch of eastern California and southern Nevada in the United States. Covering a distance of 110 miles (180 km) from Grapevine Peak to the Amargosa River, it forms a barrier between the Death Valley and the Amargosa Desert. The range comprises of three subdivisions—the ranges of Grapevine, Funeral, and Black. The area surrounding the range is drained by the Amargosa River. Zabriskie Point, a well-known feature of the Death Valley National Park, is found here. The two relatively well-known peaks in this range are the Grapevine Peak at 8,705ft (2,653m), and Dante's View at 5,475ft (1,669m); the latter provides clear views of Death Valley and the Panamint Range which lies beyond.

*A creosote bush survives in this harsh climate as wind creates patterns in the sand—Mesquite Sand Dunes, Amargosa Mountains*

- The Meteor Crater, also known as the Barringer Crater, was the first to be officially recognized out of the 160 terrestrial impact craters identified to date.
- The Meteor Crater was discovered with more than 30 tons of meteoritic iron strewn around the site for 8 to 10 miles (13 to 16km).

**Meteor Crater,** USA

# Meteor Crater

L ocated 35 miles (56km) east of Flagstaff in the northern Arizona desert, yawns the giant mouth of the Meteor Crater. Approximately 50,000 years ago, during the Pleistocene epoch, a meteorite slammed into the earth, resulting in a crater, 4,000ft (1,200m) in diameter and about 600ft (180m) deep, with its rim jutting up 120–200ft (36–60m) from the surrounding plain.

Scientists believed that an iron-nickel meteorite, possibly weighing over 300,000 tons, struck our planet causing an explosion that generated a thousand times the destructive energy of the Hiroshima atomic bomb.

As the extraterrestrial object hit the earth's surface at a speed of 12 miles (19km) per second, the intense heat generated caused the iron in the meteorite, along with some rocks in the vicinity, to vaporize. More than a few million tons of limestone and sandstone were displaced to form the cavity. The heat and pressure transformed the graphite in the meteorite and the rocks in the vicinity into miniscule diamonds. The shock of the impact is believed to have triggered off an earthquake measuring around 5.5 on the Richter scale.

*An aerial view of the Meteor Crater*

## LIVING ON

Unlike other impact craters, the Meteor Crater has remained largely unchanged by the action of the elements. The crater walls have only been slightly modified by erosion, and remnants from the original debris cloud can still to be found today. The rim stands tall around the crater, and the carpet of detritus ejected during the initial impact is still present at the site.

Geothermal volcanic mud pots

## CRATER LEGACY

The Barringer family entered into an agreement with a corporation called the Bar-T-Bar Ranch Company in 1941. The company formed Meteor Crater Enterprises Inc, 14 years later, and entered into a long-term lease with the Barringers. Today, the company continues to own the land, and along with its purpose of studying the crater, furthers the cause of science and academics, providing grants, scholarships, and instituting special awards.

Although the Pueblo people—the native inhabitants of the area—were aware of the existence of the crater, it wasn't until the late 19th century that scientists turned their attention to it, and it was only in the 20th century that the crater's origin was scientifically explained. A man named Franklin, a scout for General Custer, was the first person to write a report on the crater in 1871, and for many years it was known as Franklin's Hole. Thereafter, it was mistaken by settlers for an extinct volcano, part of the Hopi Buttes volcanic field nearby and rechristened Coon Butte. It was in 1902 that the mining engineer Daniel M. Barringer came across the crater, and certain that it was an impact crater, decided that a venture for mining iron—or even the entire meteorite—from the site would be very lucrative.

Barringer then set up the Standard Iron Company, and proceeded to secure mining rights from the government. Over the next 27 years this venture cost Barringer and his company over $600,000, a fortune in those days. Even though they dug as deep as 1,374ft (419m) into the earth's crust no significant deposit was found. Barringer was forced to abandon the mission in 1929, due to lack of funds and the fact that it was a futile excercise. He, however, did manage to convince most of the scientific community about the impact origin of the crater. It was in the 1960s that Eugene M. Shoemaker carried out further research and confirmed Barringer's hypothesis. The crater today is owned by the Barringer family, and is known as the Barringer Crater in his honor. Meteor Crater is one of Arizona's most popular tourist attractions.

Scientists are studying extremophile microbes in the Lechuguilla Cave—in the Carlsbad Caverns National Park—in the hope of generating a possible cure for cancer.

Bones of Ice Age animals such as jaguars, camels, lions, and giant sloths have been discovered in the area surrounding the entrance of caves in Carlsbad Caverns National Park.

**The Carlsbad Caverns,** USA

# The Carlsbad Caverns

## BATS

Carlsbad Caverns are home to more than 1 million Mexican freetail bats. Bat Cave, near the natural entrance to the caverns, is their favored roost. The winged mammals fly out every evening in a thick whirlwind, and then return to the caves before daybreak. These creatures are primarily responsible for the deposits of guano that are found in the caves. This section of Carlsbad is now open only to researchers.

Comprising colossal subterranean caverns and astounding cave formations, the Carlsbad Caverns lie beneath the surface of the Chihuahuan desert, near the base of the Guadalupe mountains of southeastern New Mexico and west Texas, and form one of the longest cave systems in North America. More than 80 recognized caves make up the Carlsbad Caverns National Park; these caves are famous not only for their overwhelming size but also for the beauty and diversity of their incredible natural limestone structures.

*Stalagmites, Carlsbad Caverns*

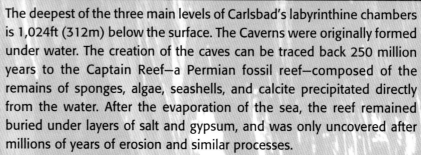

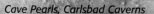

*Cave Pearls, Carlsbad Caverns*

## ANCIENT ARTIFACTS

Several caves of the Carlsbad Caverns bear pictographs left by Archaic hunters and gatherers who are believed to have settled in the area in 6,000BC. The Painted Grotto, the Upper Painted Grotto, and Slaughter Canyon contain profuse and remarkable examples of such rock art. Shards of pottery dating between AD800 and AD154 have also been discovered at several archeological sites within the Carlsbad Caverns National Park.

The deepest of the three main levels of Carlsbad's labyrinthine chambers is 1,024ft (312m) below the surface. The Caverns were originally formed under water. The creation of the caves can be traced back 250 million years to the Captain Reef—a Permian fossil reef—composed of the remains of sponges, algae, seashells, and calcite precipitated directly from the water. After the evaporation of the sea, the reef remained buried under layers of salt and gypsum, and was only uncovered after millions of years of erosion and similar processes.

Once the reef emerged above ground, the percolation and seepage of acidic rainwater through its cracks led to the dissolution of the calcite minerals and hastened the process of the formation of the great limestone chambers. The action of sulphuric acid upon limestone is believed to be the cause of the stalactites, stalagmites, and the various other extraordinary formations that we now see within the caverns. The formation of these remarkable structures started thousands of years ago, and is an ongoing process.

Human occupation of the Carlsbad Caverns area dates back to 12,000BC, with the arrival of the Palaeo-Indian people. In the late 19th century, guano mining from the caves became a thriving industry. The first extensive exploration of the caverns is credited to Jim White, who first entered the caves in 1898. Over the next 20 years, he conducted guided tours through the caverns. It was only in 1918 that Ray Davis published photographs of the stunning Carlsbad Caverns, leading to a surge in tourist activity. On October 25, 1923, the Carlsbad Caverns was declared a National Monument in the interests of conservation. It was then granted National Park status on May 14, 1930. Inscribed as a UNESCO World Heritage Site in 1995, the park is visited by tens of thousands of tourists every year.

Notable formations of the Carlsbad Caverns National Park include the Lechuguilla Cave—the deepest and third longest cave in North America, and the fifth longest in the world. Big Room—possibly formed by a partial caving in of the roof—is the largest cave chamber on the continent. There is also the Papoose Room, Ogle Cave, and the Giant Dome stalagmite. Some of the more unusual calcite shapes in Carlsbad are soda straws (hollow stalactites), cave pearls (made out of layers of calcite building up around sand grains or other tiny objects), and helictites (strange twisted shapes that appear to defy gravity). Other rare formations include delicate needle-like structures made out of aragonite.

The Carlsbad Caverns National Park also encompasses a wilderness area on the surface that provides sanctuary to a host of native plants and wildlife, including golden eagles, red-tailed hawks, elks, and cougars.

• The first oil wells in Florida were situated at Sunniland, a village in the Everglades, 40 miles (64km) southeast of Fort Myers.

• The Everglades farming district is often referred to as the Vegetable Kingdom since it is the major supplier of garden vegetables for the northern markets.

**Everglades,** Florida

# Everglades

**A** dense network of habitats with great diversity of flora and fauna characterize the Everglades in southern Florida. Spread over an area of almost 4,000sq miles (10,000sq km), this region of sawgrass marshes forms the largest expanse of subtropical rainforest in continental America. Formed almost 5,000 years ago, the Everglades occupy a shallow limestone basin, and are watered by Lake Okeechobee, the third largest freshwater lake in the United States, after Lakes Michigan and Iliamna, situated at the northern edge of the glades. The water from the lake seeps into the underlying limestone, forming a series of aquifers that feed these wetlands.

The Everglades are crisscrossed with small lakes and channels on which water lilies and bladderworts bloom. Bladderworts are specially adapted for thriving in these waters, which are low in nutrient content. The plants have small air bladders that trap insects and larvae, which are then absorbed to obtain the essential nutrients. Small low islands or hammocks are scattered across the open patches of water; cypresses, live oaks, palms, and saw palmettos are among the shrubs and tropical plants that grow in abundance on the organic

## THE FLORIDA MANATEE

Among the animals taking advantage of the abundant fish in the Everglades' coastal waters are 12 species of turtle, including giant loggerhead turtles and green turtles. The Florida manatee is a gentle, plant-eating mammal and is a member of the group of animals known as *Sirenia*, which were once believed by sailors to be mermaids.

Manatees feed on the seagrass beds in the shallow waters fringing the mangrove forests. These harmless creatures face a threat from marina developments, which decrease their feeding area and bring with them pollution and the increased danger of death or injury from boats.

*A manatee or sea cow floating at the water's surface*

soils. Formed where the underlying limestone rises above the water table, the hammocks also serve as home to many species of plants such as orchids, cacti, and ferns. Impenetrable forests of sawgrass—speckled with minute sharp teeth and growing up to 13ft (4m) in height—remain the predominant form of vegetation in the glades. A strip of red mangroves fringes the freshwater swamps toward the coast, forming North America's only forested marine wetland.

Encompassing 2,380sq miles (6,105sq km) in the southwestern section of the glades, the Everglades National Park was established in 1947 to conserve the unique ecosystem of the glades. More than 1,000 seed-bearing plants—including 25 varieties of orchid and 120 species of trees—populate the glades. Over 320 species of birds, including the wood stork, the reddish egret, and the southern race of the bald eagle nest in the area; the coastal mangrove region provides shelter to anhingas, roseate spoonbills, pelicans, wood ibis, and herons. The coastal waters host more than 150 species of fish, which serve as food for the swamp's predators such as the American alligator, the American crocodile, the rare Florida panther, and otters.

The Native Americans called the glades *pa-hay-okee*—meaning "grassy waters"—and navigated the vast expanse of the marshland as they hunted and fished. Despite such activity, the ecosystem remained intact until the arrival of non-native settlers in the middle of the 16th century. Unbalanced industrialization in the name of progress caused destructive draining of the swamps and alteration of the water flow, leading to a drastic reduction in water supply and consequently the animal population—while an estimated 1.5 million birds nested in the Everglades in the 1930s, only about 50,000 remain today. The opportunity to explore the world's largest freshwater swamp, as well as activities such as sport fishing, however, continues to lure thousands of visitors to the Everglades every year.

## THE AMERICAN ALLIGATOR

The larger of the two living species of alligators (the other is the Chinese alligator), the American alligator is the most famous of the Everglades predators. Endemic to southeastern United States, these reptiles have a diet that consists of turtles, frogs, birds, small mammals, snakes, and fish. These creatures are known to live in freshwater lakes, rivers, and swamps and only rarely in brackish water. Relentlessly hunted for its hide, the American alligator was labeled an endangered species in 1967; but conservation efforts led to a great increase in its numbers, and they were removed from the list in 1987. It is illegal, however, to feed any alligator in the Everglades, and they are protected from over-hunting by the US Fish and Wildlife Service. The largest ever alligator found in Florida measured 17ft (5.3m) in length.

*The American alligator, the Everglades main predator*

- Paricutín is located 12 miles (20km) west-northwest of Uruapan and just north of the Tancítaro Peak volcano.

- At the end of the first year of Paricutín's eruption, its cone stood 1,475ft (450 m) higher than the base elevation of 7,480ft (2,280m) above sea level; in 1952, the peak had reached an elevation of 9,210ft (2,808m).

**Paricutín , Mexico**

# Paricutín

One of the youngest volcanoes in the world, the Paricutín is located in the state of Michoacán in the central western part of Mexico. In the early 1940s, three of the largest cities in Mexico—Puebla, Guadalajara, and Mexico City—occupied this area. Situated some 200 miles (323km) west of the capital city, the area around Paricutín was mostly a serene and peaceful backwater populated by the native Tarascan Indians. The gently undulating landscape of the Paricutín region was considered one of the loveliest in the country. Though hundreds of cinder cones dotted the small valleys in the area, it had experienced negligible volcanic activity in earlier times. The only recorded eruption had occurred centuries before—the explosion of the Jorullo on September 8, 1759.

The Jorullo and Paricutín volcanoes are part of the larger Trans-Mexican Volcanic Belt, which extends almost 700 miles (1,129km) from east to west across the central-southern Mexico. According to geologists, prehistoric eruptive activity had deposited a layer of volcanic rocks almost 6,000ft (1,829m) thick, resulting in the creation of a high and fertile plateau. Moisture-laden winds from the Pacific Ocean nourish this plateau in the summer months; the consequent bountifulness of farming land has in turn made this belt the most populated region in Mexico.

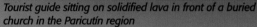
*Tourist guide sitting on solidified lava in front of a buried church in the Paricutín region*

## CINDER CONES

Cinder cones are relatively small volcanic landforms created when lava solidifies into cinder-sized fragments after ejection and forms a mountain around the crater. While some cinder cones are formed during the course of a single eruption, many are a result of multiple eruptions. However, if volcanic activity continues for thousands of years, the cinder cones tend to develop into stratovolcanoes. The cinder cone of Paricutín is a basaltic scoria that was formed as a result of a nearly continuous chain of eruptions, which is for all purposes considered one single eruption.

## RETROSPECTIVE MYTHS

Though the Tarascan people had no myths or legends associated with the volcanoes, the Paricutín eruption prompted a rather curious phenomenon. Events that had occurred a few years before the eruption were recognized as "omens," or heralds of the eruption in retrospect. The destruction of a wooden cross on a hillside in 1941, a plague of locusts in 1942, and a series of earthquakes the following year—all these events were later thought to have been announcing the imminent explosion.

*A Tarascan Indian woman weaving on a backstrap loom*

Though Paricutín is only one of the 1,400 vents that are to be found in the Michoacán-Guanajuato monogenetic field—Jorullo, too, lies in this field—what makes this small volcano extraordinary is that it is one of the rare volcanoes that have been under observation right from the time of its birth. On February 19, 1943, the day before the eruption, almost 300 earthquakes shook the entire area. On February 20, the day the eruption began, Dionisio Pulido, a farmer, saw the earth being torn apart to form a huge fissure from which clouds of smoke were emerging in the middle of a cornfield—this fumarole marked the birth of the Paricutín volcano.

The Paricutín eruption was strombolian in nature, characterized by short explosive discharges of lava. By February 22, news of the eruption had spread, and the scientists who would go on to document every moment of Paricutín's life had arrived at the scene. By then, a 164-ft (50-m) high scoria cone had already been formed by the eruptions. Within a week, the cone had grown to 328ft (100m), and ash and small fragments of lava were raining down on the nearby villages. Soon, eruption columns several feet high were being seen and the volcano would explode occasionally with canon-like blasts. By August 1944, the villages of Paricutín and San Juan had been evacuated just in time, before they were buried entirely under lava and ash. The eruption finally came to an end with a blaze of activity in 1952, nine years after it had started.

Miraculously, the Paricutín eruption did not result in any direct casualties, although it caused widespread damage to land and livestock. Today, lava covers almost 10 square miles (25sq km) surrounding the towering cone, and only a couple of church towers rise above the rugged sea of frozen lava.

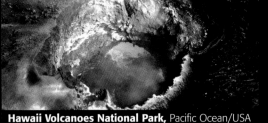

- The 450-feet (137-m) long Thurston Lava Tube was formed when molten lava continued to flow from the Kilauea even after the lava stream's outer crust had cooled and hardened.

- Imminent eruptions of the volcanoes are signaled by changes in the local electromagnetic fields; magma heated above 1,112°F (600°C) loses its natural magnetism, indicating that a large body of molten rock has developed within the volcano.

**Hawaii Volcanoes National Park,** Pacific Ocean/USA

# Hawaii Volcanoes National Park

Stretching across 377sq miles (976sq km) in the southeast of Big Island and encompassing two of the most active volcanoes in the world—Mauna Loa and Kilauea—the Hawaii Volcanoes National Park is one of the most fascinating geological sites on earth. Established in 1916, it was originally called the Hawaii National Park, and was given its present name in 1961. The area was declared an International Biosphere Reserve in 1980, and inscribed as a UNESCO World Heritage Site in 1987. The park offers its visitors an unmatched experience—the chance to watch the eruptions and lava flow from the volcanoes from close yet safe quarters.

The English explorer and navigator James Cook's arrival in Hawaii in 1778 and 1799 drew the world's attention to the Big Island. Standing at 13,677ft (4,169m) above sea level in the south central part of Big Island, Mauna Loa is the world's largest volcano. A shield volcano with a summit caldera which is 600ft (183m) deep, Mauna Loa has erupted 33 times since its first well-documented eruption in 1843. Archibald Menzies, a Scottish botanist, became the first non-native person to reach the summit of Mauna Loa in 1794. Mauna Loa's most recent eruption was in 1984.

## BEATING EVEREST

Though the height of Mauna Loa is stated as 13,677ft (4,169m), that figure is only the elevation of the volcano above sea level. The flanks of the mountain reach down an additional 16,400ft (5,000m) below the sea to the ocean bed. Because of the upward thrust of the lava, the central portion of the volcano has carved out a further depression of 26,240ft (8,000m) in the shape of an inverted cone below the ocean floor. Thus, if all three segments are considered, the true height of Mauna Loa—from its true base to its summit—crosses a staggering 56,000ft (17,169m), approximately twice the height of the Everest.

Hot lava flows from a volcano, Hawaii Volcanoes National Park

## HAWAIIAN VOLCANO OBSERVATORY

Founded in 1912 by the pioneering volcanologist Thomas Jagger, the Hawaiian Volcano Observatory was set up on the rim of the Kilauea caldera. Now under the control of the US Geological Survey, the observatory maintains a volcanic geological monitoring program. Due to their active nature, Mauna Loa and Kilauea form the focus of much of the observatory's research. Although it contributes greatly in the understanding of volcanic and seismic processes, the most important function that the observatory carries out is the identification of potential eruption and large-scale earthquake sites in order to facilitate emergency responses.

Aerial view of a lava cone in a volcano

Kilauea, at 4,078ft (1,243m) above sea level, is Hawaii's youngest volcano. Living well up to its name, which means "spewing" or "much spreading," Kilauea is believed to be the home of Pele, the goddess of Hawaii's volcanoes. The volcano has been erupting and spewing a continuous stream of lava, primarily from the volcano's east rift zone, for 24 years—since its last eruption in 1983, the volcano has been gobbling up existing parts of the island and creating new chunks of land. The Halemaumau crater and the Puu Oo and Kupaianaha are the best-known of Kilauea's vents.

More than 70 million years of volcanism, and evolution, have contributed to the creation of the Big Island. A constant process of destruction and creation has bestowed this land with eternal transience. Craters, cinder cones, spatter ramparts, fumaroles, calderas, lava tubes, black sand beaches, and thermal areas are just some of the volcanic features to be found on the island. Notable among these is the Kau Desert, a region of extraordinary lava formations, and also the Mauna Loa Trail, which winds from the peak of the Kilauea to that of the Mauna Loa.

The Hawaii Volcanoes National Park encloses an astounding volcanic area with a unique ecosystem. A treefern forest—a dense tropical area—that receives almost 100in (254cm) of annual rainfall, represents a substantial percentage of the indigenous flora. A species of bat is the only notable native mammalian inhabitant of the area; most bird species found on this island are endemic and many are endangered.

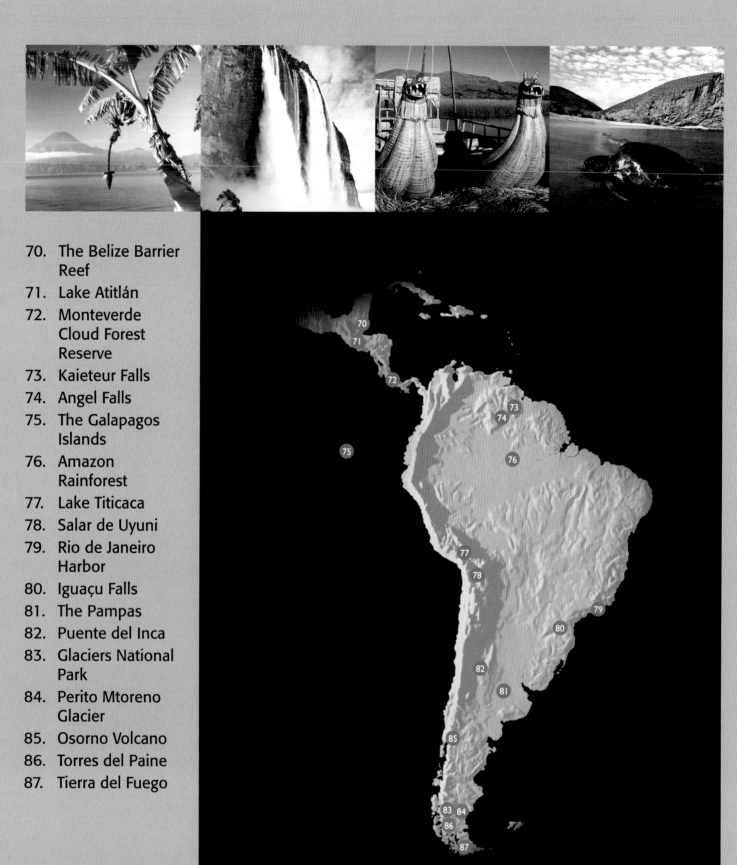

# Central & South America

Including the southern-most tip of North America, Mexico and the South American continent, Central and South America is defined by two major features: the Caribbean Plate that gave birth to various mountain ranges and geologically active sites (volcanic eruptions and earthquakes still occur here) and the incredible diversity of the Andes and the Amazon rainforest.

When writer and philosopher Aldous Huxley first saw the panoramic Lake Atitlan with its three volcanoes—San Pedro, Atitlan and Toliman—in the Guatemala Highlands, he was elated. "It's the most beautiful lake in the world!" he said. Few, who have visited this area and explored the Mayan country would dispute his remark. Charles Darwin had something similar to say, when he landed in the 5-million-year-old Galapagos Islands west of Eucador, claiming he had never expected the islands to be inhabited by so many different species—all the reptiles (including marine iguanas), half the birds, a third of the plants and a quarter of the fish are only found in this one location. It's this shock and awe that continues to inspire travelers, scientists, and naturalists that visit this incredible region.

It was ninety million years ago that the South America continent was born during massive tectonic movements that also pushed up the Andes mountain range. At about the same time, the Amazon River began to carve its way through a 2.5-million-sq mile, (6.5-million-sq km) basin—covering nearly 30 percent of the South American continent—and gave birth to the great Amazon Rainforest. While most of the Amazon Rainforest falls in Brazil, the countries of Bolivia, Peru and Guyana are as exciting—the oldest known remains of South America's culture can be found in Peru's 20,000-year-old Pikimachay Cave, and Kaieteur Falls in Guyana is magnificent.

**The Belize Barrier Reef,** The Caribbean

The Belize Barrier Reef has come under severe threat from oceanic pollution in recent years. Hurricanes and global warming, and the resultant rise in ocean temperatures, has led to acute coral bleaching and consequently endangered the marine population.

- The South Gallows Reef was named after a spot on the caye where gallows to hang criminals once stood. Originally they had been erected in Belize City, but were later moved here because the sight of public executions disturbed the citizens.

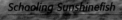

*Schooling Sunshinefish*

## THE BELIZE BARRIER REEF RESERVE SYSTEM

The Belize Barrier Reef Reserve System, the largest barrier reef in the northern hemisphere, consists of seven sites—Bacalar Chico National Park and Marine Reserve, Blue Hole Natural Monument, Half Moon Caye Natural Monument, South Water Caye Marine Reserve, Glover's Reef Marine Reserve, Laughing Bird Caye National Park, and the Sapodilla Cayes Marine Reserve. The Half Moon Caye was designated a natural monument in 1982 and became the first marine protected area in Belize and Central America.

# The Belize Barrier Reef

It was in 1842 that Charles Darwin came upon the turquoise waters of Belize after exploring many exotic lands and sailing around the world. "This is the most wonderful reef in the West Indies," he said while describing this beautiful stretch of the Caribbean in his work on the origin of coral reefs.

More than a century and a half after his visit, and despite the perceptible threat of oceanic pollution, the beauty of this stunning underground tropical forest that spans nearly 180 miles (290km) on the Atlantic–Caribbean coast of Belize, remains more or less unaffected. Even today, you can feast your eyes on innumerable varieties of brightly colored fish zigzagging in and out of the reef's millions of nooks and crannies, watch at close distance the magnificent whale sharks during diving expeditions, or spot turtles—the loggerhead, the green, and the hawksbill—glide slowly past in the tranquil waters.

The Belize Barrier Reef is believed to have been formed during the Ice Age. Second longest in the world, it is also one of the richest reefs in terms of its biodiversity. Three of the four coral atolls are said to be found here—Lighthouse Reef, Turneffe Islands, and Glover's Reef. More than 450 caves, islets, and islands across the length of the reef hide an incredible host of marine treasures.

Around 65 species of coral and over 300 species of fish have been identified on the Belize Barrier Reef, with scientists claiming discovery of still new species from time to time—remarkable figures, considering that the Caribbean as a whole boasts 70 species of coral and 500 species of fish. These statistics were partly responsible for UNESCO conferring World Heritage status upon seven areas of the reef in Belize in 1996; destruction or deterioration of this marine habitat, UNESCO felt, would impoverish the world as a whole.

Shortly after that, another biodiversity hotspot was discovered at the reef, in the semi-enclosed lagoons of what is popularly known as the Pelican Caye—a group of cayes overgrown with mangroves. Scientists today believe almost 90 percent of the reef and its inhabitants are yet to be discovered.

Archeologists studying Mayan ruins in Belize say that they have reason to believe that the people of that ancient civilization harvested the reef regularly. The reef's waters are "harvested" even today, but with conservation in mind. Tourism serves as the reef's greatest resource, with 250,000 visitors generating over $100 million each year.

### THE BLUE HOLE

The Blue Hole is almost perfectly circular, with a diameter of over 1,000ft (305m) and a depth of 400ft (122m). Formed during the Ice Age, this magnificent limestone cavern was flooded by rising in sea levels. The legendary explorer and diver Jacques Yves Cousteau charted the depths of this cavern in 1971 and declared it one of the 10 best scuba diving spots in the world.

*The Blue Hole*

**Lake Atitlán,** Guatemala

# Lake Atitlán

Nestling in the central highlands of Guatemala, 5,128ft (1,563m) above sea level, Atitlán is a lake of extraordinary natural beauty. Often called the most beautiful lake in the world—most notably by the author Aldous Huxley—Atitlán is surrounded by jagged mountains. Little villages dot the shores of the rippling lake with its vivid blue waters.

Lake Atitlán is volcanic in origin, and was formed by the Los Chocoyos eruption that took place approximately 85,000 years ago. This tremendous eruption ejected more than 72cu miles (300cu km) of ash and lava, and created a huge caldera that later filled water to form the lake that we see today. In 1976, Guatemala was wracked by an earthquake that measured 7.5 on the Richter scale. The massive tremors fractured the bed of the lake and led to subsurface drainage that caused the level of water to drop by 6.6ft (2m) within a month.

Three younger cone-shaped strato-volcanoes—Atitlán, Toliman, and San Pedro—form the spectacular backdrop for this caldera lake. San Pedro, at 9,900ft (3,020m), is the oldest of the trio. It became extinct about 40,000 years ago, around the time that Toliman, measuring 10,360ft (3,158m) today, started growing. Atitlán emerged only around 10,000 years ago. Standing tall at 11,600ft (3,535m), Atitlán last erupted in 1853 and is still considered active.

## SAN BUENAVENTURA DE ATITLÁN NATURE RESERVE

This nature reserve on the shores of Lake Atitlán occupies nearly half the valley of San Buenaventura in Panajachel. Encompassing vast tracks of native forests, the reserve is dedicated to the conservation of the natural environment of the Lake Atitlán basin. The reserve encloses a Butterfly Preserve that provides refuge to hundreds of species of butterflies and moths and has a laboratory for the breeding and study of pupae and chrysalis. The nature reserve has also been instrumental in planting thousands of trees within its boundaries.

*View of Lake Atitlán*

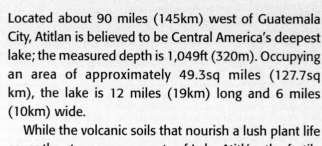

Located about 90 miles (145km) west of Guatemala City, Atitlan is believed to be Central America's deepest lake; the measured depth is 1,049ft (320m). Occupying an area of approximately 49.3sq miles (127.7sq km), the lake is 12 miles (19km) long and 6 miles (10km) wide.

While the volcanic soils that nourish a lush plant life cover the steep escarpments of Lake Atitlán, the fertile basin of the lake supports extensive cultivation of coffee and a variety of farm crops, most notably corn. The region also produces fruits and vegetables such as strawberries, avocados, the pitahaya fruit, tomatoes, cucumbers, beans, and garlic.

The small villages and towns that ring Lake Atitlán are predominantly Mayan in their culture and traditions. The Tz'utujil and Kaqchikel make up the majority of the population of the Atitlán area. Famous for its shrine to the deity Maximón, Santiago de Atitlán on the south shore is the largest of the lakeside communities. Panajachel, on the opposite side, is a small town with a booming tourism industry that caters to the needs of visitors to the lake. San Pedro la Laguna, San Marcos, and Santa Cruz la Laguna are other towns on the shores of the lake that act as quiet retreats for travelers.

The villages provide tourists with the perfect opportunity to absorb the gentle and relaxed lifestyle of the Mayans and to buy native handicrafts. There are also attractions such as lively nightspots and language schools, and the surrounding mountains provide the avid and adventurous traveler with ample opportunities for climbing or simply walking and exploring the wonderful landscape. The lake also serves as an excellent location for a wide variety of water sports such as fishing, water skiing, and boating.

*Indigenous people tying bundles of onions on the banks of the lake*

## BASS TROUBLE

The Atitlán basin, though declared a national park in 1955, used to be virtually unknown to the world. An attempt to boost tourism and the economy in general was undertaken by introducing a new fish, the black bass, into the lake. The move backfired resulting in an ecological disaster when the voracious feeder wiped out most of the lake's local species of fish. This in turn accelerated the extinction of the Atitlán giant grebe, a rare bird that would feed on the small native population of fish.

**Monteverde Cloud Forest Reserve,** Costa Rica

- Tropical forests cover only 5 percent of the earth's surface, yet they contain almost half of the plant and animal species that inhabit the planet.

- Despite measures taken to protect the species from extinction, the harlequin frog has almost vanished from the Monteverde Cloud Forest Reserve.

# Monteverde Cloud Forest Reserve

A journey through the Monteverde Cloud Forest Reserve is like walking through an exquisite canopy of green. A profusion of verdant greenery greets the eye in every direction. While the exposed ridges bear spectacularly dwarfed elfin forests that have been shaped by the winds, the protected valleys of the preserve have a prolific growth of tall majestic trees, with orchids, ferns, mosses, bromeliads, and vines trailing across them and decorating the entire forest.

Situated in the Tilaran Mountain Range in the Puntarenas province of northwestern Costa Rica, 3.7 miles (6km) east of the town of Santa Elena, the Monteverde Cloud Forest Reserve derives its name—which translates into "green mountain"—from the lush vegetation of the area. The mountain chain lies on the extreme northwestern edge of a volcanic range that runs across Costa Rica, and reaches average elevations of almost 5,000ft (1,524m) above sea level; the forest reserve encompasses over 19sq miles (50sq km) of cloud and rain forests on the slopes of this range.

The dense forests of Monteverde extend on both sides of the Continental Divide that separates the Atlantic and Pacific Oceans. The Cerro Los Amigos, at an altitude of 6,042ft (1,842m), is the highest point in the forest reserve, while the Valley of Peñas Blancas, with an elevation of 2,624ft (800m), is the lowest point within the reserve. Monteverde is made up of primarily basaltic and andesitic

## SANTA ELENA CLOUD FOREST RESERVE

One of the first community-managed reserves in Costa Rica, the Santa Elena Cloud Forest Reserve on the slopes of the Tilaran Mountains was officially opened in March 1992. It operates on the unique philosophy that the long-term sustainability of the sanctuary is the concern of the entire community. Proceeds from entrance fees, tours, and the sale of souvenirs are either invested in the management of the reserve, or used to fund educational programs in a local school. Together with the Children's Eternal Rainforest, the Arenal Conservation Area, and the Monteverde Cloud Forest Preserve, Santa Elena Cloud Forest Reserve constitutes 108sq miles (280sq km) of area under contiguous conservation. Conservation efforts concentrate heavily on establishing forest corridors to lower altitudes since many of the species protected by the reserves require large areas to breed and forage.

*A tourist taking a canopy ride through the magical cloud forest*

An Olinga crouching on a branch in the Monteverde Cloud Forest

rocks. The soil with its sandy and loamy texture, is of volcanic origin. While the low-lying areas of Monteverde have poor drainage and tend to contain swampy forests, the majority of the reserve is criss-crossed by swift clear streams that run down the mountain slopes, creating innumerable beautiful rapids and waterfalls; deep ravines and gorges have also been carved out by these streams.

Cloud forests tend to receive far less rainfall than rainforests. Their high altitude ensures conditions of far greater humidity, thus, they are actually cloudier than the rainforests. The Monteverde Cloud Forest Reserve is shrouded by a veil of mist at all times, supporting a luxuriant and abundant flora and fauna of incredible diversity.

Eight distinct biological zones can be identified within the preserve, which is home to more than 2,500 species of plants and trees, 100 species of mammals, almost 1,200 types of reptiles and amphibians, more than 400 kinds of birds, 500 species of butterflies, and thousands of varities of insects. Fortunate visitors exploring the forests can often catch a glimpse of the jaguar, puma, monkeys, ocelot, Baird's tapir, bellbirds, and the famous but elusive Resplendent Quetzal.

## THE QUAKERS

The Monteverde Cloud Forest Reserve is home to the Quaker community of Costa Rica. Made up of people who migrated to Costa Rica from the United States in the 1950s because of their refusal to register for the war draft of 1949, the Quaker community espouses a philosophy of peace and harmony. The community has been instrumental in spurring conservation efforts in the area. They raised money with the help of organizations such as the World Wildlife Fund and Nature Conservancy, and started buying off large sections of the cloud forest in 1972. This initial effort is what resulted in the formation of the Monteverde Cloud Forest Reserve.

**Kaieteur Falls,** Guyana

# Kaieteur Falls

O ne of the most spectacular waterfalls in the world, Kaieteur Falls forms a cataract on the Potaro River in west-central Guyana. Situated in one of the most diverse rainforests on the planet, the falls are the primary attraction of the Kaieteur National Park which was established in 1930.

Following a sheer plunge of 741ft (226m) over the brink of a sandstone plateau, the waterfall has carved out a gorge 5 miles (8km) long, and forms a short series of cascades that descend another 81ft (25m), making the total height of the fall a staggering 822ft (251m). The average width of this perennial waterfall is 370ft (113m).

Almost five times as high as Niagara Falls on the United States–Canada border, and more than twice the height of Victoria Falls in Africa, Kaieteur's magnificence stems from its combination of great height as well as volume— on an average, approximately 23,400cu ft (663cu m) of water tumbles over the over the edge of the Pakaraima plateau every second. The only waterfall that comes close to matching the immense volume of water discharged by Kaieteur is the Jog Falls, located in the southern state of Karnataka in India.

Charles Barrington Brown—one of the two British geologists appointed as government surveyors to the colony of British Guiana (Guyana)—was the first European to discover Kaieteur Falls. Along with his partner James Sawkins, Barrington Brown was engaged in the task of surveying and mapping the region. It was on one such expedition that Brown chanced upon Kaieteur Falls in April, 1870.

## KAIE'S FALLS

One of the most popular tales associated with Kaieteur Falls is that of the Patamona chieftain Kaie, after whom the falls have been named. According to folklore, Kaie canoed over the edge of the waterfalls and offered his life as sacrifice to the great spirit Makonaima in order to ensure that his tribe was protected from annihilation by the bloodthirsty Caribs. The word *teur* means "waterfall."

*The majestic Kaieteur Falls, Guyana*

## GUIANA SHIELD

The Guiana Shield, in which the Kaieteur National Park is located, is one of the oldest and remotest geological formations in the world, formed billions of years ago. Relatively unaffected by phenomena such as tectonic upheavals and the Ice Age, the area is considered to be one of the richest in the world in terms of biodiversity. Marked by magnificent table mountains called *tepuis* and spectacular waterfalls, the Guiana Shield also contains vast undisturbed stretches of tropical rainforests.

*Pataro River near Kaieteur Falls*

Myth and legend surround the gargantuan Kaieteur Falls, its spray creating an illusion of permanent mist at its bottom. The rainforests surrounding the falls are reputed to have provided the author Sir Arthur Conan Doyle with the inspiration for his well-known novel *The Lost World*. This region of incredible beauty has only recently begun realizing its tourism potential.

The Kaieteur National Park was one of the first areas to be so designated in South America. Today, the park occupies an area of about 242sq miles (627sq km). Thanks to the low population density of the area, the rainforests have remained relatively untouched and pristine. In recent years, with increasing awareness of the need for conservation, efforts to maintain the natural ecosystem and to properly administer the park have gained momentum. Attempts have also been made to include the park in the UNESCO World Heritage List.

Apart from encompassing an impressive white-sand forest, the park also forms a natural habitat for many species of animal, particularly amphibians and reptiles. Many of the species of plant and animal found in the national park are endemic, and sometimes endangered. The main threats posed to the area today are by humans—most significant being the problem of the illegal mining of diamonds and gold, which inevitably results in deforestation and pollution.

- Angel Falls, the world's tallest waterfall, is almost 20 times the height of Niagara Falls.
- The fractured red sandstone peak of Auyán Tepuí reaches a height of 8,250ft (2,515m)

**Angel Falls,** Venezuela

# Angel Falls

The Rio Churún, a tributary of the Caroní River, makes its way slowly across the Auyán Tepuí, a high plateau that overlooks the jungles of southeastern Venezuela. Swollen with waters from torrential tropical downpours, the river gathers pace down a short incline at the northern edge of the plateau, near the borders with Guyana and Brazil, and then plunges over the cliff as the majestic Salto Angel, or Angel Falls. From a distance, the thin white line at the cliff edge appears to gradually broaden into a blur of spray, until the water drops out of sight into the jungle below.

Angel Falls, with a total fall height of 3,212ft (979m), is the tallest cataract in the world. About 500ft (150m) wide at the base, the waterfall has an average width of 350ft (107m); the magnificent waterfall first drops 2,648ft (807m) along the precipice, barely touching the steep face of the Auyán Tepuí; then after meeting with an obstruction, it drops a further 564ft (172m) into a frothing cauldron of foam.

Thought to have been called Churún Merú by the local Pemón people, the actual Pemón name for Angel Falls is Kerepakupai-merú, which translates to "waterfall of the deepest place." In actual fact, the Churún Merú is another waterfall that occurs further up along a canyon

*A sky diver jumping from the edge of the Auyán Tepuí*

## THE PEMÓN

The forests and savannas of Canaima National Park have been inhabited by various Carib tribes—collectively known as the Pemón—for almost 10,000 years. Two archeological sites, containing handmade tools considered to be around 9,000 years old, have been discovered in the park. Today, about 10,000 Pemón people live in the area in dispersed communities of 40 to 100 members each. These people to this day continue to follow the traditional way of life, and subsist on hunting, gathering, farming, and trading artifacts.

*The magnificent Salto Angel, Jimmy Angel's accidental discovery*

## FINDING THE FALLS

The first documented sighting of Angel Falls was in 1910, when Ernesto Sánchez la Cruz reported his discovery; however, it was an American bush pilot Jimmy Angel who brought the breathtaking falls to the attention of the world. Angel was seeking gold in 1933 when he noted the falls in his logbook. After crash landing his plane he emerged from the dense jungles with the knowledge of what the local indigenous peoples had guarded for several hundred years: the Kerepakupai Merú, the world's highest waterfalls.

that bisects Auyán Tepuí, and is just about half the height of Angel Falls. Angel Falls or Salto Angel is named after the American pilot Jimmy Angel whose plane crash-landed nearby.

Angel Falls is located within the Canaima National Park in the state of Bolivar, Venezuela. Established in 1962, it is the second largest national park in the country. Spread over an area of 11,700sq miles (30,000sq km), the national park encompasses a spectacular landscape of sheer cliffs and amazing waterfalls. Almost 65 percent of the park is covered by tepuis, or table mountain formations—Auyán Tepuí is one such mesa, or flat-topped mountain. The Canaima National Park is also home to a wide range of flora, and several endemic species grow on the tepuis. Out of the 900 plant species found on the Auyán Tepuí, 10 percent are endemic to the region. The fauna of the park, too, is rich, consisting of 118 mammals, 550 birds, 72 reptiles, and 55 amphibians. The park was inscribed as a UNESCO World Heritage Site in 1994.

For a long time the entire area was virtually inaccessible to civilization, and could only be reached by the most resolute adventurers. Today, however, it is possible to reach the waterfall and view it from close range in either motorized dugout canoes or in light aircrafts. However, because of the dense thicket of forest that encircles it, Angel Falls is best viewed from the air. The area has also become a favored destination among the more adventurous visitors who arrive here to hang-glide or paraglide off the edge of the plateau.

• Lonesome George, estimated to be between 60 and 90 years old, is the last-known survivor of the Pinta Island tortoises. The Charles Darwin Research Stations' most famous resident, his death could mark the extinction of one more species from the planet.

• A service at Post Office Bay on the isle of Floreana—a major tourist attraction today—started more than 200 years ago. A wooden barrel was placed there, in which pirates and navigators would leave their mail to be collected and delivered by homeward-bound ships.

**The Galapagos Islands,** Ecuador

# The Galapagos Islands

**A**cknowledging the debt that his revolutionary theories of biological adaptation, natural selection, and evolution owed to the diverse mix of animals found in the Galapagos Islands, Charles Darwin said, "I never dreamed that islands, about 50 or 60 miles apart, formed of precisely the same rocks, placed under a quite similar climate, rising to a nearly equal height, would have been differently tenanted." An astounding range of flora and fauna thus characterizes the Galapagos Islands, which are located about 600 miles (1,000km) to the west of Ecuador in South America.

Consisting of 13 major and 6 smaller islands, the Galapagos are of volcanic origin, with the oldest estimated to have been formed 5 million years ago and the youngest around 2 million years ago. With over 50 eruptions having taken place in the past 200 years, the islands continue to evolve with volcanic activity destroying as well as creating land and isles. When British naturalist Charles Darwin

## DARWIN'S FINCHES

Galapagos finches are descended from common ancestral stock which arrived by chance from South America. They found a large number of vacant niches in various habitats throughout the islands, and have evolved into 13 species of distinguishable size, shape of bill, plumage, song, diet, and habits.

This adaptive radiation is best illustrated by the differences in the beaks of the various species. Some have the typical seed-eating bill; others, that feed on cacti, have developed a long, pointed bill; and yet more have a small tit-like bill for feeding primarily on insects.

The woodpecker finch has developed not only a specialized bill, but also a complex behavior pattern which includes the ability to use a cactus spine to prize larvae out of cracks and crevices.

visited the islands in 1835 on the HMS *Beagle*, the new pahoehoe lava—basaltic lava cooled down to form a smooth, billowy, or ropey surface—on Santiago Island had not even started forming.

Though Darwin is the first person to have scientifically studied Galapagos, archeologists have found evidence of other voyagers anchoring there. Floreana Island's first recorded human settler was an Irish crew member aboard an English vessel, which anchored there in 1807. Not much is known about his reasons for settling there or how he survived on the island. However, today about 20,000 people inhabit the Galapagos Islands.

The islands were accidentally chanced upon for the first time by Tomás de Berlanga, the Bishop of Panama, in 1535 when he was sailing for Peru but was carried to the Galapagos Islands by strong currents. Though historians contend that the Incas may have arrived here long before Berlanga, there is no evidence to support this theory.

The islands are populated by more than 5,000 species of plants and animals, including 1,900 that are not found anywhere else in the world—among them the marine iguana, Galapagos penguin, and a variety of finches, although the most famous inhabitants remain the giant tortoises. Spanish voyagers in the 16th century called these islands Galapagos—an old Spanish word for a type of saddle that the tortoises apparently resembled. In 1570, the cartographer Abraham Ortelius plotted the Galapagos, calling them the Insulae de los Galapagos or Islands of the Tortoises. After their annexation by Ecuador, the islands were given the official name Archipelago de Colon, or Archipelago of Columbus, in 1892.

Today, the Galapagos Islands are under the jurisdiction of Ecuador and are maintained as part of its national park system. Galapagos was one of the first natural sites in the world to make it to UNESCO's World Heritage List in 1978. Almost 95 percent of the islands' area is designated as reserve land.

## ISLAND REPTILES

The Galapagos Islands are the only place on earth where you can find marine iguanas. These lizards feed exclusively on seaweed, and have adapted to their marine way of life by developing partially webbed feet. Seven different species of marine iguana, each showing marked variations, have evolved on the different islands. On six of the islands, there is also a species of land iguana peculiar to the Galapagos.

The islands are also famous for another reptile, the giant tortoise. Mature individuals can weigh 300lb to 400lb (135kg to 180kg). Fifteen distinctive species have evolved to adapt to niches for which there are no other competitors—despite this, four species are now extinct and a fifth is now represented by a single male.

*Marine iguanas, Santa Cruz Island*

• There are more fish species in the Amazon river system than in the entire Atlantic Ocean.

• 70 percent of the plant species identified by the US National Cancer Institute as holding anti-cancer properties come from rainforests.

**Amazon Rainforest,** Brazil

*Military Macaw in fruiting palm tree*

## RAINFOREST PROTECTION

Since 1970s more than 230,000sq miles (600,000sq km) of Amazon Rainforest—roughly the size of France—has been destroyed. The good news is that South America's rainforests are in better shape than their African counterpart. This is largely because of the consistent pressure from environmentalists and increasingly ecologically minded governments. In December 2006, for instance, Brazil set aside some 57,915sq miles (148,500sq km) of northern Amazon—an area of land bigger than the United Kingdom—as a protected area, making it the largest protected rainforest area in the world.

# Amazon Rainforest

The richest biological incubator on the earth, the Amazon Rainforest has for long been the symbol of our planet's amazingly lush and pulsating biosphere. The dense woods take their name from the River Amazon, which winds through its forests to meet the Atlantic Ocean, and is home to millions of plant and animal species, as well as many indigenous people.

The Amazon Basin over which the rainforests grows (it was half its current size some 8,000 years ago) stretches for more than 2.3 million sq miles (5.9 million sq km) and includes most of Brazil and parts of French Guiana, Suriname, Guyana, Venezuela, Colombia, Ecuador, Peru, and Bolivia.

The Amazon Rainforest is made up of a mosaic of ecosystems that include deciduous forests and savannahs in addition to the rainforests. There was a time when the Amazon River flowed westward, believed to be part of the proto-Congo (Zaire) river system of the co-joined continents of Africa and South America, known as Gondwana. The rise of the Andes and the linkage of the Brazilian and Guyana bedrock blocked the river and caused the Amazon to become a vast inland sea. Gradually, the inland sea worked its way through the east, giving birth to the fantastic Amazon forests.

The biosphere of the Amazon is characterized by unique vegetation. Its canopy includes trees that reach

## TRANS-AMAZON HIGHWAY

Stretching some 3,286 miles (5,300km) across the Amazon region, the Trans-Amazon Highway, construction of which began in 1970s, links the city of Recife in the east to the Peruvian Andes in the west. Running on an east to west axis of the rainforest, it is crossed by north to south roads, some of which are paved. The Trans-Amazon Highway is part of an ambitious Amazon development plan by the Brazilian government. Environmentalists worry that the highway will encourage illegal logging, ranching, and mining, and endanger whatever is left of the "lungs of the world."

*Burning of tropical rainforest, Amazon Basin*

100ft to130ft (30m to 40m) above the forest floor. Below the canopy are multiple leaf and branch trees, collectively known as "understory." The lowest part of the understory is called the shrub layer and includes shrubby plants and tea saplings. This amazing topography supports the greatest diversity of living organisms in the world. Although the world's rainforests cover less than 2 percent of the earth's surface, they house an estimated 80 percent of all life on the planet. The number of creatures that inhabit tropical rainforests—an estimated 5 to 50 million species—is so great that is it is almost incomprehensible.

The Central Amazon Conservation Complex (CACC) is the largest protected area, over 23,400sq miles (60,000sq km), and the Jaú National Park is the largest national park—8,860sq miles (2,272,00sq km) in the Amazon Basin. The CACC supports varoius ecosystems, igapó forests, lakes, and channels, home to the largest array of electric fish in the world. The site protects key threatened species, including the giant arapaima fish, the Amazonian manatee, the black caiman, and two species of dolphins. The Jaú National Park protects the hydrological basin of the river, the oldest and the most recent sedimentary formation of the Amazon Basin, and an impressive range of fauna, with many species associated with blackwater river systems. It is also home to many endangered species such as the woolly spider monkey, giant anteater, South American river turtle, and giant armadillo.

**Lake Titicaca,** Bolivia/Peru

Lake Titicaca is 120 miles (190km) long and measures 50 miles (80km) at its widest point. The lake is divided into two parts by a narrow strait called Tiquina.

The only fish native to Lake Titicaca are two species of killifish and one of catfish. The trout was introduced into the lake in 1939. Its shallow portions are also inhabited by a species of frog that can grow up to a foot in length.

# Lake Titicaca

A lake of exceptional beauty and effulgence, Lake Titicaca straddles the border of Bolivia to the east and Peru to the west. It is the world's largest tropical lake, and at an altitude of 12,500ft (3,810m), the highest commercially navigable lake in the world. The second largest lake in South America after Lake Maracaibo, Titicaca has a surface area of approximately 3,200sq miles (8,300sq km).

Lake Titicaca is watered by more than 25 rivers of which the largest one, Ramis, drains almost 40 percent of the entire Titicaca basin. The lake is also fed by rainfall and melted water from glaciers on the sierras that border the Altiplano, or highlands. Although it is drained by the Desaguadero River, Titicaca loses most of its water through evaporation. Many densely populated islands dot the surface of the lake; the largest among these is the Isla de Titicaca, or Isla del Sol. The average depth of Titicaca varies between 460ft and 600ft (140m and 180m), depending on the volume of water present in the lake; the greatest depth of the lake has been recorded at 920ft (280m), near the Isla Soto in the northeastern corner of the lake. Great waves often ruffle the surface of this immense body of water.

## LAKE BALLIVIÁN

Lake Ballivián was situated on the Bolivia-Peru border during the Pleistocene Epoch. The surface of this ancient lake was at least 330ft (100m) above Titicaca's present surface. This huge lake then drained and evaporated over time, leaving behind two smaller lakes—Lake Titicaca and Minchin (predecessor to the present day Lake Poopó) in the northern and southern regions of its basin respectively.

*A view of Lake Titicaca*

## THE UROS AND THE TOTORA

The islands of Titicaca are created and recreated constantly from *totora*—a reed-like papyrus which has a dense growth in the marshy shallow sections of the lake. Protected within the Bay of Puno, these floating islands provide shelter to about 2,000 Uros, the descendants of an ancient tribe. They use the reeds to build their homes, and their famous boats, or *balsas*—made out of bundles of dried totora— resemble the papyrus craft of the ancient Egyptians. The totora is sometimes eaten as well. The Uro people protect the reeds from fire by lighting them only on a layer of stone. The Uros islands thus derive their name from these people, who subsist on fishing, weaving, and tourism.

*A traditional twin-keeled boat, Floating Islands*

Geologists are divided in their opinion on the origin of this massive lake. While a small school argues in favor of a volcanic origin, stating that the lake was originally a crater, others contend that it is the remnant of an ancient river system that flowed all the way to the Pacific Ocean. However, the most popular opinion is that the lake was created by glacial activity.

In the Aymará language, *titi* means "puma," and *caca* means "eternal city." Titicaca also translates as "rock puma" in the Bolivian tongue, and the shape of the lake is thought to resemble a puma punching a rabbit. An integral part of the development of the Inca civilization, Titicaca is surrounded by myth. According to legend, the Incas were born out of this lake. The children of the sun god, Manco Capac, and his sister-consort, Mama Ocllo, are believed to have emerged from the lake and founded the Inca dynasty. The Incas consider the lake and its waters sacred even today.

The lake and its islands are also held sacred by the Aymará Indians. Tiahuanaco, a cluster of ruins on the Bolivian side of Titicaca, showcases many aspects of this ancient civilization which predates that of the Incas. The Aymará people still live in the Titicaca basin, and sustain themselves by cultivating barley, grains, and potatoes on stepped terraces. A field of barley found near Titicaca, growing at a height of 15,420ft (4,700m) above the sea level, marks the highest cultivated plot in the world.

The naval wing of Bolivia, an otherwise landlocked country, conducts its maneuvers on Lake Titicaca. A steamer first plied the lake in 1862; today, scores of vessels travel between Puno on the Peruvian shore to the small Bolivian port of Guaqui.

• To gauge the size of this sweeping sea of salt, consider that it is roughly 25 times the size of its more famous counterpart, the Bonneville Salt Flats in the United States.

• Three breeds of South American flamingos—the Chilean, the James, and the Andean—use Salar de Uyuni as breeding grounds every November.

**Salar de Uyuni , Bolivia**

# Salar de Uyuni

An enormous white sea of salt, the Salar de Uyuni lies in the Department of Potosí in southwestern Bolivia. This arid and windswept expanse of salt is located on the Altiplano, close to the crest of the Andes, at an elevation of 11,995ft (3,656m) above sea level. Occupying approximately 4,085sq miles (10,582sq km), the Uyuni Salt Flat is the largest salt-encrusted waste land in Bolivia.

Stretching away almost endlessly until it blends into the horizon, this blinding ocean of white is separated from the smaller Coipasa Salt Flat in the north by a range of hills. Saltworks are located on the shores of Salar de Uyuni—at Salinas de Garci Mendoza in the north, at Llica on the northwestern edge, and Calcha at the southern end. It is estimated that the Salar de Uyuni contains around 10 billion tons of salt; of this vast quantity, less than 25,000 tons of salt is extracted every year.

## UYUNI

Standing 12,024ft (3,665m) above sea level, the town of Uyuni is located to the east of the vast Salar de Uyuni. The town was founded in 1890, and flourished as a market and mining center and a railroad junction under its Syrian and Slav colonists. The silver mines of Pulacayo and Huanchaca are situated just northeast of the town. A branch of Bolivia's chief north–south railroad line runs from Uyuni toward the Pacific Ocean, and provides the country with access to the port facilities of Antofagasta in Chile.

*The busy market place in Uyuni*

*Salt being harvested in the great salt flat of Salar de Uyuni*

## SALAR DE COIPASA

Salar de Coipasa, or the Coipasa Salt Flat, also lies on the bleak Altiplano area of southwestern Bolivia. Situated about 100sq miles (160sq km) to the southwest of the city of Oruro, near the Chilean border, Salar de Coipasa is located at an elevation of 12,073ft (3,680m) above sea level. Occupying approximately 856sq miles (2,218sq km), Coipasa is the second-largest salt flat in Bolivia. The dormant Coipasa Volcano, with a total elevation of 16,149 ft (4,925m), rises nearly 4,165ft (1,260m) above the floor of the salt flat.

The Uyuni Salt Flat is the crystalline residue of a gigantic saltwater lake that occupied the area roughly 40,000 years ago. Known as Lago Minchin today, most of the waters from this prehistoric lake evaporated in the blazing Andean heat over the years, leaving behind two modern lakes—Lake Poopó and Lake Uru Uru, and two salt deserts—Salar de Uyuni and the much smaller Coipasa.

The thick layers of Quaternary lake sediment of Uyuni actually serve as a record of thousands of years of wet and dry periods on the Altiplano. Thus, researchers of palaeoclimatic changes focus on and continue to explore and investigate the Salar de Uyuni. The presence of coral within limestone underneath an ancient lakeshore terrace is one of the interesting discoveries made by such research.

Waterless oases can sometimes be found breaking the monotony of the Salar landscape as it reflects the glaring Andean sun. In the middle of the salt desert lies La Isla del Pescado, or the Island of Fish; the only sign of life

for miles around, the island derives its name from the piscine shape it appears to possess. The Incuahasi Island is a fossil coral reef, from which cacti often rise as high as 30ft (9m).

Despite the incredible barrenness of the Salar de Uyuni landscape, an area of great geological activity lurks to its west along the Bolivian-Chilean border. The landscape is dotted with peaks of major late Cenozoic volcanoes, cresting above vibrantly colored lakes of brine and large oddly shaped boulders sculpted by the wind; a large number of geysers, mudpots, and hot springs attest to the geothermal activity of the region, in stark contrast to the frigid climate of the area. The extreme environmental conditions of Salar de Uyuni and its surroundings are being studied by NASA in an effort to understand the origin of early life on earth and other planets. The stunning beauty and surrealism of the Salar landscape has made it a major tourist attraction today.

- Rio de Janeiro has the world's largest natural deep-water harbor and the only replanted urban forest in the world.

- Rio de Janeiro boasts 50 miles (80km) of beaches, the most famous of which is the Copacabana, immortalized in a 1970s pop hit single and a Broadway musical of the same name by the singer-songwriter Barry Manilow

**de Janeiro Harbor,** Brazil

# Rio de Janeiro Harbor

The Harbor of Rio de Janeiro occupies one of the most stunning sites in the world. Situated on the east coast of Brazil, it encompasses the vast Guanabara Bay, which includes 42 islands, 53 beaches, and 4,000sq km of watershed. The Guanabara Bay faces the Atlantic Ocean to its south and is surrounded by the rising granite hills of Rio de Janeiro on its southwest shore and Niterói on its southeast.

The bay is about 19 miles (31km) long with a maximum width of 18 miles (29km). It has a mile-wide (1.6km) entrance that is flanked on the east by the Papagaio Peak and the Santa Cruz fortress, and on the west by the fantastically shaped Sugar Loaf Mountain and the São João fortress.

The first Europeans to reach Brazil were the Portuguese explorers in 1502. As they glided towards the entrance of the Guanabara Bay, with its backdrop of sheer rock, they were convinced that the bay was a river and named the harbor Rio de Janeiro, or the "River of January," in honor of the month in which they arrived.

The Tamoio people, the original inhabitants of the area, had long before named the bay, Guanabara (arm of the sea). A great bay that looked like a river was not the only nomenclature the Portuguese settlers invented, calling the smaller bay of Botafago a "lake." The Tamoi themselves named the bay's eastern edge Niterói (hidden waters). The strangely shaped mountain was named Pão de Açúcar since it evoked the famous sugarloaves of Madeira Island, and the highest mountain on the Rio de Janeiro coast was called Corcovado (hunchback). Today, both pre-European and Portuguese names are used interchangeably.

## PÃO DE AÇÚCAR

Pão de Açúcar, or Sugar Loaf Mountain, retains some vestiges of the Atlantic forest containing native species that have disappeared from other areas of the Brazilian coast. Visited by climbers, mountaineers, and ecologists, the mountain is also home to many rare species of plants, such as the orchid *Laelia lobata*. It is found only in two places—at Sugar Loaf and Pedra da Gávea (Gávea Rock), both in Rio de Janeiro.

*A view of Rio's harbor and Sugar Loaf Mountain*

The Guanavvbara Bay has since then shrunk, and the coastal mountains that were once carpeted with Atlantic rainforest (Mata Atlântica) and other native species of vegetation, such as semi-arid forests and tree and scrub woodlands, have all but disappeared with the exception of a few green pockets. Landfills have twice altered Guanabara Bay's contours. In the 1920s and then again in 1960s, small hills that were once home to Rio's earliest settlers were sluiced through to create land for an airport, a six-lane highway, parkland, and beaches, as well as the city's modern art museum.

Rio de Janeiro is also home to the Parque Nacional da Tijuca, the world's largest urban forest replanted by man. Covering some 12sq miles (32sq km), Tijuca is home to hundreds of species of plants and wildlife found only in Atlantic rainforests and was declared a UNESCO Biosphere Reserve in 1991. Until the 18th century the original forest spread over the region remained largely intact. As Rio de Janeiro grew into a colonial capital, the ensuing expansion decimated most of the lower forests that were used for the city's construction. Between the 18th and 19th centuries, the introduction of coffee plantations and the creation of the imperial city of Tijuca, destroyed the forest on the higher reaches of the city. By the mid-19th century, the realization of the environmental loss led Emperor D. Pedro II to appoint Major Gomes Archer to start reforestation efforts. Most of the forest that exists here today was grown from the seeds obtained from the Paineiras forest and later from nursing beds prepared in Tijuca itself.

## ISLAND OF PAQUETÁ

The tropical island of Paquetá, situated in the heart of Guanabara Bay, is home to the only Brazilian baobabs found in the Americas—an African tree that residents call Maria Gorda meaning "Fat Mary." Paqueta is close to the Pedra da Moreninha (Moreninha Rock) and the Parque Darke de Mattos (Darke de Mattos Park) known for their scenic sunsets over the bay. All motorized vehicles are banned from the island; only bicycles and horse-drawn carriages are allowed on the roads.

*The statue of Christ the Redeemer, on the summit of Corcovado, towers over the Tijuca National Park, one of the world's largest urban forests*

- The Iguaçu Falls were formed as a result of volcanic activity that shook the earth about 100 million years ago.
- The Spanish explorer Álvar Núñez Cabeza de Vaca is credited as being the first European to discover the Iguaçu Falls in 1541.

**Iguaçu Falls,** Brazil/Argentina

# Iguaçu Falls

Following a meandering course across the Paraná Plateau, the River Iguaçu tumbles over its edge in a magnificent crescent arc. The Iguaçu Falls are a constellation of as many as 275 separate cascades, with their heights varying between 200ft and 270ft (60m and 82m). The horseshoe-shaped rim of the waterfall, which stretches from Paraná in Brazil to the Misiones province in Argentina, is 1.7 miles (2.7km) long. The precise border between the two countries is marked by a narrow semi-circular chasm called La Garganta del Diablo, meaning "devil's throat" in Spanish; sprays rise approximately 500ft (150m) into the air from the bottom of this cascade.

The name of the waterfall derives from a Guaraní word meaning "great water;" it is made up of two words in the local tongue—*y* stands for "water" and *guasu* means "great." While Argentineans use the Spanish name of the waterfall, Cataratas del Iguazú, The Brazilian use the Portuguese version, Cataratas do Iguaçu. Both versions—Iguazú and Iguaçu—are accepted universally.

The River Iguaçu has its source in Serra do Mar, close to the Atlantic coast. It then travels around 820 miles (1,323km) westward, cutting across southern Brazil and gaining in strength and volume as tributaries join

## THE WORLD'S LARGEST DAM

The Paraná River, the fifth largest in the world, flows with great force, and a huge dam has been built to harness its powers and produce hydroelectric power. Itaipu, on the border between Paraguay and Brazil, was the site selected. Once the construction work had been completed, sluice gates closed for 40 days to allow the reservoir to fill, creating a new lake 100 miles (161km) long, and covering an area of 600sq miles (1,554sq km). After 14 years of work, during which million of tons of concrete were poured, the world's largest dam and hydroelectric scheme was completed in 1988. Its generators have a capacity of 12,600 megawatts—sufficient to power the whole of Paraguay and the industrial cities of Rio de Janeiro and São Paulo in Brazil.

*Iguaçu Falls*

## SALTO DOS SETE QUEDAS

On the Alto Paraná River, about 100 miles (160km) upstream of the confluence with the Iguaçu, is the Salto dos Sete Quedas or Guairá.

This waterfall, which has an average height of only 110ft (34m), may seem an unlikely contender for the world's greatest fall, but when measured on its average annual flow of water it outstrips all others.

The lip of the Salto dos Sete Quesdas is 3 miles (5km) wide and the estimated flow of water is 470,000cu ft (13,300cu m) per second. At this rate of flow, the falls could fill the dome of St. Paul's Cathedral in London in less than a second.

*Iguaçu River and Falls amid sub-tropical forest*

it along the way—its path punctuated by a series of 70 cataracts. The grandest of its falls occurs after the River Paraná joins forces with it. Leaping off the Paraná Plateau in the guise of the Iguaçu Falls, it discharges 1.4 million gal (6.5 million liters) of water every second, and then rushes onward to meet the sea. The smaller cataracts of the Iguaçu Falls are broken by rocks and ledges which disperse the waters into clouds of mist and spray; sunshine on the mist often results in the formation of exquisite rainbows.

The sprays from the waterfall, rising as high as 328ft (100m), nourish the vast tropical vegetation around it. The rock outcrops that surround the falls are covered with dense foliage that includes species of palm, bamboo, and downy tree ferns. Wild tropical flowers, such as begonias, bromeliads, and orchids, splash the landscape with vivid colors. The contiguous jungle that borders the waterfall is protected by the Iguazú National Park (established in 1934) on the Argentinean side and the Iguaçu National Park (established in 1939) on the Brazilian side. Sharing the waterfall between them, these national parks are home to more than 400 bird species, including the startlingly colorful macaw, 100 species of exotic butterfly, and a host of mammals such as jaguars, iguanas, ocelots, and peccaries. The Iguazú National Park and the Iguaçu National Park were designated UNESCO World Heritage Sites in 1984 and 1986 respectively.

**The Pampas,** Argentina

- The Pampas—*La Pampa* in Spanish—get their name from a Quechua Indian word which means "flat surface."

- Violent gales and storms common in the Buenos Aires region of the Pampas are called *pamperos*.

# The Pampas

Lushly vegetated and well-watered silted stretches set against patches of barren land and salty streams make up the great plains of the Argentine Pampas. Spread over an area of 295,000sq miles (760,000sq km), this vast plain extends westward across central Argentina from the Atlantic coast to the Andean foothills. Bounded by the Gran Chaco in the north and Patagonia in the south, the plain slopes gently from the northwest to the southeast—from an elevation of 1,640ft (500m) above sea level at Mendoza to only 66ft (20m) at Buenos Aires.

Two distinct zones can be identified in the Pampas. The drier zone occurs to the west, and occupies most of the La Pampa province. This part of the Pampas is characterized by large saline areas and sandy deserts; the water, too, is somewhat brackish. However, the humid Pampas in the east form the economic heartland of the Argentine nation. Including part of the Buenos Aires province, this region of the Pampas has temperate climes, and is the most populated area of the country. Fine sand, clay, and silt are washed down by great rivers flowing into the Atlantic, and blown into the area by stormy winds from the west. Warm air from the tropical north often meets the cool southern winds, creating disturbances that result in violent gales and heavy rains. Consequently, this area experiences high precipitation and is exceedingly fertile.

*An aerial view of agricultural fields in the Pampas. This region is also referred to as the "bread basket of Argentina"*

## THE PAMPAS IN ART

Famous for their natural bounty and beauty, the Pampas have been featured in numerous artistic pieces. They have served as the backdrop in much of Argentina's gaucho literature, including remarkable works such as *El Gaucho Martín Fierro* written by José Hernández in 1872, and Ricardo Güiraldes's 1926 novel *Don Segundo Sombra*. A fairly large segment of Argentinian musical folklore draws its inspiration from the Pampas as its theme.

## THE PAMPEAN CLIMATE

Climate in the Pampas varies between hot summers in the north to relatively cooler summers in the south. Buenos Aires, at the northern edge of the Pampas, experiences a climate akin to that of southeastern United States, with hot and humid summers and cool and mild winters; the southern areas of the Pampas are distinguished by cool summers and cold fronts advancing northward from Patagonia, accompanied by occasional snow and frosts during the winters. Rainfall, too, varies across the plain, with the humid east experiencing a mean annual rainfall of 39in (99cm).

The flat plains of the Pampas are a grassland biome. Trees occupied most of the area centuries ago; since then however, human intervention has caused much of the larger species of plants to be replaced with different species of grass like the Pampas grass, bunchgrass, and mesquite. The undulating plain is thus covered with many varieties of grass, interspersed with groves of exotic pines, oaks, eucalyptus, and poplars. The Pampas also see a profusion of plants such as cattails, water lilies, and reeds; usually found in wetland areas, these plants have adapted to the windy climate of the Pampas. The Pampas merge with the Patagonian steppe in the south; the tussock grasses intermingle with scattered bushes and spiny plants heading southward. Large sections of the Pampas have also been converted to cultivated croplands.

A variety of animals proliferate in the Pampas, among them the Geoffrey's cat, the maned wolf, and the llama-like guanaco, as well as the flightless South American bird, the greater rhea. Seed-eating birds such as the great pampas finch, the long-tailed reed finch, and the double-collared seedeater are also found in abundance.

One of the richest and most fertile lands of the world, the Pampas have been providing sustenance to both man and beast for centuries. The gently rolling grassy plains provide visitors with some of the most serene and scenic landscapes of the South American continent.

*A section of the Llalqui Pampa desert, Chile*

**Puente del Inca,** Argentina

# Puente del Inca

Puente del Inca is a natural stone bridge which crosses the Cuevas River in a town of the same name. It is located in the Andes Mountains of Argentina, not far from the border with Chile, at a height of 8,921ft (2720m) above sea level. Puente del Inca translates as "bridge of the Incas." However, it was not built by the Incas, or for that matter, by man. A creation of nature, it is a finely arched stone bridge, which forms a path 80ft (24m) above the river. An imposing sight, it is covered in snow in the winter and remains stained yellow and green by the mineral deposits of the thermals springs that flow under it for the rest of the year. The bridge is 150ft (46m) long, about 70ft (21m) wide and nearly 30ft (9m) thick, and has been further strengthened by calcareous deposits from sulphur springs at its base.

Scientists believe that erosion by the Cuevas River and the sediments from the sulphur springs played an important role in creating this stone bridge. According to another theory, the bridge was formed in the Ice Age, as a result of petrifaction of rock over ice. Charles Darwin, one of the most famous visitors to this wonder, wrote in *The Voyage Of The Beagle*: "the Incas Bridge consists of a crust of stratified shingle cemented together by the deposits of the neighboring hot springs. It appears, as if the stream had scooped out a channel on one side, leaving an overhanging ledge, which was met by earth and stones falling down from the opposite cliff."

Either way, the hot springs below the Puente del Inca play a major role in the making of this spectacle. There are five thermal mineral springs on the right edge of the bridge, which bubble to the surface at different

## AROUND AND ABOUT

Puente del Inca is best known as a stopover on climbing expeditions en route to Aconcagua in the Andes. Standing at 22,825ft (6,959m), Aconcagua is the highest peak in the world outside the Himalayas. Both are located in the province of Mendoza, which has earned renown for its wines.

## CURE ALL

Minerals in thermal springs are known to cure many maladies including gout, rheumatism, and stomach infections. The waters here contain high levels of sodium, sulphates, bicarbonates, and chlorates, which make the water a great tonic. Sulphur is known to help cure skin diseases.

*The hot springs of Puente del Inca*

temperatures ranging from a hot 98.6°F (36°C) to a tepid 57.2°F (14°C). These springs are thought to be superior to the more famous ones at Vichy because of their greater carbonic acid component. In 1925, a luxury spa was built just under the bridge to take advantage of the spring waters. Unfortunately, 40 years later a great avalanche destroyed it completely.

There are several legends attached to the Puente del Inca. According to one, a fleeing Inca king came to a dead end at the Cuevas River. Unable to cross, he began praying to the gods to show him a way. The gods, deciding to be benevolent, laid down this stone bridge for him, allowing him to escape his assassins. Another legend has an army of brave Inca warriors laying themselves down to form a human bridge for their chief to cross the river, only to be turned to stone when he crossed. The most believable story has the bridge being used by Inca warriors to cross over to Chile.

**Glaciers National Park,** Argentina

- Although the area is devoid of human habitation today, it is believed that prehistoric hunter-gatherers lived here at one time; at least 14 sites of archeological importance have been discovered within the park.

- Occupying almost half of the Glaciers National Park, the Southern Patagonian Ice Field is, at 5,460sq miles (14,000sq km), the largest ice mantle outside Antarctica. It encompasses 47 important glaciers, of which 13 drain into the Atlantic basin.

# Glaciers National Park

A stunning vista of glittering glaciers and snow-clad peaks greet the eye at the Parque Nacional Los Glaciares (or the Glaciers National Park) in Argentine Patagonia. Spread out over 1,722sq miles (4,459sq km), this national park is located in the Santa Cruz province of Argentina, along the Chilean border.

The snow-clad portion of the Andean Cordillera, portions of the Patagonian Ice Field, and a relatively ice-free section to the east make up this astounding natural park. There is a dramatic variation in altitude within the park; while the Lago Argentino and Lago Viedma—glacial troughs formed at the end of the Pleistocene Epoch—measure only 820ft (250m) above the sea level, Cerro Fitzroy rises to an imposing height of 11,236ft (3,405m). Speckled with ice caps, ice fields, glacial lakes, and towering mountains, this national park showcases one of South America's most spectacular landscapes.

Roughly divided into two parts, the northern section of the national park comprises Lake Viedma, the Viedma Glacier, and a handful of smaller glaciers. This section is also distinguished by the famous Cerro Fitzroy mountain, and the magnificent Cerro Torre which—with its pinnacles rising to a height of 10,236ft (3,102m)—matches in sheer majesty, the Torres del Paine in Chile.

The southern portion contains three major glaciers—the Perito Moreno, the Upsala and the Spegazzini, all of which drain into the Lago Argentino. Also fed by glaciers such as the Mayo, Agassiz, Onelli, and Ameghino, Lago Argentino is 15,000 years old, and Argentina's largest lake, with an area of 572sq miles (1,466sq km). The Upsala, 37 miles

## CERRO CHALTÉN

The Cerro Torre and Cerro Fitzroy mountains rise tall above the park. Called Cerro Chaltén—meaning "smoking mountain"—in the Tehuelche dialect, Mount Fitzroy was given its current name by the Moreno Expedition led by Perito Moreno in 1877, in honor of the famous captain of the HMS Beagle, which charted the channels of Tierra del Fuego and the Santa Cruz River. The local name stems from a rare aerolic phenomenon—because of which the summit always appears to be shrouded in smoky clouds. First scaled by the Frenchmen Lionel Terray and Guido Magnone in 1952, the mountain today poses an almost irresistible challenge for many climbers.

*Mount (Cerro) Torre*

## CLIMATE OF LOS GLACIARES

Annual mean temperature in the Glaciers National Park is 45.5°F (7.5°C), and the climate is thus classified as temperate. Average maximum and minimum temperatures recorded within the park hover around 53.6°F (12.0°C) and 37.9° F (3.3°C) respectively. Most of the rainfall occurs in the months of April and May. While westerly windstorms disturb the area during late spring and summer, the winters are usually marked by snowfall.

*Perito Moreno Glacier*

(60km) in length and 6 miles (10km) in breadth, is the largest glacier in South America. While tourists can travel to the Perito Moreno by land, boat excursions through waters of the lake dotted with icebergs take them to the otherwise inaccessible Upsala and Spegazzini, and the Bahia Onelli. Both the glacial lakes—Argentino and Viedma—drain into the Atlantic basin through the Santa Cruz River.

While sub-Antarctic Patagonian forests and the Patagonian steppe characterize the eastern section of the park, the ice-covered western portion is devoid of vegetation. The forested regions include species such as cypress, winter's bark, and the southern bark. The steppe region is characterized by extensive tussock grasslands interspersed with bushes and shrubs. One

hundred species of birds have been identified within the Glaciers National Park. Other animals such as guanacos, southern Andean Huemul, Argentine gray fox, and the Austral hog-nosed skunk are also found in the park. Two species of fish have been introduced into the Argentino and Viedma lakes.

Established as a national park on April 28, 1945, the Los Glaciares area was first protected in 1937. The actual boundaries of the area to be incorporated within the sanctuary were only decided in 1971. The need for conservation of this pristine natural habitat of such incredible beauty—with its skyrocketing granite peaks, silvery lakes, lagoons, and the plant and animal species which exist within it—prompted the UNESCO to designate it a Natural World Heritage Site in 1981.

- The Tehuelche were the early inhabitants of the Patagonian region.
- Glacial research of the Southern Patagonian Ice Field, which includes the Perito Moreno Glacier, has been undertaken by Japan, Chile, and Argentina since 1983.

**Perito Moreno Glacier,** Argentina

# Perito Moreno Glacier

One of only three advancing Patagonian glaciers, the majestic Perito Moreno Glacier is situated within the Glaciers National Park in the southwestern part of Santa Cruz province in Argentina, 51 miles (82km) from the town of El Calafate. The front face of the glacier, when approached from the famous Lago Argentino (the largest Lake in Argentina), appears as a massive, jagged, and twisted mass of ice that looms menacingly over its surroundings.

Among the several outlets of the Southern Patagonian Ice Field, the glacier extends for about 50 miles (80km) through the Patagonian region before terminating at the Lago Argentino in a 2-mile (3-km) wide and 165-ft (50-m) high bluish wall of ice. The snout gets its distinctive blue color from the oxygen that remains trapped in the snow.

The Perito Moreno is often called the "Crusher" or "Crushing Glacier." The epithet, bestowed on it by tourists, is largely a result of the spectacular show that occurs during the process of calving. The glacier makes explosive cracking sounds as the snout constantly fractures and casts off huge boulders of ice which tumble down and crash into the icy waters of the Lago Argentino below.

Once they fall into the lake, these ice floes of various shapes and sizes, ranging in color from white to sapphire blue, remain adrift until they melt completely into the waters of the lake. The spectacle attracts flocks of visitors, particularly during the height of summer, which is when the crushes are at their flamboyant best.

Sometimes the gigantic blocks of ice have been known to detach from the glacier and fall into the narrow Témpanos Channel, resulting in its subsequent blockage.

## LAKE PERITO MORENO

A medium-sized lake with a narrow neck that divides it into two distinct sections—the Eastern Lake and the Western Lake—makes up the Perito Moreno lake in the Bariloche region of Argentine Patagonia. Occupying an area of approximately 4.5sq miles (11.8sq km), the lake has a maximum length and width of 4 miles (6.7km) and 1.7 miles (2.9km) respectively. Several streams, including the Casa de Piedra and Goye, drain into this beautiful lake. The entire shoreline of the Eastern Lake can be traversed easily by foot, but the Western Lake is almost inaccessible from the coast. Some points along the shores provide excellent opportunities for fishing, particularly the area around the Angostura stream, which joins it to Lake Nahuel Huapi.

*Boat on the breathtakingly beautiful Lake Argentino, Glaciers National Park*

The waters then dam up in the Rico arm of Lake Argentino, with a dramatic increase in the water level. An increase of 82ft (25m) was recorded in 1988, and the maximum increase has been estimated as 98ft (30m). Eventually, the water pressure becomes so high that it breaks through the wall of ice, and normal drainage levels are restored through the Témpanos Channel. This phenomenon recurs every few years.

The Perito Moreno Glacier and its surroundings were officially designated as the Perito Moreno National Park in 1937, with the aim of conserving the glacier, two important lake systems, and the flora and fauna of the area. Covering 444sq miles (1,150sq km) in northwestern Santa Cruz, the park encompasses an area of high, rugged mountains, intersected by deep valleys. Three distinct zones of vegetation can be identified within the boundaries of the park—the Patagonian steppe in the east, comprising coironales (tussock grasses) and twisted mata; a transitional zone of short vegetation; and the forests of lenga around the Nansen and Azara lakes. The fauna within the park includes a large number of guanacos, choiques, huemul, and the endemic pilquín or orange chinchillón. The avifauna comprises both aquatic and high-altitude birds. The cultural heritage of the park includes seven caverns decorated with ancient rock art at Casa de Piedra Hill.

*Perito Moreno Glacier*

### FRANCISCO "PERITO" MORENO

The mammoth Perito Moreno Glacier has been named after the well-known Argentine scientist and explorer Dr. Francisco Pascasio Moreno, better known to the world as Perito Moreno; *perito* means "expert." This intrepid explorer traversed across much of Argentina's rugged wildernesses in the late 19th century, studying and researching the natural treasures of the country. He donated an area of land to the Argentine government, which later became the nucleus of the Nahuel Huapi National Park. The glacier was named after him in recognition of his contribution to the cause of conservation of the country's natural heritage.

- Many of Osorno's eruptions have been explosive in nature, and characterized by rapidly moving pyroclastic lava flows and surges.
- Charles Darwin once viewed one of Osorno's midnight eruptions aboard the HMS *Beagle*.

**Osorno Volcano,** Chile

### ASCENDING OSORNO

Puerto Kloker, Ensenada, and Petrohué are the points from which Osorno can be ascended. The snow does not settle on the slopes until about 6,569ft (2,000m), and bluish cracks in the snow can be observed on the southeastern slope. Mountaineering and trekking activities are concentrated on this stretch, and many sportsmen hit the slopes of the Osorno Volcano every year. Ascents usually take around 6 hours, and are carried out in the company of local guides. Tourists can also reach the top of the summit via cable cars, and then trek down to the base.

*Lake Nahuel Huapi, Bariloche in the Osorno Volcano area*

# Osorno Volcano

Towering over the large Todos los Santos and Llanquihue lakes, the graceful snow-clad peak of the Osorno Volcano rises steeply into the sky. A symmetrical, almost perfect cone, the Osorno Volcano is one of the most famous and beautiful landmarks in Chile. Situated about 37 miles (60km) northwest of the city of Puerto Varas in the south of the country, Volcán Osorno has a summit elevation of 8,730ft (2,661m) above sea level, and is thus visible from every point in the Osorno district, even from some points on the Chiloé Island.

The peak of this majestic volcano often remains obscured from view by the perennially overcast weather conditions which are typical of this region. However, the sight that is revealed when the clouds part and the mist clears is absolutely stunning. The slopes of the mountain are covered with verdant vegetation and topped by a permanent cap of pristine white snow that remains intact all the year round. The same cloud cover is also responsible for the abundant rainfall that the area receives. Squalls roll in off the South Pacific coast, bringing with them rain clouds—it rains for more than 200 days a year in the Osorno Volcano area.

Boats at Petrohué, Todos Los Santos lake in the Vicente Pérez Rosales National Park

The Osorno Volcano was formed on top of an eroded stratovolcano called La Picada. Believed to be approximately 250,000 years old, La Picada has a mostly buried caldera that is 3.7 miles (6km) wide, and lies under Osorno on the northeastern side. This ancient volcano is also marked by scoria cones and postglacial maars. One of the most active volcanoes of the southern Chilean Andes, the conical Osorno has two gray domes of dacitic lava on its northwestern and south-southeastern flanks.

Osorno has produced lava flows through fissure vents and scoria cones on its sides—particularly on the western flank—which have on occasion reached the Lago Llanquihue. Osorno has erupted frequently over the past 14,000 years, both from its summit and flank vents, producing fingers of basaltic and andesitic lava that have flowed into the Llanquihue and Todos los Santos lakes and created a series of small coves along the ragged shoreline. Osorno is composed primarily of basaltic and basaltic andesitic lava, covered by rich black soils on the middle and lower slopes, and black volcanic sands at the edges of the lakes.

The abundant rainfall ensures the proliferation of dense forests on the slopes of the volcanoes. Coihues and lengas dominate the stretches between 656ft and 3,280ft (200m and 1,000m) above sea level. Further up, the most ancient species of the forests, the Andean birch, can be found. Between 4,000 and 5,000 years old, this species is protected by regulations governing endangered species of flora. The fauna that these jungles shelter is also diverse, and includes the pudú, chingue (Patagonian skunk), culpeo (Patagonian fox), quique (a kind of ferret), and puma. Bird species that reside in these humid jungles include the hummingbird, kestrel, huet-huet, and a variety of woodpeckers.

Not surprisingly, with its picturesque landscapes and its incredible range of flora and fauna, the Osorno Volcano attracts thousands of visitors every year.

## VICENTE PÉREZ ROSALES NATIONAL PARK

The Osorno Volcano forms the primary attraction of the first national park of Chile. Established in 1926, the Vicente Pérez Rosales National Park today occupies an area of about 969sq miles (2,510sq km). The park is an incredible treasure house of volcanoes, mountains, lakes, and native flora and fauna. Apart from Osorno, other striking natural features within the park include the Todos los Santos lake, the Puntiagudo river valley, the Cayutúe valley, the Tronador Volcano, and the spectacular Petrohué river waterfalls; the latter provides the most magnificent views of Osorno.

**Torres del Paine,** Chile

- Torres del Paine literally means "Towers of Paine." The word *paine* comes from the Tehuelche Indian word meaning "blue."

- A group of five British aristocrats, guided by native horsemen, or *baqueanos*, are believed to have been the first recorded tourists to visit Torres del Paine in 1879.

# Torres del Paine

## Los Cuernos del Paine

Rising to a height of 6,300ft (1,920m), the magnificent Cuernos del Paine (Horns of Paine) consists of black granite rocks that have been given their peculiar shape by tectonic and glacial forces. Thousands of visitors arrive every year to climb and trek these impressive peaks. The origin of Cuernos del Paine is also shrouded in legend. One of the most popular myths about this mass of jagged granite is that the evil serpent Cai Cai caused massive floods in the area to kill the warrior inhabitants of Torres del Paine, and when the waters receded, he took the bodies of the greatest warriors and turned them into the stony peaks of the mountain.

*Parque Torres del Paine, seen from Lago Pehoé*

A marvelous panorama of stunning mountain scenery and exquisite blue waters, the Torres del Paine is made up of an astounding range of granite peaks that lie between the Patagonian steppe and the Andes mountains in southern Chile. The landscapes of the Paine Massif are almost surreal in their beauty, with windswept grasses and sheer frozen Andean cliffs that fill this corner of the world with breathtaking forms and vibrant colors.

The name Torres del Paine refers not only to the mountain range but also to the set of three distinctive peaks that are famous the world over, and the national park within which this range is situated. Administered by the Corporación Nacional Forestal of Chile, the Torres del Paine National Park was established in 1959. The Paine Massif, with its wealth of craggy cliffs, sculpted granite peaks, swift rivers and waterfalls, lakes fed by melt water from glaciers, green meadows, and forests, forms the primary attraction of the national park. The most staggering peaks of this mountain range include the Monte Paine Grande, the three spectacular peaks of Torres del Paine— Fortaleza, Escudo, and the distinctive horn-shaped peaks of Los Cuernos del Paine.

*A section of the breathtaking Torres del Paine*

Located at the southern edge of the Patagonian Ice Cap, this mountain range was formed at least 12 million years ago, when sedimentary rocks met hot magma, and the earth's crust crumpled and folded and was thrust upward to form the mountains. After the end of the Ice Age, when the glaciers covering the massif melted, the underlying rocks were carved by the erosive action of wind and water, and fashioned into huge towers of distinct shapes and sizes. Even today, some of the peaks remain permanently covered in ice.

The Paine Massif is located exclusively by the Rio Paine; this river originates at the Dickinson Lake at the northern edge of the park, travels through several lakes within the park, before draining into the Lago del Toro at the park's southern end. Heaped with crushed rocks and sediments from the mountains, the waters of the lakes in the Torres del Paine National Park take on a multitude of hues—from milky white and gray to intense yellows, greens, and blues. Some of the lakes, such as Laguna Azul and Laguna Verde are so named because of their characteristic colors. The Grey Glacier, Grey River, and Grey Lake together form the most extensive water system in the park.

The great diversity of fauna and flora of the area led to 7,128sq miles (18,445sq km) of the Torres del Paine National Park being declared a World Biosphere Reserve by the UNESCO in 1978. Four distinct zones of vegetation can be identified within the park— pre-Andean scrublands that cover the shores of the rivers and the lakes; Magallanes forests; Magallanes tundra, with patches of plants, and pasturelands and short bushes; and high-altitude vegetation which becomes scarcer with increasing elevations. The park also shelters about 106 species of birds, including the rare Coscoroba swan and Darwin-Nandu, 24 species of mammals, and about 570 guanacos.

## WORLD BIOSPHERE RESERVE

Since its inscription as a World Biosphere Reserve, the Torres del Paine National Park has been the focus of both national as well as international researchers. Activities include restoration of lands earlier cleared and overgrazed for rearing domestic animals. Plant succession and the reintroduction of certain rare species into the park, and their probable impact on ecology, are also being researched. The study of many species including the South Andean deer, European hare, condor, eagle, Magellan ostrich and flamingo, are also being planned.

**Tierra del Fuego,** Chile/Argentina

- Chile owns approximately 70 percent of the land of Tierra del Fuego and the rest belongs to Argentina.
- The northern part of Tierra del Fuego became Chile's only oilfield when petroleum reserves were found in Manantiales in 1945.

# Tierra del Fuego

Tierra del Fuego forms part of the hook at the tip of the South American continent, a finger of land reaching towards the vast icy wastes of Antarctica just 600 miles (965km) away. Separated from the South American mainland by the Strait of Magellan, the archipelago is spread over an area of 28,000sq miles (72,520sq km), its southernmost tip forming Cape Horn.

The Isla Grande de Tierra del Fuego forms the central island of the archipelago, with an area of 18,571sq miles (48,100sq km). While a section of this island and a clutch of isles to the west and south of it form part of Chile's Magellan Region, the eastern half of the island falls under the territory of Argentina. Until this division came about in 1881, both Chile and Argentina claimed ownership over the archipelago.

It is thought that Tierra del Fuego might have been part of what was once a land bridge that linked the Antarctic Peninsula to the South American landmass. Geological evidence suggests that this bridge broke off around 25 million years ago. Fossils discovered on the continents suggest that once upon a time Antarctica and South America were both inhabited by similar plants and animals, lending credence to the claim.

## TIERRA DEL FUEGO NATIONAL PARK

Accessible from the city of Ushuaia, the Tierra del Fuego National Park is the southernmost national park in the world. Occupying approximately 243sq miles (630sq km), the park is contained within the Argentine part of the Isla Grande de Tierra del Fuego. It is Argentina's only coastal national park, with a rich and diverse coastal wildlife including seals, walruses, and many sea birds. The park, with its stunning seascapes and beautiful fjords, offers visitors the chance to go fishing and kayaking.

*Tierra del Fuego, Argentina*

## THE LES ECLAIREURS HEADLIGHT

The excellent location of Ushuaia allows visitors to take in the impressive panorama of mountains, forests, and the sea all at the same time. On one of the many promontories along the Beagle Channel in front of the city is the Les Eclaireurs Headlight. A 36-feet (11-m) tall tower painted in red and white stripes, the headlight has a lighting device that works on solar energy. It is often mistakenly called the Headlight of the End of the World, a name that Jules Verne used for the San Juan de Salvamento Headlight at Isla de los Estados.

*Tierra del Fuego as seen from Ushuaia*

In 1520, the Portuguese navigator Fernando Magellan sailed through the strait later named after him and discovered the archipelago. It is believed that Magellan called it Tierra del Fuego, meaning "Land of Fire," because of the fires that he saw along the horizon on his approach. Magellan apparently thought that these were fires lit by the natives as they lay waiting to attack, but modern speculation gravitates towards lightning and other natural sources as the cause. Sir Francis Drake sailed through the strait 58 years after Magellan and saw the cluster of islands that was later named Cape Horn by Dutch explorers.

A complete survey of the islands was not undertaken until the 19th century by Captain Robert Fitzroy who sailed to these islands aboard the HMS *Beagle*. Twenty-two-year old Charles Darwin was the naturalist who acompanied him on his journey.

The inhospitable climate of Tierra del Fuego is classified as subpolar oceanic, characterized by short cool summers and long wet winters; while the northeast sees strong winds and little precipitation, the south and the west suffer wind, fog, and heavy rain, hail, or snowfall most of the year. The permanent snowline is only about 2,297ft (700m) above sea level and the low temperature through the year helps preserve the ancient glaciers.

Six species of tree grow in this hostile climate. Fruits such as the beach strawberry and calafate are also found in the area. The archipelago's fauna includes parrots, seagulls, guanacos, kingfishers, condors, owls, and hummingbirds. The native inhabitants of Tierra del Fuego—known as Fuegians—are primarily members of the Ona (Selk'nam), Haush, Yahgan (Yámana), and Alacaluf (Kawésqar) tribes.

# Australia & Oceania

**A**ustralia is both an island, a country, and one of the world's six continents (seven, if you include Antarctica). But, geographically, this large island is also part of the unbelievably vast waterscape known as Oceania. Besides Australia, Oceania is home to American Samoa, Fiji, Kiribati, New Caledonia, New Zealand, Papua New Guinea, the Solomon Islands, Tuvalu, Vanuatu, and Western Samoa.

Blessed with a wide range of natural attractions both on land and water, Australia boasts a remarkable gamut of coral reefs (along its northern coast) that support a variety of marine life including the dugong and the green turtle; Uluru, like the Devils Tower in America, is a natural wonder (the Anangu tribe consider it the most sacred place in Australia); the Kakadu National Park is home to an archeological and ethnological reserve that has been inhabited continuously for the last 40,000 years; the magical Blue Mountains that rise in Cumberland Plain, and the 135-million-year-old Daintree Rainforest (lest you think it's all desert and water), which houses 430 species of birds and an amazing world of reptiles, especially frogs.

Beyond Australia lie the physically most diverse marine environments on the earth. They are divided into three regions (often overlapping)—the Indo-Pacific Cradle, the Coral Triangle and the TransFly. In the Indo-Pacific Cradle, stretching from Indonesia to Solomon Islands, it's the birds and turtles that predominate; the Coral Triangle spanning Malaysia, Indonesia, the Philippines, Papua New Guinea, the Solomon Islands, Fiji and North Australia is the vast repository of corals (75 percent of all coral species), more than 3,000 species of reef fish and migrating populations of sharks and giant manta rays; and the TransFly region contains pockets of grassland, wetland and monsoon forest, where 80 species of birds not found anywhere else in the world reside.

**Kakadu National Park,** Australia

- Kakadu is the only national park in the world to encompass an entire river system within its boundaries—the South Alligator River catchment area.

- The English explorer Phillip Parker King made several forays into Kakadu between 1818 and 1822, and named the Alligator River, mistaking the large number of aggressive saltwater crocodiles for freshwater alligators.

## LIVING DINOSAURS

Saltwater crocodiles, which have roamed the planet since the age of the dinosaurs, have changed little in millions of years. Males are typically around 16 ft (5m) in length—the largest on record was said to be 29ft (8.8m). These creatures have been known to bring down animals as large as the water buffalo, with jaws more powerful than the great white shark or the tiger.

# akadu ational Park

Rugged escarpments, gorges that plummet down, lush green wetlands, meandering rivers, and cascading waterfalls are among the stunning spectacles that welcome you to the Kakadu National Park in Australia. Spread across an area of 7,724sq miles (20,005sq km) in the Northern Territory, Kakadu is Australia's largest national park. The Park was included in the UNESCO World Heritage Site list in three stages from 1981 to 1992—it is one of the very few sites in the world to be recognized for its cultural as well as its natural heritage.

The climate at Kakadu is primarily monsoonal. During the wet season, areas within the park have been known to record 60in (154cm) of rain in less than 100 days. Consequently, the area is also called the Big Wet by Australians. The extensive wetlands, formed as a result of such copious rainfall, help sustain an array of bird and animal life, and have been declared a Ramsar site. Landforms within the park include hills, savannah woodlands, plateaus, estuaries, rainforests, floodplains, billabongs, tidal flats, and coastal beaches—together, they provide habitat to a diverse range of flora and fauna.

Over 10,000 kinds of insects, 289 species of birds, 132 types of reptile, more than 60 species of mammals, 55 species of freshwater fish, and 25 frog species call the park their home, as do more than 1,600 different varieties of plants, many of them rare and endemic.

The oldest rock formations in the park are estimated by archeologists to be approximately half as old as the earth—the oldest rocks found within its range are a compound of sedimentary rocks estimated to be at least 2,500 million years old. The depression known as the Pine Creek Geosyncline exhibits the largest deposits of these rocks. The younger rocks of the region are of the igneous variety.

Drawing its name from the Gagudju language, Kakadu has one of the highest concentrations of Aboriginal rock art in the world. The earliest inhabitants of the park, the Aborigines first set foot in Australia, in the Arnhem Land Plateau adjoining Kakadu, during the Ice Age. The rich natural resources of Kakadu are believed to have supported human habitation for at least 25,000 years, and possibly even earlier, for 40,000 to 60,000 years. The theory garnered support when Mike Smith and Rhys Jones, researchers from the Australian National University, found evidence of Aboriginal residence in the Park dating back more than 50,000 years after conducting carbon dating tests.

The Aboriginal art sites make for a fascinating timeline of survival and evolution. The site provides an exceptional record of human history and interaction with nature spanning tens of thousands of years. The artwork at these sites—almost 15,000 of them are believed to be scattered throughout Kakadu—range from paintings which depict the early Aborigines hunting wild animals with spears to more recent "contact" images of Macassans and Europeans. The paintings also highlight Aboriginal legends about the Creation Time, or Dreamtime. A number of these sites are still considered potent and sacred among Aboriginal communities. The park today is jointly managed by its traditional Aboriginal owners and the government of the Northern Territory.

*Aboriginal pictographs on rock, Kakadu National Park*

*Termite mounds*

## The Six Seasons of Kakadu

Although people tend to refer only to the wet and dry seasons in Kakadu, Aboriginal legend identifies six distinct seasons: Gudjewg (monsoon season), from January to end of March; Banggerreng (storm season), in April; Yegge (cooler but still humid), from May to middle of June; Wurrgeng (cold season), from mid-June to mid-August; Gurrung (hot dry season), from mid-August to mid-October; Gunumeleng (pre-monsoon storm season), from mid-October to end of December.

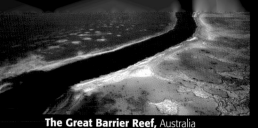

**The Great Barrier Reef,** Australia

- The flora and fauna of the Great Barrier Reef is going to change dramatically if current estimates of climate change prove to be accurate. The recent high water temperatures have caused the corals to lose their color in a process called "coral bleaching," and the Great Barrier Reef is no exception.

- Corals owe their spectacular colors to the different species of algae that grow on them. Corals are colorful only while they are alive, and all dead corals are essentially white.

# The Great Barrier Reef

Flourishing in the clear, tropical coastal waters off northeastern Australia, the stunningly beautiful Great Barrier Reef is actually a scattered labyrinth of around 2,900 exquisite reefs and more than 1,000 islands. In today's world, where human action is largely responsible for the destruction of many of natures' treasures, the relative purity of this much-visited yet well-protected reef makes it an even more extraordinary and priceless natural reserve.

The largest coral reef system in the world, the Great Barrier Reef stretches for approximately 1,250 miles (2,011 km) along the Australian coast from Lady Elliot Island to the Cape of York, and encompasses one of the world's most diverse tropical ecosystems. The individual reefs vary in size from 0.004sq miles (0.01sq km) to 39sq miles (100sq km), together occupying an area of 134,633sq miles (348,698sq km).

The Great Barrier Reef supports a complex and diverse life system that can only be rivaled by that of a tropical rainforest. It is home to more than 1,500 different fish, 4,000 species of mollusks—including chitons, snails, giant

## CORALS

Coral reefs are made up of individual coral polyps, each living inside a shell of hard calcium carbonate called aragonite. These minute organisms cluster to form colonies in shallow tropical waters where the temperature remains constant between 72°F (22°C) and 82°F (28°C). The clusters of the Great Barrier Reef are so massive that they can be seen from outer space. The magnificent and dense underwater coral forests, with striking formations such as staghorn corals, brain corals, and mushroom corals, are made up of centuries of calcareous remains. The polyps begin growing on the exoskeleton of the previous generation, often forming walls of limestone as high as 328ft (100m).

*The Great Barrier Reef*

## DARK STAR

The crown-of-thorns starfish is the greatest natural predator of living corals. An individual adult of the species is capable of wiping out 64sq ft (6sq m) of living coral in a single year. Proliferation of this species is believed to be the most dangerous natural threat posed to coral reefs. Their effect on coral colonies is potentially devastating because although they can recover from these outbreaks, coral polyps have a slow recovery rate.

*A crown-of-thorns starfish*

clams, and octopus—and more than 400 types of corals. The reef is also home to 30 species of whales, dolphins, dugongs, and porpoises in addition to several varieties of sharks and rays—warm water sharks, manta rays, and stingrays. Six of the seven species of sea turtle, all of which are endangered, depend on the remote islands of the reef for safe nesting grounds. The cays in the reef provide sanctuary to 242 species of bird including reef herons, osprey, pelicans, frigate birds, sea eagles, and shearwaters. A wide selection of sponges, anemones, worms, crustaceans, and echinoderms are also found at the Great Barrier Reef.

Declared a World Heritage Site in 1981, the Great Barrier Reef is of interest not only in terms of its scientific value because of the plethora of life-forms that it supports, but also for its immense cultural importance. Several middens and other archaeological sites of Aboriginal or Torres Strait Islander origin are located in the Great Barrier Reef, some remarkable examples of which can be found on Lizard and Hinchinbrook Islands, and on Stanley, Cliff, and Clack Islands, where there are also some impressive rock paintings.

The earliest documents describing the reef's existence come from a French naval expedition led by Louis-Antoine de Bougainville in 1768. However, it was first sited in 1770 when the British explorer James Cook's ship *The Endeavour* grounded on the reef. The process of mapping channels and passages through this spectacular maze of reefs started with Cook and continued well into the 19th and 20th centuries. The Great Barrier Reef Expedition of 1928–29 was responsible for expanding greatly the extant knowledge of coral physiology and the ecology of reefs. A research station was built on Heron Island in 1951, which to this day carries out scientific and other investigations of the reef.

Threats posed to the Great Barrier Reef include tropical cyclones, global warming, overfishing, rapid coastal development, discharge of untreated sewage into the sea, drilling for petroleum resources, shipping, and large-scale tourism. The Great Barrier Marine Park was set up in 1975 in order to combat these problems. Almost 98 percent of the Great Barrier Reef today is contained within the marine park, making it the largest protected area of ocean in the world.

- The name Bungle Bungle is believed to have originated from "bundle bundle," a variety of grass that grows in the Kimberley region.
- Western Australia's Purnululu National Park encompasses an area of 926sq miles (2,397sq km).

**Bungle Bungle Range,** Australia

# Bungle Bungle Range

It seems inconceivable that one of the most impressive landforms on this planet has become widely known in Australia and across the world only over the last two decades of the 20th century. Rising up to 1,895ft (578m) above sea level, the Bungle Bungle Range is located in the Purnululu National Park in the State of Western Australia. Despite being known to the Aborigines for centuries, it somehow managed to remain unseen by the rest of the world right up until 1980. However, once it was noticed, the impact of its discovery was so widespread and immediate that in 2003 it was conferred the status of a World Heritage Site and recognized as a "superlative natural phenomena."

It is easy to see what makes the range so special. The sight of towers that resemble beehives, their steeply sloping surfaces marked with interchanging horizontal strips of orange and black or gray, is awe-inspiring. Changing colors with the seasons, the elements, and light, the breathtaking beauty of this range is best viewed from the air. Made up of Devonian Age quartz sandstone, the conical towers of this dissected range were formed as a result of 20 million years of uplift and erosion. The colored stripes are a cyanobacterial crust (or algae) and contain deposits of orange silica; the beehive-shaped towers are the most magnificent examples of cone karst in sandstones in the world.

## ROAD TO HEAVEN

Despite remaining unknown up until the 1980s, what is even more surprising is that ground access into the remote Bungles range was achieved much later. Though a route was clearly visible from the air, there were no tracks or trails on the ground. It took the genius of an East Kimberley resident, a "spotter" plane, sacks of flour, lots of patience, and a four-wheel drive to find a trustworthy entry into the wonders of the Bungle Bungle Range. The "spotter" plane, carrying the sacks of flour, flew low over the area. On sighting the most accessible route, the sacks were thrown out, and the dusty-white left behind on the brilliant red earth was picked up by a four-wheel drive.

A stunning view of the Bungle Bungle Range reflected in a nearby pond

Contrary to its solid appearance, the sandstone is actually quite fragile. The weight of the overlying rock holds the grains of sand in the sandstone tightly in place. When removed, the stone is easily eroded. The rounded tops of the cones are a sign of the weakness in the stone. This dearth of internal strength has been ruthlessly exploited by flowing water, and, over time, it has eroded the tapering channels, thus dividing the towers.

It is water that most effectively sets off the Bungles. Narrow, meandering gorges lined with Livistona palms provide a dramatic frame to this thick and intricate labyrinth of stone towers, thrusting them into even greater prominence and earning for them the nickname of Australia's "Grand Canyon." Seasonal waterfalls and pools can be found in these sheer gorges, making them an equally attractive tourist draw. Some of the best known gorges in the park are Echidna Chasm, Frog Hole, Mini Palms, Piccaninny Creek, and the Cathedral Gorges. However, the Purnululu Park is closed to visitors from January to March—the wet season—as many of the gorges are filled with raging torrents, which transforms them into treacherous areas.

## WILD THINGS

The Purnululu National Park is lush with bird and animal life. It also hosts a variety of reptiles. Eucalyptus and spinifex monopolize the landscape, though Livistona palms can be found in many of the gorges and waterholes. More than 130 species of birds can be spotted here, including rainbow bee-eaters and flocks of budgerigars. In fact, birds are the most visible of the park's inhabitants.

*A Livistona palm near the entrance of Echidna Chasm in the Bungle Bungle Range*

• Kathleen Springs, the exquisite spring-fed waterhole at the mouth of the Kathleen Gorge in Watarrka National Park, is integral to the Aboriginal history of the area.

• The Kings Canyon area is powered by the Kings Canyon Solar Power Station. In operation since December 2003, this project is the largest single installation of its kind in Australia.

**Kings Canyon,** Australia

# Kings Canyon

Red sandstone walls soar up to the skies and pockets of lush greenery in sheltered gullies interweave to form Kings Canyon in Australia. Part of the sprawling 281sq miles (720sq km) Watarrka National Park in the Northern Territory, Kings Canyon lies at the western end of the George Gill Range, between Alice Springs and the Uluru-Kata Tjuta National Park. Rising up from the Kings Creek valley, the walls of Kings Canyon reach 886ft (270m) at their highest point.

A tourist hotspot today, the canyon is the result of 440 million years of work by the elements. Fossils discovered in areas of the canyon testify to a time when the valley was still under water. The land was formed by the process of sedimentation and cementation, followed by pressure exerted on the earth's crust by the movement of the tectonic plates; wind, rain, and streams that cut through the rock in search of a pathway then carved out the gorge. Weathered sandstone cones in areas within the canyon bear a striking resemblance to the Bungle Bungle in Western Australia. Kings Canyon is a little younger than its southern cousins, Uluru (Ayers Rock) and Kata Tjuta (the Olgas), which were formed almost 550 million years ago.

Among the bounties that Kings Canyon has to offer are the Lost City, a spectacular group of rock formations

## KINGS CANYON RIM WALK

The 3.7-mile (6-km) Kings Canyon Rim Walk is a challenging looped walk that runs along the brim of the canyon. A particularly difficult climb at the beginning of the walk has been named Heartbreak Hill or Heart Attack Hill by the locals because of its steepness. This stretch takes visitors up to the top of the canyon from where they can gaze at the spectacular landscape with its stunning gorges. A detour halfway up the walk leads to the lush Garden of Eden. The last half of the walk leads through the Lost City and then a slow descent brings visitors back to the starting point. The walk is recommended only for people who are physically fit.

*Kings Canyon, Northern Territory*

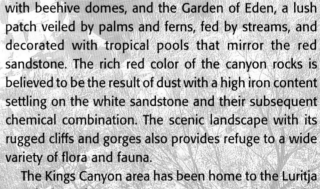

## WATARRKA NATIONAL PARK

The Watarrka National Park is home to cycads, ferns, and palms, some of which date back to the Jurassic Period. The high rock faces of Kings Canyon protect these from the surrounding desert conditions. More than 600 plant species manage to survive on the water that collects between cracks in the rocks of the canyon. The park also provides shelter to 100 varieties of birds and 60 species of reptiles. The name, Watarrka, is derived from an Aboriginal word for the umbrella bush that thrives in the area.

*Cycads* (Macrozamia macdonnellii), *growing in the MacDonnell Range, Garden of Eden, Kings Canyon*

with beehive domes, and the Garden of Eden, a lush patch veiled by palms and ferns, fed by streams, and decorated with tropical pools that mirror the red sandstone. The rich red color of the canyon rocks is believed to be the result of dust with a high iron content settling on the white sandstone and their subsequent chemical combination. The scenic landscape with its rugged cliffs and gorges also provides refuge to a wide variety of flora and fauna.

The Kings Canyon area has been home to the Luritja people for at least 20,000 years. Many sections of the canyon are considered sacred sites by the Aboriginal people. Dreamtime legends about the canyon are popular even today. The first European to set eyes upon the canyon was Ernest Giles in 1872. An explorer, Giles is also credited with the discovery of many other sites such as Mount Olga and Palm Valley, among others. The 14-mile (22-km) long Giles Track that connects Kings Canyon to Kathleen Springs, is popular with the more adventurous hikers, and has been named in his honor. Other walks in the Kings Canyon include the 1.6-mile (2.6-km) Kathleen Springs Walk and the rather difficult Kings Canyon Rim Walk.

**Uluru (Ayers Rock),** Australia

- The Uluru-Kata Tjuta National Park was inscribed as a UNESCO World Heritage Site in 1987.
- The custodians of Uluru and Kata Tjuta are the Anangu, the local Aboriginal people who live within Uluru-Kata Tjuta National Park

# Uluru (Ayers Rock)

One of Australia's most famous natural landmarks, Uluru is an enormous tor or isolated mass of weathered rock located in the middle of the continent, very close to the geographical center. Better known to the rest of the world as Ayers Rock, this gigantic monolith—one of the largest in the world—is located within the Uluru-Kata Tjuta National Park near the southwestern corner of the Northern Territory. Approximately 16 miles (24km) northwest of Uluru, is Kata Tjuta, the other attraction of the park.

Towering 1,141ft (348m) above its surroundings, Uluru is about 2.2 miles (3.6km) long and 1.2 miles (1.9km) wide. This colossal oval block of rock occupies about 1.29sq miles (3.33sq km). Erosion of the weaker layers of rock has made the lower slopes jagged, and numerous gullies and basins have been scoured on the top, which have resulted in the formation of the Mutitjulu waterhole. Caves and crevices which have been eroded into the monolith are decorated with cave paintings, which have been assimilated into Aboriginal tales of creation.

## COLORS OF ULURU

Dusty outback roads lead from Alice Springs to motels near Uluru, allowing visitors the chance to experience the fascinating spectacle of the rock changing color with the changing light of morning and evening. As the sun sets, the rock appears to glow with an inner fire as it changes from the dry brown of the day to an intense fiery orange and then blazing red, before turning into a black silhouette against the fading light. The dawn light reveals Uluru in even more beautiful pastel shades. Sunrise and sunset at Uluru are considered among the most surreal and dazzling natural displays that Australia has to offer.

*The brooding mass of Ayers Rock*

## GEOLOGICAL HISTORY

Uluru is composed from a coarse-grained sandstone, a sedimentary rock called arkose sandstone. Kata Tjuta is a conglomerate of a sedimentary rock, boulders, pebbles, and gravel held together by mud and sand. As a result, it contains many minerals and different types of rock including granite and basalt.

The distinctive red color of Uluru is attributed to weathering of the rock. Time and environmental factors such as rainwater and oxygen affect the iron minerals in the rock (imagine how iron looks when it rusts). The weathering of the feldspar minerals inside the sandstone also contributes to the beautiful color. It's also interesting to note that both Uluru and Kata Tjuta extend for several miles underground.

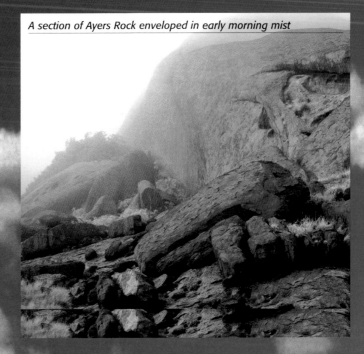

*A section of Ayers Rock enveloped in early morning mist*

The Kata Tjuta, meaning "many heads" in the Pitjantjajara language, is a cluster of 36 monoliths. The tallest of these is Mount Olga, which rises to a height of 1,790ft (546m) above the desert plain. Also referred to collectively as "the Olgas," these rocks together occupy about 13.5sq miles (35sq km). The layers of rock at Kata Tjuta are almost horizontal, unlike the close to vertical stratification of Uluru, and this accounts for the difference in patterns of erosion of the two outcrops.

Both areas have been affected primarily by two kinds of erosion—rain and heat. Despite the desert-like conditions surrounding the area, these rocks receive a plentiful rainfall every year; this precipitation occurs in the form of a few but major storms. During these infrequent rainstorms, raging torrents of water crash down the sides of the rounded rocks, often taking the form of giant cataracts, and wash away the looser chunks of rock in their path. The variations in temperature between extremely hot days and acutely cold nights is responsible for thermal erosion; the rapid and constant processes of expansion and contraction of the rocks eventually cause fragments to break away from the monoliths.

The first European to sight Uluru was the Australian explorer Ernest Giles in 1872. The first European to visit the rock and actually climb it was the surveyor Henry Gosse. He named it the Ayers Rock after Sir Henry Ayers, who was then the Chief Secretary of South Australia. However, Uluru has been a significant part of the Aboriginal Anangu culture a long time before that. The rock is of immense spiritual significance to them, and so the Anangu consider climbing the rock disrespectful, even though it is not legally prohibited. The 512sq miles (1,326sq km) Uluru-Kata Tjuta National Park—called the Ayers-Mount Olga National Park until the 1990s—today belongs to its traditional Anangu owners and is administered according to the *Tjukurpa*, a complex word that symbolizes Anangu law, religion, ethics, knowledge, and harmony.

- The remarkably Martian-like topography of the Flinders Ranges in the southern Outback region has led scientists to choose it as the location for a simulation space station.

- Temperatures in the central Outback deserts can be as high as 120°F (50°C) on summer days and as low as 15°F (-10°C) on winter nights. However, temperature variations are less extreme in the outer reaches.

**The Outback,** Australia

# The
# Outback

A vast remote land, broken only by long, lonely stretches of road, the Australian Outback is considered to be one of the last open frontiers in the world today. Though often harsh and unforgiving, this great land is also one of exquisite beauty and diversity. Sprawling across 2.5 million sq miles (6.5 million sq km) of the country, from Darwin at the rim of the Gulf of Carpentaria in the north to the southern tip of the mainland, this dry and dusty desert land is transformed by rain into a sea of color as thousands of wild plants blossom and bloom.

The sheer size and remoteness of this stretch of Australia had in the past deterred people from exploring it at length; however, it is this sense of isolation—the unearthly tranquility and desolation which it offers—that has made this fierce land such a huge tourist attraction today. The wilderness of the Outback was first conquered by pioneers who ventured out of the sheltered pleasures and comfort that the coastal settlements offered in order to carve out a new life in the wild and untamed interior of the country. The Australian Stockman's Hall of Fame and Outback Heritage Centre in Longreach,

*Eastern grey kangaroos*

## THE FLYING DOCTORS

The Royal Flying Doctors Service of Australia is a non-profit organization dedicated to providing health care and medical emergency assistance to all those who live and work in, or travel to the remote regions of Australia. First established in 1928 and developed on a national basis in the following decade, it is the world's first comprehensive aerial medical organization, and provides help to thousands of unprepared outback explorers every year. The Flying Doctors use high-frequency radio networks and telephone communication to trace imperiled travelers, and provide assistance in various emergencies, including cases of snake bite, dehydration, illness, or accident. In addition to on-the-spot medical aid, they also provide valuable safety guidelines for enthusiastic travelers starting out on their journey.

## LITCHFIELD NATIONAL PARK

One of the lesser-known Outback parks, the small Litchfield National Park is located near Darwin. A host of beautiful features adorn this tabletop plateau. The Wangi and Florence falls are the most famous of the park's four waterfalls. Other attractions include the Buley Rockholes (a series of rapids, small cascades and pools); the isolated Greenant Creek, surrounded by tall palm and monsoonal forests; the deep and narrow gorge carved out by the Tolmer Creek; and the strange and fascinating Magnetic Termite Mounds.

*The fascinating Buley Rockholes in Litchfield National Park*

Queensland pays tribute to these brave and unsung heroes of Australia.

The 1,860-miles (3,000-km) long Stuart Highway, running from north to south as it dissects the center of Australia, is the most popular road for people traversing the Outback. Other routes through this difficult and rugged terrain include the Oodnadatta, Birdsville and Tanami tracks, the Gunbarrel Highway, and the "Bomb Roads." Situated halfway down the Stuart Highway is Alice Springs, the capital of the Outback. The Ayers Rock monolith is its most famous tourist destination.

On either side of the Stuart Highway are the hot, dusty Outback deserts—the Tanami in the north, the Simpson Desert in the east, and the Great Victoria, Gibson, and the Great Sandy Desert in the west—terrifying in their barrenness. Other Outback attractions include the Nullarbor Plain—intersected by the Eyre Highway—in the north, spectacular gorges such as the Katherine Gorge, and the jagged and beautiful Kimberley Plateau in the west. The crimson cliffs of the McDonnell Ranges, the underground mining town of Cooper Pedy, the Devils Marbles boulder formations in Tennant Creek, the astonishing Gosse's Bluff impact crater, and the Mount Augustus and Kakadu national parks are also much visited.

Despite its apparent starkness, the Outback is quite fertile, and often amazes travelers with its profusion of plants and trees. The deserts of Australia receive adequate amounts of rainfall and are thus dotted with a great variety of small shrubs and bushes in some areas. The diverse range of animals that populate the Outback form one of its main attractions. Kangaroos, dingoes, wild camels, and many species of lizards form the backbone of the fauna of this region; poisonous snakes, spiders, and the Australian crocodile are among the more deadly of the Outback dwellers.

- The Pinnacles are composed of a particularly hard limestone known as the Tamala Limestone.
- Many tiny fragments of short fossil roots, called rhizoliths, cover the surface of most of the Pinnacles.

**The Pinnacles,** Australia

# The
# Pinnacles

Thousands of impressive limestone pillars rising out of a desolate landscape of ever-shifting yellow sands make up the astonishing Pinnacles Desert in Australia. Situated in the heart of the Nambung National Park in Western Australia, these columns of limestone often reach a height of 11ft (3.5m). While some of these pillars resemble domes and tombstones, others appear like giant teeth protruding from the ground, their jagged edges tapering into sharp points.

Though the formation of the Pinnacles took place over thousands of years, they were perhaps exposed only recently in terms of geological time. The denudation of the dunes by bush fires and the removal of loose quartz sands by the south-westerly winds resulted in the revelation of these odd but fascinating structures made of limestone. The discovery of Aboriginal artifacts and the lack of evidence of recent Aboriginal occupation has led archeologists to believe that the Pinnacles were exposed around 6,000 years ago. Covered by the desert's restless and rolling sands, they were re-exposed once again only a few centuries ago.

## DISCOVERING THE PINNACLES

The earliest European records of the Nambung area can be traced back to 1658, when two small hills within the park—called the North and South Hummocks—were marked on Dutch maps. The navigator Philip Parker King also mentioned these hills in his journal in 1820. However, the Pinnacles Desert remained relatively unknown until the late 1960s when the government decided to incorporate the area within the Nambung National Park, established in 1956. Today, however, the park is one of the most famous natural attractions in Australia, and almost 150,000 tourists visit the national park and the desert every year.

*The limestone columns of the Pinnacles Desert*

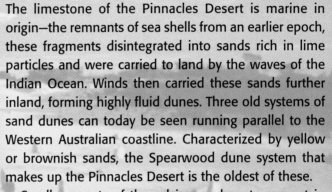

## PLANTS AND ANIMALS OF THE PINNACLES DESERT

The Pinnacles Desert teems with wildlife. Though most of the creatures stay hidden from the eyes of visitors because of their nocturnal habits, kangaroos and emus sometimes wander across the paths of visitors early in the morning. Not easily frightened, these animals can be viewed from close quarters if visitors are quiet and careful. Reptiles such as the Gould's monitor and the harmless carpet python can also be seen sheltering in the shade of the limestone pillars. The Nambung National Park is also home to a variety of plants and trees. The most common plant species that is found close to the Pinnacles is the parrotbush (*Dryandra sessilis*).

*Emus taking an early morning stroll in the Pinnacles*

The limestone of the Pinnacles Desert is marine in origin—the remnants of sea shells from an earlier epoch, these fragments disintegrated into sands rich in lime particles and were carried to land by the waves of the Indian Ocean. Winds then carried these sands further inland, forming highly fluid dunes. Three old systems of sand dunes can today be seen running parallel to the Western Australian coastline. Characterized by yellow or brownish sands, the Spearwood dune system that makes up the Pinnacles Desert is the oldest of these.

Small amounts of the calcium carbonate present in the dunes were dissolved by the slightly acidic winter rain as it percolated through the grains of sand. In summer, when the waters dried out, the calcium carbonate was precipitated in the lower levels of the dunes. Over time this precipitate cemented around tiny grains of sand. This process was repeated several times, until a hard limestone rock layer was formed. The growth of plants allowed the development of a layer of soil and humus rich in decayed organic matter over the rest of the quartzite sand, increasing the acidity of the soil and accelerating the leaching process; a layer of hard calcrete was formed over the softer limestone beneath.

Over time, plant roots and water created cracks and fissures in the limestone. Further subsurface erosion occurred, until most of the limestone was again dissolved by water, leaving only the hardiest and most resilient columns of limestone. The Pinnacles are thus the eroded remains of this earlier thick bed of limestone.

Even today, unidirectional winds are uncovering more of the limestone spires in the northern part of the desert and hiding those at the southern end. This cyclical process will probably be repeated continuously, granting an evanescent quality to this extraordinary landscape of strange and wonderful shapes. These eerie structures are best viewed at dusk and dawn, when they cast long and extraordinary shadows over the rippling sands.

• Australian pioneer William Cox is credited with laying the first road into the Blue Mountains in 1814. The road, which stretches for 101 miles (163km), was constructed in six months by about 30 convicts supervised by eight guards.

• The Lennox Bridge in the Blue Mountains is the oldest bridge in the Australian mainland. Constructed in 1832, again with the use of convict labor.

**The Blue Mountains,** Australia

# The
# Blue Mountains

According to Aboriginal legends, three sisters of the Katoomba tribe—Meehni, Wimlah, and Gunnedoo—who lived in what is today called the Jamison Valley, fell in love with three brothers of the Nepean tribe. When the girls' parents found out about the affair, they forbade marriage. Angered by the rejection, the boys decided to use force and win the girls in battle. Fearing for the girls' lives, a witch doctor cast a spell on them and turned them into rock, with plans of undoing the spell after the battle ended. Unfortunately, the witch doctor himself was killed, and the girls have remained rocks forever. This is the story of the Three Sisters—standing at 3,024ft (922m), 3,011ft (918m), and 2,972ft (906m)—the most famous of the Blue Mountain rock formations.

The Blue Mountains, a part of the Greater Blue Mountains Area, are located about 62 miles (100km) west of Sydney. Declared a World Heritage Site by UNESCO in 2000, these mountains are actually a series of deeply dissected sandstone plateaus and granite cliffs—some of them around 3,280ft (1,000m) in height—surrounding a plateau. The many gorges that run in between these are in places more than 2,460ft (750m) deep.

*The Weeping Rock Falls*

## NAMES WITH A PAST

The Marked Tree, a few miles west of Katoomba, is so named because it carries the initials of Blaxland, Lawson, and Wentworth; the pioneering explorers had supposedly carved them into the tree after reaching that point in 1813. Today, hundreds of tourists have added their names to the list. The section of highway past the Marked Tree that leads into Medlow Bath is known as Whipcord Hill. The name refers to a penal colony that used to be situated there. Behind it is Pulpit Point, where religious services were held.

Tectonic upheavals about a million years ago, followed by wind and water erosion, are what geologists believe to be the cause of the formation of the Blue Mountains. The eucalyptus trees found on these mountains secrete a volatile oil that combines with droplets of water and suspended particulate matter to form a shimmering haze which gives a blue tinge to the mountains.

The Aborigines have lived in the shadows of the Blue Mountains for more than 20,000 years; the Red Hands Cave, with well-preserved hand stencils on its walls, bears testimony to this. The name Katoomba, an area in the heart of the preserve, is the Aboriginal word for 'shiny, tumbling water.' It refers to the 656ft (200m) waterfall that thunders down the side of the mountains. Prior to 1877, this area was called The Crushers because it was the site for a stone quarry from which ballast was supplied to the railways.

The first Europeans to carve a trail through the ravines were Gregory Blaxland, William Charles Wentworth, and William Lawson. Their success is attributed to lessons learnt from earlier failed expeditions. They walked along the mountain ridges, rather than following the course of the river below. The unfolding vista from this elevated position included rich grazing lands, which were to later stand pastoralists and ranchers in good stead. Today, a string of towns have been named after these pioneers.

The Three Sisters, Blue Mountains National Park

## WORLD'S STEEPEST RAILWAY

The famous Katoomba Scenic Railway descends through sandstone cliffs via a rock tunnel, leading out into a lush green rainforest. It was initially part of the Katoomba mining tramways constructed between 1878 and 1900 for coal and shale-oil mining operations. According to the *Guinness Book of World Records*, it is the steepest funicular railway in the world, with an incline of 52 degrees over a distance of 1,361ft (415m). The railway was opened for tourism shortly before World War II, partly in an attempt to keep it from falling into disrepair, since the Katoomba Colliery had stopped operations and the tramway had been left to gather rust.

**Valley of the Giants,** Australia

- Styx Valley near Hobart, Australia, is a contender for the title Valley of the Giants. Its swamp gums, are second only to the American redwoods in terms of height.

- At over 400 years old, Grandmother Tingle is the oldest of the trees in the Valley of the Giants.

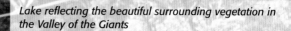

*Lake reflecting the beautiful surrounding vegetation in the Valley of the Giants*

## A DIFFERENT PERSPECTIVE

The Valley of the Giants now boasts a unique path from which to view the enormous trees. The Tree Top Walk was constructed with the purpose of minimizing the impact of humans on the forest. A swaying bridge that winds its way through the canopy of trees and rises to a height of 131ft (40m) offers breathtaking views of the forest. The design of the Tree Top Walk through the Valley of the Giants was inspired by the forest itself, more specifically by the tassel flower and sword grass, plants found in the tingle forests.

# Valley of the Giants

**N**estled in a small valley in the southwest of Western Australia is a lush forest with a towering reputation. Made up of some of the world's tallest trees that grow to heights of about 260ft (80m), this is nature at its finest. Found not far from the coast in the Walpole-Nornalup area, the forest, known as the Valley of the Giants, now lies within the Walpole-Nornalup National Park, occupying an area of approximately 78sq miles (200sq km).

The giants of this valley belong to the Eucalyptus family of the tingle (*Eucalyptus brevistylis*), the red tingle (*Eucalyptus jacksonii*) and the yellow tingle (*Eucalyptus guilfoylei*). The forest also consists of marri (*Eucalyptus calophylla*), jarrah (*Eucalyptus marginata*), and karri (*Eucalyptus diversicolor*). Karri trees can reach heights of up to 300ft (90m) and are the tallest trees found in this part of Australia. One of the most distinctive features of the tingle trees, especially the red tingle, is the size of its trunk, which can reach a girth of more than 66ft (20m). Several of them possess a hollowed-out base, making it possible for people to step inside the tree trunk. Reasons for the formation of unusual structures include fire, fungus, or insect attack. Along with their gigantic size, the age of these trees is also worth a mention, with some of them as old as a few hundred years.

Tingle and karri forests found in areas of fertile soil and abundant rainfall constitute a moist evergreen ecoregion that is a hotspot of flora and fauna. Some of these can trace their origins back to the Gondwana period more than 60 million years ago. These include the Gondwanian spider, endemic species of frogs, and freshwater fauna. Other species of animals found in the tingle forests include the quokka, southern brown bandicoot, pygmy possum, chuditch, and the western gray kangaroo. Though the birdlife does not display the richness or the endemism that would be expected in such a forest, birds like the white-tailed black cockatoo,

Western Rosella, red-winged fairy wren, golden whistler, purple-crowned lorikeet, and owlet nightjar, as well as honeyeaters and parrots can be spotted in the valley at different times of the year.

While their majesty and age may well be a misleading factor, tingle tree forests are quite vulnerable to human appreciation. Owning to their shallow root systems, the trees remain dependent on surface nutrients. However, when thousands of people come walking through the forest—the Valley of the Giants is one of the most popular natural attractions in Australia—and wear a path around the tree base, it exposes the roots and makes the tree vulnerable. One of the biggest trees in the Valley of the Giants collapsed two decades ago for this very reason. However, this mishap has prompted the park management to build alternative viewing platforms to accommodate the million or more visitors that come annually to pay homage to these giants.

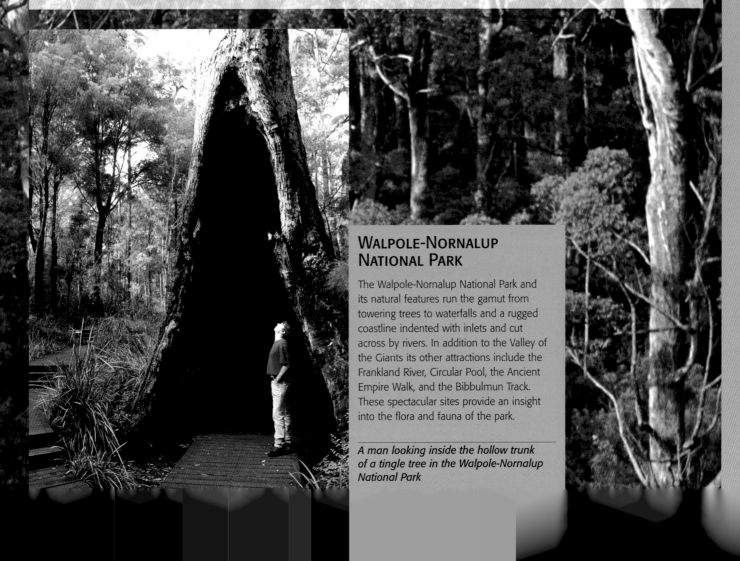

### WALPOLE-NORNALUP NATIONAL PARK

The Walpole-Nornalup National Park and its natural features run the gamut from towering trees to waterfalls and a rugged coastline indented with inlets and cut across by rivers. In addition to the Valley of the Giants its other attractions include the Frankland River, Circular Pool, the Ancient Empire Walk, and the Bibbulmun Track. These spectacular sites provide an insight into the flora and fauna of the park.

*A man looking inside the hollow trunk of a tingle tree in the Walpole-Nornalup National Park*

• The Twelve Apostles Marine National Park is located 4 miles (7km) east of Port Campbell and encompasses approximately 29sq miles (75sq km) of protected area.

• The limestone cliffs near the Twelve Apostles are being eroded at a rate of 0.8in (2cm) per year, and in the future more such stacks are likely to be formed from the rocky headlands.

**Twelve Apostles,** Australia

## SHIPWRECK COAST

The stretch of coast between Cape Otway to Port Fairy in Victoria was christened Shipwreck Coast by European explorers and settlers. The Aboriginal people were well-acquainted with this coast, and used steps cut into the steep cliffs to access marine food sources, but the jagged cliffs and rocks posed a great threat to the European ships. Though they tried to give this dangerous area a wide berth, many ships were dashed against the cliffs along this stretch. The most famous of the shipwrecks is the Loch Ard, which was wrecked in 1878 and caused around 50 casualties. The Twelve Apostles are situated along this perilous stratch.

# Twelve Apostles

Soaring high above the heaving waters of the Southern Ocean, the mighty Twelve Apostles stand guard just off the coast of Victoria. These gigantic stacks of rock are among the most amazing attractions of the Port Campbell National Park, which stretches from Princetown to Peterborough. One of the most-visited natural attractions in Australia, the Twelve Apostles are considered iconic of the natural treasures that the Great Ocean Road has to offer. The backdrop to the impressive figures of the Apostles is framed by magnificent and imposing limestone cliffs that tower almost 230ft (70m) above the seashore. The Apostles are shorter—with the tallest one reaching a height of about 148ft (45m)—but create an even more dramatic visual impact by jutting out without warning from the waves.

The origin of the Twelve Apostles can be traced back 20 million years ago, when the soft limestone cliffs of the Port Campbell coastline were being pummeled by the forces of nature. Created over the years as a result of the deposition of marine skeletons on the ocean floor, the limestone was gradually exposed as the waters of the ocean retreated. The fierce Southern Ocean continued to hew at these rocks with its strong waves, and turbulent winds constantly blasted the cliffs, until finally the limestone began to erode. This process carved caves out of the soft stone; however, erosive action over the

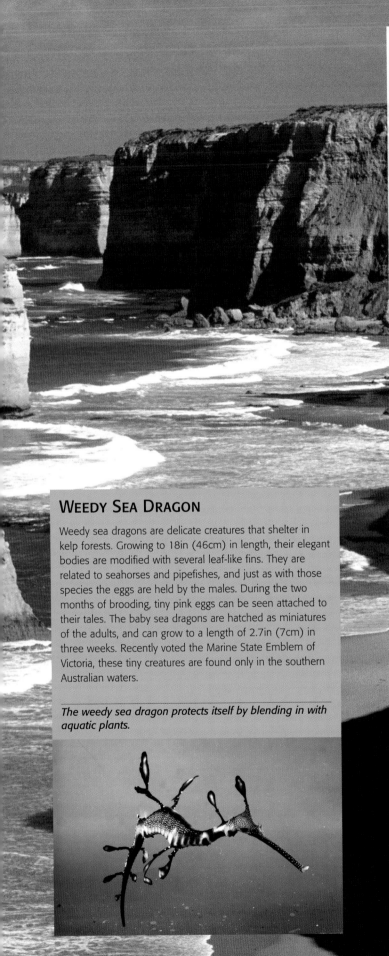

years has reduced the caves to arches. Further erosion resulted in the eventual collapse of the arches, leaving behind these isolated rock islands a short distance from the shore.

The untamed ocean also conceals a marvelous seascape beneath the waves. A remarkable labyrinth of caves, arches, canyons, fissures, and gutters have been carved out by the sea. Decorated with colorful seaweeds, ferns, and gardens of sponges, these karst features are populated by numerous sea creatures. The Twelve Apostles Marine National Park protects these underwater reaches for 11 miles (17km) along the coastline. Comprising some of the most spectacular underwater seascapes in Victoria, the undersea habitats shelter many inter-tidal and sub-tidal invertebrate colonies, including a variety of sea spiders, sea slugs, sea snails, and sea stars. Schools of reef fish and the occasional Australian fur seal can also to be found here; weedy sea dragons float gently amid the thick brown fronds of the bull kelp. While breeding colonies of seabirds inhabit the rock stacks, little penguins nest in the caves below the Twelve Apostles.

Besides the Twelve Apostles, a host of wonderful natural features have been carved out along the coast by the sea. These include the Pudding Basin Rock, Island Arch, the Razorback, Muttonbird Island, Thunder Cave, the Blowhole, Bakers Oven, London Bridge, and the Grotto, among others. Extensive viewing platforms and boardwalks have been constructed along the coast to facilitate the viewing of these awe-inspiring vistas. Though the views are magnificent at any time of the day, sunrise and sunset provide particularly stunning visual experiences, thanks to the astounding range of colors to be seen in the blazing sunlight.

## WEEDY SEA DRAGON

Weedy sea dragons are delicate creatures that shelter in kelp forests. Growing to 18in (46cm) in length, their elegant bodies are modified with several leaf-like fins. They are related to seahorses and pipefishes, and just as with those species the eggs are held by the males. During the two months of brooding, tiny pink eggs can be seen attached to their tales. The baby sea dragons are hatched as miniatures of the adults, and can grow to a length of 2.7in (7cm) in three weeks. Recently voted the Marine State Emblem of Victoria, these tiny creatures are found only in the southern Australian waters.

*The weedy sea dragon protects itself by blending in with aquatic plants.*

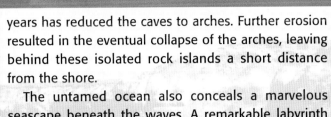

*Waves crashing against a sea stack arch at Twelve Apostles, Port Campbell National Park*

**Coromandel,** New Zealand

- The Coromandel enjoys glorious weather all year round; with average temperatures of 80°F (27°C) in summer and 55°F (13°C) in winter.

- Coromandel gets its name from the coast of the same name in southern India, which inspired the names of three Royal British Navy ships; one of these landed on the New Zealand Coast and gave its name to both a town and to the peninsula.

## GATEWAY TO THE COROMANDEL

A gold-mining and logging town from the 19th century, Thames is another place whose name can be attributed to Captain Cook; he rowed up the Waihou River and dubbed it the Thames. The Thames Coast Road that runs along the edge of the peninsula is one of the world's most scenic places.

# Coromandel

Located on New Zealand's North Island and comprising a diverse mix of pristine beaches, rainforest, hot pools, coastal scenery, secluded bays, marine wonders, mountains, and volcanic activity, the Coromandel can well be described as having an embarrassment of natural riches. A peninsula on the Island's east coast that extends 68 miles (110km) into the South Pacific Ocean, the Coromandel stretches from Cape Colville in the north to Te Aroha and Katikati in the south. More than 476 miles (145km) of mountains in the Coromandel Range run through the Peninsula, surrounded by 10 towns. This area was home to the Maori for hundreds of years before Captain James Cook's visit in 1769. Besides the naming of Mercury Bay and Cook's Beach, he is also responsible for the turn of events that followed in the peninsula's history. It was due to his report that the Coromandel region was selected for logging, which consequently led to the gold boom.

The Coromandel is famous the world over for the beauty of its beaches, which cover over 1,312 miles (400km) of this spectacular area. Pristine white sand beaches line the Peninsula's east coast, offering everything from challenging surf to gentle seas. The unique Hot Water Beach under which a river of hot water flows, is a reminder of the country's volcanic history. Hot pools can be dug up at low tide which then disappear at high tide.

## THE KAURI

The kauri is one of New Zealand's endemic species of trees found only in the Coromandel ecoregion where the humidity and warmth make for perfect growing conditions. Its abundant presence not only triggered the growth of a logging industry in the 19th century, but its gum was also one of the area's main exports. A combination of the two almost logged it out of existence. It is one of the giants of the world and can grow up to 131ft (40m) in height and live for 2,000 years.

*The giant kauri trees in the Coromandel ecoregion*

*Remains of rock arch at Cathedral Cove near Hahei, Coromandel Peninsula*

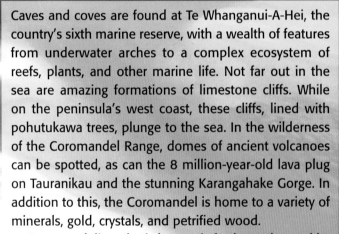

Caves and coves are found at Te Whanganui-A-Hei, the country's sixth marine reserve, with a wealth of features from underwater arches to a complex ecosystem of reefs, plants, and other marine life. Not far out in the sea are amazing formations of limestone cliffs. While on the peninsula's west coast, these cliffs, lined with pohutukawa trees, plunge to the sea. In the wilderness of the Coromandel Range, domes of ancient volcanoes can be spotted, as can the 8 million-year-old lava plug on Tauranikau and the stunning Karangahake Gorge. In addition to this, the Coromandel is home to a variety of minerals, gold, crystals, and petrified wood.

Coromandel's esthetic beauty is further enhanced by its diverse range of flora and fauna. The most famed is the kauri tree, the presence of which turned this area into one of the world's best logging destinations in the 19th century. The cloud forests on the highest peaks of the range are one of the main sites for the massive southern rata trees. Hundreds of years old pohutukawa (Christmas flower) trees, puriri, and large ferns form part of the regenerating native forests. The peninsula is also a natural sanctuary and home to many varieties of birds, including the brown kiwi, kingfisher, harrier hawk, tui, warblers, and finches; up to 74 species of shorebirds have been spotted here.

• *Hangi* is a method of Maori cooking in Rotorua, which involves ingredients being mixed together and placed in pits dug over natural thermal vents to steam and cook.

• The environmental conditions and the warmth of the waters have created a bird spa at the Motutara Point wildlife refuge and sanctuary in Rotorua.

**Rotorua Thermal Area,** New Zealand

# Rotorua Thermal Area

Situated on a volcanic plateau in the heart of the thermal belt of the North Island, New Zealand, Rotorua is famous throughout the world for its astounding geothermal activity—spouting geysers, boiling mud pools, and a phenomenal array of hot springs. More than 1,200 geothermal features dot the surface of Rotorua, including alkaline chloride springs, a host of flats, fumaroles, steaming grounds, gray and white sinter terraces, and hot lakes. Whakarewarewa, Waiotapu, Waimangu, and Tikitere are the chief thermal areas.

Located approximately 1.8 miles (3km) from Rotorua city, Whakarewarewa—which means "uprising of the war party at Waihiao"—near the banks of the Puarenga River, is Rotorua's most famous geothermal site. With its 500 or so hot springs and sinter deposits of many-hued porous silica or mineral encrustations, it is the chief tourist attraction in this area. New Zealand's largest geyser, the Pohutu, which erupts about 15 times a day and climbs to heights of 90ft (27m), is located in Whakarewarewa. Geyser activity in this area was on the decline in the 1980s because of the over-tapping of geothermal resources by bores. Following the government's ban on bores within 0.9 miles (1.5km) of Pohutu, the geothermal aquifer is regaining natural levels and geyser activity is gradually returning to its original state.

## LAKES OF ROTORUA

Lakes form an integral part of the Rotorua landscape. Lake Rotorua (Crater Lake) itself is the largest of a group of lakes, including Rotoiti and Tarawera, which were earlier called the "hot lakes." Lying at an elevation of 920ft (280m) above sea level, Lake Rotorua occupies a huge crater formed by an immense ancient volcanic explosion. The health-spa city of Rotorua is located at the edge of the lake. The volcanic Mokoia Island, which is held sacred by the Arawa Maoris, is in the middle of the lake. The largest lake in New Zealand with an area of about 234sq miles (600sq km), Lake Taupo lies 56 miles (90km) southwest of Rotorua. Created by a violent eruption about 1,800 years ago, this lake fills the crater of the ancient Taupo Volcano.

*The Waiotapu thermal wonderland*

## THE BURIED VILLAGE

Established by a Christian missionary in 1848, the Te Wairoa Village was located in a valley above Lake Tarawera. Abandoned during the land wars of the 1860s, the village was repopulated when it became the staging post to the Pink and White Terraces. However, it was wiped out entirely by the sudden and violent eruption of Mount Tarawera in 1886. Bombarding the village with rock, ash, and boiling mud for over four hours, this eruption was arguably the worst natural disaster to hit New Zealand. Besides Te Wairoa, the Terraces and two smaller villages were destroyed and buried under hot ash and mud.

*The spectacular Pohutu and Prince of Wales geysers*

The chemistry of the waters of Tikitere is quite different from that of the other geothermal sites of Rotorua. While alkali-chloride waters are more common in other North Island areas, the waters of Tikitere are described by scientists as acid-sulphate (shallow waters) or chloride-bicarbonate (deeper waters). Also called Hell's Gate, this area is extremely rich in deposits of elemental sulphur. About 5,000 tons of this bright yellow mineral has been removed through surface diggings. Sulphur lines many of the steam vents; the sulphur beds caught fire in 1881 and burnt down the bathhouses, almost suffocating the people inside.

Located about 20 minutes south of Rotorua is Waimangu (Black Water), famous for its Warbrick Terrace and Emerald Pools. The Warbrick Terrace appears to be composed of liquid rock; a combination of algae, iron oxide, hydroxides, and silicates are responsible for the rich colors of this undulating formation. The Emerald Pools, their lush green color apparently the result of sphagnum moss, are nestled in a crater caused by the 1886 eruption of Mount Tarawera. Inferno Crater and the Frying Pan—a steaming body of water that sizzles—are other attractions in this area. Waiotapu, the Maori word for "sacred waters," is situated about 30 minutes south of Rotorua, and features the spectacular Champagne Pools. Occupying a 900-year-old volcanic crater, this series of enormous hot pools is colored a rich mixture of gold, yellow, and orange.

One of the heartlands of ancient Maori culture, Rotorua has particular spiritual significance to them. The Maori consider themselves *kaitiaki* (guardians) of the geothermal resources; using the mineral waters for bathing, cooking, medicine, dyes, and rituals is an integral part of Maori tradition. As the elaborate names indicate, myth and legend surround many of these geothermal sites.

- The Aranui Cave, part of the greater Waitomo Caves system, is so named after a Maori youth who accidentally discovered it in 1910.

- The famous glowworms apart, the Waitomo Caves are also home to a variety of other insects such as the albino cave ants and giant crickets. The walls of the caves are covered with fungi, including a mushroom-like fungus called the cave flower.

**Waitomo Caves,** New Zealand

# Waitomo Caves

Epitomized by breathtaking stalactites, stalagmites, and incrustations, the Waitomo Caves are an elaborate network of subterranean limestone caverns located in the central North Island of New Zealand, about 50 miles (80km) south of Hamilton. Consisting of about 300 known caves, the Waitomo Caves were formed about 30 million years ago by geological and volcanic activity.

The Waitomo Caves were first explored in 1887 by the English surveyor Fred Mace and the Maori Chief Tane Tinorou, who stumbled upon the caverns as they followed an underground stream. Over the next few years, the two of them explored the caves thoroughly and charted them. Tane Tinorau is credited with the discovery of an easier route of access to the caves while on an individual trip.

Fossilized corals, sea shells, and fish skeletons embedded in the limestone structures testify to the underwater origin of the entire cave system. Whale bones, too, have been found in some of the underground chambers. The caves were created when tectonic plate movements caused the entire Waitomo area to thrust out and rise above the sea. Weak points in the rocks allowed the percolation of water through them; as water passed through the rocks, it left behind calcium deposits, which eventually resulted in the formation of the stalactites, stalagmites and other spectacular features. In some places, the limestone is as thick as 656ft (200m).

## THE GLOWWORMS

Celebrities in their own right, New Zealand's glowworms are not actually worms but the larvae of an insect called the fungus gnat. The glow is created as bait to lure other insects which serve as food. The glowworms' affinity for damp and dark places leads them to nest in places such as the Waitomo Caves. A specially appointed Scientific Advisory Group is responsible for the upkeep and protection of these tiny creatures. The group monitors conditions within the cave such as humidity, level of carbon dioxide, and air temperature. The collated data is then used to determine course of action regarding the caves, including imposing a restriction on the number of people at a time who are allowed to visit the Glowworm Grotto.

*Visitors looking at what resembles a night sky, but is in reality the famous Waitomo glowworms*

## CAVE ADMINISTRATION

Two years after the Waitomo Caves were first explored, Maori Chief Tane Tinorou and his wife Huti realized the tourist potential of the site and opened the area up to visitors in 1889. Visitors were given guided tours of the caverns in exchange for a small fee. However, rampant vandalism followed, leading to the government taking over the administration of the caves in 1906. The land was returned to its original inhabitants much later, in 1989. Many of the people who administer the caves today are descendants of Chief Tane Tinorou.

The Waitomo Caves are divided into two levels which are 52ft (16m) apart. The dry upper level of the caves includes formations such as the Pipe Organ, the Banquet Chamber, and the Catacombs among others. The main entrance to the cave is also through the upper level. The most remarkable of the lower level formations is the Cathedral—a 59-ft (18-m) high rough-walled enclosed cavern that has astounding acoustics owing to its contours.

The Tomo, a vertical limestone shaft which separates the two levels of the caves, was carved out by an ancient waterfall. Today, the waterfall comes to life only when it rains heavily. The magnificent vertical drop of the shaft is illuminated to highlight the many layers of limestone and the finely scalloped walls. Believed to be the newest of the Waitomo formations, the shaft connects the upper level to the lower level caves and the Waitomo River.

The most stunning of the caves is, of course, the Glowworm Grotto. Like stars studding the night sky, the ceiling and walls of the cave are lit up by millions of glowworms that rest on them. This visual experience, many visitors say, is akin to a visit to outer space. Boats ferry travelers captivated by the luminescent sight through this grotto. This was the first of the caves to be discovered by Mace and Tane on their maiden journey in 1887. Today, a trip through the grotto serves as the conclusion for a visit to the Waitomo Caves.

# Index

# Acknowledgements

Front cover: Getty Images; back cover: Getty Images.

Abbreviations for terms appearing below: (bg) background; (tl) top left; (i) inset.

Automobile Associations Developments Limited wishes to thank the following libraries and associations for their assistance in the preparation of this book.

echinaromance 69i
Eisriesenwelt Caves 28, 29
Photolibrary 26, 27, 34tl, 34–35bg, 36, 37, 52i, 58, 59, 64, 65, 68tl, 68–69bg, 82tl, 82i, 83i, 90, 91, 106, 107, 164, 164–165bg, 180–181bg, 183i, 184i, 206i, 207i, 209i, 212, 213, 216, 217, 220tl, 220–221bg
Pictures Colour Library 182tl, 182–183bg
The Legendary Black Water Rafting Co, Ruakuri Tours 220i, 221i

All other pictures are sourced from Getty Images.

# Flash CS6

## the missing manual®

The book that should have been in the box®

Chris Grover

**O'REILLY**®

Beijing | Cambridge | Farnham | Köln | Sebastopol | Tokyo

# Flash CS6: The Missing Manual

*by Chris Grover*

Published by O'Reilly Media, Inc.,
1005 Gravenstein Highway North, Sebastopol, CA 95472.

O'Reilly books may be purchased for educational, business, or sales promotional use. Online editions are also available for most titles (*http://my.safaribooksonline.com*). For more information, contact our corporate/institutional sales department: (800) 998-9938 or *corporate@oreilly.com*.

June 2012:      First Edition.

**Revision History for the 1st Edition:**

   2012-06-11      First release

See *http://oreilly.com/catalog/errata.csp?isbn=0636920022787* for release details.

ISBN-13: 978-1-449-31625-9

[M]

# Contents

## Part One: **Creating a Flash Animation**

## Part Two: **Advanced Drawing and Animation**

## Part Five: **Appendixes**

# The Missing Credits

## ABOUT THE AUTHOR

 **Chris Grover** is a veteran of the San Francisco Bay Area advertising and design community, having worked for over 25 years in print, video, and electronic media. He has been using and writing about computers from the day he first fired up his Kaypro II. Chris is the owner of Bolinas Road Creative (*www.BolinasRoad.com*), an agency that helps small businesses promote their products and services. His writing has appeared in a range of media from *Fine Homebuilding* to *Macworld.com*. He's also the author of *Office 2011 for Macintosh: The Missing Manual*, *Adobe Edge Preview 5: The Missing Manual*, and several other books in the Missing Manual series.

## ABOUT THE CREATIVE TEAM

**Nan Barber** (editor) has been working on the Missing Manual series since its inception. She lives in Massachusetts with her husband and various Apple products. Email: *nanbarber@oreilly.com*.

**Rachel Steely** (production editor) is an avid lover of books in all their forms, and can typeset, illustrate, and bind a book by hand. She enjoys traveling and speaks fluent Spanish. In her spare time, she draws Celtic knotwork, reads, and plays the violin.

**Julie Van Keuren** (proofreader) quit her newspaper job in 2006 to move to Montana and live the freelancing dream. She and her husband, M.H. (who is living the novel-writing dream), have two sons, Dexter and Michael. Email: *little_media@yahoo.com*.

**Ron Strauss** (indexer) specializes in the indexing of information technology publications of all kinds. Ron is also an accomplished classical violist and lives in northern California with his wife and fellow indexer, Annie, and his miniature pinscher, Kanga. Email: *rstrauss@mchsi.com*.

**Chris Deely** (tech reviewer) is a software developer living in Philadelphia with his wife, Nichole, and their son, Christopher Jr. He has been working with the Flash platform since 2004, building applications with ActionScript, Flex, and AIR. Chris currently leads a User Interface development team responsible for building enterprise application front-ends.

**Tina Spargo** (technical reviewer), her husband (and professional musician) Ed, their children, Max and Lorelei, and their two silly Spaniels, Parker (Clumber) and Piper (Sussex), all share time and space in their suburban Boston home. Tina juggles being an at-home mom with promoting and marketing Ed's musical projects and freelancing as a virtual assistant. Tina has over 20 years' experience supporting top-level executives in a variety of industries. Website: *www.tinaspargo.com*.

## ACKNOWLEDGMENTS

I'm always amazed at the number of pros it takes to create a book like Flash CS6: The Missing Manual. My thanks go out to everyone who worked on this book. Nan Barber has worked with me on several books and her skill and grace under fire is always appreciated. I'd also like to thank Rachel Steely for coordinating the production and Ron Strauss for writing the index. Rebecca Demarest managed to take my screenshots and crude charts and make them suitable for publication. A special thanks to the people who catch the errors that always try to sneak onto the pages: technical reviewers Chris Deely and Tina Spargo and proofreader Julie Van Keuren. And of course, thanks to Joyce, my wife, who helps me in everything I do.

— *Chris Grover*

## THE MISSING MANUAL SERIES

Missing Manuals are witty, superbly written guides to computer products that don't come with printed manuals (which is just about all of them). Each book features a handcrafted index; cross-references to specific pages (not just chapters); and RepKover, a detached-spine binding that lets the book lie perfectly flat without the assistance of weights or cinder blocks.

Recent and upcoming titles include:

- *Access 2010: The Missing Manual* by Matthew MacDonald
- *Buying a Home: The Missing Manual* by Nancy Conner
- *CSS: The Missing Manual, Second Edition*, by David Sawyer McFarland
- *Creating a Website: The Missing Manual, Third Edition*, by Matthew MacDonald
- *David Pogue's Digital Photography: The Missing Manual* by David Pogue
- *Dreamweaver CS5.5: The Missing Manual* by David Sawyer McFarland
- *Dreamweaver CS6: The Missing Manual* by David Sawyer McFarland
- *Droid X: The Missing Manual* by Preston Gralla
- *Droid 2: The Missing Manual* by Preston Gralla
- *Droid X2: The Missing Manual* by Preston Gralla
- *Excel 2010: The Missing Manual* by Matthew MacDonald
- *Facebook: The Missing Manual*, Third Edition by E.A. Vander Veer
- *FileMaker Pro 11: The Missing Manual* by Susan Prosser and Stuart Gripman
- *Flash CS5.5: The Missing Manual* by Chris Grover
- *Galaxy S II: The Missing Manual* by Preston Gralla

- *Galaxy Tab: The Missing Manual* by Preston Gralla
- *Google+: The Missing Manual* by Kevin Purdy
- *Google Apps: The Missing Manual* by Nancy Conner
- *Google SketchUp: The Missing Manual* by Chris Grover
- *HTML5: The Missing Manual* by Matthew MacDonald
- *iMovie '11 & iDVD: The Missing Manual* by David Pogue and Aaron Miller
- *iPad 2: The Missing Manual, Third Edition* by J.D. Biersdorfer
- *iPhone: The Missing Manual, Fifth Edition* by David Pogue
- *iPhone App Development: The Missing Manual* by Craig Hockenberry
- *iPhoto '11: The Missing Manual* by David Pogue and Lesa Snider
- *iPod: The Missing Manual, Tenth Edition* by J.D. Biersdorfer and David Pogue
- *JavaScript & jQuery: The Missing Manual, Second Edition* by David Sawyer McFarland
- *Kindle Fire: The Missing Manual* by Peter Meyers
- *Living Green: The Missing Manual* by Nancy Conner
- *Mac OS X Lion: The Missing Manual* by David Pogue
- *Mac OS X Mountain Lion: The Missing Manual* by David Pogue
- *Microsoft Project 2010: The Missing Manual* by Bonnie Biafore
- *Motorola Xoom: The Missing Manual* by Preston Gralla
- *Netbooks: The Missing Manual* by J.D. Biersdorfer
- *NOOK Tablet: The Missing Manual* by Preston Gralla
- *Office 2010: The Missing Manual* by Nancy Connor, Chris Grover, and Matthew MacDonald
- *Office 2011 for Macintosh: The Missing Manual* by Chris Grover
- *Palm Pre: The Missing Manual* by Ed Baig
- *Personal Investing: The Missing Manual* by Bonnie Biafore
- *Photoshop CS5: The Missing Manual* by Lesa Snider
- *Photoshop CS6: The Missing Manual* by Lesa Snider
- *Photoshop Elements 10: The Missing Manual* by Barbara Brundage
- *PHP & MySQL: The Missing Manual* by Brett McLaughlin
- *PowerPoint 2007: The Missing Manual* by E.A. Vander Veer

- *Premiere Elements 8: The Missing Manual* by Chris Grover
- *QuickBase: The Missing Manual* by Nancy Conner
- *QuickBooks 2012: The Missing Manual* by Bonnie Biafore
- *QuickBooks 2013: The Missing Manual* by Bonnie Biafore
- *Quicken 2009: The Missing Manual* by Bonnie Biafore
- *Switching to the Mac: The Missing Manual, Lion Edition* by David Pogue
- *Switching to the Mac: The Missing Manual, Mountain Lion Edition* by David Pogue
- *Wikipedia: The Missing Manual* by John Broughton
- *Windows XP Home Edition: The Missing Manual, Second Edition*, by David Pogue
- *Windows XP Pro: The Missing Manual, Second Edition*, by David Pogue, Craig Zacker, and Linda Zacker
- *Windows Vista: The Missing Manual* by David Pogue
- *Windows 7: The Missing Manual* by David Pogue
- *Word 2007: The Missing Manual* by Chris Grover
- *Your Body: The Missing Manual* by Matthew MacDonald
- *Your Brain: The Missing Manual* by Matthew MacDonald
- *Your Money: The Missing Manual* by J.D. Roth

For a full list of all Missing Manuals in print, go to *www.missingmanuals.com/library .html.*

# Introduction

Flash's evolution is unique, even for the fast-changing computer software world. First released in 1996 under the name FutureSplash, it was a tool for creating web-based animations. It's still the go-to application for that job; however, along the way it's acquired new capabilities. Today, Flash powers video websites like YouTube and Hulu (Figure I-1). It's used to develop desktop applications like eBay Desktop. As you read this, Flash/ActionScript pros are developing the next generation of apps for handheld devices like the Droid RAZR and the iPhone. Flash has grown up with the World Wide Web and managed to carve out an important niche. In fact, there are a whole slew of programs that make use of Flash technology. They include Flex, Flash Builder, and Flash Catalyst. Still, if you want to learn Flash's design and animation features as well as its programming and development features, then Flash Professional CS6 is the place to start.

Here are just some of the things you can do with Flash:

- **Animate.** You can create original artwork using Flash's tools, or you can add images from your other favorite programs. Flash recognizes the most common image, video, and sound file formats. Once your artwork is in Flash, you can add motion, sound, and dazzling effects. Surely you've spent some quality time watching JibJab cartoons (Figure I-2).

- **Multimedia websites.** Today's websites include motion, video, background music, and above all, interactive objects. Flash's built-in programming language, ActionScript, was designed to create interactive objects. You can create eye-catching, attention-grabbing websites with Flash. It's your choice whether you sprinkle Flash bits on various pages or go whole-hog and develop a 100 percent Flash site.

1

- **Tutorials.** Web-based training courses, which often include a combination of text, drawings, animations, video clips, and voice-overs, are a natural fit for Flash. By hooking Flash up to a server on the back end, you can even present your audience with graded tests and up-to-the-minute product information. You don't have to deliver your tutorials over the web, though; you can publish them as standalone projector files (Chapter 20) or AIR applications (Chapter 21) and deliver them to your students via CDs, DVDs, or mobile apps.

**FIGURE I-1**

*Sites like Hulu and YouTube have made great use of Flash's video abilities. You can check any site to see whether it's using Flash behind the scenes. Just right-click (or Control-click) an image that you think might be Flash. If it says "About Flash Player" at the bottom of the pop-up menu, you guessed right.*

- **Presentations.** PowerPoint presentations are fine...up to a point. With Flash, you can create self-running presentations that are more creative and have a higher degree of interactivity.

- **Customer service kiosks.** Many of the kiosks you see in stores and building lobbies use Flash to help customers find what they need. For example, photo kiosks walk customers through the process of transferring images from their digital cameras and ordering prints; kiosks in banks let customers withdraw funds, check interest rates, and make deposits.

- **Television and film effects.** The Hollywood set has been known to use Flash to create visual effects for TV shows and even small feature films. But where the TV and film industry is seriously adopting Flash is on promotional websites, where designers can wed Flash graphics to scenes taken from their movies and shows to present powerful trailers, interactive tours of movie and show sets, and teasers.

- **Games and other programs.** With support for runtime scripting, back-end data transfers, and interactive controls like buttons and text boxes, Flash has everything a programmer needs to create entertaining, professional-looking games.

- **Mobile apps.** With Flash CS6, the biggest change is the ease with which you can develop apps for mobile devices, from iPads to Androids.

**FIGURE I-2**

*With a little creativity, your Flash animations can capture the public's attention. Just ask the folks at JibJab.*

# What's New in Flash Professional CS6

Flash has been evolving and adding features at a breakneck pace since Adobe acquired Macromedia at the end of 2005. There are many benefits to being part of Adobe's Creative Suite, primarily the smooth interaction with applications such as Photoshop, Illustrator, and Dreamweaver. If you've used other Adobe programs, you'll also welcome the consistency in drawing, text, and color-choosing tools. By the same token, if you're new to the Adobe family, the skills you learn in Flash will come in handy if you move on to other Adobe products.

The last few versions of Flash Professional introduced a slew of new features. For example, CS4 added a more powerful, yet easy-to-use motion tween, complete with Motion Editor. New 3-D capabilities opened up the world of motion, and IK Bones (inverse kinematics) made it easy for animators to link objects for realistic movement. Flash CS5 added a new text engine called Text Layout Framework (TLF), which provides the kind of text control that you'd find in Adobe Illustrator or InDesign, and Adobe simplified the mysterious process of font embedding. IK bones were enhanced with a new Spring property. ActionScript coding was made easier with code snippets—cut and paste bits of code that are easy to drop into your document. *Code hinting* provides an instant reference and tips on what to do next. Flash CS5 also made it easier to build Adobe AIR projects that run as standalone programs on Windows, Mac, and Linux computers. An interim release, Flash CS5.5 added the ability to develop apps for iOS (iPhones and iPads) and Android devices.

Of course, all those features are covered in this book, along with the latest batch of enhancements. Flash CS6 comes quickly on the heels of the incremental release CS5.5 and refines many of the features added then. The development of mobile apps heads the list:

- **App development for multiple devices.** It's easier than ever to develop an application that works on desktops (Windows, Mac, and Linux) and mobile devices like smartphones and tablets. Flash enhancements make it easier to share files and scale projects for a variety of screen sizes.

- **Built-in iPhone and iPad App Packager.** The much-publicized squabble between Apple and Adobe is at least partially resolved. Using Flash, you can build apps for all of Apple's iDevices.

- **Built-in Android app packager.** Use your Flash skills to build apps for Android smartphones and tablets. Test your apps immediately on devices connected by USB cables.

- **The Simulator** is a new tool used when you're debugging mobile apps. It gives you the ability to test mobile features, such as touchscreen gestures, on your desktop computer.

- **Bundle AIR runtime with apps.** If you're publishing apps, now you can include the AIR runtime with your apps, saving your audience the extra step of downloading the runtime.

- **Templates and code snippets for mobile devices.** Adobe has added to the library of templates and code snippets, making it easier to develop apps for iPhones, iPads, and Android mobile devices. You'll find snippets that show how to interact with touchscreen gestures such as swipes and pinches. Templates show how to use built-in accelerometers and geo-location features.

- **Pin IK bones.** *Pinning* locks IK bones to a specific position on the stage, making it much easier to create poses and control your models.

- **Copying layers.** Flash preserves structure and other details when copying layers between files and projects.

- **Symbol rasterization.** The *cache as bitmap* feature converts vector art to bitmaps, increasing mobile device performance, CPU efficiency, and improving battery life.

- **Auto-save and file recovery.** Like your favorite word processor, Flash now has a feature that automatically saves your documents. Should disaster strike, you're less likely to lose your work.

- **Incremental compilation.** Flash is smarter when compiling (publishing) your document for testing. As a result, there's a shorter wait when you repeatedly make changes and test your work.

- **Conversion to HTML and JavaScript.** Some web animation features that were almost exclusively the domain of Flash are now possible with HTML (hypertext markup language), JavaScript, and jQuery. Flash CS6 has the ability to export part or all of an animation for use in HTML or JavaScript projects.

# Animation ABCs

Animators used to draw each and every frame by hand. Sure, they developed some shortcuts, but that's still hundreds or thousands of images depending on the length of the animation. Major animation houses employed whole armies of graphic artists, each charged with producing hundreds of drawings that represented a mere fraction of the finished work. What we chuckled at for a scant few minutes took weeks and dozens of tired, cramped hands to produce. One mistake, one spilled drop of coffee, and these patient-as-Job types would have to grab fresh paper and start all over again. When everything was done, the animation would have to be put together—much like one of those flip books where you flip pages real fast to see a story play out—while it was being filmed by special cameras.

With Flash on your computer, you have the equivalent of a design studio at your fingertips. You provide the inspiration, and Flash can help you generate pro-quality animations and full-blown interactive applications.

**UP TO SPEED**

## An Animation by Any Other Name

You may occasionally hear Flash animations referred to (by books, websites, and even Flash's own documentation) as *movies*. Perhaps that's technically accurate, but it sure can be confusing.

QuickTime's .mov files are also called movies, and some people refer to video clips as movies; but to Flash, these are two very different animals. In addition, Flash lets you create and work with movie clips, which are something else entirely. And *movie*,

with its connotations of quietly sitting in a theater balcony eating popcorn, doesn't convey one of the most important features Flash offers: interactivity.

Here's the most accurate way to describe what you create using Flash: a website, program, or app with a really cool, animated interface. Unfortunately, that description is a bit long and unwieldy, so in this book, what you create using Flash is called an *animation* or an *app*.

It's pretty incredible, when you think about it. A few hundred bucks and a few hours spent working with Flash, and you've got an animation that, just a few years ago, you'd have had to pay a swarm of professionals union scale to produce. Sweet! Naturally, if you're new to animation, it will go easier if you learn the basic terms, tricks, and techniques used by Flash animators.

## Flash in a Nutshell

Say you work for a company that does custom auto refinishing. First assignment: Design an intro page for the company's new website. You have the following idea for an animation:

The first thing you want your audience to see is a beat-up jalopy limping along a city street toward the center of the screen, where it stops and morphs into a shiny, like-new car as your company's jingle plays in the background. A voice-over informs your audience that your company has been in business for 20 years and offers the best prices in town.

Across the top of the screen, you'd like to display the company logo, as well as a navigation bar with buttons—labeled Location, Services, Prices, and Contact—that your audience can click to get more information about your company. But you also want each part of the car to be a clickable hotspot. That way, when someone clicks one of the car's tires, he's whisked off to a page describing custom wheels and hubcaps; when he clicks the car's body, he sees prices for dent repair and repainting; and so on.

Here's how you might go about creating this animation in Flash:

- Using Flash's drawing tools, you draw the artwork for every *keyframe* of the animation—that is, every important image. For example, you'll need to create a keyframe showing the beat-up junker and a second keyframe showing the gleaming, expertly refurbished result. (Chapter 2 shows you how to draw artwork in Flash; Chapter 3 tells you everything you need to know about keyframes.)

- Within each keyframe, you might choose to separate your artwork into different *layers*. Like the see-through plastic cels that professional animators used in the old days, layers let you create images separately and then stack them on top of one another to make a single composite image. For example, you might choose to put the car on one layer, your company logo on a second layer, and your city-street background on a third layer. That way, you can edit and animate each layer independently, but when the animation plays, all three elements appear to be on one seamless layer. (Chapter 4 shows you how to work with layers.)

- Through a process called *tweening*, you tell Flash to fill in each and every frame *between* the keyframes to create the illusion of the junker turning slowly into a brand-new car. Flash carefully analyzes all the differences between the keyframes and does its best to build the interim frames, which you can then tweak or—if Flash gets it all wrong—redraw yourself. (Chapter 3 introduces tweens, and Chapter 8 gives you the lowdown on advanced techniques.)

- As you go along, you might decide to save a few of the elements you create (for example, your company logo) so you can reuse them later. There's no sense in reinventing the wheel, and in addition to saving you time, reusing elements actually helps keep your animation files as small and efficient as possible. (See Chapter 7 for details on creating and managing reusable elements.)

- Add the background music and voice-over audio clips, which you've created in other programs (Chapter 11).

- Create the navigation bar buttons, hotspots, and other ways for your audience to interact with your animation (Chapters 12–18).

- Test your animation (Chapter 19) and tweak it to perfection.

- Finally, when your animation is just the way you want it, you're ready to *publish* it. Without leaving the comfort of Flash, you can convert the editable *.fla* file you've been working with into a noneditable *.swf* file and either embed it into an HTML file or create a standalone *projector* file that your audience can run without having to use a browser. Chapter 20 tells you everything you need to know about publishing.

The scenario described above is pretty simple, but it covers the basic steps you need to take when creating any Flash animation.

## The Very Basics

You'll find very little jargon or nerd terminology in this book. You will, however, encounter a few terms and concepts that you'll use frequently in your computing life:

- **Clicking.** This book gives you three kinds of instructions that require you to use your computer's mouse or trackpad. To *click* means to point the arrow cursor at something on the screen and then—without moving the cursor at all—to press and release the left clicker button on the mouse (or laptop trackpad). To *double-click*, of course, means to click twice in rapid succession, again without moving the cursor at all. And to *drag* means to move the cursor while pressing the left button continuously.

- **Keyboard shortcuts.** Every time you take your hand off the keyboard to move the mouse, you lose time and potentially disrupt your creative flow. That's why many experienced computer fans use keystroke combinations instead of menu commands wherever possible. Ctrl+B (⌘-B), for example, is a keyboard shortcut for boldface type in Flash (and most other programs).

  When you see a shortcut like Ctrl+S (⌘-S) (which saves changes to the current document), it's telling you to hold down the Ctrl or ⌘ key, and, while it's down, type the letter S, and then release both keys.

- **Choice is good.** Flash frequently gives you several ways to trigger a particular command—by choosing a menu command, *or* by clicking a toolbar button, *or* by pressing a key combination, for example. Some people prefer the speed of keyboard shortcuts; others like the satisfaction of a visual command array available in menus or toolbars. This book lists all the alternatives, but by no means are you expected to memorize all of them.

## About This Book

Despite the many improvements in software over the years, one feature has grown consistently worse: documentation. With the purchase of most software programs these days, you don't get a single page of printed instructions. To learn about the hundreds of features in a program, you're expected to use online electronic help.

But even if you're comfortable reading a help screen in one window as you try to work in another, something is still missing. At times, the terse electronic help screens assume you already understand the discussion at hand and hurriedly skip over important topics that require an in-depth presentation. In addition, you don't always get an objective evaluation of the program's features. (Engineers often add technically sophisticated features to a program because they *can*, not because you need them.) You shouldn't have to waste your time learning features that don't help you get your work done.

The purpose of this book, then, is to serve as the manual that should have been in the box. In this book's pages, you'll find step-by-step instructions for using every Flash feature, including those you may not have quite understood, let alone mastered, such as working with video or drawing objects with ActionScript. In addition, you'll find clear evaluations of each feature that help you determine which ones are useful to you, as well as how and when to use them.

> **NOTE** This book periodically recommends *other* books, covering topics that might interest Flash designers and developers. Careful readers may notice that not every one of these titles is published by Missing Manual parent company O'Reilly Media. While we're happy to mention other Missing Manuals and books in the O'Reilly family, if there's a great book out there that doesn't happen to be published by O'Reilly, we'll still let you know about it.

*Flash CS6: The Missing Manual* is designed for readers of every skill level, except the super-advanced programmer. If Flash is the first image creation or animation program you've ever used, you'll be able to dive right in using the explanations and examples in this book. If you come from an animation or multimedia background, you'll find this book a useful reference for unique Flash topics such as the motion tweens and the Motion Editor. The primary discussions are written for advanced-beginner or intermediate computer users. But if you're a first-timer, special sidebar articles called Up to Speed provide the introductory information you need to understand the topic at hand. If you're an advanced user, on the other hand, keep your eye out for similar shaded boxes called Power Users' Clinic. They offer more technical tips, tricks, and shortcuts for the experienced Flash fan. The Design Time boxes explain the art of effective multimedia design.

The ActionScript programming language is a broad, complex subject. This book isn't an exhaustive reference manual, but it gives you a great introduction to ActionScript programming, providing working examples and clear explanations of ActionScript principles.

## Macintosh and Windows

Flash Professional CS6 works almost precisely the same in its Macintosh and Windows versions. You'll find the same buttons in almost every dialog box. Occasionally, they'll be dressed up differently. In this book, the illustrations have been given even-handed treatment, rotating between Windows 7 and Mac OS X.

Shortcut keys are probably the area where the Mac and Windows versions differ the most. Often where Windows uses the Ctrl key, Macs use the ⌘ key. You'll find some other relatively minor differences, too.

Whenever this book refers to a key combination, you'll see the Windows keystroke listed first (with + symbols, as is customary in Windows documentation); the Macintosh keystroke follows in parentheses (with - symbols, in time-honored Mac fashion). In other words, you might read, "The keyboard shortcut for saving a file is Ctrl+S (⌘-S)."

## About the Outline

*Flash CS6: The Missing Manual* is divided into five parts, each containing several chapters:

- Part 1, **Creating a Flash Animation** guides you through the creation of your very first Flash animation, from the first glimmer of an idea to drawing images, animating those images, and testing your work.

- Part 2, **Advanced Drawing and Animation** is the designer's feast. Here you'll see how to manipulate your drawings by rotating, skewing, stacking, and aligning them; how to add color, special effects, and multimedia files like audio and video clips; how to slash file size by turning bits and pieces of your drawings into special elements called symbols; and how to create composite drawings using layers. Text is an increasingly important part of Flash animations and applications, so this section introduces important text topics. In Part 3, you'll learn how ActionScript works with text. In this section, you'll learn about the Motion Editor and how to use the IK Bones feature (Chapter 9).

- Part 3, **Adding Interactivity** shows you how to add ActionScript 3.0 actions to your animations, creating on-the-fly special effects and giving your audience the power to control your animations. An entire chapter is devoted to predesigned components, like buttons, checkboxes, sliders, and scrolling lists. Powerful but easy to use, these components give your animation professional functions and style. This section includes lots of examples and ActionScript code. You can copy and modify some of the practical examples for your own projects. You'll see how to loop frames and how to let your audience choose which section of an animation to play, and how to customize the prebuilt interactive components that come with Flash. You'll find specific chapters on using ActionScript with text and using ActionScript to draw.

- Part 4, **Debugging and Delivering Your Animation** focuses on testing, debugging, and optimizing your animation. You'll also find out how to publish your animation so that your audience can see and enjoy it, and how to export an editable version of your animation so that you can rework it using another graphics, video editing, or web development program. The last three chapters focus on Adobe AIR, a system for creating standalone apps using Flash. You'll learn how to deliver these apps to Windows, Mac, and Linux desktops, as well as iPhones, iPads, and Android mobile devices.

- Part 5 has two **Appendixes**: Appendix A: Installation and Help, explains how to install Flash and where to turn for help. Appendix B: Flash Professional CS6, Menu by Menu, provides a menu-by-menu description of the commands you'll find in Flash CS6.

## About→These→Arrows

Throughout this book, you'll find instructions like, "Open your Program Files→Adobe→ Adobe Flash CS6 folder." That's Missing Manual shorthand for much longer sentences like "Double-click your Program Files folder to open it. Inside, you'll find a folder called Adobe; double-click to open it. Inside that folder is a folder called Adobe Flash CS6; open it, too." This arrow shorthand also simplifies the business of choosing menu commands, as you can see in Figure I-3.

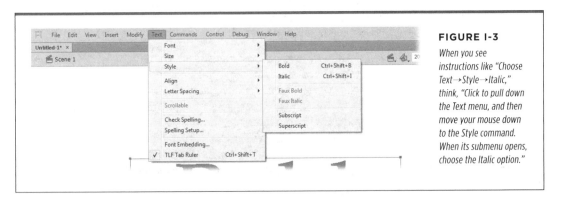

**FIGURE I-3**

*When you see instructions like "Choose Text→Style→Italic," think, "Click to pull down the Text menu, and then move your mouse down to the Style command. When its submenu opens, choose the Italic option."*

## ■ About the Online Resources

As the owner of a Missing Manual, you've got more than just a book to read. Online, you'll find example files so you can get some hands-on experience, as well as tips, articles, and maybe even a video or two. You can also communicate with the

Missing Manual team and tell us what you love (or hate) about the book. Head over to *www.missingmanuals.com*, or go directly to one of the following sections.

## Missing CD

This book doesn't have a CD pasted inside the back cover, but you're not missing out on anything. Go to *www.missingmanuals.com/cds/flashcs6tmm* to download. And so you don't wear down your fingers typing long web addresses, the Missing CD page also offers a list of clickable links to the websites mentioned in this book.

## Registration

If you register this book at *www.oreilly.com*, you'll be eligible for special offers—like discounts on future editions of *Flash CS6: The Missing Manual*. If you buy an ebook from *oreilly.com* and register your purchase, you get free lifetime updates for that edition of the ebook; we'll notify you by email when updates become available. Registering takes only a few clicks. Type *www.oreilly.com/register* into your browser to hop directly to the registration page.

## Feedback

Got questions? Need more information? Fancy yourself a book reviewer? On our Feedback page, you can get expert answers to questions that come to you while reading, share your thoughts on this Missing Manual, and find groups for folks who share your interest in Flash. To have your say, go to *www.missingmanuals.com/feedback*.

## Errata

To keep this book as up to date and accurate as possible, each time we print more copies, we'll make any confirmed corrections you suggest in both the print book and the ebook. We note such changes on the book's website so you can mark important corrections into your own copy of the book, if you like. And if you bought the ebook from us and registered your purchase, you'll get an email notifying you that you can download an updated version of that edition of the ebook. Go to *http://tinyurl.com/flashcs6-mm* to report an error and view existing corrections.

# ■ Safari®Books Online

 is an on-demand digital library that lets you easily search over 7,500 technology and creative reference books and videos to find the answers you need quickly.

With a subscription, you can read any page and watch any video from our library online. Read books on your cellphone and mobile devices. Access new titles before they're available for print, and get exclusive access to manuscripts in development and post feedback for the authors. Copy and paste code samples, organize your favorites, download chapters, bookmark key sections, create notes, print out pages, and benefit from tons of other time-saving features.

# Creating a Flash Animation

# Getting Around Flash

A s mentioned in this book's introduction, Flash performs several feats of audio-visual magic. You use it to create animations, to display video on a website, to create handheld apps, or to build a complete web-based application. So it's not surprising that the Flash workspace is crammed full of tools, panels, and windows (Figure 1-1). But don't be intimidated—you don't have to conquer these tools all at once. This chapter introduces you to Flash's main work areas and often-used toolbars and panels, so you can start creating Flash projects right away. You'll experiment with Flash's stage and timeline, and see how Flash lets you animate graphics so that they move along a path and change shape.

> **TIP** To get further acquainted with Flash, you can check out the built-in help screens by selecting Help→Flash Help. Once the help panel opens, click Using Flash Professional. It's on the left side of the somewhat busy window. You can read more about Flash's help system in Appendix A.

## ■ Starting Flash

You start Flash just as you would any other program—which means you can do it in a few different ways, depending on whether you have a PC or a Mac. Installing the program puts Flash CS6 and its related files in the folder with your other programs, and you can start it by double-clicking its icon. Here's where it's usually installed:

- **Windows.** Go to *C:\Program Files\Adobe\Adobe Flash CS6\Flash.exe*. You can create a shortcut or drag the file to the taskbar for quicker starting.

• **Mac.** Go to *Macintosh HD\Applications\Adobe Flash CS6\Adobe Flash CS6*. You can make an alias or drag the file to the Dock for quicker starting.

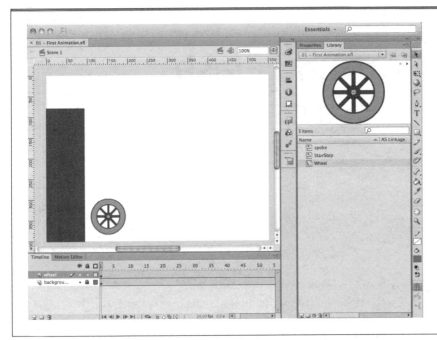

**FIGURE 1-1**

*The Flash Professional workspace is divided into three main areas: the stage, the timeline, and the Panels dock. This entire window, together with the timeline, toolbars, and panels, is sometimes called the Flash desktop, the Flash interface, or the Flash authoring environment.*

Here are some other Windows ways to start the program:

• From the Vista or Windows 7 Start menu, choose All Programs→Adobe Flash Professional CS6.

• For Windows XP, go to Start→All Programs→Adobe→Adobe Flash Professional CS6.

• If you're a keyboard enthusiast, press the Windows key and begin to type *flash*. As you type, Windows searches for a match and displays a list with programs at the top. Most likely, the Flash program is at the top of the list and already selected, so just press Enter. Otherwise, use your mouse or arrow keys to select and start the program.

Here are some Mac launching options:

• Even if you haven't added the Flash icon to the Dock, you can still find it in the Dock's Applications folder. Click and hold the Applications folder icon and choose Adobe Flash CS6→Adobe Flash CS6.

• Want to hunt down Flash in the Finder? Most of the time, it's installed in Macintosh HD→Applications→Adobe Flash CS6→Adobe Flash CS6.

- If you'd rather type than hunt, use Spotlight. Press ⌘-space and then begin to type *flash*. As you type, Spotlight displays a list of programs and files that match. Most likely, the Flash program is at the top of the list and already selected, so just press Return. Otherwise, use the mouse or arrow keys to select and start the program.

When you first start Flash, up pops the Welcome screen, shown in Figure 1-2. This screen puts all your options—like starting a new document or returning to a work in progress—in one handy place. For good measure, Adobe includes some links to help references and resources on its website.

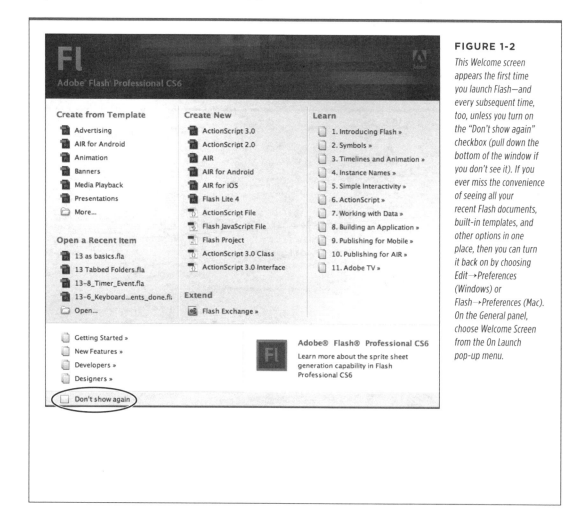

**FIGURE 1-2**

*This Welcome screen appears the first time you launch Flash—and every subsequent time, too, unless you turn on the "Don't show again" checkbox (pull down the bottom of the window if you don't see it). If you ever miss the convenience of seeing all your recent Flash documents, built-in templates, and other options in one place, then you can turn it back on by choosing Edit→Preferences (Windows) or Flash→Preferences (Mac). On the General panel, choose Welcome Screen from the On Launch pop-up menu.*

**NOTE** If Flash seems to take forever to open—or if the Flash desktop ignores your mouse clicks or responds sluggishly—you may not have enough memory installed on your computer. See page 767 for more advice.

When you choose one of the options, the Welcome screen disappears and your document takes its place. Here are your choices:

- **Create from Template.** Clicking one of the little icons under this option lets you create a Flash document using a predesigned form called a *template*. A template helps you create an animation more quickly, since a Flash developer has already done part of the work for you. You can find out more about templates in Chapter 7.

- **Open a Recent Item.** As you create new documents, Flash adds them to this list. Clicking one of the filenames listed here tells Flash to open that file. Clicking the folder icon lets you browse for and open any other Flash file on your computer.

> **TIP** The options for creating new Flash documents and opening recent documents also appear on the File menu, as shown in Figure 1-3.

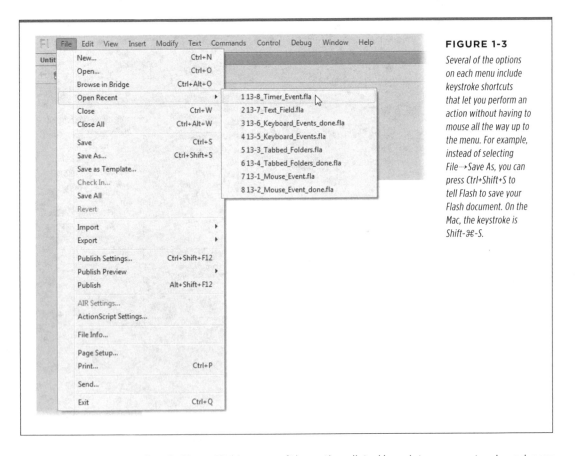

**FIGURE 1-3**

*Several of the options on each menu include keystroke shortcuts that let you perform an action without having to mouse all the way up to the menu. For example, instead of selecting File→Save As, you can press Ctrl+Shift+S to tell Flash to save your Flash document. On the Mac, the keystroke is Shift-⌘-S.*

- **Create New.** Clicking one of the options listed here lets you create a brand-new Flash file. Most of the time, you want to choose the first option, ActionScript 3.0, which is a garden-variety animation file. ActionScript is the underlying programming language for Flash animations. The current version of ActionScript is 3.0, and it's the version used for the projects in this book. You can use the ActionScript 2.0 option if you need to work with a Flash project that was created several years ago. For details on the file formats for different Flash projects, see the box below.

> **NOTE** Old programming pros—you know who you are—may have reasons to prefer ActionScript 2.0. For example, you might choose this option if you're continuing work on a project created using ActionScript 2.0, or if you're working with a team using ActionScript 2.0.

---

**FREQUENTLY ASKED QUESTION**

## Understanding Flash File Formats

*Why are there so many different options under Create New on the Welcome screen? What are they all for?*

There seem to be a bewildering number of options when you create a new Flash document. As explained above, if you're just learning Flash, you probably want to use the first option: ActionScript 3.0. The other options are for special Flash projects targeted to specific devices, like iPhones, iPads, or Android devices. Some options are for specific programming needs, like creating an ActionScript class. The details are in the appropriate sections of this book, but here's a quick rundown:

- Use *AIR* to create desktop applications using the Adobe Integrated Runtime tools (page 705). Instead of using Flash Player, these applications use AIR.

- Use *AIR for Android* if you're creating apps for Android handhelds like the Droid Razr or Samsung Galaxy.

- Creating an iPhone or iPad app? Use the *Air for iOS* option. Flash creates a document that's just the right size and

has the programming options and support for making iOS apps.

- *Flash Lite 4* is similar to the iPhone format but works for several other handheld devices.

- You can also create an *ActionScript File* (a file containing nothing but ActionScript, for use with a Flash animation); a *Flash JavaScript File* (used to create custom tools, panels, commands, and other features that extend Flash); or a *Flash Project* (useful if you're planning a complex, multifile, multideveloper Flash production and need version control).

- The last two options, *ActionScript 3.0 Class* and *ActionScript 3.0 Interface*, help programmers create reusable objects that can be used in multiple Flash projects.

---

- **Extend.** Clicking the Flash Exchange link under this option tells Flash to open your web browser and load the Flash Exchange website. There,you can download Flash components, sound files, and other goodies that you can add to your Flash animations. Some are free, some are fee-based, and all of them are created by Flashionados just like you.

- **Learn.** As you might guess, these links lead to materials Adobe designed to help you get up and running. Click an option, and your web browser opens to a page on the Adobe website. The first few topics introduce basic Flash concepts like symbols, instances, and timelines. Farther down the list, you find specific topics for building applications for mobile devices or websites (AIR). At the bottom of the Welcome screen, "Getting Started" covers the very, very basics. "New Features" explains (and celebrates) some of Flash CS6's new bells and whistles. "Developers" leads to an online magazine with articles and videos with an ActionScript programming slant. "Designers" leads to a similar resource for the Flash graphics and design community.

# ■ A Tour of the Flash Workspace

The best way to master the Flash CS6 Professional workspace is to divide and conquer. First, focus on the three main work areas: the stage, the timeline, and the Panels dock. Then you can gradually learn how to use all the tools in those areas.

One big source of confusion for Flash newbies is that the workspace is so easy to customize. You can open bunches of panels, windows, and toolbars. You can move the timeline above the stage, or you can have it floating in a window all its own. Once you're a seasoned Flash veteran, you'll have strong opinions about how you want to set up your workspace so the tools you use most are at hand. If you're just learning Flash with the help of this book, though, it's probably best if you set up your workspace so that it matches the pictures in these pages.

Fortunately, there's an easy way to do that. Adobe, in its wisdom, created the Workspace Switcher—a tool that lets you rearrange the entire workspace with the click of a menu. The thinking is that an ideal workspace for a cartoon animator is different from the ideal workspace for, say, a rich internet application (RIA) developer. The Workspace Switcher is a menu in the upper-right corner of the Flash window, next to the search box. The menu displays the name of the currently selected workspace; when you first start Flash, it probably says *Essentials*. That's a great workspace that displays some of the most frequently used tools. In fact, it's the workspace used throughout most of this book.

Here's a quick little exercise that shows you how to switch among the different workspaces and how to reset a workspace after you've mangled it by dragging panels out of place and opening new windows.

1. **Start Flash.**

   Flash opens, displaying the Welcome screen. Unless you've made changes, the Essentials workspace is used. See Figure 1-4, top.

2. **From the Workspace menu near the upper-right corner of the Flash window, choose Classic.**

   The Classic arrangement harkens back to earlier versions of Flash, when the timeline resided above the stage (Figure 1-4, bottom). If you wish, go ahead and check out some of the other layouts.

3. **Choose the Essentials workspace again.**

Back where you began, the Essentials workspace shows the timeline at the bottom. The stage takes up most of the main window. On the right, the Panels dock holds toolbars and panels. Now's the time to cause a little havoc.

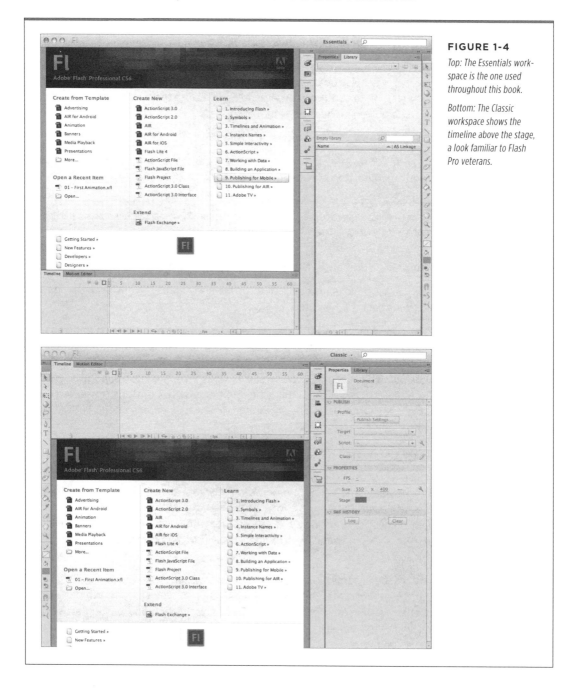

**FIGURE 1-4**

*Top: The Essentials workspace is the one used throughout this book.*

*Bottom: The Classic workspace shows the timeline above the stage, a look familiar to Flash Pro veterans.*

4. **In the Panels dock, click the Properties tab and drag it to a new location on the screen.**

Panels can float, or they can dock to one of the edges of the window. For this experiment, it doesn't matter what you choose to do.

5. **Drag the Color and Swatches toolbars to new locations.**

The Color toolbar has an icon that looks like an artist's palette at the top. Like the larger panels, toolbars can either dock or float. You can drag them anywhere on your monitor, and you can expand and collapse them by clicking the double-triangle button in their top-right corners.

6. **Go to Window→Other Panels→History.**

Flash has dozens of windows. Only a few are available now, because you haven't even created a document yet.

---

**TIP** As you work on a project, the History panel keeps track of all your commands, operations, and changes. It's a great tool for undoing mistakes. For more details, see page 34.

---

7. **From the Workspace menu, choose Reset Essentials.**

The workspace changes back to the original Essentials layout, even though you did your best to mess it up.

Anytime you want your workspace to match the one used throughout most of this book, do the "Essentials two-step": Choose Essentials from the Workspace Switcher (if you're not already there), and then choose Reset Essentials. As shown in Figure 1-4, when you use the Essentials workspace, the Flash window is divvied up into three main work areas: the stage (upper left), the timeline (lower left), and the panels dock (right). Before exploring each of these areas in detail, here are a few words about Flash's menu bar.

## Menu Bar

Like most computer programs, Flash gives you menus to interact with your documents. In traditional fashion, Windows menus appear at the top of the program window, while Mac menus are always at the very top of the screen. The commands on these menus list every way you can interact with your Flash file, from creating a new file—as shown on page 18—to editing it, saving it, and controlling how it appears on your screen.

Some of the menu names—File, Edit, View, Window, and Help—are familiar to anyone who's used a PC or a Mac. Using these menu choices, you can perform basic tasks like opening, saving, and printing your Flash files; cutting and pasting artwork or text; viewing your project in different ways; choosing which toolbars to view; getting help; and more.

To view a menu, simply click the menu's name to open it, and then click a menu option. If you prefer, you can also drag down to the option you want. Let go of the mouse button to activate the option. Figure 1-3 shows you what the File menu looks like. Most of the time, you see the same menus at the top of the screen, but occasionally they change. For example, when you use the Debugger to troubleshoot ActionScript programs, Flash hides some of the menus not related to debugging.

**TIP** You'll learn about specific commands and menu options in their related chapters. For a quick reference to all the menu options, see Appendix B.

## The Stage

As the name implies, the *stage* is usually the center of attention. It's your virtual canvas. Here's where you draw the pictures, display text, and make objects move across the screen. The stage is also your playback arena; when you run a completed animation—to see if it needs tweaking—the animation appears on the stage. Figure 1-5 shows a project with an animation under construction.

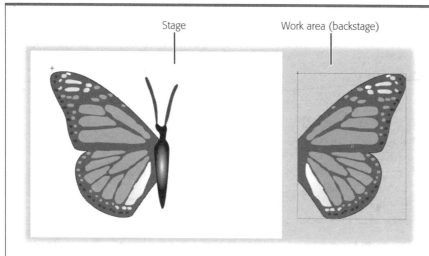

Stage    Work area (backstage)

**FIGURE 1-5**

*The stage is where you draw the pictures that will eventually become your animation. The work area (light gray) gives you a handy place to put graphic elements while you figure out how you want to arrange them on the stage. Here a text box is being dragged from the work area back to center stage.*

The *work area* is the technical name for the gray area surrounding the stage, although many Flashionados call it the *backstage*. This work area serves as a prep zone where you can place graphic elements before you move them to the stage, and as a temporary holding pen for elements you want to move off the stage briefly as you reposition things. For example, let's say you draw three circles and one box containing text on your stage. If you decide you need to rearrange these elements, you can temporarily drag one of the circles off the stage.

**NOTE** The stage always starts out with a white background, which becomes the background color for your animation. Changing it to any color imaginable is easy, as you'll learn in the next chapter.

You'll almost always change the starting size and shape of the stage depending on where people will see your finished animation—in other words, your *target platform*. If your target platform is a smartphone, for example, you're going to want a smaller stage. If, on the other hand, you're creating an animation for a ballpark's JumboTron, you're going to want a giant stage. You'll get to try your hand at modifying the size and background color of the stage later in this chapter.

## The Timeline

When you go to the theater, the stage changes over time—actors come and go, songs are sung, scenery changes, and the lights shine and fade. In Flash, you're the director, and you get to control what appears on the stage at any given moment. The timeline is the tool used to specify what's seen or heard at a particular moment. The concept is pretty simple, and if you've ever used video editing software, it will be familiar. Flash animations (or movies) are organized into chunks of time called *frames*. Each little box in the timeline represents a frame or a point in time. You use the *playhead*, shown in Figure 1-6, to select a specific frame. So when the playhead is positioned at Frame 10, the stage shows what the audience sees at that point in time.

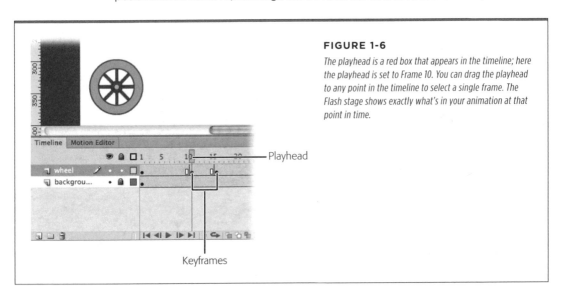

**FIGURE 1-6**

*The playhead is a red box that appears in the timeline; here the playhead is set to Frame 10. You can drag the playhead to any point in the timeline to select a single frame. The Flash stage shows exactly what's in your animation at that point in time.*

Playhead

Keyframes

The timeline is laid out from left to right, starting with Frame 1. Simply put, you build Flash animations by choosing a frame with the playhead and then arranging the objects on the stage the way you want them. The timeline uses a special tool called a *keyframe* (see Figure 1-6) to remember exactly what's on stage at that moment. You'll learn more about the keyframes and other timeline tools in Chapter 3. Most simple animations play from Frame 1 through to the end of the movie, but Flash gives you ways to start and stop the animation and control how fast it runs—that is, how many frames per second (fps) are displayed. Using some ActionScript magic, you can control the order in which the frames are displayed. You'll learn how to do that on page 522.

# Panels and Toolbars

If you followed the little exercise on page 20, you know you can put panels and toolbars almost anywhere onscreen. However, if you use the Essentials workspace, you start off with a few frequently used panels and toolbars docked neatly on the right side of the program window.

It's easy to get confused by the Flash nomenclature. Flash has toolbars, panels, palettes, and windows. Sometimes collapsed panels look like toolbars and open up when clicked—like the frequently used Tools panel. Toolbars and panels pack the most commonly used options together in a nice compact space, so you don't have to do a hunt-and-peck through the main menu every time you want to do something. Panels are great, but they take up precious real estate. As you work, you can hide certain tools to get a better view of your artwork. (You can always get them back by choosing their names from the Window menu.)

Toolbars and panels are such an integral part of working with Flash that it's helpful to learn some of their tricks early on:

- **Move a panel.** Just click and drag the tab or top of the panel to a new location. Panels can float anywhere on your monitor, or dock on an edge of the Flash program window (as in the Essentials workspace). For more details on docking and floating, see the box on page 26.

- **Expand or collapse a panel.** Click the double-triangle button at the top of a panel to expand or collapse it. Collapsed panels look like toolbars, showing a few icons that hint at the tools' purposes. Expanded panels take up more real estate, but they also give you more details and often have word labels for the tools and settings.

- **Show or hide a panel.** Use the Window menu to show and hide individual panels. Checkmarks appear next to the panels that are shown.

- **Close a floating panel.** In Windows, click the small X in the panel's upper-right corner. On the Mac, click the X in the upper-left corner.

- **Show or hide all panels.** The F4 key works like a toggle, hiding or showing all the panels and toolbars. Use it when you want to quickly reduce screen clutter and focus on your artwork.

- **Separate or combine tabbed panels.** Click and drag the name on a tab to separate it from a group of tabbed panels. To add a tab to a group, just drag it into place.

- **Reset the panel workspace.** Choose *Reset <workspace name>* from the Work-space Switcher. Instead of <workspace name>, you see the name of the current workspace—something like *Essentials* or *Classic*. You can also do a reset using the menus; choose Window→Workspace→Reset <workspace name>.

## Docked vs. Floating

A *docked* toolbar or panel appears attached to some part of the workspace window, while a *floating* toolbar or panel is one you can reposition by dragging.

Whether you want to display toolbars and panels as docked or floating is a matter of personal choice. If you constantly need to click something on a toolbar—which means it needs to be in full view at all times—docked works best. But if you usually just need a toolbar or a panel for a brief time and want to be able to move it around on the screen (so it doesn't cover up something else), then floating is the ticket.

To turn a docked panel into a floating panel:

1. Click any blank spot on the panel's top bar and hold down the mouse button. You may notice a color change

(Figure 1-7), especially as you begin to move the panel. The actual visual effect is different on Mac and Windows computers, but the mechanics work the same.

2. Drag the panel away from the edge of the workspace window and release the mouse button. Flash displays the panel where you dropped it. You can reposition it anywhere you like simply by dragging it again.

To dock a floating panel, simply reverse the procedure: Drag the floating panel to the edge of the workspace window and let go of the mouse button. You see a line or a shadow when the panel is ready to dock. When you let go, Flash docks the panel automatically.

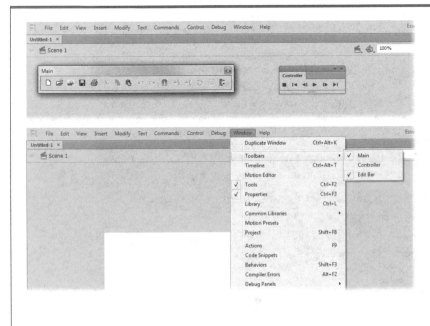

**FIGURE 1-7**

*Top: To conserve space on Flash's jam-packed desktop, only one toolbar—the Edit bar—appears automatically. It's positioned directly above the stage. To display the other two, select Window→Toolbars→Main (to display the Main toolbar, Windows only) and Window→Toolbars→ Controller (to display the Controller window).*

*Bottom: The checkmarks on the menu show when a toolbar is turned on. Choose the toolbar's name again to remove the checkmark and hide the toolbar.*

**NOTE** When you reposition a floating toolbar, Flash remembers where you put it. If, later on, you hide the toolbar—or exit Flash and run it again—your toolbars appear exactly as you left them. If this isn't what you want, use the Workspace Switcher to choose a new workspace layout or to reset the current workspace.

## Toolbars

Strictly speaking, Flash has only three toolbars: Main, Controller, and Edit. (Everything else is a panel, even if it looks suspiciously like a toolbar.) Figure 1-7 shows all three toolbars.

- **Main (Windows only).** The Main toolbar gives you one-click basic operations, like opening an existing Flash file, creating a new file, and cutting and pasting sections of your drawing.

- **Controller.** If you've ever used a DVD player or an iPod, you'll recognize the Stop, Rewind, and Play buttons on the Controller toolbar, which lets you control how you want Flash to run your finished animation. (Not surprisingly, the Controller options appear *grayed out*—meaning you can't select them—if you haven't yet constructed an animation.) With Flash Professional CS6, the Controller is a little obsolete, because now the same buttons appear below the timeline.

- **Edit bar.** Using the options here, you can change your view of the stage, zooming in and out, as well as edit *scenes* (named groups of *frames*) and *symbols* (reusable drawings).

**NOTE** The Edit bar is a little different from the other toolbars in that it remains fixed to the stage. You can't reposition it.

## Tools Panel

The Tools panel is unique. For designers, it's probably the most used of all the panels and toolbars. In the Essentials workspace, the Tools panel appears along the right side of the Flash program window. There are no text labels, just a series of icons. However, if you need a hint, just hold your mouse over one of the tools, and a tooltip shows the name of the tool. So, for example, mouse over the arrow at the top of the Tools panel, and the tooltip says "Selection tool (V)." The letter in parentheses is the shortcut key for that tool. Press the letter V while you're working in Flash, and your cursor changes to the Selection tool.

Most animations start with a single drawing. And to draw something in Flash, you need drawing tools: pens, pencils, brushes, colors, erasers, and so on. The Tools panel shown in Figure 1-8 is where you find Flash's drawing tools. Chapter 2 shows you how to use these tools to create a simple drawing; this section gives you a quick overview of the six sections of the Tools panel, each of which focuses on a slightly different kind of drawing tool or optional feature.

### ■ SELECTION AND DRAWING TOOLS

At the top of the Tools panel are the tools you need to create and modify a Flash drawing. For example, you might use the Pen tool to start a sketch, the Paint Bucket or Ink Bottle to apply color, and the Eraser to clean up mistakes.

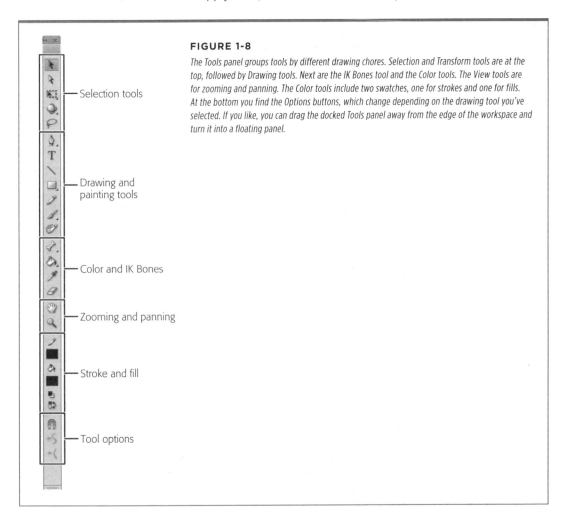

**FIGURE 1-8**

*The Tools panel groups tools by different drawing chores. Selection and Transform tools are at the top, followed by Drawing tools. Next are the IK Bones tool and the Color tools. The View tools are for zooming and panning. The Color tools include two swatches, one for strokes and one for fills. At the bottom you find the Options buttons, which change depending on the drawing tool you've selected. If you like, you can drag the docked Tools panel away from the edge of the workspace and turn it into a floating panel.*

Selection tools

Drawing and
painting tools

Color and IK Bones

Zooming and panning

Stroke and fill

Tool options

### ■ VIEW TOOLS

At times, you'll find yourself drawing a picture so enormous you can't see it all on the stage at one time. Or perhaps you'll find yourself drawing something you want to take a super-close look at so you can modify it pixel by pixel. In either of these situations, you can use the tools Flash displays in the View section of the Tools panel to zoom in, zoom out, and pan around the stage. (You'll get to try your hand at using these tools later in this chapter; see page 35.)

**NOTE** The term *pixel* is short for "picture element." Images on a computer screen are made up of lots of tiny dots emitting different colors. Each dot is a pixel.

### ■ COLOR TOOLS

When you're creating in Flash, you're drawing one of two things: a *stroke*, which is a plain line or outline, or a *fill*, which is the area within an outline. You can use these tools to choose a color from the Color palette before you click one of the drawing icons to begin drawing (or afterward to change the colors, as discussed in Chapter 2). Flash applies that color to the stage as you draw.

### ■ OPTIONS TOOLS

Which icons appear in the Options section at any given time depends on which tool you've selected. For example, when you select the Zoom tool from the View section of the Tools panel, the Options section displays an Enlarge icon and a Reduce icon that you can use to change the way the Zoom tool works (Figure 1-9).

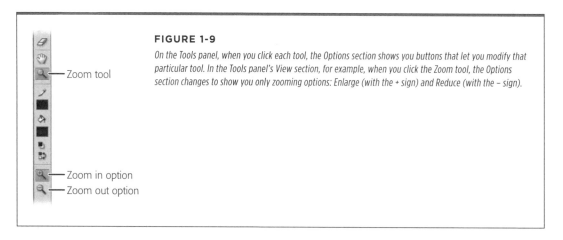

**FIGURE 1-9**

*On the Tools panel, when you click each tool, the Options section shows you buttons that let you modify that particular tool. In the Tools panel's View section, for example, when you click the Zoom tool, the Options section changes to show you only zooming options: Enlarge (with the + sign) and Reduce (with the − sign).*

Zoom tool

Zoom in option
Zoom out option

## Properties Panel

In many ways, the Properties panel is Command Central as you work with your animation, because it gathers all the pertinent details for the objects you work with and displays them in one place. Select an object, and the Properties panel displays all of its properties and settings. It's not just an information provider; you also use the Properties panel to change settings and tweak the elements in your animation. When there's fine-tuning to be done, select an object and adjust the settings in the Properties panel. (You can learn more in the "Test Drive" section on page 35.)

The Properties panel usually appears when you open a new document. Initially, it shows information about your Flash document, like the stage dimensions and the animation's frame rate. Whenever you select an individual object in your animation, the Properties panel shows that object's details. For example, if you select a text field, the Properties panel lists the typeface, font size, and text color. You also see information on the paragraph settings, like the margins and line spacing. Because the Properties panel crams so many details into one place, you'll find yourself using the collapse and expand buttons to show and hide some of the information in its subpanels, as shown in Figure 1-10.

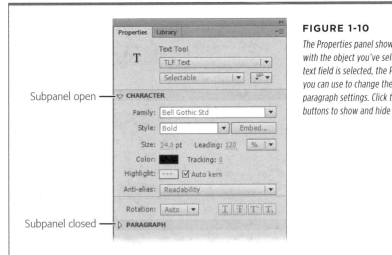

Subpanel open

Subpanel closed

**FIGURE 1-10**

*The Properties panel shows only those properties associated with the object you've selected on the stage. Here, because a text field is selected, the Properties panel gives you options you can use to change the typeface, font size, font color, and paragraph settings. Click the triangular expand and collapse buttons to show and hide details in the Properties panel.*

**NOTE** If you don't see the Properties panel, you can display it by selecting Window→Properties or by pressing Ctrl+F3 (⌘-F3 on a Mac).

### ■ PROPERTIES SUBPANELS

On the Properties panel, you see different subpanels depending on the object you've selected. Some objects have a lot of settings, and subpanels are Flash's way of giving you access to all of them. Fortunately, the various panels and tools work consistently. For example, many objects have settings that determine their onscreen positions and define their width and height dimensions. These common settings usually appear at the top of the Properties panel, and you set them the same way for most kinds of objects. If you want to change colors or add special effects like filters or blends, you'll find that the tools work the same way throughout Flash.

## Library Panel

The Library panel (Figure 1-11) is a place to store objects you want to use more than once. Let's say, for example, that you create a picture-perfect bubble, sun, or snowflake in one frame of your animation. (You'll learn more about frames on page 91.) Now, if you want that bubble, sun, or snowflake to appear in 15 additional frames, you *could* draw it again and again, but it really makes more sense to store a copy in the current project library and then just drag it to where it's needed on those other 15 frames. This trick saves time and ensures consistency to boot. The Library panel has quite a few other important tricks, and you'll learn more about it on page 248. To show the Library panel, click Window→Library, or press Ctrl+L (Windows) or ⌘-L (Mac).

> **TIP** In the upper-right corner of most panels is an Options menu button. When you click this button, a menu of options appears—different options for each panel. For example, the Color Swatch panel lets you add and delete color swatches. You'll find many indispensable tools and commands on the Options menus, so it's worth checking them out. You'll learn about different options throughout this book.

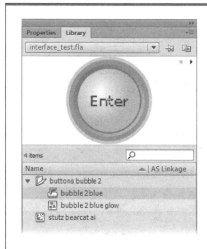

**FIGURE 1-11**

*Storing simple images as reusable symbols in the Library panel does more than just save you time: It saves you file size, too. (You'll learn a lot more about symbols and file size in Chapter 7.) Using the Library panel you see here, you can preview symbols, add them to the stage, and easily add symbols you created in one Flash document to another.*

## Other Flash Panels

As you can see from the examples on the preceding pages, each Flash panel performs specific functions, and most of them deserve several pages to describe them fully, as you'll find throughout this book. For now, Table 1-1 gives a thumbnail description and notes the page where the panel is described in detail. If you're eager to get started actually using Flash, jump to page 35 to start the Flash CS6 Test Drive.

**TABLE 1-1** *Flash Panels and their uses (in order as they appear on the Window menu)*

| PANEL NAME | KEYBOARD SHORTCUT | PURPOSE |
|---|---|---|
| Timeline | Windows: Ctrl+Alt+K Mac: Option-⌘-T | Technically, the timeline is just another panel. You can move, hide, expand, and collapse the timeline just as you would any other panel. See page 91 for more. |
| Motion Editor | none | A powerful tool used to create and control animation effects. See page 311 for more. |

| PANEL NAME | KEYBOARD SHORTCUT | PURPOSE |
|---|---|---|
| Tools | Windows: Ctrl+F2<br>Mac: ⌘-F2 | Perhaps the most frequently used panel of all—it holds drawing, selecting, and coloring tools. The Tools panel also includes specialized tools like the IK Bones tools and the 3D Rotation tool. See page 60 for more. |
| Properties | Windows: Ctrl+F3<br>Mac: ⌘-F3 | Everything that appears on the stage has properties that define its appearance or characteristics. Even the stage has properties, like width, height, and background color. You can review and edit an object's properties in the Properties panel. See page 29 for more. |
| Library | Windows: Ctrl+L<br>Mac: ⌘-L | Holds graphics, symbols, and entire movies that you want to reuse. See page 248 for more. |
| Common Libraries | none | When you want to share buttons, classes, or sounds among several different Flash documents, use the common libraries. That way, they'll be available to all your projects. See the tip on page 274 for more. |
| Motion Presets | none | Serves up dozens of predesigned animations. See page 295 for more. |
| Actions | Windows: F9<br>Mac: Option-F9 | You use this panel to write ActionScript code. The Actions panel provides a window for code, a reference tool for the programming language, and a visual display for the object-oriented nature of the code. See page 415 for more. |
| Code Snippets | none | Contains predesigned chunks of code—someone else sweated the details so you don't have to. Specific bits of code perform timeline tricks, load or unload graphics, handle audio-visual tasks, and program buttons. See the box on page 445 for more. |
| Behaviors | Windows: Shift+F3<br>Mac: Shift-F3 | The earlier version of ActionScript (version 2.0) uses this panel to provide predesigned bits of code. |
| Compiler Errors | Windows: Alt-F2<br>Mac: Option-F2 | Here's where you troubleshoot ActionScript code. Messages explain the location of an error and provide hints as to what went wrong. See page 665 for more. |
| Debug Panels | none | Additional panels to help you find errors in your ActionScript programs. See page 662 for more. |

| PANEL NAME | KEYBOARD SHORTCUT | PURPOSE |
|---|---|---|
| Movie Explorer | Windows: Alt+F3<br>Mac: Option-F3 | Helps you examine the elements in your Flash animation, including separate scenes if you've created them. The display uses a tree structure to show the relationship of the elements. |
| Output | Windows: F2<br>Mac: F2 | Another place to debug ActionScript programs. The Output panel is used to display text messages at certain points as a program runs. See page 657 for more. |
| Align | Windows: Ctrl+K<br>Mac: ⌘-K | Lets you align and arrange graphic elements on the stage. See page 78 for more. |
| Color | Windows: Shift+F9<br>Mac: Shift-⌘-F9 | Lets you select and apply colors to graphic elements. See page 198 for more. |
| Info | Windows: Ctrl+I<br>Mac: ⌘-I | Provides details about objects, like their location and dimensions. The Info panel also keeps track of the cursor location and the color immediately under the cursor. See page 104 for more. |
| Swatches | Windows: Ctrl+F9<br>Mac: ⌘-F9 | Colors and gradients that you can apply to graphic elements. You can create your own swatches for colors you want to reuse. See page 203 for more. |
| Transform | Windows: Ctrl+T<br>Mac: ⌘-T | Lets you change the size, shape, and position of graphic elements on the stage. You can even use the Transform panel to reposition or rotate objects in 3-D space. See page 174 for more. |
| Components | Windows: Ctrl+F7<br>Mac: ⌘-F7 | Holds predesigned components you can use in your Flash projects. You'll find user interface components like buttons and checkboxes, components that can be used to create data tables, and components used to control movie and sound players. See page 543 for more. |
| Component Inspector | Windows: Shift+F7<br>Mac: Shift-F7 | Provides compatibility with older animations. (Flash CS6 displays component properties in the Properties panel. Earlier versions of Flash used the Component Inspector. See the box on page 560 for more.) |
| Accessibility (under Other Panels) | Windows: Alt+Shift+F11<br>Mac: Shift-⌘-F11 | Tools that help you ensure that vision- and hearing-impaired folks can enjoy the animations you create using Flash. See the box on page 34. |

| PANEL NAME | KEYBOARD SHORTCUT | PURPOSE |
| --- | --- | --- |
| History (under Other Panels) | Windows: Ctrl+F10 Mac: ⌘-F10 | Lets you backtrack or undo specific steps in your work. Flash keeps track of every little thing you do to a file, starting with the time you created it (or the last time you opened it). You can also use this panel to save a series of commands you want to reuse later. |
| Scene (under Other Panels) | Windows: Shift+F2 Mac: Shift-F2 | Helps you organize and manage your scenes. (You can break long Flash animations into separate scenes, as described on page 529.) |
| Strings (under Other Panels) | Windows: Ctrl+F11 Mac: ⌘-F11 | Need to create an animation or application that works in different languages? Using the Strings panel, you can create and manage multi-language versions of the text. (This book doesn't cover multi-language Flash.) |
| Web Services (under Other Panels) | Windows: Ctrl+Shift+F10 Mac: Shift-⌘-F10 | Used only with ActionScript 2.0 projects that connect to the Internet. (This book doesn't cover ActionScript 2.0.) |

**WORD TO THE WISE**

## Why Accessibility Matters

The term *accessibility* refers to how easy it is for folks with physical or developmental challenges (like low or no vision) to understand or interact with your animation.

As you can imagine, a Flash animation—which often includes audio in addition to video and still images—isn't going to be experienced the same way by someone who's blind or deaf as it is by someone who isn't impaired. But there is help. One of the features that conscientious Flashionados build into their animations is alternative information for those who can't see or hear. Often, sight-and hearing- impaired folks use assistive devices to "report back" on what they otherwise can't access, so Flash animators build content into their animations that these assistive devices can access and translate.

Thanks to U.S. legislation referred to as Section 508, local, state, and federal websites absolutely have to be accessible and useable to the public. But if you're a private individual planning to incorporate your animation into a website, you shouldn't ignore the issue of accessibility just because nobody's looking over your shoulder. If you ignore accessibility, you eliminate a whole audience who might otherwise benefit from your content.

For more information on accessibility, check out these websites:

- *www.adobe.com/accessibility/products/flash/*
- *www.Section508.gov*
- *www.paciellogroup.com*
- *www.WebAIM.org*
- *www.w3.org/wai*

# ■ The Flash CS6 Test Drive

For the tutorials in this section, you need a Flash animation to practice on. There's one ready and waiting for you on the Missing CD page at *www.missingmanuals. com/cds/flashcs6mm*. The file is named *01-1_First_Animation.fla*.

> **NOTE** In case you're wondering, the number *01* at the beginning stands for Chapter 1, and the *-1* indicates it's the first exercise in the chapter. Other Missing CD files for this book are named the same way. You can download all the exercise files in a single ZIP file or you can grab them chapter by chapter. The Missing CD also includes links to all the web-based resources mentioned in this book.

## Open a Flash File

Get the file *01-1_First_Animation.fla* and save it on your computer. You may want to create a FlashMM folder in your My Documents or Documents folder to hold your Missing Manual exercises. Launch Flash, and then choose File→Open. When the Open dialog box appears, navigate to the file you just downloaded, and then click Open. When you open a document, the Welcome screen disappears. Flash shows you the animation on the stage, surrounded by the usual timeline, toolbars, and panels. If you're using the Essentials workspace, it should look like Figure 1-12.

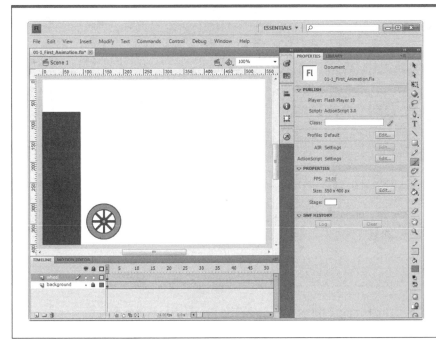

**FIGURE 1-12**

*After you open the exercise in Flash, your screen should look like this. At the bottom, the timeline shows two layers—one named* background *and the other,* wheel. *The stage shows (surprise, surprise) a background and a wheel. To the right, the Properties panel displays the properties for the document.*

## Explore the Properties Panel

The Properties panel appears docked to the right side of the stage when you open a new document. As shown in Figure 1-13, it shows the Property settings for objects. Initially, it shows the properties for the Flash document itself. Click another object, such as the wheel, and you see its properties. Why are properties so important? They give you an extremely accurate description of objects. If you need to precisely define a color or the dimensions of an object, the Properties panel is the tool to use. It not only reports the details, but it also gives you the tools to make changes, as shown in this little exercise:

1. **At the top of the Tools panel, click the Selection tool (solid arrow).**

   As an alternative, press V, the keyboard shortcut for the Selection tool.

2. **Click the white part of the stage.**

   The Properties panel shows the properties for your Flash document. At the top, you see the word "Document," and underneath, you see the filename.

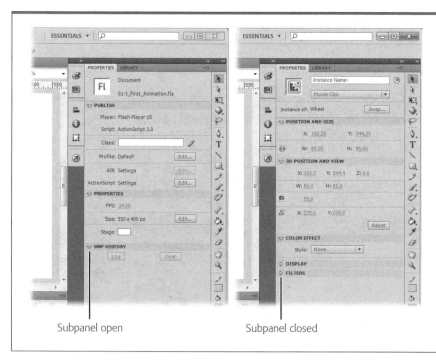

Subpanel open     Subpanel closed

**FIGURE 1-13**

*Left: When you first open a document, the Properties panel shows property settings for the document.*

*Right: Select the wheel in the document, and you see its properties. Click the triangle buttons to expand and collapse the subpanels.*

3. **Click the triangle button to open the Properties subpanel.**

   The button works like a toggle to open and close the subpanel. The subpanel displays three settings: FPS (frames per second), Size, and Stage.

4. **Click the white rectangle next to Stage.**

   A panel opens with color swatches.

5. **Click a color swatch—any color will do.**

   The background color of the stage changes to the color you chose.

6. **Click the wheel.**

   Information about the wheel fills the Properties panel. The wheel is a special type of object called a *Movie Clip symbol*. You'll learn much more about Movie Clips and other reusable symbols in Chapter 7.

**NOTE**  You may notice that you can't select anything else in this document. That's because the other objects are in the background layer, which is locked. (For more details on locking layers, see page 148.)

## Resize the Stage

In Flash, the size of your stage is the actual finished size of your animation, so setting its exact dimensions is one of the first things you do when you create an animation, as you'll see in the next chapter. But you can resize the stage at any time.

Here's how to change the size of your stage:

1. **With the Selection tool, click on a blank area of the stage (to make sure nothing on the stage is selected).**

   Alternatively, you can click the Selection tool and then choose Edit→Deselect All.

2. **In the Properties panel, open the Properties subpanel, and then click the Edit button.**

   The Document Settings window appears, as shown in Figure 1-14. At the top of the window are boxes labeled Dimensions. That's where you're going to work your magic.

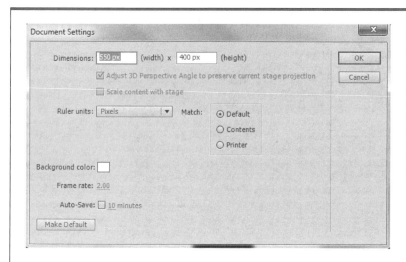

**FIGURE 1-14**

*The Document Settings dialog box puts several related settings in one place. At the top are the document's dimensions. In the lower-left corner are settings for the stage's background color and the frame rate. Click "Ruler units" to choose among Inches, Points, Centimeters, Millimeters, and Pixels.*

3. **Click in the width box (which currently reads "550 px"), and then type *600*.**

   You can change both the width and the height. The changes won't take place until you click OK. So if you have second thoughts and don't want to make any changes, then just click Cancel.

---

**TIP** If you want to change the stage back to its original dimensions after you've clicked OK, you can do that by choosing Edit→Undo or pressing Ctrl+Z (⌘-Z on a Mac). Undo works like it does in most programs, undoing your last action, and you can press it multiple times to work your way back through your recent actions.

---

4. **Click OK when you're done.**

   The stage resizes according to your instructions.

## Zoom In and Out

When your Flash project gets big or complicated, you may want to focus on just a portion of the stage. If you've used other graphics programs—from Windows Paint to iPhoto or Photoshop—there's not much mystery to the process. In the Tools panel, click the Zoom tool, which looks like a magnifying glass (Figure 1-15). Initially, the Zoom tool shows a + sign, meaning it's all set to zoom in. Click any spot you want to zoom in on, and you get a closer view. As an alternative, you can click and drag over an area to zoom in with more precision. As you drag, a rectangle appears to mark the area of interest.

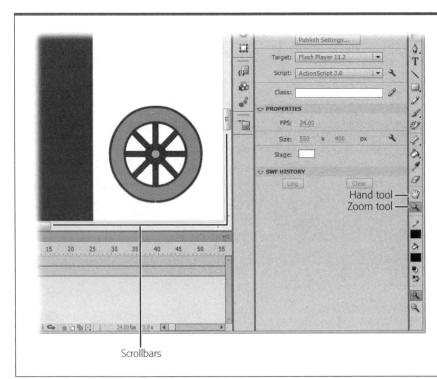

**FIGURE 1-15**

*Choose the Zoom tool and then click the stage to zoom in on your Flash document. Hold the Alt (Option) key down to zoom out. Once you're zoomed in, you can move around using either the scrollbars or the Hand tool (H).*

Hand tool
Zoom tool

Scrollbars

Using the Zoom tool, you can get so close that you see individual pixels in your artwork. Very handy for some operations. Once you're zoomed in, you can use the scroll bars at the right and bottom of the stage to reposition the stage in the viewing area. Even easier, choose the Hand tool (H) and then click and drag the stage within the viewing area.

Want to zoom out? Hold down the Alt (Option) key as you use the Zoom tool. Each time you click, you see more and more of the stage. Directly above the stage is the Edit bar. (If you don't see it, select Window→Toolbars→Edit Bar.) A menu on the Edit bar sets the Magnification or Zoom property as a percentage, as shown in Figure 1-16.

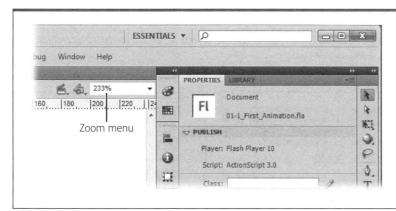

**FIGURE 1-16**

*The Magnification menu in the Edit bar gives you a quick readout on the Zoom factor. Click the menu to choose from several presets, including "Fit in Window," which shows the entire stage, or Show All, which zooms in or out to show all the objects drawn on the stage.*

## Make It Move

If you've followed along in the exercises up to this point, you deserve a taste of the Flash magic to come. Enough studying panels and tools—Flash is an animation program. It's time to make something move, or more precisely, to make something bounce. With the help of a little feature called Motion Presets, it's easier than you think:

1. **In the Magnification menu, choose "Fit in Window."**

   This gives you a view of the entire stage.

2. **With the Selection tool (V), drag the wheel to the top of the stage.**

   All the parts of the wheel (tire, spokes, hub) move as a single unit because they're grouped within a Flash symbol, called a Movie Clip.

3. **Choose Window→Motion Presets.**

   A floating panel appears, as shown in Figure 1-17. Motion Presets are covered in detail on page 295, but for this exercise, you just need a couple of basic steps.

4. **Click the triangle next to Default Presets.**

   The Default Presets folder opens, showing many predesigned motions.

5. **Click the words "bounce-smoosh."**

At the top of the panel, the preview window gives you an idea of how the bounce-smoosh preset works.

6. **Make sure the wheel is selected on the stage and that "bounce-smoosh" is selected in the Motion Presets panel, and then click the Apply button.**

A green line appears hanging from the bottom of the wheel. This line is called the *motion path*, and it shows you how the wheel will move over the course of the animation. In the timeline, the wheel layer turns to blue to indicate that it's now a *motion tween*.

**NOTE** *Tween* is an animation term that comes from all those in-between frames that animators have to draw to create a smooth animated motion.

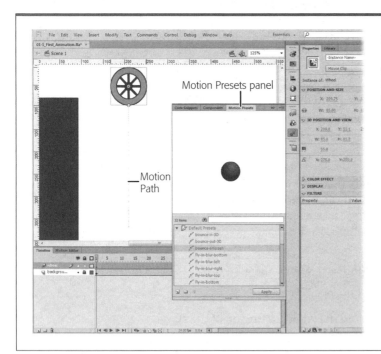

**FIGURE 1-17**

*The Motion Presets window has two folders. The one called Default Presets (shown open here) holds presets designed by Adobe. The other folder holds presets that you design and save. The "tail" hanging down from the wheel is the motion path.*

7. **Close the Motion Presets panel.**

That's all it takes to animate the wheel, so you might as well close the Motion Presets window. You can always bring it back later if you want to try out some of the other presets on the wheel.

## Play an Animation

Naturally, after you've animated an object in Flash, you want to see the results. You'll be checking your work frequently, so Adobe makes it easy to play an animation. Just press Enter (Return), and your animation bounces and smooshes as advertised. In the timeline, notice how the playhead moves along frame by frame as your animation plays. You can see your animation at all the different stages by dragging the playhead up and down the timeline—a process sometimes called *scrubbing*.

New in Flash CS6, the animation controller is fixed to the bottom of the timeline (Figure 1-18). That's the perfect place because it's always available.

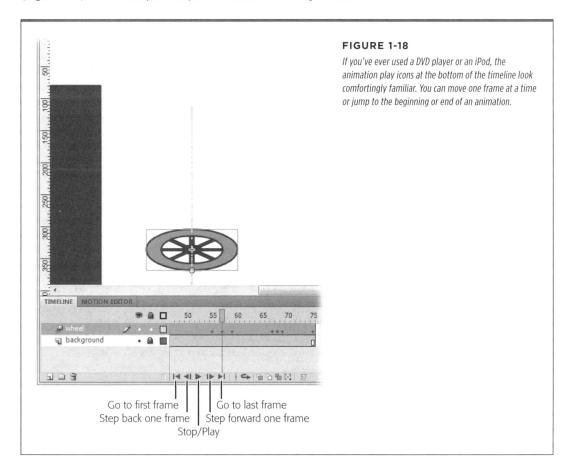

**FIGURE 1-18**

*If you've ever used a DVD player or an iPod, the animation play icons at the bottom of the timeline look comfortingly familiar. You can move one frame at a time or jump to the beginning or end of an animation.*

Go to first frame | Go to last frame
Step back one frame | Step forward one frame
Stop/Play

## Save a File

Saving your work frequently is important in any program, and Flash is no exception. You don't want to have to go back and recreate that perfect animated sequence because the power went out. The minute you finish a sizable chunk of work, save your

Flash file by pressing Ctrl+S (⌘-S). The Save command also appears on the menu bar: File→Save. Both maneuvers save the animation with the current name. So, if after following the exercises in this chapter, you use the Save command, you end up with a single Flash document using the original filename: *01-1_First_Animation.fla*.

If you want to save the file under a different name, use Save As or Ctrl+Shift+S (Shift-⌘-S). A standard window opens where you can choose a folder and give your document a name. When you use Save As, you end up with two documents, the original and one saved with the new name. The newly named document is the one that remains open in the Flash workspace.

If you close a document (File→Close) after you've made changes, Flash automatically asks if you want to save it. You're given three options. Choose *Save* to save your work and close the document. Choose *Don't Save* to close the document without saving your work. Choose *Cancel* if you don't want to save and don't want to close the document.

**NOTE** Flash Professional CS6 provides a new life-saving feature for files. When you create a new document you can turn on Auto-Save. This feature saves your document periodically even if you forget. You even get to choose the period. Initially, the Auto-Save period is set to every 10 minutes. To change that, click the number and type a new value.

---

**UP TO SPEED**

### Don't Be Afraid to Play

This first chapter introduced some important basics to help you get started working in Flash. Here's the most valuable Flash tip of all: Don't be afraid to play. This book is full of exercises that carefully show you how to build animations, but that doesn't mean you shouldn't head off the beaten path from time to time. The more you experiment and say, "What happens if I try this?" the faster you'll learn. It's true of all computer programs, but it's especially true with a graphics program like Flash. So download some of the animations from *www.missingmanuals.com/cds/flashcs6mm*. Open them in Flash, and then disassemble them. Alter the artwork. Mess with the tweens. Add new parts. You won't break anything. You can always make copies or download the originals again. For a start, why not go back and check out how some of the other motion tweens work with that wheel?

# Creating Simple Drawings

O ver the years, Flash has acquired many new features, but at heart it's still an animation tool. The best way to learn Flash is to jump in and start drawing. So that's exactly what you'll do in this chapter. It starts with tips for planning your animation and then moves on to specific tools like the Pen, the Pencil, the shape tools, the Line tool, and the Brush. You'll draw a simple picture and see how to use Flash to draw in different styles, from cartoons to mechanical drawings. Once you've created some drawings, you'll learn more about moving and arranging objects on the stage.

In the next chapter, you'll add a few more drawings and string them together to create a simple animation.

## ■ Plan Before You Draw

If you're just creating a simple banner ad, you probably already have a concept in mind and are itching to start drawing and animating. On the other hand, if you're creating a new feature for the Cartoon Network, then you need to think like a movie director. If you're creating a tablet or smartphone app or a rich Internet application (RIA), then you need to think like a graphic user interface (GUI) designer. Whatever you're producing, it pays to plan. In the case of an ad, what do you want your audience to do? What sales message will motivate it? If your goal is to entertain, then you need to think about how to tickle people's funny bones or how to move them emotionally. If the story is complicated, then you need to break it down into scenes and use the entire storyteller's toolkit to be effective. To learn some of the tricks of the storytelling trade, try the techniques animators and graphic novelists use. If you're designing an application, whether it's for a handheld device or a full-size web page, you need to think about the needs of the app's users. What do they want to do? What tools do they expect to use?

Drawing a single picture is relatively easy. But creating an effective animation—one that gets your message across, entertains people, or persuades them to take an action—takes a bit more up-front work. And not just because you have to generate dozens or even hundreds of pictures: You also have to decide how to order them, how to make them flow together, when (or if) to add text and audio, and so on. With its myriad controls, windows, and panels, Flash gives you all the tools you need to create a complex, professional animation, but the creativity comes from you. You can avoid pitfalls and wasted time by planning before you draw.

## Creating a Storyboard

Say you want to produce a short animation to promote your company's great new gourmet coffee called Lotta Caffeina. You decide your animation would be perfect as a banner ad. Now, maybe you're not exactly the best artist since Leonardo da Vinci, so you want to keep it simple. Still, you need to get your point across—BUY OUR COFFEE!

Before you even turn on your computer (much less fire up Flash), pull out a sketch pad and a pencil and think about what you want your animation to look like.

For your very first drawing, you might imagine a closeup of a silly-looking face on a pillow, belonging to a guy obviously deep in slumber, eyes scrunched tight, mouth slack. Next to him is a basic bedside table, empty except for what appears to be a jangling alarm clock.

OK, now you've made a start. After you pat yourself on the back—and perhaps refuel your creativity with a grande-sized cup of your own product—it's time to plan and execute the frame-by-frame action. You do this by whipping out six quick pencil-and-paper sketches. When you finish, your sketch pad may look something like this:

- The first sketch shows your initial idea—Mr. Comatose and his jangling alarm clock.

- Sketch #2 is identical to the first, except for the conversation balloon on the left side of the frame, where capped text indicates that someone is yelling to your unconscious hero (who remains dead to the world).

- In sketch #3, a disembodied hand appears at the left side of the drawing, placing a cup bearing the Lotta Caffeina logo on the bedside table next to Mr. Comatose.

- Sketch #4 is almost identical to the second, except that the disembodied hand is now gone, and Mr. Comatose's nose has come to attention as he gets a whiff of the potent brew.

- Sketch #5 shows a single eye open. Mr. Comatose's mouth has lost its slackness.

- The last sketch shows a closeup of the man sipping from the cup, his eyes wide and sparkling, a smile on his lips, while a "thought bubble" tells viewers, "Now, *that's* worth getting up for!"

**DESIGN TIME**

## Tips from the Trenches

Starting out on a learning curve as steep as Flash's can be daunting. Sometimes it's helpful to hear what the pros think—to get advice from folks who've been there, done that, and want you to know that you can, too.

Here are the top 10 recommendations from Flash experts:

1. **Analyze other people's animations.** As you begin to explore Flash content on other websites, think about it critically. Don't just focus on whether the result is dazzling or colorful, but also consider whether it's effective. Does it do what it was designed to do: Help you keep track of the baseball pool? Provide advice and recipes for Thai cuisine? Get you to buy something? Did it work? If not, why not? What detracts from the overall effect? Keep a notebook so you can apply what you learn to your own efforts.

2. **Don't sell yourself short.** Don't think you can't create great animations just because you're not a professional artist with a background in design. You'll find that Flash helps you through lots of tough spots (like correcting your shaky lines), and frankly, you're probably not shooting for a Picasso- or Tarantino-level result anyway. You get better at everything with practice; Flash is no exception.

3. **Start with a storyboard.** When you're working with anything but the simplest design (anything more than a couple of frames), create a storyboard (page 44). It can be as rough or as detailed as you want; some folks just jot notes to themselves. Every minute you spend planning saves you hours of hair-pulling.

4. **Practice, practice, practice.** There are many programs out there that you can sit down and nail in 20 minutes. Flash isn't one of them. And while reading is a great way to begin learning Flash, no amount of book learning is a substitute for rolling up your sleeves and producing an animation or two. (That's why this book includes hands-on examples.)

5. **Join an online Flash community.** Real-time help from knowledgeable Flashionados is a beautiful thing. Use the online resources outlined in Appendix A to join a Flash community where you can ask questions, get help, and share ideas.

6. **Don't throw anything away.** You might be tempted to discard your mistakes. But if the "mistake" is interesting or useful, save it; you may be able to use it later for a different project. (While you're at it, write down a few quick notes about how you achieved the result so you can recreate it if you want to.)

7. **Spread yourself thin.** Many Flash pros have several projects of various types going at once. They can switch around when they get stuck on one. Keeping a lot of balls in the air can be an excellent way to help you think about things from different angles, which will help develop your skills. Often the best way to solve a problem is to give yourself a break and not think about it for a while. The next time you tackle the problem, the solution is right there.

8. **Always test your work in a live environment.** Don't rely on Flash's testing environment. If you're creating a Flash animation to display on a smartphone, test it on a smartphone before you go live. If you're targeting a website, upload your animation to a web server and test it in a browser, or better yet, several different browsers, like Internet Explorer, Firefox, Safari, and Chrome.

9. **Solicit (and incorporate) viewer feedback.** When you finish an animation, ask for feedback. Choose people you know will take the time to look at your work carefully and give you an honest evaluation.

10. **Never, ever sacrifice content for the sake of coolness.** The purpose of tools like Flash is to help you get your message across, not to see how many special effects you can cram into a 5-second spot. Pay more attention to whether you're creating an effective animation than to whether you're adding enough colors, shapes, or audio clips.

In the animation world, your series of quick sketches is called a *storyboard*.

Figure 2-1 shows a basic storyboard.

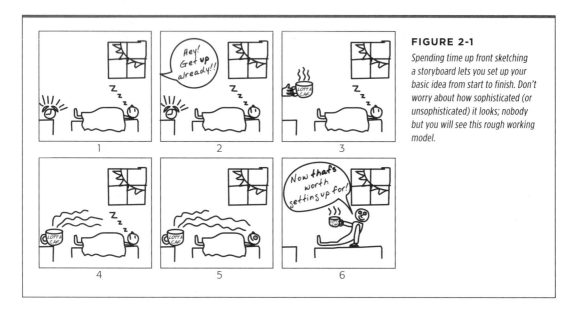

**FIGURE 2-1**

*Spending time up front sketching
a storyboard lets you set up your
basic idea from start to finish. Don't
worry about how sophisticated (or
unsophisticated) it looks; nobody
but you will see this rough working
model.*

## Five Questions for a Better Result

Creating your Flash animation will go more smoothly if you can answer these five basic questions:

- **What do you want to accomplish with this Flash creation?** Give yourself a mission statement, just as if you were in one of those tedious business meetings. You want something like "Generate 1,000 hits for the Lotta Caffeina website" or "Create a 22-minute animation set on the planet Galactrix" or "Sell an iPhone app to movie lovers."

- **Who's your audience?** Different types of people require different approaches. For example, kids love all the snazzy effects you can throw at them; adults aren't nearly as impressed by animation for animation's sake. The better sense you have of the people most likely to view your Flash creation, the better you can target your message and visual effects specifically to them.

- **What third-party content (if any) do you want to include?** *Content* is the stuff that makes up your Flash animation: the images, text, video, and audio clips. Perhaps you want your animation to include only your own drawings, like the ones you'll learn how to create in this chapter. But if you want to add images or audio or video clips from another source, then you need to figure out where you're going to get them and how to get permission to use them. (Virtually anything you didn't create—a music clip, for example, or a short scene from a TV show or movie—is protected by copyright. Someone somewhere owns it, so you need to track down that someone, ask permission, and—depending on the content—pay a fee to use it. Chapter 11 lists several royalty-free, dirt-cheap sources of third-party content.)

- **How many frames is it going to take to put your idea together, and how do you want them to be ordered?** For a simple banner ad, you're looking at anywhere from a handful of frames to around 50. A tutorial or product demonstration, on the other hand, can easily require 100, 200, or more frames. Whether you use storyboarding or just jot down a few notes to yourself, getting a feel for how many frames you'll need helps you estimate the time it's going to take to put your animation together.

**TIP** Try to get your message across as succinctly as possible. Fewer frames (and therefore images) typically mean a smaller file size, which is important if you plan to put your Flash animation up on the Web. (Folks surfing with dial-up or on a smartphone often have trouble viewing large files.)

- **How will you distribute it?** In other words, what's your target platform? If you plan to put your animation up on a website, then you need to keep file size to a minimum so people with slow connections can see it; if you plan to make it available to hearing-impaired folks, then you need to include an alternative way to communicate the audio portion; if you're creating an animation you know will be played on a 100-inch monitor, then you need to draw large, bold graphics. Your *target platform*—the computer (or device) and audience most likely to view your project—always affects the way you develop your animation.

**NOTE** Page 762 provides advice for designing a single animation that works with several different target devices such as web pages, smartphones, and tablets.

# ■ Preparing to Draw

Even if you're familiar with animation software (but especially if you aren't), you need to know a few quick things before you roll up your sleeves and dive into Flash—sort of like the quick where's-the-turn-signal once-over you do when you jump into a rental car for the first time.

In this section, you'll find out how to get around the stage and how to customize your Flash document's properties. You'll also learn a couple of basic Flash terms you need to understand before you use the drawing tools (which you'll see how to do on page 65).

But first you need to open a new Flash document page so you can follow along at home. To do so, launch Flash. Unless you've turned it off (page 17), the first thing you see is Flash's Welcome screen. Under Create New, choose ActionScript 3.0. If you've turned off the Welcome screen, you can create a new file using the Flash main menu. Here's how:

1. **From the main menu, choose File→New.**

   The New Document window opens. If the window doesn't show the General tab, as in Figure 2-2, then click that tab to make it active.

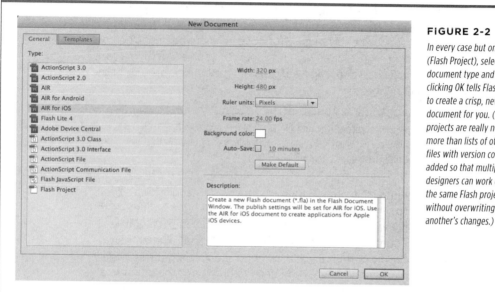

**FIGURE 2-2**

*In every case but one (Flash Project), selecting a document type and then clicking OK tells Flash to create a crisp, new document for you. (Flash projects are really nothing more than lists of other files with version control added so that multiple designers can work on the same Flash project without overwriting one another's changes.)*

2. **In the Type list, select the type of new file you want to create, and then click OK.**

   (If you're not sure what file type you want, choose ActionScript 3.0; see the box on page 19 for the reason why.) The New Document window disappears, and Flash displays a brand-new blank document. You can tell it's a new document by the name Flash gives it—for example, *Untitled-1*.

## Setting Document Properties

The stage, as you may recall from Chapter 1, is your electronic canvas: It's where you draw your lines and shapes and add your text. Figure 1-1 shows what the stage looks like the first time you create a new document in Flash. There's certainly nothing wrong with it, but you may want to change the size or color. Or, as described on page 50, you might want to make other changes to the stage to help you draw. For example, you can tell Flash to display guidelines that help you align objects and draw accurately. These guides show while you're creating, but your audience won't see them in the final animation. This section shows you how.

### ■ CHANGING THE SIZE OF THE STAGE

The size of your stage is also the size of your finished animation. The standard 550 x 400 pixel Flash stage, which worked well in the past, is pretty small by today's web standards. You may want to bump it up to 800 x 600 or even larger, depending on your target audience. If you're creating something for a smartphone or a tablet, you need to shrink the stage accordingly. In the case of the Lotta Caffeina banner ad, you want a wide, short stage (typically somewhere around 729 x 90).

The best way to ensure that your finished animation is the right size is to start with the right size stage out of the gate. Figure 2-3 shows how to change the stage dimensions using the Document Settings dialog box. There are several ways to open this box, which contains settings related to the stage and your animation:

- Press Ctrl+J (⌘-J).

- Right-click the stage. From the shortcut menu that appears, choose Document Properties.

- In the menu bar, choose Modify→Document.

- Press Ctrl+Shift+A (Shift-⌘-A) to make sure nothing is selected—that way, the Properties panel shows the document settings. If necessary, open the Properties subpanel. (Yep, there's a Properties subpanel in the Properties panel.) Click Edit.

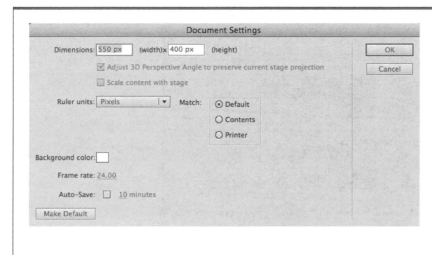

**FIGURE 2-3**

*You use the Document Settings window to set the size and color of your stage (which will also be the size and background color of your finished animation). When you type the dimensions, you can type the units of measurement (px, or even pixels, for example). But it's not necessary: The value in the Ruler units menu tells Flash which unit of measurement you're using.*

Once the Document Settings window is open, you can type new height and width numbers in the Dimensions box. The Match radio buttons let you automatically set the stage size. By selecting Default, you can change the stage size by typing new values. Choose Contents, and Flash automatically sizes the stage to fit the elements on it—a nice snug fit, no more, no less. If you know you're going to be printing your work, choose the Printer option, and the stage will fit nicely on a single sheet of paper.

In the center of the Document Settings box, there's a menu where you set the units used to measure the stage. These units are used for rulers, guidelines, and grids—all of which are covered later in this chapter. Out of the box, Ruler units is set to pixels, which is good for animations that your audience will view on a computer screen or a handheld device. In other cases, you may prefer points, inches, or metric units.

This dialog box is also where you change the stage color by clicking the Background color box and selecting a new color, as shown in Figure 2-4. (You'll learn more about frame rates in Chapter 15, but for now, just note that this is one of the places where you can change that setting. For now, leave it at 24.00 frames per second.)

> **TIP** If you save your work frequently, you're less likely to have to recreate animations that get lost due to lightning strikes or wild dog attacks. If you need help remembering to save, click the Auto-Save checkbox in the Document Settings window (Figure 2-3) and type a time period. Flash starts you off with a 10-minute interval, which works well for many Flash designers.

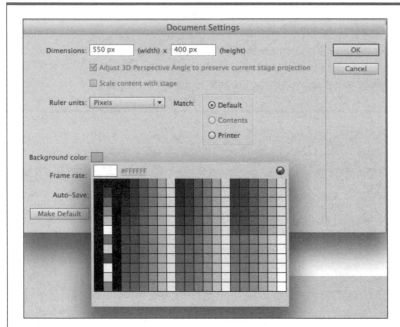

**FIGURE 2-4**

*Changing the color of the stage is an easy way to change the way your drawing looks. It can also make constructing your drawing easier. For example, if you're working with light-colored shapes, a nice dark background will help you see what you're doing—even if you end up changing the stage back to a lighter color when your design is finished.*

> **NOTE** Because the background color changes the way foreground objects appear, you may want to experiment with the color of the stage, beginning with one color and changing it as you add objects to the stage until you get the effect you want. (You can change the color of the stage at any time, even after you've completed your drawing.) When you're working on your animation, it may be easier to change the stage background color in the Properties panel. Go to Properties→Properties→Stage, and then choose a color from the color picker.

## Adding Measurement Guides

Even professional artists can't always draw a straight line or estimate 3 inches correctly. Fortunately, with Flash, they don't have to, and neither do you. Flash has several tools that help you spot precisely where your objects are on the stage and how much space they take up: rulers, a grid, and guides. You can see an example of these tools as they appear on the stage in Figure 2-5.

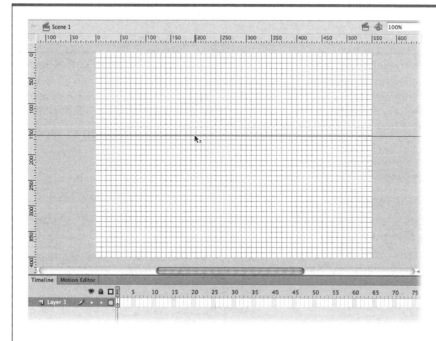

**FIGURE 2-5**

*Grids, guides, and rulers are Flash's answers to graph paper and a T square. To change the unit of measurement for the ruler, press Ctrl+J (⌘-J) to open the Document Settings box. From the "Ruler units" menu, select whatever measurement unit you want. You can also change the unit of measurement for the guides and the grid. To do so, right-click (Control-click) the stage, and then choose Guides→Edit Guides or Grid→Edit Grid.*

You can fine-tune your ruler, grid, and guides using the View menu or the shortcut menu that pops up when you right-click (or, on a Mac, Control-click) the stage. Here's what each tool does and how to display each of them:

- **Rulers.** This tool displays a ruled edge along the left and top of the stage to help you determine the location and position of your objects. To turn on rulers, right-click (or Control-click) the stage. Then, from the shortcut menu, choose Rulers.

- **Grid.** This tool divides the stage into evenly sized rectangles, which is great for helping you to position objects with precision. To turn on the grid, right-click (Control-click) the stage. Then, from the shortcut menu, choose Grid→Show Grid. You can fine-tune the grid to your taste; right-click the stage, and choose Edit Grid. Among your options: You can set the width and height of the grid rectangles; you can have the grid appear over or under graphics on the stage; and you can have lines and shapes automatically "snap to" the grid as you draw.

- **Guides.** If you want a tool that helps with straight-edge alignment—like the grid—but if you want more control over where the straight edges appear on the stage, then you want guides. To add guides, you first have to turn on rulers (see the first item in this list). Then, right-click (Control-click) the stage and, from the shortcut menu, choose Guides→Show Guides. A checkmark appears next to Show Guides to indicate that they're turned on, but you don't actually see any guide lines until you drag them onto the stage. You can drag as many guides as you want down from the top ruler or over from the left ruler. To add a guide, click a ruler (don't let go of the mouse) and then drag your cursor to the stage. Release the button when you get to the spot where you want your guide to appear.

**TIP** Grids and guides would be helpful enough if all they did was help you eyeball stuff, but Flash takes them one step further. If you turn on *snapping* and then drag, say, a circle around the stage, Flash helps you to align the circle precisely with either a grid or a guide mark. When the circle is close to a grid or guide line, it snaps into position. To turn on snapping, simply right-click (Control-click) the stage, and then choose Snapping→"Snap to Guides" (or Snapping→"Snap to Grid"). For more on the joys of snapping, see page 190.

**FREQUENTLY ASKED QUESTION**

## Taking Advantage of Templates

*How can some template designers I've never even met possibly know what kind of drawings I want to put in my animation, or how long I want my animation to be, or what kinds of sounds I want to add? They can't—so how on earth can Flash templates save me time?*

The predesigned templates that come with Flash can save you time on the grunt work associated with several commonplace kinds of animations. For example, the Interactive Advertising Bureau (*www.iab.net*) recommends certain dimensions for certain types of web ads, including pop-up windows and banner ads. When you open a template for a pop-up ad, for example, the stage is already preset to the dimensions for a standard-sized pop-up in a standard-sized browser window. You don't have to research the issue, and you don't have to customize the stage yourself.

Or say you want to create a slideshow in Flash, complete with buttons that let folks click forward and backward through your pictures. Putting an interactive animation like this together from scratch would require a fair bit of work, but if you use a photo album template, all you have to do is add your images and captions. The template takes care of the rest.

Over the years, different templates have come and gone in Flash. One of the complaints in Flash Professional CS4 was that many templates, like the ones for photo albums, mysteriously disappeared. Well, they're back in Flash Professional CS6, along with other truly useful templates. Now you'll find more time-saving templates for lots of different projects. In particular,

the Sample Files templates offer great examples for common or complicated tasks.

To see the templates Flash has, select File→New to display the New Document window, and then click the Templates tab. Here are the main categories:

- **Advertising.** Pop-up, skyscraper (skinny vertical), banner (skinny horizontal), and full-page ads.

- **AIR for Android.** These templates set the stage to the correct dimensions for Android devices, as well as get you started with techniques for using Android's accelerometer and swipe gestures.

- **Animation.** Predesigned buttons, masks, and animated effects like candle glow, rain, and snow.

- **Banners.** Standard-sized ads for the tops and sides of web pages.

- **Media Playback.** Photo albums and standard-sized documents for TV displays.

- **Presentations.** Predesigned presentation documents— think PowerPoint meets Flash.

- **Sample Files.** Perhaps the most interesting templates of them all. These templates show you how to tackle specific Flash projects, from creating menus to making a stick figure walk naturally. You can learn a lot by opening these templates and dissecting the elements to see how they work.

To lock the guides so you don't accidentally move them as you're drawing, right-click (Control-click) the stage and choose Guides→Lock Guides. When Lock Guides is set, you can't move any existing guides, but you can still add new ones. To remove a guide, make sure Lock→Guides is turned off, and then just drag the doomed guide back to the ruler. Poof, it's gone.

## Drawing a Shape

Flash graphics are made up of two primary elements: *strokes* and *fills*. Strokes may vary in thickness, but they look like lines. A stroke may be a single straight line, a curved line, or a complex series of connected lines. Strokes can also be dotted or dashed lines. Fills are colored shapes or surface areas. A fill may take on a common shape, such as a rectangle or an oval, or a fill may be a complex shape, such as a cartoon character's head. When you're drawing, you can create strokes and fills independently or together. For example, using the Rectangle tool, you can create a rectangle that has a stroke outline and a fill that colors the surface. Here's how to do it:

1. **With a new Flash document open, click the Rectangle tool in the Tools panel, or just press the shortcut key, R.**

   When a tool is selected, the button in the Tools panel has a distinctive pushed-in look. The Properties panel changes to display Rectangle Tool properties, as shown in Figure 2-6. A subpanel displays fill and stroke properties.

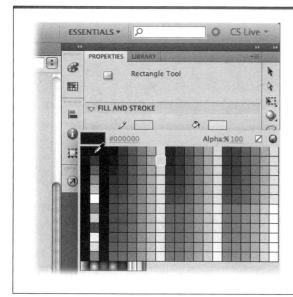

**FIGURE 2-6**

*When you choose the Rectangle tool (R), the label at the top of the Properties panel says "Rectangle Tool," and the panel displays properties related to a rectangle, such as the color of the stroke and fill. Here the color for the rectangle's stroke is being changed.*

2. **Click the color swatch next to the pencil.**

When you click the color swatch, a panel filled with different colors appears, and the cursor changes into an eyedropper—your signal that it's time to pick a color. The colors in the leftmost column are standard hues and shades of gray.

3. **In the upper-left corner, click the black swatch.**

The color picker panel closes, and the color for the rectangle's stroke is set to black.

4. **Click the color swatch next to the Paint Bucket, and choose blue from the color picker panel.**

The color for the rectangle's fill is set to blue.

---

**TIP** Sometimes as you work in the Properties panel, you may wonder what property a particular color swatch, text box, slider, or menu controls. If you move your cursor over the mystery setting, a tooltip appears with its name, such as "Stroke color," "Fill color," or "Stroke height."

---

5. **In the "Fill and Stroke" subpanel, drag the slider next to the word "Stroke" until the number in the "Stroke height" box is about 3 or 4.**

As you drag the slider, the number in the box to the right changes to show the *stroke height* (you may prefer to think of it as thickness). The Stroke slider goes from 0.10 pixels to 200 pixels, a huge range that makes the slider a little touchy. If you have trouble getting the number you want, you can just type a number in the text box.

6. **Click a spot on the stage and then, holding down the mouse button, drag to create a rectangle.**

As you drag, you see an outline that indicates the size and shape of the object you're drawing. As long as you hold the mouse button down, you can continue to change the size and shape.

7. **Release the mouse button.**

The finished rectangle appears on the stage, as shown in Figure 2-7. The stroke is black and about 3 or 4 pixels thick. It forms the outline for the rectangle. The fill is blue and appears inside the stroke.

As advertised, your rectangle is made up of two graphic elements, a stroke and a fill. You could have just as easily made a rectangle that was only a stroke outline or a solid fill. When you're drawing a shape, you can eliminate the stroke or the fill by choosing a "no color" option in the color picker. The no color option appears in the upper-right corner of the color picker as a white box with a red diagonal line drawn through it, as shown in Figure 2-6.

Flash gives you several tools to draw shapes. You'll find them all in the Tools panel (Figure 2-10). Just click the Rectangle tool and continue to hold the mouse button down. A fly-out menu shows Rectangle tools, Oval tools, and the PolyStar tool. You'll learn all the ins and outs of these tools throughout this book, but if you want to experiment, go right ahead. Just like the Rectangle tool, the other shape tools can create both strokes and fills. Other drawing tools create *either* strokes or fills. For example, the Line (L), Pencil (Y), and Pen (P) tools create strokes, while the Brush (B) and the Deco (U) tools create fills.

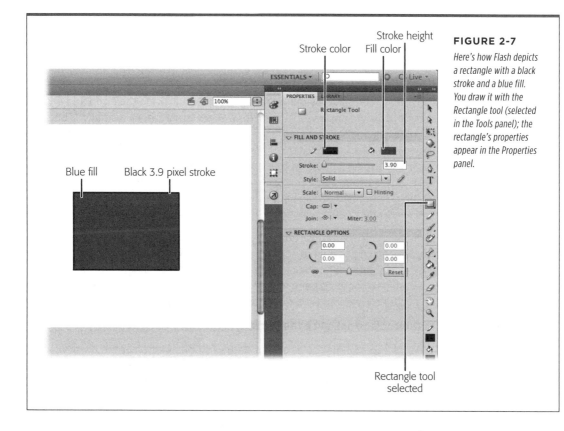

**FIGURE 2-7**

*Here's how Flash depicts a rectangle with a black stroke and a blue fill. You draw it with the Rectangle tool (selected in the Tools panel); the rectangle's properties appear in the Properties panel.*

## Choosing a Drawing Mode

If you're new to Flash, here's a tip that will save you hours of frustration. Write these words on a sticky note on your monitor: *Flash has two drawing modes*—merge mode *and* object mode. *When drawings don't behave as expected, I'm suffering from mode confusion.*

Lines and shapes drawn in merge mode behave differently from those drawn in object mode. This phenomenon becomes apparent when you try to move drawings around the screen or arrange them in front of or behind other graphics. You use a simple toggle button or shortcut key to change from one mode to the other. Keep in mind that you can use both drawing modes in a single Flash document, and there's a good chance you'll want to work that way. You can even have graphics drawn in merge mode in the same layer and frame as graphics drawn in object mode. Both types of graphics retain their native characteristics and eccentricities unless you purposely convert them to the other format.

---

**NOTE**    Want to check out the differences between the two modes? The Missing CD (www.missingmanuals. com/cds/flashcs6mm) has two example files. *02-1_Merge_Drawing_Mode.fla* shows an oval and a rectangle drawn in merge drawing mode. *02-2_Object_Drawing_Mode.fla* shows a similar oval and rectangle drawn in object mode.

---

## Merge Drawing Mode

Originally, Flash offered only merge mode. It's unlike drawing tools you find in most programs, but merge mode works great for web and smartphone animations because it keeps file sizes small and animations fast. Flash assumes you want to use the merge drawing mode unless you tell it otherwise. Graphics drawn in merge mode are called *shapes*. In this mode, if one shape overlaps another shape, Flash erases the hidden portion of the bottom shape underneath—a fact you discover when you move the overlapping shape, as shown in Figure 2-8 (bottom). Many Flash veterans love merge mode, because they can draw quickly, using overlapping shapes like cookie cutters.

Out of the box, Flash assumes you want to work in merge drawing mode, so you don't have to do anything special to activate it the first time you use Flash. But if you (or someone you share your copy of Flash with) have activated object drawing mode, then you need to toggle it back to merge mode. In the following steps, you'll learn how to make sure you're in merge mode and discover some of its idiosyncrasies.

1. **In the Tools panel, click the Rectangle tool (or press the R key).**

   When the Rectangle tool is selected, the Options section at the bottom of the Tools panel displays the Object Drawing icon (Figure 2-9, left). If the icon (a circle in a square) appears pressed down, then you're in object drawing mode and need to switch back to merge drawing mode.

2. **If necessary, click the Object Drawing button (or press J) to deselect object mode.**

   When the Object Drawing button is deselected, you're in merge mode.

3. **Draw a rectangle on the stage.**

   You can set the stroke and fill however you want before you draw the rectangle.

4. **Select the Oval tool (O) and then change the fill and stroke color.** Set the stroke height to about 3 or 4 pixels.

   If you need a refresher on setting the stroke and fill properties, see page 53.

5. **Draw an oval that partially overlaps the rectangle, as shown at the top of Figure 2-8.**

   The oval is drawn on top of the rectangle. In general, Flash places the most recently drawn graphic on top of previous graphics; however, there are some gotchas when you mix and match merge and object graphics.

6. **With the Selection tool (V), click the middle of the oval.**

   The fill portion of the oval displays a dotted highlight. When you see a dotted highlight like this, it's a signal that the graphic was drawn in merge mode. And, sure enough, the Properties panel identifies the selection as a Shape.

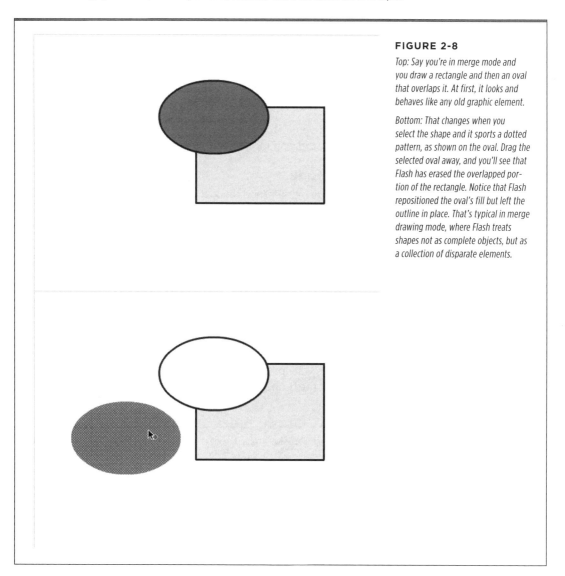

**FIGURE 2-8**

*Top: Say you're in merge mode and you draw a rectangle and then an oval that overlaps it. At first, it looks and behaves like any old graphic element.*

*Bottom: That changes when you select the shape and it sports a dotted pattern, as shown on the oval. Drag the selected oval away, and you'll see that Flash has erased the overlapped portion of the rectangle. Notice that Flash repositioned the oval's fill but left the outline in place. That's typical in merge drawing mode, where Flash treats shapes not as complete objects, but as a collection of disparate elements.*

**7. Drag the oval away from the rectangle.**

As you drag, the fill moves away from the rectangle, leaving the empty stage beneath. When shapes drawn in merge mode overlap, the bottom shape is erased. Notice that the stroke portion of the oval remains behind. A single click on the fill selects *only* the fill portion of the oval. If you want to select the fill and the stroke, then double-click the fill. There are more tips on using the Selection tool on page 61.

### ■ WHEN TO USE MERGE DRAWING MODE

As shown in Figure 2-8 (bottom), when you overlap objects in merge drawing mode, Flash erases the hidden portions of the objects underneath. You'll probably want to use merge mode if you fall into one of the following three categories:

- You want to be able to select portions of objects or create a deliberate "cutout" effect by overlapping objects and letting Flash do the cutting for you.

- You plan to create no more than one shape or object per timeline layer, so overlapping isn't an issue. For more details on layers, see page 135.

- You're familiar (and comfortable) with an older (*really* older) version of Flash. Merge was the *only* drawing mode before Flash 8.

## Object Drawing Mode

The object drawing mode tells Flash to think of shapes the way most humans naturally think of them: as individual, coherent objects. Overlapping shapes in object mode doesn't erase anything, and when you select a shape, you select the *entire* shape—not just the fill, or line, or portion of the shape you selected. If you've used Adobe Illustrator or the drawing tools in Microsoft Office, this drawing mode will seem familiar. To get a feeling for object mode characteristics, repeat the steps that begin on page 56. In step 2, toggle object drawing mode on by making sure the Object Drawing button is depressed, as shown at left in Figure 2-9. As you draw, your shapes look similar to the ones drawn in merge mode. However, when you select the oval in step 6, you won't notice the dotted selection pattern. Instead, you see a rectangular outline around the oval, as shown at bottom right in Figure 2-9. That's the object mode's way to show that an object is selected. The words "Drawing object" at the top of the Properties panel are another clue that you selected an object mode graphic.

> **TIP** The selection box for graphics drawn in object mode is rectangular. That makes it a little difficult to spot when the selected object is a rectangle or a straight line. In those cases, if you need to double-check, look for the words "Drawing object" in the Properties panel.

### ■ WHEN TO USE OBJECT DRAWING MODE

If you want to overlap objects and move them around with impunity—without putting them on separate layers—simply activate object drawing mode. Bingo—Flash lets you stack and overlap your objects on a single layer as easily as a deck of playing cards.

- Choose object mode if you want to work with entire objects (as opposed to portions of them).

- Choose object mode if you're used to working in programs like Adobe Illustrator and want a familiar graphics editing environment.

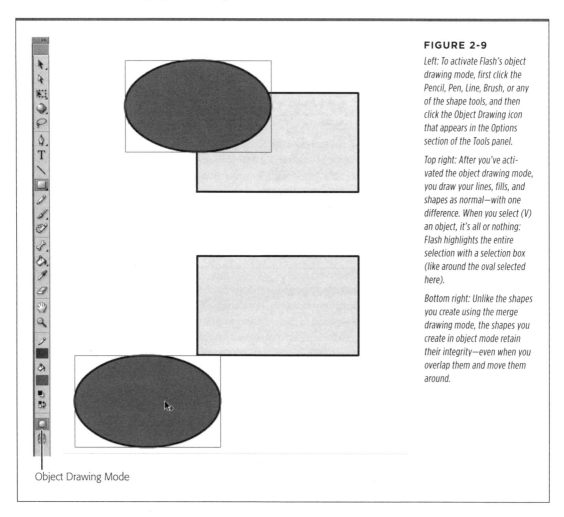

**FIGURE 2-9**

*Left: To activate Flash's object drawing mode, first click the Pencil, Pen, Line, Brush, or any of the shape tools, and then click the Object Drawing icon that appears in the Options section of the Tools panel.*

*Top right: After you've activated the object drawing mode, you draw your lines, fills, and shapes as normal—with one difference. When you select (V) an object, it's all or nothing: Flash highlights the entire selection with a selection box (like around the oval selected here).*

*Bottom right: Unlike the shapes you create using the merge drawing mode, the shapes you create in object mode retain their integrity—even when you overlap them and move them around.*

Object Drawing Mode

Merge drawing mode, is unlike most other programs' drawing tools, while the object drawing mode will seem familiar if you're coming from other programs, like Adobe Illustrator. Even if this is your first adventure with a computer-based drawing program, you may find the object drawing mode easier to learn and use. Each exercise in this book will clearly explain which drawing mode is used.

**TIP** You can mix and match modes in a single document. For example, you can use object drawing mode for some shapes and merge drawing mode for others. The drawing mode button on the Tools panel is a toggle, so the mode you choose remains in effect until you change it. Flash even remembers the setting from one document to another. So if you decide to use only object drawing mode, you can set it once and forget it.

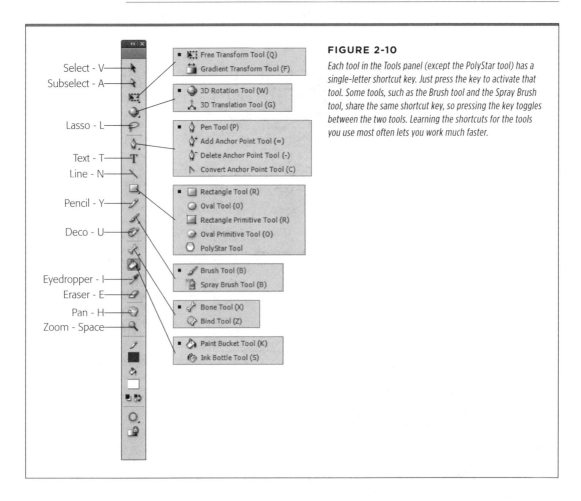

Select - V
Subselect - A

Lasso - L

Text - T
Line - N

Pencil - Y

Deco - U

Eyedropper - I
Eraser - E
Pan - H
Zoom - Space

Free Transform Tool (Q)
Gradient Transform Tool (F)

3D Rotation Tool (W)
3D Translation Tool (G)

Pen Tool (P)
Add Anchor Point Tool (=)
Delete Anchor Point Tool (-)
Convert Anchor Point Tool (C)

Rectangle Tool (R)
Oval Tool (O)
Rectangle Primitive Tool (R)
Oval Primitive Tool (O)
PolyStar Tool

Brush Tool (B)
Spray Brush Tool (B)

Bone Tool (X)
Bind Tool (Z)

Paint Bucket Tool (K)
Ink Bottle Tool (S)

**FIGURE 2-10**

*Each tool in the Tools panel (except the PolyStar tool) has a single-letter shortcut key. Just press the key to activate that tool. Some tools, such as the Brush tool and the Spray Brush tool, share the same shortcut key, so pressing the key toggles between the two tools. Learning the shortcuts for the tools you use most often lets you work much faster.*

## Using Merge Mode and Object Mode Together

You can use merge mode shapes and object mode graphics together in the same Flash document. Here are a few tips that will make life with mixed graphics a little easier:

- Merge mode shapes always appear underneath object mode graphics if they're on the same timeline layer. To make merge mode shapes appear on top of object graphics, place them on a separate timeline layer, as described on page 135.

- If you've already created a drawing object using the object mode, you can convert it to a shape by selecting it and then choosing Modify→Break Apart.

- If you've already created a shape in merge drawing mode and want to convert it to a drawing object, select the shape and then choose Modify→Combine Objects→Union. The entire selection becomes an object.

## Selecting Objects on the Stage

Once you draw a line or a shape on your stage, you need to select it to do anything else to it—for example, if you want to change its color, make it bigger, move it, or delete it.

As you can see in Figure 2-11, the Tools panel has three tools that let you select an object on the stage—Selection, Subselection, and Lasso. How these tools behave depends on whether you've created your drawings in merge or object drawing mode (see the previous section).

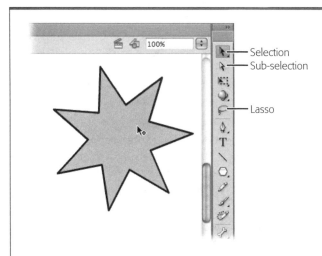

**FIGURE 2-11**

*Selecting an object on the stage to work with should be easy—and most of the time, it is; all you have to do is click the Selection tool and then either click your object or click near it and drag a selection box around it. But if your stage is crowded and you're trying to pick out just one little tiny angle of a line or a portion of a drawing to manipulate, you may need to use either the Subselection tool or the Lasso tool.*

■ **SELECTION TOOL (SHORTCUT KEY: V)**

This tool lets you select entire shapes, strokes, and fills, as well as symbols and bitmaps. (If you've created objects in merge mode, the Selection tool also lets you select rectangular portions of those objects.) After you've made your selection, you can then work with it—move the object around the stage by dragging, for example.

- **Using the Selection tool in merge mode.** To select a symbol, a bitmap, or one element of a shape (just the fill portion of a rectangle, for example), simply click the symbol, bitmap, or element. To show that an object is selected, Flash covers the selected merge mode graphic with a dotted pattern. To select both the fill *and* stroke of a merge mode graphic, double-click the fill. In merge mode, a single click on the stroke portion of a shape selects one line segment. Double-clicking selects the entire stroke.

To select a rectangular portion of a shape you've drawn in merge mode, click near (but not on) the shape and drag your cursor to create a selection box around just the portion you want to select. To select an entire shape, create a selection box around the whole shape, or double-click the shape.

- **Using the Selection tool in object mode.** To select an object created in object mode, click it. A rectangular outline appears around the selected object.

### ■ SUBSELECTION TOOL (SHORTCUT KEY: A)

The Subselection tool lets you reposition the individual points that define and control your strokes and fills. These points are called *anchor points*, and the connecting lines are called *segments*.

- **Using the Subselection tool in merge mode.** To select a stroke or a fill created in merge mode, click the Subselection tool, and then click the stroke or edge of the fill you want to move or change. Flash automatically redisplays that line as a bunch of individual anchor points and segments. As you move your cursor over the selection, the arrow cursor displays either a black or a white box. To move the entire stroke or fill, click and drag when a black *move box* appears on the cursor. To change the shape of an object, click and drag when a white *edit box* appears on the cursor. (See page 164 for details on editing graphics with anchor points.)

- **Using the Subselection tool in object mode.** The Subselection tool works in a similar way on objects drawn in object mode. You can use it to move or change the shape of an object. Move the cursor over the stroke or edge of an object, and you see the black move box or the white edit box.

> **TIP** You can't select an object's fill with the Subselection tool; however, you can "open up" an object graphic and edit it as if it were a merge shape. Double-click the object with the Selection (V) tool. When you do, other graphics on the stage fade, and the drawing object opens in edit mode. At this point, it behaves like a merge shape. When you're finished editing, close the graphic by clicking the left-pointing arrow in the upper-left corner of the work window.

### ■ LASSO TOOL

The Lasso tool is the one to use when you want to select a weirdly shaped portion of an object—say, you want to create a hand-shaped hotspot in the middle of a square bitmap—or when you need to select a weirdly shaped object that's super-close to another object.

- **Using the Lasso tool in merge mode.** To select a nonrectangular portion of an object drawn in merge mode, first click the Lasso tool; then click near (or on) the object and drag your cursor (as if you were drawing with a pencil) to create a nonrectangular shape.

- **Using the Lasso tool in object mode.** To select an entire object drawn in object mode, select the Lasso tool, click near the object, and then drag your cursor over the edge of the object. In object mode, dragging over a portion of the object selects the whole object.

CHOOSING A DRAWING MODE

> **TIP**  If you need to deselect an object after you've selected it (say, you changed your mind and don't want to change the object's color after all), you have several choices. You can press Esc, you can press Ctrl+Shift+A (Shift-⌘-A), you can click an empty spot on the stage, or you can select Edit→Deselect All.

Special note to Photoshop fans Ctrl+D (⌘-D on the Mac) works differently in Flash than it does in other Adobe programs. In Photoshop or Photoshop Elements, Ctrl+D (⌘-D) is the keyboard shortcut that deselects an object. In Flash, the same keystroke creates a duplicate of the selected object.

## Essential Drawing Terms

In Flash, a cigar isn't just a cigar. A circle isn't even just a circle. As explained earlier, every drawing you create using Flash's drawing and painting tools is composed of strokes and fills. As shown in Figure 2-12, you create strokes and fills with a variety of drawing tools:

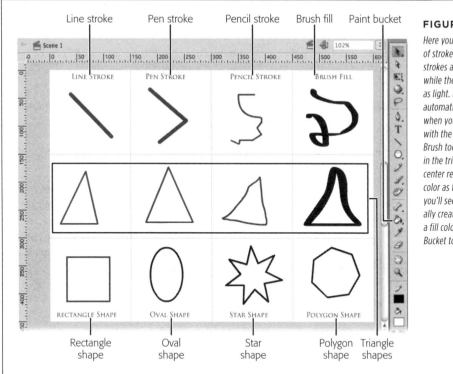

**FIGURE 2-12**

*Here you see examples of strokes and fills. The strokes appear dark, while the fills show as light. Flash doesn't automatically create fills when you create shapes with the Line, Pencil, and Brush tools, so as you see in the triangle shapes, the center remains the same color as the stage. Later you'll see how to manually create a fill or change a fill color with the Paint Bucket tool (page 87).*

- **Strokes.** A *stroke* in Flash looks just like the stroke you make when you write your name on a piece of paper. It can either be a plain line or the outline of a shape. Strokes can be dotted or dashed lines. You draw strokes in Flash using the Pen, Pencil, and Line tools. When you use one of the shape tools (for example, to create a square or polygon), Flash includes a stroke outline free of charge.

---

**TIP**  You can quickly add a stroke to outline a shape that doesn't have a stroke. Choose the Ink Bottle tool (S), and then click the shape. If you don't see the Ink Bottle on the Tools panel, click the Paint Bucket and continue to hold down the mouse button. The Ink Bottle appears on a pop-out menu.

---

- **Fills.** Flash recognizes two kinds of *fills*: the marks you make with the Brush tool, and the interior of a shape (in other words, everything inside the strokes that form the outline of a shape).

In a lot of cases, your shapes comprise both strokes and fills. You can create fill- and stroke-containing shapes in one fell swoop using Flash's shape tools—Oval, Rectangle, and PolyStar. If you draw a shape by hand using the Pen, Pencil, or Line tools, then you need to manually add a fill if you want one using the Paint Bucket tool. That process is described on page 87.

Why the emphasis on the technical terms "stroke" and "fill" when all you want to do is draw a smiley face? For one very important reason: Flash treats strokes and fills differently. You use different tools to create them and different tools to modify them. If you don't know the difference between a stroke and a fill, you won't be able to do a whole lot with the drawing and painting tools described in this chapter.

**DESIGN TIME**

## To Thine Own Self Be True

When asked about her artistic process, a celebrated 20th century painter said that in order to create, she had to toss aside everything she knew about matching colors, standard techniques, and even the way she held her pencil and her paintbrush. As a right-handed person with a strongly ana-lytical mind, she discovered her ability to create only after she started drawing with her *left* hand. She learned to ignore what everyone else told her about how she *should* be working.

There's a moral to this story: Just because one person finds the Pencil or Brush the easiest tool to use and sticks to it almost exclusively, that doesn't mean you should do the same. Experiment and find what works best for *you*!

To help get your juices flowing, the stick figure you see in this chapter shows several ways you can use Flash's painting and drawing tools. Each of these tools has its pros and cons, so try them all out for yourself. After all, the Flash police aren't going to arrest you if you sketch a beard and moustache on your stick figure using the Brush tool instead of the Pencil.

# ◼ Creating Original Artwork

Before you can create an animation, you have to have something to animate. You start with one drawing and then create a bunch more (often by altering the first drawing slightly). For example, if you want to create an animation showing a raccoon marching in place, you need to draw a picture of a raccoon standing still; another picture of the same raccoon lifting its left foot; and still more pictures showing the raccoon putting its left foot down, lifting its right foot, and so on. Put them all together using Flash's timeline (Chapter 3), and you've got yourself an animation.

**NOTE**  You're not limited to using your own drawings. Flash lets you *import*, or pull in, existing drawings and photos—and even sound and video clips. Page 351 shows you how to import files.

This section shows you how to use basic Flash tools to create a simple stick person drawing. You'll see the Line, Pencil, Pen, Brush, and shape tools (Oval, Rectangle, and PolyStar) in action and learn the differences among them (some are better for creating certain effects than others). You'll also find out how to add color to a Flash drawing and how to erase your mistakes.

## Drawing and Painting with Tools

One of the true beauties of creating digital artwork—besides not having to clean up a mess of paint spatters and pencil shavings—is that you don't have to track down your art supplies—the one pen that feels good in your hand, the right kind of paper, the sable brush that smells like paint thinner. Instead, all you need to do is display Flash's Tools panel.

In this section, you'll see Flash's drawing and painting tools in action: the Line, Pen, Pencil, Brush, and shape tools. You'll have a chance to use the Selection, Subselection, and Lasso tools. And finally, you'll get a quickie introduction to color—specifically, how to change the colors of strokes and fills.

### ◼ LINE TOOL

You use the Line tool in Flash to draw nice, straight lines—perfect all by themselves or for creating fancy shapes like exploding suns and spiky fur.

Make sure you're in object drawing mode, and then follow these steps to start drawing your stick figure using the Line tool:

1. **In the Tools panel, click the Line tool, as shown in Figure 2-13.**

   Flash highlights the Line tool in the Tools panel to let you know you've successfully selected it. When you move your cursor over the stage, you see it's turned into crosshairs.

2. **Click anywhere on the stage and drag to create a short horizontal line.** To end your line, let go of the mouse.

   Your line (technically called a *stroke*) appears on the stage.

3. **Click above the horizontal line, and drag down to create a vertical line.**

   The result is a cross. Next, you'll add legs by drawing diagonal lines.

4. **Click the bottom of the vertical line and drag down and to the left; then click the bottom of the vertical line again and drag down and to the right.**

   Figure 2-13 shows the result. It doesn't look like much yet, but it's actually the basis for a stick figure you'll create as you experiment with Flash's drawing and painting tools in the following sections.

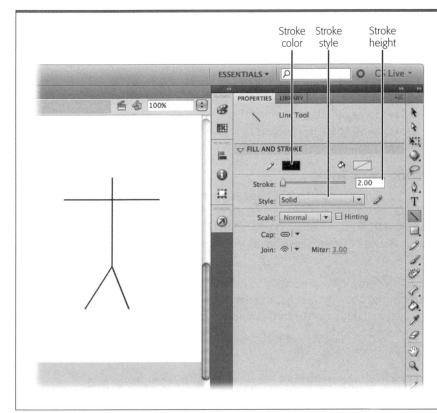

**FIGURE 2-13**

*The Line tool is the easiest, quickest way to create straight lines in Flash (like the four straight lines you see here). If you'd like to customize the way your lines look, head to the Properties panel. There you find options that let you make a line thicker, change it to a different color—even turn it into a dashed or dotted line, instead of a plain solid line. (If you don't see the Properties panel, choose Window→Properties to display it.)*

### ◾ PENCIL TOOL

The Pencil tool lets you draw free-form strokes on the stage, similar to the way you draw using a regular pencil on a regular sheet of paper. Unlike the Line tool, the Pencil tool doesn't make you stick to the straight and narrow, so it lends itself to curving lines and fine details, like hands and faces. Here's how to use the Pencil tool:

1. **In the Tools panel, click the Pencil tool.**

   Flash outlines the Pencil tool to let you know you've successfully selected it, and Pencil-related options appear in the Options section at the bottom of the

Tools panel. When you move your cursor over the stage, you see it's turned into a miniature pencil.

2. **In the Options section at the bottom of the Tools panel, click the Pencil Mode button.**

    A fly-out menu appears.

3. **In the fly-out menu, turn on the checkbox next to Smooth.**

    The *Smooth* option gently corrects any jiggles you make as you draw with the pencil—essential when you're trying to draw small lines, like this stick figure's face and hands.

4. **Click the stage and drag to draw a little face, hands, and feet similar to the ones in Figure 2-14.**

    While you're on the Options section, there are other ways you can modify how the Pencil tool works: The *Straighten* option emphasizes the corners you draw with the Pencil (for example, turning squarish circles into squares or roundish squares into circles—definitely *not* what you want when you're trying to draw the feet you see in Figure 2-14), and the *Ink* option leaves your Pencil strokes just as they are, jiggles and all.

---

**UP TO SPEED**

### Mouse vs. Graphics Tablet

If you expect to do a lot of Flash work, do yourself a favor: Ditch your mouse and get yourself a *graphics tablet* (sometimes referred to as a *digitizing tablet, graphics pad,* or *drawing tablet*). A graphics tablet is basically an electronic sketch board with a stylus that doubles as a pen, pencil, and brush. Today's graphics tablets connect through the Universal Serial Bus (USB) port, typically located at the front or back of your computer, so they're a snap to connect and remove.

With a graphics tablet, drawing and painting feels a whole lot more natural. Your results will look a lot better, too.

When you use a graphics tablet, Flash recognizes and records subtle changes, like when you change the pressure or slant of the stylus—something you don't get with a plain old mouse. (In fact, if you install your graphics tablet correctly, Flash displays extra icons on the Tools panel that relate only to graphics tablets. For example, you can adjust how the tablet behaves when more or less pressure is applied.)

Expect to spend anywhere from $100 to $500 on a good graphics tablet.

---

Here are some tips for drawing with the Pencil tool:

- If the object you're drawing with the Pencil is small, press Ctrl+= (⌘-=) to get a better view. You can use the Hand tool (H) to position the stage where you want it. When you're ready to zoom out, press Ctrl+hyphen (⌘-hyphen). For more tips on changing the view, zoom over to page 38.

- Don't do the same work twice. For example, in Figure 2-14, a hand and shoe were drawn once, then duplicated (Ctrl+D or ⌘-D). While still selected, they were flipped horizontally using Modify→Transform→Flip Horizontal.

- You can also straighten or smooth a line you've already drawn. To do so, select the line you want to modify using any selection tool—the Lasso tool (page 62) works great. When a line is selected, buttons for the Straighten and Smooth commands also appear in the Options section of the Tools panel. You can click multiple times to increase the effect.

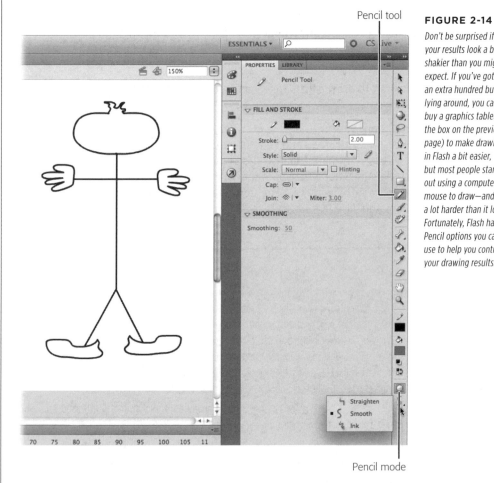

Pencil tool

**FIGURE 2-14**

*Don't be surprised if your results look a bit shakier than you might expect. If you've got an extra hundred bucks lying around, you can buy a graphics tablet (see the box on the previous page) to make drawing in Flash a bit easier, but most people start out using a computer mouse to draw—and it's a lot harder than it looks. Fortunately, Flash has Pencil options you can use to help you control your drawing results.*

Pencil mode

■ **PEN TOOL**

If you want to create a complex shape consisting of a lot of perfect arcs and a lot of perfectly straight lines, then the Pen tool is your best choice.

To create straight lines with the Pen tool, click the stage to create *anchor points*, which Flash automatically connects using perfectly straight *segments*. The more times you click, the more segments Flash creates—and the more precisely you can modify the shape you draw, since you can change each point and segment individually (see Chapter 5). When you want to stop creating anchor points, double-click the mouse or press the Esc key.

If you drag the Pen tool (instead of just clicking), the Pen lets you create perfectly curved arcs.

**NOTE** Working with the Pen tool is a lot (a *whole* lot) less intuitive than working with the other Flash drawing tools. Because you can easily whip out a triangle with the Line tool or a perfect circle with the Oval tool, save the Pen tool for when you're trying to draw a more complex shape—like a baby grand piano—and need more control and precision than you can get freehanding it with the Pencil or Brush.

As you can see in the Tools panel in Figure 2-15, the Pen tool icon looks like the nib of an old-fashioned fountain pen.

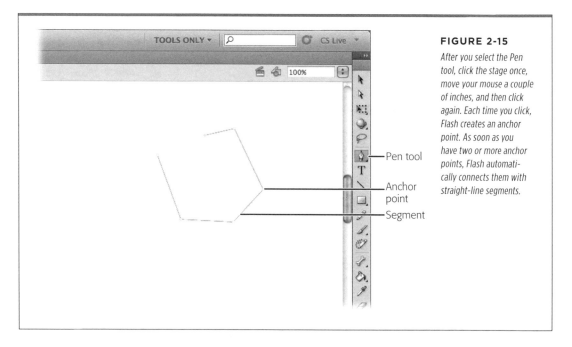

**FIGURE 2-15**

*After you select the Pen tool, click the stage once, move your mouse a couple of inches, and then click again. Each time you click, Flash creates an anchor point. As soon as you have two or more anchor points, Flash automatically connects them with straight-line segments.*

To draw a straight line with the Pen tool:

1. **Select the Pen tool.**

   Your cursor changes into a miniature pen nib.

2. **Click the stage, move your cursor an inch or so to the right, and then click again.**

   Two anchor points appear, connected by a straight segment.

3. **Move the cursor again, stopping where you want to anchor the line, and then change direction again.**

Figure 2-15 shows the results of several clicks. Flash keeps connecting each anchor point every time you click the stage. To break a line and start a new one, double-click where you want the first line to end.

To draw a curve with the Pen tool:

1. **Select the Pen tool.**

Your cursor changes into a miniature pen nib.

2. **Click the stage once, and then move your cursor an inch or so to the right.**

A single anchor point appears.

---

**NOTE**   Flash lets you change the way it displays anchor points, as well as the way your cursor appears, when you're using the Pen tool. You can even tell Flash to preview line segments for you, much as it previews curves. To change any of these preferences, select Edit→Preferences (Flash→Preferences for the Mac). Then, in the Preferences window, select the Drawing category. The Pen tool preferences appear at the top of the Preferences window.

---

3. **Click again, but this time, without letting go of the mouse button, drag the cursor around.**

As you drag, the anchor point you create sprouts two control lines, and your cursor turns into an arrow. As you can see in Figure 2-16, something different is happening. Flash displays a preview curve and a control line that lets you adjust the angle of the curve. Drag the end of the control line, and the shape of the curve changes.

4. **Release the mouse button.**

When you let go of the mouse button, Flash draws the curve on the stage. The control lines disappear when you choose another tool. Using the Pen tool, you can create both straight lines and curves, as shown in Figure 2-17.

5. **Continue drawing connected lines by clicking other points on the stage.**

Click, move, and click to draw straight lines. Click, move, and drag to create curves. Adjust the curves using the handles on the end of the curve control lines. If you've never used tools like these before, don't worry; you'll get better with a little practice.

6. **Create a closed loop shape by clicking the first point you created in step 2.**

When the cursor is over a point that closes the loop, you see a small circle to the right of the Pen tool cursor.

**TIP** If you want to adjust a curve after the fact, choose the Subselection tool and then click an anchor point adjacent to the curve. The control lines appear, and you can change the shape of the curve by dragging the control points.

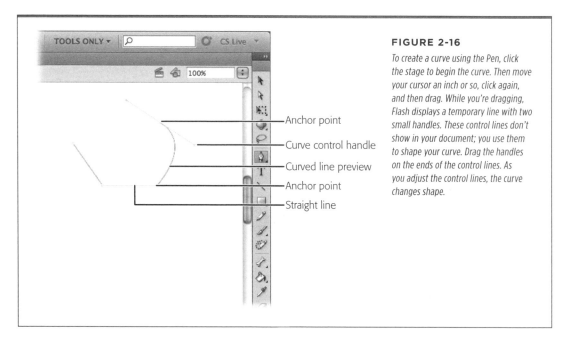

**FIGURE 2-16**

*To create a curve using the Pen, click the stage to begin the curve. Then move your cursor an inch or so, click again, and then drag. While you're dragging, Flash displays a temporary line with two small handles. These control lines don't show in your document; you use them to shape your curve. Drag the handles on the ends of the control lines. As you adjust the control lines, the curve changes shape.*

7. **Once you feel comfortable drawing straight lines and curved lines, use curves to create a cartoon head, similar to the one in Figure 2-17. Then use straight lines to make a hat for your creation.**

Drawing curves can be a bit tough until you get the hang of controlling the shape of the curves as you draw. One of the great things about the Pen tool is that you can make adjustments after the fact. Here are some tips for working with the Pen tool:

- You can change the path of a line or the shape of an object by moving anchor points with the Subselection tool (A).

- To change the arc of a curve, click an adjacent anchor point with the Subselection tool. The anchor point sprouts control lines, and you can adjust the curve by dragging the points on the end of the control lines.

- Use the Convert Anchor Point tool (C) to turn hard angles into curves and vice versa.

- Use the Add Anchor Point tool (=) to—you guessed it—add anchor points to a line segment. The Delete Anchor Point tool (-) removes anchor points but leaves a line segment between the remaining anchor points.

Once you get used to the Pen tool's drawing system, you'll find that you can draw very precise shapes. (Plus, all your practice with the Pen tool will pay off if you ever use Adobe Illustrator or similar programs that use the same *Bezier curves* to draw complex shapes.)

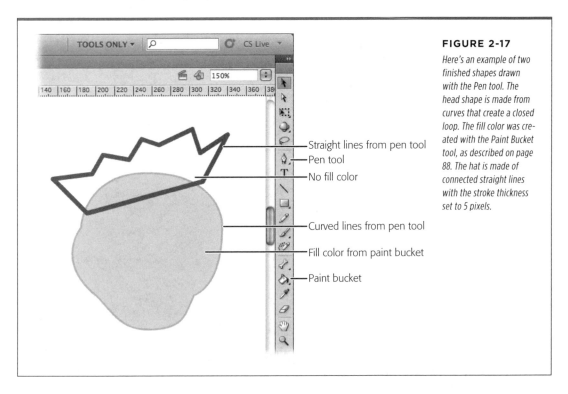

**FIGURE 2-17**

*Here's an example of two finished shapes drawn with the Pen tool. The head shape is made from curves that create a closed loop. The fill color was created with the Paint Bucket tool, as described on page 88. The hat is made of connected straight lines with the stroke thickness set to 5 pixels.*

Labels in figure:
- Straight lines from pen tool
- Pen tool
- No fill color
- Curved lines from pen tool
- Fill color from paint bucket
- Paint bucket

### ■ BRUSH TOOL

You use the Brush tool to create free-form drawings, much like the Pencil tool described on page 66. The differences between the two include the following:

- You can change the shape and size of the Brush tool. You can choose a brush tip that's fat, skinny, round, rectangular, or even slanted.

- The Brush tool creates fills, while the Pencil tool creates strokes. This distinction becomes important when it comes time to change the color of your drawings (see page 84).

**NOTE** The Brush tool really shows its stuff when you use it with a graphics tablet, as described in the box on page 67. That's because the Brush tool makes great use of the tablet's ability to sense pressure. Press hard for thick, bold lines. Lessen the pressure for thin, delicate lines. With practice, you can create great calligraphic effects.

To use the Brush tool:

1. **On the Tools panel, click the Brush tool (the little paintbrush icon).**

   Flash displays your Brush options—including Brush Mode, Brush Size, and Brush Shape—in the Options section of the Tools panel. If you have a graphics tablet, you also see Brush Pressure and Use Tilt buttons.

2. **From the Brush Size drop-down menu (Figure 2-18), select the third- or fourth-smallest brush size.**

   The larger brushes let you paint great, sweeping strokes on the stage. But in this example, you'll be drawing hairs on your fellow's head, so a modest brush size is more appropriate. Your cursor changes to reflect your choice (you can see this change if you mouse over the stage).

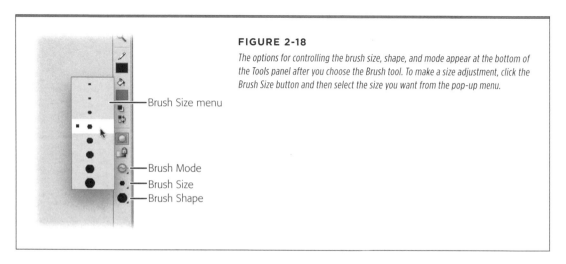

**FIGURE 2-18**

*The options for controlling the brush size, shape, and mode appear at the bottom of the Tools panel after you choose the Brush tool. To make a size adjustment, click the Brush Size button and then select the size you want from the pop-up menu.*

Brush Size menu

Brush Mode
Brush Size
Brush Shape

> **TIP** Whenever you make a mistake, or simply want to wipe out the very last thing you did in Flash, Press Ctrl+Z (⌘-Z) or select Edit→Undo.

3. **From the Brush Shape drop-down menu, choose the round brush shape.**

   Each brush shape gives you a dramatically different look. To draw hair, as in this example, you may choose round because it most closely approximates the results you get with a real brush. Once again, your cursor changes to reflect your choice.

4. **Click the Brush Mode button and then, from the pop-up menu that appears, choose Paint Normal.**

   Brush modes change the way the Brush tool paints over or under strokes and fills already in your drawing. Figure 2-19 shows the different effects. Here you choose Paint Normal to draw hair that shows over the head shape and the hat. Later, you'll see how to tuck that hair under the hat.

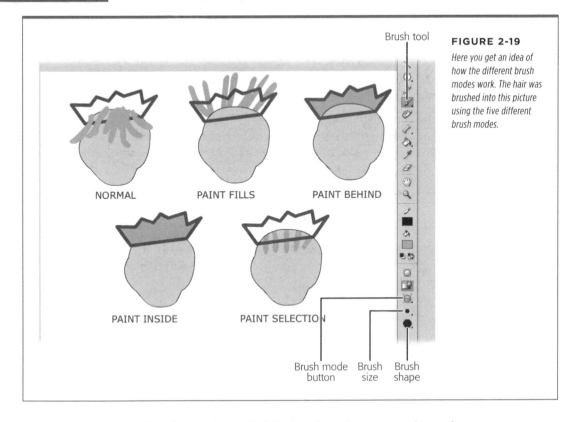

Brush tool

**FIGURE 2-19**

*Here you get an idea of how the different brush modes work. The hair was brushed into this picture using the five different brush modes.*

NORMAL        PAINT FILLS        PAINT BEHIND

PAINT INSIDE        PAINT SELECTION

Brush mode    Brush    Brush
button       size     shape

Here's a rundown of all the brush modes you can choose from:

- **Paint Normal.** Flash uses this mode unless you tell it otherwise. If you brush over an existing object on the stage using Paint Normal, your brush stroke appears on top of the shape.

- **Paint Fill.** When you brush over an existing object on the stage using Paint Fill, your brush stroke appears on top of the fill portion of the object, behind the stroke, and on the stage.

- **Paint Behind.** When you brush over an existing object on the stage using Paint Behind, your brush stroke always appears behind the object.

- **Paint Selection.** When you brush over an existing object on the stage using Paint Selection, your brush stroke appears only on the parts of the shape that are both filled and that you've previously selected.

- **Paint Inside.** If you brush over an existing object on the stage using Paint Inside and begin *inside* the stroke outline, your brush stroke appears only inside the lines of an object (even if you color outside the lines). If you begin *outside* the lines, then your brush stroke appears only outside (even if you try to color inside them).

5. **Click the stage just about where your stick person's hair should be and drag your mouse upward; release the mouse button when the hair is the length you want it.**

   Your paintbrush stroke appears on the stage.

6. **Repeat to create additional locks of hair.**

   You should see a result similar to the one shown in Figure 2-19.

■ **ARRANGING DRAWN OBJECTS FORWARD AND BACKWARD**

When you draw in object mode, each part of your drawing (the head, the hat, the hair) is an object, and you can place it in front of or behind the other objects. Imagine that the head, hat, and hair are each cardboard cutouts that you're placing on your desktop. You set them down so that the head is at the bottom, the hair cutout covers the top of the head, and the hat covers part of the hair. Perfect! Flash works the same way. When you draw objects, Flash places each new object in front of the last. But what if you don't draw them in the proper order? Suppose, in the cartoon face example, that you drew the hair on top of the hat? Flash can help. Follow these steps to move the hat to the front.

**NOTE** If you don't have a drawing handy for this exercise, you can download *02-3_Arrange_Objects.fla* from the Missing CD page at *www.missingmanuals.com/cds/flashcs6mm.*

1. **With the Selection tool, click the hat's outline.**

   Before you can rearrange the stacking order, you need to select an object to move.

2. **Go to Modify→Arrange→"Bring to Front" or press Shift+Ctrl+up arrow (Windows) or Shift-Option-up arrow (Mac) to move the hat to the front.**

   The hat moves in front of both the head shape and the hair, as shown in Figure 2-20. You can still move the hat, hair, or head around the stage with the Selection tool. They stay in the same stacking order (head on bottom, hair in middle, hat on top) until you make another change using the Modify→Arrange commands.

There are four commands that help you arrange the stacking order of the objects you've drawn:

- **Bring to Front.** Moves the selected object to the very front of the stack.

- **Bring Forward.** Moves the selected object forward one level in the stack.

- **Send to Back.** Moves the selected object to the very back of the stack.

- **Send Backward.** Moves the selected object back one level in the stack.

As an alternative to using menu commands, you can select an object and then use Ctrl+up arrow or Ctrl+down arrow (⌘-up arrow or ⌘-down arrow) to move the selected object forward or backward. Add the Shift key (Shift+Ctrl+up arrow or Shift+Ctrl+down arrow for PCs; Shift-⌘-up arrow or Shift-⌘-down arrow for Macs) to move all the way to the front or all the way to the back.

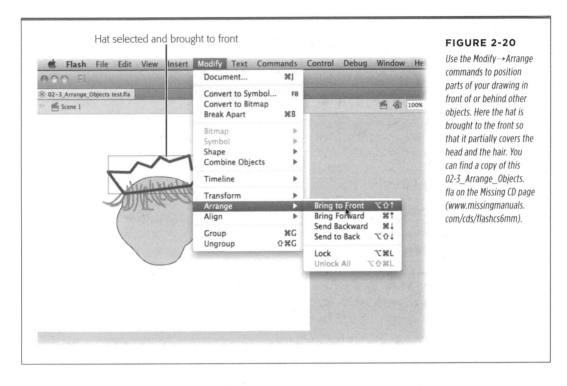

Hat selected and brought to front

**FIGURE 2-20**

*Use the Modify→Arrange commands to position parts of your drawing in front of or behind other objects. Here the hat is brought to the front so that it partially covers the head and the hair. You can find a copy of this 02-3_Arrange_Objects. fla on the Missing CD page (www.missingmanuals. com/cds/flashcs6mm).*

**TIP** Remember, shapes drawn in merge drawing mode always appear behind objects drawn in object drawing mode. If you want to rearrange mixed graphics, then you need to use the timeline layers, as explained in Chapter 4.

### ■ SHAPE TOOLS: OVAL, RECTANGLE, AND POLYSTAR

Flash gives you quick ways to create basic shapes: the Oval tool, which lets you draw everything from a narrow cigar shape to a perfect circle; the Rectangle tool, which lets you draw rectangles, from long and skinny to perfectly square; and the PolyStar tool, which you can use to create multisided polygons (the standard five-sided polygon, angled correctly, creates a not-too-horrible side view of a house) and star shapes.

You can see the Oval, Rectangle, and PolyStar tools in Figure 2-21; Figure 2-22 shows you how to configure the PolyStar tool.

**TIP**  You can always create a circle, a square, or a star using one of the other drawing tools, like the Pencil or the Line tool. But most people find the shape tools quicker and easier.

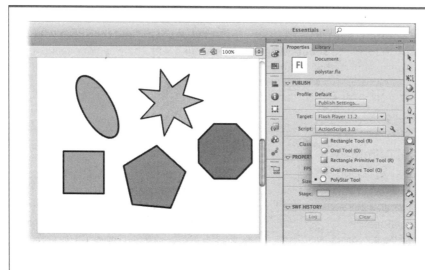

**FIGURE 2-21**

*The Oval, Rectangle, and PolyStar tools are all tucked under the same button on the Tools panel. The icon and related tooltip for the last-used shape appear on the button. The small triangle in the lower-right corner of the button is your clue that there are more options. To see the other shape options, click and hold down the button. A small menu appears showing all the options.*

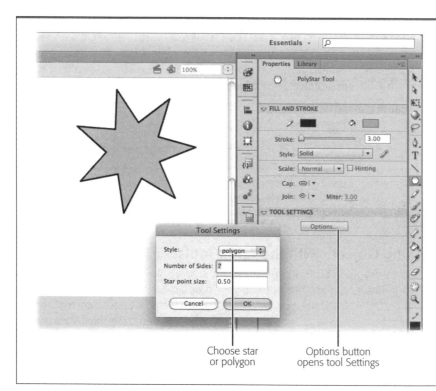

Choose star
or polygon

Options button
opens tool Settings

**FIGURE 2-22**

*One of the shape tools is called PolyStar because it creates polygons and stars. After choosing PolyStar on the Tools panel, click the Options button in the Properties panel. Then, in the Tool Settings box, choose either "polygon" or "star" from the drop-down menu.*

To create a shape:

1. **Click the shape tool you want (choose from Oval, Rectangle, or PolyStar, as shown in Figure 2-21).**

   Your cursor changes into a cross.

2. **Click the stage where you want to start your shape, and then drag your cursor to form the shape.** When you're satisfied with the way your shape looks, release your mouse button.

   Flash displays your shape on the stage.

---

**POWER USERS' CLINIC**

## Rectangle and Oval Primitives

Flash has two special shapes: the rectangle and oval *primitives*. What makes these guys so primitive, and where and how should you use them? When you draw a rectangle or an oval using the standard tools, Flash just considers them shapes. You see one as having corners and the other curves, but to Flash they're pretty much the same. When you draw them in merge mode, you can chop standard ovals and rectangles into little irregularly shaped pieces.

Primitives behave like graphics drawn in object mode. And as with the shapes drawn in object mode, you can adjust the width and height of the objects by typing measurements in the Properties panel. When they're in the hands of an ActionScript programmer, these primitives can really jump through hoops.

Primitives are different in that you can't erase part of a primitive or break it into parts. It's all or nothing. In spite of their object-drawn nature, primitives have some special features that you also find in merge-mode graphics. For example, using the Properties panel, you can add rounded or beveled corners to your rectangle primitives. With the Oval primitive, you can create pie slices by defining the arc angles. You can perform these feats with merge-mode shapes and primitives, but not with object-mode shapes.

Draw a rectangle, and then select it. Look in the Properties panel. If you drew it in object mode, then the Properties panel lists it as a drawing object. Otherwise, it describes it as a shape. Now draw a rectangle using the Rectangle Primitive tool. Sure enough, the Properties panel describes it as a rectangle primitive.

---

**TIP**   To create a perfectly round circle or a perfectly square square, simply hold down the Shift key while you drag to create your shape. If you want to create beveled or rounded corners, then before you release the mouse button, press the up or down arrow keys.

---

## Aligning Objects with the Align Tools

Sometimes dragging stuff around the stage and eyeballing the result works just fine. Other times, you want to position your graphic elements with pinpoint precision. Using the Align panel, you can align graphic elements based on their edges (top, bottom, right, left) or by their centers. And you can base this alignment on the objects themselves (for example, you can line up the tops of all your objects) or relative to the stage (useful if you want to position, say, several Freddy Flash heads precisely at the bottom of the stage, as shown in Figure 2-23). You can even distribute individual objects evenly with respect to one another.

To display the Align panel, select Window→Align or press Ctrl+K (Windows) or ⌘-K (Mac).

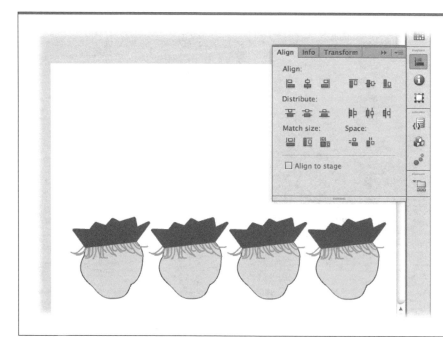

**FIGURE 2-23**

*The Align panel gives you the opportunity to align a single object (or whole groups of selected objects) along the left side, right side, top, or bottom of the stage, and more. First select Modify→Align→To Stage. Select the objects you want to align, and then click the alignment icon from the Align panel.*

## Erasing Mistakes with the Eraser Tool

Only in the digital realm does an eraser work so effectively. Try erasing a goof on paper or canvas, and you not only have shredded eraser everywhere, but you're also left with ghostly streaks of paint, lead, or charcoal.

Not so in Flash. Using the Eraser tool (Figure 2-24), you can effectively wipe anything off the stage, from a little speck to your entire drawing.

> **NOTE**  Using the Eraser tool is similar to selecting Edit→Undo only in the sense that they both remove objects from your drawing. The difference: Edit→Undo tells Flash to work sequentially backward to undo your last actions or changes, the most recent one first. The Eraser tool, on the other hand, lets you wipe stuff off the stage regardless of the order in which you added it.

To use the Eraser tool:

1. **In the Tools section of the Tools panel, click the Eraser tool to select it.**

   Your cursor changes to the size and shape of eraser Flash assumes you want. To make your eraser larger or smaller, head to the Options section at the bottom of the Tools panel and, from the Eraser Shape pop-up menu (Figure 2-25), select the eraser size and shape you want. (You want a nice fat eraser if you have a lot to erase, or a skinny one if you're just touching up the edges of a drawing.)

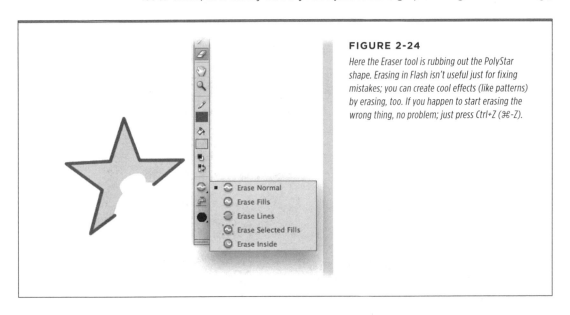

**FIGURE 2-24**

*Here the Eraser tool is rubbing out the PolyStar shape. Erasing in Flash isn't useful just for fixing mistakes; you can create cool effects (like patterns) by erasing, too. If you happen to start erasing the wrong thing, no problem; just press Ctrl+Z (⌘-Z).*

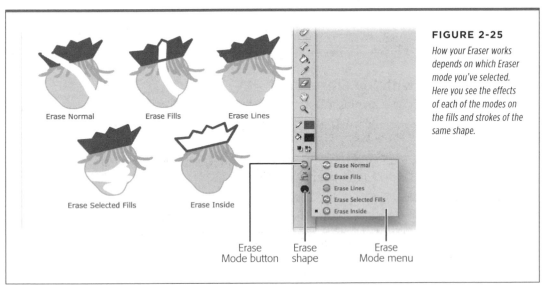

**FIGURE 2-25**

*How your Eraser works depends on which Eraser mode you've selected. Here you see the effects of each of the modes on the fills and strokes of the same shape.*

2. **On the stage, click where you want to begin erasing, and drag your cursor back and forth.**

Flash erases everything your cursor touches (or not, depending on the Eraser mode you've chosen—see the following section for details).

**TIP** To erase a line or a fill in one fell swoop, click the Faucet option, and then click the line or fill you want to erase. To erase everything on the stage and the Pasteboard (the area surrounding the stage), double-click the Eraser icon on the Tools panel.

### ■ CONFIGURING THE ERASER

Flash has a ton of Eraser modes you can use to control how the Eraser tool works (and what it erases).

**NOTE** The Eraser tool works only on editable objects. It doesn't work on closed groups or symbols. To remove grouped objects and symbols, click them with the Selection tool and then press Delete.

To see them, click the Erase Mode button in the Options area (Figure 2-25), and then, from the fly-out menu that appears, select one of the following modes:

- **Erase Normal.** Flash uses this mode unless you tell it otherwise. When you erase over an existing object on the stage using Erase Normal, Flash erases everything, fill and stroke included.

- **Erase Fill.** When you erase over an existing object on the stage using Erase Fill, only the fill portion of the object disappears.

- **Erase Lines.** When you erase over an existing object on the stage using Erase Lines, only the stroke portion of the object disappears.

- **Erase Selected Fills.** When you erase over an existing object on the stage using Erase Selected Fills, you erase only those parts of the object that are both fills and that you've previously selected (using one of the selection tools described on page 61).

**NOTE** Oddly enough, if you configure your eraser to Erase Selected Fills and then rub your virtual eraser over *non*-selected fills, Flash pretends to erase them—until you let up on your mouse, when they pop right back onto the stage.

- **Erase Inside.** If you erase over an existing object on the stage using Erase Inside, Flash erases the inside (fill) of the object as long as you begin erasing inside the stroke outline; if you begin erasing outside the line, it erases only outside the line.

### ■ CUTTING OUT AN IRREGULAR SHAPE FROM ANOTHER OBJECT

You can cut an irregular shape out of the middle of an object using the Eraser tool. If you're going for precision, for example, then you can use an eraser with a small head to outline the area you're erasing and then use the Faucet tool to quickly erase the rest. For example, say you want to draw a donut. Here's how:

1. **Select the Oval tool on the Tools panel.**

   If you don't see the Oval tool, it's probably hiding under the Rectangle tool or the PolyStar tool. Notice the little triangle that indicates that there are more options on the menu? Make sure you choose the Oval tool and not the Oval Primitive tool. The Oval Primitive tool has a dot in the center.

2. **Drag out a decent-sized oval on the stage.**

   You're drawing a donut, so there's no need to make a perfect circle, but do make it large enough so that you can cut out a donut hole.

3. **On the Tools panel, click the Eraser tool.**

   When you move the cursor over the stage, you see that it's changed to a black dot. That's the Eraser, and the dot cursor shows how big the eraser head is.

4. **In the Options section at the bottom of the Tools panel, choose a small eraser head.**

   At the bottom of the Tools panel is the drop-down menu that sets the size and shape of the Eraser.

5. **Using the Eraser, draw a circle within your oval to outline the donut hole.**

   As you drag, the fill color disappears, and you see the stage color beneath. (Make sure you complete the circle, or the Faucet will erase the entire fill color in your donut.)

6. **On the Tools panel, click the Faucet, and then click the donut hole.**

   The rest of the donut hole disappears as the Faucet tool erases all the fill color from inside the cutout.

# ■ Copying and Pasting Drawn Objects

Copying graphic elements and pasting them—into the same frame, into another frame, or even into another document—is much faster than drawing new objects from scratch. It's also the most familiar. If you've ever copied text in a word processing or spreadsheet document and pasted it somewhere else, then you know the drill.

A simple copy-and-paste is the best way to go when you're experimenting—for example, when you want to see whether the blue-eyed wallaby you drew for one animation looks good in another. But if you're trying to keep your animation's finished file size as small as possible, or if you plan to include more than one copy of that wallaby, copying and pasting *isn't* the best way to go. Instead, you'll want to look into symbols (page 248).

To copy and paste an image:

1. **On the stage, select the image you want to copy.**

   Page 61 gives you an overview of the selection tools. In Figure 2-26, Freddy Flash is selected.

2. **Choose Edit→Copy (or press Ctrl+C in Windows, ⌘-C on the Mac).** Then select the keyframe into which you want to paste the image.

   You can paste the image in the keyframe you're in, or you can select another one. Flash doesn't restrict you to the document you currently have open; you can open another document to paste the image into.

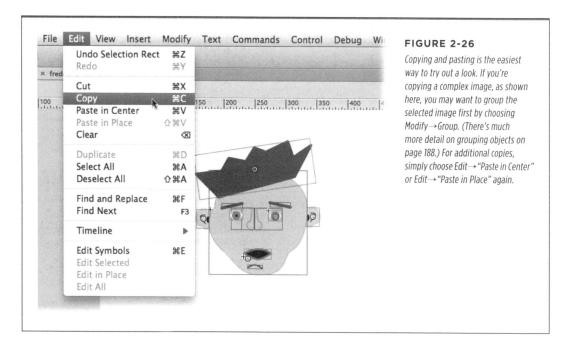

**FIGURE 2-26**

*Copying and pasting is the easiest way to try out a look. If you're copying a complex image, as shown here, you may want to group the selected image first by choosing Modify→Group. (There's much more detail on grouping objects on page 188.) For additional copies, simply choose Edit→"Paste in Center" or Edit→"Paste in Place" again.*

3. **Choose one of the Paste commands.** Here are your options:

   - **Edit→Paste in Center.** Tells Flash to paste the image in the center of the viewing area.

   - **Edit→Paste in Place.** Tells Flash to paste the image in the same spot it was on the original stage. (If you choose this option to paste an image to the same stage as the original, then you need to drag the pasted copy off the original to see it.)

   - **Edit→Paste Special (Windows only).** Displays a Paste Special dialog box that lets you paste an image as a device-independent bitmap (an uneditable version of your image with a fixed background the size and shape of the selection box).

Flash pastes your image based on your selection, leaving your original copy intact.

**NOTE** If all you want to do is make a quick copy of an image on the same stage as the original, then Flash gives you an easier way than copying and pasting. Select Edit→Duplicate (or press Ctrl+D in Windows, ⌘-D on the Mac). When you do, Flash pastes a copy of the image just a little below and to the right of your original image, ready for you to reposition as you see fit. For the fastest duplication method of all, with the Selection tool, just Alt-drag (Option-drag) the item you want to copy. The original stays put, and you have a duplicate attached to your cursor. You can then drag the duplicate wherever you want on the stage.

# ■ Adding Color

The Colors section of the Tools panel lets you choose the colors for your strokes and fills. Before you click one of the drawing icons to begin drawing (or afterward, to change existing colors), you can click either of the Stroke or Fill icons in the Colors section to bring up a color palette, as shown in Figure 2-27. Choose a color from the color palette, and Flash applies that color to the objects you draw.

**FIGURE 2-27**

*Before you begin drawing with the Pen or Pencil tools (both of which let you create strokes), you can choose the color of the Pen or Pencil by clicking the Stroke Color icon and then selecting a color from the palette that appears. If you want to change that color when you use the Brush tool (which creates fills), then you need to click the Fill Color icon (and select a color) before you click the Brush tool and begin to draw.*

## Changing the Color of a Stroke (Line)

One of the best things about drawing in Flash is how easy it is to change things around. If you draw a bright orange line using the Pencil tool, for example, you can change that line an instant later to spruce, chartreuse, or puce (and then back to orange again) with just a few simple mouse clicks.

**NOTE** In Flash, all lines are made up of strokes. The Flash drawing tools that produce strokes include the Pencil, the Pen, the Line, and the shape tools (Oval, Rectangle, and PolyStar).

Flash gives you two different ways to change the color of a stroke: the Properties panel and the Ink Bottle tool.

## COLORING STROKES WITH THE PROPERTIES PANEL

Changing the color of a stroke using the Properties panel is best for situations when you want to change the color of a single stroke or when you want to change more than just the color of a stroke (for example, you want to change the stroke thickness or the color of the fill inside the stroke).

To change the color of a stroke using the Properties panel:

1. **On the stage, select the stroke you want to change.**

   A highlight appears around or on the selected stroke.

2. **If the Properties panel isn't open, press Ctrl+F3 (⌘-F3).**

   The Properties panel shows settings related to the stroke, as shown in Figure 2-28.

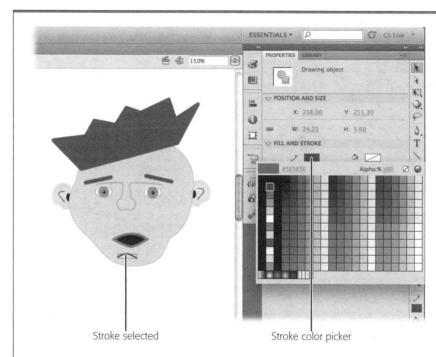

Stroke selected          Stroke color picker

**FIGURE 2-28**

*Using the Properties panel is a quick and easy way to change the color of a single stroke. First, select the stroke you want to recolor; then, in the Properties panel, click the Stroke Color icon. When you do, the color picker appears, complete with any custom color swatches you've added to it (if any). The instant you choose a color, the color picker disappears and the selected stroke changes to the new color. Here the Fill Color icon has a slash through it, meaning that no fill color is currently selected.*

3. **In the Properties panel, click the Stroke Color icon.**

   The color picker appears.

4. **Click a new color for your selected stroke.**

   The color picker disappears, and Flash displays your stroke using the new color you chose.

## ■ COLORING STROKES WITH THE INK BOTTLE TOOL

The Ink Bottle tool is great for situations when you want to apply the same color to a bunch of different strokes in one fell swoop.

To change the color of a stroke (or several strokes) using the Ink Bottle tool:

1. **In the Tools panel, click the Ink Bottle or press S.**

   The Ink Bottle and the Paint Bucket share the same Tools panel button. If the Ink Bottle isn't showing, click and hold the Paint Bucket until you see the fly-out menu, as shown in Figure 2-29, and then select the Ink Bottle tool. Now, as you mouse over the stage, you notice that your cursor looks like a little ink bottle.

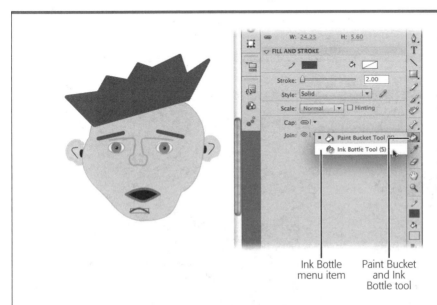

**FIGURE 2-29**

*Use the Ink Bottle tool to change the color strokes. To change the color of strokes one by one, you don't need to select them first; simply click them with the Ink Bottle tool. If you want to change several strokes at once, preselect the bunch, and then click on any one with the Ink Bottle.*

Ink Bottle menu item

Paint Bucket and Ink Bottle tool

2. **In the Properties panel, click the Stroke Color swatch (Figure 2-30).**

   The color picker appears, and as you mouse over the different colors, you notice that your cursor looks like a tiny eyedropper.

3. **Click a color to choose it.**

   The color picker disappears, and Flash changes the Stroke Color swatch to match your selection.

4. **Click the strokes you want to recolor.**

   Flash changes the color of the strokes to match the stroke color in the Properties panel.

# Changing the Color of a Fill

If you change your mind about the color of any of the fills you add to the stage, no problem. Flash gives you several ways to change the color of a fill, including the Properties panel and the Paint Bucket tool.

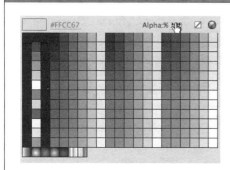

**FIGURE 2-30**

*Clicking the Stroke Color icon displays the color picker. All of Flash's color pickers work the same. Here you can change not just the hue, but also the transparency of the color. To do so, click the number in the Alpha box and type in a new percentage or drag right or left to "scrub" in a new value. Numbers from 0%, (completely transparent) to 100% (completely opaque) are valid.*

> **NOTE** The Flash drawing tools that produce fills include the Brush tool and all the shape tools (Oval, Oval Primitive, Rectangle, Rectangle Primitive, and PolyStar).

## ■ COLORING FILLS WITH THE PROPERTIES PANEL

Using the Properties panel to change the color of a fill is great for situations when you want to change more than just fill color—for example, you want to change both the fill color and the color of the stroke outline surrounding the fill.

To change the color of a fill using the Properties panel:

1. **On the stage, select the object you want to change.**

   The selected object is highlighted.

2. **If the Properties panel isn't open, go to Window→Properties to open it.**

   The Properties panel, similar to the one in Figure 2-31, appears.

3. **In the Properties panel, click the Fill Color icon.**

   The color picker appears.

4. **Click to choose a new color for your selected fill.**

   As soon as you let go of your mouse button, the color picker disappears, and Flash displays your fill using the color you chose.

**NOTE** To change the color of a bunch of fills quickly, select the fills you want to recolor, and then select the Fill Color icon and choose a new color. When you do, Flash automatically displays all your selected fills using your new color.

### ■ COLORING FILLS WITH THE PAINT BUCKET TOOL

The Paint Bucket tool is great for situations when you want to apply the same color to one or more fills on the stage, either one fill at a time or all at once.

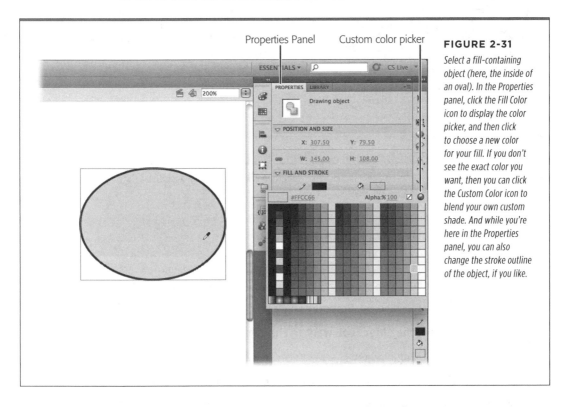

Properties Panel    Custom color picker

**FIGURE 2-31**

*Select a fill-containing object (here, the inside of an oval). In the Properties panel, click the Fill Color icon to display the color picker, and then click to choose a new color for your fill. If you don't see the exact color you want, then you can click the Custom Color icon to blend your own custom shade. And while you're here in the Properties panel, you can also change the stroke outline of the object, if you like.*

To change the color of a fill using the Paint Bucket tool:

1. **In the Tools panel, select the Fill Color icon (Figure 2-32).**

   The color picker appears, and as you mouse over the different colors, you notice that your cursor looks like a tiny eyedropper.

## 2. Click a color to choose it.

The color picker disappears, and Flash redisplays the Fill Color icon using the color you just selected.

## 3. On the stage, click the fill(s) you want to recolor.

Flash recolors each fill you click, as shown in Figure 2-32.

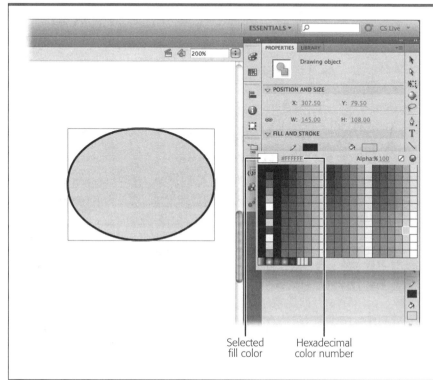

Selected fill color

Hexadecimal color number

**FIGURE 2-32**

*Click the Fill Color icon to choose a new color for your fills. As you move your cursor around the color picker, you notice that the Preview window displays the color your cursor happens to be over at any given time.*

**NOTE** If you don't have a completely closed outline around your fill, Flash might not let you apply a fill color. To tell Flash to ignore small gaps (or medium or even relatively large gaps) surrounding your fill, in the Options section of the Tools panel (Figure 2-33), click Gap Size. Then, from the pop-up menu that appears, turn on the checkbox next to Close Small Gaps, Close Medium Gaps, or Close Large Gaps. Then try to modify your fill again. (You may also want to consider closing the gap yourself using one of Flash's drawing tools.)

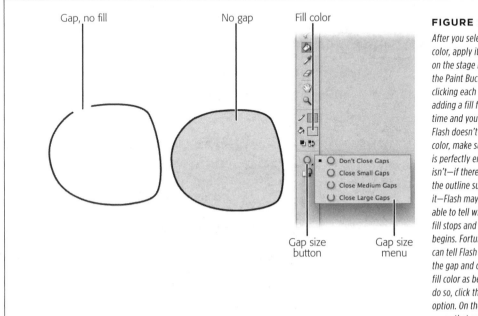

Gap, no fill    No gap    Fill color

Gap size button    Gap size menu

Don't Close Gaps
Close Small Gaps
Close Medium Gaps
Close Large Gaps

**FIGURE 2-33**

*After you select a new fill color, apply it to the fills on the stage by clicking the Paint Bucket and clicking each fill. If you're adding a fill for the first time and you find that Flash doesn't add your fill color, make sure your fill is perfectly enclosed. If it isn't—if there's a gap in the outline surrounding it—Flash may not be able to tell where your fill stops and the stage begins. Fortunately, you can tell Flash to ignore the gap and change your fill color as best it can. To do so, click the Gap Size option. On the fly-out menu that appears, choose Close Small (or Medium, or Large) Gaps.*

# Animate Your Art

I n the olden days of animation, artists had to create a drawing for each frame of a movie by hand. Sure, they had their shortcuts, but since most movie frames click by at 24 frames per second, that's a labor-intensive endeavor. To keep costs down, animation production companies had their best, highest-paid artists draw the most important images, where major changes took place, and then had lesser talents and beginners draw the in-between images. Those most important images are known as *keyframes*. The in-betweeners are called *tweens*.

This chapter is your introduction to keyframes and tweens from Flash's point of view. In this case, you're the high-paid artist who gets to create the keyframes, while your computer does the grunt work of drawing all the tweens. You'll learn about two types of tweens—the motion tween and the shape tween. But first, you need to understand the various types of frames you see in Flash's timeline.

**NOTE** "Tween" is one of those words that makes you smile—it just sounds funny. It's even funnier when you realize that it's used as both a noun and a verb. Not only can you create a tween, but you can also tween a drawn object, such as a car: "I tweened the car to make it drive down the road."

## ■ Frame-by-Frame Animation

An *animation* is nothing more than a series of framed images displayed one after the other to create the illusion of motion. If you want to, you can use Flash to make your animation the old-fashioned way, by drawing each frame individually. Whether you animate frame by frame or use computer-generated tweens, you need to be able to decode the timeline symbols to understand how your animation works. Figure 3-1 shows some of the hieroglyphics you'll find on the timeline. Here are some more details:

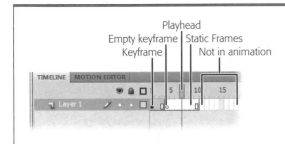

**FIGURE 3-1**

*From left to right on this little strip of timeline you see several frames. Frame 1 is a keyframe with a solid circle. Frame 4 is an empty keyframe, shown as a hollow circle. The playhead is positioned at Frame 7, and the entire animation ends at Frame 10. The rectangles from Frame 11 on are not part of this animation, even though they're visible in the timeline.*

- **Static frames** represent a unit of time. If your animation runs at 24 frames per second, then that unit is one twenty-fourth of a second. You control the timing in your animation by adding or removing frames. For example, if you want an image to remain on screen for a longer period of time, then you insert frames into the timeline. Static frames appear to be empty in the timeline—that is, they don't display any special symbol, as keyframes do.

- **Keyframes** are the important frames—the frames you designate to hold distinct images. Keyframes mark changes in your animation. For example, if you want to add text to your animation at a certain point in time, you create a keyframe in the timeline and then add the text to the stage at that point of the timeline. On the timeline, keyframes are shown as a solid circle. If there's no visible content on the stage, then you see a blank keyframe, as explained next.

- **Blank keyframes** are keyframes with no visible graphics or text in the frame. As soon as you add text or graphics to a blank keyframe, it becomes a plain old keyframe. On the timeline, a blank keyframe is shown as a hollow circle.

- **Property keyframes** come into play when you create a *motion tween*, as described on page 103. Motion tweens change the appearance of a graphic or movie clip symbol. Property keyframes are shaped like small diamonds, and they mark a change to one of the symbol's properties. On the timeline, the frames devoted to a motion tween are tinted light blue.

- **Frames not in animation.** You can't move the playhead beyond the last frame in your animation. Beyond that point, you see rectangles that represent frames not in your animation. If you want to make your animation run longer, you can add or insert frames, as explained on page 101.

As you work with your animation, you use the playhead to manage time and build your animation. Drag the playhead to Frame 15, and you see the contents of the stage at that moment in time.

## Creating a Frame-by-Frame Animation

Flash lets you animate virtually any visible object you place on the stage. You can animate cartoon-style drawings, photos, videos, or even text.

Follow these steps to see how frame-by-frame animation works:

1. **Open a blank Flash document by choosing File→New and then selecting ActionScript 3.0 and pressing OK.**

   You have a spanking new Flash document. As the timeline in Figure 3-2 shows, Flash starts you out in Layer 1, Frame 1, because initially, a Flash document has only one frame, a keyframe at Layer 1, Frame 1.

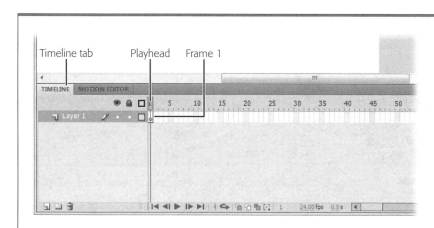

**FIGURE 3-2**

*When you create a new Flash document, Flash automatically designates Frame 1 as a blank keyframe. You can tell that Frame 1 contains a blank keyframe by the hollow circle in Frame 1 and the fact that nothing appears on the stage when the playhead is at Frame 1.*

**TIP**  If you don't see the timeline, then select Window→Timeline or use the shortcut Ctrl+Alt+T (Option-⌘-T).

   The red rectangle over Frame 1 is the *playhead*. It marks the current frame—the one displayed on the stage. When you begin a new document, you can't move the playhead until you add more frames, as described in step 3.

2. **Using Flash's painting and drawing tools, draw an image on the stage.**

   Figure 3-3 shows an example drawing of a frog with a tempting fly overhead, but you can use any drawing or shape for this exercise. As soon as you add a drawing or any visual content to a keyframe, the hollow circle fills in, becoming a solid circle. The hollow circle marks an empty keyframe (no content). The solid circle marks a keyframe with content—in other words, there are graphics displayed on the stage.

**NOTE** If you have an existing image stored on your computer, you can bring it onto the stage. Select File→Import→"Import to Stage," and then, in the Import window that appears, type in (or browse to) the name of the file you want to pull in. When you finish, click Open (Import on a Mac). (Chapter 10 covers importing files in more detail.)

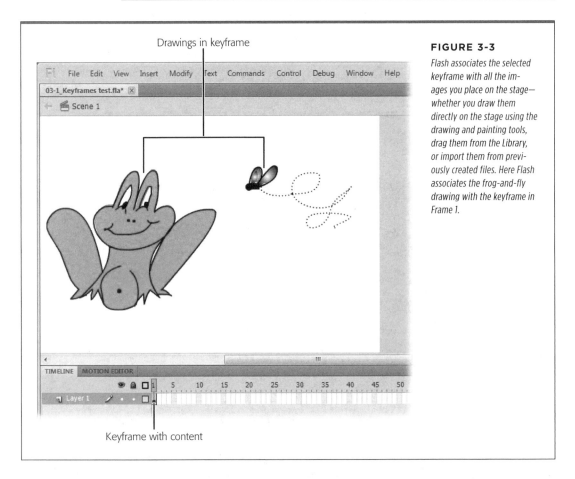

Drawings in keyframe

Keyframe with content

**FIGURE 3-3**

*Flash associates the selected keyframe with all the images you place on the stage—whether you draw them directly on the stage using the drawing and painting tools, drag them from the Library, or import them from previously created files. Here Flash associates the frog-and-fly drawing with the keyframe in Frame 1.*

3. **In the timeline, click the rectangle under the number 20.**

   Flash highlights the rectangle, as shown in Figure 3-4. Notice that the playhead doesn't move, because at this point your animation contains only one frame.

4. **Turn the selected frame into a blank keyframe by pressing F7.**

   Flash moves the playhead to the selected frame (Frame 20 in Figure 3-4), inserts a keyframe icon, and clears the stage.

**TIP** In Flash, you often have several ways to do the same thing, and that's true with inserting frames and keyframes. You can use the menu: Select Insert→Timeline and then choose Frame, Keyframe, or Blank Keyframe. Or you can right-click (Control-click) a frame in the timeline and choose one of the options from the pop-up menu.

### To Tween or Not to Tween

The great thing about creating an animation frame by frame is that it gives you the most control over the finished product. If you're looking for a super-realistic effect, for example, you may not be satisfied with the frames Flash generates when you tell it to tween (page 103). Instead, you may prefer to lovingly handcraft every single frame, making slight adjustments to lots of different objects as you go.

Say, for instance, you're creating an animation showing an outdoor barbecue. Over the course of your animation, the sun will move across the sky, which is going to change the way your characters' shadows appear. Bugs are going to fly across the scene. When one character opens his mouth to speak, the other characters won't remain static: Their hair might ripple in the breeze, they'll start conversations of their own, and they'll drop pieces of steak (which the host's dog will streak over to wolf down). You can't leave realistic, director-level details like this to Flash; you've got to create them yourself.

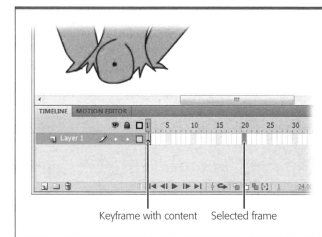

**FIGURE 3-4**

*When you click a frame in the timeline, Flash highlights it, as shown in Frame 20. At this point, the animation consists of a single frame, and it's not possible to move the playhead beyond Frame 1.*

Keyframe with content    Selected frame

5. **Draw a second image on the stage.**

   The second keyframe in Figure 3-5 shows the frog drawn again, with a thought balloon instead of a fly. But if your two images are fairly similar, then you can avoid having to completely redraw the image for your second keyframe, as you'll see in the next step.

6. **Click further out in the timeline (Frame 40, say), and press F6.**

Just as when you inserted the blank keyframe, Flash moves the playhead and inserts a keyframe icon; but instead of clearing the stage, Flash carries over the content from the previous keyframe, all ready for you to tweak and edit.

7. **Repeat the previous step to create as many keyframes as you want.**

To get the hang of frame-by-frame animation, adding two or three keyframes is plenty. But when you're building an actual animation, you'll likely need to add dozens or even hundreds of keyframes (or even more, depending on the length and complexity you're shooting for).

**FIGURE 3-5**

*Here the playhead is over the second keyframe, which tells Flash to place the content on the stage in the second keyframe (Frame 20). When it detects a new keyframe, Flash displays only the new contents, so Frames 2–19 carry forward the content from Frame 1 (the first keyframe). You can verify this behavior by dragging the playhead from Frame 20 back to Frame 1.*

Adding frames, keyframes, and blank keyframes is a recurring activity as you work in Flash. As explained in the tip on page 95, you can use menus to do the job, but it's faster and easier to remember the three function keys that do the job:

- F5: Insert a frame.

- F6: Insert a keyframe.

- F7: Insert a blank keyframe.

**NOTE** You can review the sample frog-and-fly frame-by-frame animation. Simply download *03-1_Frame-by-Frame.fla.*

## Make the Timeline Easier to Read

The timeline serves as a kind of indispensable thumbnail sketch of your animation, showing you at a glance which frames contain unique content (the keyframes) and which don't (the static frames), how many layers your animation contains (page 135), which sections of your animation contain tweens (page 103), and so on.

If you find it hard to read the timeline because everything's too small, or if you have trouble remembering what graphics are controlled by certain keyframes, there's a solution.

In the timeline's upper-right corner, click the Options menu (Figure 3-6) and experiment with some of the different options. You can make the timeline's frames larger or smaller, for example. Using the Preview options, you can set keyframes to display miniature images of the stage contents. The "Preview in Context" option shows the entire frame, while the Preview option zooms in on the visual content, sometimes making it a little larger.

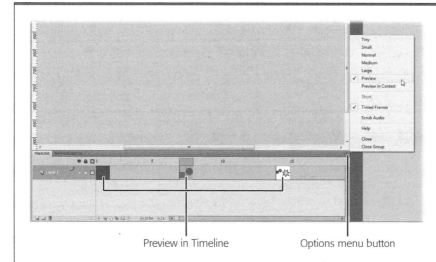

**FIGURE 3-6**

*Click the Options menu button to see the menu shown here. Use the Tiny through Large options to change the timeline's frame size. Use the Preview options to display thumbnail images in the keyframes, as shown here.*

Preview in Timeline      Options menu button

## Test Your Frame-by-Frame Animation

Sooner or later you'll want to test your animation. Sometimes you'll want to take a quick peek at a few frames to see if the mechanics are in order. Other times you'll want to review the entire animation exactly the way your audience will see it. Flash has options for both situations:

- Press **Enter (Return** on a Mac) for a quick view of your animation action. The animation plays out on the same stage where you built it. The playback begins at the playhead's position, so you don't have to watch the entire animation when you want to review only a few frames. If you prefer, you can use the menu option Control→Play.

This view doesn't always give you the same view your audience will see. For example, selected objects still appear selected, ruler guides remain visible, and objects on the backstage are still visible. If you want a more accurate view of your finished animation, then use the next viewing option.

**TIP**   Flash CS6 adds another quick way to view your animation on the stage. Click the Play button below the timeline to begin playing your animation starting from the playhead's position. In addition to the other DVD-like controls, you can use the Loop button to repeat a selected group of frames.

• Press **Ctrl+Enter (⌘-Return)** to view your animation from beginning to end for the most accurate preview. Or you can use the menu option Control→Test Movie→"in Flash Professional." Your animation opens in a window that uses *Flash Player* to display the images. This "display engine" is called a *runtime*, and it's similar to the engine that your audience's computers use to show your animation. Your animation starts playing at the first frame and plays all the way through to the end. When it reaches the last frame, it starts over again. This is called *looping*, and you can turn it off in the Flash Player window by choosing Control→Loop (Figure 3-7) or right-clicking (Control-clicking) the animation.

This viewing method takes a little longer, but it's the most accurate way to view your animation. You're actually seeing what your audience will eventually see, from beginning to end.

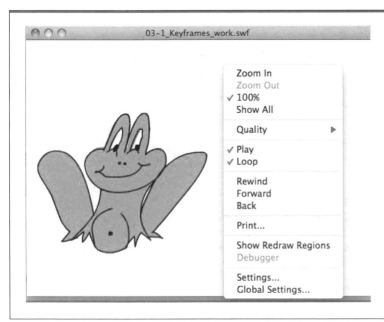

**FIGURE 3-7**

*The first time you run your animation in Flash Player, Flash assumes that you want to run it over and over (and over and over). Fortunately, you can rid Flash of this annoying assumption. Right-click (Control-click) your animation, and then click Loop to remove the checkmark. Other useful options include stopping your animation, rewinding it, and even stepping through it frame by frame. Chapter 19 covers animation testing in depth.*

# ■ Editing Your Frame-by-Frame Animation

It's rare that your first crack at any given animation will be your last. Typically, you'll start with a few keyframes, test the result, add a few frames, delete a few frames, and so on until you get precisely the look you're after.

This section shows you how to perform the basic frame-level edits you need to take your animation from rough sketch to finished production: inserting, copying, pasting, moving, and deleting frames.

## Selecting Frames and Keyframes

Selecting a single frame or keyframe is as easy as zipping down to the timeline and clicking the frame or keyframe you want to select.

But if you want to select multiple frames, Flash gives you four additional selection alternatives:

- **To select multiple contiguous frames.** Drag your mouse over a group of frames you want to select. The selected frames show a highlight, as shown in Figure 3-8. Be careful though: If the first frame you click is already selected, you may move that frame instead of selecting multiples. Alternatively, click the first frame you want to select, and then Shift-click the last frame.

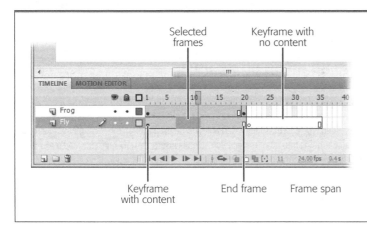

Selected frames     Keyframe with no content

Keyframe with content     End frame     Frame span

**FIGURE 3-8**

*To select a single frame (including a keyframe), simply click the frame. To select multiple frames, drag or choose one of Flash's other two multiple-frame-selection options. A frame span comprises a keyframe, an end frame, and all the frames in between. If you've added multiple layers to your animation, then make sure you select frames from the correct layer.*

**NOTE**   Sometimes dragging to select frames can be hazardous to your animation's health. You can move frames in the timeline by clicking and dragging. If you're not careful, you may end up moving frames when you simply meant to select them.

- **To select multiple noncontiguous frames.** Ctrl-click (⌘-click) each frame you want to select.

- **To select an entire frame span.** Double-click any frame in the *frame span*. A frame span starts with a keyframe and ends with the end frame marker, as shown in Figure 3-8.

- **To select all the frames on a layer.** Click the name of the layer. In the example in Figure 3-8, clicking Fly automatically selects all the frames in the Fly layer.

No matter which method you use, Flash highlights the frames to let you know you've successfully selected them.

## Inserting and Deleting Keyframes and Frames

The smoothness of your finished animation depends on timing, and timing is controlled by the number of keyframes and regular frames you've included. This section shows you how to add and delete both.

### ■ INSERTING KEYFRAMES

Typically, you'll start with a handful of keyframes and need to insert additional keyframes to smooth out the animation and make it appear more realistic (less herky-jerky).

For example, say you're working on an animation showing a dog wagging its tail. You've got a keyframe showing the tail to the left of the dog, one showing the tail straight behind the dog, and a final keyframe showing the tail to the right of the dog. You test the animation and it looks okay, but a little primitive.

Inserting additional keyframes showing the dog's tail in additional positions (just a bit to the left of the dog's rump, a little bit further to the left, a little further, and then all the way to the left) will make the finished sequence look much more detailed and realistic.

---

**NOTE** Technically speaking, you don't actually *insert* a keyframe even though the Flash menus call it that. In most cases, you turn a regular frame into a keyframe. If you actually inserted a new keyframe, you'd be making your timeline longer and changing the timing of your animation.

---

To insert a keyframe into an existing animation:

1. **In the timeline, select the regular frame you want to turn into a keyframe.**

   If you want to add a keyframe midway between Frame 1 and Frame 20 on Layer 1, for example, then click in Layer 1 to select Frame 10, as shown in Figure 3-9.

   Flash moves the playhead to the frame you selected.

2. **Press F6 (or choose Insert→Timeline→Keyframe) to tell Flash to carry over the content from the previous keyframe so you can edit it.** As an alternative, press F7 or (or choose Insert→Timeline→Blank Keyframe) to tell Flash to clear the stage.

   On the stage, Flash either displays the image associated with the previous keyframe or, if you inserted a blank keyframe, displays nothing at all.

3. **Using the drawing and painting tools, add content for your new keyframe to the stage.**

If you've already created drawings in another program, you can import them, as described on page 351.

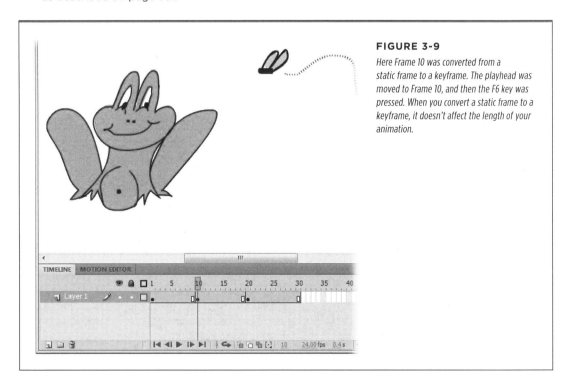

**FIGURE 3-9**

*Here Frame 10 was converted from a static frame to a keyframe. The playhead was moved to Frame 10, and then the F6 key was pressed. When you convert a static frame to a keyframe, it doesn't affect the length of your animation.*

### ■ INSERTING STATIC FRAMES

Regular frames in Flash act as placeholders; they mark time while the contents of the previous keyframe are displayed. Without regular frames to stretch it out, your audience would have only a twenty-fourth of a second to see the image! Insert additional frames when you want to slow down the action a little. In fact, inserting frames is sort of like having a director yell, "Hold camera!" with the contents of the last keyframe remaining onscreen.

To insert a frame into an existing animation:

1. **In the timeline, click to select the frame after which you want to add a frame.**

   Flash moves the playhead to the frame you selected. Make sure the stage shows the graphics you want to hold onscreen.

2. **Choose Insert→Timeline→Frame (or press F5).**

   Flash inserts a new frame *after* the frame you selected, bumping up the total number of frames in your animation by one.

If your animation runs at the standard 24 frames per second, then inserting a single frame doesn't change the timing all that much. Often you want to insert several static frames. If you want to insert five static frames, select any five regular frames and then press F5. (When you insert multiple frames, they're always inserted at the beginning point of your selection.)

### ■ CLEARING A KEYFRAME

As explained on page 93, keyframes mark the points in your animation where you've added unique content to the stage. If you want to remove that unique content, you *clear* the keyframe. Once cleared, the frame and the following frame span show the content from the previous keyframe. Clearing a keyframe doesn't change the length of the animation—that is, you aren't removing any frames.

To clear a keyframe and turn it back into a static frame:

1. **Right-click (Control-click) the keyframe you want to clear.**

   The playhead moves to that keyframe, and the frame is highlighted. A pop-up menu appears with several frame-related options.

2. **Choose Clear Keyframe.**

   Flash demotes the frame from a keyframe to a plain old static frame. Any special content the frame had is relegated to the bit bucket.

---

**TIP**  Clearing a keyframe means you lose anything you've drawn or imported to the stage for that keyframe. If your immediate reaction after clearing a keyframe is "Oops!" then press Ctrl+Z (⌘-Z) to undo the action. Then you can save that worthy drawing or graphic to a symbol (page 248) or a separate file (page 699).

---

### ■ DELETING FRAMES

Deleting frames—like inserting them—lets you control the pace of your animation. But instead of making your animation run longer, the way inserting frames does, deleting frames shrinks the timeline and makes your animation run shorter.

For example, say you're working on the animation showing a frog catching a fly. You've created three keyframes: one showing the frog noticing the fly, one showing the frog actually catching the fly, and one showing the frog enjoying the fly. If you space out these three keyframes evenly (say, at Frame 1, Frame 15, and Frame 30), then all three images spend the same amount of time onscreen. That's perfectly serviceable—but you can create a much more realistic effect by shortening the number of frames between the second and third keyframes (in other words, by deleting a bunch of frames between Frame 15 and Frame 30 to speed up the portion of the animation where the frog's tongue snags the fly).

To delete frames:

1. **In the timeline, select the frame (or frames) you want to delete.**

   Flash highlights the selected frame(s) and moves the playhead to the last selected frame.

2. **Right-click (Control-click) the selection, and choose Remove Frames from the pop-up menu.**

Flash deletes the selected frames and shortens the timeline by the number of deleted frames.

## Making It Move with Motion Tweens

There are a lot of fun things you can do in Flash, but one that's sure to put a smile on your face is the *motion tween*. Using the motion tween, it's surprisingly easy to make the objects in your animation move, change shape, change color, or fade to nothingness. The first step is to convert the graphics you want to tween to Flash symbols; then you can change the properties of the symbols at any given point in time—or more specifically, at any point along the timeline. For example, if you have a redwood tree and you want to make it grow, you'd change the height (H) property. Next, in Frame 12 you might set the H property to, say, 100 (pixels), and then set it to 150 in Frame 24, 200 in Frame 36, and so on. The tree appears to grow before your audience's eyes. Want to move a car across the stage? Just change the X and Y properties, which set the position on the stage, to create the illusion of movement. (For a rundown on the X/Y coordinate system, see the box below.)

Chapter 1 showed you how to apply the bounce-smoosh motion preset to a wheel symbol. Motion presets are motion tweens that are predesigned to create certain effects. In the case of bounce-smoosh, it made the wheel drop from the top of the stage to the bottom. When it hit ground, it squashed like a cartoon character and then bounced a couple of times until it came to rest. In the next few exercises, you will create your own version of the bounce-smoosh tween.

---

**UP TO SPEED**

### Use X/Y Coordinates to Set Stage Position

In the computer world, it's a common practice to use the letters X and Y to locate a point in two-dimensional space. X marks the horizontal position, while Y marks the vertical position. It's exactly like the graphs you learned about in algebra class.

Every point on the Flash stage has a specific X/Y coordinate, as shown in Figure 3-10, and the unit of measurement is pixels. The numbering starts in the upper-left corner, where X = 0 and Y = 0. That's usually expressed as *0,0* with the X coor-

dinate coming first. So, if your stage is 550 x 400 pixels, the upper-right corner is 550,0. Dead center is 275,200. Anything displayed on the stage, whether it's an image, symbol, or text block, has a *registration point*, which looks like a tiny cross (+) and positions the object on the stage. When you set the X and Y properties for a line, shape, symbol, or text block, you're positioning that registration point. Page 253 has more details on registration points.

---

1. **Open *03-2_Motion_Tween.fla*.**

The new document opens, and you see an empty stage.

**NOTE** As always, you can find the sample file on the Missing CD page: *www.missingmanuals.com/cds/flashcs6mm.*

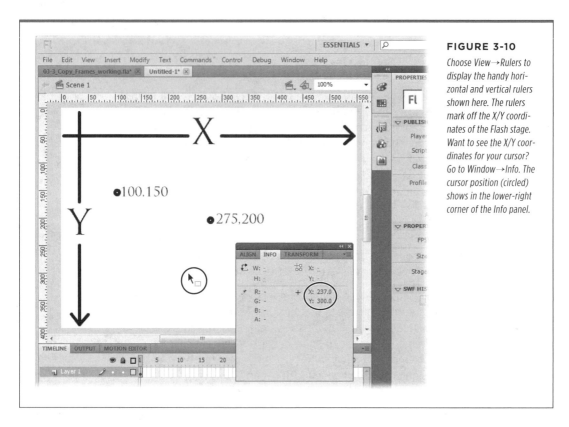

**FIGURE 3-10**

*Choose View→Rulers to display the handy horizontal and vertical rulers shown here. The rulers mark off the X/Y coordinates of the Flash stage. Want to see the X/Y coordinates for your cursor? Go to Window→Info. The cursor position (circled) shows in the lower-right corner of the Info panel.*

2. **In the Panels dock, click the Library tab.**

   As shown in Figure 3-11, the Library is your warehouse for graphics you want to reuse. There are three items in this Library. For now, focus your attention on the Wheel symbol.

3. **In the Library, click the word "Wheel."**

   The wheel appears in the Library's preview window. Notice that images in the Library have different icons next to their names. The gear icon indicates that the wheel is a movie clip symbol. The icon for StairStep shows three different shapes, indicating that it's a graphic icon. You'll learn about the subtle differences between symbols on page 248.

4. **Drag the wheel to the top of the stage.**

   When you drag a symbol from the Library to the stage, you're creating an *instance* of the symbol. The original remains safe in the Library, where it can be used again. You can change the size, color, and other properties of your wheel instance without affecting the original.

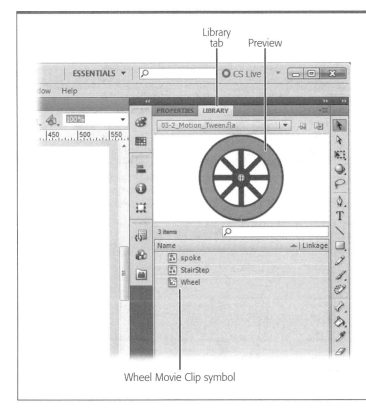

Library
tab    Preview

Wheel Movie Clip symbol

**FIGURE 3-11**

*Click the Library tab to see the symbols stored in your Flash document. Click a symbol's name to see it previewed at the top of the panel. In Flash, symbols can be movie clips, graphics, or buttons. They have a number of special abilities, one of which is the ability to work with the motion tween.*

5. **With the wheel on the stage selected, choose Insert→Motion Tween.**

   In the timeline, several frames are added to Layer 1, and the background color for the span changes to blue, the color for a motion tween. The playhead automatically moves to the last frame in the tween.

   **NOTE**  Flash can't tween an image unless it's a symbol (page 248). If you try to apply a tween to an object that's not a symbol, Flash asks if you want it converted to a symbol.

6. **Drag the wheel to the bottom of the stage.**

   After you drag the wheel to a new position, a dotted line marks the path from the first position to the last (Figure 3-12). This is the motion path, and each dot represents a frame in the animation. A small diamond appears in the last frame of the timeline. The diamond marks the point for a *property keyframe*, indicating that one of the wheel's properties changed.

**7. Press Enter (Return).**

You see the result of your first motion tween as the wheel moves along the motion path. You can drag the playhead along the timeline to see the position of the wheel at any frame—or in other words, at any point in time. Animators and filmmakers call dragging the playhead manually *scrubbing*.

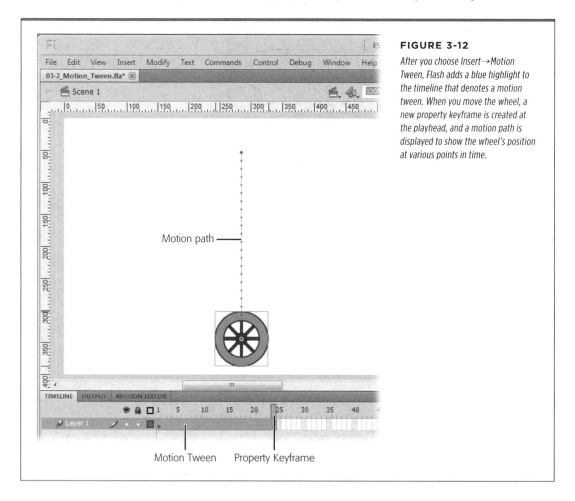

**FIGURE 3-12**

*After you choose Insert→Motion Tween, Flash adds a blue highlight to the timeline that denotes a motion tween. When you move the wheel, a new property keyframe is created at the playhead, and a motion path is displayed to show the wheel's position at various points in time.*

For another way to grasp how the motion tween works, examine your symbol's properties. Click the Properties tab and then click the wheel on the stage. In the Properties panel, the Y property (under Position and Size) marks the vertical position of the wheel on the stage. Drag the playhead to a new position, and then select the wheel again. The value of the Y property changes to show the wheel's current position.

The motion tween uses property keyframes, which are similar to standard keyframes except that they track all the individual properties of an object during a tween. For example, property keyframes keep track of the wheel symbol's X and Y coordinates. You animate the symbol by making adjustments to these properties in different frames. It's a two-step process: Move the playhead to mark the point in time, and then change the property. When you change the property, Flash automatically creates a property keyframe in the timeline. In the previous example, Flash automatically moved the playhead when you created the motion tween. You manually changed the Y (position) property when you moved the wheel. In the next example, you'll change the shape of the wheel by adjusting the W (width) and H (height) properties in the Properties panel.

## Tweening a Symbol's Dimension Properties

The steps on page 103 showed how to animate the beginning of the bounce-smoosh—the drop. The next step is to add some smoosh. To do so, you need to make the wheel wider and shorter at the moment of impact. To begin, you want to extend the tween and the timeline beyond the bottommost point of the bounce.

> **NOTE** This exercise continues the exercise begun on page 103.

1. **Click the frame that's four frames beyond the end frame of the tween.**

   The tween ends where the blue highlight ends.

2. **Choose Insert→Timeline→Frame or press F5.**

   Frames are added to the end of the animation, and the blue highlight of a motion tween extends to the new end point.

3. **Drag the playhead to the last frame in the tween.**

   On the stage, the wheel looks like it did in the previous frame. That won't last long as you begin to fiddle with the properties in the next step.

4. **Click the Properties tab, and then click the wheel on the stage.**

   The Properties panel displays the wheel's properties, as shown in Figure 3-13. Note that the H and W properties for the perfectly round wheel are 85 pixels—you'll use this number later.

> **TIP** Don't forget to click the wheel if you want to examine the wheel properties. Otherwise, you may be looking at the properties for the document, the frame, or even the tween itself.

5. **In the Properties panel, under Position and Size, change the W property to 150.** Then change the H property to *60*.

   You can change properties by clicking and typing in a new number, or you can click and drag to scrub in a new value.

6. **Press Enter (Return) to test the animation.**

   The wheel gradually changes shape from a perfect circle to an oval (Figure 3-14); however, it begins changing shape at the very beginning of the animation. For a proper smoosh, it should change shape on impact with the ground. You can accomplish that with a couple of property tweaks.

7. **Drag the playhead back to the first diamond-shaped property keyframe.**
Select the wheel and change the W and H properties to 85 by 85 pixels.

The wheel returns to its pristine, perfectly round shape.

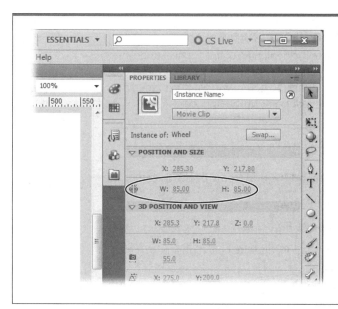

**FIGURE 3-13**

*Select an object on the stage, and you see the W (width) and H (height) properties in the Properties panel. Here the wheel X and Y properties (circled) are set to 85 pixels. When the chain link icon to the left is broken, you can change the W and H properties independently; otherwise, changing one dimension automatically changes the other, keeping an object's proportions. Click the chain link to toggle it on or off.*

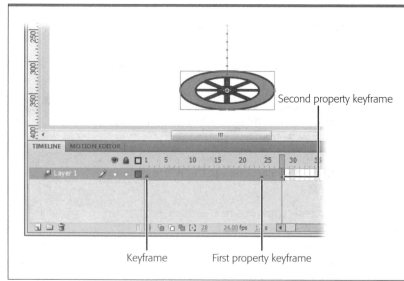

Second property keyframe

Keyframe          First property keyframe

**FIGURE 3-14**

*Every animation begins with a keyframe (round icon). This motion tween also has two property keyframes (diamond icon) that hold values for the position and shape of the wheel. With the playhead positioned at the second property keyframe, you see the wheel smooshed because the W (width) property is set to 150 and the H (height) property is set to 60.*

8. **Press Enter (Return) to test the animation.**

Now, when the animation plays, the wheel retains its roundness until it reaches the bottom of the motion. Then it appears to flatten as it hits the ground.

Flash automatically makes the height and width changes occur smoothly and evenly. Originally, that transition started in Frame 1 and continued through the final frame of the tween. By making the H and W properties identical in Frame 1 and the first property keyframe, the height and width remain the same at the beginning, and the shape change at the end of the animation is faster and more dramatic.

### ■ CHANGING DIMENSIONS WITH THE TRANSFORM TOOL

The steps on page 107 show how to change an object's dimensions using the H and W properties, which are accurate down to the pixel. But what if you prefer to eyeball it? In that case, you can change a symbol's dimensions using the Transform tool. Just make sure the playhead is at the right frame, and then press Q to choose the Transform tool. Click the symbol you want to reshape, and it sprouts handles like the ones shown in Figure 3-15. Drag the handles to modify your symbol, and Flash stores the dimensions with the property keyframe.

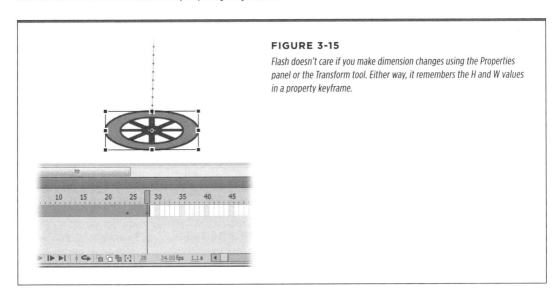

**FIGURE 3-15**

*Flash doesn't care if you make dimension changes using the Properties panel or the Transform tool. Either way, it remembers the H and W values in a property keyframe.*

Not only can you work faster and get the benefit of visual feedback with Transform, but it's also the Swiss Army knife of Flash tools. It does a lot more than just change dimensions. You can use it to skew and rotate an object, too. Go ahead and make those changes in your motion tween, and the changes are stored in the property keyframe.

## Copying and Pasting Frames

As any school kid can tell you, for every action there's a reaction. Your wheel needs to bounce back from its precarious state. In a word, it needs to de-smoosh. Ideally, you want the next five frames in the animation to be the reverse actions of the last five frames of the tween. You could do that manually, but why reinvent the wheel? (Sorry about the pun.) Instead, you can copy the last five frames, paste them back in at the end of the tween, and then reverse their order. This may sound more complicated than it really is.

> **NOTE** The next exercise follows from the steps begun on page 103. You can use the same Flash document, or download *03-3_Copy_Frames.fla* from *www.missingmanuals.com/cds/flashcs6mm*.

Here's how to copy and paste frames:

1. **Ctrl-click (⌘-click) the first property keyframe, and then drag to the last frame in the timeline.**

   The selected frames at the end of the tween show a dark blue highlight.

2. **Right-click (Control-click) the selected frames, and then choose Copy Frames from the shortcut menu.**

   There's no visual response when you copy frames in the timeline, but rest assured that the selected frames are copied and stored so you can paste them somewhere else on the timeline.

3. **Right-click (Control-click) the first frame after the tween, and then choose Paste Frames from the shortcut menu (Figure 3-16).**

   The copied frames are pasted on the end of the timeline. If you press Enter (Return) to preview your animation now, you see that the squashing frames are repeated at the end of the animation.

When you paste the frames on the end of the timeline, Flash creates a second motion tween in Layer 1. You can tell by the solid vertical line followed by a circle keyframe symbol. If you click any frames in either motion tween, you can see the dark blue highlight. The unselected tween has a light blue highlight.

## Reversing Frames in a Frame Span

Swapping the order of keyframes in a motion tween lets you do cool things like make a smooshed wheel round again. Simply right-click (Control-click) any frame in the tween and then choose Reverse Keyframes, as shown in Figure 3-17. In the case of your bouncing wheel, the keyframes at the beginning and end of the tween trade places. Preview your animation, and it looks pretty good: The wheel drops down, smooshes, and then recovers its round shape.

## ■ Editing the Motion Path

When it comes to moving objects around the stage, the motion path rules. That means you need to know how to change the path. As explained back on page 103, you make symbols move on the stage using the X and Y position properties. If the values change from one property keyframe to the next, then the symbol moves. You set the X and Y properties by moving the playhead to a frame and then moving the object or changing the X and Y properties in the Properties panel. Either way, your symbol moves, and it sprouts a motion path, like the one shown in Figure 3-18.

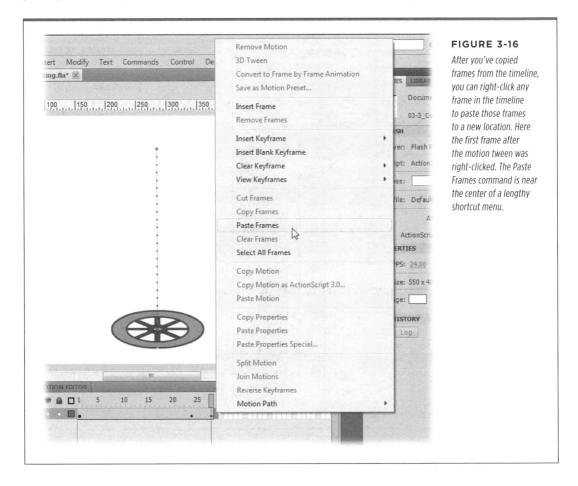

**FIGURE 3-16**

*After you've copied frames from the timeline, you can right-click any frame in the timeline to paste those frames to a new location. Here the first frame after the motion tween was right-clicked. The Paste Frames command is near the center of a lengthy shortcut menu.*

## Moving the Motion Path

Suppose you've got the perfect motion, and everything's working just the way you want. The only problem is that it's on the wrong place on the stage. You can move the entire motion path and the symbol that's being animated in one fell swoop. Here are the steps:

1. **With the Selection tool (solid arrow), click anywhere on the motion path.**

   The path becomes slightly thicker—that's its version of a selection highlight.

2. **Move the cursor over any point on the path.**

The cursor shows the move icon—a cross with four arrows.

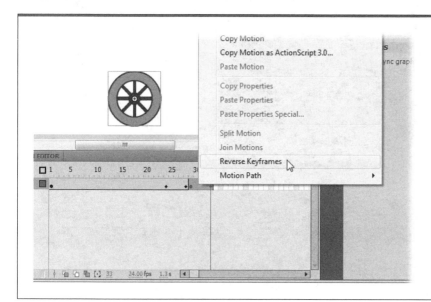

**FIGURE 3-17**

*When you right-click (Control-click) a motion tween, you see a lengthy shortcut menu. The Reverse Keyframes command is near the bottom. Reverse Keyframes is a handy command when you're developing repetitive, pendulum-like motions. Here reversing the pasted frames at the end of the animation makes the smooshed wheel round again.*

3. **Click, drag, and then release the mouse button.**

The motion path and the symbol move as a single unit. Once you release the mouse button, the path is in a new location, but everything else about the tween (the timing and the property changes) is the same.

Moving an entire motion path is easy for you, but Flash is working hard behind the scenes. It's changing all the X and Y properties for every property keyframe and calculating the new values for the tween.

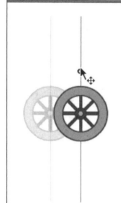

**FIGURE 3-18**

*Use the Selection tool to select a motion path before you move it to a new location. The cross with four arrows is Flash's Move icon.*

## Adding Curves to the Motion Path

The shortest distance between two points is a straight line, and that's exactly what Flash uses when you first make a symbol move. You're not stuck with that choice, though—it's easy to make the line curve.

1. **With the Selection tool, move the cursor to an _unselected_ motion path.**

   If the path is unselected, you see the curve cursor shown in Figure 3-19. The key here is that the path must not be selected. If it's selected, Flash shows the move cursor (the cross with four arrows).

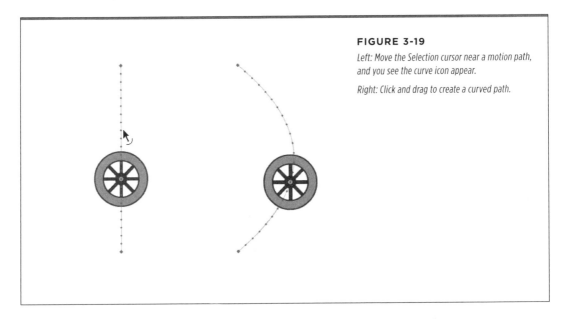

**FIGURE 3-19**

_Left: Move the Selection cursor near a motion path, and you see the curve icon appear._

_Right: Click and drag to create a curved path._

2. **Click, drag, and then release the mouse button.**

   As you drag, you see a preview of the new curved motion path. When you release the mouse button, the path is set.

This method for creating curves works well, but it takes some practice to create just the path you want. You can also combine the curve technique with fixed property keyframes along the motion path. For example, to create a double curve, start with a straight path and pull it into a curve, as shown at right in Figure 3-19. Move the playhead to a frame so that the wheel is centered on the path. Then, drag the wheel in the opposite direction of the curve. Moving the wheel creates a new property keyframe on the path and creates a motion path similar to the one in Figure 3-20.

## Moving End Points on the Motion Path

If you want to reposition one of the end points without moving the rest of the motion path, use the Subselection tool (A), which looks like a hollow arrow. Click the motion path with the Subselection tool, and the path end points appear as hollow squares. With the Subselection tool, you can click and drag these points to a new location.

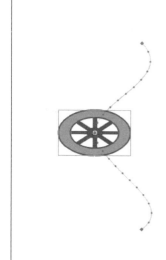

**FIGURE 3-20**

*Moving the tweened symbol (in this case, the wheel) at any point along the motion path creates a new property keyframe that stores the X and Y position values. This double curve is formed by three property keyframes—one at each end of the path and one in the middle.*

## Copying and Pasting a Motion Path

Here's one last motion path trick to learn. Suppose you want to create a complex motion path with lots of curves or lots of sharp angles. You can do that manually, using the techniques already described in this chapter, but there's a faster method. You can draw a line and then paste it into your tween. You can't draw directly in the tween, so you need to draw the path in a separate layer or even in a separate Flash document.

1. **Draw a line using either the Pencil, Pen, or Line tool.**

   The Pencil is best for freehand paths. The Pen works best for paths where you need precise control. The line must be simple, with a clear starting and ending point. For example, an X will not work as a motion path, and a line that crosses over itself may not work as expected.

2. **Select the entire path, and then press Ctrl+C (⌘-C).**

   Flash copies the line to the Clipboard. If you've got a long, twisty, curvy line, then you may have to double-click to select the entire line.

3. **Select the path in your tween, and press Ctrl+V (⌘-V).**

   The new path replaces the old path. It uses the same starting point as the original, so you may need to move the entire path (as described on page 110) to position it properly on the stage.

You can also paste a hand-drawn path into a motion tween that doesn't yet have a path. Just select the symbol you want to move, and then press Ctrl+V (⌘-V). There's an extra benefit to drawing a path with the Pencil or Pen tool. As shown in Figure 3-21, drawn paths have anchor points within the line. You can use these points to accurately reshape the line.

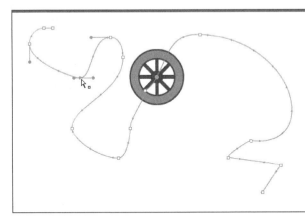

**FIGURE 3-21**

*One advantage of drawn lines for motion paths is that they have anchor points you can use to fine-tune the path. Click the path with the Subselection tool, and you can reshape the line as you would any other line drawn with the Pen.*

## ■ Copying and Pasting Properties

Sometimes you want to copy the properties from one property keyframe to another. For example, in the exercise on page 107, you used identical W and H properties to keep the wheel the same size and shape. The first keyframe and the first property keyframe had the same values. Anytime you want different keyframes to have the same properties, you can copy and paste property settings, just as you copy and paste words in a word processor. Follow these steps:

1. **Ctrl-click (⌘-click) the property keyframe with the properties you want to copy.**

   The selected cell shows a dark blue highlight.

2. **Right-click (Control-click) the selected frame.**

   A shortcut menu appears—the copy and paste properties commands are near the bottom.

3. **Choose Copy Properties from the shortcut menu.**

   All the properties related to the property keyframe are stored, so you can paste them into another frame.

4. **Ctrl-click (⌘-click) the frame where you want to paste the properties.**

   A shortcut menu appears (Figure 3-22). You can paste the properties to any frame; it doesn't have to be a property keyframe.

5. **Choose Paste Properties to paste all the properties to the new property keyframe.**

If necessary, a new keyframe is created, and all the properties are transferred to the new keyframe. Your work is done. If you want to paste only some of the properties, then see the next steps.

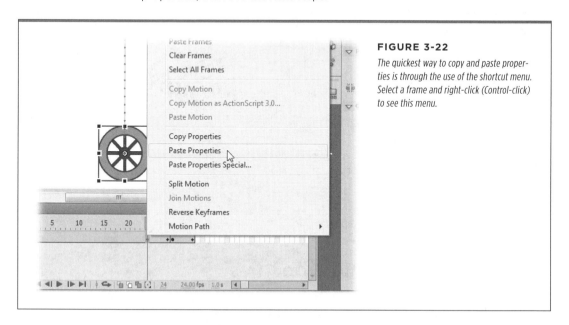

**FIGURE 3-22**

*The quickest way to copy and paste properties is through the use of the shortcut menu. Select a frame and right-click (Control-click) to see this menu.*

6. **Or choose Paste Properties Special to select a few of the properties to paste.**

The Paste Properties Special dialog box appears, as shown in Figure 3-23.

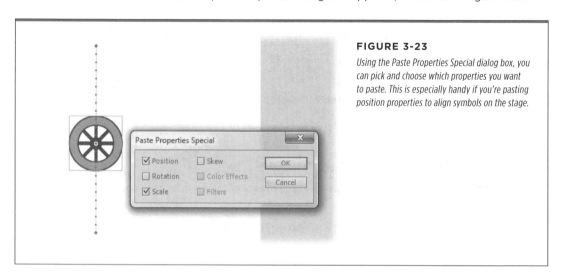

**FIGURE 3-23**

*Using the Paste Properties Special dialog box, you can pick and choose which properties you want to paste. This is especially handy if you're pasting position properties to align symbols on the stage.*

7. **Check the properties you want to copy, and then press OK.**

The selected properties are copied to the frame. If necessary, a new keyframe is added to the timeline.

# ◼ Shape Tweening (Morphing)

*Shape tweening*—sometimes referred to as *morphing*—lets you create an effect that makes one object appear as though it's slowly turning into another object. Often, shape tweening is one job that can't be done easily by simply changing properties with the motion tween, so Flash has a special tween tool for the job.

To make a shape tween, you draw the beginning object and the ending object, and Flash does all the rest. For example, say you create a keyframe containing a yellow ball. Then, 24 frames along the timeline, you create another keyframe containing a green star. You then apply a shape tween to the frame span, and Flash generates all the incremental frames necessary to show the ball slowly—frame by frame—transforming itself into a star when you run the animation.

**TIP** *Shape tweens* work only on editable graphics. If you want to tween a symbol (page 103), then you need to use a *motion tween*. If you want to tween a group of objects or reshape characters of text, then you need to ungroup the objects (page 161) or break apart the text (Modify→Break Apart) and then apply the shape tweens to the individual elements.

Shape tweening lets you change more than just an object's shape over a series of frames. Using a shape tween, you can also change an object's size, color, transparency, position, scale, and rotation.

To create a shape tween:

1. **Select the frame where you want your tween to begin (for example, Frame 1).**

Flash highlights the selected frame.

2. **If the selected frame isn't a keyframe (if you don't see a dot in the frame), then turn it into a keyframe by selecting Insert→Timeline→Keyframe (or pressing F6).**

Flash displays a dot in the frame to let you know it's a keyframe.

**NOTE** Shape tweens use the standard keyframe (circle icon). They don't use property keyframes (diamond icons). Property keyframes are used exclusively with motion tweens (page 103).

3. **On the stage, draw the shape you want to begin your tween.**

In Figure 3-24, the beginning shape is a ball—a yellow fill with a black stroke.

4. **Select the frame where you want your tween to end (for example, Frame 24).**

   Flash highlights the selected frame.

5. **Insert an ending point for your tween (and a clean, fresh stage on which to draw your ending shape) by selecting Insert→Timeline→Blank Keyframe.**

   The stage clears, the playhead moves to the selected frame, and Flash displays a hollow dot in the selected frame to let you know it's a keyframe.

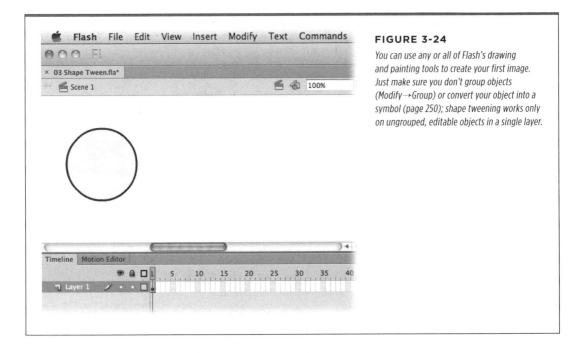

**FIGURE 3-24**

*You can use any or all of Flash's drawing and painting tools to create your first image. Just make sure you don't group objects (Modify→Group) or convert your object into a symbol (page 250); shape tweening works only on ungrouped, editable objects in a single layer.*

**TIP** As explained on page 96, you can carry over your beginning image from the first keyframe and make changes to it by choosing Insert→Timeline→Keyframe (instead of Insert→Timeline→Blank Keyframe).

6. **On the stage, use Flash's drawing and painting tools to draw the shape you want to end your tween.**

   Your ending shape can differ from your first shape in terms of position, color, transparency, rotation, skew, and size—so feel free to go wild. In Figure 3-25, the ending shape is a green, five-pointed star.

7. **On the timeline, right-click (Control-click) any frame in the middle of the frame span, and then choose Create Shape Tween from the shortcut menu.**

   When you right-click, Flash moves the playhead and highlights the frame you clicked. When you choose Shape Tween, the frame span changes to a nice lime color and inserts an arrow to let you know that you've successfully added a shape tween (Figure 3-26). A new tweening section appears in the Properties panel. (If the Properties panel isn't showing, choose Window→Properties.)

**NOTE** If you have Tinted Frames turned off, then Flash doesn't change the color behind the tweened frames. To turn on Tinted Frames, click the Options menu (the tiny, striped icon on the far right of the timeline, just above the frame numbers, as shown in Figure 3-25) and then select the Tinted Frames option. A checkmark indicates that the option is turned on.

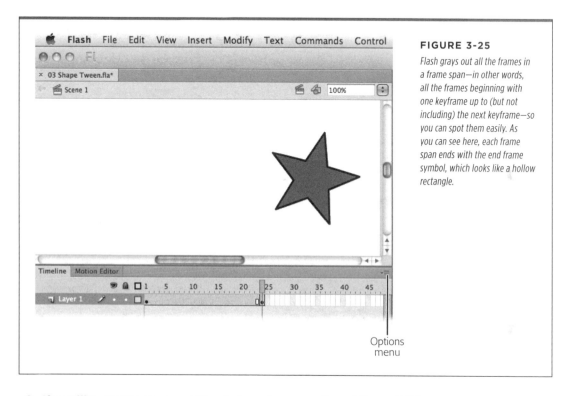

**FIGURE 3-25**

*Flash grays out all the frames in a frame span—in other words, all the frames beginning with one keyframe up to (but not including) the next keyframe—so you can spot them easily. As you can see here, each frame span ends with the end frame symbol, which looks like a hollow rectangle.*

Options menu

8. **If you like, set the Ease and Blend shape tween options (Figure 3-27).**

Here's what the options do:

- *Ease* tells Flash to speed up (or slow down) the tween. To change the Ease value, type a number or drag to change the number. If you want your tween to start out normally but speed up at the end, then set the Ease value to a negative number. To tell Flash to start your tween normally but slow down at the end, use a positive number. (Zero means that when you play your animation, the tween appears to be the same speed throughout.)

- *Blend* tells Flash how picky you want it to be when it draws its in-between frames. If you want to preserve the hard angles of your original shape, click the Blend drop-down box and then select *Angular*; if you want Flash to smooth out the hard edges so that the tween appears softer, select *Distributive*.

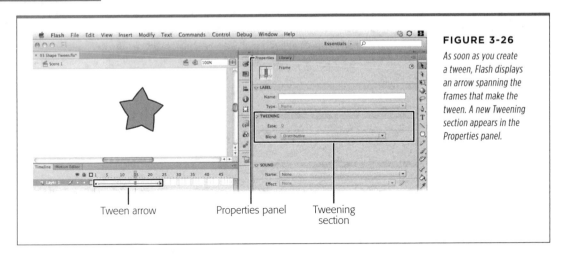

**FIGURE 3-26**

*As soon as you create a tween, Flash displays an arrow spanning the frames that make the tween. A new Tweening section appears in the Properties panel.*

Tween arrow          Properties panel          Tweening section

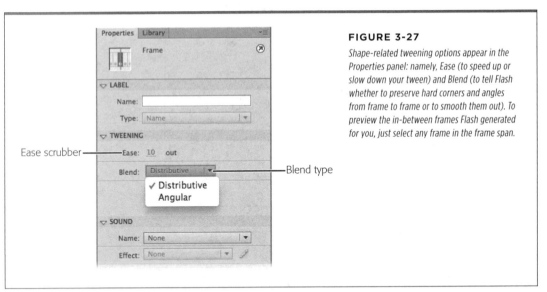

**FIGURE 3-27**

*Shape-related tweening options appear in the Properties panel: namely, Ease (to speed up or slow down your tween) and Blend (to tell Flash whether to preserve hard corners and angles from frame to frame or to smooth them out). To preview the in-between frames Flash generated for you, just select any frame in the frame span.*

Ease scrubber          Blend type

9. **Test your shape by selecting Control→Play.**

Flash plays your shape tween on the stage (Figure 3-28).

Want to see the finished example of the ball-morph-to-star shape tween? Go to *www.missingmanuals.com/cds/flashcs6mm* and download *03-4_Shape_Tween.fla*.

## Shape Hints

Flash does a bang-up job when it comes to tweening simple shapes: circles, squares, stars, raindrops. But the more complicated the images you want to tween, the harder Flash has to work to calculate how to generate the in-between images.

And if you think about it, that difficulty makes sense. Because complex beginning and ending images like a stylized acorn and tree (Figure 3-29) contain a bunch of editable lines, shapes, and colors, Flash has to guess at which elements are most important and how you want the morph to progress from the first keyframe to the last.

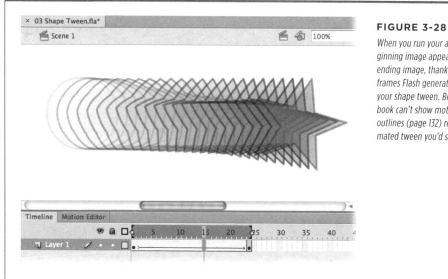

**FIGURE 3-28**

*When you run your animation, your beginning image appears to morph into your ending image, thanks to the in-between frames Flash generates when you create your shape tween. Because the pages of a book can't show motion, here, onionskin outlines (page 132) represent the animated tween you'd see on the stage.*

**FIGURE 3-29**

*1. The original acorn drawing: so far, so good.*

*2. Flash's first attempt at generating an in-between frame is a little scary.*

*3. Clearly, the acorn is changing and growing, but that's about all you can say for this generated image.*

*4. You can almost make out the outline of a tree now.*

*5. This one's getting there.*

*6. And finally, at the end of the tween, Flash makes it to your original image.*

Sometimes Flash guesses correctly; other times, you need to give it a few hints. Adding *shape hints* to your tweens tells Flash how you want it to create each in-between frame. This makes your finished tween appear more realistic—more how *you* want it to be.

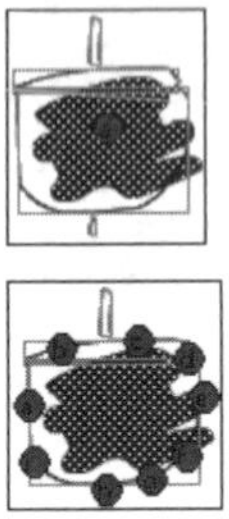

**FIGURE 3-30**

*Top: When you add a shape hint, Flash places it at the center of your object. All you have to do is drag it to the edge of your object.*

*Bottom: The more shape hints you use (and the more accurately you place them around the edge of your object), the more closely Flash attempts to preserve your shape as it generates the tween frames. Make sure you place the hints in alphabetical order as you outline your shape. If you find after several tries that Flash doesn't seem to be taking your hints, your shapes might be too complex or too dissimilar to tween effectively. In that case, you'll want to create additional keyframes or even consider replacing your tween with a frame-by-frame animation.*

In short, shape hints give you more (but not complete, by any means) control over the shape-tweened sections of your animation.

**NOTE** Shape hints are especially valuable when you're working on an animation that moves at a relatively slow frame rate—in other words, in situations when each separate frame will be visible to your audience's naked eye.

To add shape hints to a shape tween:

1. **Select the first frame of your tween.**

   Flash highlights the selected frame.

2. **Choose Modify→Shape→Add Shape Hint, or press Ctrl+Shift+H (Shift-⌘-H).**

   Flash displays a hint (a red circle containing a letter from A to Z) in the center of your shape, as shown in Figure 3-30 (top).

3. **Drag the hint to the edge of your shape.**

   Figure 3-30 (bottom) shows the result of dragging several hints to the edge of your shape.

4. **Repeat as many times as necessary, placing hints around the outline of the object in alphabetical order.**

   The bigger or more oddly shaped your object, the more hints you need. Placing a hint at each peak and valley of your object tells Flash to preserve the shape of your beginning object as much as possible as it morphs toward the shape of your ending object.

5. **Go to the last frame of the shape tween and adjust the shape hints to match the final shape.**

When the animation runs, Flash uses the hints in both the beginning and the ending keyframe to control the shape of the morphing object.

**FIGURE 3-31**

1. The original acorn is the same here as it was in Figure 3-29.

2. Using hints, this attempt at generating a first in-between frame is better than the one in Figure 2-39. It's not exactly a prize pig, but it's better.

3. Already you can see the form of the tree taking shape.

4. Here the already-pretty-well-shaped tree looks as thought it's about to burst out of the acorn outline.

5. Compared to tweening without hints (see Figure 3-29) this tween appears much smoother; you don't see the Flash generated squiggly lines.

6. The final frame of any tween appears the same whether or not you use hints.

6. **Test your animation by clicking Control→Play.**

The tweened frames of your animation conform, more or less, to the hints you provided. Figure 3-31 show you an example.

## Using Multiple Layers for Shape Tweens

It's easier for Flash to morph two simple shapes than one complex shape. So if shape hints don't help Flash solve shape tween confusion, then try tweening parts of your drawing separately. For example, put the cap of an acorn on a layer by itself, and put the bottom shell in a separate layer. Then you can shape tween the cap into the leaves of the tree and shape tween the shell into the trunk of the tree, with results as shown in Figure 3-32. There's an example of this technique on the Missing CD page (*www.missingmanuals.com/cds/flashcs6mm*). The file is called *03-5_Shape_Acorn.fla*. You'll learn more about creating timeline layers in the next chapter.

## Classic Tween

You may have noticed that Flash has a third type of tween listed on the Insert menu—Classic Tween. In the olden days, before Adobe developed the new and improved motion tween with its control of individual properties, the Classic tween was called Motion tween, and it was used to tween symbols. The new Motion tween is so much better and powerful that there aren't many reasons to use Classic tween on a new project. Here are the main two reasons you might want to use Classic tween:

- You need to work on a project developed with an earlier version of Flash.

- You're a Flash veteran and aren't ready to learn the newfangled motion tween.

In any case, Adobe wisely kept the Classic tween as part of Flash so you can use it if you need it. This book doesn't cover the Classic tween, but it was covered in Chapter 3 of *Flash CS4: The Missing Manual*. If you want, you can download a PDF of the chapter at *www.missingmanuals.com/cds/flashcs6mm*.

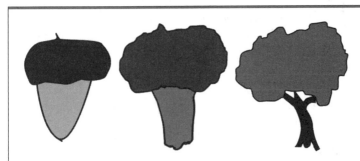

**FIGURE 3-32**

*If you add a shape tween to a layer with more than one object, the results usually aren't pretty. It's best to place objects on separate layers. Here the cap of the acorn tweens into the leaves of the tree, and the shell tweens into the trunk and branches. Using tweens on multiple layers gives you more control over your animation.*

# Advanced Drawing and Animation

# Organizing Frames and Layers

art 1 of this book gets you started launching Flash, creating your own draw-ings, and transforming them into moving animations. Most animation work, though, takes place after you've got all the frames and layers in place. Like a film director slaving away in the cutting room, as an animator you spend most of your time testing, editing, and retesting your movie.

This chapter is your crash course in Flash animation editing. Here you'll learn how to reorganize your animation horizontally (over time) by cutting, pasting, and rear-ranging frames in the timeline. You'll also see how to reorganize your animation vertically by shuffling and restacking the layers you've added to it.

## ■ Working with Frames

When you create an animation, you build it from frames and keyframes. Editing your document is a simple matter of moving, cutting, and pasting those frames until they look good and work well. You can perform these operations on individual frames or on multiple frames by combining them into groups, as you'll see at the end of this section.

### Copying and Pasting Frames

Copy and Paste are the world's favorite computer commands for good reason. These functions let you create a piece of work once (a word, line, shape, drawing, or what have you) and then quickly recreate it to build something even more complex with a minimum of effort. Well, Flash lets you cut, copy, and paste not just the content of your frames but also your frames themselves from one part of your timeline to another.

Copying and pasting frames is a great way to cut down on your development time. Here's how it works. Say you have a series of frames showing a weasel unwrapping a stick of chewing gum. It's a gag scene, one you want to repeat throughout your animation for comic effect. Instead of having to insert all the keyframes and regular frames every time you want to slip in the weasel gag, all you need to do is copy the weasel frames once and then paste them into your timeline wherever you want them to go.

Furthermore, copying and pasting isn't just useful for those times when you want a carbon copy of a scene. If you want to change something in each pasted scene—the brand of chewing gum the weasel is unwrapping, for example—you can do that, too, after you've pasted the frames. Copying and pasting frames works almost exactly like copying and pasting words or drawn objects—with a few twists. Here are some points to keep in mind:

- As usual, you have to select what you're going to copy before you set off the command. See page 99 for a refresher on selecting frames in the timeline.

- If the frames you're selecting span more than one layer, then make sure you select all the layers for each frame, as shown in Figure 4-1. (If the frames you're selecting are part of a motion tween, then you need to use a different technique, as explained on page 109. Ctrl-click [⌘-click] to select the first frame, and then drag to select adjacent frames.)

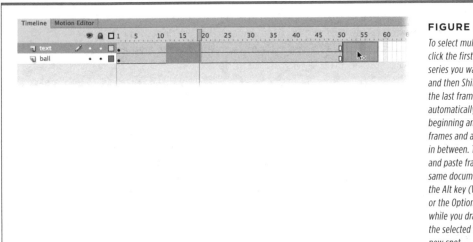

**FIGURE 4-1**

*To select multiple frames, click the first frame of the series you want to select, and then Shift-click the last frame. Flash automatically selects the beginning and ending frames and all the frames in between. To copy and paste frames in the same document, press the Alt key (Windows) or the Option key (Mac) while you drag a copy of the selected frames to a new spot.*

- Copying and pasting tweened frames varies depending on the type of tween— motion or shape. While tweened frames are displayed as separate, distinct images, they're not; only keyframes contain distinct images. If you want to copy and paste an entire shape tween, then you have to select the beginning and end keyframes. The motion tween is much easier-going when it comes to copying and pasting frames. You can select any frames from the middle of a motion tween and paste them (as a tween) into another layer.

**NOTE** Classic tweens (page 124) work more like shape tweens. You have to select the beginning and ending keyframes of what you want to copy and paste. You can't take a chunk of frames from the middle.

- Flash doesn't limit you to pasting within the same document. After you copy, you can open any other Flash animation and paste the frames right in.

**NOTE** Although Cut, Copy, and Paste usually travel as a threesome, things work a little differently in Flash. The Cut Frames command on the Edit→Timeline submenu doesn't actually cut *frames*; instead, it cuts the *contents* of the selected frame. To get rid of the frame itself, you need to use Edit→Timeline→Remove Frames, as described in the box on page 131.

The process of copying and pasting frames follows the same basic steps every time:

1. **In the timeline, select the frames you want to copy.**

   You probably want to make sure that the set of frames you choose begins with a keyframe, as described in the third bullet point above. Either way, Flash highlights the selected frames and moves the playhead to the last selected frame. You can select frames on more than one layer, as long as the layers are adjacent to each other.

2. **Press Ctrl+Alt+C (Option-⌘-C).**

   Flash stores the frames so you can paste them at another spot on the timeline or even to a different Flash document. Keep in mind, the timeline copy and paste commands are different from the standard Copy (Ctrl+C or ⌘-C) and paste (Ctrl+V or ⌘-V).

**TIP** There are three ways to use the Copy Frames and Paste Frames commands. For most Flash folk, the shortcut keys shown in these steps are the fastest method. You'll use the commands often enough that they'll become second nature. As an alternative, you can right-click (Control-click) the timeline to see a shortcut menu with the commands. Probably the least convenient method is the main menu (Edit→Timeline→Copy Frames).

3. **Select the keyframe where you want to begin pasting the copied frames.**

   In other words, select the frame after which you want to add the copied frames.

4. **Press Ctrl+Alt+V (Option-⌘-V on the Mac).**

   Flash pastes the copied frames, replacing the currently selected keyframe with the first copied frame. If you pasted frames into the middle of a timeline, Flash repositions your existing frames *after* the last pasted frame. If your selection in step 1 included more than one layer, then Flash adds extra layers as needed.

## Moving Frames and Keyframes

The timeline is serial: When you run your animation, Flash displays the content in Frame 1, followed by the content in Frame 2, followed by the content in Frame 3, and so on. If you change your mind about the order in which you want frames to appear, all you need to do is move them.

Simple in theory—but moving frames in Flash isn't quite as cut and dried as you might think. As you may recall if you've had a chance to read through Chapter 3, only keyframes can contain actual images; regular frames, technically called static frames, contain either tweened or "held over" copies of the images placed in the previous keyframe. So whether you move a frame or a keyframe, you end up with a keyframe. Here's how it works:

- **Moving a keyframe.** When you move a keyframe, what Flash actually moves is the keyframe's content and keyframe designation; Flash leaves behind a static frame in the original keyframe's place. (And that static frame may or may not be empty, depending on what precedes it.)

- **Moving a static frame.** Flash moves the static frame but turns the moved frame into a keyframe. (If you move a series of regular frames, then Flash turns just the first moved frame into a keyframe.)

---

**TIP** There's another way to change the order in which Flash plays frames: by creating an ActionScript action, as described in Chapter 15. Creating an action lets you tell Flash how to play your frames: backward, for example, or by rerunning the first 10 frames three times and then moving on. You want to use ActionScript (as opposed to moving frames) to give your audience the choice of viewing your animation in different ways.

---

Here are the steps in detail:

1. **In the timeline, select the frame(s) you want to move.**

   Flash highlights the selected frame (or frames) and moves the playhead to the last selected frame.

2. **Drag the selected frame(s) to the frame after which you want to place the selected frames.**

   As you drag the selected frames, Flash highlights the frames you're moving to help you position them (Figure 4-2). If your selection includes a keyframe, then Flash clears the selected frames from their original position and then inserts them in their new location. If your selection doesn't include a keyframe, then Flash copies the content and creates a new keyframe at the point of insertion.

---

**TIP** To select multiple frames, drag in the timeline. You have to release the mouse button to complete the selection. Then you can drag the selected frames to move the whole bunch of highlighted frames to a new location. If dragging your frames isn't working, you can always copy and paste the frames you want to move (page 115). Then use Edit→Timeline→Remove Frames to delete them from their original location (see the box on page 131).

---

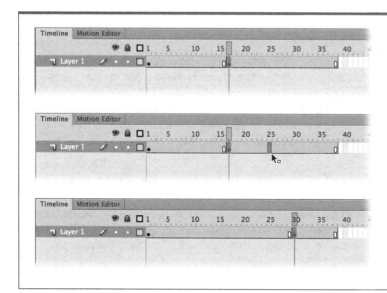

**FIGURE 4-2**

*Top: Click to select the frame you want to move, and then let go of your mouse. Then drag to move the frame.*

*Middle: As you make the move, Flash displays a highlighted frame, or a group of frames if you selected more than one.*

*Bottom: Here you can tell the frame moved to Frame 30 because the keyframe and end frame indicators have disappeared from their original locations (Frames 16 and 17) and reappeared in their new locations (Frames 29 and 30).*

## Remove vs. Cut vs. Clear

Flash has three commands you can use to get rid of your frames (and the content associated with those frames): Remove, Cut, and Clear. When you're new to Flash, it may not be immediately clear which command does what. Here's what these commands do to selected frames:

- **Edit→Timeline→Remove Frames (Shift+F5).** Removing a frame deletes that frame or group of frames from the timeline, as if you'd reached into the timeline and yanked them out. When a keyframe is involved, the result is a little different. If you attempt to remove a keyframe followed by a regular frame, Flash deletes the frame immediately to the right of the keyframe instead (go figure). To be safe, if you want to remove a keyframe—in other words, if you want to delete a keyframe from the timeline—then you first want to clear the keyframe with Shift-F6. That strips

the frame of its keyframe status. Then you can remove the frame itself.

- **Edit→Timeline→Cut Frames (Ctrl+Alt+X or Option-⌘-X).** Cutting a frame deletes the content on the stage associated with that frame (in other words, turns the frame into a blank keyframe). If the immediately succeeding frame is a regular frame, then Flash turns that succeeding frame into a keyframe. Flash stores the contents of the cut frames on the Clipboard, so you can restore them by choosing Edit→Timeline→Paste Frames.

- **Edit→Timeline→Clear Frames (Alt+Delete or Option-Delete).** Clearing frames is just like cutting them, but with one difference: Flash doesn't store the contents of the cleared frames (so you can't restore them).

# Editing Multiple Frames

Imagine you've just completed a 250-frame animation showing a character in a red T-shirt demonstrating your company's latest product, an electronic egg slicer. Suddenly, your boss comes in and declares that red is out. (Red is the color your competitor is using for *its* egg slicer launch.) You have, your boss declares, until the end of the day to change all 250 frames.

Now, if you had to change all 250 frames one at a time, you'd never be able to meet your deadline, and even if you did, you'd probably make a few mistakes along the way, like accidentally repositioning the T-shirt in a couple of frames or missing a few frames altogether. But it's precisely this kind of en masse editing job that Flash's multiple-frame editing capability was designed to handle. (By the way, you can also edit multiple frames using Flash's Find and Replace commands. See the box below for more.)

Using a technique called *onion skinning*, you can see the contents of several frames at once. There are three modes for onion skinning: Onion Skin, Onion Skin Outlines, and Edit Multiple Frames. Each is helpful for a different type of task. Use the buttons at the bottom of the timeline to choose an onion skin mode, as shown in Figure 4-3; use the *onion markers* in the timeline to choose which frames are displayed.

---

**GEM IN THE ROUGH**

## Editing Multiple Frames with Find and Replace

Another way to edit the content of multiple frames is to use Flash's Find and Replace function. Similar to the Find and Replace you've undoubtedly used in word processing programs, this function lets you search every frame of your animation for a specific bit of text (or even a certain color or bitmap file) and either replace the occurrences yourself or tell Flash to replace them for you using the text (or color or bitmap file) you tell it to use.

To use this function, select Edit→"Find and Replace." Then, in the "Find and Replace" window that appears, head to the

*For* drop-down menu and select the item you want to find. Your choices include Text, Font, Color, Symbol, Sound, Video, and Bitmap.

To change the occurrences yourself, click Find Next or Find All (and then make your changes on the stage). To tell Flash to change the occurrences, add a Replace With option (for example, the color or text you want to insert), and then click Replace or Replace All.

---

The Edit Multiple Frames mode makes it easy to deal with that red T-shirt issue, because you can quickly identify (and change) the frames containing red T-shirts. Onion skinning is also useful for those times when you want to hand-draw an "in-between" frame, because you can see both the preceding and succeeding frames on the stage at the same time.

**NOTE** Technically speaking, when you edit multiple frames in Flash, you're actually editing multiple *keyframes.* Keyframes are the only frames that contain unique, editable art. (Regular frames just "hold over" the contents of the previous keyframe, and Flash stores tweened frames not as editable images, but as a bunch of calculations.)

To edit multiple frames using onion skinning:

1. **In the timeline, click the Edit Multiple Frames icon.**

   Flash displays multiple frames on the stage and adds onion markers to the frame display (Figure 4-3, bottom). These beginning and ending onion markers tell Flash which frames you want it to display on the stage.

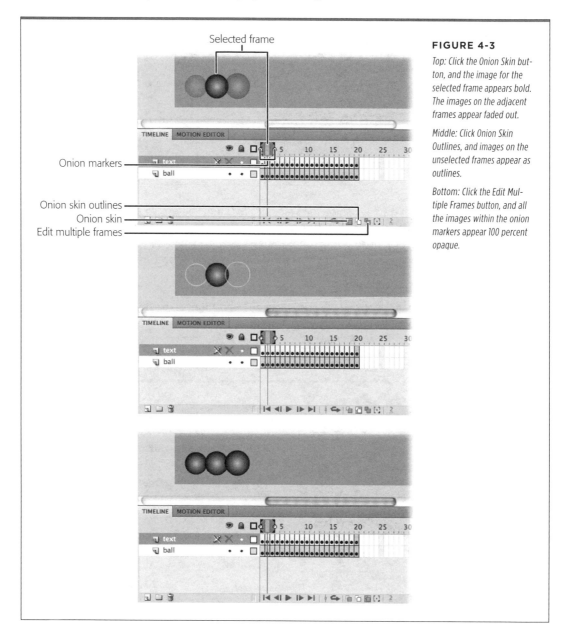

Selected frame

Onion markers

Onion skin outlines
Onion skin
Edit multiple frames

**FIGURE 4-3**

*Top: Click the Onion Skin button, and the image for the selected frame appears bold. The images on the adjacent frames appear faded out.*

*Middle: Click Onion Skin Outlines, and images on the unselected frames appear as outlines.*

*Bottom: Click the Edit Multiple Frames button, and all the images within the onion markers appear 100 percent opaque.*

2. **Click the Modify Markers icon.**

   Flash displays a pop-up menu.

3. **From the pop-up menu, select Marker Range All (Figure 4-4).**

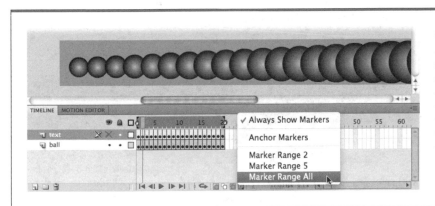

**FIGURE 4-4**

*Here you see the result of selecting Marker Range All. The onion markers surround the entire frame span (Frame 1 through Frame 20), and all 20 images appear on the same stage, ready for you to edit en masse.*

Flash displays onion markers from the beginning of your timeline's frame span to the end and shows the contents of each of your frames on the stage. (If you don't want to edit all the frames in your animation, you can drag the onion markers independently to surround whatever subset frames you want.)

4. **Edit the frames.**

   Because you can see and select all the content on a single stage, you can make your edits more easily than having to hunt and peck individually through every frame in your animation. In Figure 4-5, four frames are selected with the onion markers.

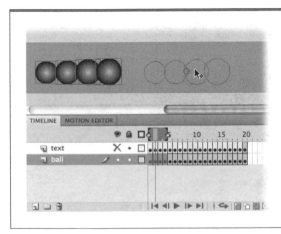

**FIGURE 4-5**

*You can work with multiple images just as easily as single images. For example, you can select several (or all of them) and apply whatever edits you like—moving them, coloring them, reshaping them, and so on.*

The contents are first recolored and then moved in one fell swoop. When the move is complete, your stage looks like Figure 4-6.

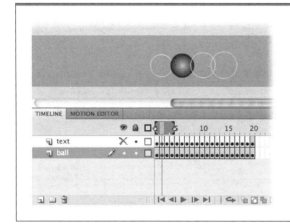

**FIGURE 4-6**

*With onion skinning turned on, you can see multiple frames, but you can edit only the content of the selected frame. Use the Edit Multiple Frames mode when you want to see and edit several frames at once.*

5. **Click Edit Multiple Frames again.**

   Flash returns to regular one-frame-at-a-time editing mode and displays only the contents of the current frame on the stage.

> **NOTE** You can't edit multiple frames on a locked layer (page 148). In fact, when you click Edit Multiple Frames on a locked layer, Flash doesn't even show you the content of the frames in the locked layer (not even in onion skin form).

# ■ Working with Multiple Layers

A layer is a named sequence of frames in the timeline. When you work with a single layer, adding content to frames is easy: You just click a keyframe and use Flash's drawing, painting, and text tools to create an image on the stage. But when you work with multiple layers, you need to keep track of the layers' order and what objects are on each layer. For example, suppose you're creating a composite drawing with mountains in the background, a car driving by in the foreground, and a separate layer for your sound clips. You may find adding content a bit trickier, because you have to be aware of the layer to which you're adding your content. Fortunately, as you'll see in the steps below, the timeline's Show/Hide icon helps you keep track of which content you've placed on which layer.

To add content to multiple layers:

1. **Open the file *04-1_Multiple_Layers.fla*.**

   You can find this file (and all the other example files) on this book's Missing CD page at *www.missingmanuals.com/cds/flashcs6mm*.

2. **Click the first keyframe in Layer 1.**

   Flash highlights the selected frame, as well as the layer name. You also see a little pencil icon that lets you know this frame is now ready for editing.

3. **Use Flash's drawing and painting tools to draw a fence on the stage.**

   Your fence doesn't have to be fancy; a quick "wooden" fence like the one in Figure 4-7 is fine.

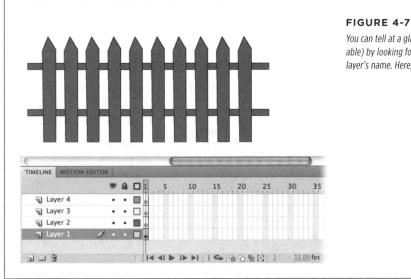

**FIGURE 4-7**

*You can tell at a glance which layer is active (editable) by looking for the pencil icon next to the layer's name. Here, Layer 1 is active.*

4. **Hide Layer 1 by clicking the Show/Hide button next to Layer 1.**

   The content on the stage temporarily disappears. Flash replaces the Show/Hide icon with an X and draws a slash through the pencil icon next to Layer 1 to let you know this layer is no longer editable.

> **NOTE** Technically, you don't *have* to hide the contents of one layer while you're working with another; in fact, in some cases, you want to see the contents of both layers on the stage at the same time (page 138). But for this example, hiding is the best way to go.

5. **Click the first keyframe in Layer 2.**

Flash highlights the selected frame, as well as the layer name (Layer 2). Now the pencil icon is next to Layer 2.

6. **Use Flash's drawing and painting tools to draw a few flowers on the stage.**

Your workspace should now look like the one in Figure 4-8. You can make multiple flowers by copying and pasting a single flower.

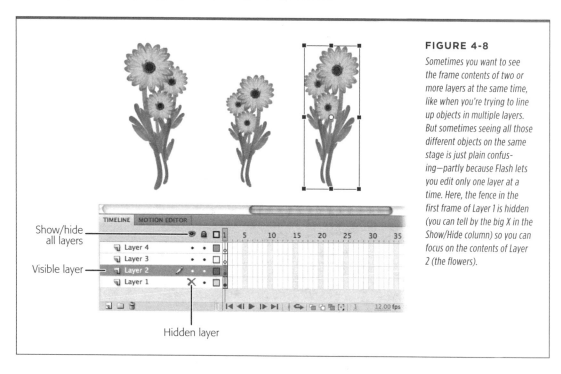

Show/hide all layers

Visible layer

Hidden layer

**FIGURE 4-8**

*Sometimes you want to see the frame contents of two or more layers at the same time, like when you're trying to line up objects in multiple layers. But sometimes seeing all those different objects on the same stage is just plain confusing—partly because Flash lets you edit only one layer at a time. Here, the fence in the first frame of Layer 1 is hidden (you can tell by the big X in the Show/Hide column) so you can focus on the contents of Layer 2 (the flowers).*

7. **Hide Layer 2 by clicking the Show/Hide icon next to Layer 2.**

The content on the stage temporarily disappears. Flash replaces the Show/Hide icon with an X and draws a slash through the pencil icon next to Layer 2 to let you know that this layer is no longer editable.

8. **Repeat steps 4–6 for Layers 3 and 4, adding some gray clouds to Layer 3 (Figure 4-9) and some flying birds to Layer 4 (Figure 4-10).**

9. **To see the content for all four layers, click to remove the Show/Hide X icon next to Layer 3, Layer 2, and Layer 1, as shown in Figure 4-11.**

Flash displays the content for all four layers on the same stage.

## Showing and Hiding Layers

This section shows you how to use Flash's layer tools (including locking/unlocking and hiding/showing) to keep from going crazy when you're editing content in multiple layers (Figure 4-12). Two layers aren't so bad, but if you need to add 6, 8, 10, or even more layers, it's pretty easy to lose track of which layer you're working in. Then in the following section you'll see how to edit the content in your layers.

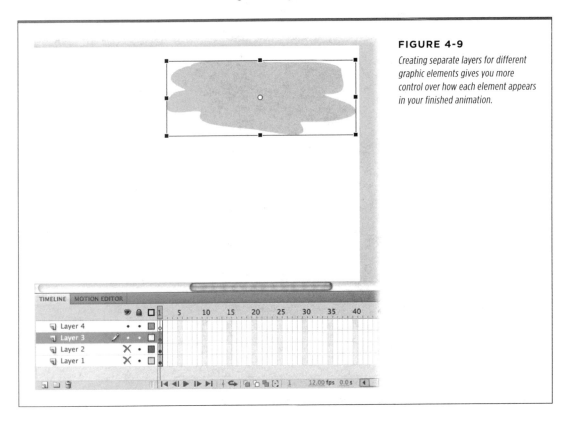

**FIGURE 4-9**

*Creating separate layers for different graphic elements gives you more control over how each element appears in your finished animation.*

Whether or not you want Flash to show the contents of your layered frames on the stage depends on the situation. Typically, when you're creating the content for a new layer, you want to hide all the other layers so you can focus on what you're drawing without any distractions. But after you've created a bunch of layers, you want to see them all at once so you have an idea of what your finished animation looks like and make adjustments as necessary.

Flash shows all layers until you tell it otherwise.

**FIGURE 4-10**

*In this example, the images are static, but you can place everything from motion and shape tweens to movie clips, backgrounds, actions, and sounds on their own layers. Hiding layers affects only what you see on the stage; when you select Control →Test Movie to test your animation, Flash displays all the layers, whether or not you've checked them as Hidden.*

**GEM IN THE ROUGH**

## Distribute to Layers

If you have a bunch of graphic elements on one layer that you want to put on separate layers (perhaps you want to tween them individually), you can save time by telling Flash to do the work for you. First, select the objects you want to put on different layers and then select Modify→Timeline→Distribute to Layers.

Unfortunately, like any automatic process, this approach may not create the precise results you want. Flash can't possibly

know that you want both an eye and an eyebrow to go on the same layer, for example. And this trick doesn't break apart bitmaps, symbols, or grouped objects.

If you want to distribute the elements of a bitmap or symbol to individual layers, you first need to break up that bitmap, symbol, or grouped object by selecting it and then choosing Modify→Break Apart or Modify→Ungroup.

### ■ HIDING A LAYER

The eyeball in the timeline is the Show or Hide All Layers button. It works like a toggle. Beneath that eye are buttons to show or hide layers individually. So to hide a single layer, click the dot in that layer. When you do, Flash replaces the dot with a red X and temporarily hides the contents of the layer (Figure 4-13).

**FIGURE 4-11**

*Here's what the composite drawing for Frame 1 looks like: the fence, the flowers, the cloud, and the birds, all together on one stage. Notice the display order: The flowers (Layer 2) appear in front of the fence (Layer 1), and the birds (Layer 4) in front of the cloud (Layer 3). You can change the way these images overlap by rearranging the layers, as you'll see on page 146.*

### ■ SHOWING A LAYER

In the timeline, click the X in the layer you want to show. When you do, Flash replaces the X with a dot and displays the contents of the layer on the stage.

### ■ HIDING (OR SHOWING) ALL LAYERS EXCEPT THE ONE YOU'RE EDITING

In the timeline, Alt-click (Option-click) the Show/Hide button next to the layer you're editing. Flash immediately hides (or shows) all the layers, except the one you're editing.

**TIP** If you try to edit a hidden layer by drawing on the stage, Flash displays a warning dialog box that gives you the opportunity to show (and then edit) the layer. Not so if you try to drag a symbol onto the stage—Flash just refuses to let you drop the symbol on the stage. Oddly enough, however, Flash *does* let you add and remove frames and keyframes in a locked layer.

## Working with Layers

The more layers you have, the more important it is to keep them organized. In this section, you'll see how to give your layers meaningful names so you'll know which images, sounds, or actions they hold. You'll learn how to arrange your layers so that your images and objects overlap the way you want. And you'll learn how to copy and paste layers, an important skill that saves time and cuts down on repetitive tasks.

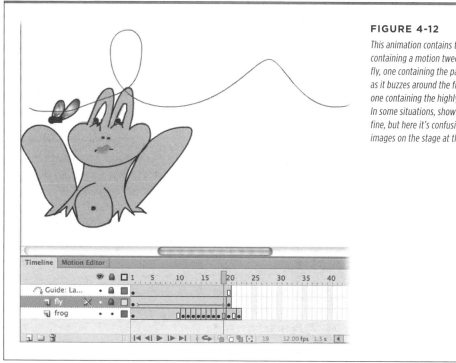

**FIGURE 4-12**

*This animation contains three layers: one containing a motion tween of a buzzing fly, one containing the path the fly takes as it buzzes around the frog's head, and one containing the highly interested frog. In some situations, showing all layers is fine, but here it's confusing to see all those images on the stage at the same time.*

## Renaming Layers

The names Flash gives the layers you create—Layer 1, Layer 2, Layer 3, and so on— aren't particularly useful when you've created 20 layers and can't remember which layer contains the ocean background you spent 10 hours drawing. Get into the habit of renaming your layers as soon as you create them, and you'll have an easier time locating the specific elements you need when you need them.

This section builds on the example you created earlier in this chapter. If you haven't had a chance to work through that section, you can download *04_2_Flowers.fla* from this book's Missing CD page (*www.missingmanuals.com/cds/flashcs6mm*) and use it instead.

## Why Layer?

In addition to making it much, much easier for you to change your animations, working with layers gives you the following benefits:

- **You can create multi-tweened animations.** Often if you're tweening more than one object, it helps to put each of those objects on a separate layer. Sometimes, it's the only way to get the job done. For example, if you want to show two baseballs bonking a parked car—one ball sailing in from the right and one from the left—then you need to either draw the entire animated sequence for each ball by hand or use separate layers for each tween.

- **You can create more realistic effects.** Since you can shuffle layers, putting some layers behind others and even adjusting the transparency of some layers, you can add depth and perspective to your drawings. And because you can distribute your drawings to layers at whatever level of detail you want, you can create separate layers that give you independent control over, say, your characters' facial expressions and arm and leg movements.

- **You can split up the work.** In the olden days, TV and movie animators used layers (technically, they use transparent sheets of plastic called cels, but it's the same concept) to divvy up their workload, and so can you. While you're crafting the dog layer, one of your teammates can be working on the cloud layer, and another two can be working on the two character layers. When you're all finished, all you need to do is copy everyone's layers and then paste them into a single timeline. Bingo—instant animation.

- **You can organize your animations.** As you begin to create more sophisticated animations, which may include not just images and animated effects but also symbols (Chapter 7), sounds (Chapter 11), and actions (Chapter 12), you'll quickly realize that you need to organize your work. Layers help you get organized. If you get into the habit of putting all your animation's ActionScript code into a single layer (called "actions"), all the sounds into a single layer (called "sounds" or "soundtrack"), all the text into a single layer (called "text"), and so on, then you can quickly spot the element you're looking for when it comes time to edit your animation.

To rename a layer:

1. **Open the file *04_2_Flowers.fla*.**

   If you created your own Flash document when you worked through "Working with Multiple Layers" (page 135), you can use that document instead.

2. **Double-click the name Layer 4.**

   Flash displays the layer name in an editable text box (Figure 4-15). On the stage, you see the content for this layer (the birds) selected.

**NOTE** Instead of double-clicking the layer name, you can use the Layer Properties dialog box to rename your layer. Check out the box on page 144 for details.

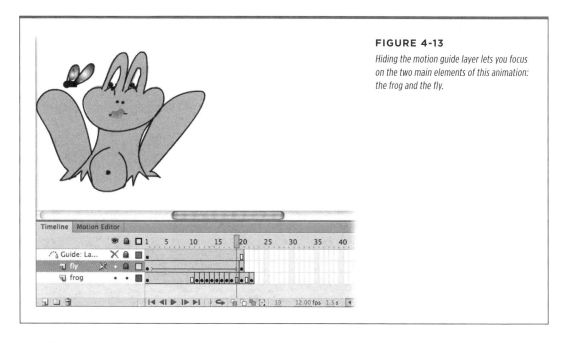

**FIGURE 4-13**

*Hiding the motion guide layer lets you focus on the two main elements of this animation: the frog and the fly.*

3. **Click inside the text box, type** *birds*, **and then click anywhere else in the workspace.**

   Flash displays the new name for your layer.

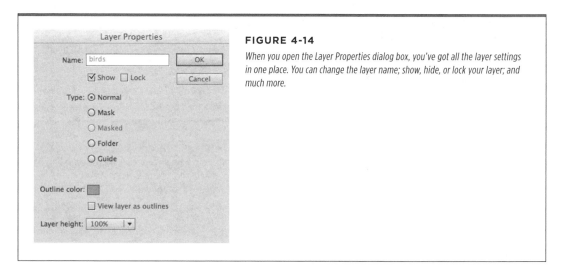

**FIGURE 4-14**

*When you open the Layer Properties dialog box, you've got all the layer settings in one place. You can change the layer name; show, hide, or lock your layer; and much more.*

4. **Repeat steps 1 and 2 for Layers 3, 2, and 1, renaming them *cloud, flowers,* and *fence*, respectively.**

## Layer Properties

Flash gives you two ways to change the properties associated with your layers—for example, the name of your layer, whether you want to show the content of a layer on the stage or hide it, whether you want to lock a layer or leave it editable, and so on.

One way is clicking the Show/Hide button in the timeline. (That's the approach described in this chapter.) The other way is by using the Layer Properties dialog box shown in Figure 4-14.

To display the Layer Properties dialog box, click to select a layer, and then do one of the following:

- Double-click the layer icon you find just to the left of the layer name. Right-click the layer name, and then choose Properties from the shortcut menu that appears.

- Select Modify→Timeline→Layer Properties.

The Layer Properties dialog box lets you change several properties in the selected layer in one fell swoop:

- **Name.** Type a name in this text box to change the name of your layer.

- **Show.** Turn on this checkbox to show the contents of this layer on the stage; turn it off to hide the contents of this layer.

- **Lock.** Turn on this checkbox to prevent yourself (or anyone else) from editing any of the content in this layer; turn it off to make the layer editable once again.

- **Type.** Click to choose one of the following layer types:

    - **Normal.** The type of layer described in this chapter.

- **Mask.** A type of layer you use to carve out "portholes," through which the content on an underlying masked layer appears (page 151).

- **Masked.** A regular layer that appears below a mask layer (page 152).

- **Folder.** Not a layer at all, but a container you can drag layers into to help you organize your animation (page 150).

- **Guide.** A special type of layer that you use to position objects on a guided layer, and which doesn't appear in the finished animation (page 192).

- **Outline color.** Click to choose the color you want Flash to use when you turn on the "View layer as outlines" checkbox.

- **View layer as outlines.** Turning on this checkbox tells Flash to display the content for this layer on the stage as wireframe outlines (instead of the way it actually looks when you run the animation). Find out more on page 149.

- **Layer height.** Click the arrow next to this drop-down list to choose a display height for your layer in the timeline: 100% (normal), 200% (twice as big), or 300% (three times as big). You may find this option useful for visually setting off one of your layers, making it easier to spot quickly.

After you make your changes, click OK to tell Flash to apply your changes to the layer.

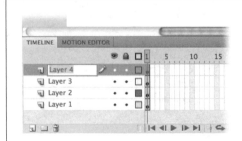

**FIGURE 4-15**

*If you can't remember what a particular layer contains, then check the stage: When you double-click a layer name to rename it, Flash automatically highlights the content associated with that layer.*

When you're done, your renamed layers should look like Figure 4-16.

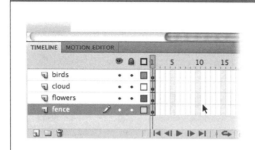

**FIGURE 4-16**

*The Layers area of the timeline isn't particularly big, so it's best to keep your layer names short and sweet. If you need more room, just drag the bar that separates the names from the frames.*

## Copying and Pasting Layers

Earlier in this chapter, you saw how to copy and paste individual series of frames. But Flash also lets you copy and paste entire layers—useful when you want to create a backup layer for safekeeping or when you want to create a duplicate layer you'll later change slightly from the original.

For example, if you want your animation to show an actor being pelted with tomatoes from different angles, you can create a layer that shows a tomato coming in from stage right—perhaps using a motion or shape tween (Chapter 3). Then you can copy that layer, paste it back into the Layers window, rename it, and tweak it so that the tomato comes from stage left. Maximum effect for minimum effort—that's what copying and pasting gives you.

To copy and paste a layer:

1. **In the timeline, click the name of the layer you want to select.**

   Flash highlights the layer name, as well as all the frames in the layer.

2. **Select Edit→Timeline→Copy Frames.**

   If you don't have a layer waiting to accept the copied frames, then create a new layer now before going on to the next step.

3. **In the Layers window, select the name of the destination layer.** Then choose Edit→Timeline→Paste Frames.

   Flash pastes the copied frames into the new layer, beginning with the first frame. It also pastes the name of the copied layer into the new layer.

**TIP** It's also possible to copy and paste layers between Flash documents. That's a process used on one of the last exercises in the book (page 760), where layers from an iPhone app are pasted into an Android project.

## Reordering (Moving) Layers

You can change the way images, text fields, and other objects overlap on the stage by rearranging the layers in the timeline. For example, in Figure 4-17, the fence seems to be behind the flowers because, in the timeline, the fence layer is below the flowers layer. If you'd rather have the flowers behind the fence, just drag the flowers layer below the fence. Figure 4-18 shows you an example.

**FIGURE 4-17**

*Flash treats layers the same way you treat a stack of transparencies: The image on the bottom gets covered by the image above it, which gets covered by the image above it, and so on. Stacking isn't an issue if none of your images overlap. But when they do, you need to decide which layers you want in front and which behind.*

## Deleting a Layer

Flash gives you three ways to delete a layer:

- In the timeline, right-click (Control-click) the layer you want to delete and then, from the shortcut menu that appears, choose Delete Layers.

- Drag the layer you want to delete to the trash can (see Figure 4-19).

- Click the layer you want to delete to select it (or Shift-click to select several layers), and then click the trash can.

Whichever method you choose, Flash immediately deletes the layer or layers (including all the frames associated with that layer or layers) from the Layers window.

**TIP** If you delete the wrong layer by mistake, choose Edit→Undo Delete Layer or press Ctrl+Z (⌘-Z).

**FIGURE 4-18**

*Moving a layer is easy: Just click to select a layer, and then drag it to reposition it (and change the order in which Flash displays the content of your frames). Here the cloud layer has been moved to the bottom of the list, so it now appears behind the other images. The birds layer is in the process of being moved; you can tell by the thick gray line you see beneath the cursor.*

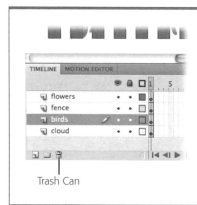

Trash Can

**FIGURE 4-19**

*The quickest way to dispose of a layer is to select it and then click the trash can. All Flash animations have at least one layer, so you can't delete the last layer. If you try, Flash doesn't display any error—it just quietly ignores you.*

## Locking and Unlocking Layers

Working with layers can be confusing, especially at first. So Flash lets you lock in-dividual layers as a kind of safeguard, to keep yourself from accidentally changing content you didn't mean to change:

- **To lock a layer,** click the dot under the padlock, as shown in Figure 4-20. When you do, the dot turns into a little padlock icon and deselects any objects that you'd selected on the stage in that layer. If you locked the active layer, Flash draws a slash through the pencil icon next to the layer's name as a visual re-minder that you can't edit it.

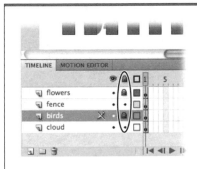

**FIGURE 4-20**

*Here the cloud and fence layers are unlocked, and the flowers layer (and the selected birds layer) are locked. Some people get into the habit of locking all the layers they're not cur-rently editing. That way, they can't possibly add a shape or a tween to the wrong layer.*

- **To unlock a layer,** click the padlock (Figure 4-20). Instantly, the padlock turns into a dot, Flash reselects your objects, and you can edit them once again on the stage.

- **To lock (or unlock) all your layers all at once,** click the Lock or Unlock All Layers icon (padlock at the top). Click the icon again to return to unlocked (or locked) layers. Ctrl-clicking (⌘-clicking) on any Show/Hide button also locks or unlocks all layers.

- **To lock (or unlock) all layers except one,** Alt-click (Option-click) the dot or padlock in the layer you want to edit.

**NOTE** If you try to edit a locked layer, Flash displays a warning dialog box that gives you the opportunity to unlock (and then edit) the layer.

# ■ Organizing Layers

Flash gives you a couple of options that help you organize your layers while you're working. The *Outline view* removes the fill from drawings, showing only a wireframe outline. Outline view is helpful when you want to simplify the artwork on a clut-tered screen. *Layer folders* help you organize your layers into a hierarchy, which is helpful when you're working with dozens of layers. The ability to put several layers in a single folder makes it easier to lock and hide related materials.

## Outline View

Flash lets you display the contents of your layers in outline form. Instead of seeing solid pictures on the stage, you see wireframe images, as in Figure 4-21. Looking at your layer content in outline form is useful in a variety of situations—for example, when you want to align the content of one layer with respect to the content of another.

- **To display the content of all your layers as outlines,** click the Show All Layers As Outlines icon (next to the padlock). Clicking it again displays your layers normally.

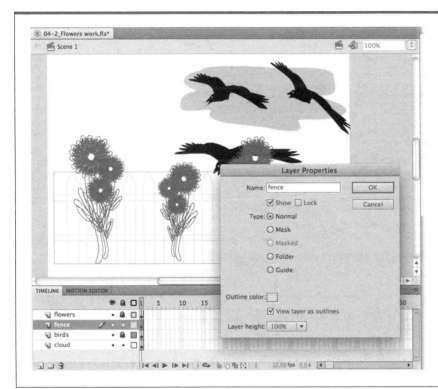

**FIGURE 4-21**

*Depending on the visual effect you're going for, you might want to align the centers of your flowers with the crosspieces of your fence. But when you look at the content normally, it's hard to see the alignment, because both your flowers and your fence are opaque. Here Flash displays the flowers and fence layers in outline form so you can concentrate on shape and placement without being distracted by extraneous details.*

**TIP** You can change the color Flash uses to sketch your outlined content. For example, you can change the color from light to dark so that you can more easily see the outline against a light background or so that there's more contrast between two overlapping outlines. To change the outline color for a layer, first select the layer, and then select Modify→Timeline→Layer Properties. From the Layer Properties dialog box (Figure 4-21) that appears, click the Outline Color swatch and then select a color from the color picker that appears.

- **To show a single layer's content in outline form,** click the filled square, as shown in Figure 4-20. When you do, Flash changes the filled square to a hollow square (the Outline icon) and displays your layer content in outline form on the stage. To return your layer to normal, click the square again.

- **To outline the contents of every layer except one,** Alt-click (Option-click) the outline icon for that layer.

## Organizing Layers with Folders

When your animation has only a handful of layers, organization isn't such a big deal. But if you find yourself creating 10, 20, or even more layers, you'll want to use layer folders to keep your layers tidy (and yourself from going nuts).

A *layer folder* is simply a folder you can add to the Layers window. Layer folders aren't associated with frames; you can't place images directly into them. (If you try, you'll see the error message shown in Figure 4-22.)

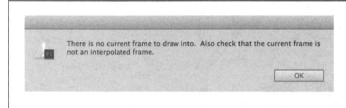

There is no current frame to draw into. Also check that the current frame is not an interpolated frame.

OK

**FIGURE 4-22**

*If you try to draw on the stage when you've selected a folder instead of a layer, Flash lets you know in no uncertain terms. (An interpolated frame is a tweened frame; as you learned in Chapter 3, you can't place images in a tweened frame, either.)*

Instead, layer folders act as containers to organize your layers. For example, you might want to put all the layers pertaining to a certain drawing (like a logo or a character) into a single layer folder and name the folder *logo* or *Ralph*. That way you don't have to scroll through a bunch of layers to find the one image you're looking for.

**NOTE** As you might expect, showing, hiding, locking, unlocking, and outlining a layer folder affects every layer inside that folder.

Each folder you add takes up a line in the timeline, and eventually there's not enough room to display all the layers and folders in the panel. You can use the scroll bar on the right side of the timeline to find your layers, or you can increase the height of the timeline panel by dragging the panel's top edge.

### ■ CREATING LAYER FOLDERS

To create a layer folder:

1. **Click the name of a layer to select it.**

   When you create a folder, it appears above the selected layer; but you'll be able to drag your folder and its contents to a new location.

2. **Click the Insert Layer Folder icon.** (If you prefer, you can choose Insert→ Timeline→Layer Folder or right-click the layer, and then, from the shortcut menu that appears, choose Insert Folder.)

Flash creates a new layer folder named Folder 1, as shown in Figure 4-23.

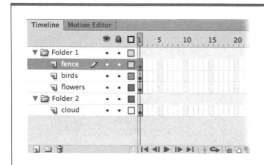

**FIGURE 4-23**

*Newly created layer folders appear expanded, like Folder 1 here (note the down arrow). Clicking the down arrow collapses the folder and changes the down arrow to a right arrow. When you drag layers into an open folder (or expand a collapsed folder), the layers appear beneath the folder. You rename a layer folder the same way you rename a layer: by double-clicking the existing name and then typing in one of your own. You can move layer folders around the same way you move layers around, too: by dragging.*

3. **Drag layers onto the layer folder.**

   If the folder is already expanded, you see the layers appear beneath it. If the folder is closed, then click the triangle button to view the layers inside.

**TIP** You can place layer folders inside other layer folders, but don't go wild; the point is to organize your layers so that you can find them easily, not to see how few folders you can display in the Layers window.

### ■ DELETING A LAYER FOLDER

To delete a layer folder, *and all the layers and folders inside*, right-click the layer folder, and then, from the shortcut menu that appears, select Delete Folder. Flash pops up a warning message informing you that you're about to delete not just the folder, but also everything in it. If that's what you want, then click Yes; otherwise, click No.

## ■ Spotlight Effect Using Mask Layers

Imagine placing a sheet of red construction paper containing a cutout of a star over a piece of green construction paper. The result you see, when you look at the two sheets stacked on top of each other, is a green star on a red background. That's the concept behind mask layers, a special type of layer that lets you create shaped "portholes" through which an underlying (masked) layer appears.

At a masquerade ball, masks hide the important stuff—your face. It's a little different in Flash and other graphic arts endeavors. Masks hide part of a picture in order to reveal the important stuff—the subject. You use masks to direct the eye of your audience. And when you apply a classic tween to the porthole, you can create an effect that looks like a spotlight playing over an image—mighty cool, indeed.

Here's how you go about it:

1. **Open the file 04-3_Mask_Layer.fla.**

   You can download this file, a working example of the file (*04-4_Mask_Layer _done.fla*), and all the other examples shown in this chapter from the Missing CD page at *www.missingmanuals.com/cds/flashcs6mm*.

2. **Click Layer 1 to select it.**

   In the example file for this section (*04-3_Mask_Layer.fla*), Layer 1 contains a bitmap image.

3. **Click the Insert Layer button.** (The Insert Layer button is on the bar below the layer names and looks like a folded-over page.)

   Flash creates a new layer named Layer 2 and places it above Layer 1.

4. **Double-click the layer icon next to Layer 2.**

   The Layer Properties window appears (Figure 4-24).

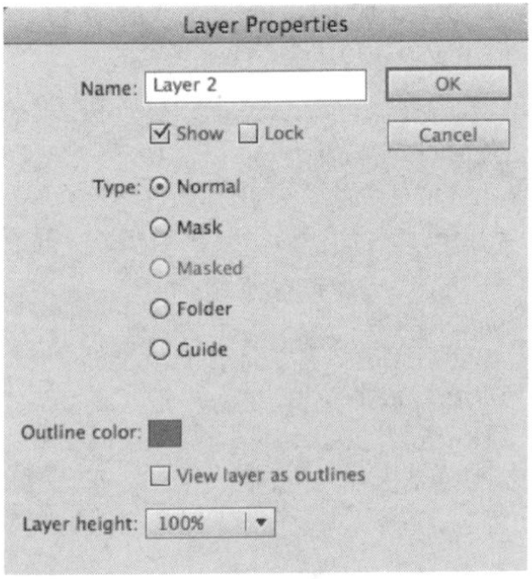

**FIGURE 4-24**

*Use the Layer Properties window to change the layer from one type to another. In this example, you create a mask layer and a masked layer.*

5. **In the Layer Properties window, turn on the Mask checkbox, and then click OK.**

   Flash displays the mask icon next to Layer 2.

6. **Double-click the layer icon next to Layer 1.**

   The Layer Properties window appears again.

7. **This time, turn on the checkbox next to Masked, and then click OK.**

   Flash displays the masked icon next to Layer 1.

8. **Select Frame 20 in both Layer 1 and Layer 2, and then select Insert→Timeline→ Frame.**

Flash extends both layers to Frame 20.

9. **Click to select the first frame in Layer 2 (the mask layer).** On the stage, click the Oval tool, and then draw a circle in the upper-right corner of the stage (Figure 4-25).

**FIGURE 4-25**

*The shape you use as a portal has to be either a fill (like the circle shown here) or a symbol. Because the Brush tool creates fills, you can use the Brush to draw a freehand portal. (Strokes on the mask layer have no effect.)*

The oval can be any color you choose, since it won't appear in the finished effect; instead, it'll act as a see-through portal.

Flash gives you a bunch of ways to create masks and masked layers (by right-clicking an existing layer, and then choosing Mask or Masked, for example), but one thing doesn't change: Masked layers have to appear directly below mask layers in the Layers window for the effect to work. If you create a mask layer and a masked layer in the wrong order, just drag the mask layer above the masked layer.

10. **With the circle still selected, choose Modify→"Convert to Symbol" or press F8.**

A "Convert to Symbol" box appears. If you want to animate a mask with a motion tween, you need to use a symbol.

11. **In the Name box, type *Circle Mask*.** Choose Movie Clip for type and then press OK.

Now, the circle symbol on the stage is an instance of the Circle Mask movie clip symbol.

12. **Right-click Layer 2 and choose Create Motion Tween.**

Layer 2 shows the blue motion tween highlight.

13. **Move the playhead to Frame 20.** Then, with the Select tool (V), drag the circle to the lower-right corner of the stage (Figure 4-26).

**FIGURE 4-26**

*In this example, you're creating a simple tween in Layer 2 so that the portal moves across the bitmap image showing only a circle's worth of image at any one time (a spotlight effect). But you can create static portals (masks), too. The simplest is a circle or a square, but nice thick letters also make a compelling effect.*

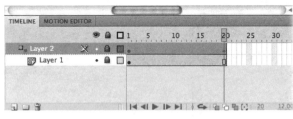

14. **Right-click the layer name (Layer 2) and then choose Show Masking from the shortcut menu.**

    With the mask in effect, everything in the photo is hidden except the portion covered by the circle. Flash automatically locks both layers when you choose Show Masking.

15. **Press Return to test your animation.**

    The circle mask moves across the photo, revealing different portions of the image, as shown in Figure 4-26.

You can animate your mask using the standard motion tween tricks described in Chapter 3 and Chapter 8. For example, filmmakers sometimes use an iris effect, where the visible part of an image shrinks down to a small circle. You can use the X/Y properties to change the size of the mask symbol as it moves. Keep in mind that before you can make changes to the mask's properties, you need to unlock the mask layer. When you click the padlock button to unlock the layer, Show Masking is turned off, so you see the entire photo as well as the circle mask.

# Advanced Drawing and Coloring

There's a difference between using a pencil to create stick drawings and using a pencil to create a carefully shaded portrait. Chapter 2 covered drawing basics, explaining exactly how the Pencil, Pen, Brush, Line, and shape tools work. This chapter explains how to use the tools in a more creative and nuanced manner. In real life—whether you're pounding out Flash animations for your boss or for your own personal website—you're rarely going to be satisfied with a simple drawing. For each keyframe of your animation, you're going to want to start with a basic sketch and then play with it, changing its color, moving a line here and there, adding a graphic element or two, and repositioning it until it looks exactly the way you want it to look.

In this chapter, you'll get more acquainted with Flash's *selection* tools—the tools you use to tell Flash which specific part of a drawing you want to change. Then you'll apply Flash's editing tools from basic (copying, pasting, and moving) to advanced (scaling, rotating, stacking, grouping, and more). You'll also do more with color in Flash drawings than you saw in Chapter 2. After a quick background in color theory, this chapter covers applying color effects like brightness and transparency, and even creating custom colors. The chapter wraps up with some special tools that let you create complex patterns with a click of your mouse.

## ◼ Selecting Graphic Elements

With few exceptions, before you can modify an object on the stage, you first have to *select* the object. It's the same in a word processor, where you have to highlight a word with your cursor before you can edit or delete it. Since Flash deals with more complex objects than words, it gives you a variety of selection tools for different purposes. The Tools panel (Figure 5-1) has three different selection tools. Each is good for selecting a different type of objects.

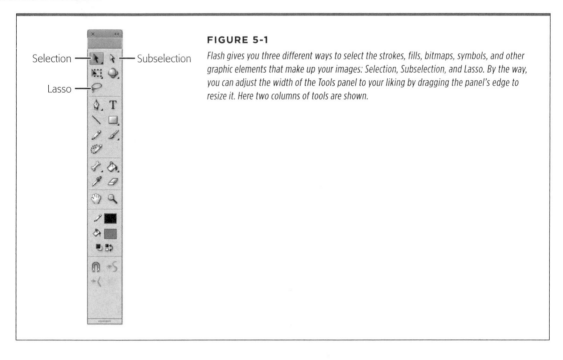

Selection — Subselection

Lasso

**FIGURE 5-1**

*Flash gives you three different ways to select the strokes, fills, bitmaps, symbols, and other graphic elements that make up your images: Selection, Subselection, and Lasso. By the way, you can adjust the width of the Tools panel to your liking by dragging the panel's edge to resize it. Here two columns of tools are shown.*

There are a couple of exceptions to this rule: specifically, modifying fill color using the Paint Bucket tool (page 87) and reshaping lines and curves using the Selection tool (next page). But in general, you need to select stuff in Flash before you can work with it.

**TIP** To select everything on the stage, choose Edit→Select All or use the shortcut key Ctrl+A (⌘-A).

- **Selection.** The black arrow selects entire strokes, fills, shapes, and objects (like bitmaps and symbols), as well as individual portions of those strokes, fills, shapes, and objects.

- **Subselection.** The white arrow lets you select the individual points that make up lines and curves.

- **Lasso.** This tool, which looks like a miniature lasso, is great for selecting groups of objects, oddly shaped objects, or portions of objects. When objects are close together on the stage, you can use the lasso to carefully select around them.

The following sections describe each of these tools in detail.

**NOTE** The selection tools behave differently depending on whether you've drawn your objects on the stage using object drawing mode or chosen to stick with merge drawing mode (which Flash assumes you want until you tell it differently). See page 55 for a rundown on the two drawing modes.

## The Selection Tool

The aptly named Selection tool (V) is the workhorse of Flash's selection tools; with it, you can select individual graphic elements like strokes, fills, shapes, symbols, text blocks, and grouped objects. You can also use the Selection tool to select a portion of any object, as shown in Figure 5-2, or to move or reshape an object (a process sometimes referred to as *transforming* an object).

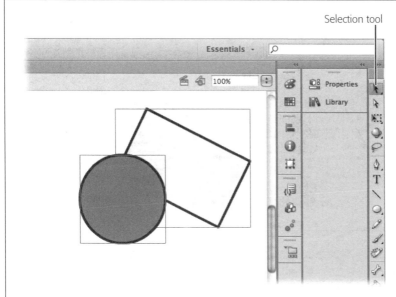

Selection tool

**FIGURE 5-2**

*Using the Selection tool is the easiest way to select just about any object, whether it's a shape, a stroke, a bitmap, a fill, or a text block. To use the Selection tool: In the Tools panel, click the tool; then, on the stage, click the object you want to select. To select groups of objects, you have a choice: You can either Shift-click each object, or click outside the group and then drag until Flash displays a selection box around your group.*

### ■ SELECTING A GRAPHIC ELEMENT

The most common thing you're going to want to do with the Selection tool is select an entire graphic element—a circle, a line, a block of text, a bitmap, a hand-drawn kangaroo—so that you can apply color to it, copy it, skew it, or make some other modification to it.

**NOTE** To deselect a selected object (regardless of which tool you used to select it), simply click any blank spot on the stage or press Ctrl+Shift+A (Shift-⌘-A).

To select an entire graphic element (or group of elements) using the Selection tool:

1. **In the Tools panel, click the Selection tool.**

   Flash highlights the Selection tool, and Selection tool–specific options appear in the Options section at the bottom of the Tools panel (Figure 5-3).

2. **Either click the object you want to select, or (best for lines and groups of objects) click near the object, and then drag your cursor until the selection box surrounds the object.**

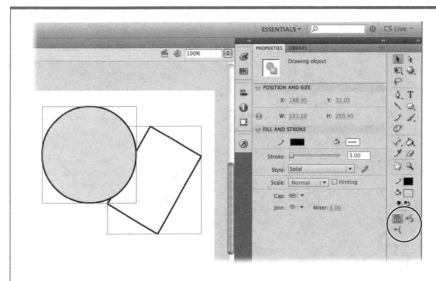

**FIGURE 5-3**

*Flash displays a selection box around selected objects (like the circle and rectangle shown here), symbols, and text blocks to let you know you've successfully selected them. When you're using the Selection tool, you see special options at the bottom of the Tools panel. For example, the magnet button toggles the "Snap to Objects" option described on page 192.*

---

**TIP** You can also select more than one object with the Selection tool. Select the first object, and then Shift-click each additional object you want to select.

---

Flash highlights the selected object—either by displaying a selection box around the object as shown on the left in Figure 5-4 or by covering the selected area with the selection pattern shown on the right. Either way, the Properties panel changes to reflect the object you've selected.

---

**NOTE** When you select a straight line or a rectangular object, you may find it tough to see the selection box because Flash draws it so closely around the line that it almost looks like part of the line itself. A quick look at the Properties panel will tell you what is selected.

---

With the object selected, you can make any modifications you want to the object using the main menu options, Flash's Color or Transform tools (pages 84 and 109), or any of the panels, like the Properties panel.

**NOTE** If you use the Selection tool to select an ungrouped line or shape, Flash displays the Straighten and Smooth options (check out the Options section of the Tools panel). These options let you tweak your lines and shapes—useful if you've got a shape almost the way you want it, but not quite (and you don't want to have to start over and redraw the whole thing). To incrementally straighten a curved line, with the line selected, click the Straighten option. To incrementally turn a series of straight-line angles into a curve, with the line selected, click the Smooth option.

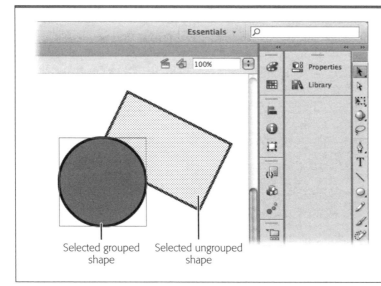

**FIGURE 5-4**

*Grouped shapes and ungrouped shapes behave differently when it comes to selection tools. They even look different when you select them. The circle here is a selected grouped shape; it shows a marquee. The rectangle is a selected ungrouped shape; it shows the dotted highlight pattern on the selected portions.*

Selected grouped shape

Selected ungrouped shape

### ■ SELECTING PART OF A SHAPE OR OBJECT

Here's yet another case when shapes drawn in object drawing mode behave differently from shapes drawn in merge mode. Select a shape created in object drawing mode and it's an all-or-nothing deal. Flash thinks of those shapes as a unit. However, if you create a shape in merge mode, it's easy to select just a portion of the shape. A single click selects the fill or the stroke—maybe just a segment of the stroke. That's why shapes drawn in merge mode are sometimes called *ungrouped* shapes. Because they're ungrouped, you can select or carve a chunk off the shape. Maybe you want to apply a gradient effect to a portion of the shape. Or maybe you want to sculpt a complex shape from a rectangle or oval by removing bits and pieces. Using the Selection tool, you can drag a rectangle anywhere over an ungrouped shape to tell Flash to select just a portion.

So is it impossible to edit parts of a shape drawn in object mode? No, not at all. Double-click a *drawing object*, and it opens for editing as an ungrouped shape. Other objects on the stage are dimmed and unselectable. The Edit bar above the stage lists "Drawing Object" to indicate that you're editing a drawing object. To close the object, click the scene name or the blue Back arrow in the Edit bar. The drawing object closes, and no matter how you've changed its appearance, it still behaves as a drawing object. For example, a single click selects the object, and the Properties panel describes it as a drawing object.

**TIP** While it's open for editing, you can cut a drawing object into two or more parts. You can even add a separate, unconnected shape to the drawing. Once you're through editing and the object is closed, Flash still treats it as a single drawing object.

If you want, you can convert a drawing object into an ungrouped shape. Select the shape, and then choose Modify→Ungroup. Flash gives you visual clues so you can tell a grouped shape from an ungrouped shape, as shown in Figure 5-4. Your object drawing becomes an ungrouped shape, as if it had been drawn in merge mode. You can confirm this by selecting the shape and checking the Properties panel, where it's listed as a Shape.

**NOTE** If you want to select a free-form portion of an object—for example, you've drawn a jungle scene and you want to cut the shape of a baboon's head out of it—you need the Lasso tool (page 62). The Selection tool lets you select only a rectangular shape.

To select just a portion of an ungrouped shape using the Selection tool:

1. **In the Tools panel, click the Selection tool.**

   Flash highlights the Selection tool.

2. **Click near the object, and then drag your cursor until the selection box surrounds just the portion of the ungrouped object you want to select (Figure 5-5).**

   When you let go of the mouse, Flash highlights the selected portion of the object, as shown in Figure 5-5.

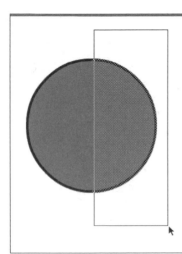

**FIGURE 5-5**

*The Selection tool lets you select using only a rectangular selection box. You can make it a large rectangle or a small one, but it's still a rectangle. If you need to select an irregular portion of an object, then you need the Lasso tool. If Flash insists on selecting the entire shape (or bitmap) when all you want to do is select a piece of it, then ungroup the shape (or break apart the bitmap).*

**NOTE** To select a portion of a grouped shape or a drawing object, you need to ungroup it first (Modify→Ungroup). To select a portion of a bitmap (like a photograph), you need to break it apart first (Modify→Break Apart).

### ▮ MOVING AND RESHAPING (TRANSFORMING) WITH THE SELECTION TOOL

The Selection tool does more than just select objects. It also moves and reshapes, or *transforms*, them. This is great—as long as you know what to expect. (Many's the budding Flashionado who's sat down to select part of an image and been totally dismayed when the object suddenly, inexplicably, developed a barnacle-like bulge.)

**NOTE** Whether or not Flash treats your shape as a single cohesive entity or independent elements depends on whether you drew that shape in object or merge drawing mode, as explained on page 161.

Here's how it works: If you click the Selection tool and then position your cursor directly over an unselected fill or stroke, Flash displays, next to your cursor, one of three icons: a cross with arrowheads, a curve, or an angle.

- **Moving (cross with arrowheads).** The cross with arrowheads (Figure 5-6) tells you that you can drag the selected object to move it.

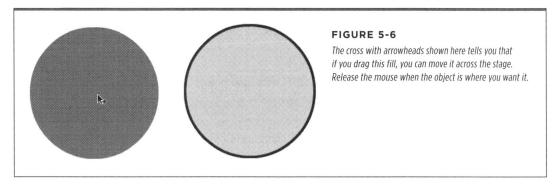

**FIGURE 5-6**

*The cross with arrowheads shown here tells you that if you drag this fill, you can move it across the stage. Release the mouse when the object is where you want it.*

- **Reshaping (curve).** When you see the curve icon shown in Figure 5-7, dragging reshapes the stroke or edge beneath your cursor (in other words, it lets you add or modify a curve).

- **Reshaping (angle).** Dragging the angle icon (Figure 5-8) lets you reshape one of the corners of your object.

**TIP** To add an angle rather than a curve, when you see the curve icon, press Alt (Option) before dragging.

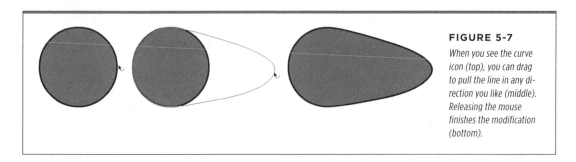

**FIGURE 5-7**

*When you see the curve icon (top), you can drag to pull the line in any direction you like (middle). Releasing the mouse finishes the modification (bottom).*

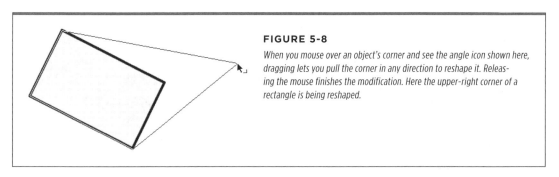

**FIGURE 5-8**

*When you mouse over an object's corner and see the angle icon shown here, dragging lets you pull the corner in any direction to reshape it. Releasing the mouse finishes the modification. Here the upper-right corner of a rectangle is being reshaped.*

## The Subselection Tool

When you want to modify the individual points and segments that make up your shapes, use the Subselection tool: the white arrow in the Tools panel.

Click a stroke or the edge of a fill with the Subselection tool, and you see the anchor points that define the stroke or shape. To change the stroke or shape, drag one of the anchor points. To adjust a curved line segment, click an anchor point adjacent to the curve, and you see control handles connected to the anchor. These control handles work like the ones used with the Pen tool (page 68). To change a curve, drag a control handle, and the curve changes its path. You can move a fill or stroke using the Subselection tool—just make sure you don't click on an anchor point. The cursor shows a hollow square when it's over an anchor point and a solid square when it's over a line segment.

To use the Subselection tool to move an object:

1. **In the Tools panel, click the Subselection tool (Figure 5-9).**

   Flash highlights the Subselection tool, and the cursor becomes a white arrow.

2. **Click the object you want to modify (or click near the object, and then drag your cursor until the selection box surrounds the object).**

Flash redisplays the object as a series of segments and selectable points.

3. **Mouse over any of the line segments in the object.**

The cursor displays a black square when it is over a line segment but displays a hollow square when it is over an anchor point.

4. **While the cursor displays a black square, click and drag to move the object.** When you're satisfied, let go of the mouse.

Flash displays your moved object.

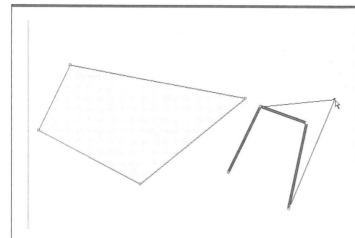

**FIGURE 5-9**

*If you click the Subselection tool and then click an object you've created using any drawing tool (Pen, Pencil, Brush, Line, or shape), Flash redisplays the line as a series of segments and points. Click any segment (the cursor displays a tiny black square as you mouse over a segment), and Flash lets you move the entire object. Click a point (a hollow square) instead, and Flash lets you change the object's shape.*

To use the Subselection tool to move an anchor point (and, by association, the segments attached to that point):

1. **In the Tools panel, click the Subselection tool.**

Flash highlights the Subselection tool.

2. **Click the object you want to work with (or click near the object, and then drag your cursor until the selection box surrounds the object).**

Flash redisplays the object as a series of segments and selectable points.

3. **Mouse over the point you want to modify.**

Flash displays a hollow square.

4. **Drag the anchor point to reshape your object.** When you're satisfied, let go of the mouse.

Flash displays your modified object. You can see an example in Figure 5-10.

**TIP** If the anchor point defines a curve (in other words, if you see a hollow square at the end of a curved line), clicking the point tells Flash to display *control handles* that define the curve. You can drag one of the control handles to adjust the curve. To convert a straight line segment to a curve, hold the Subselection tool over an anchor point and then press Alt (Option), and you can drag a control handle from the anchor point. Use the new control handles to form the curve.

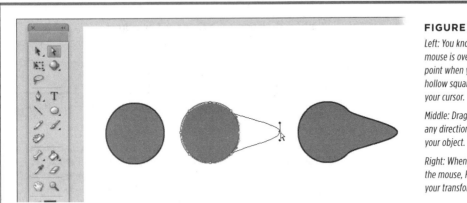

**FIGURE 5-10**

*Left: You know your mouse is over a selectable point when you see the hollow square next to your cursor.*

*Middle: Drag the point in any direction to reshape your object.*

*Right: When you let go of the mouse, Flash displays your transformed object.*

## The Lasso Tool

Sometimes a rectangular selection just can't encompass the objects you want to select. Say you want to select an irregular shape inside an oval so you can recolor it or remove it. Or perhaps your stage is so jam-packed with images that you can't select the image you want with the Selection tool without inadvertently selecting parts of images you *don't* want. Those situations call for the Lasso tool (L). Draw a line around your selection with the Lasso tool and you can grab it, as shown in Figure 5-11. The lasso has two modes—freehand mode and polygon mode. You'll learn how to use both here.

**TIP** As explained earlier in this chapter (page 161), you can only select portions of ungrouped shapes. If it's a drawing object, then double-click the object to open it for editing, or convert it to an ungrouped shape with Modify→Ungroup.

### ■ FREEHAND SELECTING WITH THE LASSO

Depending on how steady your hands are, drawing a freehand lasso around an object (or around the portion of an object you want to select) is the quickest way to select what you want. Straight out of the box, this is how the Lasso works.

To use the Lasso tool to select objects (and portions of objects) freehand:

1. **In the Tools panel, click the Lasso tool (Figure 5-11, left).**

   Flash highlights the Lasso tool, and in the Options section of the Tools panel, the Lasso-related options appear.

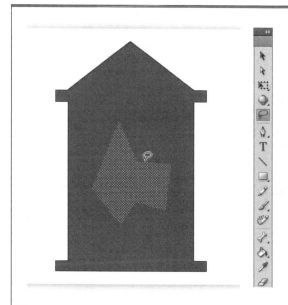

**FIGURE 5-11**

*Use the Lasso tool when you want to select an irregular shape. With the Lasso, you draw a line around the objects or parts that you want to select. Then you can modify, move, or remove the selection.*

2. **Click near the object you want to select, and then drag your mouse to encircle the object.**

   Figure 5-12 (right) shows you an example.

3. **When you've completely encircled your object, let go of the mouse button.**

   Flash selects everything inside the loop you drew with the Lasso tool.

> **TIP** You can have a tricky time drawing a precise loop using the Lasso, especially if you're using a mouse instead of a graphics tablet. Fortunately, Flash has got your back; if you don't completely close the loop, Flash closes it for you, using a straight line. If this action isn't what you want, just select Edit→Undo Lasso, and then start over. If you're still having trouble, try using the Zoom tool to enlarge the stage, or try the Lasso's polygon mode, described in the following section.

### ◼ POLYGON SELECTING WITH THE LASSO

The Lasso is great for those irregular shapes, but sometimes you may want to outline your selection with straight lines.

In these cases, freehand just doesn't cut it; one slip, and you have to start over. You're better off taking advantage of the Lasso tool's polygon mode, which lets you click to surround an area. (Flash takes care of filling in the straight lines between your clicks so you don't have to.)

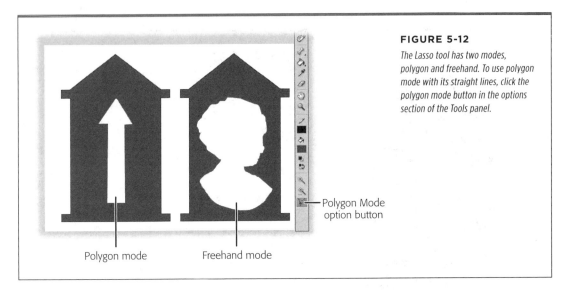

**FIGURE 5-12**

*The Lasso tool has two modes, polygon and freehand. To use polygon mode with its straight lines, click the polygon mode button in the options section of the Tools panel.*

Polygon Mode
option button

Polygon mode

Freehand mode

To use the Lasso tool to select objects (and portions of objects) by pointing and clicking:

1. **In the Tools panel, click the Lasso tool.**

   Flash highlights the Lasso tool. In the options section of the Tools panel, the Lasso-related options appear.

2. **Click the polygon mode option (Figure 5-12).** Then, using a series of clicks, enclose the object you want to select.

   Flash automatically connects your clicks with straight-line segments.

3. **Double-click to complete your selection.**

   Flash selects everything inside the loop you drew with the Lasso tool.

#### ■ COMBINING FREEHAND AND POLYGON MODES

Just because you start out in freehand or polygon mode doesn't mean you're stuck with it for the entire selection. For example, you can start off your selection in freehand mode by dragging the mouse to trace lines. Then, hold down the Alt (Option) key to switch to polygon mode. Continue your selection by clicking on points to create straight lines. Double-click when you're ready to finish off your selection, and Flash draws the last straight line to connect the beginning and end points.

**TIP** You may find that the Lasso—especially in polygon mode—doesn't want to quit when you do. In other words, when you go to use the main menu or a panel or another drawing tool, you find you can't because Flash keeps insisting that you need to keep lassoing. The best way to get rid of a sticky Lasso is to double-click and then press Ctrl+Shift+A (Shift-⌘-A) to deselect all.

### ■ SELECTING RANGES OF COLOR IN BITMAPS WITH THE MAGIC WAND

Flash treats *bitmaps*—for example, photos in the JPEG format—differently from the way it treats the shapes you create using its drawing tools. And if you take a look at Figure 5-13, you'll see why.

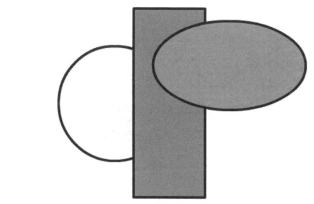

**FIGURE 5-13**

*Top: The drawing is clearly composed of three shapes, each of which you can click to select separately.*

*Bottom: The bitmap image is much more complex, with no easily identifiable shape outlines. When you click to select the image on the bottom, Flash highlights the entire rectangular image; it makes no distinction among the colors and shapes inside.*

While you can't manipulate bitmaps in Flash anywhere near as easily or as completely as you can manipulate the shapes and lines you draw directly onto the stage, Flash does have a special tool specifically for selecting ranges of colors in bitmaps: the Magic Wand. After you select color ranges, you can then recolor them or cut them out of the bitmap completely.

To select color ranges in a bitmap using the Magic Wand:

1. **On the stage, select the bitmap you want to work with.**

   Flash displays a light-colored border around the selected bitmap.

2. **Choose Modify→Break Apart.**

   Flash redisplays the bitmap as a selected fill.

3. **From the Tools panel, select the Lasso.** Then, in the Options section at the bottom of the Tools panel, click the Magic Wand (Figure 5-14, top).

   As you mouse over the bitmap, your cursor turns into a tiny magic wand.

4. **Click the bitmap to select a color range.**

   Flash highlights bits of selected color.

5. **Click the bitmap again (click a similarly colored area).**

   Flash highlights the bits of color that match your selection. You can modify the highlighted bits of fill color as you go (cut them, recolor them using the Eyedropper tool described on page 211, and so on), or continue to click the bitmap as you did in step 4 to add to the selection.

In Figure 5-14 (bottom), the designer first selected, and then cut (Edit→Cut), the pixels, the start of turning a foggy sky to blue.

# ■ Manipulating Graphic Elements

Flash gives you a gazillion tools to modify the drawings that make up your animations. You can stack, rearrange, and reposition each individual graphic element, transform (shrink and squish) them, move them, apply color effects, and more until you're completely satisfied with the way they look. It's a cliché, but it's true: When it comes to drawing in Flash, you're pretty much limited only by your imagination. This section acquaints you with the most powerful tools Flash has for modifying the lines, shapes, bitmaps, symbols, and other graphic elements you add to your drawings.

## Modifying Object Properties

Flash's Properties panel is a beautiful thing. Select any element on the stage, and the Properties panel responds by displaying all the characteristics, or *properties*, that you can change about that element.

In Figure 5-15, for example, you see several graphic elements on the stage: a brush-drawn squiggle (fill), a bitmap of a ship, a block of text, and a star. When you select the star, the Properties panel shows all the properties associated with the star: the color, width, and type of outline; the fill color; and so on. When you select the text, the Properties panel changes to reflect only text properties.

**FIGURE 5-14**

*Top: The first time you click the Magic Wand, Flash notes the color you choose.*

*Middle: The second (and subsequent) times you click the Magic Wand, Flash selects the bits of color nearby that match your first selection. Selecting colored areas of bitmaps with the Magic Wand can be slow going. Don't expect the precision you enjoy when you're working with primitive shapes, like squares and circles. Still, depending on the effect you're after, the Magic Wand can be useful.*

*Bottom: Here most of the background was selected with the Magic Wand tool and primed for repainting.*

Select a shape, and you can change the properties for the fill and stroke. If it's a merge mode graphic, you can select the fill and stroke independently. If it's an object mode graphic, the fill and stroke are both selected with a single click. In either case, the properties for the selection appear in the Properties panel. For example, you can change the color, the thickness, and the style of a stroke. Select the fill, and you can change the color, the opacity (alpha), or the gradient. These color options are explained on pages 198 and 206.

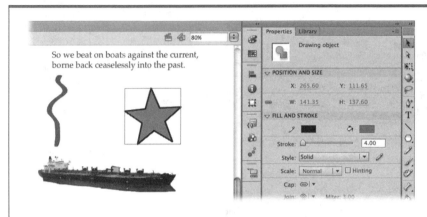

**FIGURE 5-15**

*Selecting an object tells Flash to display that object's properties right there in the Properties panel. Here the star shape is selected, so the properties all relate to the star. As long as the property isn't grayed out, you can change it in the Properties panel.*

## Moving, Cutting, Pasting, and Copying

After you have an object on the stage, you can move it around, cut it (delete it), paste it somewhere else, or make copies of it.

> **TIP** All the things you can do to an object—cutting, pasting, copying, and moving—you can also do to a piece of an object. Instead of selecting the entire object, just select whatever portion of the object you want to work with, and then go from there.

### ■ MOVING GRAPHICS

To move an object, simply select it (page 61), and then drag it around the stage. Figure 5-16 shows an example of using the Selection tool to select a group of objects, and then move them together.

### ■ CUTTING GRAPHICS

To cut an object, select the object (page 61), and then choose Edit→Cut. Flash deletes the object from the stage and turns on the Paste functions.

> **NOTE** Choosing Edit→Clear deletes the selected object, too, but doesn't turn on the Paste functions. In other words, after you choose Edit→Clear, it's gone, baby, gone (unless you quickly choose Edit→Undo Delete).

## COPYING GRAPHICS

To copy an object, select the object (page 61), and then choose Edit→Copy. Flash leaves the object on the stage and turns on the Paste functions (see the next section).

> **TIP** You can perform a quick copy-and-paste operation by selecting an object and then choosing Edit→Duplicate. Flash displays a movable copy of the selected object just above the selected object. For even faster duplication, press Alt (Option) as you drag the object.

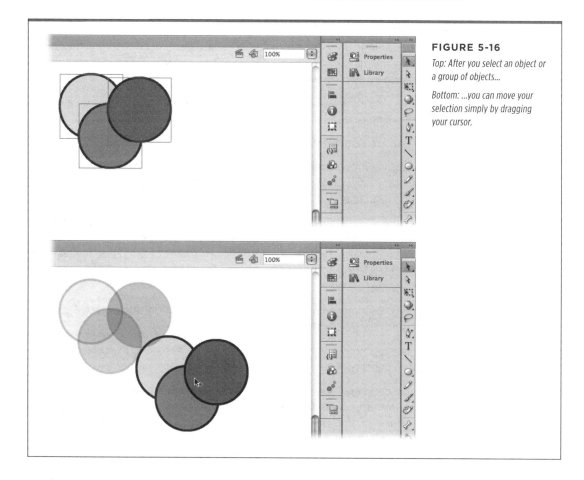

**FIGURE 5-16**

*Top: After you select an object or a group of objects...*

*Bottom: ...you can move your selection simply by dragging your cursor.*

## PASTING GRAPHICS

To paste an object that you've either cut or copied, choose one of the following:

- **Edit→Paste in Center.** This tells Flash to paste the cut (or copied) object smack in the middle of the stage's visible area, on top of any other image that happens to be there.

- **Edit→Paste in Place.** This tells Flash to replace the cut object, or to put the copied object square on top of the original. This command is especially useful when you want to move an object from one frame to another and place it in exactly the same position in the new frame.

> **TIP** For many Flash designers, the quickest way to cut, copy, and paste objects is to right-click (Control-click) the stage and then choose the command off the shortcut menu.

## Transforming Objects

In the graphics world, *transforming* an object doesn't just mean changing the object; transforming means applying very specific shape and size changes to the object. These changes—called *transforms*—include some fun tricks:

- **Scaling**. Among graphic designers, scaling means shrinking or enlarging a selected shape based on its width, height, or both.

- **Rotating.** You can rotate (turn) an object as far as you want, in any direction.

- **Skewing.** A limited kind of distortion, skewing means slanting an object either horizontally or vertically. For example, *italic text* appears skewed when compared to regular text.

- **Distorting and enveloping.** You distort an object by pulling it out of shape—in other words, by repositioning one or more of the object's angles. The envelope transform is similar, but it doesn't preserve the lines of the shape the way distortion does; instead, it lets you pull any angle, line, or curve out of shape to create fantastic effects.

- **Flipping.** Flipping an object creates a mirror image of the object. Flash has commands for flipping both horizontally and vertically.

You have several choices when it comes to applying a transform to a selected object (or group of objects):

- You can click the Free Transform tool (Figure 5-17), choose the appropriate option from the Options section of the Tools panel, and then, on the stage, drag your selection to apply the transform. This approach is described in the following sections.

- You can open the Transform panel (Window→Transform) and then type information (for example, the number of degrees you want to rotate an object) directly into the Transform panel.

- You can choose Modify→Transform, and then, from the pop-up menu that appears, turn on the checkbox next to the transformation you want to apply.

- You can right-click an object and choose Transform from the shortcut menu.

## ■ SCALING OBJECTS

To resize a drawn object, first select the object on the stage, and then proceed as follows:

1. **Select the Free Transform tool's Scale option.**

   Black squares appear at the corners and sides of your selection.

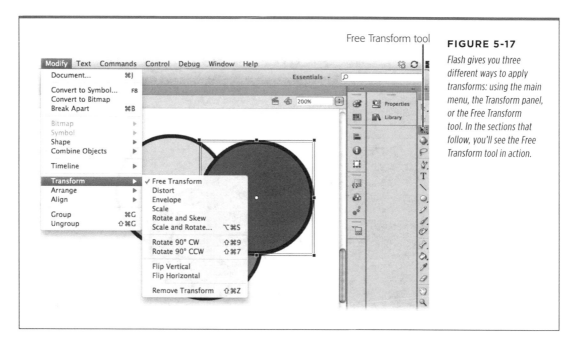

Free Transform tool

**FIGURE 5-17**

*Flash gives you three different ways to apply transforms: using the main menu, the Transform panel, or the Free Transform tool. In the sections that follow, you'll see the Free Transform tool in action.*

2. **Position your cursor over one of the black squares.**

   Your cursor turns into the double-headed *scale arrow* (Figure 5-18, top).

3. **Drag to scale the selection.**

   As you drag outward, the selection gets larger; as you drag inward, the selection gets smaller. You can see an example of a scaled object at the bottom of Figure 5-18.

**TIP**   You can use modifier keys to constrain objects as you scale them. For example, press Shift to lock the proportions or press Alt (Option) to scale an object around its transformation point (indicated by a circle).

### ■ ROTATING OBJECTS

To rotate a drawn object around its axis, first select the object on the stage, and then proceed as follows:

1. **Select the Free Transform tool's Rotate and Skew option.**

   Flash displays a black bounding box around your selection.

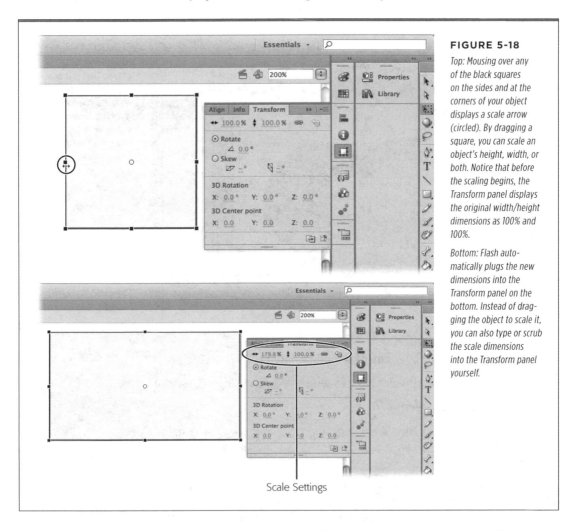

**FIGURE 5-18**

*Top: Mousing over any of the black squares on the sides and at the corners of your object displays a scale arrow (circled). By dragging a square, you can scale an object's height, width, or both. Notice that before the scaling begins, the Transform panel displays the original width/height dimensions as 100% and 100%.*

*Bottom: Flash automatically plugs the new dimensions into the Transform panel on the bottom. Instead of dragging the object to scale it, you can also type or scrub the scale dimensions into the Transform panel yourself.*

Scale Settings

2. **Position your cursor over one of the black squares you see at the corners of your selection.**

   Your cursor turns into a circular *rotation arrow* (Figure 5-19, top).

3. **Drag to rotate the selection.**

If you drag your cursor to the right, the entire selection rotates right; if you drag your cursor to the left, the selection rotates to the left. There's a rotated object in Figure 5-19 (bottom). Shift-drag to make an object rotate 45 degrees at a time. Alt-drag (Option-drag) to make your selection rotate around the anchor point on the opposite side from the cursor.

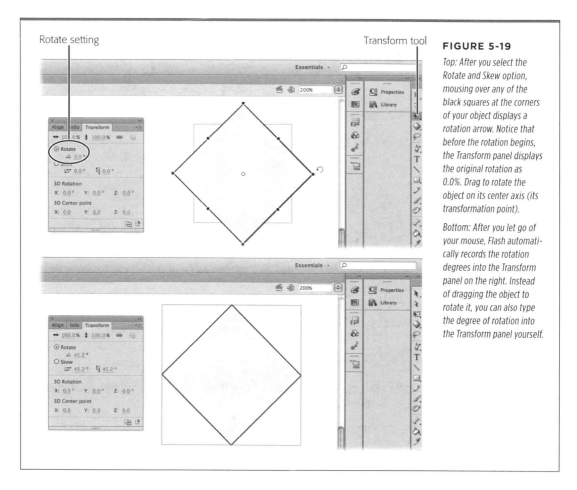

**FIGURE 5-19**

*Top: After you select the Rotate and Skew option, mousing over any of the black squares at the corners of your object displays a rotation arrow. Notice that before the rotation begins, the Transform panel displays the original rotation as 0.0%. Drag to rotate the object on its center axis (its transformation point).*

*Bottom: After you let go of your mouse, Flash automatically records the rotation degrees into the Transform panel on the right. Instead of dragging the object to rotate it, you can also type the degree of rotation into the Transform panel yourself.*

**TIP** You can flip your objects, too, by using Modify→Transform→Flip Vertical and Modify→Transform→Flip Horizontal. The effects are a little different from rotating, as explained in Figure 5-20.

■ **SKEWING OBJECTS**

To give your drawing a slanted shape, first select the object on the stage, and then proceed as follows:

1. **Select the Free Transform tool's Rotate and Skew option.**

   Flash displays a black bounding box around your selection.

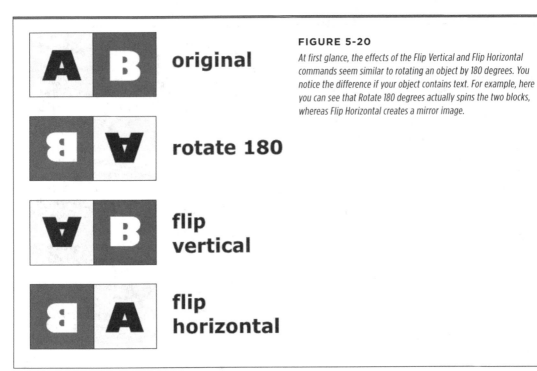

original

rotate 180

flip
vertical

flip
horizontal

**FIGURE 5-20**

*At first glance, the effects of the Flip Vertical and Flip Horizontal commands seem similar to rotating an object by 180 degrees. You notice the difference if your object contains text. For example, here you can see that Rotate 180 degrees actually spins the two blocks, whereas Flip Horizontal creates a mirror image.*

2. **Position your cursor over one of the lines of the bounding box, but avoid the square handles.**

   When the cursor is over the bounding box lines, you see the *skew arrow* (Figure 5-21, top). If your cursor is over one of the bounding box handles, you see the scale arrow.

3. **Drag to skew the selection.**

   Dragging slants the selection along one of its axes (the one marked by the skew arrow you clicked) in the direction you're dragging. Figure 5-21 (bottom) shows a skewed object. Alt-drag (Option-drag) to make the selected object skew around the transformation point, which is usually the center.

## ■ DISTORTING OBJECTS

For more freedom than simple skewing, you can distort your drawn objects in any way or direction:

1. **First, select the object you want to distort, and then select the Free Transform tool's distort option (Figure 5-17).**

   Flash displays black squares around the sides and corners of your selection.

2. **Position your cursor over one of the black squares.**

   Your cursor turns into a tailless *distortion arrow* (Figure 5-22, top).

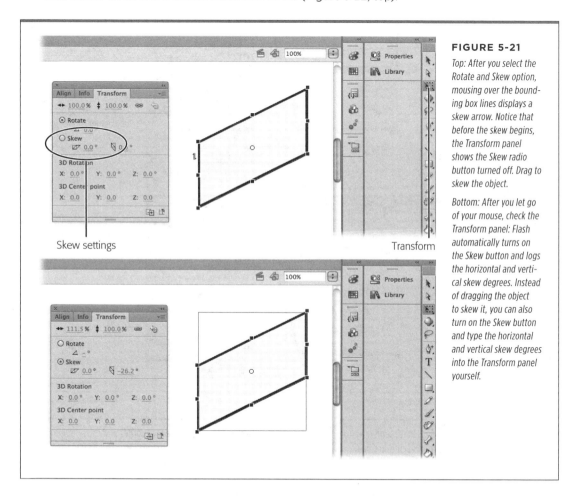

**FIGURE 5-21**

*Top: After you select the Rotate and Skew option, mousing over the bounding box lines displays a skew arrow. Notice that before the skew begins, the Transform panel shows the Skew radio button turned off. Drag to skew the object.*

*Bottom: After you let go of your mouse, check the Transform panel: Flash automatically turns on the Skew button and logs the horizontal and vertical skew degrees. Instead of dragging the object to skew it, you can also turn on the Skew button and type the horizontal and vertical skew degrees into the Transform panel yourself.*

Skew settings          Transform

### 3. **Drag to distort the selection.**

As you drag outward, the shape bulges outward; drag inward, and the shape dents inward. Figure 5-22 (bottom) shows a distorted object.

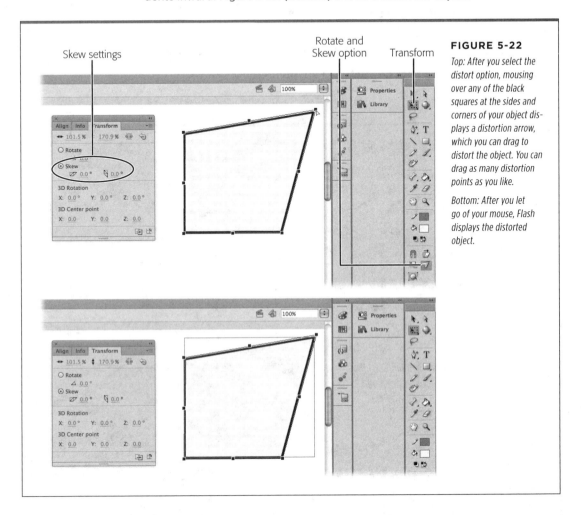

**FIGURE 5-22**

*Top: After you select the distort option, mousing over any of the black squares at the sides and corners of your object displays a distortion arrow, which you can drag to distort the object. You can drag as many distortion points as you like.*

*Bottom: After you let go of your mouse, Flash displays the distorted object.*

> **TIP** Shift-dragging a corner point lets you taper a shape; that is, move that corner and the adjoining corner apart from each other an equal distance.

#### ■ APPLYING AN ENVELOPE TRANSFORM

As discussed on page 174, an envelope transform is the most radical distortion. It gives you more distortion points than the regular Distort option, and also gives you finer control over the points by letting you drag inward or outward to create rounded bulges or dents (not just pointy ones). Here's how to use the envelope distortion:

1. **Click the Free Transform tool.**

   The Free Transform options appear in the Options section of the Tools panel.

2. **Select the object you want to distort.**

   Flash highlights the selected object with a black bounding box and tiny black squares.

3. **Click the envelope option.**

   The selected object appears surrounded by a series of black squares and circles.

4. **Position your cursor over one of the black squares or circles (distortion points).**

   Your cursor turns into a tailless *distortion arrow*.

5. **Drag to pull the selection into a new shape (Figure 5-23).**

   You'll notice that the envelope transform gives you a lot more distortion points to choose from than the distort transform; it also gives you finer control over the points you choose to distort (by dragging inward or outward).

You can see the results of modifying several distortion points in Figure 5-23.

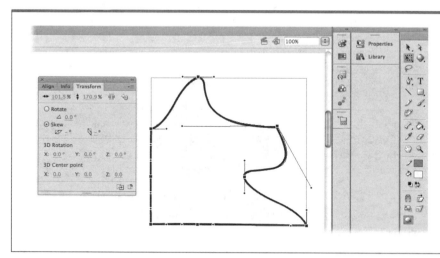

**FIGURE 5-23**

*This shape began life as a square. The top and right side were transformed using the Envelope option. Mousing over any of the black squares or circles at the sides and corners of your object displays a distortion arrow. Drag to reshape your object. The squares remain attached to the outline as you drag. The circles are curve control handles.*

## Moving and Rotating Objects in 3-D

Until Flash CS4 came along, it wasn't easy to make an object look as if it were moving in three dimensions. For example, if you wanted to make an image look as if it were traveling away from the viewer, about all you could do was move it slightly on the stage and make it smaller. There was no real science to the effect; the best you could do was eyeball it. Creating a 3-D rotation effect was even more difficult. But no more. Flash now has tools that automatically create exactly these two effects. Next to the selection tools, there's another tool that looks like a globe with some circles drawn around it, shown in Figure 5-24. Press and hold that button, and you find the two tools that turn the stage into a 3-D world. The globe lets you rotate an object three-dimensionally, while the tool with three arrows lets you move an object around in 3-D space.

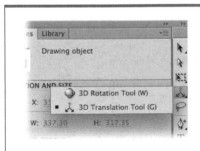

**FIGURE 5-24**

*Flash has two tools that let you move movie clip symbols in three dimensions. The tool that looks like a globe rotates movie clips. The tool with the three arrows lets you move movie clips in three dimensions.*

One catch is that the object has to be a movie clip or a TLF text field. (For details on text fields, see page 215.) This isn't too much of a catch, because you can put any object inside a movie clip—like your logo or some text—and then make it fly and spin in 3-D. The other catch is a bit more limiting, since Flash's drawing tools create only two-dimensional images. For example, you can create squares but not cubes, and circles but not spheres. The text tool creates only two-dimensional type, not 3-D letters. But once these objects are placed inside movie clips, you can move those movie clips around in three dimensions. It's sort of like moving a photo of a car around in 3-D space as opposed to moving a model car around the same space. But even with those limitations, you can create some pretty snazzy effects.

**NOTE** Because the 3-D tools are relative newcomers to Flash, they won't work if you choose the ActionScript 2.0 option (page 18), and they rely on Flash Player 10 or greater—an option you choose when you publish your animation (page 667).

### ■ ROTATING (TRANSFORMING) OBJECTS THREE-DIMENSIONALLY

The 3-D pros refer to rotating an object as *transforming* an object or a *transformation*. Here are the steps for rotating a movie clip in 3-D:

1. **Select the object or group of objects you want to spin, and then press F8 to convert them into a movie clip symbol.**

   You can combine objects in a movie clip. For example, Figure 5-25 shows a circle and text combined in one movie clip.

2. **On the stage, select the movie clip, and then click the 3-D Rotation tool in the Tools palette.**

A globe-like image appears near the movie clip, made up of colored circles. Each color represents a 3-D axis. The small circle in the center marks the point around which the rotation happens.

3. **Drag the center point to change the point around which the rotation takes place.**

   You can drag the center point to any location on the stage or even off the stage.

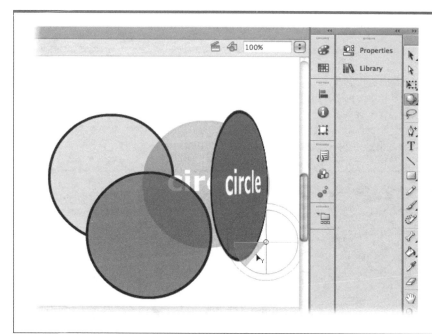

**FIGURE 5-25**

*Use the transform tools to rotate movie clip symbols in three dimensions. The sphere represents the directions you can spin a selected object. The object spins around the transformation point indicated by the small circle at the center of the sphere.*

4. **Click one of the colored lines in the 3-D rotation tool to rotate the movie clip along that axis.**

   As you hold the cursor over one of the colored axes, a tooltip appears indicating the axis around which the object will rotate. For example, move the cursor near the green line and a Y appears on the cursor, meaning that the selected object will rotate around the Y axis. You can think of the Y axis as a line that runs from the top of the stage to the bottom. The red line in the sphere represents the X axis, and the blue circle represents the Z axis, which you can think of as a line running from the viewer back into the stage. The easiest way to get your bearings is to experiment. Try the different options and click Undo (Ctrl+Z or ⌘-Z) if you don't like the results. If you don't want to be limited to spinning along a standard XYZ axis, then drag the orange ring around the outside of the other circles. That way, the object is free to follow your mouse movement in any direction.

### ■ MOVING (TRANSLATING) OBJECTS IN THREE DIMENSIONS

The 3-D pros refer to moving an object in three dimensions as *translating* an object or a *translation*. Here are the steps for moving a movie clip in 3-D:

1. **On the stage, select the movie clip you want to move in 3-D.**

   Make sure the object you want to move is a movie clip symbol. If not, press F8 to make it into one.

2. **In the Tools palette, click and hold the button for 3-D rotation tools, and then choose the 3D Translation tool from the menu.**

   In the tools panel, the 3D Translation tool looks like three arrows pointing in different directions. After you click the button, a 3-D translation icon appears over the selected movie clip on the stage. The 3D Translation icon looks like a red and green arrow protruding from a large dot. As shown in Figure 5-26, each arrow is a different color to represent an axis along which the movie clip can be moved. Green moves the object vertically (the Y axis). Red moves it horizontally (the X axis). The big black dot represents the Z axis.

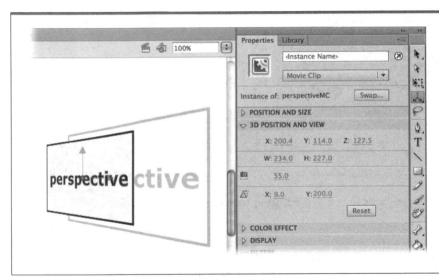

**FIGURE 5-26**

*The 3D Translation tool lets you move movie clips along the X, Y, or Z axes on the stage. Drag along one of the colored arrows representing each of the axes. Here the object is being dragged along the Z axis, which makes it smaller as it moves away from the viewer.*

3. **Drag one of the colored arrowheads or the dot to move the movie clip along that axis.**

   When you hold the cursor over one of the arrowheads or the dot, a tooltip appears indicating the direction of the axis: X, Y, or Z. In addition to using the 3D Translation tool, you can also use the Properties panel to move objects along the three axes (Figure 5-27). Select the movie clip you want to position, and then use the "3D Position and View" X, Y, and Z settings to move it around the stage. Click a setting and type a number, or drag to scrub in a number.

## ■ ADJUSTING THE PERSPECTIVE AND VANISHING POINT IN 3-D

You can set two 3-D properties in the Properties panel: Perspective and Vanishing Point (Figure 5-28). Choosing a perspective setting is similar to choosing a lens for your camera. Flash starts you off at 55, a "normal" point of view similar to a 55 mm lens on a camera. Set the number higher, and it's like you're zooming in or attaching a telephoto lens. Choose a lower setting, and it's as if you attached a wide-angle lens. You can add some creative distortion to your images using the Perspective setting, along with some of the other 3-D tools.

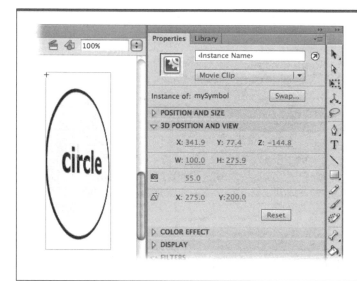

**FIGURE 5-27**

*Use the "3D Position and View" panel to dial in numbers for the perfect 3-D view. You can adjust the position, the perspective, and the vanishing point for objects on the stage.*

Think back to your art class days when you learned how to add a vanishing point to your drawings to help you draw in perspective. The vanishing point is that place way off in the distance where all parallel lines seem to converge. In Flash, you can move the vanishing point around in your animation using the X/Y settings in the Properties panel (Figure 5-28).

**NOTE** You can add these same 3-D effects to your motion tweens when you use the Motion Editor. For the details, see page 311.

## Stacking Objects

In Chapter 4, you learned how to stack objects to create composite drawings using layers. But you don't need layers to place one item on top of another. You can overlap two or more objects on the same layer, but there are a few issues to consider:

• You can't stack ungrouped shapes, which includes any lines and fills you've created in merge mode, because the cookie cutter effect takes place. See the box on page 188 for details.

- Objects drawn in merge mode always appear below objects drawn in object mode.

- If you try to tween two objects that aren't grouped or enclosed in a single symbol, you get unexpected results.

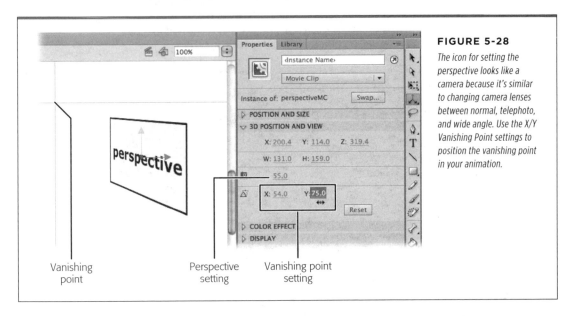

**FIGURE 5-28**

*The icon for setting the perspective looks like a camera because it's similar to changing camera lenses between normal, telephoto, and wide angle. Use the X/Y Vanishing Point settings to position the vanishing point in your animation.*

Vanishing point

Perspective setting

Vanishing point setting

The instant you create two or more overlapping object drawings on the stage, though, you need to think about *stacking*, or arranging them. Stacking tells Flash which object you want to appear in front of the other.

In Figure 5-29, for example, you see three object drawings: a rectangle, a circle, and a star. They were drawn in object mode in that order, so Flash stacks them one on top of the other with the rectangle first, then the circle on top of the rectangle, and the star at the top of the stack. Flash keeps track of the stacking order even if the shapes aren't overlapping one another. So, when you drag the rectangle and drop it on top of the star, Flash displays the rectangle *behind* the star. Then, when you drag the circle and drop it on top of both the rectangle and the star, Flash displays the circle behind the star, but in front of the rectangle, as shown in Figure 5-29. If that's the effect you want, great; if not, you can change the stacking order of all three shapes.

To stack objects on the stage:

1. **Select the object you want to rearrange (either to push behind or pull in front of another object).**

   In Figure 5-30, the circle is selected.

2. **Choose Modify→Arrange, and then, from the submenu, change the object's stacking order.**

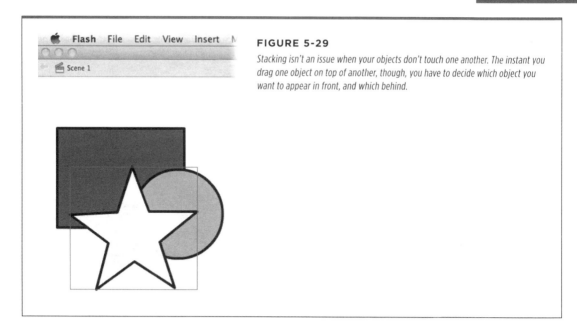

**FIGURE 5-29**

*Stacking isn't an issue when your objects don't touch one another. The instant you drag one object on top of another, though, you have to decide which object you want to appear in front, and which behind.*

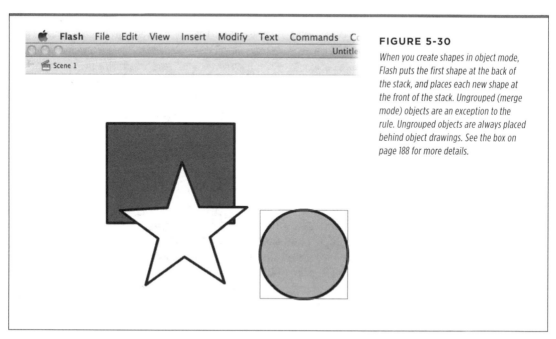

**FIGURE 5-30**

*When you create shapes in object mode, Flash puts the first shape at the back of the stack, and places each new shape at the front of the stack. Ungrouped (merge mode) objects are an exception to the rule. Ungrouped objects are always placed behind object drawings. See the box on page 188 for more details.*

Here are your options:

- **Bring to Front.** Pulls the selected object all the way forward until it's on top of all the other objects.

- **Bring Forward.** Pulls the selected object forward one position, in front of just one other object.

- **Send Backward.** Pushes the object back one position, behind just one other object.

- **Send to Back.** Pushes the selected object all the way back, until it's behind all the other stacked objects.

> **TIP** To quickly move a selected object forward and backward, use Ctrl+up arrow or Ctrl+down arrow (⌘-up arrow and ⌘-down arrow). Ctrl+Shift+up arrow (Shift-Option-up arrow) brings the selected object all the way to the front and Ctrl+Shift+down arrow (Shift-Option-down arrow) sends it all the way to the back.

**WORKAROUND WORKSHOP**

### Safety in Groups

If you plan to move your graphic elements around a lot—stack them, unstack them, and reposition them on the stage—you can make your life easier by putting them in *groups*. In general, groups behave more like objects drawn in object mode. A group can contain any number of objects, from a simple shape with a stroke to complex shapes like a car or a city background scene with buildings, trees, and fire hydrants. Groups can include text fields and just about anything that's visible on the stage. If you want to edit the individual elements, you can open the group with a double-click. When you're done editing, close it using the buttons on the Edit bar.

Suppose you've drawn a car made up of different parts: spinning wheels, fenders, and a windshield. If you place all those parts inside a group, you can move the car around the stage as a single object. All the pieces of the car maintain their positions relative to one another, and you don't have to worry about accidentally dragging a wheel or some other part away from the group. As a bonus, you can arrange the stacking order of groups on the stage using the Modify→Arrange commands like "Bring Forward" or "Send to Back." That way, the car can drive behind some buildings and in front of others. Perhaps the best thing about groups is that they give you a way to manage fewer objects when your animation is filled with hundreds of individual fills, strokes, and other elements.

Figure 5-31 shows you an example of choosing Bring Forward with the circle selected. If you've drawn shapes in merge mode, there's a way to make them behave like object drawings when you stack them: The trick is to group them. Select the fill, stroke, and anything else you want to include in a group. Then choose Modify→Group (Ctrl+G or ⌘-G). The selected objects are now part of a group that you can position using commands like Bring Forward or "Send to Back." For details, see the box on page 188.

## Converting Strokes to Fills

As you saw in Chapter 2 (page 55), Flash treats lines and fills differently when you're working in merge drawing mode. For example, take a look at Figure 5-32, which shows a line drawn with the Pencil and a line drawn with the Brush.

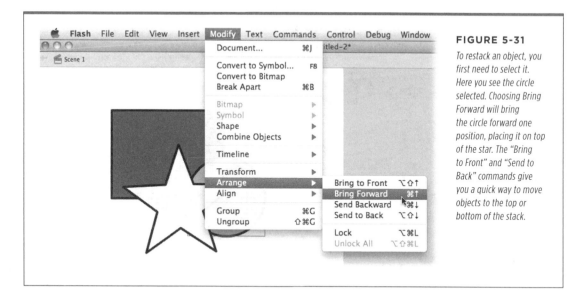

**FIGURE 5-31**

*To restack an object, you first need to select it. Here you see the circle selected. Choosing Bring Forward will bring the circle forward one position, placing it on top of the star. The "Bring to Front" and "Send to Back" commands give you a quick way to move objects to the top or bottom of the stack.*

If you click the Selection tool and then click to select the Pencil-drawn line, Flash highlights just one segment of the line. But performing the very same operation on the similar-looking Brush-drawn line selects the *entire* line.

When you convert a line into a fill, Flash lets you interact with the line just as you would with any other fill. This technique is especially useful when you're working with shapes, no matter which drawing mode you're using. That's because when you create a shape using one of Flash's shape tools—a star, say, or a circle—Flash actually creates two separate elements: the inside of the shape (a fill), and the outline of the shape (a stroke). If you want to change the color of the entire shape, you need to use two tools: the Paint Bucket tool (which lets you change the color of fills), and the Ink Bottle tool (which lets you change the color of strokes, or add a stroke to an existing fill). When you convert the outline to a fill, Flash lets you manipulate both the outside and the inside of the shape in the same way using the same tools. Converting also lets you create scalable shapes (images that shrink evenly) and nice, straight corners (thick strokes appear rounded at the corners; thick fills shaped like lines don't).

To convert a line into a fill:

1. **Select the line (or outline) you want to convert into a fill.**

   Flash highlights the selected line.

2. **Choose Modify→Shape→"Convert Lines to Fills."**

Flash redisplays the line as a fill, and the Properties panel changes to display fill-related properties (as opposed to line-related properties).

**FIGURE 5-32**

*Top: When you're working with ungrouped objects (which is what you create in merge drawing mode), the Selection tool behaves differently. Here you see the results of clicking the Pencil-drawn line: Flash selects only a portion of the line (a single stroke).*

*Bottom: Clicking the Brush-drawn line, on the other hand, selects the entire line. This behavior is just one example of how Flash treats strokes and fills differently.*

## Aligning Objects

In Chapter 2 (page 50), you saw how to use Flash's grid, guides, and rulers to help you eyeball the position of objects as you drag them around on the stage. You also saw how to use the Alignment panel to line up objects with respect to one another or to one of the edges of the stage.

Both these approaches are useful—but Flash doesn't stop there. Snapping and guide layers give you even more control over where you place your objects with respect to one another on the stage.

### ■ SNAPPING

*Snapping* is one of those features people seem to love or hate. The key to snapping is to turn it on when you need consistent alignment and to turn it off when it cramps your style. Here's how it works: When you turn snapping on, you tell Flash to help you out when you're positioning objects on the stage. Snapping helps in a few ways. For one, it provides guidelines when elements are aligned. And, it makes items snap into place when they're close. You don't have to be a mouse marksman.

For example, in Figure 5-33, you see an oval being dragged across the stage. Because Snap Align is turned on, Flash displays a dashed line (top) when the circle is dragged so that one or more of its edges is aligned with another object in your animation. Snapping also creates a *snapping point* at the point clicked or, if you click close to the center of an object, in its center.

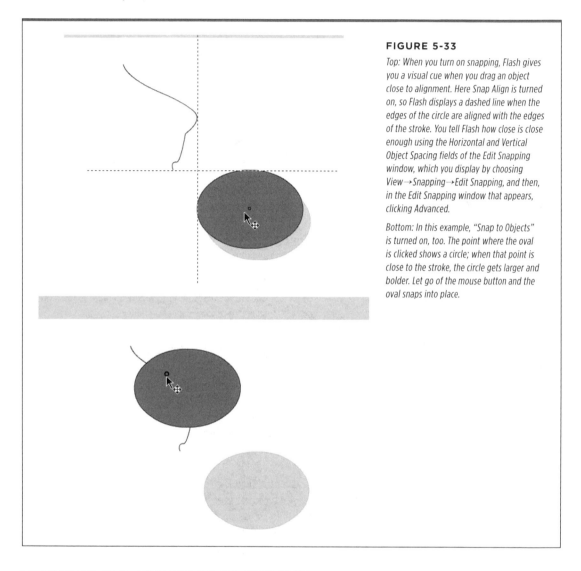

**FIGURE 5-33**

*Top: When you turn on snapping, Flash gives you a visual cue when you drag an object close to alignment. Here Snap Align is turned on, so Flash displays a dashed line when the edges of the circle are aligned with the edges of the stroke. You tell Flash how close is close enough using the Horizontal and Vertical Object Spacing fields of the Edit Snapping window, which you display by choosing View→Snapping→Edit Snapping, and then, in the Edit Snapping window that appears, clicking Advanced.*

*Bottom: In this example, "Snap to Objects" is turned on, too. The point where the oval is clicked shows a circle; when that point is close to the stroke, the circle gets larger and bolder. Let go of the mouse button and the oval snaps into place.*

---

**TIP** For snapping to work, you can't speed around the stage; if you do, you'll miss Flash's cues. Instead, drag your objects slowly.

---

To turn on snapping, select View→Snapping, and then, from the shortcut menu that appears, choose from the following:

- **Snap Align.** Displays a dashed line when you drag an object within a certain number of pixels (you see how to change this number in the box on this page) of another object or of any edge of the stage.

- **Snap to Grid.** Displays a small, thick circle where you select an object. This point snaps to points in the grid. See page 51 for details about displaying a grid. If you click near the center, Snap assumes you meant to select the center of the object, so that's where it places puts the circle snapping point.

- **Snap to Guides.** Works similarly to Snap to Grid except that the snapping action works with guides that you drag out from the rulers and place individually. For more on guides, see page 50.

- **Snap to Pixels.** Useful only if you want to work at the single-pixel level (your stage has to be magnified to at least 400% for this option to work). This option prevents you from moving an object in any increment less than a whole pixel. (To magnify your stage by 400%, select View→Magnification→400%; when you do this with "Snap to Pixels" selected, a single-pixel grid appears.)

---

**FREQUENTLY ASKED QUESTION**

### Object Snapping: How Close Is Too Close?

*Everybody says Snap Align is so great, but I'm not sure why I'd use it or how close I should set the snapping range.*

Whether or not you'll find Snap Align useful depends entirely on you (some folks prefer to freewheel it, while others appreciate hints and advice) and what you're trying to create on the stage. Snap Align is most useful in situations where you're trying to custom-position objects down to the pixel. For example, say you've drawn a row of different-sized flowers, and you're trying to position a row of bees, one bee at a time, exactly 25 pixels above the flowers. You can use the Align panel for a lot of basic alignment tasks, but this kind of custom alignment isn't one of them: Snap Align is your best option.

Initially, Flash has all the Snap Align settings set to 0. To change either of these buffer zones:

1. Choose View→Snapping→Edit Snapping. The Edit Snapping window appears, as shown in Figure 5-34.

2. In the Edit Snapping window, click Advanced to display expanded Edit Snapping options.

In the Object Spacing fields, type the buffer zone you want in pixels (you can specify both horizontal and vertical). For example, under Object Spacing, if you type 20 px in the Horizontal and Vertical boxes, the edge of one object will snap to the edge of another when they're within 20 pixels of each other.

---

- **Snap to Objects.** Displays a small, thick circle on your object when you select it. As you drag that object close to another object on the stage, Flash uses that point for snapping. The actual location of the snapping circle depends on where you click the object you're moving. Flash does its best to guess whether you want to select the center, the edge, or some other point.

#### ■ GUIDE LAYERS

If you've ever traced a drawing onto a piece of onionskin paper, you understand the usefulness of guide layers in Flash.

A *guide layer* is a special kind of layer that doesn't appear in your finished animation, but that you can hold beneath your stage while you're drawing to help you position and trace objects. Say, for example, you want to align objects in a perfect circle, or on a perfect diagonal, or you want to arrange them so that they match a specific background (say, an ocean scene). You create a guide layer and, on it, draw your circle or diagonal or ocean scene. Then, when you create your layer, your guide layer shows through so you can position your objects the way you want them. When you go to run your animation, though, you don't see your guide layer at all; it appears only when you're editing in Flash.

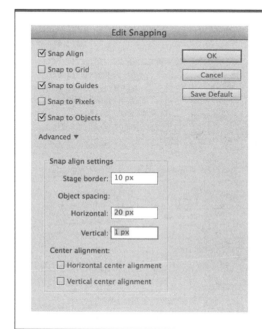

**FIGURE 5-34**

*Use the Edit Snapping settings to fine-tune the way Flash behaves when you're aligning objects on the stage. Use the checkboxes to choose the types of objects that have snapping behaviors. And then use the Snap Align settings to determine when the alignment cues kick in.*

To create a guide layer:

1. **On the stage, draw your guide shapes or lines, or add a tracing image, as shown in Figure 5-35.**

   This first layer contains the "guide" material. Later, you'll add one or more layers with the images you want to appear in your animation.

2. **Position your cursor over the name of the layer you want to turn into a guide layer, and then right-click.**

   Flash displays a pop-up menu.

3. **From the pop-up menu, select Guide.**

   Flash displays a little T-square just before the layer name, as in Figure 5-35.

4. **With the guide layer still selected, create a new, regular layer for your objects by choosing Insert→Timeline→Layer.**

   Flash creates a new layer and places it above the guide layer, as shown in Figure 5-35.

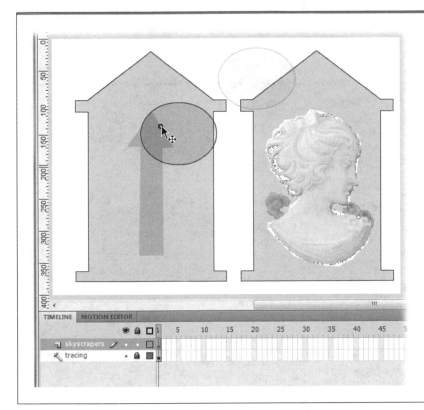

**FIGURE 5-35**

*Here the guide layer is used in two different ways: for alignment and as a tracing tool. The arrow and the cameo profile are both on the guide layer. On the left, the oval is being dragged, and it snaps to the edge of the arrow. On the right, the cameo was used to trace the shape of the head with the freehand Lasso.*

**TIP** Working with layers—especially guide layers—can be confusing if you're not used to it (and, frankly, it can be confusing even if you are used to it, especially if you're working with a lot of layers). To make sure you don't inadvertently modify your guide layer, you can *lock* it (tell Flash not to let you edit it temporarily). To lock your guide layer, click the dot beneath the padlock icon. The dot changes to a padlock. Then, when you click to select your regular layer, you can align away without worrying about accidentally changing your (locked) guide layer.

5. **Select View→Snapping, and then, in the context menu that appears, turn on the checkbox next to "Snap to Objects."** You've turned snapping on.

   Turning snapping on helps you position your objects on your guide layer. Both "Snap to Objects" and Snap Align are helpful when you work with a guide layer.

6. **With the regular layer selected, draw, trace, or move your objects.**

You can then drag objects to your guideline (or guide object, or guide background) or use objects in the guide layer for tracing. When tracing a cutout, as in Figure 5-35, temporarily adjust the alpha (transparency) setting of objects you want to see through.

## Spray Painting Symbols

Instead of simply spraying blobs of color, the Spray Brush tool can spray complex images, by using emphasis symbols as its paint source. Symbols, as you'll see in Chapter 7, are reusable images and objects stored in the Library (Window→Library). When you know you're going to use a graphic, a movie clip, or a button more than once, you save it as a symbol so you can reuse it to save time later.

The Spray Brush tool takes the concept of reusing a copy of something to an extreme. Suppose you want a sky filled with flashing yellow stars. You can load the Spray Brush tool with a movie clip of blinking stars, and then spray them across the horizon. In the Tools panel, the Spray Brush tool is hidden underneath the Brush tool. (You can use the B shortcut key to toggle between these two tools.)

**NOTE**  For the following steps, you can download the file *05-01_Spray_Brush.fla* from the Missing CD page at *www.missingmanuals.com/cds/flashcs6mm*.

1. **Open the file *05-01_Spray_Brush.fla.***

The background color of the stage is a nice midnight blue. There are two symbols in the Library: a graphic called Star and a movie clip called BlinkingStar.

2. **In the Tools panel, select the Spray Brush tool (it shares a fly-out menu with the Brush tool), or press B until your cursor changes to the Spray Brush cursor, as shown in Figure 5-36.**

The Spray Brush tool looks like a spray paint can. When the Spray Brush tool is selected, the Properties panel (Window→Properties) shows related settings.

3. **Under Properties→Symbol, click the Edit button.**

The Swap Symbol dialog box opens, displaying the symbols you can use with the Spray Brush tool.

4. **Select the BlinkingStar symbol, and then click OK.**

The BlinkingStar symbol is loaded in the Spray Brush tool, and its name is displayed next to the "Spray:" label.

**TIP**  If you plan to spray the same symbol frequently, then turn on the Default checkbox and it will load automatically when you choose the Spray Brush tool.

5. **In the same Symbol subpanel, set both the "Scale width" and the "Scale height" to 25%.**

   Use the "Scale width" and "Scale height" to adjust the size of the symbol as it's sprayed. Often symbols are drawn at a size larger than needed for spraying.

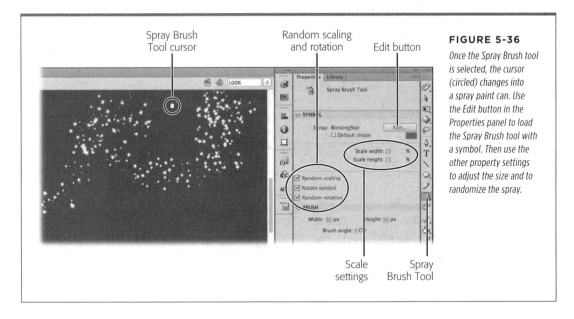

Spray Brush Tool cursor

Random scaling and rotation

Edit button

**FIGURE 5-36**

*Once the Spray Brush tool is selected, the cursor (circled) changes into a spray paint can. Use the Edit button in the Properties panel to load the Spray Brush tool with a symbol. Then use the other property settings to adjust the size and to randomize the spray.*

Scale settings

Spray Brush Tool

6. **Turn on the checkboxes for "Random scaling," "Rotate symbol," and "Random rotation."**

   Starry skies (and many other natural patterns) don't have standard sizes. Using random settings creates a much more natural effect for your starry sky.

7. **Click the sky, and then spray in some stars.**

   Drag to spray stars across the sky. Hold the mouse button down for as long as you want to create new stars.

## Drawing with the Deco Tool

The Deco tool lets you draw multiple complex shapes easily. In that way, it's similar to the Spray Brush tool, described above (page 195). After you select the tool in the Tools panel, the Properties panel shows you the settings and options for the tool. Click the drop-down menu in the Drawing Effect subpanel (Figure 5-37), and you see that the Deco tool is actually three different tools: Vine Fill, Grid Fill, and Symmetry Brush. The designs created by each brush are different, but they all work by creating repeating patterns. For example:

- Use *Vine Fill* to create patterns on the stage or a selected symbol. Used on a background, the Vine Fill tool could create wallpaper for an interior scene. Used on a shape, Vine Fill could create the gift wrap for a present. Flash comes loaded with a leafy vine that you can use, as shown in Figure 5-37. Or you can provide your own symbols for the leaf and flower parts of the vine.

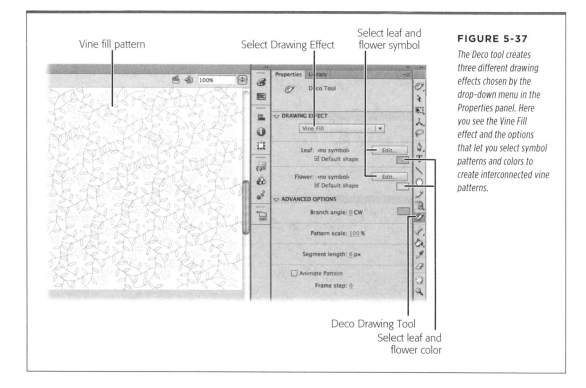

Vine fill pattern · Select Drawing Effect · Select leaf and flower symbol · Deco Drawing Tool · Select leaf and flower color

**FIGURE 5-37**

*The Deco tool creates three different drawing effects chosen by the drop-down menu in the Properties panel. Here you see the Vine Fill effect and the options that let you select symbol patterns and colors to create interconnected vine patterns.*

- Use the *Grid Fill* effect to create a repeating effect that's more uniform than the Vine Fill. For example, you could use your company logo as the symbol and apply the Grid Fill effect to a background layer in your animation. Then you can adjust the alpha (transparency) to soften its appearance and make the logo fade into the background, giving text or images in other layers precedence.

- Use *Symmetry Brush* to arrange symbols symmetrically around a central point. If you've ever seen a Busby Berkeley movie with all those symmetrical dancers, you have an idea of the kaleidoscope effects you can create with symmetry. If you're not feeling quite so Hollywood, you can use the Symmetry Brush tool to create clocks, speedometers, or other circular gauges. As with the Vine Fill and Grid Fill tools, you can load the Symmetry Brush with any symbol. If you want to experiment and don't have a shape handy, use the preset rectangle to create patterns. When you drag on the stage, the Symmetry Brush creates multiple images using the loaded symbol. Use the drop-down menu in the Advanced subpanel to select a pattern. You have several options: Rotate Around Point,

Reflect Across Line, Reflect Around Point, and Grid Translation. Select the Test Collisions button to keep symbols from overlapping.

The best way to learn about the Deco tool is to create a new document and experiment. Adobe continues to create new deco brushes. With some brushes, you can tweak the colors by clicking on color swatches. With others, you can replace the standard symbols with your own creations. So go ahead and play with the Deco tool, and then the next time you need a repeating pattern, you'll know where to turn.

# Advanced Color and Fills

Color is one of the most primitive and powerful communicative devices at your disposal. With color, a skillful animator can engender anxiety or peacefulness, hunger or confusion. She can jar, confuse, delight, soothe, entertain, or inform—all without saying a word.

Color theory is too large a topic to cover completely here. What you *will* find in this chapter is a quick introduction to basic color theory, as well as tips on how to work with color in Flash. You'll see how to change the colors of the shapes, lines, and images you create with Flash's drawing tools; how to create and reuse custom color palettes (especially useful if you're trying to match the colors in your Flash animation to those of a corporate logo, for example, or to a specific photo or piece of art); and how to apply sophisticated color effects including gradients, transparency, and bitmap fills.

## Color Basics

The red you see in a nice, juicy watermelon—or any other color, for that matter—is actually made up of a bunch of different elements, each of which you can control using Flash's Color panel:

- **Hue** is what most people think of when someone says "color." Red, orange, yellow, green, blue, indigo, and violet are all hues. Out of the box, Flash has 216 different hues. These are sometimes called *web-safe* hues because, in the early days of the Web, they were the colors most computers could display. You can also blend your own custom hues by mixing any number of these basic 216 hues.

- **Saturation** refers to the amount of color (hue) you apply to something. A light wash of red, for example, looks pink; pile on more of the same color and you get a rich, vibrant red.

- **Brightness** determines how much of any given color you can actually see. A lot of light washes out a color; too little light, and the color begins to look muddy. At either end of the spectrum, you have pitch black (no light at all) and white (so much light that light is all you can see). In between these two extremes, adding light to a hue creates a tint. For example, if you add enough light to a rich strawberry-ice-cream pink, you get a delicate pastel pink.

- **Transparency** refers to how much background you can see through a color, from all of it (in which case the color is completely transparent, or invisible) to no background at all (in which case the color is opaque). In Flash, you set the transparency (technically, the *opacity*) for a color using the Alpha field.

## RGB and HSB

Color doesn't exist in a vacuum. The colors you get when you mix pigments aren't the same as the colors you get when you mix different-colored lights (which is how a computer monitor works). Artists working in oil paint or pastel use the red-yellow-blue color model, for example, and commercial printers use the cyan-magenta-yellow-black color model. In the world of computer graphics and animation, though, the color model you use is *red-green-blue,* or *RGB*.

This model means you can tell Flash to display any color imaginable just by telling it precisely how much red, green, and blue to display. But if you don't happen to know how much red, green, and blue make up, say, a certain shade of lilac, Flash gives you three more ways to specify a particular color:

- **HSB.** You can tell Flash the hue, saturation, and brightness you want it to display.

- **Hexadecimal.** You can type the hexadecimal number (see page 203) for the color you want Flash to display. Because hexadecimal notation is one of the ways you specify colors in HTML, you can use hexadecimal numbers to match a web page color precisely to a color in Flash.

- **Selection.** In the Color panel, you can drag your cursor around on the color picker (Figure 5-38) until you find a color you like. This option is the easiest, of course, and the best part is, after you decide on a color, Flash tells you the color's RGB, HSB, and hexadecimal numbers (all of which come in handy if you want to recreate the color precisely, either in another Flash animation or in another graphics program altogether).

In the next section, you'll see how to specify a custom color using Flash's Color panel.

## Creating Custom Colors

Out of the box, Flash has 216 web-safe colors. But if you can't find the precise shade you want among those 216 colors, you're free to mix and match your own custom colors using Flash's Color panel.

Here's how:

1. **Select Window→Color.**

   The Color panel shown in Figure 5-38 appears, with the Color tab selected.

2. **On the Color tab, click either the Fill icon or the Stroke icon, depending on whether you plan to apply your custom color to a fill or a stroke.**

   Page 53 gives you the lowdown on the differences between the two.

3. **Select a custom color.** You can do this one of these ways:

- You can drag around on the color picker circle and slider until you see a color you like in the Preview window (Figure 5-38).

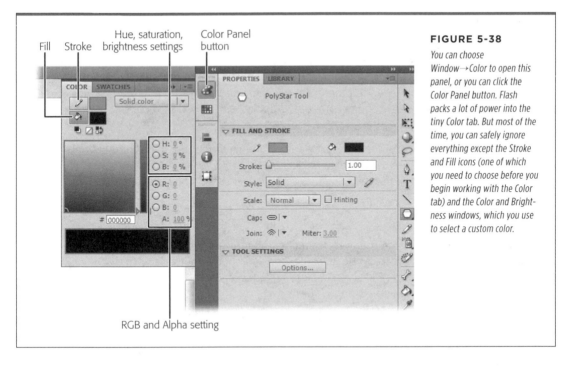

Fill   Stroke   Hue, saturation, brightness settings   Color Panel button

RGB and Alpha setting

**FIGURE 5-38**

*You can choose Window→Color to open this panel, or you can click the Color Panel button. Flash packs a lot of power into the tiny Color tab. But most of the time, you can safely ignore everything except the Stroke and Fill icons (one of which you need to choose before you begin working with the Color tab) and the Color and Brightness windows, which you use to select a custom color.*

- If you know them, you can type values for the RGB (red, green, and blue) or HSB (hue, saturation, brightness) colors next to their respective letters in the Color panel. (See the box on page 201.)

- You can type a hexadecimal value in the Hexadecimal Color Designator box. (Hexadecimal, or base 16, values can contain only the following digits: 0–9 and A–F. Folks who spend a lot of time writing HTML code are usually comfortable with hex numbers; if you're not one of them, you can safely skip this option.)

4. **To customize your color even further, you can use the drop-down menu to specify its color type.**

Choose from *Solid* (what you want most of the time), *Linear* (a type of gradient effect described on page 206), *Radial* (another type of gradient also described on page 206), and *Bitmap* (lets you color an object using an image rather than a hue, as on page 204).

5. **To change the opacity (transparency) of your color, change the percentage in the A setting.**

   Zero percent tells Flash to make your color completely transparent (see-through); 100% tells Flash to make your color completely opaque (Figure 5-39).

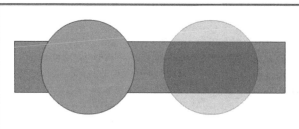

**FIGURE 5-39**

*When you use a transparent color, background objects and the stage itself show through, giving the appearance of a different color altogether. Here the two ovals are actually the same color, but they don't look like it: The selected oval on the right is 50% opaque, while the oval on the left is 100% opaque.*

**TIP**   Invisible color sounds like an oxymoron, but zero percent opacity actually has a place in your bag of Flash tricks. As you'll see on page 318, you can create a nifty appearing/disappearing effect using see-through color and a shape tween by changing Alpha settings.

6. **In the Tools panel, select a drawing tool, and then begin drawing on the stage.**

   Your strokes (or fills, depending on which icon you selected in step 1) appear in your brand-new custom color.

**UP TO SPEED**

## Specifying RGB Colors

RGB is a funky system based not on the way humans think, but on the way computers think. So the numbers you type in the Color Mixer to describe the red, green, and blue components of a color aren't in percentages, as you might expect, but instead need to range from 0 (no color at all) to 255 (pure color).

This table shows a handful of common colors expressed in RGB terms:

| RED | GREEN | BLUE | RESULT |
|-----|-------|------|--------|
| 0 | 0 | 0 | Black |
| 255 | 255 | 255 | White |
| 255 | 0 | 0 | Red |
| 0 | 255 | 0 | Green |
| 0 | 0 | 255 | Blue |
| 255 | 255 | 0 | Yellow |
| 0 | 255 | 255 | Cyan |
| 255 | 0 | 255 | Magenta |

**TIP** You don't have to create a custom color before you draw an object. You can draw an object first, select it, and then create a custom color. When you create a color, Flash automatically changes the object's color to your new custom color.

## The Six Commandments of Color

Whether you're using Flash to create an interactive tutorial, an animated art short, a slick advertisement, or something else entirely, you need to be aware of color and how it supports (or detracts from) the message you're trying to get across. Color is at least as important as any other design element, from the fonts and shapes you choose to the placement of those shapes and the frame-by-frame timing of your finished animation.

Although the psychology of color is still in its relative infancy, a few color rules have stood the test of time. Break them at your own risk.

1. **Black text on a white background is popular for a reason.** Any other color combination produces eyestrain after as little as one sentence.

2. **Color is relative.** The human eye perceives color in context, so the same shade of pink looks completely different when you place it next to, say, olive green than it does when you place it next to red, white, or purple.

3. **For most animations, there's no such thing as a web-safe color.** Web-safe colors—the handful of colors that supposedly appear the same on virtually all computers, whether they're Mac or Windows, laptop or desktop, ancient or new—were an issue in the old days. If you chose a non-web-safe color palette, your audiences might have seen something different from what you intended (or might have seen nothing at all, depending on how their hardware and software were configured). But time marches on, and any computer newer than a few years old can display the entire range of colors that Flash lets you create. Of course, if you know for a fact that your target audience is running 15-year-old computers (as a lot of folks in other countries and in schools are), or if you suspect they might have configured their monitor settings to display only a handful of colors (it happens),

then you should probably play it safe and stick to the web-safe colors that Flash already has. (To display web-safe colors, choose Window, and then, in the pop-up menu that appears, turn on the checkbox next to Swatches. In the Swatches panel, click the Options menu (upper-right corner), and then, from the pop-up menu that appears, select Web 216. The Swatches tab displays 216 web-safe colors.)

4. **Contrast is at least as important as color.** Contrast—how different or similar two colors look next to each other—affects not just how your audiences see your animation, but whether or not they can see it at all. Putting two similar colors back-to-back (putting a blue circle on a green flag, for instance, or red text on an orange background) is unbearably hard on your audience's eyes.

5. **Color means different things in different cultures.** In Western cultures, black is the color of mourning; in Eastern cultures, the color associated with death and mourning is white. In some areas of the world, purple signifies royalty; in others, a particular political party; in still others, a specific football team. In color, as in all things Flash, knowing your audience helps you create and deliver an effective message.

6. **You can never completely control the color your audience sees.** Hardware and software calibration, glare from office lighting, the amount of dust on someone's monitor—a lot of factors affect the colors your audience sees. So unless you're creating a Flash animation for a very specific audience and you know precisely what equipment and lighting they'll be using to watch your masterpiece, don't waste a lot of time trying to tune your colors to the nth degree.

## Specifying Colors for ActionScript

ActionScript is Flash's programming language. As you'll learn in later chapters, you can use ActionScript to automatically perform the same tasks that you do by hand—including specifying colors. Suppose your animation is selling cars. Using ActionScript, you can let your audience change a car's color with the click of a button. ActionScript uses the RGB color system described in the previous section but identifies individual colors using hexadecimal numbers. *Hexadecimal* numbers are base 16 instead of the base 10 numbers people use. (How's that for a flashback to math class?) The hexadecimal number system uses 16 symbols to represent numbers instead of the usual 0–9. When the common numeric symbols run out, hexadecimal uses letters. So, the complete set of number values looks like this: 0, 1, 2, 3, 4, 5, 6, 7, 8, 9, A, B, C, D, E, F.

Hexadecimal RGB numbers use six places to describe each color. The first two numbers represent shades of the color red, the second two numbers represent shades of the color green, and the final two numbers represent shades of the color blue. So a color specification might look like this: 0152A0. Or this: 33CCFF. At first, it seems odd to see the letters in numbers, but after a while you get the hang of it. So, the hexadecimal number FF0000 is a bright, pure red, while 0000FF is a bright blue. When you choose a color from a color picker, or Flash's Color panel (Window→Color) as shown in Figure 5-40, you're actually choosing an RGB color, whether you know it or not. Select a color, and then find the hexadecimal number in the box below.

You usually use the hexadecimal notation to specify RGB colors in ActionScript. Notice that the hexadecimal number in the color picker box is preceded by a pound sign (#), which is one common way to indicate that this is a hexadecimal number. (Not all hexadecimal numbers include letters, so this notation prevents hexadecimal numbers from being confused with regular numbers.) ActionScript code uses another method to indicate that a number is a hexadecimal number. In ActionScript, you precede all color codes with two characters: *0x*. So, if you want to use the color shown in Figure 5-40 in your ActionScript code, you'd specify the color as *0xFF0000*. You'll see plenty of other examples of specifying colors in ActionScript, starting with Chapter 12.

## Saving Color Swatches

After you go to all the hard work of creating a custom color as described in the preceding section, you're probably going to want to save that color as a virtual *swatch* so you can reuse it again without having to try to remember how you mixed it.

To save a custom color swatch, first create a custom color, as described in the preceding section. You see your custom color displayed in the rectangle at the bottom of the Color panel. In the upper-right corner, click the panel's Options menu and choose Add Swatch. Your color is automatically added to the Swatches panel. Click the Swatches tab and you see your new swatch at the bottom of the list next to the gradients, as shown in Figure 5-41.

After you've saved a custom swatch, you can use it to change the color of a stroke or a fill, as you see in Figure 5-41.

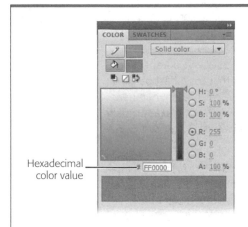

**FIGURE 5-40**

*Flash's color pickers display the hexadecimal color value in the box marked with the pound (#) sign. You can use any color picker to look up the hexadecimal value for use in your ActionScript code.*

Hexadecimal color value

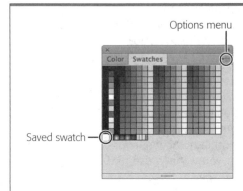

Options menu

Saved swatch

**FIGURE 5-41**

*Saving a specific color as a color swatch—whether it's one you custom-mixed or a standard color you found on the palette and liked—is kind of like saving the empty paint can after you paint your kitchen. The next time you want to use that particular color, all you have to do is grab the swatch (instead of relying on your memory or spending hours trying to recreate the exact shade). If you work with color a lot, swatches can make your life a whole lot easier.*

## Using an Image as a Fill "Color"

Instead of choosing or blending a custom color, you can select an image to use as a fill "color," as shown in Figure 5-42. You can select any image in Flash's Library panel (page 30), or from anywhere on your computer and apply that image to any size or shape of fill to create some pretty interesting effects.

As you can see in the following pages, the result depends on both the size and shape of the fill and the image you choose.

To use an image as a fill color:

1. **Select all the fills you want to "color."**

   Figure 5-42 shows an example of two fills: a star, and a free-form fill created using the Brush.

2. **In the Color panel, click the arrow next to Type, and then, from the drop-down list that appears, choose Bitmap fill (Figure 5-43).**

Flash displays the "Import to Library" window (Figure 5-44).

---

**TIP** To import additional image files to use as fills, in the Color panel, click the button marked Import. Then, with the fill on the stage selected, click the image you want to use.

---

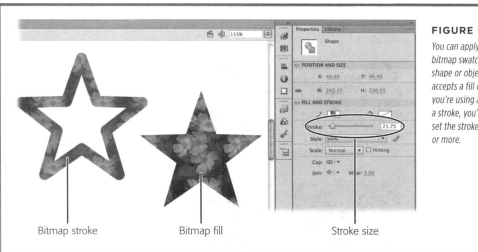

**FIGURE 5-42**

*You can apply your bitmap swatch to any shape or object that accepts a fill or stroke. If you're using a bitmap on a stroke, you'll want to set the stroke size to 30 or more.*

Bitmap stroke    Bitmap fill    Stroke size

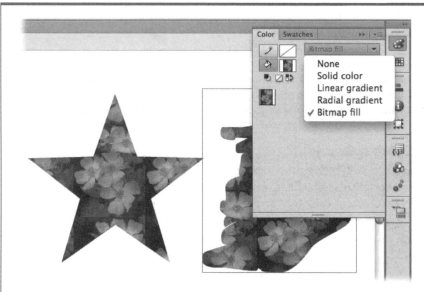

**FIGURE 5-43**

*Click the Type drop-down menu in the Color panel, and then choose Bitmap to see your bitmap swatches. After you've added a bit-map, it appears as a swatch in your Color panel.*

3. **In the "Import to Library" window, select the image file you want, and then click Open.**

Flash displays the image in the bottom of the Color panel, as well as next to the Fill icon, and "paints" your image with the bitmap. You can apply the bitmap to both fills and strokes, as shown in Figure 5-42. If your fill is larger than your image, Flash tiles the image (Figure 5-45).

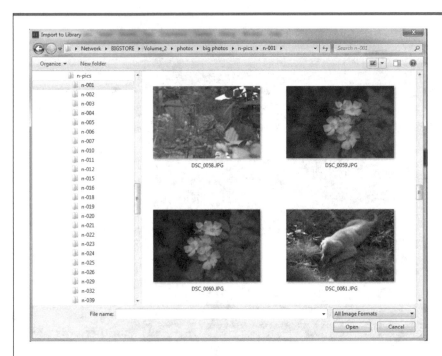

**FIGURE 5-44**

*The first time you head to the Color panel and set the Type menu to Bitmap, Flash pops open this "Import to Library" window. Despite the name (Bitmap), Flash lets you import JPEG and other types of image files; you're not limited to .bmp files. Browse your computer for the image file you want, and then click Open.*

> **TIP** If you apply the new fill "color" to an image by clicking the Paint Bucket icon and then clicking the fill, Flash tiles super-tiny versions of the image inside the fill to create a textured pattern effect.

## Applying a Gradient

A *gradient* is a fill coloring effect that blends bands of color into one another. Flash has *linear gradients* (straight up-and-down, left-to-right bands of color) and *radial gradients* (bands of color that begin in the center of a circle and radiate outward).

By applying a gradient to your fills, you can create the illusion of depth and perspective. For example, you can make a circle that looks like a sphere, a line that looks like it's fading, and text that looks like it's reflecting light (Figure 5-46). See the tip on page 210 for applying gradients to text.

You can apply a gradient swatch to your fills, or you can create your own custom gradients in Flash, much the same way you create your own custom colors (page 199).

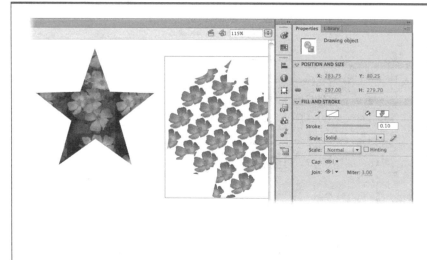

**FIGURE 5-45**

*How Flash applies your image to your fill depends on the size of your fill and the size of your image (and whether you select the fill, and then change the Style type to Bitmap, or vice versa). Here the star is smaller than the image imported into Flash, so Flash shows a single image framed by the star's outline. Because the freeform fill is larger than the image, Flash tiles the image inside the freeform fill. Note, too, that Flash sticks the image you imported into the Library panel.*

**FIGURE 5-46**

*Applying one of the preset radial gradients that Flash provides turns this circle into a ball, and makes this text look shiny, like it's reflecting light. The thin rectangle beneath the text is sporting a linear gradient; its bands of color blend from left to right.*

To apply a gradient swatch to an object:

1. **On the stage, select the object to which you want to add a gradient.**

   Flash highlights the selected object.

2. **Click the Fill Color icon.**

   Flash displays the color picker (Figure 5-47).

3. **From the color picker, choose one of the seven gradient swatches that come with Flash.**

   Flash automatically displays your object using the gradient swatch you chose. Figure 5-47 shows a red radial gradient applied to a plain circle to create a simple 3-D effect.

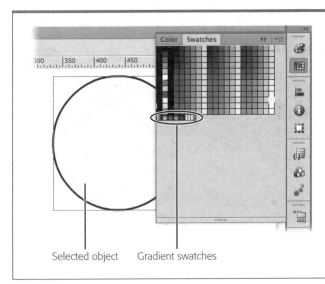

**FIGURE 5-47**

*Applying a gradient swatch is just as easy as applying a color. Flash comes with four radial gradient swatches (white, red, green, and blue) and three linear gradient swatches (white/black, blue/yellow, and rainbow). If one of these creates the effect you want, great. If not, you can change any of them to create your own custom gradient effects, as you see on page 210.*

Selected object     Gradient swatches

To create a custom gradient:

1. **On the stage, select the object to which you want to apply a custom gradient.**

   Flash highlights the selected object.

2. **Apply a gradient swatch to the object (see page 206).**

   If you like, change the color of the gradient, as described next.

3. **In the Color panel, double-click the first color pointer to select it.**

   Flash displays a color picker.

4. **In the color picker, click to select a color.**

   In your selected object, Flash turns the color at the center (for a radial gradient) or at the very left (for a linear gradient) to the color you chose. Repeat these two steps for each color pointer to change the color of each band of color in your gradient. If you like, change the thickness and definition of your gradient's color bands, as described next.

5. **In the Color panel, drag the first color pointer to the right.**

   The farther to the right you drag it, the more of that color appears in your custom gradient. The farther to the left you drag it, the less of that color appears in your custom gradient. Repeat this step for each band of color in your gradient.

   Next, if you like, you can add a new band of color to your custom gradient.

6. **In the Color panel, click anywhere on the Gradient edit bar.**

   Flash creates a new color pointer (see Figure 5-48), which you can edit as described in step 3. You can add as many as 15 color pointers (new bands of color) to your gradient.

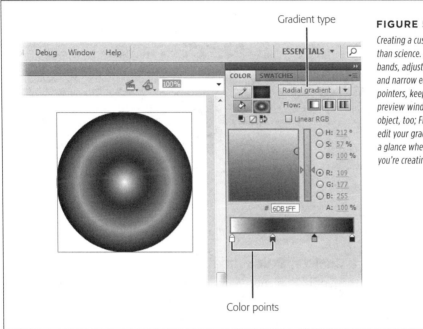

Gradient type

Color points

**FIGURE 5-48**

*Creating a custom gradient is more art than science. As you create new color bands, adjust the colors, and widen and narrow each band using the color pointers, keep an eye on the gradient preview window and on your selected object, too; Flash updates both as you edit your gradient, so you can see at a glance whether you like the effects you're creating.*

For even more excitement, apply one or more gradient transforms to your object, as described next.

7. **In the Tools panel, choose the Gradient Transform tool (F).** It shares a fly-out menu with the Free Transform tool.

   Flash displays a rotation arrow, a stretch arrow, and a reposition point.

   You can drag the rotation arrow to rotate the gradient; drag the stretch arrow to stretch the bands of color in your gradient, as shown in Figure 5-49; or drag the reposition point to reposition the center of the gradient, also shown in Figure 5-49.

**TIP** In Flash, text is usually a single color, so you need to take some extra steps to apply a gradient. If you aren't planning on editing the text or changing it on the fly using ActionScript, you can turn the text into an image and *then* apply the gradient. Select the text and press Ctrl+B (⌘-B). That breaks strings of characters into individual characters. Press Ctrl+B (⌘-B) a second time to turn those letters in to graphics. At this point you can apply gradients to individual letters or groups of letters.

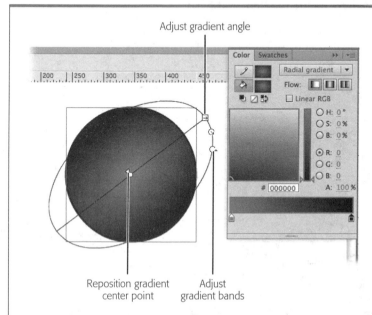

Adjust gradient angle

Reposition gradient
center point

Adjust
gradient bands

**FIGURE 5-49**

*Just as regular transforms let you poke and prod regular images to create interesting effects, gradient transforms let you manipulate gradients (with respect to the shapes you originally applied them to) to create interesting effects. Here dragging the stretch arrow pulls the bands of color, widening the bands at the center and discarding the bands at the edges. Use the circular rotate control to adjust the gradient angle. Drag the reposition point to move the center of the gradient away from the center of the object. This effect is especially useful for creating the illusion that the object is reflecting light streaming in from a different angle.*

## Importing a Custom Color Palette

Depending on the type of animation you're creating in Flash, you might find it easier to import a custom color palette than to try to recreate each color you need. For example, say you're working on a promotional piece for your company, and you want the colors you use in each and every frame of your animation to match the colors your company uses in all its other marketing materials (brochures, ads, and so on). Rather than eyeball all the other materials or spend time contacting printers and graphics teams to try and track down the RGB values for each color, all you need to do is import a GIF file into Flash that contains all the colors you need: a GIF file showing your company's logo, for example, or some other image containing the colors you need to match.

To import a custom color palette:

1. **In the Swatches panel (Window→Swatches), click the Options menu.**

   A pop-up menu appears.

2. **From the pop-up menu, select Clear Colors.**

Flash clears out the entire color palette on the Color Swatches tab, leaving just black, white, and a gradient (Figure 5-50, right).

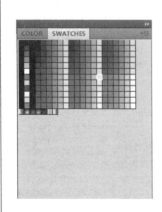 

**FIGURE 5-50**

*Left: Here's what the typical Swatches tab looks like before you clear it (by clicking the Options menu and then selecting Clear Colors). Think twice before you clear the palette: You can get back Flash's basic color palette, but you lose any custom color swatches you've saved in this document.*

*Right: After you clear the color palette, you're left with black, white, and a gradient.*

3. **Once again, click the Options menu.**

The pop-up menu reappears.

4. **From the pop-up menu, select Add Colors.**

Flash displays the Import Color Swatch window.

5. **In the Import Color Swatch window (Figure 5-51), click to choose a GIF file, and then click Open.**

Flash imports the custom color palette, placing each color in its own swatch in the Swatches panel (Figure 5-50, left).

> **NOTE** To restore the standard Flash color palette: From the Swatches panel, click the Options menu, and then, from the pop-up menu that appears, select Load Default Colors.

## Copying Color with the Eyedropper

Tying color elements together is a subtle—but important—element of good design. It's the same principle as accessorizing: Say you buy a white shirt with purple pinstripes. Add a pink tie, and you're a candidate for the Worst Dressed list. But a purple tie that matches the pinstripes somehow pulls the look together.

In Flash, you may find you've created a sketch and colored it just the right shade of green, and you want to use that color in another part of the same drawing. Sure, you could slog through the Color panel, write down the hexadecimal notation for the color and then recreate the color. Or, if you know you're going to be working a lot with that particular color, you could create a custom color swatch (page 203). But if you want to experiment with placing bits of the color here and there on the fly, the Eyedropper tool is the way to go. The Eyedropper tool lets you click the color on one image and apply it instantly to another color on another image.

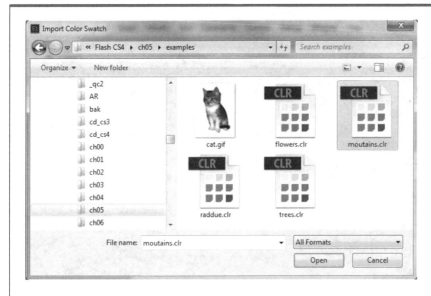

**FIGURE 5-51**

*When you head to the Swatches panel, click the Options menu, and then choose Add Colors to import a custom color palette, Flash displays an Import Color Swatch window that should look pretty familiar if you've ever had occasion to open a file on a computer. Here you click to browse your files. When you find the .clr file containing your custom color palette, click Open. Flash brings you back to your Color Mixer panel, where you see that Flash has pulled in each separate color in your .clr file as a separate swatch, ready for you to use.*

**NOTE**  The Eyedropper tool lets you transfer color only from a bitmap or a fill to a fill, and from a stroke to another stroke. If you want to transfer color to a bitmap, you need the Magic Wand (Lasso).

To copy color from one object to another:

1. **Select Edit→Deselect All.**

   Alternatively, you can press Ctrl+Shift+A (Shift-⌘-A) or click an empty spot on the stage.

2. **From the Tools panel, click to select the Eyedropper (I) tool.**

   As you mouse over the stage, your cursor appears as an eyedropper while it's over a blank part of the stage; an eyedropper and a brush when it's over a fill (as shown in Figure 5-52, top); and an eyedropper and a pencil when it's over a stroke.

3. **Click the bitmap, fill, or stroke color you want to copy from (imagine sucking the color up into your eyedropper).**

If you click to copy from a fill or a bitmap, your cursor turns immediately into a paint bucket; if you click to copy from a stroke, the cursor turns into an ink bottle.

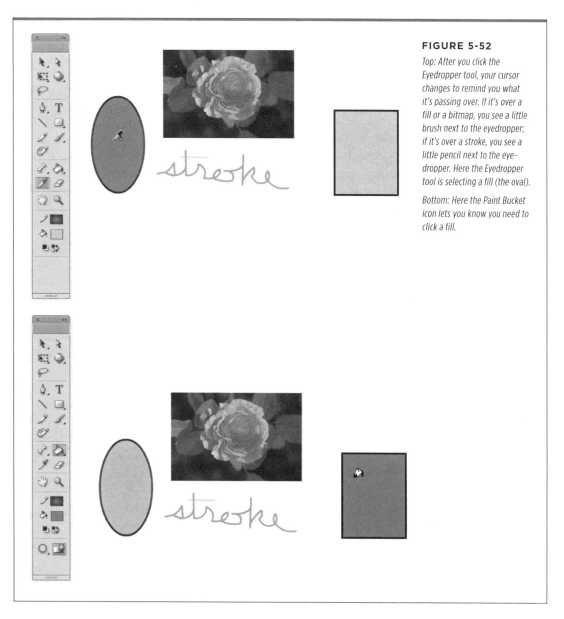

**FIGURE 5-52**

*Top: After you click the Eyedropper tool, your cursor changes to remind you what it's passing over. If it's over a fill or a bitmap, you see a little brush next to the eyedropper; if it's over a stroke, you see a little pencil next to the eyedropper. Here the Eyedropper tool is selecting a fill (the oval).*

*Bottom: Here the Paint Bucket icon lets you know you need to click a fill.*

**NOTE** You can copy from a stroke, a fill, or a bitmap using the Eyedropper tool; you can't copy from a symbol or a grouped object without opening it or breaking it apart.

4. **Click the bitmap, fill, or stroke you want to copy to (imagine squeezing the color out of your eyedropper).** If you copied color from a bitmap or a fill, you need to click a fill; if you copied color from a stroke, you need to click a stroke.

Flash recolors the stroke, fill, or bitmap you click, applying the *from* color to the *to* color, as shown in Figure 5-52, bottom.

## Kuler: Color Help from the Community

In an office full of designers, water cooler discussion often revolves around color palettes. What color combinations best represent autumn, or the Rocky Mountains, or surfing in Hawaii. Kuler is Adobe's way of providing that kind of designer know-how to everyone (Figure 5-53). To open Kuler, go to Window→Extensions→Kuler. Simply put, Kuler is a panel that shows named color combinations with five colors to a palette. Anyone can provide a color palette, even you. All these color combinations are stored online, so when you use Kuler, your computer connects to the Web.

Using the buttons and menus on the Kuler panel, you can browse through all the color combinations provided by the Kuler community. You can choose a palette, edit the colors, and then save it under a different name. You can create your own color palettes and then upload them for others to review and use. If you see the perfect color combination for your project, you can add the palette to your Swatches panel by clicking Add to Swatches.

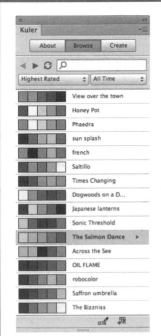

**FIGURE 5-53**

*When you find a palette that you want to use in your Flash project, click the "Add to Swatches" button, and those colors appear in your Swatches panel. If you want to create your own theme for the Kuler community, click the button in the upper-right corner.*

# Choosing and Formatting Text

Flash isn't just about moving pictures. Text is a big part of many projects, and with Flash you can do remarkable things with text and type. You can label buttons, boxes, and widgets with small, helpful text, and make page headlines pop with big, bold type. When you use large blocks of text—as in newspaper articles or how-to instructions—you can add scroll bars so your readers can see all the text in one place, or you can create hyperlinks that lead to other pages. And of course, Flash can do things to type that wouldn't enter Microsoft Word's wildest dreams: morphing paragraphs as they move across the screen; exploding words and letters into dozens of pieces. You can also create the same kind of effects that you see in the opening credits of TV shows. To handle all this variety, Flash provides different text tools. As with any craft, it's important to choose the right tool for the job.

Text handling is another feature that has grown and evolved with new versions of Flash. In fact, a couple of versions ago Flash Professional introduced a brand-new and powerful way of handling text, officially named *Text Layout Framework*, but usually called *TLF text*. If you're comfortable working with Flash's tried-and-true text tools, don't panic. Flash provides backward compatibility with *Classic text*, too. You can even mix and match text in the same document, layer, and frame. So, each time you click the Text tool, you need to choose which text engine you want to use.

How do you know which to use? That's what you'll learn in this chapter. First, you'll get tips on choosing the right tools. Then you'll learn how to work with text and create special effects. Finally, at the end of the chapter (page 239), you'll find a subpanel-by-subpanel description of text properties, including which properties work with which text engines and text types. (Interested in using ActionScript to make text jump through hoops? Turn to Chapter 17.)

# ■ Text Questions

When you add text to your Flash animation, you have a specific job in mind. You may want to put a headline at the top of the page, label a widget on the screen, or provide instructions. If you're creating the next great eBook reader, your needs are different than if you're creating a splashy intro sequence like the ones on *The Daily Show* or *American Idol*. Because these text jobs vary so much, ask yourself a few questions before you click the Text tool:

- Is the text a single line or a paragraph?
- If the block of text is several lines, should it have scroll bars?
- Should the text be selectable by the audience, or is it read-only?
- Will the audience be able to change or add to the text?
- Do I want to animate the text?
- Do I want to make changes to the text using ActionScript?
- Do I need to provide text in multiple languages?

As you'll see in the following section, the answers to these questions help you choose the right text engine and text type. Flash designers have always had to consider these questions, and even with a new way of handling text (TLF), the questions are still valid. Read on to learn which text tools best accomplish these jobs.

# ■ Choosing TLF or Classic Text

Click the text tool—it looks like a big capital T in the Tools panel (Figure 6-1). The Properties panel changes to show all the different text properties available to you, the designer. Starting at the top, the first drop-down menu gives you a choice between two text engines—TLF Text and Classic Text. These text-handling routines are called *engines* because they're the mechanisms used to display text in Flash Player—the tool your audience uses to watch your Flash animation. In previous versions of Flash, the text options were much more limited than those provided by programs like InDesign, Illustrator, and Photoshop. TLF text goes a long way toward closing that gap. *Classic text* is still an option for a number of reasons, including compatibility.

**Choose TLF text if:**

- You're new to Flash. It's the text engine of the future, so you may as well start learning it. It gives you the most control over your text. In spite of the many options, it's fairly easy to use.
- You want to animate your text in three dimensions. It's much easier to spin and rotate TLF text fields.

- You want to use fancy typographic features such as ligatures (special characters that represent two letters). TLF text provides many more of the features that print typographers expect.

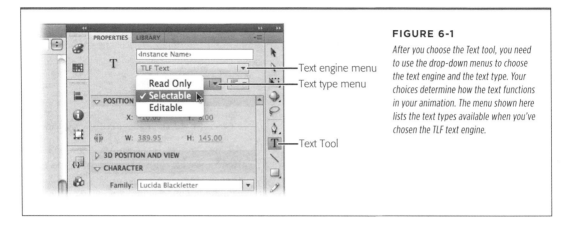

**FIGURE 6-1**

*After you choose the Text tool, you need to use the drop-down menus to choose the text engine and the text type. Your choices determine how the text functions in your animation. The menu shown here lists the text types available when you've chosen the TLF text engine.*

- You want to provide text in different languages, including those where text doesn't flow from left to right. TLF text is much more cosmopolitan than Classic.

**Choose Classic text if:**

- You need to be compatible with older versions of Flash. You can open and work on older projects in Flash Professional CS6. You can even mix Classic and TLF text in the same project.

- It's critically important to make your animation files (SWFs) as small as possible. If you're using text simply as labels on the stage and you aren't changing it with ActionScript or giving your audience a chance to add and edit, then Classic static text takes up the least room in your SWF file.

- You're a Flash veteran and the old ways are just fine, thank you very much. There's nothing wrong with sticking with what you know will work, especially when there's a deadline looming.

## Choose a Text Type

Once you've chosen either TLF Text or Classic Text, the Properties panel changes to display settings for that text engine. You notice right away that TLF includes many more options. Immediately below the "Text engine" menu, the first setting is the "Text type" menu. Below that, there are several subpanels filled with widgets to help you manage your text. The choices you make at the top of the Properties panel determine which properties are available as you work your way down. For example, TLF has different text types from Classic.

### ■ TLF TEXT TYPES

- Use **Read Only** when you want to display text on the stage, but you don't want the audience to edit the text.

- Use **Selectable** when you want to give your audience the ability to select and perhaps copy and paste text.

- Use **Editable** when you want to give your audience the ability to change or add their own text. For example, choose this option when you're creating "fill-in" forms.

### ■ CLASSIC TEXT TYPES

Classic text continues to offer the three options familiar to Flash veterans (Figure 6-2):

- Use **Static Text** when you want to display text on the stage for simple chores like headlines and labels. Your audience can't change static text, and you can't change it using ActionScript. Static text is actually converted to images when it's stored in your final SWF file.

- Use **Dynamic Text** when you want to make changes using ActionScript. Creating a program that continuously updates basketball scores? That's a job for dynamic text.

- Use **Input Text** when you want to give your audience the ability to change or add their own text, perhaps through the use of a text input box or form. Input text can also be used in conjunction with ActionScript.

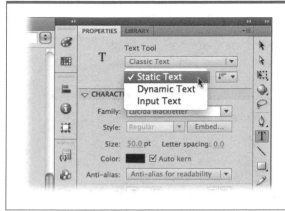

**FIGURE 6-2**

*If you're a Flash veteran, you'll recognize the Classic Text options. As shown here, you can choose the following text types: Static Text, Dynamic Text, and Input Text. Because static text is converted to an image before your audience sees it, you can't edit the text (change the words or letters) when the animation is running.*

Some options, such as your choice of typeface, size, and color, remain the same no matter which text engine or text type you choose. Other options, such as highlight, ligatures, and baseline shift, appear or disappear from the Properties panel based on your choices. So, if a particular setting you need is unavailable, go back and choose a different text engine or text type. In general, TLF text gives you more typographic control. You can mix TLF and Classic text in the same document and even in the same layer or frame.

# ■ About Typefaces and Fonts

Choosing a typeface for your project should be fun—just not too much fun. There are two paths to the available typefaces installed on your computer. Using the menus, go to Text→Font, or in the Properties panel, find the Character subpanel, and then click the Family menu. Either way, you see a list like the one in Figure 6-3. Make your typeface decisions based on the job at hand, and you can't go wrong. Think about what you expect your type to do, and then help it do that job by choosing the right typeface, size, color, container, and background. Beginning designers often treat text as yet another design element and let the desire for a cool look override more practical concerns. Designers sometimes talk about a text block like just another shape on the page. But cool type effects can torture your readers' eyes with hard-to-read backgrounds, weird letter spacing, or hopelessly small font sizes. (For more advice on readability, see the box on page 220.)

**NOTE** If you want to be technical in a Gutenbergian fashion, typefaces are families of fonts. Times Roman is a typeface, while "Times Roman, bold, 12 point" is a font. Somewhere along the line, as type moved from traditional typesetters to computer desktops, the meaning of the word "font" came to be synonymous with "typeface." That's okay, but knowing how the terms originated makes great cocktail party banter.

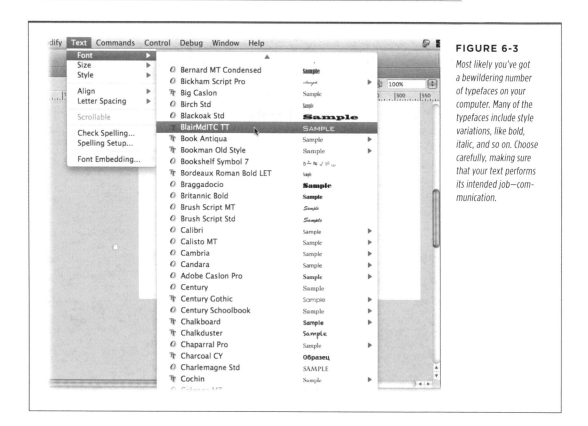

**FIGURE 6-3**

*Most likely you've got a bewildering number of typefaces on your computer. Many of the typefaces include style variations, like bold, italic, and so on. Choose carefully, making sure that your text performs its intended job—communication.*

# ■ Adding Text to Your Document

Enough theory—it's time to put some words on the stage. Just as Flash has tools for adding shapes and lines to your drawings, it also has a tool specifically designed to let you add text to your drawings—the Text tool (T). The following steps describe the basic method for putting read-only text on the stage.

---

**FREQUENTLY ASKED QUESTION**

### Small Is Beautiful

*How can I use small type and make sure it stays readable?*

For most people, reading text on a computer or smartphone screen is more difficult than reading it off a piece of paper. In fact, most people simply won't read text if it's too hard to see. If your Flash project includes text with small font sizes (12 points or less), there are a few things that you can do to keep your audience from straining their eyes:

- If possible, bump the type up to a larger size (Properties→ Character→Size). At small sizes, a point or even half a point makes a big difference.

- Black text on a white background is the most readable combination. If you want to use different colors, opt for very dark text on a very light background. If you have to use light text on a dark background, then make sure there's a great deal of contrast between the colors.

- Use sans-serif type, like Verdana, Helvetica, or Arial, for small sizes. Sans-serif type looks like the text in this box; it doesn't have the tiny end bars (serifs) you find in type like the body text in this book. Computer screens have a hard time creating sharp serif type at very small sizes.

- Use both upper- and lowercase type for anything other than a headline. Even though all-uppercase type looks bigger, it's actually less readable. The height differences in lowercase type make it more readable. Besides, too much uppercase type makes it look like you're shouting.

- Avoid bold and italic type. Often bold and italic type are hard to read at small font sizes. But this varies with different typefaces, so it doesn't hurt to experiment.

- If your text isn't going to be animated, then turn on "Anti-aliasing for readability" (Properties→Character→ Anti-alias→"Anti-alias for readability"). Antialiasing is a bit of computer magic and fool-the-eye trickery that gives type nice, smooth edges.

- Choose "Anti-aliasing for animation" (Properties→ Character→Anti-alias→"Anti-alias for animation") if you're going to be pushing that text around the screen with tweens or ActionScript.

It never hurts to get second and third opinions. If you've got eyes like an eagle, you may want to get some opinions from your less-gifted colleagues when it comes to readability. You want your Flash project to be accessible to as wide an audience as possible.

---

To use the Text tool:

1. **In the Tools panel, select the Text tool.**

   Flash highlights the Text tool; when you mouse over to the stage, your cursor changes to crosshairs accompanied by a miniature letter T, as shown in Figure 6-4.

2. **Using the two menus at the top of the Properties panel, choose TLF Text and then, below, choose Read Only.**

Armed with this information, Flash is ready to create a text field that meets those specs. By choosing Read Only, you create text that can't be changed by your audience. It works well for simple labels or headlines.

> **TIP**   In the Properties panel, many of the text widgets, including the "Text engine" and "Text type" menus, aren't labeled. However, if you're ever in doubt, move the cursor over a widget, and a tooltip appears with the official name.

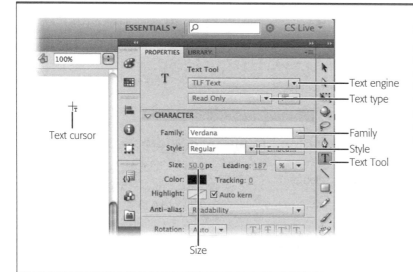

**FIGURE 6-4**

*After you select the Text tool, the cursor changes to crosshairs with a T symbol, and the Properties panel shows the available options. At the top, you choose a text engine and text type. Farther down, you can choose a font family, style, and size.*

3. **In the Character subpanel, choose a family, style, and size.**

These are the familiar settings that you use every time you create text. The choices are similar to those you'd use in your word processor. In Figure 6-5, the settings are for *Verdana* family, *bold* style, and *50-point* type size.

4. **Click the stage and drag to create a text field.**

If you simply click once, Flash displays a squished-up, empty text field. If you drag, you create a rectangle. Either method works, because the box resizes as you type your text, and you can resize the box at any time.

5. **Type some headline text, like *Breaking News!***

Your text appears on the stage, showing the specs you chose in step 3.

**TIP** If the type you specified looks different on someone else's computer, then you've got a font-embedding problem. It most often happens when you let your audience add or edit text, or when you create text with ActionScript. Font embedding is covered in the chapter on animating text with ActionScript, page 582.

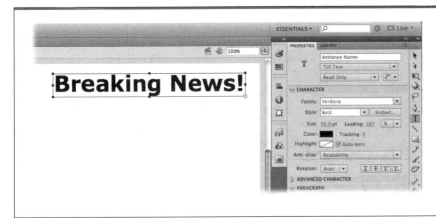

**FIGURE 6-5**

*You can modify text using several different subpanels in the Properties panel. The Position and Size settings work the same as they do with other objects on the stage. Using the Character and Paragraph subpanels, you can fine-tune your type as you would in a page layout program.*

## Changing Text Position, Height, and Width

Once you have a block of text on the stage, you can make changes as you would with any other graphic element:

- To move the text field, use the Selection tool (V). Drag to reposition the text.

- To resize the text field, use the Selection tool (V) to drag one of the handles around the edge of the box.

- To stretch or squash the type, use the Free Transform tool (Q) and drag one of the handles, as shown in Figure 6-6.

When resizing the text field, you can drag the handles whether you're using the Text tool or the Selection tool (solid arrow). The container holds the text and changes size, but the text itself remains the same size. Some text fields can be changed to automatically expand to accommodate the text they hold. When you resize a text field that's set to automatically expand, Flash changes it to a fixed-width field. To change a fixed-width text field to one that automatically resizes to fit the text, double-click the hollow square handle. The handle changes to a hollow circle.

As with shapes and other graphics, you can make position and dimension changes directly in the Properties panel. Want to change the height of the text field? Just type a new number. TLF text and Classic text fields behave in the same way when you move them or change their width and height.

## Rotating, Skewing, and Moving in 3-D

Naturally, Flash lets you spin your type around in different directions—after all, it is an animation program. To spin text in two dimensions, use the Transform tool (Q).

Select the text, and then move the cursor near one of the corners. When you see a circular arrow, click and drag. The steps are similar for skewing text, except that you position the cursor near one of the edges of the text field. A slanted double-arrow appears when it's time to click and drag.

Position Properties    Free Transform Tool

Text box handles

**FIGURE 6-6**

*You can use the same tools to position and transform blocks of text that you use to work with other graphics. Here the headline was stretched dramatically by increasing the Height property for the text field. Note, however, that the font size is still 50. Transforming distorts the text but doesn't change the underlying typographic properties.*

If you want to rotate a text field in 3-D, you need to use TLF text, as shown in Figure 6-7. Then, you can use the 3D Rotation tool (W) and the 3D Translation tool (G), as you would with any other graphic. The 3D Translation tool lets you move the text field in 3-D space, as in text zooming in at you from far away.

**FIGURE 6-7**

*You can use the Transform tool (Q) to rotate text in two dimensions. For 3-D rotation or motion, use TLF text and the 3D Rotation tool (shown here) or the 3D Translation tool.*

## Changing Text Color

Colorful text puts pizzazz into your animation; just make sure you don't sacrifice readability. You can change the color of an entire block of text, or you can choose certain characters and change their color, as shown in Figure 6-8:

- **To change the color of an entire block of text,** use the Selection tool (V) and click the text. Once you see the familiar text box and handles, head over to the Properties panel. In the Character subpanel, click the Color swatch. A color picker opens, similar to the ones you use to specify colors for shapes. You won't see any gradient settings for text, but you can change its opacity using the Alpha percentage in the upper-right corner.

**FIGURE 6-8**

*You use Flash's familiar color picker to select a color for your text. To change the color for specific characters within a block of text, select the characters before you make your color selection.*

- **To change the color of individual characters,** use the Text tool (T). Click the text block, and you see a blinking line similar to ones used in word processors. This line marks the insert position. So, if you start typing, new characters appear in the text. Just as in a word processor, you drag to select text. Select the text you want to change, and then choose a color in Properties→Character→Color.

- **With text, you set the color for the entire character**—unlike shapes, where you choose separate stroke and fill colors. However, TLF text gives you an extra color option called Highlight. As the name implies, this gives you a way to make your text stand out through the use of a background color, as if you had highlighted the text with a marker.

**TIP** You can create additional color effects using the Color Effect, Display, and Filters subpanels at the bottom of the Properties panel. These settings work the same for shapes, objects, and text, and they're described on page 245.

**WORKAROUND WORKSHOP**

### Applying a Color Gradient to Text

Flash lets you apply a gradient to graphics (page 206) but not text. But if you insist, and promise to use this effect in moderation, you have a couple of ways to get it.

The most obvious solution is to turn the text into a graphic and then add a gradient. Start by selecting the text and pressing Ctrl+B (⌘-B) to break blocks of text into separate letters; then press Ctrl+B (⌘-B) a second time to break the letters into graphic elements. The drawback with this technique is that the text is, well, no longer text. It still looks like text, but you can't edit it like text.

Alternatively, you can adapt the masking technique described on page 151: You create a block of Classic text on one layer and then, on another layer beneath that, use the rectangle tool to create a block with a gradient color, as shown at the top of Figure 6-9. To turn the layer with the text into a mask, right-click (Control-click) the layer's name, and then choose Mask from the shortcut menu. The block with the gradient disappears, except for the color that shows through the text. Flash automatically locks masked and masking layers. You'll find that this text is editable inside of Flash—just unlock the layer and make your changes. You can also change the text using some of the ActionScript techniques discussed in Chapter 17. Want to color your text with a photographic image? Simply place a photo in the layer below the text.

## Creating a Text Hyperlink

You can add hyperlinks to your text with or without using ActionScript to generate the code. Using TLF text, you can add a link to an entire text block, or you can add the link to a few words or characters. Hyperlinks often open web pages or documents, but with some ActionScript code, they can perform other feats, too. To create a link that opens a web page or document, you provide a *URL* address. URL stands for Universal Resource Locator. You usually hear this term in relation to the Internet, but a URL can just as well point to a file on your computer. The key is in the prefix: Instead of beginning with *http://*, a link that points to a file on your computer begins with *file://*. Keep in mind, this only works when the animation (SWF file) and the linked file are on the viewer's computer. It won't work if the animation is on a web page or stored on the Internet.

Here are the steps for creating a link when you're using TLF text:

1. **Use the Select tool (V) to select an entire text block, or use the Text tool (T) to select text inside a text block.**

   Either method determines the clickable link text your audience clicks to open a web page or a document.

2. **In Properties→Advanced Character→Link, type the complete URL, such as www.missingmanuals.com.**

You can use other standard URLs to open files or to create emails such as *file:///documents/missingmanual.txt* or *mailto://george@washington.edu.*

3. **Optional: In Properties→Advanced Character→Target, choose an option.**

Target options are used, as they are in HTML, to tell the browser how to open the linked web page: *_self* (the standard option) opens the page in the current browser window; *_blank* opens the page in a new window; *_parent* opens the page in the parent of the current frame; and *_top* opens the page in the top-level frame of the current window. If you don't choose an option, the menu remains set to None, and the standard behavior is to open the page in the current browser window.

**FIGURE 6-9**

*You can create a mask with text so the color of the graphic or photo underneath shows through the letters.*

*Top: Here are the two layers before the mask is turned on. The rainbow rectangle is beneath the text.*

*Bottom: When the mask is turned on, the layers are locked and the rectangle with the gradient disappears except for the color that shows through the text.*

4. **Press Ctrl+Enter (⌘-Return) to test your movie.**

Flash plays your movie. When you move your cursor over the linked text, it changes to the pointing finger, indicating a link. Click the text, and your linked web page, document, or addressed email message should appear.

## Creating a Hyperlink Using Classic Text

Creating a link using Classic text is a little more convoluted than with TLF text. As is often the case with Classic text, static text behaves one way and non-static text (dynamic text and input text) behaves differently. If you want to highlight a couple of words inside a paragraph of text, you need to use static text, as shown in Figure 6-10. When you add a hyperlink to dynamic text, Flash applies a link to the entire text field. You can get around this behavior by selecting the text and then, in the Properties→Character panel, clicking the "Render text as HTML" button. (There's no text label for the button, which looks like HTML angle brackets: < >.)

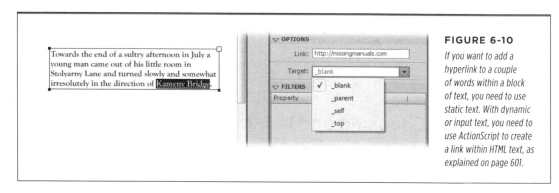

**FIGURE 6-10**

*If you want to add a hyperlink to a couple of words within a block of text, you need to use static text. With dynamic or input text, you need to use ActionScript to create a link within HTML text, as explained on page 601.*

Here are the steps for applying a link to Classic static text:

1. **With the Text tool, drag to select the words within the static text you want to link.**

   If you prefer to navigate by keyboard, you can use the Shift and arrow keys to select text, too—just as in a word processor.

2. **In Properties→Options→Link, type the link details.**

   You need to include the path for the file, unless you're certain that it's going to be in the same folder as the .swf file when the animation runs. A complete link to a file on the Internet might look like this:

   *www.missingmanuals.com/cds/flashcs6mm/text_scram_finished.fla*

3. **If you want your link to open in a new browser window or tab, select Properties→Options→Target→ _blank.**

   If you don't change the target setting, the new page replaces your animation in your audience's browser. The other target settings let you open documents in different sections of an HTML page using *frames*—a web design technique that's fallen out of fashion.

4. **Highlight the hyperlinked text so your audience knows it's a link.**

   If you want the linked words to be highlighted so your audience will know they're a link, you'll have to do it yourself by changing the text color. Don't be fooled; when you create a link, you see a line beneath the linked words in the Flash authoring program, but when your animation runs in Flash Player, there's no line, no highlight, no indication that the words are linked. The only clue your audience has that the words are linked is the changing cursor if they chance to move the mouse over the words.

If you want to link an entire block of dynamic text, the technique is similar. You can use the Selection tool (arrow) to select the text field, and then provide the link details in the Properties→Options→Link box.

**TIP** You can create an email link—great for a "contact us" button. Instead of *http://*, type *mailto:*, and then add your email address to the end. For example, a complete address might look like this: *mailto:harry@ stutzmotors.com*. When your audience clicks the link, their email program of choice starts and creates an email using that address in the link.

## ■ Choosing and Using Text Containers

At design time, when you click in a text field with the Text tool, you can select and edit the existing text. You may also notice that the handles around the text box change. One of the handles on the right or bottom of the text box appears larger than the rest, as shown in Figure 6-11. This handle always provides some helpful information about the text box's characteristics and behavior.

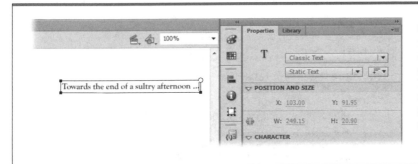

**FIGURE 6-11**

*The handles on a text box provide details about the type of text field and the way it's sized. The hollow, round handle in the upper-right corner of this text field shows that it's static text that expands with the box.*

Here's your secret text field handle decoder ring for horizontal text:

- Handle at upper right means it's Classic static text.

- Handle at lower right means it's Classic dynamic or input text.

- Hollow circle means the text field expands as text is added.

- Hollow square indicates that the text has a fixed width (as shown in Figure 6-12).

- Solid square means the dynamic text is scrollable.

The codes for vertical text are similar, except that the handle providing information is always at the bottom of the text box. It appears at bottom left for static text and at bottom right for dynamic and input text.

When you click inside a TLF text container, it displays square handles on the left and right side. As described on page 232, you use these handles to flow text from one container to another.

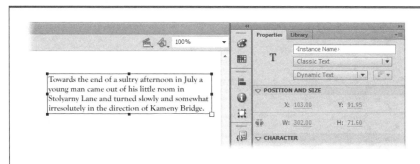

**FIGURE 6-12**

*The handle shown in the lower-right corner of this text box indicates that this dynamic text has a fixed width.*

## Creating Vertical Text Containers

You can change the orientation of TLF text and Classic static text using the Properties panel. As shown in Figure 6-13, the "Change orientation of text" menu is at the top, next to the Text type menu. Your choices are "Horizontal," "Vertical," and "Vertical, left to right." You edit text that's been turned with the orientation options as with any other text. Choose the Text tool from the Tools panel, and click the text field. It may take a moment or two for you to get your bearings if you're not used to working with vertical text. But you'll soon find it's easy to drag to select text. The arrow keys help you navigate back and forth. When you type, text appears vertically and follows the paragraph's orientation properties.

When you use TLF text, you can rotate characters within the lines of text. This technique is handy if you want, for example, to create vertical text like the neon signs that attach to the sides of buildings. Set the "Change orientation of text" menu to Vertical, and then change the Rotation to 270 degrees, as shown in Figure 6-14.

## Multiline and Single-Line Text Containers

In Flash, text containers are either multiline or single line. Multiline containers are great for big paragraphs of text, while single-line containers work well for headlines, labels, and input text.

When you're working with TLF text, go to Properties→"Container and Flow"→Behavior. The menu gives you these choices: "Single line," "Multiline," "Multiline no wrap," and "Password." The available options depend on the text type. For example, Password is available only with editable text. You use it to conceal the characters someone types into a password box.

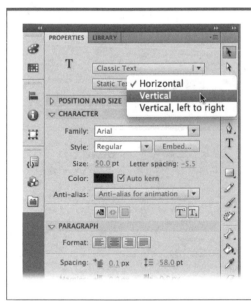

**FIGURE 6-13**

*Use the "Change orientation of text" menu to create vertical text. Then, use the Rotate button to change the direction the vertical text points.*

When you're working with Classic text, you have similar options, but the Properties panel tools are slightly different. With Classic static text, you create multiline text boxes by pressing Enter (Return). If you're using dynamic or input text, you find the single-line and multiline options in the Paragraph subpanel.

## Applying Advanced Formatting to Text

Typographers and art directors are as particular about text as winemakers are about wine. With Adobe, the Ministry of Fonts, as its publisher, Flash has lots of tools to keep type connoisseurs smiling. You can delve into these features if you like, but right out of the box, Flash has some pretty good settings:

■ **TLF TEXT TYPOGRAPHY**

• **Tracking (Properties→Character→Tracking).** Tracking determines how much space surrounds individual letters. In most cases, you can leave the tracking at zero for the best readability. Enter a negative number for tighter tracking, where letters can bump up against one another or even overlap. A positive number creates larger spaces between letters, a style sometimes used for logos and other artsy effects.

• **Auto kern (Properties→Character→"Auto kern").** Kerning also affects the space between characters, but its purpose is different. Some letters, like A and V, look better when they're tucked a little closer together, to eliminate the awkward gaps that are especially noticeable at larger type sizes. Flash's

Auto-kern feature is on when you first begin using Flash. If you want to turn it off, turn off the "Auto kern" checkbox.

- **Leading (Properties→Character→Leading).** Back in the days of metal type, printers called the space between lines *leading*, because they actually used lead slugs to set the space. The name is still used to set the space between lines. With TLF text, you can set the leading as a percentage of the line height or as a specific point size.

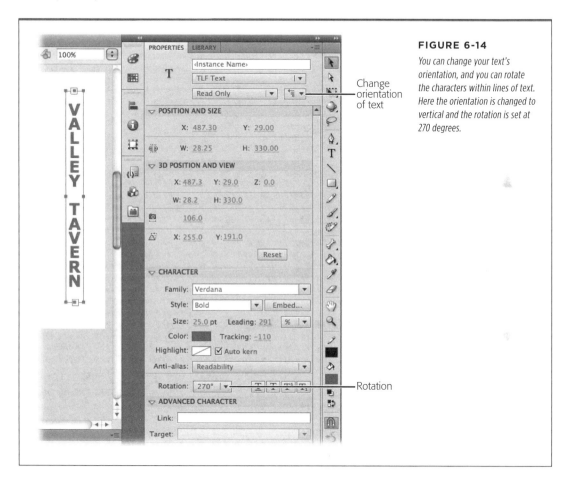

**FIGURE 6-14**

*You can change your text's orientation, and you can rotate the characters within lines of text. Here the orientation is changed to vertical and the rotation is set at 270 degrees.*

### CLASSIC TEXT TYPOGRAPHY

- **Letter spacing (Properties→Character→Letter spacing).** Works the same as TLF text tracking.

- **Auto kern (Properties→Character→Auto kern).** Works the same as TLF auto kern.

- **Line spacing (Properties→Paragraph→Line Spacing).** Works the same as TLF leading.

## Create a Multicolumn Text Container

Before Adobe developed TLF text, you created multiple newspaper-style columns of text by creating multiple containers and carefully putting the right amount of text in each container. With TLF text, you can create up to 10 columns of text in any container. Simply go to Properties→"Container and Flow" and type a number from 1 to 10 for the Columns setting, as shown in Figure 6-15. Then use the box at the right to specify the distance between columns.

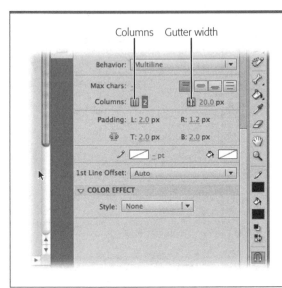

**FIGURE 6-15**

*With TLF text, you can create up to 10 columns in a text container. Use the box to the right to specify the gutter width—that is, the distance between columns.*

## Flow Text from One Container to Another

Another TLF text specialty is making text flow from one container to another. If you know your text is always going to be seen at the same size or with the same typeface, you might not worry about automatically flowing text. However, if you give your audience the option to change the text size or font, the text may need more or less space. That's when automatically flowing text comes in handy.

The following steps demonstrate how flowing text works:

1. **Using TLF text, create two text boxes on the stage.**

   You can use any text type: read only, selectable, or editable.

2. **Copy and paste several paragraphs of text.**

   You can type directly into the text boxes, but it's faster to copy and paste text from a letter or other document.

3. **In the lower-right corner of the first text container, click the red square.**

   The cursor changes—it looks like it has a paragraph of text attached.

4. **Move the cursor over the second text container.**

When the cursor is over an empty text container, it changes to a chain link.

5. **Click in the second container.**

Text flows automatically from the first container to the second, as shown in Figure 6-16. A blue line connects the two text boxes, indicating how the text flows.

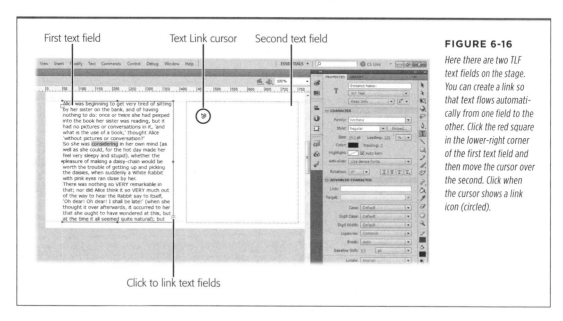

First text field      Text Link cursor      Second text field

**FIGURE 6-16**

*Here there are two TLF text fields on the stage. You can create a link so that text flows automatically from one field to the other. Click the red square in the lower-right corner of the first text field and then move the cursor over the second. Click when the cursor shows a link icon (circled).*

Click to link text fields

Not only does any extra text fill the second container, but it also makes automatic adjustments if you change the size of the text containers or change the type specifications.

### ◼ DISCONNECT FLOWING TEXT

Sooner or later, you'll want to break the link between two text containers. To do that, just double-click the text flow button in either container where the connecting line meets the box.

# ◼ Animating Text Without ActionScript

You can animate text using the usual Flash tools, or you can use ActionScript. Which technique you choose depends on your own skills and inclinations. This section explains how to create some interesting animation effects for text using only Flash.

**NOTE**    If you'd like to see the finished animation before you begin, you can download *06-1_Text_Scram.fla* from *www.missingmanuals.com/cds/flashcs6mm*.

The following steps show you how to make text move using frames and Flash's Modify commands.

1. **Select File→New→Flash File (ActionScript 3.0).**

   Make the document size 550 x 400 pixels, the frame rate 12 fps, and choose a light-colored background.

2. **Use the Text tool to create a line of Classic static text with a font size of about 36 in a darker color that complements the document background color.**

   You can use any word or phrase you want. "Make this text scram," for example.

3. **Click Frame 12 in the text layer, and then press F5 to insert a frame.**

   The text layer now has 12 frames. Equally important, when you create new layers, they'll automatically be 12 frames long, saving you a click or two of work.

4. **With the text selected, choose Modify→Break Apart.**

   The Break Apart command comes in very handy when you want to animate text. It puts each letter in its own text field, which gives you an opportunity to move the letters independently.

5. **While the text is still selected, choose Modify→Timeline→"Distribute to Layers."**

   Flash places each letter in its own layer in the timeline and thoughtfully names each layer by the letter, saving you a lot of cut, paste, and layer creation work. Layer 1 is empty at this point, and you can remove it if you want to tidy things up. Click the layer, and then click the Delete icon (trash can) below the layer names.

6. **Click the M layer (the capital M in "Make"), right-click the M layer in the timeline, and then choose Create Motion Tween.**

   The 12 frames of the M layer take on the blue hue that indicates a motion tween.

7. **Ctrl-click (⌘-click) Frame 12, and then drag the letter M off the right edge of the stage.**

   Press the Shift key as you drag to create a perfectly straight motion path. The letter M displays a motion path. If you scrub the playhead, you see that it moves from the left side of the stage until it exits stage right.

8. **With the letter M still selected and the playhead still at Frame 12, select the Transform tool, and then scale the letter so it's about five times its original size.**

   If, after you resize it, part of the letter is still visible on the stage, pull it a little more to the right.

---

**TIP** If you want to accurately resize the letter, use the Motion Editor to handle the scaling (Window→Motion Editor→Transformation→Scale X). (Motion Editor details are on page 311.)

---

9. **With the M still selected in Frame 12, open the Properties→Filters panel.**

Click the small triangle next to the word "Filters" to open the panel. Initially the panel is empty.

10. **Click the "Add filter" button in the lower-left corner, and then choose Blur from the pop-up menu.**

The menu lists all the filters you can apply to the selected object—in this case, the oversized letter M. When you click Blur, the properties for the filter appear in the Filter panel, as shown in Figure 6-17.

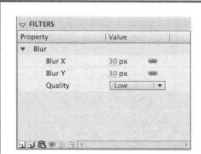

**FIGURE 6-17**

*You apply filters to selected objects. Each filter has different properties. Here the Blur filter shows three different properties to control the direction and the quality of the blurring effect.*

11. **Click the Blur X setting and type *30*.**

Doing so changes both the Blur X and Blur Y settings, which initially are linked together. Sometimes you can create a better speeding blur effect by limiting the blur to one axis. If you want to unlink one of the settings, click the link icon to the right of the setting; the icon changes to a broken link. Then you can enter a separate value for each property.

12. **Move the playhead to Frame 1, and then with the letter M selected, type *0* in the Blur X and Blur Y filter settings.**

You need to re-select the letter M after scrubbing the Playhead. Setting the Blur filter in Frame 12 also affects the letter in Frame 1. Setting Blur X and Blur Y to 0 creates a nice, sharp letter again.

13. **Move the playhead to Frame 6, and with the letter M still selected, type *0* in the Blur X and Blur Y filter settings.**

As explained on page 107, you can change just about any property, at any point, along a motion path. In this case, you're changing the Blur filter so that the letter stays focused for the first part of its trip and then becomes blurry as it leaves the stage.

You're done with the motion tween effect. If you test your animation at this point (Ctrl+Enter or ⌘-Return), you see the letter M move from left to right, becoming larger and blurry as it makes its journey, as shown in Figure 6-18. In the next steps, you'll copy the motion tween from the letter M and paste that motion into the layers with the other letters. (Admit it—you were worried you were going to have to create all those tweens by hand.)

1. **Right-click the motion tween in the M layer, and then choose Copy Motion.**

   Flash stores a copy of the tween on the Clipboard. It includes that carefully constructed motion and all its property changes.

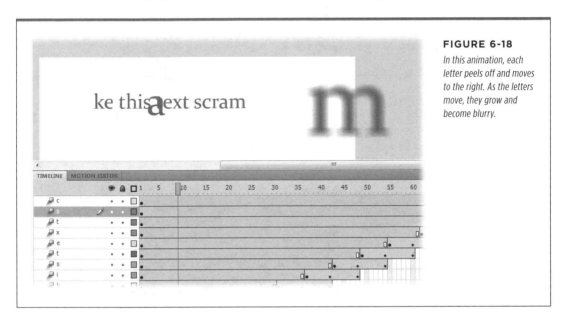

**FIGURE 6-18**

*In this animation, each letter peels off and moves to the right. As the letters move, they grow and become blurry.*

2. **Click the first frame of the "a" layer, and then Shift-click the first frame of the "m" layer in the word "scram."**

   The first frame of each layer (except for M in the word "Make") is selected.

3. **Right-click one of the selected frames, and then choose Paste Motion from the shortcut menu.**

   Flash pastes the tween into the each of the selected layers. Obediently, the letters now follow the same motion, scale, and blurring changes as dictated by the tween.

4. **Press Ctrl+Enter (⌘-Return) to test your animation.**

   The letters rush off the right side of the stage in a large blurry clump. Kinda cool, but your audience will appreciate the effect even more if the letters peel off one by one across the stage. You can do that by staggering the frames on each layer, as detailed in the next steps.

5. **In the "a" layer, click the motion tween, and then drag all 12 of the selected frames down the timeline a distance of six frames.**

The motion tween for "a" begins its action on Frame 7. This creates about a half-second gap between the time when the M starts moving and when the "a" starts moving. After the move, there are six blank frames at the beginning of the "a" layer.

6. **Select the letter "a" in Frame 7, and then paste it into Frame 1 using Edit→ "Paste in Place" (Ctrl+Shift+V or ⌘-Shift-V).**

After you move the tween, you need to put a copy of each letter back in the first frame of the animation. Using "Paste in Place" displays the letter in the right position in the frames before the tween takes effect.

7. **Repeat steps 18 and 19 to create a six-frame offset between each of the letters.**

When you're done, the timeline looks something like Figure 6-19.

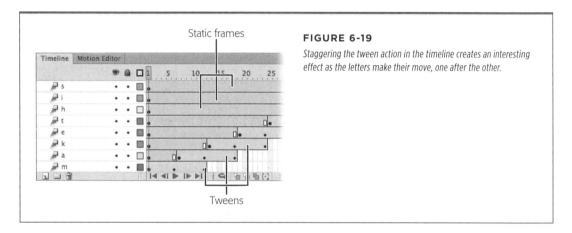

Static frames

**FIGURE 6-19**

*Staggering the tween action in the timeline creates an interesting effect as the letters make their move, one after the other.*

Tweens

## Experimenting with Animated Text

Applying motion tweens to text can really capture your audience's attention. It works great for headlines, intros, and transitions, but like anything else, it's possible to have too much of a good thing. No one likes to wait these days, so be careful not to strain your audience's patience. That said, you can pack more effects into the previous animation without making it run longer. You can add other moving objects to the animation, like more text or shapes. If you turn each of the letters into a movie clip, you can take advantage of Flash's 3-D capabilities. Then your tweens can twist and flip the letters as they move through three-dimensional space. Experiment—let your imagination run wild! If you're looking for inspiration, study the techniques used by some of the network and cable news programs. They love to use moving text and other visuals to make the news seem more exciting than it really is.

Store the techniques that work in your Flash toolkit and remember the lessons you learn from the ones that flop. As with any craft, you're likely to learn as much from your mistakes as from your successes.

## Moving Text in Three Dimensions

Want to make a block of text spin in the air or float off into the distance the way it does at the beginning of *Star Wars* movies? You can perform those feats of typographic magic with TLF text and the "3D Position" and View subpanels.

To create a spinning block of text, follow these steps:

1. **Click the Text tool, and then in the Properties panel, choose TLF Text and Read Only.**

   Read-only text works best here, because you wouldn't want your audience to select or edit spinning text. It would make them dizzy.

2. **Click the stage and add text to the text container.**

   You can type in your own text or copy and paste it from some other source.

3. **Click Frame 48 in the timeline, and then press F5.**

   The timeline for your movie is now 48 frames long.

4. **Right-click the timeline, and then choose Create Motion Tween.**

   In the timeline, the frames show the light-blue highlight that indicates a motion tween.

5. **Move the playhead to the last frame in the tween.**

   That should be Frame 48.

6. **Select the 3D Rotation tool (W), and then click the text box.**

   The 3D Rotation sphere appears on top of the text box.

7. **Drag one of the sphere axes to rotate the text.**

   For complete details on the 3D Rotation tool, see page 222. If you want to rotate the text with more precision, check out page 311, which explains how to use the Motion Editor.

8. **Press Enter to preview your animated text.**

For the most part, you can manipulate TLF text just as you would a movie clip symbol. That gives you lots of opportunities for spinning, distorting, and changing colors. As shown in the previous steps, you use the 3D Rotation tool (W) to spin text around a single point. If you want to move text forward or backward in 3-D space, use the 3D Translation tool (G). If you're up for a challenge, try creating an animated *Star Wars*–style block of text like the one shown in Figure 6-20. Here are some tips to help you complete the project:

- Create a TLF text container.

- Use the 3D Rotation tool to spin the text so it's leaning backward.

- Create a motion tween.

- Use 3D Position Vanishing Point X and Vanishing Point Y settings to adjust the vanishing point for your animation.

- Use the Perspective Angle setting to adjust the text angle.

- Create property keyframes and change the "3D Position and View"→Z property to move the text block away from the audience.

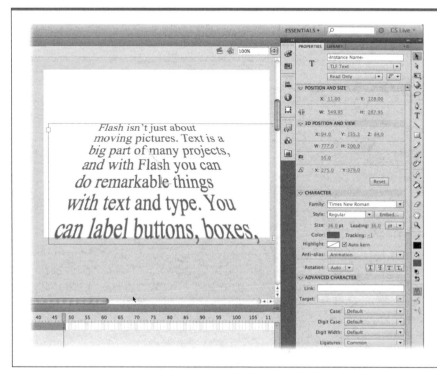

**FIGURE 6-20**

*Using TLF text and the "3D Position and View" settings, you can create text in space that looks similar to a popular science fiction epic.*

## Text Properties by Subpanel

So far, this chapter has only scratched the surface when it comes to tweaking type. Printers, graphic artists, and typographers have dozens of methods for arranging and positioning type—and, with TLF text, so do you. These settings determine the space between individual letters, between words, and between lines and paragraphs. There are settings to set margins and to justify or center text. The possibilities may boggle your mind if you're not up to speed with printing jargon. And the fact is, you may never use some of the text tools provided in Flash. Still when you need them, it's helpful to know where the tools are, so here's a subpanel-by-subpanel description of the text properties.

**NOTE**  Keep in mind, some properties are available to only a specific text engine or text type.

## Text Engine Properties

As explained on page 216, the top of the Text Properties panel has menus for choosing the text engine (TLF Text or Classic Text) and the text type (Figure 6-21). For every text type except Classic static text, there's an Instance Name box. Give your text an instance name, and then you can refer to it in ActionScript code. This gives you the opportunity to change text properties as your Flash animation runs. In the lower-right corner, use the "Change orientation of text" box to change the direction the text flows when you're working with different languages. This option is not available for Classic dynamic text or Classic input text.

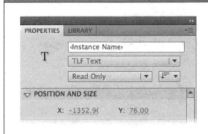

**FIGURE 6-21**

*Menus to choose the text engine and text type appear at the top of the Properties panel after you select the Text tool.*

## Position and Size

For Classic text, you use standard X and Y coordinates to position text on the stage. (For TLF text, use the "3D Position and View" subpanel.) The upper-left corner of the text box is the registration point (page 253). The W and H properties set the width and height of the text block. Use the chain link to lock the values and maintain proportions. Changing the width and height doesn't change the font size specification; it distorts the text.

## 3D Position and View (TLF Text Only)

With TLF text, you can control the position of your text blocks in three dimensions. Use the "3D Position and View" subpanel (Figure 6-22), where you find controls similar to those used with movie clip symbols. The X and Y properties represent horizontal and vertical positioning. Use the Z property to move the text block toward or away from your audience. As you use the 3D Rotation tool (W) to make text blocks spin around, you automatically change the "3D Position and View's" W and H settings. The Perspective Angle setting (camera) changes the apparent angle of the view. The Vanishing Point (X and Y) settings control the orientation of the Z axis by relocating the vanishing point (the point where parallel lines appear to merge in the distance).

## Character

Use the Character subpanel (Figure 6-23) for the standard type specifications: Family (font), Style, Size, and Color. With TLF text, you also have the option to set the highlight (background) color. Leading sets the space between lines of text. Tracking sets the distance between individual characters (or *glyphs*, as the typographers say). Turn on the "Auto kern" checkbox to have Flash automatically adjust the space between certain characters. For example, in some cases auto-kerning pushes the letters A and V closer together to avoid an unsightly gap.

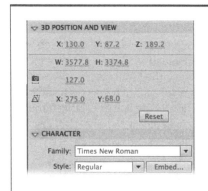

**FIGURE 6-22**

*For TLF text, use the "3D Position and View" settings to display your text with 3-D effects.*

**FIGURE 6-23**

*Many of the settings on the Character subpanel are shared for both text engines and all types of text. Here you can choose a font family, text size, color, and style.*

The *Anti-alias* settings require a little explanation. It's not always easy to make type look good on a computer screen, especially when displaying a complex typeface at a small size. Anti-aliasing is one of those fool-the-eye tricks used to make small type look less jagged. Flash gives you a few options depending on the text type you've selected:

- **Device fonts.** This option uses the fonts installed on the computer where the Flash animation is viewed. Usually, these fonts will be readable at most sizes.

- **Bitmap text [no anti-alias] (Classic text only).** This option turns off anti-aliasing because the fonts are converted to bitmap images. This increases the size of the Flash file, and the text may appear jagged when it is resized.

- **Anti-alias for animation (called Animation for TLF text).** As the name implies, this option is good for text that you want to reposition and resize on the fly.

Some typographic details, such as alignment and kerning, are ignored to create smoother animation.

- **Anti-alias for readability (called Readability for TLF text).** The best option for large blocks of small text. All the anti-aliasing tricks are used to make it easier for your audience to read.

- **Custom anti-alias (Classic text only).** If you think you can do a better job than Flash, you can use your own anti-alias settings, such as sharpness and smoothness. Some additional text styles are available in the Character subpanel, such as buttons that let you toggle superscript and subscript characters (like ™). As usual, TLF text offers some extra features, like Underline and Strikethrough. Using the Rotation menu, you can rotate characters within the text line. For more details, see "Creating Vertical Text Containers" on page 229.

TLF text offers more advanced character options than Classic text. In fact, there are enough new features that they get their own Advanced Character subpanel (see the next section). The more modest Classic text features are placed in the Character subpanel, where they've always been. They include these choices:

- **Selectable.** Click to let your audience select text at runtime. This option is always on for input text.

- **Render text as HTML (dynamic text and input text only).** Tells Flash to interpret any HTML code it encounters as dynamic text instead of just displaying it.

- **Show Border Around Text (dynamic text and input text only).** Select to place a border around dynamic or input text to set it off from other text.

## Advanced Character (TLF Text Only)

The Advanced Character options (Figure 6-24), which are available only with TLF text, change depending on the text type selected. The TLF text types include Read Only, Selectable, and Editable. For example, settings used to create hyperlinks aren't available in editable text—it wouldn't make sense.

The Link and Target options are used to create hyperlinks. Type a URL (like *http://www.missingmanuals.com*) to display text in your finished animation as a clickable link. Target options are used, as they are in HTML, to tell the browser how to open the linked web page: *_self* (the standard option) opens the page in the current browser window; *_blank* opens the page in a new window; *_parent* opens the page in the parent of the current frame; and *_top* opens the page in the top-level frame of the current window.

The rest of the options in the Advanced Character panel are typographic features.

For example, use the Case options to change the text to uppercase, lowercase, or small caps. The Digit Case options change the baseline positioning of numbers. Use the Digit Width options to control the horizontal spacing of characters. This is useful when you want numbers to line up vertically in columns. Printers sometimes use special characters called *ligatures* in place of letter pairs, like œ and æ. You have a few choices when it comes to ligatures: Minimum, Common, Uncommon, and Exotic. Use Baseline Shift to change the vertical position of selected text. Positive numbers move the text up above the natural baseline, while negative numbers move text down. The Advanced Character Locale menu is used to choose different languages and their different character sets.

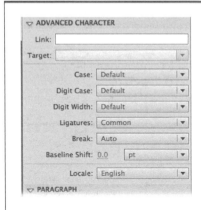

**FIGURE 6-24**

*The Advanced Character subpanel works exclusively with the TLF text engine. Using these tools, you can create hypertext links and shape your text like a master printer.*

## Paragraph

For the most part, the Paragraph subpanel contains the usual suspects. Because TLF text is designed to accommodate several different languages, the nomenclature may seem a little unfamiliar. So, for English and other European languages, "Align to start" lines up text on the left side, leaving the right side ragged. Other options include "Align to center" and "Align to end," which is ragged left and aligned to the right side. There are four justify options, which force the text to fill the line, except for the last line. The options are "Justify with last line aligned to start," "Justify with last line aligned to center," "Justify with last line aligned to end," and "Justify all lines." When you justify text, you can use the Text Justify menu to add spacing between letters (letter spacing) or between words (word spacing).

Using the Paragraph properties, you can set the "Start margin," "End margin," and "First line indent." The two *Spacing* properties determine the space before and after paragraphs.

## Options (Classic Text Only)

The Options subpanel appears only when you've chosen the Classic text engine. (These same hyperlink tools are available to TLF text in the Advanced Character subpanel.) The *Link* and *Target* options are used to create hyperlinks. Type a URL (like *http://www.missingmanuals.com*) to display text in your finished animation as a clickable link. Target options are used, as they are in HTML, to tell the browser how to open the linked web page: _self (the standard option) opens the page in the current browser window; _blank opens the page in a new window; _parent opens the page in the parent of the current frame; and _top_ opens the page in the top-level frame of the current window.

## Container and Flow (TLF Text Only)

The Container and Flow settings control some nifty new text features, such as the ability to create multiple columns of text within a single container (text box) and the ability to flow text from one container to another. Using the Behavior menu (Figure 6-25), you can create text containers that are single-line, multiline, or "Customize for Passwords." (For details, see page 229.)

There are two color swatches at the bottom of the Container and Flow subpanel, which you use to select the border and background colors for the text container. Use the Padding settings to create space between text and the edge of the container.

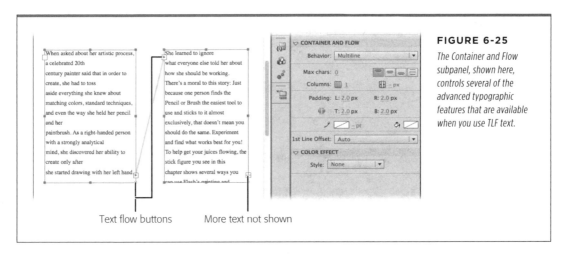

**FIGURE 6-25**

*The Container and Flow subpanel, shown here, controls several of the advanced typographic features that are available when you use TLF text.*

Text flow buttons    More text not shown

## Color Effect (TLF Text Only)

The Color Effect subpanel appears when you choose TLF text. The settings here give you control over the brightness, tint, and opacity of the text and the text container. Choose the color effect you want to apply, and then use the sliders in the panel to make your adjustments. As you'll see in Chapter 17, you can control these same features using ActionScript.

## Display (TLF Text Only)

Use the Display subpanel to add and manage blends and other special effects. Blends are created by overlapping images. Flash uses mathematical calculations to create different effects with descriptive names like Darken, Lighten, Multiply, Difference, Add, Invert, Erase, and Alpha. The best way to get a handle on these special effects is to use them. Create a shape or other graphic object with a color fill or a pattern. Then create a text field over that shape. With the text container selected, go to Properties→Display→Blending and choose an option such as Lighten, Screen, or Erase.

## Filters

Filters perform a number of color effect chores. They work with both TLF text and Classic text. So, if you want to add a drop shadow to separate text from the background, then go to the Filters subpanel. Other options include Drop Shadow, Blur, Glow, Bevel, Gradient Glow, Gradient Bevel, and Adjust Color. You can apply multiple filters to your text, so it would be possible to have bevel characters that cast a shadow. As you pile on special effects, keep in mind that someone may want to actually read the text.

In general, you apply filters to the entire text container. If you want to apply filters to individual letters, choose Modify→Break Apart to break the text container into multiple text containers. To turn an individual character into a shape so you can tween it or distort it to the *n*th degree, select the individual character and then choose Modify→Break Apart again. That turns the character into a shape, just like any other Flash shape and it is no longer editable text. Once you've done that, you can change the stroke and fill color independently. Use Modify→Transform→Envelope to distort the character. And, of course, you can use the Shape Tween tool to animate these changes.

---

**TIP** As a designer, the color effects like blends, filters and gradients give you an opportunity to add visual drama to your project. However, if your work is destined for handheld devices like smartphones and tablets, it's best to use these effects sparingly because they gobble up CPU resources, memory, and battery life.

# Reusable Flash: Symbols and Templates

The secret to productivity is to work smarter, not harder. And the secret to smart work is to avoid doing the same thing more than once. Flash understands. The program gives you ways to reuse bits and pieces of your animations—everything from simple shapes to complex drawings, multiframe sequences, and even entire animations. Create something once; reuse it as many times as you like. Reusing animation elements can save you more than just time and effort—Flash lets you store pieces of animation as reusable master copies that can actually whittle the size of your finished animation file. That's great news if you plan to put your animation up on a website or shoot it out to handhelds. The smaller your file size, the faster it downloads, which makes *you* less likely to lose your audience to impatience.

Templates are another work- and time-saving feature in your Flash arsenal. You can use these predesigned Flash documents as starting points for your own projects. Even better, you can save documents as templates. You can also save templates containing the pictures, logos, and other elements that appear in just about all your documents. Then you don't have to start from scratch next month when you have a similar project.

> **TIP** With Flash Professional CS6, Adobe has included several templates that serve as hands-on learning tools. Want to learn how to create random movement? Check out the templates in the Animation category. You'll find several button examples, as well as techniques for creating rain and snow effects. In the Sample Files category, some of the examples include handwriting simulations, menu navigation tools, and walking figures. Chapter 23 includes an exercise that shows how to use an "AIR for Android" template that senses the position of the smartphone or tablet.

# ■ Symbols and Instances

Copying and pasting is the most obvious way to reuse something you've created, but while that time-honored technique saves time, it doesn't save *space*. Say, for example, you need to show a swarm of cockroaches in the Flash advertisement you're creating for New and Improved Roach-B-Gone. You draw a single cockroach, then copy and paste it 100 times. Congratulations: You've got yourself 101 cockroaches... and one massive Flash document.

Instead, you should take that first cockroach and save it in Flash as a *symbol*. Symbols give you a way to reuse your work and keep your animation's finished file size down to a bare minimum. When you create a symbol, Flash stores the information for the symbol, or master copy, in your document as usual. But every time you create a copy (an *instance*) of that symbol, all Flash adds to your file is the information it needs to keep track of where you positioned that particular instance and any modifications you make to it on the stage.

So, to create the illusion of a swarm of roaches, you drag instances of the symbol onto the stage. Neither you nor Flash have to duplicate the work of drawing each roach. You can even vary the roach instances a little for variety and realism (so important in a pesticide ad) by changing their color, position, size, and even their skew. If symbols offered only file optimization, they'd be well worth using. But symbols give you additional benefits:

- **Consistency.** By definition, all the instances of a symbol look pretty much the same. You can change certain instance characteristics—color and position on the stage, for example—but you can't redraw them; Flash simply won't let you. (You can't turn a roach into a ladybug, for example.) For situations where you really need basic consistency among objects, symbols help save you from yourself.

- **Instantaneous update.** Suppose you want to change the roach color from brown to black. Edit the "master" roach stored in your Library, and Flash automatically updates all the instances of that symbol. So, for example, say you create a symbol showing the packaging for Roach-B-Gone. You use dozens and dozens of instances of the symbol throughout your animation, and then your boss tells you the marketing team has redesigned the packaging. If you'd used Copy and Paste to create all those boxes of Roach-B-Gone, you'd have to find and change each one manually. But with symbols, all you need to do is change the symbol in the Library. Flash automatically takes care of updating all the symbol's instances for you.

  Does that mean you can't make changes to *one* of the roaches already on the stage? No, not at all. You can change an instance without affecting any other instances or the symbol itself. (You can turn one roach light brown, for example, without affecting any of the dark-brown roaches.)

- **Nesting.** Symbols can contain other symbols. Sticking symbols inside other symbols is called nesting symbols, and it's a great way to create unique, complex-looking images for a fraction of the file size you'd need to create them individually. Suppose you've drawn the perfect bug eye. You can turn it into a symbol and place it inside your symbols for roaches, ladybugs, and any other insect you want.

Flash lets you create three types of symbols: graphic symbols, movie clip symbols, and button symbols. As you see in Figure 7-1, Flash stores all three types of symbols in the Library.

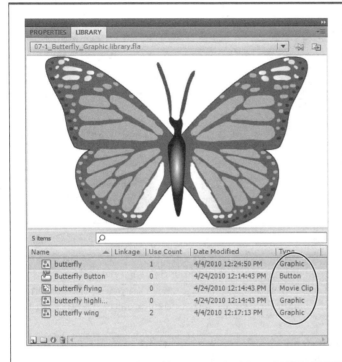

**FIGURE 7-1**

*The Library is your one-stop shop for symbols. From this panel, you can create symbols, edit them, and drag instances of them onto the stage. Note the icons and descriptions that tell you each symbol's type—graphic, button, or movie clip. If you don't see the Library panel, press Ctrl+L (⌘-L) or go to Window→Library. To display all the information in the Library panel, you may want to undock the panel by dragging the tab away from the Properties dock. Then, you can resize it.*

## Graphic Symbols

You can tell Flash to turn everything from a simple shape (like a circle or a line) to a complex drawing (like a butterfly) into a symbol. You can also nest graphic symbols. For example, you can nest butterfly wing symbols inside a butterfly symbol, as shown in Figure 7-2.

A graphic symbol isn't even limited to a static drawing. You can save a series of frames as a *multiframe* graphic symbol that you can add to other animations.

**NOTE** Another kind of symbol that contains multiple frames is a movie clip symbol (page 267). But there are big differences between the two, as described in the box on page 251.

**FIGURE 7-2**

*If you're really serious about paring down the size of your animation file, consider nesting your symbols. Here a single wing symbol is used for both the butterfly's wings. The wing instance on the left was flipped horizontally (Modify→Transform→Flip Horizontal). Flash lets you flip, resize, and recolor symbol instances, so you can create surprisingly different effects using just a few basic shapes—all while keeping your animation's file size as small as possible.*

Flash gives you two options for creating a graphic symbol:

- You can create a regular image on the stage and then convert it to a graphic symbol. This is the best approach for those times when you're drawing an image (or a multiframe animated scene) and suddenly realize it's so good that you want to reuse it.

- You can create your symbol from scratch using Flash's symbol editing mode. If you know going in that you want to create a reusable image or series of frames, it's just as easy to create it in symbol editing mode as it is to create it on your main animation's stage and timeline—and you get to save the conversion step. The following sections show you both approaches.

### ■ CONVERTING AN EXISTING IMAGE TO A GRAPHIC SYMBOL

If you've already got an image on the stage that you'd like to turn into a symbol, you're in luck: The process is quick and painless.

To convert an existing image on the stage to a graphic symbol:

1. **On the stage, select the image (or images) you want to convert.**

   Flash's selection tools are described on page 61. Converting a grouped or editable image into a graphic symbol is quick and easy. Figure 7-3 shows three separate images selected that, all together, form a star.

2. **Select Modify→"Convert to Symbol."**

   The "Convert to Symbol" dialog box appears.

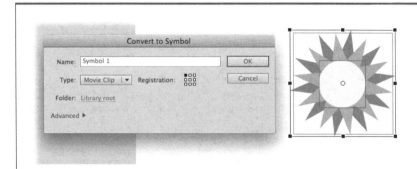

**FIGURE 7-3**

*You use the little grid labeled Registration to position the registration point of your symbol. Most of the time, it's fine to leave the registration point in the upper-left corner; see the box on page 253 for the full story. If necessary, you can reposition it later by editing your symbol (page 257).*

**FREQUENTLY ASKED QUESTION**

## Multiframe Graphic Symbol vs. Movie Clip

*A movie clip symbol is a series of frames, but a graphic symbol can have multiple frames, too. So what's the difference between the two?*

Leave it to the Flash development team (the people who let you add motion to a shape tween and manipulate shapes with a motion tween) to refer to a multiframe animation clip as a *graphic* symbol (instead of a movie clip symbol). The truth is, there are some big differences between a multiframe graphic symbol and a movie clip. For the programmer, the biggest difference between multiframe graphics and movie clips is that movie clips can be controlled in ActionScript while multiframe graphics cannot. Here are two other differences:

- **A multiframe graphic symbol has to match the animation to which you add it, frame for frame.** For example, suppose your main timeline has 20 frames and you add a 15-frame graphic symbol to Frame 1. Frame 1 in the main timeline shows Frame 1 of your graphic symbol. Frame 2 in the main timeline shows Frame 2 of the graphic symbol, and so on. If your main timeline has only five frames,

you'd see only five frames of the graphic symbol. A movie clip symbol, on the other hand, doesn't have to match the animation you add it to frame by frame because movie clips have their own timelines. So, if you add a 15-frame movie clip symbol to a main timeline with only a single frame, you still see all 15 frames of the movie clip symbol. It loops unless it encounters a keyframe with an ActionScript statement telling it to stop playing.

- **A multiframe graphic symbol can't include sound or interactivity; a movie clip symbol can.** Movie clip symbols take up just one frame in the main timeline, so you can drop instances of them into button symbols and other movie clip symbols to create interactive nested symbols. Because they're not tied frame for frame to the animation you drop them into, they're able to hang fire while your animation plays and spring into action only when an audience member clicks them.

Chapter 11 and Chapter 12 show you how to add sounds and ActionScript actions to your symbols, respectively.

3. **In the Name text box, type a name for your symbol.**

Because you'll be creating a bunch of instances of this copy over the course of the next several hours, days, or weeks (and because you may end up with dozens of symbols before you're finished with your animation), you want a unique, short, descriptive name.

4. **Set the Type drop-down menu next to Graphic, and then click OK.**

Flash creates the new graphic symbol, places it into the Library, and automatically replaces the selected image on the stage with a selected instance of the symbol (Figure 7-4). Notice the instance's single bounding box (the original three images in this example had three).

> **TIP** If you're already poking around the Library panel, you can create a new graphic symbol quickly by clicking the Library panel's New Symbol button (at the bottom of the panel) or by clicking the Library panel's Options menu, and then, from the pop-up menu that appears, selecting New Symbol. Either way tells Flash to display the Create New Symbol dialog box.

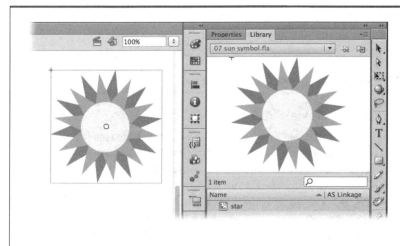

**FIGURE 7-4**

*You get two clues that Flash has converted your image on the stage to an instance of the newly created symbol: the cross in the upper-left corner of the instance (the instance's registration point) and the little round circle (the instance's transformation point). Flash uses the transformation point if you decide to transform the instance, as described in Chapter 5. You'll learn more about these points in the box on page 253.*

### ■ CREATING A GRAPHIC SYMBOL IN SYMBOL EDITING MODE

If you want to create a symbol from scratch without going through the conversion step described on page 250, you can use Flash's symbol editor—the same symbol editor you use to modify your symbols.

To create a graphic symbol in symbol editing mode:

1. **Select Insert→New Symbol.**

The Create New Symbol dialog box shown in Figure 7-6 (top) appears.

2. **In the Name text box, type a name for your symbol.**

Shoot for something unique, short, and descriptive.

**UP TO SPEED**

## Registration Point vs. Transformation Point

Flash associates two different points with each symbol you create: a transformation point and a registration point. Both reference a specific point in the symbol, but you use them in very different ways. Here's the scoop:

- **The symbol's transformation point is the little circle Flash displays in every symbol and graphic element.** Flash uses the symbol's transformation point when you transform a symbol—for example, when you rotate a symbol, it spins around the transformation point. You can move the transformation point to any spot in or even outside of your symbol. The center of your symbol is a good starting spot for the transformation point, until you have a reason to place it elsewhere. If you want to reposition the transformation point, select a symbol or graphic element, and then click the Free Transform tool. The transformation point appears as a circle, usually on or near the symbol. Reposition the point by dragging it to a new location.

- **The symbol's registration point appears as a little cross on the symbol.** The registration point is the set of coordinates Flash uses to position an instance of a symbol on the stage. Often called X/Y coordinates, X equals the distance from the left side of the stage, and Y is the distance from the top. You can place a symbol precisely on the stage by typing in the position coordinates in the Properties panel, as shown in Figure 7-5. You also use

the position coordinates when you position and move objects on the stage with ActionScript programming, as explained in Chapter 12. When you create new visual elements, like shapes and text, Flash automatically places the registration point in the upper-left corner. That's a good place to have the registration points for the symbols you create, unless you have a particular need to place it elsewhere. For example, if you want to align several symbols on their center point, you may prefer to have the registration point in the center. To reposition the registration point for a symbol, double-click the symbol to edit it. The image opens in symbol edit mode, as described on page 257, and the registration point appears as shown on the bottom of Figure 7-6. If you want the registration point centered, move your graphic element over the registration point, so it's centered. If you want the registration point in the lower-right corner, position your graphic above and to the left of the registration point.

In most cases, you don't have to think twice about the registration point. Let Flash put it in the upper-left corner and leave it there. If you're planning to manipulate the symbol in ActionScript, be aware that you can reposition the registration point if that upper-left corner doesn't work for your project, as described on page 255.

3. **From the drop-down menu, choose Graphic, and then click OK.**

Flash displays the symbol editing workspace shown in Figure 7-6 (bottom). The symbol editing workspace looks very much like an animation workspace, even down to the background color. Here are the key differences that indicate you're in symbol editing mode:

- The name of the symbol you're currently editing appears in the Edit bar. To see the Edit bar, select Window→Toolbars, and then turn on the checkbox next to Edit Bar. There's no "stage" when you're editing symbols, so you won't see any backstage work area either.

- The Back arrow and Current Scene icons in the Edit bar appear clickable, or active.

- A cross (the registration point for the symbol you're about to create) appears in the middle of the symbol editing workspace. The registration point is the reference point Flash uses to position your symbol on the stage, as explained in the box on page 253. Technically, you can position your symbol anywhere you like with respect to the registration point; but out of the box, Flash puts the registration point for most graphics in the upper-left corner. For consistency's sake, you may want to do the same when you create symbols. Just create your artwork below and to the right of the registration point.

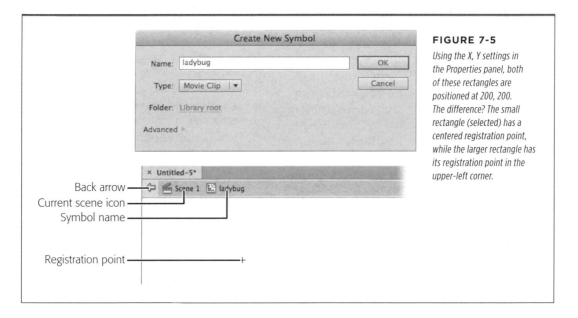

**FIGURE 7-5**

*Using the X, Y settings in the Properties panel, both of these rectangles are positioned at 200, 200. The difference? The small rectangle (selected) has a centered registration point, while the larger rectangle has its registration point in the upper-left corner.*

4. **On the symbol editing workspace, create a graphic symbol.**

   You can use Flash's drawing tools, instances of other symbols, or even an imported image (Chapter 10), just as you can on the main stage. As you draw, Flash displays a thumbnail version of your symbol in the Library preview window, as shown in Figure 7-7. Note that the use count is zero, until you drag an instance of the symbol onto the stage. The *use count* is the number of instances of this symbol that have been dragged onto the main animation stage.

5. **When you're finished creating your symbol, head to the Edit bar, and then click the Back arrow or click the current scene icon.** (Or use the menu command Edit→Edit Document.)

   Flash brings you back to your main animation workspace.

## ■ USING A GRAPHIC SYMBOL (CREATING AN INSTANCE OF A GRAPHIC SYMBOL)

After you've created a symbol, you use it by creating an instance of that symbol and then placing the instance somewhere in your animation.

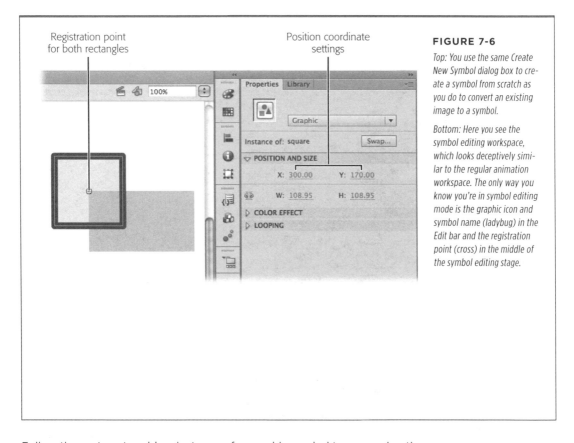

Registration point for both rectangles

Position coordinate settings

**FIGURE 7-6**

*Top: You use the same Create New Symbol dialog box to create a symbol from scratch as you do to convert an existing image to a symbol.*

*Bottom: Here you see the symbol editing workspace, which looks deceptively similar to the regular animation workspace. The only way you know you're in symbol editing mode is the graphic icon and symbol name (ladybug) in the Edit bar and the registration point (cross) in the middle of the symbol editing stage.*

Follow these steps to add an instance of a graphic symbol to your animation:

1. **Make sure the Library panel containing the graphic symbol you want is visible.** If it isn't, select Window, and then turn on the checkbox next to Library.

   Flash displays the Library panel.

2. **On the timeline, click to select the keyframe and layer where you want to put the instance.**

   Flash highlights the selected keyframe.

3. **In the Library panel, click the name of the symbol you want to use.**

   A thumbnail version of the symbol appears in the Library's preview window.

4. **Drag the thumbnail onto the stage (Figure 7-8).**

   Flash creates an instance of the symbol and places it on the stage. You can transform or recolor this instance, as shown in the following section, without affecting any other instances or the symbol itself.

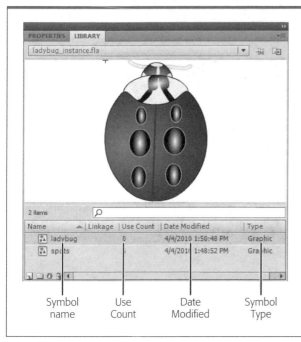

**FIGURE 7-7**

*The ladybug symbol here was just created, so the Library is showing a use count of 0. The registration point appears in the upper-left corner. The Library panel provides other details, including when the symbol was last changed and how it's linked to other Flash and ActionScript documents.*

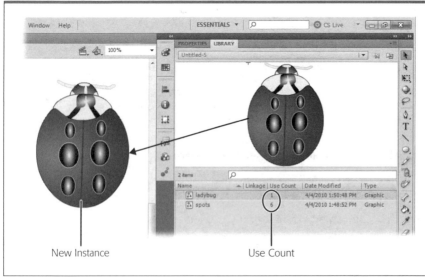

**FIGURE 7-8**

*Creating an instance of a symbol is as easy as dragging the symbol from the Library and dropping it onto the stage. Flash has bumped up the use count for the ladybug symbol by 1. Because the ladybug uses spots symbols, the count for spots has bumped up to 6.*

**TIP** You can always convert an instance of a graphic symbol back into an editable image—perhaps because you want to use a symbol as a starting point for a brand-new image. To convert an instance of a graphic symbol back into an editable image, first select the instance, and then choose Modify→Break Apart. If your instance contains nested instances, you may want to choose Modify→Break Apart once for each nested instance to convert the entire symbol into editable pixels.

### ■ EDITING AN INSTANCE OF A GRAPHIC SYMBOL

The whole point of graphic symbols is to help you reuse images (and to help Flash keep down file size while you're doing it). So it should come as no surprise that you can't completely rework the instances you create. You can't, for example, create an instance of a ladybug, erase it, draw a toad in its place, and expect Flash to consider that toad an instance of the ladybug symbol.

### In the Mode

It's astonishingly easy to get confused about where you are when you're working in symbol editing mode. If you think you're in your main animation when you're actually in symbol mode, for example, you get frustratingly unexpected results when you try to test your animation by selecting Control→Play or Control→Test Movie→Test.

The easiest way to find your bearings is to check the Edit bar. First, make sure it's visible (Window→Toolbars→Edit Bar). Then, if your symbol's name appears in the Edit bar, you're in symbol editing mode; if it doesn't, you're not.

But while you can't use Flash's drawing and painting tools to change your instance, you *can* change certain characteristics of an instance, including color, transparency, tint, and brightness using the Properties panel; and scale, rotation, and skew using the Transform panel.

**NOTE** When you transform or recolor an instance, only that instance changes; the other instances you've added to your animation aren't affected, and neither is the symbol itself. If you want to change all instances en masse, you need to edit the original symbol, as described below.

You can also edit an instance by swapping one instance of a graphic symbol for another. Say, for example, that you've created a nature backdrop using multiple instances of three symbols: a tree, a bush, and a flower. If you decide you'd rather replace a few trees with bushes, Flash gives you a quick and easy way to do that, as shown in the following steps:

1. **On the stage, select the instance you want to replace.**

   Flash displays the Properties panel to show instance-related properties. (If you don't see the Properties panel, choose Window→Properties to display it.)

2. **In the Properties panel, click Swap (Figure 7-9).**

   The Swap Symbol dialog box appears.

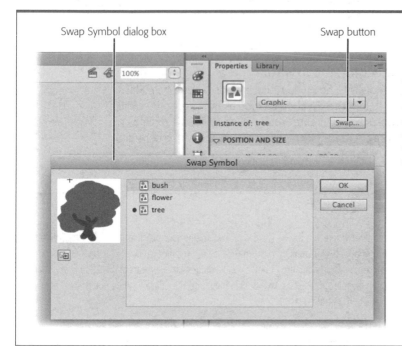

Swap Symbol dialog box

Swap button

**FIGURE 7-9**

*The Swap button is active only when you have a single instance selected on the stage. The Swap Symbol dialog box is misnamed; it should be called the Swap Instance dialog box. That's because you use it to replace an instance of one symbol with an instance of another symbol; the symbols themselves don't change.*

3. **In the Swap Symbol dialog box, click to select the symbol with which you'd like to replace the original.** When you finish, click OK.

   On the stage, Flash replaces the selected instance with an instance of the symbol you chose in the Swap Symbol dialog box.

### ■ EDITING A GRAPHIC SYMBOL

Recoloring or transforming an instance changes only that instance, but editing a symbol changes *every single instance* of that symbol, immediately, wherever you've placed them in your animation.

The good news about editing symbols, of course, is that it can save you a boatload of time. Say you've added hundreds of instances of your company's logo to your animation and the brass decides to redo the logo. Instead of the mind-numbing chore of slogging through your animation finding and changing each instance by hand, all you have to do is edit one little image—your logo symbol. The minute you do, Flash automatically ripples your changes out to each and every instance of that symbol.

The bad news, of course, is that you might edit a symbol by mistake, thinking you're editing an instance (page 266). Editing a symbol is for keeps. You can select Edit→Undo if you realize your mistake in time, but once you close your Flash document and Flash erases your Undo history, it's all over but the crying: You're stuck with your edited symbol, for better or for worse.

**TIP** If the thought of editing a symbol makes you leery—say you've got 500 instances of your symbol scattered around your animation and you don't want to have to redraw it if you goof up the edit job—play it safe and make a duplicate of the symbol before you edit it. In the Library panel, click the Options menu in the upper-right corner. Then, from the pop-up menu that appears, select Duplicate. When you do, Flash displays the Duplicate Symbol window, which lets you give your backup copy a unique, descriptive name (like *logo_backup*).

---

**UP TO SPEED**

## Exchanging Symbols Between Documents

Flash puts all the symbols you create in a Flash document—as well as all the bitmaps, sound files, and other goodies you import into that document—into the Library panel, which you display by choosing Window→Library.

Technically speaking, the stuff you put in the Library is good only for that Flash document or project (unlike the Common Libraries, which you access by choosing Window→Common Libraries, and which always list the same preinstalled files, no matter which document you have open).

But you can pull a symbol from one document's library and put it into another by copying and pasting. To do so:

1. Open the two documents between which you want to exchange symbols (File→Open).

2. Open the Library panel from which you want to copy a symbol (Window→Library), and then choose the document from the drop-down list in the Library panel.

3. In the Library panel, right-click the name of the symbol you want to copy, and then, from the pop-up menu that appears, choose Copy.

4. Above the stage, click the tab displaying the name of the other document.

5. In the new document, click to select the keyframe where you want to paste the symbol.

6. Choose Edit→Paste in Center. Flash pastes a copy of the other document's symbol on the stage.

To open a document's Library without having to open the document itself: Select File→Import→Open External Library, choose the document whose symbols you want to copy, and then click Open. When you do, Flash opens the document's Library (but not the document). With two libraries open, you can drag symbols directly from one Library to another.

---

Flash gives you three ways to edit symbols: Edit, Edit in Place, and Edit in New Window.

- **Edit** is the most common way to edit symbols, and it's the method Flash uses when you right-click a symbol name in the Library and then choose Edit. You can also use the menu command Edit→Edit Symbols or keyboard shortcut Ctrl+E (⌘-E). The stage temporarily disappears, to be replaced by a window showing only the contents of the symbol. If you have the Edit toolbar showing (Windows→Toolbars→Edit Bar), you see the symbol's name, as shown in Figure 7-10. After you finish your edits, click the Scene name or the Back button to return to the stage.

- **Editing in place** lets you edit a symbol right there on the stage, surrounded by any other objects you may have on the stage. (Flash grays out the other objects; they're just for reference. The only thing you can edit in this mode is the symbol.)

If you're not ready for it, this option is right up there with the more confusing features the Flash design team has ever come up with. As you can see in Figure 7-11, mixing the symbol editing mode with the appearance of the main stage makes it incredibly easy to assume you're changing an *instance* of a symbol (instead of the symbol itself), with frustrating results. Double-clicking a symbol on the stage or selecting Edit→Edit in Place from the main menu or from the pop-up menu that appears when you right-click an instance on the stage all tell Flash that you want to edit in place.

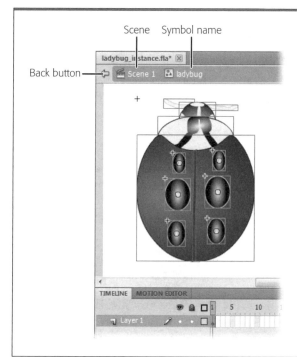

Scene    Symbol name

Back button

**FIGURE 7-10**

*When you edit your symbol in its very own window, there's no ambiguity: You know you're editing a symbol (and not merely an instance). You edit a symbol using the same tools and panels you use to edit any other image. As you make your changes, Flash automatically updates the symbol in the Library, as well as all the instances of that symbol, wherever they may be in your Flash document.*

**NOTE**  One man's meat is another man's poison. If you absolutely have to see your symbol in context (surrounded by all the other stuff on the stage) to be able to edit it properly, then editing in place is just what you want.

- **Edit in New Window** creates a new window tab where you edit your symbol, as shown in Figure 7-12. Right-click (Control-click) a symbol on the stage, and then choose Edit in New Window from the pop-up menu. Flash opens the symbol under a new tab, and your work area looks similar to the basic Edit mode. As you make changes, Flash updates all existing instances to match the newly edited symbol. This makes it easy to jump back and forth between the symbol editing workspace and the stage, so you can see how the edited symbol looks in context. When you're finished making changes, just click the Close button.

In a nutshell, to tell Flash you want to edit a symbol, do any of the following.

In the Library panel:

- Double-click the symbol, either in the list or in the preview window. The symbol opens in Edit in Place mode.

- Select a symbol from the list, and then click the Options menu. From the pop-up menu that appears, choose Edit. The symbol opens in Edit mode, where you see the symbol by itself.

- Right-click a symbol in the list. From the pop-up menu that appears, choose Edit, Edit in Place, or Edit in New Window. The pop-up menu lets you select exactly how you'd like to view the symbol while editing.

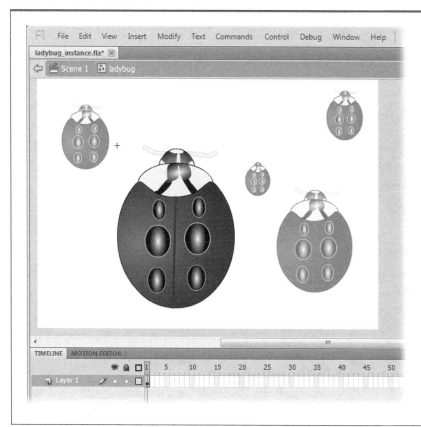

**FIGURE 7-11**

*It's hard to tell that the large ladybug (the one that's not grayed out) is a symbol and not just an instance of a symbol. (Your one clue: the symbol name "ladybug" that Flash displays above the stage.) Editing a symbol when you mean to edit an instance can have pretty serious consequences, so if you find yourself second-guessing, then stick to editing in a new window, as described in Figure 7-10.*

On the stage:

- Select Edit→Edit Symbols.

- Select an instance of the symbol, and then choose Edit→Edit Selected.

- Right-click an instance of the symbol, and then, from the pop-up menu that appears, choose Edit, Edit in Place, or Edit in New Window.

- In the Edit bar (Window→Toolbars→Edit Bar), click Edit Symbols (the icon on the right that looks like a jumble of shapes).

No matter which method you choose—editing, editing in place, or editing in a new window—you get out of symbol editing mode and return to the main stage the same way: by selecting Edit→Edit Document (Ctrl+E on a PC or ⌘-E on a Mac).

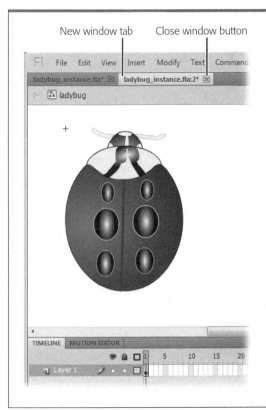

New window tab    Close window button

**FIGURE 7-12**

Edit in New Window is one of three ways that Flash gives you to edit a symbol. Both the Edit and Edit in New Window options give you a nice, uncluttered view of your symbol.

### ■ DELETING A GRAPHIC SYMBOL

You can delete the graphic symbols you create. Just remember that when you do, *Flash automatically deletes all the instances of that symbol*, wherever you've placed them in that document.

To delete a graphic symbol:

1. **In the Library panel, click to select the graphic symbol you want to delete.**

   Flash highlights the selected symbol's name and type.

2. **Right-click the graphic symbol icon, and then, from the pop-up menu that appears, choose Delete.**

Flash removes the graphic symbol from the Library panel. It also removes all the instances of that symbol from your animation. Another option is to click the trash can icon at the bottom of the Library panel.

## Multiframe Graphic Symbols

Multiframe graphic symbols are a kind of hybrid symbol, halfway between single frame graphic symbols and movie clip symbols. Multiframe graphic symbols can't contain sounds or actions the way movie clip symbols can, but they *can* contain multiple frames, which regular single-frame graphic symbols can't. As explained in the box on page 251, multiframe graphic symbols synchronize frame-for-frame to the animation in which you place them.

> **TIP** For many common Flash chores, it makes sense to use movie clips instead of multiframe graphics. As a designer, you have more control over movie clips, and you don't have to worry about the synchronization issues that come with multiframe graphics. Movie clips are the symbols to choose if you want animate or control them with ActionScript. However, one small advantage multiframe graphic symbols have over movie clips is that they may take up slightly less space in the SWF file when you publish your animation.

### ■ CREATING A MULTIFRAME GRAPHIC SYMBOL

Flash gives you the same two options for creating multiframe graphics symbols as it does for single-frame graphic symbols: You can create a series of frames as usual and then convert it into a reusable symbol, or you can use Flash's editing mode to create a multiframe graphic symbol from scratch and save yourself the conversion step. This section shows both approaches.

To convert a series of frames to a multiframe graphic symbol:

1. **On the timeline, select the frames you want to convert.**

   You can easily select a series by clicking at one end of the series and then Shift-clicking at the other end. Flash automatically selects all the frames in between.

2. **Choose Edit→Timeline→Copy Frames or press Ctrl+Alt+C (Option-⌘-C).** Then choose Insert→New Symbol.

   The Create New Symbol dialog box appears.

3. **In the Create New Symbol dialog box, turn on the Graphic radio button.** Type a short, descriptive name for your symbol, and then click OK.

   The name of your symbol appears in the Library panel and in the Edit bar above your stage to let you know you're in symbol editing mode. In addition, Flash replaces your animation stage with the symbol editing stage. You can recognize the symbol editing stage by the cross (your symbol's registration point) that appears in the middle of the symbol editing stage.

4. **In the symbol timeline, click to select the first keyframe (Frame 1).**

Flash highlights the selected keyframe.

5. **Select Edit→Timeline→Paste Frames.**

Flash pastes the copied frames in the symbol's timeline. The Library panel's preview window shows you the contents of your new symbol's first keyframe (along with a minicontroller, as shown in Figure 7-13).

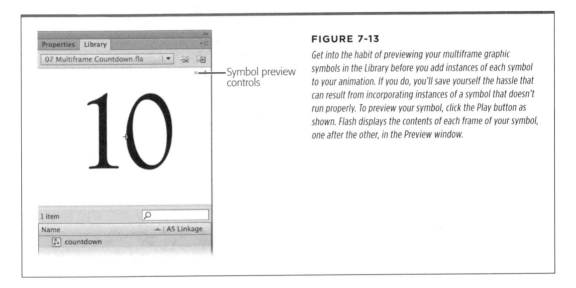

**FIGURE 7-13**

*Get into the habit of previewing your multiframe graphic symbols in the Library before you add instances of each symbol to your animation. If you do, you'll save yourself the hassle that can result from incorporating instances of a symbol that doesn't run properly. To preview your symbol, click the Play button as shown. Flash displays the contents of each frame of your symbol, one after the other, in the Preview window.*

6. **Preview your symbol by clicking the minicontroller's Play button.**

Flash runs a thumbnail version of the symbol in the preview window.

7. **Get out of symbol editing mode by choosing Edit→Edit Document.**

Flash hides the symbol editing stage and brings you back to your main animation's stage and timeline. To create a multiframe graphic symbol from scratch in symbol editing mode, follow the steps you see on page 252, adding the content for as many frames as you need in step 5.

### ■ CREATING AN INSTANCE OF A MULTIFRAME GRAPHIC SYMBOL

Creating an instance of a multiframe graphic symbol is like creating an instance of a movie clip symbol, but it's not identical. When you insert a multiframe graphic symbol into a timeline, the graphic synchronizes frame-for-frame with that timeline. If the timeline doesn't have enough frames, Flash lops off any frames of the graphic that don't fit. If the timeline has more frames than the graphic, Flash loops the graphic frames unless you provide other instructions in the Properties panel. If it's important that every frame of the graphic plays, make sure the timeline has enough frames. The following steps show you how.

To create an instance of a multiframe graphic symbol:

1. **In your main animation, click to select the keyframe where you want to place an instance of a multiframe graphic symbol.**

   Only keyframes can contain new content (see page 99 for the skinny on keyframes). So if you try to place a symbol in a regular frame, Flash "backs up" and places your symbol in the keyframe immediately preceding the selected frame anyway.

2. **Make sure you have exactly as many frames after the selected keyframe as you need for this instance.**

   If you're creating an instance of a symbol that contains 10 frames, make sure 10 frames exist, including the selected keyframe. If the symbol contains 20 frames, make sure 20 frames exist. To add frames after your selected keyframe, choose Insert→Timeline→Frame (or press F5) once for each frame you want to add.

---

**WARNING** If you forget this step and add a multiframe graphic symbol to a timeline that doesn't contain exactly as many frames as the symbol, Flash doesn't issue any warnings. Instead, it matches as many of the instance frames to your timeline frames as it can. If you don't have enough room on your timeline, Flash quietly snips off the instance frames that don't fit. If you have too much room, Flash repeats the instance frames until all your main animation's frames are filled.

---

3. **In the Library, click to select the multiframe graphic symbol of which you want to create an instance.**

   You can either click the symbol's icon from the list or click the symbol's thumbnail in the preview window. The Library lists the type of both single and multiframe graphics the same—Graphic—but you can always tell a multiframe graphic by the minicontroller that appears along with the symbol's content in the Library's preview window, as shown in Figure 7-13.

4. **Drag the symbol to the stage.**

   Flash creates an instance of the symbol and places it in the keyframe you selected in step 1. As you see in Figure 7-14, Flash colors your frames a nice solid gray to let you know that they now contain content. But Flash *doesn't* display the individual keyframes of your instance in your main timeline. (By the same token, if your symbol contains multiple layers, you don't see those on your main timeline, either. This visual simplification is one of the benefits of using symbols, as opposed to just copying and pasting frames.) To preview your instance, select Control→Test Movie→Test.

---

**NOTE** You can also test an instance of a multiframe graphic symbol by choosing Control→Play, or by dragging the playhead on the main timeline.

---

## ■ EDITING AN INSTANCE OF A MULTIFRAME GRAPHIC SYMBOL

If you need the flexibility to individually change each keyframe of a multiframe graphic instance, you're out of luck, but you can use the Transform tool and the Properties panel to make tweaks that affect every frame of your multiframe graphics. Use the Properties panel to change the size, position, and color of your graphic, as shown in Figure 7-15. Changes you make here affect every frame in the multiframe graphic.

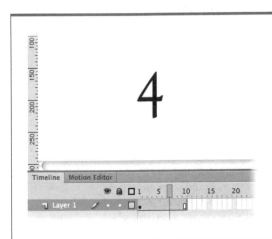

**FIGURE 7-14**

*The solid gray bar you see beginning with the keyframe (Frame 1) lets you know that Frames 1–10 now contain content: in this case, an instance of a multiframe graphic symbol. If testing your animation yields an unexpected result, check to make sure that the frame span to which you've added the symbol matches your symbol frame for frame.*

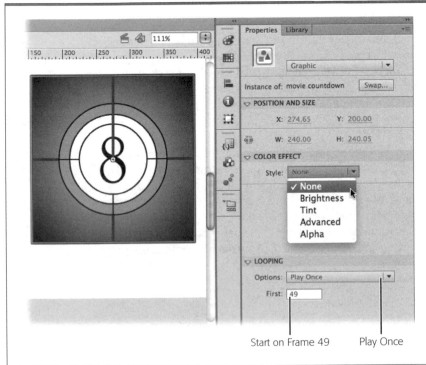

**FIGURE 7-15**

*This multiframe graphic shows a countdown similar to the ones that appear before old movies. In the Properties panel, the Looping→First option is set to Frame 49, so that the countdown begins with the number 8.*

Start on Frame 49          Play Once

Flash lets you change the contents of the first keyframe of your instance, just the way you can an instance of a single-frame graphic (page 257). But Flash automatically applies those changes to the contents of *every* keyframe in your instance. Skew the frog in your first keyframe and turn it blue, for example, and every image in every frame of your instance appears skewed and blue.

Using the Properties panel, you can tweak the playback settings for a multiframe graphic. Under Looping→Options, you can choose between Loop, Play Once, and Single Frame. In the First box, you can choose the first frame that Flash displays. For example, suppose you have a nifty countdown multiframe graphic like the ones at the beginning of old newsreels. Your graphic counts down from 10, but for this project you'd like to start it at 8, like in the movies. Simply adjust the starting frame so that it begins when the 8 is showing, as shown in Figure 7-15.

**NOTE** The file *07-1_Multiframe_Countdown.fla*, shown in Figure 7-15, is available at *www.missingmanuals. com/cds/flashcs6mm*. It shows how multiframe graphic symbols can be made up of several different graphic elements, layers, and symbols. A second file, *07-2_Movie_Clip_Countdown.fla*, shows the differences between multiframe graphic symbols and movie clip symbols.

■ **EDITING A MULTIFRAME GRAPHIC SYMBOL**

You edit a multiframe graphic symbol the same way you edit a single-frame graphic symbol: by switching to symbol editing mode (page 257). In both cases, Flash immediately applies the changes you make to the symbol to all the instances of that symbol.

■ **DELETING A MULTIFRAME GRAPHIC SYMBOL**

You delete a multiframe graphic symbol the same way you delete any other symbol in Flash: through the Library panel. Just remember that when you delete a symbol, *Flash automatically deletes all the instances of that symbol*, wherever you've placed them.

To delete a graphic symbol:

1. **In the Library panel, click to select the graphic symbol you want to delete.**

   Flash highlights the selected symbol's name and type.

2. **Right-click the graphic symbol icon, and then, from the pop-up menu that appears, choose Delete.**

   Flash removes the graphic symbol from the Library panel. It also removes all the instances of that symbol from your animation.

## Movie Clip Symbols

A *movie clip* symbol (Figure 7-16) is a reusable, self-contained chunk of animation, which you can drop into a single frame in another animation.

Unlike multiframe graphic symbols, you can add sounds (Chapter 11) and actions (Chapter 12) to movie clip symbols. Also unlike multiframe graphic symbols, movie clip symbols run independently from the animations to which you add them.

So movie clips give you the opportunity to create nonsequential effects like repeating, or *looping*, scenes, as well as interactive graphics—for example, buttons, checkboxes, and clickable images that tell Flash to display something different, depending on what your audience clicks.

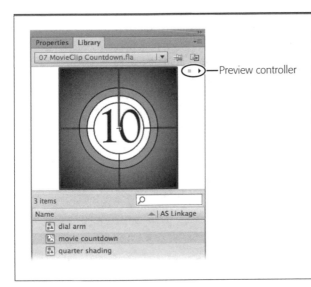

**FIGURE 7-16**

*When you select a movie clip symbol in the Library, the Library panel's preview window shows you the first frame of the symbol, as well as a minicontroller you can use to play (and stop) the movie clip right there in the Library before you go to all the trouble of dragging an instance of the movie clip to the stage. (You see this same minicontroller when you select a multiframe graphic in the Library.)*

As you'll see in the following section, movie clip symbols have their very own time-lines, so an instance of a movie clip symbol always takes up just one frame in the animation to which you add it, no matter how many frames the movie clip symbol actually contains.

### ■ CREATING A MOVIE CLIP SYMBOL

Creating a movie clip symbol in Flash is similar to creating a multiframe graphic symbol (page 263). You can either create a series of frames (including sounds and actions, if you like) and convert it into a movie clip symbol, or you can use Flash's editing mode to create a movie clip symbol from scratch and save yourself the conversion step.

In fact, as the following steps show, only one minor but important difference exists between creating a multiframe graphic symbol and creating a movie clip symbol, and that's selecting the correct drop-down menu option in step 4.

---

**WARNING** Modify→Convert to Symbol works only when you're converting an image to a single-frame graphic symbol; it doesn't let you convert a series of frames into a movie clip symbol. But if you try it, Flash won't give you an error. Instead, it'll chug along happily, pretending it's creating a movie clip symbol. But in reality, the symbol you create this way contains just one frame.

---

To convert a series of existing frames to a movie clip symbol:

1. **On the timeline, select the frames you want to convert.**

   It's easy to select a series of frames. Click at one end of the series, and then Shift-click at the other end of the series. Flash automatically selects all the frames in between. If your frames contain layers, make sure you select all the layers in each frame.

2. **Choose Edit→Timeline→Copy Frames or press Ctrl+Alt+C (Option-⌘-C).**

   Flash copies the frames.

3. **Choose Insert→New Symbol.**

   The Create New Symbol dialog box appears.

4. **In the Create New Symbol dialog box, make sure to choose Movie Clip from the drop-down menu.**

   If it's not selected, click to select it.

5. **Type a name for your movie clip symbol, and then click OK.**

   The name of your movie clip symbol appears in the Library panel, and in the Edit bar above your stage, to let you know you're in symbol editing mode. Another tip-off that you're in symbol editing mode is the cross, or registration point, that appears in the middle of the symbol editing stage.

6. **In the symbol timeline, click to select the first keyframe (Frame 1).**

   Flash highlights the selected keyframe.

7. **Select Edit→Timeline→Paste Frames.**

   Flash pastes the copied frames onto the symbol's timeline and displays the first keyframe of the new symbol (along with a minicontroller) in the Library panel's preview window.

8. **In the Library panel, preview your symbol by clicking the minicontroller's Play button.**

   Flash runs a thumbnail version of the movie clip symbol in the preview window.

9. **Get out of symbol editing mode by choosing Edit→Edit Document.**

   Flash brings you back to the workspace and your main animation.

To create a movie clip symbol from scratch in symbol editing mode, follow the steps on page 252, adding the content for as many frames as you need.

### ■ CREATING AN INSTANCE OF A MOVIE CLIP SYMBOL

Because movie clip symbols have their own timelines, they're completely self-contained. You don't have to worry about matching your movie clip symbol to your main animation's timeline the way you do with a multiframe graphic symbol (page 263);

movie clip instances live on a single frame in your main animation, no matter how many frames the instances themselves contain. As a matter of fact, as you'll see next, creating an instance of a movie clip symbol is as easy as dragging and dropping.

To create an instance of a movie clip symbol:

1. **In your main animation, click to select the keyframe where you want to place an instance of a movie clip symbol.**

    Only keyframes can contain new content. So if you try to place a symbol in a regular frame, Flash "backs up" and places your symbol in the keyframe immediately preceding the selected frame anyway.

2. **In the Library, click to select the movie clip symbol of which you want to create an instance.**

    You can either click the symbol's icon from the list or click the symbol's thumbnail in the preview window.

3. **Drag the symbol to the stage.**

    Flash creates an instance of the symbol and places it in the keyframe you selected in step 1, as shown in Figure 7-17.

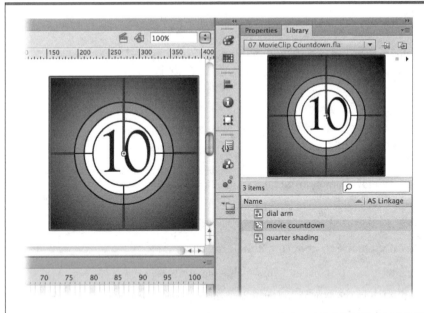

**FIGURE 7-17**

*Dragging a movie clip symbol from the Library to the stage tells Flash to create an instance of the symbol. No matter how many frames (or layers) your movie clip instance contains, it takes up only one frame on your animation (circled), which makes movie clips perfect for creating animated buttons.*

4. **To preview your instance, select Control→Test Movie→Test.**

    You'll notice that even if you turn looping off in the Control panel (which you do by selecting Control, and then, from the pop-up menu that appears, turning off the checkbox next to Loop) your movie clip instance continues to loop. The movie clip behaves this way because it's running on its own timeline (not the timeline Flash associates with your main animation). One way to tell Flash to stop looping your movie clip instance is to add a keyframe to your timeline *after* the keyframe that contains your movie clip instance. It can be a blank keyframe or a keyframe with content other than the movie clip you intend to stop.

**NOTE** Flash automatically loops the movie clip instance (plays it over and over again) until it encounters a keyframe that removes the movie clip, or until it encounters an ActionScript statement that tells it to stop (like *stop()* or *goToAndStop(), for example*). You can see an example of controlling playback with ActionScript in Chapter 15.

### ■ EDITING A MOVIE CLIP SYMBOL

You edit a movie clip symbol the same way you edit a single-frame graphic symbol: by switching to symbol editing mode (page 258). In both cases, Flash immediately applies your changes to all the instances of that symbol.

### ■ EDITING AN INSTANCE OF A MOVIE CLIP SYMBOL

Similar to multiframe graphic symbols, Flash lets you change the contents of the first keyframe of your movie clip instance, just the way you can an instance of a single-frame graphic (page 257). But Flash automatically applies those changes to the contents of *every* frame in your instance. So, for example, if you apply a sepia tint to the first keyframe, your entire movie clip instance looks old-timey. You can also apply filters (page 276) and blending effects to movie clip instances.

**DESIGN TIME**

### Reuse Deluxe: Repurposing Symbols

When you think about it, it's the simple, classic shapes you use most often in drawing.

Sure, it's great to have a sun, flower, or cockroach symbol hanging around in the Library, but it's the ovals, wedges, and sweeps that you find yourself coming back to again and again. And because Flash lets you resize, reposition, and recolor each instance, you can create radically different drawings using the same handful of simply shaped graphic symbols. Working this way lets you optimize the size of your finished animation, and, as a bonus, you get to focus on design at the graphic element level. (Even accomplished animators can find fresh ideas by limiting themselves to a handful of shapes.)

Expand and flip a raindrop symbol and then add a tail, for example, and you've got yourself a whale, as shown in Figure 7-18.

## Button Symbols

The easiest way to make your animation interactive is to add a button someone can click at runtime to perform a task, like replaying your entire animation, choosing which of several scenes to play, loading a web page, and so on.

To make creating a button easy, Flash has button symbols (Figure 7-19). A *button symbol* has four frames. Each frame has a specific function that helps you control the appearance of the button as it's being used by your audience:

- **Up**. In this frame, you draw the button as you want it to appear *before* your audience mouses over it.

- **Over**. In this frame, you draw the button as you want it to appear *after* your audience mouses over it.

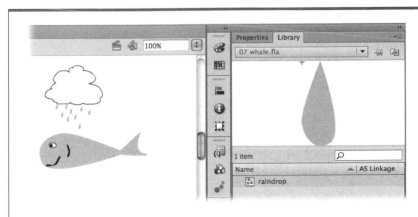

**FIGURE 7-18.**

*You'll find that simple shapes are the easiest to reuse because they're the most adaptable. In this image, a raindrop is resized and rotated to become the body of a whale. Creative repurposing saves time and reduces the size of your Flash files.*

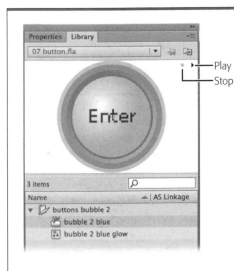

**FIGURE 7-19**

*Because button symbols are like specialized movie clip symbols, you see the same minicontroller in the Library's preview window when you click a button symbol as you see when you select a movie clip or multiframe graphic symbol. Clicking Play cycles through the button symbol's four frames, so you get to see 1) how the button looks before the cursor mouses over it, 2) how it looks after the cursor mouses over it, 3) how it looks when clicked, and 4) the button's clickable area. When you create a button symbol, Flash spots you the four frames; all you have to do is customize them, as shown in the following sections.*

- **Down**. In this frame, you draw the button as you want it to appear when your audience clicks it.

- **Hit**. In this frame, you draw the active, or "clickable," area of your button. In most cases, you want the active area to be identical to the button itself. But in other cases—for example, if you want to create a bullseye-shaped button that responds only when your audience clicks the tiny red dot in the center—you draw that center dot here, in the fourth frame (the Hit frame). You can also use this frame to create invisible buttons, as explained on page 277, or buttons that are the shape of an image in your animation, like a car.

For the designer, button symbols are handy. Flash automatically gives you the four Up, Over, Down, and Hit frames—all you have to do is plug in your drawings and go. As you'll see in the following section, Flash also gives you a handful of built-in graphic effects, called *filters*, which you can apply to your buttons to get professional-looking results. Button symbols aren't the only way to provide clickable interactivity to your projects. ActionScript coders often create their own buttons or use button components (page 544).

---

**NOTE** To get your button to actually do something when someone clicks it—to display a different section of the timeline, for example, or some dynamic text—you need to tie a snippet of ActionScript code to your button. Chapter 13 shows you how.

---

### ■ CREATING A BUTTON SYMBOL

When you create a button symbol, you start out basically as if you're creating any graphic symbol from scratch (page 252), but since button symbols have those four possible states, you can create up to four different graphics. When you choose Button in the New Symbol dialog box, Flash gives you a separate frame to hold each drawing so that you won't get confused.

In this example, you'll create a round, red button that turns yellow when your audience mouses over it and green when your audience clicks it.

1. **Click Insert→New Symbol.**

   The Create New Symbol dialog box appears.

2. **In the Name text box, type *bullseye*.** Make sure the drop-down menu is set to Button, and then click OK.

   When you create a new button symbol, Flash gives you four named frames (Figure 7-20). It's up to you which frames you want to modify, but at the very least, you need to add a drawing to the Up frame, to show the button before it's clicked or moused over. For a more sophisticated button, you'll also add a drawing to the Over frame (as shown below) to let someone know when his mouse is over the button.

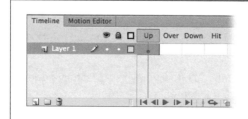

**FIGURE 7-20**

*Flash pops you into symbol editing mode. In the symbol's timeline, you see four named frames: Up, Over, Down, and Hit.*

**TIP** Flash comes with a blue million button symbols already spiffed up and ready for you to drop into your animations. So before you get too carried away drawing your own button, choose Window→Common Libraries→Buttons to see if Flash already has a button symbol that fits your bill. (You still have to write ActionScript code to tell Flash what you want to do when your audience clicks your button. Find out how in Chapter 13.)

3. **Draw your button as you want it to appear initially by using the Oval tool to add a red circle to the first keyframe (the Up frame).**

   Keep the registration point (the cross) in the upper-left corner of your button image as you draw. When you finish, your workspace should look similar to the one in Figure 7-21.

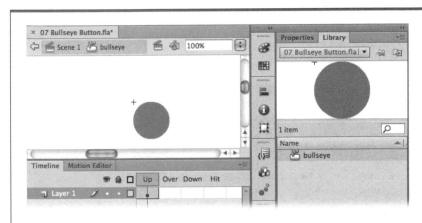

**FIGURE 7-21**

*Your button doesn't have to look like a button; it can be an image, a shape, a line—anything you like. But most people are used to circular buttons, so a circle's a good place to start. Notice that as you create your image, Flash automatically updates the Library's preview window.*

4. **Right-click Frame 2 (the Over frame), and then, from the pop-up menu that appears, select Insert Keyframe.**

   Flash displays a circle in Frame 2 to let you know you've successfully added a keyframe. On the stage, you see a copy of the button you drew in Frame 1.

5. **Here's how you make the button change when a cursor passes over it: On the stage, select the circle.** In the Properties panel, click the Fill Color icon, and then, from the color picker that appears, choose a yellow swatch.

   Flash recolors the circle yellow. If you don't see the Properties panel, select Window→Properties. If you still don't see it, make sure you've selected the circle on the stage.

6. **Right-click Frame 3 (the Down frame), and then, from the pop-up menu that appears, select Insert Keyframe.**

   Flash displays a circle in Frame 3 to let you know you've successfully added a keyframe (and, therefore, can change the content of the frame).

7. **Here's how you draw the button as you want it to appear when a cursor clicks it: Select the button.** In the Properties panel, click the Fill Color icon once again, and then, from the color picker that appears, choose a green swatch.

Flash recolors the circle green.

8. **Right-click Frame 4 (the Hit frame), and then, from the pop-up menu that appears, select Insert Keyframe.**

Flash displays a circle in Frame 4 to let you know you've successfully added another keyframe. As you can see on the stage, Flash assumes you want the entire button to respond to a mouse click—and in a lot of cases, that's exactly what you do want. But you can make the clickable portion of your button smaller or larger. To do so:

9. **On the stage, click the circle to select it.** Then choose Window→Transform to display the Transform panel.

In the Transform panel, type *50* into the Width and Height boxes, and then press Enter or Return. Figure 7-22 shows you a scaled-down circle that should look similar to the one you see on your workspace.

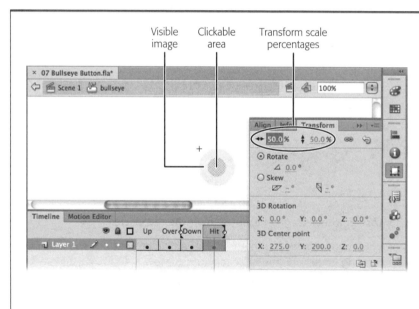

**FIGURE 7-22**

*Normally, you want to draw the same size shape in the Hit frame as you do in the other frames so that the entire button responds to mouse clicks. Drawing a smaller (or even different-shaped) image for the Hit frame lets you create more sophisticated buttons: click-able images, for example, or invisible buttons that let the content of your frame itself appear to respond to mouse clicks (see the box on page 277). Here, the clickable por-tion of the button is exactly half the size of the visible portion.*

10. **Return to your animation by choosing Edit→Edit Document.**

Flash hides your symbol editing workspace and displays your animation workspace.

### ■ USING A BUTTON SYMBOL (CREATING AN INSTANCE OF A BUTTON SYMBOL)

You can find the work file from the previous exercise *07-3_Bullseye_Button.fla* at *www.missingmanuals.com/cds/flashcs6mm*.

To create an instance of a button symbol:

1. **Click to select the first keyframe (Frame 1) in your animation.**

   Flash highlights the selected frame.

2. **In the Library panel's preview window, drag your button symbol's thumbnail onto the stage.**

   On the stage, Flash creates an instance of the button symbol and surrounds it with a selection box.

3. **Test your button instance.** To do so, choose Control→Test Movie→Test.

   A red circle appears in the middle of the test window (Figure 7-23).

> **TIP**   To test your button instance on the stage, select Control→Enable Simple Buttons. When you do, your button responds to mouse movement and clicking right there on the stage.

**FIGURE 7-23**

*Whatever you drew in Frame 1 (the Up frame) appears first.*

4. **In the test window, drag your mouse over the red circle.**

   When your mouse nears the center of the red circle, your arrow cursor turns into a pointing finger, and the red circle turns yellow.

5. **With your pointing-finger cursor, click the yellow circle.**

   The yellow circle turns green.

> **NOTE**   Chapter 13 shows you how to add an action to your button so that clicking it does something useful.

### ■ EDITING AN INSTANCE OF A BUTTON SYMBOL

You can't change the individual frames of your button instance individually. But Flash does let you apply the same changes to *all* the frames of your button instance.

Page 273 shows you the steps you can take to apply color, transparency, and transforms to your button instances. (The steps are identical to those you take to edit a single-frame graphic instance.) But you can also apply *filters*, or visual effects, to your buttons. Filters can turn even a plain oval button into something that looks like you spent hours tweaking it.

### Oddly Shaped (and Invisible) Buttons

*Why would I want to make my Hit frame smaller than the button itself? Won't that just make it harder for people to click?*

One popular situation when you might want to make the Hit frame smaller than the button itself is when you're creating a hotspot. For example, say you're creating an interactive web-based game for kids. On the stage, you've drawn several different animals: a pig, a duck, and a lamb.

The audio file you've attached to your animation tells the player which specific part of each animal to click: the duck's bill, for instance, or the pig's tail. In this case, you want to limit the clickable portion of the image to the bill (or tail).

A situation when you might consider making the Hit frame larger than the button is when you want to give your audience a larger target. Instead of making someone center her cursor precisely over a teeny-tiny button, for example, you can let her click as soon as her cursor comes anywhere close to the button. This option is great for text-only buttons, too.

Otherwise, only the actual letters are clickable. (Obviously, this strategy works best when you have only a few buttons on the stage and they're not near one another.)

Finally, you can create invisible buttons by drawing a shape in the Hit frame and leaving the rest of the button frames empty. Suppose you have a picture and you want to make a car inside that picture a clickable button, as shown in Figure 7-24. Bring the entire picture into your button symbol. In the Hit frame, trace and fill the portion you want to be clickable—say, the car. Then delete the original picture, leaving only the filled shape. Exit symbol editing mode, and then drag your invisible button over the picture in the main timeline. To help you out in placing an invisible button on the stage, Flash provides a transparent blue hotspot shape. You can see this shape when you're working in Flash, but it doesn't appear in your published animation. For a working example of an invisible button, download *07-4_Invisible_Button.fla* from the Missing CD at *www.missingmanuals.com/cds/flashcs6mm*.

**NOTE** Filters aren't just for buttons. You can also apply filters to text blocks (Chapter 6) and movie clip instances.

To apply a filter to a button instance:

1. **On the stage, select the button instance.**

   Flash draws a blue selection box around the instance.

2. **In the Properties panel, click the Filters subpanel.**

   If the Filters subpanel is closed, click the triangular button to expand it.

3. **Click the Add Filter button (lower-left corner).**

   A pop-up menu appears (Figure 7-25), listing the following filter options:

- **Drop Shadow.** Displays a shadow on the right and bottom edges of the button.

**FIGURE 7-24**

*You can tell the car is a clickable button in this Flash animation, because the cursor changes to the well-known pointing finger. This clickable hotspot, or invisible button, was created by placing a graphic the shape of the car in the Hit frame of a button symbol.*

- **Blur.** Redraws the surface of the button so that it appears soft and blurred.

- **Glow.** Similar to a drop shadow, creates a fuzzy aura in the color of your choosing.

- **Bevel.** Applies brightness and shadow on opposite sides of the button to create a 3-D effect.

- **Gradient Glow.** Similar to Glow (above), but lets you specify bands of different colors (instead of just one color).

- **Gradient Bevel.** Similar to Bevel (above), but lets you choose bands of different colors for the brightness and shadow.

- **Adjust Color.** Lets you individually adjust the brightness, contrast, saturation, and hue of your button.

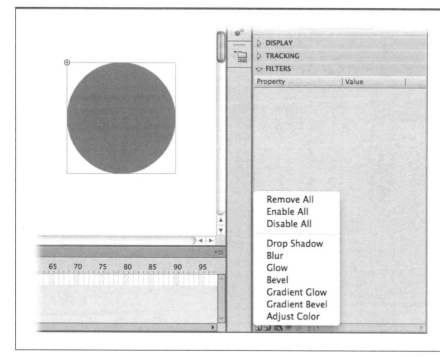

**FIGURE 7-25**

*When you click the Add Filter icon in the Filters panel, this pop-up menu appears, showing you all the effects you can add to your button instance.*

4. **From the menu, select Glow.**

   A red, glowing effect appears around your button, and the Filter panel displays the Glow properties.

5. **Click the down arrow next to Blur X, and then drag the slider to 40.**

   On the stage, the glow diffuses.

6. **Click the Shadow Color icon, and then, from the color picker that appears, click the black swatch.**

   On the stage, the glow turns from red to black, yielding a subtle 3-D effect (Figure 7-26).

7. **Test your newly edited button by selecting Control→Test Movie→Test.**

   In the test window that appears, you see your button with the Glow effect applied.

8. **In the test window, move your mouse over your button.**

   Flash applies filters to the entire instance (not just the contents of the keyframe to which you apply them), so the Glow effect remains even when you mouse over the button.

TIP With filters, you can quickly make a button instance look both unique and spiffy. Flash lets you change the properties of your filters—for example, you can change the size of a blur or the color of a drop shadow—so the drop shadow you apply to one instance doesn't have to look the same as the drop shadow you apply to another instance of the same symbol.

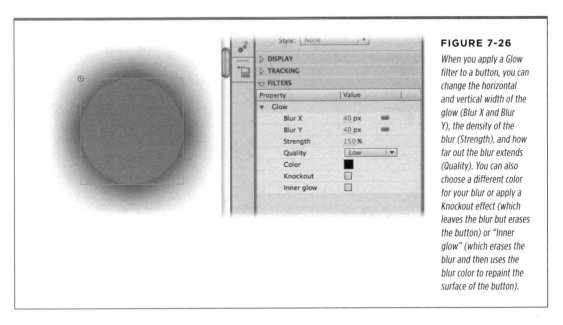

**FIGURE 7-26**

*When you apply a Glow filter to a button, you can change the horizontal and vertical width of the glow (Blur X and Blur Y), the density of the blur (Strength), and how far out the blur extends (Quality). You can also choose a different color for your blur or apply a Knockout effect (which leaves the blur but erases the button) or "Inner glow" (which erases the blur and then uses the blur color to repaint the surface of the button).*

To remove a filter you've applied: In the Filter panel, select the filter you want to remove, and then click the Delete Filter button (trash can).

**TIP** Applying a filter isn't an either/or proposition. You can add multiple filters to the same instance to create different effects: For example, you can add both a glow and a drop shadow, as shown in Figure 7-27.

### ▒ EDITING A BUTTON SYMBOL

You edit a button symbol, the same way you edit a single-frame graphic symbol: by switching to symbol editing mode (page 258). In both cases, Flash immediately applies the changes you make to the button symbol itself, as well as all the instances of that button symbol.

## ▒ Templates

While symbols let you reuse images and series of frames, *templates* let you reuse entire Flash documents. In this section, you see how to use Flash's prebuilt templates and how to create your own. In Flash CS6, templates are helpful in several ways:

- **Use Adobe's predesigned templates as a project starting point**. For example, the Advertising templates start you off with the stage set to web advertising standards like 160 x 600 Wide Skyscraper or 728 x 90 Leaderboard. Among the Media Playback templates, you'll find templates to create photo albums.

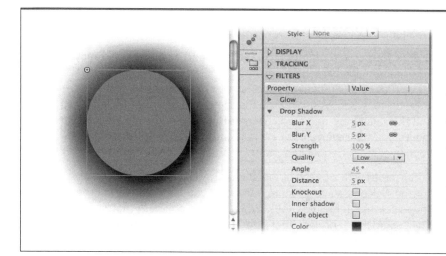

**FIGURE 7-27**

*Flash applies filters in top-down order, so adding a glow and a drop shadow yields a different result than adding a drop shadow and then a glow. You can even add the same filter more than once to compound the effect. To change the order of your filters, simply drag them to reposition them in the Filter panel.*

**DESIGN TIME**

## Organizing Your Symbols

If you do a lot of work in Flash, chances are you're going to create a lot of symbols. But in Flash, as in life, if you can't see what you've already got, you're apt to recreate it or go without it—both of which defeat the purpose of using symbols for in the first place.

The answer? Organize your symbols into folders.

Flash lets you create folders inside the Library. You can use these folders to organize your symbols. For example, you might want to keep all your movie clip symbols in one folder, all your graphic symbols in another, and so on. Or you might want to keep all the symbols related to a composite drawing (like a cartoon character or a corporate logo) in a separate folder. Use whatever organization makes sense to you; you can always reorganize your files and folders later.

To create a folder in the Library:

1. In the Library, click the Options menu. From the pop-up menu that appears, choose New Folder.

2. A folder named "untitled folder 1" appears in the Library beneath your symbols.

3. Replace the folder name by typing in a new, more meaningful name, like logo, spaceman, or intro_scene. Flash selects the folder name automatically when it creates a new folder, but if you need to change the name after the fact, double-click it.

4. Drag all the logo-related symbols into the logo folder, all the spaceman-related symbols into the spaceman folder, and so on.

If you need more levels of organization, you can place folders inside folders.

- **Use Adobe's predesigned templates as learning examples**. The Animation and Sample Files templates show how to use advanced techniques such as tweens, masks, and easing. These are working examples, which you can learn from by experimenting and analyzing them (as of this writing, these templates contain no written instructions). Still, if you want to learn how to create random effects with ActionScript, you can study the code in the Scripted Rain or Scripted Snow templates.

- **Create your own templates to save time and ensure consistency**. Suppose you create marketing animations for display on your corporate website. You always use your company's logo and copyright notice, the same stage size and color palette, a copyright notice, the same sound clips of your CEO speaking, and the same intro and credit scenes. By creating a template with these elements, you can save yourself a lot of time, and you ensure consistency among your animations (highly important in certain corporate circles).

Flash CS6 comes with a bunch of templates all ready for you to customize. You see them on the Welcome screen (Figure 7-28) when you start Flash (or choose File→New and then click the Templates tab). While they're obviously not specific to your particular company or project, they *can* save you time on a lot of basic animations, including banner ads, slideshows, and presentations. They're also great examples for learning new Flash skills. Here's a quick rundown of the major template categories.

- **Advertising** templates are sized according to web advertising standards. Other than setting the stage to a specific size, they don't provide that much help.

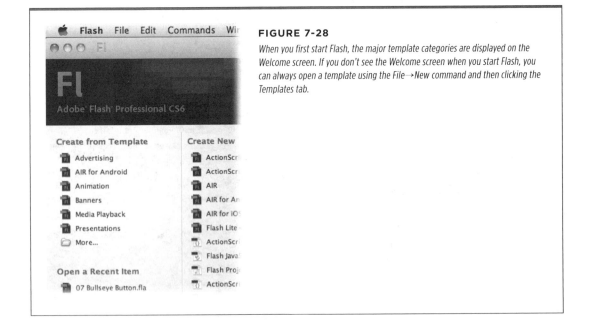

**FIGURE 7-28**

*When you first start Flash, the major template categories are displayed on the Welcome screen. If you don't see the Welcome screen when you start Flash, you can always open a template using the File→New command and then clicking the Templates tab.*

- **AIR for Android** templates are great learning tools. As you'll see in Chapter 23, they include example for handling common mobile device behaviors such as touch screen gestures and accelerometer events.

- **Animation** templates are more helpful both as a starting point and as learning examples. You'll find working buttons and examples of graphic masks—a method where part of an image that's concealed is gradually revealed. The animation template examples shown use an *ease*—that is, an effect that starts off at one speed and then increases or decreases. The Animation templates also include several examples that include random movement and timing.

- **Banners** holds templates similar to the ones in the Advertising group. There are fewer examples, but they include some ActionScript programming. For example, the 160 x 600 Simple Button AS3 template includes code to link to a web page.

- **Media Playback** templates come in two flavors—photo album templates (always popular) and TV title-safe templates. The TV templates give you a presized stage, with rectangles marking the safe areas for titles and action. If your work goes outside the safe area, some TVs may not display all your beautiful animation.

- **Presentations** are predesigned to help you create PowerPoint-style presentations in Flash.

- **Sample Files** are a grab bag of templates that are great learning tools. You'll find examples that use Flash's IK Bone tool (Figure 7-29).

> **NOTE** Flash's templates are useful—*if* you can figure out what they're supposed to do and how to customize them. You're at the mercy of the people who created the templates. If you're lucky, they provided a helpful name and description that appears in the dialog box where you choose a template. If you're very, very lucky, they provided instructions, comments, and notes in the template itself.

## Opening a Prebuilt Template

Starting a document from a template is similar to opening an existing document. There's one big difference, though. When you use a template to create a new document, the original template remains untouched. It's as if you opened an existing document and immediately used Save As to save it under a new name. Here are the steps for using one of the prebuilt templates that come with Flash:

1. **Select File→New.**

   The New Document window appears.

2. **In the New Document window, click the Templates tab.**

   The New from Template window opens (Figure 7-30).

3. **In the Category box, select Animation.**

   Several animation templates appear in the Templates box.

**4. At the top of the list, click Animated Button Highlight.**

The Preview window shows the stage for the selected template. Sometimes you won't see anything but the shape of the stage. For the Animated Button Highlight, you see the button. The description gives you some hints about the template and what it is designed to do.

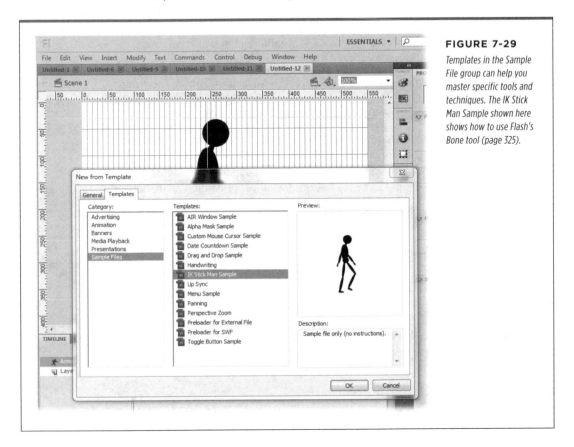

**FIGURE 7-29**

*Templates in the Sample File group can help you master specific tools and techniques. The IK Stick Man Sample shown here shows how to use Flash's Bone tool (page 325).*

**5. Click OK.**

Flash opens the template, and you're ready to roll. Several of the prebuilt templates have instructions, including this one. The instructions are in the top layer of text on the stage. After you've read them, you can delete or hide the layer. These instructions explain how to change the button's appearance and behavior.

With many templates, the best way to start is with a test drive. Watch the animation, then examine its timeline, symbols, and any ActionScript code that makes it work. In the Animated Button Highlight template, press Ctrl+Enter (⌘-Return) to see how the animation works in the Flash Player test window. It's pretty basic: There's one big button on the center of the stage labeled "click". When you mouse over the button, its appearance subtly changes—it starts to blink. Click the button, and its appearance changes again—it stops blinking and has a pressed-down appearance. The Output panel down near the timeline reads, "Button clicked".

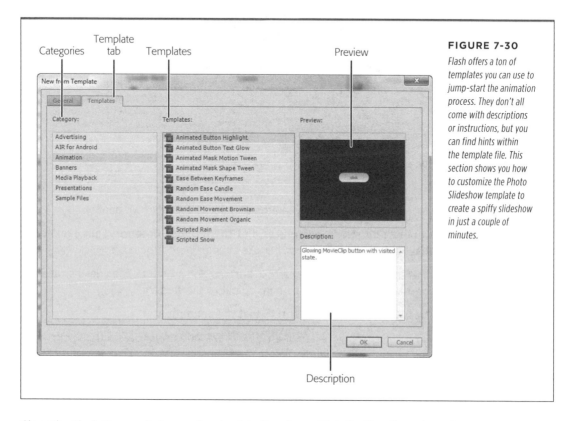

TEMPLATES

**FIGURE 7-30**

*Flash offers a ton of templates you can use to jump-start the animation process. They don't all come with descriptions or instructions, but you can find hints within the template file. This section shows you how to customize the Photo Slideshow template to create a spiffy slideshow in just a couple of minutes.*

Close the Flash Player window and go back to the stage. Click the Timeline tab, and you can start to explore the mysteries of this template. For example, select the button on the stage, and then check out the Properties. You see the button is a movie clip symbol rather than a button symbol. Double-click the button on the stage, and it opens so you can see the timeline for the symbol, as shown in Figure 7-31. This particular template uses some Flash tools that you'll learn about later in this book: ActionScript (page 407) and timeline labels (page 523). But that's one of the cool things about templates—you don't have to know exactly how they work to use them. In many cases, you can make simple modifications without getting knee-deep in the mechanics.

## Customizing the Photo Album Template

The Simple Photo Album template (Figure 7-32) is a perfect example of a template you can use without completely understanding all the ActionScript code and other techniques that make it work. You can even customize it, which this section shows you how to do.

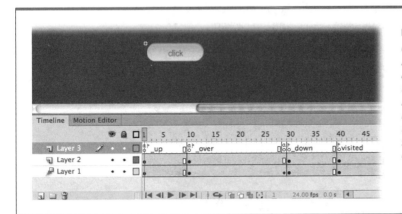

**FIGURE 7-31**

*Open the button symbol in the Animated Button Highlight template, and you see why the button behaves the way it does. Layer 3 contains ActionScript code and timeline labels. Layer 2 holds the text that appears on the button. Layer 1 holds the button shape with the color changes that display the highlights.*

Here are the steps for customizing the template with your own photos:

1. **Choose File→New→Templates and then, under Category, choose Media Playback.** Under Templates, choose Simple Photo Album, and click OK.

   The template opens, showing text, buttons, and an image. The brief instructions for using the template appear in red below the stage.

2. **Press Ctrl+Enter (⌘-Return) to test the animation.**

   Flash Player shows an image that looks like video color bars with the big number 1. The text above the image says "Image Title 1". Three familiar-looking buttons control the animation. The center button is a Play/Pause button, and the other buttons move the album forward or backward one image.

3. **Close the Flash Player window.**

   When Flash Player closes, you're back in Flash Professional.

4. **In the timeline, click the Show/Hide button for the instructions.**

   A red X appears when the instructions are hidden.

5. **Click the Show/Hide button for the Controls layer.**

   A red X appears when the three control buttons are hidden. When you're investigating a new template, you can learn what's on each layer by toggling the Show/Hide button for each layer. In this case, you learn that the controls are on one layer and that the images and text are on the Images/Titles layer. The Matte layer is a rectangle that's partially hidden by the image. When the image is visible, it looks like a border around the image. The background creates the dark-gray stage color.

6. **Drag the playhead to Frames 2, 3, and 4.**

    Each frame on the timeline corresponds with one of the images. That means you can swap your own images for the numbered color bar pics.

7. **Move the playhead to Frame 1, and then click the color bar image on the stage.**

    When the image is selected, the Properties panel shows that it's a bitmap, and it's an instance of *image1.jpg*.

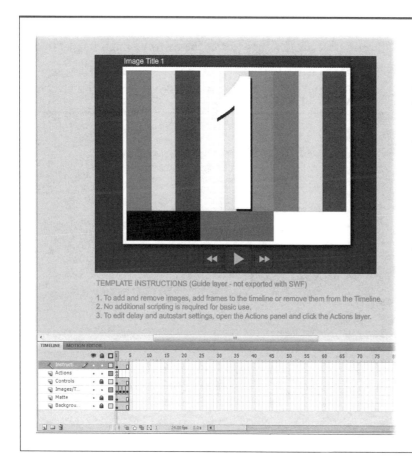

**FIGURE 7-32**

*The Simple Photo template displays photos one by one. Your audience can move through the photo collection using the Play/ Pause and the Back and Forward controls. It's a perfect example of a template that can be used for many different projects.*

8. **Examine the Position and Size properties.**

    Adobe may change the templates from time to time, but the position is probably something like X: 70 and Y: 35. Those settings indicate the position of the upper-left corner. The size properties are probably about: W: 500 and H: 376. If you want to add your own pics, they should be about the same size or at least the same proportions: 500 x 376 pixels.

9. **Prepare your own images for a new album.**

   You can resize photos or images within Flash, but you'll probably have best results if you crop your images before you bring them into Flash using a program like Photoshop, the GIMP, or iPhoto.

10. **Choose File→Import→Import to Library and then select your photos and click Open.**

    Shift-click or Ctrl-click to select more than one photo for importing. After you click Open, the Import to Library window closes, and your photos are added to the Library.

11. **In the Library, select your photos and drag them to the Sample Images folder.**

    Click to open the Sample Images folder, and you can see the individual color bar photos. You might as well put your own pics in there, too, as shown in Figure 7-33.

**FIGURE 7-33**

*The album photos are stored in the Sample Images folder in the Library. Here you see a combination of the photos that came with the template and new photos that have been added: car, duck, gremlin, puppy, and rose.*

12. **Select the instance of *image1.jpg* on the stage.**

Make sure the playhead is on Frame 1 in the timeline and the Properties panel says "Instance of: image1.jpg" as shown in Figure 7-34.

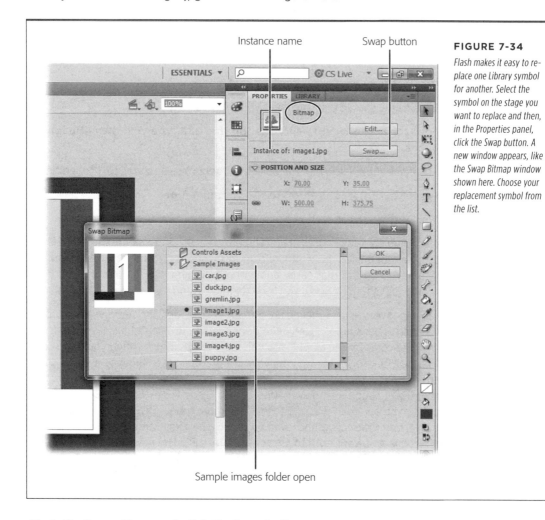

Instance name     Swap button

**FIGURE 7-34**

*Flash makes it easy to replace one Library symbol for another. Select the symbol on the stage you want to replace and then, in the Properties panel, click the Swap button. A new window appears, like the Swap Bitmap window shown here. Choose your replacement symbol from the list.*

Sample images folder open

13. **In the Properties panel, click the Swap button.**

The Swap Bitmap window opens.

14. **Open the Sample Images folder and select one of your new images.** Then click OK.

    Your image appears on the stage. If it doesn't look exactly right, you may need to tweak the size or position settings.

15. **Set the size and position to match the settings you noted in step 8.**

    This example had a position of X: 70 and Y: 35, and a size of W: 500 and H: 376.

16. **Repeat the swapping process for each photo you want to add.**

    Each frame should display one of your photos.

17. **For each frame, double-click the top title and type your own title for the image.**

    You can double-click with the Selection tool (V) to open the text for editing.

18. **Press Ctrl+Enter (⌘-Return) to test the animation.**

    Your customized animation plays, showing your own photos and text.

The preceding steps work great if you want to create a photo album with exactly the same number of pics as the template. Suppose you want to add one more image to the album. You can do that easily and without digging into the ActionScript code that makes the album work. All you have to do is extend the timeline in a few places.

The top two layers in the timeline are named Instructions and Actions. You can delete the Instructions layer once you're done reading it. The Actions layer holds the ActionScript code for the album. You can learn more about writing your own code on page 407, but for now, you can leave the Actions layer the way it is. The next layer moving down is the Controls layer. You want the Play/Pause and Forward and Back controls to appear with every photo, so you need to extend the Controls layer. Select Frame 5 and then press F5 to insert a frame (page 100). Do the same for the Matte layer and the Background layer. You need a new keyframe in the Images/Titles layer because you want both to change, so press F6. The newly created keyframe holds that last image and title in the album. All you need to do now is swap them for the new photo. You can repeat this process to add as many photos as you want to the album (Figure 7-35).

## Create Your Own Template

Once you start cooking in Flash, you'll have a bunch of animations that you want to turn into templates. As they say, why reinvent the wheel? Templates are great timesavers, and it's easy to create your own. For now, you may want to experiment with a file from the Missing CD (*www.missingmanuals.com/cds/flashcs6mm*), such as *07-5_Photo_Gallery.fla*. This example, shown in Figure 7-36, is a lightbox-style photo gallery. Click a thumbnail image, and it flips around a bit and then fills the stage. Another click, and the photo shrinks back to a thumbnail. The gallery holds nine photos total. If you save the photo gallery as a template, you can open it and swap the sample photos with your own masterpieces.

**FIGURE 7-35**

*Here the timeline in the Simple Photo Album template is extended to accommodate a new image and title. New frames were added to the Controls, Matte, and Background layers. A new Keyframe was added to the Images/Titles layer.*

First, open the standard .fla file. It's all ready to go, and it even has some instructions in the top layer that appear above the stage. If you want to see the photo gallery in action, press Ctrl+Enter (⌘-Return).

07-5_Photo_Gallery.swf

**FIGURE 7-36**

*The Photo Gallery template is another pre-designed Flash document that you can download from the Missing CD. Follow the steps in this section to turn it into a reusable template. Then you can swap the gallery photos with your own.*

To save the Flash document as a template, choose File→Save As Template. A dialog box appears with a warning that explains that the "SWF history" will be cleared when the file is saved as a template. Go ahead and click the Save As Template button. The next thing you see is the Save as Template box shown in Figure 7-37, where there's room for a Name, Category, and Description. The Preview window shows the stage for the template. Fill in the details you want, and then click Save. Flash saves your file as a template. The next time you choose File→New and click the Templates tab, you'll see your saved template along with all the others.

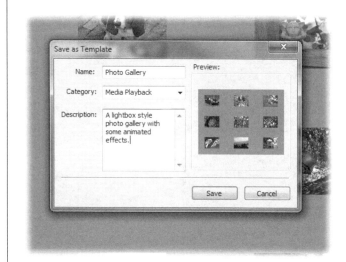

**FIGURE 7-37**

*Use the Save as Template dialog box to give your template a name, a category, and a description. This information comes in handy when you or someone else tries to figure out how to use your creation.*

---

## Building a Better Template

Sometimes, you'll find yourself creating a template almost by accident. For example, imagine that you're hard at work on one animation when your boss comes in, peeks over your shoulder, and tells you to create another one "just like that one" for another client. Choose File→Save As Template, continue with the instructions on page 291, and you're on your way.

But if you know *beforehand* that you're creating a template, you can plan for its reuse. And planning always results in a more useful template. Here are a few planning tips for creating a template you'll use over and over again:

- **Include only reusable stuff**. If you save a working animation as a template (complete with company-specific elements), you'll need to delete any unusable elements each time you reuse the template. Consider up front which elements apply across the board, and include only those in your template.

- **Name your layers**. Giving your layers meaningful names that describe what each layer contains (like actions, sounds, background, buttons, and so on) is always a good

idea. But it's even more important when you're creating a template, because it gives you (or your colleague, or whoever's reusing the template two weeks from now) an easy way to find and change the elements that need to be changed.

- **Document, document, document**. Have pity on the person who tries to reuse your template a month from now, and tell him up front what the template's for (a product demonstration combined with an order form, for example) and what needs to be changed (the company logo, demo movie clip, and three form fields). The quickie description you type when you create your template is rarely enough. Instead, provide an Instructions layer at the top of the timeline. Add a labels layer with words that help other people understand the animation's structure. If you're including ActionScript code, use comments to explain how the code works and how someone can make simple changes.

---

# Advanced Tweens with the Motion Editor

Tweens have always been a big tool in Flash's animation toolbox, and, as explained in Chapter 3, these days you have more control over tweens than ever. Flash's motion tween (page 103) can do more than just show a car moving down a street—it can make the car stretch out and turn blazing red when it's going really fast and scrunch up when it stops. It can even make the car's shadow change position as the car and sun move across the screen.

You accomplish these sophisticated tweens by making multiple property changes at multiple points in time. Want precision control over every aspect of a tween? Turn to the Motion Editor. This chapter shows you in detail how to apply and fine-tune your motion tweens, focusing in particular on Motion Editor control. You'll start with a refresher on motion presets, which are simply predesigned tweens that you can apply to objects with a couple of mouse clicks. Then you'll learn some of the different ways you can edit your tweens on the stage, in the timeline, and using the Motion Editor. Along the way, you'll learn how to apply filters for special effects and how to create more realistic motion (easing).

> **NOTE** If you need a primer on motion tween basics, or tweens in general, head back to page 103.

## ■ Applying Motion Presets

Designing a perfect tween can be a lot of work. It's not so much that it's difficult, but creating a complex motion tween where several properties change at different points in time can be time-consuming. Fortunately, right out of the box, Flash gives you a head start. Open the Motion Presets panel (Window→Motion Presets), and you see a handful of predesigned tweens, as shown in Figure 8-1. Initially, the Motion Presets panel comes with two folders: Default Presets, where the Adobe-designed presets live, and Custom Presets, where you can store tweens you've perfected as motion presets (see page 298). Just click a motion preset to see a minipreview at the top of the panel.

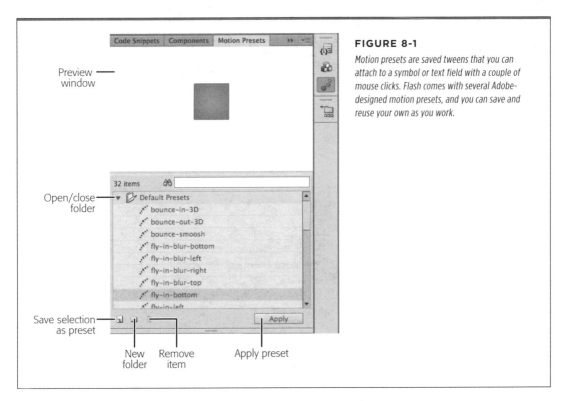

**FIGURE 8-1**

*Motion presets are saved tweens that you can attach to a symbol or text field with a couple of mouse clicks. Flash comes with several Adobe-designed motion presets, and you can save and reuse your own as you work.*

Not only are motion presets useful design tools, but they're also great learning tools. By dissecting some of the professionally designed presets that come with Flash, you can see how certain effects are created. After you've applied presets in your project, you can modify them, examine them, and steal some of their ideas for your own tweens. To get started, the following steps show how to apply and modify a motion preset called *flyin-pause-flyout*. As with most presets, the name gives you a pretty good hint at the action.

First, the easiest part: applying a motion preset. Like any motion tween, a preset can be applied only to a symbol or a text field. For this exercise, you can draw your own simple circle, or you can use the Missing CD document *08-1_Flyin_Preset.fla* from *www.missingmanuals.com/cds/flashcs6mm*.

1. **Open the Motion Presets panel by choosing Window→Motion Presets.**

   The Motion Presets panel is small, so you can easily let it float over your work area while you're making a selection, and then close it after you've applied a preset. You won't need it again until you need another preset. If you're working in the Essentials workspace, the Motion Presets panel appears at the bottom of the collapsed panels to the right of the stage.

2. **Select the symbol you want to tween; in this case, your circle or the car from the example file.**

   The symbol or text field you tween has to be by itself in a layer in the timeline. If the layer holds more than one object, then Flash creates a new layer for the object before it applies the tween. If the object can't be tweened (perhaps it's not a symbol), you see a warning like Figure 8-2.

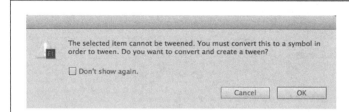

**FIGURE 8-2**

*If you try to apply a motion tween to an object other than a symbol or a text field, you see this warning.*

3. **In the Motion Presets panel, click the *flyin-pause-flyout* preset, and then click Apply.**

   A motion path appears attached to the object on the stage, and a blue tween appears in the main timeline, as shown in Figure 8-3.

4. **Press Enter to preview your tween in Flash.**

   More often than not, you'll make changes to a preset motion after you apply it. Start by taking a look at how the motion preset behaves. The *flyin-pause-flyout* preset blurs the symbol while it's moving, giving it a sense of speed. It slows for a bit and then speeds on. As you'll learn in this chapter, once you've applied the preset you can change the position of the tweened symbol, its size, and even its appearance. For example, you can increase or decrease the blurriness of the image.

5. **Modify the tween just as you would any tween you created from scratch.**

   For example, often the tween is working right, but you need to fine-tune the position of both the object and the motion path. With the Selection tool, drag a box around both the object and the motion path to select everything. Then you can drag the whole kit and caboodle to a new position on the stage.

**NOTE** In different places, this book explains how to make changes to the tween using the motion path (page 300), the timeline (page 307), the Motion Editor (page 311), and the Properties panel (page 107).

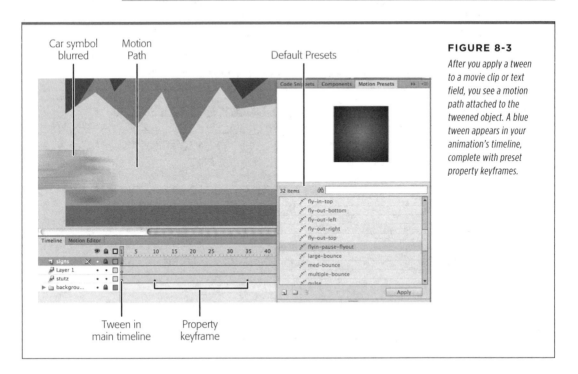

Car symbol blurred

Motion Path

Default Presets

**FIGURE 8-3**

*After you apply a tween to a movie clip or text field, you see a motion path attached to the tweened object. A blue tween appears in your animation's timeline, complete with preset property keyframes.*

Tween in main timeline

Property keyframe

Once you've applied a tween using a motion preset, it's no different from a tween you create from scratch. Also, there's no connection between the tween and the presets panel. If you make changes to the tween in your animation, it has no effect on the one stored in the Motion Presets panel. The opposite is true, too. Unlike with symbols in the Library, making changes to or deleting the tween in the Motion Presets panel has absolutely no effect on animations to which you've applied the preset.

## Saving a Custom Motion Preset

Setting up the perfect motion tween can take time. Perhaps you've got a text banner with some 3-D effects. Or maybe you spent time getting a basketball to bounce just right. With all that time invested, you want to be able to reuse that work, and as usual, Flash helps you do just that. You can save your carefully crafted tween as a motion preset, and then, in the future, apply it to new symbols and text fields with a click or two. Furthermore, because you modify the tweens created by presets, they're very versatile and adaptable to different uses. For example, a badminton shuttlecock might not bounce like a basketball, but it's probably faster to apply the basketball-bounce preset to the shuttlecock and then tweak it a bit than to create a new motion tween from scratch.

Saving a preset is easy, and you have a couple of ways to do the job. Which one you use may depend on your own preferences or where your mouse happens to hover at the moment. You can choose one of these methods to save a motion preset:

- Right-click the tween or motion path, and then choose "Save as Motion Preset" from the pop-up menu.

- Select the tween or motion path, and then click the "Save selection as preset" button on the Motion Presets panel (Figure 8-1).

In either case, a dialog box opens where you name the preset and then click OK. Once that's done, your newly named preset appears in the Custom Presets folder in the Motion Presets panel. (Your custom preset won't have an animated preview like the ones that come with Flash, but you can create one as instructed in the box below.)

---

**FREQUENTLY ASKED QUESTION**

### DIY Preview

*Can I create a preview for my custom motion preset?*

If you've gone to the work of creating a custom motion preset, you may want it to have its own nifty preview animation just like the presets Adobe designed. As it turns out, you can do that easily. First, publish your preset to create an SWF file that shows the animation. (SWF files are final files created to display animations. The details for publishing SWF files are on page 677.) Then place the SWF file in the folder that holds your motion presets.

That last bit is the tricky part. The motion presets storage location is different for different computers, as shown in the following examples. (The words in brackets, like <hard disk> and <your name>, represent the disk drives and user names

on your computer, while <locale> represents the locale or language for the computer; for example "en" is used for English.)

- Mac OS X: *<hard disk>/Users/<your name>/Library/ Application Support/Adobe/Flash CS6/<locale>/ Configuration/Motion Presets/*

- Windows 7 and Vista: *<hard disk>\Users\<your name>\ AppData\Local\Adobe\Flash CS6\<locale>\Configuration\ Motion Presets*

- Windows XP: *<hard disk>\Documents and Settings\<your name>\Local Settings\Application Data\Adobe\Flash CS6\<locale>\Configuration\Motion Presets\*

---

### ■ DELETING MOTION PRESETS

If you decide that a particular motion preset isn't worthy, you can delete it from the Motion Presets panel. In the Motion Presets panel, click to select the offending preset, and then click the trash can icon at the bottom of the panel. The stored preset disappears from the panel, but throwing it away has no effect on any tweens that were created using the preset.

## ■ Modifying a Motion Preset

As discussed earlier in this chapter, Adobe gives you a bunch of snazzy motion tweens with Flash. But one designer's perfect tween is another designer's, well... nearly perfect tween. Fortunately, you can customize presets after you apply them. In fact, tweaking a motion preset is great learning ground for designing and perfecting your own tweens. Editing a motion preset is no different from editing a tween you created yourself, so the following sections "Changing the Motion Path" (below) and "Editing a Tween Span" (page 307) apply to both motion presets and the tweens that you create from scratch.

## Changing the Motion Path

Whether you use a motion preset or create your own tween, chances are you'll want to tweak the motion path. Perhaps the ball doesn't bounce in just the right places, or that car looks like it's driving off the road. The motion path looks like a line trailing off from the tweened object. As you drag the playhead in the timeline, you'll notice that the tweened object follows the motion path. If you need a practice file, download *08-2_Motion_Path.fla* from the Missing CD (*www.missingmanuals. com/cds/flashcs6mm*).

You can change this path on the stage using the same Selection tool that you use to modify any line:

- **Move the entire motion path.** With the Selection tool, drag a box around any part of the path. Then drag everything to a new spot.

- **Move the starting point for the motion path.** With the Selection tool, drag the diamond-shaped selection point at the beginning of the motion path to a new location. The end of the path remains anchored where it was, while the motion path stretches or shrinks to accommodate the move.

- **Move the ending point of the motion path.** Select the diamond-shaped end point of the path and drag it to a new location. The starting point of the tween remains anchored in place, and the motion path adjusts to the move.

- **Create a curve in the motion path.** First, make sure the motion path is not selected, by clicking some empty spot on the stage. Then with the Selection tool, point to the path; when you see a curve appear next to the cursor arrow, drag to create a curved path (Figure 8-4). You can reshape the path by dragging different points along the path.

- **Change the tweened object's position at any point of the motion path.** In the main timeline, move the playhead to the frame where you want to reposition the tweened object, and then drag the object to a new position. Flash creates a new property keyframe in the timeline and adjusts the motion path to the new position. To use this method to move the start or end point, make sure that the playhead is on the first or last frame of the tween. This action also creates a diamond-shaped control point in the motion path. You can use the point and the accompanying control handles to change the shape of the motion path. It's similar to any line you draw using the Pen tool (page 68).

The example file *08-2_Motion_Path.fla* includes a wheel with the bounce-smoosh tween applied. The animation would be much more interesting if the wheel rolled along the high step, dropped to the ground, and then bounced in a forward motion. Here's how to change the path for that effect:

1. **Move the playhead to Frame 1 and make sure nothing is selected.** Then drag the wheel so it sits on the step, as shown in Figure 8-5.

   If the entire path moves with the wheel, you've selected both the path and the object. To deselect everything, click an empty spot or press Shift+Ctrl+A (Shift-⌘-A).

2. **With the Selection tool, adjust the curve so that the wheel appears to roll along the top of the stairstep.**

   When you move the cursor close to the path, it changes to show a curved line next to the arrow. Drag to adjust the curve in the motion path. The solid line shows the general arc of the motion, while the small dots show the actual position of the tweened object at different points in time.

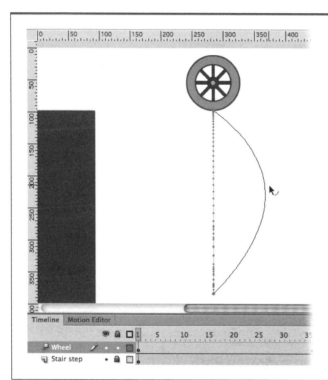

**FIGURE 8-4**

*Use the Selection and Subselection tools to modify a motion path just as you would any other line.*

3. **Adjust the end of the motion path so the wheel moves to the right as it bounces.**

   You can stretch the path to the right side of the stage, giving the wheel a feeling of increased forward motion as it bounces.

4. **Preview the animation and fine-tune it as necessary.**

If you got it perfect the first time, great! If not, try zooming in a little and fine-tuning the motion path as described in step 2.

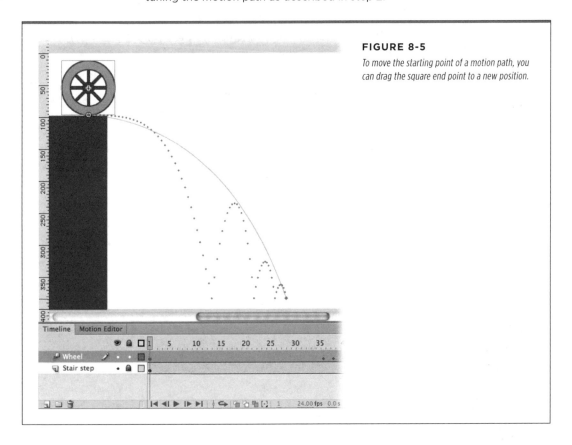

**FIGURE 8-5**

*To move the starting point of a motion path, you can drag the square end point to a new position.*

## Deleting a Motion Path

You can delete a motion path from a tween by simply selecting it and then pressing Delete. The consequence, of course, is that your tween isn't going anyplace. The tweened object remains stranded at its starting point until you provide further instructions. For example, you can copy and paste in a new path, as described next.

## Copying and Pasting a Motion Path

Flash gives you tools to create perfect shapes like circles, rectangles, polygons, and stars, not to mention the precise control that comes with the Pen tool. You can use any of these drawing tools to create a motion path. If you need a path that matches a perfect shape or is extremely complex, it's faster and easier to use Flash's drawing tools, rather than dragging tween objects around the stage to modify a motion path. First you need to create the path with one of the tools that creates a stroke—that is, any of the shape tools, the Pen, the Pencil, or the Line tool. Then, you paste that stroke into an existing tween that doesn't have a motion path.

> **NOTE** A file with a completed version of this project, *08-3_Path_Orient.fla*, is available at *www.missingmanuals.com/cds/flashcs6mm*.

Here are the steps:

1. **In a new Flash document, create two layers, each with 48 frames.**

   After you create the second layer, Shift-click to select the 48th frame in both layers, and then press F5 to add new frames on both layers.

2. **Create a text field with the words *not oriented*, and then rename the layer *not oriented*.**

   Make the text nice and bold and about 32 points in size. Double-click the layer name so you can edit it.

3. **Right-click a frame in the timeline of the "not oriented" layer, and then choose Create Motion Tween from the pop-up menu.**

   You now have a motion tween with no motion and no tween, because you haven't yet made any changes to the tweened object's properties.

4. **In the other layer, use the Oval tool to draw a circle, and then rename that layer circle.**

   Set the oval fill color to none by clicking the swatch with the Paint Bucket, and then, in the upper-right corner of the panel with color swatches, click the square with a stroke through it. Make the circle about 200 pixels in diameter. If necessary, you can set the size in the Properties panel.

5. **Use the Eraser tool, with a small eraser size, to erase a little bit of the circle.**

   You can't use a closed shape as a motion path, so you need to break the path at some point. When you're done erasing, your stage should look something like Figure 8-6.

6. **Using the Selection tool, drag a box around the circle to select the entire circle.** Copy it (Ctrl+C or ⌘-C), click the "not oriented" tween layer, and then paste it (Ctrl+V or ⌘-V) into the tween.

   As soon as you paste the circle into the tween layer, the text field attaches itself to the path. At this point, it's easier to examine your tween if you hide the original circle by clicking the Show/Hide button in the "circle" layer (Figure 8-6).

7. **Press Enter or Return to preview the animation.**

   Your not oriented text field moves in a circular motion, but the text isn't oriented to the circle. It remains right-side up and oriented to the stage. That looks a little odd, but don't fret. You'll learn how to orient the text to the circle in the next section.

You can use any stroke as a motion path, even complex strokes created using the Pen tool with multiple complex Bezier curves. Just make sure you're not using a closed path. Even though the circle isn't a closed path, the motion of the text looks like it's making a complete circle. When the movie clip loops, no one in your audience will ever know there's a break in the circle.

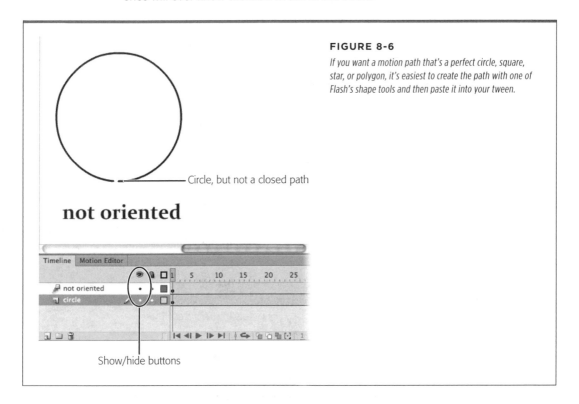

**FIGURE 8-6**

*If you want a motion path that's a perfect circle, square, star, or polygon, it's easiest to create the path with one of Flash's shape tools and then paste it into your tween.*

Circle, but not a closed path

not oriented

Show/hide buttons

## Orienting Tweened Objects to a Motion Path

Orienting text fields and symbols to a motion path is as simple as clicking a checkbox. In this section, you'll learn how to do that, as well as another handy technique—copying and pasting a motion from one layer to another in the same animation. When you're done, you'll have one Flash file with two examples of circular motion. In one, the text field is oriented to the circle; in the other, it's not (Figure 8-7).

1. **Click the Insert Layer button in the timeline's lower-left corner.**

   A new layer appears in the timeline.

2. **Rename the new layer *oriented*.**

   Double-click the layer, and then type the new name.

3. **Click the "not oriented" layer name to select all the frames in that layer, and then copy the frames (Edit→Timeline→Copy Frames).**

When you click the layer name, Flash automatically selects all the frames in the layer. You can also Ctrl-drag (Control-drag) over the frames to select multiple frames.

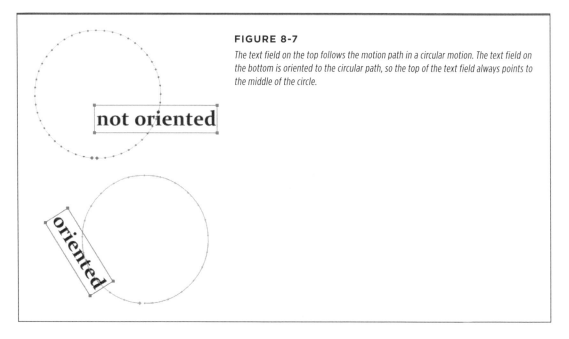

**FIGURE 8-7**

*The text field on the top follows the motion path in a circular motion. The text field on the bottom is oriented to the circular path, so the top of the text field always points to the middle of the circle.*

4. **Click the first frame of the "oriented" timeline, and then paste the frames (Edit→Timeline→Paste Frames).**

When you paste frames into the timeline, Flash inserts the pasted frames, pushing any existing frames on down the timeline.

> **TIP** You can also right-click the timeline to see a shortcut menu that has both the Copy Frames and Paste Frames commands.

5. **Shift-drag the end of the "oriented" timeline to the 48th frame so it matches the length of other layers.**

At this point, your oriented timeline is almost identical to the not-oriented layer.

6. **Edit the text field to read "oriented."**

With the Text tool still selected, you can resize the text field to fit the text by double-clicking the box in the text field's upper-right corner.

7. **Click the motion path, and then, in the Properties panel, turn on the "Orient to path" checkbox.**

If the "Orient to path" checkbox isn't showing, click to open the Rotation subpanel in the Properties panel, as shown in Figure 8-8. Notice that in the timeline, Flash has added a property keyframe to every frame of the tween, since the rotation of the text field changes in every single frame.

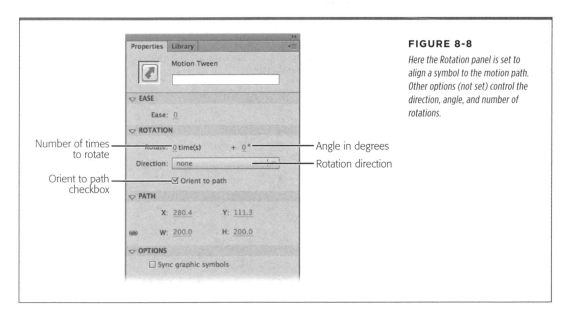

Number of times
to rotate

Angle in degrees

Rotation direction

Orient to path
checkbox

**FIGURE 8-8**

*Here the Rotation panel is set to align a symbol to the motion path. Other options (not set) control the direction, angle, and number of rotations.*

8. **Preview your animation (Ctrl+Enter or ⌘-Return).**

Your animation has two text fields that follow a circular path. The text that says "oriented" is oriented toward the circle and rotates as it makes its rounds. The text that says "not oriented" remains upright while it follows the motion path.

■ **OTHER THINGS YOU CAN DO IN THE ROTATION SUBPANEL**

The Rotation subpanel in the Properties panel has a few other settings in addition to "Orient to path." You can use the Direction drop-down menu to choose clockwise (CW) or counterclockwise (CCW) rotation for a tweened symbol or text field. This rotation refers to the tweened object rotating around its center point, not to its path around the circular motion path; in other words, it makes a text field or symbol spin during the tween. Above the Direction drop-down menu, you can set the number of times the object spins and its angle at a particular point in time.

**NOTE** If you turn on "Orient to path," these other settings are reset, as shown in Figure 8-8. Vice versa is true, too. Setting Direction to any setting other than "none" deselects the "Orient to path" option.

## Swapping the Tweened Object

Suppose you create the perfect tween for a logo or a text banner. It spins, it moves in 3-D, and even the transparency changes so it fades in and out at just the right moments. Then your client informs you of a big change—there's a new company logo or different text. Before you pull your hair out, read on to see how easy it is to swap the object of a motion tween. Remember, a motion tween is applied to a single object, so it's simply a matter of shifting all the property value changes over to a new movie clip or text field. To swap a symbol for a tweened object, follow these steps:

1. **In the original tween, select the symbol.**

   The symbol's properties appear in the Properties panel.

2. **In the Properties panel, click the Swap button.**

   The Swap button appears beneath the symbol's name and type.

3. **In the Swap Symbol box, select the new symbol, and then click OK.**

   The new symbol replaces the old symbol and performs all the same property changes.

# ■ Editing a Tween Span

The tween span in the timeline deserves a closer look (Figure 8-9), since it gives you a good overview of what's going on in a tween. When you create a motion tween, Flash colors it blue to set it off from the other layers, so you can easily find your way around. Property keyframes are diamond-shaped in the timeline to distinguish them from the circle-shaped standard keyframes. Clicking anywhere on the tween selects the entire tween and moves the playhead to that frame in the tween. What if you need to select a single frame in a tween? Perhaps you want to copy a tweened symbol's properties at that point in the timeline. In that case, Ctrl-click (⌘-click) the timeline to select a single frame. Then, right-click the frame and choose Copy Properties from the shortcut menu.

When you apply a motion tween to an object, Flash automatically sets aside a certain number of frames for the tween, marking them with the blue highlight. If there's only one keyframe in the layer, Flash uses all the layer's frames for the tween. Otherwise, if there are several keyframes on a layer, Flash uses all the frames between two keyframes. So, being the clever designer you are, you take this into account when you create your motion tweens; you lengthen or shorten the available space in the timeline to make your tweens just the right length. Still, there are times when you need to make a tween longer or shorter after the fact. The main thing to consider when you change the number of frames in your tween is the effect the change has on your carefully positioned property keyframes. For example, suppose you have the perfect tween for a basketball bouncing, but it seems to be running too slowly. You want to speed up the bouncing motion but keep the relative positions of the property keyframes the same. In that case, use the first option in Table 8-1—drag the end of the timeline. In another case, you may want to trim a few frames off the end of your timeline, making it shorter, but you don't want the property keyframes to change position at all. To do that, Shift-drag the end of the timeline.

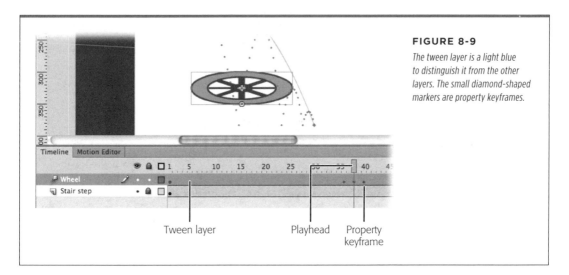

**FIGURE 8-9**

*The tween layer is a light blue to distinguish it from the other layers. The small diamond-shaped markers are property keyframes.*

Tween layer    Playhead    Property
keyframe

**TABLE 8-1** *Want to lengthen or shorten the timeline of your motion tween? Here are the commands and the way they affect the property keyframe.*

| ACTION | HOW TO DO IT... | EFFECT ON PROPERTY KEYFRAMES |
|---|---|---|
| Make a motion tween longer or shorter. | Drag the end of the timeline. | Property keyframes move proportionately, keeping their relative positions along the tween. |
| Keep a tweened object on the stage after its motion is complete. | Shift-drag the end of the timeline. | Has no effect on property keyframes. |
| Remove frames from a tween. | Ctrl-drag (⌘-drag) to select the frames to be deleted. Then press Shift-F5 to remove frames. | The number of frames between property keyframes stays the same, except for the segment where the frames are removed. |
| Insert frames into a tween. | Ctrl-drag (⌘-drag) to select the number of frames to insert in the timeline. Then right-click the selected frames. Choose Insert Frame from the timeline. | Inserts frames at the point of selection. Keyframes before the insertion point remain in the same position. Keyframes beyond the insertion point move down the timeline. |
| Move a tween span in the same layer. | Drag the tween span to a new point in the timeline. | The relationship of all the keyframes stays the same; however, the move erases the existing frames at the new location. |

| ACTION | HOW TO DO IT... | EFFECT ON PROPERTY KEYFRAMES |
|---|---|---|
| Change the breakline between two adjacent tween spans. | Drag the breakline to a new point. | Property keyframes move proportionately, keeping their relative positions along the tween. |
| Delete a tween span. | Right-click the tween span, and then choose Remove Frames or Clear Frames to replace the selection with standard frames. | Deletes all the property keyframes. |

## Viewing and Editing Property Keyframes in the Timeline

Property keyframes appear in the tween span at the point when any property changes. Those properties can include the following:

- Position shown as X/Y coordinates in the Properties panel.
- Scale shown as H/W (height and width) coordinates.
- Skew, created with the Transform tool.
- Rotation around the transformation point.
- Color, including tint, brightness, and alpha (transparency).
- Filters, like Drop Shadow, Blur, and Glow.

Suppose you want to change the width of a symbol or text field in the middle of a motion tween. So you drag the playhead to the point in the timeline where you want the change to happen. Then, with the tweened object selected, you make the width change using the W setting in the Properties panel. Flash automatically adds a diamond-shaped property keyframe to the tween span to mark the change. As seen on page 307, a single tween span can end up with bunches of property keyframes scattered all up and down the timeline. Single property keyframe markers can represent more than one property change, too; for example, you may have both a color change and a scale change in the same frame. Sometimes when you're working with your tween, you want to zero in on property keyframes for specific types of changes. Perhaps you want to double-check all the color property keyframes. In that case, right-click the timeline, and then choose View Keyframes from the shortcut menu, as shown in Figure 8-10. Toggle the different options until only the Color option is checkmarked.

---

**TIP** As you're trying out different effects with the Motion Editor, you may experiment your way from a good motion tween to a not-so-good motion tween. Don't forget about the History panel (Windows→Other Panels→History), where you can backtrack to a previous (and better) point in your work. Just drag the arrow handle on the left side of the panel back to where things looked good.

---

## Copying Properties Between Property Keyframes

There may be times when you want to duplicate the properties in one property keyframe to another elsewhere in the tween span, or perhaps to an entirely different tween span. For example, it's a great way to freeze the action for a certain number of frames. (Create two motion keyframes with identical properties. Insert frames in between the keyframes to lengthen the amount of time the action freezes. Or remove frames to make it shorter.)

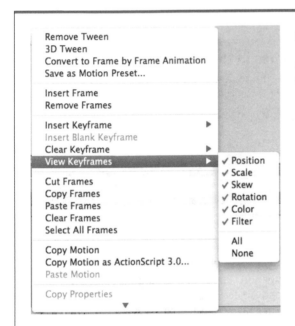

**FIGURE 8-10**

*You can select which property keyframes you want marked in the timeline. Right-click a tween span, and then choose View Keyframes to see this menu.*

---

**FREQUENTLY ASKED QUESTION**

### No Longer a Tween

*Can I change a tween to a frame-by-frame animation?*

Yes. Sometimes you may want to work with the individual frames inside a tween. Perhaps you want to copy and use them in another scene. Before you can do that, you need to convert the tween to a frame-by-frame animation. What you're basically doing is changing every frame in your tween to a keyframe that contains a copy of the tweened object with all the adjusted position, scale, rotation, and color properties.

Keep in mind, though, that doing so substantially increases the size of your Flash animation.

Right-click the tween span you want to convert. Choose "Convert to Frame by Frame Animation" from the shortcut menu. The blue tween highlight disappears from the timeline and is replaced with keyframes lined up like dominoes, as shown in Figure 8-11. These are standard keyframes, mind you, not property keyframes.

---

Start by Ctrl-clicking (⌘-clicking) the property keyframe you want to copy to select a single frame. Right-click that frame, and then choose Copy Properties from the shortcut menu. Head over to the destination frame where you want to paste the

properties and select that single frame using a Ctrl-click (⌘-click). Then, right-click
that selected frame; you can then choose Paste Properties to paste in all the properties, or Paste Properties Special, where you can specify which properties to paste.

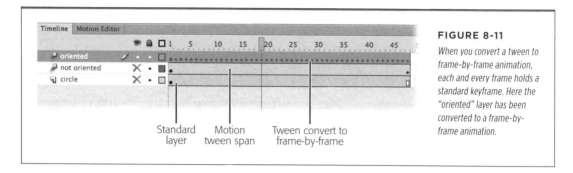

**FIGURE 8-11**

*When you convert a tween to
frame-by-frame animation,
each and every frame holds a
standard keyframe. Here the
"oriented" layer has been
converted to a frame-by-
frame animation.*

Standard layer   Motion tween span   Tween convert to frame-by-frame

# ■ A Tour of the Motion Editor

The Motion Editor is like a powerful microscope that lets you examine a motion
tween's innards. Combining the features of the timeline and the Properties panel,
the Motion Editor focuses on a single tween span, showing you its workings at a
seemingly molecular level. Not only that, but the Motion Editor also gives you the
power to make a change to any tweenable property at any point in time. With all
this firepower, you can create very complex tweens and control them with better
precision than ever before.

To open the Motion Editor, go to Window→Motion Editor. The Motion Editor won't
show its stuff unless you select either a tweened object on the stage or a tween span
in the timeline. (If you want to experiment with an existing tween, you can download
*08-4_Motion_Editor.fla* from the Missing CD page at *www.missingmanuals.com/
cds/flashcs6mm*.) At first glance, the Motion Editor may look a little intimidating,
with lots of properties, numbers, widgets, and graph lines. Don't be put off—it's not
tough to master these elements and bend those motion tweens to your iron will. If
you've used Flash's custom easing feature before (it's been around since Flash 8),
you have a head start.

**TIP**   Using the Essentials workspace, which this book uses throughout, the Motion Editor appears as a tab
below the stage, next to the timeline (Figure 8-12). If you have room, though, you may want to drag the tab to a
new location—like a second monitor. Giving the Motion Editor more room makes your work easier and faster.

There's a lot going on with the Motion Editor, so it's best to introduce yourself a
section at a time. At the very top, there are labels for each of its sections:

- Below the **Property** label, you see the same properties that you've used in the
  Properties panel, like the X/Y position coordinates, the W/H (width and height)
  properties, and so on.

- The **Value** settings should look familiar by now. For each property, you can click and type a new value, or you can drag to scrub in a value.

- The **Ease** tools (covered on page 320) let you speed up or slow down specific portions of your tweens. For example, you could make a moving car start off slowly and then gain speed.

- The triangle buttons under **Keyframe** give you a way to jump forward and backward among the property keyframes. You use the diamond button to add and delete property keyframes.

- The **Graph** gives you a visual representation of the way properties change over time, showing the property values as they increase and decrease. The vertical axis displays property values, while the horizontal axis measures time—just the way things are in the main timeline. The squares on the graph represent property keyframes. The graph isn't just some way to show you the geeky innards of your tween; it's a design tool. You can drag the graph elements around to make changes in your animation. (More on that on page 320.)

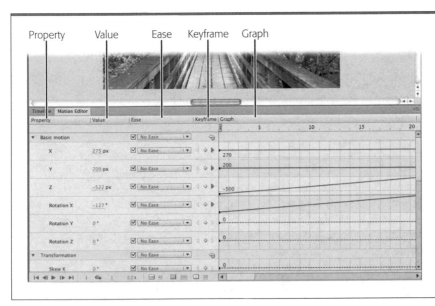

**FIGURE 8-12**

*At first, the Motion Editor may seem more like a tool for math geeks than one for graphic artists. Give it a chance, though. Master a couple of Motion Editor principles, and you'll enjoy the control and precision it provides.*

## Workflow for Common Tweens

You won't see anything at all in the Motion Editor unless you select a tween span in the timeline or a tweened object on the stage. Most of the time, you want to set up the basic framework of your tween in the main timeline before you work with the Motion Editor. That way, you can establish the timing for the major events in the tween, using some of the steps described on page 307. Using a famous cartoon example, you might have a coyote chase a roadrunner run off a cliff at Frame 6; then up to Frame 12, the coyote hangs in midair, feet churning; from Frame 12 to Frame 18, the coyote drops to the desert floor; and so on. After you have the basic timing for these major positions worked out, you can turn to the Motion Editor to perfect the details. The Motion Editor breaks down all the tweenable properties into five categories:

- "Basic motion" is where you change the X, Y, and Z properties, positioning tweened objects in two and three dimensions. (You can move only movie clips and text fields in three dimensions, so those are the only types of objects to which you can apply the Z property.)

- Under Transformation, you tween properties like Scale X (width), Scale Y (height), Skew X, and Skew Y.

- Color Effect includes properties for Alpha, Brightness, Tint, and Advanced Color (a combination of color effects).

- Use the Filters panel to apply filters like Glow, Blur, and Drop Shadow.

- Eases give you the ability to speed up or slow down property changes at specific points in the timeline. The details are on page 320.

Within each of those categories you can do the following:

- Add and remove property keyframes (page 313).

- Move property keyframes to change values and timing (page 314).

- Fine-tune and smooth property changes using Bezier curves (page 315).

- Add and remove color effects and filters (page 315).

- Apply easing to change the timing of property changes (page 320).

---

**TIP**   Keep in mind that a visual effect, like the aforementioned coyote, can be composed of several different tweened objects. The spinning legs can be a movie clip that stretches as gravity takes effect—the legs keep spinning but become elongated. Facial features like the mouth and eyes can be separate tweened objects on different layers, giving you the opportunity to create lots of different facial expressions.

---

## Adding and Removing Property Keyframes

In the Motion Editor, every property has its own graph line, as shown in Figure 8-13. Move from left to right along that graph line, and you're marking the passage of time. Like the main timeline, it's measured in frames on a scale at the top of the Motion Editor. The vertical axis of the graph tracks changes in value for that particular property. The units used differ according to the property. For example, if it's the Y coordinate in the "Basic motion" panel, the value relates to the vertical position of an object on the stage, and it's measured in pixels. If it's the alpha value in the Color Effect group, it's a percentage indicating the transparency (0%) or opacity (100%) of an object.

You apply tweens to values by placing property keyframes along the timeline; Flash calculates the changes for all the values between two property keyframes (Figure 8-13). To add a property keyframe, move the playhead to the frame where you want to record a change in value, and then click the diamond-shaped button under Keyframe. This button is a toggle: If there aren't any keyframes at that position, Flash creates one. If there's a keyframe at that position, Flash removes it.

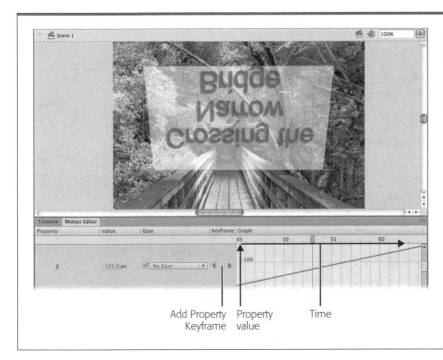

**FIGURE 8-13**

*Each property has a graph where the horizontal axis marks time in frames and the vertical axis shows the change in property values.*

Add Property Keyframe    Property value    Time

There are other ways to add property keyframes to a graph line. One of the quickest is simply to right-click at a point in the graph line and then choose Add Keyframe from the shortcut menu. Another way to add keyframes is to drag the playhead to a specific frame, and then make a change in a property's value. Flash automatically creates the property keyframe.

The Motion Editor uses a solid line in the graph to indicate values in between key-frames—values that are changing. A dashed line indicates that the values of the property aren't changing—static, in Flash-speak.

## Moving Property Keyframes

When you work with tweens, timing is everything. Whether you're controlling the movement of a jumping cheetah or changing the color of a building as it explodes, you control the timing by moving property keyframes left and right along the timeline. You reposition property keyframes in the Motion Editor's graph by dragging them with the Selection or Subselection tools. By moving the property keyframe up and down, you increase or decrease the value of that property. If you drag a property keyframe left or right along the graph's timeline, you change the frame (time) at which the property change happens.

There's another way you can move property keyframes along the timeline—with roving keyframes. Using this method, Flash keeps track of the relationship of keyframes even as you make changes to the timeline. See the box on page 324 for the details.

> **TIP** Sometimes when you move a property keyframe, the entire graph line moves. That's because you've somehow selected more than one property keyframe. To deselect all the property keyframes, just click an empty spot on the graph, and then try your move again.

## Fine-Tuning Property Changes

In the Motion Editor, the basic motion properties X, Y, and Z go everywhere hand in hand. Whenever you change one of the properties, the Motion Editor registers the values for the other two. It's Flash's way of keeping tweened objects pinned down in time and space. The basic motion properties are also the only properties that you can't fine-tune using Bezier line tools.

For any properties other than the basic motion properties, you can use Bezier controls in the Motion Editor graph to create smooth changes that increase or decrease over time. It's just like editing a line that you draw on the stage. The property keyframes can be either sharp-angled corner points where a value changes abruptly, or they can be gradual curves. Initially, property keyframes are corner points. Right-click a property keyframe to change a corner point to a curve, as shown in Figure 8-14. If there are property keyframes on both sides of the one you click, you can choose whether to add a single Bezier control handle ("Smooth left" or "Smooth right") or add two handles ("Smooth point"). If you right-click a property keyframe that's already a curve, you can turn it back into a corner point.

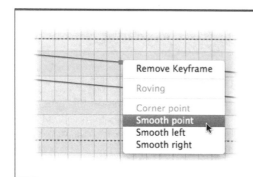

**FIGURE 8-14**

*Right-click a property keyframe to change a corner point to a curve. The menu shows different options depending on the position of the property keyframe.*

## Adding and Removing Color Effects

Your tween span has no color effects until you apply them (in the Properties panel or the Motion Editor). To add a color effect using the Motion Editor, position the playhead on the frame where you want to make a change, click the + button, and then choose the effect you want to add: Alpha, Brightness, Tint, or Advanced Color. Once you choose an effect, its subpanel appears under Color Effect. Click the Value setting to the right of the property name, and then type a new value.

**NOTE** Alpha sets the transparency for an object. If you want to apply a combination of alpha, brightness, and tint, use the Advanced Color option.

To remove a color effect, click the – button, and then choose the name of the effect from the pop-up menu. Flash removes the property changes from the tweened object, and the effect's subpanel goes away.

## Using Filters in Tweens

Flash includes a handful of standard filters that you apply to movie clips and text fields, and when you apply filters using the Motion Editor, you can change the values of these filters over time. Want a drop shadow to change its angle as the sun moves across your animation? You can do it with the Motion Editor (Figure 8-15).

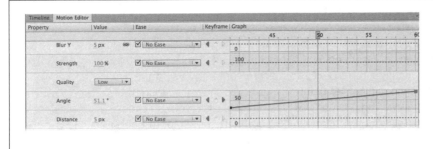

**FIGURE 8-15**

*Filters sometimes have multiple properties. The Drop Shadow filter shown here has properties for the shadow's blurriness, strength, quality, and angle. Not shown, there are even more properties for the color and type of shadow created.*

Don't be afraid to experiment with the filter effects. A single filter can create dramatically different effects, as shown in Figure 8-16.

## Customizing Your Motion Editor View

Working with Flash, you fight a constant battle to get a good view of the stage, the timeline, and all the panels and windows. It's a balancing act where you're constantly expanding this and shrinking that. Adding the Motion Editor to the mix just makes the problem tougher. It's so packed with properties, graphs, and widgets that it requires tweaking to achieve a workspace that works for you. If you plan to do a lot of work in Flash and you don't have a two-monitor system, think seriously about upgrading to one. With two monitors, you can leave your Motion Editor open on one monitor and keep your stage and main timeline open on another. To move the Motion Editor, or remove it from a docked position, drag it by the tab with its name on it.

Initially, Flash gives you a fairly skimpy view of each property. Some of the panels are closed, depending on the kinds of changes in your tween. To open and close panels, click the triangle toggle buttons, as shown in Figure 8-17.

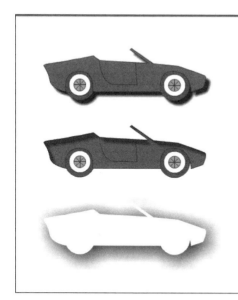

**FIGURE 8-16**

*You don't have to settle for the first effect a filter gives you. The Drop Shadow filter, for example, gives some remarkably different effects.*

*Top: When you first apply a drop shadow, it looks like this.*

*Middle: Adjusting the inner shadow gives the car a more 3-D look.*

*Bottom: The Knockout property makes the car look like a paper cutout.*

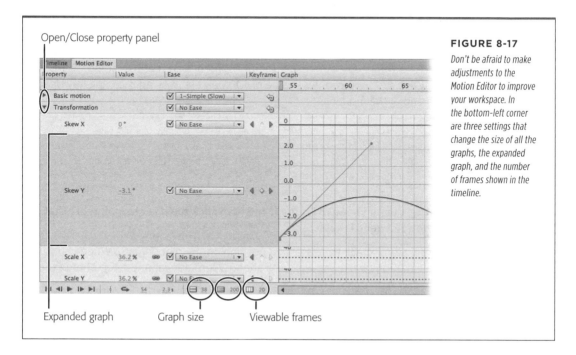

**FIGURE 8-17**

*Don't be afraid to make adjustments to the Motion Editor to improve your workspace. In the bottom-left corner are three settings that change the size of all the graphs, the expanded graph, and the number of frames shown in the timeline.*

### ■ GETTING THE BEST VIEW PROPERTY GRAPHS

Unlike some windows, you can't change the amount of horizontal space occupied by labeled sections like Property, Value, and Ease, but you can change the vertical space in a number of ways. That vertical space is what's important when you're trying to get a good view of the property graphs while you perfect, for example, a custom ease (page 323). You can expand a single property graph by clicking anywhere in the panel to the left of the graph. That graph remains expanded until you click the panel again. Two settings in the lower-left corner of the Motion Editor control the height of graphs. A third setting controls the number of frames displayed in the Motion Editor timeline:

- Graph Size sets the height of all the graphs.

- Expanded Graph Size sets the height of the one expanded graph.

- Viewable Frames sets the number of frames showing in the graph timeline.

## ■ Changing Transparency with the Motion Editor

Now it's time to turn some of that Motion Editor theory to practice. By now, you know how to tween dimensions (page 107) and position (page 103); now you'll learn how to change the transparency of a tweened symbol. As shown in Figure 8-18, the Missing CD file *08-5_Tween_Alpha.fla* shows an animated sign for a car company, but you can use your own symbol if you prefer. In the sample file, the sign spins and bounces as it gets bigger, giving the impression that it's coming at the audience. In the following steps, you adjust the transparency so that the sign goes from an alpha value of 20 percent to a value of 100 percent, making it completely opaque at the end of the motion.

---

**NOTE** Techies often refer to transparency as the *alpha channel*. Typically, computer video has RGB channels for red, green, and blue. To store information about the opacity and transparency of an image, programmers needed another channel, and they dubbed it the alpha channel, because they needed another letter and why not start at the beginning of the alphabet?

---

1. **Drag the playhead to Frame 1, and then click the layer to make sure that the motion tween is selected.**

   Your sign is back to its starting position on the motion path. When you select the motion tween, the words "Motion Tween" appear at the top of the Properties panel.

2. **Click the Motion Editor tab next to the Timeline tab.**

   If you don't see the Motion Editor tab, choose Window→Motion Editor to make it visible, as shown in Figure 8-19.

3. **In the Motion Editor window, find the Color Effect section, and then click the + button to add an alpha color effect to the tween.**

   If some of the panels are expanded, you may not see the Color Effect panel right away. Either close the open panels by clicking their expand/collapse triangles, or use the scroll bar to find the Color Effect panel. When you click the + button, a shortcut menu gives you four color-related choices: Alpha, Brightness, Tint, and Advanced Color. After you choose Alpha, a new subpanel opens, showing an alpha amount as a percentage.

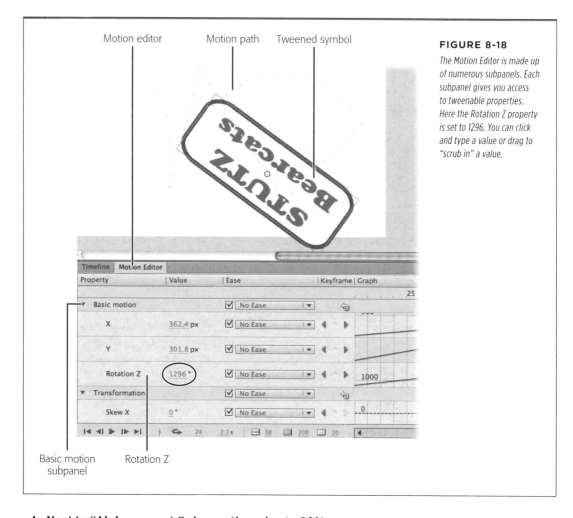

**FIGURE 8-18**

*The Motion Editor is made up of numerous subpanels. Each subpanel gives you access to tweenable properties. Here the Rotation Z property is set to 1296. You can click and type a value or drag to "scrub in" a value.*

4. **Next to "Alpha amount," change the value to 20%.**

   You can click the number and type *20*, or you can scrub the value until 20 appears in the box. Notice how the graph to the right changes as you change the value.

5. **Click the Timeline tab, and then drag the playhead to the last frame.**

By moving the playhead to a new location, you can enter a different alpha value to create the tween.

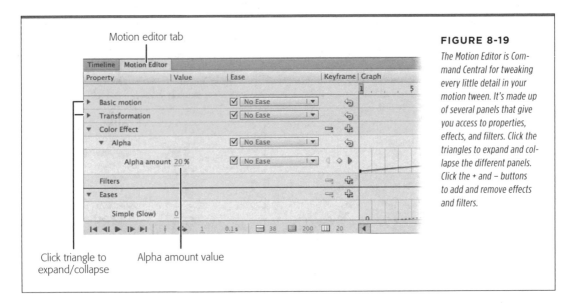

Motion editor tab

Click triangle to expand/collapse

Alpha amount value

**FIGURE 8-19**

*The Motion Editor is Command Central for tweaking every little detail in your motion tween. It's made up of several panels that give you access to properties, effects, and filters. Click the triangles to expand and collapse the different panels. Click the + and – buttons to add and remove effects and filters.*

6. **Click the Motion Editor tab, and then change the Alpha amount to 100%.**

Setting the Alpha amount to 100% makes the sign symbol completely opaque.

7. **Test your animation in Flash or using the Flash Player.**

At this point, the animation looks pretty much the same whether you run it inside Flash (Enter) or you compile the animation and test it in the Flash Player (Ctrl+Enter or ⌘-Return). Position, size, and alpha properties are all visible inside Flash, but that's not always the case with some filters, components, timeline effects, and ActionScript code.

# ■ Easing Tweens

When Flash creates a tween, it doesn't use an artist's eye; it uses an accountant's calculator. If a cartoon roadrunner sprints across the desert, it moves exactly the same distance in each frame, even though we all know that cartoon roadrunners start slowly, build up speed, and then slow as they skid to a stop, usually with a little thwang motion at the end. It's up to you to add realistic (or, if you prefer, cartoonistic) motion to your animations, and fortunately, the Ease tools are there to help. When you apply an *ease* to one of the properties in your tween span, Flash recalculates how much of a change takes place in each frame. Suppose you want an object, like a moving car, to roll gradually to a stop. You can apply an ease that makes the car move farther in the first few frames, and then shorter distances in the final frames until it stops, as shown in Figure 8-20.

**FIGURE 8-20**

*These two tweens are onion-skinned to show the car in several different frames. The tween on the top has no ease. The Simple (Fastest) ease was applied to the tween on the bottom.*

## Applying an Ease Preset

Flash comes with several ease presets, as shown in the menu in Figure 8-21. Ease presets aren't limited to changing the position of an object; you can apply them individually to specific properties. For example, if you have a lamp shining a yellow light, you can make that light blink on and off by applying a Square Wave ease to the alpha value (transparency) of the light. (A square wave is binary; it's either on or off.)

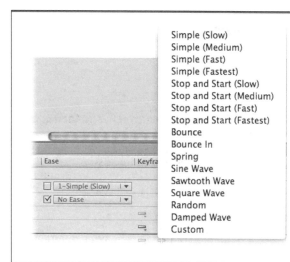

Simple (Slow)
Simple (Medium)
Simple (Fast)
Simple (Fastest)
Stop and Start (Slow)
Stop and Start (Medium)
Stop and Start (Fast)
Stop and Start (Fastest)
Bounce
Bounce In
Spring
Sine Wave
Sawtooth Wave
Square Wave
Random
Damped Wave
Custom

**FIGURE 8-21**

*Flash gives you ease presets that you apply in the Motion Editor's Eases panel.*

There are a couple of steps for applying an *ease preset*. First, you need to add the ease preset to the Motion Editor's Eases panel. Then you apply the ease to one or more properties, using the drop-down menus that appear in the Ease section of each property. Here are the step-by-step details for adding the Square Wave ease to make a light blink. You can create your own lamp and light, or you can use the simple desk lamp provided in *08-6_Ease_Tween.fla* found at *www.missingmanuals.com/cds/flashcs6mm*. In either case, make sure the light emanating from your lamp is a movie clip on its own layer, and give yourself about 48 frames for the tween span.

1. **With the light's tween selected, as shown in Figure 8-22, open the Motion Editor (Window→Motion Editor).**

   The Motion Editor panel opens, with the Eases panel at the bottom.

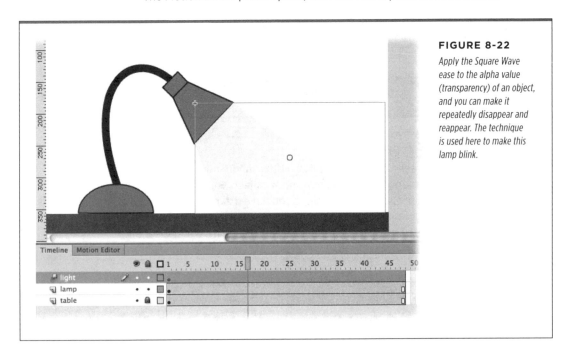

**FIGURE 8-22**

*Apply the Square Wave ease to the alpha value (transparency) of an object, and you can make it repeatedly disappear and reappear. The technique is used here to make this lamp blink.*

2. **In the Eases panel, click the + button to add a new tween, and then choose Square Wave from the shortcut menu.**

   When you click the + button, you see the Eases menu (Figure 8-21). After you select the Square Wave ease, a subpanel for Square Wave appears under the Eases panel (with any other eases belonging to the tween span).

3. **In the Square Wave property subpanel, set the value to 6.**

   Eases have a related value, but the function of the value may be different depending on the ease. The Square Wave's value controls the number of changes. In this case, it controls the number of times your lamp blinks on or off.

4. **In the Color Effect panel, click the + button, and then choose Alpha from the pop-up menu.**

   An Alpha subpanel appears under the Color Effect panel.

5. **In the Motion Editor's timeline, move the playhead to the last frame of the tween, and then set the alpha value to 0.**

   Without any easing, this causes the light to gradually dim from 100% to 0%.

6. **In the Color Effect→Alpha panel, in the Ease section, choose Square Wave, as shown in Figure 8-23.**

The Square Wave ease is applied to all the Color Effect properties. You can see that the Alpha property subpanel is also set to Square Wave. You can apply an ease in some of the category panels, like the Transformation category, where it applies to all the properties in that category, or you can apply it individually to each property.

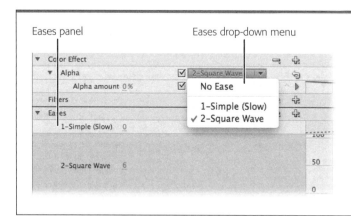

**FIGURE 8-23**

*Once you've added an ease to the Eases panel, you can apply it to any property, using the Ease drop-down menu.*

7. **Test your animation.**

The light flashes from on to off and then back again. It changes six times, matching the value in the Square Wave subpanel.

After you've applied an ease to a property, the graph shows two lines, as shown in Figure 8-24. The solid line shows any property changes that were originally in that tween span. The dotted line shows the property changes after you apply the tween.

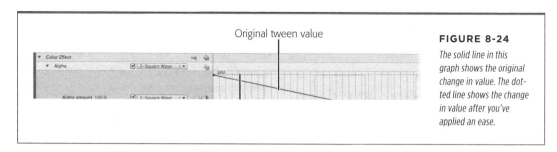

**FIGURE 8-24**

*The solid line in this graph shows the original change in value. The dotted line shows the change in value after you've applied an ease.*

## Creating a Custom Ease Preset

You can create your own ease presets and store them in your Flash file. Once you've created a preset, you apply it just as you would any other ease preset. Flash names your preset for you, so you'll have to remember what your 3-Custom and 5-Custom ease presets do. Flash saves the presets in your Flash file, so you can use them with any property and they'll be there the next time you open the file. However, you can't use your custom ease in other Flash documents; they're available only in the document in which you created them.

To create a custom ease, click the + button in the Eases panel, and instead of choosing one of Adobe's predesigned ease presets, choose Custom at the bottom of the menu. A custom preset appears in the panel with any other eases you may be using in your document. There's a line in the graph ready for you to edit (Figure 8-25). You use Flash's standard line and Bezier tools to change the shape of the line, and subsequently change the values of any property, once the ease is applied. Page 71 has some tips on editing Bezier curves that were created with the Pen tool. You can use those same techniques with Motion Editor graphs.

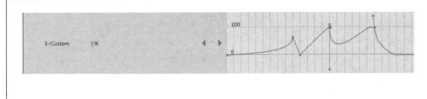

**FIGURE 8-25**

*Use Flash's Bezier tools to modify the graph line in a custom ease preset. It may take some trial and error to become proficient in designing custom ease presets.*

**FREQUENTLY ASKED QUESTION**

## The Keyframe Rovers

*What's a roving keyframe...and why do I care?*

Roving keyframes are a concept that migrated from Adobe's After Effects program to Flash. Roving keyframes apply only to properties in the "Basic motion" category (X, Y, and Z). You can think of a roving keyframe as a keyframe that's not tied down to a specific frame. You're letting Flash move that keyframe horizontally along the timeline so the speed of a motion remains consistent throughout the tween.

As for the second part of your question, roving keyframes are especially helpful if you've messed with the motion path on the stage by dragging the tweened object to different locations.

Often, this type of editing changes the path segment in a way that affects its timing.

You can change an entire motion path to roving keyframes by right-clicking the motion path on the stage, or right-clicking the tween span in the timeline and then choosing Motion Path→"Switch keyframes to roving" in the shortcut menu. Using the same technique, you can remove all the roving keyframes by choosing Motion Path→"Switch keyframes to non-roving." If you want to convert a single keyframe, select the single frame in the timeline with a right-click (Control-click), and then choose the option from the Motion Path submenu.

# Realistic Animation with IK Bones

Everywhere you look in the real world, you see things that are linked together: a dog and its tail, a ribbon and a bow, a train engine and its caboose. And then, of course, there's that song about the thigh bone connected to the hip bone. When objects are connected, they move differently than they do in isolation, since the movement of each linked part influences the movement of the others. Flash gives you a special tool—the Bone tool—that lets you link these kinds of objects, so when you move the hip bone, the thigh bone automatically moves in a realistic manner. The animation tool you use is appropriately called a *bone*; specifically an *IK bone*. IK stands for *inverse kinematics*, which is the type of animation algorithm at work here, but you don't have to remember that. You can just call them "bones," and know that you're using the same technology that computer game developers use to make onscreen characters move realistically.

In this chapter, you'll learn about the two different ways you can use Flash's IK Bones tool—with symbols, and with shapes. When you use bones with symbols, you link one symbol to another. For example, suppose you have a train in your animation. Each car is a separate, carefully drawn symbol. Using bones, you can link the engine to the coal car, the coal car to the boxcar, and so on, all the way down to the caboose. The other way you can use bones is with shapes. In the past, if you wanted to draw a snake, you'd have a hard time getting that snake to squirm and slither properly. You'd have had to painstakingly reposition, distort, or even redraw several versions of the snake to make a good animation. Now you can draw a snake, place bones inside that single shape, and then bend the shape into realistic poses, which makes it easy to reposition or pose your snake for some realistic slithering and sliding.

When you use bones in your animation, you spend a lot of time creating "poses" where each element is in just the right position. Flash Professional CS6 has tools to make the posing process go smoothly. You can use constraints and pins, for example. If those options sound restrictive...well, they are. The purpose of these tools is to keep your animated elements from flopping around, making it much easier to create the proper pose.

---

**NOTE** When you use IK Bones, make sure you start off with an ActionScript 3.0–compatible document. For example, after you go to File→New, choose ActionScript 3.0, Air, "AIR for Android," or "AIR for iOS." If you choose ActionScript 2.0, you get no bones.

---

## ■ Linking Symbols with Bones

What better way to show how IK bones link one symbol to another than with a chain made up of separate links? Just to show that all the linked symbols don't have to be identical, you can throw in a padlock at the end. If you want to get a feeling for the end result, then open the file *09-2_Simple_Bones_Done.fla*. If you're ready to start earning your bones, then open the file *09-1_Simple_Bones.fla*. You'll find both files on the Missing CD page at *www.missingmanuals.com/cds/flashcs6mm*.

1. **Open the Flash document *09-1_Simple_Bones.fla*.**

   There are six hollow ellipses on the stage that look like the links in a chain. In the Library, there are two movie clips: link and padlock. The links on the stage are different colors. Click a link to select it, and then in the Properties panel under Color Effect, you see that it's colored using the Tint color effect.

2. **Drag the padlock symbol from the Library and position it on the stage so the lock's shackle overlaps the rightmost link in the chain, as shown in Figure 9-1.**

   Before you start linking symbols together, you need to make sure you have every symbol on the stage. You can't add new symbols to the bones layer after you've created a bone with the IK Bone tool.

3. **Select View→Snapping→"Snap to Objects" to turn "Snap to Objects" off.**

   It's easier to position bones precisely in objects if you turn off the cursor's snapping action.

4. **Click the Bone tool (or press M, the hot key for the Bone tool).**

   The Bone tool is in the middle of the Tools palette, and there are two tools under the Bone icon. The one on the top is the Bone tool; the one on the bottom is the Bind tool. The cursor for the Bone tool is a bone and a plus sign. When the Bone tool is over an object to which you can attach a bone, the solid black bone turns into a hollow bone.

5. **Click the left side of the leftmost link and, while holding the button down, drag to the right until you reach the left side of the next link, as shown in Figure 9-2.**

You may want to zoom in so that you can carefully place each bone. You drag to create a bone. The first place you click creates the head of the bone; when you release the mouse button, you create the tail of the bone. The head, indicated by the large circle, becomes the registration point for the bone, and the symbol to which it's attached. That means that the bone symbol pivots around the head of the bone. When you create a series of bones, known in Flash-speak as an *armature*, the first bone is known as the *root* bone. The head of the root bone takes on special importance, since it's the registration point for the entire armature or family of symbols.

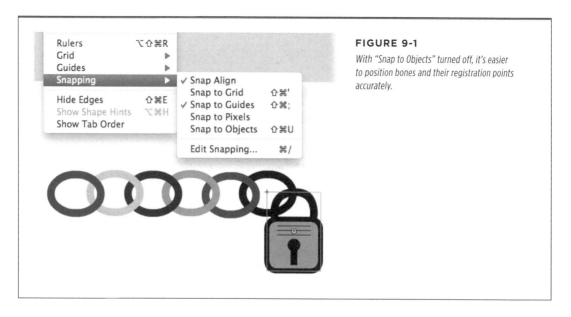

**FIGURE 9-1**

*With "Snap to Objects" turned off, it's easier to position bones and their registration points accurately.*

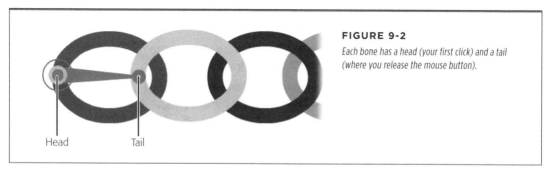

**FIGURE 9-2**

*Each bone has a head (your first click) and a tail (where you release the mouse button).*

If you glance at the timeline, you notice that adding the first bone creates a new armature layer (also called *pose layer*) in the timeline (Figure 9-3). Similar to a motion tween layer, the pose layer has special properties.

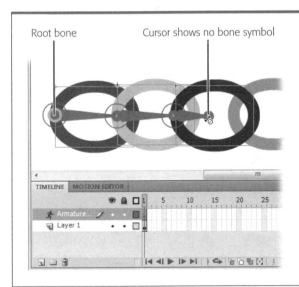

Root bone    Cursor shows no bone symbol

**FIGURE 9-3**

*When you create a bone, Flash automatically creates an "arma-ture" or pose layer. The pose layer is similar to a motion tween layer, but with a couple of twists to make it work with bones.*

6. **From the tail of the first bone, drag to create another bone that connects to the next link in the chain.**

    You can attach bones to either the head or the tail of the first bone. In this case, you attach a second bone to the tail. As you drag, notice that the cursor shows a "no" symbol (a circle with a line through it) when you're over the empty stage or some other object where it's not possible to link your bone. It turns back to a + when the cursor is over a suitable target. In this case, that target is another symbol.

    When you link to a new symbol, Flash automatically repositions the transforma-tion point to the point where the bones connect. The transformation point is the point around which the symbol rotates.

7. **Repeat this process for the remainder of the chain links until you finally connect the last bone to the padlock's shackle.**

    In this animation, all the links in the chain are instances of the same symbol, but often you'll use bones with lots of different symbols. For example, if you were applying bones to the symbols that make up a human body, there'd be sepa-rate symbols for the head, neck, torso, parts of the arms and hands, and so on.

    **TIP** If necessary, you can switch to another tool, like the Hand tool, to get a better view of your work. You can then go back to the Bone tool and add more bones. The one thing you can't do is add new symbols or drawings to the pose layer.

8. **In the pose layer, click Frame 30, and then press F5 to create a frame.**

   The pose layer extends to become 30 frames long. You can make the pose layer any length you wish, and you can add and remove frames from the pose layer as you would any other layer.

9. **With the Selection tool, click Frame 5, and then drag the padlock to a new position (Figure 9-4).**

   The pose layer is similar to a motion tween layer (page 103). When you reposition the padlock in Frame 5, Flash creates a tween to animate the motion from Frame 1 to Frame 5. The frame where you create a new pose is marked with a small diamond, and it's called a pose frame.

   The bones connecting all the links in the chain and the padlock constrain the movement of each symbol, giving the entire family of symbols a connected sense of motion. Not only that, but it's also easier for you, the artist, to position the symbols, because they really are connected to one another.

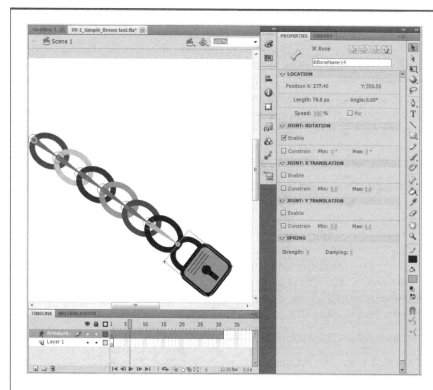

**FIGURE 9-4**

*Pose the chain by dragging the lock or by dragging individual links. When you drag a link, the links up to the top rotate around their transformation points; the links down to the lock don't rotate.*

10. **Click Frame 10 and reposition one of the middle links in the chain.**

    Bones have a parent-child relationship. When you move one of the middle links, the motion is different, in that the links on the tail end of the chain move as one group. With a little practice, you'll learn to use the parent-child relationship of the bones to quickly pose linked symbols.

11. **Every five frames or so, continue to pose the chain and padlock.**

Experiment to get a feeling for the motion. You can create a new pose by dragging either a bone or the symbol attached to the bone. You can use either the Selection tool or the Bone tool to create a pose. If you want a quick preview, press Enter to see the animation play. You can make it swing back and forth, like a chain attached to a wall or a door, or you can make it move like a snake charmer's cobra. Try some different techniques and positions.

12. **Press Ctrl+Enter (⌘-Return) to test the animation.**

The chain links and the padlock move. The head of the root bone acts as an anchor. The entire armature can pivot around the head, but it remains fixed at that point.

## Changing the Pose Layer

Creating just the right motion is more art than science. Think about how many movement details there are in a running cheetah, or a swinging pendulum, or a slithering snake. Chances are, you'll fiddle with the pose layer after you finish using the Bone tool. For example, you may want to slow down or speed up the action. You may want to hold the armature (that is, all the linked bones and their related symbols) in a certain position for a few beats, and then continue the motion. You may want to smooth the motion or make it more erratic. You can make those changes by changing the relationship of the pose frames in the pose layer. For example, adding or removing frames changes the timing of the animation. Copying and pasting frames can freeze the action for an interval.

For most actions, you need to select specific frames in the pose layer before you cut, copy, paste, and so on. In many respects, you manage the pose layer and its frames the same way you manage other layers. Its behavior is similar to that of motion tween layers. The pose layer is colored green so you can distinguish it from normal layers and tween layers, which are shaded with other colors. There's also a little figure of a person to the left of the layer name. Each frame with a small diamond is a *pose frame*. These frames are similar to keyframes in a normal standard layer; they mark a point in the timeline where you've defined exactly how the animated object is positioned. Flash is responsible for positioning (tweening) the other frames.

Here's the lowdown on some common operations you can perform in the pose layer:

- **Speed up or slow down animation.** Move the cursor to the end of the pose layer. When the cursor is over the right edge, the cursor changes to show arrowheads pointing left and right. Drag to extend or shorten the pose layer. Flash inserts or removes frames, making the playing time longer or shorter. As much as possible, Flash keeps the pose frames in the same position relative to one another. Of course, if you really shrink the layer, all the pose frames get bunched together.

- **Select frames.** Click to select a single frame in the pose layer. Double-click to select all the frames in the pose. Click and drag to select a sequence of frames. Selected frames show a different highlight color. Once the frames are selected, you can copy, paste, or delete them.

- **Remove frames.** After you've selected the frames you want to remove, right-click (or Control-click) the selected frames. A shortcut menu appears, displaying options related to the pose layer, as shown in Figure 9-5. Click Remove Frames to remove all the selected frames. (This action removes the standard frames in the pose layer as well as the pose frames.)

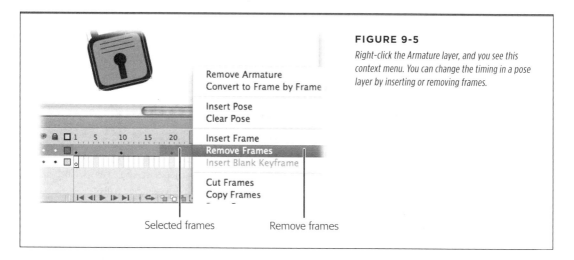

**FIGURE 9-5**

*Right-click the Armature layer, and you see this context menu. You can change the timing in a pose layer by inserting or removing frames.*

Selected frames          Remove frames

- **Insert a pose.** The pose layer has two types of frames. The pose frames, which display a small diamond, are like keyframes for the armature, where you position every part of the armature just the way you want. The other frames are tweened frames, where Flash determines the position of the armature. You can turn a tweened frame into a pose frame in a number of ways. First, move the playhead to the frame you want to change, and then press F6. Flash turns the frame into a pose frame. You can also right-click the frame in the pose layer and then choose Insert Pose from the shortcut menu. Inserting a pose doesn't add any frames to the timeline; it simply converts the frame at the playhead to a pose.

- **Clear a pose.** If you want to clear a specific pose frame in your timeline but leave the rest of it intact, click the frame you want to change. You don't need to Ctrl-click (or ⌘-click) in this case. The playhead moves to the clicked frame. Right-click (or Control-click), and then choose Clear Pose from the shortcut menu. This action removes the pose but doesn't remove the frame. The position of the armature changes because it's now controlled by the closest pose frames before or after the displayed frame. If you want to clear several pose frames at once, you can Ctrl-drag (⌘-drag) to select several frames, right-click, and then choose Clear Pose to convert the pose frames to standard frames. Clearing a pose doesn't remove frames from the pose layer.

• **Copy a pose.** If you want your carefully positioned armature to remain in the same position for a few frames, one way to do that is to copy the desired pose and then paste it back into the pose layer. The frames in between two identical pose frames will all be the same. To copy a pose, Ctrl-click (⌘-click) to select a frame in the pose layer, right-click it, and then choose Copy Pose from the shortcut menu.

• **Cut a pose.** Similar to copying a pose, except that it actually removes the pose from the frame at the playhead. You can then paste it somewhere else (earlier or later) in the pose layer. To cut a pose, Ctrl-click (⌘-click) to select a frame in the pose layer, right-click it, and then choose Cut Pose from the shortcut menu.

• **Paste a pose.** When you copy or cut a pose, the next logical action is to paste that pose into the pose layer on a different frame. Ctrl-click (⌘-click) to select the frame where you want to place the pose. Then, right-click (Control-click) and choose Paste Pose from the shortcut menu.

---

**FREQUENTLY ASKED QUESTION**

### Combining Bones and Tweening

*How do I tween color, dimensions, and other properties when I use IK Bones?*

There's one important difference between a pose layer and a motion tween layer: A pose layer tweens only the position of the symbols or shapes; you can't tween colors, dimensions, or any of the other properties that you can change in a motion tween. If you want to change those properties, too, the solution is to create your animation in the pose layer, and then wrap the entire animation in a movie clip or graphic symbol (Modify→"Convert to Symbol" or F8).

Once the bone's animation is contained in a symbol, you can add it to your main timeline as you would any symbol. Just drag it onto the stage. At that point, you apply a motion tween to the entire movie clip or graphic. This trick also lets you use filters or blends on the animation.

So wrapping your pose layer in a movie clip or graphic symbol gives you the best of both worlds: IK Bones' help in creating an animation and all the power of a motion tween to transform your animated object.

---

## Creating Branching Armatures

In the lock and chain example earlier in this chapter (page 326), the armature linked symbols together in one long chain. Often, though, you want to create an armature that branches out at different points. The classic example is a human body. The less classic example, as in this case, is a robot. For this exercise, start with a new copy of the file *09-3_Branch_Armature.fla* from the Missing CD page at *www.missingmanuals.com/cds/flashcs6mm*.

In this example, you'll operate on a robot with a somewhat human shape. As shown in Figure 9-6, the armature for the robot isn't quite complete.

1. **Open the file *09-3_Branch_Armature.fla*.** If you don't see the robot's bones (armature), use the Selection tool to click the robot's chest.

   When you click the robot with the Select, Subselect, or Bone tools, you see the armature that holds it together.

2. **In the "right arm" layer, click the Show/Hide button (beneath the eye icon) twice to hide and then unhide the layer.**

All the pieces for the arm on the right are in a separate layer from the pose layer and the armature. You can't draw directly in a pose layer with an existing armature, but you can add symbols from another layer to an existing armature, which is what you'll do in the next step.

3. **With the bone tool, click the thick circle in the root bone, and then drag a new branching bone to the right shoulder, as shown in Figure 9-6.**

When you connect from the root bone to the upper arm (technically called the *humerus*), the symbol is automatically moved from the "right arm" layer to the pose layer, and the bone is connected.

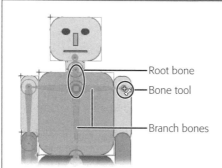

**FIGURE 9-6**

*The root bone (circled) goes from the upper torso to the neck. Branch bones are already created to the left arm and down to the hips. Here a new branch is being created to the right shoulder.*

Root bone

Bone tool

Branch bones

4. **Continue to create bones for the robot's right arm and hand.**

As each bone is added, the connected symbol is moved from the "right arm" layer into the pose layer.

You can add bones that branch from the head or tail of any bone, and, as you see in this example, you can create multiple branches from the same joint. So if you want to create a spider, for example, you can create eight legs that all connect to the same joint.

**NOTE** One thing you can't do is reconnect the tail of a bone to an existing bone. For example, you can't connect a bone from the hand to the hipbone.

## Controlling the Degree of Rotation

Bodies, even robot bodies, have their limits. You don't want your robot flapping around like a rag doll. In terms of IK Bones, that means you don't want every bone in the robot armature to have full movement to rotate 360 degrees. Constraining rotation is one of the ways you can create realistic movement when you're using bones. Once you put constraints on rotation, it's easier for you to set up pose frames, too.

Also, by turning off "Joint: Rotation," you can prevent bones from pivoting around specific joints. If you want to provide a certain degree of motion around a point, you leave the "Joint: Rotation" turned on, but constrain the motion by providing a minimum and maximum number of degrees for rotation.

> **TIP** When you work with more complex armatures with lots of branching bones, it's sometimes hard to control all the flopping parts. When you're just getting started, it's helpful to save (File→Save As) multiple copies of your file with different names, like *robot_arms_down.fla* or *robot_running.fla*. Save a few versions where you're happy with the poses. Then if things get out of hand as you're working on your file, you have a saved file as a backup.

In the next few steps, you'll see how to prevent rotation and how to constrain rotation:

1. **In the *09-3_Branch_Armature.fla* from the previous section, click the bone you created in step 3 on page 333.**

   When you select the bone that connects the root bone to the top of the right arm, the Properties panel shows settings specific to that bone. There are four subpanels: Location, "Joint: Rotation," "Joint: X Translation," and "Joint: Y Translation."

2. **In Properties→"Joint: Rotation," click to turn off the Enable checkbox.**

   Once you turn off the Enable checkbox for "Joint: Rotation," the armature won't pivot around that joint. You want the robot's arms to pivot around a joint near the shoulder, not in the center of the torso.

3. **With the bone still selected, click the Child button at the top of the Properties panel (shown in Figure 9-7), to select the bone that connects to the right forearm.**

   The humerus bone is selected, and the Properties panel shows the related settings.

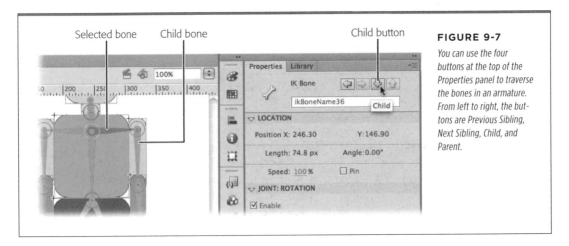

Selected bone    Child bone                    Child button

**FIGURE 9-7**

*You can use the four buttons at the top of the Properties panel to traverse the bones in an armature. From left to right, the buttons are Previous Sibling, Next Sibling, Child, and Parent.*

4. **Drag the selected bone to examine its movement.**

The horizontal bone from the torso to the top of the arm remains locked in place, in effect creating a shoulder. The humerus pivots around the joint at the top of the bone. It can pivot a full 360 degrees.

5. **Under Properties→"Joint: Rotation," click the Constrain button.**

With a check in the Constrain checkbox, the Min and Max settings come to life.

6. **Enter a value of −45 in the Min box and a value of 45 in the Max box.**

Min and Max settings are displayed as degrees. You can click and type in a value, or you can scrub in a value. Scrubbing is a good option, because Flash shows the joint's angle as you scrub, as shown in Figure 9-8. With the constraints, the robot arm has a more appropriate range of movement. (Well, appropriate for a robot, not what you'd want in a major league pitcher.)

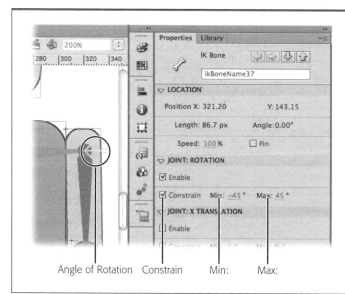

**FIGURE 9-8**

*As you type or scrub in a Min and Max "Joint: Rotation" value, Flash shows you the angle of rotation superimposed over the joint.*

If you want to create a well-behaved robot, you can repeat these steps to turn off or constrain the rotation in the other joints. Once you've done that, you can make your robot dance a jig by creating different poses in the pose layer.

## Moving Bones

No matter how talented or lucky you are, it's unlikely you're going to get your IK Bones animations exactly right the first time you set them up. You can, and probably will, edit the pose layer (as shown on page 330), and edit the armature (as described in this section).

Here's a good example of a problem and solution continuing from the exercise begun on page 326. If you drag the padlock down as far as it can reach, it ends up beyond the bottom of the stage. The next few steps show how to move the entire chain and padlock up higher in the animation.

Here are the steps to move the entire armature to a new location:

1. **Open the Flash document *09-1_Simple_Bones.fla*.**

   If you haven't done the steps on page 326, do so now. Then continue here with step 2.

2. **Click the first frame in the pose layer.**

   The playhead moves to the first frame in the layer.

3. **Select the root bone.**

   The root bone is the first bone you created, and in this case, you need to actually select the bone; just selecting the symbol attached to the bone won't do the trick. A selected bone is highlighted in a different color. The color depends on your preference settings in Edit→Preferences→General (Flash→Preferences→General). When you move the root bone to a new location, the other bones (sometimes referred to as *children* or *child bones*) move with the root.

   When you select any bone, the Properties panel displays settings related to the bone. The subpanels include Location, "Joint: Rotation," "Joint: X Translation," and "Joint: Y Translation" (Figure 9-9).

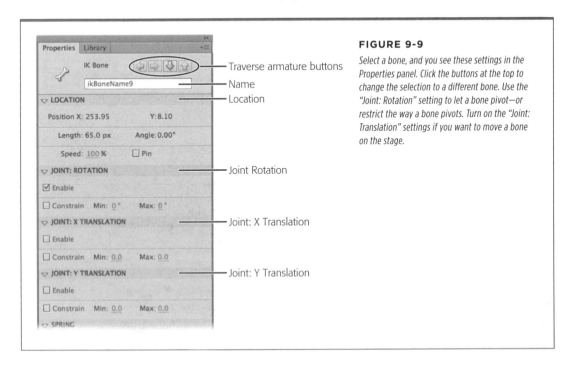

**FIGURE 9-9**

*Select a bone, and you see these settings in the Properties panel. Click the buttons at the top to change the selection to a different bone. Use the "Joint: Rotation" setting to let a bone pivot—or restrict the way a bone pivots. Turn on the "Joint: Translation" settings if you want to move a bone on the stage.*

4. **In Properties→"Joint: Rotation," click to turn off the Enable checkbox.**

When you first create a root bone, "Joint: Rotation" is turned on and "Joint: X Translation" and "Joint: Y Translation" are turned off. These initial settings keep the entire armature rooted to one spot on the stage.

Turning off "Joint: Rotation" on this bone prevents the entire armature from spinning around when all you want to do is move it.

5. **In Properties→"Joint: X Translation," turn on the Enable checkbox.** Do the same in Properties→"Joint: Y Translation."

With "Joint: X Translation" and "Joint: Y Translation" turned on, you can move the root bone and the entire armature along the X and Y axes.

6. **Drag the root bone up to the top center of the stage.**

The root bone and the armature move slowly as you drag them to a new location. There may be some rotation around the joints of some of the child bones as you move the armature. You can prevent this movement by turning off "Joint: Rotation." Remove the checkmark from Properties→"Joint: Rotation"→Enable.

7. **Turn Properties→"Joint: Rotation" back on.** Turn both Properties→"Joint: X Translation" and Properties→"Joint: Y Translation" back off.

Now that you've moved the armature, these changes reset the properties of the root bone to their previous settings.

8. **Drag the padlock and some of the links on the chain.**

Notice that the armature's movement and action hasn't changed, just the location.

In these steps, you changed the location of the chain in Frame 1. If you move the playhead along the timeline, you see that this move didn't change the chain's position in the other pose frames. This setup probably isn't what you want for this particular animation, but it shows a point: One way to create movement about the stage when you're working with an armature is to move the root bone between poses. Another way to animate movement is to wrap your armature inside a movie clip or graphic symbol, and then use a motion tween to create movement around the stage.

## Repositioning Symbol Instances

You don't always want your symbols to move in lockstep. There are times when you want some of the symbols to rotate on their own or even move away from the rest of the armature. For example, suppose you have a clown cartoon character who keeps losing his hat. The hat bounces around his head at different angles and perhaps even flies off, only to snap back into place. When you connect symbols to one another using bones, you can reposition the symbols independently using the usual transform tools. For example, you can "break" the chain in the previous example, as shown in Figure 9-10. Select the Transform tool, and then rotate one of the links in the middle of the chain. The link pivots around its transformation point. Using the Transform tool to rotate an instance of a symbol doesn't change the length of the bones in the armature.

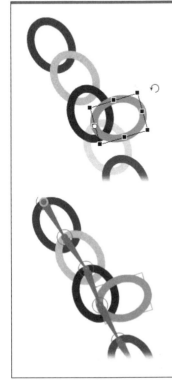

**FIGURE 9-10**

*Top: To reposition a symbol relative to the bone armature, use the Transform tool.*

*Bottom: The link has pivoted around its transformation point, but it still moves with the rest of the armature.*

## Changing the Length of a Bone

If you want to move the symbol, including its transformation point, you have to change the length of the connected bones. That's also a job for the Transform tool. Select the Transform tool, and then move the cursor over the symbol that you want to move. Drag the symbol to a new position. As an alternative, you can use the Selection tool to move a symbol; just press Alt (Option) as you drag.

Flash doesn't display the armature when you use the Transform tool. When you're done, select the symbol to see how the length of the bones have changed to accommodate the move, as shown in Figure 9-11.

**NOTE** Test the file *09-2_Simple_Bones_Done.fla* to see examples of the different bone techniques. Examine the armature to see movement and joint constraints. The last few frames of the animation show bones that were "lengthened," which makes the chain links appear disconnected.

## Deleting Bones

Deleting bones from an armature is a pretty straightforward procedure. Just select the bone, and then press Delete. The bone disappears, along with any child bones connected to it. The symbols that were connected by the bone remain in the pose layer, but they're no longer connected to the armature, so they aren't animated with the other symbols.

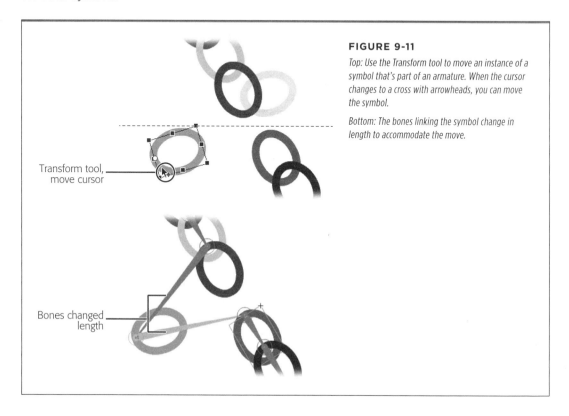

**FIGURE 9-11**

*Top: Use the Transform tool to move an instance of a symbol that's part of an armature. When the cursor changes to a cross with arrowheads, you can move the symbol.*

*Bottom: The bones linking the symbol change in length to accommodate the move.*

Transform tool, move cursor

Bones changed length

# Perfect Posing with Control Handles

As you work with IK Bones, you spend your time creating a pose, moving down the timeline, and creating another pose. Anything that helps you arrange an armature faster makes you more efficient. One problem you encounter when you're trying to force your animation into the perfect pose is that all those bones and attached symbols tend to fly and flop all over the place. As explained earlier, the "Joint: Rotation" and "Joint: Translation" settings help you control and constrain movement. Want to keep a joint from spinning? Turn off "Joint: Rotation." Want to restrict the rotation? Leave rotation turned on, but also turn on the Constrain checkbox and enter a Min and Max value as explained on page 333. But what about that last joint?

The "Joint: Rotation" settings affect the head of a bone, but there's no way to set the Min and Max rotation for the joint at a bone's tail.

For an example of this dilemma, open *09-4_Chris_Army_Knife.fla*. You see a handy multitooled knife like the one made famous by a certain Alpine nation (Figure 9-12). If you move the knife blade, it opens just the right amount and closes neatly into the knife's handle. Click the bone along the knife blade and in the Properties panel, you see that "Joint: Rotation" and Constrain are both turned on, and Min and Max values are set. The scissors don't behave nearly as well. The short scissor blade spins like a top, because the tail of the last bone creates the joint where the two scissors blades meet. What's the difference between these two examples? It's that little green dot at the end of the knife blade. In essence, you overcome the last bone dilemma by creating another bone and attaching it to a "dummy" symbol—in this example, a green dot. When it's time to publish your animation, you can make that green dot disappear by going to the Library panel and editing the symbol. Set the fill Alpha to *0*, and all the green dots in your animation become invisible. Later, if you want your handles back for posing, you reverse the process.

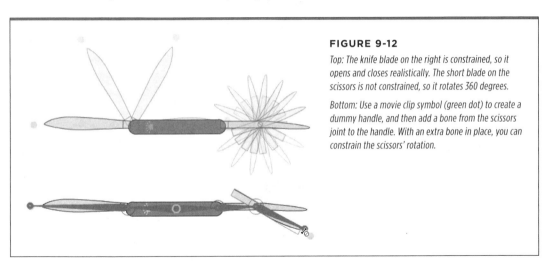

**FIGURE 9-12**

*Top: The knife blade on the right is constrained, so it opens and closes realistically. The short blade on the scissors is not constrained, so it rotates 360 degrees.*

*Bottom: Use a movie clip symbol (green dot) to create a dummy handle, and then add a bone from the scissors joint to the handle. With an extra bone in place, you can constrain the scissors' rotation.*

If you're in the mood for some practice, drag another green dot out of the library and place it near the tip of the short scissors blade. Create a new bone from the scissors joint to the green dot. At that point, send the short scissors blade to the back (Modify→Arrange→"Send to Back"). The knife looks better that way. Lastly, adjust the "Joint: Rotation Constrain" settings for the scissors so they behave properly.

Homemade control handles like these have many uses. In the knife example, they give you a way to move the blades even when they're hidden behind the red knife handle. If you want to rotate part of your armature with precision, create an extra-long bone for your control handle. The further the handle is from the rotating joint, the more precise your control.

**NOTE**  The finished knife project *09-05_Chris_Army_Knife done.fla* is available on the Missing CD (*www.missingmanuals.com/cds/flashcs6mm*).

## Baby Steps with Pins

Flash CS6 has another time-saving feature for IK Bones—*pinning*. This feature lets you literally pin the tail of any bone to a point on the stage, preventing the armature from flying and flopping while you arrange a pose. Best of all, pinning a tail joint couldn't be simpler, so it's fast and easy to use. To practice with a simple example, open *19-6_Pin_Bones.fla* from the Missing CD (*www.missingmanuals.com/cds/flashcs6mm*). The animation consists of three popsicle sticks, connected with an armature. The armature makes use of homemade control handles like the ones described in the previous section. With the help of pins, you can make the stick figure crab-walk across the stage.

To pin the tail of a bone to the stage, follow these steps:

1.  **With the Select tool (V), click the bone.**

2.  **Move the cursor to the tail of the selected bone.**

3.  **When the cursor changes to a pushpin, click the tail of the bone.**

Pinning fixes the tail in place but lets the bone rotate around the spot. The pin feature works like a toggle, so you can turn it off with the same steps. Tail joints that are pinned show a big X over the joint, as shown in Figure 9-13. You can pin more than one tail joint in the armature. Get used to quickly pinning and unpinning joints, and your posing sessions will go much faster.

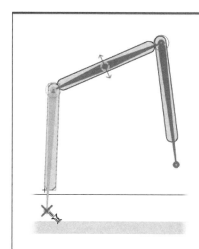

**FIGURE 9-13**

*Move the cursor over the tail of a selected bone, and it turns into a pushpin. Click to toggle pinning on and off. Here the left leg is pinned, making it easier to arrange the other bones for the walking popsicle sticks.*

To make the sticks walk across the stage, move the playhead two or three frames down the timeline where you want to create a new pose. Pin the tail of the left leg in place, and then rearrange the pose by raising the right leg as if it's beginning a step (Figure 9-13). Move down the timeline a few more frames and bring the right leg down to its new foothold further to the right. Now, pin the tail of the right leg in place and unpin the left. Create a couple of poses to bring the left leg down. Repeat the process a few times, and the popsicle sticks will walk off the edge of the stage.

You could make the three sticks walk across the stage without the help of pins, but it would take a bit longer. Consider a more complex, legged model, like a person or a dog, with hips, shoulders, knees, and elbows. With just a couple of clicks, pinning gives you a quick way to freeze parts of the armature in place while you fiddle with the rest.

**NOTE**   The finished walking sticks animation is named *19-7_Pin_Bones done.fla* on the Missing CD (*www.missingmanuals.com/cds/flashcs6mm*).

## ■ Making Shapes Move with Bones

There are two ways to use bones. You can use IK Bones to link symbols together, creating a chain of objects (as described on page 326), or you can add bones to the *inside* of a shape, making that shape bendable and flexible. It's kind of like dressing up a group of bones inside a costume. Though both of these methods rely on an armature made up of bones, the techniques you use to make them work are quite different.

You can add bones to a single shape, or you can add bones to more than one shape. The word "group" isn't used here, since you can't combine the shapes using the Group commands. The way you add bones to more than one shape is to select all the shapes that you're going to include *before* you add the first bone. Flash then automatically places those selected shapes in the pose layer.

In this exercise, you'll animate a snake by placing several bones inside it. Unlike a robot, snakes don't have limbs, but you can still give them plenty of bones. Download *09-8_Shape_Bones.fla* from the Missing CD page at *www.missingmanuals. com/cds/flashcs6mm*.

1. **Open *09-8_Shape_Bones.fla*.**

   The lovely rattlesnake is made up of several shapes: a body, a tongue, and two eyes.

2. **Zoom in on the front section.**

   To place bones precisely inside a shape, it helps to zoom in for a close view. Then, if you need to get a view of a different part of the shape, you can use the Hand tool to reposition the object on the stage. As mentioned earlier, it also helps to turn off object snapping (View→"Snapping→Snap to Objects").

3. **Press Ctrl+A (⌘-A) to select the tongue, the body, and the eyes.**

   You can add bones to more than one shape, but you can't group those shapes with the Modify→Group command when you add the bone. Instead, you have to select all the shapes you want to include in the IK shape object.

4. **With the Bone tool, drag to create a bone from the snake's head to the tongue.**

   When you create the first bone, Flash converts all the selected shapes and the bone into an IK shape object and places the object in a pose layer. Why start with the head? Your first click sets the transformation point for the entire armature—better to center the snake on its head rather than its forked tongue.

5. **Create a bone from the root bone down the body of the snake.**

   You can attach bones to both the head and tail of the root bone. You can also create branches in shapes. (Page 332 describes creating branching armatures when linking symbols.)

6. **Create several more bones inside the body of the snake down to the tail.**

   Use a total of about eight or nine bones for the snake's armature (Figure 9-14). If you use too many bones, it's more work for you when you try to pose the snake. Too few bones, and you won't be able to create the desired snaky slithering.

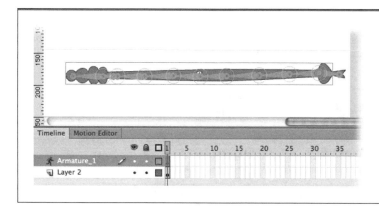

**FIGURE 9-14**

*The root bone in the snake starts at the head. One bone extends to the tongue. The rest of the bones extend down the body of the snake to the tail.*

7. **In the pose layer, click Frame 50, and then press F5.**

   The green pose layer shows 50 frames for you to create some snaky movement.

8. **Create several poses to animate the snake so that it moves across the stage from left to right.**

   Here are some suggestions: In Frame 1, start with the snake offstage to the left. In Frame 5, pose the snake with just the head coming on to the stage. In Frames

10, 20, 30, and 40, pose the snake in different S-shaped curves to simulate snake propulsion across the stage. In Frame 45, show just the snake's rattle with the rest of the snake body already offstage. In Frame 50, move the snake entirely off stage to the right.

9. **Test the animation.**

If you're not pleased with the movement at any stage, then try to reposition the adjacent poses or create more intermediate poses.

You use the pose layer to animate the position and location of the armature. In many ways, the pose layer seems like a motion tween; however, you can't use the pose layer to tween properties like color, transparency, or dimensions. If you want to change these properties, you need to select the pose layer, and then wrap it in either a movie clip or a graphic symbol. There are more details in the box on page 332.

## Working with Control Points

When you place bones inside shapes, Flash automatically creates control points around the contour of the shape, as shown in Figure 9-15. The control points establish the perimeter of the shape as you create different poses. Some shapes, especially more complex and branched shapes, can get contorted in unexpected ways. You can solve the problem by repositioning the control points. With the Subselection tool, click the boundary of the shape. The control points and the edge of the shape appear highlighted. Then just drag the control points to adjust the shape. Control points at a curve show Bezier-style curve control handles that you can use to modify the curve.

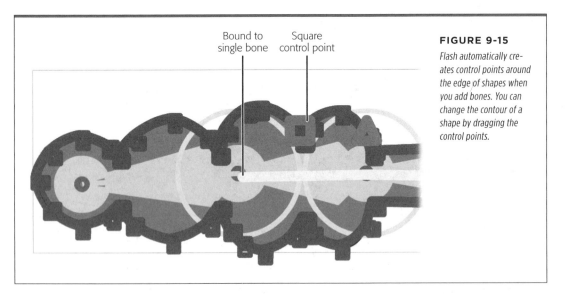

Bound to
single bone

Square
control point

**FIGURE 9-15**

*Flash automatically creates control points around the edge of shapes when you add bones. You can change the contour of a shape by dragging the control points.*

When you add bones to a shape, Flash binds the control points on the perimeter of the shape to the nearest bone. In some cases, a control point may be bound to more than one bone, as shown in Figure 9-16. If the control points aren't configured the way you'd like, you can edit them using the following techniques:

- **View control points bound to a bone.** Choose the Bind tool in the Tools panel, and then click a bone in the armature. The selected bone shows a red highlight. The control points bound to the selected bone are highlighted in yellow. The other control points in the armature are colored blue.

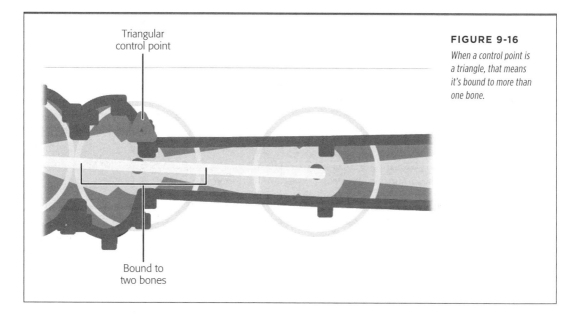

Triangular
control point

Bound to
two bones

**FIGURE 9-16**

*When a control point is a triangle, that means it's bound to more than one bone.*

- **View bones bound to a control point.** Choose the Bind tool in the Tools panel, and Flash displays the bones and control points in the armature. Square control points are bound to a single bone. Triangular control points are bound to more than one bone. Click a control point, and it shows a red highlight. Bones bound to the control point are highlighted in yellow.

- **Bind a control point to a bone.** Choose the Bind tool in the Tools panel, and then click a bone. The control points bound to the bone appear highlighted in yellow. With the Bind tool, Shift-click a control point that doesn't show a yellow highlight, and Flash binds it to the selected bone.

- **Remove (unbind) control points from a bone.** Use the Bind tool to select a bone. Ctrl-click (Option-click) a control point that's highlighted in yellow. The control point changes from yellow to blue, indicating that it's no longer bound to the selected bone.

- **Bind a bone to a control point.** Select a control point with the Bind tool, and then drag to the bone you want to bind to. As an alternative, Ctrl-clicking (Option-clicking) acts as a toggle, binding and unbinding control points to adjacent bones.

- **Remove (unbind) a bone from a control point.** Select a control point with the Bind tool, and then drag away from the shape to unbind the control point. As an alternative, Ctrl-clicking (Option-clicking) acts as a toggle, binding and unbinding control points to adjacent bones.

## ■ Apply Spring to a Motion

An A-flat played on a guitar sounds different from an A-flat on a trumpet. The note may be the same, but the differences in overtone and timbre make music beautiful and endlessly entertaining. Motion in the real world is like a symphony orchestra. A pencil, a feather, and a cooked noodle may move the same distance and arrive at the same resting point, but the subtleties of their motion are entirely different. Your audience subconsciously recognizes these differences. When you want to fine-tune a motion's subtleties in Flash, turn to the Spring properties: Strength and Damping, which you find in the Properties panel when you select an IK Bone.

Here's a simple experiment that shows how Spring works. If you want to skip the first few steps for creating a rectangle shape with bones, use the file *09-9_Spring_Settings.fla* from the Missing CD (*www.missingmanuals.com/cds/flashcs6mm*).

1. **Choose File→New→ActionScript 3.0.**

   A new Flash document opens.

2. **Select the Rectangle tool (R) and then make sure object drawing mode (J) is toggled off.**

   A simple shape works great for this demonstration.

3. **In the Properties panel, set Stroke to None and Fill to a color of your choice.**

   Again, simplicity works just fine.

4. **Draw a skinny, horizontal rectangle across the top of the stage, as shown in Figure 9-17.**

   In this animation, one side of the rectangle drops to the floor. The shape of the rectangle and the fluidity of the motion change depending on the Spring properties.

5. **Select the Bone tool (M), and then add two bones to the shape.**

   Make the bone on the left shorter than the bone on the right.

6. **In the timeline, click Frame 24 and then press F5.** With the Selection tool (V), drag the right end of the rectangle down to the bottom of the stage.

Make sure that you're in the final frame of the animation (Frame 24) and that the rectangle is pulled tight with no bends in it, as shown in Figure 9-17.

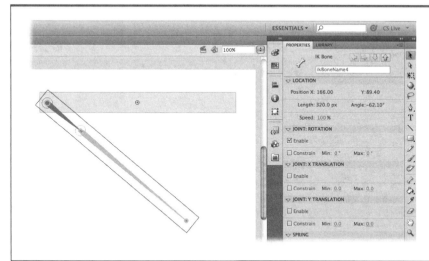

**FIGURE 9-17**

*You apply Spring properties to individual bones in a armature. The settings affect the motion and interaction between the bones. Spring makes a child bone resist the movement of a parent bone. How much resistance? Well, that's up to you and the Strength and Damping properties.*

7. **Press Enter (Return) to preview the motion.**

On the stage, the movement of the rectangle is similar to a pencil. The shape remains pretty much unchanged through the entire motion.

8. **Select the bone on the right, and then change Properties→Spring→Strength to 70 (Figure 9-18).**

A setting of 70 makes the relationship between the parent and child bones pretty loose.

9. **Press Enter (Return) to preview the motion.**

This time, the motion is more fluid. The rectangle flutters more like a feather or some other flexible object.

You apply Spring properties to individual bones, and they change the way the shape moves. There's a reaction when the parent bone moves. The child bone resists the movement, and that resistance changes the shape. See Figure 9-19. Set the Spring→Strength property to 0, and the joint is rigid. Set the value to 100 and the joint is very loose. Damping affects the motion, too. In the real world, movement like springiness is often more dramatic initially and then gradually loses its power until the object comes to rest. Think about a jack-in-the-box when it pops out. There's lots of movement at first, but then there's a little less distance with each bounce. In Flash, you use the Damping setting to set the difference between the initial movement and the movement when an object comes to rest.

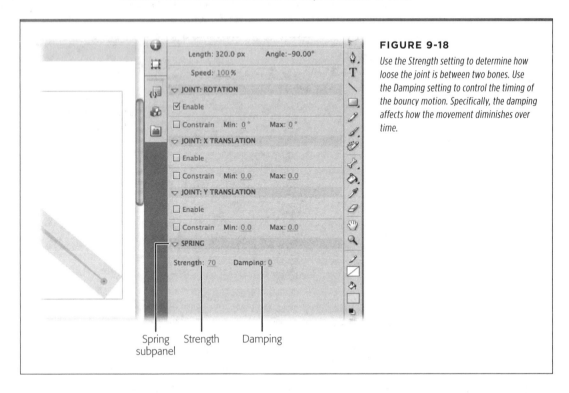

**FIGURE 9-18**

Use the Strength setting to determine how loose the joint is between two bones. Use the Damping setting to control the timing of the bouncy motion. Specifically, the damping affects how the movement diminishes over time.

Spring subpanel    Strength    Damping

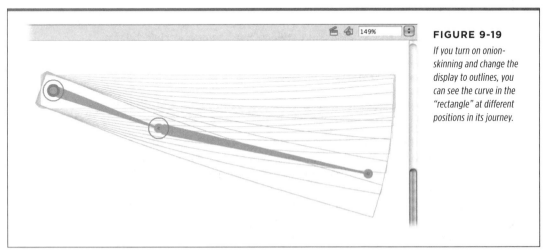

**FIGURE 9-19**

If you turn on onion-skinning and change the display to outlines, you can see the curve in the "rectangle" at different positions in its journey.

# ■ Animating an Armature with ActionScript

Though it's not covered in this book, you can use ActionScript 3.0 to animate IK Bones armatures. The IK armature has to be connected to either shapes or movie clip symbols. You can't use ActionScript to animate graphic symbols. To prepare an armature for use with ActionScript, create a pose layer with only a single pose. If there's more than one pose in the layer, then you can't use it with ActionScript.

1. **Select a frame in the pose layer.**

   The settings for the pose layer appear in the Properties panel (Figure 9-20).

**FIGURE 9-20**

*Change the Properties→Options→Type to Runtime if you want to use ActionScript to control the movement of your IK Bones armature.*

2. **In Properties, under Options→Type, choose Runtime from the drop-down menu.**

   When you first create an armature, Properties→Options→Type is set to Authortime, meaning you create the animation in the timeline as you design the animation. Once you change it to Runtime, you can use ActionScript code to control the movement of the armature and its elements.

3. **Change the instance name for the armature to *amtrChain*.**

   You can change the name of the armature to match your ActionScript naming conventions. Initially, Flash gives the armature instance the same name as the pose layer. You can change the name in either the layer in the timeline or in the Properties panel.

# Incorporating Non-Flash Media Files

Flash gives you a ton of drawing and painting tools you can use to create original artwork, as you saw in Chapter 2 and Chapter 5. But if you've already got some cool logos or backgrounds that you created in another program (like Adobe Illustrator and Photoshop), you don't have to redraw them in Flash. All you have to do is pull them into Flash—*import* them. Once you do, you can work with them nearly as easily as you do the images you create directly on the stage.

This chapter introduces you to the different types of graphics and still images that Flash lets you work with. You'll learn how to import files while preserving just the features you need in Flash. (If you're looking for tips on how to work with audio and video media, turn to Chapter 11.)

> **NOTE** After you've incorporated non-Flash media into your animation, you can control that media using ActionScript. For more details, flip to Chapter 12.

## ■ Importing Graphics

Theoretically, you can cut or copy graphic elements from any other program you have open, paste them into Flash, and then tweak them. For example, say you've created a drawing in Autodesk SketchBook Pro. In SketchBook, you can choose Edit→Copy. Then, in Flash, you can choose Edit→"Paste in Center" to transfer the image from SketchBook to your stage, and then edit it using Flash's drawing and painting tools. When you import or paste an image onto the stage, Flash stores a copy in your Library, as shown in Figure 10-1.

Copying and pasting usually works, and it's quick and easy. It's not surprising that Adobe tweaked Flash so that Cut and Paste work smoothly with its own programs—Illustrator, Photoshop, and Fireworks. In fact, the cut-and-paste process opens the same Import dialog box that you'd see if you'd used the File Import command. That handy tool helps you import graphics exactly the way you want them in Flash. On the other hand, using non-Adobe programs, you may get hit-or-miss results by using the system Clipboard. Flash may decide to flatten (group) the drawing, limiting your ability to edit it. Flash may also decide to ignore certain effects (like transparency and gradients) so that the image you paste onto your stage doesn't quite match the image you cut or copied.

Properties button

**FIGURE 10-1**

*After you import a bitmap, Flash throws a backup copy of the image into the Library as a convenience so you have the option of dragging another copy onto the stage without going through all the trouble of importing the file again. To see the properties of your newly imported bitmap, click the information icon.*

A safer alternative: In your non-Adobe programs, save your graphic elements as separate files, and then import those files into Flash. Flash lets you import most popular graphics file formats, including .jpg, .gif, .png, and .bmp formats. If you're a Flash veteran, you may notice that the list of importable file formats is actually shorter than it used to be. Adobe has retired some older and less-common formats, like Macromedia Freehand, Silicon Graphics, Targa, and Windows metafiles. If you're working in one of these formats, you need to save your files in one of the formats listed in Table 10-1.

One of the major improvements in recent versions of Flash is the way it imports Adobe Photoshop and Adobe Illustrator files. These programs use layers much like the layers in Flash, as explained on page 135. When you import Photoshop and Illustrator files into Flash, you can choose which layers you want to import, and the program converts them into Flash layers. Say you're creating a business presentation and you've got a Photoshop file of a map. The Photoshop (.psd) file has the map on one layer, city names on another layer, and stars on another layer to highlight where you've had increased sales. Flash imports the map, the city names, and the stars on separate layers, making it easy for you to show and hide these elements separately in your Flash animation. Also, if you need to make changes after you pull Photoshop or Illustrator files into Flash, you can edit the shapes and text within Flash.

**TABLE 10-1** *Graphics file formats you can import into Flash*

| FILE TYPE | EXTENSION | NOTE |
|---|---|---|
| Adobe Illustrator | .ai | Instead of automatically pulling these files in as flat, rasterized bitmaps, Flash lets you set import settings that help preserve the original images' layers and editable text. |
| Portable Network Graphic | .png | Instead of automatically importing PNG files created in Fireworks as flat, rasterized bitmaps, Flash lets you set import settings that help preserve the original images' layers, editable objects, and editable text. |
| Photoshop | .psd | You must have QuickTime 4 (or later) installed before you can import Photoshop files into Flash. |
| Adobe FXG | .fxg | This is Adobe's new open source, MXML-based file format. It works well with Photoshop, Illustrator, Flash, and Flex. For more details, see the box on page 354. |
| AutoCAD DXF | .dxf | Flash imports 2-D DXF files, but not 3-D DXF. Font confusion can happen when Flash tries to match AutoCAD's nonstandard font system. Flash imports only ASCII (text-based) DXF files. Binary DXF files have to be converted to ASCII before they're imported to Flash. |
| Windows Bitmap | .bmp, .dib | If you're running a Mac, you must have QuickTime 4 (or later) installed on your computer to import Windows bitmap files into Flash. |
| Flash and FutureSplash (pre-Flash) | .swf | These are Flash movies that have been published (also known as *compiled*) for distribution. |
| Graphic Interchange Format (including animated GIF) | .gif | This format, originally developed by CompuServe (one of the earliest online information services), is good for simple drawings. |
| Joint Photographic Experts Group | .jpg, .jpeg | The most popular format for displaying photos on the Web. |
| QuickTime Image | .qtif | You must have QuickTime 4 (or later) installed before you can import QuickTime Image files into Flash. |
| Tagged Image File | .tif, .tiff | You must have QuickTime 4 (or later) installed before you can import TIFF files into Flash. |

**NOTE** If you're looking for third-party graphics files to import into Flash, check out the box on page 382.

---

**FREQUENTLY ASKED QUESTION**

## New File Formats for Flash? Why?

*With all the file formats floating around, why did Adobe create two new ones: XFL for Flash and FXG for images?*

It's a reasonable question. If you use Flash, you're expected to keep track of dozens of different types of files and understand their capabilities and shortcomings. Over the years, Flash has matured from a simple animation tool to an application-building tool. Branches of that growth include Flex and AIR—development tools that use Flash files to create full-blown applications. Adobe created the new file formats to accommodate the needs of these new app-building tools.

At the same time, there's an industry trend toward open-source tools and file formats. In the past, companies like Microsoft and Adobe created proprietary file formats that only their programs could open. Once the competition figured it out, the company would come out with a new version, protecting their corner of the market. This system wasn't so great for the consumer. The trend these days is to develop file formats made of separate components that are compressed like a ZIP file, often using the XML scripting language to define the separate parts. Microsoft went this direction when creating file formats for Office 2007 and 2008, and now Adobe is using a similar method for Flash and other programs.

**Flash Files (.fla and .xfl).** Now, when you save a Flash file (File→Save), the program automatically stores it in the new format and squashes it using ZIP compression. You can see for yourself—use a tool like WinZip or StuffIt to open a Flash file. (You may need to change the file extension to ".zip" before you can open it.) Once it's open, it looks like Figure 10-2. Flash

developers who work in teams will love this approach. Artists can design buttons and widgets somewhat independently of programmers who write the ActionScript code. Then, each team member can pop her work into the Flash document without messing up any other part of the project. Folks who develop Flash extensions and add-ons will also be fans of the new, easily accessible file format.

When you save your Flash documents (File→Save), you can choose Flash CS6 Uncompressed Document (*.xfl) from the "Save as type" menu. When you choose this option, Flash forgoes the compression. Instead, it saves your file as a folder with subfolders to hold all of its parts (called *assets*). For example, a Library subfolder holds any symbols you've created. This setup makes asset swapping and sharing even easier.

**FXG file format.** There's more than one way to operate on a Flash animation. For example, you can use Flash Professional with all its bells and whistles. If you're a designer but not a programmer, you may want to use Flash Catalyst. On the other hand, if you're a developer *and* a programmer, you may want to use Flash Builder. These last two tools are useful when an entire team is working on a project. Adobe developed the FXG file format to ease the cooperation between these programs, as well as Photoshop, Illustrator, Flash, and Flex. FXG uses XML-type descriptions to define an image. Technically, this code is a subset of Flex's MXML language. To see the innards of an FXG file, open it using Notepad or TextEdit. You'll find text descriptions of the image. It looks a little like the code that underlies web pages, because XML and HTML have shared roots.

---

## ■ Importing Illustrator Graphics Files

Flash lets you import graphics files you've created with another image-editing program (like Adobe Illustrator or Photoshop) and then stored on your computer. After you import a graphics file, you can either edit the image it contains using Flash's tools and panels, or just add it directly to your animation.

**NOTE** Table 10-1 (page 353) shows you a complete list of all the different graphics file formats you can import into Flash.

As you see in the steps below, after you've imported a graphics file, Flash stores a copy of the image in the Library panel (page 30) so you can add as many instances of the image to your animations as you like.

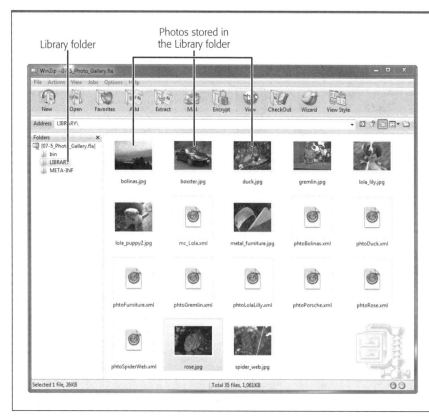

Library folder

Photos stored in
the Library folder

**FIGURE 10-2**

*Flash Professional CS6 uses a new file format that's easier for everyone to open and understand. Here a Flash file is uncompressed and opened in WinZip, so you can see its contents stored in separate folders. These images are part of the Photo Gallery file (07-5_Photo_Gallery.fla on the Missing CD page at www.missingmanuals. com/cds/flashcs6mm).*

Of course, there's no such thing as a free lunch. Depending on the format of your graphics file (see page 353), Flash either pulls the image in as a collection of editable shapes and layers—which you can work with just as you work with any image in Flash—or as a flattened bitmap, which limits your editing choices a bit. (Page 364 gives you tips for working with flattened bitmaps.) Flash does its best to give you all the bells and whistles of the original file format. Flash really excels when you import a file from one of Adobe's Creative Suite programs, like Illustrator. As the example below shows, you get to choose the way Flash imports layers, shapes, and text. As a result, if you're importing Illustrator files, Flash lets you go ahead and modify the shapes (vector graphics) and edit the text after import.

**TIP**  Adobe Illustrator files are frequently saved for printing on paper using a color space called CMYK (cyan, magenta, yellow, black). Before you import these files, use Illustrator to convert them to the RGB (red, green, blue) color space used by Flash. To check and change the color space setting in Illustrator, choose File→Document Color Mode. Less frequently, you may find Adobe Photoshop files using the CMYK color space. In Photoshop, to check and change the color space, go to Image→Mode RGB.

**UP TO SPEED**

## Flash/QuickTime Cross-Pollination

Since the good old days of Flash 4, Flash has enjoyed a symbiotic relationship with Apple's QuickTime. Back then, you could import a QuickTime movie into Flash and then add some Flash content (for example, buttons that web surfers can press to start and stop the QuickTime movie). And you still can import QuickTime movies into Flash and link the two together, as you see on page 396.

But the relationship between Flash and QuickTime goes beyond video integration—it also affects your ability to import media files into Flash. If you have QuickTime installed on your computer, for example, Flash lets you import more types of graphic file formats than it does if you don't have QuickTime installed (see Table 10-1 for details).

The bottom line is, if you're working with others who use both Macs and PCs, it's well worth installing QuickTime. When this was written, the current version was QuickTime 10. Fortunately, QuickTime is easy to install. It's free, too. To download a copy, visit *www.apple.com/quicktime/download*.

1. **Choose File→Import→"Import to Stage."**

   Your standard file dialog box appears. If you're using a PC, it looks like Figure 10-3, for example.

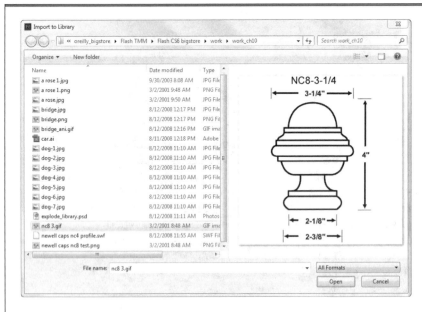

**FIGURE 10-3**

*You can import a graphic to the stage and the Library, as you see in the numbered steps, or just to the Library (by choosing File→Import→"Import to Library"). Either way, you first have to tell Flash which file contains the graphic you want to import—and that's exactly what you do here, in the Import dialog box.*

**NOTE** Looking for an Adobe Illustrator practice file? Go to the Missing CD (*www.missingmanuals.com/cds/flashcs6mm*) and download either *10-1_Sports_Car.ai* or *10-2_Stutz_Bearcat.ai*.

2. **In the "File name" field, type the name of the Adobe Illustrator (.ai) file you want to import (or, in the file window, click the file to have Flash fill in the name for you).**

   Use the drop-down menu at the bottom to see all the different types of files you can import. Initially the drop-down menu is set to All Formats.

3. **Click Open.**

   The Import dialog box disappears, and then Flash displays an extra Import Settings window that lets you tell it how much editability you want to preserve: whether you want it to convert the original frames into Flash frames or Flash layers, to pull in all the frames or just a few, to include invisible layers or not, and so on. Figure 10-4 shows the Import Settings windows you see when you import files created with Adobe Illustrator.

4. **When you see the "Import to Stage" dialog box (Figure 10-4), click to select one or more of the following options, and then click OK.**

   - **Select Illustrator Artboard.** You can create multiple artboards within an Illustrator file. They're similar to having multiple pages in a word processing document. Use the drop-down menu to choose which artboard (page) you want to import.

   - **Check Illustrator layers to import.** Flash gives you a scrolling list of all the layers in the Illustrator file, with icons and labels describing the contents of the layers. Place checkmarks next to the layers and artwork you wish to import. To the right of the scrolling list, you see Layer Import Options that change depending on the content of the layer.

On the right site of the Import window, you see "Layer import options for '<Path>':" or Group, or Text, or whatever you selected on the left. Here's your opportunity to fine-tune the import process. Suppose you have a drawing of a car. You can import the wheels as movie clips with the registration points centered, so you can create rotating wheels in your Flash animation. Here are examples of the import options:

- **Layer import options for paths.** If the layer includes lines and shapes, you can choose to import the content as an *editable path*, meaning that you can change it later within Flash. Or you can import it as a bitmap, which gives you fewer editing options.

- **Layer import options for text.** You have three options for importing text. Choose "Editable text" if you want to edit or rewrite the text. Choose "Vector outlines" if you want to change the shapes of letters in the same way you change the shapes of polygons and circles within Flash. Choose Bitmap if you're happy with the text as is and don't plan to change it other than perhaps tweaking the color and size a bit.

**TIP**  If you see a yellow triangle with an exclamation point (!), Flash is warning you that one of the graphic elements may not be imported as expected. For example, you may see an incompatibility warning if you try to import text that has been rotated in Illustrator. Click the layer, and Flash explains that the best option is to import the text as vector outlines. Once you fix the problem, the warning sign disappears.

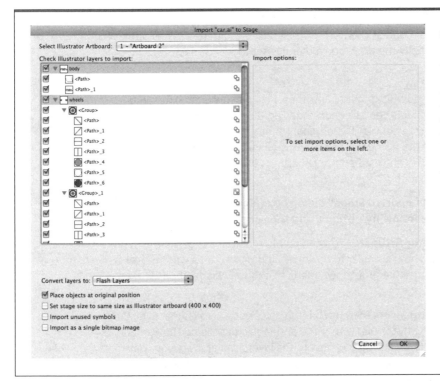

**FIGURE 10-4**

*When you try to import certain types of vector files, Flash lets you specify how much edit-ability you're willing to sacrifice for good-quality images. Here you see the dialog box Flash displays when you try to import an Adobe Illustrator file.*

- **Create movie clip.** Use this option to instantly turn the graphics in the selected layer into a Flash movie clip symbol. Check the box, and then give the clip an Instance name that's used for the copy of the movie clip symbol that Flash places on the stage. If your Illustrator artwork uses effects like filters or blends, choose the "Create movie clip" option. In Flash, only movie clips can have filters and blends. At the bottom of the "Import to Stage" dialog box, you see options that affect all the layers you're importing.

- **Convert layers to: Flash Layers/Keyframes/Single Flash Layer.** This option tells Flash to keep the layering structure of the original file intact, to place the content of each layer in a separate layer or keyframe. If you don't need to work with the image's layers separately, you can flatten the content of all layers onto a single Flash layer.

- **Place objects at original position.** This option keeps the different elements in a graphic positioned the same way they were in Illustrator.

- **Set stage to same size as Illustrator artboard/crop area.** Turning on this box automatically changes the Height and Width document settings in Flash to match the page settings in the Illustrator file you're importing.

- **Import unused symbols.** Illustrator has a Symbols panel that's similar to Flash's Library. Turn on this option if you want to import all the symbols in the Illustrator panel, even if they don't appear in the document's page.

- **Import as a single bitmap image.** Sometimes you're not interested in multiple layers, editable shapes, and editable text. All you want is a single picture in your Library that you don't want to change. Turn on this box to import the Illustrator file as a single bitmap picture.

After you've made your choices and then clicked OK, the Import settings window disappears. Flash imports your file, placing it on the stage (or in multiple frames and layers, based on the options you selected above) and in the Library, as shown earlier in Figure 10-1.

---

**TIP** You can import files into your Library without placing them on the stage. Just choose File→Import→"Import to Library."

---

# Importing Photoshop Graphic Files

Photoshop files have a special relationship with Flash, and the import process is very similar to importing Illustrator files, described on page 354. The Import dialog box (Figure 10-5) has the same look and layout, but when you look closely at the options, you see some differences. That's not surprising, since Photoshop specializes in raster or bitmap images, while Illustrator focuses on vector graphics (sometimes called *drawings*).

The "Import to Stage" dialog box for Photoshop files shows you a scrolling list of Photoshop layers. Turn on the checkbox for each layer you want to include in the import process. Click the layer name to highlight the layer, and you see options listed on the right. The options differ depending on the content of the layer.

Here's the rundown on the import options you find in the Photoshop "Import to Stage" dialog box:

## Import Options for Bitmaps

- **Import this layer as.** You have two choices for importing bitmap layers. Choose "Bitmap image with editable layer styles" if you want to tweak the layer settings in Flash. If all you need is a picture, choose "Flattened bitmap image."

- **Create movie clip for this layer.** Use this option to instantly turn the graphics in the selected layer into a Flash movie clip symbol. Turn on the box, and then give the clip an Instance name (which Flash uses for the copy of the movie clip symbol it places on the stage).

- **Publish settings.** You can adjust the quality of bitmaps as you import them into Flash. This option gives you control over the size of your Flash files, which is important when you're posting Flash movies on the Internet (better quality equals bigger files). Using the Compression drop-down menu, you can choose between Lossy and Lossless. If you choose lossy compression (similar to JPEG images), you get a compact file size at the risk of degraded image quality. Lossless compression retains all the digital information, even when resized. As with JPEG images, you can adjust the quality of lossy compression images by setting them to match your Flash publish settings (page 681) or by entering a number in the Custom box.

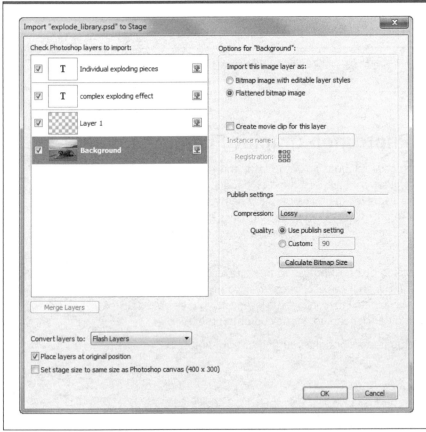

**FIGURE 10-5**

*When you import Photoshop graphics, Flash gives you a boatload of control over the process. Using the "Import to Stage" dialog box, you can tweak the settings on individual layers of the Photoshop file so you get exactly the tools you need for your animation.*

## Import Options for Text

- **Editable text.** Photoshop places text on separate layers from photographs so that the text can be edited, like it's in a word processor. Choose this option if you want to edit text after you've brought it into Flash.

- **Vector outlines.** The letters in text are drawn on the screen in the same way that circles and polygons are drawn. If you want to be able to modify those letters as if they were any other shape, choose "Vector outlines" as your import option. You'll be able to distort your letters in all sorts of fun ways, but you won't be able to edit them like editable text.

- **Flattened bitmap image.** This option turns your text into a bitmap picture, like a photograph. You can't do much more than tweak the color and resize it a bit.

## Other Photoshop Import Options

The "Import to Stage" dialog box has several other options you can adjust before you import files:

- **Create movie clip for this layer.** Select one or more layers, and you can turn them into a Flash movie clip symbol.

- **Merge layers.** Below the scrolling list of layers is a Merge Layers button. Shift-click or Ctrl-click (⌘-click) to select multiple layers, and then click Merge Layers. Flash creates a new merged layer right in the scrolling list that you can import into your Flash document. (This process doesn't affect the original Photoshop file on your computer.)

- **Convert layers to: Flash layers/Keyframes.** This option tells Flash to keep the layering structure of the original file intact, to place the content of each layer in a separate layer or keyframe.

- **Place layers at original position.** This option keeps the different elements in a graphic positioned the same way they were in Photoshop.

- **Set stage to same size as Photoshop canvas.** Turn on this box to automatically change the Height and Width document settings in Flash to match the page settings in the Photoshop file you're importing.

## ■ Importing Fireworks Graphics

Fireworks is another program that's part of Adobe's Creative Suite family. Fireworks's specialty is performing all sorts of graphics tricks for people who design websites. It has tools for creating buttons, rollover images, and other web graphics. For example, Fireworks can take a photo file and shrink it down to a very small file size, so it'll look fine on a website, but maybe not so great in print. Fireworks creates most of its magic using the standard web language (HTML), and graphics files (JPEG, GIF, PNG), with a little JavaScript for programming chores. Although Flash produces SWF files and uses ActionScript for programming, these two programs play well with each other, and you'll often find reasons for swapping files back and forth between them.

**NOTE** Flash and Fireworks have a working relationship that precedes the Adobe era. Both were published by Macromedia until Adobe purchased the company.

Fireworks is a hybrid in that its working file format (PNG) holds both photographic images like Photoshop and vector drawings like Adobe Illustrator. Designers often create complex images in Fireworks that may include photographs, text, and shapes. They *save* their work in PNG files, but they *export* the files to smaller, simpler formats to use on the Web. Flash can import almost any of the files that Fireworks saves or exports. This section shows you how.

---

**WORKAROUND WORKSHOP**

## Importing Unimportable Graphics

If you're not importing Adobe Illustrator, Photoshop, or Fireworks files, don't expect perfection when you're importing complex graphics. That's especially true if you're trying to preserve the ability to edit your graphics in Flash. Flash does the best it can, but there are an awful lot of variables involved, from the specific effects you applied, to the graphics, to the specific version of the program you used to create them.

If the graphics you import into Flash don't look or behave the way they do in the original program, try one or more of the following:

• **Ungroup the imported image.** You do this by selecting the image on the stage, and then choosing Modify→Ungroup.

• **Try using the Clipboard.** First, choose Edit→Preferences→ Clipboard (Windows) or Flash→Preferences→Clipboard (Mac) to display the Preferences window. You can choose the color depth and resolution for the image you're cutting and pasting. Higher numbers are more likely to match the original artwork, while lower numbers reduce the file size.

• **Return to the original program and see if you can simplify the image.** Reduce the number of colors you're using, as well as the number of layers, and flatten (group) as much of the image as you can. Then try the import process again.

---

**TIP**   The PNG (Portable Networks Graphic) file format is a standard that was developed to replace GIF files on the Internet for both copyright and techie reasons. In Fireworks, you can save files as PNGs, or you can export files as PNGs. Exported files are very small and great for use on websites.

---

There are three ways to bring graphics from Fireworks into Flash. Before you choose a method, ask yourself a couple of questions: Do I want the entire image or do I just want parts of it? Do I want the image in one solid chunk or do I want to animate individual pieces? After you know the answer to those questions, choose one of these methods for importing the graphic:

• Use Flash's File→Import command to import a complete Fireworks graphic. Whether you saved it as a GIF, JPG or PNG the image will be imported as a flattened bitmap—that is, one solid image. Even if it had separate layers in Fireworks, that's not the case once it's imported into Flash.

- Drag images from Fireworks to Flash, as shown in Figure 10-6. Before you drag, select the graphics you want to copy. Make sure any graphics you want to copy are visible and on unlocked layers. As with the Import method, you graphic in Flash is a flattened bitmap. The advantage of this option is you can pick can choose the parts of the image you need in Flash.

Adobe Fireworks

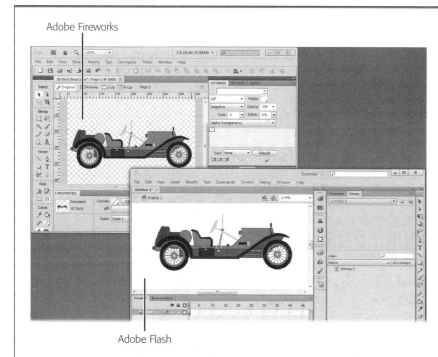

**FIGURE 10-6**

*With Adobe Creative Suite programs, like Fireworks, you can drag and drop graphics from one program to another. An Import dialog box opens, letting you choose among the import options.*

Adobe Flash

- Copying and pasting works, too, and sometimes it's easier than arranging your windows for a drag operation. The same rules apply; make sure any graphics you want to copy are visible and on unlocked layers. Sometimes, you'll want the pieces of a Fireworks graphic to be separate objects in your Flash animation. For example, if you have a car, you may want to animate the wheels so the they turn. In that case, choose Edit→Copy as Vectors in Fireworks. Then choose Edit→Paste in Flash. A dialog box, like the one in Figure 10-7 appears. Choose the Paste Using AI Importer preferences. Translation: I want to import this as if it were an Adobe Illustrator file. Check the box Maintain layers. That way, each the elements is appear in Flash timeline layers. At this point, work with the graphics just as if you created them in Flash. That means you can move them to different layers or you can turn them into symbols for animation.

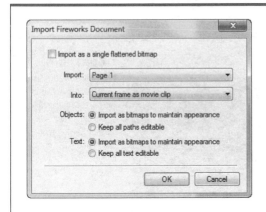

**FIGURE 10-7**

*If you want to import a Fireworks graphic but as individual elements on separate layers, use the Edit→Copy as Vectors command in Fireworks. Then when you Edit→Paste the image into Flash, you see this dialog box giving you different options for the way the graphic is added to your Flash animation.*

# ■ Editing Bitmaps

Depending on the graphics file format you import into Flash, you may be able to edit the image using Flash's tools, or you may not. If Flash recognizes the image as a *vector* image, with distinct strokes and fills, you're good to go. Just open the Tools panel, choose a selection, drawing, or painting tool, and then get to work.

But if the image comes through as a bitmap, then you need to do a bit of finagling, because Flash treats bitmaps as big blobs of undifferentiated pixels. (See the box on page 365 for more details.)

With bitmaps, Flash's selection tools don't work as you might expect. Say, for instance, you import a scanned-in photo of the Seattle skyline. Flash treats the entire photo as a single entity. When you click the Space Needle, Flash selects the entire scanned-in image. When you try to use the Lasso tool to select the half of the image that contains Mount Rainier, Flash selects the entire image. When you try to repaint the sky a lighter shade of gray, Flash paints around or behind the imported bitmap, but not the sky.

Fortunately, Flash gives you a few options when it comes to working with bitmaps: You can break them apart, you can turn them into vector graphics, or you can turn them into symbols. The following sections describe each option.

## Turning Bitmaps into Fills

*Breaking apart* a bitmap image transforms the image from a homogenous group of pixels into an editable fill. You still can't click the Space Needle and have Flash recognize it as a distinct shape (you can do that only with vector art), but you *can* use the Selection, Subselection, and Lasso tools to select the Space Needle, and then either cut it, copy it, move it, repaint it, or otherwise edit it separately from the rest of the scanned-in image.

To break apart a bitmap:

1. **On the stage, select the bitmap image you want to break apart.**

   Flash displays a selection box around the image.

2. **Choose Modify→Break Apart.**

   Flash covers the image with tiny white dots to let you know it's now a fill.

At this point, you can use the Selection, Subselection, and Lasso tools to select portions of the image (something you *couldn't* do before you broke the bitmap apart).

---

**UP TO SPEED**

### Vector vs. Bitmap Images

Flash lets you import and work with two different types of graphics files: vector and bitmap. You can't tell what type an image is by looking at it—the difference is in the structure of the information that makes up the image. Here are the main points:

Computer programs, including Flash, store vector graphics (such as the original artwork you create on the stage) as a bunch of formulas. Vector graphics have the advantage of being pretty modest in size compared with bitmaps, and they're scalable. In other words, if you draw a tiny blackbird and then decide to scale it by 500 percent, your scaled drawing will still look like a nice, crisp blackbird, only bigger.

In contrast, computer programs store *bitmap*, or *raster*, graphics (such as a digital or scanned-in photo) as a bunch of pixels. Bitmap doesn't refer just to files with the Windows bitmap (.bmp) extension; it refers to all images stored in bitmap format, including gif, .jpg, .png, and .tif. (You can find a complete list of the file formats Flash lets you import on page 353.)

The good thing about bitmap graphics is that they let you create super-realistic detail, complete with complex colors, gradients, and subtle shadings. On the downside, bitmaps typically take up a whopping amount of disk space, and they're *not* particularly scalable: If you scale a photo of a blackbird by 500 percent, it appears blurry because all Flash can do is enlarge each individual pixel: It doesn't have access to the formulas it would need to draw the additional pixels necessary to keep the detail crisp and sharp at five times the original image size.

Why do you care whether a graphics file is a vector or a bitmap? Because you work with imported bitmap files differently in Flash than you do with imported or original vector files. As you see on page 364, you need to break bitmap images apart before you can crop them in Flash. Depending on your export settings, you may need to optimize the bitmaps to reduce the size of your finished animation. (Chapter 20 provides the details.)

---

## Turning Bitmaps into Vectors

*Tracing* a bitmap transforms it into a vector graphic. You can check out the box above for a rundown of the differences between the two, but basically, turning a bitmap into a vector gives you three benefits:

- It can produce a cool, stylized, watercolor effect.
- It may reduce the file size associated with the image (but only in cases where the image doesn't have a lot of different colors or gradients).

- It turns a nonscalable image into a scalable image—one you can "zoom in" on without it turning all fuzzy on you.

> **NOTE** The fewer colors your bitmap has, the more faithful your bitmap-turned-vector is likely to be to the original. Tracing a bitmap of a hand-drawn sketch done in black charcoal, for example, is going to result in a vector graphic that resembles the original bitmap much more closely than a bitmap trace of a scanned-in photo. (Even photos that look to the naked eye as though they have only a handful of colors usually contain many, many more at the pixel level.)

To trace a bitmap, select the bitmap you want to turn into a vector graphic, and then select Modify→Bitmap→Trace Bitmap. Figure 10-8 shows you an example.

### ■ TURNING BITMAPS INTO SYMBOLS

Suppose you want to add an old-timey sepia color to a photo or you want your bitmap to gradually fade and then disappear. You can't change the color, brightness, or transparency (*alpha*) of an imported bitmap, but you *can* change them for a symbol. So if all you want to do is tint or fade a bitmap, you can use a quick and easy fix, and transform it into a symbol.

To turn a bitmap into a symbol:

1. **Select the bitmap, and then choose Modify→"Convert to Symbol."**

   The "Convert to Symbol" dialog box appears.

2. **In the "Convert to Symbol" dialog box, choose Movie Clip from the drop-down menu, and then click OK.**

   In the Properties panel, click the drop-down list next to Color Effect to set the symbol's brightness, tint, and alpha (transparency) settings. If you convert bitmaps to movie clip symbols, then you can apply filter effects in the Properties panel (page 276). If you don't intend to apply a filter and you want to create the smallest possible file size, choose Graphic from the drop-down menu.

> **NOTE** For the skinny on symbols, check out Chapter 7; for more on color, brightness, and transparency, see Chapter 5.

## ■ Editing Bitmaps with Photoshop

Photoshop is a much more powerful tool than Flash when it comes to editing bitmap images. If you have experience with Photoshop, Fireworks, or some other image editor, you probably prefer using it for some chores. These days, that's not hard to do provided you have the programs installed on your computer. Right-click (Control-click) the bitmap image in Flash's Library and choose Edit with Photoshop. If you prefer another image editor, such as Fireworks, click the Edit With option and find the program you want to use. In either case, your bitmap editor of choice opens with the image ready for editing. When you're done, save and close the file and return to Flash, where you see the changes already in place. No File Import commands needed. With each version of the Creative Suite, Adobe adds features to make this kind of round trip editing easier.

**FIGURE 10-8**

*Top: Here's the way a scanned-in image looks as a bitmap.*

*Middle: Here's how it looks after Flash has traced it (turned it into vector art). Depending on your settings, the results may be artistic than, rather than realistic. Here the color threshold and the minimum area are both set to 60.*

*Bottom: With the layer set to show outlines, you see the edges for each swath of color.*

# ▪ Importing a Series of Graphics Files

At times, you may have a series of graphics files you want to import into Flash. Say, for example, you have a series of images you took with a digital camera showing a dog leaping through the air to catch a tennis ball. If you import all these images into Flash, one per frame, you've got yourself an animation. (How herky-jerky or smooth the animation appears depends on how many images you have; the more images, the smoother the animation.)

If you give your graphics files sequential names like *dog_01.gif, dog_02.gif, dog_03. gif*, and so on, Flash is smart enough to recognize what you're trying to do and asks if you want to import the entire series.

To import a series of graphics:

1. **Make sure the names of the files you want to import end with sequential numbers.**

   For example, *file1.bmp, file2.bmp*, and *file3.bmp*.

2. **Choose File→Import→"Import to Stage."**

   The Import dialog box you see in Figure 10-9 (top) appears.

**FIGURE 10-9**

*When you tell Flash to open the first in a series of sequentially numbered files (top), the program asks if you'd like to import the entire series (bottom). This trick works only if the numbers appear at the end of the filename just before the extension and if you don't skip any numbers in the series. And since Flash begins importing with the numbered file you chose, it doesn't go back and pick up files containing lower numbers.*

3. **In the Import dialog box, click to select the first file in the series, and then click Import.**

The confirmation dialog box you see in Figure 10-9 (bottom) appears.

4. **Click Yes.**

The confirmation dialog box disappears, and Flash imports the series of files. In the timeline, you see one image (and one keyframe) per frame.

If you check the Library panel (Window→Library), you see that Flash has placed each of the image files in the Library.

---

**DESIGN TIME**

## Using Bridge as a File Manager

A Flash chapter that discusses different graphics file formats isn't complete without a mention of Bridge, Adobe's program for managing media files of all types (Figure 10-10). If you got Flash as part of an Adobe Creative Suite collection, you probably have Bridge installed on your computer. If you think you're perfectly happy managing files with Mac's Finder or Windows's Explorer, you don't know what you're missing. Bridge is much more powerful and customizable than either of those handy and necessary utility programs. Because Bridge is devoted to media files and because Adobe has the proprietary key to some of the most important file formats (Photoshop and Illustrator), Bridge is a more powerful graphics program than your typical OS utility.

Like Finder and Explorer, you can select a file from a thumbnail in Bridge, and then launch a program to open it. But Bridge is much more versatile and flexible when it comes to organizing media files and showing you the files you want at a given moment. Bridge tracks all sorts of information about the photos, graphics, videos, and sound files on your computer, and you get to decide exactly how those details are displayed. For example, if you manage a large collection of photographs, Bridge excels at managing photos' descriptive *metadata*. (Cameras automatically store details about a photograph in the photo file. That

includes details like the date a picture was snapped or edited, the exposure used, and the type of lens. As a photographer or photo archivist, you can also add other metadata tags to photos to make them easier to find in searches.) Bridge gives you the tools to read the metadata in photos, and to find, sort, and view photos based on those details.

There's not enough room here to fully describe Bridge, but here's a short list of some of the things it can do:

- Organize media assets including photos, graphics, video, and audio files.
- Show media files from different computer folders in a single catalog.
- Preview Flash SWF files, while using the file catalog.
- Compare and preview most media files.
- Show/hide/find files based on criteria that you provide.
- Automatically import, name, and store photos from digital cameras and card readers.
- Run automated tasks from programs like Photoshop.
- Manage the tags (metadata) embedded in photos and other graphics files.

---

# Exporting Graphics from Flash

Sometimes you have artwork in Flash that you'd like to use in another program. Perhaps it's a single image that you want to place on a web page, or maybe it's an entire animation that you want to save in a format other than Flash's SWF format. In either case, it's easy to save that artwork in a format that other programs can use. As you might expect, Flash plays especially well with other Adobe programs like Illustrator, Photoshop, and Fireworks.

**FIGURE 10-10**

*Bridge is Adobe's program for managing, organizing, cataloging, and previewing media files of all flavors. You can customize the program to show the details you need for your media files.*

To Export graphics from Flash, go to File→Export, and then choose either Export Image or Export Movie. Flash opens a box similar to Figure 10-11, where you can name your file and choose its format. After you click Save, Flash displays another box, where you can choose options specific to the movie or image file format you selected. The complete details for exporting single images and animations from Flash are covered in Chapter 20.

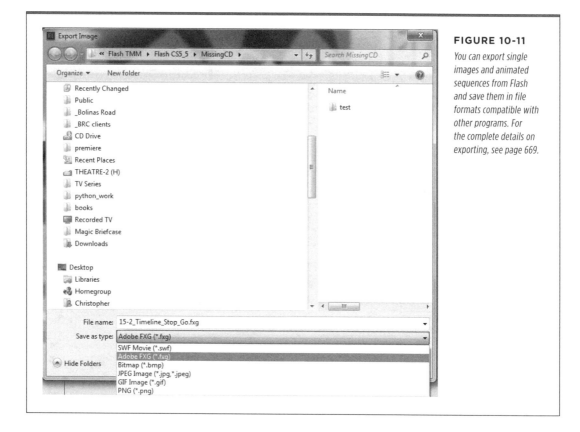

**FIGURE 10-11**

*You can export single images and animated sequences from Flash and save them in file formats compatible with other programs. For the complete details on exporting, see page 669.*

# Incorporating
# Sound and Video

You can create almost any kind of picture or effect in Flash, but sometimes you already have the perfect piece of sound or video...and it's in another file. No problem: Flash lets you pull in all kinds of other media files—like songs in MP3 files or QuickTime videos. Whether you're showcasing your band's performances, creating an employee training website, or creating an online wedding album, Flash has all the multimedia tools for the job.

When Flash was born, it was a big deal to have moving pictures on the Internet. Most folks had pretty slow Internet connections, so it was a kick to see pictures move, even if they were simple, cartoonish images. The same was true of even the most basic sound effects. Today, we expect to use the Net to watch our favorite movies, sports, and TV shows. Sounds have gone from beeps and bells to radio broadcasts, audiobooks, and entire albums of music. Things have changed, and Flash is often at the center of the revolution. Apple's resistance to Flash on its handheld devices has been an epic battle between two tech heavyweights. One reason it's been so controversial is the fact that so many websites use Flash to broadcast video.

As the number of people with fast Internet connections grew, web developers began to use Flash video (FLV) to broadcast. Most of the web browsers in the world have Flash capabilities—Adobe's estimates are way above 90 percent. For you, the good news is that when you wrap your audio and video offerings in Flash, you don't have to force your audience to download and install yet another plug-in. This chapter explains how to add sound to your animations and how to edit that sound for the best fit. You'll also learn how to present video in a predesigned component that gives the audience playback controls.

# ■ Incorporating Sound

Flash lets you score your animations much the same way a filmmaker scores a movie. You can add a soundtrack that begins when your animation begins and ends when it ends. Or you can tie different sound clips to different *scenes* (series of frames) of your animation. For example, say you're creating an instructional animation to demonstrate your company's egg slicer. You can play music during the opening seconds of your animation, switch to a voice-over to describe your product, and then end with realistic sounds of boiling, peeling, and slicing to match the visual of cooks using your product in a real-life setting.

You can also tie sounds to specific *events* in Flash. For example, say you want your instructional animation to contain a button someone can press to get ordering information. You can tie the sound of a button clicking to the Down state of your button, so when someone clicks your button, she actually *hears* a realistic clicking sound.

**NOTE**   Looking for the perfect sound effect? Start your search in the Sounds library. It's crammed full of noises made by animals, machines, and nature. To add a Library sound to your animation, choose Window→Common Libraries→Sounds, and drag a sound to the stage.

## Importing Sound Files

Before you can work with sound in Flash, you need to import a sound file either to the stage, the Library, or both. Flash lets you import a variety of sound files, as you can see in Table 11-1.

**TABLE 11-1** *Audio file formats you can import into Flash*

| FILE TYPE | EXTENSION | NOTE |
|---|---|---|
| WAV sound | .wav | Works on Windows only, *unless* you have QuickTime 4 (or later) installed; then you can import .wav files into Flash on the Mac, too. |
| MP3 sound | .mp3 | Works on both Mac and Windows. |
| Adobe Sound Document | .asnd | Sound files used by Adobe's Soundbooth editing and mixing program. |
| Audio Interchange File format | aiff, .aif | Works on Mac only, *unless* you have Quick-Time 4 (or later) installed; then you can import AIFF files into Flash running in Windows, too. |
| Sound Designer II | .sd2 | Only works on Mac, and only if you have QuickTime 4 (or later) installed. |
| Sound-only QuickTime movies | .mov, .qtif | Works on both Windows and Mac, but only if you have QuickTime 4 (or later) installed. |
| Sun AU | .au | Works on both Windows and Mac, but only if you have QuickTime 4 (or later) installed. |

To import a sound file:

1. **Select File→Import→"Import to Library."**

   The "Import to Library" dialog box appears.

2. **In the "File name" field, type the name of the sound file you want to import (or, in the file window, click the file to have Flash fill in the name for you).**

   To see the different types of sound files you can import, you can either click the drop-down menu at the bottom of the "Import to Library" dialog box, or check out Table 11-1.

3. **Click Open ("Import to Library" on a Mac).**

   The "Import to Library" dialog box disappears, and Flash places a copy of the imported sound file into the Library (Figure 11-1). When you click to select any of the frames in your timeline, the Sound subpanel appears in the Properties panel.

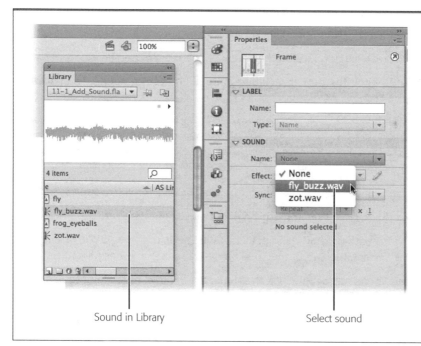

Sound in Library

Select sound

**FIGURE 11-1**

*The visual representation Flash displays when you select an imported sound clip is called a waveform. (As discussed on page 382, you use this waveform when you're editing a sound clip in Flash.) When you click the Play button that Flash displays along with the waveform, you can preview the sound. Flash puts a copy of your imported file in the Library and makes the imported file available in the Properties panel.*

## Adding an Imported Sound to a Frame (or Series of Frames)

You can tell Flash to play an animated sound beginning with any frame of your animation. Depending on the settings you choose, Flash keeps playing the sound file either until it finishes (regardless of whether your animation is still playing) or until you tell it to stop.

This example shows you how to use the *stream* option to synchronize a short sound clip of a fly buzzing with an animated sequence showing—what else?—a buzzing fly. Then you'll learn how to start and stop a second sound (the sound of the fly becoming a frog's lunch).

To add an imported sound to a series of frames:

1.  **Open the file *11-1_Add_Sound.fla.***

    This file includes a simple animated sequence with a frog and a fly. The library already includes a couple of previously imported sounds. You can find this file on the Missing CD page at *www.missingmanuals.com/cds/flashcs6mm*. (To see a working version, check out *11-2_Add_Sound_done.fla*.)

2.  **In the Layers window, click to select the topmost layer (fly).**

    Flash highlights the layer name, as well as all the frames in that layer.

3.  **Select Insert→Timeline→Layer.**

    Flash creates a new layer and places it above the selected layer.

4.  **Double-click the new layer name, and then type in *sounds*, as shown in Figure 11-2.**

---

**TIP**   You add a sound to a button the same way you see shown here, but with two exceptions: You typically add a sound file for a button to the button's third, or Down, frame (so that the sound plays when your audience clicks *down* on the button) and you leave the synchronization option set to Event. To see an example, check out the file *11-3_Button_Sound.fla* on the Missing CD page.

---

5.  **Click the first keyframe in the newly created sounds layer.**

    In the Properties panel, Flash activates the Frame properties. With a sound file in the Library, the Sound subpanel appears in the Properties panel.

6.  **In the Sound subpanel, click the Name drop-down menu, and then choose the imported sound file *fly_buzz.wav*.**

    Alternatively, you can drag the sound file symbol from the Library to the stage. Either way, the sound properties for the file appear at the bottom of the Properties panel, and the waveform for the buzzing fly sound appears in the soundtrack layer (Figure 11-3).

7. **In the Properties panel, click the Sync field, and then, from the first drop-down list that appears, choose Stream.**

   Your synchronization choices include these:

   - **Event.** Tells Flash to give the sound its very own timeline. In other words, Flash keeps playing the sound until the sound finishes, regardless of whether or not the animation has ended. If you repeat (or loop) the animation in the Controller, Flash begins playing a new sound clip every time the animation begins again—with the result that, after a dozen or so loops, you hear a dozen flies buzzing! Flash assumes you want your sound to behave this way unless you tell it otherwise.

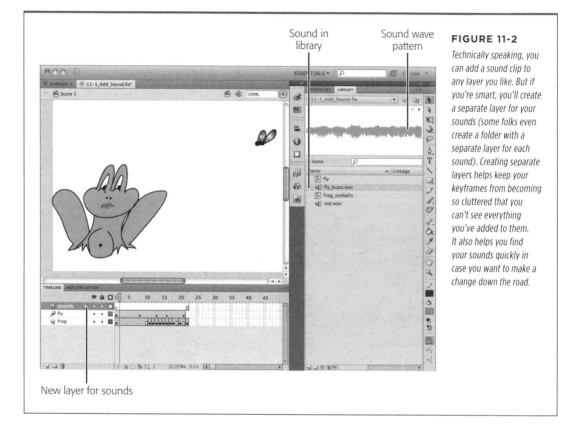

Sound in
library

Sound wave
pattern

New layer for sounds

**FIGURE 11-2**

*Technically speaking, you can add a sound clip to any layer you like. But if you're smart, you'll create a separate layer for your sounds (some folks even create a folder with a separate layer for each sound). Creating separate layers helps keep your keyframes from becoming so cluttered that you can't see everything you've added to them. It also helps you find your sounds quickly in case you want to make a change down the road.*

   - **Start.** Similar to Event, but tells Flash *not* to begin playing a new sound if the animation repeats.
   - **Stop.** Tells Flash to stop playing the sound.

- **Stream.** Tells Flash to match the animation to the sound clip as best it can, either by speeding up or slowing down the frames-per-second that it plays the animation. This option is the one you want for *lip-synching*, when you're trying to match a voice-over to an animated sequence featuring a talking head. Because choosing this option also tells Flash to *stream* the sound file (play it before it's fully downloaded in those cases where you've put your animation on a website), someone with a slow connection can get a herky-jerky animation.

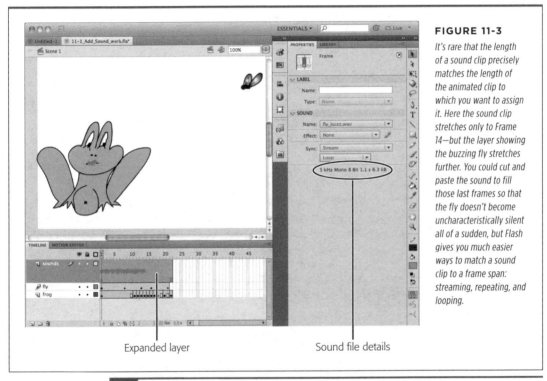

**FIGURE 11-3**

*It's rare that the length of a sound clip precisely matches the length of the animated clip to which you want to assign it. Here the sound clip stretches only to Frame 14—but the layer showing the buzzing fly stretches further. You could cut and paste the sound to fill those last frames so that the fly doesn't become uncharacteristically silent all of a sudden, but Flash gives you much easier ways to match a sound clip to a frame span: streaming, repeating, and looping.*

Expanded layer

Sound file details

**TIP** With your sound set to stream, you can preview your newly added sound on the stage, drag (*scrub*) the playhead along the timeline. You can scrub forward or backward. To hear just the sound in a specific frame, Shift-click the playhead over that frame. Flash keeps playing the sound until you let up on either the Shift key or the mouse.

## Using Sound Effectively

If you've ever watched a movie that had a breathtakingly beautiful (or laughably cheesy) musical score, you've experienced the power of sound firsthand. Effective sound can elevate a decent visual experience into the realm of art. Ineffective sound can turn that same visual experience into a nerve-shredding mess.

If you're thinking about adding sound to your animation, consider these points:

- **Why do you want to add sound?** If your answer is to add emotional punch; to cue your audience aurally to the interactive features you've added to your animation, like buttons that *click* or draggable objects that *whoosh*; or to deliver information you can't deliver any other way (like a voice-over explaining an animated sequence or realistic sounds to accompany the sequence); then by all means go for it. But if your answer is "Because I can," then you need to rethink your decision. Sound—as much as any graphic element—needs to add to the overall message you're trying to deliver or it'll end up detracting from that message.

- **Are you sure your audience will be able to hear your sound?** Sound files are big. They take time to download. If you're planning to put your animation on a website, Flash gives you a couple of different options for managing download time—but keep in mind that not everyone in your audience may have a fast connection or the volume knob on her speaker turned up. (For that matter, some folks can't hear. Check out the box on page 34 for tips on providing hearing-impaired folks with an alternate way of getting your information.)

- **How important is it that your soundtrack matches your animation precisely?** Flash gives you options to help you synchronize your sound clips with your frames. But you can't match a 2-second sound clip to a 10-second animated sequence without either slowing down the sound or speeding up the animation. If you want to match a specific sound clip to a specific series of frames, you may need to edit one (or both) to get the balance right before you begin synchronizing them in Flash.

8. **From the second drop-down menu next to the Sync field, choose Loop.**

   Loop tells Flash to repeat the sound clip until the timeline ends. Repeat lets you tell Flash how many times you want it to play the sound clip (regardless of the length of the frame span).

9. **Test the soundtracked animation by choosing Control→Test Movie.**

   You hear a buzzing sound as the fly loops its way across the test movie.

Add a second, short sound clip to your animation to make the scene more realistic. To do so:

1. **In the "sound" layer, click Frame 20.**

   On the stage, you see the frog's tongue appear (Figure 11-4).

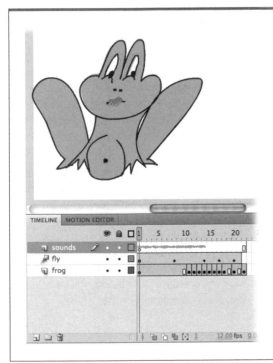

**FIGURE 11-4**

*Beginning sound clips in individual keyframes let you change the soundtrack at the exact moment your visuals change. Here you see the frog's tongue appear in Frame 20 of the frog layer, and it doesn't change until Frame 22 (which contains the final keyframe of the animation). So to match the "zot!" sound to the tongue action, you want to tell Flash to start playing the zot.wav file on Frame 20 and stop playing it on Frame 22.*

2. **Select Insert→Timeline→Blank Keyframe, or press F6.**

   Flash places a blank keyframe (a hollow circle) in Frame 20.

3. **With Frame 20 selected, in the Sound subpanel, click the arrow next to Name, and then, from the drop-down list that appears, choose *zot.wav.***

   Flash places the waveform for the sound file into the timeline, beginning with Frame 20.

---

**TIP**  If you need a better view of the sound's waveform in your timeline, right-click the layer with the sound, and then choose Properties. The Properties panel opens. At the bottom, set the layer height to either 200% or 300%, as shown in Figure 11-3.

---

4. **In the Properties panel, click the arrow next to Sync, and then, from the drop-down list that appears, choose Start.** Then, in the soundtrack layer, click to select Frame 22.

   On the stage, you see a very satisfied frog (Figure 11-5).

**FIGURE 11-5**

*Because the synchronization option for the "zot!" sound was set to start in Frame 20, Flash automatically stops playing the zot.wav sound file when the animation ends. Still, it's good practice to tell Flash specifically when you want it to stop playing a sound file. You'll be glad you did when you come back to the animation a week or two later, because you won't have any cleanup to do before you add additional sounds to the timeline.*

5. **Select Insert→Timeline→Blank Keyframe or press F6.**

   Flash places a blank keyframe (a hollow circle) in Frame 22.

6. **In the Sound subpanel, click the Name drop-down menu, and then choose *zot.wav.*** Click the arrow next to Sync, and then, from the drop-down list that appears, choose Stop.

   You're done!

7. **Test the new sound by choosing Control→Test Movie.**

   You hear a buzzing sound as the fly loops its way across the test movie. But as the frog's tongue appears, the buzzing stops and you hear a satisfying "zot!"

---

**TIP** If you don't hear any sounds, select Control and see whether the checkbox next to Mute Sounds is turned on. If it is, click it to turn it off.

---

## Editing Sound Clips in Flash

You can change the way your imported sound clips play in Flash. You can't do anything super-fancy, like mix down multiple audio channels or add reverb—Flash isn't a sound-editing program, after all—but you *can* crop the clips, add simple fade-in/fade-out effects, and even choose which speaker (right or left) your sounds play out of.

### Stock Images, Sounds, and Video Clips

If you're using Flash to create stuff for work—presentations, tutorials, web advertisements, marketing materials, or what have you—then you or someone else on your team is probably going to be creating all your content from scratch. But there's a place in every Flash fan's toolkit for *stock media*: generic images, sound clips, and video clips that you purchase (or, more rarely, get for free) from companies whose job it is to produce such items.

Typically, you pay a modest fee to use stock images, sounds, and video clips. Sometimes, you also pay a royalty fee based on the number of times you use a stock element in your animation.

If you're using Flash to jazz up your personal website, you may find that stock media is just what the doctor ordered: You get something cool that you can use for a relatively low price without having to invest time and money buying audio and video equipment or taking drawing lessons.

But even professional animators have been known to rely on stock media occasionally because it lets them test out a concept quickly and cheaply.

Places to find stock images, sound clips, and video clips abound on the Web. Here are a few you might want to check out:

> www.freestockfootage.com
>
> www.wildform.com/videolibrary
>
> www.flashkit.com/soundfx
>
> www.gettyimages.com

First, import the sound clip you want to edit, as described on page 374. To edit it, follow these steps:

1. **In the timeline, click any frame that contains a portion of the sound clip's waveform.**

    Flash activates the sound options you see in the Properties panel.

2. **In the Properties panel, click the drop-down box next to Effect, and then choose from the following menu options:**

    - **Left channel.** Tells Flash to play the sound through the left speaker.

    - **Right channel.** Tells Flash to play the sound through the right speaker.

    - **Fade left to right.** Tells Flash to begin playing the sound through the left speaker and then switch midway through the clip to the right speaker.

    - **Fade right to left.** Tells Flash to begin playing the sound through the right speaker and then switch midway through the clip to the left speaker.

    - **Fade in.** Tells Flash to start playing the sound softly, and then build to full volume.

- **Fade out.** Tells Flash to start playing the sound at full volume, and then taper off toward the end.

- **Custom.** Tells Flash to display the Edit Envelope window you see in Figure 11-6, which lets you choose the *in point* (the point where you want Flash to begin playing the sound) and the *out point* (where you want the sound clip to end). You can also choose a custom fading effect; for example, you can fade in, then out, then in again.

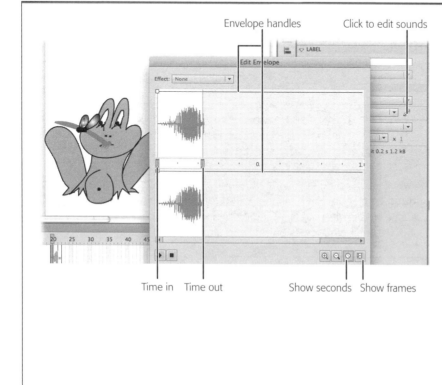

Envelope handles     Click to edit sounds

Time in   Time out     Show seconds   Show frames

**FIGURE 11-6**

*The sound file you see here is a two-channel (stereo) sound, so you see two separate waveforms, one per channel. To crop the sound clip, drag the time in and time out control bars left and right. Flash ignores the gray area during playback and plays only the portion of the waveform that appears with a white background, so here Flash plays only the second half of the waveform. To create a custom fading effect, you can drag the envelope handles separately. These settings tell Flash to fade out on the left channel while simultaneously fading in on the right channel. To preview your custom effect, click the Play icon.*

**TIP**   Clicking the Property panel's Edit button displays the same Edit Envelope window you see when you choose the Custom option.

If you want to do more extensive sound editing, you need a separate program like Adobe's Audition. It comes with some, but not all, of the Creative Suites. If you need a sound editor but have cash flow concerns, check out Audacity (*http://audacity. sourceforge.net*). It's free and works on Windows, Mac, and Linux computers.

# ■ Incorporating Video

In the past years, Flash has become the video champion of the Internet. You find Flash video on sites from YouTube to Hulu to CNET. The major networks ABC, CBS, and NBC also use Flash video. It wasn't long ago that a battle royale raged among Microsoft, Apple, and RealMedia for web video bragging rights. Flash was seldom mentioned in the contest; after all, it was just for making little animations. But, like the Trojans with their famous horse, Flash Player managed to sneak onto about 90 percent of today's computers. And guess what? Flash does video, too. It's easy for you to add video to a web page or any other project by adding it to a Flash animation. It's easy for your audience, too, since they don't have to download and install a special plug-in to watch your masterpiece. Flash is also fueling the surge in video blogging, or *vlogging*—adding video clips to plain-vanilla blogs. You can find out more at sites like *http://mashable.com/2009/10/09/video-blogging*.

> **TIP** If you're watching a video on the Web and wondering whether the site uses Flash to publish it, right-click (Control-click) the video. If you see "About Flash Player" in the shortcut menu, you know Flash is working behind the scenes.

May as well face it: Sometimes video footage is more effective than even the most well-crafted animation. For example, video footage showing a live product demonstration, a kid blowing out the candles on his birthday cake, or an interview with a CEO can get the point across quickly and directly.

> **TIP** Neither Flash nor the Adobe Media Encoder let you do extensive editing. At best, they let you crop a segment out of a larger video clip. If you're interested in piecing together different video segments to create a movie or a scene, turn to a specialized video editing program like Adobe Premiere or Apple Final Cut Pro. If your needs are more modest, you can probably get by with Premiere Elements, Apple's iMovie, or Microsoft's MovieMaker.

There are two basic steps to creating Flash video:

- **Convert your video to the Flash video file format: .flv or .f4v.** Before you can add video to your Flash animation, you have to convert it to a special file format. The process, which video techies call *encoding*, creates small files that can travel quickly over the Internet. Flash comes with the Adobe Media Encoder, which lets you convert most types of video into Flash video format. The next section describes the encoding process.

- **Import your video into a Flash animation.** Once your video clip is in Flash video format, you can import it into your project. Flash stores a copy of the video in the Library, and you can drag the video to the stage like any other graphic. It's remarkably easy to add video playback controls to your Flash video. If you have a video that's already in the Flash video format (.flv or .f4v), you can jump ahead to page 396 to learn how to import it into your Flash file.

# Encoding: Making Flash Video Files

Video files are notoriously huge, which means they take a long time to travel the Internet. To solve this problem, Flash uses special video formats that shrink or compress video into smaller files. The quality might not be what you'd expect from your 60-inch LED HDTV, but it's certainly acceptable for web delivery. The process of converting a video from its original format to Flash video (.flv or .f4v) is called encoding. If you already have a file in the Flash video format, or if someone else is responsible for this part of the job, you can jump ahead to page 396.

---

**UP TO SPEED**

## Overcompression: Too Much of a Good Thing

The final destination for many Flash projects is a website. One of Flash's great virtues is the ability to present animations, video, and sound over the Web without making the audience wait while humongous files travel the Internet. Flash makes big files small by compressing them. It uses different compression methods for images, sound files, and video files. Some types of compression actually degrade the image, sound, or video quality. It's a tradeoff, but it's the best way to create really small files that travel the Net quickly. The idea is to keep as much information as is needed to maintain acceptable quality and throw out the extra bits. These types of compression schemes are called lossy formats because they lose data and, as a result, lose quality. Examples of lossy formats are JPEG photo files, MP3 audio files, and FLV or F4V Flash video files. While compression is a good thing because it keeps the file size down and helps web-based Flash animations load quickly, it's possible to overcompress a file. One way that happens is when you compress a file that's already been compressed.

If you repeatedly compress photos, sound files, and video files, you can end up with media mush. For example, take a

JPEG and save it five times using 50% quality—you'll find that the last copy is much poorer in quality than the first. You can do the same thing to MP3 audio files and video files. Ideally, it's best to bring uncompressed files into Flash, and then let Flash do the compression once, when it publishes an SWF file.

For audio files, that means it's best to use uncompressed AIFF files on a Mac or WAV files on a PC. For video files, use video that hasn't already been compressed. On a PC, you can use uncompressed AVI files; on a Mac, use uncompressed QuickTime MOV files. If you're working in another video editing program and there's an option to encode directly to Flash Video (.flv or .f4v), choose that. Then you can skip the step with Media Encoder. With video, the compression takes place when you use the Adobe Media Encoder to make .flv or .f4v files. So, if you just shot the video with your camcorder, feed the raw .dv file to Adobe Media Encoder for the best results. If the file is coming from someone else, ask him to give you the best quality possible.

---

Using the Adobe Media Encoder, you can encode any of the common video files listed in Table 11-2. As explained in the box on page 385, it's best to start off with a high-quality, uncompressed video. You can add prebuilt controls that let your audience control the playback and adjust the volume. You can even apply effects to a video clip in Flash; for example, skewing and tinting.

**TABLE 11-2** *Some of the most popular video file formats you can convert to Flash Video with Adobe Media Encoder*

| FILE TYPE | EXTENSION | NOTE |
|---|---|---|
| QuickTime movie | .mov | The audio/video format Apple's video player uses. A free version of QuickTime player is available for both Macs and PCs. |
| Audio Video Interleaved | .avi, .wav | Microsoft audio/video formats. |
| Motion Picture Experts Group | .mpg, .mpeg | MPEG-1 is an early standard for compressed audio and video media. |
| | .mp2, m2v | MPEG-2 is what standard DVDs use. |
| | .mp4, .m4v, .m4a, .mts | MPEG-4 Part 2 is used by the DivX and Xvid codecs. |
| | .264 | MPEG Part 10 is used by QuickTime 7 and the H.264 codec. |
| Digital video | .dv | Many camcorders use this digital video format. |
| Windows Media | .asf, .wmv, .wma | These Microsoft formats are for compressed audio/ video files. |
| Flash video | .flv, .f4v | Flash's video format employs a lossy compression technique to produce very small files suitable for broadcast over the Internet. |

The hardest part of encoding video files is the wait. It takes time to encode large video files, but it's getting better with today's faster computers. Flash CS6's installer automatically puts Adobe Media Encoder on your computer. Fire it up, and it looks like Figure 11-7. There are two basic things you need to do: Locate the file you want to encode, and give Adobe Media Encoder instructions about how to process it. Here are the steps:

1. **In Adobe Media Encoder, click the + button in the upper-left corner.**

   Flash displays a standard Open window similar to the one you use to open a Flash document.

2. **Navigate to the file on your computer that you want to encode, and then click Open.**

   The name of the video file appears in the Queue panel.

3. **Under Format, choose the Flash video format: FLV or F4V.**

   Choose F4V if your target is one of the newer smartphones or tablets. The FLV format is useful for websites with a slower transmission rate. It works with Flash Player 8 and later. The F4V formats show better quality video in smaller files, but they work only in Flash Player 9 and later. You can get an idea of the suitability of a format by examining the available presets, described in the next step. Flash gives you these presets (predetermined settings) because choosing all the settings to encode video can be ridiculously complicated. Even when you choose a file format like FLV or F4V, there are still dozens of settings you can choose based on how the video is to be distributed and viewed. Adobe helps you wade through the swamp of video settings by providing presets for common video needs.

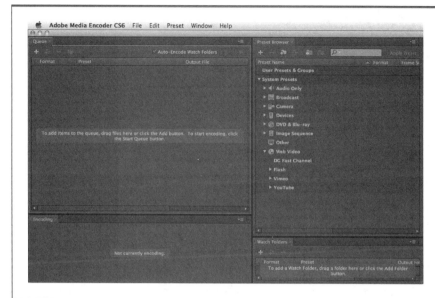

**FIGURE 11-7**

*Adobe Media Encoder is a multipurpose conversion tool that comes with several different Adobe products, including Flash. You add media files to the queue and tell Flash what type of file you want it to produce.*

4. **Under Preset, choose a preset format that matches your project.**

   The Media Encoder has what may seem like a bewildering number of presets, as shown in Figure 11-8. The names are descriptive: "Phone & Tablet wifi," "PC & TV High," "16x9." Experienced videographers may want to tweak the encoding settings or trim the video clip before it's encoded.

5. **Under Output, you can change the name or location of the file.**

   If you don't make any changes under Output, then the encoded file appears in the same folder as the original video file. It has the same name, but will end with either .flv or .f4v.

6. **Click the Start Queue button in the upper-right corner.**

   Adobe Media Encoder starts to encode your file. A bar tracks the progress (Figure 11-9). If you have several files to encode, then add them all to the queue before you hit Start Queue. The encoder makes no changes to the original file. When the encoder is finished, a checkmark appears next to the file in the queue, and you have a new file with an *.flv* or *.f4v* extension.

**TIP**   Want to see some details about the encoding process while you wait? Click the Current Encode tab near the bottom of the window.

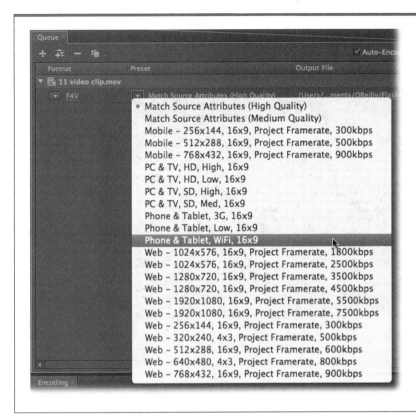

**FIGURE 11-8**

*When you first use Adobe Media Encoder, it's best to use one of the presets that match your project. Later, you may want to create your own settings by clicking Edit Export Settings. The presets shown here are for the F4V format.*

## ■ BATCH ENCODING TO SAVE TIME

No matter how you cut it, encoding video takes time and can slow down your computing workflow. If you have lots of video to encode, prepare several video clips for encoding using the steps described in this section. You can add several encoding jobs to the encoding queue and then run them all at the same time when you click Start Queue. Why not do all that encoding overnight or when you head out to lunch?

One way to encode batches of video is to create a *watch folder*. In essence, you tell the media encoder to automatically encode any video file that's dropped in your watch folder. If the Watch Folders panel isn't visible, go Window→Watch Folders. Click the + Add Folder button and choose one or more folders. You choose the file format and preset for each folder individually, making it possible to automatically encode to different settings. Once your folders are set up, make sure that the Auto Encode Watch Folders box at the top of the Queue panel is checked. At that point all you need to do to encode a video is drag it to one of your watch folders.

## Encoding Part of a Video Clip

There are a few reasons why you might want to dig into Adobe Media Encoder's export settings before you encode a file. One of the most common scenarios is that you have a long video and you need to bring only a small part of it into your Flash project. To do so, follow the encoding steps that begin on page 386. When you reach step 4, instead of choosing one of Adobe's presets, right-click (Control-click) the filename of your video and choose Export Settings. The next thing you see looks like a video editing window, shown in Figure 11-10. You can't do extensive editing in this window like you can with Adobe's Premiere or Apple's Final Cut, but you can select a portion of a video clip to encode. Encoding is pretty slow business, and there's no reason to waste time converting video that you won't use.

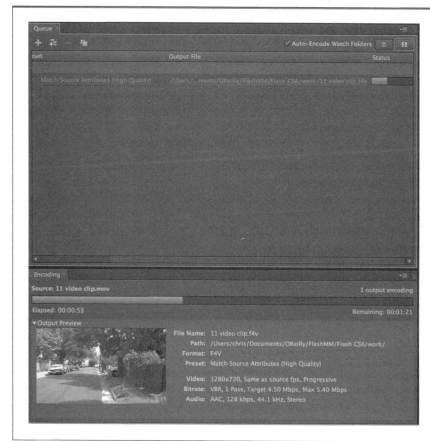

**FIGURE 11-9**

*While the Media Encoder processes your file, it keeps you updated with a progress bar and the estimated remaining time. The video also appears in a preview window.*

In the upper-left corner of the Export Settings window is a small preview screen. Below the screen is a timeline with a playhead similar to Flash's. Drag the playhead to see different frames in your video. The two markers in the timeline below the playhead are called the *in point* and the *out point*. You use these two points to select a segment of the video. As you drag either point, the preview window shows the image (or video frame) for that point in time. A highlight appears on the selected segment of video.

If you want to use one of Adobe's encoding presets, you can choose one in the upper-right corner of the Export Settings window. (If you'd rather tweak the export settings on your own, see page 390.) Click OK, and you're back at the Media Encoder, where you can change the name and location for your encoded file, as described in step 5 on page 387.

Preview source or output

Export video and/or audio

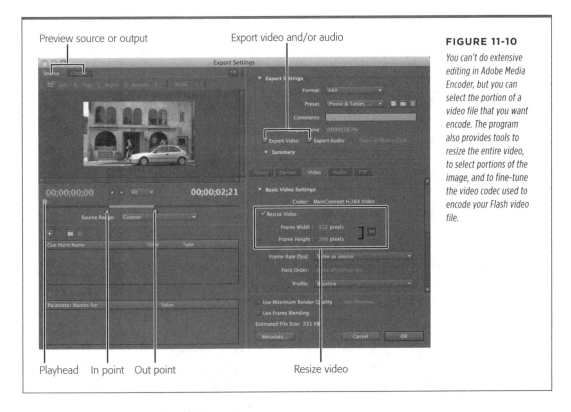

Playhead    In point    Out point

Resize video

**FIGURE 11-10**

*You can't do extensive editing in Adobe Media Encoder, but you can select the portion of a video file that you want encode. The program also provides tools to resize the entire video, to select portions of the image, and to fine-tune the video codec used to encode your Flash video file.*

## Resizing and Cropping a Video Clip

When you choose an encoding preset in Adobe Media Encoder, the preset determines the dimensions of the video image. For comparison, a wide-screen TV might show a high-definition image that's 1920 pixels wide by 1080 pixels high. When you choose the "Web–512x288" setting, the preset encodes an image that's 512 pixels wide by 288 pixels high. When you're in Export Settings, you can choose any size you want. Understandably, large dimensions, like those for that hi-def TV, mean much larger files. If your video is traveling the Internet, you can dramatically reduce the travel time by reducing the video dimensions. The 512 x 288 size of the "Web 512x288" preset is a nice, compact size for the Net. If you know everyone in your audience is going to have a fast cable or DSL connection, you can go ahead and bump the dimension up to a larger dimension.

After you've opened Adobe Media Encoder and added a video to the encoding queue, as described on page 386, follow these steps to choose a custom size for the encoded video:

1. **Instead of choosing one of Adobe's presets, right-click (Control-click) the video filename and choose Export Settings.**

   The Export Settings window appears, where you can fine-tune many aspects of the encoding process.

2. **On the right side of the Export Settings window, click the Video tab.**

   This tab displays details about frame size, frame rate, and bitrate, as shown in Figure 11-11.

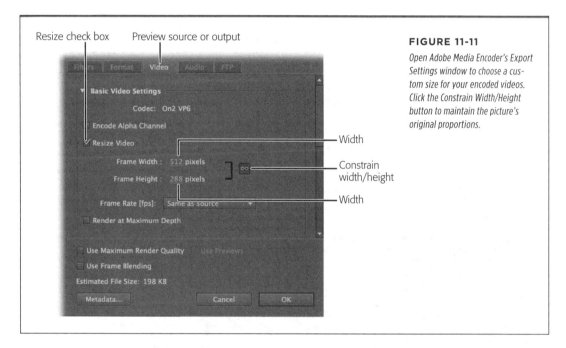

Resize check box    Preview source or output

**FIGURE 11-11**

*Open Adobe Media Encoder's Export Settings window to choose a custom size for your encoded videos. Click the Constrain Width/Height button to maintain the picture's original proportions.*

3. **Click the Resize Video checkbox.**

   Once you've checked the Resize Video box, the encoder uses the size dimensions entered in the next step.

4. **Change the height and width dimensions.**

   Most of the time, you want to maintain your video's proportions to keep the images from looking too tall or too fat. To constrain the proportion, make sure the Constrain Width/Height button is depressed. Then you can enter either a width or a height dimension, and the other dimension automatically sizes itself.

**5. Click OK.**

The Export Settings window closes, and you see the Adobe Media Encoder queue.

### ■ CROPPING A VIDEO WHILE ENCODING

Cropping a video is just like cropping a photo. Instead of resizing the entire image, you select a portion of the image that you want to view. With moving pictures, it's a little trickier, because the image is changing at multiple frames per second. The crop that looks great for the first 20 seconds of a clip might not look as good a minute later. Also keep in mind that when you crop a video, you're changing the dimensions and the quality of the image. When you crop into an image too far, you end up with a blurry picture.

To crop your video, follow the preceding steps to open the Export Settings window in Adobe Media Encoder. Above the preview window, click the Crop button. A frame appears around the video image with handles at the corner. Drag the handles to frame the portion of the picture you want to keep, as shown in Figure 11-12. A tooltip shows the dimensions of your video image in pixels. You can click the Crop dimension numbers and then type new values, but keep in mind that these numbers are showing the number of pixels being trimmed from the edges of the picture.

Crop button     Crop dimensions                        Crop box

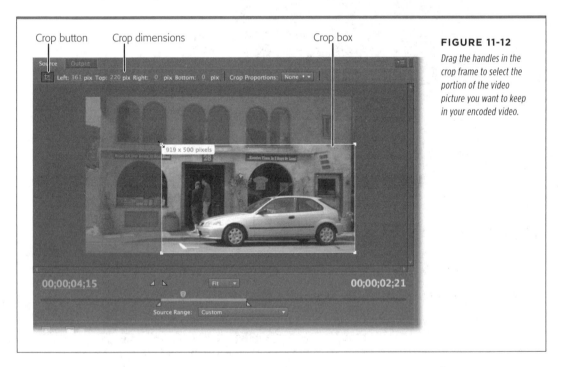

**FIGURE 11-12**

*Drag the handles in the crop frame to select the portion of the video picture you want to keep in your encoded video.*

## Adding Cue Points to Your Video

Flash lets you place *cue points* (markers) in your video clips, which you can then use to trigger other actions in your Flash animation. For example, perhaps you'd like to show text on the screen at a certain point in the video, or perhaps you'd like to trigger a certain sound or narration track. You give cue points names—like "narration"—as you create them. Then you use ActionScript code to identify the cue points and trigger the actions you want performed. (There's more on ActionScript starting in Chapter 12.)

You add cue points in Adobe Media Encoder, using the same Export Settings window that you use to resize or crop your video.

1. **In Media Encoder, select Edit→Export Settings to open the Export Settings window.**

   You see a preview window showing your video, with a timeline underneath, as shown in Figure 11-13. Just as in Flash, the timeline has a playhead. Drag the playhead to a point in the timeline, and you see that frame in your video. Below the preview, there are two panels: one for cue points and one for parameters.

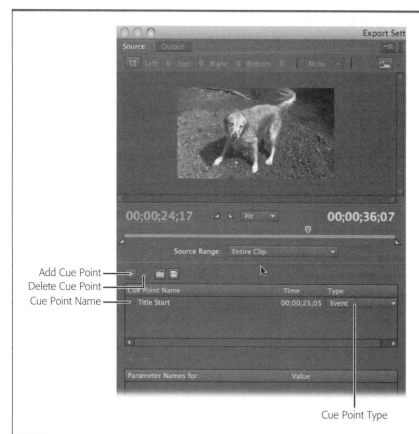

**FIGURE 11-13**

*You use cue points to place markers in your video. With the help of ActionScript, you can use the cue points to trigger events in your animation.*

2. **Drag the playback head to the point in your video you want to mark.**

   The video image changes as you move the playback head.

3. **Click the + button to add cue points; click the – button to remove them if you make a mistake.**

   Flash creates a cue point in the list and gives it a name, a time setting, and a type. The time setting is determined by the playback head's position in the video clip. In the next steps, you'll change the name and type of the cue point.

4. **Click the name, and then type a descriptive name for your cue point.**

   Flash names all cue points "cue point" when it creates them. It's up to you to type something more descriptive.

5. **Choose the type of cue point you want to create—Event or Navigation.** If you're an ActionScript hotshot, set parameters.

   Event cue points trigger an action when the video reaches them. Navigation cue points let you locate and play certain portions of your video. Both Event and Navigation cue points require ActionScript to work their magic.

6. **Click the + button to add parameters to your cue point; click the – button to remove them if you make a mistake.**

   Parameters are key-value pairs that programmers use to store and retrieve information. So the parameter values are available to ActionScript programs when the video reaches the cue point.

7. **Repeat steps 2–6 to add more cue points, or click OK to go back to the encoder queue.**

## Other Techniques for Reducing Video File Sizes

No one likes to wait while a web page loads. So when you're publishing video on the Web, life is a constant quest to shrink the size of your video files so they'll travel the Net faster. In addition to the encoding tricks already mentioned, here are some tips for shrinking those files while still providing a good video experience. Some of these techniques are related to creating the video, and others are related to Adobe Media Encoder and Export Settings.

■ **VIDEO TECHNIQUES FOR REDUCING FILE SIZES**

- **Use a tripod and keep pans and zooms to a minimum.** Steady shots make for better compression results.

- **Start out with good-quality video.** When possible, use uncompressed video before you encode to Flash video. If your video has blips and glitches (called "noise" by videographers) before you encode it, the video file ends up bigger.

- **Avoid fancy effects and transitions.** Special effects like fancy wipes or spiral transitions don't work as well in Flash video as a plain cut from one scene to the next. Even dissolves add to the size of your video file.

## ▪ ENCODING TECHNIQUES FOR REDUCING FILE SIZES

- **Reduce the dimensions of the video.** It's great to have a high-resolution video that looks beautiful when the audience clicks the full-screen button. But if it takes too long to download over the Internet, you won't *have* an audience. As described on page 390, you can change the dimensions of your video to reduce the file size.

- **Consider using a lower frame rate.** You can set the frame rate in the Video tab of the Export Settings window. The standard frame rate for American TV is 29.97 frames per second (don't ask about the decimal; it's a long story). The standard for film is 24 fps. Test your videos at 18, 15, or even 12 fps to see whether the quality/file size tradeoff is worth it.

- **Use mono sound where possible.** If your video is a musical performance, it may be important to have stereo sound, but otherwise you can save precious file space by clicking the Audio tab in the Export Settings window and then choosing Mono.

- **Use a lower bit rate for sounds that are mostly voices or don't require high fidelity.** Go to the Audio tab in Export Settings, and then use the drop-down menu to reduce the bit rate for sound. The encoder has bit rates from 16 to 256. A bit rate of 64 works for many Flash videos. You can go even lower if the sound track is primarily voice, with no music.

## Preparing to Import Video Files

It's obvious that before you can import a video clip into Flash, you need to know where it is: on your computer or somewhere in the Net. It's also important to know up front how you expect to link the video file to your finished Flash animation file at runtime: by embedding the video file directly into your Flash timeline, or by linking to the video file at runtime, and so on.

This cart-before-the-horse consideration isn't quite as odd as it seems at first blush. Video files tend to be so huge that you don't usually want to embed them directly into your Flash document the way you embed graphics (page 351) and sound files (page 374). The process of setting up your Flash animation and Flash video files for the public to view them is called *deploying*. First you tell Flash where to find the file at design time, and then you tell Flash how the video will be accessed by your audience.

---

**NOTE** Chapter 20 tells you all you need to know about publishing Flash files, including Flash files containing video clips.

---

Your deployment options include the following:

- **Progressive download from a web server.** This option is one of the most popular because all you need to publish video on the Internet is a regular, garden-variety web server. Your Flash animation files (SWF) and Flash video files (FLV, F4V or mp4) are stored on the server. It's called progressive because the video starts playing for your visitors before the entire video file is downloaded. The downside to this option is the fact that the entire video is eventually stored on your visitor's computer, giving her the ability, if she's clever, to make a copy of your video. If you aren't comfortable with bootleg copies, then consider one of the next two options.

- **Stream from Flash Video Streaming Service.** This option is the most popular way to show videos without letting others copy them. Basically, you hire a company to stream your video from their computers to your website visitors. Your visitors never have a complete copy on their computers, making it more difficult (but not impossible) for them to swipe it. You can find a long list of companies that provide this service on Adobe's website (*www.adobe.com/ products/flashmediaserver/fvss/*). These companies have a program called Flash Media Server on their computers, which detects the speed of your web visitor's Internet connection and sends the video at a speed it can handle. Your visitor gets a higher-quality video experience, and you get added security for copyrighted material. All you have to do is pay for the service.

- **Stream from Flash Media Server.** This option is similar to the second option above, except that you (or, more likely, your organization's IT department) buy the server hardware, install the server software, and maintain the resulting system. This option is best if you have deep pockets and don't mind the hassle of maintaining a media server. Flash Media Server options start at about $250 and go up from there depending on the features.

**NOTE** If you have your own web server and want to dip your toe in the Media Server water, you may want to investigate Red5, an open source (free) Flash Server (*http://osflash.org/red5*).

- **A mobile device video bundled in SWF.** Use this option in combination with Flash's templates for consumer devices and handsets to create animations for small handheld devices. This option is used to place video inside SWF files used with phones and handsets.

- **Embed video in SWF and play in timeline.** This option represents the simplest way to embed video into your animation, but it works only for very short video clips (somewhere between 5 and 10 seconds or less). Any more than that, and the size of your animation file grows so large that you have trouble editing the file in Flash *and* your audience has trouble viewing it in their Flash Players.

# ◼ Importing Video Files

Once you have access to a video in the Flash video format (.flv or .f4v), you're ready to begin importing the video file into Flash. When you begin this process, your video can be on your computer or it can be on the Web, where it's served up by a Flash Media Server. In this section, you see step-by-step examples for both scenarios.

# Importing a Flash Video File Stored on Your Computer

When you have a video on your computer in one of Flash's video formats (.flv, .f4v, or .mp4), it's easy to import it into your Flash project. By making a couple of choices along the way, you can give your Flash audience standard controls to play and pause your video, and adjust its sound. To work on the following exercise, you can download the video *11-4_Building_Implode.flv* from the Missing CD page at *www.missingmanuals.com/cds/flashcs6mm.*

> **NOTE** If you need to convert a video to one of the Flash video formats (.flv, .f4v, or .mp4), see page 385.

When you add video to your Flash project using this method, Flash creates a link between the Flash file and your project. Even after you publish a Flash .swf file for final distribution, the Flash file and your video file remain separate. If the project is for a website, you need to place both the Flash .swf file and the video file (.flv or .f4v) on the website, ideally in the same folder. To make things easy for yourself, it's best to put your Flash video in the same folder where you save your Flash work file (.fla) and publish your Flash animation (.swf).

1. **Create a new Flash document, and then save it.**

   It's always good to name and save your Flash projects at the beginning. It's even more helpful when you work with external video files, as you do in this project. A name like *building_bye_bye.fla* might be appropriate for this one.

2. **Place the Flash video *11-4_Building_Implode.flv* in the same folder where you save your Flash file (.fla) and your published Flash file (.swf).**

   This step makes it easier for Flash to create a link to the video file. After publishing the .swf, as long as both files are located in the same folder, the link between the two will continue to work.

3. **In Flash, select File→Import→Import Video.**

   The Import Video dialog box appears, as shown in Figure 11-14, with several options you can choose using radio buttons. The question is: Where is your video file? Either it's on your computer, or it's stored on a web server with Flash Media Server software.

4. **Select "On your computer."**

   Flash wants to know where the file is right now, so it can load it into your project. At this step, don't jump ahead and start thinking about where the final project is going to be published.

5. **Click the Browse button, and then locate and select your video file.**

   Flash displays a standard Open window similar to the one you use to open a Flash document. It should be easy to locate *11-4_Building_Implode.flv*, because it's in the same folder as your Flash file. After you select the file, its name and path show up under the Browse button. Now that Flash knows where the file is located, it can work with the video.

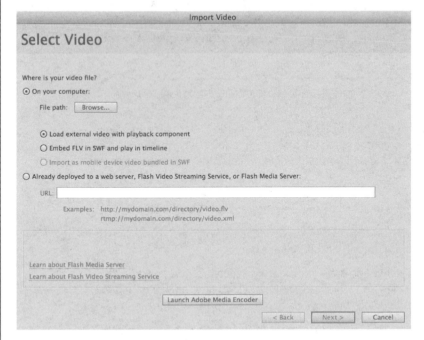

**FIGURE 11-14**

*The large Import Video dialog box walks you through adding video to your Flash project. In the first step, shown here, you answer questions about the location of the video file and how you want to use it in your project.*

**NOTE** The video of the imploding building is copyrighted and was provided by *www.freestockfootage.com*.

6. **Tell Flash how you want to work with the video by clicking the radio button labeled: "Load external video with playback component."**

    • **Load external video with playback component** creates a link between your Flash file and an external video file. When Flash gets a command to play the video, it finds and plays the external file.

    The other two options are used less frequently, but they're useful for special cases:

    • **Embed FLV in SWF and play in timeline.** This option embeds video into your animation. Each frame of video becomes a frame in the Flash timeline. The result is that the Flash file gets huge very fast, and your audience will be frustrated trying to download and play the video. Don't try this option with clips any longer than 5 or 10 seconds.

- **Import as mobile device video bundled in SWF.** Use this option in combination with Flash's templates for consumer devices and handsets to create animations for handheld devices (a topic not covered in this book).

7. **Click Continue to move to the next Import Video step.**

The Import Video box changes to show skinning options for your video. A *skin* is a sort of container that adds Play/Pause/Stop type controls to your video, as shown in Figure 11-15.

**FIGURE 11-15**

*There are two basic types of skins for Flash video. "Over" skins like the one shown here sit on top of the video image, hiding some parts of the picture. "Under" skins are completely outside the image.*

8. **From the Skin drop-down box, choose SkinOverAll.swf.**

Use the drop-down menu to choose an Adobe predesigned skin, as shown in Figure 11-16. Adobe supplies a whole slew of skins with different combinations of controls. SkinOverAll includes all the controls, so this exercise shows you what's available. When you tackle a real-world project, you may find you don't need quite so many gadgets on your videos.

There are also options to provide no controls at all (usually not the best option) or to use a custom-designed skin. For example, you might want to put your client's logo on the video skin as another way to establish his brand.

9. **Click Next.**

Flash displays the Import Video: Finish Video Import dialog box you see in Figure 11-17. The details shown may not seem that important until it's time to publish your Flash project on a web page. Here's a translation for each of the lines:

- **The video you are using is located at:** This line lists the folder where the video file lives. If your final project is going on a web server, you have to give both *11-4_Building_Implode.flv* and *building_bye_bye.swf* to your webmaster.

- **The video will be located at:** (relative paths are relative to your .swf). This line explains the relationship of your files when you publish your Flash animation. It shows you the path that has to exist between the .swf and your video file (*11-4_Building_Implode.flv*). In this case, there is no path (just a filename) because you're planning on keeping both the .swf and the .flv in the same folder, whether it's on your computer or a web server.

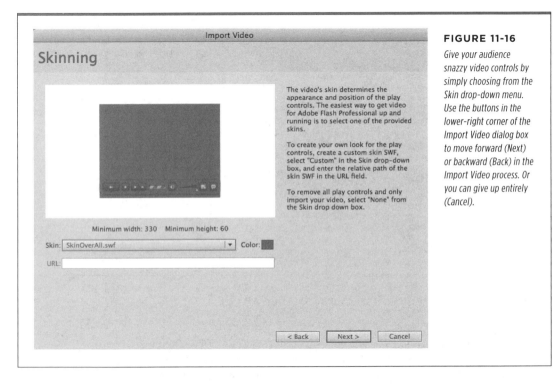

**FIGURE 11-16**

*Give your audience snazzy video controls by simply choosing from the Skin drop-down menu. Use the buttons in the lower-right corner of the Import Video dialog box to move forward (Next) or backward (Back) in the Import Video process. Or you can give up entirely (Cancel).*

- **A Flash video component will be created on the stage and configured for local playback.** This line simply tells you that your video and whatever skin you selected will appear on the stage in your Flash document.

- **The video component uses a skin that has been copied next to your .fla. This file will need to be deployed to your server.** These sentences are a roundabout way of saying that the skin for your video is stored in a separate .swf file. Flash places it in the same folder on your computer with *building_bye_bye.fla*. This skin has a name similar to the name you chose in step 8. In this case, it's named *SkinOverAll.swf*, and it has to be in the same folder with *building_bye_bye.swf* and *11-4_Building_Implode.flv* when you publish your Flash animation.

- **Before exporting and deploying your .swf you may need to...** If *building_ bye_bye.swf* and *11-4_Building_Implode.flv* aren't in the same folder when you put your animation on a web server, you need to change the path in the video component. For more on video components, see the next section, page 403.

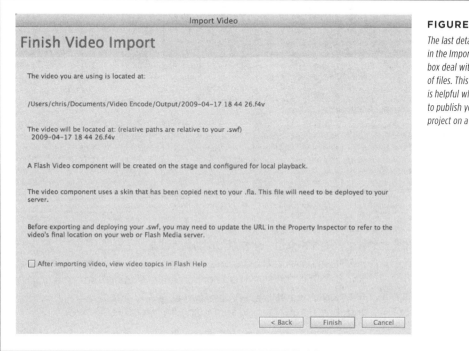

**FIGURE 11-17.**

*The last details displayed in the Import Video dialog box deal with the location of files. This information is helpful when it's time to publish your Flash project on a web page.*

10. **Click Finish.**

The "Import Video: Finish Video Import" dialog box disappears. As promised, you see the video player on your stage along with the skin (video controls). If you embed the video, rather than load it as described in this example, there's also a copy of the video in the Library, as shown in Figure 11-18.

11. **Press Ctrl+Enter (⌘-Return on a Mac) to test your Flash project and view the video.**

In the Flash animation, you see your video running. Using the skin controls, you can start and stop the playback.

**NOTE** One of Flash's relatively new tricks is the ability to test video within the Flash workspace. If you want, you can press Enter (Return) to watch your video instead of Ctrl+Enter (⌘-Return).

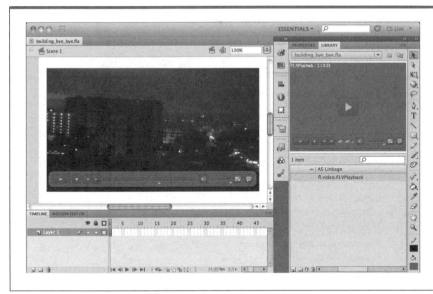

**FIGURE 11-18**

*When you finish importing your video to Flash, it shows up in the Library, and there's an instance already placed on the stage. If you need another instance of the video, say in another scene, you can simply drag it from the Library to the stage in that scene.*

### ■ DEPLOYING YOUR FLASH VIDEO ON THE WEB

Most of the time, Flash projects that incorporate videos end up on the Web. Whether you're uploading the video to a web page or someone is doing it for you, make sure that all the files make the journey: the Flash animation (.swf), the Flash video file (.flv or .f4v), and the skin file (named something like *SkinOverAll.swf*).

## Importing a Flash Video from the Web

Surprisingly, importing a video file that's stored on the Web isn't much different from importing one that's on your computer, as described on page 396. The Flash video file may be in a standard web server or one that has Flash Media Server software. (Don't worry if you don't have a video file stored on a web server; there's an example file you can practice with, as you'll see in the following steps.)

The only differences in the importing process happen at the very beginning.

1. **Select File→Import→Import Video.**

   The "Import Video: Select" window appears.

2. **Turn on the radio button next to "Already deployed to a web server, Flash Video Streaming Service, or Flash Media Server" (Figure 11-14).** In the URL box, type the web address where the file lives, and then click Continue.

   The URL for the practice file is *http://examples.oreilly.com/flashcs4mm/11-4_ Building_Implode.flv.* When you click Continue, the "Import Video: Skinning" window you see in Figure 11-16 appears.

The rest of the steps are identical to those for importing a Flash video file on your own computer. You can pick up the process at step 8 on page 399.

## Customizing the Video Playback Component

In Flash-speak, once your video is added to your Flash file, it's called the FLVPlayback component. Components are prebuilt widgets that you drop into your animations. Someone else went to all the trouble of building (and hopefully testing) the component. All you have to do is drop a component into your Flash project and let it do its stuff. Components save you design and programming time, so it's worthwhile to learn about them. There's a whole chapter on components (Chapter 16), but since you're already using one in this example, it's worth covering some of the specific ways you can customize the FLVPlayback component.

Most components provide a few options that let you customize them for your nefarious purposes. For example, in the case of the FLVPlayback component, you can change the playback behavior of the video and the appearance of the video controls. You can even change the video source file if you have a newly edited and improved video. You change the settings for a component by changing its parameters. Here's how to view and edit the FLVPlayback parameters:

1. **In Flash, click the FLVPlayback component on the stage.**

   As with other objects, you select the video playback component and then modify it using the settings in the Properties panel.

2. **In the Properties panel, open the Component Parameters subpanel.**

   The Component Inspector panel opens in Flash. The name of each parameter (setting) is listed on the left, and its value is shown on the right.

3. **Make changes to the FLVPlayback parameters.**

   You can change multiple parameters. For example, to change the appearance of the skin (video playback controls), click skinAutoHide, and then set the value to "true." To change the color of the skin, click the skinBackgroundColor swatch, and then choose a new color from the color picker.

Here's a complete description of the parameters for the FLVPlayback component:

- **align.** Determines the alignment of the video image when the video scaleMode (below) isn't set to exactFit.

- **autoPlay.** If set to "true," the video automatically plays when the Flash animation frame that holds it is loaded.

- **cuePoints.** You can add cue points to your video when it's encoded, as explained on page 393. Or you can add them using the FLVPlayback component. Click the magnifying glass to open a window where you can add manual cue points by typing in a name and a time.

- **islive.** Used with a Flash Media Server, this value is set to "true" when streaming a live performance.

- **preview.** Used for the live preview feature that helps you test the parameter settings. Click the magnifying glass to see your video with the current settings.

- **scaleMode.** This setting determines how the video image sizes itself after it's loaded. There are three options: *noScale*, where the video uses the size of the Flash video source file; *maintainAspectRatio*, where the video retains its proportions when enlarged or shrunk; and *exactFit*, which forces the video to fit the dimensions of the component as shown in the Properties panel.

- **skin.** The name and path for the .swf file that adds playback controls to the video.

- **skinAutoHide.** If set to "true," the playback controls disappear unless the mouse is hovering over the video image.

- **skinBackgroundAlpha.** Playback controls can be transparent. A value of 1.0 = opaque and 0 = invisible. So, a value of 0.8 provides an 80 percent opacity effect.

- **skinBackgroundColor.** Click the color swatch, and then choose a new color from the color picker.

- **source.** The name and path for the Flash video file.

- **volume.** Sets the audio volume for video playback. A value of 1.0 = full volume and 0 = no volume. So a value of 0.5 provides half the available volume for audio playback.

# Adding Interactivity

# Introduction to ActionScript 3.0

When your Flash document is on your computer, you're in control. You can make it do whatever you want, whenever you want. But eventually, your creation has to strike out on its own. You won't be there to tell your animation what to do when someone clicks a button or to remind it to turn off the sound after the first three times through. You need to provide instructions to make your animation perform automatically—that is, *automate* it.

To automate your animation or make it interactive, you use ActionScript—Flash's built-in programming language—to act on, or *script*, the different parts of your animation. For example, you can instruct your animation to load a web page when someone clicks a button you've added, to start playing an audio clip at the beginning of a certain scene, to play your animation in reverse, to loop certain sections of your animation, and so on.

Flash calls the chunks of ActionScript code you attach to your animation *actions*, which is a great reminder that ActionScript exists to help your audience *interact* with your animation.

The first part of this chapter explains how ActionScript has grown up from a simple macro language for animations into a full-blown programming language. After that, the chapter introduces you to some of ActionScript's basic concepts, with examples each step of the way. Follow the examples and try some experiments of your own. Go ahead, you won't break anything. You're on your way to a whole new level of Flash animation.

# ■ Getting to Know ActionScript 3.0

ActionScript is a serious programming language. As explained in the box below, folks in cubicles use ActionScript to develop major programs—like ticket purchasing and reservation systems. ActionScript incorporates geeky programming concepts like variables, functions, parameters, and so on. Delve deep and you find the scripting *object model* (the internal, Flash-designated names of all the parts of your animation). But none of that will stop you from using ActionScript for your own needs. In fact, Flash has some great tools to ease you into programming, like the Actions panel and Code Snippets introduced in this chapter. The visual nature of Flash gives you instant feedback, letting you know when your script works and when it doesn't. Combine those features, and you've got a great way to dip your toe in the programming waters. You can even apply the skills you gain with ActionScript to other programming languages, including that web developer favorite, JavaScript.

### ActionScript on the Desk, in the Phone

Believe it or not, now is an exciting time to learn ActionScript. Not only is ActionScript the programming language Flash uses to control animations, but it also lets you create lots of other programs that run via the Internet, on a smartphone, or on your desktop, just like your wordprocessor or spreadsheet. Adobe is taking advantage of the fact that nearly every computer on earth plays the SWF files that Flash creates. ActionScript programs can sit on a website and run in people's browsers. Adobe calls these programs *rich Internet applications* (RIAs), and they're at the forefront of a big wave in computer software. Traditional (non-artist) programmers use Flex SDK (now an Apache Open Source project) and Flash Builder to create these RIAs.

It doesn't end with the Internet. Flash Player is the little unit that plays Flash movies on your computer desktop. The pocket-protector set calls it a *runtime* program, since Flash Player provides all the support needed to run programs in a given computer operating system. There are Flash Players for Windows, Mac, and Linux computers, making it a virtually universal system. So if you create your program in Flash, it can run just about anywhere. Adobe has expanded this universality into a standard dubbed *Adobe Integrated Runtime* (AIR). AIR combines several standards to produce desktop programs: Flash, ActionScript, JavaScript, PDF (Adobe Acrobat), and HTML. You can build AIR programs using Flash, Dreamweaver, Flash Builder, and other tools. Depending on your program's version, it may require either an upgrade or an extension.

There's icing on the AIR cake, too. You can build applications for Android devices and Apple's iOS devices. Yes, that means you can use Flash to create apps for iPhone, iPad, and all sorts of Android smartphones and tablets. You may remember all the furor, gnashing of teeth, and blog space devoted to Apple's refusal to allow Flash Player on the iPhone, which meant web pages that use Flash Player wouldn't work on iPhones and iPads. What hasn't gotten as much press is the fact that Adobe has done an end run around the issue. That's right: With AIR, Flash Pro now lets you create apps and turn the code into the native language for iOS as well as Android. You can build apps, test them on mobile devices, and sell them through the Apple and Android app stores. The last few chapters in this book get you started.

### The Flash/ActionScript Partnership

ActionScript is a great name for a programming language. All computer programs perform actions, but the cool thing about Flash and ActionScript is that those actions are so visible. You're not just "assigning a value to a variable," as you would in typical computer lingo—you're making the moon move across the sky, or playing a video clip, or turning up the volume of the music. ActionScript programming is satisfying because many of the actions it performs are so apparent.

In the earliest versions, ActionScript was sort of tacked on to the Flash animation machine, the way macro programming was added to early word processors and spreadsheets. You used drop-down menus and dialog boxes to move parts of your drawing around the stage. You could start and stop animations on specific frames using familiar programming techniques like loops and conditionals (more on those later). In short, you could create some pretty snazzy visual effects.

At first, programming and animation seemed a curious match, since artists and programmers often seem to be such different people. But when you think about it, programming and drawing are both creative activities. Just like the artist, a programmer needs imagination and a vision. And animation is a very programmatic visual art, complete with reusable chunks of action that branch off into separate scenes. Today, there are Flash artist/programmers responsible for both the artwork and the programming code in their projects. There are also large teams producing Flash projects where artists create the objects that the programmers animate.

**NOTE** In recent years, Adobe developed separate tools for Flash development teams. Flash Catalyst is a tool for designers, while Flash Builder is a tool for programmer/developers. When you work in Flash Pro, you have access to both sides of the coin.

**UP TO SPEED**

## About ActionScript 1.0, 2.0, or 3.0

Today's Adobe Flash Player can run programs written with any version of ActionScript (1.0, 2.0, or 3.0), but it uses an entirely different engine to run the ActionScript 3 programs. More important, ActionScript 3 programs run faster. ActionScript 3.0 programs also work better with XML, a popular, nearly universal way to store data, and with CSS (Cascading Style Sheets), used to format web pages.

**ActionScript 1.0 (2000).** Flash 5 was the first version to introduce the term "ActionScript," and for the first time, animators could type in code like real programmers. Before that, Flash kept track of commands chosen from drop-down menus and dialog boxes.

The ActionScript language was based on ECMAScript, which was a great move, since the popular JavaScript also has the same roots. Web programmers who know JavaScript can easily pick up ActionScript.

**ActionScript 2.0 (2003).** Flash MX 2004 introduced ActionScript 2.0 a few months prior to the date implied by its moniker.

ActionScript 2.0 adopted additional object-oriented programming concepts, making it a better tool for larger projects and projects developed by teams of programmers. Some concessions were made so that both ActionScript 1.0 and ActionScript 2.0 animations would run in the same Flash Player that was installed on so many computers.

**ActionScript 3.0 (2006).** Adobe introduced ActionScript 3.0 with Adobe Flex 2.0 (a programming system that makes use of the Flash Player but doesn't use the Flash Authoring program)—a sure sign that the language had matured beyond a simple macro language for controlling Flash animations. ActionScript 3.0 follows established object-oriented programming concepts very closely, bringing benefits as well as changes from the previous versions. Adobe Flash CS3 was the first version to include ActionScript 3.0 as an option. With Flash Pro CS5.5, Adobe added the ability to create apps for iOS and Android. These apps are translated into the devices' native language so they do not require Flash Player.

## ActionScript 3.0

Each version of Flash has introduced new, more sophisticated features, like better video handling à la YouTube. For example, Flash CS4 introduced a powerful new Motion Editor for creating and adjusting tweens. Flash CS5 introduced the Text Layout Framework. All along, ActionScript has kept pace. (The box on page 409 details some of the history.) With ActionScript 3.0, Flash's programming language has matured quite a bit, adopting the latest and best programming concepts. As a result, ActionScript is more powerful, more consistent, and a better tool for team-based projects. If you're a lone artist/programmer, does that mean ActionScript 3.0 doesn't have any benefits for you? Not at all. You'll benefit from ActionScript 3.0's consistency and power. Tools like the Display List and the Event Listener system will help you write better programs and keep your sanity in the process.

## ActionScript vs. JavaScript and Other Languages

ActionScript and JavaScript have a lot in common. They're both *scripting* languages, meaning that they're programming languages that run inside other programs. Specifically, ActionScript runs inside Flash Player, and JavaScript runs inside a web browser. On top of that, ActionScript and JavaScript sprouted from the same programming language specification, ECMA-262.

> **NOTE** Since you're just dying to know, ECMA stands for European Computer Manufacturers Association, the standards group that established the spec.

Initially, programmers used both ActionScript and JavaScript in snippets to perform quick and easy chores. For example, in ActionScript, you'd write something like the following:

```
on (press) {
startDrag(this);
}
```

You would literally attach code to a drawn object on Flash's stage. JavaScript uses similar chunks of code to control the behavior of buttons and rollover images. However, JavaScript is often interspersed throughout the HTML code that describes web pages. From a technical point of view, ActionScript and JavaScript are considered high-level languages because they're closer to human language than the 1's and 0's of machine language.

As human nature kicked in and Flash animations became more elaborate, ActionScript snippets got tucked in all over the place. As a result, if an animation didn't work as expected, it was hard to find the misbehaving code. It could be almost anywhere. ActionScript writers started to use more disciplined programming techniques, and new versions of ActionScript encouraged better programming practices. The idea of attaching ActionScript code to any old object became frowned upon. Instead, programmers tried to keep all their code in one place, usually a single layer in the timeline. At the same time, *object-oriented programming* was becoming more popular and better-defined in programming circles, from the Visual Basic coders to the C programming crowd. ActionScript added object-oriented concepts in version 2.0 and even more in ActionScript 3.0.

## ActionScript 3.0 Spoken Here

The ActionScript chapters in this book focus entirely on ActionScript 3.0. If you're already versed in one of the earlier versions, you may be pleased to know that Flash CS6 still supports ActionScript 1.0 and 2.0, but you can't *mix* code from ActionScript 3.0 with code from earlier versions in the same SWF file. The reason is that the Flash Player now includes two completely separate *virtual machines* (the software that interprets ActionScript code and turns it into actions). The original one runs ActionScript versions 1.0 and 2.0. A completely new virtual machine handles ActionScript 3.0 code, which tends to run faster.

---

**CODERS' CLINIC**

### Diving Deeper into ActionScript

This book introduces ActionScript 3.0 and covers many of the common elements of ActionScript programming. The goal is to make you comfortable writing ActionScript code so you can use it to control your Flash animations. But don't stop there—experiment with ActionScript code and branch out from the examples in this book. If you're in the midst of a project and have an ActionScript question, try Flash's help (Help→Flash Help). Click the ActionScript topic near the top of the page. That jumps to a section of the page with ActionScript help topics. For a compendium of geeky ActionScript details, click the link that says "ActionScript 3.0 Reference" (middle Figure 12-1). At that point, you see the ActionScript reference that provides details on every single object, property and method. There are three panels; click an item in the top left panel to see its details. Then to fine tune your selection, click an item in the lower left

panel. The details are always shown in the large panel on the right. If you do a lot of ActionScript 3.0 coding, this reference is probably the one you'll use the most. For more details on setting up and using Flash's help files, see page 770.

In an effort to get you up and programming quickly, this book doesn't cover everything you'd learn in an advanced computer science course. There are great books that go into more detail on ActionScript topics. *Learning ActionScript 3.0* by Rich Shupe and Zevan Rosser (O'Reilly) is a clearly written guide for beginners. For a more advanced reference, *Essential ActionScript 3.0* by Colin Moock (O'Reilly) is ideal. If you're an old hand with ActionScript 2.0 and want to make the move to ActionScript 3.0, consider *ActionScript 3.0 Quick Reference* (O'Reilly) to ease you through the transition.

---

**TIP** If you're interested in learning more about ActionScript 2.0, find a copy of *Essential ActionScript 2.0* by Colin Moock.

---

If you're new to ActionScript, no problem. As the language of the future, ActionScript 3 is the version to learn. If you're an experienced ActionScript programmer, it's worth a little relearning to gain the advantages that ActionScript 3.0 gives you.

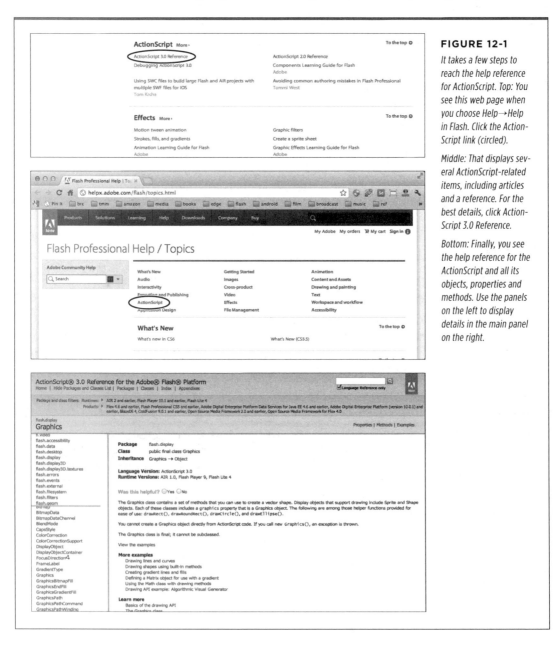

**FIGURE 12-1**

*It takes a few steps to reach the help reference for ActionScript. Top: You see this web page when you choose Help→Help in Flash. Click the Action-Script link (circled).*

*Middle: That displays several ActionScript-related items, including articles and a reference. For the best details, click Action-Script 3.0 Reference.*

*Bottom: Finally, you see the help reference for the ActionScript and all its objects, properties and methods. Use the panels on the left to display details in the main panel on the right.*

# ■ Beginning Your ActionScript Project

When your Flash project includes ActionScript programming, you have some decisions to make at the outset. As explained in the previous section, you need to decide whether you're using ActionScript 2.0 or ActionScript 3.0, since you can't mix version 3.0 with earlier versions. The exercises in this book all use ActionScript 3.0, so that fact alone may make your decision easier. Once you've decided, you choose the type of Flash file you want to create in the intro screen or in the File→New dialog box (Figure 12-2). If you choose one of the AIR options, you're automatically creating an ActionScript 3.0 document.

---

**CODERS' CLINIC**

## Timeline Programming: Pros and Cons

Ask more than one script writer where it's best to place code—the Flash timeline or an ActionScript file—and you're likely to start an energetic debate. If you plan on a long ActionScript career, it's worth learning both techniques.

Originally, ActionScript was considered a helper tool for animations. If you wanted the moon to rise at a certain point in an animation, you'd attach a snippet of ActionScript code to the moon or to a specific frame in an animation. Before you knew it, you had bits and pieces of code tucked in every nook and cranny of your timeline and Flash file. That situation is bad enough if you're the only one working on the project, but it was really a problem for team projects. Eventually, it became a common practice to keep one timeline layer devoted to ActionScript code. That way, at least most code was in one place. In recent years, the growing trend is to store ActionScript code in a separate file, making it easier for teams to work on the same project. Artists can work on the drawing in an .fla document, and programmers can write code in .as documents.

If you're working on a team project, chances are your team leaders will tell you exactly where and how to add ActionScript to the project. If you're working on your own, you can choose the method that's best for you. In some cases, particularly with smaller projects or projects that need to be hammered out quickly, it may make perfect sense to attach code to the Flash timeline. Here are more details about both methods:

**Timeline programming** is the way everyone used to write ActionScript. You attach scripts to individual frames in the Flash timeline. Quick and easy, this method gives a certain amount of instant gratification. If you want to quickly test an idea, the tendency is to attach some code to the timeline. The problem is that you may end up with snippets of ActionScript code in many different places, which makes it more difficult to troubleshoot the code if something goes wrong. It's even worse if you (or someone else) return to a project years later to make some changes.

**ActionScript file programming** is the preferred method for large projects and true object-oriented programming. One of the goals of object-oriented programming is to create code that's easily reusable. First of all, it has to be readable and understandable. Second, the chunks of code have to be somewhat independent. Placing all your code in a separate .as file forces you to provide more thorough definitions of the objects in your Flash project. As a result, you write more lines of code, but there's a better chance that you can reuse that code for other projects. When teams of programmers work on the same project, it's much easier this way to update the code and keep track of each updated version.

In the end, it comes down to the needs of your project and, if you're the project boss, your personal preference.

---

Next, you need to decide where you're going to place your ActionScript code. You have two choices. You can place your ActionScript code in frames in the Flash timeline, or you can place your code in one or more separate ActionScript (.as) files:

- To place ActionScript code in the timeline of your Flash file, create a Flash document (.fla) by choosing File→New→ActionScript 3.0. You have a choice between creating a Flash document based on ActionScript 2.0 or ActionScript 3.0. When Flash creates a new .fla file, it includes information that (ultimately through the .swf file) tells the Flash Player what flavor of ActionScript to use. You can use timeline programming for smaller projects and when you're not working with a team of other programmers. Just remember that it's more difficult to reuse your ActionScript code if it's embedded in a Flash document's timeline.

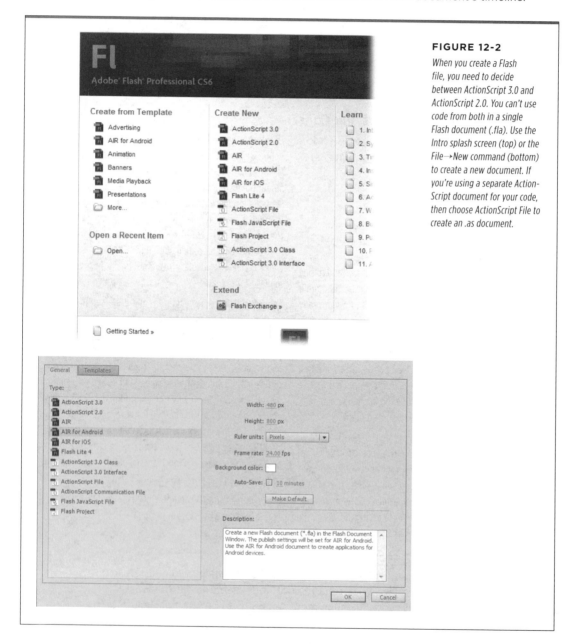

**FIGURE 12-2**

*When you create a Flash file, you need to decide between ActionScript 3.0 and ActionScript 2.0. You can't use code from both in a single Flash document (.fla). Use the Intro splash screen (top) or the File→New command (bottom) to create a new document. If you're using a separate Action-Script document for your code, then choose ActionScript File to create an .as document.*

- To place ActionScript code in a separate ActionScript file, create an ActionScript document (.as) by choosing File→New→ActionScript File. When you work with teams of programmers and artists, it's likely the team manager will tell you to keep ActionScript code in a separate file. Even if you're working alone, you may want to keep code in a separate *.as* file so that your work can be reused with other Flash projects. There's a bit more programming overhead when you keep your ActionScript code in a separate file. On the plus side, that overhead leads to better object-oriented practices, making your code easier to reuse.

For more details on making the choice between timeline programming and keeping your code in a separate ActionScript file, see the box on page 413.

---

**NOTE** Most of the examples in this book use timeline programming to show ActionScript programming principles.

---

## Writing ActionScript Code in the Timeline

If you've got a Flash document open, you're ready to begin adding ActionScript code to the timeline. Here are the steps to get you started:

1. **Create a new layer in the timeline to store your code.**

   To make your life easier later, keep your ActionScript code in one place—a single layer at the top of the timeline that holds only ActionScript code. You can use any name you want for this layer, but for clarity's sake, call it *actions* or *scripts*.

2. **Click a keyframe where you want to add your code, and then press F9 (Option-F9) to open the Actions panel.**

   The Actions panel is divided into three main parts, as shown in Figure 12-3. The Script pane is where you type your ActionScript code. The Actions toolbox holds a list of ActionScript objects, properties, methods, and events. The Script navigator shows a list of objects that have ActionScript code attached.

3. **Type your statements in the Script pane, or choose statements from the Actions toolbox.**

   You can type code directly into the Script pane, or you can double-click or drag the ActionScript elements in the Actions toolbox. As you add code to individual frames, you see them listed in the Script navigator (in the toolbox, located on the left side of the Actions panel), giving you a running list of the objects that have code attached. To view or edit code for a particular object, click the object in the Script navigator, and you see the code in the Script pane.

**TIP** You can collapse and expand the Actions toolbox and its panels. If you don't see the item you're looking for, click the rectangular buttons with the triangles to open and close the panels.

Actions toolbox    Script pane

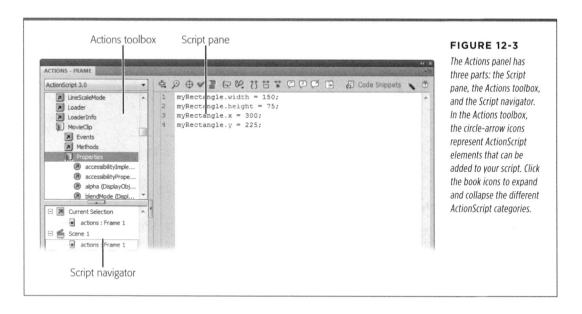

**FIGURE 12-3**

*The Actions panel has three parts: the Script pane, the Actions toolbox, and the Script navigator. In the Actions toolbox, the circle-arrow icons represent ActionScript elements that can be added to your script. Click the book icons to expand and collapse the different ActionScript categories.*

Script navigator

## Using the Script Pane Toolbar

The toolbar above the Script pane provides helpful tools for working with your ActionScript code (Figure 12-4). The buttons aren't labeled, but you can see their names when you mouse over them. From left to right, these are the buttons:

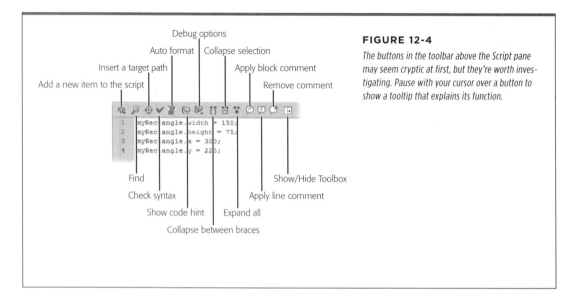

**FIGURE 12-4**

*The buttons in the toolbar above the Script pane may seem cryptic at first, but they're worth investigating. Pause with your cursor over a button to show a tooltip that explains its function.*

- **Add a new item to script.** Provides access to the same elements as the Actions toolbox. Useful if you've hidden the toolbox using the Show/Hide toolbox command (last in this list of buttons).

- **Find.** Searches your script for words and characters.

- **Insert a target path.** Click this button, and then choose your target object from a list, and this tool writes the proper code identifying it.

- **Check syntax.** Inspects your code for obvious errors.

- **Auto format.** Formats your script, making it easier to read, by using colors and indents. To set formatting options, go to Edit→Preferences→ActionScript (Flash→Preferences→ActionScript on a Mac).

> **TIP** Some coders have reported that in some cases autoformatting has broken their otherwise serviceable code. To avoid this, test your code before and after autoformatting. If you run into trouble, you can undo the formatting.

- **Show code hint.** Displays tooltips with suggestions for your script.

- **Debug options.** Inserts and removes breakpoints in your code. Breakpoints stop your program from running, giving you an opportunity to examine the workings of your program.

- **Collapse between braces.** Hides the text between a set of curly braces {}, making it easier to read and understand your code. Similar to collapsing an outline in a word processor.

- **Collapse selection.** Select the text you want to hide, and then click this button to hide it. Hold down the Alt (Option) key when you click this button, and the Actions panel collapses the code not selected.

- **Expand all.** Expands collapsed portions of your script after you've used one of the two previous commands.

- **Apply block comment.** Inserts the /* and */ used to create a block comment.

- **Apply line comment.** Inserts the // used to create a line comment.

- **Remove comment.** Removes the comment characters from a comment.

- **Show/Hide toolbox.** If you need more room to see your Script pane, use this button to hide the Actions toolbox. When the toolbox is hidden, you can use the "Add a new item to script" button to insert elements.

> **TIP** If you need more room to see your script, use the "Show/Hide toolbox" button on the far right to temporarily hide the Actions toolbox. When the toolbox is hidden, you can use the "Add a new item to script" button (far left) to insert ActionScript elements.

# Writing Code in an ActionScript File

When you want to store all your code in an ActionScript (.as) file, the first thing you need to do is create the file:

1. **Create a new ActionScript file (File→New→ActionScript File).**

   A new window opens, as shown in Figure 12-5. Initially, the window has a tab that reads Script-1 or something similar. When you save the ActionScript file with a name of your choice, that name appears on the tab. The Script window has two sections, a Script pane and the Actions toolbox. The toolbar above the Script pane is identical to the one described on page 416.

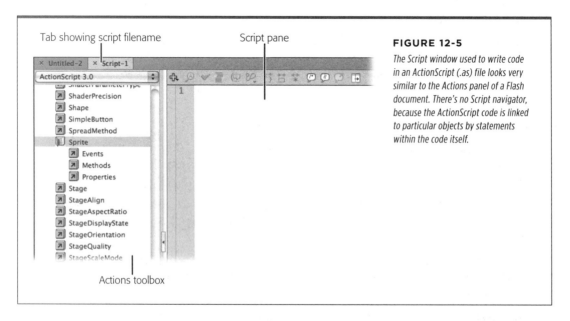

Tab showing script filename      Script pane

**FIGURE 12-5**

*The Script window used to write code in an ActionScript (.as) file looks very similar to the Actions panel of a Flash document. There's no Script navigator, because the ActionScript code is linked to particular objects by statements within the code itself.*

Actions toolbox

2. **Save your ActionScript file in the same directory as your Flash file (File→Save).**

   A dialog box opens where you can select a folder and then name your document. You want to save your file in the same directory as your Flash file. This way, Flash's compiler can find it when it creates an .swf file for distribution. Another option is to save your file in a folder that's designated as the ActionScript class folder; the steps for doing so are described in the box on page 419.

3. **Type your statements in the Script pane or choose statements from the Actions toolbox.**

   You can type code directly into the Script pane, or you can double-click or drag the ActionScript elements in the Actions toolbox.

When you separate your ActionScript code from a Flash document, it's up to you to establish links between your code and the objects in the Flash document. Because this chapter focuses on the basics, the following examples use timeline programming.

# ■ Object-Oriented Thinking

When programmers talk about object-oriented programming, they're referring to specific programming techniques—a way of looking at the parts of a program and the overall design. The idea is to create chunks of programming code that do a specific job. If you design them all, those chunks can fit together with other pieces of code. Think for a second about a typical home theater system that has an amplifier/receiver, a DVD player, a TV screen, and maybe a cable box. Each unit is an object. The folks who designed the DVD player don't have to know how to build a TV screen; they just have to make a DVD player that can plug into a TV. You can plug the same DVD player into another home theater system, and it'll work perfectly well. Programmers strive for that kind of modularity when they build objects.

The benefits are obvious. As long as the objects have an agreed-upon method for interacting, different programmers can work on different objects. When they all come together, they'll play well with one another. If the objects are truly useful and flexible, you can reuse them in future projects. Future programmers won't have to understand how the DVD player works; all they need to know is how to plug it in and how to send and receive signals from it.

---

**CODERS' CLINIC**

## Creating an ActionScript Class Folder

If you're working on several ActionScript projects over time, you want to reuse as much of your ActionScript code as possible. So you may create objects that work with a variety of Flash projects.

Perhaps you have some great shopping cart code that you can use for several different clients. You can put your shopping cart code in one ActionScript file (.as), and then put code for each of your clients in separate files. Your client files need to reach out and use that shopping cart code, but it's probably in a different file folder. The solution is to create one or more ActionScript class folders, where you store code that's used by many different Flash projects.

Then you need to tell Flash and ActionScript where to find those class folders.

You do that through Flash preferences. Go to Edit→Preferences→ ActionScript→ActionScript 3.0 Settings (on a Mac, go to Flash→Preferences→ActionScript→ActionScript 3.0 Settings).

Figure 12-6 shows the box that opens to let you set file paths for three different types of ActionScript files. Use the middle tool labeled "Folders containing ActionScript class files." Click the + button to add a new path to the list; you may have more than one Library path. Click the folder icon to browse to the directory that holds the class files.

---

In addition to reusability, there are a handful of other concepts that define object-oriented programming. Some of them don't make a lot of sense until you understand the basics of ActionScript, but here are a few of the basics for reference:

- **Classes.** A class describes an object in the abstract, like the concept of DVD players. A class is like a generalized blueprint for building an object.

- **Instances.** An instance is a specific object, like a Sony DVD Player Model N55.

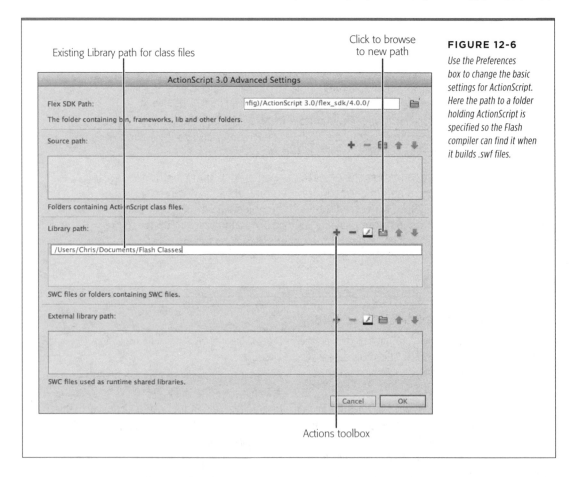

**FIGURE 12-6**

*Use the Preferences box to change the basic settings for ActionScript. Here the path to a folder holding ActionScript is specified so the Flash compiler can find it when it builds .swf files.*

- **Properties.** Properties are characteristics that define an object. For example, color may be a property of the Sony DVD player; that property may be set to black or silver. Properties are part of an object's definition, so they're called *members* of the object.

- **Methods.** Methods are actions that an object can perform. To continue the DVD player example, Play, Pause, and Fast Forward are methods of the DVD player class. These methods also belong to the Sony N55 instance of the DVD player class. Methods are part of an object's definition so, like properties, they're members of the object.

- **Events.** Events act as triggers. Someone presses the Play button on the DVD player—the event—and the Play method runs. Events are also part of an object's definition.

- **Encapsulation.** It's not necessary or wise to expose all the inner workings of an object. It's important for people to be able to play, pause, and eject discs in the DVD player, but they don't need to control the rotation speed or the intensity of the laser that reads the discs. In object-oriented programming, encapsulated features are those your audience can't mess with.

**CODERS' CLINIC**

### Is ActionScript a True Object-Oriented Language?

If you use the strictest definition for object-oriented programming languages, ActionScript doesn't make the cut. In true object-oriented programming, everything is an object and derives from objects. Even ActionScript 3.0, with its enhanced object-oriented features, has a few loopholes that you won't find in a language like Java (not to be confused with JavaScript). For example, timeline programming in Flash breaks some of the accepted rules of object-oriented programming. ActionScript permits functions that exist outside of an object, referred to as *function closures*.

ActionScript doesn't force you to always use object-oriented programming techniques. Instead, it takes advantage of many object-oriented concepts and lets you choose how strictly you want to use them.

Flash itself gives you a good head start toward object-oriented thinking. Consider a lowly rectangle you draw on the Flash stage. That's an *object*. All rectangles share some of the same properties. For example, they have four sides defined by four points, and they have a surface or face between those sides. All the corners of a rectangle are right angles.

Once you understand the basics, you can describe a Flash rectangle using a few properties:

- Width
- Height
- Stroke thickness
- Stroke color
- Fill color

Taking it a step further, you can place that rectangle anywhere on the stage by placing its upper-left corner on a particular point. That location is another property of a Flash rectangle.

## ActionScript Classes

If you're working in Flash, chances are you're going to use more than one rectangle, and you don't have to build every rectangle from the ground up. You can take certain rectangular characteristics for granted—four sides, right-angled corners. Other properties you need to define separately for each rectangle—width, height, color, location on the stage. So you need a class that defines rectangles in general, and you can then create specific instances of rectangles by defining their individual properties. And that's exactly how Flash works. *Class, instance*, and *property* are all fundamental terms for object-oriented programming and thinking.

## Changing an Object's Properties

In Flash, you change a rectangle's height or width using the Modify→Transform→Scale command. To change its location, you drag it to a new place. In ActionScript, by contrast, you change the height, width, and location by changing the properties in your ActionScript code:

```
myRectangle.width = 150;
myRectangle.height = 75;
myRectangle.x = 300;
myRectangle.y = 225;
```

> **NOTE** It's common practice to refer to locations on a computer screen as *x/y* coordinates. The *x* refers to the horizontal position, and the *y* refers to the vertical position. If you need something to help you remember which is which, remember that a lowercase *y* extends farther in a vertical direction.

Want to put some of these programming concepts to work? Try this:

1. **In a new document, draw a rectangle of any size and shape.**

   You can think of this step as defining an object.

2. **Select the rectangle, and then convert it to a symbol (Modify→"Convert to Symbol"), choosing Movie Clip as the type.**

   Movie clip is a great catch-all symbol for ActionScript programming. Movie clips can be as simple or complicated as you want.

3. **Create a new layer, double-click the layer name, and then type *actions*.**

   It's good programming practice to create a separate layer in the timeline for your ActionScript code. Naming it *actions* or *scripts* makes it clear that the layer is reserved for code.

4. **For consistency, rename the rectangle layer *drawings*.**

   Your timeline now has two layers with descriptive names.

5. **Make sure the instance on stage is selected, and then in the Properties panel, type *myRectangle* in the "Instance name" box, as shown in Figure 12-7.**

   This step is important. If you don't give objects on the stage a name, there's no way to tell ActionScript exactly which object you're talking about.

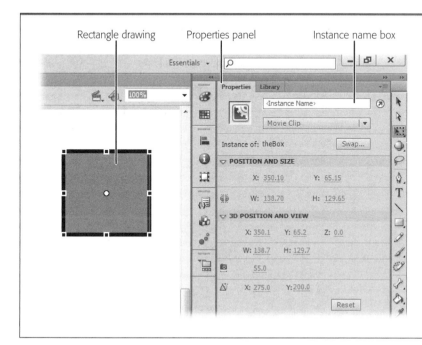

Rectangle drawing   Properties panel   Instance name box

**FIGURE 12-7**

*Before you can control objects on the Flash stage with ActionScript, you have to convert them to movie clip or button symbols, and then name them in the "Instance name" box on the Properties panel.*

6. **Open the Actions panel.**

   The Actions panel looks pretty busy when you first see it, as shown earlier in Figure 12-3. All the details are described on page 415. For now, focus on the big blank area in the middle, where you type ActionScript code.

7. **Select the first frame of the actions layer in the timeline, and then type the following lines in the Actions panel:**

```
myRectangle.width = 150;
myRectangle.height = 75;
myRectangle.x = 300;
myRectangle.y = 225;
```

   When you're done, the Script pane should look like Figure 12-8.

---

**TIP** Uppercase and lowercase spelling make a difference to ActionScript. Objects named myRectangle, MyRectangle, and myrectangle are completely different things to ActionScript. ActionScript programmers use certain typographic conventions that make it easier to read and understand code. One of those conventions is to use *camel case* for instances of objects. Camel case uses an initial lowercase letter and then uppercase for the first letter of additional words. For example: thisIsCamelCase.

---

8. **Click the Check Syntax button (the checkmark) at the top of the Actions panel to check for typos in your code.**

The check syntax feature in ActionScript 3.0 isn't as picky as it could be. Still, it helps you find major bloopers in your code, so it's worth using, especially when you're just starting out.

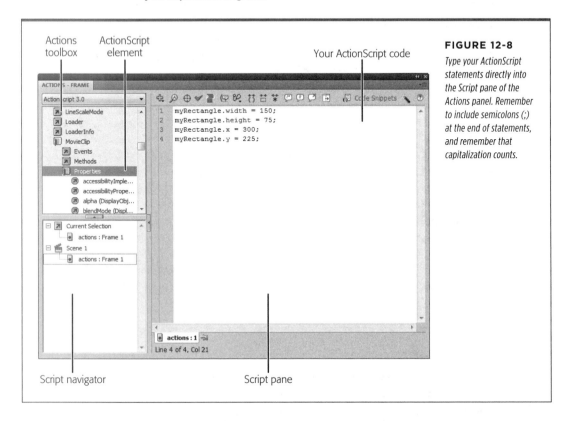

Actions toolbox

ActionScript element

Your ActionScript code

Script navigator

Script pane

**FIGURE 12-8**

*Type your ActionScript statements directly into the Script pane of the Actions panel. Remember to include semicolons (;) at the end of statements, and remember that capitalization counts.*

9. **Test your movie.**

After a little churning, the Flash Player or your browser appears on your screen. If everything is working right, your rectangle changes its shape and size. No matter what dimensions and location your rectangle had to begin with, it takes on the properties you defined in your ActionScript code. It's 150 pixels wide and 75 pixels high, and it's located 300 pixels from the left (x) of your screen and 225 pixels from the top (y).

You can probably guess what you need to do to animate this baby. Just add new frames, including a keyframe, to your timeline, and then type some instructions similar to the ones in step 7 on page 423. Here are the specific steps:

1. **Click the 40th frame in both layers of your timeline, and then press F5 to insert frames.**

You've just added 39 new blank frames to each layer of the timeline. Blank frames show whatever is on the stage in the previous keyframe without changing anything.

2. **Click the 20th frame in the timeline's actions layer, and then press F6 to insert a keyframe.**

Pressing F6 here places a second keyframe in the middle of the timeline, where you can change the look of myRectangle using another snippet of ActionScript. When you're done, the timeline should look similar to Figure 12-9.

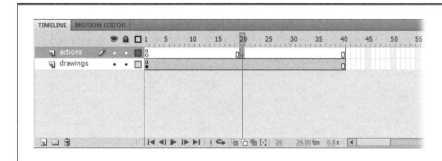

**FIGURE 12-9**

*The timeline shows where ActionScript is attached to frames with a small "a" icon. To prevent confusion, keep your ActionScript code on a layer of its own at the top of the timeline.*

3. **In the Actions panel, type the following lines:**

```
myRectangle.width = 200;
myRectangle.height = 200;
myRectangle.x = 100;
myRectangle.y = 225;
```

Or, to avoid duplicate effort, use the Copy (Ctrl+C or ⌘-C) and Paste (Ctrl+V or PCs ⌘-V) commands to steal the code from Keyframe 1 to Keyframe 20. Just copy, paste, and then change the numbers. It's faster than typing in new code, and you're less likely to create a typo.

4. **Click the Check Syntax button.**

You never know!

5. **Test your movie.**

Halfway through your animation, the rectangle turns square and moves to the left—exactly as you programmed it. Not terribly exciting, but you can use these same methods to dress it up a bit more, which you'll do in the next section.

**TIP**  When you're starting out in any programming language, the most common error is misspelling. Computers are worse than your second-grade teacher. They want everything spelled and punctuated perfectly. If something goes wrong, double-check your spelling and punctuation first. You can save yourself some grief by copying and pasting words, like myRectangle, to avoid typos.

# Functions and Methods Put the Action in ActionScript

As explained on page 419, properties define the characteristics of objects. Methods are the actions. Methods explain how a particular object can do something. If you, as a human being, are an object, then your height, hair color, and gender are your properties. Walking, talking, and keyboarding are your functions and methods.

> **NOTE** In ActionScript, methods are actions that are a defined part of an object, just like its properties. Functions are actions that are independent of any particular object.

In the exercise in the previous section, your code moved myRectangle to the left 200 pixels. What if you want to move to the left by 5 pixels at several different points along the timeline? The script writer's way to do that is to write a *moveLeft()* function, and then run that function whenever the object needs to be moved. Here's the code for a function that handles the move:

```
function moveLeft(anyMovieClip:MovieClip):void
{
  anyMovieClip.x = anyMovieClip.x -5;
}
```

Go ahead and type the function below the ActionScript code on the first frame of your document. Start on line 6, so that there's a little room between the different parts of your code. Click the Check Syntax button and double-check your spelling and punctuation. When you're done, it should look like Figure 12-10.

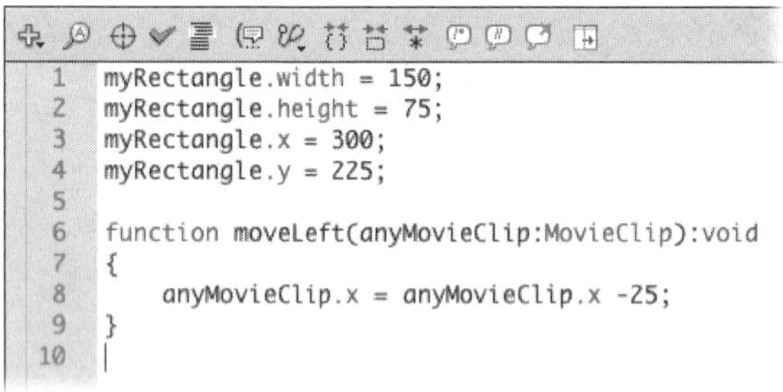

**FIGURE 12-10**

*Compared to the object's properties, a function is just a tad more geeky and complicated. The first word, function, explains that the code that follows is a function. The next word is the name of the function, moveLeft(). You'll use this name every time you want to run the function.*

```
1   myRectangle.width = 150;
2   myRectangle.height = 75;
3   myRectangle.x = 300;
4   myRectangle.y = 225;
5
6   function moveLeft(anyMovieClip:MovieClip):void
7   {
8       anyMovieClip.x = anyMovieClip.x -25;
9   }
10  |
```

Your function *moveLeft()* is an *action*, and as such it needs an *actor*. Something's gotta move, and that something is named inside the parentheses. You're moving anyMovieClip. That's probably a clear enough explanation for you, but it's not for your computer. To your computer, "anyMovieClip" might as well be "joeJones." They're both names it's never heard of. Your computer needs to know exactly what kind of object it is that you're moving. So, on the other side of the colon (:), you explain that anyMovieClip is in fact a MovieClip object. With that explanation, ActionScript can look up the definition for MovieClips, and it knows exactly what anyMovieClip can and can't do. Your computer also knows how much memory it needs to devote to anyMovieClip—an issue that becomes more important as your programs grow bigger.

Following the parentheses is the mysterious *:void*—another bit of ActionScript housekeeping. This code tells ActionScript that *moveLeft()* doesn't perform a calculation and provide a value in return. Suppose you created a function to find the area of a rectangle; *getArea()* would do its calculation, and the result would be a number. Instead of expecting the ominous-sounding *:void*, you'd tell ActionScript to expect *:Number.*

The actual instructions for your *moveLeft()* function have to be between curly brackets *{...}*, like the ones you see on the second and fourth lines. The brackets don't have to be on lines by themselves, but sometimes it's easier to read your code when it's written that way.

The action in your code is all on one line; everything else was just the necessary ActionScript overhead used to create every function.

```
anyMovieClip.x = anyMovieClip.x -5;
```

Remember how myRectangle.x was shorthand for "the horizontal position of myRectangle?" You're using the same shorthand here with anyMovieClip. ActionScript knows what you mean by *x*, because it's one of the built-in properties of the MovieClip class. What's more, if you change the value of *x*, the movie clip changes position. You saw that in the example on page 422. Changing a value is also called *assigning a new value*. And while you may know the = symbol as *equals*, in ActionScript it's called the *assignment operand*, because it assigns the value on the right side to the property or variable on the left.

When you wrote:

```
myRectangle.x = 100;
```

you were assigning the value *100* to the *x* property of myRectangle. Your *moveLeft()* function's code is just a little bit more complicated. You're saying "take the value that's currently assigned to anyMovieClip.x, subtract 5, and then put the result back in the anyMovieClip.x property." This method of reassigning a value is very common in ActionScript and almost any programming language.

So you may be wondering why your function used the word *anyMovieClip* instead of using *myRectangle* as the object of this *moveLeft()* action. The function is literally for moving *any* movie clip, so it's not hardcoded for a single rectangle like *myRectangle*. The name in the parentheses is a parameter of the function, so when you run *moveLeft()*, you tell ActionScript specifically which movie clip you want to move. Here's how it's done:

```
moveLeft(myRectangle);
```

It's that simple to run a function, or as the fellow with the pocket protector and tape on his glasses would say, "to call a function and pass it a parameter." To put your function into action, go back to your timeline. Add keyframes (press F6) every fifth frame from Frame 5 to Frame 25. Delete all the code that's on Frame 20. In the keyframes from 5 onward, type a call to your function:

```
moveLeft(myRectangle);
```

With the code inserted, your timeline looks like the one in Figure 12-11.

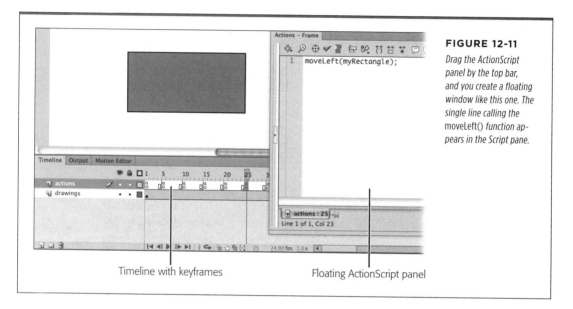

**FIGURE 12-11**

*Drag the ActionScript panel by the top bar, and you create a floating window like this one. The single line calling the moveLeft() function appears in the Script pane.*

Timeline with keyframes          Floating ActionScript panel

Check syntax, spelling, punctuation, and then test your movie by pressing Ctrl+Enter ⌘-Return. If the scripting deities smile upon you, myRectangle should move left in 5-pixel increments, and then pause for a bit.

Here's another great thing about using functions instead of *hardcoding* everything. Suppose you decide that 5-pixel steps isn't quite the grand, sweeping motion you had in mind. All you have to do is change one number in the original function. Change the code:

```
anyMovieClip.x = anyMovieClip.x -5;
```

to the following:

```
anyMovieClip.x = anyMovieClip.x -25;
```

and then test the results.

The complete geeky moniker for *moveLeft()* in this example is *function closure*. In ActionScript, functions that are part of an object definition are called *methods*. Functions that aren't part of an object definition are called function closures. (Often, in other languages, they're referred to simply as functions.) If *moveLeft()* was part of the definition for a rectangle object, it would be called a method of *myRectangle*.

**NOTE** To see the completed file, download *12-1_Move_Rectangle.fla* from the Missing CD page (*www. missingmanuals.com/cds/flashcs6mm*).

## Events

In the olden days of programming, programs simply ran through a series of statements. The experience was similar to watching an animation with no way to change it. All you could do was watch it run from beginning to end. The concept of events helped change all that. When a person clicks a button in a Flash animation, that's an event. The response to that event might be a number of things: Perhaps a new shape appears on the stage, or maybe the animation jumps to a new scene or frame.

ActionScript programmers create methods that *listen* for a particular event, like that mouse click, and then *handle it* with a particular action, like jumping to a new scene. It's a great, tried-and-true method of interaction that lots of programming languages use.

When you write an ActionScript program, you decide what *events* your program will listen for. Those events can include any of the following:

- Mouse events, like mouse clicks or mouse movements.

- Touch events, like finger taps or two-finger swipes

- Keyboard events, like pressed keys.

- Frame events, like the Flash playhead moving into or out of specific frames.

- Load events, which report on the progress when loading external files.

Once you've identified the events you want your ActionScript program to respond to, you write *event handlers* to spring into action. Your event handlers will run through a series of ActionScript statements, which may be made up of functions like the *moveLeft()* function from the previous section. Your event handlers can also change an object's properties.

You can use events to hand the controls over to the folks watching your Flash animations, which makes events an important tool in your Flash/ActionScript toolbox. Events are so important they have their own chapter (Chapter 13).

**NOTE** Previous versions of ActionScript handled events in a few different ways, including the well-known *on* statements. ActionScript 3.0 has only one method for handling events—*event listeners*, as introduced here and covered in more detail on page 443.

# ■ Using Data Types, Variables, and Constants

Flash animations are made up of different elements, like drawings, text, frames, timelines, and movie clips. Some of these elements serve as containers for the others. For example, frames can hold drawings and text, and timelines hold frames. ActionScript is similar. A few basic elements, like *numbers* and *strings*, are the building blocks for more complicated data containers. Many programming languages use similar data types but have slightly different rules about the way they're used.

This section introduces the most common data types that you use in ActionScript and explains how they're used. If you've worked your way through this chapter, you've used some of these already. In examples in the following chapters, you'll have an opportunity to give these data types a workout.

**TIP** This book isn't an exhaustive reference on ActionScript. It gives you a solid introduction to the language and shows you how to put it to work right away. If you're hungry for more details on the subject, check out the recommendations in the box on page 411.

## Numbers

Numbers are one of the data building blocks ActionScript uses. For example, you may want to tell Flash to play the same movie clip three times. As you saw earlier, Flash uses numbers to identify positions on the stage, to identify certain frames in a timeline, and to identify colors. Numbers are so important that Flash has three different data types for numbers. Why have more than one? Well, numbers that include fractions like 2.5 or 3.14159 require more computing power than integers like 3 or –1. Choose the right type of number for the job, and you can make your computer do less work so that your programs run faster.

### ■ NUMBER

In ActionScript, a *Number* can be any type of number, including fractions. In many programming languages, integer data types—like int and uint, described next—are preferred over numbers when fractions aren't needed. That's not necessarily the case in ActionScript. For some fairly technical reasons having to do with how ActionScript is designed, many programmers use the Number data type most of the time.

### ■ INT

The *int* (think *integer*) data type can represent any whole number from –2,147,483,648 to 2,147,483,647. The int type can't represent fractions. If you need a fraction or a number outside this range, use the Number data type.

### ■ UINT

The *uint* (think *unsigned integer*) data type can represent numbers from 0 to 4,294,967,295. If you need a negative whole number, use the *int* data type. If you need a fraction, use the Number data type. The *uint* is particularly useful to identify colors, since colors are always positive whole numbers.

### ■ NUMBERS AND OPERATORS

When you work in ActionScript, you can and probably will perform mathematical operations with numbers. To perform these feats, you use *operators*, the characters that indicate addition, subtraction, multiplication, and so on. Table 12-1 shows the operators you can use in ActionScript.

*Table 12-1. This table lists the operators you can use in ActionScript 3.0. Examples on the right show each operator in action.*

| OPERATOR | FUNCTION | EXAMPLE |
|----------|----------|---------|
| + | Adds two numbers | 2+3 |
| - | Subtracts number on right from number on left | 3-2 |
| * | Multiplies two numbers | 2*3 |
| / | Divides number on left by number on right | 6/2 |
| > | Expresses greater than (which may make a statement true or false) | 6>2 |
| < | Expresses less than (which may make a statement true or false) | 2<6 |
| >= | Expresses greater than or equal to (which may make a statement true or false) | 6>=2 |
| <= | Expresses less than or equal to (which may make a statement true or false) | 2<=6 |
| == | Expresses equality (which may make a statement true or false) | 12==6*2 |
| != | Expresses inequality (which may make a statement true or false) | 3!=2 |
| = | Assignment operator | myNumber = 6*2 |

Notice the difference between the equality operator and the assignment operator. The equality operator is used to make a statement: The data on the right side of the equality operator is equal to the data on the left. That statement may be true or false. The assignment operator has a different job. The assignment operator changes the value of the *variable* on the left. (There's more on variables on page 435.)

### ■ PRECEDENCE AND PARENTHESES

Some statements are simple and unambiguous, like this one:

```
myNumber = 3 + 12
```

But a statement can include more than one operator:

```
myNumber = 3 + 12 / 3
```

When there's more than one operator, it's a little harder to anticipate the value. In general, ActionScript multiplies and divides before it adds and subtracts. But you can make things easier for yourself (and others) to read and understand your work by using parentheses to dictate the order of operations. So the following statement forces ActionScript to perform the addition before it performs the division:

```
myNumber = (3 + 12) / 3
```

## Strings

In geek-speak, strings are sequential lists of letters, numbers, and symbols—strings of characters. For example, this very sentence is a string. "Foo" is a string with three characters. You identify strings by placing them inside either single or double quotes:

```
myCar = "Stutz Bearcat";
visitorName = "Erwin Baker";
```

If you want to include quotes within your string, you have a couple of options. For example, you can use single quotes to enclose your string when you want to use double quotes *in* the string, like so:

```
famousQuote = 'He said, "My name is Erwin Baker."'
```

### ■ STRINGS AND OPERATORS

You can't do math with strings, not even if some of the characters are numbers. But there are other types of operations that work with strings. One very common operation is to build up longer strings by adding words or characters. Usually this is called *concatenation*, and it looks a lot like string addition:

```
carModel = "Stutz" + " " + "Bearcat";
```

The previous statement adds three strings together. First, it adds a *space* character (between the two empty quotes) to the word *Stutz*. Spaces, punctuation, and numbers are all part of the String data type. Then it adds *Bearcat* onto the string. So, the value of the stored variable carModel reads *Stutz Bearcat*.

Just to prove the point that you can't do math with strings, consider these two statements:

```
parkingTicket = 50 + 25;
parkingTicket = "50" + "25";
```

In the first example, parkingTicket is an unpleasant but reasonable number, *75*. In the second example where two strings are concatenated, you end up with a string value in parkingTicket of *5025*.

It's also fairly common to compare two strings to see if they're the same, which you have to do every time someone types in a password. To do that type of comparison, you use the equality operator (==), not the assignment operator (=). Here's an example:

```
visitorPassword == textFieldPassword;
```

You can use a statement like that to test whether a password typed into a Flash text field matches the password the visitor previously supplied.

These aren't the only operations you can perform with strings, just two of the most common. You'll see examples using strings throughout the rest of the book. Chapter 17 covers several common string programming techniques, beginning on page 581.

# Boolean

A *Boolean* is a data type that has one of two values: true or false. The *Boolean* is very handy, because programs often test conditions and then report on the results. For example, parkingMeterExpired could be a Boolean data type. In that case, you might see an expression:

```
if (parkingMeterExpired == true)
{
ticketVehicle();
}
```

In human-ese, this translates to "If the value of parkingMeterExpired equals *true*, then run the function *ticketVehicle()*." The equality operator creates a statement that's either true or false. You're not assigning a value to parkingMeterExpired; you're creating a statement that ActionScript can test.

### ■ BOOLEANS AND OPERATORS

The most common Boolean operator has been used several times in this chapter; that's the equality (==) operator that's used to test if two statements are equivalent. So, if parkingMeterExpired is a Boolean data type, then it has one of two values: *true* or *false*. That makes the statement:

```
parkingMeterExpired==true
```

either true or false.

For the times when it's more convenient to test for a false statement, use the inequality operator (!=) as shown in this example:

```
parkingMeterExpired!=true
```

# Arrays

Unlike the simple data types, *arrays* are containers that can hold more than one item. Those items don't even need to be the same data type. For example, a single array can hold Numbers and strings, which makes them a great way to keep related information together. Imagine you want to collect different tidbits of information about people who belong to your Stutz Bearcat auto club. For example, you might want to record first name, last name, age, number of speeding tickets, and whether their club dues are paid up:

```
memberDetailsArray = ["Erwin", "Baker", 38, 12, true]
```

Each tidbit of data is called an *element*, so the above array has five elements. In the example, the first two elements of the array are strings. The following two are numbers. The last item is a Boolean, so it can have only two values: true or false. An array can even hold another array as one of its elements. Individual elements are separated by commas, and the entire array is enclosed in square brackets. You can access individual elements in the array by number, but there's one "gotcha" to remember. The first element in an array is referred to as number *0*. So, if you want to change the last name "Baker" to "Paxton" you assign a new value, like so:

```
memberDetailsArray[1] = "Paxton";
```

In ActionScript, arrays are a type of object, and there are a whole crop of methods (functions) you can use to work with them. For example, there are methods to do all of the following:

- Add a new element to an array.

- Remove an element from an array.

- Report the number of items in an array.

- Sort and reorder the elements in an array.

Earlier in this chapter (page 426), you saw examples of ActionScript *functions*. Methods are also functions—they're actions; they do something. What makes methods special is that they're part of the definition of an object. For example, one method that adds a new element to an array is called *push*. You can think of it as pushing another plate on a stack of dishes. You use the dot (.) nomenclature to connect it to the function. Suppose you want to add a new element to your memberDetailsArray that represents the year a member's car was built. Here's the statement that does the job:

```
memberDetailArray.push(1937);
```

The dot (.) nomenclature looks familiar because ActionScript also uses it to access an object's properties. Arrays are used in examples in the following chapters.

## ActionScript Built-In Data Types

ActionScript has a number of built-in data types that are made up of some of the simple data types. Some examples include familiar Flash objects, like the following:

- MovieClip

  A symbol (from the Flash Library) that's a movie clip.

- TextField and TLFTextField

  A field (or box) that holds text. You can set and change the contents, or your audience can type them when your program is running.

- SimpleButton

  A special type of graphic that's preprogrammed to behave like a button. Click it, and your program does something.

- Date

  The Date data type represents a specific moment in time. ActionScript code can access the month, day, hour, and second.

# Variables

If you followed some of the exercises earlier in this chapter, you may have noticed that programming is the fine art of swapping one value for another. Move an object, change a color, start playing a movie clip at a certain point—those actions require providing a new value for a color, stage position, and timeline position.

Like buckets or baskets, variables are the containers that hold these changing values.

## ■ DECLARING VARIABLES

Before you can use a variable, you have to tell ActionScript 3.0 what to expect. You introduce the name you're planning on using and you explain whether it's a number, string, or some other data type. It's called *declaring a variable*, and here are some examples:

```
var minutesOnMeter : Number;
var carModel : String;
var licensePlate: String;
var meterExpired: Boolean;
```

If you want, you can assign a value to your variable when you declare it.

```
var minutesOnMeter : Number = 60;
var carModel       : "Stutz Bearcat";
var meterExired    : Boolean = false;
```

---

**TIP** In general, ActionScript isn't fussy about white space. If you want to include extra spaces to line things up as shown in previous examples, that's fine. Just don't make mistakes with your spelling and punctuation or you'll get a virtual ruler to the back of your hand.

---

Once you've declared that the variable *minutesOnMeter* is a Number, you can't store a different type of data in it. For example, if you try to assign a string to minutesOnMeter, an error message appears in the Compiler Error panel, like the one in Figure 12-12: "Implicit coercion of a value of type Number to an unrelated type String." Sentences like that may make you feel like you should call a lawyer, but you can usually figure out the problem. Double-click the error message, and Flash takes you directly to the line in your code that caused the error.

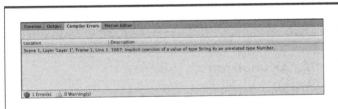

**FIGURE 12-12**

*ActionScript's Compiler Error panel provides about the problem. Location tells you where the error is, Description names the type of error.*

## Constants

A constant is a value that never changes through the course of the program. It might be the color of a stoplight (red) or the boiling point of water (100 degrees Celsius). Use constants when it's easier or more readable to refer to something by name (Stop, BoilingPoint) rather than value. ActionScript programs use variables more often than constants.

### ■ DECLARING CONSTANTS

As with variables, you have to declare constants, and it makes sense to provide their value at the same time:

```
const PARKING_TICKET : Number = 50;
```

Most programmers use all caps for constants to differentiate them from variables. If you accidentally try to assign a value to a constant, you get one of those nasty compiler error messages.

# ■ Conditionals and Loops

Using conditions and loops, you can teach your Flash animations how to make decisions, and viewers will think both you and your animations are very smart. ActionScript provides a few different decision-making statements that you can use depending on your needs. In human-ese, they work like this:

- If (this condition exists) do (these actions)
- While (this condition exists) do (these actions)
- For (X number of times) do (these actions)

Those three forms of decision-making may seem very similar, but as you'll see in the following explanations and examples, there are some important basic differences. You'll hear programmers refer to these decision-making statements using different terms, like "program flow controls," "conditionals," and "loops." These tools have one thing in common: They all help you dictate whether or not ActionScript runs some specific lines of code.

## Conditionals: *if()* and *switch()* Statements

Two of ActionScript's statements tackle the "If (this condition exists) do (these actions)" situations. The first and simplest state is appropriately called an *if* statement.

### ■ IF() STATEMENTS TEST A CONDITION

The most basic *if* statements are built like this:

```
if (this is true) {do this}
```

So, if you're writing an ActionScript statement for a parking meter cop, it might look like this:

```
if (parkingMeterExpired==true) {writeTicket();}
```

It works like this: If the condition within the parentheses is true, then your code performs the statements within the curly brackets. If the expression in the parentheses is false, then your code ignores the statements within the curly brackets. In this example, if the parking meter has expired, the cop writes a ticket. If the parking meter hasn't expired, the cop doesn't do anything. (Well, maybe she goes for donuts.)

**NOTE** The parentheses *()* after *writeTicket* are part of any function including the *writeTicket()* function. The following semicolon is the proper way to end a statement.

In some cases, you may want to provide some additional alternatives. Suppose you're sending your assistant to the auto store. You want him to buy a Stutz Bearcat, but in the unlikely event that the store doesn't have any Bearcats, you want him to buy a Packard Roadster. In ActionScript, that instruction takes the form of an *if...else* statement.

```
if (storeHasStutzBearcat==true) {
 buyStutzBearcat();
} else {
 buyPackardRoadster();
}
```

### ■ IF...ELSE IF STATEMENTS CHOOSE FROM MANY OPTIONS

You can string *if...else* statements together to handle several different conditions. The result looks like this:

```
if (storeHasStutzBearCat==true) {
buyStutzBearcat();
} else if (storeHasPackardRoadster==true) {
 buyPackardRoadster();
}
 else if(storeHasHudson==true) {
 buyHudson();
}
```

There's a statement that should resolve any out-of-stock issues at the car store. ActionScript works through the statements from top to bottom. When it finds a car in stock, it buys the car. Using this *if...else if* structure, your assistant will purchase only one car. For example, you won't end up with both a Packard Roadster and a Hudson. If the Packard is in stock, the function *buyPackardRoadster()* runs and the *else if(storeHasHudson...)* portion is ignored. If none of the conditions are met, then your assistant buys no car.

## ■ SWITCH() STATEMENTS CHOOSE FROM MANY OPTIONS

You can string together as many *if...else if* conditions as you want, but at some point the code gets a little awkward and hard to read. The *switch()* statement makes a good alternative when you have more than three conditions to check. Suppose you want to create a system where a parking ticket costs more depending on the number of tickets the scofflaw has received. The variable numberOfTickets holds a Number value. A *switch()* statement might look like this:

```
switch (numberOfTickets) {
 case 1 :
 parkingTicket = 25;
 break;
 case 2 :
 parkingTicket = 50;
 break;
 case 3 :
 parkingTicket = 75;
 break;
 case 4 :
 parkingTicket = 100;
 break;
 case 5 :
 parkingTicket = 125;
 break;
 default :
 parkingTicket = 0;
 }
```

The switch statement takes the variable numberOfTickets and, starting at the top, compares it to the first *case*. If the offender has a single parking ticket, then the value of parkingTicket is set to 25. When ActionScript gets to the word *break*, it jumps to the end of the *switch()* statement and doesn't run any of the other cases. The default case is used when none of the other cases match.

## Loops: *while()* and *for()* Statements

There's a good rule of thumb to remember with computers. If *you're* doing the same chore over and over again, there's probably some way your computer can do it more efficiently. Computers are great at repetitive tasks, and that's certainly true of ActionScript, which has two great ways to repeat statements in your programs. Using the *while()* statement, you can have your computer repeat a task as long as a certain condition exists. Using the *for()* statement, you can tell your computer exactly how many times to repeat a task.

## ■ WHILE() STATEMENTS REPEAT TASKS AS LONG AS A CONDITION IS MET

The *while()* statement checks to see if a condition is met. If it is, then the code within the curly brackets runs. If the condition isn't met, then ActionScript moves on to the next statement. It's very common to use the *while()* statement with a variable that's incremented. So, if you want your assistant to pop down to the auto store and buy six Stutz Bearcats (enough for you and a few close friends), you'd put together a statement like this:

```
while (myStutzBearcats < 6) {
 buyStutzBearcat();
 myStutzBearcats = myStutzBearcats + 1;
}
```

Like the *if()* statement, the condition for the *while()* statement is inside parentheses, and if the condition is met, then the statements inside curly brackets {} run. In this example, the second line runs a function that buys a Bearcat. The third line *increments* the variable that keeps track of how many Bearcats you own. As long as that number is less than 6, the program loops; you buy another and add 1 to the number of Bearcats you own.

The whole idea of incrementing a value, like myStutzBearcats, is so common that there's even a shorthand way of adding one to a variable. The third line could also read:

```
myBearCats++;
```

There's no assignment operator (=), but the statement is assigning a new value to myBearcats. When you want to count down, you can use the decrement operator (--). Here's a statement that sells off your Stutz Bearcats until you have only three left.

```
while (myStutzBearcats > 3 {
 sellStutzBearcat();
 myStutzBearcats--;
}
```

> **NOTE** If you're reading ActionScript code for pleasure and you come across *i++*, don't be surprised. The *i* usually stands for *iterator* or *integer*. It's the programmer's way of saying, "I need an integer to operate this loop, but it can be any old integer, it doesn't need a fancy variable name." Using the lowercase *i* as a stand-in isn't a rule, just a programmers' tradition.

### ■ FOR() STATEMENTS REPEAT TASKS A SPECIFIC NUMBER OF TIMES

The *for()* loop gives you a very compact way to repeat a portion of your program. The mechanics that make a *for()* statement run are all packed in the first line. It's so compact and down to business that it reads a little more like machine talk than human talk. Here's an example:

```
for (var myStutzBearcats:Number = 0; myStutzBearcats < 6; myStutzBearcats++)
{
 buyStutzBearcat();
}
```

Like the earlier statement, this loop buys six Stutz Bearcats. A lot goes on in that very first line of code. From left to right, here's what happens:

- The word *for* indicates a *for()* statement.

- The beginning parenthesis is your clue that the condition follows.

- The word *var* means that a variable is being declared.

- *myStutzBearcats:Number* is the name of that variable and its data type.

- The assignment operator (=) immediately gives the variable a value of zero.

- Following the semicolon, you finally arrive at the condition that's being tested: Are there fewer than six Bearcats?

- The semicolon ends that statement, and in the next *myStutzBearcats* is *incremented*.

The *for()* statement is very compact, and it puts everything you need to know right up front. Script writers often create *for()* statements using the variable *i* for the condition (see the note on page 439). You'll often see something like:

```
for (var i = 0; i < 6; i++) {
  buyStutzBearcat;
}
```

Just like the earlier *for* statement, this one purchases six of those beautiful Bearcats.

> **NOTE** For an example of the *for()* statement in action, download *12-2_For_Statement.fla* from the Missing CD page (*www.missingmanuals.com/cds/flashcs6mm*).

# ■ Combining ActionScript's Building Blocks

This chapter covered a lot of ActionScript theory, and you may be itching to put some of these concepts into action. In the following chapters, there are many examples that show you how to do just that.

Here's a recap of the topics covered in this chapter:

- *Classes* are blueprints for objects.

- *Instances* are specific objects, in use.

- ActionScript objects may have *properties, methods,* and *events*.

- *Properties* are the characteristics of objects; by changing values, your programs can change those characteristics.

- *Methods* and *functions* are the actions in ActionScript.

- *Methods* are included in the definition of an object.

- *Functions* (technically called function closures) are independent of objects.

- *Events* are used to make Flash projects interactive.

- *Events* have two parts: 1) *event listeners* that wait for events like mouse clicks; and 2) *event handlers* that run ActionScript statements in response to the event.

- *Variables* are containers for values. *Constants* are named values that never change.

- Variables can be one of several different data types: *number, int, uint, string, Boolean*, and *array.*

- *Arrays* can hold multiple values and different types of data.

- *Operators* are used to perform math functions, assign values, and compare values.

- *Conditional* statements, like (*if, if...else if*, and *switch*) test to see if a condition exists, and then, based on the result, run or ignore portions of ActionScript code.

- *Loop* statements (like *while* and *for*) run portions of ActionScript code either a specified number of times, or while a condition exists.

# Controlling Actions with Events

In the previous chapter, you learned how to use ActionScript to move, transform, and change parts of your animation. But *when* something happens is just as important as the action itself. For example, you may want a movie object to start playing as soon as the web page opens, or you may want to let your audience decide when to watch it. You use *events* to control the actions in your animation. It's as if your ActionScript program tells Flash: "When this (event) happens, do this (action)." The classic example is a button on the stage. The action statement says something like: "When this button gets clicked, go to Frame 25 of the movie clip, and then start playing." You provide the programming that puts the people who view your Flash creations in the driver's seat. Using events and event handlers, you can send your programs off into the world on their own, confident that they'll behave.

This chapter explains how to use ActionScript to detect events when they happen and how to get your animations to perform specific actions as a result. Unlike previous versions, ActionScript 3.0 has one single way of handling all kinds of events. So, once you learn the basics, you're all set to handle any event.

## ■ How Events Work

There are many different types of events. Some events—like a mouse click—are triggered by the people viewing your animation. Other events are simply occurrences in a Flash animation—like a movie clip reaching the last frame. The button is one of the easiest events to understand, and, not surprisingly, it's one of the most common. Someone clicks a button, and then an action takes place. To the person clicking, it appears that the button makes something happen. That's true to some extent, but there are some additional gears and levers behind the scenes.

The object related to the event is called the *event target*. So in the button example, the button is the event target. When an event like a button click happens, an *event object* is created. The job of this new event object is to deliver information to an *event listener*, which has instructions about what to do when that event happens. So how does the event target know where to deliver the information carried within the event object? That detail is handled by *registering* the event. In effect, the code that registers an event says, "When this event happens, send that event object to this location." Figure 13-1 shows the major elements involved in event handling.

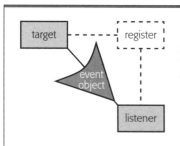

**FIGURE 13-1**

*When an event related to the target happens, ActionScript sends a message, in the form of the event object, to the event listener, which performs the actions. You register specific events, like a mouse click, beforehand, so the target knows where to send the event object.*

Like most things in ActionScript, an event is considered an object. Obviously, it's not an object in the sense that a rectangle or a circle on your stage is an object. It's an object by the strict ActionScript definition of an object because it has properties where it stores information about the event, and it has methods (functions) that let you perform actions related to the event. The Event class is the definition of events in a very general sense—similar to the class definition of a rectangle as a four-sided object. The Event class is the basis for other, more specific Event objects. Different types of events, such as mouse events, keyboard events, and error events, have properties and methods that serve their specific needs.

---

**FLASHBACK**

## Past Events

As ActionScript matured with each version of Flash, it sprouted several different ways to handle events. Having various ways to handle events may not have been a bad thing at the time, but at some point in ActionScript's evolution, it became a problem. Some methods were easy to use but made Action-Script code harder to maintain and troubleshoot. One obvious problem, from an ActionScript programmer's point of view,

was remembering which event-handling routines to use in different circumstances.

One of the welcome changes that ActionScript 3.0 brings is a single, consistent way to deal with events. This chapter explains in detail how to handle events using ActionScript 3.0.

---

# ■ Mouse Events

The mouse is the most common way your audience interacts with your Flash creation, so a lot of events center around the mouse. The MouseEvent class detects all sorts of mouse events, including a variety of clicks and mouse movements, like mouse over (when the cursor moves over an object) and mouse out (when the cursor moves away from an object). Such events are the stuff that buttons and other smart objects are made of. So roll up your sleeves and get ready to create a mouse event listener. If you have a project deadline looming and just need bulletproof code for a simple mouse-over event, see the box below.

**NOTE** A mouse event refers to an event generated by *any* kind of pointer device, whether it's a mouse, a trackpad on a laptop, or a drawing pad. Touch and gesture events for smartphones and tablets are managed by their own event objects.

---

**FREQUENTLY ASKED QUESTION**

### Create an Event Handler in a Snap

*I need an ActionScript 3.0 event handler now! Where can I find some cut-and-paste code?*

Events and event handlers are fundamental to most ActionScript projects, so it's great to have a thorough understanding of their workings. You'll get that in the following pages. But if you don't have time to look up references and write the code, Flash CS6 can help you out with Code Snippets. These predesigned chunks of ActionScript 3.0 code are ready for you to drop into your project. So, if you need a mouse-over event handler, select a movie clip symbol and then choose Window→Code Snippets. Expand the Event Handler, and then click Mouse Over Event. Flash adds several lines of code to your project and displays it on the Actions panel. The code has comments and instructions to help you customize the snippet to work in your project.

---

This first example uses two movie clip objects: a circle and some text. The goal is to create an event listener that recognizes when the mouse is over the circle and when it's not—your basic rollover action. When the mouse moves over the circle, the text changes to say "mouse over." When the mouse moves out of the circle, the text changes back to the original message, "mouse out." Not an earthshaking event, but you have to start somewhere.

**NOTE** You can create your own movie clip as described in the following steps, or you can download *13-1_Mouse_Event.fla* from the Missing CD page at *www.missingmanuals.com/cds/flashcs6mm*. If you want to see how the final project works, download and test *13-2_Mouse_Event_done.fla*.

Here are the steps to set up a Flash document with the necessary symbols for the mouse event experiment.

1. **In a new Flash document, draw a circle, and then create some static text that reads "mouse out."**

   When you're done, you have two objects in Frame 1 of your movie, as shown in Figure 13-2.

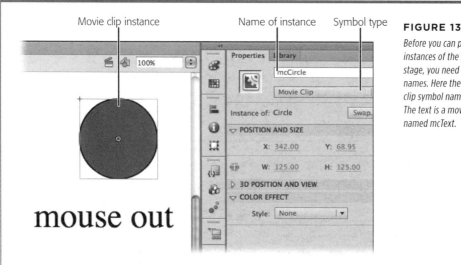

Movie clip instance    Name of instance    Symbol type

**FIGURE 13-2**

*Before you can program the instances of the symbols on the stage, you need to give them names. Here the circle is a movie clip symbol named mcCircle. The text is a movie clip symbol named mcText.*

2. **Convert both the circle and the text to movie clip symbols (Modify→"Convert to Symbol").**

   This creates two symbols in the Library and leaves instances of the symbols on your desktop. As you create the symbols, use whatever names seem appropriate, like *Circle* and *Text*. The symbol names in the Library aren't as critical as the *instance* names described in the next step. Your ActionScript code will use these instance names.

3. **Select the circle movie clip instance on the stage, and then, using the Properties panel, name it *mcCircle*, as shown in Figure 13-2.** Select and then name the text movie clip instance *mcText*.

   You can use any name you want for instances on your desktop, but it's helpful to add something to the name that identifies the type. Here, *mc* indicates that the symbol instances are movie clips.

4. **Double-click mcText to open the movie clip symbol for editing.**

   As shown in Figure 13-3, the Text movie clip opens. At the top of the window you see "breadcrumb" navigation buttons: Scene and mcText. These are helpful when you open symbols within symbols. The new button displays the Library symbol name (not the instance name). On the stage, the text remains boldly colored to indicate that it's part of the symbol you're editing. The circle is faded to indicate that it's not part of the symbol you're editing.

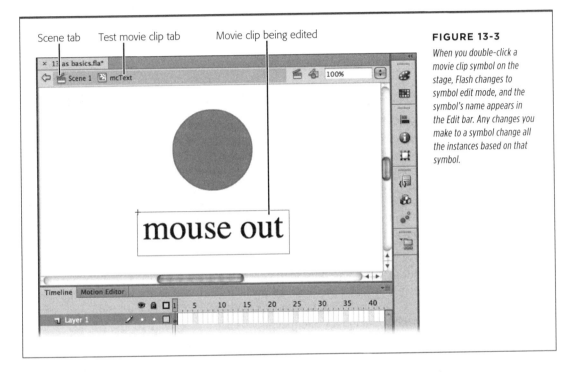

**FIGURE 13-3**

*When you double-click a movie clip symbol on the stage, Flash changes to symbol edit mode, and the symbol's name appears in the Edit bar. Any changes you make to a symbol change all the instances based on that symbol.*

5. **Click Frame 2 in the timeline, and then press F6 to add a keyframe that includes content from the previous frame.**

   A new keyframe appears containing your text.

6. **Use the text tool to change the text in Frame 2 to read *mouse over*.**

   Click anywhere in the text to begin editing. When you're done, just click outside the text or choose another tool from the Tools palette.

7. **Use the Properties panel to label Frame 1 *out*, and then label Frame 2 *over*.**

   You can use either labels or frame numbers as references in ActionScript programming. In many ways, labels are the best choice because they make your code easier to understand when you read it. A good label explains more than a number any day. Also, if you insert new frames in the timeline, the frame numbers in your ActionScript will no longer be valid.

8. **Click Scene 1 to exit the mcText movie clip and go back to your main movie clip.**

   The symbol closes, and you're back on the main timeline.

9. **Add a new layer to your main movie clip, and then name it *actions*.**

   It's always best to create a special, well-labeled layer to hold your ActionScript code.

# ■ Getting Help for Events and Event Listeners

Now that the Flash document is ready to go, it's time to write and register an event listener, but where do you start? Computers are fussy beasts and won't work properly unless everything is done their way. ActionScript is the same. Event handling uses specific words, punctuation, and even capitalization. Everything has to be just so, or your event will be a nonevent. For beginning ActionScript coders, one of the challenges is learning the right words to use to define and register particular events. This section explains what questions you need to ask as you're coding and where to find the answers.

The first question to ask is this: What type of event is going to serve as the trigger to set your actions in motion? In this case, the event is the movement of the mouse over an object named mcCircle, so this is a mouse-related event. With that bit of knowledge, you can consult ActionScript reference tools that list different types of events. You're looking for one that sounds like it deals with mouse events.

The best reference tool that's close at hand while you're ActionScripting is the *ActionScript 3.0 Reference.* Open it through the help menu: Help→Flash Help. A web page opens with many different help topics. Click the ActionScript topic near the top of the page, then click ActionScript 3.0 Reference. The help systems shows packages (groups of ActionScript classes) in the top left panel and specific classes in the lower left panel. Details for a class appear in the large right panel.

This electronic reference book provides details on every object, function, and element of ActionScript. Click the names on the left to open up descriptions and examples in the main window. Events are in the list of "packages" in the upper-left corner. The packages that begin with "fl." are related to Flash components, video, multi-language tools, motion classes, tweens, and transitions. Some of these you can't use unless you've added the related components to your Flash document. The packages that begin with "flash." are built into Flash Player and work in any Flash document.

Scroll down and click "flash.events." The main window fills with classes and descriptions. Under the heading Classes, you see all the different types of event classes. Some may seem a little mysterious, like AsyncErrorEvent. But other names—like KeyboardEvent and MouseEvent—sound more helpful. One click on MouseEvent, and your journey is over. The window fills with all the programmer's details you need to handle a MouseEvent, like the public constants that mouse events use (see the box below).

**TIP** It's kind of a lengthy trip to hunt down the help details on a specific event type, but it's worth remembering. If you end up writing a lot of event listeners, you'll probably remember the details for the events you use all the time. Occasionally, though, you'll need to look up the details for some oddball and unfamiliar event type. So leave some breadcrumbs (or fold down the corner of this page) to remind yourself how to look up events in the *ActionScript 3.0 Reference*.

The reason for mucking through all this programming gobbledegook is about to become apparent. Scroll down and look at the items under Public Constants. These are the names of the actual events that MouseEvent can recognize: CLICK, DOUBLE_CLICK, and so on, including MOUSE_OUT and MOUSE_OVER—the two events you need for your script. Each event type (MouseEvent, KeyboardEvent, ErrorEvent) has related *constants* that you use when you create event listeners. You have to type these constants exactly as they're defined (including capital letters, underscores, and so on) for your event listener to work. In addition to the constants, the events have properties you can use in your programs. For example, MouseEvent has properties called altKey, ctrlKey, and shiftKey. These are Booleans, and they can tell you whether a particular key is being pressed during a mouse event. You can use them to define, say, a special action for Shift-click and a different one for Alt-click.

**CODERS' CLINIC**

## Mouse Events: Public Constants

Here's the complete list of constants used by MouseEvent, as shown in *ActionScript 3.0 Reference*. The first word, in capital letters, is the constant you use to identify the event. The word after the colon, *String*, indicates that the constant is of the string type. The word in quotes is the constant's actual value. The most important part of this definition is the word in caps, because that's the word you use to register listeners for a particular mouse event, as explained in the next section. You can think of these constants as the specific triggers for a MouseEvent.

```
CLICK : String = "click"
DOUBLE_CLICK : String = "doubleClick"
MOUSE_DOWN : String = "mouseDown"
MOUSE_MOVE : String = "mouseMove"
MOUSE_OUT : String = "mouseOut"
MOUSE_OVER : String = "mouseOver"
MOUSE_UP : String = "mouseUp"
MOUSE_WHEEL : String = "mouseWheel"
ROLL_OUT : String = "rollOut"
ROLL_OVER : String = "rollOver"
```

**TIP** You can ignore the items with the red triangles next to their names unless you're planning on doing some AIR (Adobe Integrated Runtime) programming. The triangles indicate that these classes, properties, and methods are available only in AIR. For more details on AIR projects, see Chapter 21.

## Creating a Rollover with a Mouse Event

So you know you want to listen for a mouse event; specifically, you want to trigger some actions when the mouse is over the mcCircle movie clip. That makes mcCircle the *event target*, because it's the object where the event takes place. As described earlier and as shown in Figure 13-1, the event target creates an event object, and then sends it to an event listener. The event object delivers information about the event that happened. Often, all that's necessary is notification that the event took place. As programmer, it's your job to tell the event target the name of the event that serves as a trigger and where to deliver the event object. This process is called *registering* an event, and it's done with a line of code like this:

```
mcCircle.addEventListener(MouseEvent.MOUSE_OVER, mouseOverListener);
```

> **NOTE**   As usual, create an actions layer in your timeline and use the Actions panel (Window→Actions) to write your code.

In ActionScript-speak, this statement "registers an event listener." Almost all events use a similar method to register event listeners, so it's worthwhile to examine the statement completely. The first chunk of code, *mcCircle.addEventListener*, is nearly recognizable. The dot syntax indicates that mcCircle is an object, and that makes addEventListener either a property or a method of the object. The action verb "add" in the name hints that it's a method, because methods are actions, while properties are characteristics. In fact, addEventListener is a method that's included with just about every object in Flash. That means you can use nearly any object to register an event listener. The details in the parentheses are the *parameters* for the method.

The first parameter is the event the listener is listening for. In this case, it's a MouseEvent, and the specific type of event is named by the constant MOUSE_OVER. As you know from your extensive research in the Flash help files, those capital-lettered constants *are* the specific triggers for a MouseEvent. A comma separates the parameters of the method. In this statement, there are two parameters. The second parameter, *mouseOverListener*, is the name of the event listener. An *event listener* is simply a function—a series of statements or actions—that run when the event happens. You get to name (and write all the code for) the event listener. It's helpful to use a name that shows that this is an event listener and that describes the event that triggers the actions; hence the name "mouseOverListener."

The event listener is a function, much like the functions described on page 426. The most significant detail is that the function has to list the event object in its parameters. You can think of the event object as the message sent from the event target to the event listener. Here's the code for mouseOverListener:

```
function mouseOverListener (evt:MouseEvent):void
{
  mcText.gotoAndStop("over");
}
```

The first line begins with the keyword *function*, indicating that what follows defines a function—a list of actions. Next comes the name of the function: *mouseOverListener*. The function's parameter is the event object; in this case, the event object's name is *evt*. That's followed by a colon (:) and the object class *MouseEvent*. The name doesn't matter—it can be *evt, e,* or *george.* As always, it's helpful to choose a name that means something to you now and will still make sense 5 years from now when you're trying to remember how the code works. You do have to accurately define the class or type of event, which in this case is MouseEvent. The term *:void* indicates that this function doesn't return a value. If you need to brush up your function-building skills, see page 426.

Once the curly brackets begin, you know that they contain the list of statements or actions that the function performs. In this case, there's simply one line that tells the movie clip mcText to go to the frame labeled "over" and stop there. All in all, here's the complete code so far, with accompanying line numbers:

```
1  mcCircle.addEventListener(MouseEvent.MOUSE_OVER, mouseOverListener);
2
3  function mouseOverListener (evt:MouseEvent):void
4  {
5    mcText.gotoAndStop("over");
6  }
```

What you have at this point is one complete and registered event listener. Line 1 identifies mcCircle as the event target for a MOUSE_OVER event. It also registers the event listener as mouseOverListener. Beginning on Line 3, you have the code for mouseOverListener. Any actions you place between those curly brackets will happen when the mouse cursor is over mcCircle.

You can go ahead and test your movie if you want, but it's not going to behave all that well. It needs a few more lines of code to make it presentable. If you test your movie at this point, you'll see a lot of movie clip flickering. If you mouse over the circle, the flickering stops and the text changes to "mouse over." That much works well. When you move the mouse out of the circle...nothing happens. The text still reads "mouse over." That's because you haven't written the mouse-out event. Fortunately, it's very similar to the mouse-over code. In fact, all you have to do is copy and paste the mouse-over code, and then make changes where needed, as shown in bold text in this example:

```
7
8      mcCircle.addEventListener(MouseEvent.MOUSE_OUT, mouseOutListener);
9
10     function mouseOutListener (evt:MouseEvent):void
11  {
12     mcText.gotoAndStop("out");
13  }
```

By now, you should be able to read and understand most of the code. Like the first example, the event is registered using the mcCircle object. The event in this case is MOUSE_OUT, and the event listener is named accordingly: mouseOutListener. The action part of the event listener sends the timeline playhead to the frame labeled "out," which displays the text "mouse out"—back where it was when the program started. Perfect.

Well, almost perfect. If you test the movie now, you'll find that it behaves well when you mouse over the circle and when you mouse out of the circle. At the beginning though, there's still a bunch of movie clip flickering, unless the mouse starts off over the circle. Time for a little Flash troubleshooting. Unless they're told otherwise, movie clips play one frame, and then the next, and so on, until they reach the last frame, and then they play over again. And again. And again. Your main movie has only one frame, so it's not causing the flickering. mcCircle only has one frame, so it's not causing the flickering either. The mcText clip has two frames, and those are the ones doing the dance when you start your animation. You need a line of code that stops the movie clip on Frame 1. Then it will be up to the mouse events to control which frame is shown. All you need is one line that says:

```
mcText.gotoAndStop(1);
```

The method *gotoAndStop()* is part of every movie clip. This bit of code tells mcText to go to Frame 1 and stop. The parameter inside the parentheses has to refer to a specific frame. You can do that with a frame number, as shown here, or you can do it with a frame label, as you did in your event listeners. If you're wondering how you can find out about the properties and methods for particular classes and objects, see the box below.

**CODERS' CLINIC**

## Getting Help for ActionScript Classes

On page 448, the section "Getting Help for Events and Event Listeners" explained how to find an event and all its programming details in the *ActionScript 3.0 Reference*. You can use the same reference to look up the properties and methods of particular classes and objects. For example, if you can't remember the exact spelling for the "goto and stop" method, you can look up the MovieClip class, and you see all the methods associated with the class.

After opening the *ActionScript 3.0 Reference* (see the box on page 441), look for MovieClip in the scrolling box at the bottom left under Classes. Click the word "MovieClip," and you see the complete and formal definition of the class, including the public properties that you can change through ActionScript programming. Below that, you see the public methods including *gotoAndStop()*. There's a short description that describes what the method does and the type of parameters it requires. Scroll down far enough, and you'll see examples of how to use the MovieClip class, along with its properties and methods.

As a statement on the first frame of your main movie clip, *mcText.gotoAndStop(1)* runs when the animation begins. It doesn't really matter whether it comes before or after the other lines of code. Those other bits of code don't do anything until an event happens. Not so with the statement above. There's nothing to prevent it from running as soon as Frame 1 of the main movie clip loads.

In ActionScript programming, the order in which different functions and statements appear isn't always important. It doesn't matter which event listener appears first in your code. The order in which the event listeners *run* is determined by the order in which someone mouses over or out of mcCircle. So whenever possible, you may as well arrange your code so it's easy to read and understand. In this case, it's probably best to register all your event listeners in the same spot, and then put the event listener functions together. You may also want to put the code that isn't dependent on a listener at the very top. So here, with a little rearranging for readability, is the code up to this point:

```
1   mcText.gotoAndStop(1);
2
3   mcCircle.addEventListener(MouseEvent.MOUSE_OVER, mouseOverListener);
4   mcCircle.addEventListener(MouseEvent.MOUSE_OUT, mouseOutListener);
5
6   function mouseOverListener(evt:MouseEvent):void
7   {
8     mcText.gotoAndStop("over");
9   }
10
11  function mouseOutListener(evt:MouseEvent):void
12  {
13    mcText.gotoAndStop("out");
14  }
```

Line 1 stops mcText in its tracks before it has a chance to start flickering between its two frames. Lines 3 and 4 register event listeners. Beginning on line 6 are the functions that make up the event listeners. At this point, you can test your program, and it should behave pretty well. If something unexpected happens, double-check your spelling and make sure you have semicolons at the end of the statements.

## Add Statements to an Event Listener

So far in this example you've seen how an event listener attached to one object (mcCircle) can effect a change in another object (mcText). A single event listener can change any number of objects, including the object that registers the listener. After all, any statements you put between the curly brackets of an event listener will run when the event happens.

So the next steps change the mcCircle object to give it a rollover-style behavior. Once you make these changes, both the text and the circle will change in response to MOUSE_OVER and MOUSE_OUT events. Before you can indulge in ActionScript programming fun, you need to create a new keyframe in the mcCircle movie clip with a different image. Then you get to add statements to the two event listeners, mouseOverListener and mouseOutListener, to describe the actions.

Here are the steps to set up mcCircle's timeline:

1. **On the stage, double-click mcCircle to open it for editing.**

   The circle symbol opens, showing a single frame in the timeline.

2. **Click Frame 2 in the timeline, and then press F7 to add a blank keyframe.**

   A new empty keyframe appears in Frame 2 of the circle timeline.

3. **Draw a star in Frame 2 using the Polystar tool.**

The circle timeline now has a circle on Frame 1 and a star on Frame 2.

4. **In the Properties panel, label Frame 2 *over*, and then label Frame 1 *out*.**

It's good to get in the habit of labeling frames you refer to in ActionScript code.

5. **In the Edit bar above the stage, click Scene 1 to close the movie clip.**

The circle movie clip symbol closes, and you're back at the main movie clip's timeline.

In your ActionScript, you need to add the lines that control the behavior of the mcCircle movie clip. They're all of the *gotoAndStop()* variety. Start off with a line that stops the movie clip from flickering when the animation begins.

```
mcCircle.gotoAndStop(1);
```

Then, between the curly brackets of mouseOverListener, add code to change the circle to a star when a MOUSE_OVER event happens.

```
mcCircle.gotoAndStop("over");
```

Last but not least, between the curly brackets of the mouseOutListener, add code to change the star back to a circle when the mouse moves away from mcCircle.

```
mcCircle.gotoAndStop("out");
```

When you're done, the complete code should look like this:

```
1   mcText.gotoAndStop(1);
2   mcCircle.gotoAndStop(1);
3
4   mcCircle.addEventListener(MouseEvent.MOUSE_OVER, mouseOverListener);
5   mcCircle.addEventListener(MouseEvent.MOUSE_OUT, mouseOutListener);
6
7   function mouseOverListener(evt:MouseEvent):void
8   {
9     mcText.gotoAndStop("over");
10    mcCircle.gotoAndStop("over");
11  }
12
13  function mouseOutListener(evt:MouseEvent):void
14  {
15    mcText.gotoAndStop("out");
16    mcCircle.gotoAndStop("out");
17  }
```

Now is a good time to test your movie. If everything runs as it should, you enjoy a high-quality mouse-over and mouse-out experience. Both the graphics and the text change with the mouse events. On the other hand, if you're getting somewhat different results, you may want to download *13-2_Mouse_Event_done.fla* from the Missing CD page at *www.missingmanuals.com/cds/flashcs6mm* to look for places where your code doesn't match the downloaded file.

### ■ APPLYING MOUSE EVENTS TO OTHER PROJECTS

As it stands now, your mouse event project isn't the flashiest thing on the block (pun intended). Still, it's worth considering how you can take the same rollover style behaviors and create larger, more impressive projects. For example, using the same mouse events, it would be easy to create a photo gallery that has half a dozen or more photo thumbnails and one large "feature" image, like the one in Figure 13-4. When the mouse moves over one of the thumbnails, the thumbnail changes to display a highlight, and the feature image changes to match the thumbnail. You can even add a text caption that changes for each picture. Once you've created one photo gallery, it's easy to reuse your code by simply swapping in new photos. The variations are limited only by your time and imagination. For example, the photo gallery animation mentioned in Chapter 7 (*7-5_Photo_Gallery.fla*), uses mouse-click events. When a thumbnail is clicked, the playhead moves to a different point on the timeline, where a tween moves the photo in 3-D space until it finally fills the stage. Another click, and it shrinks back to size.

**FIGURE 13-4**

*Using the mouse-event techniques described so far, you can create a photo gallery like this one. When the mouse is over a thumbnail, a large version of the picture is shown to the right.*

# Creating a Tabbed Window with Mouse Events

So far this chapter has covered two types of mouse events: MOUSE_OVER and MOUSE_OUT. The technique for using other events is nearly identical. The most frequently used mouse event is probably the CLICK event. If you understand the previous examples with MOUSE_OVER and MOUSE_OUT, you'll have no problem putting CLICK to work. Suppose you want to create a Flash project that's organized with tabs. You've seen a similar system on websites and in programs including Flash. You click a tab, and it reveals different information or a panel of tools.

Using the ActionScript programming tools introduced in this chapter and the preceding one, you can create a tabbed window like the one shown in Figure 13-5. Here are the tools you need in your Flash and ActionScript toolbox:

- Three mouse events: MOUSE_OVER, MOUSE_OUT, and CLICK.

- A few IF..ELSE conditional statements to control tab behavior.

- Four movie clips to serve as tabs.

- One movie clip that holds the "content" shown under each tab.

## Setting the Stage for Tabbed Folder Display

The tabbed bar in Figure 13-5 is made up of four movie clips, one for each tab subject: dog, cat, flower, and Porsche. You can make the graphic part of the tab any shape you want. In this example, the tabs are created with a rectangle primitive. The top corners are rounded to give it that old-fashioned, tabbed-folder look. The Classic static text was created with the text tool. The important thing is that each tab is a separate movie clip, and each movie clip has three frames: over, out, and selected. In the example, the tabs are 137.5 pixels wide so that four tabs fit snugly in a 550-pixel horizontal space.

> **NOTE**  You can follow the instructions in this section to set up your tabbed folder document, or you can download *13-3_Tabbed_Folders.fla* from the Missing CD page (*www.missingmanuals.com/cds/flashcs6mm*). If you want to see a finished and working copy of the project, download *13-4_Tabbed_Folders_done.fla*.

As the mouse moves and clicks, you want to change the tabs' appearance to provide some interactive feedback for your audience. In this example, when the mouse is "out," the tab contrasts in color with the color of the content's folder. It looks as if the tab is behind another open folder. When the mouse moves over the tab, it changes size and color and the text is bold, providing a highlight effect.

When the tab is selected and its content is showing, the color of the tab matches the background color of the folder, giving it the appearance of an open folder. The frames are labeled *out, over*, and *selected* as shown in Figure 13-6. The ActionScript code uses the labels to identify particular frames.

**FIGURE 13-5**

*You can make a tabbed window interface using three simple mouse events.*

*Top: The dog tab is selected, and the content area below shows a dog.*

*Bottom: Clicking the cat tab changes the tab's appearance and the content below.*

The main movie clip has only one frame, but it organizes the actions, tabs, and content into three layers, as shown in Figure 13-7.

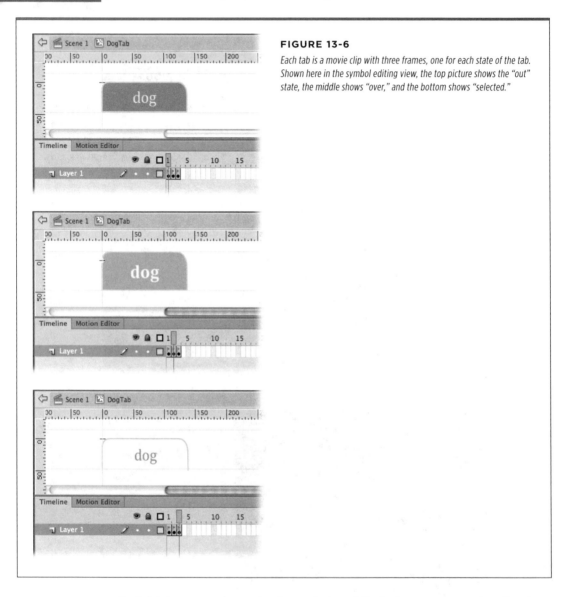

**FIGURE 13-6**

*Each tab is a movie clip with three frames, one for each state of the tab. Shown here in the symbol editing view, the top picture shows the "out" state, the middle shows "over," and the bottom shows "selected."*

Each tab is a separate movie clip symbol, and the instances arranged on the stage are named mcDogTab, mcCatTab, mcFlowerTab, and mcPorscheTab. There's one other movie clip in this project, called mcContent. You guessed it—that's a movie clip that covers most of the stage and shows the contents for each of the tabs. The mcContent movie clip has four frames with labels that match each tab: dog, cat, flower, and Porsche. So, when the "cat" tab is clicked, the playhead in mcContent moves to the "cat" frame. In the example file, there's a matching photo for each mcContent frame. If you don't have photos of your favorite dog, cat, flower, and Porsche, a static text word will do.

**FIGURE 13-7**

*The timeline for the main movie clip in this project has three layers: actions, tabs, and content. It's not absolutely necessary to use three layers, but it's helpful to organize your project using layers.*

**TIP** It's easy to line up and arrange the tabs on the stage using the Align commands. Use Modify→ Align→Bottom to line up all the bottom edges. Then use Modify→Align→Distribute Widths to space them evenly.

## Planning Before Coding

As projects become more complicated, you can save a lot of time by thinking things through before you start writing code. It's a lot like doing a rough pencil sketch or storyboard (page 44) before you draw. With programming, it helps to list the actions that need to take place for your program to work. You can put these down in the human language of your choice, but it certainly helps to keep in mind the ActionScript tools you'll be using to build your project. Here's an example of planning notes for the tabbed window project:

- On startup, the *dog tab* should be selected, and *dog content* should be showing. The other tabs should show the "out" frame.

- If the mouse rolls over or out of the *dog tab*, it shouldn't change its appearance; it should stay "selected."

- If the mouse rolls over any of the *non-selected tabs*, they should highlight, showing the "over" image when the mouse is over, and they should change back to "out" when the mouse moves away.

- When the mouse clicks *any tab*, the clicked tab should change to "selected" and all the *other tabs* should change to "out." The *content* should change to match the selected tab.

These points present a pretty good sketch of how the tabbed window should behave, and they give you some programming goals. To help grapple with the elements in your program, the words indicating movie clips are in italics, and the words indicating frames are in quotes. In your sketch, use any tools (typographic effects, colors, circles, and arrows) you want that help you understand the project.

The first bullet point in the sketch is easy to tackle, especially if you warmed up by completing the rollover project outlined earlier in this chapter (page 448). Here's the code you need to start with the dog tab selected and the other tabs set to the "out" frame:

```
1   // Start with the Dog tab selected and Dog content showing
2   mcDogTab.gotoAndStop("selected");
3   mcContent.gotoAndStop("dog");
4   // Stop the other tab movie clips from playing on
5   mcCatTab.gotoAndStop("out");
6   mcFlowerTab.gotoAndStop("out");
7   mcPorscheTab.gotoAndStop("out");
```

Because this project involves more lines of code and is a bit more complicated, it's good programming practice to use line numbers and to add comments to the code. If you don't have line numbers in your Actions window, click the Options button in the upper-right corner of the Actions window, and then choose Line Numbers near the bottom of the menu. In the code shown, the lines that begin with two slashes (//) are comments. ActionScript ignores anything from the slashes to the end of the line, so you're free to put whatever words will help you and others understand the logic behind your program.

Looking over the "sketch" of your program, you can see that each tab needs to react to three different mouse events: MOUSE_OVER, MOUSE_OUT, and CLICK. So each tab needs to register event listeners for those mouse events. (If you need a refresher on registering an event listener, the details are on page 450.) It may look like a lot of code, but each line uses the same form, or as programmers like to say, *syntax*, to register an event listener.

```
8
9    // Register mouse event listeners for mcDogTab
10   mcDogTab.addEventListener(MouseEvent.MOUSE_OVER, dogOverListener);
11   mcDogTab.addEventListener(MouseEvent.MOUSE_OUT, dogOutListener);
12   mcDogTab.addEventListener(MouseEvent.CLICK, dogClickListener);
13
14   // Register mouse event listeners for mcCatTab
15   mcCatTab.addEventListener(MouseEvent.MOUSE_OVER, catOverListener);
16   mcCatTab.addEventListener(MouseEvent.MOUSE_OUT, catOutListener);
17   mcCatTab.addEventListener(MouseEvent.CLICK, catClickListener);
18
19   // Register mouse event listeners for mcFlowerTab
20   mcFlowerTab.addEventListener(MouseEvent.MOUSE_OVER, flowerOverListener);
21   mcFlowerTab.addEventListener(MouseEvent.MOUSE_OUT, flowerOutListener);
22   mcFlowerTab.addEventListener(MouseEvent.CLICK, flowerClickListener);
23
24   // Register mouse event listeners for mcPorscheTab
25   mcPorscheTab.addEventListener(MouseEvent.MOUSE_OVER, porscheOverListener);
26   mcPorscheTab.addEventListener(MouseEvent.MOUSE_OUT, porscheOutListener);
27   mcPorscheTab.addEventListener(MouseEvent.CLICK, porscheClickListener);
```

**NOTE**     Some lines in this script are left empty on purpose. ActionScript doesn't mind, and a little white space makes the code easier to read and understand, especially when viewed in the Actions panel.

Now that the event listeners are registered, you have a roadmap for the action part of your code. The last word in each of those statements—like dogOverListener, catOutListener, and porscheClickListener—is a reference to an event listener, and it's up to you to write the code that defines the actions. For example, lines 10, 11, and 12 show that mcDogTab needs three listeners, so that's a good place to start.

Looking back at the sketch, you have a rough outline of how the dog tab is supposed to behave. Those two middle bullet points from page 456 describe what's supposed to happen:

- If the mouse rolls over or out of the *dog tab*, it shouldn't change its appearance; it should stay selected.

- If the mouse rolls over any of the *non-selected tabs*, they should be highlighted, showing the "over" image when the mouse is over, and they should change back to "out" when the mouse moves away.

The word "if" is a good clue that you've got an *if...else* situation here. At this point, it may help to refine your human language describing the actions; however, if you're feeling confident, you can jump in and start to code. Here's a refined version of what should happen when the mouse moves over the dog tab:

- If the movie clip *mcDogTab* is selected, then the movie clip *mcDogTab* should remain on the frame labeled "selected."

- Else if the movie clip *mcDogTab* isn't selected, then the movie clip *mcDogTab* should change to the frame labeled "over."

With the refined description, it's just a hop, skip, and a jump to the ActionScript code for the mouse-over event listener. Remember, the lines with double slashes (///) are just comments, not statements:

```
28
29   // Event listeners for mcDogTab
30   function dogOverListener(evt:MouseEvent):void
31   {
32     // if the tab is selected, leave it selected on mouse over
33     // else if the tab isn't selected, show the out frame
34     if (mcDogTab.currentLabel == "selected")
35     {
36       mcDogTab.gotoAndStop("selected");
37     }
38     else
39     {
40       mcDogTab.gotoAndStop("over");
41     }
42   }
```

The *if...else* conditional statement for mcDogTab follows this form:

```
if (condition)
   {
   do these statements;
   }
   else
    {
   do these statements;
   }
```

The *if...else* structure works well for the tabs because it helps you manage the possibility that the tab may already be selected when the mouse moves over it. (There are more details on conditional statements like *if...else* on page 437.)

---

**NOTE**    When you write the *(condition)* part of the statement (line 34), you want to use ActionScript's equality operator, which is two equal signs (= =). You use the equality operator to test whether a statement is true or false. A single equals symbol (=) is the *assignment operator* in ActionScript and is used to change values.

---

The next event listener for mcDogTab handles the MOUSE_OUT event. Similar to the MOUSE_OVER event, you want the tab to do nothing if the tab is selected. If it's not selected, then you want the tab to change back to the "out" state. Another job for *if...else*, and the form for the listener is very similar:

```
43
44   function dogOutListener(evt:MouseEvent):void
45   {
46     // if the tab is selected, leave the tab selected
47     // else if the tab isn't selected, show the out frame
48     if (mcDogTab.currentLabel == "selected")
49     {
50       mcDogTab.gotoAndStop("selected");
51     }
52     else
53     {
54       mcDogTab.gotoAndStop("out");
55     }
56   }
```

The actions that need to be performed for the CLICK event were listed in the sketch as follows:

- When the mouse clicks *any tab*, the clicked tab should change to "selected" and all the *other tabs* should change to "out." The *content* should change to match the selected tab.

There's no *if...else* situation here. There's simply a series of actions that need to take place when a tab is clicked. Those actions position the playhead on specific frames of the "tab" and "content" movie clips. Here's the dogClickListener code:

```
57
58   function dogClickListener(evt:MouseEvent):void
59   {
60     // when clicked change the tab to selected
61     mcDogTab.gotoAndStop("selected");
62     // when clicked change the mcContent to show related frame
63     mcContent.gotoAndStop("dog");
64     // Set all the other tabs to the "out" frame
65     mcCatTab.gotoAndStop("out");
66     mcFlowerTab.gotoAndStop("out");
67     mcPorscheTab.gotoAndStop("out");
68   }
69
```

When the dog tab is clicked, line 61 changes the dog tab to "selected," and line 63 displays dog stuff in the content movie clip. The other three lines of code, 65-67, change the other tabs to the "out" state.

### ■ TESTING YOUR WORK SO FAR

You've finished writing the event listeners for the dog tab. You've got three more tabs to go; however, if you use the "copy and tweak" coding technique described in this section, the last three tabs will go quickly. Before you copy and reuse code, you want to make sure it's working properly. There's no benefit in copying mistakes, so this is a good time to test the code for the dog tab.

The first thing to do is to check for typos and obvious errors with the Check Syntax tool. At the top of the Actions window, click Check Syntax, as shown in Figure 13-8. A box appears, telling you whether or not there are errors in the code. If there are errors, you see them listed by line number in the Compiler Errors tab next to the timeline. Double-click an error, and Flash highlights the offending line of code. The explanations of errors may seem a little cryptic. If you don't understand what Flash is saying, then compare your code to the code in this book. Check spelling, capitalization, and punctuation carefully. Punctuation errors can include missing semicolons at the ends of statements or missing parentheses and brackets. Sometimes, bracket confusion includes using an opening bracket ({) when you should use a closing bracket (}).

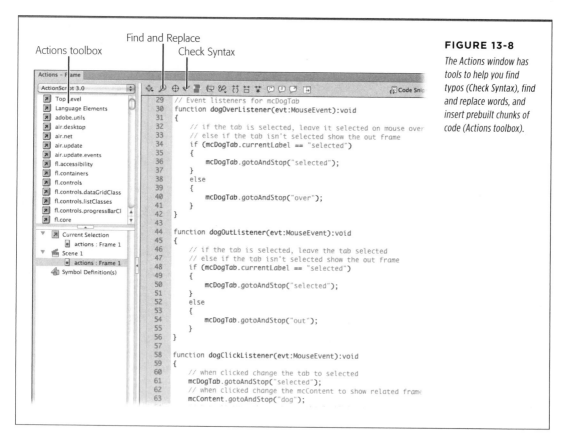

Actions toolbox

Find and Replace

Check Syntax

**FIGURE 13-8**

*The Actions window has tools to help you find typos (Check Syntax), find and replace words, and insert prebuilt chunks of code (Actions toolbox).*

It takes a little extra effort to test part of your code before your program is complete, but the process gives you a better understanding of how it works. If you're copying and reusing code, testing is worth the effort, and it's likely to save you time in the long run.

If you test your movie at this point, you just get a lot of flickering, and the Compiler Errors panel fills up with errors with descriptions like the ones in Figure 13-9: "Access of undefined property catOverListener" and so on. In the Compiler Errors panel, double-click the error, and Flash highlights line 15 in your code. The problem is this line (and others) register event listeners and point to functions that you haven't written yet. This confuses ActionScript. Often, if one part of your code doesn't work (or isn't complete), the rest of the code doesn't run properly—hence the flickering when you test your program.

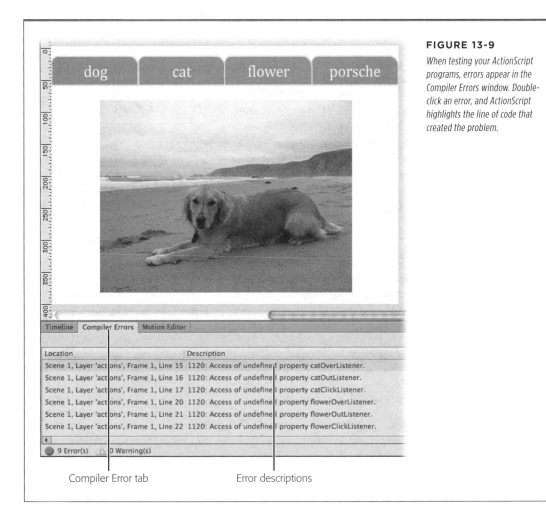

**FIGURE 13-9**

*When testing your ActionScript programs, errors appear in the Compiler Errors window. Double-click an error, and ActionScript highlights the line of code that created the problem.*

The solution is to temporarily remove these lines from your program while you test the dog tab. You don't want to delete lines you've already written—that would be a waste of time. Instead you can *comment them out*. In other words, when you place double slash lines in front of the code, ActionScript ignores the lines because they look like comments. After testing, you remove the comment marks and turn your code back into legitimate statements.

So, to comment out line 15, which registers the catOverListener, place two slash marks at the beginning so that it looks like this:

```
// mcCatTab.addEventListener(MouseEvent.MOUSE_OVER, catOverListener);
```

Problem solved. Place comment marks in front of the lines for the mcCatTab (15, 16, and 17); for the mcFlowerTab (20, 21, and 22); and for the mcPorscheTab (25, 26, and 27).

---

**TIP**   When you want to comment out more than one line of code, you can use the block comment characters. Put /* at the front, and then put */ at the end. Everything between those markers is considered a comment, no matter how many characters, words, or lines there are. Two buttons on the Actions panel toolbar make it easy to add comment marks to your text. To use the "Add block comment" button, select the text you want to "comment out," and then click the button. The "Apply line comment" button places slash marks at the cursor.

---

Now you can test the dog tab part of your movie; press Ctrl+Enter (⌘-Return). If everything is working properly, there shouldn't be any flickering when the animation runs, because all the movie clips are told to *gotoAndStop()* at a specific frame. The dog tab should be selected, and the other tabs should be showing the "out" movie clip frame. When you mouse over any of the tabs, nothing should happen. The dog tab doesn't change when you mouse over and out of it, because that's what you programmed it to do. The other tabs don't change because you haven't programmed their actions yet.

It would be nice to test the MOUSE_OVER and MOUSE_OUT events on the dog tab before you copy the code and use it for the other tabs. To do that, you have to tweak your code so that mcDogTab isn't "selected" when you test the program. Change line 2 to read:

```
mcDogTab.gotoAndStop("out");
```

And then change the mcCatTab so it's selected by changing line 5 to:

```
mcCatTab.gotoAndStop("selected");
```

Now, when you test your movie, the dog tab should change when you mouse over it. If everything works as expected, great. If not, you need to search and destroy any typos that appear in your code. You can download the file *13-4_Tabbed_Folders_ done.fla* from the Missing CD page (*www.missingmanuals.com/cds/flashcs6mm*) to compare coding. Open the Actions window in the downloaded file, and you see the tabbed folders statements with the proper lines commented out and tweaked for testing. If you compare the code line by line to your project, you should be able to identify any errors.

Once your code has passed the testing phase, you need to undo the changes you made. So, change line 2 back to its original form:

```
mcDogTab.gotoAndStop('selected');
```

And, likewise, change line 5 back to:

```
mcCatTab.gotoAndStop("out");
```

Remove the comment marks from the lines that register event listeners: 15, 16, and 17 for the mcCatTab; 20, 21, and 22 for the mcFlowerTab; and 25, 26, and 27 for the mcPorscheTab.

With your code tested and working properly, you can copy and tweak with confidence, as described in the next section.

## Copy-and-Tweak Coding

If you've typed all of the 60-plus lines of code shown so far in this example, you probably agree that writing and testing code can be a little tedious. The good news is, if you've gotten this far, you can use the copy-and-tweak technique to develop code for the other three tabs. When you have some code that works properly and you need to write nearly identical code for another part of your program, it makes sense to copy the code and then change a name or word here and there. In this example, all the tabs have very similar behavior. You can copy the event listeners for mcDogTab, and then paste that code to the bottom of your script. Then, all you need to do is swap a few names. For example, where it says *mcDogTab*, change it to *mcCatTab*.

First copy and paste the code you want to modify:

1. **Select and copy the code between line 29 and line 68, inclusive.**

2. **Move to line 70, and then paste the code back into your script.**

At this point, you need to rewrite the code for mcCatTab. You can do so in a couple of ways, but for learning purposes, this exercise will walk you through the changes one at a time. See Table 13-1.

**TABLE 13-1** *This table shows how to convert the code for the event listener dogOverListener to catOverListener. Elements in bold were changed.*

| LINE # | CODE AS WRITTEN FOR MCDOGTAB | CODE REVISED FOR MCCATTAB |
|---|---|---|
| 70 | `// Event listeners for mcDogTab` | `// Event listeners for `**`mcCatTab`** |
| 71 | `function dogOverListener`<br>`(evt:MouseEvent):void {` | `function `**`catOverListener`**<br>`(evt:MouseEvent):void {` |
| 75 | `if (mcDogTab.currentLabel ==`<br>`"selected") {` | `if (`**`mcCatTab`**`.currentLabel ==`<br>`"selected") {` |

| LINE # | CODE AS WRITTEN FOR MCDOGTAB | CODE REVISED FOR MCCATTAB |
|---|---|---|
| 77 | mcDogTab.gotoAndStop("selected") | **mcCatTab**.gotoAndStop("selected") |
| 67 | // else if the tab isn't select-ed, change it on mouse over | // else if the tab isn't select-ed, change it on mouse over |
| 81 | mcDogTab.gotoAndStop("over") | **mcCatTab**.gotoAndStop("over") |

**TIP** Reading your code line by line, thinking through the actions that the code performs, and then making changes is the safest way to rewrite your code. You can also employ ActionScript's find-and-replace tool; however, it's awfully easy to get carried away and make bad changes. To use find and replace, click the magnifying glass at the top of the Actions window, as shown in Figure 13-8.

The event listener, catOverListener, is very similar to the previous example. You need to change "dog" to "cat" in the function name and everywhere the tab movie clip symbol appears. When you're finished, the code should look like this example:

```
function catOutListener(evt:MouseEvent):void
{
    // if the tab is selected, leave the tab selected
    // else if the tab isn't selected, show the out frame
    if (mcCatTab.currentLabel == "selected")
    {
        mcCatTab.gotoAndStop("selected");
    }
    else
    {
        mcCatTab.gotoAndStop("out");
    }
}
```

To rewrite the code for the CLICK event, think back to the tasks the code has to perform. When *any* tab is clicked, it should change to "selected," and all the *other* tabs should change to "out." The content needs to be changed to match the selected tab. With those concepts clearly in mind, it's fairly easy to adapt the dogClickListener code to work for catClickListener. Below is the code as it should read after you've made changes. The bolded words have been changed.

```
function catClickListener (evt:MouseEvent):void
{
    // when clicked change the tab to selected
    mcCatTab.gotoAndStop("selected");
    // when clicked change the mcContent to show related frame
    mcContent.gotoAndStop("cat");
    // Set all the other tabs to the "out" frame
    mcDogTab.gotoAndStop("out");
```

```
        mcFlowerTab.gotoAndStop("out");

        mcPorscheTab.gotoAndStop("out");
}
```

That finishes the changes that transform the dog tab code to work for the cat tab.
Now you need to repeat the process for the remaining two tabs: flower and Porsche.
When you've done that, the rest of your code should look like this:

```
1   // Event listeners for mcFlowerTab
2   function flowerOverListener(evt:MouseEvent):void
3   {
4       // if the tab is selected, leave it selected on mouse over
5       // else if the tab isn't selected, show the out frame
6       if (mcFlowerTab.currentLabel == "selected")
7       {
8           mcFlowerTab.gotoAndStop("selected");
9       }
10      else
11      {
12          mcFlowerTab.gotoAndStop("over");
13      }
14  }
15
16  function flowerOutListener(evt:MouseEvent):void
17  {
18      // if the tab is selected, leave the tab selected
19      // else if the tab isn't selected, show the out frame
20      if (mcFlowerTab.currentLabel == "selected")

21      {
22          mcFlowerTab.gotoAndStop("selected");
23      }
24      else
25      {
26          mcFlowerTab.gotoAndStop("out");
27      }
28  }
29  function flowerClickListener(evt:MouseEvent):void
30  {
31      // when clicked change the tab to selected
32      mcFlowerTab.gotoAndStop("selected");
33      // when clicked change the mcContent to show related frame
34      mcContent.gotoAndStop("flower");
35      // Set all the other tabs to the "out" frame
36      mcCatTab.gotoAndStop("out");
37      mcDogTab.gotoAndStop("out");
38      mcPorscheTab.gotoAndStop("out");
```

```
39   }
40   // Event listeners for mcPorscheTab
41   function porscheOverListener(evt:MouseEvent):void
42   {
43       // if the tab is selected, leave it selected on mouse over
44       // else if the tab isn't selected, show the out frame
45       if (mcPorscheTab.currentLabel == "selected")
46       {
47           mcPorscheTab.gotoAndStop("selected");
48       }
49       else
50       {
51           mcPorscheTab.gotoAndStop("over");
52       }
53   }
54
55   function porscheOutListener(evt:MouseEvent):void
56   {
57       // if the tab is selected, leave the tab selected
58       // else if the tab isn't selected, show the out frame
59       if (mcPorscheTab.currentLabel == "selected")
60       {
61           mcPorscheTab.gotoAndStop("selected");
62       }
63       else
64       {
65           mcPorscheTab.gotoAndStop("out");
66       }
67   }
68
69   function porscheClickListener(evt:MouseEvent):void
70   {
71       // when clicked change the tab to selected
72       mcPorscheTab.gotoAndStop("selected");
73       // when clicked change the mcContent to show related frame
74       mcContent.gotoAndStop("porsche");
75       // Set all the other tabs to the "out" frame
76       mcCatTab.gotoAndStop("out");
77       mcFlowerTab.gotoAndStop("out");
78       mcDogTab.gotoAndStop("out");
79   }
```

When you test the code, using Ctrl+Enter (⌘-Return), it should work as advertised. On startup, the dog tab is selected. Mouse over any of the other tabs, and they should show a highlight. Click a tab, and it becomes the selected tab, showing related content in the main part of the window. If your project isn't working exactly as expected, compare your code with *13-4_Tabbed_Folders_done.fla* from the Missing CD (*www.missingmanuals.com/cds/flashcs6mm*).

### ■ MODIFYING TABBED WINDOWS FOR PROJECTS

The tabbed window project creates a container. You can rename the tabs and put anything you want in the "content" movie clip. The example in this chapter holds a single picture, but each tab could hold an entire photo collection or a collection of widgets that work with a database. The tabs simply provide a way to organize the elements of a project.

You can easily change the tabs themselves for a different look. Metallic high-tech tabs, perhaps? All you have to do is change the shape or the color of the graphics in the tab movie clips. For example, if you'd like a look that emulates colored file folders, you can coordinate the color of the tabs with the background of the content movie clip. If it works better for your project, you can use the same ActionScript code to manage tabs that run vertically along the edge of the content area.

# ■ Keyboard Events and Text Events

ActionScript 3.0 uses a single technique for handling events, so if you know how to register an event listener for a mouse event, it's not difficult to handle events for keyboards or other objects. All events use the same event register and event listener duo. For example, the keyboard event has two constants: KEY_DOWN and KEY_UP. You can use the Flash stage itself to register keyboard events.

> **NOTE**  You can download the Flash document for this example, *13-5_Keyboard_Events.fla*, from the Missing CD page at *www.missingmanuals.com/cds/flashcs6mm*.

Here's a simple example that shows you how to start and stop a movie clip from running using the KEY_DOWN and KEY_UP events. The movie clip simply shows a number for each frame as it's running. This example references an instance of the Stage class. The stage represents the drawing area in a Flash animation. As a result, the stage has properties, like width and height, and like other objects, it has an addEventListener method.

Create a new document. Add a layer, and then name one layer *actions* and the other layer *counter*. At the first frame of the counter layer, add a movie clip symbol to the stage. Open the movie clip, and put a big number 1 on the stage. Add four more keyframes with the numbers 2 through 5 on the stage. In the Properties panel, name the movie clip mcCounter. Click the first frame in the actions layer, open the Actions window, and then type this short script:

```
stage.addEventListener(KeyboardEvent.KEY_DOWN, keyDownListener);
stage.addEventListener(KeyboardEvent.KEY_UP, keyUpListener);
```

```
function keyDownListener(evt:KeyboardEvent):void
{
  mcCounter.stop();
}


function keyUpListener(evt:KeyboardEvent):void
{
  mcCounter.play();
}
```

When you test the animation (Control→Test Movie), it quickly runs through the frames showing the numbers 1 through 5 on the stage. Press and hold the space bar, and the numbers stop. Release the space bar, and the numbers start again.

> **NOTE** When you test keyboard events inside Flash, you may notice some odd behavior. That's because Flash itself is trapping some keyboard events, and it tends to catch the letter keys. If you actually publish your Flash project, and then run the SWF in Flash Player or a browser, you get a more accurate experience.

## Using Event Properties

Like most things in ActionScript, an event is actually an object. The event object is passed to the event listener as a parameter inside parentheses. Take this line of code:

```
function keyDownListener(evt:KeyboardEvent):void {
```

The *evt* is an instance of the keyboard event that was created when a key was pressed. You can use any name you want in place of *evt*. The colon and the word "KeyboardEvent" indicate the type of event.

The KEY_DOWN and KEY_UP constants are parts of the KeyboardEvent class. Keyboard events also have properties that store changeable values. Properties can be passed to the event listener and used in the event listener's actions. For example, the charCode property holds a value that identifies the specific keyboard character of KEY_DOWN and KEY_UP events. Programs use character codes to identify the characters shown on a screen or sent to a printer. By adding a couple of lines to your keyboard event listeners, you can view character codes as you press keys:

```
stage.addEventListener(KeyboardEvent.KEY_DOWN, keyDownListener);
stage.addEventListener(KeyboardEvent.KEY_UP, keyUpListener);

function keyDownListener(evt:KeyboardEvent):void {
  mcCounter.stop();
  trace("Key Down");
  trace(evt.charCode);
}

function keyUpListener(evt:KeyboardEvent):void {
  mcCounter.play();
```

```
    trace("Key Up");
    trace(evt.charCode);
}
```

The *trace()* statement is a remarkably handy programmer's tool that's used to display values in the Output panel, as shown in Figure 13-10. If your Output panel is closed, you can open it with Window→Output or the F2 key. Like any function, you pass values to the *trace()* statement by placing them inside the parentheses. If you put a string inside the parentheses, like ("Key Down"), Flash shows that string in the Output panel when it reaches the *trace()* statement in your code. The two strings "Key Down" and "Key Up" are called *string literals* by programmers, because the value of the string is defined. It's not a variable or a property that changes.

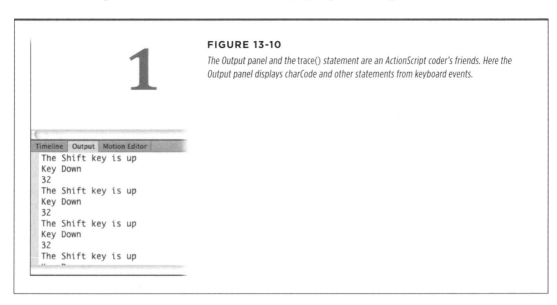

**FIGURE 13-10**

*The Output panel and the* trace() *statement are an ActionScript coder's friends. Here the Output panel displays charCode and other statements from keyboard events.*

---

**NOTE**  The *trace()* statement doesn't have any use in final Flash animations. The most common use of *trace()* is to examine the value of variables while testing a program. Sometimes a *trace()* statement is used to simply determine whether a program reaches a certain point in the script.

---

The second *trace()* statement shows the value of a property in the Output window. As explained previously, *evt* is the event object that's passed to the event listener, and charCode is a property of *evt*. Like all good properties, it's shown with dot syntax as *evt.charCode*. So the second *trace()* statement shows the value of *evt*'s charCode property. Each time a key is pressed, a new instance of the KeyboardEvent is created and passed to the listener keyDownListener. Each instance holds a single value in the charCode property that corresponds to the key that was pressed.

When you test the program, as you press keys, string literals (Key Down and Key Up) and numbers appear in the Output panel. If you press the space bar, the keyDown-Listener sends the "Key Down" string, and then the value 32. Because keyboards repeatedly send character codes when a key is held down, you may see multiple 32s while you hold the key down and one final 32 on KEY_UP.

Keyboard events have six properties called *public* properties, because you can access them from your ActionScript program (see Table 13-2).

**TABLE 13-2** *Public properties of KeyboardEvents*

| PUBLIC PROPERTY | DATA TYPE | DESCRIPTION |
| --- | --- | --- |
| altKey | Boolean | True if the Alt key is pressed |
| charCode | uint (unsigned integer) | Value of the character code for key up or key down |
| ctrlKey | Boolean | True if the Ctrl key is pressed |
| keyCode | uint (unsigned integer) | Value of the key code for key up or key down |
| keyLocation | uint (unsigned integer) | Indicates the location of the key on the keyboard |
| shiftKey | Boolean | True if the Shift key is pressed |

Like charCode, keyCode, and keyLocation are used to determine what key was pressed on a keyboard. The other three properties are used specifically to determine whether the Alt, Ctrl, or Shift keys are down or up. Add this *trace()* statement to your keyboard event program to see how the shiftKey property works:

```
trace(evt.shiftKey);
```

As a Boolean, the value of shiftKey is *true* when the Shift key is pressed and *false* if it's not pressed. You can use an *if* conditional statement to test if the Shift key is pressed. For example, you can replace the preceding statement with this *if...else* statement:

```
if (evt.shiftKey==true)
{
  trace("The Shift key is down");
}
else
{
  trace("The Shift key is up");

}
```

The result is a more complete description than the bare-bones *true* and *false* reports.

# Capturing Text Input with TextEvent

*KeyboardEvent* works fine for detecting whether or not keys are pressed on the keyboard, but it's not very good at capturing the actual text or characters typed into a program. The best tool for that job is the *TextEvent*. You use the TextEvent with an object like an input text box.

1. **Open a new document.**

2. **Click the Text tool in the Tools palette, and then choose TLF Text and Editable from the two drop-down lists, as shown in Figure 13-11.**

3. **Draw a text box on the stage, and then add some preliminary text to the text box, like *Your name here*.**

4. **In the Properties panel, name the Input Text box *tfName*.**

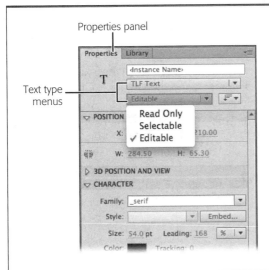

Properties panel

Text type menus

**FIGURE 13-11**

*As explained on page 216, Flash text can be TLF text or Classic text. TLF text can be read only, selectable, or editable. Classic text can be static text, dynamic text, or input text. You can name, and then access, TLF text, dynamic text, and input text using ActionScript.*

5. **Open the Actions window, and then type this code:**

```
tfName.addEventListener(TextEvent.TEXT_INPUT, textInputListener);

function textInputListener(evt:TextEvent):void
{
    trace(evt.text);
}
```

When you test the Flash program, you see a text box on the stage with the words "Your name here." Select the text, and then type your own name in its place; any key you press while the text box is *in focus* appears in the Output panel. The text box captures each letter and stores it in the *text* property of the Text Event object *evt.* The TextEvent is passed to textInputListener, which uses the *text* property in the statement:

```
trace(evt.text);
```

> **NOTE** You can download the Flash document for this example, *13-7_Text_Event.fla*, from the Missing CD page at *www.missingmanuals.com/cds/flashcs6mm*.

# ■ Keeping Time with TimerEvent

All the events explored in this chapter so far rely on audience input. There are other types of events that occur as part of a process and don't involve audience input. A good example is the TimerEvent, which triggers an event when a specified amount of time has passed. Suppose you're developing a quiz and you want to give students 30 seconds to answer each question. You could use a TimerEvent to move to the next question every 30 seconds. Sounds merciless, doesn't it?

Here's an example that's not quite so cruel. All it does is change the text on the screen after a certain interval. Open a new document, and then add a TLF read-only text field to the stage. Put some placeholder text in the field, like the word "blank." In the Properties panel, name the dynamic text field *tfTimerText*. Using ActionScript, you can create a Timer object. Using the properties of the timer object, you can set it to trigger an event after a certain amount of time has passed. This example uses the event to change the text in the dynamic text box. Initially, it says, "It's not yet time." The color of the type is blue. After the timer event, the text reads "Now it's time!" as shown in Figure 13-12, and the color of the type changes to red:

```
1    var timer:Timer = new Timer(1000,3);
2
3    tfTimerText.text = "It's not yet time.";
4    tfTimerText.textColor = 0x0066FF;
5
6    timer.addEventListener(TimerEvent.TIMER_COMPLETE, timerCompleteListener);
7    timer.start();
8
9    function timerCompleteListener(evt:TimerEvent):void
10   {
11       tfTimerText.text = "Now it's time!";
12       tfTimerText.textColor = 0xFF0000;
13   }
```

**FIGURE 13-12**

*In this example, a timer event is used to change the text displayed in a dynamic text field.*

You can't just drag a timer out of the Tools palette like a circle or a text box, so you have to use ActionScript code to create a new object. That's exactly what the code in line 1 does. From left to right it creates a variable called *timer* (lowercase *t*) which is of the data type Timer (uppercase *T*). The = *new Timer* portion of the line creates the timer object. The numbers inside the parentheses are the parameters you use to set the timer. The first number sets the *delay* property, and the second number sets the *repeatCount* property. The ActionScript Timer measures time in milliseconds, so 1000 equals a second. With repeatCount set to 3, the timer waits 3 seconds before triggering the TIMER_COMPLETE event. Setting these two numbers is sort of like winding up a kitchen timer to a specified interval.

In line 3, a new string of characters is displayed in the text box: "It's not yet time." The following line sets the color of the text to blue. If you've read from the beginning of this chapter, line 6 probably looks familiar. It registers the event listener called timerCompleteListener. As you can probably guess, line 7 starts the countdown. Lines 9 through 13 are the event listener for TIMER_COMPLETE. The function displays the new message in the text box, "Now it's time!" And it changes the type to red for added dramatic effect.

**NOTE**  You can download the Flash document for this example, *13-8_Timer_Event.fla*, from the Missing CD page at *www.missingmanuals.com/cds/flashcs6mm*.

# ■ Removing Event Listeners

When you create an event listener, it sits there constantly waiting for the event to happen. You may forget it's even there; but still, it sits patiently, waiting, listening, and using up computer resources in the process. There are a couple of good reasons why you should remove event listeners when they're no longer needed. One is the computer resource issue. It's also possible for a forgotten event listener to foul up some other process when you least expect it.

Ideally, you should remove an event listener whenever your program no longer needs it. For example, in the preceding TimerEvent, you can remove the listener after the TIMER_COMPLETE event triggers. You can place the code to unregister the timer within timerCompleteListener:

```
timer.removeEventListener(TimerEvent.TIMER_COMPLETE, timerCompleteListener);
```

The code to remove an event listener is very similar to the code used to register it in the first place. The *removeEventListener()* function is a method of any object that has a method to *addEventListener()*. The same parameters that define the event type and the event handler identify the event listener being removed.

## ■ In Case of Other Events

The events covered in this chapter are just a few of the many events defined in Flash and ActionScript. There are events to handle error messages and events to track the process of a file or web page loading. There are events specific to components like scroll bars, sliders, context menus, text lists, and color pickers. The good news is that you use the same statements to register an event listener and to specify the actions that are to take place when an event happens.

Table 13-3 gives a partial list of some of the event classes recognized by Flash Player.

*Table 13-3. Examples of the events available in ActionScript 3.0.*

| CLASS | DESCRIPTION |
|---|---|
| Activity Event | Used by cameras and microphones to indicate they're active. |
| AsyncErrorEvent | Used to indicate an error in network communication. |
| ContextMenuEvent | Indicates a change when the audience interacts with a context menu. |
| DataEvent | Indicates raw data has completed loading. |
| ErrorEvent | Used to indicate a network error or failure. |
| Event | The base class for all other events classes. |
| FocusEvent | Triggers an event when the audience changes focus from one object to another. |
| FullScreenEvent | Indicates a change from or to full-screen display mode. |
| HTTPStatusEvent | Creates an event object when a network request returns an HTTP status code. |
| IOErrorEvent | Indicates an error when trying to load a file. |
| KeyboardEvent | Indicates keyboard activity. |
| MouseEvent | Indicates mouse activity. |

| CLASS | DESCRIPTION |
|---|---|
| NativeDragEvent | Used to acquire details about a drag-and-drop event. |
| NetStatusEvent | Reports on the status of a NetConnection, NetStream, or SharedObject. |
| ProgressEvent | Reports on the progress while a file loads. |
| SampleDataEvent | Used when the Flash Player requests audio data. |
| SecurityErrorEvent | Reports a security error. |
| ShaderEvent | Indicates the completion of a shader operation. |
| StatusEvent | Used by cameras and microphones to report on their status and connection. |
| SyncEvent | Used by SharedObjects to indicate a change. |
| TextEvent | Indicates a change when the audience enters text. |
| TimerEvent | Indicates the passing of a timing interval. |

## Smartphone and Tablet Events

Smartphones and tablets have their own unique set of events (not events like getting left in a taxi; that's another matter entirely). These devices have capabilities that we've all come to take for granted. For example, because the iPhone has a sensor called an *accelerometer*, you can shake the phone to clear the screen or reset the letters in a game. When you make a turn, your location and heading change on your gadget's map—if it has a GPS antenna. And of course, all those 1-, 2-, and 3-fingered swipes are part of the mobile device language. ActionScript continues to add new classes that register these events. Just as with the mouse and keyboard events, you write code that "listens" for the event to occur and that shoots a message off to some other object in your application to take action.

Here are some of the events related to these handheld devices:

| EVENT | DESCRIPTION |
|---|---|
| Accelerometer Event | Triggered when the accelerometer in a mobile device is updated. In other words, the gadget was moved, tilted or shaken. |
| Geolocation Event | Updates details on longitude, latitude, heading, speed, and altitude when it receives updates from the GPS sensor. |
| Gesture Event | Used by touchscreen devices that handle multitouch (two-fingered) gestures. |
| Gesture Phase | Provides information on the type of gesture being performed. Is it a tap? Is it a swipe? |
| PressAndTapGestureEvent | Handles press and tap gestures. Often used to trigger pop-up, contextual menus. |

| EVENT | DESCRIPTION |
|---|---|
| SoftKeyboardEvent | Dispatches a message when a software-driven keyboard (like the iPad's touchscreen keyboard) is activated or deactivated. |
| SoftKeyboardTrigger | Reports on the event that triggered the SoftKeyboard. Was it the user? Was it content? |
| StageOrientationEvent | Stage object sends a StageOrientationEvent object when the device is rotated or changed due to softkeyboard activation or other event. |
| TouchEvent | Detects user contact with the touchscreen. Used with the other classes to determine the type of event. |
| TransformGestureEvent | Used to detect swipes and report on their type. As always, the object's Public Constants give good clues as to the object's purpose: GESTURE_PAN, GESTURE_ROTATE, GESTURE_SWIPE, and GESTURE_ZOOM. |

**TIP**   If you're just beginning to write code for smartphone and tablet apps, you can learn a lot by studying the code snippets that come with Flash CS6. Go to Window→Snippets and check out the snippets under Mobile Touch Events, Mobile Gesture Events. Pop some of that code into your Actions window and you'll see how the wizards at Adobe expect you to use the event classes they created for handhelds.

# Organizing Objects with the Display List

When you create your animation using the Flash authoring tool, you draw objects on the stage or drag them from the Library. Often, you put one object inside another. For example, you might place a shape and some text inside a movie clip that's on the stage. Then you can move or transform the movie clip and its content as a whole. When you want one displayed object to appear in front of or behind another, you use Flash's Modify→Arrange commands. To a designer, it all seems pretty natural. But what happens when you put on your ActionScript programmer's hat and want to do those same display-related chores using only ActionScript? The key is the Display List, and that's the sole topic of this chapter.

The Display List is exactly what its name implies. It's a running list of the objects displayed during a Flash animation. You make things visible by adding them to the Display List and make them disappear by removing them from the list. The Display List keeps track of the stacking order of objects on the stage, managing the way they overlap one another. This chapter shows you how to add and remove items from the Display List and how to manage the stacking order. You'll learn a lot about the DisplayObject and DisplayObjectContainer classes. At the end of the chapter (page 507), there's a handy reference for some of the most common properties and methods related to Display List tasks.

## ■ The Display List: Everything in Its Place

Simply put, anything that appears on the stage in Flash Player is a *display object*. That includes shapes, lines, text fields, and movie clips. Because they're displayable, these objects have a lot of similar properties, including x/y coordinates that mark their position on the stage. They have width and height properties, which you can see in the Properties panel whenever you select them. If you're following the ActionScript discussion that began in Chapter 12, then it's probably clear that displayable objects inherit these similar properties from some ancestor class (page 422). In fact, they're all descendants of a class called, appropriately enough, *DisplayObject*. As you work in ActionScript, you'll find lots of objects that get important, much-used properties and methods from DisplayObject.

## When Display Objects are Display Object Containers

Suppose you create a new Flash document, with nothing on the stage, and you publish it or test it with Ctrl+Enter (⌘-Return on a Mac). From Flash Player's point of view, that empty .swf has two display objects: the stage itself (yep, it's a display object) and the animation's main timeline. Even if there's only a single frame, the main timeline is considered a display object that's placed on the stage. It works like this: Though the Flash Player's stage looks empty, it still has a couple of displayable features, like a background color and the width and height of the stage. Equally important, the stage is a container. When you put display objects on the stage, they become visible. Along the same lines, the main timeline is also a display object. Anything you put in a frame of that main timeline is displayed in the Flash animation. So it, too, is a container for other display objects. So, before you even start the process of building your animation, Flash always starts out with two display objects, which are also containers, as shown in Figure 14-1.

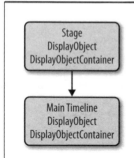

### FIGURE 14-1

*Every Flash document starts off with two display objects that are also display object containers. You build your animation by placing additional display objects and display object containers inside those two original containers.*

---

**NOTE**    Technically, the main timeline for any .swf is referred to as the .swf's *main class instance*, but it's easier to think of it as the main timeline, and that's what it's called in this chapter.

---

Now, suppose you place something on that stage. Perhaps you've already drawn a playing card and saved it as a movie clip in the Library. Drag that card from the Library onto the stage, and now you've got three display objects. The stage is a container holding the main timeline, and the timeline is a container holding the playing card movie clip. Everything that appears in a Flash animation has to be in a container, and ultimately those containers are held in the main timeline, which is held in the stage. Objects that can hold or contain other objects are a special type of display object—they're *display object containers*. Objects that descend from the DisplayObjectContainer class have special properties and methods that are uniquely suited to acting as containers for display objects.

---

**NOTE** If you're eager to see a list of some of DisplayObjectContainer's special properties and methods, go ahead and flip to page 507. If you'd like a gradual introduction, just keep on reading.

---

All display object containers are also display objects, but there are display objects that don't have the special properties of a display object container. For example, a rectangle can't contain another object. You can group a rectangle with another object, but technically it doesn't contain the other object. Table 14-1 shows which objects inherit properties from the DisplayObjectContainer class and which don't.

**TABLE 14-1** *Display objects that can hold or contain other objects inherit the special properties of the DisplayObjectContainer class.*

| DISPLAYOBJECT AND DISPLAYOBJECTCONTAINER CLASS | DISPLAYOBJECT CLASS ONLY |
| --- | --- |
| Stage | Shape |
| Sprite | TextField |
| MovieClip | SimpleButton |
| Loader | Bitmap |
| | Video |
| | StaticText |
| | MorphShape (tween) |

In practical terms, you won't spend a lot of time fretting over the stage and the main timeline as display objects or display object containers. They're always there. You can count on them being there. And there aren't many ways you can change them. If you're approaching ActionScript 3.0 with a Flash designer's background, you probably consider the act of placing something in the main timeline as "placing an object on the stage." On the other hand, you need to be aware of the properties and methods available when you're working with the movie clips, buttons, shapes, and text that you place on that stage.

## ■ Adding Objects to the Display List

Enough theory! It's time to get back to that empty stage and the task of displaying an object. The following exercises use a file called *14-1_Display_List.fla* that's available on the Missing CD page at *www.missingmanuals.com/cds*. Several of the examples in this chapter gradually add ActionScript code to this Flash document.

1. **Select File→Open, and then browse to *14-1_Display_List.fla*.**

   When you open this document, there's nothing on the stage.

2. **If the Library isn't visible, go to Window→Library to display it.**

   The Library holds seven movie clips. Five of the movie clips look like simple playing cards, and are named PlayingCard1 through PlayingCard5. No suits, just numbers. There are two simple rectangles that represent card tables: GreenCardTable and BlueCardTable.

3. **Open the Actions window by pressing F9 (Option-F9) or Window→Actions.**

   The Actions window appears without any code. If the Line Number option is turned on, you see the number 1 in the left margin. If line numbering isn't turned on, click the Options button in the upper-right corner, and then choose Line Numbers from the menu.

---

**CODERS' CLINIC**

## Making Library Objects Available to ActionScript

In the exercises in this chapter, you use ActionScript to display instances of objects in the Library on the stage using Action-Script code. When you drag a symbol out of the Library and then place it on the stage, Flash knows what object you're referring to because, well, you dragged it. ActionScript 3.0, on the other hand, knows only classes and objects. Every object has to derive from a class. In this chapter, the objects in your Library are movie clips, but that's not specific enough to distinguish one from the other. So, in the Flash documents created for this chapter, each of the movie clips in the Library represent *classes* that *extend* the MovieClip class. In other words, they represent custom classes derived from ActionScript's built-in MovieClip class.

It's not that hard to associate a movie clip symbol in the Library with a custom class that's accessible to ActionScript. In the Library, right-click the symbol's name, and then choose

Properties from the pop-up menu. The Symbol Properties dialog box opens with details about that particular symbol, as shown in Figure 14-3. Turn on the appropriately named Export for ActionScript checkbox, and then type in a class name for the new class you're creating in the Class text box. Immediately below the Class text box is the name of the base class. In the example shown in Figure 14-3, the PlayingCard1 class *extends* the MovieClip class. When you click OK, the Symbol Properties dialog box closes. Flash can't find an existing definition for the PlayingCard1 class, so it displays an alert mentioning the fact, but because a de facto definition exists in the Library, Flash can create a definition and place it in the *.swf*, which is what it does.

In the document *14-1_Display_List.fla*, each of the cards and the card tables represent custom classes created using this same technique.

---

4. **In the ActionScript window, type in the following code:**

```
1   var card1:PlayingCard1 = new PlayingCard1();
2   addChild(card1);
```

The first line is called a "variable declaration." It creates a new instance of the *PlayingCard1 class* and stores it in the variable *card1*. (If you want to learn more about how PlayingCard1 became a class, see the box on page 490.) The second line adds card1 to the Display List.

5. **Press Ctrl+Enter (⌘-Return) to test your ActionScript code.**

   When the Flash Player runs, a single card with the number 1 appears in the upper-left corner of the stage.

The second line of code shown in step 4 adds card1 to the Display List, making it visible on the stage, as shown in Figure 14-2. It's almost as if you dragged the card out of the Library. You may be wondering why the method for adding an object to the Display List is called "addChild." It has to do with the hierarchical relationship of displayed objects. (ActionScript just loves hierarchical relationships.) In the case of the Display List, an object contained in another object is considered a child of the container. The *addChild()* statement adds card1 as a child to the main timeline DisplayObjectContainer.

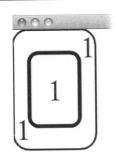

**FIGURE 14-2**

*When you add this playing card to the Display List using ActionScript, you'll see it on the stage when you preview the Flash document (Ctrl+Enter or ⌘-Return).*

## Add a Second Object to the Display List

You can add a second card using the same two steps in your code. First create an instance of PlayingCard2 using the variable name card2. Then add card2 to the Display List using the *addChild()* method. Here are the steps:

1. **In the Actions panel, press Enter or Return to create a new empty line, and then type two more lines:**

   ```
   var card2:PlayingCard2 = new PlayingCard2();
   addChild(card2);
   ```

   The main timeline now has two children, as shown in Figure 14-4.

## 2. Press Ctrl+Enter (⌘-Return) to test your ActionScript code.

When Flash Player runs, you see the second playing card in the stage's upper-left corner. It looks as if only the card2 movie clip is on the stage. That's because the second card was placed directly over the first. So far, your ActionScript code adds cards to the Display List, making them visible. You haven't provided any instructions about where to place the cards. Without instructions, ActionScript places the registration point of an object at 0, 0 on the stage—that's the upper-left corner.

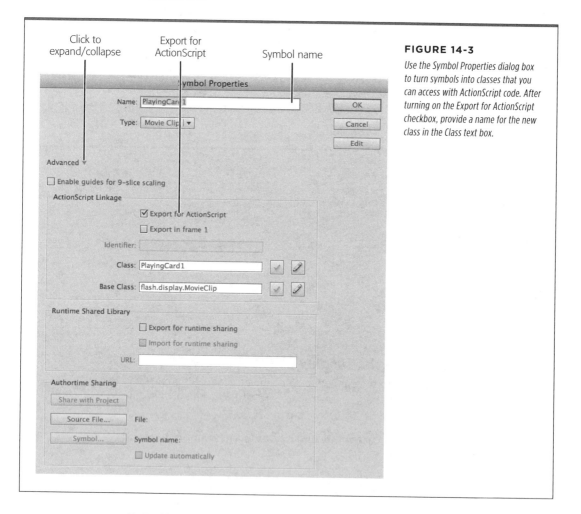

Click to expand/collapse

Export for ActionScript

Symbol name

**FIGURE 14-3**

*Use the Symbol Properties dialog box to turn symbols into classes that you can access with ActionScript code. After turning on the Export for ActionScript checkbox, provide a name for the new class in the Class text box.*

## 3. In the Action panel on the next available line, type the following code:

```
card2.x = 50;
card2.y = 50;
```

These lines reposition the card2 movie clip so it appears 50 pixels from the top and left margins.

4. **Press Ctrl+Enter (⌘-Return) to test your ActionScript code.**

This time when Flash Player shows your document, you see both cards (Figure 14-5). The first card movie clip you placed, card1, appears to be underneath card2.

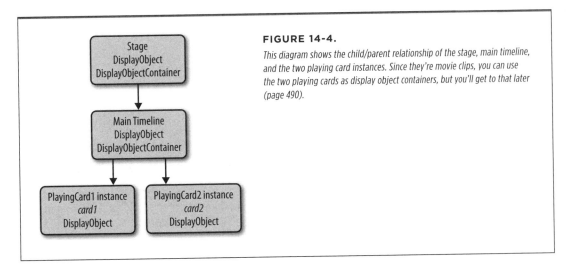

**FIGURE 14-4.**

*This diagram shows the child/parent relationship of the stage, main timeline, and the two playing card instances. Since they're movie clips, you can use the two playing cards as display object containers, but you'll get to that later (page 490).*

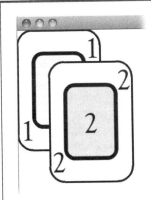

**FIGURE 14-5**

*The card2 movie clip is positioned using x/y coordinates. Because card1 was added to the Display List first, it appears beneath card2.*

At this point, the complete code for your project may look like this:

```
1 var card1:PlayingCard1 = new PlayingCard1();
2 addChild(card1);
3
4 var card2:PlayingCard2 = new PlayingCard2();
5 addChild(card2);
6
7 card2.x = 50;
8 card2.y = 50;
```

The empty lines aren't necessary they're there for housekeeping purposes only, making the code a little easier to read. As your projects get bigger, you may be inclined to keep the variable declarations together. So go ahead and rearrange your code so it looks like this:

```
1 var card1:PlayingCard1 = new PlayingCard1();
2 var card2:PlayingCard2 = new PlayingCard2();
3
4 card2.x = 50;
5 card2.y = 50;
6
7 addChild(card1);
8 addChild(card2);
```

Now, when you test the animation, you see card1 peeking out from behind card2.

You can make a couple of interesting conclusions from the code. Display List factoids so far include these:

- Objects added to the Display List are placed on top of each other. Just like cards dealt onto a card table, the second object you add to the Display List covers the first.

- You can apply properties to an object before you display it. In lines 4 and 5, you define the x/y coordinates for card2 before you display the card using the *addChild()* method in line 8.

You can use both points to your advantage when you develop projects using ActionScript. Every visible object has a position index number (sometimes called the Z-order) that tracks its position (or depth) in the stack. No two objects in a container share the same position index number. When the way objects overlap is important, you can control their appearance by adding them to the Display List in a specific sequence. If you're thinking that's not always possible, don't worry—this chapter shows plenty of other ways to shuffle cards. Also, you can change the properties of objects before they're displayed. For example, you can set the x/y coordinates prior to displaying the card2 movie clip on the stage. You can work with an object in code without showing the object to your audience. You can set its position, change its dimensions and colors, and add transformations and filters without adding it to the Display List. When you finally place that object on the Display List, it's essentially preformatted.

## Using trace() to Report on the Display List

As mentioned on page 473, the *trace()* statement is a multipurpose tool that ActionScript programmers use to double-check their code and report on variables and objects. It never hurts to trace some of the objects in your code to understand how ActionScript sees them. A good first step is to place one of your cards inside the trace statement's parentheses and see what shows up in the Output panel, as shown in Figure 14-6. Trace shows the following text: *[object PlayingCard1]*. From this you can deduce that the variable card1 is an object of the PlayingCard1 class.

```
trace(card1);
```

Helpful, but what happens if you check the name property for card1?

```
trace(card1.name);
```

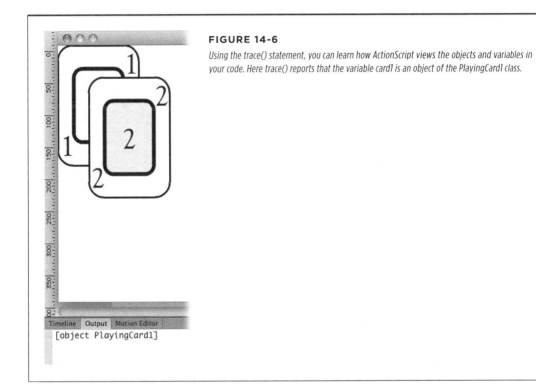

**FIGURE 14-6**

*Using the trace() statement, you can learn how ActionScript views the objects and variables in your code. Here trace() reports that the variable card1 is an object of the PlayingCard1 class.*

The message that appears in the Output panel is: *instance1*. Not so helpful. If you don't specifically give names to objects as you add them to your ActionScript code, Flash names them for you, and you end up with names of the instance1 variety. So, the next step for *this* project is to modify your code a little and add names for both card1 and card2. (If you find the differences between class names, variable names, and the name property of an object a little confusing, see the box on page 490.) You can assign any string you want to the name property of card1 and card2, but there's no need to be *too* creative. Something like the following works just fine. Create new lines, and then add:

```
card1.name = "Card 1";
card2.name = "Card 2";
```

Now the trace statements show the names of the objects in the Output panel. Instead of getting "instance1" and so forth, you get "Card 1" and "Card 2." Much better, but you can fashion your *trace()* statements into something even more helpful by adding some more explanatory text. Anything that appears in quotes in a *trace()* statement is displayed literally in the Output panel. If you write a statement like *trace("dog")*, you see the word dog displayed in the Output panel. So you can modify your *trace()* statement a bit to make a descriptive sentence about your card variables:

```
trace(card1.name, " is ", card1);
```

This statement displays an "almost sentence" that's a little easier to understand: *Card 1 is [object PlayingCard1]*. Creating this statement might seem like a lot of unnecessary work at this point, but as your ActionScript becomes more complicated, statements like this are a big help in understanding what's going on inside your code. The next section uses *trace()* statements to report on the parent or display object containers that hold the cards.

---

**CODERS' CLINIC**

### Naming Conventions and Your Sanity

In ActionScript, everything gets named. There are class names, object names, variable names, and more. Sometimes, when you're up to your neck in code, you have one of those can't-see-the-forest-for-the-trees moments. One of the ways experienced coders tell class names apart from variable names is by the way they spell the names.

Flash gives you a fair amount of freedom in how you name the classes that you create; however, it's a convention to use an initial uppercase letter for class names like PlayingCard1.

It's also a convention to use an initial lowercase letter for a variable name like card1. In this example, the names for instances of cards are Card 1, Card 2, and so on. (Class names and variable names don't permit a space in the name, but instance names do.) This makes the *trace()* statements a little more readable, plus it's different from the class and variable names. Obviously, once you decide on a naming convention, stick to it. It'll make your code easier to read and understand.

---

## Placing Objects Inside Display Containers

So far, the code that adds the two cards to the Display List isn't specific about the container that holds the objects. When no specific container is identified, ActionScript places the object in the timeline that holds the code. As you might expect, if your card is referred to as a "child," the display object container holding the card is referred to as a "parent." You can use the trace statement to show the name of the parent (the display object container) that holds your cards.

> **NOTE**  If you look up the class description for DisplayObject in the ActionScript 3.0 Reference, you find that it has a property called *parent*. Every display object is held in a display object container, so every display object has a parent.

Add these lines to the end of the code in the Actions panel:

```
trace(card1.name, " is ", card1);
trace("The parent of ", card1.name," is ", card1.parent);
trace(card2.name, " is ", card2);
trace("The parent of ", card2.name," is ", card2.parent);
```

Placing *card1.parent* inside the trace statement parentheses causes Flash to show the object class of the parent in the Output panel—in this case, MainTimeline. The Output panel displays the words in the quotation marks verbatim. You can include these words to make the output a little clearer for humans. As shown in Figure 14-7, both of the cards have the same parent, meaning they're both held in the same display object container.

| Timeline | Output | Motion Editor |
| --- | --- | --- |

```
Card 1  is  [object PlayingCard1]
The parent of  Card 1  is  [object MainTimeline]
Card 2  is  [object PlayingCard2]
The parent of  Card 2  is  [object MainTimeline]
```

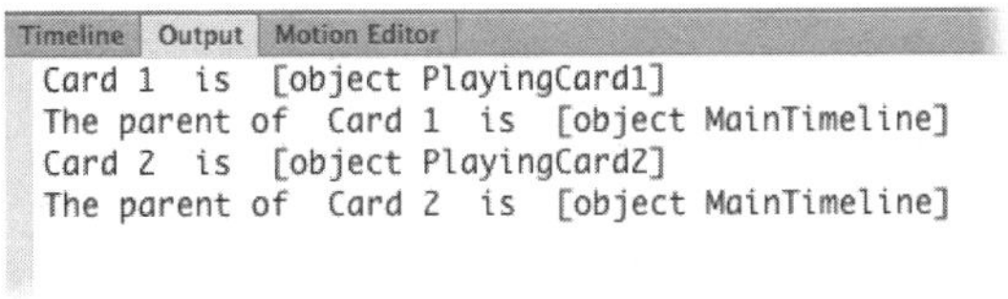

**FIGURE 14-7**

*The trace() statement shows that the main timeline is the parent of both cards. Programmers often use trace() to make sure code is behaving as expected.*

Once your animations get more populated, you're likely to place display objects inside other display object containers. To show that point, the next example adds a card table to the Display List. The card table is a movie clip, so it has all the properties and methods of the DisplayObjectContainer class. Using the *addChild()* method, you can move one of the cards into the card table display object container. Finally, you'll add some additional trace statements at the end of the code to gain more understanding about how the code works.

Follow these steps to update *14-1_Display_List.fla*:

1. **On new lines, type the following two lines of code.** (You may want to keep that first line with the other variable declarations):

   ```
   var greenTable:GreenCardTable = new GreenCardTable();
   greenTable.name = "Green Table";
   ```

   The first line creates a new variable, *greenTable*. It's an instance of the GreenCardTable symbol in the Library. (The drawing is a bit primitive, but think of it as one of those professional green felt card tables.) The second line changes the name property of this instance to "Green Table."

2. **To position the table, type the following line of code:**

   ```
   greenTable.x = 250;
   ```

   This code positions greenTable so that it's 250 pixels from the left margin. That way, it won't cover up the other items on the stage.

3. **Next, add the following two lines of code:**

```
addChild(greenTable);
greenTable.addChild(card2);
```

The *addChild()* method in the first line adds greenTable to the Display List. No parent is designated, so greenTable is in the main timeline. In the second line, you're using the *addChild()* method a little differently from the previous examples. Since you're running it specifically as a method of greenTable, *addChild()* adds card2 to the Display List as a child of greenTable. In other words, greenTable is a display object container that holds card2. Figure 14-8 shows a diagram of the relationships among the objects on the stage.

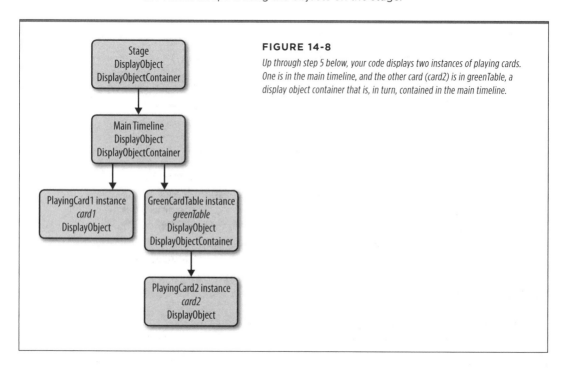

**FIGURE 14-8**

*Up through step 5 below, your code displays two instances of playing cards. One is in the main timeline, and the other card (card2) is in greenTable, a display object container that is, in turn, contained in the main timeline.*

4. **Beginning on line 18, update the trace statements to match the following code:**

```
trace(card1.name, "is", card1);
trace("The parent of", card1.name,"is", card1.parent);
trace(card2.name, "is", card2);
trace("The parent of", card2.name,"is", card2.parent.name);
trace(greenTable.name, "is", greenTable);
trace("The parent of", greenTable.name, "is", greenTable.parent);
```

5. **Press Ctrl+Enter (⌘-Return) to test your animation.**

When you test the code, the display looks like Figure 14-9. In the Output tab, you see that now the parent of card2 is Green Table. The parent of Green Table is an object of the MainTimeline class.

The complete text in the Output panel reads:

Card 1 is [object PlayingCard1]
The parent of Card 1 is [object MainTimeline]
Card 2 is [object PlayingCard2]
The parent of Card 2 is Green Table
Green Table is [object GreenCardTable]
The parent of Green Table is [object MainTimeline]

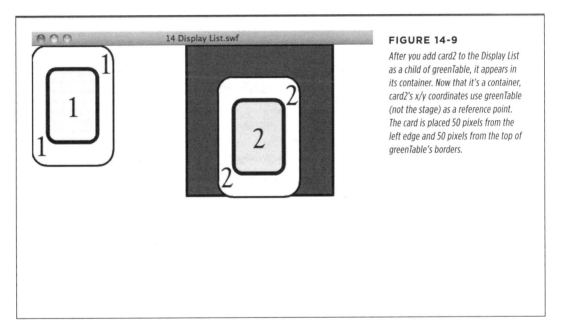

**FIGURE 14-9**

*After you add card2 to the Display List as a child of greenTable, it appears in its container. Now that it's a container, card2's x/y coordinates use greenTable (not the stage) as a reference point. The card is placed 50 pixels from the left edge and 50 pixels from the top of greenTable's borders.*

If you've been following the examples in this chapter, then at this point your code looks something like this:

```
1   var card1:PlayingCard1 = new PlayingCard1();
2   var card2:PlayingCard2 = new PlayingCard2();
3   var greenTable:GreenCardTable = new GreenCardTable();
4
5   card1.name = "Card 1";
6   card2.name = "Card 2";
```

```
7    greenTable.name = "Green Table";
8
9    card2.x = 50;
10   card2.y = 50;
11   greenTable.x = 250;
12
13   addChild(card1);
14   addChild(card2);
15   addChild(greengreenTable.addChild(card2);
16
17   trace(card1.name, " is ", card1);
18   trace("The parent of ", card1.name," is ", card1.parent);
19   trace(card2.name, " is ", card2);
20   trace("The parent of ", card2.name," is ", card2.parent);
21   trace(greenTable.name, "is", greenTable);
22   trace("The parent of", greenTable.name, "is", greenTable.parent);
```

The main thing the new code does is create and display a new display object container—the greenTable movie clip instance. A new *addChild()* statement places card2 inside greenTable. If you're keeping track of interesting Display List factoids, here are some more for you:

- You can move display objects from one display object container to another with the *addChild()* statement. There are two *addChild()* statements related to card2. The first places card2 in the main timeline. The *greenTable.addChild(card2)* statement moves card2 from the stage into the greenTable DisplayObjectContainer. A single instance, like card2, can appear in only one place at a time, so the latter statement takes precedence.

- A display object's position coordinates are relative to the display object container that holds it. Initially, card2 was positioned 50 pixels from the top and 50 pixels from the left border of the stage. After moving it to greenTable, the code displays card2 relative to greenTable's borders.

### ■ MODIFYING DISPLAY CONTAINERS

The objects inside a display object container are pretty much at the mercy of any transformations that happen to the container. For example, suppose you move or scale the width of greenTable while card2 is contained within it. Those changes and transformations affect card2, since it's a child of greenTable. You can test this process by inserting these lines into your code beginning on line 12.

```
greenTable.y = 75;
greenTable.scaleX = 1.5;
```

The first line moves greenTable down from the top margin 75 pixels. The second line scales the display object container, greenTable, making it one and one half times its original width. When you test the code after these changes, you see that both the move and the transformation affect card2 as well as greenTable (Figure 14-10).

It's interesting to note that it doesn't matter whether the code places card2 in the greenTable container before or after transforming the table: card2 is transformed in either case.

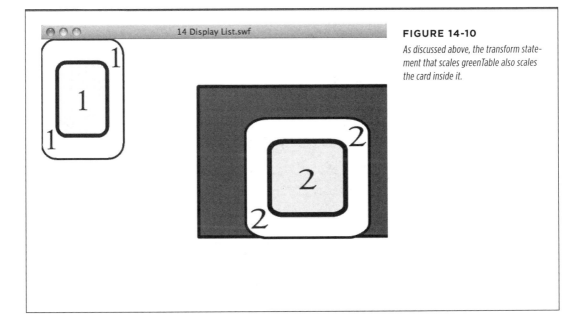

FIGURE 14-10

As discussed above, the transform statement that scales greenTable also scales the card inside it.

## Moving Objects from One Container to Another

It's not unusual for a Flash animation to have more than one container, and you'll often want to move display objects from one container to another, just as you'd move a document from one folder to another on your computer. The following updated ActionScript code expands on the cards and card table theme. It adds a second table to the stage (blue this time). It then places card1 on the new, blue table. *Trace()* statements at the end of the code report on blueTable.

> **NOTE** If you're following along, add the bold lines to your project. If you'd like to start from here, you can use *14-2_Move_DisplayObjects.fla* from the Missing CD (*www.missingmanuals.com/cds*).

```
1 var card1:PlayingCard1 = new PlayingCard1();
2 var card2:PlayingCard2 = new PlayingCard2();
3 var greenTable:GreenCardTable = new GreenCardTable();
4 var blueTable:BlueCardTable = new BlueCardTable();
5
6 card1.name = "Card 1";
7 card2.name = "Card 2";
8 greenTable.name = "Green Table";
9 blueTable.name = "Blue Table";
```

```
10
11   card2.x = 50;
12   card2.y = 50;
13   greenTable.x = 250;
14   greenTable.y = 75;
15   greenTable.scaleX = 1.5;
16
17   addChild(card1);
18   addChild(card2);
19   addChild(greenTable);
20   addChild(blueTable);
21   greenTable.addChild(card2);
22   blueTable.addChild(card1);
23
24   trace(card1.name, " is ", card1);
25   trace("The parent of ", card1.name," is ", card1.parent);
26   trace(card2.name, " is ", card2);
27   trace("The parent of ", card2.name," is ", card2.parent);
28   trace(greenTable.name, "is", greenTable);
29   trace("The parent of", greenTable.name, "is", greenTable.parent);
30   trace(blueTable.name, "is", blueTable);
31   trace("The parent of", blueTable.name, "is", blueTable.parent);
```

In this code, line 4 declares the blueTable variable, and line 9 gives it the name "Blue Table." Line 20 adds blueTable to the Display List, and then line 22 puts card1 in the blueTable DisplayObjectContainer. The code is nearly identical to the code used for greenTable (page 493). When you test the code, Flash Player displays it, as shown in Figure 14-11.

So at this point you have two tables and two cards. One of the tables is distorted a bit by scaling. Suppose you want to move a card from one table to another. That would be a good job for a mouse click. You can add an event listener to the blue table that waits for a mouse click and then moves card2 from the green table to the blue table. Here's the code for the event listener and the function that runs on a mouse click. You can insert this code so it begins on line 24:

```
blueTable.addEventListener(MouseEvent.CLICK, clickTableListener);

function clickTableListener(evt:MouseEvent):void
{
    blueTable.addChild(card2);
}
```

Now when you test your animation, you first see the blue table with card1 and the green table with card2. If you click the blue table, card2 moves from the green table to the blue table. It works as planned, but it's kind of a one-shot deal and pretty dull. One click, and the fun is over. It would be more exciting if you could click either table to make card2 jump over to that table. It's not hard to modify the event listener to do the job. In fact, the MouseEvent class has a special property—called *target*—that identifies the object that's clicked.

**NOTE**   It's worth noting that clicking on the cards when they're held in the "table" display object containers triggers the event listener. When the cards can't perform the function an error message appears. That's not an issue for this exercise, but would need to be accounted for in a finished project.

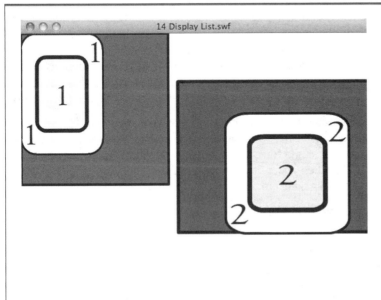

**FIGURE 14-11**

*In the code that defines this page, there are two display object containers representing tables, with cards in them. A scaleX() method has transformed the green table (right). The transformation affects both the table and the card in the table.*

As explained in Chapter 12, this process involves a listened-for event and an event object. Like any object, the event object has properties, one of which is *target*. This property stores the name of the object that initiates the event. In this case, blueTable initiated the event, so it's the target. To modify the code so that card2 jumps to whichever table is clicked, you need to modify the *clickTableListener()* function so it identifies the clicked target object. Then you need to add an event listener to greenTable.

Here are the changes you need to make to the code (shown in bold):

```
blueTable.addEventListener(MouseEvent.CLICK, clickTableListener);
greenTable.addEventListener(MouseEvent.CLICK, clickTableListener);
function clickTableListener(evt:MouseEvent):void
{
    evt.target.addChild(card2);
}
```

Remember, *evt* is the variable name that identifies the MouseEvent in *clickTableListener()*. Like any variable, the actual name is up to you. It could be *event* or simply the letter *e*. The property *target* identifies the object that triggered the event. With the modified code, either of the tables can listen for the click event. There's nothing in the *clickTableListener()* function that's specific to either the blue or the green table, so it behaves relative to the container that's clicked. When you test the animation, card2 moves to the table you click. If it's already on the table you're clicking, nothing happens.

Now that a display object (card2) is shuffling around between display object containers (greenTable and blueTable), it makes the *trace()* statements that report on parent and child relationships a little more interesting. Unfortunately, the trace statements run only once, and they don't provide any updates when the *clickTableListener()* function runs. One solution would be to copy and paste all the *trace()* statements so they're inside the *clickTableListener()* function's brackets, but that adds a lot of extra lines to your code. For a more elegant solution, you can turn all the trace statements into a single function, and then simply call that function whenever you need it.

Turning the *trace()* statements into a single function is relatively easy. Create a line that defines the function with the keyword *function*, and a name you supply, like *traceDisplayList*. Place all the trace statements inside the curly brackets that hold the function's code. When you're done, it looks like the following. The bold line at the top and the curly brackets are the only changes that need to be made:

```
function traceDisplayList():void
{
    trace(card1.name, "is", card1);
    trace("The parent of", card1.name,"is", card1.parent);
    trace(card2.name, "is", card2);
    trace("The parent of", card2.name, "is", card2.parent.name);
    trace(greenTable.name, "is", greenTable);
    trace("The parent of", greenTable.name, "is", greenTable.parent);
    trace(blueTable.name, "is", blueTable);
    trace("The parent of", blueTable.name, "is", blueTable.parent);
}
```

Throughout this chapter, you've added *trace()* statements as the code developed and grew. If, as you're working, you want to add more *trace()* statements, just place the new lines inside the curly brackets. They'll run with the other statements whenever your code calls *traceDisplayList()*.

---

**NOTE** There are more details about creating functions and methods on page 426.

---

Now, to show the results of the *trace()* statements in the Output window, you need only one line of code:

```
traceDisplayList();
```

For example, if you add this line to the *clickTableListener()* every time someone clicks one of the tables, the Output panel shows all the *trace()* statements. Here's the *clickTableListener()* code with the call to *traceDisplayList()* included:

```
function clickTableListener(evt:MouseEvent):void
{
    evt.target.addChild(card2);
    traceDisplayList();
}
```

Test your project now with Ctrl+Enter (⌘-Return), and card2 jumps to whichever table you click. Keep an eye on the Output panel, and you see that card2's parent is updated with each click.

## Removing Objects from the Display List

The statement that removes a display object from the Display List is pleasingly consistent with the statement that adds objects. It looks like this:

```
displayObjectContainer.removeChild(child);
```

So, if you want to remove card1 from the blue table, you write:

```
blueTable.removeChild(card1);
```

If you don't specifically define the display object container, Flash assumes that you're referring to the main timeline. That's the same assumption it makes with the *addChild()* statement. For example, if you want to remove the blue table, you write:

```
removeChild(blueTable);
```

That removes blueTable from the main timeline. If blueTable is a display object container holding other objects, those contained objects also get removed. Everything from the container on down disappears from view. If blueTable isn't contained in the main timeline—if it's contained in another display object container, for example—the code won't find it and won't remove it. The result is an error message, specifically *Error #2025: The supplied DisplayObject must be a child of the caller.*

The previous section explained how to use a MouseEvent to move a card from one table to another. That code used the *target* property to identify the table that was clicked. To remove a card from the Display List when it's clicked, you need to identify both the target (card1) and the target's parent (blueTable). It may look a little convoluted, but the code that does the trick looks like this:

```
evt.target.parent.removeChild(evt.target);
```

Here's how that statement works, moving from left to right. As explained in the previous section, *evt.target* identifies the object that was clicked, initiating the event. By tacking the *.parent* onto that, you identify the container of the object that was clicked. That's all you need to invoke the *removeChild()* method. Remember, *removeChild()* is a method of the display object container. Because the child you want to remove is the object that was clicked, you can place *evt.target* inside the parentheses of the *removeChild()* statement.

Here's the event listener for card1, with a call to run *traceDisplayList()* at the end of the function:

```
card1.addEventListener(MouseEvent.CLICK, clickCardListener);

function clickCardListener(evt:MouseEvent): void
{
    evt.target.parent.removeChild(evt.target);
    traceDisplayList();
}
```

As you see, there's nothing in the function *clickCardListener()* that mentions card1. It simply identifies the target that was clicked and the container of that target. So it's easy to add an event listener to card2 so that it works in exactly the same manner and removes card2 from the Display List.

> **NOTE** Removing display objects from the Display List removes them from the main timeline and the stage, but it doesn't remove them from memory. As your programs increase in both size and their demands on computer resources, it becomes important to remove them from memory when they're no longer needed. To delete all references to an object from memory you can use a statement like *card2=null;*.

It may not be the most entertaining card game in the world, but at this point when you test your animation and code, it performs two basic card tricks:

- Click one of the tables, and card2 jumps to that table, if it's not there already.
- Clicking card1 removes the card from the Display List.

In the next section, you'll learn how to stack the deck the ActionScript way.

## ■ Managing the Stacking Order

As mentioned earlier, when you add display objects to the Display List, it's like laying cards on a card table. The first card appears on the table, and the next card is placed on top of it (Figure 14-12). Each card placed on the table is at a specific position in the stack. Like a lot of programming lists, the Display List position index begins at 0. So the first object placed in a display object container is at position 0. The second object is placed at position 1, and so forth. The position is known as the *index*, and it's represented by a number that's an *int* type (integer). As the display objects in your Flash animation become more numerous, it's harder to keep track of them. There are times when it might be easier for you, the ActionScripter, to identify an object by its position in the stack rather than by its instance name. For example, you might have a card game where you want to deal the top five cards in the deck. In this case, the cards' names don't matter as much as their position in the deck.

## Adding Display Objects by Index Position

Just as display object containers have methods for working with child display objects by name, they have other methods for working with them by their index. For example, when you used the *addChild()* method earlier in this chapter, it looked like this:

```
greenTable.addChild(card1);
```

This statement adds the display object *card1* to the display object container *greenTable*. Suppose there were already five cards on greenTable and you want to place card1 in the second-from-the-bottom position. You use the *addChildAt()* method:

```
greenTable.addChildAt(card1, 1);
```

The *addChildAt()* method needs two parameters to work: the variable name of the display object (card1) and the index position (1). Because the position index starts with 0 at the bottom, you use the *int* 1 to place the card in the second position from the bottom.

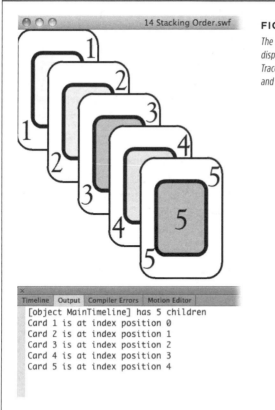

**FIGURE 14-12**

*The code in the box on page 506 places cards on the main timeline display object container. Card 1 was placed first, then Card 2, and so forth. Trace statements show that Card 1 is at position 0, Card 2 is at position 1, and so forth.*

The Flash document *14-3_Stacking_Order.fla* (on the Missing CD page at *www.missingmanuals.com/cds*) shows this example. The code below is similar to the previous examples in this chapter. Here's a rundown on how the code works:

- The lines with double slashes (//) are comments; they have no effect on the way the program runs.

- Lines 2 through 6 declare the playing card variables.

- Lines 9 through 13 give each variable an instance name.

- Lines 16 through 25 use the x/y properties to set the position for each card so that they overlap, making their stacking order easily visible, although the cards aren't displayed yet.

- Lines 28 through 31 add card2 through card5 to the Display List using the *addChild()* method. This way, each new display object gets placed on top of the previous one. As the code adds them, it gives each card a position index starting with 0. So, card2 index = 0, card3 index = 1, card4 index = 2, card5 index = 3. Because no display object container is explicitly defined, it places the display objects in the main timeline. Card1 has not yet been displayed.

- Line 34 adds card1 to the Display List at index position 1, using the *addChildAt()* method. When card1 is added at index position 1, any card at or above that index gets bumped up by one, to make room for the new card. No two cards (DisplayObjects) can have the same index in the main timeline (DisplayObjectContainer). All the cards, except for card2, are repositioned in the stacking order.

- Line 36 calls the *traceDisplayList()* function.

- Lines 39 through 47 define the *traceDisplayList()* function. The first trace statement uses *card1.parent* to identify the display object container holding card1; that is, the main timeline. The statement also uses the numChildren property to display a value showing the number of children held in the display object container. The rest of the statements use the *getChildIndex()* method of the DisplayObjectContainer:

```
1    // Declare variables for the playing cards
2    var card1:PlayingCard1 = new PlayingCard1();
3    var card2:PlayingCard2 = new PlayingCard2();
4    var card3:PlayingCard3 = new PlayingCard3();
5    var card4:PlayingCard4 = new PlayingCard4();
6    var card5:PlayingCard5 = new PlayingCard5();
7
8    // Give the playing cards instance names
9    card1.name = "Card 1";
10   card2.name = "Card 2";
11   card3.name = "Card 3";
12   card4.name = "Card 4";
```

```
13  card5.name = "Card 5";
14
15  // Set the card's position on the stage
16  card1.x = 0;
17  card1.y = 0;
18  card2.x = 50;
19  card2.y = 50;
20  card3.x = 50;
21  card3.y = 100;
22  card4.x = 50;
23  card4.y = 150;
24  card5.x = 50;
25  card5.y = 200;
26
27  // Place card2 through card5 on the stage (add to Display List)
28  addChild(card2);
29  addChild(card3);
30  addChild(card4);
31  addChild(card5);
32
33  // Insert card1 at a specific index position
34  addChildAt(card1,1);
35
36  traceDisplayList();
37
38  //Function to show Display List details in Flash's Output panel
39  function traceDisplayList()
40  {
41  trace(card1.parent, "has", numChildren,"children");
42  trace(card1.name, "is at index position",getChildIndex(card1));
43  trace(card2.name, "is at index position",getChildIndex(card2));
44  trace(card3.name, "is at index position",getChildIndex(card3));
45  trace(card4.name, "is at index position",getChildIndex(card4));
46  trace(card5.name, "is at index position",getChildIndex(card5));
47  }
```

Test the animation, and you see a Flash stage that looks like Figure 14-13. The Output
panel shows a report on the number of display objects in the main timeline and the
index position of each card:

[object MainTimeline] has 5 children
Card 1 is at index position 1
Card 2 is at index position 0
Card 3 is at index position 2
Card 4 is at index position 3
Card 5 is at index position 4

You can experiment with the code by changing the index number in line 34. As a result, you see card1 at different levels in the pile, and the Output panel reports a different index position.

## Removing Display Objects by Index Position

Display object containers have a method for removing the display objects they hold by referencing their index position. You don't need to mention the variable name; just identify the index position by number. You can give the method a try in *14-3_Stacking_Order.fla*. At line 35, insert a line with this statement:

```
removeChildAt(0);
```

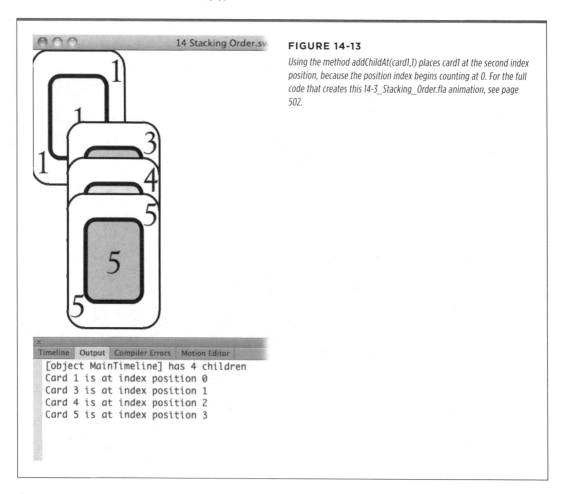

**FIGURE 14-13**

*Using the method addChildAt(card1,1) places card1 at the second index position, because the position index begins counting at 0. For the full code that creates this 14-3_Stacking_Order.fla animation, see page 502.*

This statement removes card2, the first card that was placed in the main timeline. Comment out the line with the *trace()* statements for card2, so it won't produce an error, by placing two slashes in front of the line so that it looks like this:

```
//trace(card2.name, "is at index position",getChildIndex(card2));
```

Test the code, and you find that card2 isn't displayed (Figure 14-14), and the index position numbers for all the cards have changed:

[object MainTimeline] has 4 children

Card 1 is at index position 0

Card 3 is at index position 1

Card 4 is at index position 2

Card 5 is at index position 3

## Getting the Name or Index Position of a Display Object

A major part of the battle in writing ActionScript code is identifying a particular object that you want to change or manipulate. Display object containers give you two ways to identify the objects that they hold: You can identify them either by their variable names or by their index positions. If you have either the name or the index, the DisplayObjectContainer will provide the other descriptor. For example, suppose greenTable is a display object container holding several cards. You can get the index for card1 with a statement like this:

```
greenTable.getChildIndex(card1);
```

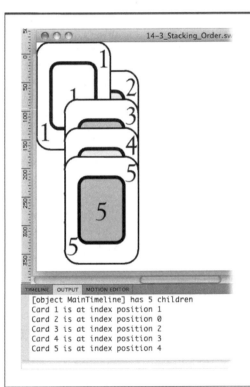

**FIGURE 14-14**

*In this example, card2 was removed from the display, so only four cards are displayed.*

Attacking it from the other direction, if greenTable is a display object container holding several cards and you want to know the name of a card at a specific index position, you can use a command like this:

```
greenTable.getChildAt(2).name;
```

In *14-3_Stacking_Order.fla*, the *getChildIndex()* method is used in the *trace()* statements to report on the index position of the various cards. It may be a little redundant, but you can add statements using the *getChildAt()* method to display the names of display objects at different index levels. To do so, add these lines before the last curly brace of the traceDisplayList function:

```
trace("The name of the object at index position 0 is",getChildAt(0).name);
trace("The name of the object at index position 1 is",getChildAt(1).name);
trace("The name of the object at index position 2 is",getChildAt(2).name);
trace("The name of the object at index position 3 is",getChildAt(3).name);
```

**CODERS' CLINIC**

## Using a *while* Loop to Eliminate Repetitive Code

In this chapter, you see lots of nearly identical statements grouped together, like the *trace()* statements in the example above. The examples in this book use this method to clarify how the code works. There's nothing wrong with these statements, and they produce fine results. But when you see repetitive code like that, it's important to know that there's almost always a more elegant way to handle the job. Usually, a *while* or a *for* loop (page 438) will do the trick. For example, you can replace the code above with the following:

```
var positionIndex:int = 0;


while (positionIndex < numChildren)
    {
        trace("The name of the object at
index position", positionIndex, "is",
getChildAt(positionIndex).name);
    positionIndex++;
    }
```

The first line creates a variable named *positionIndex* of type *int* and stores the value 0 in it. The next line starts a *while* loop. It says "while positionIndex is less than the number of children in the display object container, run the code between the curly brackets." There are two statements in between

the curly brackets. The first is a *trace()* statement that uses positionIndex to identify a child of the display object container. That statement ends with the semicolon (;). The first time positionIndex is used, it displays a number, and the second time it's the index for a *getChildAt()* method. The second and last statement before the closing curly bracket increments the positionIndex. So, on the first trip through the loop, positionIndex starts with a value of 0 and ends with a value of 1. The loop continues to run until the value of positionIndex is greater than or equal to the number of children in the display object container. If you replace the *trace()* statements above with this *while* loop, the lines displayed in the Output panel are identical. They look like this:

The name of the object at index position 0 is Card 2
The name of the object at index position 1 is Card 1
The name of the object at index position 2 is Card 3
The name of the object at index position 3 is Card 4
The name of the object at index position 4 is Card 5

One major advantage that this *while* loop has over the more literal code is that it works no matter how many children are held in the display object container. You don't have to know in advance and write specific code for each child.

## Swapping the Position of Two Children

If you're into multitasking, you'll be glad to know you can reposition two display objects at once using the *swapChildren()* or the *swapChildrenAt()* methods. As you might anticipate at this point, the *swapChildren()* method uses the variable names of the child display objects, while the *swapChildrenAt()* method uses the index positions.

Going back to the tried-and-true green card table, here are a couple of examples that show how to swap the positions of two child display objects. The following code swaps positions using the variable names of the children:

```
greenTable.swapChildren(card1, card4);
```

To swap children by referencing their index positions, you provide an *int* value, like this:

```
greenTable.swapChildrenAt(0,3);
```

Swapping children makes a pretty good mouse-click event. You can try it by adding the following lines to the code in *14-3_Stacking_Order.fla*. Adding the *traceDisplayList()* function to *clickSwapListener()* updates the Output panel after the swap has taken place:

```
card2.addEventListener(MouseEvent.CLICK, clickSwapListener);

function clickSwapListener(evt:MouseEvent):void {
    swapChildrenAt(0,4);
    traceDisplayList();
}
```

Test the animation after you've added the event listener, and you find a little inter-activity in the animation. Click card2, and it swaps position with the card at index position 4. Click card2 again, and the cards move back to their original positions. The *trace()* statements send updated reports to the Output panel.

## ■ Summary of Properties and Methods

This section gives you a summary of the properties and methods covered in this chapter. This list isn't exhaustive, but it includes some of the handiest and most frequently used tools. You can find a complete list in the Flash CS6 help files: Help→Flash Help→ActionScript 3.0 and Components→ActionScript 3.0 Language and Components Reference. Look for the DisplayObjectContainer class, and then scroll down to find the properties and methods. If you see a method and want more details about it, click its name.

## DisplayObjectContainer Properties

All display object containers are also descendants of the DisplayObject type. They have all the properties you'd expect in a displayable object, like x/y position coordinates, height, and width. In addition, they have a few properties that are particularly useful in their role as containers. The summary below lists the name of the property in bold, followed by a description, explaining the characteristics of the property and a few details about its use. The formal description is the description found in Adobe's ActionScript 3.0 Reference. It lists the property name, and then on the right side of the colon, it shows the data type stored in the property. The formal description is helpful but a little abstract, so this list also provides an example, which is a little more concrete and follows the card table and card theme used throughout this chapter. The examples show how you'd use the property, assuming that the display object container is an instance of a movie clip named greenTable.

- **name.** You can assign a name to a display object container using the *name* property. You can use just about anything for a name. In the examples in this book, the *name* property was used with the *trace()* statement. Be careful not to confuse the *name* property with variable names or class names. See page 488 for more details about the *name* property.

  *Formal description*: name: String

  *Example*: greenTable.name

- **numChildren.** A property that keeps track of the number of children in a display object container. The value is an *int* data type. This value is helpful when you're writing routines that identify specific child objects in a container. If you use *numChildren* along with the position index of the children, keep in mind that the index begins its count at 0, while *numChildren* starts its count at 1. See page 502 for an example that uses the *numChildren* property.

  *Formal description*: numChildren: int

  *Example*: greenTable.numChildren

- **parent.** Display object containers can have parents, too. Use the *parent* property to show the parent of the display object container, which has to also be a DisplayObjectContainer type. When you work with the Display List, the methods used most are those that belong to the display object container. Often the easiest way to identify the display object container is with the *parent* property. See page 490 for more details about the *parent* property.

  *Formal description*: parent: DisplayObjectContainer

  *Example*: card1.parent. In this example, if *card1* is a display object held in the display object container *greenTable*, the result identifies *greenTable* as the parent.

## DisplayObjectContainer Methods

When you work with the Display List, you're working with the methods of display object containers. Methods like *addChild()* and *removeChild()* are indispensable.

The summary list below is made up of three parts. The first part shows the name of the method in bold, and then gives a description, explaining what the method does, and the result or value that comes from the method. There may also be a page reference pointing you to a place in this chapter that provides more details about the method and related issues.

The second part of the summary shows the formal description of the method as provided by Adobe in the help system's *ActionScript 3.0 Language and Components Reference*. From left to right, the formal description begins with the method name, and then in parentheses shows the parameters required by the method. Parameters include a descriptive word on one side of the colon and the data type on the other side of the colon. Some methods have more than one parameter. On the right side of the parentheses is another colon and a word that describes the data type or class that the method returns. The formal description is somewhat abstract. The examples at the end of each summary are more concrete, showing you how you'd write a statement using the method. The examples continue using the card table and card theme used in this chapter. The assumption is that the display object container in the example is an instance of a movie clip named greenTable. The display object is an instance of a movie clip named "card1." Where a *name* property is used, card1 has a *name* property of "Card 1."

- **addChild().** Adds a display object to the Display List using the variable name of the display object. Adding a display object to the Display List makes it visible in the animation. The display object is added as a child of the display object container and then placed on the top of the visual stack, giving it the highest position index number. See page 501 for more details about the *addChild()* method.

  *Formal description*: addChild(child:DisplayObject): DisplayObject

  *Example*: greenTable.addChild(card1);

- **addChildAt().** Adds a display object to the Display List using the variable name of the child and a specified index position. The child is positioned at the exact index included in the method parameters. Objects already on the Display List at that index level or above are bumped up by one. The position index doesn't permit empty spots. So, for example, if a display object container has only four children and you attempt to add a new child at index position 7, your animation won't run, and you see an error message with the words, "The supplied index is out of bounds." For more examples using the *addChildAt()* method, see page 501.

  *Formal description*: addChildAt(child:DisplayObject, index:int):DisplayObject

  *Example*: greenTable.addChildAt(card1,3);

- **contains().** Determines whether a display object is held in a DisplayContainerObject. The result is true if the display object is in the display object container.

  *Formal description*: contains(child:DisplayObject):Boolean

  *Example*: greenTable.contains(card1);

- **getChildAt().** Returns the child display object instance at a particular position index. After identifying the instance, you can use the properties and methods of the object. See page 506 for more details.

  *Formal description*: getChildAt(index:int):DisplayObject

  *Example*: greenTable.getChildAt(3);

- **getChildByName().** Returns the child display object by identifying the *name* property. After identifying the instance, you can use the properties and methods of the object.

  *Formal description*: getChildByName(name:String):DisplayObject

  Example: greenTable.getChildByName("Card 1");

- **getChildIndex().** Returns the position index of a display object using the variable name. The result is a value of type *int*. See page 502 for more examples using the *getChildIndex()* method.

  *Formal description*: getChildIndex(child:DisplayObject):int

  *Example*: greenTable.getChildIndex(card1);

- **removeChild().** Removes a display object from the Display List and from its display object container. A child removed from the Display List is no longer visible in the animation. The object is referenced by its variable name. If the object is itself a display object container, then the display objects it holds are also removed. For more details, see page 504.

  *Formal description*: removeChild(child:DisplayObject):DisplayObject

  *Example*: greenTable.removeChild(card1);

- **removeChildAt().** Removes a display object from the Display List and from its display object container. The object is referenced by its positionIndex; its name or variable name isn't required. If the object is itself a display object container, then the display objects it holds are also removed. For another example of the *removeChildAt()* method, see page 504.

  *Formal description*: removeChildAt(index:int):DisplayObject

  *Example*: greenTable.removeChildAt(2);

- **swapChildren().** Swaps the position of two display objects in their display object container. This changes the visual stacking order—the way objects appear to overlap one another as well as other display objects in the container. For more on *swapChildren()*, see page 507.

  *Formal description*: swapChildren(child1:DisplayObject, child2:DisplayObject): void

  *Example*: greenTable.swapChildren(card1, card2);

- **swapChildrenAt().** Swaps the position of two display objects in their display
object container. This changes the visual stacking order—the way the objects
appear to overlap one another as well as other display objects in the container.
There are more details on the *swapChildrenAt()* method on page 507.

*Formal description*: swapChildrenAt(index1:int, index2:int):void

*Example*: greenTable.swapChildrenAt(1,3);

# Controlling the Timeline and Animation

O rdinarily, Flash assumes you want to play your animation in sequential order from the first frame in your timeline to the last. But sometimes "start at the beginning and quit at the end" isn't exactly what you want. Fortunately, by using a combination of scenes, frame labels, and ActionScript (Chapter 12), you can control your animation virtually any way you like.

For example, say you're putting together an instructional animation. You want to start with an introductory section, move on to the meat of your topic, and then wrap up with a question-and-answer section. If you organize these sections into separately named scenes, then you can play with the order of your animation quickly and easily. If you decide to reposition the question-and-answer scene directly after the introduction as a kind of pretest, for example, you can do that with a simple drag of your mouse. You can even add buttons that the trainee can click to replay the question-and-answer scene over and over, as many times as she likes.

In this chapter, you'll see how to stop and start playback using ActionScript code. You'll see how to use Flash labels, scenes, and ActionScript to make the most common types of nonsequential playback effects, including *looping* (replaying a section of your animation over and over again). To make these effects easy to test, you'll also see how to add interactive buttons to your animations. To start it off, this chapter describes how to control the overall speed at which Flash plays your animation on your audience's computers.

# ▅ Slowing Down (or Speeding Up) Animation

As you saw in Chapter 1, animations are nothing more than a series of content-containing frames that Flash plays one after another so quickly that your eyes interpret the overall effect as continuous movement.

You get a pretty good idea of how it will appear to your audience when you test it on your own computer. But the speed at which Flash actually displays your frames on *someone else's* computer depends on several factors, many of which you can't control:

- **Your audience's computer hardware.** Both processor speed and memory affect animation playback, especially if the animation is very long or includes multimedia, like bitmaps, sound, or video clips (Chapter 11). You have no control over this factor unless you're developing an animation for playback on a specific set of machines: for example, if you're creating a tutorial in Flash that you know will be played only on the computers in your company's training room.

- **Your audience's Internet connection.** If you've added your animation to a web page, the speed of your audience's Internet connection affects how quickly your animation downloads and plays on their computers. You have little or no control over this factor (beyond *preloading*, which you can learn about in Chapter 19) because, even if you're targeting your animation for specific machines with slower connections, Internet congestion may force download speeds of much less than that.

- **The delivery option you've chosen (if you've added video).** If you've incorporated a video clip into your animation (Chapter 11), you've had to tell Flash whether you want to:

  - **Embed the video into your Flash document.** If you've chosen this option, your animation won't begin to play until the person has downloaded the entire (enormous) Flash document, video clip and all. When the animation *does* begin to play, however, neither his Internet connection speed nor overall Internet traffic affect playback.

  - **Stream the video at runtime.** If you've chosen not to embed the video clip into your Flash document, the person's Flash Player begins playing the animation as soon as a few frames' worth of the animation file have finished downloading to his computer. When the animation *does* begin to play, however, it might run in fits and starts, depending on his computer hardware, Internet connection speed, Internet traffic, and the size of your animation or video file.

- **The size and configuration of your finished animation file.** Large animation files—files containing complex animated effects, lots of gradients, and transparent images, video clips, and so on—take longer than small files to download or stream over the Internet. They can also take longer to play, because large files tend to suck up all the memory on a computer or handheld device. You can control this factor by optimizing your animation to keep the file size as small as possible and by *preloading* sections of your animation. (Chapter 19 shows you how.)

- **The frame rate you've applied to your animation.** In your animation's timeline, you can tell Flash the maximum frame rate you want it to shoot for, in frames per second (fps).

The easiest factor to control—and the only one covered in this chapter—is the last one: the frame rate. The following section shows you how to set a new frame rate for an animation.

## Setting a Document Frame Rate

When you create a new animation, Flash assumes a maximum frame rate of 24 *fps* (frames per second). In other words, given the constraints listed in the previous section, Flash tries its best to display one frame every 1/24th of a second. Here's another way to look at frame rate: If your animation spans 240 frames, you're looking at roughly 10 seconds of screen time.

**NOTE** Previous versions of Flash started out using 12 fps because most people had slower Internet connections. At 24 fps, Flash matches the frame rate used for years by motion pictures.

In many cases, the standard 24 fps works just fine, but if you're planning to put your animation up on a website, you may want to consider a slower rate, like 12 fps. Your rule of thumb should be to use the lowest frame rate that still provides smooth action for your animation. Usually, you decide on a frame rate when you create a new Flash document. But you can change the frame rate at any time using the document properties (as shown in Figure 15-1) or using ActionScript. Changing the frame rate has some pretty significant side effects. First and most importantly, higher frame rates speed up your document. If you have a 4-minute animation with a 12 fps frame rate and you change it to 24 fps, your animation now finishes in 2 minutes. Too high a frame rate can make animation look blurry. Too slow a frame rate creates herky-jerky movements and may cause audio syncing problems.

The next few examples use a Flash document, *15-1_Frame_Rate.fla*, that you can find on the Missing CD page at *www.missingmanuals.com/cds/flashcs6mm*.

To see the effects of different frame rates, follow these steps and feel free to add some of your own experiments:

1. **Open *15-1_Frame_Rate.fla*, and then press Ctrl+Enter (⌘-Return) to test the animation.**

   The Stutz Bearcat auto races across your screen at a blazing 12 fps. The car is the only animated object in the movie and uses a motion tween to move from left to right across the screen.

2. **Below the timeline, click the Frame Rate setting (fps), and then type** *8*
   **(Figure 15-2).**

   You can click the Frame Rate and then type a new number, or you can drag to
   change the setting.

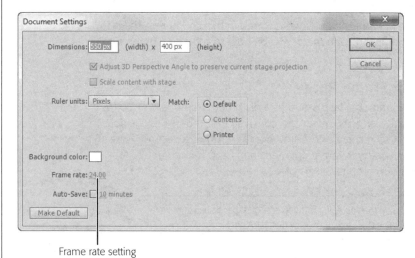

Frame rate setting

**FIGURE 15-1**

*Flash can play your movies at frame rates from 0.01 frames per second (that is, a super-slow 100 seconds per frame) to a blistering 120 frames per second. Going with a super-low or super-high frame rate, though, can cause audio synchronization problems. Also, setting a frame rate doesn't ensure that your animation will actually play at that frame rate; it's just a suggested maximum. Several other factors (page 514) affect playback, regardless of the frame rate you set.*

3. **Test the animation by pressing Ctrl+Enter (⌘-Return).**

   The car moves across the screen in a decidedly herky-jerky fashion.

4. **Click Modify→Document to open the Document Properties box, as shown in**
   **Figure 15-1, and then for Frame rate, type a number from 24 to 120.** Click OK.

   Flash lets you type in a frame rate of anything between 0.01 and 120. But in
   most cases, you want to stick with a frame rate of somewhere between 12 and
   24 (the standard Hollywood movie frame rate). Every animation is different, of
   course, and you might actually *want* to create an unusual effect. The Document
   Properties window disappears. In the timeline, you see the new frame rate.

5. **Test your new frame rate by choosing Control→Test Movie.**

   If you type in a frame rate greater than 24, then the car moves noticeably faster
   and may even look a bit blurry.

---

**NOTE** Frame rate affects the playback speed of the entire animation. Base your frame rate decisions on how smooth you want the animation to be and the capabilities of your intended audience, as explained on page 515. If you want to speed up (or slow down) only certain sections of your animation, change the rates by removing (or adding) frames, as described on page 100.

---

## Setting a Frame Rate with ActionScript

ActionScript gives you the tools to change the frame rate for your animation, too, since the stage has a frameRate property. (If you need more basics on ActionScript and properties, see Chapter 12.) When you use ActionScript to set the frameRate property for the stage, it has the same effect as setting a new frame rate in the timeline when you're designing your animation.

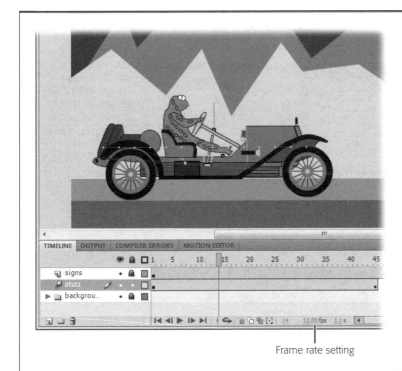

**FIGURE 15-2**

*In addition to clicking the Frame Rate setting (circled) in the timeline, Flash gives you two additional ways to set your animation's frame rate. You can select Modify→Document (which pops up the window in Figure 15-1) or click the stage and then change the frame rate directly in the Properties panel (Properties→Properties→FPS). Flash doesn't prevent you from changing your frame rate in the middle of building an animation, but it's such a basic characteristic that you typically want to set it once up front and change it later only if you absolutely have to.*

Frame rate setting

1. **Add a new layer for actions to the timeline.**

   If you're going to add code to the timeline, it's good practice to add a special layer at the top just for code and to name it something like "actions." That way, it's much easier later if you have to hunt down and debug your code.

2. **In the actions layer, click the first frame, and then open the Actions panel (Window→Actions).**

   The Actions panel opens, as shown in Figure 15-3. For more details about the tools available in the Actions panel, see page 416.

3. **In the Actions panel, type the following line of code:**

   ```
   stage.frameRate=60;
   ```

Even though you're changing the frameRate in ActionScript, the rate showing below the time line still shows a frame rate of 24 fps (or whatever you used in the last setting). In fact, the frameRate doesn't officially change until the actions on Frame 1 of the timeline are processed.

4. **Click the 22nd frame in the actions layer of the timeline, and then press F7.**

   Flash inserts a blank keyframe in the timeline.

Click to open/close panels      ActionScript code

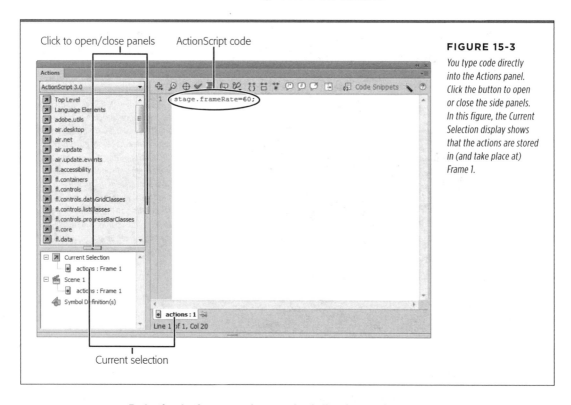

**FIGURE 15-3**

*You type code directly into the Actions panel. Click the button to open or close the side panels. In this figure, the Current Selection display shows that the actions are stored in (and take place at) Frame 1.*

Current selection

5. **In the Actions panel, type the following code:**

   ```
   stage.frameRate=6;
   ```

   Make sure that the 22nd frame in the timeline is selected when you type in the code, because you want the frame rate to change at that point in the animation. The Current Selection tab should change to show a frame symbol and the words *actions: Frame 22*.

6. **Test your animation using Ctrl+Enter (⌘-Return).**

   The Stutz Bearcat races up to the stop sign and performs a Hollywood stop, slowing down and rolling through the intersection, and then off the stage.

**TIP** Though you can change the frame rate of a timeline midstream, as shown in this example, in most cases, it's better to keep your frame rate at a single speed. Instead, to speed up the action, remove frames from the sequence; if you want to slow things down, add frames. If you want to slow down or speed up a tweened motion, that's easy to do using the Motion Editor, as described on page 311.

# ◼ Timeline Stop and Go

Starting and stopping an animation is similar to hitting the Pause and Play buttons on a DVD player. If your audience is viewing your animation in the desktop version of Flash Player, then they can pause and play the animation by pressing Enter or Return, just as you start and stop the playback when you're working in the Flash authoring environment. ActionScript gives you the tools to start and stop animations programmatically. There are all sorts of ways you can put this feature to use. Suppose you want the Stutz Bearcat to make a real stop at that stop sign, instead of the kind of stop that'll get you a ticket. You can place a *stop()* command in the timeline at the frame where you want the animation to stop.

**NOTE** The *stop()* and *go()* examples in this section also use the car-driving frog graphics. If you're continuing to use your document from the previous exercises, delete the code on Frames 1 and 22 that changes the timeline speed. If you want to start with a new sample document, download *15-2_Timeline_Stop_Go.fla* from the Missing CD page at *www.missingmanuals.com/cds/flashcs6mm*.

Here's how to tell your animation when to stop using ActionScript:

1. **Open *15-2_Timeline_Stop_Go.fla*.**

   The actions layer at the top of the timeline has keyframes at Frame 1 and Frame 22, but there's no code in the frames.

2. **Right-click Frame 22, and then choose Actions from the shortcut menu.**

   The Actions panel opens, and the current selection is set to Frame 22.

3. **Type the following code:**

   ```
   stop();
   ```

   This line of code is a little more complex than it may appear. In essence, it tells the main timeline of the animation to stop playing. A more complete version of this statement would read *this.stop()*. In that case, "this" refers to the main timeline. If you don't explicitly reference the timeline you're stopping, ActionScript assumes you mean the current timeline, which in this case is the main timeline.

4. **Test your animation using Ctrl+Enter (⌘-Return).**

   When the main timeline reaches the 22nd frame, it stops. Oddly, the wheels of the Stutz Bearcat keep on spinning (Figure 15-4). (That's got to be hard on the tires!) The car on the stage is an instance of the StutzBearcatFrog symbol in the Library. The symbol is a movie clip made up of two frames that make the car's wheels spin. To stop the wheels from turning, you need to stop the StutzBearcat animation, too.

**FIGURE 15-4**

*In this scene, the animation of the main timeline stops, but the animation in the car's movie clip keeps running, so the wheels spin even when the car is stopped. To restore the laws of physics, you have to stop both the main timeline and the car's movie clip using ActionScript statements.*

5. **In the Actions panel, add the following line of code:**

```
stutzBearcat.stop();
```

Now Frame 22 has two *stop()* statements. The first stops the main timeline, and the second stops the instance of the stutzBearcat movie clip.

6. **Test your animation using Ctrl+Enter (⌘-Return).**

When the animation runs, the car *and* the car's wheels make a legal stop in front of the stop sign.

## Using ActionScript to Start a Timeline

As you saw in the previous steps, the *stop()* command stops an animation nicely. But what about getting that Bearcat rolling again? You stopped the animation by putting the *stop()* statement in the frame where you wanted to stop, but putting a *play()* statement in the following frame, as logical as it sounds, will do you no good. The Flash Player will never reach the next frame—it's stopped. So you have a couple of choices, depending on what you want to trigger the starting and stopping. If you want your audience to control it, then you can give them clickable buttons or controls. If you want the animation to resume on its own, then a TimerEvent is the best tool in your toolbox. You can add a TimerEvent to the same frame where the *stop()* happened, as shown in Figure 15-5. When the timer is complete, it can trigger a *play()* statement for both the main timeline and the stutzBearcat movie clip. Modify the code on Frame 22 of the actions layer to read as follows:

```
1    stop();
2    stutzBearcat.stop();
3
4    var carTimer = new Timer(400,1);
5    carTimer.start();
6
7    carTimer.addEventListener(TimerEvent.TIMER_COMPLETE,
     timerCompleteListener);
8
9    function timerCompleteListener(evt:TimerEvent):void
10   {
11       play();
12       stutzBearcat.play();
13   }
```

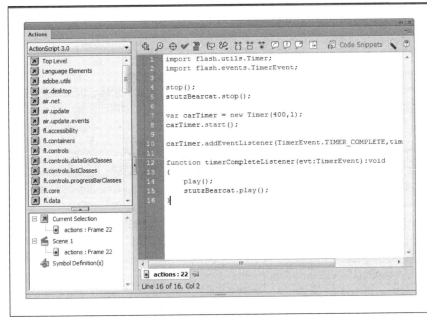

**FIGURE 15-5**

*The tab at the bottom of the Actions panel provides details about the location of the code shown. In this case, the code resides on the 25th frame of the actions layer.*

The first two lines were already in the code. Line 4 creates a new timer called *carTimer*. The first number in parentheses (400) sets the timer to wait a little less than half a second (400 thousandths of a second). The second number (1), sets the timer to run once. Line 5 starts the timer. The remainder of the code sets up the event handler.

Line 7 registers the event listener to run the function *timerCompleteListener()* when the timer runs out. (For more details on events and event listeners, see page 460.) The code between the curly brackets (line 11 and line 12) are the statements that start the main timeline and the stutzBearcat movie clip. For the completed exercise, download *15-3_Timeline_Stop_Go_done.fla* from the Missing CD (*www.missingmanuals.com/cds/flashcs6mm*).

> **NOTE**  In 1915, Erwin "Cannonball" Baker set a record driving from Los Angeles to New York in 11 days, 7 hours, and 15 minutes in a Stutz Bearcat.

# ■ Organizing Your Animation

As you see in a lot of the examples earlier in this book, you don't have to do a thing to your standard timeline, organization-wise. You can let Flash play your animation sequentially, from Frame 1 right through to Frame 500 (or whatever number your last frame is) with no problems.

If you need your animation to jump around and play out of sequence, though, there are a few ways you can do it. Which method is best depends on what you're trying to do. Here are three methods, along with their pros and cons:

- **Use labels to create bookmarks in the timeline.** If you break an animation into named chunks with frame labels, then you give your animations the potential to be flexible and more interactive, because you can write ActionScript actions that *target* (act on) each individual chunk. For example, you can let your audience decide whether to play the ralph_reacts scene first, last, or skip it altogether. This method is one of the most popular, especially with the ActionScript crowd. It's easy to create labels and easy to use them in ActionScript. In short, wherever you use a frame number to refer to a specific frame in a timeline, you can also use a frame label.

- **Divide your animation into separate .swf files and load them as needed.** This method is great if you have different teams working on a long animation. Team members can create movie clips independently, and then a master movie clip can load the other movie clips as needed. One of the advantages of this method is that it's faster, especially if you're sending .swf files over the Internet. Your audience needs to download only the .swf files they actually want to view.

- **Create scenes within your Flash document.** Scenes have more benefits for the Flash designer than they do for either the Flash coder or the Flash audience. If you break an animation into scenes, then you can find what you're looking for quickly; you can also easily rearrange your animation, using the Scene panel. Scenes make it easy to focus on a small section of your animation while you're creating and previewing it. You don't have to preview an entire animation when all you want to see is one small section. All the scenes are stored in a single .swf file, so your audience has to download the complete file, even if they're viewing only one or two of the scenes.

> **TIP** Both scenes and labeled frames are a natural fit for creating a website in Flash because they let you organize your content nonsequentially. Page 456 shows you an example of linking content to navigation buttons.

## Working with Labeled Frames

*Labeled frames* are like named bookmarks. Once you label a frame, you can jump to that specific point in the timeline using the label's name. Labeled frames are great tools to use when you want to give your audience an opportunity to interact with the animation. For example, if you're creating a series of lessons, you can create a label for each lesson. You can then give your students a table of contents, where they can jump to any lesson with the click of a button. Or, suppose you're using Flash to build an animated website and you want to display a different web page when someone clicks a button on your navigation bar. If she clicks the Contact Us button, for instance, you want to display a web page showing your company's contact information.

Technically, you don't have to label your frames in order to do this. You can create an *event listener* for your Contact page button that uses code like this:

```
gotoAndPlay(15);
```

The problem with this approach is that if you go back and add frames to the beginning of your timeline, it muffs up your code. If you add 10 frames to the beginning of your animation, for example, the old Frame 15 is now the new Frame 25. So, to make your button work again, you'd have to change the ActionScript code to this:

```
gotoAndPlay(25);
```

A much better approach is to give Frame 15 a meaningful label, like *contact*, and write the ActionScript code this way:

```
gotoAndPlay("contact");
```

When you label a frame like this, Flash always associates the same frame with the label—no matter what number that frame ends up being. So you can edit your timeline to your heart's content without ever having to worry that you're breaking your actions. As a significant side benefit, using words rather than numbers makes your code easier to read and understand.

The following sections show you how to label frames, and how to reference those labels in ActionScript code. This exercise uses a file called *15-4_Frame_Labels. fla*, which you can find at the Missing CD page at *www.missingmanuals.com/cds/ flashcs6mm*. The completed project is in a file named *15-5_Frame_Labels_done.fla*.

### ■ ADDING A FRAME LABEL

Labeling a frame is easy. All you have to do is select a frame and then, in the Properties panel, type a name for the label.

**NOTE** As with all content (images, sounds, actions, and so on), the label you attach to a keyframe stays in force until the next keyframe.

To label a frame:

1. **Open *15-4_Frame_Labels.fla* in Flash, and then press Enter to play the animation.**

   This rather abbreviated movie is made up of three words: Intro, Main, and Credits. Each word is animated using shape tweens. There are new words at Frame 1, Frame 16, and Frame 46. The animation has three layers: words, buttons, and labels. You can label any keyframe in a timeline, but if you place all your labels in a single layer, they're easier to find.

2. **In the timeline, in the labels layer, click the first frame.**

   Flash highlights the selected frame, and the Properties panel shows properties associated with Frame 1. (If the Properties panel isn't showing, then go to Window→Properties.)

3. **In the Properties panel, click the Label→Name box (Figure 15-6), and then type *intro*.**

   Your first label is complete. In the timeline, Flash displays a little red flag in the frame you attached the label to, followed by the label itself. In the Properties panel, you may need to click the triangle button next to Label to expand the Label subpanel.

**FIGURE 15-6**

*Flash assumes a label type of Name, and that's exactly what you want in most circumstances. (The other label types Flash has are Comment, which displays your label in the timeline but doesn't let you access it using ActionScript, and Anchor, which lets you designate the frame as a separate HTML anchor page that your audience can return to using the browser's Back button.)*

4. **In the labels layer, click Frame 16, and then press F6.**

   A new keyframe appears at Frame 16. Only keyframes can have labels. So to attach a new label to Frame 16, you need to create a keyframe first.

5. **In the Properties panel, click the Label→Name box, and then type *main.***

The second label named *main* appears in the labels layer.

---

## The Difference Between Scenes and Labeled Frames

*It sounds like scenes and frame labels do the same thing: Both let me break up my animation into chunks and make the chunks interactive, and both let me target a frame using a name instead of just the frame number. So if they both do the same thing, when do I use one over the other?*

Using labeled frames *is* very similar to using scenes. But there are three big differences between the two:

- Simply dragging scenes around in the Scene panel rearranges the way Flash plays your animation. It doesn't work that way with frame labels. (You can rearrange the way your animation plays using labeled frames, but you have to write the ActionScript code to do it.)

- It's harder to break up scenes than to add labels. When you use scenes, you need to either add new content for each scene as you build your animation, or—if you've already created your animation and want to break it into scenes after the fact—you need to cut and paste frames from the original Scene 1 into your new scenes. Hardly rocket science, but it is extra work. Adding or changing frame labels is much quicker.

- As a designer, you see separate timelines when you work with scenes. When you work with frames, you see one big timeline. This difference is usually the deal breaker: Some people love working with content in separate timelines; some people hate it. It's interesting to note that no matter which method you use, Flash stores everything in one big timeline in the published SWF file.

---

6. **In the labels layer, click Frame 46, and then press F6.**

A new keyframe appears at Frame 46.

7. **In the Properties panel, click the Label→Name box, and then type *credits.***

The third label named "credits" appears in the labels layer.

### ■ TARGETING A FRAME LABEL WITH ACTIONSCRIPT

After you've labeled a frame, you can reference that label in an ActionScript action. This section shows you how to program three buttons that jump to a specific frame label in the timeline.

---

**NOTE** The example in this section is identical to the one on page 532 except for two differences: This example shows ActionScript targeting labeled frames in a single timeline, while the one on page 532 shows ActionScript targeting separate scenes.

---

To target a labeled frame:

1. **Open the Flash file, and then move the playhead to Frame 1.**

   On the stage you see the word "Intro" and three buttons with the text "Play Intro," "Play Main," and "Play Credits."

2. **Test the animation by choosing Control→Test Movie.**

   In the test window, you see the word "Intro" recede, the word "Main" approach and recede, and the word "Credits" approach. Clicking the Play Intro, Play Main, and Play Credits buttons turns the buttons from red to yellow but has no other effect on the animation.

3. **Below Flash's timeline, click the New Layer button.** Then click the name and type *actions*, as shown in Figure 15-7.

   A new layer named *actions* appears in the timeline. You'll use this layer to hold all of your ActionScript code. As a rule of thumb, it's best to keep your ActionScript code as close together as possible. When snippets of code are tucked away in different layers or movie clips, it's harder to troubleshoot.

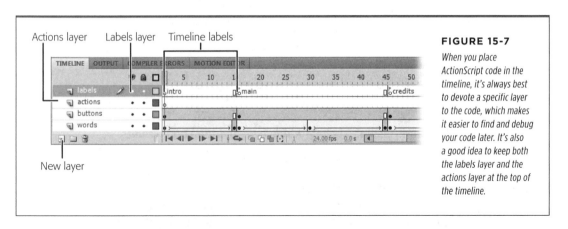

**FIGURE 15-7**

*When you place ActionScript code in the timeline, it's always best to devote a specific layer to the code, which makes it easier to find and debug your code later. It's also a good idea to keep both the labels layer and the actions layer at the top of the timeline.*

4. **In the actions layer, create a keyframe at Frame 15 by selecting the frame and then pressing F6.**

   An empty circle appears in Frame 15, indicating a keyframe.

5. **With Frame 15 still selected, type the following ActionScript statement in the Actions panel:**

   ```
   stop();
   ```

   This statement stops the animation from playing when it reaches Frame 15. This marks the end of the "intro" segment of the animation.

6. **Create keyframes and *stop()* statements for Frames 44 and 60, similar to what you did in steps 4 and 5.**

At this point, each of the three animation segments (intro, main, credits) has a *stop()* statement at the end. If you test your animation now, it will stop at the end of the Intro. In the following steps, you'll write code for each of the three Play buttons.

7. **Click the outside edge of the Play Intro button.**

The button shows a selection box, and a button icon appears in the Properties panel, as shown in Figure 15-8. If you see the letter T in the Properties panel, it means you selected the Play Intro text, not the Play Intro button, so try again.

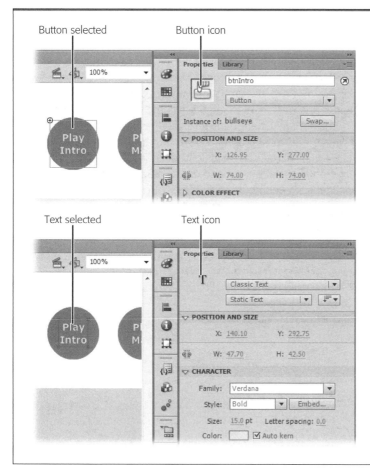

Button selected    Button icon

Text selected    Text icon

**FIGURE 15-8**

*These buttons are made up of two parts: a button symbol, plus text placed over the symbol. To select just the button, click the edges outside the text. You can tell whether you've selected the button symbol or the text by checking the icon that shows in the Properties panel.*

8. **In the Properties panel, name the button instance *btnIntro*.**

There are three instances of buttons on the stage: Play Intro, Play Main, and Play Credits. They're all instances of the BullsEye button in the Library. Before you can write ActionScript code for each button, you have to name it.

9. **Repeat steps 7 and 8 to name the remaining two buttons.**

   Using a consistent naming convention, name the Play Main button *btnMain*, and the Play Credits button *btnCredits*.

10. **Click Frame 1 in the actions layer, and then type the following code to create an event listener for btnIntro:**

```
1   btnIntro.addEventListener(MouseEvent.CLICK, clickIntroListener);
2
3   function clickIntroListener(evt:MouseEvent)
4   {
5       gotoAndPlay("intro");
6   }
```

   Line 1 registers a MouseEvent listener for btnIntro. Lines 3 through 6 comprise the function *clickIntroListener()*. This function holds the code that runs when someone clicks the btnIntro button. (For more details on handling events and event listeners, see page 448.) Line 5 holds the important action for the function. The *gotoAndPlay()* statement tells the Flash Player to jump to the frame labeled "intro" and to begin playing from that point forward. You can place either a label, like "intro," or a specific frame number, like "16," inside the *gotoAndPlay()* parentheses. As explained on page 523, labels are much more flexible than specific frame numbers.

11. **Add event listener code for the remaining two buttons.** When you're through, it should look like this:

```
btnIntro.addEventListener(MouseEvent.CLICK, clickIntroListener);
btnMain.addEventListener(MouseEvent.CLICK, clickMainListener);
btnCredits.addEventListener(MouseEvent.CLICK, clickCreditsListener);

function clickIntroListener(evt:MouseEvent)
{
    gotoAndPlay("intro");
}

function clickMainListener(evt:MouseEvent)
{
    gotoAndPlay("main");
}

function clickCreditsListener(evt:MouseEvent)
{
    gotoAndPlay("credits");
}
```

When you have several similar statements, like these mouse event listeners, you can save time by writing and testing one statement. Then, with a little copy, paste, and modify magic, you can quickly create the similar statements. If things don't work as planned, double-check the way you modified the code. In this case, you'd carefully examine all the code where "intro," "main," and "credits" appear.

12. **Test your animation using Ctrl+Enter (⌘-Return).**

If your code is working properly, the animation plays the "intro" and then stops. When you click any of the Play buttons, Flash plays that segment and then stops. If your code isn't working quite right, compare your project with *15-5_Frame_Labels_done.fla*.

As this example shows, frame labels and *gotoAndPlay()* statements are powerful tools for animations that play out of sequence. Labels give you an easy and convenient way to mark off segments in a timeline, and you can add as many of them as you want. There's another related statement, *gotoAndStop()*, which does exactly what you imagine. It jumps to a specific frame and stops Flash Player from moving on to the next frame. The next section of this chapter explains how to use *scenes* to accomplish the same tasks.

## Working with Scenes

A *scene* in Flash is a series of frames to which you assign a name of your choosing. When you're working in Flash, each scene has its own timeline. In the preceding example using labels, a single timeline was marked off into three parts: intro, main, and credits. Each segment occupied frames in the same timeline. The first 15 frames made up the "intro," the next 30 frames were labeled "main," and the final 15 frames were labeled "credits." You can use scenes to break a larger animation into smaller chunks that can be targeted with ActionScript.

Each time you create a new scene, Flash displays a brand-new timeline for you to fill with content. Then, when you play your animation, Flash plays each scene in top-down order, beginning with the first scene listed in the Scene panel (Figure 15-9), and ending with the last.

As the following sections show, after you create scenes, you can rename them and reorganize them with the click of a button.

> **TIP**  As an alternative to using scenes, you may want to consider publishing separate .swf files and loading them into your main animation as needed. This method can be helpful when teams of animators produce a long animation. Each team works with separate Flash documents and publishes its own .swf files.

### ■ CREATING A SCENE

Flash automatically starts you out with one scene (cleverly named Scene 1) each time you create a new Flash document.

To create additional scenes:

1. **In the timeline, create content for the frames you want in your first scene.**

   If you're using the example file *15-6_Scenes.fla*, you see two layers, buttons, and words, each of which extends from Frame 1 through Frame 15. (You can download this example file from the Missing CD page at *www.missingmanuals.com/cds/flashcs6mm*.)

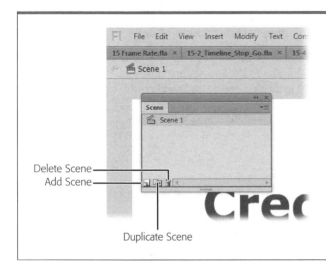

Delete Scene
Add Scene
Duplicate Scene

**FIGURE 15-9**

*Every animation you create has at least one scene (named Scene 1, unless you tell Flash differently). By using the Scene panel to create and name new scenes, you can organize long animations into manageable chunks. Flash displays the timeline for each scene separately, so it can be easy to forget which scene you're in at any given time. In fact, your only cue is the scene name Flash displays in the Edit bar. If you don't see it (along with the little clapper icon), choose Window→Toolbars→Edit Bar.*

2. **Choose Window→Other Panels→Scene.**

   The Scene panel appears.

3. **Click the Add Scene icon.**

   In the Scene panel, Flash creates a new scene and then places it directly below Scene 1. Flash also displays a brand-new timeline and a clean, fresh stage (Figure 15-10).

4. **In the timeline, create content for the frames you want in your new scene.**

   When you're done, you may want to rename the scene (as discussed in the next section), and then test it by choosing Control→Test Scene. Or, to create additional scenes, simply repeat steps 3 and 4.

### ■ RENAMING A SCENE

The names Flash gives each scene you create—Scene 1, Scene 2, Scene 3, and so on, as you see in Figure 15-10—aren't particularly useful if you're using scenes as a way to find the frames you need quickly. Fortunately, Flash makes it easy for you to rename scenes. Here are the steps:

1. **Choose Window→Other Panels→Scene.**

   The Scene panel appears.

2. **In the Scene panel, double-click the name of the scene you want to change.**

Flash displays the scene name in an editable text box.

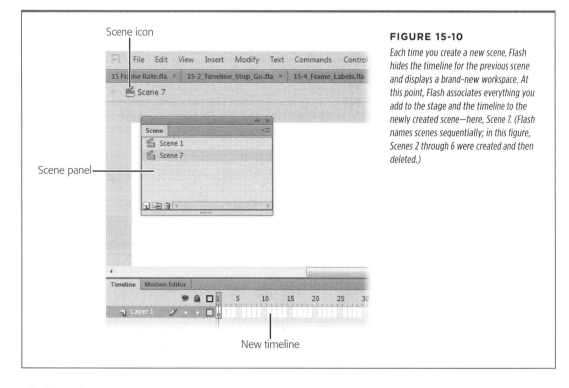

Scene icon

Scene panel

New timeline

**FIGURE 15-10**

*Each time you create a new scene, Flash hides the timeline for the previous scene and displays a brand-new workspace. At this point, Flash associates everything you add to the stage and the timeline to the newly created scene—here, Scene 7. (Flash names scenes sequentially; in this figure, Scenes 2 through 6 were created and then deleted.)*

3. **Type the new name.**

You'll need to refer to this name in ActionScript code if you're planning to make your animation interactive, so short and meaningful is best. For example, you might choose *intro* for an introductory scene, *main* for the meat of your animation, and *credits* for the last few wrap-up frames that display your company's name and contact info.

### ■ REORGANIZING SCENES

Flash always plays scenes in order from the scene that appears at the top of the Scene panel down to the scene that appears in the bottom. To change the order in which Flash plays your scenes:

1. **Choose Window→Other Panels→Scene.**

The Scene panel appears.

---

**NOTE** Another way to change the order in which Flash plays your scenes and frames is by using ActionScript, as shown in the next.

---

2. **In the Scene panel, click the name of the scene you want to move, and then drag it above or below the other scenes, as shown in Figure 15-11.**

   The instant you let up on your mouse, Flash reorders the scenes in the Scene panel. The new order is the order in which Flash plays your animation when you choose Control→Test Movie.

---

Change scene sequence

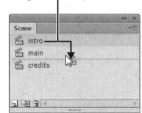

**FIGURE 15-11**

*Dragging a scene to a new location in the Scene panel automatically reorganizes the sequence in which Flash plays your animation—no ActionScript necessary. The line that appears as you drag a scene lets you know where Flash will put the scene when you let up on your mouse.*

---

**NOTE** To play just the scene currently on the stage, select Control→Test Scene (instead of Control→Test Movie).

---

### ■ TARGETING A SCENE WITH ACTIONSCRIPT

In Flash-speak, *targeting* a scene means writing ActionScript code that performs some action on a scene. The example in this section shows how to program the buttons to jump to a new scene and begin playing the animation at that point. The tools you use are similar to those used with labels: event listeners and the *gotoAndPlay()* statement. Figure 15-12 gives you a quick overview of how the finished example looks.

---

**TIP** For more information on creating button symbols, see page 271.

---

3. **Open the file *15-7_Scenes_Actions.fla*.**

   In the Scene panel (Window→Other Panels→Scene), notice that the animation contains three scenes (intro, main, and credits). The stage has three corresponding buttons labeled Play Intro, Play Main, and Play Credits.

---

**NOTE** You can download the example files for this section from the Missing CD page at *www.missingmanuals.com/cds/flashcs6mm*. The file *15-7_Scenes_Actions.fla* is the starting point, and *15-8_Scenes_Actions_done.fla* is the completed animation with ActionScript.

---

4. **Test the animation by selecting Control→Test Movie.**

   In the test window, the word "Intro" recedes; the word "Main" approaches and recedes; and the word "Credits" approaches. The Play Intro, Play Main, and Play

---

Credits buttons turn from red to yellow when you move your mouse over them and turn green when clicked. But none of the buttons affect the animation.

**FIGURE 15-12**

*You may want to break an animation into scenes so that you can give your audience the ability to play the scenes independently. Here, pressing the Play Credits button plays the credits scene, pressing the Play Main button plays the main scene, and pressing the Play Intro button plays the (you guessed it) intro scene. To put together an interactive animation, you have to first create named scenes, and then tie those scenes to buttons using ActionScript code.*

5. **Click the Edit Scene icon (Figure 15-13), and then choose "intro" if it's not already chosen.**

The Edit bar displays "intro" to let you know you're about to edit the intro scene. On the stage, you see the three buttons shown in Figure 15-12.

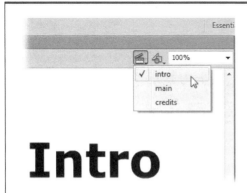

**FIGURE 15-13**

*You can switch from scene to scene in your animation using the Scene panel, but you'll probably find clicking the Edit Scene icon much handier, because the Edit Scene icon doesn't disappear while you're working.*

6. **Below Flash's timeline, click the New Layer button.** Then click the name and type "actions," as shown earlier in Figure 15-7.

A new layer named actions appears in the timeline. You use this layer to hold all your ActionScript code. As a rule of thumb, it's best to keep your ActionScript code as close together as possible. When snippets of code are tucked away in different layers or movie clips, it makes it hard to troubleshoot.

7. **In the actions layer, create a keyframe at Frame 15 by selecting the frame and then pressing F6.**

An empty circle appears in Frame 15, indicating a keyframe.

8. **With Frame 15, still selected, type the following ActionScript statement in the Actions panel:**

stop();

This statement stops the animation from playing when it reaches Frame 15. Without a *stop()* statement here, the Flash Player automatically plays the next scene.

9. **Repeat steps 3 through 6 to create action layers, keyframes, and stop() statements on the last frames of the main scene and the credits scene.**

Use the Edit Scene icon to move from one scene to another.

10. **Go back to the intro scene, and then click the first frame in the actions layer.**

Flash displays the timeline for the intro scene.

11. **In the Actions window, type the following code:**

```
1    btnIntro.addEventListener(MouseEvent.CLICK, clickIntroListener);
2    btnMain.addEventListener(MouseEvent.CLICK, clickMainListener);
3    btnCredits.addEventListener(MouseEvent.CLICK, clickCreditsListener);
4
5    function clickIntroListener(evt:MouseEvent):void
6    {
7        gotoAndPlay(1,"intro");
8    }
9
10   function clickMainListener(evt:MouseEvent):void
11   {
12       gotoAndPlay(1,"main");
13   }
14
15   function clickCreditsListener(evt:MouseEvent):void
16   {
17       gotoAndPlay(1,"credits");
18   }
```

If you've been following the ActionScript code sections in this and previous chapters, the event listeners used in this code should look pretty familiar. If you need to brush up on event listeners, check out page 448. The only differences between this code and the code used to target labels is in the way the *gotoAndPlay()* method is used. In this example, *gotoAndPlay()* has two parameters inside the parentheses. The first parameter is a frame number, but it could just as easily be a label like "start" or "intro." The second parameter is the name of a scene. Like labels, the name of the scene has to be inside quotes. Each of the statements on lines 7, 12, and 17, tell Flash Player to go to a scene and begin playing the animation at the first frame of that scene.

12. **Select lines 1 through 3 in the Actions panel, and then press Ctrl+C (⌘-C).**

The three statements that register event listeners for the buttons are copied and stored on your computer's Clipboard.

13. **Go back to the main scene, and click the first frame in the actions layer.**

Flash displays the timeline for the main scene.

14. **Click the first line in the Actions panel, and then press Ctrl+V (⌘-V).**

You've just copied the three statements that register event listeners into the Actions panel. Each scene is shown on a new timeline beginning with keyframes at Frame 1 for each layer. The statements that register event listeners in the intro scene don't register event listeners for the other scenes. Note that you don't need to (and shouldn't) copy the functions, just the code that uses the *addEventListener()* method.

15. **Go back to the credits scene, and click the first frame in the actions layer.**

Flash displays the timeline for the main scene.

16. **Click the first line in the Actions panel, and then press Ctrl+V (⌘-V).**

The three statements that register event listeners are copied into the Actions panel.

17. **Test your animation using Ctrl+Enter (⌘-Return).**

If your code is working properly, the animation plays the intro and then stops. When you click any of the Play buttons, Flash plays that segment and then stops.

---

**NOTE** With a long exercise like this, it's super-easy to miss a step. To see a working example, check out the finished file *15-8_Scenes_Actions_done.fla*.

---

# ■ Looping a Series of Frames

*Looping*—replaying a section of your animation over and over again—is an efficient way to create long-playing effects for a modest investment of effort and file size.

Say, for example, you want to create a repetitive background effect like sunlight glinting off water, palm fronds waving in the breeze, or flickering lights. You can create the frames necessary to show the effect briefly (a couple seconds' worth or so), save the frames as a movie clip, and place an instance of that movie clip in one of the layers of your animation so that the effect spans your entire animation. Flash automatically replays the movie clip until you tell it otherwise, so you get an extended effect for a just a few frames' worth of work—and just a few frames' worth of file size, too. What a deal! (For a more in-depth look at movie clip symbols, check out Chapter 7.)

> **NOTE**  You've seen this kind of looping background effect in action if you've ever watched *The Flintstones*—or just about any other production cartoon, for that matter. Remember seeing the same two caves shoot past in the background over and over again as Fred chased Barney around Bedrock? Earlier in this chapter, the car's spinning wheels were made up of a two-frame movie clip that looped.

To loop a series of frames using a movie clip symbol:

1.  **Open the file *15-9_Loop_Frames.fla*, which you can download from the Missing CD page at *www.missingmanuals.com/cds/flashcs6mm*.**

    On the stage, you see a sprinkling of white stars on a blue background. In the Library, you see four symbols, including the blink_lights movie clip symbol (Figure 15-14).

    Since you've never seen this movie clip before, take a look at the preview.

> **NOTE**  To loop a section of your *main* timeline, all you have to do is attach the following action to the last frame of the section you want to loop: *gotoAndPlay(1)*. (If you want your loop to begin at a frame other than Frame 1, replace the 1 in the preceding ActionScript code with the number of the frame at which you want Flash to begin looping.)

2.  **In the Library, select the blink_lights movie clip.** Then, in the Library's preview window, click the Play icon.

    You see the lights on the cactus change from red to yellow, pink, and blue in rapid succession.

3.  **Preview the main animation by selecting Control→Test Movie.**

    In the test window, you see a lone shooting star streak across the background.

4. **Close the test window to go back to the workspace.**

First stop: Add an instance of the blink_lights movie clip symbol to the animation.

5. **In the xmas_cactus layer, click the first keyframe (Frame 1) to select it.** Then drag the blink_lights movie clip from the Library to the stage.

Choose Control→Test Movie again to see the results. In the test window that appears, you see the lights on the cactus blink repeatedly as the shooting star moves across the screen. In the test window, you can stop the main timeline from looping by choosing Control→Loop. The shooting star on the main timeline stops looping, but the lights on the cactus continue to blink because they're in a separate timeline in the blink_lights movie clip. If you *don't* want your embedded movie clip to loop, you need to tell Flash to stop playing the movie clip after the first time through. To so instruct it, attach the *stop()* action to the last frame of your movie clip symbol (*not* to the movie clip instance).

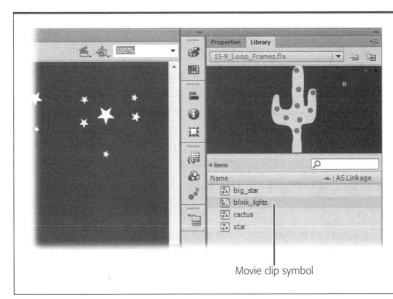

**FIGURE 15-14**

*Looping a series of frames using a movie clip is super-easy because Flash does all the work. In fact, Flash always assumes you want to loop the movie clips you add to your animations. (If you don't want to loop them, then you can tell Flash to stop playing a movie clip after the first time through by attaching the stop() action to the last frame of your movie clip symbol.)*

Movie clip symbol

## Looping Part of the Timeline

Sometimes, you'll want to loop just a portion of the timeline. Usually in this kind of situation, you provide buttons or some other means for letting the viewer switch between looping portions of the animation. The file *15_10_Loop_Partial.fla* is a simple (some might say silly) animation with two sections. In this exercise, you'll create two looping segments on the timeline using the *gotoAndPlay()* main timeline method.

Then you'll add two button symbols to the stage and use code snippets to program the buttons to play the different segments.

1. **Open the file *15_10_Loop_Partial.fla*.**

   You can download the file from the Missing CD at *www.missingmanuals.com/cds/flashcs6mm*.

2. **Press Ctrl+Enter (⌘-Return) to review the animation.**

   You can't preview all the action for this animation by simply playing the timeline. That's because it uses movie clip symbols that contain tweens. For the first 48 frames of the animation, you see squares marching across the stage. From Frame 49 to Frame 96, you see circles marching.

3. **Add a new layer and name it *actions looping*.**

   The actions looping layer will hold the ActionScript code that makes these two segments loop. At the end of each segment, a single *gotoAndPlay()* method will send the playhead back to the beginning of that segment.

4. **Move the playhead to Frame 48, and then press F6 to create a keyframe.**

   The *gotoAndPlay()* methods must be anchored to specific frames in the timeline.

5. **Press F9 to open the Actions window and add the following code:**

   ```
   gotoAndPlay("squares");
   ```

   The *gotoAndPlay()* method works with either frame numbers or labels. In this example, you'll use labels. Don't forget the quotes.

6. **Move the playhead to Frame 96, and then press F6 to create a keyframe.**

   At this frame, you'll add code to loop the second segment.

7. **Press F9 to open the Actions window, and add the following code:**

   ```
   gotoAndPlay("circles");
   ```

8. **Select the buttons layer and move the playhead to Frame 1.** Then drag instances of ButtonCircle and ButtonSquare from the Library onto the stage.

   These buttons were premade using Flash's button symbol. All you need to do is place them on the stage and program them with ActionScript.

9. **Select the ButtonSquare instance.** Then go to Window→Code Snippets to open the snippets window (Figure 15-15).

   You must select an object before you can use the Timeline Navigation snippet. If you haven't selected an object, then Flash prompts you to do so.

10. **Open the Timeline Navigation folder and double-click "Click Go to Frame and Play."**

There are several other navigation snippets worthy of later investigation in this folder.

11. **When prompted to set the instance name, type *btnSquare* and then press OK.**

    If you followed these steps to the letter, you didn't name the button instance when you dragged it to the stage. ActionScript needs an instance name, so it prompts you to provide one.

12. **In the function named "fl_ClickToGoToAndPlayFromFrame," change the *gotoAndPlay()* method to read:**

    gotoAndPlay("squares");

13. **Select the ButtonCircle instance on stage.** Then go to Window→Code Snippets to open the snippets window.

    The next few steps repeat the snippet process for the ButtonCircle symbol.

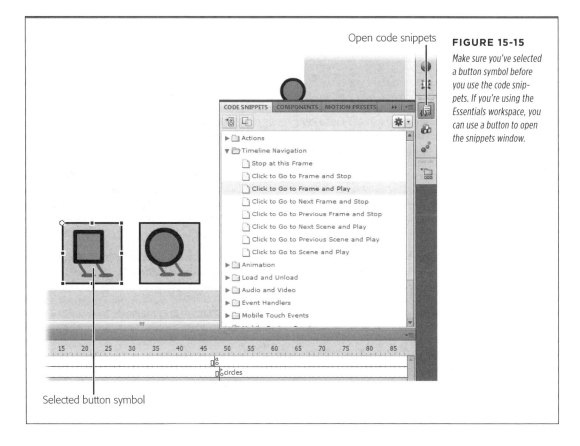

Open code snippets

**FIGURE 15-15**

*Make sure you've selected a button symbol before you use the code snippets. If you're using the Essentials workspace, you can use a button to open the snippets window.*

Selected button symbol

14. **Open the Timeline Navigation folder and double-click "Click Go to Frame and Play."**

15. **When prompted to set the instance name, type *btnCircle* and then press OK.**

    You're adding the same snippet twice to your code, so Flash has to give the second listener function a distinguishable name. In this case, it simply adds "_2" to the name.

16. **In the function named "fl_ClickToGoToAndPlayFromFrame_2," change the gotoAndPlay() method to read:**

    ```
    gotoAndPlay("circles");
    ```

17. **Press Ctrl+Enter (⌘-Return) to review the animation.**

    When you play the animation this time, the squares segment loops until you click the circle button. You can jump back and forth between segments with a click of the button. If your squares and circles aren't behaving, then compare your animation to *15-11_Loop_Partial done.fla*.

## Power to the People

Early on, one of the beefs people had with Flash advertising and splash screens (intro pages) was the inability to control the animations. It wasn't easy to stop, start, bypass, or control the sound on some of those pages. It gave Flash a bad name.

Things have changed. You can use Flash to create entire web-based environments with ingenious and creative navigation systems. If you don't, even though your audience can right-click (or Control-click) your animation to view a context menu that lets them interact with your animation, context menus aren't particularly useful when it comes to providing consistent playback control. For one thing, few audience members know about them. Also, Flash gurus who also happen to be expert ActionScript coders can modify, rearrange, add to, and delete menu options.

Don't be one of them. Consider the Flash experience from your audience's point of view. You won't go wrong by giving power to the people. Giving your audience as much control as possible is always a good idea, but it's crucial if you're planning to put your Flash animation on the Web. You can't possibly know your web audience's hardware configuration.

Say, for example, you create a splash page animation with a stage size of 550 x 400 pixels, and a file size of 10 MB. Someone accessing your animation on a handheld, over a slow connec-tion, or on a machine that's already maxed out running 10 other resource-hogging programs won't be able to see the animation you see on *your* machine.

But even if everyone on the planet had a high-speed connection and the latest computer hardware, giving your audience control would still be important. Why? Because no matter how kick-butt your animation is, by the 23rd time through, it's going to wear a little thin. If you don't offer at least one of the options listed below, you risk turning away repeat visitors:

- The ability to bypass intro splash screens and advertising and go straight to the site's home page.

- The ability to stop and restart the animation.

- The ability to turn off or turn down the audio.

- The ability to choose which sections of your animation to play.

- The ability to choose a low-bandwidth, reduced length, or small-screen version of your animation.

You can accomplish these feats using a combination of buttons, components, and some ActionScript code. So be merciful to your audience and let them choose the Flash experience that works on their end.

# Reversing a Series of Frames

Reversing a series of frames is a useful effect. A basketball bouncing up and down, a flag waving side to side, a boomerang advancing and receding: These things are all examples of reversing a single series of frames.

Instead of creating the two complete series of frames by hand—one showing a ball falling, for example, and another showing the same ball bouncing back up—you can copy the frame series, paste it, and use Modify→Timeline→Reverse Frames to reverse the pasted frames.

**NOTE** If you need a file for reverse frame experiments, you can download *15-12_Reverse_Frames.fla* from the Missing CD (*www.missingmanuals.com/cds/flashcs6mm*).

## Reversing Frames in the Timeline

When you use Modify→Timeline→Reverse Frames in conjunction with Flash's copy-and-paste function, you can create the reverse of a series of frames quickly, right in the timeline.

To create a reversed series of frames using Modify→Timeline→Reverse Frames:

1. **Click the first frame in the series you want to reverse.** Then Shift-click the last frame in the series you want to reverse.

   Flash highlights every frame in the series, from first to last.

2. **Select Edit→Timeline→Copy Frames.** In the timeline, click the first frame where you want to insert the reversed series of frames.

   Flash highlights the selected frame.

3. **Select Edit→Timeline→Paste Frames.**

   Flash pastes the copied frames onto the timeline, beginning at the selected frame.

4. **If the pasted frame series isn't highlighted, select it.**

5. **Choose Modify→Timeline→Reverse Frames (Figure 15-16).**

   Flash reverses the frames in the timeline.

**TIP** You can reverse the action in a motion tween by selecting the frames you want to change. Right-click the selected frames and then choose Reverse Keyframes from the shortcut menu.

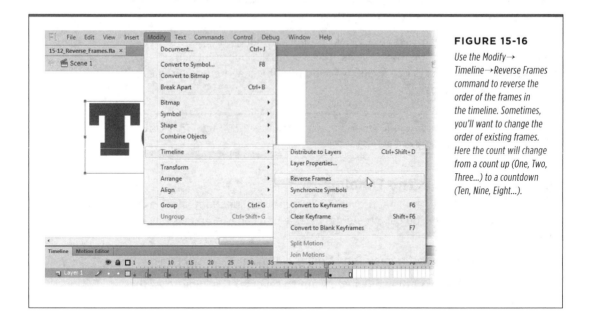

**FIGURE 15-16**

*Use the Modify→
Timeline→Reverse Frames
command to reverse the
order of the frames in
the timeline. Sometimes,
you'll want to change the
order of existing frames.
Here the count will change
from a count up (One, Two,
Three...) to a countdown
(Ten, Nine, Eight...).*

# Components for Interactivity

Creating common Flash elements like playback controls (Play and Pause buttons), text fields, checkboxes, and buttons can add up to a lot of grunt work. Since they pretty much look the same in every animation, some kind Flash developers did the grunt work for you and put ready-made versions of these Flash bits and pieces—called *components*—right into the program.

A component is a compiled, prebuilt movie clip that you can drag onto the stage and customize. Flash comes with dozens of components (Figure 16-1). If you do a lot of work in Flash, you'll appreciate the time components can save you. But another great thing about components is the consistency they give. For example, the user interface components discussed in this chapter all look like they belong together. If you don't like their style, Flash gives you some convenient ways to change their appearance. So, if you're working in a design shop, you can add time-tested components to your projects and still give each client a look that matches her image and brand.

There's a consistency in the way you work with components, which also makes them easy to use. This chapter starts off showing you how to add, modify, and write code for the Button and ColorPicker components. By the time you're done, you'll not only know how to work with Button components, but you'll also be 90 percent of the way to knowing how to use the other Flash components.

After you learn how to add, modify, and program a couple of components, you'll learn about the different types of components available and what they can do for you. To wrap it all up, you'll learn how to find and install components that come from sources other than Adobe.

**NOTE**  Using components requires a fair amount of ActionScript knowledge. But *creating* your own components is an even more ActionScript–intensive proposition. If you'd like to explore creating your own components,
check out both the *ActionScript 3.0 Language and Components Reference* you find in Flash Help (see page 448),
and a good book that covers both ActionScript and object-oriented design. Colin Moock's *Essential ActionScript
3.0*, and *ActionScript 3.0 Cookbook* by Joey Lott et al. (both O'Reilly) are two of the best on the market.

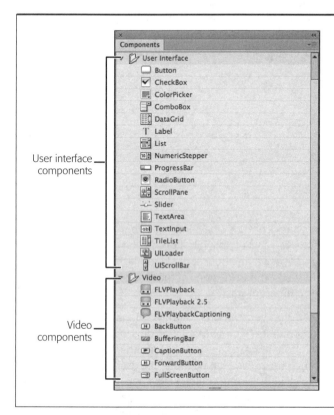

User interface
components

Video
components

**FIGURE 16-1**

*Flash CS6 Professional comes with dozens of compo-
nents. Components for ActionScript 3.0 documents
include user interface controls to create interactive buttons, boxes, and lists (similar to HTML form controls (not
shown); and video controls, as discussed on page 403.*

# ■ Adding Components

Adding a component to your animation is the first step in using that component.
As you'll see in the following sections, adding an instance of a component to the
stage is similar to adding an instance of a symbol: All you have to do is drag and
drop. But instead of dragging components from the Library panel, you drag them
from the Components panel.

To add a component to your animation:

1. **Select Window→Components.**

   The Components panel appears.

2. **In the Components panel, click to select the component you want, and then drag it to the stage.**

As Figure 16-2 shows, Flash displays an instance of the component on the stage. It also places a copy of the component in the Library (Window→Library).

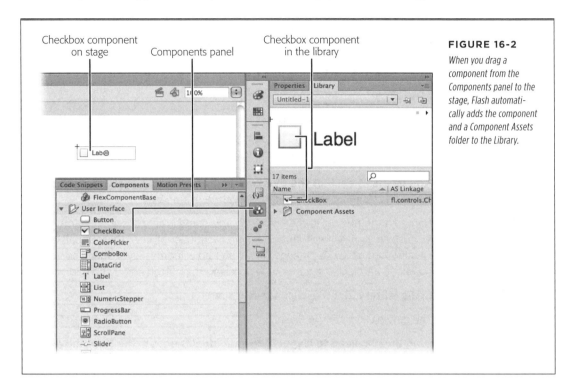

Checkbox component on stage

Components panel

Checkbox component in the library

**FIGURE 16-2**

*When you drag a component from the Components panel to the stage, Flash automatically adds the component and a Component Assets folder to the Library.*

> **TIP**  Flash gives you another way to add a component: In the Components panel, double-click the component. When you do, Flash immediately places an instance of the component on the center of your stage.

In most cases, adding a component to the stage is just part of the process. After you add the component, you still need to customize it and—depending on the component you choose—add ActionScript code to make it work with the other parts of your animation. That's exactly what you'll do in the following steps. In this example, you'll learn how to add buttons to an animation and then use those buttons to control both the main timeline and the timeline of a movie clip that's added to the main timeline.

This project uses a file, *16-1_Button_Component.fla*, that you can download from the Missing CD page (*www.missingmanuals.com/cds/flashcs6mm*). If you'd like to see the completed project, you can download *16-3_Map_Components_done.fla*. The first steps in this example set up the Flash document so it works with Button components and the ActionScript code that makes the buttons work. That involves creating new layers for actions, labels, and buttons.

1. **In Flash, open *16-1_Button_Component.fla*.**

   There's a layer named "words" containing five keyframes. In the last four key-frames are the names of famous cities. There's a second empty layer called "maps." In the Library, there's a folder called "map jpgs" and a movie clip called "Maps."

2. **Click the New Layer button in the lower-left corner of the timeline to add three layers.** From top to bottom, name them *actions, labels,* and *buttons.*

3. **In the labels layer, click Frame 1, and then Shift-click Frame 5.**

   Flash selects all five frames.

4. **With the frames selected, press F6.**

   Empty keyframes are created in each of the frames. You need to have keyframes to create labels in each of the frames.

5. **Add labels to each of the five keyframes by clicking each frame and then typing its name in the Properties→Label→Name box.**

   Name Frame 1 *world*; name Frame 2 *paris*; name Frame 3 *london*; name Frame 4 *moscow*; and name Frame 5 *beijing*. ActionScript uses these labels to find specific frames in the timeline. You won't be using this layer again, so you can go ahead and lock the contents by clicking the button under the padlock.

6. **In the Library, double-click the Maps movie clip.**

   The movie clip opens in Flash.

7. **Drag the playhead to inspect the individual frames in the Maps movie clip, and then click the Scene 1 button.**

   As you move the playhead, each frame shows a different map. The labels in the timeline name the map. When you click the Scene 1 button, the movie clip closes and brings you back to the main timeline.

8. **Click the maps layer in the main timeline, and then drag the Maps movie clip to the stage.**

   The Maps movie clip appears in all five frames of the main timeline because there's only one keyframe in the maps layer.

   You don't have to sweat positioning the movie clip by hand; you can do the job with the Properties panel, as shown in Figure 16-3.

9. **With the Maps movie clip selected, in the Properties panel, type the instance name *maps*.**

   You have to name the instance of the Maps movie clip before you can control it with ActionScript.

Once the Maps movie clip is positioned and named, lock the maps layer so you don't accidentally move it when you're repositioning other elements on the stage.

If you test your animation at this point (Ctrl+Enter or ⌘-Return on a Mac), you'll see the maps and city names flash by rapidly. So far, your steps have set up a sort of slideshow with labels that you can use as bookmarks for your buttons and ActionScript code. In the next steps, you'll add buttons and use ActionScript to control both the main timeline and the Maps movie clip timeline.

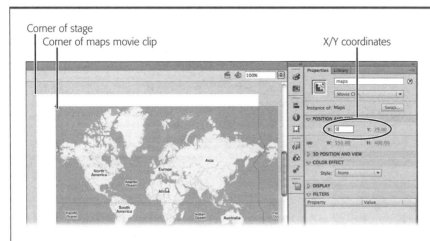

**FIGURE 16-3**

*The Maps movie clip is exactly the same size as the Flash document, 550 x 400 pixels. Here, the Maps movie clip isn't lined up with the stage, but setting the X/Y coordinates in Properties to 0,0 positions it perfectly to cover the entire stage. © 2008 Google Maps*

Corner of stage
Corner of maps movie clip
X/Y coordinates

10. **In the timeline, click the buttons layer.**

You want to place all the new buttons in the buttons layer of the timeline.

11. **Select Window→Components to open the Components panel, and then drag the Button component to the stage.**

The button appears on the stage, and two items appear in the Library: a button symbol and the Component Assets folder.

> **NOTE** When you add your first component to a Flash project, it increases the file size of the published *.swf* file by about 20 to 50 kilobytes. This isn't a whopping leap in file size by today's standards, but it's good to know that if you add more components, they usually won't increase your file size by the same amount. They'll add only a few more kilobytes for each component. That's because most components share a certain amount of underlying code. Once the basic code is added to the .swf file, it's available to any components that need it.

12. **With the button selected, in the Properties panel, type the instance name _btnParis_.**

When you select the button, the Instance Name box is at the top of the Properties panel. As with other symbols, you have to name the Button components before ActionScript can work with them.

**13. Select the button on the stage, and then in the Properties panel, if neces-sary, expand the Component Parameters subpanel.**

The Component Parameters subpanel shows the two parts of each parameter: its name and its value, as shown in Figure 16-4. You customize components for your project by changing the parameter values. Some parameters, like those with true/false values, have checkboxes. Other parameters, like the label parameter for buttons, have text boxes where you can type a new label.

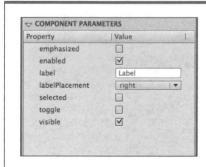

**FIGURE 16-4**

*Use the Component Parameters subpanel to make changes to the component parameters. The names of parameters appear on the left. Use the text boxes, menus, and checkboxes on the right to change the parameters' values.*

**NOTE** In earlier versions of Flash, you used the Components Inspector (Shift-F7) to set component parameters. In Flash Professional 6, those responsibilities appear in the Component Parameters subpanel in the Properties panel. Not a bad move, since it puts all your property and parameter settings in the same neighborhood, and you have one less window cluttering the screen.

**14. Click the text box for the label parameter, and then type *Paris*.**

What you type in this text box changes the word that appears on the button. You don't need to change any of the other parameters right now, but here's a rundown on their uses:

- **emphasized.** If this value is checked, or in programmer-speak *true*, it changes the button's appearance. Use it when you want to make one but-ton stand out from a group of buttons.

- **enabled.** If this value is deselected, the button won't work. It's helpful in situations where you don't want your audience to use a button but you still want it to be visible.

- **labelPlacement.** As it sounds, this parameter gives you several choices for the way a label is positioned: left, right, top, or bottom.

- **selected.** Like "emphasized," this parameter changes the button's appear-ance to show that it's selected.

- **toggle.** If this value is *true*, then the button works like a toggle, and its appearance changes to reflect that.

- **visible.** You can hide a button by deselecting the "visible" parameter.

**NOTE** Components are sometimes called *black boxes* because you can't inspect their inner workings. The only things you can look at or change are the characteristics that the developer *exposes* (lets you access) through the Properties panel, the Component Parameters, or ActionScript classes.

15. **Drag three more buttons from the Library to the stage.** Give them the instance names "btnLondon," "btnMoscow," and "btnBeijing," and then label them "London," "Moscow," and "Beijing."

    As shown in Figure 16-5, you don't have worry too much about how the buttons are arranged. In the next steps, you'll use the Align tool to position them precisely.

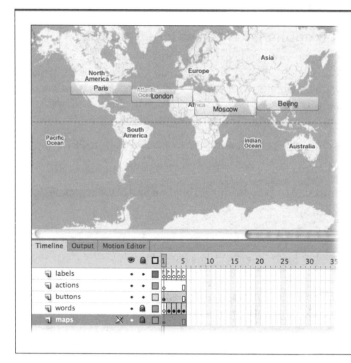

**FIGURE 16-5**

*Arrange the buttons so that they're roughly, end to end, in a left-to-right order: Paris, London, Moscow, and Beijing. Then use Flash's Modify→Align tools to tidy them up. © 2008 Google Maps*

16. **Select all the buttons, and then select Modify→Align→Distribute Widths.**

    The Distribute Widths command evenly lines the buttons up end to end.

17. **Select Modify→Align→To Stage, and then Select Modify→Align→Bottom.**

    A checkmark appears next to To Stage on the menu, meaning that subsequent align commands will be relative to the stage; the Bottom command pushes all the buttons to the bottom of the stage.

18. **Press Ctrl+G (⌘-G) to group the buttons, and then select Modify→Align→ Horizontal Center.**

    This command centers the buttons at the bottom of the stage. You won't be doing anything immediately with single buttons, but you may as well ungroup them now with a Ctrl+Shift+G (⌘-Shift-G).

At this point, you've got everything positioned on the stage and you've labeled all the necessary frames. The only thing that's missing is the ActionScript code that glues it all together. If you test the animation at this point, it's pretty clear what that code needs to do. The first thing it needs to do is stop the movie clips from playing when the animation starts. The second thing the code needs to do is program the buttons to jump to specific frames in the main timeline and the Maps movie clip timeline.

## Making Button Components Work with ActionScript

If you've followed the ActionScript code exercises earlier in this book, chances are you've been introduced to ActionScript 3.0's event listeners. Unlike previous versions, ActionScript 3.0 uses a single method for recognizing and reacting to events. The following example uses event listeners to react to clicks on the Button components. If you need to brush up on using event listeners, see page 448.

1. **In the actions layer, click Frame 1, and then press F9 (Option-F9).**

   The Actions panel opens.

2. **Type the following code to stop the main timeline and the Maps movie clip.**

   ```
   stop();
   maps.stop();
   ```

   The first line stops the main timeline. The second line stops the Maps movie clip from playing.

3. **Type the following code to register an event listener for the Button component with the variable name *btnParis*, as shown in Figure 16-6.**

   ```
   btnParis.addEventListener(MouseEvent.CLICK, clickParisListener);
   ```

   Event listeners come in two parts. This first part registers an event listener. In other words, it tells ActionScript to wait for a mouse click on btnParis. When there's a click, the *clickParisListener()* function runs.

4. **Type the code for the clickParisListener() function:**

   ```
   function clickParisListener(evt:MouseEvent):void
   {
       gotoAndStop("paris");
   ```

```
    maps.gotoAndStop("paris");
}
```

The *clickParisListener()* function has two lines of code that control movie clip timelines. As you might guess, the *gotoAndStop()* method moves to a specific frame and then prevents the playhead from moving beyond that frame. The first line inside the curly brackets moves the playhead on the main timeline to the frame labeled "paris," which displays the word "Paris" on the stage. The second line inside the curly brackets moves the playhead on the Maps movie clip to a frame also labeled "paris." This displays the map of Paris background, as shown in Figure 16-7.

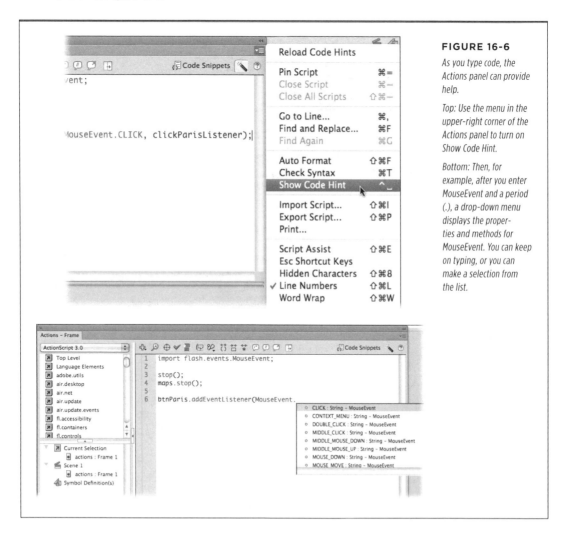

**FIGURE 16-6**

*As you type code, the Actions panel can provide help.*

*Top: Use the menu in the upper-right corner of the Actions panel to turn on Show Code Hint.*

*Bottom: Then, for example, after you enter MouseEvent and a period (.), a drop-down menu displays the properties and methods for MouseEvent. You can keep on typing, or you can make a selection from the list.*

5. **Press Ctrl+Enter (⌘-Return) to test the animation.**

   When the animation runs, it stops on the first frame showing the world map. Click the Paris button, and the word "Paris" appears and the background map changes to a city map of Paris.

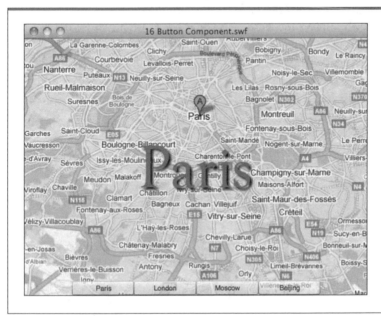

**FIGURE 16-7**

*ActionScript code controls the main timeline, which displays the word "Paris," and the Maps movie clip, which displays the Paris city map background. © 2008 Google Maps*

6. **Add event listeners for the remaining three buttons with the following code.**

   When you're done, the code in Frame 1 in the actions layer should look like this:

```
1    stop();
2    maps.stop();
3
4    btnParis.addEventListener(MouseEvent.CLICK,clickParisListener);
5    btnLondon.addEventListener(MouseEvent.CLICK,clickLondonListener);
6    btnMoscow.addEventListener(MouseEvent.CLICK,clickMoscowListener);
7    btnBeijing.addEventListener(MouseEvent.CLICK,clickBeijingListener);
8
9    function clickParisListener(evt:MouseEvent):void
10   {
11       gotoAndStop("paris");
12       maps.gotoAndStop("paris");
13   }
14   function clickLondonListener(evt:MouseEvent):void
15   {
16       gotoAndStop("london");
17       maps.gotoAndStop("london");
```

```
18  }
19  function clickMoscowListener(evt:MouseEvent):void
20  {
21      gotoAndStop("moscow");
22      maps.gotoAndStop("moscow");
23  }
24  function clickBeijingListener(evt:MouseEvent):void
25  {
26      gotoAndStop("beijing");
27      maps.gotoAndStop("beijing");
28  }
```

7. **Test the animation again.**

When you test the animation, button clicks display the city name and a matching background map.

In this example, it would have been easier to use a single timeline for both the words and the background maps, but the point is to show how buttons or events can control multiple timelines—in this case, the main timeline with the words and the Maps movie clip timeline with the maps.

## Modifying Components in the Properties Panel

There are several ways you can modify components after you've added them to your project. The most straightforward way is to change the properties of the component in the Component Parameters subpanel. Suppose you'd like to make the buttons in the previous example wider, so they run all the way across the bottom of the stage. Select btnParis, and in the Properties panel's "Position and Size" section, click the link button "Lock width and height values together." When the link is broken, you can change width and height independently. Change the width setting to 137.5 (a fourth of the width of the stage). The width of btnParis changes, but all the other properties (position, height, and color) remain the same, as shown in Figure 16-8.

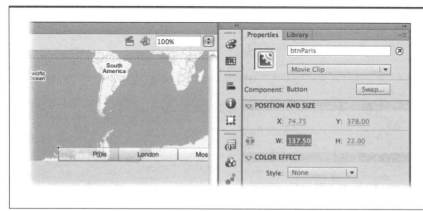

**FIGURE 16-8**

*Changing the properties of an instance of a component changes that single instance. Notice that the other buttons, btnLondon, btnMoscow, and btnBeijing, remain the same width. © 2008 Google Maps*

For this example, go ahead and make all the instances of the Button component the same width: 137.5. Then use the Align commands to align them along the bottom of the stage, so it looks like Figure 16-9.

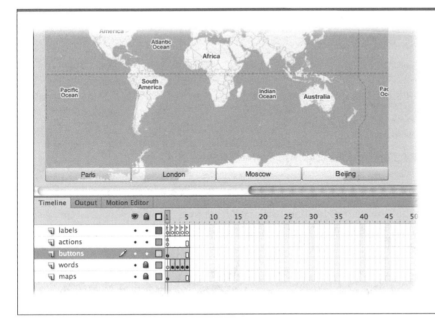

**FIGURE 16-9**

*Using the Properties panel, you can change the properties of the instances on the stage. Here the width of the Button components has been changed. © 2008 Google Maps*

## Adding a ColorPicker Component

One of the great things about Flash components is their consistency. Once you know how to add and customize one component, like the Button component, it's easy to apply that knowledge to other components. For example, the ColorPicker tool appears in an animation as a little color swatch. When your audience clicks the swatch, it displays a palette of colors to choose from, as shown in Figure 16-10. Using this handy tool, you can give your audience the power to change the colors of elements in your animation. Even though components like buttons and color pickers have very different purposes, the steps for adding them to the stage, setting their parameters, and creating event listeners to react to them are very similar.

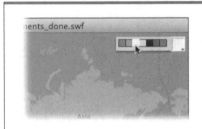

**FIGURE 16-10**

*The ColorPicker is one of those components that's fun for your audience. It gives them a way to customize elements in your animation to suit their own tastes. © 2008 Google Maps*

In this example, you'll add a ColorPicker component to the animation so your audience can choose a background color for the main timeline.

**NOTE** This example continues exercises that started at the beginning of this chapter. If you didn't work on those examples but would like to jump in at this point, download the file *16-2_Color_Picker.fla* from the Missing CD page at *www.missingmanuals.com/cds/flashcs6mm*. To see the final version, get *16-3_Map_Components_done.fla*.

1. **In the timeline, unlock the maps layer.**

   The maps layer is a good place to put the ColorPicker because there are no keyframes. Placing the ColorPicker in the maps layer makes it available in every frame in the animation.

2. **Select Window→Components, and then drag a ColorPicker component on the stage.**

   You can place the ColorPicker anyplace you like, but the upper-right corner is a good spot if you can't decide. In addition to the instance on the stage, a ColorPicker gets added to the Library. If you delve into the Library folder named Component Assets, you find that folders and items specific to the ColorPicker have been added as well.

3. **With the ColorPicker selected, type *cpBackground* in the Properties panel for the instance name.**

   It's good to identify object types as you create instance names. In this case *cp* is used to identify the object as a ColorPicker. Background indicates what the ColorPicker is changing.

4. **Press F9 (Option-F9) to open the Actions window, and then type the following code to import the ColorPickerEvent.**

   ```
   import fl.events.ColorPickerEvent;
   ```

   When you create documents with Flash, you automatically have access to the most commonly used ActionScript classes, like the MovieClip class, the Shape class, and so on. The ColorPickerEvent isn't included, so you need to import the packages that define those classes. If you try to run your program without importing the package, you see an error that says "Error 1046: Type was not found...".

5. **Continue your code by registering an event listener for the ColorPicker and a function that runs when the ColorPicker changes:**

   ```
   cpBackground.addEventListener(ColorPickerEvent.CHANGE,changeColorPicker);

   function changeColorPicker(evt:ColorPickerEvent):void
   {
           opaqueBackground = evt.color;
   }
   ```

This code follows the standard event listener format. One statement registers the event listener for an object, and the function explains what to do when the event happens. If you're already familiar with event listeners, the juicy bit of this example is the line that says *opaqueBackground = evt.color;*. This line changes the background color of the main timeline. The opaqueBackground property is inherited by all DisplayObjects. The ColorPicker event has a property, appropriately called *color*, that holds the value of the color that was selected. (If you need to brush up on events and event handling, see page 448.)

6. **With the ColorPicker selected, in the Component Parameters, change the selectedColor and the showTextField parameters.**

    At first the selectedColor parameter is set to *black*. If you want folks to notice that they can change the color, it's best to set this to something more colorful. Note that this command changes only the color displayed in the ColorPicker. It doesn't actually change the background color at this point; that's done by the code within the event listener.

    The showTextField parameter gives the audience a text box where they can type a color's hexadecimal value. You can assume that your audience would rather click a color swatch, so set this parameter to *false*.

7. **Select the Maps movie clip on the stage, and then select Properties→Color Effect→Alpha and type *50*.**

    The Maps movie clip becomes semi-transparent, letting the background color show through, as explained in Figure 16-11.

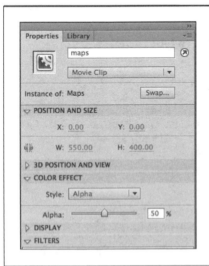

**FIGURE 16-11**

*The background color won't show through if there's a completely opaque movie clip covering the stage. Setting the movie clip's alpha value to 50% lets the background color show through, giving the image on top a pleasing color effect.*

8. **Press Ctrl+Enter (⌘-Return) to test the animation.**

When the animation first runs, there's no background color, since the code that sets the background color is inside the ColorPicker event. The color changes when you select a new color in the ColorPicker. If you use the buttons to jump from city to city, the background color remains constant until a new color is selected.

As this example shows, the steps for putting the ColorPicker component into action are similar to those for using the Button component. Adding an instance of the component to the stage, creating an event listener, and changing the component parameters are much the same. The only differences are related to the components' purpose and behavior.

■ **MODIFYING THE COLORPICKER WITH ACTIONSCRIPT**

Components have properties just like any other objects. When you change the parameters of a component, you're changing properties that the author of the component has made available to designers. (Other component properties are hidden, where you can't mess with them.) You can change those properties using ActionScript, too. Specifically, you can change a component's properties while an animation is running, or as coders like to say, "You can change the properties at runtime."

Here's an example that changes the ColorPicker using ActionScript code. The ColorPicker's palette shows bunches of colors, many of them very similar. There may be times when you don't want to offer so many color choices. For example, if you're letting customers choose the color for their new Stutz Bearcat automobile, you may offer only a handful of color options. Using ActionScript, you can specify each color shown on the palette, as long as you know the hexadecimal code that identifies the color.

Add this to the code for your ColorPicker project (step 5 on page 555). You can place it following the line that begins with the word "import":

```
cpBackground.colors =
[0xFF0000,0xFF7700,0xFFFF00,0x00FF00,0x000044,0x0000FF,0x0066FF];
```

The colors property of the ColorPicker is an array. The values held inside an array are enclosed in square brackets and separated by commas. The odd-looking numbers, like 0xFF7700, are hexadecimal values. Now, when you test the animation, the ColorPicker shows a palette of only seven colors, as shown in Figure 16-10.

---

**TIP** Use Flash's color panel (Window→Color) to look up the hexadecimal numbers for the colors you need. Select a color, and the hexadecimal value appears in the text box, as shown in Figure 16-12. Replace the # with ActionScript's identifier for hex values, *0x*.

---

You can use similar code to change the properties of the ColorPicker (or other components). In step 6 on page 556, you used the Component Parameters subpanel to change the ColorPicker's showTextField property. To change that setting using ActionScript, use a statement like this:

```
cpBackground.showTextField = false;
```

**FIGURE 16-12**

*Drag the crosshairs to choose a hue, and then adjust the brightness of the color using the vertical slider on the right. When you're happy with the color previewed at the bottom, select and copy the hexadecimal number that appears in the box. To use the number in ActionScript, replace the # with 0x (ActionScript's identifier for hex values).*

## ■ The Built-In Components

Choose Window→Components, and you see a panel full of built-in components that you can drag and drop into your Flash document. Well, it's almost that easy. You see different components depending on whether your document is based in ActionScript 2.0 or ActionScript 3.0. Like any ActionScript code, you can't mix version 2.0 components and version 3.0 components in the same document. This forward-looking chapter focuses on the ActionScript 3.0 components. The ActionScript 3.0 built-in components fall into three main categories:

- **Flex components.** Flex is a programming tool that, like Flash Professional, creates applications using ActionScript and SWF files. Also, like Flash, Flex programs can make use of prebuilt components, which are saved in SWC files.

- **User interface components.** Similar to HTML components, Flash user interface components include buttons, checkboxes, lists, text fields, and windows—everything you need to create a Flash form and collect data from your audience.

- **Video components.** These components give you tools to work with video clips. For example, they work with streaming video (where a movie begins to play before the entire file is downloaded). These components are an indication of Flash's growing role as a tool to provide web-based video.

**NOTE** This chapter focuses on the user interface components, because they're by far the most popular Flash components. For an introduction to the video components, see page 403.

## User Interface Components

Similar to HTML form components, Flash's popular *user interface components* (Figure 16-1) let you interact with your audience, display information, and gather information. Examples of user interface components include buttons, checkboxes, text fields, and drop-down lists. In this section, you'll find details about ActionScript 3.0 user interface components. For each component, there's a Component Parameters subpanel that lets you tweak the component. If you use components a lot, some of the parameters will become very familiar, because they work with several different components. Other parameters are specific to the purpose of a particular component, and you may need to refer to this section for the full explanation. See the box on page 560.

**NOTE** There's a companion file for this section, *16-4_Component_Index.zip*. You can see it in Figure 16-13, and download it from the Missing CD page (*www.missingmanuals.com/cds/flashcs6mm*). The ZIP-compressed file holds a Flash document and some other assets used to demonstrate the various user interface components. Test the document with Ctrl+Enter (⌘-Return), and you'll see buttons for each component, as shown in Figure 16-13. Click a button to see a component in action. Want to see the ActionScript code behind the component? Click the frame code button, and you'll find the code with lots of explanatory comments. Use the button at the bottom of the window to return to the main index.

frame code button

**FIGURE 16-13**

*There's a lot to learn about components—more than can fit in the pages of this chapter. Working examples can be a big help, so there's a companion file for this section, download it from the Missing CD page (www.missingmanuals.com/cds/flashcs6mm). For each component example, you can see the underlying ActionScript code. Just click the "frame code" button.*

## ■ BUTTON

The Button component hardly needs introduction. It's a multipurpose component you can use to receive input from your animation's audience. The process of using a Button component is covered in detail beginning on page 545, and you see an example of the clickable Button component in Figure 16-14.

**FIGURE 16-14**

*Similar to HTML buttons, Button components are straightforward, no-nonsense, clickable buttons you hook up to ActionScript. For example, you can customize a Button component's label to read Add Text or Clear, as shown here, and then write the code necessary to carry out those tasks.*

---

**UP TO SPEED**

### Learning the Parameters

Back in the days when you used the Component Inspector to set parameters, you had type in the proper words for a parameter. Words like *true, false, left, right, top,* and *bottom.* The problem was, it wasn't always obvious what word the component expected. That meant you had to look up the component in the Flash docs or your handy Missing Manual. In Flash CS6 Professional, component parameters are friendlier.

Now, with the Component Parameters subpanel, you use checkboxes for true and false values. If you have a positioning choice, such as left, right, top, or bottom, they're presented in a handy drop-down menu. If a color is expected, you can choose it from a panel of color swatches. Hooray for progress and helpful widgets!

---

You may be wondering when it's best to use a Button component and when it's best to use Flash's button symbol from the Common Libraries. If you're into customizing a button with, say, animations and other snazzy effects, then go for the button symbol from the Common Libraries or design your own button symbol. The symbol gives you a movie clip timeline where you can do your magic—for all the details, see page 546. The Button component is a predesigned button that you don't have to fiddle with too much to make it useful. The button is a good alternative if you're using other components, because they'll all have a similar look. As you see in the Button Parameters table (Table 16-1), one handy built-in feature of the Button component is the *toggle* parameter. When you set this parameter to "true," the button displays on/off characteristics. Clicking the button turns it on, and the button stays down. Click it again, and it pops back up into position.

Table 16-1. Parameters for the Button component.

| BUTTON PARAMETERS | EXPECTED VALUE | PURPOSE |
|---|---|---|
| emphasized | selected or deselected | Changes appearance of button to stand out from other buttons. |
| enabled | selected or deselected | If deselected, the button doesn't accept audience input. |
| label | a string of characters | Explanatory text label for button. |
| labelPlacement | left, right, top, bottom | Positions label relative to button. |
| selected | selected or deselected | Changes appearance of a toggle button to show it's selected. |
| toggle | selected or deselected | Gives the button on/off functions. |
| visible | selected or deselected | If deselected, the component is hidden. |

## ◼ CHECKBOX

The checkbox is another familiar friend to anyone who has completed an online survey or filled out a questionnaire. The CheckBox component lets you offer your audience an easy way to choose multiple options, as shown in Figure 16-15. With checkboxes, folks can make several selections in a group of options. If you want to limit your audience to a single choice, use the RadioButton component. Checkboxes are common in computer programs, on the Web, and in print, so your audience will easily understand how to use them. You can customize the CheckBox component at design time using the following parameters (Table 16-2). For example, if you check the *selected* parameter in the Component Parameters subpanel, a checkmark appears in the checkbox when your animation first runs.

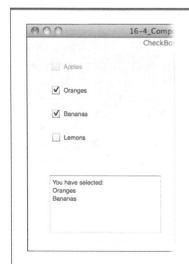

**FIGURE 16-15**

*Unlike RadioButton components (page 571), CheckBox components let your audience make multiple selections.*

**NOTE** For ActionScript coders, there are two distinct categories for time: *design time* and *runtime*. Design time is where you are now, when you have Flash open on your computer and you can control events, drawings, and all details in Flash. Runtime is when your Flash project is out there in the world, where your audience is viewing it and controlling it.

Using ActionScript, you can change components' properties while the animation is running. For example, examine the following code, which could appear at any time within your animation:

```
cbApples.enabled = false;
cbOranges.visible = false;
cbBananas.selected = true;
```

This code turns off the CheckBox *cbApples*, making it appear grayed out and un-clickable. The CheckBox *cbOranges* is hidden entirely, and *cbBananas* is selected, so it sports a handsome checkmark.

*Table 16-2. Parameters for the CheckBox component.*

| CHECKBOX PARAMETERS | EXPECTED VALUE | PURPOSE |
| --- | --- | --- |
| enabled | selected or deselected | If deselected, CheckBox doesn't accept audience input. |
| label | a string of characters | Explanatory text for CheckBox. |
| labelPlacement | left, right, top, bottom | Positions label relative to component. |
| selected | selected or deselected | Makes a checkmark appear in the checkbox. |
| visible | selected or deselected | If deselected, the component is hidden. |

### ■ COLORPICKER

The ColorPicker component (shown in Figure 16-16) displays a palette of colors, giving your audience an opportunity to select a single color. You can give your audience a way to customize, text, background colors, and just about any other elements in the display. For example, suppose you're selling laptop computer cases. You can limit the colors shown in the ColorPicker to just those you have available. (You can learn how to use the ColorPicker tool in detail on page 557.) Select ColorPicker, and in the Component Parameters subpanel, you see the parameters shown in the following table (Table 16-3).

Table 16-3. Parameters for the ColorPicker component.

| COLORPICKER PARAMETERS | EXPECTED VALUE | PURPOSE |
|---|---|---|
| enabled | selected or deselected | If deselected, ColorPicker doesn't respond when clicked. |
| selectedColor | hexadecimal color value | The currently selected color that's displayed when the palette is closed. ActionScript code can work with the hexadecimal value of this color. |
| showTextField | selected or deselected | If selected, a text field displays the hexadecimal value of the selectedColor parameter, and your visitors can type a new hexadecimal value. |
| visible | selected or deselected | If deselected, the component is hidden. |

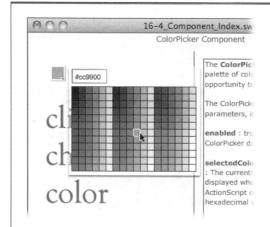

**FIGURE 16-16**

*The ColorPicker component makes it easy for your audience to select a single color from an entire palette of options. Using ActionScript code, you can limit the colors shown in the palette.*

### ■ COMBOBOX

As Figure 16-17 shows, the ComboBox component lets you display a drop-down list of options. Use this component when you want to offer people an easy way to choose a single option (like which animation they want to play, or which web page they want to hop to) from a predefined list. You can customize the ComboBox component at design time using the Component Parameters subpanel to change the parameter values (Table 16-4). Flash automatically adds a scroll bar to your ComboBox component if you create a long list (over five options). Short list or long, the ComboBox component lets your audience choose only one option. If you want to offer people a list from which they can Shift-click or Ctrl-click multiple options, use the List component (page 567). The ComboBox uses a DataProvider as the source for its list. You can point to an external file or create the DataProvider in ActionScript within your document. For more details, see the box on page 566.

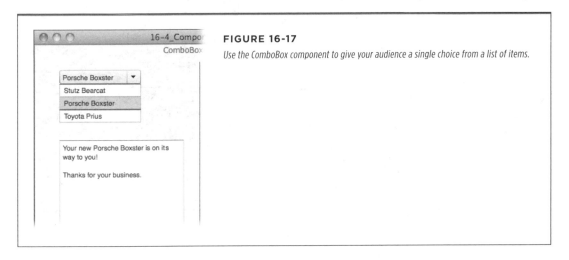

**FIGURE 16-17**

*Use the ComboBox component to give your audience a single choice from a list of items.*

*Table 16-4. Parameters for the ComboBox component.*

| COMBOBOX PARAMETERS | EXPECTED VALUE | PURPOSE |
|---|---|---|
| dataProvider | a DataProvider object (for more details, see the box on page 566) | Points to a data source to provide the items in the list. The DataProvider object can come from an external source, or you can create one using ActionScript code. You can also manually add values by clicking the Value box in the Component Inspector. |
| editable | selected or deselected | If deselected, your audience can't make changes to the ComboBox. |
| enabled | selected or deselected | If deselected, your audience can't use the ComboBox. |
| prompt | a string of characters | The words that appear before your visitor uses the ComboBox. |
| restrict | a string of characters | Limits the characters that a visitor can enter in the text field. |
| rowCount | a number value | Sets the number of items displayed in the list. If the list has more items, a scroll bar appears. If the list has fewer items, the list is sized to fit. |
| visible | selected or deselected | If deselected, the component is hidden. |

## ■ DATAGRID

The DataGrid component lets you display a table containing multiple rows and columns of data, similar to a spreadsheet, as shown in Figure 16-18. DataGrid parameters are listed in Table 16-5.

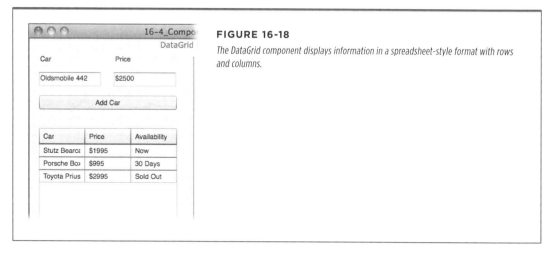

**FIGURE 16-18**

*The DataGrid component displays information in a spreadsheet-style format with rows and columns.*

Table 16-5. Parameters for the DataGrid component.

| DATAGRID PARAMETERS | EXPECTED VALUE | PURPOSE |
| --- | --- | --- |
| allowMultipleSelection | selected or deselected | If selected, allows the selection of more than one list item in the data grid. |
| editable | selected or deselected | If deselected, your audience can't change the DataGrid. |
| headerHeight | a number value | Sets header height in pixels. |
| horizontalLineScrollSize | a number value | The amount of content to be scrolled, horizontally, when your audience clicks a scroll arrow. |
| horizontalPageScrollSize | a number value | The number of pixels the scroll marker moves when your audience clicks the scroll bar track. Similar to a Page Up or Page Down command. |
| horizontalScrollPolicy | ON, OFF, AUTO | Controls whether a scroll bar appears in the component. |
| resizableColumns | selected or deselected | If deselected, your audience can't change column widths. |
| rowHeight | a number value | Sets the height of the rows in pixels. |

| DATAGRID PARAMETERS | EXPECTED VALUE | PURPOSE |
| --- | --- | --- |
| showHeaders | selected or deselected | If deselected, the DataGrid doesn't display headers. |
| sortableColumns | selected or deselected | If deselected, your audience can't sort the data in the columns. |
| verticalLineScrollSize | a number value | The amount of content to be scrolled, vertically, when a scroll arrow is clicked. |
| verticalPageScrollSize | a number value | The number of pixels the scroll marker moves when your audience clicks the scroll bar track. Similar to a page up or page down command. |
| verticalScrollPolicy | ON, OFF, AUTO | Controls whether a scroll bar appears in the component. |

**FREQUENTLY ASKED QUESTION**

## Providing Data

*What's a DataProvider?*

Several Flash components—notably List, DataGrid, TileList, and ComboBox—use DataProvider objects to fill in the blanks. The DataProvider class is like any other ActionScript class; it has properties and methods, all of which relate to storing and retrieving data. You can use methods like AddItem and AddItemAt to fill a DataProvider with a list of items. When it's time to use a component, you can assign your prefilled DataProvider to the dataProvider parameter (or property) of a component. For example, here's the code that adds fine wines to a DataProvider named wineList:

```
wineList.addItem({label:"Chateau Thames
Embankment", data:24});


wineList.addItem({label:"Domaine Dogtown
Reserve", data:18});


wineList.addItem({label:"Cuvee Cuyahoga",
data:21});
```

In this example, each item consists of two parts: label and data. Label stores a text string representing the name of the wine, while data stores a number value representing the wine's quality rating. (Yes, that's 24 out of a possible 100.) If you're familiar with XML, the paired format consisting of a name and a value may look familiar.

In this format, you can add the items to a List component. The List component expects to receive a name and a data element for each item. To make these fine wines appear in a list component, you assign the *wineList* DataProvider to the *lstFineWine* List component:

```
lstFineWine.dataProvider = wineList;
```

The DataProvider is one more way that Flash Components achieve consistency even though their purposes and functions are different.

Typically, you use this component when you want to transfer data from your server (for example, product names, descriptions, and prices) and display it in Flash in table form. But you can also use it to display the data you collect (or create) in your Flash animation. You can populate the cells in the data grid from an external source, or you can create a DataProvider and store values in it, using ActionScript (see the box on page 566).

## ■ LABEL

A Label component lets you add noneditable, nonclickable text to your Flash creation. To use the Label component, add the text you want displayed to the *text* parameter in the Component Inspector. If you're using ActionScript code, then assign a string to the *text* property of the label (Table 16-6). As an alternative, you can display HTML-encoded text using the *htmlText* parameter or property.

> **TIP** For most Flash designers, using Flash's Text tool is easier and keeps .swf files smaller. Even if you want to change text during runtime with ActionScript, you can do that with a text field.

*Table 16-6. Parameters for the Label component.*

| PARAMETERS | EXPECTED VALUE | PURPOSE |
| --- | --- | --- |
| autoSize | selected or deselected | If selected, the label shows all of its text, regardless of the W and H properties. |
| condenseWhite | selected or deselected | When selected, this removes extra white space from HTML text. |
| enabled | selected or deselected | If deselected, your audience can't access the component. |
| htmlText | HTML-encoded text | Displays HTML encoded text, showing formatting, hyperlinks, and other features. |
| selectable | selected or deselected | If checked, your audience can select the text in a label. |
| text | a string of characters | The text shown in the display. |
| visible | selected or deselected | If deselected, the component is hidden. |
| wordWrap | selected or deselected | Controls line breaks in large chunks of text. |

## ■ LIST

You use the List component (Figure 16-19) to create a clickable, scrollable list from which your audience can Shift-click to select multiple options. The List uses a DataProvider as the source. You can point to an external file, or you can create the DataProvider in ActionScript within your document. For more details, see the box on page 566. The items that make up each row in a list consist of a label and data. The label appears in the list display; the data is the part that's invisible to your audience but accessible to ActionScript. So, for example, you can create a list where someone can choose an employee by name; that selection can then pass the employee's ID number to another part of your program.

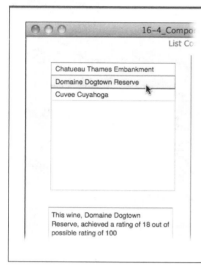

**FIGURE 16-19**

*The List component is similar to multiple checkboxes (see page 561) in that both let your audience select multiple options (once you customize the List component by setting allowMultipleSelection to true in the Component Parameters, Table 16-7). But because List components are scrollable, they tend to take up less screen real estate than checkboxes, and so they're helpful when your stage is already packed with graphics and other components.*

*Table 16-7. Parameters for the List component.*

| LIST PARAMETERS | EXPECTED VALUE | PURPOSE |
|---|---|---|
| allowMultipleSelection | selected or deselected | If deselected, your audience can select only one item from the list at a time. |
| dataProvider | a DataProvider object (for more details see the box on page 566) | Points to a data source to provide the items in the list. The DataProvider object can be an external source, or you can create one using ActionScript. |
| enabled | selected or deselected | If deselected, your audience can't use the List component. |
| horizontalLineScrollSize | a number value | The amount of content to be scrolled, horizontally, when your audience clicks a scroll arrow. |
| horizontalPageScrollSize | a number value | The number of pixels the scroll marker moves when your audience clicks the scroll bar track. Similar to a Page Up or Page Down command. |
| horizontalScrollPolicy | ON, OFF, AUTO | Controls whether a scroll bar appears in the component. |
| verticalLineScrollSize | a number value | The amount of content to be scrolled, vertically, when a scroll arrow is clicked. |

| LIST PARAMETERS | EXPECTED VALUE | PURPOSE |
| --- | --- | --- |
| verticalPageScrollSize | a number value | The number of pixels the scroll marker moves when your audience clicks the scroll bar track. Similar to a Page Up or Page Down command. |
| verticalScrollPolicy | ON, OFF, AUTO | Controls whether a scroll bar appears in the component. |
| visible | selected or deselected | If deselected, the component is hidden. |

### ■ NUMERICSTEPPER

You use the NumericStepper component to create a clickable list of numbers, as shown in Figure 16-20. Simpler for people to use than a type-in-your-own-number text field, this component makes it easy for you to limit your audience's choices to a predefined set of valid numbers. See Table 16-8 for the parameters used with the NumericStepper component.

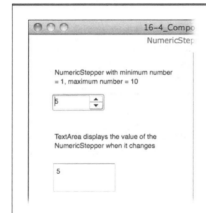

**FIGURE 16-20**

*When you use the NumericStepper component, your audience gets an easy way to specify a number, and you don't have to use ActionScript to examine the number and see whether it's valid (as you would have to if you let them type any number they want).*

*Table 16-8. Parameters for the NumericStepper component.*

| PARAMETERS | EXPECTED VALUE | PURPOSE |
| --- | --- | --- |
| enabled | selected or deselected | If deselected, your audience can't use the component. |
| maximum | a number value | Sets the highest number the component can display. |
| minimum | a number value | Sets the lowest number the component can display. |

| PARAMETERS | EXPECTED VALUE | PURPOSE |
|---|---|---|
| stepSize | a number value | Sets the amount the value changes with each click. |
| value | a number value | The current value selected by the NumericStepper. |
| visible | selected or deselected | If deselected, the component is hidden. |

### ■ PROGRESSBAR

The ProgressBar component, shown in Figure 16-21, is a visual indicator that a file—like a Flash .swf file—is loading. There are two ways a ProgressBar can work. If you're loading a file and have no way of knowing how big the file is, then you can't very well say the file is, for example, 50 percent loaded. In that case, the progress bar is considered *indeterminate*. In other words, it provides some motion, kind of like a barber's pole, to show that something's going on. On the other hand, if you know how big the file is, you can give your audience more detail on the process. You've probably seen the ProgressBar in action when Flash animations are loading from web pages. To have the ProgressBar report on the progress of loading a file, type the name and path of the file in the *source* parameter (Table 16-9). In ActionScript, you assign the name to the source property of the ProgressBar. You can also use ActionScript to access the percentComplete property, giving you a way to create a companion line of text.

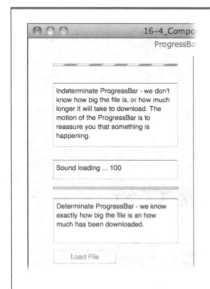

**FIGURE 16-21**

*The ProgressBar component lets you give your audience a visual indication of how long they have left to wait for an animation (or a web page) to load.*

*Table 16-9. Parameters for the ProgressBar component.*

| PARAMETERS | EXPECTED VALUE | PURPOSE |
| --- | --- | --- |
| direction | left or right | Sets whether the bar fills from the left or from the right. |
| enabled | selected or deselected | If deselected, your audience can't access the component. |
| mode | event, polled, manual, | Selects different methods for providing progress information. Event and polled are the most common modes. |
| source | an object that's being loaded; for example, a Loader instance | Sets the source for the object that's being loaded. |
| visible | selected or deselected | If deselected, the component is hidden. |

### ■ RADIOBUTTON

When you want to make sure your audience chooses just one of several mutually exclusive options, use a group of RadioButton components (Figure 16-22). Radio buttons are frequently used in programs and on the Internet, so it's likely your audience will be familiar with them. See Table 16-10 for a list of parameters to use with the RadioButton component.

**FIGURE 16-22**

*RadioButton components let you offer your audience mutually exclusive options, so you always use RadioButton components in groups of two or more. (If you think you want a single radio button, you probably want to use a checkbox.) Turning on one radio button tells Flash to turn off all the other radio buttons with the same groupName.*

*Table 16-10. Radiobutton parameters.*

| RADIOBUTTON PARAMETERS | EXPECTED VALUE | PURPOSE |
| --- | --- | --- |
| enabled | selected or deselected | If deselected, your audience can't use the component. |
| groupName | RadioButtonGroup | Identifies the group of buttons from which your audience can make a single selection. |

| RADIOBUTTON PARAMETERS | EXPECTED VALUE | PURPOSE |
|---|---|---|
| label | a string of characters | Explanatory text for the RadioButton component. |
| labelPlacement | left, right, top, bottom | Positions the label relative to the button. |
| selected | selected or deselected | Changes the appearance of the RadioButton to show it's checked. |
| value | An object like a string or a number | Defines the values represented by radio buttons. |
| visible | selected or deselected | If deselected, the component is hidden. |

### ■ SCROLLPANE

The ScrollPane component helps you include an image that's too big to fit into your animation. Think about some of those map programs that let you move a map image inside a frame. You can let your audience position an image using scroll bars or by dragging in the image. Figure 16-23 shows you the ScrollPane in action, and Table 16-11 lists the multitude of parameters you find in the Component Inspector. There are two parameters for each type of scroll bar: horizontal and vertical. These parameters determine how far the window scrolls when you click the scroll bar's arrows and when you click the body or track of the scroll bar. A ScrollPolicy lets you define scrolling behavior and assign that behavior to many objects and components. The ScrollPolicy settings can get a little involved, but in most cases, you can leave *horizontalScrollPolicy* and *verticalScrollPolicy* set to AUTO without adverse effects.

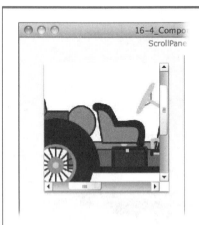

**FIGURE 16-23**

*When you display an animation or image using the ScrollPane component, Flash automatically tacks on scroll bars that people can use to choose which part of the animation they want to see through the window.*

*Table 16-11. Parameters for the ScrollPane component.*

| SCROLLPANE PARAMETERS | EXPECTED VALUE | PURPOSE |
|---|---|---|
| enabled | selected or deselected | If deselected, your audience can't use the component. |
| horizontalLineScrollSize | a number value | The amount of content to be scrolled, horizontally, when your audience clicks a scroll arrow. |
| horizontalPageScrollSize | a number value | The number of pixels by which to move the scroll marker on the horizontal scroll bar when your audience clicks the scroll bar track. |
| horizontalScrollPolicy | ON, OFF, AUTO | Controls whether a scroll bar appears in the component. |
| scrollDrag | selected or deselected | If selected, your audience can drag an image within the ScrollPane. |
| source | name and path to the file to be displayed; this can be an Internet address | Sets the source for the file to be displayed in the ScrollPane. |
| verticalLineScrollSize | a number value | The amount of content to be scrolled, vertically, when your audience clicks a scroll arrow. |
| verticalPageScrollSize | a number value | The number of pixels by which to move the scroll marker on the vertical scroll bar when your audience clicks the scroll bar track. |
| verticalScrollPolicy | ON, OFF, AUTO | Controls whether a scroll bar appears in the component. |
| visible | selected or deselected | If deselected, the component is hidden. |

## ■ SLIDER

The Slider component gives your audience an easy way to select a value. Better still, it helps you prevent them from choosing a useless value. (Ever had someone type his name into a box where you expected a number?) Sliders are a natural for controlling volume or sizing an image, and there are lots of creative ways to use them. Use the maximum and minimum parameters to set the range (Table 16-12). Use the *snapInterval* parameter to count by fives or twos if you want. The *tickInterval* parameter refers to a visual scale that appears above the slider, as shown in Figure 16-24.

Table 16-12. Parameters for the Slider component.

| SLIDER PARAMETERS | EXPECTED VALUE | PURPOSE |
| --- | --- | --- |
| direction | horizontal or vertical | Sets the Slider's orientation. |
| enabled | selected or deselected | If deselected, your audience can't access the component. |
| liveDragging | selected or deselected | If selected, lets your audience drag to change the Slider's value. If you deselect the parameter, it's up to you to move the Slider through ActionScript to display a value. |
| maximum | a number value | The high number on the Slider's scale. |
| minimum | a number value | The low number on the Slider's scale. |
| snapInterval | a number value | Sets the precision available on the Slider's scale. |
| tickInterval | a number value | Shows visual tick marks above the Slider. |
| value | a number value | The value represented by the Slider's position. |
| visible | selected or deselected | If deselected, the component is hidden. |

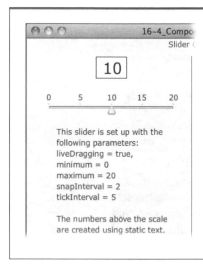

**FIGURE 16-24**

*The slider component doesn't automatically provide numbers for its scale. Here the numbers were added using Flash text.*

### ▓ TEXTAREA

The TextArea component (Figure 16-25) is an all-purpose, multiline, scrollable text field that's useful for presenting text to your audience. It's also useful when you want your audience to be able to type a long comment, or any other information longer than a few words. You can modify the text property through ActionScript, which means you can change the text that appears in a text field while your animation is running. (See Table 16-13 for a list of TextArea parameters.)

*Table 16-13. Parameters for the TextArea component.*

| TEXTAREA PARAMETERS | EXPECTED VALUE | PURPOSE |
|---|---|---|
| condenseWhite | selected or deselected | When selected, removes extra white space from HTML text. |
| editable | selected or deselected | If deselected, your audience can't make changes to the component. |
| enabled | selected or deselected | If deselected, your audience can't access the component. |
| horizontalScroll-Policy | ON, OFF, AUTO | Controls whether a scroll bar appears in the component. |
| htmlText | HTML-encoded text | Displays HTML encoded text, showing formatting, hyperlinks, and other features. |
| maxChars | a number value | Limits the number of characters that the TextArea component can contain. The setting 0 means there's no limit. |
| restrict | a string of characters | Lets you specify which characters your audience can type into the TextArea component. For example, you can limit input to the numbers 0–9 if you expect a phone number. |
| text | a string of characters | The text to be displayed in the TextArea. |
| verticalScrollPolicy | ON, OFF, AUTO | Controls whether a scroll bar appears in the component. |
| visible | selected or deselected | If deselected, the component is hidden. |
| wordWrap | selected or deselected | Controls line breaks in large chunks of text. |

**FIGURE 16-25**

*The TextArea and TextInput components both let your audience type text, but the TextArea component (shown here) lets them type multiple lines of text. Flash automatically adds scrollbars if someone types in more text than the TextArea component's dimensions can display.*

### ■ TEXTINPUT

The TextInput component lets you create a single-line text field, used mostly as a field in a form. (See Table 16-14 for the list of TextInput parameters.) Using this component lets you give your audience a free-form text field just long enough to type what you want them to type (for example, a name, phone number, or email address).

*Table 16-14. Parameters for the TextInput component.*

| TEXTINPUT PARAMETERS | EXPECTED VALUE | PURPOSE |
|---|---|---|
| displayAsPassword | selected or deselected | When selected, disguises the actual characters in the display. |
| editable | selected or deselected | If deselected, your audience can't change the text. |
| enabled | selected or deselected | If deselected, the component can't be accessed by the audience. |
| maxChars | a number value | Limits the number of characters that can be contained in a TextInput component. If it's set to 0, then there's no limit. |
| restrict | a string of characters | Used to limit the characters that can be typed into the TextInput component; for example, you can limit input to numbers if you expect a phone number. |
| text | a string of characters | The text shown on the display. |
| visible | selected or deselected | If deselected, the component is hidden. |

### ■ TILELIST

The TileList is used to display several images in a grid (Figure 16-26). For example, you may want to show several thumbnail images in a row. When your audience clicks a thumbnail, a larger version of the image is displayed (See Table 16-15).

*Table 16-15. Parameters for the TileList component.*

| TILELIST PARAMETERS | EXPECTED VALUE | PURPOSE |
|---|---|---|
| allowMultipleSelection | selected or deselected | If selected, your audience can select more than one image. |
| columnCount | a number value | Sets the number of columns in the grid. |
| columnWidth | a number value | Sets the width of the columns in pixels. |
| dataProvider | a DataProvider object (for more details, see the box on page 566) | Points to a data source to provide the items in the list. The DataProvider object can come from an external source, or you can create one using ActionScript code. |
| direction | horizontal or vertical | Sets whether the TileList scrolls horizontally or vertically. |

| TILELIST PARAMETERS | EXPECTED VALUE | PURPOSE |
|---|---|---|
| enabled | selected or deselected | If deselected, your audience can't use the component. |
| horizontalLineScrollSize | a number value | The amount of content to be scrolled, horizontally, when your audience clicks a scroll arrow. |
| horizontalPageScrollSize | a number value | The number of pixels by which to move the scroll marker on the horizontal scroll bar when your audience clicks the scroll bar track. |
| rowCount | a number value | Sets the number of rows in the grid. |
| rowHeight | a number value | Sets the height of the rows in pixels. |
| scrollPolicy | ON, OFF, AUTO | Controls whether a scroll bar appears in the component. |
| verticalLineScrollSize | a number value | The amount of content to be scrolled, vertically, when your audience clicks a scroll arrow. |
| verticalPageScrollSize | a number value | The number of pixels by which to move the scroll marker on the vertical scroll bar when your audience clicks the scroll bar track. |
| visible | selected or deselected | If deselected, the component is hidden. |

**FIGURE 16-26**

*Usually TileList components are filled with images and captions. In honor of this chapter's topic, this TileList is filled with images of other components.*

### ■ UILOADER

Think of the UILoader (user interface loader) as a container for images (.jpg, .gif, and .png) and Flash animations (.swf) that are outside of your Flash application. You provide the name and path of the file you want to load into the source parameter (Table 16-16). If you're ActionScripting, you can assign the name to the *source* property of the UILoader. Through ActionScript, you can also access the *percentLoaded* property.

*Table 16-16. Parameters for the UILoader component.*

| UILOADER PARAMETERS | EXPECTED VALUE | PURPOSE |
|---|---|---|
| autoLoad | selected or deselected | If deselected, the UILoader waits until it receives a *load()* statement. |
| enabled | selected or deselected | If deselected, your audience can't access the component. |
| maintainAspectRatio | selected or deselected | Determines whether an image maintains its proportions; usually left set to true. |
| scaleContent | selected or deselected | If selected, the UILoader automatically scales the image to fit the loader's dimensions. |
| source | name and path to the file to be displayed; this can be an Internet address | Sets the source for the file to be loaded. |
| visible | selected or deselected | If deselected, the component is hidden. |

### ■ UISCROLLBAR

The UIScrollBar component is a fancy, color-customizable scrollbar you can add to a TextField or TextArea field to make your text fields match your overall color scheme (see Table 16-17 for parameters).

*Table 16-17. Parameters for the UIScroller component.*

| UISCROLLBAR PARAMETERS | EXPECTED VALUE | PURPOSE |
|---|---|---|
| direction | horizontal or vertical | Sets the orientation of the scroll bar. |
| scrollTargetName | instance name of a textArea or textInput component | Identifies the text field to be scrolled. |
| visible | selected or deselected | If deselected, the component is hidden. |

# Finding Additional Components

In addition to the components that ship with Flash, you can also find components on the Web (try searching for "Flash components" using your favorite search engine).

Below are a few of the most popular sources for Flash components as this book goes to press:

- Flash Exchange (*www.adobe.com/cfusion/exchange/index.cfm*). Adobe hosts a website called Flash Exchange (see Figure 16-27). Adobe itself doesn't create the components on the Flash Exchange; instead, regular folks and third-party software companies submit the components, and the site categorizes and rates them. To visit the Flash Exchange, select Help→Flash Exchange.

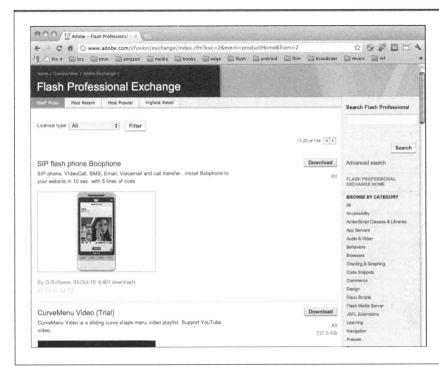

**FIGURE 16-27**

*The Flash Exchange website (which you can surf to by selecting Help→Flash Exchange) lists hundreds of components in nearly a dozen different categories, from Navigation to Commerce and Accessibility. Some you pay for; others you can download for free. Use the component specifications, number of downloads, and rating associated with each component to help you decide which ones to try.*

- The Flash Components Network (*www.flashcomponents.net*). Similar to Adobe's Flash Exchange, this site lists and rates Flash components submitted by a variety of Flash enthusiasts and software companies.

- ActionScript.org (*www.actionscript.org*). This everything-Flash site lists dozens of freely downloadable components.

**NOTE** Because anyone with the time, inclination, and ActionScript experience can create a Flash component, Flash enthusiasts (as opposed to established software companies) create most of the Flash components on the Web. Many of the components are free, but there's a downside: Components don't always come with the documentation you need to customize them, and they virtually never come with a guarantee. They may *not* work as promised, and they *may* harbor viruses that can damage your computer. Don't be afraid to try out useful components, but do exercise the same care and caution you use when you download and install any other software program.

## Installing Third-Party Components

After you find and download a component (page 572 lists several online component resources), you need to install the component so you can use it in Flash:

1. First, exit Flash if you've got it running.

2. Place the .swc or .fla file containing the component in the folder where you keep components.

3. For PCs, use *C:\Program Files\Adobe\Adobe Flash CS6\language\Configuration\Components*. For Macs, use

*Macintosh HD:Users:username:Library:Application Support:Adobe:Flash CS6:language:Configuration:Components*.

4. Start Flash.

5. Open the Components panel (Window→Components) and check to make sure the new component is available.

## Getting a Component's Version Number

Like programs, components get updates from time to time. Perhaps the folks who designed the component added new features, or maybe they needed to make changes so that the component would be compatible with an updated version of Flash. In any case, there may come a time when you'll want to find out the version number of a component that you're using in your Flash project. Fortunately, every component has a version property, so there's a consistent way to check. All you need to

do is drag an instance of the component onto the stage, and then add this ActionScript code to the timeline:

```
trace(component_instance_name.version);
```

Replace "component_instance_name" with the actual instance name of the component you added to the stage. Press Ctrl+Enter (⌘-Return) to test your document. The component's version number appears in the Output panel (Figure 16-28).

**FIGURE 16-28**

You can display the version number of a component in the Output panel simply by placing a snippet of code in the Actions panel.

# Choosing, Using, and Animating Text

Text plays a big part in many Flash projects, and you can put it there in a few ways. As explained on page 220, you can use the Text tool to create text fields and then alter the text's appearance using the Properties panel. But if you want your text to undergo changes over the course of an animation, you need the power of ActionScript. This chapter shows you how to use ActionScript to edit, format, and manipulate text fields as your animation runs. First, you need to know about font embedding, to ensure that your audience sees exactly the typefaces you specify. Then, to edit text on the fly, you'll learn how to add and remove characters from strings of text. The remainder of the chapter explains how to create text fields using ActionScript and how to format and animate text.

## ■ What Font Does Your Audience Have?

When you create your Flash masterpiece, you use the fonts installed on your computer. Dozens of fonts show up in the Properties→Character→Family list. Franklin Gothic or French Script, anyone? Whenever a program like Flash needs a font, it gets the font description from the file on your computer. Font files mathematically describe the outlines of each character. Flash uses this description to display type at all different sizes, just like resizing a vector image (page 357).

When your project is finished and you publish it, you create an SWF file (page 7). There are two ways that Flash handles text. It can look up the font description and then draw the image, or it can turn the text into a raster image. Raster images are fine, but because the text is converted to a graphic, you can't edit the words or characters when the animation is running on your audience's computer. It looks like text, but it's really just another graphic. If Flash stores the name of the font in the SWF file, then Flash Player looks up the font description and has everything it needs to draw those beautiful, complicated glyphs that make up a typeface. You can change the text on the fly using ActionScript, and your audience can even add and edit text if you let them. There's only one snag with using the font name in your Flash projects: If your audience's computer doesn't have the font file for Franklin Gothic or French Script, Flash Player uses another font in its place. In the best cases, the difference doesn't show. In the worst cases, your text looks strange and doesn't fit properly in the space you've provided.

## Embedding Fonts in Your SWF file

It's not always possible to anticipate the fonts your audience will have. (Heck, these days it's hard to guess whether your audience will be watching on a computer, a smartphone, a tablet, or a television screen.) So Flash provides a way to put the font descriptions *in the SWF file.* In Flash-speak, that's called *embedding* the font. With the font description in the animation file, Flash Player has everything it needs. Of course, embedding adds to the size of the SWF file, but at least your audience sees the animation as you designed it. In earlier versions of Flash (before CS5), you had to remember to embed all the fonts you used in your animation. Now, Flash automatically embeds any characters used in text fields. However, if you want to generate new text on the fly or give your audience the ability to add text, you need to embed additional font descriptions.

You need to embed fonts if:

- You create new text objects, like text fields, on the fly using ActionScript.

- You edit text with ActionScript using new characters, numerals, or punctuation.

- You give your audience a way to add or edit text with TLF editable, Classic dynamic, or Classic input text.

If you're using Flash CS4 or earlier, it's best to manually embed fonts unless your project meets one of the criteria below.

You don't need to embed fonts if:

- You place your text in fields at design time and use TLF read only, TLF selectable, or Classic static text.

- All the text in your project is in text fields, and it won't change when the animation runs.

- You choose device fonts: _sans, _serif, or _typewriter. This specification automatically uses fonts already installed on your audience's computer, phone, or tablet.

As mentioned earlier, embedding font descriptions in your SWF files adds to the file size—and you want to keep those SWF files as small as possible. Flash lets you embed only the necessary fonts and characters—no extras. You wouldn't want to embed Zapf Chancery, for example, if you're not using that font, and you don't need to embed character descriptions for Q, z, #, and | if they don't appear in your text and there's no potential for them to be used when your animation runs. The Font Embedding dialog box (Figure 17-1) gives you the tools to embed just the right fonts and characters.

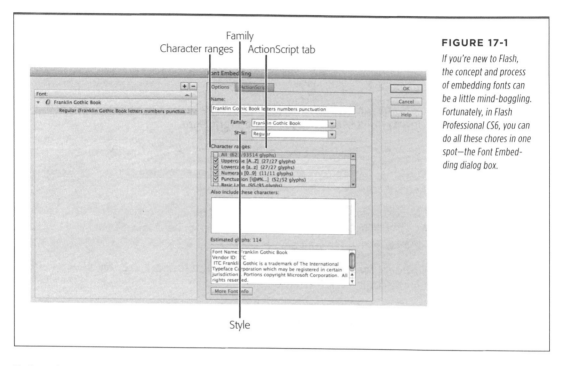

**FIGURE 17-1**

*If you're new to Flash, the concept and process of embedding fonts can be a little mind-boggling. Fortunately, in Flash Professional CS6, you can do all these chores in one spot—the Font Embedding dialog box.*

Follow these steps to embed specific characters from a font in your SWF file:

1. **With your Flash document open, choose Text→Font Embedding.**

   The Font Embedding dialog box opens.

2. **Make sure the Options tab is selected, and then use the Family menu to select the Family and Style you want to embed.**

   The family is the common name you use for a font, like Times, Arial, or, as shown in Figure 17-1, Franklin Gothic Book. The style includes Regular, Bold, Italic, and other characteristics.

3. **In the Name box, type a name for the font, like *Franklin Gothic Book letters numbers punctuation*.**

   Use a name that helps you identify the font description later. This name appears in the Library panel.

4. **Use the "Character ranges" list to choose the specific characters you want to embed.**

Here's where you control how much data goes into the SWF file. So if you need only lowercase letters, no numbers or punctuation, you can choose *Lowercase [a..z] (27/27 glyphs)*. The more characters you add, the bigger your SWF gets. *Glyph* is another word for character; it also includes numerals and punctuation.

5. **Optional: Add characters to the "Also include these characters" box.**

   Suppose you need to include the dollar sign, a comma, and periods, but don't need to include all 52 punctuation glyphs. Just type the necessary punctuation into this box, and don't select the punctuation option in the "Character ranges" list.

6. *Optional for ActionScript:* **If you're going to use create text fields on the fly with ActionScript, click the ActionScript tab.**

   The ActionScript tab has three sections: "Outline format," Linkage, and Sharing.

7. *Optional for ActionScript:* **In the Linkage section, turn on "Export for ActionScript."**

   The buttons and boxes in the ActionScript tab change from grayed out to available. Flash automatically turns on "Export in frame 1," making your font available at the beginning of your animation.

8. *Optional for ActionScript:* **In the "Outline format" section, choose either Classic (DF3) or TLF (DF4).**

   Your choice here must match the choices you make when you create text fields. If you happened to use the Palatino font in both Classic text fields and TLF text fields, then you need to embed the Palatino font for both text engines.

9. *Optional for ActionScript:* **In the Class box, type a name, like *Franklin-GothicBook*.**

   Like everything in ActionScript, your font description is an object based on a class. In this step, you provide the name for a new class, which is based on the flash.text.Font class.

10. *Optional for ActionScript:* **Click the green checkmark button.**

    Flash displays a message: "A definition for this class could not be found in the classpath, so one will be automatically generated in the SWF file upon export." Translation: This is a new class that didn't previously exist, so Flash will create the necessary code to create the class when you publish your SWF file.

11. **On the left in the Font area, click the + button.**

    Flash creates a font symbol and adds it to your Flash document. The name you provided in step 3 appears in the Font list in the Embedded Font dialog box, and the font symbol is shown in the Library.

There are a few technical details when you embed fonts in your SWF files. If the font's appearance isn't important to your project, then consider using system fonts, as described in the box below. Create separate font symbols for each style, such as Bold, Italic, and Regular. Remember, TLF text and Classic text are two different beasts where Flash and ActionScript are concerned. You can use both types of text in a single Flash document, but when you export text for ActionScript, you need to make sure it matches the text type.

**FREQUENTLY ASKED QUESTION**

### Device Fonts: _sans, _serif, and _typewriter

*At the top of the list in Properties→Character→Family, there are fonts called _sans, _serif, and _typewriter. What are they, and how do I use them?*

These three font options are known as device fonts. Device fonts include three generic styles: _sans is similar to Helvetica or Arial, _serif is similar to Times or Times New Roman, and _typewriter is similar to Courier or Courier New. You find these choices at the top of the font lists in the Properties→Character panel and the Text→Font menu. If you specify device fonts when you create text fields, then Flash Player always looks for

a font that's installed on the device (computer, smartphone, or whatever) that's playing the animation. Sometimes, small file size is an overriding concern. Perhaps you know that your audience will be using a slow Internet connection or handheld devices. When you choose device fonts for your animation, no fonts are embedded in the .swf file. On the Web, this makes for smaller, faster Internet transmission. On handhelds, this conserves resources such as CPU power and battery life. In both cases, you give up some control over the appearance of the type.

## Controlling Text with ActionScript

If you're used to using a word processor, it probably seems pretty natural to format your text with menus and the Properties panel. After all, they aren't that much different from Microsoft Word menus and dialog boxes. On the other hand, if you want to make major changes to text on the fly, or if you want to format text with HTML or CSS, you have to use ActionScript to produce your text. You saw some text and ActionScript examples in Chapter 12 (page 432). You'll find more here. First, the elementary basics, which begin with string theory.

### ActionScript Text: String Theory

Flash has lots of text containers, like TLF editable and Classic dynamic text. And then there are the components: Label, TextArea, and TextInput. All of these text-displaying tools use the String data type (page 432). As far as ActionScript is concerned, a string is similar to an array, in that it's a list of characters. The list can be a single character or hundreds of characters. Each character is in a specific position in the list—its index number (page 488). Arrays and strings both begin counting at position zero (0). So if the string is "Stutz Modern Motorcars," that capital S is at position 0.

**NOTE** Strings are common to most programming languages, and there are loads of books that explain how to perform string manipulation magic. Most Flash programs don't require such trickery. This chapter explains some of the most common techniques used by Flash designers. However, if you're an aspiring string magician, you may want to start out with *ActionScript 3.0 Cookbook* or *Essential ActionScript 3.0*, both published by O'Reilly.

## Creating a New String

You want to use the name of your company, "Stutz Modern Motorcars," in an ActionScript program. The typical way to do so is to create a variable with the data type string, and then store the name of your company inside that variable. Whenever you need the company name to appear in your program, you can provide the name of the variable. Here's the way you'd create a string variable for your company name:

```
var strCompanyName:String = "Stutz Modern Motorcars";
```

This statement does a few things in a single line. It creates and names a String variable strCompanyName, and then it assigns a string value to the variable. You only have to create the variable with the *var* statement once, and then you can use it as many times as you want. In this case, the variable name begins with the three letters "str" to indicate that it's a string, but that's not necessary. The variable name could be a single letter.

**NOTE** String values, like "Stutz Modern Motorcars", are always shown within either double or single quotes. One of the reasons you can use either type of quotes is that it provides an easy way to include quotes within your string. So here are examples of valid strings:

```
strDont = "don't";
strQuote = 'Ed said, "I love my Stutz Bearcat. I drive it everywhere."';
```

The important rule is that you have to begin and end the string with the same type of quotation mark.

Because you assign your strings to variables, you can change the strings' values. For example, if the boss changes the name of Stutz Modern Motorcars to the simpler (and even more modern) Stutz Motor Company, you can update your ActionScript code by assigning the new name to the strCompanyName variable, like so:

```
strCompanyName = "Stutz Motor Company";
```

## Joining Strings

One of the most common ways to modify a string is to add more text to it. In geek-speak that's called concatenation, but you can think of it as joining strings. Suppose your boss finally gets around to filling out those incorporation papers, and your company has yet another new name. If you want to add the word "Incorporated" to the existing strCompanyName, here's how you'd do it:

```
strCompanyName = strCompanyName + ", Incorporated";
```

As you can see, you're adding a new string value to the end of the existing string. The end result is a complete name, "Stutz Motor Company, Incorporated." Joining strings is such a common and popular task that there's a shortcut to help you do so with fewer keystrokes. It looks like this:

```
strCompanyName += ", Incorporated";
```

That line of code does exactly the same thing as the preceding example, just with fewer keystrokes. Make sure you keep the + sign to the left of the = sign. When you do it the other way around, the code has an entirely different meaning to ActionScript.

> **NOTE** If you want to test some of these string examples, you can use the *trace()* statement to display the string in the Output panel. For example, to display strCompanyName, add this line to your ActionScript code:
>
> ```
> trace(strCompanyName);
> ```
>
> Make sure all the string variables are declared with a var statement like this:
>
> ```
> var strCompanyName:String = "Stutz Modern Motorcars";
> ```
>
> If they're not declared before they're used, you'll get an error.

When you have a string inside quotes, like ", Incorporated," it's known as a *string literal*. The string is *literally* what's inside the quotes, similar to a constant. When a string is represented by a variable, like strCompanyName, it's a *string variable*. In most situations, you can use either representation. For example, here's another way you can construct the new company name:

```
var strCompanyName:String = "Stutz Motor Company";
var strInc:String = ", Incorporated";
strCompanyName += strInc;
```

You can use a combination of string literals and string variables when you're joining a string. You see this technique in use when websites greet you by name. An ActionScript example looks like this:

```
var strVisitorName = "Chris Grover";
strGreeting = "Hello, " + strVisitorName + ". What can I do to put you in a
Stutz Bearcat today?";
```

When you join strings with the concatenation operator (+ or +=), everything inside the quotes has to be on a single line. That's one of the reasons you see multiple assignment statements when an ActionScripter is creating a long paragraph of text.

```
var strSalesPitch:String = "The legendary Stutz Bearcat. ";
strSalesPitch += "It's your best value in high-performance ";
strSalesPitch += "sport cars today. ";
strSalesPitch += "At the Stutz Motor Company, we want to know, ";
strSalesPitch += "what can we do to put you in a Stutz Bearcat today?";
```

This block of text produces a single long string. Even though there were line breaks in the ActionScript code, those have no effect on the string when it is displayed. The line breaks are dictated by the properties and size of the text container. To see how you specifically place line breaks in a string, see the next section.

> **NOTE** This last example is shown in *17-1_Join_Strings.fla* in the Missing CD (*www.missingmanuals.com/cds/flashcs6mm*). A trace statement added to the code displays the completed string in the Output panel.

## Using TextField's *appendText()* Method

When you're using objects of the TextField class, you can use the *appendText()* method. In fact, *appendText()* is preferred because it runs faster than the concatenation operator. Here's some code that shows *appendText()* in action:

```
1    var tfBearcatBanner:TextField = new TextField();
2    var strSalesPitch:String = new String();
3    strSalesPitch = "Stutz Motor Company\nHome of the legendary Stutz
     Bearcat\n";
4    tfBearcatBanner.text = strSalesPitch;
5    tfBearcatBanner.appendText("What can we do to put you in a Bearcat
     today?");
6
7    tfBearcatBanner.x = 40;
8    tfBearcatBanner.y = 40;
9    tfBearcatBanner.width = 280;
10   tfBearcatBanner.height = 160;
11
12   addChild(tfBearcatBanner);
```

The first two lines create a text field and a string. The third line puts some text in the string strSalesPitch. Line 4 assigns that string to the text property of the text field. Line 5 is where the *appendText()* method comes in. The text in the parentheses is a string literal, but it could just as easily be a variable. Lines 7 through 10 position and size the text field on the stage. The last line adds the text field to the Display List, which makes it visible on the stage. When you run this bit of code, Flash Player displays the text as shown in Figure 17-2. This example is called *17-2_Append_Text.fla* in the Missing CD (*www.missingmanuals.com/cds/flashcs6mm*).

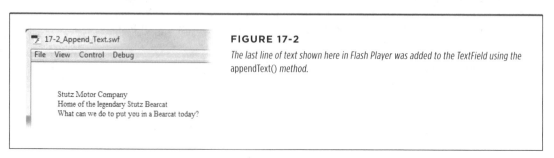

**FIGURE 17-2**

*The last line of text shown here in Flash Player was added to the TextField using the appendText() method.*

## Adding Line Breaks to a String

When you're typing text into a text field, you hit the Enter (or Return) key to begin a new line, but that doesn't work when you're creating a string in ActionScript. You need to insert a special signal within the string. It's a backslash with a lowercase n, which stands for new line. Here's an example:

```
strSalesPitch = "Stutz Motor Cars \n Home of the legendary Stutz Bearcat";
```

If placed in a multiline text field and given enough room to display, this string appears as two lines:

Stutz Motor Cars
 Home of the legendary Stutz Bearcat

There's a space after the word "Cars" and before the word "Home," because, after all, strings are literal. To avoid the extra space at the beginning of the second line, you have to eliminate the space characters on both sides of \n. It looks strange to us humans, because we see individual words, but that's not the way ActionScript sees a string. ActionScript just sees a long line of characters: letters, numbers, spaces, and punctuation. The only thing that really grabs its attention is the sequence \n. When ActionScript sees that backslash followed by a lowercase n, it knows that's the signal for a new line.

## Finding a String Within a String

Suppose your Flash animation is more like a computer program. It's so complex that you've provided 200 pages of help text to help your audience learn how to use it. You want to create some sort of search function so folks can zero in on the help they need. A string that's inside another string is often called a *substring*, and ActionScript provides some methods to help you find a substring inside a larger string.

To make it simple, this example is going to search for the word "legendary" within the longer string "Home of the legendary Stutz Bearcat." Not quite hundreds of pages, but you get the idea. All strings inherit the same properties and methods from the string class. Two of those methods are *indexOf()* and *lastIndexOf()*, and they're specifically used to search for substrings. As with any good method, you put them to work by tacking them onto the end of an object. Here's some code to show how it works:

```
var strSalesPitch:String = "Home of the legendary Stutz Bearcat."
strSalesPitch.indexOf("legendary");
```

The first line creates the string variable named strSalesPitch. The second line runs the string method *indexOf()*. The method needs to know what substring you're searching for, so you provide that as a parameter. You can put the string literal right inside the parentheses, as shown here with "legendary," or you can provide a string variable, which, of course, wouldn't include the quotes.

So what does the *indexOf()* method do? It gives you back a number. Specifically, it gives you the index number where the searched-for string begins. In the case above, *strSalesPitch.indexOf("legendary")* is equal to 12, because if you start counting at zero, and you count the letters and spaces, you find that the letter "l" is at index 12. The *lastIndexOf()* method works in a similar manner, except that it starts searching from the end of the string rather than the beginning. If either method is unable to find the substring, it gives back the number –1. That result is actually helpful, since you can use it with conditional statements. For example, this code would work:

```
if (strSalesPitch.indexOf("legendary ") == -1) strComment = "Not legendary.";
```

The *if()* statement tests to see if the string "legendary" is part of strSalesPitch. If the statement doesn't find that string, then the *indexOf()* method returns –1. When that condition exists, the words "Not legendary" are assigned to strComment. It's also useful to partner the "does not equal" (!=) operator with *indexOf()* and *lastIndexOf()*. So you can write code that says something like the following:

```
if (strSalesPitch.indexOf("legendary") != -1) strComment = "This is a
legendary automobile.";
```

In other words, if the code finds the substring, it assigns the string "This is a legendary automobile." to strComment.

## Replacing Words or Characters in a String

Search and replace go hand in hand in the computer world. Suppose there were changes at the car dealership and you needed to make changes to your sales pitch: "Home of the legendary Stutz Bearcat." You can use the replace method. It works like this:

```
strSalesPitch = strSalesPitch.replace("Stutz Bearcat","Toyota Prius");
```

As usual with methods, you tack *replace()* onto the end of the object, in this case, a string. For parameters, you provide the search words or letters, and then you provide the replace words or letters. Also, as usual, you use a comma to separate parameters when there's more than one. The *replace()* method works with both string literals, like the ones shown here, or string variables.

## Converting Strings to Uppercase or Lowercase

You can change the case of a string using the *toUpperCase()* or *toLowerCase()* methods. Part of the String class, you use these the same way as the other methods. Continuing with the car dealership theme, here are some examples that use *trace()* to display the strings in the Output panel:

```
var strSalesPitch = "Home of the legendary Stutz Bearcat";
trace("This is the initial string: \n" + strSalesPitch);
trace("\nThis is toUpperCase: \n" + strSalesPitch.toUpperCase());
trace("\nThis is toLowerCase: \n" + strSalesPitch.toLowerCase());
```

The first line creates the strSalesPitch variable and assigns the words "Home of the legendary Stutz Bearcat" to the variable. The next line uses *trace()* to send the string to the Output panel. (As mentioned on page 473, the *trace()* statement is a favorite debugging tool of ActionScripters.) The first string inside the *trace()* statement's parentheses is a string literal that explains what's to follow: "This is the initial string:." The \\n is the newline character that forces the following text to start on a new line. It works in the Output panel the same way it works in a text field. The + (concatenation operator) joins the two strings. The last string is the variable strSalesPitch. The final two lines are nearly identical to the second line. They add one more \\n to provide some additional, helpful white space. Finally, the methods are applied to the strings. What appears in the Output panel comes as little surprise:

This is the initial string:

Home of the legendary Stutz Bearcat

This is toUpperCase:

HOME OF THE LEGENDARY STUTZ BEARCAT

This is toLowerCase:

home of the legendary stutz bearcat

Enough with the string theory. The next sections show how to create text on the fly using ActionScript and how to format that text using a few different tools. This example is named *17-4_Change_Case.fla* in the Missing CD (*www.missingmanuals. com/cds/flashcs6mm*).

# Creating Text Fields with ActionScript

You've seen how to create and then display objects using ActionScript (page 481), and text fields are no different. You create, and if needed, format the object, and then you use the *addChild()* method to add the text field to the Display List. Objects added to the Display List are on the stage, and they're visible unless you've programmed them otherwise.

ActionScript has two text field classes. The TextField class is the basis for Classic text: static, dynamic, and input. Use the TLFTextField class to create TLF text. Fortunately, the properties and methods in both classes are nearly identical, so if you know how to use one, then you can use the other, too. For example, both text fields use the .text property to define the characters displayed in the text field—more on that later. The following examples use the new TLFTextField, which offers more bells and whistles, but it shouldn't be hard to translate the techniques to a Classic TextField.

**NOTE** The properties and methods related to TLF text fields are defined by the TLFTextField class. That means if you ever have a question, or if you're ever digging deeper for details about text, you can look up "TLFTextField" in the *ActionScript 3.0 Language and Components Reference* (page 448), where you'll find a listing of all the properties, methods, and events that are part of the TLFTextField class. This section will familiarize you with quite a few of these features.

You create a new text field like you create an instance of any ActionScript class, using its constructor method. Here's some code that creates a text field and displays it. Try this demonstration yourself to create a TLFTextField:

1. **In a new ActionScript 3.0 document, open the Actions panel (Window→Actions).**

   At this point, there's nothing on the stage and a single frame in the timeline.

2. **Type the following code and press Enter (Return):**

   ```
   var tlfBanner:TLFTextField = new TLFTextField();
   ```

   Somewhere as you type or when you hit Enter (Return), Flash generates its own line of code at the top of your document:

   ```
   import fl.text.TLFTextField;
   ```

   Cleverly, Flash knows you need to import the class to create a TLFTextField object.

3. **Continue your code with the following lines:**

   ```
   tlfBanner.text = "Stutz Motor Company\nHome of the legendary Stutz Bearcat";

   addChild(tlfBanner);
   ```

4. **Press Ctrl+Enter (⌘-Return) to test your code.**

   The result looks like Figure 17-3—not pretty, but at least there's some text on the screen. Obviously, a little formatting comes next.

**FIGURE 17-3**

*Text created in ActionScript usually requires some formatting before it's ready for prime time. Here the typeface is small and a bit blah. The text doesn't fit in the 100 x 100 pixel text field that ActionScript provides unless you specify different dimensions. And because there was no code to position the text field, it showed up in the upper-left corner.*

If you've followed the earlier ActionScript examples in this book, the code may seem pretty familiar. The first line you typed creates a variable called tlfBanner that's an instance of TLFTextField. At that point, ActionScript automatically wrote the code to import the TLFTextClass. In step 3, you created a string literal: "Stutz Motor Company\nHome of the legendary Stutz Bearcat," and assigned it to the text field's .text property. The last line of code adds the text field to the Display List, making the text field visible on the stage. Without a single Flash tool touching the stage, you made text, albeit a bit dull and truncated, appear in a Flash animation. In the next few steps, you'll spruce it up.

This example used a string literal to set the text property. In some cases, especially if you want to perform some string magic, as explained earlier in this chapter, you may want to use a string variable. That works, too. For example, you could get the same result in the text field using these lines:

```
var strSalesPitch:String = new String();
strSalesPitch = "Stutz Motor Company\nHome of the legendary Stutz Bearcat";
tlfBanner.text = strSalesPitch;
```

The first line creates an instance of the String class. The next line assigns a value to the string variable. You could use any of the string tricks, like append or replace, at this point. The last line assigns the string variable to the text field's .text property.

# ■ Positioning, Sizing, and Formatting a Text Field

You position and size your text field on the stage as you do other visual elements. In fact, because text fields are rectangular, it's very similar to working with a rectangle. You use the *x* and *y* properties to put the text field in a certain spot on the stage, and then you use the *width* and *height* properties to size the text field. So, the first step for the Bearcat banner is to move away from that upper-left corner, and then give it enough width to show all the text. Here's the code you add before the *addChild()* statement:

```
tlfBanner.x = 40;
tlfBanner.y = 40;
tlfBanner.width = 240;
tlfBanner.height = 160;
```

## Formatting the Text Field's Background and Border

In addition to positioning and sizing text fields, you can format text fields by changing their properties. For example, you can add colored backgrounds and borders for text fields. These are the same properties you change in the Properties panel using color pickers and text boxes. The difference here is that you're accessing the properties with your code. In the case of backgrounds and borders, not only do you have to set the color and size, but you also need to set the background and border properties to true so that they display something like this:

```
tlfBanner.border = true;
tlfBanner.borderColor = 0x993300;
tlfBanner.borderWidth = 5;
tlfBanner.background = true;
tlfBanner.backgroundColor = 0xFFFFCC;
```

**TIP** Here's an important point to keep in mind when you're learning to work with text and ActionScript: Formatting a text field is different from formatting text. You use TLFTextField properties to change the appearance of the box that holds text, but you can't change the typeface or font size using text field properties. There's an extra step and an extra object when it comes to specifying type, as explained on page 596.

Those aren't the only color tricks you can perform on a text field. You can set the alpha (transparency/opacity) property for the text (.alpha), the border (.borderAlpha), or the background (.backgroundAlpha). As usual with alpha properties, you use a number between 0 and 1 to set the opacity, where 0 is completely transparent and 1 is completely opaque. So a statement like this:

```
tlfBanner.backgroundAlpha = .20;
```

makes the background 20 percent opaque.

## Adjust the Space Between Text and Border

If you're going to go to the trouble of giving your text field a background color and a border, you probably don't want your text scrunched up against the edge. To create some breathing room, use the text field's *padding* properties. There's a property for each edge—top, bottom, left, and right—so you use a different setting for each. In this example, 24 pixels is used for all the edges:

```
tlfBanner.paddingTop = 24;
tlfBanner.paddingLeft = 24;
tlfBanner.paddingRight = 24;
tlfBanner.paddingBottom = 24;
```

When you want to change something in your text field but don't know the exact name of the property, you can use code hinting to help. So, in the previous example, you can type the variable name for the text field, *tlfBanner*, and press period (.). After you do that, code hinting displays a scrollable list of properties for the object, which in this case is a TLFTextField, as shown in Figure 17-4. Scroll through the list and look for a property that sounds like it might handle the chore at hand. Most property names are pretty descriptive, as is the case with the padding properties. If you double-click the property name, Flash adds it to your code. If you begin typing letters, code hinting automatically scrolls to properties beginning with those letters. So, if you're working with a TLFTextField, hit *.pa* to see the padding options.

## Autosizing a Text Field

It's hard to set the dimensions for a text field when you don't know how much text it's going to hold. The ideal solution to this common dilemma is to pin one or more of the edges of the text field down to the stage and let the other edges shrink and grow to accommodate the text. ActionScript lets you do just that with the help of two tools: the TextField's autoSize property and the TextFieldAutoSize class. First, you use the value of one of the TextFieldAutoSize constants to define the edge of the text field you want to pin down. Then you pass that value to your TextField's autoSize property. It sounds more complicated than it is: The good news is you can take care of the whole job with a single line of code:

```
tlfBanner.autoSize = TextFieldAutoSize.LEFT;
```

On the right side of the assignment operator (=), TextFieldAutoSize is set to the constant LEFT. Then the value is assigned to txtBanner's autoSize property. The autoSize property expects this value to come packaged with the TextFieldAutoSize object. It won't work if you just try to assign the LEFT constant by itself. There are four constants that control the sizing behavior of a text field:

• **TextFieldAutoSize.NONE** is what you use if you don't want to set autosizing in your code. The text field doesn't resize at all. If there's more text than can be displayed in the text field, it simply doesn't show.

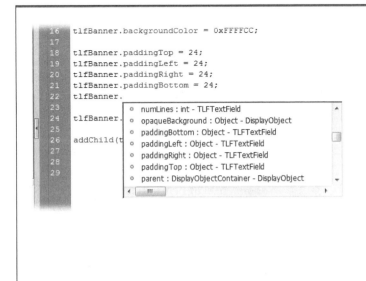

**FIGURE 17-4**

*When in doubt about the properties you can apply to an object, give code hinting a try. After the field name, you see a colon (:) and the type of object used to set the property. It could be a number, string, Boolean, or other type. Next is a hyphen (-) and the name of the class that defines the property. You might see TLFTextField listed or one of the classes from which it inherits properties, such as DisplayObject or Sprite.*

• **TextFieldAutoSize.LEFT** is one of the most common settings. In this case, the left edge of the text field stays anchored. The right edge can resize to accommodate text (see Figure 17-5). If it's a multiline text field and there are line breaks, the bottom can resize, too. When wordWrap is used, only the bottom is resized. The left, right, and top edges stay put. To turn wordWrap off, add a line of code like this:

```
tlfBanner.wordWrap = false;
```

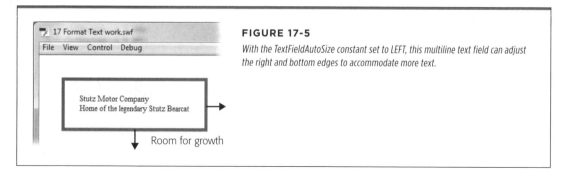

**FIGURE 17-5**

*With the TextFieldAutoSize constant set to LEFT, this multiline text field can adjust the right and bottom edges to accommodate more text.*

- **TextFieldAutoSize.RIGHT** is used less frequently, because it behaves as if the text is right-justified and flowing to the left. The right edge stays anchored. When a single line runs long, the left edge resizes. If it's a multiline text field and there are line breaks, the bottom resizes, too. When wordWrap is used, only the bottom is resized.

- **TextFieldAutoSize.CENTER** comes in handy for headers or other cases where you want your text right in the middle. Resizing is equally distributed to both the left and right edges. For multiline text fields with line breaks, the bottom resizes to accommodate the new lines. If wordWrap is set to *true*, then the bottom resizes and the left, right, and top edges stay put.

## Formatting Characters and Paragraphs

Formatting text is such a noble endeavor that ActionScript devotes an entire class to the job. Once you learn the ins and outs of the TextFormat class, you can do it all. It works the same for TLF and Classic text and all the text types they encompass. You can apply a single format to an entire text field and then fine-tune specific words or phrases with special formatting like bold, italic, or color highlights. Some formatting properties you apply to specific characters, while others you apply to entire paragraphs.

Most of the action takes place using the properties of the TextFormat class. As you'd expect, the TextFormat class has character-level properties that set font names, size, style, and color. It also includes paragraph-level properties that control the alignment, margins, indents, kerning, leading (line spacing), and bullets.

TextFormat is an object itself, so you need to create an instance of the TextFormat class to use in your program. Here's an example of code that does that:

```
var txtFormat:TextFormat = new TextFormat();
```

The next step is to choose the format options you want to include in this specific instance of the class. For example, you can choose the typeface and font size using the TextFormat's properties:

```
txtFormat.font = "Cooper Black";
txtFormat.size = 20;
txtFormat.align = "center";
```

As explained earlier, when you use ActionScript to create text fields, you need to choose fonts that you know are on your audience's computers, or you need to embed the fonts in the SWF file (see page 568). If the font isn't available, then the Flash Player finds a substitute. In this example, the big, bold Cooper Black font is specified. The number in the size property refers to points, the traditional typographic measurement also used in programs like Microsoft Word. The actual size and readability of typefaces at the same size can vary, so it's good to review and experiment when choosing a typeface and size. The .align property centers the text in the text field.

Once you've established your type specs in the TextFormat object, you need to use the text field's *setTextFormat()* method and provide your newly created format as the parameter. That means you put it inside the parentheses, like this:

```
tlfBanner.setTextFormat(txtFormat);
```

This statement registers the format for the entire txtBanner text field. A TextFormat object can include as many or as few properties as you want.

You can use more than one instance of the TextFormat class. Suppose you want to apply special formatting to a word or two. You can create formats that make type bold, italic, or change its color. Here's code that creates two new TextFormat objects, one for bold text and one for italic text.

```
var txtFormatBold:TextFormat = new TextFormat();
txtFormatBold.bold = true;

var txtFormatItalic:TextFormat = new TextFormat();
txtFormatItalic.italic = true;
```

If you want to apply formatting to a word or phrase inside a text field, you need to tell ActionScript exactly which characters to format, which you do using the index numbers in the string. For example, if you want to italicize the word "legendary" in the text "Home of the legendary Stutz Bearcat," you need to count characters. Don't forget to start that count at 0. Then, when you use the *setTextFormat()* method, you also provide a starting point and ending point for the formatting. It looks like this:

```
tlfBanner.setTextFormat(txtFormatItalic,12,20);
```

Formatting with ActionScript is similar to setting properties in the Properties panel. When you apply the txtFormatItalic format, it doesn't mess with any of the other formatting properties. It leaves the font and size settings as they were, changing only the properties that it specifically defines.

Here's a chunk of ActionScript code that uses most of the TLFTextField and TextFormat coding tricks covered so far. The lines beginning with // are comments. You can download this code from the Missing CD (*www.missingmanuals.com/cds/ flashcs6mm*). The file is named *17-5_Format_Text.fla*:

```
1    import fl.text.TLFTextField;
2    import flash.text.TextFormat;
3
4    // Define variables, instances of TLFTextField and TextFormat
5    var tlfBanner:TLFTextField = new TLFTextField();
6    var txtFormat:TextFormat = new TextFormat();
7    var txtFormatItalic:TextFormat = new TextFormat();
8    var txtFormatBold:TextFormat = new TextFormat();
9
10   // Assign a string literal to the .text property of the TLFTextField
11   tlfBanner.text = "Stutz Motor Company\nHome of the legendary Stutz
Bearcat";
12
13   // Position and size properties
14   tlfBanner.x = 40;
15   tlfBanner.y = 40;
16   tlfBanner.width = 220;
17   tlfBanner.height = 160;
18
19   // Background and border properties
20   // Remember to set the .background and .border properties to "true"
21   tlfBanner.border = true;
22   tlfBanner.borderColor = 0x993300;
23   tlfBanner.borderWidth = 5;
24   tlfBanner.background = true;
25   tlfBanner.backgroundColor = 0xFFFFCC;
26   tlfBanner.backgroundAlpha = 1;
27
28   // Padding properties determine the distance between the text
29   // and the edge of the text field
30   tlfBanner.paddingTop = 24;
31   tlfBanner.paddingLeft = 24;
32   tlfBanner.paddingRight = 24;
33   tlfBanner.paddingBottom = 24;
34
35   // Autosize permits the text field to grow to accommodate the text
36   tlfBanner.autoSize = TextFieldAutoSize.LEFT;
```

```
37    // Turn off wordWrap for this banner; you might want it on
38    // for paragraph text where line breaks aren't as critical
39    tlfBanner.wordWrap = false;
40    // Turn multiline on so the text box displays more than one line
41    tlfBanner.multiline = true;
42
43    // Define text specifications like font, size, and color
44    // through the txtFormat an instance of the TextFormat class
45    txtFormat.font = "Times";
46    txtFormat.size = 20;
47    txtFormat.align = "center";
48
49    // Heres are two more TextFormat objects that set italics and bold
50    txtFormatItalic.italic = true;
51    txtFormatBold.bold = true;
52
53    // Assign the format using the text field's .setTextFormat() method
54    // The second text format makes specific characters in the
55    // text field italic
56    tlfBanner.setTextFormat(txtFormat);
57    tlfBanner.setTextFormat(txtFormatItalic,32,41);
58    tlfBanner.setTextFormat(txtFormatBold, 42,55);
59
60    // The addChild method adds the text field to the Display List
61    // making it visible on the stage.
62    addChild(tlfBanner);
```

Line 5 creates the text field called tlfBanner, and line 11 assigns a string literal to its text property. The lines from 14 through 35 tweak various text field properties, changing its appearance and behavior. Lines 45 through 51 focus on setting properties for TextFormat objects. On lines 56 through 58, TextFormat objects are applied to the tlfBanner text field using the .setTextFormat method. The first one is applied to the entire text field, while the other two target specific characters by position. The last line adds tlfBanner to the display list, making it visible on the stage.

When all is said and done, the text field looks like Figure 17-6 (shown in Flash Player).

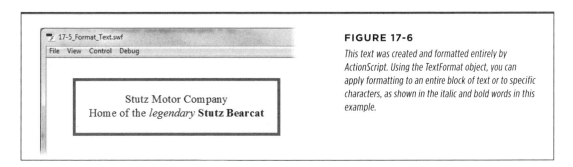

**FIGURE 17-6**

*This text was created and formatted entirely by ActionScript. Using the TextFormat object, you can apply formatting to an entire block of text or to specific characters, as shown in the italic and bold words in this example.*

# ■ Formatting with HTML and CSS

When you're working in ActionScript, there's more than one way to format text. The previous technique using ActionScript's TextFormat object works well when you're working on a project on your own. The properties and methods are familiar if you're used to working with Flash's Properties panel. Flash also lets you use the same formatting tools used by web designers: HTML (hypertext markup language) and CSS (Cascading Style Sheets). There are a few reasons why you might want to go this route for a project. Perhaps your project uses lots of text and it's already formatted using HTML. In some cases, you may be working on a large project where some people are responsible for generating the text and others are responsible for presenting it on the Web or in a Flash-based program.

## HTML and CSS Philosophical Differences

Before you make a decision about using either HTML or CSS for your Flash formatting chores, it helps to understand their approaches to formatting text. HTML embeds formatting codes inside the text. For example, the second line in the tlfBanner text field of the previous example might look like this if you formatted it in HTML:

```
<font face="Times" size="3"> Home of the <em>legendary</em> <strong>Stutz
Bearcat</strong></font>
```

When a web browser like Internet Explorer, Safari, or Chrome reads this text, it knows how to display the text in the browser window. It applies the formatting instructions and shows the text. It displays the proper typeface if it's available; otherwise it uses a substitute font. So HTML coding works fine from the audience point of view. For designers, it can be a bit of a pain. One of the problems of HTML coding is that the message gets a bit lost in the formatting tags. Complicated HTML coding is hard for human eyes to read, and that makes it easy to foul up. When you want to make changes, it's a lot of work to go in there and tweak all those bits of embedded code.

These days, the fashionable technique is to use CSS to format web pages. The underlying philosophy is that it's best to separate the formatting from the content. You create styles (type specs) for body text, major headlines, subheads, captions, and so forth. You store those definitions in a style sheet. Then, in the text, you tag different portions, indicating the styles they should use. In effect, you say: This is a major headline, this is body text, and this is a caption. When the browser goes to display your web page, it comes to the text tagged as a headline, and then it looks up the type specs in the style sheet. It does the same thing for the body text and the captions. From a designer's point of view, this system is a tremendous timesaver. If you want to change the caption style for a website that has 400 captioned pictures, all you need to do is edit one definition in the style sheet. If all those type specs were embedded HTML code, you'd need to make 400 separate edits.

**NOTE** Most web pages designed today use a combination of HTML and CSS to format pages. HTML is still the basic, underlying code for web pages. CSS, JavaScript, and Flash are technologies built on top of the HTML foundation.

## Using HTML Text in Flash

There are two steps to using HTML encoded text in Flash. First, you need to create strings with the HTML codes embedded. Then you need to assign those strings to the htmlText property of the text field that will display the formatted text.

When you want to use HTML with its embedded codes in a Flash project, you need to build strings of text that include all the HTML codes. That means you end up with a lot of angle brackets, equals signs, and quotes inside your strings. The quotes present a small challenge, because your string needs to be wrapped in quotes when it's assigned to a variable or a text field (page 586). Fortunately, Flash accepts either single or double quotes. So if the HTML you're embedding looks like this line:

```
<p><font face="Times" size="3"> Home of the <i>legendary</i> <b>Stutz
Bearcat</b></font></p>
```

You can place it inside single quotes when you use it in Flash. For example, this statement assigns the HTML coded string to the txtBanner text field. It uses single quotes to define the string:

```
tlfBanner.htmlText = '<p><font face="Times" size=24> Home of the
<em>legendary</em> <strong>Stutz Bearcat</strong></font></p>';
```

HTML is like Flash in that it can use either single or double quotes in most places. Most of the time, you'll use double quotes, but be aware that you may sometimes see single quotes used to assign values in HTML code. In that case, you'd use double quotes to define your string in Flash.

Once you've stored your text in a string, you need to assign that string to a text field. Lucky for you, all TextField objects have an htmlText property, as shown in the code example above. It works just like the regular text property except that it understands how to read and then display text with HTML codes. As with any text field, you need to use the *addChild()* method to add your text field to the Display List and show it on the stage.

## Creating a Hyperlink with HTML

If there's one thing that made HTML king of the World Wide Web, it's the hyperlink. Hyperlinks are the threads that form that web. Click a linked word, and suddenly you're in a different part of the universe (or at least, the Web). On page 225, you saw how to create hyperlinks using the standard Flash authoring tools. The ability of text fields to use HTML encoded text also enables them to use HTML links. You create the links using the usual HTML codes: <a> anchor tags. Here's an example of an HTML hyperlink:

```
<a href="http://www.stutzbearcat.net">click me</a>
```

Like most HTML tags, the anchor tag comes in pairs: *<a>in between stuff</a>*. The slash is the defining mark of an end tag. In HTML, you stuff that first tag with any necessary parameters. In this case, the parameter is a web address. The *href* stands for hypertext reference; the equals sign assigns a value to the reference inside double quotes. The specific value here is a web address. The words in between the two <a> tags, "click me," are visible in the browser window. Depending on the tag's formatting, they may appear underlined or highlighted in some way to show that they're a link.

Beyond that there's no magic to adding and using HTML hyperlinks in Flash. Here's an example of the same link included in a string that's passed to the htmlText property of a text field:

```
txtBanner.htmlText = '<p>To visit our website <a href="http://www
.stutzbearcat.net">click me</a> </p>';
```

Flash Player isn't a web browser, so when your audience clicks the link, their browser opens and then loads the web page specified in the link. The link can just as easily point to a file on the local computer. In that case, instead of the *http://* reference, you'd use a *file://* reference. Keep in mind that in most cases, file system access is only available when the SWF animation and the file are on same local computer. For security reasons, file access is severely restricted on web servers.

---

**NOTE**    You can find HTML examples in *17-6_HTML_Text.fla* in the Missing CD (*www.missingmanuals.com/cds/flashcs6mm*). There are a lot of HTML tags and keywords, and Flash works with only some of them. A complete list of HTML tags that work with Flash is included in the help document *ActionScript 3.0 Reference for the Adobe Flash Platform*. Look up the *Textfield* class and its *htmlText* property.

---

## Using CSS to Format Classic Text in Flash

CSS is the acronym for *Cascading Style Sheets*—an ingenious system for formatting HTML text. If you want to read up on how CSS works, you can get an excellent introduction in David Sawyer McFarland's *CSS: The Missing Manual* (O'Reilly). You need to have a basic understanding of CSS to use it with Flash. This book provides a quick overview of CSS and an example or two to get you started.

CSS style sheets are a little like those wooden Russian dolls where one object is nested inside another. Starting from the outside and working in, here's what you find in a CSS style sheet. A style sheet is a list of formatting specifications. Each formatting spec has a selector that identifies the HTML tag that it formats. That tag could be the paragraph tag <p>, or the heading tag <h1>, or an anchor tag <a>. In CSS lingo, the formatting spec is called a *declaration block*. The declaration block is contained inside curly braces {}. Within those curly braces are specific declarations that define fonts, styles, colors, sizes, and all the other properties that can be defined in CSS. (Flash works with only some of these properties.) The declarations have two parts: a property and a value. So in CSS, if that property is *font-size*, then the value is a number representing point size. A CSS definition to format an <h1> heading tag might look like this:

```
h1 {
font-family: Arial;
font-size:18;
font-weight: bold;
color: red;
}
```

The first line has the selector for *h1* headings, usually the biggest, boldest heading on a web page. The next four lines show pairs of properties and values. On the left side of the colon is the property, which is hyphenated if it's made up of more than one word. On the right side is the value assigned to that property.

In Flash, you can recreate the function of a CSS style sheet using the StyleSheet object. It gives you a way to create selectors and then assign values to the properties Flash recognizes. You can't use style sheets with TLF text, so here's Flash's version of the specification shown above using a Classic TextField:

```
1    var txtBanner:TextField = new TextField();
2    var styleSheet:StyleSheet = new StyleSheet();
3    var h1Style:Object = new Object();
4    var pStyle:Object = new Object();
5
6    h1Style.fontFamily = "Arial";
7    h1Style.fontSize = "24";
8    h1Style.fontWeight = "bold";
9    h1Style.color = 0x800000;
10
11   pStyle.fontFamily = "Arial";
12   pStyle.fontSize = "12";
13   pStyle.fontWeight = "normal";
14
15   styleSheet.setStyle("h1", h1Style);
16   styleSheet.setStyle("p", pStyle);
17   txtBanner.styleSheet = styleSheet;
18
19   txtBanner.x = 60;
20   txtBanner.y = 120;
21   txtBanner.width = 200;
22   txtBanner.height = 120;
23   txtBanner.autoSize = TextFieldAutoSize.LEFT;
24   txtBanner.background = true;
25   txtBanner.backgroundColor = 0xFFFFFF99;
26   txtBanner.border = true;
27
28   txtBanner.htmlText = '<h1>Home of the legendary Stutz Bearcat</h1>
     <p>What can we do to put you into a Bearcat today?</p>';
29   addChild(txtBanner);
```

Here's a line-by-line rundown on the ActionScript. As in the other examples, line 1 creates the TextField object called txtBanner. The next three lines also create objects. Line 2 creates an instance of the StyleSheet class, and lines 3 and 4 create instances of the more generic Object class. You use these objects to hold the CSS declarations. That's exactly what's going on in lines 6 through 13. Values are being assigned to the h1Style object, and then the pStyle object.

Note that the property names have been changed slightly. That's because Action-Script jumps into action when it sees a minus sign (-). Instead, these properties eliminate the hyphen and use an uppercase letter for the word following the hyphen. So where the CSS property is named font-family, the ActionScript property is named fontFamily. Lines 15 and 16 use styleSheet's *setStyle()* method. The first parameter in the parentheses defines the selector: *h1*, the heading style, in line 15 and *p*, the paragraph style, in line 16. The second parameter in each case is the object that was created to hold the declarations. These are ActionScript's substitute for a declaration block with those paired sets of properties and values.

The styleSheet Object now has formatting instructions for two tags that it's likely to encounter in an HTML document. Line 17 assigns the styleSheet object to txtBanner's styleSheet property. Lines 19 through 26 are the ActionScript code that formats the text field. There's no CSS here; it's just straight ActionScript. Line 28 gets back into the CSS business. When you format with CSS, you pass the string to the text field using the htmlText property. The string itself is formatted like HTML, but instead of embedding formatting specs, it uses style tags. This little snippet uses two tags, first the <h1> tag for the heading, and then the <p> tag for its rather skimpy paragraph. With CSS, you need to assign the StyleSheet property before you put text in the text field. The last line adds the txtBanner to the Display List for the world to see. Figure 17-7 shows how the CSS-formatted text looks.

**NOTE**   Flash is very fussy about its style sheets. If it's unable to read or use any of the styles, it tends to ignore the entire style sheet. The result is that no formatting is applied.

---

### Home of the legendary Stutz Bearcat
What can we do to put you into a Bearcat today?

**FIGURE 17-7**

*This text is formatted with CSS. Styles are applied to the paragraph <p> tag and to the heading 1 <h1> tag. You can create CSS styles within your ActionScript code, or you can load an external CSS file.*

There are quite a few things missing from Flash's version of CSS. First of all, you can assign only one StyleSheet at a time to a text field's styleSheet property. One of the handy things about CSS is the way you use multiple style sheets for the formatting chores. Another feature missing from Flash's HTML capabilities is tables, causing moans among web-savvy designers. Web designers like to use tables to format and organize text and pictures.

## Formatting Text with an External CSS File

One of the great features of CSS for designing web pages is that you can use a single external file (called a CSS style sheet) to format many web pages. Want to change the color of a heading? Simply change the definition in the style sheet, and that changes the look of all the web pages. You can use external CSS style sheets with Flash projects, too—just keep in mind the limitations of HTML and CSS in Flash mentioned in the previous section.

> **NOTE**    There are two files for this project, *17-7_External_CSS.fla* and *17-8flashText.css*. You can find both at *www.missingmanuals.com/cds/flashcs6mm*. Both files need to be in the same folder to test the code.

To start this exercise, you need a file that defines CSS styles. You can download *17-8flashText.css* from the Missing CD site or create your own using a text editor. It's short and sweet:

```
p {
    font-family: Arial;
    font-size: 12px;
    font-weight: normal;
}
h1 {
    font-family: Arial;
    font-size: 24px;
    font-weight: bold;
    color: #800000;
}
```

This external CSS file defines the same CSS styles that were used in the previous example—the paragraph <p> tag and the heading 1 <h1> tag. Most CSS style sheets are more complicated than this, but as an example, this works just fine.

The ActionScript code that uses this external file needs to do a few things:

- Load the external CSS file.
- Read (parse) and store the CSS style instructions.
- Apply the CSS styles to a text field rendered as HTML.
- Display the text field.
- Assign text with HTML tags to the htmlText property of the text field.

Here are the steps to load an external CSS style sheet and use the styles with code created in ActionScript:

1. **Create an instance of the URLLoader class.**

   ```
   var loader:URLLoader = new URLLoader();
   ```

   The URLLoader class is used to load external files that reside on a computer or on the Internet.

2. **Register an event listener that triggers when the CSS file has completed loading.**

   ```
   loader.addEventListener(Event.COMPLETE, loadCSSListener);
   ```

   The URLLoader class triggers an event when a file has loaded. When that event triggers, the function *loadCSSListener()* will run.

3. **Create an instance of the URLRequest class to identify the CSS file to be loaded.**

   ```
   var request:URLRequest = new URLRequest("17-8flashText.css");
   ```

   The URLRequest class is used to identify files by filename and if needed, a path. In this case, just the filename is used because *17-8flashText.css* is to be stored in the same folder as the Flash project.

4. **Use the *load()* method to load the CSS file.** Use "request" as the parameter for the load method.

   ```
   loader.load(request);
   ```

   Adding an extra blank line here sets the function for the event listener off from the rest of the code.

5. **Create the function that runs when the loader event is complete.**

   ```
   function loadCSSListener(evt:Event):void {
   ```

   The rest of the statements in this exercise are part of this function, which ends with the closing curly bracket.

6. **Create an instance of the StyleSheet class.**

   ```
   var cssFlashStyles:StyleSheet = new StyleSheet();
   ```

   The StyleSheet class holds CSS style definitions.

7. **Read the data in the external CSS file (*flash_text.css*) and store the data in the style sheet cssFlashStyles.**

   ```
   cssFlashStyles.parseCSS(URLLoader(evt.target).data);
   ```

8. **The process of reading and processing the CSS definitions is called *parsing*.**
   The method parseCSS is part of the StyleSheet class. Create an instance of the TextField class with the variable name *txtBanner*.

   ```
   var txtBanner:TextField = new TextField();
   ```

The text field txtBanner displays text stored in one of two properties—the *text* property or the htmlText property.

9. **Position and size the txtBanner, and then format the background and border.**

```
txtBanner.x = 60;
txtBanner.y = 120;
txtBanner.width = 200;
txtBanner.height = 120;
txtBanner.autoSize = TextFieldAutoSize.LEFT;
txtBanner.background = true;
txtBanner.backgroundColor = 0xFFFF99;
txtBanner.border = true;
txtBanner.borderColor = 0x800000;
```

These statements aren't related to CSS, and their formatting applies to the entire text field.

10. **Add txtBanner to the Display List.**

```
addChild(txtBanner);
```

Adding txtBanner to the Display List makes it visible on the stage.

11. **Assign the cssFlashStyles to the styleSheet property of txtBanner.**

```
txtBanner.styleSheet = cssFlashStyles;
```

It may seem a little backward, but the style sheet needs to be applied before the text is assigned to txtBanner.

12. **Assign a string of text to txtBanner's htmlText property.**

```
txtBanner.htmlText = '<h1>Home of the legendary Stutz Bearcat</h1> <p>
What can we do to put you into a Bearcat today?</p>';
}
```

The text assigned to the htmlText property of txtBanner is a string literal. The HTML tags <p> and <h1> are embedded within the string.

13. **Save your Flash file *17-7_External_CSS.fla* in the same folder as the CSS file *17-8flashText.css*.**

If you don't store the two files in the same folder, then you need to provide complete path information in the URLRequest, as in step 3.

When you test the movie, Control→Test Movie, you see text formatted as shown in Figure 17-8. The style definitions are identical in this example and the previous example, where CSS styles were written into the ActionScript code, so the results look the same.

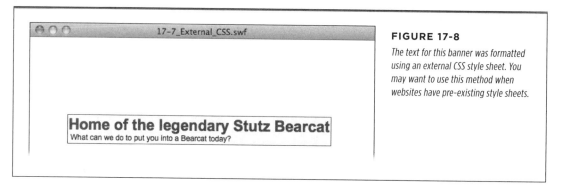

**FIGURE 17-8**

*The text for this banner was formatted using an external CSS style sheet. You may want to use this method when websites have pre-existing style sheets.*

In general, using external CSS style sheets gives you more flexibility, because you can change the appearance of text inside of your Flash project by simply editing the style sheet. As long as the name and location of the external CSS file stay the same, you don't even need to fire up Flash or ActionScript or republish your .swf files. How cool is that?

# Choosing the Right Text Formatting System

So far this chapter has described four different ways to format text in Flash animations. How do you choose the right technique for your project? Here are some general guidelines about when to use Flash's Properties panel, ActionScript's TextFormat object, HTML, or CSS to format text in your Flash projects:

- Use the Properties panel for its ease of use and when you make all your formatting decisions as you design the animation.

- Use ActionScript's TextFormat object when you need to make changes to your text while the animation is running.

- Use ActionScript's TextFormat object when you want to work quickly and your project creates TextField objects on the fly.

- Use HTML if you have lots of text already formatted in HTML or if your workgroup requires it.

- Use HTML or CSS when you want to embed hyperlinks in dynamic text.

- Use CSS if you're working on a large web-based project that already has established CSS type specs.

- Use CSS if you're working with lots of text and there are timesaving benefits to be gained by separating formatting from content.

**NOTE** When you use HTML and CSS in Flash, you can use only a few of the most common tags and properties. It's not surprising that these are the tags and properties that are matched by the TextFormat object. If you're choosing HTML or CSS for a specific feature, make sure that you can use that feature in Flash and ActionScript. You can find a complete list in the *ActionScript 3.0 Reference for the Adobe Flash Platform* in Flash's help system. Look under flash.text, and then choose the TextField class. Then choose the *htmlText* property, and you see a table that lists the tags Flash supports. For CSS, look under flash.text for the StyleSheet class. In its help pages, you see a table listing the CSS properties supported in Flash and ActionScript.

# Drawing with ActionScript

I f you were one of those kids who loved the Etch-A-Sketch, then you're probably going to love this chapter. With ActionScript, you can draw lines and shapes in your Flash animations. The great advantage of drawing with ActionScript is that your animations can draw new objects on the fly.

This chapter will introduce the Graphics class and all the power it puts at your fingertips. To start with, you'll learn how ActionScript works with points and lines. You'll learn about the virtual pen and how, as it moves from one spot to another, you can tell it to draw lines (or not). Then you'll learn how to draw and display Flash's built-in shapes, including ellipses, rectangles, and rounded rectangles. There are times when prebuilt shapes won't do the job, so you'll see how to draw more complex and irregular shapes using nothing but ActionScript code. To wrap things up, this chapter shows how to move the shapes you've drawn about the stage using ActionScript's TimerEvent to trigger the motion.

## ▩ What's the Point?

It all comes down to the point. Flash's stage is a mass of points measured by x/y coordinates. In the upper-left corner, there's a point that's referenced by 0, 0, which means it's at the 0 point on the horizontal axis and the 0 point of vertical axis. ActionScript describes the point as x = 0 and y = 0. If you put something on the stage and don't tell Flash or ActionScript where you want to place it, chances are that something will end up at 0, 0. If your stage is one of Flash's standard sizes, say 550 x 400 pixels, the lower-right corner is 550, 400 or x = 550 and y = 400. When drawing with ActionScript, you can bet that you'll be dealing with a lot of x/y coordinates and a lot of points. If you want to draw a line from one place to another, you need to define two points. If you want to draw a trapezoid, you need to define, at least by inference, the four corner points.

Since the point is a building block for all the lines, shapes, and drawings to follow, ActionScript has a special Point class. Not only does the class give you a place to store information about specific points, but it also provides some helpful methods that you can use when you're working with points and their relationships. For reference, the Point class is part of the *flash.geom* package. You create instances of the Point class the same way you create other objects in ActionScript, like so:

```
var ptNear:Point = new Point();
```

When you enter this line of code, you're doing a couple of things at once. First of all, you're creating a new variable and providing a variable name, ptNear. The word after the colon declares the data type—in this case, Point. Then, after the assignment operator (=), you use the reserved word *new* to explain that you're creating a new instance of an object. The word *Point()* with its parentheses is the constructor for the Point class. When all is said and done, you've got yourself a new instance of the Point class that's addressed by the variable name ptNear.

As you might guess, Point objects have two properties, *x* and *y*. You can assign values to these properties to set a point's location, and if you have the name of a point but you don't know where it is, you can read these properties to learn its location.

```
ptNear.x = 20;
ptNear.y = 20;
trace("The location of ptNear is:",ptNear);
```

The first two lines assign values to ptNear, an instance of the Point class. The third line uses that handy *trace()* statement to place information in the Output panel. In this case, the *trace()* statement reports:

```
The location of ptNear is: (x=20, y=20)
```

The Point class has just one other property, oddly called *length*. Thankfully, it's not referring to the length of the point. That would confuse everyone, including Euclid. In this case, *length* refers to the length of a line from 0, 0 to the point. It's a *read-only* property, meaning you can't assign a new value to length; all it does is report on its value.

Most of the interesting and useful features of the Point class are the methods:

- *distance()*. Calculates the distance between two points. Example:

  ```
  distanceBetweenPoints = Point.distance(ptNear,ptFar);
  ```

- *add()*. Adds the coordinates of two points and returns another point in x, y values.

  ```
  sumOfPoints = ptNear.add(ptFar);
  ```

- *subtract()*. Subtracts the coordinates of two points and returns another point in x, y values.

      differenceOfPoints = ptNear.subtract(ptFar);

- *equals()*. Tests to see if two points are equal. Useful for creating conditional statements, like *if ptBall* equals *ptGround*, then bounce.

      if (ptBall.equals(ptGround)) bounce(); //run the function Bounce()

- *interpolate()*. Calculates a point between two end points. You use a third parameter, with a value between 0 and 1, to find a point and to determine how close that point is to one or the other of the end points. Think of it as a percentage.

      ptHalfWay = Point.interpolate(ptNear, ptFar, 0.5);
      ptQuarterWay = Point.interpolate(ptNear, ptFar, 0.75);

The *interpolate()* method uses three parameters, which as usual make their appearance inside the parentheses. The first two parameters have to be points. The third parameter is a number between 0 and 1; that's a common ActionScript technique for indicating a percentage. In this case, the closer the number is to 1, the closer the point is to the first point. The closer the number is to zero, the closer it is to the second point. So, in the examples above, the value 0.5 finds the midpoint between ptNear and ptFar. The value 0.75 is closer to the first point, so it finds a point a quarter of the way between the two points.

The best way to understand how these methods work is to use them in ActionScript. Follow these steps to see how to run the Point class through some of its paces.

---

**NOTE**   You can download *18-1_Point_Methods.fla* with the following code from the Missing CD (*www. missingmanuals.com/cds/flashcs6mm*).

---

1. **Select File→New and choose ActionScript 3.0.** Select the first frame on the timeline, and then press F9 (Option-F9).

   The Actions panel opens. Figure 18-1 shows the Actions panel with some code entered.

2. **Type the following code (but not the line numbers at left):**

       1  var ptNear:Point = new Point();
       2  var ptFar:Point = new Point();
       3  var distanceBetweenPoints:Number;
       4  var sumOfPoints:Point;
       5  var differenceOfPoints:Point;
       6  var pointBetweenPoints:Point;
       7  var ptHalfWay:Point;
       8  var ptQuarterWay:Point;
       9  var ptBall:Point = new Point();
      10 var ptGround:Point = new Point();

```
11
12 ptNear.x = 0;
13 ptNear.y = 20;
14 ptFar.x = 100;
15 ptFar.y = 20;
16
17 distanceBetweenPoints = Point.distance(ptNear,ptFar);
18 sumOfPoints = ptNear.add(ptFar);
19 differenceOfPoints = ptNear.subtract(ptFar);
20 ptBall.x = 200;
21 ptBall.y = 350;
22 ptGround.x = 200;
23 ptGround.y = 350;
24 ptHalfWay = Point.interpolate(ptNear,ptFar,0.5);
25 ptQuarterWay = Point.interpolate(ptNear,ptFar,0.75);
26
27 trace("The location of ptNear is:",ptNear);
28 trace("The location of ptFar is:",ptFar);
29 trace();
30 trace("A line from 0, 0 to ptNear is",ptNear.length, "long.");
31 trace("The distance between ptNear and ptFar
is:",distanceBetweenPoints);
32 trace("If you add ptNear to ptFar you get:", sumOfPoints);
33 trace("If you subtract ptFar from ptNear you get:",differenceOfPoints);
34 trace("This point is half the way between ptNear and ptFar:", ptHalf-
Way);
35 trace("This point is a quarter of the way between ptNear and ptFar:",
   ptQuarterWay);
36 trace();
37 trace("The location of ptBall is:",ptBall);
38 trace("The location of ptGround is:",ptGround);
39 if (ptBall.equals(ptGround))
40 {
41     bounce();
42 }
43
44 function bounce():void
45 {
46     trace("I'm bouncing");
47 }
```

The first 10 lines in the code create instances of objects. All except one are Point class objects. The data type for distanceBetweenPoints is *Number*. Lines 12 through 15 assign values to the x and y properties to ptNear and ptFar. The next block of statements (lines 17 through 25) show the Point methods discussed in this section.

If you want to experiment with these methods, you can use these examples as a model. From line 27 to line 38 there are *trace()* statements that send text to the Output panel. The text inside quotes is displayed literally; the items outside the quotes are the variable names. Most of the variables refer to points, so the Output panel lists the values of their x and y properties. In some cases the output is a distance, which is a number. Line 39 is a conditional *if()* statement that demonstrates the Point class's *equals* property. The two points are equal, because they have the same values for the x and y properties, so the value of the statement *ptBall.equals(ptGround)* is *true*. With the condition *true*, the if statement calls the *bounce()* function, which is written on lines 44 through 47. The bounce function sends the words "I'm bouncing" to the Output panel, as shown in Figure 18-2.

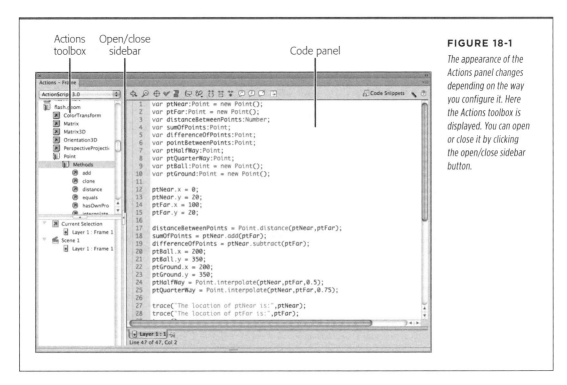

Actions toolbox    Open/close sidebar    Code panel

**FIGURE 18-1**

*The appearance of the Actions panel changes depending on the way you configure it. Here the Actions toolbox is displayed. You can open or close it by clicking the open/close sidebar button.*

Working with points is a little abstract, because you can't really add a point instance to the display list in Flash. It's good to understand how points work in ActionScript and to be aware of the methods of the Points class, but the fun really begins when you start drawing lines and shapes.

## Beginning with the Graphics Class

With ActionScript, you can draw lines, curves, shapes, fills, and gradients. As with most ActionScript features, this ability comes to you courtesy of a class—in this case, the *flash.display.Graphics* class. Using the Graphics class, you can draw on instances of these three classes: Shape, Sprite, and MovieClip. Each of these classes has a graphics property, which, in turn, provides all the properties and methods of the Graphics class. So, for example, if you want to define how a line looks, you use the *graphics.lineStyle()* method. It looks like this:

```
spriteLine.graphics.lineStyle(3,0x00FF00);
```

Or, if you want to actually draw a line, it looks like this:

```
spriteLine.graphics.lineTo(20,150);
```

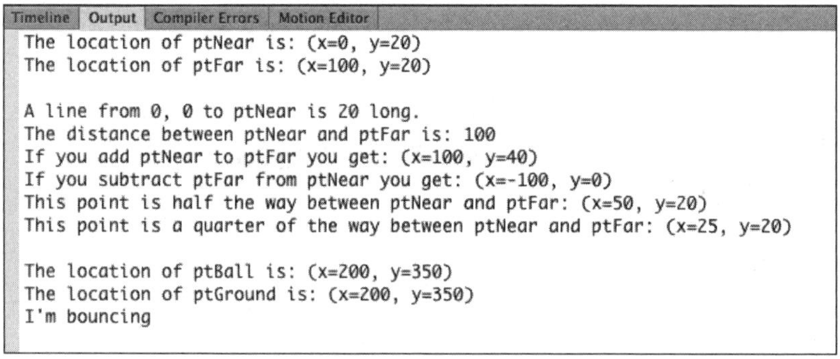

| Timeline | Output | Compiler Errors | Motion Editor |

```
The location of ptNear is: (x=0, y=20)
The location of ptFar is: (x=100, y=20)

A line from 0, 0 to ptNear is 20 long.
The distance between ptNear and ptFar is: 100
If you add ptNear to ptFar you get: (x=100, y=40)
If you subtract ptFar from ptNear you get: (x=-100, y=0)
This point is half the way between ptNear and ptFar: (x=50, y=20)
This point is a quarter of the way between ptNear and ptFar: (x=25, y=20)

The location of ptBall is: (x=200, y=350)
The location of ptGround is: (x=200, y=350)
I'm bouncing
```

**FIGURE 18-2**

*When you put a reference to a point in a trace() statement, Flash automatically shows the values of the x and y properties. This Output panel shows the results of several Point class methods.*

The important point to notice about the Graphics class is that it's a read-only property of the Shape, Sprite, or MovieClip classes. You reference the Graphics class by referencing one of those classes, then the Graphics class itself, and then the property or method of the Graphics class that you want to use.

# ◼ Drawing Lines

Think about the steps you take when you draw a line in the real world. You probably have your piece of paper in front of you. You pick up a pen, pencil, or marker. You place the writing instrument down on a specific point on the paper and drag it to another point. If you don't want to continue with another line, you pick up your pen and the job is done. You pretty much follow those same steps when you draw a line using ActionScript. Here's a list of the ActionScript steps:

- Open a Flash document and the Actions panel. The stage is your paper.

- Choose a line style. It's similar to choosing a pen, pencil, or whatever.

- Move to a specific point on the stage. Here's where you put pen to paper.

**NOTE** The code for the next line-drawing exercise is included in *18-2_Draw_Line.fla* in the Missing CD (*www. missingmanuals.com/cds/flashcs6mm*).

- Move to another point, drawing a line in the process, dragging the pen across the paper.

- Stop drawing lines. Lift the pen from the paper.

With those generalizations in mind, here are the specific steps to draw a line on the Flash stage:

1. **Select File→New and choose ActionScript 3.0.**

   A new, empty Flash document appears.

2. **Press F9 (Option-F9).**

   The Actions window opens, where you can enter ActionScript code.

3. **In the Actions panel, create an instance of the Sprite class by typing the following.**

   ```
   var sprtLine:Sprite = new Sprite();
   ```

   A Sprite is a container like a MovieClip, except it doesn't have a timeline. Using a Sprite instead of a MovieClip when you don't need a timeline keeps the size of your .swf slightly smaller.

4. **Use the *lineStyle()* method to set the style for the line you want to draw.**

   ```
   sprtLine.graphics.lineStyle(16,0x00FF00);
   ```

   The first parameter inside the parentheses sets the thickness of the line. In this case, setting the value to 16 draws a monster line 16 pixels thick. It's just as if you typed *16* in the Properties→"Fill and Stroke"→Stroke box. The second number is a color value shown in hexadecimal format. (For more on colors and the hexadecimal format, see page 203.)

   The *lineStyle()* method has other parameters that define properties like the opacity of the line or how lines meet at the corners. Often, all you need are the first two parameters, and if that's the case, you don't need to worry about the *lineStyle()* parameters. But in case you do, here's a rundown on all the *lineStyle()* parameters:

   - **thickness.** Provides a number (0-255) for the thickness of the stroke in points.

   - **color.** Provides a color value in hexadecimal format.

   - **alpha.** Provides a number from *1* to *0* that indicates a percentage of transparency.

   - **pixelHinting.** Provides *true* or *false* to change the way Flash Player displays corners. Flash usually has this option set to *false*, and you seldom need to change it.

   - **scaleMode.** Provides one of the following constants to determine how a stroke changes when an object is scaled. *NORMAL* means the line is scaled with the object. *NONE* means the line keeps its thickness when scaled. *VERTICAL* means the line keeps its thickness if the object is scaled vertically only. *HORIZONTAL* means the line keeps it thickness if the object is scaled horizontally only.

- **caps.** Provides the constants *NONE, ROUND,* or *SQUARE* to set the way the ends of lines appear.

- **joints.** Provides the constants *MITER, ROUND,* or *BEVEL* to set the way lines appear when they meet at corners.

- **miterLimit.** Provides a number from *1* to *255* to indicate the limit at which a miter is cut off. The miter in effect trims off the end of a corner when two lines meet.

The *lineStyle()* method does expect to receive these values in a particular order. So, for example, you'd get a confused result if you swapped the color value for the stroke thickness. Or, for example, if you want to provide a *NONE* constant for scaleMode, you need to provide values for the alpha and pixelHinting parameters, too. It looks like this:

```
sprtLine.graphics.lineStyle(3,0x00FF00,1,false,"NONE");
```

5. **Move the virtual pen to the line's starting point:**

```
sprtLine.graphics.moveTo(20,50);
```

Think of this statement as moving your pen to a position on the page without drawing a line. Flash expects a value for x and y for parameters for the *moveTo()* method. Unlike the *lineTo()* method, *moveTo()* is similar to picking the pen up from the paper and moving it to a new location. This action doesn't draw a line.

6. **Draw a line to another point.**

```
sprtLine.graphics.lineTo(500,380);
```

Think of this move as dragging your pen across the paper. The *lineTo ()* method draws a line from the current point to the point specified in the parentheses.

7. **Add the sprtLine Sprite to the Display List.**

```
addChild(sprtLine);
```

Until you use the *addChild()* method to add sprtLine to the Display List, nothing actually appears in the Flash Player.

8. **Test the animation.**

You see a Flash Player stage with a big fat green line running diagonally across the stage, as shown in Figure 18-3.

While you might not draw lines as frequently as you draw rectangles and other shapes, it's still good to have a thorough understanding of lines and the *lineStyle()* property, because the stroke outline for other shapes works the same way. If you want to draw an irregular shape, as described on page 625, then you need to draw a series of connected lines.

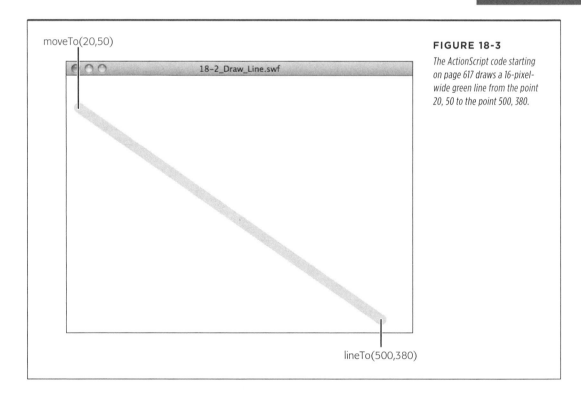

**FIGURE 18-3**
*The ActionScript code starting on page 617 draws a 16-pixel-wide green line from the point 20, 50 to the point 500, 380.*

## Drawing Curves

When you draw a curve using ActionScript, you need to add one more point to the mix. Think about the way you draw curves in Flash or Adobe Illustrator. You have a line with two anchor points, and you drag control handles from the anchors to create a curve. The line doesn't travel through the control handles, it's just geometrically influenced by the position of the handles. ActionScript uses a similar method to create curves, but you have to imagine that there's a single control point connected to both endpoints. Figure 18-4 shows the concept. By repositioning that control point, you change the shape of the curve. The *curveTo()* method is similar to the *lineTo()* method described in the previous section. You're creating a line from the current position of the virtual pen (one anchor point) to the end point of the curve (another anchor point). The shape of that line is influenced by a control point.

When you draw a curve in ActionScript, the control point isn't visible; it's defined but doesn't get displayed on the stage. In the code example here, the control point is marked with an X, and it's displayed in a text field. It shares the control point's x and y values. This code appears in *18-3_Draw_Curve.fla* in the Missing CD (*www. missingmanuals.com/cds/flashcs6mm*).

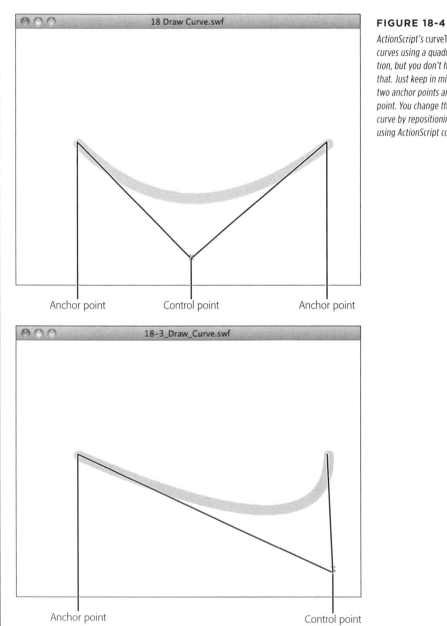

**FIGURE 18-4**

*ActionScript's* curveTo() *method draws curves using a quadratic Bezier equation, but you don't have to remember that. Just keep in mind that there are two anchor points and one control point. You change the shape of the curve by repositioning the control point, using ActionScript code, naturally.*

```
1   var shpLine:Shape = new Shape();
2   var ptAnchor1:Point = new Point();
3   var ptAnchor2:Point = new Point();
4   var ptControl:Point = new Point();
5   var tfControl:TextField = new TextField();
6
7   ptAnchor1.x = 100;
8   ptAnchor1.y = 180;
9   ptAnchor2.x = 500;
10  ptAnchor2.y = 180;
11  ptControl.x = 500;
12  ptControl.y = 350;
13
14  tfControl.text = "X";
15  tfControl.x = ptControl.x;
16  tfControl.y = ptControl.y;
17  addChild(tfControl);
18
19  shpLine.graphics.lineStyle(16,0x00FF00);
20  shpLine.graphics.moveTo(ptAnchor1.x,ptAnchor1.y);
21  shpLine.graphics.curveTo(ptControl.x,ptControl.y,ptAnchor2.x,ptAnchor2.y);
22  addChild(shpLine);
23
24  shpLine.graphics.moveTo(0,0);
```

The first line in this example creates a shape. You can create vector drawings in Sprites, Shapes, and MovieClips. Shapes use even less space than Sprites in your Flash animation. The three lines from 2 through 4 create points. The names could be anything, but in this example there's a hint that two of them are going to serve as anchor points and one will serve as a control point. Line 5 creates a text field that's named tfControl. Lines 7 through 12 position the three points. You can tell from their y values that ptAnchor1 and ptAnchor2 appear on the same horizontal axis. The ptControl y value is quite a bit below that axis. Line 14 stores an X in the text property of tfControl. (Think: *X* marks the spot.) Then, the code assigns *x* and *y* values of the text box the same values that are in ptControl.x and ptControl.y. Line 17 displays the tfControl text field when it's added to the Display List using the *addChild()* method. Line 19 defines a *lineStyle()*. The *moveTo()* method on line 20 positions the virtual pen at the first anchor point for the line. Then the *curveTo()* method is used. The first anchor point was already established by the preceding *moveTo()* method, so the *curveTo()* method needs two points. The x and y values of the control point come first, and then come the x and y values of the second anchor point. The *addChild()* method in line 22 displays the curve. When you test the curve code, it draws a curve similar to the one at the bottom in Figure 18-4. If you want to experiment, you can go ahead and change the *x* and *y* values of ptControl in lines 11 and 12. That changes the shape of the curve, and it also moves the x in the text field to mark the new position of the control point.

# ■ Drawing Built-In Shapes

When you graduate from lines to shapes, you get to fill your shapes with a color. The *lineStyle()* method becomes optional, because shapes don't have to have an outline stroke. You can draw simple shapes using ActionScript's built-in methods. The technique is very similar to drawing lines and curves with the addition of the *beginFill()* method that lets you choose a color and transparency percentage for the fill color. Here's the step-by-step for drawing a rectangle and a circle in a MovieClip. You can find all the code in *18-4_Draw_Shape.fla* in the Missing CD (*www.missingmanuals. com/cds/flashcs6mm*):

1. **Select File→New and choose ActionScript 3.0.**

   A new, empty Flash document appears.

2. **Press F9 (Option-F9).**

   The Actions panel opens, where you can enter ActionScript code.

3. **Type this line into the Actions panel to create an instance of the mcShapes MovieClip class:**

   ```
   var mcShapes:MovieClip = new MovieClip();
   ```

   MovieClip is one of three data types that let you draw vector graphics. The other two classes are Sprite and Shape.

4. **Define a *lineStyle()* for your first shape:**

   ```
   mcShapes.graphics.lineStyle(4,0x003300,.75);
   ```

   This statement uses the Graphics class, which is a property of the MovieClip class. As explained on page 617, the *lineStyle()* method can accept several parameters. This code uses three parameters, and the remaining ones are left unchanged from their original values. The first parameter sets the line or stroke thickness to 4 pixels. The second parameter provides a hexadecimal color value (dark green) for the line color. The third and last parameter sets the transparency for the line to 75%.

5. **Define a fill style for your shape:**

   ```
   mcShapes.graphics.beginFill(0x339933,.75);
   ```

   The method to fill a shape is *beginFill()*. The *beginFill()* method uses only two parameters. The first sets the fill color, a lighter green, and the second sets the transparency to 75%.

6. **Position the mcShapes movie clip on the stage:**

   ```
   mcShapes.x=mcShapes.y=50;
   ```

   This line sets both the x and y properties of mcShapes to 50 in one statement. You can use this form or use separate statements for each property.

7. **Use the built-in *drawRect()* method to define a rectangle.**

   ```
   mcShapes.graphics.drawRect(0,0,300,250);
   ```

   The first two parameters for *drawRect()* set the x and y values for the rectangle. Set at 0, 0, the rectangle is positioned in the upper-left corner of the mcShapes movie clip; but keep in mind that the movie clip is positioned at 50, 50 on the stage. The next two parameters set the rectangle's width and height values. In this case, the rectangle is 300 pixels wide and 250 pixels high. As with the other vector drawings, even though you've defined the object, it won't be visible until you add it to the Display List.

8. **Use the *endFill()* method to stop filling the shape:**

   ```
   mcShapes.graphics.endFill();
   ```

   The *endFill()* method doesn't use any paramaters.

9. **Use the *addChild()* method to display the movie clip mcShapes:**

   ```
   addChild(mcShapes);
   ```

   The *addChild()* method adds the movie clip to the Display List, which makes its contents visible.

10. **Test the animation.**

    When the animation runs, the rectangle appears with its registration point (upper-left corner) at 50, 50 on the stage. Though you gave the stroke and fill some transparency, the rectangle looks pretty solid because it's on a plain white background.

11. **Set new colors for the stroke and fill for a second shape, the circle:**

    ```
    mcShapes.graphics.lineStyle(4,0x0033CC,.5);
    mcShapes.graphics.beginFill(0x003333,.5);
    ```

    These are the same methods used in steps 4 and 5, but you're changing the color values to shades of blue and setting the transparency to 50 percent.

12. **Use the built-in *drawCircle()* method to define a circle and then use the *endFill()* method to stop filling the shape.**

    ```
    mcShapes.graphics.drawCircle(275,100,75);
    mcShapes.graphics.endFill();
    ```

    To define a circle, you need to provide the *drawCircle()* method with a center point and a radius. The first two parameters are the x and y values of the center point. The third parameter is the radius, which means this circle will be 150 pixels in diameter. The *endFill()* method stops filling the shape.

13. **Test the animation.**

    When the animation runs, the circle appears overlapping the rectangle as shown in Figure 18-5. The rectangle (the first shape you defined) appears on the bottom. Both the rectangle and the circle are positioned relative to their container mcShapes, not to the stage.

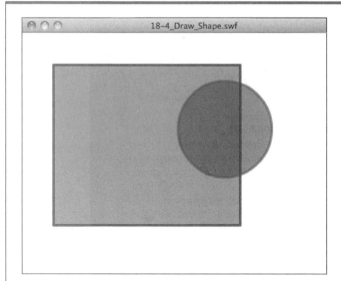

**FIGURE 18-5**

*These two shapes are drawn on a movie clip that's positioned at 50, 50 on the stage. The rectangle was defined first, so it appears underneath the circle.*

ActionScript includes two other built-in shapes, and you use them the same way: Define the stroke and fill, use one of the drawing methods to create the shape, and then use the *addChild()* method to display the shape. All that varies from shape to shape are the parameters you use to describe them. Here are definitions and a brief explanation for each built-in shape:

- **drawEllipse(x:Number, y:Number, width:Number, height:Number).** The first two parameters position the center of the ellipse. The next two parameters set the dimensions for the ellipse.

- **drawRoundRect(x:Number, y:Number, width:Number, height:Number, ellipseWidth:Number, ellipseHeight:Number).** The first two parameters are numbers that position the rectangle using its registration point. The next two parameters set the rectangle's width and height. The last two parameters, ellipseWidth and ellipseHeight, define the curve for the rounded corners. If the curves are equal, you can set just the first number, ellipseWidth, and ignore the second value. If the curve isn't equal, use both parameters to set different width and height values.

If you entered the statements in this exercise line by line, following the instructions, the code in your Actions panel looks something like this:

```
var mcShapes:MovieClip = new MovieClip();

mcShapes.graphics.lineStyle(4,0x003300,.75);
```

```
mcShapes.graphics.beginFill(0x339933, .75);
mcShapes.x=mcShapes.y=50;
mcShapes.graphics.drawRect(0,0,300,250);
mcShapes.graphics.endFill();

addChild(mcShapes);

mcShapes.graphics.lineStyle(4,0x0033CC,.5);
mcShapes.graphics.beginFill(0x003333,.5);
mcShapes.graphics.drawCircle(275,100,75);
mcShapes.graphics.endFill();
```

The order of the statements in this code is worth a closer look. First of all, even though the *addChild()* statement precedes the definition for the circle, the circle appears in the movie clip when it's added to the Display List. This is because its parent, mcShapes, has already been added to the stage. Also, the first shape defined, the rectangle, appears beneath the circle. You can change its position by changing its position in the code. If you want the rectangle to appear on top of the circle in the movie clip, move the code that defines the rectangle to follow the code that defines the circle.

# ■ Drawing Irregular Shapes

When you draw the built-in shapes, ActionScript does a lot of the work for you, but you're limited to the shapes that ActionScript offers. Sometimes you need to draw irregular shapes. For example, suppose you needed to draw a floor plan for a modern home with a number of odd angles and curves. In that case, you need to draw each line and curve separately. To fill the shape with a color, use the *beginFill()* method when you begin drawing lines. Then, when you're finished with the shape, use *endFill()*.

For example, here's some code that draws a very irregular shape that includes a variety of angles and one curved edge (see Figure 18-6). Open a new document and type the following into the Actions panel—or you can use *18-5_Draw_Irregular_Shape.fla* from the Missing CD (*www.missingmanuals.com/cds/flashcs6mm*):

```
1  var mcShapes:MovieClip = new MovieClip();
2
3  mcShapes.graphics.lineStyle(4,0x330000,.5);
4  mcShapes.graphics.beginFill(0xFF3300,.5);
5  mcShapes.graphics.moveTo(200,50);
6  mcShapes.graphics.lineTo(300,150);
7  mcShapes.graphics.lineTo(400,150);
8  mcShapes.graphics.curveTo(425,175,400,200);
9  mcShapes.graphics.lineTo(200,200);
10 mcShapes.graphics.lineTo(200,150);
```

```
11 mcShapes.graphics.lineTo(100,150);
12 mcShapes.graphics.lineTo(200,50);
13 mcShapes.graphics.endFill();
14
15 addChild(mcShapes);
```

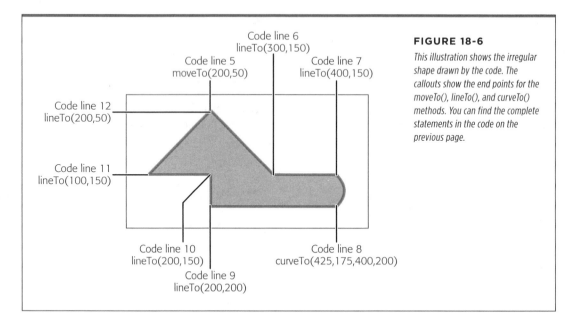

Code line 6
lineTo(300,150)

Code line 5
moveTo(200,50)

Code line 7
lineTo(400,150)

Code line 12
lineTo(200,50)

Code line 11
lineTo(100,150)

Code line 10
lineTo(200,150)

Code line 8
curveTo(425,175,400,200)

Code line 9
lineTo(200,200)

**FIGURE 18-6**

*This illustration shows the irregular shape drawn by the code. The callouts show the end points for the moveTo(), lineTo(), and curveTo() methods. You can find the complete statements in the code on the previous page.*

If you worked your way through the previous sections in this chapter, most of this will look familiar. The first two lines set the line style and the fill color. The third line moves the virtual pen to point 200, 50. Following that are several *lineTo()* methods with one *curveTo()* method added for good measure. If you want to match up the code with the lines in the shape, see Figure 18-6. These lines form a closed path when the last *lineTo()* method ends up back at the beginning: 200, 50. The final line runs the *endFill()* method.

**NOTE** Flash fills shapes even if they aren't entirely enclosed. So, even if line 12 (the line that closes the shape) was missing in the example above, Flash would still apply a fill to the shape that's defined by the rest of the lines.

When you test your animation (Ctrl+Enter on a PC or ⌘-Return on a Mac), you see an image like Figure 18-6.

## ▇ Making Drawings Move

As shown earlier in this chapter, you draw lines and shapes on three classes of objects: Shape, Sprite, and MovieClip. In effect, these objects are canvases for the drawings. To make drawings move from one location to another, you move the canvas. You can think of the Shape, Sprite, and MovieClip containers as transparent sheets of film with the drawings inked on top. You place the film on the stage. Then to create motion, you reposition the film on the stage. If you want to move objects together, you can place them on the same piece of film. If you want to move them independently, you have to place them on separate pieces of film.

To make Shapes, Sprites, and MovieClips move, you change those good old friends, the x and y properties. You can make them move in response to mouse clicks or other input from your audience. If you want them to move without prompting, you need to set up the mechanism.

## Using ActionScript's TimerEvent to Animate Drawings

One popular animation technique makes use of Flash's TimerEvent. It's sort of like setting one of those kitchen minute timers, and each time it goes "ding!," you move the drawing. ActionScript's Timer class uses two constants: *TIMER_COMPLETE* and *TIMER*. In earlier examples (page 476), you saw *TIMER_COMPLETE* in action. It triggers an event when the time has completely run out. You use the *TIMER* constant when you want to trigger repeated events at regular intervals.

Here's how it works: When you create an instance of the Timer class, you provide two parameters. The first parameter is called the *delay*. Think of it as the time in milliseconds before the timer goes "ding!" The second parameter is the repeatCount. Think of it as the number of times you want to reset the timer to run again.

So suppose you want to move a drawing every half-second, and you want it to move across the stage in 12 steps. You can set a timer with a delay of *500* and a repeatCount of *12*. Then every time the timer sends a TIMER event (ding!), you move the drawing by changing its x and/or y properties. Follow these steps to perform this feat of animation in code.

---

**NOTE**  You can find a copy of this code in the Flash file *18-6_Animate_Shape.fla* on the Missing CD page at *www.missingmanuals.com/cds/flashcs6mm*.

---

1. **Select File→New and choose *ActionScript 3.0.***

   A new, empty Flash document appears.

2. **Press F9 (Option-F9).**

   The Actions panel opens, where you can enter ActionScript code.

3. **Type this line into the Actions panel to create an instance of the MovieClip class named mcShapes:**

   ```
   var mcShapes:MovieClip = new MovieClip();
   ```

   MovieClip is one of three data types that let you draw vector graphics.

4. **Create an instance of the Timer class.**

```
var tmrMover:Timer=new Timer(500,12);
```

The parameters set the timer's delay value to 500 milliseconds and the repeatCount to 12.

5. **Define the line and fill style for the circle.**

```
mcShapes.graphics.lineStyle(4,0x000033);
mcShapes.graphics.beginFill(0x0099FF,.5);
```

You've set the line and fill colors to shades of blue. The code sets no alpha value (transparency) in the line style, so ActionScript assumes it should be 100%—that is, opaque. The fill has an alpha value of .5, making its transparency 50%.

6. **Draw the circle with the *drawCircle()* method and then stop the fill with *endFill().***

```
mcShapes.graphics.drawCircle(250,100,75);
mcShapes.graphics.endFill();
```

The first two parameters place the center of the circle at 250, 100 in the movie clip. (You haven't positioned the movie clip, so Flash automatically positions it at 0, 0.)

7. **Add the movie clip to the Display List.**

```
addChild(mcShapes);
```

This code adds the movie clip to the Display List, making it visible.

8. **Start the timer.**

```
tmrMover.start();
```

The timer starts.

9. **Register a TimerEvent listener.**

```
tmrMover.addEventListener(TimerEvent.TIMER,timerMoverListener);
```

10. **Write the function for the TimerEvent listener.**

```
function timerMoverListener(evt:TimerEvent):void
{
    mcShapes.x = mcShapes.x + 10;
}
```

The *timerMoverListener()* function assigns a new value to the *x* property of the mcShapes movie clip, which makes it move horizontally. To calculate the new value for *x*, the function takes the current value of *x* and adds 10 to it. Each time the *TIMER* event triggers, the movie clip moves.

11. **Test the animation.**

When the animation runs, the blue circle moves across the stage 10 pixels at a time. It moves 12 times and then stops, as shown in Figure 18-7.

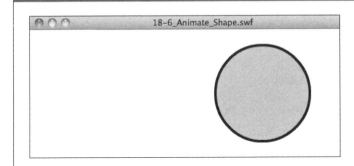

**FIGURE 18-7**

*This circle is animated to move across the stage through the use of a TimerEvent and the x property of the object that contains the circle—a movie clip.*

In the example above, if you want to move another object along with the circle, all you need to do is add that object to the movie clip. Suppose you want to move a small square along at the same speed. All you need to do is add one line to step 6 to define the position and size of the square.

```
mcShapes.graphics.drawRect(100,300,75,75);
```

Now, if you test the animation, both the circle and the square move across the stage in sync.

## Moving Objects Independently

The world and your animations don't always move in lockstep. So to make objects move independently, you can place them in different containers. Here's a variation on the previous example that places a circle, a rectangle, and a triangle in separate containers. The code uses the Shape class as a container because it keeps the size of the published .swf file at a minimum, but you can do the same thing with Sprites, MovieClips, or any combination.

**NOTE**  You can find a copy of this code in the Flash file *18-7_Move_Three_Shapes.fla* on the Missing CD page at *www.missingmanuals.com/cds/flashcs6mm*.

```
1  var shpCircle:Shape = new Shape();
2  var shpRectangle:Shape = new Shape();
3  var shpTriangle:Shape = new Shape();
4
5  shpCircle.graphics.beginFill(0x000077,1);
6  shpCircle.graphics.drawCircle(250,100,75);
7  shpCircle.graphics.endFill();
8
```

```
 9  shpRectangle.graphics.beginFill(0x009900,1);
10  shpRectangle.graphics.drawRect(200,100,150,100);
11  shpRectangle.graphics.endFill();
12
13  shpTriangle.graphics.moveTo(200,150);
14  shpTriangle.graphics.beginFill(0x880000);
15  shpTriangle.graphics.lineTo(300,250);
16  shpTriangle.graphics.lineTo(100,250);
17  shpTriangle.graphics.lineTo(200,150);
18  shpTriangle.graphics.endFill();
19
20  addChild(shpRectangle);
21  addChild(shpTriangle);
22  addChild(shpCircle);
23
24  var tmrMover:Timer = new Timer(250,30);
25  tmrMover.start();
26
27  tmrMover.addEventListener(TimerEvent.TIMER,timerMoverListener);
28
29  function timerMoverListener(evt:TimerEvent):void
30  {
31      shpCircle.x += 3;
32      shpRectangle.x -= 3;
33      shpTriangle.y += 3;
34  }
```

What distinguishes this example from the previous one is that the first three lines create three instances of the Shape class, appropriately named shpCircle, shpRectangle, and shpTriangle. Lines 5 through 18 define the objects. None of them have a *lineStyle()* definition, so they're all fill and no stroke. The alpha value is set to 1, so they're completely opaque. The circle and the rectangle are drawn using built-in shapes, but the triangle is drawn line by line. Lines 20 through 22 use the *addChild()* method to place each shape on the stage.

The TIMER portion of the code is similar to the previous example. On line 24 when the tmrMover is created, the delay is set to 250 and the repeatCount is set to 30. This means this timer will tick off events twice as quickly as the earlier example, where the delay was set to 500. Line 27 registers the event listener *timerMoverListener()*. By using the *TIMER* constant instead of the *TIMER_COMPLETE* constant, this timer will trigger 30 events, instead of just one. (For more details, see page 476.) The function *timerMoverListener()* from line 29 through the last line of the code runs each time the event triggers.

To move the circle 3 pixels from left to right, this line:

```
shpCircle.x += 3;
```

increments the value of the shpCircle's x property by 3. It's simply an abbreviated way of saying:

```
shpCircle.x = shpCircle.x + 3;
```

The other two lines in the function work similarly, except that by decrementing the *x* property, line 31 moves the rectangle from right to left. Line 32 operates on the *y* property of shpTriangle, so it moves down the stage.

Each time the clock ticks, the objects move. There are a couple of ways to make them move at different rates of speed. Make the values smaller, and the objects will move a shorter distance in the same time period. Or, for the most versatility, you can create separate timers for each object. That way, you can change the delay and the intervals, as well as the distance that the objects move.

# ■ Shapes, Sprites, and Movie Clips for Drawings

When you create drawings on Shapes, Sprites, and MovieClips, it's tempting to think you're placing the drawings inside containers—but you're not. At least, not in the true ActionScript sense of the word "container." As explained back in Chapter 14 (page 483), Sprite and MovieClip objects are DisplayObjectContainers, meaning that by using the *addChild()* method, you can put objects inside a Sprite or MovieClip and the objects will be displayed. Shape, on the other hand, isn't a DisplayObjectContainer, so how can it show the drawn objects as shown in this chapter?

The fact of the matter is, when you draw as described in this chapter, you're drawing lines and shapes on the canvas or the background of the Shape, Sprite, or MovieClip. It's not the same thing as using the *addChild()* method, which adds an object to a DisplayObjectContainer. For example, you can't position a drawing to appear in front of an object that's added to a MovieClip using the *addChild()* method. Here's an example; the code appears in *18-8_Canvas_Drawing.fla* in the Missing CD (*www. missingmanuals.com/cds/flashcs6mm*):

```
1  var tfPoem:TextField = new TextField();
2  var mcCanvas:MovieClip = new MovieClip();
3
4  tfPoem.text = "Twas brillig, and the slithy toves";
5  tfPoem.x = 110;
6  tfPoem.y = 110;
```

```
 7  tfPoem.autoSize=TextFieldAutoSize.LEFT;
 8  mcCanvas.addChild(tfPoem);
 9
10  mcCanvas.graphics.beginFill(0x99FFFF);
11  mcCanvas.graphics.drawRect(100,100,200,150);
12  mcCanvas.graphics.endFill();
13
14  addChild(mcCanvas);
```

This example has only two objects: a TextField called tfPoem and a MovieClip called mcCanvas. Note that the rectangle isn't an object in its own right. Lines 4 through 7 define the text field, adding text, positioning it, and setting its *autoSize* property to accommodate the text. Line 8 places the txtField inside mcCanvas. The text field is now contained in the movie clip, a DisplayObjectContainer. The technique for creating and displaying the drawing is different, though. The rectangle is defined in lines 10 and 11, but that's done through the graphics property of mcCanvas. It never uses the *addChild()* method in mcCanvas. This means the rectangle has no index value, and you can't reposition it in the Display List using a command like *addChild()* or *addChildAt()*.

The last line of the code adds mcCanvas to the main timeline. When mcCanvas is placed in the main timeline (also a DisplayObjectContainer), then both the rectangle drawn on mcCanvas and the text field that's contained by mcCanvas are displayed.

## ■ Removing Lines and Shapes

So far, this chapter has shown several ways to draw lines and shapes. This section tells how to make them disappear. The Graphics class has a *clear()* method. When you use this method, it erases the drawings that were created in the object, resets the line and fill style settings, and moves the virtual pen back to the 0,0 position. The *clear()* method is a multipurpose cleanup tool. Here's an example of the *clear()* method in action. A text field is added to the code that begins on the previous page. This text field serves as kind of a button that, when clicked, triggers the *clear()* method to remove the drawings on the mcCanvas movie clip. For the complete code, check out *18-9_Clear_Graphic.fla* in the Missing CD (*www.missingmanuals. com/cds/flashcs6mm*):

```
 1  var tfPoem:TextField = new TextField();
 2  var mcCanvas:MovieClip = new MovieClip();
 3
 4  tfPoem.text = "Twas brillig, and the slithy toves";
 5  tfPoem.x = 110;
 6  tfPoem.y = 110;
 7  tfPoem.autoSize = TextFieldAutoSize.LEFT;
 8  mcCanvas.addChild(tfPoem);
 9
```

```
10 mcCanvas.graphics.beginFill(0x99FFFF);
11 mcCanvas.graphics.drawRect(100,100,200,150);
12
13 addChild(mcCanvas);
14
15 var txtRemoveRectangle = new TextField();
16 txtRemoveRectangle.text = "Click here to remove the rectangle";
17 txtRemoveRectangle.x = 110;
18 txtRemoveRectangle.y = 250;
19 txtRemoveRectangle.autoSize = TextFieldAutoSize.LEFT;
20 addChild(txtRemoveRectangle);
21
22 txtRemoveRectangle.addEventListener(MouseEvent.CLICK,clickListener);
23 function clickListener(evt:MouseEvent):void
24 {
25     mcCanvas.graphics.clear();
26 }
```

There are no changes to the code until line 15. A new text field, *txtRemoveRectangle*, is created, and on the following line, text is assigned to the *text* property. The text field is positioned on the stage, and the *autoSize* property is set. On line 20, the *addChild()* method adds the txtField to the main timeline. Lines 22 through 26 create and register an event listener.

When you test this code, it looks like Figure 18-8.

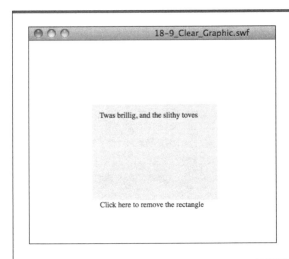

**FIGURE 18-8**

*Click the words at the bottom of this animation, and the rectangle disappears. The clear() method removes the vector graphics from the movie clip. Drawings in the movie clip disappear, but items contained by the movie clip, like the text field, remain.*

# Debugging and Delivering Your Animation

# Testing and Debugging Your Animation

The odds are against you. When you're designing an animation and writing Action-Script code, there may be several ways to do it and have it come out right. Unfortunately, there are many more ways you can do it wrong. Maybe you chose a motion tween when you meant to choose a shape tween, or you added content to a frame instead of a keyframe. In ActionScript, a tiny error like using a capital letter in the wrong place or a misplaced semicolon can ruin everything. The more complex your project is, the more errors you're likely to encounter.

The only way to find—and fix—your mistakes before your audience sees them is to test and debug your projects. Yes, troubleshooting can be tedious, time-consuming, and not nearly as much fun as designing and creating a brilliant animation. But if you approach troubleshooting as solving a puzzle or a mystery, it can be fun. Furthermore, Flash Professional CS6 comes with some pretty powerful testing and debugging tools to help you find and squash those bugs.

Throughout this book, you've seen examples of testing an animation using the Control→Test Movie option (for an example, look ahead to Figure 19-3). This chapter expands on that simple test option, plus it shows you how to test animation playback at a variety of connection speeds. And if you've added ActionScript to your animation, this chapter shows you how to unsnarl uncooperative ActionScript code using Flash's debugging tools.

## Testing Strategies

All your audience ever sees is the finished product, not your intentions. So no matter how sophisticated your animation or how cleverly constructed your ActionScript code, if you don't test your animation and make sure it works the way you want it to, all your hard work will have been in vain.

The following section shows you how to prepare for testing from the very beginning by following good Flash development policies. Also, you'll find out the differences between testing on the stage and testing in Flash Player, along with tips for testing your animation in a web browser.

## Planning Ahead

The more complex your animation, the more you need a thorough plan for testing it. Few of the guidelines in the next two sections are specific to testing in Flash. Instead, they're tried-and-true suggestions culled from all walks of programming life. Following them pays off in higher-quality animations and reduced time spent chasing bugs.

Ideally, you should begin thinking about testing before you've created a single frame of your animation. Here are some pre-animation strategies that pay off big:

### ■ SEPARATE POTENTIALLY TROUBLESOME ELEMENTS

ActionScript actions are very powerful, but they can also cause a lot of grief. Get into the habit of putting them into a separate layer named "actions" at the top of your list of layers, so that you'll always know where to find it. Putting all your labels into a separate layer (named "labels") is a good idea, too. With sounds, you may be able to put them in a single layer, or a sounds folder.

### ■ REUSE AS MUCH AS POSSIBLE

Instead of cutting and pasting an image or a series of frames, create a symbol and reuse it. That way, if a bug raises its ugly head, you'll have fewer places to go hunting. You can cut down on bugs by reusing ActionScript code, too. Instead of attaching four similar ActionScript actions to four different frames or buttons, create a single ActionScript method or function and call it four times.

### ■ BE GENEROUS WITH COMMENTS

Before you know it, you'll forget which layers contain which images, why you added certain actions to certain objects, or even why you ordered your ActionScript statements the way you did. In addition to adding descriptive comments to all the actions you create, get in the habit of adding an overall comment to the first frame of your animation. Make it as long as you want, and be sure to mention your name, the date, and anything else pertinent you can think of. You create a comment in ActionScript two different ways, as shown below:

```
// This is an example of a single-line ActionScript comment.

/* This type of ActionScript comment can span more than one line. All you
   have to remember is to begin your multiline comment with a slash-asterisk
   and end it with an asterisk-slash, as you see here. */
```

### ■ STICK WITH CONSISTENT NAMES

Referring to a background image in one animation as "bg," in another animation as "back_ground," and in still another as "Background" is just asking for trouble. Even if you don't have trouble remembering which is which, odds are your office teammates will—and referring to an incorrectly spelled variable in ActionScript causes your animation to misbehave quietly. In other words, type *Backgruond* instead of *Background*, and Flash may not pop up an error message; your animation just looks or acts odd for no apparent reason. Devise a naming convention you're comfortable with and stick with it. For example, you might decide always to use uppercase, lowercase, or mixed case. You might decide always to spell words out, or always to abbreviate them the same way. The particulars don't matter as much as your consistency in applying them. Keep in mind that capitalization counts. Because ActionScript is case-sensitive, Flash treats "background," "Background," and "BACKGROUND" as three different names.

## Techniques for Better Testing

The following strategies are crucial if you're creating complex animations as part of a development team. But they're also helpful if it's just you creating a short, simple animation all by your lonesome.

- **Test early, test often.** Don't wait until you've attached actions to 16 different objects to begin testing. Test the first action, and then test each additional action as you go along. This iterative approach helps you identify problems while they're still small and easy to pinpoint.

- **Test everything.** Instead of assuming the best-case scenario, see what happens when you access your animation over a slow connection or using an older version of Flash Player. What happens when you type the wrong kind of data into an input text field or click buttons in the wrong order? (Believe this: Your audience will do all of these things, and more.)

- **Test on different computers.** It's very important to test on a computer other than the one that writes the code. For example, an alien computer may have different fonts installed or a different version of Flash Player or some other support file. Use as much variety as possible in testing. Use Macs and PCs. Use old clunkers and the latest, greatest state-of-the-art machine you can get your hands on. Then test on an underpowered netbook, a smartphone, and a tablet.

- **Test in different web browsers.** If your animation is going to be viewed over the Internet, try it out in different browsers. These days, Microsoft's Internet Explorer, Apple's Safari, Firefox, and Google's Chrome are the most widely used browsers. It's best to test in each browser. Each of these browsers has several versions in use. For the fewest surprises and complaints, test in the last two or three available versions.

- **Test blind.** In other words, let someone who's unfamiliar with how your animation is supposed to work test it. In programming circles, this type of testing is known as *usability testing*, and it can flush out problems you never dreamed existed.

- **Test in "real world" mode.** Begin your testing in the Flash authoring environment, as described in the next section, but don't end there. Always test your animation in a production environment before you go live. For example, if you're planning to publish your animation to a website, upload your files (including your .swf file and any external files your animation depends on) to a web server, and then test it there, using a computer running the operating system, connection speed, browser, and Flash Player plug-in version you expect your audience to be running. (Sure, transferring a few files isn't *supposed* to make a difference—but it often does.) Chapter 20 covers publishing to the Web, as well as other publishing options.

---

**UP TO SPEED**

## Testing on the Stage vs. Testing in Flash Player

Flash gives you several options for testing your animation. You can test on the stage using the Control→Play command, or you can test in Flash Professional, Air Debug Launcher (desktop or mobile), or Device via USB. Testing on the stage is the fastest option, and it's good for checking your work as you go along, but in order to try out your animation exactly as your audience will see it, you have to choose one of the other options. Here's some more advice on when to choose each.

Testing on the stage is the quick and easy option, using the Controller below the timeline and the associated menu options (Control→Play, Control→Stop, Control→Rewind, Control→Step Forward One Frame, Control→Step Backward One Frame, and Control→"Go to End"). Testing on the stage is quicker than testing in Flash Player, because you don't have to wait for Flash to compile (*export*) your Flash document and then load it into the player. Instead, when you test on the stage, Flash immediately plays the timeline frame by frame. Use the loop button and its associated timeline brackets to repeatedly play a selected group of frames. For simple animations and to review a portion of your animation, testing on the stage is easier and quicker than the other testing methods.

The downside to testing on the stage is that it doesn't always test what you think it's testing. For example, if you test a frame

containing a movie clip instance, you don't see the movie clip playing; you need to dig down into symbol editing mode to test the movie clip symbol. And if your animation contains a button instance and you forget to turn on the checkbox next to Control→Enable Simple Buttons, then the button doesn't work on the stage—even though it may work perfectly well in a published animation.

To test your animation in an environment similar to that of the intended audience, use one of the Control→Test Movie options. When you test an animation by selecting Control→Test Movie→"in Flash Professional" or Control→Test Scene, Flash generates an .swf file. For example, if you're testing a Flash document named *myDocument.fla*, Flash generates a file called *myDocument.swf* (or *myDocument_myScene.swf*, if you're testing a scene) and automatically loads it into a testing environment (powered by Flash Player). This option usually shows you exactly what your audience will see, not counting computer hardware and connection differences (page 646).

If you started your project from one of the AIR templates, you have the option to use the AIR Debug Launcher for either Desktop or Mobile. Use the "On Device via USB" option to test using a smartphone or tablet connected to your computer.

---

# Testing on the Stage

If all you want to do is check out a few simple frames' worth of action, this is the option to use. It's also the best choice if you want to see your motion path or *not* see the layers you've marked as hidden. (For the skinny on hiding and showing layers, check out page 138.)

The timeline controller buttons under the timeline (Figure 19-1), make it easy to test your animation as you build it. This addition makes the older floating controller (Window→Toolbars→Controller) obsolete. There are some handy menu options that work with the controllers:

- **Control→Loop Playback.** Tells Flash to loop playback over and over again after you click Play on the Controller. Flash keeps looping your animation until you click Stop. If you don't turn on this option, Flash just plays the animation once.

- **Control→Play All Scenes.** Tells Flash to play all the scenes in your animation, not just the scene currently visible on the stage.

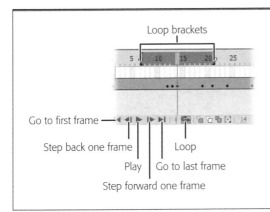

**FIGURE 19-1**

*The easiest way to test part of your animation is with the controller embedded below the timeline. Click the Loop button and position the brackets over the section you want to test.*

- **Control→Enable Simple Frame Actions.** Tells Flash to play the actions you've added to frames in the timeline. If you don't turn on this option, then Flash ignores all frame actions.

- **Control→Enable Simple Buttons.** Tells Flash to make your buttons work on the stage. (If you don't turn on the checkbox next to this option, mousing over a button or clicking it on the stage has no effect.)

- **Control→Enable Live Preview.** Tells Flash to display any components you've added to the stage the way they'll appear in Flash Player. (The components don't work on the stage, but you see how they're supposed to look.) If you have components on the stage and you don't choose this option, then only the outlines of your components appear.

- **Control→Mute Sounds.** Tells Flash not to play any of the sound clips you've added to your animation.

If you want to test a particular scene, for example, click the Edit Scene icon in the Edit bar, and then choose a scene to display the timeline for that scene. If you want to test a movie clip symbol, select Edit Symbols to display the timeline for that movie clip.

Whether you use the timeline controller or the floating controller, you'll find the standard play options, similar to your DVD player or iPod:

- **Stop.** Clicking this square button stops playback. (Found only on the floating controller.)

- **Go to first frame.** Clicking this button rewinds your animation. That is, it moves the playhead back to Frame 1.

- **Step back one frame.** Clicking this button moves the playhead back one frame. If the playhead is already at Frame 1, this button has no effect.

- **Play/Pause.** Clicking this right-arrow toggle button alternately runs your animation on the stage and pauses it. Playback begins at the playhead. In other words, playback begins with the frame you selected in the timeline and runs either until the end of your animation, or until you press the Stop button.

- **Step forward one frame.** Clicking this button moves the playhead forward one frame (unless the playhead is already at the last frame, in which case clicking this icon has no effect).

- **Go to last frame.** Clicking this button fast-forwards your animation to the very end. That is, it sets the playhead to the last frame in your animation.

> **NOTE**  You can also drag the playhead back and forth along the timeline to test your animation on the stage (a technique called *scrubbing*).

## ◾ Using the Test Movie Commands

Flash's test modes show you a closer approximation of how your animation will actually appear to your audience than testing on the stage. When you choose one of the Test Movie commands, your animation plays in one of the target environments: Flash Professional, AIR, or "Device via USB." Test Movie is your best bet if your animation contains movie clips, buttons, scenes, hidden layers, or ActionScript, since it shows you *all* the parts of your animation—not just the parts currently visible on the stage.

> **NOTE**  Motion paths (the lines) don't appear when you test your animation in Flash Player, for good reason: Flash designed them to be invisible at runtime. If you want to see your motion paths in action, you need to test your animation on the stage.

Here are the steps for testing an animation in Flash Professional. You use this mode for animations destined for websites or Flash Player:

1. **Select Control→Test Movie→"in Flash Professional."**

   The Exporting SWF Movie dialog box in Figure 19-2 appears, followed by your animation running in the Flash Player test window, similar to the one in Figure 19-3.

> **NOTE** If you're working on an AIR project, you can choose one of the AIR options: "in AIR Debug Launcher (Desktop)" or "in AIR Debug Launcher (Mobile)." Flash remembers your selection, so the next time you can test your animations with Ctrl+Enter (⌘-Return).

**FIGURE 19-2**

*When you see this dialog box, you know Flash is exporting your animation and creating an .swf file. If you've tested this particular animation before, Flash erases the .swf file it previously created and replaces it with the new one. Finishing an export can be fast or slow depending on the size and complexity of your animation and your computer's processing speed and memory.*

**FIGURE 19-3**

*Normally, when you select Control→Test Movie or Control→Test Scene, Flash opens up Flash Player in its own window. To control playback, you have a couple of choices: You can choose options from the File, View, Control, and Debug menus, or you can right-click (Control-click) the window, and then choose options from the shortcut menus that appear.*

2. **To control playback—to stop the animation, and then rewind it, for example—choose options from the Control menu.**

   If you're running Windows, the Control menu appears in your movie test window; on a Mac, you get the Control menu in Flash itself. (In Windows, you can also see the Control menu in Flash itself if you turn on tabbed viewing in Preferences. See the box below for details.)

3. **To close Flash Player, select File→Close or click the X in the upper-right corner of the window (Windows) or the red button in the upper-left corner of the window (Mac).**

> **NOTE** Testing your animation with Test Movie gives you a great sense of what your audience will see. But factors like connection speed and hardware differences come into play when you actually publish your animation, so you'll want to test your animation in a real-life production setting (using the same kind of computer, same connection speed, and same version browser as you expect your audience to use) before you go live.

## ■ Testing Inside a Web Page

In addition to letting you test your animation, Flash lets you test your animation embedded in a web page. This option lets you see how your animation looks in a web browser based on the animation alignment, scale, and size options Flash lets you set.

Here's how it works. You tell Flash in the Publish Settings window (Figure 19-4) that you want to embed your animation in a web page. Use the settings on the right side of the Publish Settings window to control the behavior of your animation when it runs in a web page. When you choose File→Publish Preview→HTML, Flash constructs an HTML file containing your animation, and then loads it automatically into the web browser on your computer.

> **NOTE** Tucking your animation into a web page is a popular publishing option, but it's certainly not the only one. The other publishing options, including publishing your animation as a QuickTime movie and as a standalone Flash projector file, are covered in detail in Chapter 20.

---

**GEM IN THE ROUGH**

### Test Multiple Animations

Some folks find a tabbed page—like the tabs in some web browsers—easier to pop back to, especially if they're trying to test several different animations at once. If you'd rather Flash Player appear in a tabbed page, select Edit→Preferences (Windows) or Flash→Preferences (Mac).

In the Preferences window that appears, click the General category. Turn on the checkbox next to "Open test movie in tabs." Then choose Control→Test Movie. This time, Flash Player appears as a tab. When you click the tab, the Flash Developer menu options change to the Flash Player options.

---

To test your animation inside a web page:

1. **Choose File→Publish Settings.**

   The Publish Settings window appears, as shown in Figure 19-4.

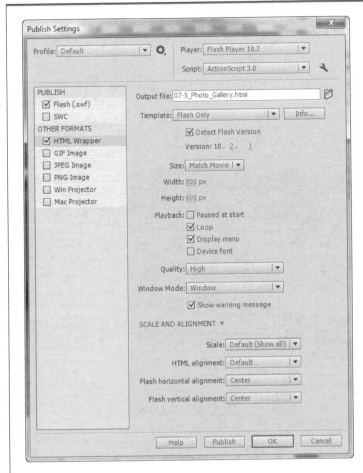

**FIGURE 19-4**

*Flash gives you several publishing options, one of which is embedding your animation inside of an HTML wrapper. The name Flash uses for your HTML file is the name of your Flash document, but with an .html extension.*

2. **Under Other Formats, turn on HTML Wrapper.**

   Flash displays the HTML options in the right side of the window.

3. **Click the Template drop-down menu, and then choose "Flash only."** Click OK.

   Flash accepts your changes and closes the Publish Settings dialog box.

**NOTE** For a description of each of the settings on this tab, see page 685.

4. **Choose File→Publish Preview→HTML.**

   The Publishing dialog box appears briefly to let you know Flash is creating an HTML file. When the dialog box disappears, Flash loads the completed HTML, including your embedded animation, into the web browser on your computer (Figure 19-5).

Right-clicking (Windows) or Control-clicking (Mac) the running animation shows you standard menu options you can use to control playback inside the browser, although how many options you see depends on whether you turned off the checkbox next to "Display menu" in the Publish Settings dialog box.

**FIGURE 19-5**

*In addition to creating an HTML file, choosing File→Publish Preview→HTML launches your web browser preloaded with that file.*

# Testing Download Time

If you're planning to publish your animation on the Web, you need to know how long it takes your animation to download from a web server to somebody's computer. Chapter 20 gives you several optimization techniques, including tips for preloading content and reducing your animation's file size; but before you begin to optimize your animation, you need to know just how bad the situation is and where the bottlenecks are. The following sections show you how.

## Simulating Downloads

You *could* set up a bank of test machines, each connected to the Internet at a different transfer speed, to determine the average download time your audience will eventually have to sit through. But Flash gives you an easier option: simulating downloads at a variety of transfer speeds with the click of a button. The simulation takes into consideration any additional, non-Flash media files that you've included in your animation, like sound and video clips.

To simulate different download speeds:

1. **Choose Control→Test Movie→"in Flash Professional."**

   The Flash Player (test window) appears.

2. **Select View→Download Settings (Figure 19-6), and then, from the submenu, select the connection speed you expect your audience to be running.**

   Your choices range from 14.4 (1.2 KB/s) to T1 speed (131.2 KB/s). If you need to simulate a faster speed, check out Figure 19-7.

**FIGURE 19-6**

*If you're used to testing your animation inside the Flash development environment, you may be shocked when you see how long it takes to download and play your animation over the web. Flash automatically adjusts for standard line congestion to give you a more realistic picture. So, for example, when you choose the 14.4 KB/s setting, Flash actually simulates the transfer at the slightly lower rate of 12.0 KB/s.*

3. **Choose View→Simulate Download.**

   The test window clears, and Flash plays your animation at the rate it would play it if it had to download your file from a web server at the connection speed you chose in step 2.

**FIGURE 19-7**

*To keep up with the latest advances in transfer technology, you can select a faster transfer rate than any of the options Flash has. To do so, select View→Download Settings→Customize, and then type a label and the new transfer speed you want to test (from 1 byte per second to 10,000,000).*

4. **Repeat steps 2 and 3 for each connection speed you want to test.**

   Often, you'll find that your animation takes too long to play at one—or even all—of the simulated connection speeds you test. Fortunately, Flash gives you additional tools to help you pinpoint which frames take longest to download (so that you know which frames to optimize). Read on for details.

### ■ PINPOINTING BOTTLENECKS WITH A BANDWIDTH PROFILER REPORT

Simulating downloads at different connection speeds gives you a general, overall feel for whether you'll need to optimize your animation or give your audience a low-bandwidth alternative (or both). But to get more precise information, like which frames represent the greatest bottlenecks, turn to the *bandwidth profiler report* (Figure 19-8).

To generate a bandwidth profiler report:

1. **Choose Control→Test Movie→"in Flash Professional."**

    The Flash Player (test window) appears containing your running animation.

---

**CODERS' CLINIC**

### Size Reports

Flash has a second statistical report called a *size report*. To create a size report, choose File→Publish Settings→Flash→Advanced, and then turn on the "Generate size report" checkbox. Make sure you can see the Output window (Window→Output). Then, when you choose File→Publish, Flash displays the size report in the Output window. It also automatically generates a text file named *yourFlashFile Report.txt* that you can pull into a text editor or word processor.

This report provides detailed information about the elements that add to the size of the published .swf file. It thoroughly breaks down the details frame by frame, giving a running total of the file size in bytes. A summary lists scenes, symbols, and fonts and shows how the shapes, text, and ActionScript code add to the heft of your published file. If you're suffering from file bloat, generate a report to see which images, symbols, sounds, or other elements are causing the problem.

---

2. **In the test window, select View→Bandwidth Profiler.**

    In the top half of the window, Flash displays a report similar to the one in Figure 19-8.

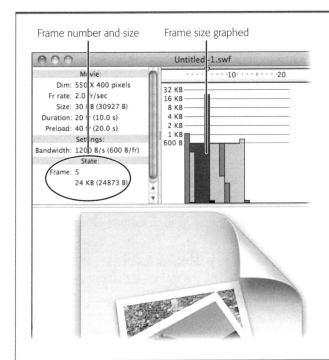

Frame number and size    Frame size graphed

**FIGURE 19-8**

*Flash assumes you want it to display your bandwidth reports in Streaming Graph format, as shown here, unless you tell it otherwise. Unfortunately, analyzing the graph on this kind of report can be tricky; to match a stacked segment to a particular frame, you have to click the stacked segment. When you do, Flash displays the associated frame in the Frame field on the left side of the report.*

### 3. Select View→Frame By Frame Graph.

The graph Flash displays when you choose the Frame By Frame option makes detecting rogue frames much easier than if you stick with Flash's suggested View→Streaming Graph option shown in Figure 19-8. Figure 19-9 has an example of a Frame By Frame graph.

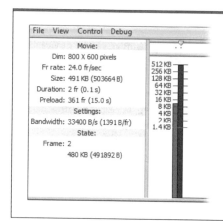

**FIGURE 19-9**

*On the left side of this Frame By Frame bandwidth profiler report, you see animation properties pertinent to playback, including the .swf file size and the stage dimensions and frame rate you set in Flash. The right side of the report shows you a frame-by-frame picture of the download process. Frame bars that appear above the red line (here, Flash has drawn the red line at 1.4 KB) mean a wait for data. So Frame 2 is the obvious slow-playing culprit in this animation.*

### 4. Select View→Simulate Download.

The progress bar at the top of the bandwidth profiler report moves as Flash simulates a download.

The report gives you information you can use to figure out which frames of your animation are hogging all the bandwidth. You'll find a timeline and a playhead at the top of the report. As your animation plays, the playhead moves along the timeline to help you see at a glance which frames are causing Flash to display those tall bandwidth-hogging frame bars. *Preload*, the most useful number, tells you how long your audience has to sit and wait before your animation begins. These are the details you'll find in the bandwidth profiler report:

- **Dimensions (Dim).** The width and height of the stage in pixels.

- **Frame rate (Fr rate).** The frame rate you set for this animation.

- **Size.** The size of the .swf file Flash created when you exported (began testing) the movie.

- **Duration.** The number of frames in this animation, followed by the number of seconds the frames take to play based on the frame rate you set.

- **Preload.** The total number of seconds it takes Flash to begin playing the animation at the bandwidth setting you chose.

- **Bandwidth.** The connection simulation speed you chose by selecting View→Download Settings.

- **Frame.** The frame Flash is currently loading.

If your animation played just fine, try testing it using a slower simulated connection. (Your goal is to make sure as much of your potential audience can enjoy your animation as possible—even folks running over slow connections and congested networks.) To do this test, redisplay the bandwidth profiler report, this time using a different connection simulation speed:

1. **Choose View→Download Settings.**

   A submenu appears, showing a list of possible connection simulation speeds, like 28.8, 56K, and T1.

2. **Choose the new simulation speed you want to test.** Then choose View→Simulate Download again.

   A new bandwidth profiler report appears, based on the new connection speed.

---

**UP TO SPEED**

### The Flash Player View Menu Options

Flash Player has several menu options that you can use to change the way your animation appears as it's playing. If you turn on the checkbox next to *Display menu* in the Publish Settings→HTML dialog box (coming up in Figure 20-1), your audience can see some of these same options, by right-clicking (Windows) or Control-clicking (Mac).

If you're running a Mac, the following menu options don't appear directly in Flash Player; instead, they appear in the Flash menu:

- **View→Zoom In.** Tells Flash to enlarge your animation. This option is useful if you want to examine your artwork close up.

- **View→Zoom Out.** Tells Flash to shrink your animation.

- **View→Magnification.** Displays a menu of percentage options you can choose from to tell Flash to enlarge or shrink your animation.

- **View→Bandwidth Profiler.** Creates a bandwidth profiler report.

- **View→Streaming Graph.** Tells Flash to display download data in stacked bars when it creates a bandwidth profiler report (Figure 19-8).

- **View→Frame By Frame Graph.** Tells Flash to display the download time for each frame separately when it creates a bandwidth profiler report (Figure 19-9).

- **View→Simulate Download.** Tells Flash to pretend to download your animation from a web server based on the download settings you select using View→Download Settings.

- **View→Download Settings.** Displays a list of connection speeds, from 14.4 to T1, to test the download speed of your animation on a variety of different computers.

- **View→Quality.** Tells Flash to display your animation's artwork in one of three different quality modes: low, medium, or high. Flash assumes you want high quality unless you tell it differently. (Choosing low or medium quality doesn't reduce simulation download time, but reducing image quality in the Flash authoring environment does reduce your animation's file size, which in turn speeds up download time.)

- **View→Show Redraw Regions.** Displays borders around the moving images in your animation.

# The Art of Debugging

Imagine, for an instant, that your animation isn't behaving the way you think it should. Testing it on the stage or in Flash Player, and then eyeballing the results, as described in the previous section, is a good place to start tracking down the problem. But if you've added ActionScript to your animation, chances are you need more firepower. You need to be able to examine the inner workings of your ActionScript code—the variables, instance names, methods, and so on—to help you figure out what's wrong. Debugging is one of those activities that's part art, part craft, and part science. Flash and ActionScript provide several tools that help you track down and eliminate those pesky bugs of all types. These are some of the tools at your disposal:

- The **Check syntax** button catches the most obvious typos. If you've got too many parentheses in a line or you misplaced a comma or semicolon, the syntax checker is likely to notice. Still, it lets lots of the bad guys through.

- The **Compiler Errors** panel is the next layer of defense against bugs. If there's a flaw in your code's logic (for example, a reference to some object that doesn't exist or is misnamed), a message is likely to appear in the Compiler Errors panel. Sometimes your animation will run anyway; other times it won't.

- The **Output panel** displays messages. Using the *trace()* statement, you can display the values of variable and object properties in the Output panel. So you get to tell ActionScript what to report on.

- The **Debugger** is your debugging power tool. It's kind of like the diagnostic machine your mechanic connects to your car to see what's going on inside. The debugger combines the usefulness of the other tools with the all-important ability to stop your animation and code in its tracks. That gives you an opportunity to examine the critical variables, property settings, and values.

> **NOTE**   The debugger for ActionScript 3.0 is different in a few ways from the debugger for ActionScript 2.0 and 1.0 code. For details on the older debugger, see *Flash CS3: The Missing Manual*.

You're likely to use the first three tools as you're writing and testing your animation. As your code gets more complex, with multiple timelines, multiple objects, and multiple functions and methods, you'll turn to the debugger. This section starts off with the quick and easy bug squashers, and then moves on to the more complex. The troublesome program attached to that diagnostic machine is called *19-1_Debug_Code.fla*, and you can download it from the Missing CD page at *www.missingmanuals.com/cds/flashcs6mm*. If you'd like to see how the program is supposed to behave, check out *19-2_Debug_Code_done.fla*.

## Checking with the Syntax Checker

The animation *19-1_Debug_Code.fla* isn't behaving the way it should—pretty ornery for a snippet of code that's only 20 lines long. It's supposed to draw lines on the screen from one random point to another. The lines are supposed to randomly vary in thickness, color, and transparency. There are four text fields in the display that are supposed to flash the x/y coordinates of the points used to draw the lines. If you try to test the program with Ctrl+Enter (⌘-Return), nothing much happens. The first step to putting things on track is to use the "Check syntax" button in the Actions panel, as shown in Figure 19-10.

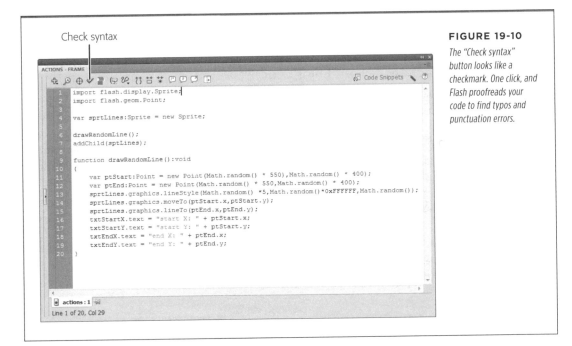

Check syntax

**FIGURE 19-10**

*The "Check syntax" button looks like a checkmark. One click, and Flash proofreads your code to find typos and punctuation errors.*

```
1   import flash.display.Sprite;
2   import flash.geom.Point;
3
4   var sprtLines:Sprite = new Sprite;
5
6   drawRandomLine();
7   addChild(sptLines);
8
9   function drawRandomLine():void
10  {
11      var ptStart:Point = new Point(Math.random() * 550,Math.random() * 400);
12      var ptEnd:Point = new Point(Math.random() * 550,Math.random() * 400);
13      sprtLines.graphics.lineStyle(Math.random() *5,Math.random()*0xFFFFFF,Math.random());
14      sprtLines.graphics.moveTo(ptStart.x,ptStart.y);
15      sprtLines.graphics.lineTo(ptEnd.x,ptEnd.y);
16      txtStartX.text = "start X: " + ptStart.x;
17      txtStartY.text = "start Y: " + ptStart.y;
18      txtEndX.text = "end X: " + ptEnd.x;
19      txtEndY.text = "end Y: " + ptEnd.y;
20  }
```

ACTIONS - FRAME

Code Snippets

actions : 1

Line 1 of 20, Col 29

1. **With *19-1_Debug_Code.fla* open in Flash, select Window→Actions.**

   The Actions panel opens. The Actions panel can look different depending on how you've set up your workspace. It also remembers some of the settings, like which panels are open and closed, from the last time you used it.

2. **If you don't see code in the Actions panel, then in the animation's timeline, click Frame 1 in the actions layer.**

   The Actions panel shows the code associated with particular frames in the timeline. It's not a problem with this little snippet, but with larger animations if you don't see the actions you want to debug, make sure you've selected the frame that holds the code.

3. **In the Actions panel, click the "Check syntax" button.**

   The "Check syntax" button looks like a checkmark. After a little deep thinking, you hear a ding, which occurs whether there's an error or not.

**4. Click the Compiler Errors panel, and look for an error message.**

If everything is okay, you won't see any message. If "Check syntax" found an error, a message appears in the panel. The Compiler Errors panel's location may vary depending on how you've organized your workspace. If you're using the Essentials workspace, it appears beneath your animation. (And if you're wondering what the heck a compiler is, see the box on page 655.)

## Deciphering the Actions Panel's Color Code

One quick way to spot problems in your ActionScript code is to examine the colors Flash uses to display your code in the Actions panel.

Right out of the box, Flash displays ActionScript keywords and identifiers in blue, comments in light gray, text strings (text surrounded by quotes) in green, and stuff it doesn't recognize in black. So if you notice a function call or a property that appears black, you know there's a problem. A properly spelled function call or property should appear blue (unless it's a custom function), so if it's black, chances are your finger slipped.

If Flash's ActionScript coloring scheme is too subtle for your tastes, you can change the colors it uses.

To change colors:

1. Select Edit→Preferences (Windows) or Flash→Preferences (Mac).

2. In the Preferences panel that appears, select the ActionScript category. Make sure the checkbox at "Syntax colors: Code coloring" is turned on.

3. Click the color pickers next to Foreground, Keywords, Identifiers, Background, Comments, and Strings to choose different colors for each of these ActionScript code elements.

For example, if you have trouble making out the text strings in your scripts due to red-green color blindness, you can change Strings to a different hue.

For this animation, the message in the Compiler Errors panel looks like Figure 19-11. As helpful as these details are, sometimes your view of the issue and the compiler's view aren't coming from the same direction, so the messages may seem a bit cryptic. In this case, you're told the error is on Line 11. The error's description is:

```
1086: Syntax error: expecting semicolon before dot.
```

That's a little on the cryptic side, but it means there's probably something wrong with the way the line is punctuated. Double-clicking the error message puts your cursor in the offending line in the Actions panel.

**5. Examine the highlighted line for a syntax error.**

Here's where you get into the grunt work of debugging: looking through your code to find out where there might be a problem. Flash is a lot fussier about punctuation than your third-grade teacher, so double-check to make sure there are commas between parameters and a semicolon at the end of the line. Parentheses are another place where it's easy to make a mistake. In any statement (from the beginning of the line to the semicolon), there should be an equal number of left parentheses and right parentheses. And yes, they all need to be in the right spots, too. But it's so easy to mess up on parentheses that counting is a legitimate debugging technique. In the code in line 11, there's one extra closing parenthesis before the comma:

```
var ptStart:Point = new Point(Math.random() * 550),Math.random() * 400);
```

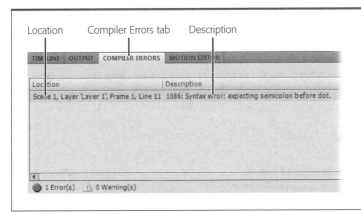

**FIGURE 19-11**

*The messages in the Compiler Errors panel have two parts. The Location part tells you where the error is, and the Description part tells you how the compiler sees the error.*

6. **Delete the error, and then click "Check syntax" again.**

   This time, you hear the ding, but there's no error message. That's fine as far as it goes. With ActionScript 3.0 code, all the syntax checker does is check the punctuation and a few other details of your code. The Syntax checker works quickly because it doesn't actually compile your code. That means it doesn't catch nearly as many errors as you find when you test your animation using Ctrl+Enter (⌘-Return).

---

**UP TO SPEED**

## What's a Compiler and Why Does It Err?

When you write ActionScript code, you name objects and write statements in a language that's relatively understandable by humans. Your computer, however, speaks a different language altogether. When Flash compiles your ActionScript code, it translates the code from your human language to the computer's machine language. When Flash comes across statements that don't make sense, it says "Aha! A compiler error!" For example, one very common compiler error is the simple misspelling of an object's name.

Flash and ActionScript are very literal. If there's a misplaced letter or even an error in capitalization in a word, that's an error. For example, if your program has a variable named *myBall* and you mistakenly type in *myball*, ActionScript sees that second reference as an undefined object and a compiler error. Anything that prevents the compiler from successfully identifying all the objects and values and performing all the methods in your program results in an error.

## Finding Errors with the Compiler Errors Panel

When you test your animation using Control→Test Movie or by pressing Ctrl+Enter
(⌘-Return), Flash creates an .swf file. That's the same as the finished file you distribute or put on a website so the world can see your animation. In the process, your
ActionScript code is translated into a computer language that's smaller and faster
than your ActionScript. The process of compiling your code is likely to catch mistakes
that the "Check syntax" button misses. (See the box on page 655 for more details.)

> **NOTE** This example continues debugging the file *19-1_Debug_Code.fla*. The entire process began on page 652.

1. **Test your animation using Ctrl+Enter (⌘-Return).**

   An error appears in the Compiler Errors panel, as shown in Figure 19-12. (It could
   be worse; sometimes you see seven or eight errors stacked up in the panel.) This
   error didn't appear when you clicked the "Check syntax" button in the previous exercise, because "Check syntax" doesn't compile the code. Obviously, the
   compiler choked on something you're trying to feed it. The Compiler Errors panel
   reports that the location of the error is "Scene 1, Layer 'actions', Frame 1, Line
   7." That's very helpful information, and what's more, when you double-click the
   error message in the panel, Flash zips you to the Actions panel and finds that
   point in your code. But before you double-click, read the description of the error:

   ```
   1120: Access of undefined property sptLines.
   ```

   That's also a good clue, which explains the problem, at least as far as the compiler sees it. The compiler thinks you're trying to make a change to a property
   that doesn't exist. That property has something to do with sptLines.

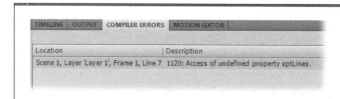

**FIGURE 19-12**

*Here the Compiler Errors pane is reporting an unde-
fined property. This type of error is often the result
of misspelling an object or a variable's name.*

2. **Double-click the error message in the Compiler Errors panel.**

   Flash zips you to the Actions panel and highlights line 4, which reads:

   ```
   addChild(sptLines);
   ```

3. **Examine the highlighted line for a syntax error.**

   At first this might seem a little puzzling. It's a simple statement that adds sptLines
   to the Display List, which should make its contents visible on the stage. The
   compiler error said something about a property, but this line doesn't seem to

be changing a property. You know, however, that the compiler sees something it can't identify, and that's *sptLines*. It makes sense to check the code that precedes the error for previous references to *sptLines*. There aren't any, and that's exactly the problem. The variable sprtLines is defined in the first line of the code, and the reference to "sptLines" is a typo.

4. **In line 7, correct the spelling of sprtLines, and then test the animation.**

   This time, *19-1_Debug_Code.fla* is a little more entertaining. The animation draws random lines on the stage. The lines vary in thickness, color, and transparency. But the text boxes, like the one that reads *start X*, don't change or provide any other information. Looks like there's more debugging to do.

**NOTE** The animation *19-1_Debug_Code.fla* uses a very slow frame rate of 2 fps so that each line appears slowly on the screen. If you want to speed up the action, go to Modify→Document and change the frame rate. If you have the Bandwidth Profiler open and the animation doesn't play as expected, try turning and you have the Bandwidth running the animation with the Bandwidth Profiler closed.

Stop the *19-1_Debug_Code.fla* when you're sufficiently entertained. Because there's no automatic end to the animation, Flash can conceivably draw so many lines that your computer will run out of memory trying to display them.

## Using the Output Panel and *trace()* Statement

The ActionScript *trace()* statement is one of the easiest ways to debug your programs—and it delivers a lot of bang for your debugging buck. You get to tell ActionScript exactly what variable value or object you want to keep track of, and Flash obligingly sends the details to the Output panel. *Trace()* is such an important code-writing tool that it's used throughout the ActionScript examples in this book. Here's another good example of the way you can use *trace()* to understand why your program isn't behaving as expected.

**NOTE** This example continues debugging the file *19-1_Debug_Code.fla*. The entire process begins on page 652.

When you tested *19-1_Debug_Code.fla* in step 4 above, the drawing lines part of the program worked, but the text fields didn't display information about the points used to start and end the lines. Text fields display strings of text in your animation. There are a few different types of text fields, and you can format them in a number of ways. (For all the details, see page 217.) In this case, the text fields show some of the information that you want displayed, but not all of it.

The *trace()* statement works kind of like a text field. You put the information that you want displayed inside the *trace()* statement's parentheses. If you want to display a string of text, put it inside quotes, like this:

```
trace("show this text");
```

When your ActionScript code gets to that line, the words "show this text" appear in the Output panel (without the quotes). If you have a variable named strMsg, and its value is "show this text," then you can write a *trace()* statement like this:

```
trace(strMsg);
```

This statement would also send the words "show this text" to the Output panel. The Output panel isn't at all fussy about the data types. Put the name of a variable, an instance of an object, or just about anything inside a *trace()* statement, and something is bound to appear in the Output panel. If the value is a number, that's what you see. If it's a reference to an object, you see the object's name.

Following are some steps to gain a little insight into the problem with the text fields in the file *19-1_Debug_Code.fla*.

1. **Test the animation as it worked at the end of the previous section.**

   When you test the animation, you see the random lines drawn properly, but you see only part of the text that should be displayed in the text fields, as shown in Figure 19-13. Don't forget to stop the animation (Control→Stop) or close the window (File→Close).

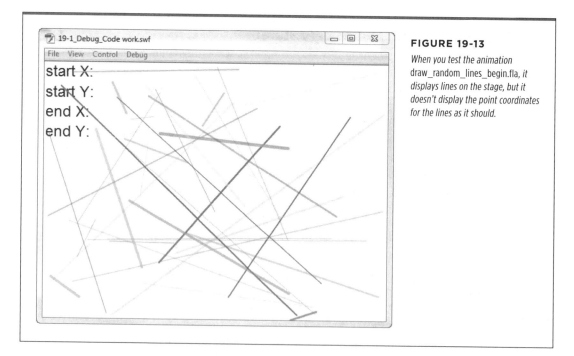

**FIGURE 19-13**

*When you test the animation draw_random_lines_begin.fla, it displays lines on the stage, but it doesn't display the point coordinates for the lines as it should.*

2. **On the stage, click the text fields, and then, in the Properties panel, check the names of the text fields.**

   In your Flash document, the text fields on the stage show text, like "start X" and "start Y." When you select a text field, you see its name at the top of the

Properties panel. For example, the text field with the text "start X" is named txtStartX. The others are named txtStartY, txtEndX, and txtEndY. These are the names of misbehaving text fields, so you'll look for references to them in your code.

3. **Select Window→Actions to open the Actions panel.**

The Actions panel displays this code, which amounts to only 20 lines:

```
1   import flash.display.Sprite;
2   import flash.geom.Point;
3
4   var sprtLines:Sprite = new Sprite;
5
6   drawRandomLine();
7   addChild(sprtLines);
8
9   function drawRandomLine():void
10  {
11      var ptStart:Point = new Point(Math.random() * 550,Math.random() *
400);
12      var ptEnd:Point = new Point(Math.random() * 550,Math.random() *
400);
13      sprtLines.graphics.lineStyle(Math.random() *5,Math.
random()*0xFFFFFF,Math.random());
14      sprtLines.graphics.moveTo(ptStart.x,ptStart.y);
15      sprtLines.graphics.lineTo(ptEnd.x,ptEnd.y);
16      txtStartX.text = "start X: " + ptStart.x;
17      txtStartY.text = "start Y: " + ptStart.y;
18      txtEndX.text = "end X: " + ptEnd.x;
19      txtEndY.text = "end Y: " + ptEnd.y;
20  }
```

4. **Search for lines with references to the misbehaving text fields: txtStartX, txtStartY, txtEndX, and txtEndY.**

In lines 16 through 19, values are assigned to the text fields' properties. Each value is made of two parts, a string literal with text like "start X:" and then the string concatenation operator (+) and a reference to an object's property, like *ptStart.x*. Looking back up in the code, you see on line 11 that the data type for ptStart is Point. The reference ptStart.x is a reference to the *x* property of a point. That value is a number. Still, there's nothing apparently wrong with the code.

5. **Insert a line after line 15, and then type the following *trace()* statement:**

```
trace("start X: " + ptStart.x);
```

The text inside the parentheses is exactly the text that's supposed to appear in the text field. In fact, you can copy and paste to create the line. Copying and pasting is a good technique for an operation like this, because you'll be sure the text in the two statements is identical.

---

**TIP** If you don't see your *trace()* statement in the Output panel, select File→Publish Settings→Flash, and make sure the "Omit trace actions" checkbox is turned off.

---

6. **Test your animation using Ctrl+Enter (⌘-Return) and examine the Output panel.**

When you run your animation, the Output window starts to fill up with lines like:

start X: 549.6419722447172

start X: 499.13692246191204

start X: 239.57312640268356

start X: 64.5334855420515

Comparing the Output panel details, you see that your text fields display the string literals, like *start X:*, but they aren't displaying the numbers with all those decimal places. Those long numbers are generated by the *random()* method used earlier in the code. For example, the value for ptStart.x is created in line 11 with the statement:

```
var ptStart:Point = new Point(Math.random() * 550,Math.random() * 400);
```

This line creates a new variable called *ptStart*. Its data type is Point, which includes x and y properties. At the same time that the new instance of Point is being created, values are assigned to those *x* and *y* properties. Instead of providing specific numbers, you want to provide random numbers that change every time the *drawRandomLine()* method runs. So the statement uses a method that's provided by the Math class. The section of the statement that reads *Math.random() * 550* is in effect saying, give me a random number between zero and 550 (the width of the stage). Likewise, the next bit of code is providing a number for the y property that matches the height of the stage. *Math.random()* is providing a number with a little more precision than is necessary for this snippet of a program. In fact, the number is too long to fit in the text field.

7. **Select the txtStartX text field on the stage, and then in the Properties panel, change the width to 550.**

The width of the text field expands so it's the length of the stage.

8. **Test your animation using Ctrl+Enter (⌘-Return).**

When the animation runs, the entire number is displayed in the txtStartX text field, as shown in Figure 19-14. The *x* and *y* properties aren't displayed in the other text fields.

Mystery solved. You figured out what's gone wrong with the code. The solution is a little less than satisfactory—you don't really need a number that long for this animation. Fortunately, that gives you an opportunity to explore the Debugger in action, as you'll see in the next section.

You can delete the *trace()* statement from your code or you can temporarily leave it in. It doesn't change the appearance of the animation in any way. A third alternative is to use a handy programmer's trick called *commenting out*; see the box below.

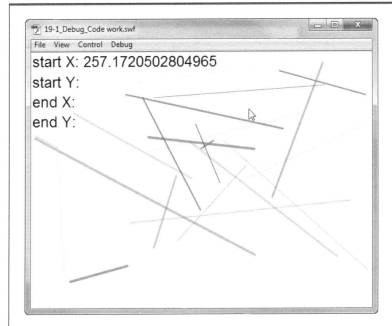

**FIGURE 19-14**

*After changing the width of the text field, Flash displays the very long number that represents the x property for your line's starting point.*

---

**TRICK OF THE TRADE**

## Comment Me Out

If you're planning to keep working on your ActionScript code and think you'll need to reuse these *trace()* statements at some point down the road, you don't have to delete them and then type them in again later. Instead, you can "comment them out" by placing two slashes in front of each line, like this:

```
// trace("start X: " + ptStart.x);
```

When you stick two slashes at the beginning of a line of Action-Script code, Flash ignores everything it finds on the line after

those slashes. In other words, it treats the code as if it were a plain old comment. Later, when you want to use that *trace()* statement again, all you have to do is remove the slashes and you're back in business.

It's a good idea to remove or comment out *trace()* statements when you no longer need them. Not only will you avoid cluttering up your Output panel, but there's a performance boost, too.

---

## ■ Analyzing Code with the Debugger

When you need as much debugging muscle as Flash can provide, click Debug→Debug Movie→"in Flash Professional." You may think you've fired up a different program, but actually, Flash has merely closed some panels, opened others, and rearranged your view of your animation (Figure 19-15). It also automatically compiles and runs your animation. Your first visit to the debugger can be a little intimidating, but don't worry. Look around for familiar landmarks, and you'll soon figure out the purposes of the multiple panels and the messages within:

- The Debug Console in the upper-left corner shows buttons (Figure 19-15). You use these to move through your code and to end the debug session. You can also open the Debug Console using menus: Window→Debug Panels→Debug Console.

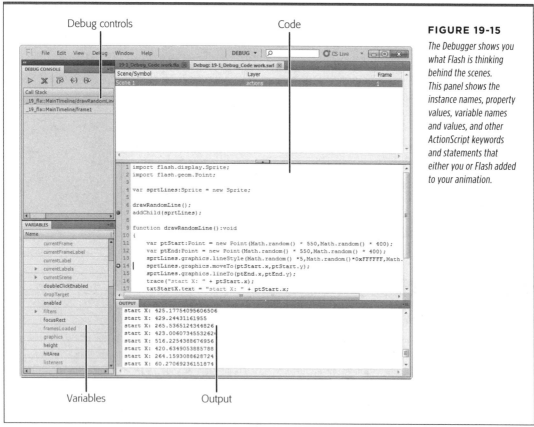

**Debug controls**

**Code**

**FIGURE 19-15**

*The Debugger shows you what Flash is thinking behind the scenes. This panel shows the instance names, property values, variable names and values, and other ActionScript keywords and statements that either you or Flash added to your animation.*

**Variables**

**Output**

- The Variables panel below the Debug Console is where you really learn what's going on in your program. As you work in the debugger, you'll see variable and object names here, along with their related values. There are probably a lot of unfamiliar words in there, because this panel keeps track of every property for every object in your animation. You don't need to worry about many of these, because Flash takes care of them perfectly well. But when something goes wrong, look up the name of the offending text box, variable name, or object in this list, and you'll be on your way to a solution. You can also open the Variables panel using menus: Window→Debug Panels→Variables.

- In the upper-right corner, the Scene/Symbol panel is pretty straightforward. It tracks your animation's current position in the main timeline, scene, or symbol timeline. You see the name of the scene or symbol, the layer that contains code, and the frame number.

- The middle panel shows the ActionScript code you wrote, similar to the Actions panel. You can force your program to stop at certain places in your code to give you a chance to inspect the inner workings of the objects. More on that in the next section.

- At the bottom is the Output panel, covered earlier in this chapter (page 657). If you've used the *trace()* statement while you were writing code and experimenting with ActionScript, you know how helpful the Output panel can be.

## Setting and Working with Breakpoints

One of the most important debugging tools in any well-stocked ActionScript programmer's arsenal is the *breakpoint*. A breakpoint is an artificial stopping point—sort of a roadblock—that you can insert into your ActionScript code to stop Flash Player in its tracks. Setting breakpoints lets you examine your animation at different points during playback so that you can pinpoint where a bug first happens.

Flash lets you set breakpoints at specific lines in your ActionScript code. Setting a breakpoint lets you play the animation only up until Flash encounters that breakpoint. The instant Flash encounters a line with a breakpoint, it immediately stops the animation so that you can either examine object property values (as described in the previous section) or step through the remaining code in your action slowly, line by line, watching what happens as you go.

Setting breakpoints is a great way to track down logic errors in your ActionScript code. For example, say you've created a chunk of code containing a lot of *if* and *switch* conditionals or *while* and *for* looping statements. Stopping playback just before you enter that long stretch of code lets you follow Flash as it works through the statements one at a time. By stepping through statements in the order Flash actually executes them (as opposed to the order you thought Flash was supposed to execute them), you may find, for example, that the cause of your problem is that Flash never reaches the *else* section of your *if...else* statement, or never performs any of the statements inside your *while* block because the *while* condition is never met.

**NOTE** For more information on using *if...else, do...while*, and other logical statements in ActionScript, check out Colin Moock's *Essential ActionScript 3.0*, and *ActionScript 3.0 Cookbook*, by Joey Lott, et al. Both books have detailed coverage of more advanced ActionScript topics that are beyond the scope of this book.

So far, this chapter has shown how to clean up the buggy code in the file *19-1_Debug_Code.fla*. In this section, you can make further improvements to the animation while learning how to stop your animation and code in its tracks and examine individual properties using the debugger.

---

**NOTE**  This example continues debugging the file *19-1_Debug_Code.fla*. The entire process began on page 652.

---

To get started, follow these steps:

1. **With *19-1_Debug_Code.fla* open in Flash, click Debug→Debug Movie.**

   A Flash Player window opens and begins playing your animation. The panels in Flash change to show the Debug Console, the Variables panel, the Scene/Symbol panel, your code, and the Output panel. There's no information showing in either the Debug Console or the Variables panel at this point. If you followed the steps in the previous example, some information appears in the Output panel.

2. **In the Flash Player window, select the Play toggle, Ctrl+Enter (⌘-Return).**

   The animation stops playing.

3. **In the panel with the ActionScript code, click to the left of the line numbers 11 and 12.**

   A red dot appears next to the line number, indicating a breakpoint. These dots appear next to the lines:

   ```
   var ptStart:Point = new Point(Math.random() * 550,Math.random() * 400);
   var ptEnd:Point = new Point(Math.random() * 550,Math.random() * 400);
   ```

4. **In the Flash Player window, press Ctrl+Enter (⌘-Return).**

   The Flash Player may be hidden by the debugger. If necessary, use Alt+Tab (or ⌘-Tab) to bring it to the front. When you press Ctrl+Enter (⌘-Return), the animation runs for a moment and then stops. A small arrow appears in the breakpoint next to line 11, indicating that the animation is at this point in the ActionScript code. You see more details in both the Debug Console (Figure 19-16) and the Variables panel.

   There are two items displayed in the Debug Console. You may need to drag the right edge of the panel to read the entire lines. The line at the top references the *drawRandomLine()* method in your code. The bottom line references the main timeline in the animation. When you click different items in the Debug Console, the items listed below in the Variables panel change. Click the top line before examining the Variables panel in the next step.

5. **In the Variables panel, click the expand button next to the word "this," and then scroll the panel to view all the variables.**

   Initially, there are three items in the variables panel: *this, ptStart*, and *ptEnd*. *This* refers to the main timeline; *ptStart* and *ptEnd* are variables inside the *drawRandomLine()* function. At this point, the value for both variables is undefined. When you click the + button next to *this*, a list expands beneath, showing all the properties and variables related to the main timeline. Some of the items are familiar, like alpha, height, and width. Others may be a bit mysterious, especially if they're properties you haven't yet used in ActionScript. In Flash, there are a lot of preset values, which you may never need to worry about. If you look carefully in the list, you find the names of the text fields in your animation: txtStartX, txtStartY, txtEndX, and txtEndY.

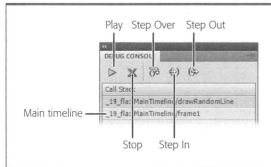

**FIGURE 19-16**

*Here, the Debug Console shows two items: the main timeline and the* drawRandomLine() *method. Using the buttons at the top of the console, you can start and stop your animation and the processing of ActionScript code.*

6. **Click a second time to close the list.**

   The lists closes, leaving just the three items showing: *this, ptStart*, and *ptEnd*.

7. **In the Debug Console, click the green Continue button.**

   Flash moves ahead just one step in the code because there's a breakpoint at line 12. In the Variables panel, you see that the ptStart item has changed. The value is no longer undefined; there's some weird-looking text and numbers there. And there's an expand button next to the name.

   When you place a breakpoint in your code, the debugger stops before that line is executed. That's why, with a breakpoint at line 12, ptStart has newly assigned values, but ptEnd is still undefined.

8. **Click the expand button next to ptStart and examine its properties.**

   As explained on page 611, the Point class has three properties: *length, x*, and *y*. Now that ptStart is defined, the variables panel shows values for each. More of those are really long decimal numbers.

9. **Double-click the x value for ptStart and type *300*.** Then, double-click the y value and type *200*.

   One of the extremely handy features of the Debugger is that you can change values of properties when the animation is stopped at a breakpoint.

10. **Click the green Continue button.**

The animation moves through its two frames, and then it runs the *drawRandomLine()* method again. It stops again at line 11 in the code.

11. **Examine the animation in the Flash Player window.**

The two text fields at the top of the animation show the values you entered in the Variables panel: 300 and 200, as shown in Figure 19-17. This small test proves that if you round the numbers to whole numbers, they'll fit in the text fields.

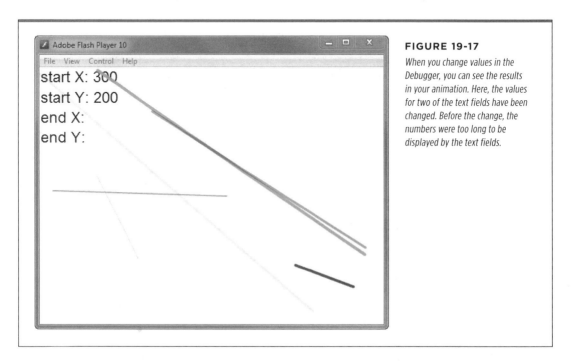

**FIGURE 19-17**

*When you change values in the Debugger, you can see the results in your animation. Here, the values for two of the text fields have been changed. Before the change, the numbers were too long to be displayed by the text fields.*

12. **In the Debug Console, click the red X, also known as the End Debug Session button.**

Flash restores your project to its appearance before you entered the debugger.

So, one solution to making the numbers fit in the text fields is to round them off to whole numbers. You can do that with another method that's part of the Math class. Here's what the finished code looks like. The two bold lines show the changes using the *Math.round()* method:

```
var sprtLines:Sprite = new Sprite();

drawRandomLine();
addChild(sprtLines);
```

```
function drawRandomLine():void
{var ptStart:Point = new Point(Math.round(Math.random() * 550),Math.
round(Math.random() * 400));
var ptEnd:Point = new Point(Math.round(Math.random() * 550),Math.round(Math.
random() * 400));
    sprtLines.graphics.lineStyle(Math.random()*5,Math.random()*0xFFFFFF,
      Math.random());
    sprtLines.graphics.moveTo(ptStart.x,ptStart.y);
    sprtLines.graphics.lineTo(ptEnd.x,ptEnd.y);
    txtStartX.text = "start X: " + ptStart.x;
    trace("start X: " + ptStart.x);
    txtStartY.text = "start Y: " + ptStart.y;
    txtEndX.text = "end X: " + ptEnd.x;
    txtEndY.text = "end Y: " + ptEnd.y;
}
```

Now the animation runs as it was intended. It draws lines that are random in position, color, thickness, and transparency. The x/y coordinates for the start and end points of the lines are shown in the upper-left corner of the animation. Not only do the whole numbers fit in the text fields, but they're also a little easier to discern than the monster decimals. The debugged version of the animation is in the Missing CD (*www.missingmanuals.com/cds/flashcs6mm*), named *19-2_Debug_Code_done.fla.*

**NOTE** Flash lets you debug your animations remotely after you've uploaded them to a web server. This book doesn't cover remote debugging, but you can find out more about it in Flash's help files.

# Publishing and Exporting

You're done designing, developing, and debugging. Your animation is ready for its audience. You've decided whether you want them to view it on a web page, a smartphone, a tablet, a CD, or on their computers. The next step is to *publish* the animation, which means packaging it in a form your audience can play. As another alternative, you may *export* the animation, so you (or someone else) can further edit and develop it using another graphics or animation program (like Adobe Illustrator or Adobe Fireworks). In this chapter, you'll learn how to do both.

Using Flash's publishing settings (Figure 20-1), you'll see how to tell Flash to publish your animation as part of a web page, and as a standalone *projector*. You'll also see how to export the artwork in your animation as editable image files. But before you publish or export, you need to learn how to *optimize* your animation (reduce your animation's file size) so that it runs as quickly and efficiently as possible—a real concern if you're planning to publish your animation on the Web or a handheld with limited memory.

## ■ Optimizing Flash Documents

It's a fact of the digital world—big files take longer to travel the Web and load, and that creates a bottleneck for many Flash animations. The longer your audience waits, the more likely you are to lose them to another web page, or app, or quick peek at Facebook. No one has the patience to wait for a stop-and-start animation. With that in mind, you should make every effort to keep your published files small. The process is called *optimization* because you're seeking the optimal tradeoff between quality and file size. (If you're still tempted to skip this step, read the box on page 671.)

Ideally, you've kept file size in mind from the moment you started planning your project and throughout the entire production process. That's why there are tips scattered throughout this book about reducing file size. You can think of optimization as low-fat cooking for the animation set: The goal is to get rid of the fat without getting rid of the flavor. And, as with low-fat cooking, Flash doesn't have a single approach to optimization. Your animation may include graphics, sound, and video, and there are ways to optimize each element. On top of that, every animation and target audience is different—you need to experiment, tweak, and retest using the strategies outlined next.

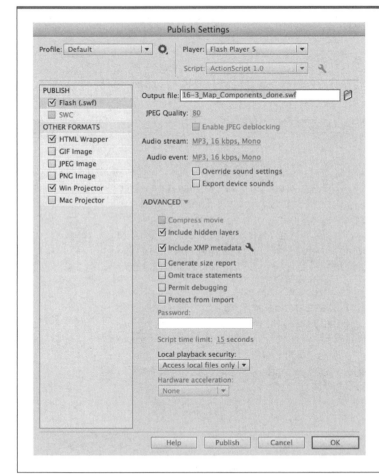

**FIGURE 20-1**

*Flash lets you choose how to deliver your compiled animation. The options shown here produce a plain .swf that plays in most browsers. You can also publish it as a standalone projector file (a self-contained executable file you double-click to run, with no need for a web browser or a separate Flash Player), an image file, or embedded in a web page.*

**TIP** As you check out the optimization strategies in this section, keep in mind that effective optimization is always a balancing act. You may decide some effects are worth the bloated file size they require, and some aren't. In still other cases, you'll want to compromise. For example, you might choose to remove half of the gradient effects you've applied to your images so that you reduce file size, but keep the other half. In Flash, you're the director, so you get to decide how much is enough.

# Ten Optimization Strategies

Here are 10 tried-and-true strategies for reducing file size. Apply as many as you can while you're developing your animation. You can use any of these techniques to trim down a completed animation. Better yet, keep them in mind as you create your next animation. That way, you'll end up with a streamlined animation without a lot of extra, after-the-fact work.

---

**FREQUENTLY ASKED QUESTION**

## The Importance of Being Optimized

*In an era where lightning-fast connections, high-speed processors, and multimegabyte memory cards abound, why should I bother optimizing my Flash documents?*

Here's why: Not everyone has access to the latest, greatest equipment and Internet service. In many parts of the world, people don't have access to affordable T1 connections, for example. Also, folks relying on the computers at their schools or jobs don't have control over their equipment. And, of course, not everyone has the time, money, or patience necessary to upgrade every time a new "revolution" in hardware or software technology hits the market.

There's a tendency among some animators to resist the extra effort that optimizing their animations requires. But here's the fact: If people can't see your animation, nothing else matters. Not the beauty or cleverness of your artwork, nor the sophistication of your animated sequences, nor the appropriateness of your perfectly synchronized background music.

Here's a short list of the most common excuses some animators give for not optimizing their animations (and the reasons why these excuses don't fly):

- *It looks great on my machine. If my audience doesn't have a fast enough connection, they need to upgrade.* Animators and others using Flash tend to be running high-end equipment—much faster and more powerful than the equipment their audiences are running. The trend toward smartphones, tablets, and underpowered netbooks as an on-the-road option reinforces the need for optimized animations. That's why testing your animation at a variety of connection speeds (as discussed on page 671) and even on a variety of machines, if possible, is so important. As

noted above, not everyone *can* upgrade, and not everyone *wants* to. But even if they do, chances are they're not going to do it just to see your animation.

- *So what if it takes 5 minutes to download my animation file? My animation is so fantastic it's worth waiting for.* It doesn't matter if your animation is in line for the next Webby Award: If your audience can't run it (or surfs away impatiently instead of waiting for it to download and stutter across their screens), you haven't communicated effectively—and communicating effectively is, or should be, the goal of every animation you create in Flash.

- *The big boys (Hollywood trailer-makers, high-end advertisers, and super-sophisticated, high-traffic sites) don't worry about optimization. Why should I?* It's true that some folks would still check out the latest Hollywood teaser even if it took all day to download. But they don't have to because the big boys pay an army of professional testers and software designers to optimize their animations using the techniques in this chapter.

The bottom line, as you've read over and over in this book, is to determine the needs of your target audience *first*, and then construct your animation to meet those needs. If you're delivering your animation as a standalone file on DVD, you're absolutely sure that your audience will be running high-end equipment, and you know for a fact that they're highly motivated to run your animation (for example, they have to work through the Flash training tutorial you created in order to keep their jobs), then by all means take optimization with a grain of salt. But if your audience fits any other profile, ignore optimization at your own risk.

### ■ 1. USE AS FEW KEYFRAMES AND PROPERTY KEYFRAMES AS POSSIBLE

Flash stores data for every keyframe, which adds to the size of your .swf file. The regular and tweened frames add very little to file size, so creating an effect with a tween is more efficient than creating the same effect with frame-by-frame animation.

### ■ 2. CHOOSE THE PENCIL TOOL OVER THE BRUSH TOOL

In general, brush tool fills are more complex than the lines you create with the Pencil tool, so brush strokes take up more file space. When you feel both strokes are equally acceptable, choose the Pencil.

### ■ 3. CHOOSE SOLID OVER DASHED OR DOTTED LINES

Through the Property Inspector, Flash lets you apply a handful of dash-and-dot effects to the lines you draw on the stage using the Pencil, Pen, Line, and Shape tools. But do so sparingly, because these line effects increase file size.

### ■ 4. OPTIMIZE CURVES AND SHAPES

The fewer anchor points used to define curves and fills, the less information Flash has to track. Flash even gives you a special Optimize command to remove superfluous points from your shapes. Here's how to use it:

1. **Select the curved line or fill outline you want to optimize, and then choose Modify→Shape→Optimize.**

   The Optimize Curves dialog box you see in Figure 20-2 (top) appears.

2. **Type or scrub in a new number to tell Flash how much optimization to apply, from 0 to a maximum of 100, and then click OK.**

   Flash displays a message (Figure 20-2, bottom) letting you know what percentage of the selected line or outline it was able to dispense with.

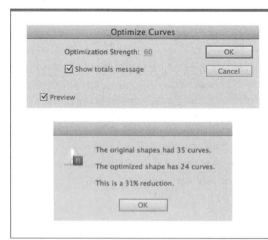

**FIGURE 20-2**

*Top: Optimizing a line doesn't straighten it out or even smooth it the way that Modify→Shape→Advanced Straighten and Modify→Shape→Advanced Smooth do; instead, it ever-so-subtly shifts the points that make up the line. If you want to see how successful the optimization is, make sure you leave the "Show totals message" checkbox turned on.*

*Bottom: Because optimization is a final tweak meant for you to do after your image already looks the way you want it to look, you don't see a huge reduction in size here. Still, depending on the number of curved lines and fill outlines your animation contains, the saved bytes can add up.*

3. **Click OK.**

   On the stage, you see the (subtle) results of the optimization.

### ■ 5. USE SYMBOLS

Creating a reusable symbol (page 248) lets you add multiple instances of a shape or drawing to your animation without dramatically increasing file size. Even shrinking, rotating, or recoloring your instances costs less in file size than creating separate images. This strategy can result in big benefits.

### ■ 6. TEST BITMAPS AND VECTORS, AND THEN CHOOSE THE MOST EF-FICIENT OPTION

Often bitmaps, especially photos, are expensive in terms of file size. If you can do without them, do so; if not, crop them (so that you use as little of them as possible) or optimize them by choosing a higher-than-standard compression option, as described below. On the other hand, overly complicated vector graphics also use a lot of space. If in doubt, test both options and compare the sizes by generating a size report (see the box on page 649).

> **NOTE**  You can also optimize bitmaps in the Publish Settings dialog box (page 685).

To optimize a bitmap:

1. **Import the bitmap into your document's Library panel.**

   The steps, if you need a refresher, are in Chapter 10 (page 359).

2. **In the Library, double-click the icon next to the imported bitmap's filename.**
   (Or select the bitmap, and then, from the Options menu in the upper-right corner of the Library, choose Properties.)

   Either way, the Bitmap Properties window you see in Figure 20-3 appears.

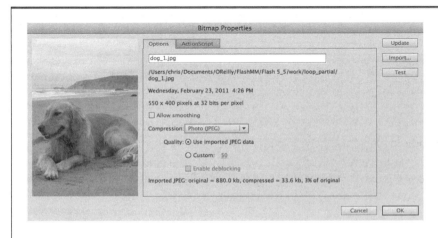

**FIGURE 20-3**

*Everything in life is a tradeoff, and bitmap optimization in Flash is no exception. If you find you can't balance image quality with compression—for example, by the time you reach an acceptably high compression rate, your image appears nearly unrecognizable—consider cropping the bitmap or turning it into a vector drawing (page 365).*

3. **From the Compression drop-down list, choose either "Photo (JPEG)" or "Lossless (PNG/GIF)".**

Choose the first option if your image contains a lot of different colors or transparent effects; choose the second if it contains a few solid lumps of color. Find out more about JPEGs, PNGs, and GIFs beginning on page 351.

Flash calculates a percent compression rate and displays it near the bottom of the Bitmap Properties window.

If you chose Photo (JPEG), you can compress the image further. Click the Custom radio button, and then type a number into the box (Figure 20-3). A value of 100 is the highest quality and the least compression.

---

**TIP** Flash starts you out with a quality rate of 80. You need to experiment to find out the lowest number that gives you an acceptable tradeoff between file size and quality, but one way to begin is to jot down the current file size (Flash displays it just below the Quality field), type 25, and then click OK. When you open the Bitmap Properties window again, Flash displays the new file size for the bitmap based on a file quality of 25. If the image looks OK, type a lower number; if not, type a higher number. The higher the number, the larger the file size; the lower the number, the lower the file size.

---

4. **Take a look at your newly optimized image by clicking the Test button.**

The preview area shows the way the image looks using the optimization settings you chose. Near the bottom of the Bitmap Properties window, you see the percent compression rate Flash has calculated based on the Quality setting you typed in. If the image quality looks horrible, repeat step 2 with a higher quality setting; if the quality looks OK but the compression rate doesn't seem low enough, try again with a lower quality setting. (Sometimes, depending on your image, a lower quality setting will look practically identical to a slightly higher quality setting.)

5. **When you're satisfied with the quality-vs.-file-size tradeoff, click OK.**

Flash hides the Bitmap Properties window and brings you back to your workspace.

---

**NOTE** The image doesn't appear optimized in the Library preview area. But you can preview the effects of different optimization settings when you drag the image to the stage.

---

■ **7. KEEP SOUND CLIPS TO A MINIMUM (OR OPTIMIZE THEM)**

Sound clips can quickly swell your animation size, so use them sparingly. Naturally, sound effects like a bell's ding or a thunderclap use less space than a high-quality music soundtrack. A narrator's voice also takes up less space than most music. As a rule, use the shortest clips you can and compress them as much as the quality can bear. Here are the steps to optimize a sound file that's already in your Library:

1. **In the Library, double-click the icon next to the imported sound file's name.**

   This icon is the quickest of three ways to open the properties for a symbol. You can also use the Options menu in the upper-right corner of the Library panel or right-click (Control-click) a symbol.

   Either way, the Sound Properties dialog box you see in Figure 20-4 appears.

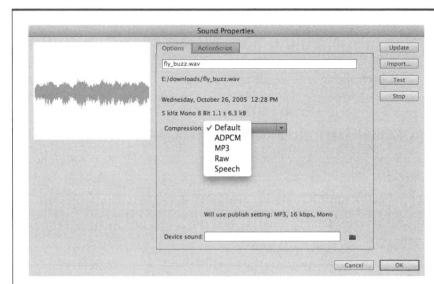

**FIGURE 20-4**

*If you leave compression set to Default, Flash uses the Compression option you set in the Publish Settings dialog box (page 685) to figure out how to compress this sound clip. Otherwise, Flash applies the Compression option you set here (unless you've told Flash to override this compression setting; see page 682 for details).*

2. **Press Update, if you think the sound has been edited.**

   The file may have been trimmed or changed, using an editor like Soundbooth, since it was imported.

3. **From the Compression drop-down list, choose a compression scheme.**

   Flash gives you several options. Choosing the right compression scheme gives you the best size/quality optimization:

   - The **Default** settings are defined in the panel that appears when you go to File→Publish Settings and click the Flash tab. There are separate settings for audio streams (longer sounds like music and narration) and events (like sound effects). You can change these settings by clicking the *Set* buttons.

   - **ADPCM** is good for short event sounds. You can reduce file size by checking the "Preprocessing: Convert stereo to mono" box. Sample rates range from a primitive 5 kHz to CD-quality 44 kHz. You can also set the ADPCM bits from 2 to 5 bits, with larger numbers increasing file size. Below the menus you see the setting and the effect they have on reducing or increasing the file size.

- **MP3** is the familiar compression format for music. It has the ability to dramatically reduce the size of long streams of sound. You can choose the bit rate (higher numbers, bigger files) and the quality: Fast, Medium, or Best. (These options refer to the length of time it takes to compress the files.) In most cases, you'll want to choose Best because it achieves the best sound quality for the file size.

- **Raw** provides no compression, so you'd normally not use it for a web-based animation. As with ADPCM, you can reduce the size of the sound file by selecting "Convert stereo to mono" and by reducing the sample rate.

- **Speech** applies compression that's suitable for voice, but isn't full enough for a symphonic orchestra. You can further tweak the setting by changing the sample rate (smaller numbers for smaller files).

4. **As you experiment with the settings, click the Test button.**

   You hear the sound file with the compression applied. Click the Stop button when you've heard enough.

5. **When you're satisfied with the quality-vs.-file-size tradeoff, click OK.**

   Flash hides the Sound Properties dialog box and brings you back to your workspace.

---

**NOTE** To make sure Flash uses the Compression option you set in the Sound Properties dialog box, turn off the "Override sound settings" checkbox in the File→Publish Settings→Flash dialog box. Page 682 has details.

---

### 8. GROUP ELEMENTS

Grouping shapes, lines, and other portions of your drawings (by selecting them, and then choosing Modify→Group) cuts down on file size because Flash can streamline the information it needs to store. Page 192 has full instructions.

### 9. AVOID THE EXTRANEOUS

The more you add to your animation, the larger your file size. If you absolutely, positively need to pare down your file, consider removing or simplifying some (or all) of your drawings, multimedia files, and graphic effects, paying particular attention to these space hogs:

- Sound files, embedded video clips, and bitmaps

- Gradient effects

- Alpha (transparency) effects

- Custom colors

Make sure your .swf files don't include any unnecessary symbols. Look in the Library panel. If it says Export under Linkage, the symbol is being exported for use with ActionScript and will definitely be added to the .swf. If the symbol isn't needed for the final animation, right-click the symbol, and then choose Properties from the shortcut menu. In the Symbol Properties dialog box, deselect "Export for ActionScript."

> **TIP** If you can't bring yourself to do without media files altogether, go ahead and use them—but abbreviate them. For example, instead of using a long sound clip, loop a short one. Or use a single sound clip a bunch of different ways (soft, loud, the first half, the second half) to create multiple sound effects for minimal overhead. Instead of embedding a video clip as is, try adjusting the in and out points to clip off any nonessential intro or outro frames when you import it into Flash (page 389). And if you're using a mask layer, make sure you clip off every scrap of the background image not revealed by the mask.

### ■ 10. TELL FLASH TO KEEP YOUR FILE SIZE DOWN

One of the options you want to make sure you set when you're ready to publish your animation is the "Compress movie" option in the Publish Settings dialog box (page 685). (Out of the box, Flash turns on this option, but do double-check that you haven't inadvertently turned it off.) Choosing this option tells Flash to squeeze your animation file as much as it can without sacrificing content. How much Flash compresses your file depends on the specific elements and effects you've included in your animation; the more text and ActionScript code your animation contains, for example, the more "bloat" Flash can squeeze out of your file.

# ■ Publishing Your Animations

When you publish your animation, Flash Professional reads the images and sounds in your .fla file, applies compression according to the settings you chose, and then writes a noneditable file (.swf) that your audience will view.

The kind of noneditable file Flash produces depends on how you decide to publish your animation. These are your choices:

- **A compiled Flash file (.swf).** Flash Players, including the Flash Player plug-ins that come with most browsers, play .swf files. If you plan to include your Flash animation in a hand-coded HTML file (or to import it into a website creation program like Adobe Dreamweaver), you want this option.

- **A compiled SWC file (.swc).** If you're working with a team on a Flex project, you can archive components and assets in a SWC file. Flex applications can access the embedded SWF and the other assets.

- **A web page (.html, .swf).** Choose this option if you want Flash to put together a simple web page for you that includes your animation. (You can always tweak the HTML file later, either by hand or using a web design program like Dreamweaver.)

- **An image file (.jpg, .gif, or .png).** You can export an individual frame, or if you use the GIF format, you can export a series of image files that play as a frame-by-frame animation—useful for those times when your audience doesn't have Flash Player. (For more advice on using ActionScript to detect your audience's Flash Player at runtime and offer alternatives, see the box on page 690.)

---

**POWER USERS' CLINIC**

## Preloading Large, Slow-to-Load Content

If your animation is large (approaching a megabyte or more) and you're delivering it over the Web, it takes some time for your audience to download. You need to let them know that something is happening behind the scenes and give them an idea how soon they'll be entertained. That's the job of a preloader—a bit of ActionScript and some simple images. You've seen them before when web pages display a "Loading" message and report on the progress. In essence, a preloader is a small Flash animation that's designed to load a larger animation. The smaller program shows a simple animation to let the audience know their computer hasn't frozen. Many preloaders also report on the progress as a percentage of the download. You can think of a preloader as a "wrapper" that holds the larger, slow-loading animation.

Flash CS6 includes a simple preloader template that you can use for your project. Go to File→New→Templates and click Sample Files. Near the bottom of the list choose "Preloader for SWF." There's no documentation with the template, but with a couple of tips, it's easy to use. All you have to do is place your larger SWF, larger picture, or other slow-loading content in the second frame of the layer named "Content." Test the animation (Control→Test Movie) and you may not notice the preloader, because everything runs so quickly when it's all on one computer. To see the preloader in action, you need to make some adjustments in the test environment. Set View→Download Settings to 56K or one of the slower settings. Then choose View→Simulate Download. The "Loading" text pulses while the download percentage is shown in numbers.

If the template doesn't quite match the style of your project, it's easy to swap in your own graphics. The pulsing loading text is a movie clip symbol in the Library made of a 31-frame tween. To examine the movie clip, right-click (Control-click) "loading clip" in the Library and choose Edit. Replace the "Loading" animation in the symbol but make sure you don't change its name. Feel free to change the length of the movie clip if it suits your needs.

If you want to examine the ActionScript code that powers the preloader, just click Frame 1 in the actions layer and open the Actions window. You'll see that the code stops the animation. At that point, two event listeners take over. The listeners' functions are named: onLoading and onComplete. The onLoading listener displays the pulsing text and download percentage. The onComplete listener moves the animation to the second frame in the animation, where the larger, now fully downloaded content is displayed. The "onComplete" function also does a little housekeeping, removing the two listeners from memory because they're no longer needed.

If you're interested in learning more about preloading, you can find more information on the Web; Christopher Skyi's article on ActionScript.org is a good place to start (*www.actionscript.org/resources/articles/869/1/Preloading-in-ActionScript-30-the-Easy-Way/Page1.html*).

---

- **A standalone projector file (.exe, .app).** A *projector* file is a self-contained Flash-Player-plus-your-animation file. Your audience can run a projector file to play your animation even if they don't have a copy of Flash Player installed. You might choose this option if you're creating a CD or DVD (as opposed to delivering via the web). You can create projector files for Windows (.exe) or the Mac (.app).

**NOTE**  Flash gives you another way to turn your artwork into an image file: by *exporting* it (page 370).

You can choose more than one publishing option at a time simply by turning on as many checkboxes as you like in the Publish Settings dialog box. For example, you can publish your animation as a compiled Flash file, a web page, and a standalone projector file all at once when you click Publish.

The following sections show you each of these publishing options in detail.

## Publishing as a Compiled Flash (.swf) File

When you publish your animation as an .swf file, your audience can run it using a Flash Player—either a standalone version of Flash Player, or a web browser plug-in version. Publishing as an .swf file gives you the flexibility of including your animation in a from-scratch web page.

**NOTE**  If you've worked through any of the examples in this book, you're already familiar with .swf files. Each time you test your animation using Control→Test Movie, Flash automatically generates an .swf file and plays it in the Flash Player that's built into the test environment.

To publish your animation as a compiled Flash (.swf) file:

1. **Choose File→Publish Settings.**

   A Publish Settings panel, similar to the one in Figure 20-5, appears. Here's where you tell Flash what kind of files to publish, and you can choose as few or as many as you like. Click on a file format to adjust the settings for that particular file.

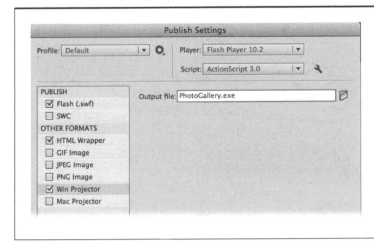

**FIGURE 20-5**

*Each time you turn on a Type checkbox, Flash adds a new file type to the publish process; for example, SWF, HTML, or JPG. Click the format name to display the settings for that type of file. With these settings, the publish process produces an SWF, an HTML wrapper, and a standalone Windows projector file. The Win Projector format name is currently selected.*

2. **Turn on the checkbox next to "Flash (.swf)," and then turn off all the other checkboxes.**

   The Flash tab appears next to the Formats tab.

> **NOTE** You can use almost any animation to experiment with the Publish and Export settings. If you don't have one handy, use *20-1_Publish_Settings.fla* from the Missing CD (*www.missingmanuals.com/cds/flashcs6tmm*). It's identical to one of the Chapter 8 motion tween files.

3. **Click the words "Flash (.swf)" next to the checkbox.**

The Flash settings in Figure 20-6 appear.

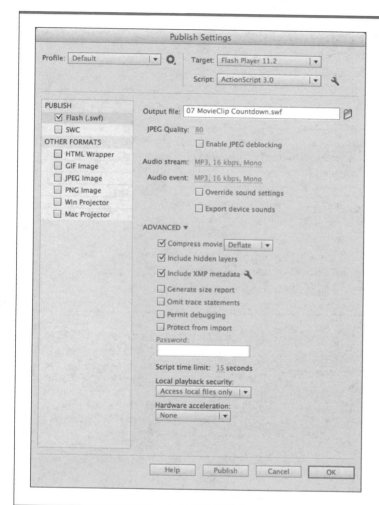

**FIGURE 20-6**

*The settings here let you fine-tune the .swf file that Flash generates when you click Publish. Normally, you don't have to make any changes to these settings. But in some cases—for example, when you know your target audience is running an older version of Flash Player—you do want to change them. These pages explain each setting.*

4. **Change one or more of the following settings:**

- **Player.** Lets you select the version of Flash Player you want to run your animation. Choose the latest version (Flash Player 11.2) if you've included any of the new-in-Flash-11.2 features or if you're not sure whether you've included any new features. If you know your audience is running an earlier version of Flash Player (for example, Flash Player 8) and you know you won't be using any new-in-Flash-11 features, then you can choose the earlier version.

If you choose Flash Player 11, and it turns out that your audience is running an earlier version of the player, like Flash Player 8, they will need to download and install the newest version, which isn't as troublesome as it sounds. Adobe makes a free downloadable copy of the latest Flash Player available at *www.adobe.com/products/flashplayer.* The box on page 690 explains how to create a web page that automatically checks to make sure the proper version of Flash Player is present on your audience's computers.

**NOTE** On this menu, you'll also find options for Adobe AIR, iPhone, and Flash Lite players. Usually, if you're developing an animation for one of these platforms, you start your animation using one of the related templates. The templates size the stage to match the device and automatically choose the right player.

- **Script.** Tells Flash which version of ActionScript to use. You already made this decision when you chose File→New to start your animation. So, if you started with ActionScript 3.0, that's the only option available here.

- **JPEG quality.** The quality of your JPEGs is controlled in two different places, and sometimes this leads to confusion. You can set the quality for individual images in the Library by right-clicking the library item and choosing Properties (Figure 20-7). Choose a Custom setting for the image and that's the final word. However, if you choose "Use imported JPEG data" then the image quality is controlled by the Publish Settings (Figure 20-6). In both cases, you can type or scrub in a quality value from 1 to 100. For highly compressed images (50 or less) it may help to turn on JPEG deblocking.

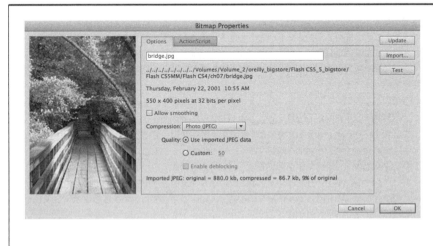

**FIGURE 20-7**

*If you choose "Use imported JPEG data" as shown here, Flash lets you set bitmap quality using the JPEG quality number in the Publish Settings window's Flash tab. If you set the quality of your bitmap using the Bitmap Properties dialog box, however, Flash ignores the JPEG quality number in the Publish Settings window. In other words, you can't tell Flash to compress the same image twice.*

- **Audio stream.** Tells Flash which compression scheme to use for streaming audio clips for which you haven't already specified a compression scheme (page 675). Flash displays the compression scheme it assumes you want. To specify another one, click the current compression name, and then, in the Sound Settings dialog box that appears (Figure 20-8), choose the compression scheme you want.

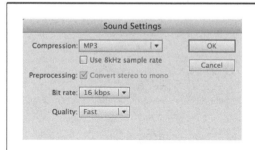

**FIGURE 20-8**

*In the Publish Settings window, clicking the name next to "Audio stream" or "Audio event" to opens this Sound Settings dialog box. Here, you can choose from a variety of compression schemes (like MP3, suitable for long, continuous clips like soundtracks) and lower-quality, byte-saving schemes (like Speech). Choosing Raw tells Flash not to compress your sounds at all.*

- **Audio event.** Tells Flash which compression scheme to use for audio events for which you haven't already specified a compression scheme, using the Sound Properties dialog box. Flash displays the compression scheme it assumes you want. To specify another one, click the current compression name next to "Audio event" and then, in the Sound Settings dialog box that appears, choose another compression scheme. Your options are identical to the options Flash gives you for setting "Audio stream" (see Figure 20-8), and they don't override individual sound properties unless you turn on "Override sound settings."

**NOTE** Flash gives you two ways to specify a compression scheme for your sound clips. You can specify a compression scheme for individual sound clips using the Sound Properties dialog box (page 675) or you can specify one for all the sound clips in your animation using the Audio Stream and Audio Event options you find in the Publish Settings window. (See below for more detail on the difference between audio streams and audio events.)

- **Override sound settings.** Tells Flash to ignore the individual compression schemes you set for your sound clips using the Sound Properties dialog box (page 675) and use the compression schemes (both streaming and event) you set in the Publish Settings window instead. If you *don't* turn on this checkbox, Flash uses the compression settings you set in the Publish Settings window only for those sound clips assigned a Default setting in the Sound Properties dialog box.

**NOTE** Flash can only work with what you give it. Specifying a high-quality compression scheme doesn't improve a low-quality sound clip.

- **Export device sounds.** Tells Flash to include MIDI and other device sound files with the .swf file. Turn on this option only if you're targeting mobile devices.

- **Compress movie.** Tells Flash to reduce .swf file size as much as possible without sacrificing your animation's quality. Make sure this option is turned on. (Flash can't compress animations targeting pre-6 versions of Flash Player, but odds are you aren't doing that anyway.)

- **Include Hidden Layers.** Flash's factory settings export all the layers in your animation, even those that are hidden or nested in movie clips. Uncheck this option if you want to test or create different versions of your animation by hiding layers in the Flash file.

- **Include XMP metadata.** Publishes all the details about your animation included in the File Info box. Metadata is a standard method for storing details about a media file. To create metadata in the first place, choose File→File Info, and then fill in whatever information you want your audience to see.

- **Generate size report.** Tells Flash to list the bytes in your .fla file by frame, scene, action, object, and so on. This report is also useful for keeping track of the content you've added to your animation.

- **Omit trace actions.** Tells Flash to ignore any *trace()* statements you've added to your ActionScript actions (page 473). It's best to turn this on before publishing an .swf that's going out in public. You don't need other folks with a Flash debugger seeing your trace details, and trace statements can slow down playback.

- **Permit Debugging.** Tells Flash to let you debug your animation remotely (over the web) using the special Flash Debug Player browser plug-in. This option also gives you more detailed error messages when you debug locally. This book doesn't cover remote debugging, but you can find out more about it using Flash Help (see Appendix A: Installation and Help).

- **Protect from import.** Theoretically, this option tells Flash to encode your .swf file so other folks can't import it into Flash and edit (steal!) your animation. Unfortunately, human nature being what it is, you can find programs floating around the Web to bypass this encoding. So if you need to reference sensitive information in your Flash animation (like passwords or confidential company info), don't store that information in Flash; instead, store it safely on a protected server and get it at runtime.

- **Password.** If you've chosen "Protect from import" or "Debugging permitted," type a password in this box. Typing a password lets anyone with the password import the compiled .swf file into Flash at a later date, and then edit it—a potential security risk if your ActionScript code contains confidential company information. Typing a password also lets anyone with the password debug the .swf file remotely. (This book doesn't cover remote debugging.)

- **Script time limit.** Sets the maximum time that scripts can take to run before there's a stage update. If a script runs longer, Flash Player stops the script from running.

- **Local playback security.** Lets you tell Flash whether you want your .swf to be able to exchange information with *local files* (files located on your audience's computers) or *network files* (files located elsewhere on the Web).

- **Hardware Acceleration.** These settings let your animation take advantage of any advanced video hardware capabilities your audience's computers may have. The *Direct* option bypasses the computer browser and draws directly to the screen. The *GPU* option uses advanced graphics processing units if they're available.

5. **Click Publish.**

The Publish Settings window disappears, and Flash generates an SWF file using the name you provided. If you didn't type a name of your own choosing, Flash names the file based on your .fla filename. For example, if the name of your Flash document is *myAnimation.fla*, Flash generates a file named *myAnimation.swf.* If you click OK, Flash saves your settings and uses them later when you're ready to publish.

---

**TIP** You don't have to go through the Publish Settings window every time you want to publish your animation. Once you've got the settings the way you want them, all you have to do is select File→Publish.

---

## Publishing as a Web Page

If you want to put your animation on a web page, an .swf file by itself isn't sufficient: It's always best to create an HTML file (a web page) that embeds that .swf file. You can create the HTML file either by using your favorite HTML editor or by telling Flash to generate a simple HTML file for you.

---

**POWER USERS' CLINIC**

### Create a Publish Profile

Customizing Flash's publishing settings can be time-consuming. If you plan to reuse a batch of options, you can save time by saving your settings in a profile. So you could create one profile for publishing Flash CDs or DVDs and another for your website.

That way, when you want to publish a web-page version of your animation, for example, all you have to do is specify myWebPageProfile or myCD-DVDprofile.

To create a publish profile:

1. In the Publish Settings dialog box, click the gear-shaped button next to Profile and choose Create Profile.

2. In the Create New Profile dialog box that appears, type a name for your profile, and then click OK.

3. Flash saves all your current settings to that profile. As you continue to make changes in the Publish Settings window, Flash continues to save those changes to your profile.

4. You can create as many profiles as you like. To change profiles, click the Profile menu, and then select a new name.

---

At a minimum, the HTML file needs to tell the web browser how to display the .swf file: at the top of the page or in the middle, whether you want the animation to begin playing immediately or wait until the audience clicks a button, and so on.

Because many people who use Flash want to put their animations on the web, the Publish Settings dialog box makes it easy to create an .swf in addition to a simple web page (.html) in one fell swoop.

To publish your animation as a web page (.html and .swf):

1. **Choose File→Publish Settings.**

   The Publish Settings dialog box appears.

2. **Make sure the checkboxes next to "Flash (.swf)" and HTML Wrapper are turned on; if they're not, turn them both on now.**

   You can choose to publish several different types of files at once, as shown in Figure 20-9. To publish an SWF file and a web page that holds the SWF file, check the boxes: Flash (.swf) and HTML Wrapper. Click the words next to the check-box to display the file settings in the dialog box.

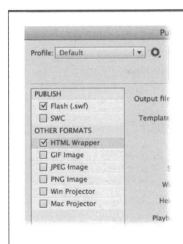

**FIGURE 20-9**

*To publish an SWF file and a web page that holds the SWF file, turn on the Flash (.swf) and HTML Wrapper checkboxes. Click the words next to the checkbox to display the file settings shown in Figure 20-10.*

3. **Click the words "Flash (.swf)," and then set up your .swf file.**

   For the details, see step 4 on page 680.

4. **Click the words "HTML Wrapper."**

   The HTML publish settings you see in Figure 20-10 appear.

5. **If you like, change the template setting.**

   Most of the time, you want to stick with the "Flash only" template that Flash assumes you want. But if you've added certain elements to your animation, or if you want to target a specific web browser, Flash needs to insert special HTML tags into the template it uses. In that case, you may need one of the following options:

- **Flash for Pocket PC 2003.** Creates an HTML file that runs on Pocket PC 2003.

- **Flash HTTPS.** Choose this option if you plan to upload your HTML and SWF file to a secure web server (https://).

- **Flash Only.** Creates a basic HTML file that runs in any web browser.

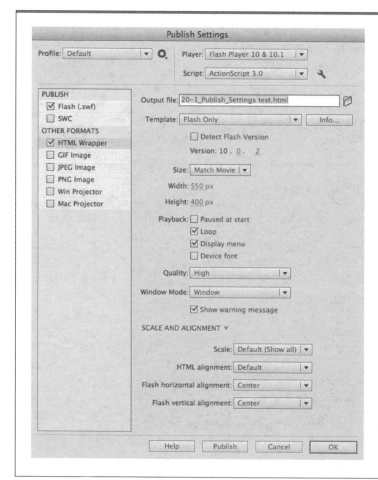

**FIGURE 20-10**

*These settings let you tell Flash how you want your animation to be included in your web page. This option is great for testing the way your animation looks on the web, as well as for creating simple pages. But if you want a really sophisticated web page, you need to edit the HTML file that Flash produces—either in a text editor, or in a web page creation tool like Dreamweaver.*

- **Flash Only—Allow Full Screen.** Used only with Flash Player 9 or later. This option adds a parameter to the HTML code that lets Flash content run in Full Screen mode. The animation can fill an entire monitor without menus, borders, or the other usual computer paraphernalia.

- **Flash with AICC Tracking.** Choose this option if you've added Learning Interaction components (Window→Common Libraries→Learning Interactions) to your animation and plan to have these components interact with an AICC learning management system. (AICC stands for Aviation Industry CBT Committee.)

- **Flash with FSCommand.** Choose this option if you've included the ActionScript *fscommand()* statement in your animation. (*fscommand()* lets your Flash animation call a JavaScript statement. JavaScript is the scripting language supported by most web browsers. Adobe warns that *fscommand()* may not work with Flash Player 10 and later.) The alternative ExternalInterface should be used instead. Details are available in the ActionScript 3.0 Reference.

- **Flash with Named Anchors.** Choose this option if you've organized your animation into named scenes (Chapter 15). Flash generates the tags necessary to let people surf directly from scene to scene using their browsers' Back buttons.

- **Flash with SCORM 1.2 Tracking and Flash with SCORM 2004 Tracking.** Choose one of these options if you've added Learning Interaction components (Window→Common Libraries→Learning Interactions) to your animation, and plan to have these components interact with a SCORM learning management system. (SCORM stands for Shareable Content Object Reference Model.)

- **Image Map.** Choosing this option tells Flash to create an HTML image map (which an HTML-savvy person can turn into hotspots). For this option to work, you need to have added the frame label *#map* to the frame you want Flash to turn into an image map, and you need to have chosen GIF Image (.gif), JPEG Image (.jpg), or PNG Image (.png) in addition to HTML (.html) in the Formats tab of the Publish Settings window. (Chapter 15 explains how to add frame labels.)

6. **If you chose Flash Only, "Flash Only – Allow Full Screen," or Flash HTTPS in the previous step, you can now turn on Detect Flash Version to help make sure your audience has the correct version of Flash Player to view your animation.**

    When you turn on the checkbox for this option, if your audience has a version of Flash Player older than the one you specified, they see a message, which explains that they need a newer version and gives them a link to download the latest version. (See the box on page 690 for further advice.)

7. **Turn on any of the following settings if you'd like to tweak how your animation appears in the web page—which may be different from how it appears in Flash on the stage:**

    - **Size.** Lets you tell Flash how large you want your animation to appear in the web page. Your options are Match Movie, which tells Flash to use the dimensions of the stage you specified in the Document Properties window (page 516); Pixels, which tells Flash you want to specify new height and width dimensions in pixels; and Percent, which tells Flash you want to specify new height and width dimensions as a percentage of the web page display (see below).

- **Width/Height.** Lets you specify your animation's width and height in the web page in pixels or as a percentage of the web page.

- **Paused at start.** Tells Flash *not* to begin playing your animation as soon as your audience loads your web page into their browser. If you choose this option, make sure you either turn on Display menu (see below) or—a better solution—make sure you've included an obvious Play button in your animation. Otherwise, your audience won't be able to play your masterpiece.

- **Loop.** Tells Flash to automatically play your animation over and over again.

- **Display menu.** Tells Flash to include a shortcut menu for your animation so that when your audience right-clicks (Windows) or Control-clicks (Mac), they see animation controller options like Zoom In, Zoom Out, Play, Loop, Rewind, Forward, and Back.

- **Device font.** This option applies only to Windows computers. It provides antialiased (smoothed) system fonts for fonts that aren't on your audience's computers.

- **Quality.** Tells Flash how precisely (and how processor-intensively) you want it to *render*, or draw, your animation on your audience's computers. Your options range from Low to Best.

- **Show Warning Messages.** Initially, this option is turned on to display messages if there are conflicts with the HTML tags that are used in your project.

8. **Choose one of the following Window Mode settings to tell Flash how you want your animation to appear with respect to HTML/DHTML content that you add to your .html file:**

    - **Window.** This standard mode tells Flash to place your animation in a rectangular area on the web page. HTML content can appear around the animation.

    - **Opaque Windowless.** Tells Flash to place your animation on top of HTML content.

    - **Transparent Windowless.** Tells Flash to erase the background of your animation (the blank parts of the stage) so that HTML and DHTML content can show through.

9. **Choose from the Scale and Alignment options to size and position your animation with respect to the rest of your page.**

- **Default (Show All).** Fits as much of the animation into the height/width dimensions you set as possible without stretching or distorting the animation. If there's extra room left over, Flash fills in the empty spaces with black bands, letterbox style.

- **No border.** Fits as much of the animation into the height/width dimensions you set as possible without stretching or distorting the animation. If there's extra room left over, Flash crops it.

- **Exact fit.** Stretches (or squishes) the animation to fit the height/width dimensions you set.

- **No scale.** Tells Flash to preserve the stage height/width dimensions you set in the Document Properties dialog box.

- **HTML alignment** options include Default (center), Left, Right, Top, or Bottom.

- **Flash horizontal alignment.** Tells Flash how you want to align your animation with respect to the dimensions you set in the Publish Settings dialog box—in other words, how you want to position your animation horizontally inside the width-and-height box you're adding to your web page. Your options include Left, Center, and Right.

**NOTE** See step 7 if you want to align the width-and-height box with respect to your web page (as opposed to aligning your animation with respect to the width-and-height box, which you do using "Flash alignment," as described on this page).

- **Flash vertical alignment.** Tells Flash how you want to align your animation with respect to the dimensions you set in the Publish Settings dialog box; in other words, how you want to position your animation vertically inside the width-and-height box you're adding to your web page. Your options include Top, Center, and Bottom.

**NOTE** You need to know when Flash encounters problems so that you can fix them, so make sure the "Show warning messages" option is always turned on. Turning on this option tells Flash to pop up any errors that happen during the publishing process.

10. **Click Publish.**

The Publish Settings window disappears, and Flash generates both an HTML file and a Flash file based on the names you provide. If you don't type names of your own choosing, Flash names both files based on your .fla filename. For example, if the name of your Flash document is *myAnimation.fla,* Flash generates a file named *myAnimation.html* and *myAnimation.swf.* To make your HTML file and Flash animation available on the Web, you need to upload both of these files to your web server.

**TIP**     Sometimes, after you've published your .html and .swf files, you may want to change the name of your web page (.html) to match the other pages on your website. You can do that without a problem, as long as you don't change the extension (.html). On the other hand, if you change the name of your animation (.swf), say from *myAnimation.swf* to *thatAnimation.swf*, the HTML code won't know how to find it, and it won't run in the web page.

---

**DESIGN TIME**

## The Problem with Detecting Your Audience's Flash Version

If you create an animation that uses only Flash 11 (or greater) features, your audience won't be able to play it in an earlier version of Flash Player. But how do you know which version of Flash Player your audience has installed? And if it turns out they *are* running an earlier version, how can they see your animation?

The easiest approach to this dilemma is the one most Flash-ionados opt for: using the Detect Flash Version publishing option described on page 687.

But making people jump through hoops before they can see your animation isn't always the best design choice. For one thing, not everyone wants to stop what they're doing and download yet another plug-in. For another, folks in many corporate settings aren't allowed to download and install software of any kind, even a free Flash Player.

Fortunately, hoop-jumping isn't necessary: Computers excel at this kind of automatic detect-this-and-do-that process. With

a little bit of elbow grease, you can devise a more seamless, professional approach, like one of these:

- Detecting your audience's installed Flash Player and automatically displaying a version of your animation that runs in that player.

- Having your HTML file substitute a static image or animated GIF file if it doesn't find the correct Flash Player.

- Having your animation download and install the correct version of Flash Player for your audience so they don't have to.

Many Flash programming folks use another option, called SWFObject, to detect the presence of a Flash Player in their audience's browsers. A small chunk of JavaScript code— SWFObject 2—is easy to use and works with both HTML and XHTML. You can find SWFObject and more details at *www.adobe.com/devnet/flashplayer/articles/swfobject.html*.

---

## Publishing a Frame as a Static Image File

It may seem odd that Flash lets you publish a frame of your animation as a single, static image—after all, the point of using Flash is creating animations, not images. But publishing your animation as an image file (in addition to publishing it as a Flash file) can be a savvy design choice: If some people don't have Flash Player installed on their machines and so can't see your animation, at least they can see your opening frame. Also, sometimes web designers use static images produced by Flash as graphic links to the animation.

**NOTE**     When you *do* choose to publish an image file, you're the one who needs to create the HTML to display that image file; Flash doesn't do it for you when you select the HTML Wrapper option in the Formats tab of the Publish Settings window.

---

## ▦ PUBLISHING A STATIC GIF

GIF (Graphic Interchange Format) files are super-small, thanks in part to the fact that they limit your image to 256 colors. GIF files are the best choice for vector images containing just a few areas of solid color.

> **NOTE** Another way to create static images is to export them by choosing File→Export→Export Image (page 701).

To publish a frame of your animation as a static GIF file:

1. **In the timeline, click to select the frame you want to publish.**

   Flash highlights the selected frame. On the stage, you see the image you're about to publish.

> **NOTE** Another way to tell Flash which frame you want to publish is to add the frame label *#Static* to the frame you want to publish. Make sure you've selected a file type (like GIF, JPEG, or PNG) for the image as described in step 3. Chapter 15 (page 524) shows you how to label a frame.

2. **Choose File→Publish Settings.**

   The Publish Settings dialog box appears.

3. **Turn on the checkbox next to "GIF Image."**

   The GIF settings appear in the dialog box as shown in Figure 20-11. If you don't see the GIF settings, click the words "GIF Image" next to the checkbox.

4. **Choose one or more of the following publishing options:**

   - **Match movie.** Tells Flash to create a GIF image the same size as the stage.

   - **Size (Width/Height).** Tells Flash how large you want the GIF file to be, in pixels. These options are available only if you haven't turned on "Match movie" (see above).

   - **Playback (Static/Animated).** Tells Flash whether to create a static GIF file or an animated GIF file. Make sure you turn on Static. (Page 697 shows you how to create an animated GIF file.)

   - **Loop Continuously** and **Repeat times** are used only with animated GIFs.

   - **Optimize colors.** Lowers file size as much as possible without sacrificing image quality. Always make sure you turn this option on.

   - **Interlace.** Tells Flash to create a GIF that downloads in several passes, so that a fuzzy version appears first, then a clearer version, then a still clearer version, and so on. Turning on this option doesn't reduce download time, but it does give your audience quick successive "tastes" of the image while they're waiting—useful for very large images.

- **Smooth.** Tells Flash to smooth (antialias) your image. Turning on this option may improve the look of any text your image contains; it can also save a few bytes.

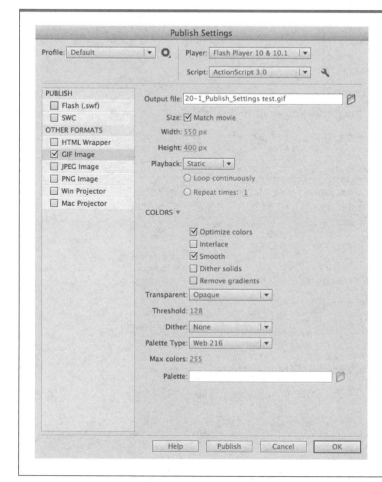

**FIGURE 20-11**

*GIFs are generally the most compact of the three static image file formats, but they're also the most restrictive: They can display at most 256 colors. (If the image you're exporting contains a bunch of custom colors, your GIF may look slightly off.) Two different types of GIFs exist: static and animated. In this section, you see how to publish frame content to a static GIF.*

- **Dither solids.** Tells Flash to attempt to match any solid custom colors you've used as closely as it can by combining two colors. If you don't turn on this option, Flash chooses the nearest-in-shade solid color in its palette.

- **Remove gradients.** Tells Flash to convert the gradients in your image to solid colors. (Gradient effects don't translate well to the GIF format anyway, so if your image contains gradient effects, you probably want to turn on this option.)

- **Transparent.** Lets you specify the transparency of your image background (the blank area of the stage). Your options include Opaque (a regular, solid background), Transparent (no background), or Alpha and Threshold (lets you choose how transparent you want the background to appear).

- **Dither.** Tells Flash to *dither* (mix two colors) to try to match all the non-solid areas of your image as closely as possible. Your options include None (no dithering), Ordered (minimal dithering, minimal file size increase), and Diffusion (maximum dithering, maximum file size increase).

- **Palette Type.** Lets you tell Flash which 256 colors to use to create the GIF image. (GIFs are limited to 256 colors, but you get to pick which 256.) Your options include Web 216 (web-safe colors), Adaptive (non-web-safe colors), Web Snap Adaptive (a mix of web-safe and non-web-safe colors), and Custom (lets you specify a color palette you've saved as an .act file, using a program like Fireworks). Depending on the image you're publishing, one of these options may yield better-looking results—although in most cases, you want to leave this option set to Web 216.

- **Max colors.** Available only if you've selected a palette type of Adaptive or Web Snap Adaptive (see above), this option lets you specify a maximum number of colors lower than 256 to save on file size.

- **Palette.** Available only if you've selected a palette type of Custom (see above), this option lets you type the filename of your own custom color palette. The palette has to have been created using another program, like Fireworks, and saved with the .act file extension. If you prefer, you can click the file icon to browse your computer for the palette filename.

5. **Click Publish.**

   The Publish Settings window disappears, and Flash generates a GIF file based on the name you set in the Formats tab. If you didn't type a name, Flash names the GIF file based on your .fla filename. For example, if the name of your Flash document is *myAnimation.fla*, then Flash generates a file named *myAnimation.gif*.

### ■ PUBLISHING A JPEG

JPEG (Joint Photographic Experts Group) files typically don't end up being as small as GIF files, but they can contain many more colors. Sometimes referred to as the "photo format," JPEG is the best choice if your image, like a scanned-in photograph, contains lots of colors, subtle shading, or gradient effects.

To publish a frame of your animation as a JPEG file:

1. **In the timeline, click to select the frame you want to publish.**

   Flash highlights the selected frame. On the stage, you see the image you're about to publish.

2. **Choose File→Publish Settings.**

   The Publish Settings dialog box appears.

3. **Turn on the checkbox next to JPEG Image.**

The JPEG publishing settings shown in Figure 20-12. appear. If you don't see the JPEG settings, click the words "JPEG image" next to the checkbox.

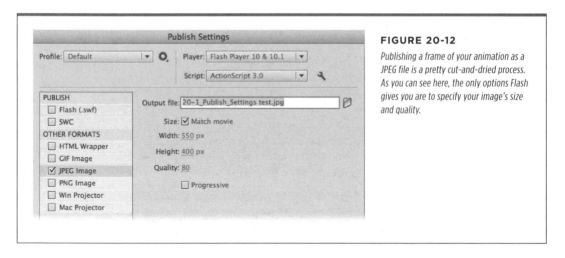

**FIGURE 20-12**

*Publishing a frame of your animation as a JPEG file is a pretty cut-and-dried process. As you can see here, the only options Flash gives you are to specify your image's size and quality.*

4. **Choose one or more of the following publishing options:**

- **Size: Match movie** tells Flash to create a JPEG image the same size as the stage.

- **Width/Height.** Tells Flash how large you want the JPEG file to be, in pixels. These options are available only if you haven't turned on "Match movie," described on page 687.

- **Quality.** Tells Flash how much detail you want it to include. The larger the number you type (or specify by dragging the slider), the better your JPEG image will look, and the larger your JPEG file size will be. (Depending on your particular image, the image quality may appear similar enough at different quality levels that you can get away with a lower number, thereby whittling away at your animation's finished file size. See page 671 for more on optimization.)

- **Progressive.** Similar to the GIF Interlace option (page 691), turning on this option tells Flash to create a JPEG that downloads in several passes, so that a fuzzy version appears first, then a clearer version, then a still clearer version, and so on. Turning on this option doesn't reduce download time, but it does give your audience quick successive "tastes" of the image while they're waiting, which some audiences appreciate.

5. **Click Publish.**

The Publish Settings window disappears, and Flash generates a JPEG file based on the name you set in the Formats tab. If you didn't type a name, then

Flash names the JPEG file based on your .fla filename. For example, if the name of your Flash document is *myAnimation.fla*, Flash generates a file named *myAnimation.jpg*.

### ■ PUBLISHING A PNG

Developed to replace and improve on the GIF file format (back when it looked like web developers would have to pay royalties for every GIF they produced), the PNG (Portable Network Graphics) file format offers the best of both worlds: the tiny file size of a static GIF with the support for 24-bit color of a JPEG. PNG files can include transparent (alpha) effects, too.

To publish a frame of your animation as a PNG file:

1. **In the timeline, click to select the frame you want to publish.**

   Flash highlights the selected frame. On the stage, you see the image you're about to publish.

2. **Choose File→Publish Settings.**

   The Publish Settings dialog box appears.

3. **Turn on the checkbox next to PNG Image.**

   The PNG publishing settings shown in Figure 20-13 appear. If you don't see the PNG settings, click the words "PNG Image" next to the checkbox.

4. **Choose one or more of the following publishing options:**

   - **Size: Match movie.** Tells Flash to create a PNG image the same size as the stage.

   - **Width/Height.** Tells Flash how large you want the PNG file to be, in pixels. These options are available only if you haven't turned on "Match movie," described on page 691.

   - **Bit depth.** Tells Flash how many colors you want the PNG to be able to render. Your options include 8-bit (256 colors, the same as GIF), 24-bit (16.7 million colors), and 24-bit with Alpha (16.7 million colors, plus the ability to render your image background as transparent). The more colors, the larger the file size.

   - **Optimize colors.** Reduces file size without sacrificing the quality of your image. You always want to turn this option on.

   - **Interlace.** Tells Flash to create a PNG that downloads in several passes, so that a fuzzy version appears first, then a clearer version, then a still clearer version, and so on. Turning on this option doesn't reduce download time, but it does give your audience quick successive "tastes" of the image while they're waiting—useful for very large images.

- **Smooth.** Tells Flash to smooth (antialias) your image. Turning on this option may improve the look of any text your image contains; it can also save a few bytes of file size.

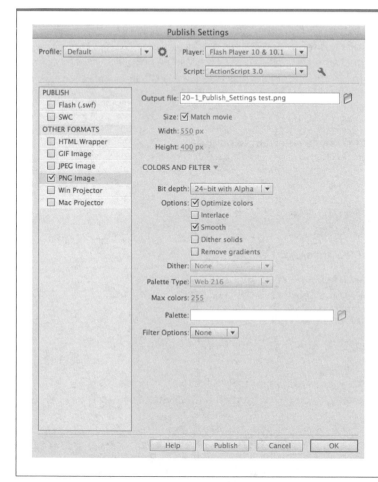

**FIGURE 20-13**

*Some older web browsers—for example, Internet Explorer versions 6 and earlier— don't completely support PNG files. If you want to publish a static image but you're not sure which browser your audience has installed, you may want to opt for GIF or JPEG instead.*

- **Dither solids.** Tells Flash to attempt to match any solid custom colors you've used as closely as it can by combining two colors (only necessary if you choose a bit depth of 8-bit, as described above). If you don't turn on this option, then Flash chooses the nearest-in-shade solid color in its palette.

- **Remove gradients.** Tells Flash to convert the gradients in your image to solid colors to save on file size.

- **Dither.** Tells Flash to *dither* (mix two colors) to try to match all the nonsolid areas of your image as closely as possible (necessary only if you've chosen a bit depth of 8-bit). Your options include None (no dithering), Ordered (minimal dithering, minimal file size increase), and Diffusion (maximum dithering, maximum file size increase).

- **Palette Type.** Available only if you chose a bit depth of 8-bit (see page 695), this option lets you tell Flash which 256 colors to use to create the PNG image. Your options include Web 216 (web-safe colors), Adaptive (non-web-safe colors), Web Snap Adaptive (a mix of web-safe and non-web-safe colors), and Custom (lets you specify a color palette you've saved as an .act file, using a program like Fireworks). Depending on the image you're publishing, one of these options may yield better-looking results—although in most cases, you want to leave this option set to Web 216.

- **Max colors.** Available only if you've selected a Palette Type of Adaptive or Web Snap Adaptive (see above), this option lets you specify a maximum number of colors lower than 256 to save file size.

- **Palette.** Available only if you've selected a Palette Type of Custom (see above), this option lets you type the filename of your own custom color palette. The palette has to have been created using another program, like Fireworks, and saved with the .act file extension. If you prefer, you can click the file icon to browse your computer for the palette filename.

- **Filter options.** This option lets you tell Flash to apply an additional compression algorithm when it's creating your PNG file. Normally, you don't use this option unless you're trying to pare down your PNG file by a few bytes. Your options include None, Sub, Up, Average, Paeth, and Adaptive.

5. **Click Publish.**

The Publish Settings window disappears, and Flash generates a PNG file based on the name you provide. If you don't type a name, Flash names the PNG filename based on your .fla filename. For example, if the name of your Flash document is *myAnimation.fla*, Flash generates a file named *myAnimation.png*.

## Publishing as an Animated GIF

In addition to static images, the GIF file format lets you create animated images. Animated GIFs are mini-animations that play right in the web browser, with no need for a Flash Player add-in. The quality isn't always stellar, and your audience can't interact with them (which is why Flash was invented). But depending on how long your animation is, and what quality of playback you're shooting for, they can be an impressive alternative.

To publish your animation as an animated GIF file:

1. **Choose File→Publish Settings.**

The Publish Settings dialog box appears.

2. **Turn on the checkbox next to GIF Image.**

The GIF publishing options shown in Figure 20-14 appear.

3. **Set the publishing options you see in Figure 20-14 just as you would for a static GIF file (page 691), except for the following:**

- **Static/Animated.** This option tells Flash whether to create a static or animated GIF file. Make sure you turn on Animated.

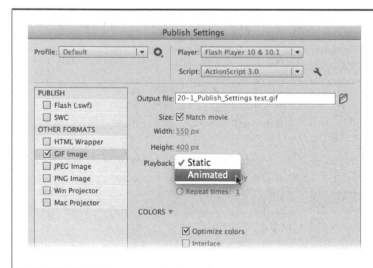

**FIGURE 20-14**

*Animated GIFs are amazing creatures: small, decent quality (especially if you're only talking about a few frames), and as easy to include in an HTML file as a static GIF file (the basic line of HTML code you need is <img src="yourGIF.gif"/>). The only extra settings you have to specify for an animated GIF, as opposed to a static GIF, are whether you want the animated GIF to loop continuously, loop a few times, or not loop at all.*

- **Loop continuously.** Turn on this option to tell Flash to replay the animated GIF over and over again.

- **Repeat times.** Tells Flash to create an animated GIF that automatically plays the number of times you type into the "times" box.

4. **Click Publish.**

The Publish Settings window disappears, and Flash generates a GIF file based on the name you set in the Formats tab. If you didn't type a name, then Flash names the GIF file based on your .fla filename. For example, if the name of your Flash document is *myAnimation.fla*, then Flash generates a file named *myAnimation.gif*.

## Publishing as a Standalone Projector

A *projector* is the equivalent of an .swf file and a copy of Flash Player all rolled up into a single executable file. When you create a projector, your audience doesn't need to have either a web browser or Flash Player installed on their computers: All they need to do to play your animation is to run the projector file.

You'll want to choose this option if you want to deliver your animation on a CD or DVD (as opposed to over the web). Tutorials, product demonstrations, and program mock-ups (as well as the programs themselves) are all examples of the kinds of animations you might want to publish as projectors.

**NOTE** If you plan to distribute a Flash projector to folks outside your company, take a look at the Adobe Player Distribution License, a legalese description of what you can and can't do with your projector files. Adobe may change the location of this document, but the time of this writing, you can find a copy online at *www.adobe.com/ products/players/fpsh_distribution1.html*.

To publish your animation as a standalone projector:

1. **Choose File→Publish Settings.**

   The Publish Settings dialog box appears.

2. **Turn on the checkbox next to one or both of the following, depending on the operating system you expect your audience to be running:**

   - **Windows Projector (.exe)** to create a projector that runs on Windows.

   - **Macintosh Projector** to create a projector that runs on the Mac.

3. **Click Publish.**

   If you chose "Windows Projector (.exe)," Flash generates an .exe file. If you chose Macintosh Projector, Flash generates an .app file. Flash names the files based on the names displayed in the Formats tab. For example, if the name of your Flash document is *myAnimation.fla*, Flash generates files named *myAnimation.exe* or *myAnimation.app*.

# Exporting Flash to Other Formats

*Exporting* your entire animation—or one or more of the individual frames that make up your animation—is very similar to publishing. In both cases, you get to specify which file format you'd like Flash to write, and in both cases, you get to tweak file settings based on the file format you choose. Flash designates the most common file formats (.html, .swf, .gif, .jpg, .png, and projector files) as publishing destinations, and all other file formats as export destinations. Most of the time, you'll export (rather than publish) an image, sound, or your entire animation when you want to work with it in another graphics or animation program.

To export to a single frame image, select File→Export→Export Image. To export to an animation (multiframe) file format or an audio format, select File→Export→Export Movie. In Flash Professional CS6, there are very few differences in the available formats for Macs and PCs. The most significant is that Windows computers can write to the Windows BMP, AVI, and WAV formats. Table 20-1 shows the available formats.

**TABLE 20-1** *File formats to which you can export your Flash animation*

| FORMAT | EXTENSION | NOTE |
|---|---|---|
| SWF movie | .swf | Single frame image |
| Adobe FXG | .fxg | Single frame image |

| FORMAT | EXTENSION | NOTE |
|---|---|---|
| Bitmap | .bmp | Single frame image |
| JPEG image | .jpg | Single frame image |
| GIF image | .gif | Single frame image |
| PNG image | .png | Single frame image |
| SWF movie | .swf | Animation |
| Windows AVI (Windows only) | .avi | Animation |
| QuickTime | .mov | Animation |
| Animated GIF | .gif | Animation |
| WAV audio (Windows only) | .wav | Audio |
| JPEG sequence | .jpg | Animation |
| GIF sequence | .gif | Animation |
| PNG sequence | .png | Animation |

**GEM IN THE ROUGH**

### Exporting to HTML5 with CreateJS

As web standards evolve, HTML5, CSS and JavaScript have taken on some of the functions that were originally in Flash's domain. What's a Flash designer/developer to do with all those hard earned Flash skills. Well, one new thing you can do is develop projects in Flash and export them to HTML5 with a third party extension called CreateJS (*www.createjs.com*). It won't be suitable for every project you create. For example, the CreateJS extension knows how to work with Classic tweens, but at the time this was written it couldn't handle motion tweens.

To use CreateJS, you need to download the extension and then install it using the Adobe Extension manager. After you've done that, you'll find the Toolkit for CreateJS panel under Windows→Other Panels→Toolkit for CreateJS.

You can run the extenstion by going Command→Publish to CreateJS.

## Exporting the Contents of a Single Frame

Exporting the contents of a single frame of your animation lets you create a one-frame animation or (more commonly) an image file you can edit with another image-editing program.

**NOTE** Exporting an image from one animation and then importing the image into another animation is one way to share images between Flash documents. You can also share by saving the image as a graphic symbol in one animation, and then using the Library panel's drop-down list to add the symbol to another animation, as described in Chapter 7.

1. **On the stage, click to select the frame you want to export.**

   Flash highlights the selected frame.

2. **Choose File→Export→Export Image.**

   The Export Image dialog box you see in Figure 20-15 appears.

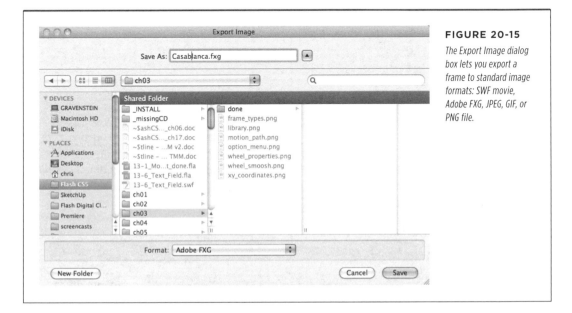

**FIGURE 20-15**

*The Export Image dialog box lets you export a frame to standard image formats: SWF movie, Adobe FXG, JPEG, GIF, or PNG file.*

3. **From the pop-up menu, choose the file format to which you want to export.**

   In Windows, this menu is called "Save as type"; on the Mac, it's called Format.

4. **In the Filename (Save As) box, type a name for your exported file.**

   Leave the file extension Flash suggests.

5. **Click Save.**

   Flash displays an Export window containing format-specific settings, as shown in Figure 20-16.

6. **In the Export window, set one or more export options, and then click OK.**

Flash exports the contents of your frame to the file format you chose in step 3.

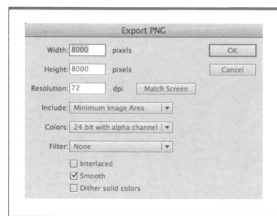

**FIGURE 20-16**

*The settings window you see after you click Save (and even whether you see one or not) depends on the format you're exporting to. Here, you see the settings window for the PNG format.*

## Exporting an Entire Animation

Exporting your animation to another file format lets you edit the animation using another animation program, like Apple's QuickTime. You might want to do this if, for example, you want to combine frames from Flash and QuickTime animations into a single animation.

1. **Choose File→Export→Export Movie.**

The Export Movie dialog box you see in Figure 20-17 appears.

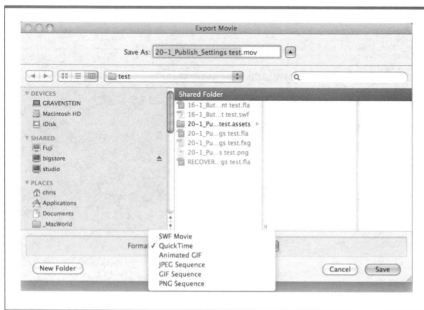

**FIGURE 20-17**

*The Export Movie dialog box lets you export your animation to a variety of formats, several of which will be familiar to you if you've had a chance to check out the section on publishing (page 677).*

2. **From the pop-up menu, choose the file format to which you want to export.**

In Windows, this menu is called "Save as type"; on the Mac, it's called Format.

3. **In the Save As box, type a name for your exported file.**

Leave the file extension Flash suggests.

4. **Click Save.**

Flash displays an Export window containing format-specific settings, as shown in Figure 20-18.

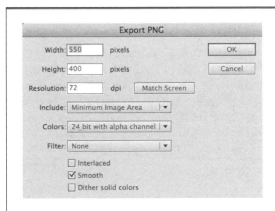

**FIGURE 20-18**

*When you export your animation, Flash displays the same settings you see when you publish your animation. From Flash's perspective, the two processes are the same, but you may appreciate the convenience of publishing over exporting. For example, when you publish your animation, Flash lets you save your settings in an easy-to-reuse publish profile (see the box on page 684). Not so when you export your animation.*

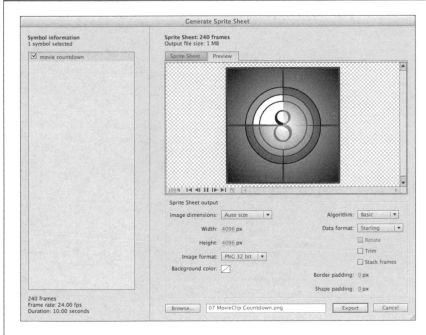

**FIGURE 20-19**

*You can create sprite sheets from the symbols in your library. Sprite sheets and their accompanying JavaScript code are used for creating animated web pages using HTML5, CSS and JavaScript.*

5. **In the Export window, set one or more export options, and then click OK.**

Flash exports the contents of your frame to the file format you chose in step 2.

**FREQUENTLY ASKED QUESTIONS**

### Generating Sprite Sheets from Flash

**What's a sprite sheet and why would I want to generate one?**

In the olden days of the web you almost always turned to Flash to create animations. These days there are more options because HTML, CSS and JavaScript have new capabilities. If you're working with a team or on an HTML only website you may want to export a Flash animation to an HTML and JavaScript project.

So, what's a sprite sheet and how does it fit in? Perhaps you have an animated character such as a large desert bird that likes to run down the highway. You have all it's foot motions animated and they're stored in a Flash symbol. You could export each frame of that animation as individual images (gif, png or jpeg). However, that's not the best way to serve up an animated image on the web. It takes less time to download one large image than it does to download lots of small images. This is particularly important when developing games or other time-dependent animations. Sprite sheets take advantage of this. Each frame of your running bird animation is placed in a single image and JavaScript code is produced to identify each frame.

You can generate a sprite sheet for a symbol, by right-clicking it in the Library panel and choosing Generate Sprite Sheet. A window appears (as shown in Figure 20-19) where you can adjust settings like size and background color and choose the image format. Clicking Export generates both the sprite sheet and the necessary JavaScript code.

# Introducing Adobe AIR

Flash began life as a program for creating cool animations in files small enough to send over the Internet. Flash has evolved since then, gaining the ability to create interactive animations using ActionScript. During the same period, the Internet grew up, and the line between desktop applications and web-based services has blurred. The next step in Flash's evolution is the ability to create desktop and mobile applications. After all, not all computers are connected to the Internet *all* the time. Better still, desktop programs don't have the limitations of browser-based apps, which are, for safety's sake, restricted in the ways they can read and write to files on your computer.

And so Adobe developed the AIR system for creating applications that run outside a web browser. AIR lets you develop powerful applications using your Flash and ActionScript skills, and do it quickly. This chapter introduces the concepts behind Adobe AIR and shows you how to create a bare-bones AIR application. You'll learn how to convert your existing Flash animations into an AIR desktop application. Throughout, you'll find tips explaining where you can learn more about AIR and how other developers are using it. The following chapters show how to apply your AIR skills when building apps for the iPhone operating system (iOS) and Android handhelds.

## Meet Adobe AIR

If you're interested in developing desktop applications or applets that can run on Windows, Mac, and even Linux computers, read on. AIR stands for Adobe Integrated Runtime. In programmer-speak, a *runtime*, sometimes called a runtime environment, works sort of like a translator. You can write a program in a relatively human language like ActionScript, and the runtime translates your code into the 1s and 0s that a PC understands. For example, you can display an object on a computer screen using ActionScript's *addChild()* method—one line of code. Flash Player (the runtime environment) pushes around a bunch of bits and bytes to manipulate specific pixels on the screen. The fact that Adobe has Flash Players for Windows, Mac, and Linux computers means you can write *one* Flash animation that plays everywhere. You don't have to worry about all the differences among those operating systems. Adobe has done that work for you. The same runtime concepts apply to AIR.

Like Flash Player, AIR is a runtime environment, but there are significant differences between AIR and Flash Player, making each suited for different types of projects. From the beginning, AIR was designed to let Flash designers and web developers use their expertise to build programs that run on computer and mobile desktops instead of within web browsers. Many AIR programs retrieve and store data on a web server, but they also have the ability to work with the local files on a computer in ways not available to a browser-based app. For example, eBay Desktop (Figure 21-1) is an AIR app that lives on the desktop and shuffles data stored on a web server when there's an Internet connection. But other AIR applications can browse through a computer's file system and then open a file in the associated application; for example, Word docs in Word, and MP3s in media players. AIR applications can be designed to recognize when cameras, thumb drives, or other storage devices are connected or disconnected. You can use input from microphones in your AIR app to create audio notes or other features.

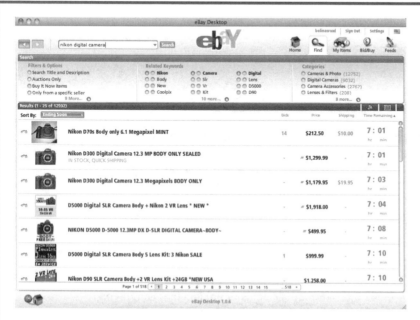

**FIGURE 21-1**

*The eBay Desktop is an example of an AIR application. You install it to run like a desktop program, but it uses web-based data to give you real-time updates on auctions and other eBay services.*

The *Integrated* part of the Adobe Integrated Runtime name comes from the fact that AIR was designed as a system that gives developers the opportunity to use the skills they've already learned. It's not limited to Flash and ActionScript. If you're an HTML and JavaScript wizard, you can create an entire AIR application using those tools. If you're proficient in JavaScript and ActionScript, you can use a combination of those tools to build your app. Naturally, Adobe hopes you'll use its tools to create your apps, so you'll find AIR capabilities built into lots of its tools, not just Flash and Flex. For example, Dreamweaver and Fireworks have AIR capabilities, too.

## Differences Between AIR and Flash

Both AIR and Flash are available for Windows, Mac, and Linux computers, so you can focus on developing one great program and you don't have to sweat the details of different operating systems. In spite of that, there are many ways AIR applications and Flash animations differ. Here's a list of the main differences:

- AIR uses the Adobe AIR runtime. Flash uses the Flash Player (also a runtime environment).

- Most AIR applications run in a desktop window. Flash usually uses a browser window.

- AIR programs can be developed using a combination of tools: Flash, Flex, HTML, XML, and JavaScript. Flash animations are most often developed using Flash Professional, Flash Builder, or Flex.

- An AIR application must be installed on a computer like any other desktop application. Flash animations simply require that the Flash Player be present. According to Adobe, Flash Player is installed on well over 90 percent of computers.

- Because it's installed on a computer like any old program, an AIR application requires a code signing certificate. This bit of security verifies the source of the program (see page 710). Flash animations don't require a code signing certificate.

---

**TIP**  Want to see some snazzy examples of AIR programs? Go to *http://www.adobe.com/cfusion/marketplace/* and click OSMF Marketplace. (OSMF stands for Open Source Media Framework.) As shown in (Figure 21-2) you'll see a variety of apps to download. They're displayed with descriptions and ranked by users.

---

# ■ Creating Your First AIR Application

Developing a bare-bones AIR application is simple. If you've worked through a fraction of the exercises in this book, you have the skills to build an AIR app. By doing a simple "Hello, World" exercise, you'll learn that you already have all the computer resources and programming skills you need to produce a working application. Follow these steps to create an animator's version of the old, reliable "Hello, World" program that's given so many people their first taste of a new programming language.

1. **Choose File→New→AIR, as shown in Figure 21-3.**

   Flash creates a new document with a stage and timeline that looks just like your usual Flash workspace. Behind the scenes, there are differences, because Flash creates a document that uses the AIR runtime instead of Flash Player.

**FIGURE 21-2**

*Taking a page from the iTunes App Store, Adobe created the AIR Marketplace, where developers can showcase and sell their creations. Want to learn what others are doing with AIR? Go to www.adobe.com/cfusion/ marketplace/. Already have a finished AIR app? Maybe yours will make the Highest Rated or Most Popular lists.*

2. **Click the Text tool, and then in the Properties panel, choose TLF Text and Read Only.**

   You use the same tools for AIR apps as you use for Flash animations.

3. **Click the stage and type some text, such as *Hello Adobe AIR World*.**

   Change the font, color, and size so that it's large and attractive on the stage.

4. **In the timeline, click Frame 48 and then press F5.**

   Flash adds new frames to the timeline.

5. **Right-click (Control-click) the timeline and then choose Create Motion Tween.**

   The timeline changes to light blue, indicating a motion tween.

6. **Move the playhead to Frame 48.**

In the next step, you'll create a new property keyframe at this location.

7. **In the Transform panel (Window→Transform), set Rotate to 720.**

That's enough to make the text field spin twice.

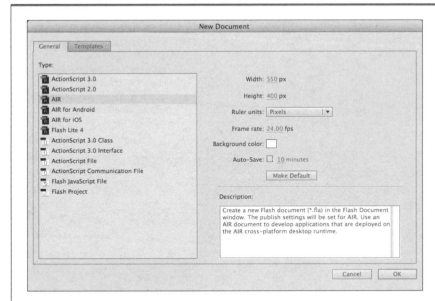

**FIGURE 21-3**

*Starting an AIR project in Flash Professional is similar to starting any project, but instead of choosing ActionScript 3.0, choose AIR 2. This way Flash knows your project will use the AIR runtime instead of the Flash Player.*

8. **Click the New Layer button and name the new layer actions.**

Time to add a smidgen of ActionScript, just to prove that it works in AIR. Keep in mind, your AIR applications use ActionScript 3.0 and won't work with ActionScript 2.0 or earlier.

9. **Right-click the 48th frame of the actions layer and press F6.**

A blank keyframe appears in the timeline, where you can add some code.

10. **Press F9 (Option-F9) or choose Window→Actions to open the Actions panel.**

You have access to the same ActionScript coding tools, including code hinting and code snippets.

11. **Type *stop();*.**

This line simply stops the animation when it reaches the last frame.

12. **Press Ctrl+Enter (⌘-Return).**

After a little computing, your animation runs in a standard window that matches your Windows or Mac operating system, as shown in Figure 21-4. Additional details about the app appear in the Output panel.

Your first attempt at an AIR project proves that the various parts work. You use the standard tools, including tweens and ActionScript, to build applications that run in the Adobe Integrated Runtime.

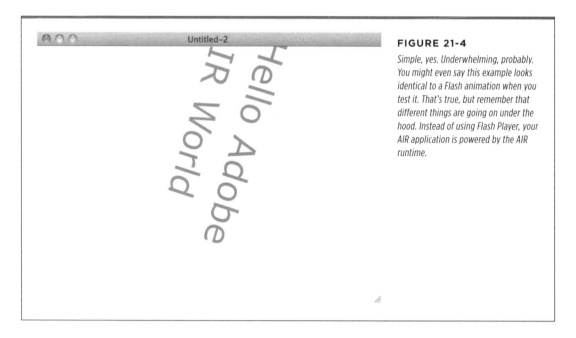

**FIGURE 21-4**

*Simple, yes. Underwhelming, probably. You might even say this example looks identical to a Flash animation when you test it. That's true, but remember that different things are going on under the hood. Instead of using Flash Player, your AIR application is powered by the AIR runtime.*

**NOTE** Interested in the process of developing a complex AIR app? There's a story on Adobe TV about an application developed by the Fiat car company. Its program uses data that's recorded to a thumb drive while your car is running. Plug the thumb drive into your computer at home, and the AIR app provides details on how to drive more economically to reduce your carbon emissions. Your data is pooled with other drivers in the Fiat community. According to the developers, the AIR app was developed in about five to six months. To find the video, go to *http://tv.adobe.com* and search for the word Fiat. The video runs about 20 minutes, describing the project from both the client's and the developer's point of view.

## Create a Code Signing Certificate

In the previous exercise, you wrote an AIR app that you can test inside Flash, but that's about all it can do. You can't save it in a format that runs outside Flash or share it with your friends. If you want to produce a program that runs as a standalone desktop app and distribute it, you need to give people a way to confirm where it's coming from. In other words, you need to get a *code signing certificate*. After all, if you're going to send this app to other people's computers, they need to make sure it's really coming from you—a known and trusted source.

In the bad old days when the Internet was young, just about any website you visited could install and run (or trick you into running) an evil program on your computer. There are still bad folks out there trying to push malware onto unsuspecting computers, but life online is somewhat safer. The safer environment is due in part to *certificates*—a system that authenticates the source of a program. If a program asks you to install it on your computer, you can check its certificate to see if it's genuinely from, say, Adobe or Microsoft and not from 16-year-old Todd, aka GrimHackerOfAnarchy. If you expect strangers to install your apps on their computers, you should get a code signing certificate from a company like Thawte (*www. thawte.com*). You'll find they aren't cheap—about $300 for a year or $550 for two years. When you distribute your software, people can check with Thawte or some other certificate authority (CA) to see if you're really who you say you are. And of course, if something goes wrong, they'll be able to hunt you down through the CA.

All AIR programs require a certificate before you can publish them. That certificate can be a third-party code signing certificate from a CA, or if you're not ready for the big time, you can create what's known as a *self-signed certificate*. With a self-signed certificate, you're vouching for yourself, which is good enough for testing or for distributing an app among friends and colleagues who know and trust you.

If you decide to go the self-signed route for now, here's how:

1. **Choose File→New→AIR.**

   Flash creates a new Adobe AIR document. This step also activates some menu options specific to AIR projects.

2. **Choose File→"AIR 3.2 for Desktop Settings."**

   The "Application & Install Settings" panel opens. It includes tabs labeled General, Signature, Icons, and Advanced. (AIR 3.2 was the latest version when this was written. It's likely that AIR 3.3 or some other version will appear here in the future.)

3. **Click the Signature tab.**

   The Signature tab displays a form where you can enter details related to code signing certificates, as shown in Figure 21-5. The More Info button leads to the Adobe website.

4. **Next to Certificate, click the Create (New on a Mac) button.**

   A form like the one in Figure 21-6 appears, where you create and issue your own certificate.

5. **Fill in the form details, and then click OK.**

   Use your name or company name as the Publisher. All the fields need to be filled in, but you can repeat your name in the Organization name field and use something like *Company* or *Developer* for the Organization unit. Provide a password and leave the Type set to 1024-RSA. Click the folder next to "Save as," and navigate to a folder on your computer where you want to store the certificate.

When you click OK, if all is well, you see a message telling you that a certificate was created. If you missed a field or made some other mistake, you see an alert message.

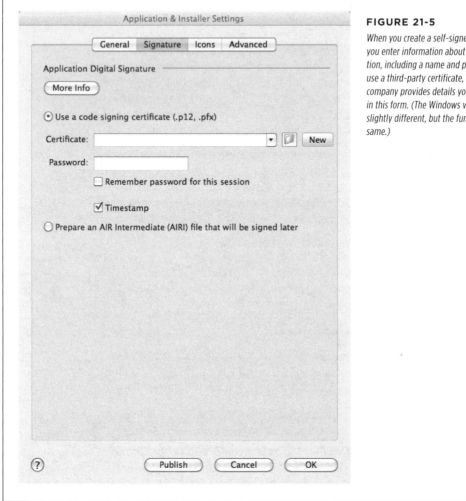

**FIGURE 21-5**

*When you create a self-signed certificate, you enter information about your organization, including a name and password. If you use a third-party certificate, the issuing company provides details you can enter in this form. (The Windows version looks slightly different, but the functions are the same.)*

6. **Click OK.**

   You return to the Signature tab, where your new certificate is listed in the Certificate field. Unless you provided a new name, it's named something like *mycert.p12*.

7. **In the Password box, type the password you created in step 5 and turn on "Remember password for this session."** Click OK.

Your audience's computers will use the certificate you create to authenticate the files included in your AIR project. You can go ahead and Publish—that is, compile and package—an AIR application. If you don't have a certificate, Flash won't let you publish in AIR.

8. **Optional: If you're ready to publish, then instead of clicking OK, click Publish.**

Flash creates the files for your AIR project, which at a minimum include a main *.swf* file and an *.xml* descriptor file. These are stored in a single *.air* file, which is the one you distribute to your audience. If your project includes other assets like sound or video, they're also stored in the *.air* file. Your completed AIR app can be distributed as a download from a website, a file on a disk, or an attachment to an email. For more details on publishing, see page 677.

**FIGURE 21-6**

*Creating a self-signed certificate is pretty much a fill-in-the-blanks job. Flash creates a certificate and stores it on your computer. With this kind of certificate, you can publish AIR apps and give them to people, but your self-signed certificate might not be enough if you want to distribute your app to the world at large.*

# ■ Convert a Flash Animation to AIR

If you follow the steps on page 707, you can create a new AIR application from scratch. You can use all your Flash tools and skills to build a new application. On the other hand, you may have a great Flash animation that you'd like to convert to AIR. That's not hard to do. It's really just a matter of creating a new AIR document and then opening your Flash project in another tab. Then you can copy content from the Flash animation to the AIR project. To give it a try, you can use the Photo Gallery project from Chapter 7. The file in the Missing CD (*www.missingmanuals.com/cds/flashcs6mm*) is named *21-1_Flash_Gallery.fla*.

1. **Choose File→New→Adobe AIR.**

A new AIR document opens in Flash.

2. **Choose Modify→Document.** Then in the Document Settings, change the document width to *800 px* and the height to *600 px*. Set the background color to a light gray (#999999). Click OK.

   After you change the dimensions and click OK, the stage changes to the new color and larger size.

3. **Choose File→Save As, and save this empty document using the name AIR_Gallery.fla.**

   The tab for this project changes from "untitled" to its new name: AIR_Gallery.fla.

4. **Choose File→Open and then find *21-1_Flash_Gallery.fla*.**

   You have two documents in the Flash workspace, the AIR document and the Flash Photo Gallery animation. As shown in Figure 21-7, the workspace holds two projects.

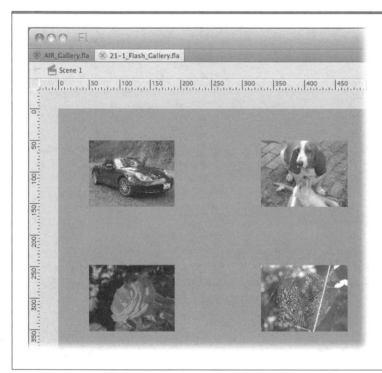

**FIGURE 21-7**

*When you have two projects open, you can jump back and forth between them by clicking on their tabs. In this case, one project is a Flash animation, and the other is an AIR project.*

---

**NOTE** The Photo Gallery consists of nine photos which, when clicked, spin around and expand to fill the stage. A second click reduces them to their former thumbnail size. Motion tweens create the animation, and event listeners handle the mouse clicks. You'll find *stop()* methods in the code to keep the animation from continuing to play at key points. Labels (page 524) are used as timeline markers for the *gotoAndPlay()* methods.

---

5. **In the *21-1_Flash_Gallery.fla* animation, drag the edge between the timeline and the stage so you can see all the layers in the timeline.**

   Once all layers are visible, you see the top layer named "instructions" and the bottom layer named "Gallery."

6. **Right-click (Control-click) any frame in the animation, and then choose Select All Frames from the shortcut menu.**

   Once selected, all the frames in the animation show a blue highlight.

7. **Right-click (Control-click) a second time and then choose Copy Frames from the shortcut menu.**

   The contents of every frame in your animation are stored on the Clipboard.

8. **Click the AIR_Gallery.fla tab.**

   The empty AIR project fills the workspace.

9. **Right-click the first frame (the only frame) in the first layer of the timeline.** Then choose Paste Frames.

   The timeline in the AIR project fills with the frames and layers that were in the Flash animation. All the tweens and labels show in the timeline. All the layers are named as they were in the Flash animation.

10. **Click the Library or go to Window→Library.**

    The symbols and JPEG photos used in this project are listed in the Library.

11. **Press Ctrl+Enter (⌘-Return).**

    The AIR project behaves like the original Flash animation.

Your AIR document now has all the assets and functions that were in the original project. If you want to examine the code in the project, press F9 (Option-F9) and take a peek. If you're happy with the project, save it and go on to the next section to publish it. If you want, you can make changes such as swapping some of the pictures or developing some new features. AIR projects have capabilities not available to Flash animations, so in the Actions panel, you'll find AIR packages with classes, properties, methods, and events, like those shown in Figure 21-8. For more details and documentation, go to *http://labs.adobe.com/technologies/air.*

# ◾ Publish Your AIR Application

Once you've got your AIR project squared away, you'll want to test it, debug it, and ultimately distribute it to your audience, just like a Flash animation. In Flash-speak, that means you need to publish your project. The process for publishing an AIR project is different from publishing a Flash animation. For one thing, as explained on page 710, you need a *code signing certificate.* Usually, Flash animations consist of one or more SWF files and sometimes some HTML code to create a web page. On the other hand, AIR applications are distributed as a single *.air* file, which holds all the project's stuff. Your audience uses that *.air* file to install the program and all the necessary files on their computers. As part of that process, the installation routine checks to make sure the AIR runtime is on the local computer. If it isn't, your user is prompted to install it. The following steps show you how to publish your AIR project. (You can use your own project or the example from page 707.)

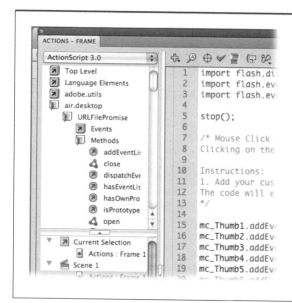

**FIGURE 21-8**

*There are special packages and classes you can use with AIR projects. Open the Actions panel, and you see several packages that begin with the name "air." AIR methods have a special icon (circled) next to their names in the Actions window and in the ActionScript documents.*

1.  **With your AIR project open in Flash, choose File→"Adobe AIR 3.2 for Desktop Settings."**

    The "Application & Installer Settings" window opens, displaying the General tab. Parts of the form are probably already filled in, such as the Output filename. In any case, here's a rundown on all the text boxes and widgets:

    -   **Output file.** The name of the file that you distribute to people who want to install and run your application. The filename ends in *.air* to indicate that it's an Adobe AIR application/installation file. Click the folder icon to choose a folder for the file that Flash creates during the publish process. Turn on the Windows or Mac installer box to create an *.exe* installer for Windows computers or a *.dmg* installer for Macs.

    -   **Output as.** You have three choices: An "AIR package" contains all the files necessary to run your application except for the AIR runtime; use this option if you think your target audience will already have AIR runtime installed. "Windows installer" (or "Mac installer") lets you create a standard installation program for your app. "Application with runtime embedded" creates a standalone application.

- **App Name** (**Name** on the Mac). The application name that appears on the window when the program is running.

- **Version.** The version number for your application. You need to update this when you make improvements to your program.

- **App ID.** The name AIR uses for this application. By convention, AIR developers use the reverse of their website address and the app name. For example, something like *com.MissingManuals.AIR_Gallery* would be appropriate.

- **Description.** Your description of your program. What does it do? Who would find it helpful?

- **Copyright.** Protect your work with a copyright notice and date.

- **Window style.** This option determines the appearance of the window that holds your application, called *chrome* in geekspeak. Choose System Chrome to have the window match the Windows, Mac, or Linux system it runs on. As an alternative, you can choose Custom Chrome (opaque) or Custom Chrome (transparent).

- **Profiles.** Choose where your program is intended to run. Options are Desktop, Mobile Device, Extended Desktop, Extended Mobile Device, TV, and Extended TV.

- **Included files.** Flash automatically adds files needed for your AIR app. In the Photo Gallery project, it adds *AIR_Gallery.swf* and *AIR_Gallery-app.xml* (the descriptor file). If your project needs additional assets, like photos, videos, or sound files, you can add them by clicking the + button, as shown in Figure 21-9.

2. **Click the Signature tab and add your certificate name and password.**

   If you created a self-signed certificate, as explained on page 710, you can use that here. Use the password you assigned to the certificate. If you have a certificate from a third-party certificate authority, use the details it provided for the certificate name and password.

3. **Click the Icons tab.**

   You use the Icons tab, shown in Figure 21-10, to define program icons used by the various operating systems (Windows, Mac OS X, Linux) to represent your application. In pixels, icons are expected to be the following sizes: 16 x 16, 32 x 32, 48 x 48, and 128 x 128. Use a program like Fireworks or Photoshop to create and size your icons. For this exercise, you can create your own or use the icons found on the Missing CD (*www.missingmanuals.com/cds/flashcs6mm*) in the file *21-2_Gallery_Icon.zip*. The examples are named *gallery_icon_16.png*, *gallery_icon_32.png*, *gallery_icon_48.png*, and *gallery_icon_128.png*.

4. **In the Icons tab, select "icon 128x128."** Then click the folder button to find and open the file *gallery_icon_128.png*.

After you click Open, the selected icon appears in the Preview pane at the bottom.

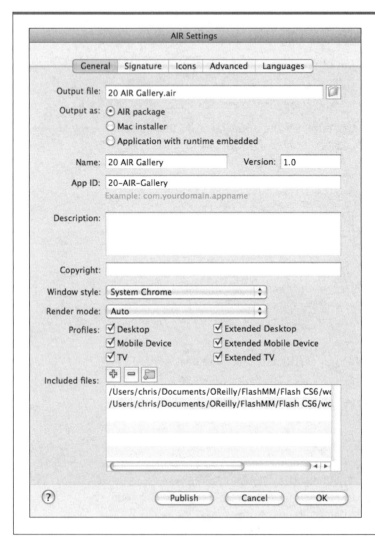

**FIGURE 21-9**

*The .air files created during the publishing process hold all the items needed to install an AIR application. You can add files or remove files and folders using the buttons in the "Included files" section of the "Application & Installer Settings."*

5. **Repeat the process to add all four icon sizes to your project.**

When you're finished, four icons of different sizes are associated with your project. When your AIR app is installed on someones desktop, their operating system will uses the icons to represent the program. Different sizes are used for different OS contexts.

6. **Click the Advanced tab.**

You use the advanced options to create file associations, to manage the program window size and behaviors, and to designate the folder for installation files and menus. This simple test program doesn't use any of the advanced features, so there's no need to make changes unless you're feeling adventurous.

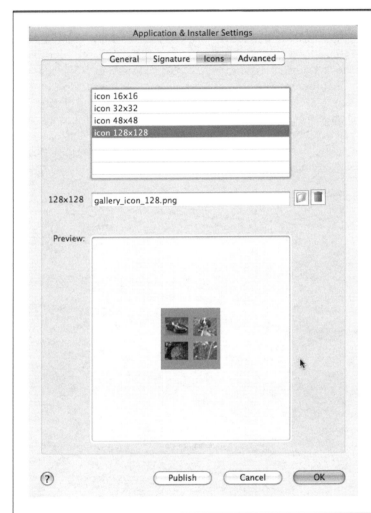

**FIGURE 21-10**

*Use the Icons tab to associate program icons with your AIR application. The host operating system uses these images to display thumbnails at various sizes.*

7. **Click Publish.**

You can use the Publish button on the "Application & Installer Settings" window, or you can use the standard File→Publish command. In either case, Flash creates an .air file that holds all the assets needed to run your application. If you selected the installer option, then Flash creates either an .exe installer for Windows or a .dmg installer for Macs.

Once your project is published, you can distribute the .air file or one of the installer files (.exe or .dmg). When your fans double-click the file, your application installs itself. If the AIR runtime is not present on the local computer, the installer prompts the person to download and install it.

## ■ Manually Install Adobe AIR Runtime

The strategy for AIR is similar to the one for Flash Player. Hopefully, your audience will already have AIR installed on their computers because they've used some other AIR program. If AIR isn't present, the program invites your audience to install AIR when they install your program. The process is simple—all they have to do is answer a couple of questions to accept the installation. It makes the installation of your program a little longer, but in most cases it won't be more than 10 to 30 seconds. And most of the time you won't need to provide any special instructions for installing the AIR runtime environment. For any unusual circumstances that may come up, it's good to know you can always find the latest version of AIR at *http://get.adobe.com/air*.

# Making iPhone Apps

I n spite of some well-publicized squabbling between Apple and Adobe, it *is* possible to use your Flash tools and know-how to create apps for the iPhone, iPod Touch, and iPad. You can use either the Mac or Windows version of Flash CS6 to create and package apps that use iOS (Apple's operating system) for Apple handhelds. The iOS packager that's built into Flash Professional CS6 translates your animation and ActionScript code into a language that Apple devices understand. Once your app is converted to the right file format, you can test it on Apple gadgets. When it's perfected, you can submit your masterpiece to the App Store. (Then all you have to do is play Angry Birds while you wait for the big checks to roll in.)

In this chapter, you'll start off with a simple "Hello iPad" app and test it in the AIR Debug Launcher (Mobile). If you want to test your app on an iPhone, iPod Touch, or iPad, you have to become a registered developer ($99) and jump through some of Apple's security-related hoops. Those details take up a substantial chunk of this chapter, but once they're out of the way, you can create and test iOS apps that include iPad/iPhone gestures and touchscreen behaviors.

> **NOTE** There's a difference between the AIR apps created with the techniques described in this chapter and Flash content embedded in a web page. Your AIR for iOS apps are actually translated into the language iDevices understand. Flash content on websites requires a browser with a Flash Player plug-in. At this writing, Safari for iPhone, iPodTouch, and iPad didn't display Flash Player content, because they don't permit the Flash Player plug-in. However, there are third-party browsers such as Skyfire (*www.skyfire.com*) that display Flash video and other content on iDevices.

# ■ Your First "Hello iPad" App

Creating a "Hello World" app is a rite of passage for any new coding endeavor, and your iPad or iPhone project is no different. As the following steps show, creating this simple demonstration using AIR for iOS isn't much different from creating any simple animation or AIR project.

1. **Choose File→New.**

   The New Document window opens.

2. **Choose AIR for iOS and click OK.**

   When you click "AIR for iOS," the width and height for the stage are automatically set to 640 x 960, as shown on the left of Figure 22-1. In future iOS projects, you may want to make changes to the background color or frame rate, but for now leave them as they are. When you click OK, your new iOS stage appears. It looks like an iPhone held in the vertical position.

3. **Click the Text tool, and in the Properties Panel set the Text engine to TLF and the text type to Read Only text.**

   No frills for Hello iPad—all it does is display text on one page so you don't need the overhead of Selectable or Editable text.

4. **In the Character settings, set the Family (font) to _serif and the size to 108.**

   In many cases, it's best to use the device fonts (_sans, _serif, and _typewriter) when you're working with iOS. This means the iPad will use the system fonts already installed on the device, which maximizes performance and minimizes your app's size.

5. **Drag to create a text box on the stage and type Hello iPad or a similar message.**

6. **Press Ctrl+S (⌘-S) to save your work.**

7. **Go to Control→Test Movie→"in AIR Debug Launcher (Mobile)."**

   Your minimalist app displays your message in its own little window. That small window is officially called the AIR Debug Launcher. See the right of Figure 22-1.

As the name implies, the AIR Debug Launcher is a special tool for viewing AIR animations on your computer. Its limitations for testing iOS apps are immediately apparent. No matter how much you tap, swipe, or give your computer screen the two-finger squeeze, the Hello iPad app just sits there. However, if your app was an animation with multiple frames of content, you could use the AIR Debug Launcher to inspect the animation. Fortunately, Adobe includes the Simulator, a special panel devoted to iOS features including touch and gestures, geolocation, and the accelerometer. For more Simulator details, see the box on page 737.

To give your app a real-world test, you need to move it to a real iPad. That's not as easy as installing one of your AIR apps on a new computer. The stumbling block is Apple's security system for the iPhone, iPod Touch, and iPad: You need to join Apple's Developer program and acquire security certificates. Unfortunately, this step is required even if all you want to do is test your app on your own equipment.

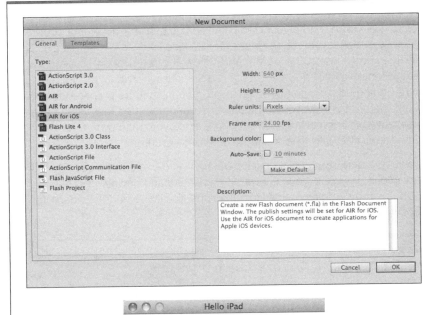

**FIGURE 22-1**

*Left: To create an app for the iPhone or iPad, you start off with the "AIR for iOS" setting in the New Document window.*

*Right: You can test your app on your computer in the AIR Debug Launcher, but it's usually a less-than-complete iOS experience.*

**NOTE**  The operating system for Apple's popular mobile devices is referred to as iOS. The current version as of this writing is iOS 5.1. Flash Professional CS6 can produce apps that work with version 3.0 and higher.

## ■ Joining the iOS Developer Program

Apple is the gatekeeper when it comes to putting apps on the various iDevices. If you want to share, sell, or even test your app on an iPhone, iPod Touch, or iPad, you must join Apple's iOS Developer program. A yearly subscription for an individual costs $99 (plus tax). Once you've joined, you have access to Apple developer tools, help pages, instructional videos, and developer forums. But for Flash developers, the vital materials are the certificates and IDs required to move apps from your computer onto test devices.

It's easy to sign up. Just grab your credit card and go to *http://developer.apple.com*. There are separate developer programs for iOS, Mac, and Safari. To create apps for handhelds, choose the iOS program and follow the registration procedures. For individual, lone-wolf developers, choose the Standard Individual program for $99. If you're signing up for a company, choose Company and be prepared to provide additional details to prove your company exists and that it's a responsible entity. If you're a really big company, say 500 or more employees, and want to develop and distribute apps internally, check out the Enterprise program.

Once you're a paid-up, official developer, log in and explore the site. Though it's not covered in this book, you may want to go ahead and download Xcode and the iOS SDK, the tools Apple provides to build apps. You'll also find the videos, forums and documentation helpful.

> **NOTE** If you're interested in developing iPhone apps using Apple's tools, Craig Hockenberry's *iPhone App Development: The Missing Manual* (O'Reilly) is a great place to start learning.

## The Purpose of Developer Certificates and App IDs

Apple's success in selling phones, MP3 players, and tablets relies on more than manufacturing cool gadgets. Experts agree that iTunes and the App Store give Apple products an edge over the competition. People flock to Apple products because they make it easy to buy and organize music, videos, and apps. In the case of apps, whether they're free or pay-to-play, customers are confident that there's no malware hidden inside, thanks to Apple's security system. As gatekeeper to the store, Apple can both certify the individuals and companies offering apps and ensure that customers can't legally (or accidentally) add apps to their devices without going through iTunes or some sort of security checking system.

> **NOTE** Some iPhone and iPad power users *jailbreak* their devices, which frees the devices so they can install apps without going through Apple. This process voids the warranty and is, naturally, frowned on by the powers that be, who constantly find ways to disable jailbroken devices. Jailbreaking isn't covered in this book, but you can find instructions on the Web in seconds.

As an app developer, you need to jump through at least four security-related hoops before you can test your app on an iDevice. The requirements are the same whether you're using Flash or Apple's tools to create apps. In broad terms, you need to:

1. **Get a developer's certificate.**

2. **Assign devices for testing.**

3. **Create an App ID for your project.**

4. **Create and install a provisioning profile on testing devices.**

If the system sounds complicated and potentially confusing, it is. It might even sound like a lot of rigmarole, when all you want to do is see if your Flash app will actually run on an iPad. The good news is, you can handle all the certificate-creating business on the iOS Provisioning Portal of Apple's Developer site (Figure 22-2). You apply the certificates and other details to your application within Flash (File→"AIR for iOS Settings"). Once those chores are done, it's easy to add your app to iTunes and then install it on a testing device.

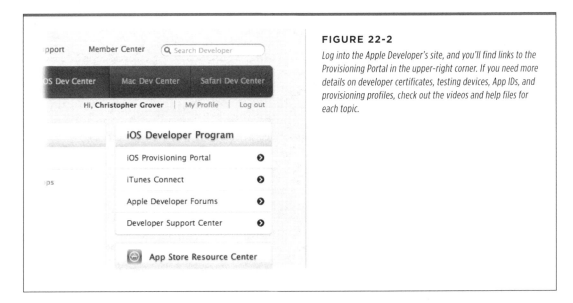

**FIGURE 22-2**

*Log into the Apple Developer's site, and you'll find links to the Provisioning Portal in the upper-right corner. If you need more details on developer certificates, testing devices, App IDs, and provisioning profiles, check out the videos and help files for each topic.*

The following sections describe the procedures for the four security requirements: developer's certificate, testing devices, app IDs, and provisioning profiles.

## Getting a Developer's Certificate

The developer's certificate is your way of proving you are who you say you are. You only need one certificate to develop multiple apps. Apple, the certification authority, identifies you through your credit card information when you pay to join the Developer program. Apps you design will be signed with the name that is on that credit card. (Keep this in mind if you're thinking of using someone else's card to pay for your Developer subscription.) For companies, Apple requests additional business information to prove that the company exists and to establish an address. In either case, you're held accountable for the apps you develop and distribute.

Once you're a paid-up, official developer, follow these steps on your Macintosh to get your certificate.

**NOTE** Apple would prefer that everyone use Macs to develop iDevice apps, but you can use Windows computers and Flash to develop your apps. The trickiest part is setting up your Windows computer to supply the developer's certificate when it's needed. For details, see the box on page 728.

### ■ AUTHORIZE APPLE AS A CERTIFICATE AUTHORITY

1. **Log into your developer account at** *https://developer.apple.com/devcenter/ios.*

2. **In the upper-right corner, click Provisioning Portal.**

   The left side of the Provisioning Portal has links to pages for certificates, devices, app IDs, provisioning profiles, and distribution. Go ahead and create a bookmark for this page. You'll be back.

**TIP** The right side of the Provisioning Portal has How-To links. Some are text, and some are audio/visual. Later, if you need a refresher on how to get a certificate, a device or app ID, or a provisioning profile, you might find them helpful.

3. **Click the Certificates link.**

   The web page displays your developer certificate if you have one. If not, it's empty.

**TIP** The layout for each of the major sections in the Provisioning Portal is similar. So whether you're working on a certificate, a device ID, an app ID, or a provisioning profile, the body of the page has tabs at the top. The tab on the far right is labeled How To. If you're stumped about the procedure at hand, take a look. You're likely to find some answers.

4. **At the bottom of the page, click the link that reads: "If you do not have the WWDR intermediate certificate installed, click here to download now (*https://developer.apple.com/certificationauthority/AppleWWDRCA.cer*)."**

   The intermediate certificate that downloads to your computer is named *AppleWWDRCA.cer.* This is your way of telling your computer that Apple is a certification authority. (You might be able to skip this step and the next ones if you've already used your computer for Apple development projects.)

5. **Once the download is complete, double-click the *AppleWWDRCA.cer* file.**

   Your Keychain Access application opens, and the Add Certificates dialog box appears.

6. **Set the menu to *login* and click the Add button.**

   The Apple World Wide Developer Relations Certification Authority certificate appears in Keychain Access, in the Certificates category, as shown in Figure 22-3.

**NOTE** The *keychain* is a security system on Macintosh computers that stores passwords and other security related information in one place. The keychain then supplies security-related data to websites and programs as needed. For example, once you're an authorized iOS developer, information saved in your keychain is used to sign the apps you create.

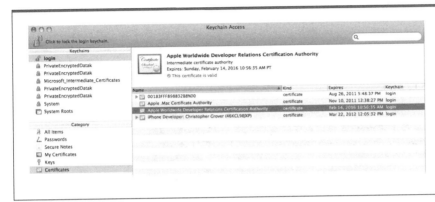

**FIGURE 22-3**

*By downloading and installing the Apple World Wide Developer Relations Certificate Authority certificate to your keychain, you identify Apple as an authority worthy of providing certificates.*

## ■ REQUEST YOUR DEVELOPER CERTIFICATE

Now that you've authorized Apple as a certificate authority, it's time to have it give you a certificate. You use the Keychain Access program to create a *certificate request*, which you will then upload to the Provisioning Portal.

1. **Go to Keychain Access→Certificate Assistant→"Request a Certificate From a Certificate Authority."**

   The Certificate Assistant (Figure 22-4) opens, which will walk you through the process of creating a certificate request.

2. **Type the email address and name you used to join the Apple Developer program.** Leave the CA email address blank. Click "Saved to disk."

3. **Click Continue.**

   The Certificate Assistant prompts you for a name and location for your certificate request file. You can leave the name as is and save the file to your desktop. It's not needed after you upload a copy to the Provisioning Portal.

4. **Click Done to close the Certificate Assistant.**

Head on back to the Provisioning Portal using that handy bookmark you created earlier. On the left side of the page, click Certificates. A message appears that says you don't have a certificate. Click Request Certificate, and use Choose File to find the certificate request you saved on your desktop. When you click Choose, the box closes. On the web page, click Submit, and you'll see a message letting you know your request has been submitted. On the certificate page, the status of your request is set to Pending Approval. If you're the boss of a team of developers, you'd approve each of their certificate requests for your company. Working alone, you get to approve your own request by clicking the Approve button.

It doesn't take long for a certificate to be issued. So if you wait a minute or two and then refresh the web page, you'll probably see a Download button. Click the Download button to save the *developer_identity.cer* file on your computer. Once the download is complete, double-click the file to add it to your keychain certificates. Choose "login" from the menu and click Add.

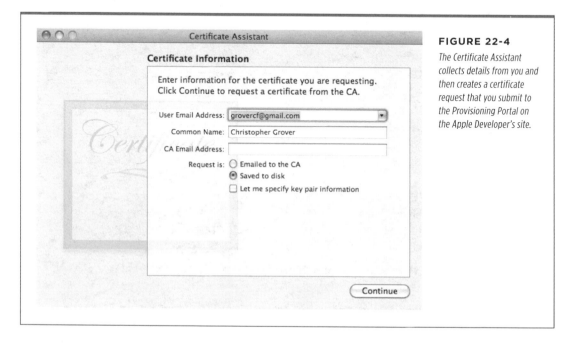

**FIGURE 22-4**

*The Certificate Assistant collects details from you and then creates a certificate request that you submit to the Provisioning Portal on the Apple Developer's site.*

## Getting a .p12 Certificate for Your Windows Computer

Apple expects everyone to use Macs when they want to build an app for iDevices, but if you're creating apps with Flash, you can do your development on a Windows PC. The tricky part comes when it's time to sign your app with your developer's certificate. Macs use OS X's keychain program to install and safeguard the certificate. On a Windows computer, double-clicking the *developer_identity.cer* file doesn't do the job because Windows computers don't have a keychain access program. The easiest solution is to download and install the developer's certificate on a Mac and then export a .p12 certificate from the keychain access program. Right-click (Control-click) the certificate name and then choose the Export option. The

.p12 certificate can then be moved to a Windows computer and identified in Flash's AIR for iOS settings.

If you don't have access to a Mac, there's another solution, but it's not nearly as easy. You can use OpenSSL (Open Secure Socket Layer) to manage certificates on a Windows computer. OpenSSL can also convert the *developer_identity.cer* file from Apple into a .p12 certificate. The process involves command line tools and is too lengthy to cover in this chapter; however, there's a YouTube video that patiently explains how to do it: *www.youtube.com/watch?v=4GteMgFvA1Y.*

When you're done, you'll see an iPhone Developer certificate in the Certificates category of Keychain Access. If you click the expand arrow next to its name, your name appears under the iPhone Developer certificate with a key symbol. Under the kind column, you see "private key." It's that private key that officially identifies you, giving you Apple developer's rights. No one else has access to your private key. Apps you create are signed with a related "public key."

As you'll see later, Flash requires a .p12 certificate to publish the IPA file that's used by iPhones and iPads. Keychain Access can export this for you. Right-click (Control-click) the certificate name and then choose the Export option. You choose a folder and name for the .p12 file, but remember both; you'll need this info when you fill out the AIR for iOS settings (page 738). Keychain Access needs two passwords to complete the export process. First, it asks for a password that's used with the certificate; it then asks for your keychain password.

## Assigning Devices for Testing

A major goal of security is to keep bad apps from being installed on good iDevices. On the other hand, developers need to test apps they're developing. Apple requires developers to identify *specific, individual* devices that are used to test *specific* applications under development. As a developer, you register the devices in your account on the Apple Developer site; you can then associate them with apps.

Each, Apple iDevice has a special identifier called a *UDID*. (It's *not* the same as the device's serial number.) The easiest way to find this identifier is to connect your device to your computer and fire up iTunes. When you see your gadget listed in iTunes under Devices, click its name and then go to the summary page. Next to the picture of your snazzy device, you see its name and details like capacity, software version, and serial number. Click the serial number, and it changes to display the UDID, which is a 40-character string of numbers and letters (Figure 22-5, top). You could memorize the UDID, but it's probably easier just to press Ctrl+C (⌘-C) to copy it.

Now, head back to the Provisioning Portal and, on the left side of the page, choose Devices. The Manage tab lists the testing devices that you've registered. All it takes to add a new device is to provide a descriptive name and that 40-character UDID. Click the Add Device button and fill in the blanks (Figure 22-5, bottom). Apple lets you register up to 100 devices each year, which should be enough for anybody. (You can remove devices from your list, but they'll still count toward that annual total.)

## Creating an App ID for Your Project

Apps that you develop are given a unique ID that connects you, the developer, to the app. In addition, encrypted information stored inside the app makes it easy to see if the code has been altered from the original. This prevents other individuals with bad intentions from adding malware or Trojan horses to your perfectly innocent app. Where do you create your App ID? You guessed it—the Provisioning Portal.

1. **On the Apple Developer site (*http://developer.apple.com/iphone*), go to the Provisioning Portal and click App IDs.**

   As a developer, you can create multiple app IDs. Once they're created, you see them all listed at the bottom of this page.

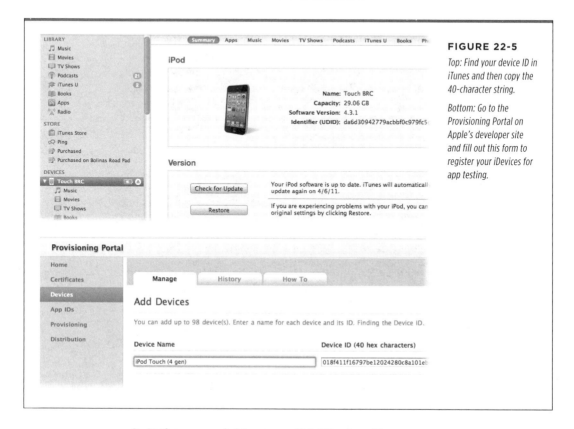

**FIGURE 22-5**

*Top: Find your device ID in iTunes and then copy the 40-character string.*

*Bottom: Go to the Provisioning Portal on Apple's developer site and fill out this form to register your iDevices for app testing.*

2. **In the upper-right corner, click New App ID.**

   A new page appears, where you provide a name and other details for the app you're building.

3. **Under Description, give your app a name.** You might want to call this app *AngryArmadillos*.

   This name identifies your app in iTunes and on iDevices when it's installed.

4. **Leave Bundle Seed set to *Generate New*.**

   The bundle seed is a unique identifier provided by Apple. In addition to Generate New, the menu displays bundle seeds from your previous projects. If you want several of your apps to share the same keychain access on a user's computer, you can set the menu to use the same bundle seed.

5. **Set Bundle Identifier to *com.MyName.AngryArmadillos*.**

This is the name that you use in Flash's iOS Settings to identify your app. It's common practice to use a *reverse domain* as an identifier. So, for example, if your website is *www.MassiveCorp.com*, you'd name the app *com.MassiveCorp .AngryArmadillos*. Folks who don't have a website often use their complete name instead of a domain. For example, *com.ChrisGrover.AngryArmadillos*.

Unlike certificates and provisioning profiles, you don't have to download a file to use the app ID. The details for your app IDs remain on Apple's Provisioning Portal. You will use the ID without the bundle identifier in "Flash AIR for iOS Settings," as described in the next section.

## Creating and Installing a Provisioning Profile

You've added a developer's certificate to your keychain, identifying you as an official iOS developer. You've registered the devices you plan to use for testing, and you've acquired an ID for the app you're developing. The last step is to create a provisioning profile that ties all these elements together. Without a provisioning profile, Flash can't translate your Flash project into code that works with iOS. Apple's provisioning profile connects you the developer, your testing devices, and your application. The provisioning profile is installed on the device you use for testing, making it possible for you to install the app using iTunes.

To create a provisioning profile, follow these steps:

1. **On Apple's Developer site (*https://developer.apple.com/devcenter/ios*), go to the Provisioning Portal and click Provisioning.**

The page where your provisioning profiles live opens. You can create more than one provisioning profile. In fact, you need a provisioning profile for every app you test, distribute, or sell.

---

**TIP** You can come back to this page to make changes to a provisioning profile and to download your profiles. Why would you want to make changes? Perhaps you're creating a new app or you added a new device for testing. In either case, you'll want to add those items to your profile and download the new, improved profile to your computer.

---

2. **In the upper-right corner, click New Profile.**

A page like Figure 22-6 opens, where you provide details for the provisioning profile.

3. **Next to Profile Name, type a name, such as *AngryAardvarks*.**

4. **Next to Certificates, turn on the box with your certificate name.**

You must have already created your developer certificate. For details, see page 727.

5. **Next to App ID, use the menu to select the app you're developing.**

   Page 729 explained how to create app IDs. Once they've been created, the IDs appear in this drop-down menu.

**FIGURE 22-6**

*You get to choose a name for your provisioning profile, but the rest of the settings depend on the certificate, device, and app IDs that you've already created.*

6. **Next to Device, select the testing devices you want to use with this app.**

   Your registered testing devices automatically appear in the list. You can add several testing devices to your provisioning profile. If you need to register a new testing device, see page 729.

7. **Click Submit.**

   It takes only a moment for your submission to be processed. Click your web browser's Refresh button, and you should see your new provisioning profile listed at the bottom of the page with a Download button next to it.

8. **Click Download.**

   Provisioning profiles are small files (about 8 K), so they don't take long to download.

You'll probably want to move the file from your Downloads folder to a more convenient spot, such as the folder with the FLA file for your app. It doesn't really matter where you keep the file as long as you know where it is. You need to locate and identify your provisioning profile in the iOS settings for your app. See page 731.

# Creating an iOS App that Responds to Gestures

iPhones and iPads don't come with mice. That's why Apple had to create a whole new operating system for its handheld devices. iOS responds to a variety of user inputs: taps, swipes, and shakes. In general, mouse clicks translate easily to single finger taps on the iPhone, but if you're writing code for an iDevice, you want to employ the other commonly used gestures, too. Fortunately, Adobe developed ActionScript objects that understand gestures, and they went one step further, creating code snippets that "listen" for those iOS events.

Handling iOS gestures isn't the only thing to consider when you create an app for iDevices. You need to rethink the size and placement of buttons, menus, and other user interface widgets. Also, when it makes sense to do so, take advantage of the device's geolocation and gyroscopic abilities. Here are some more technical considerations:

- Test your application for performance on the device you expect your audience to use. iOS devices use slower processors and less memory than most laptops or desktop computers. Also, remember that older iPhones are slower than the latest iPad.

- Only ActionScript 3.0 code works with the iOS packager. You cannot use ActionScript 1.0 or ActionScript 2.0 code in your projects.

- For best results, use system fonts in your apps (_sans, Helvetica; _serif, Times New Roman; _typewriter, Courier New).

- If your app is destined to be used by iPhones as well as iPads, make sure the elements are properly sized for the small screen.

## Using the Swipe to Next/Previous Code Snippet

Suppose you're a manufacturer who wants to create a product catalog. You want shoppers to thumb through the pages to learn details about individual products. Follow these steps to create a new app for a manufacturer of wooden finials—the type of ornament you see on the top of gazebos or porch railings. You'll add ActionScript code to enable swipe left and swipe right gestures that move from one frame (page) to another. Your handy app also orients itself to a portrait or landscape format when the iPhone or iPad is rotated.

1. **Open 22-1_iOS_Swipe_Pages.fla.** Then choose Save As and name the new file *Finials.fla*.

   This FLA file was created using the "AIR for iOS" option described on page 738. You can find the *22-1_iOS_Swipe_Pages.fla* on the Missing CD at *www.missingmanuals.com/cds/flashcs6mm*.

2. **Examine the handful of frames in the Flash document.**

The first frame (Figure 22-7) shows a photo of a finial on top of a newel post and displays some introductory text. The user won't interact with this text, so TLF Read Only text was used. The font specified is *_serif*. The same text settings are used throughout this project. The following frames (catalog pages) show line drawings of finials. There are three layers in the timeline: actions, text, and profiles.

**FIGURE 22-7**

*This iOS project creates a manufacturer's catalog. Shown here, the introductory page displays a photo of the product (a finial) in use. The following pages show designs and specs for other finials.*

3. **Click Frame 1 in the actions layer on the timeline and then open the Actions window (Window→Actions).**

4. **On the first line in the actions, type *stop()*;**

This method prevents the animation from moving to the next frame until it receives a specific command.

5. **Press Enter (Return) to create a new line, and then open Code Snippets**

You can use the button in the upper-right corner of the Actions window, or you can use the palette button if it's visible. The button for Code Snippets looks like a page of text with two curly brackets above it.

6. **Expand the Mobile Actions snippets and click *Swipe to* "Swipe to Go to Next/Previous Frame and Stop."**

When you select a snippet, the buttons for the Code Snippets heads-up display (HUD) appears. The "i" button leads to general information. In this case it says: "Swiping the stage moves the playhead to the next/previous frame in the timeline and stops the playhead."

7. **Click the bracket button, and after examining the description, click the Insert button.**

The bracket button {} display more details about the snippet, including the actual code. After you click the Insert button, there's a little animated flourish, and the snippet is copied to your code in the Actions window (see Figure 22-8). In some cases, you need to select an object on the stage before you insert a code snippet. That's not the case for this particular gesture.

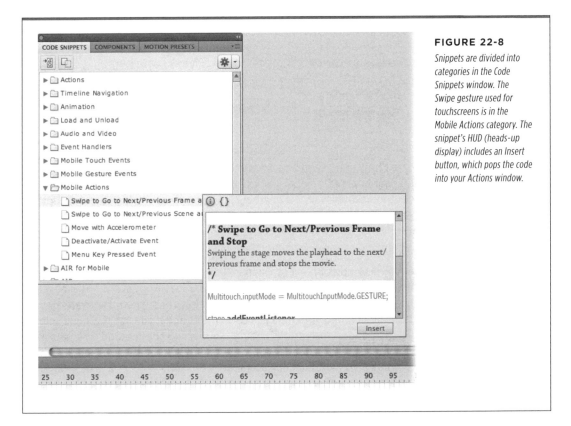

**FIGURE 22-8**

*Snippets are divided into categories in the Code Snippets window. The Swipe gesture used for touchscreens is in the Mobile Actions category. The snippet's HUD (heads-up display) includes an Insert button, which pops the code into your Actions window.*

**8. Open the Actions window (Window→Actions) to examine the code.**

You can usually learn something by examining code snippets. In some cases, you'll pick up new techniques. In other cases, you may want to modify or copy the code for use elsewhere. Here's the snippet you added to your project:

```
/* Swipe to Go to Next/Previous Frame and Stop
Swiping the stage moves the playhead to the next/previous frame and stops
the movie.
*/


Multitouch.inputMode = MultitouchInputMode.GESTURE;


stage.addEventListener (TransformGestureEvent.GESTURE_SWIPE, fl_SwipeToGo-
ToNextPreviousFrame_2);


function fl_SwipeToGoToNextPreviousFrame_2(event:TransformGestureEvent):vo
id
{
 if(event.offsetX == 1)
 {
        // swiped right
        prevFrame();
 }
 else if(event.offsetX == -1)
 {
        // swiped left
        nextFrame();
 }
}
```

The text between /* and */ is a comment that explains the purpose of the snippet. In some cases, snippet comments offer tips for modifying and using the code. The next line sets the MultitouchInputMode to *Gesture*. ActionScript has three modes that are used with MultitouchInput: none, Gesture, and TouchPoint. Only one multitouch mode is in effect at a time, so ActionScript can't listen for a Gesture event and a TouchPoint event simultaneously.

The next line adds an event listener. The first parameter in the parentheses defines the event "TransformGestureEvent.GESTURE_SWIPE." The next parameter identifies the method (function) that runs when the event occurs. Methods are named automatically by snippets and if you use the same snippet more than once, Flash starts adding numbers to the method's name simply to differentiate them. That's why in this example there's a "_2" at the end of *fl_SwipeToGoToNextPreviousFrame*. In your code, you may see a different number or no number at all.

The body of the method takes the form of an "if..else if" statement. In effect it says, if the event was "swiped right," go to the previous frame; else if the event was "swiped left," go the next frame.

The familiar methods *prevFrame()* and *nextFrame()* do the heavy lifting, flipping between pages. The page content in this example is in the main timeline, so there's no need to designate a specific movie clip or timeline. Later in this chapter (page 745), you'll see how to flip pages in a movie clip symbol that's been added to the stage.

> **NOTE** If you want to learn more about multitouch events, you can find all the details in the *ActionScript Reference for the Adobe Flash Platform*. You can open that document by going to Help→Flash Help and then choosing "ActionScript 3.0 and Components."

9. **Press Ctrl+S (⌘-S) to save your work.**

   Flash saves your work as an FLA file.

At this point, you can go ahead and test your application in the AIR Debug Launcher (Mobile). When tested, you see the first frame of the animation but have no way to move beyond that frame because your computer won't respond to a swipe gesture. Instead, you want to test your app on an iPhone, iPodTouch, or iPad that you've registered as a test device. If you've followed the steps beginning on page 727 to get a developer's certificate, set up test devices, get app IDs, and get provisioning profiles, then you're ready to fill in the AIR for iOS settings. Once that's done, you can test your app on an iDevice.

**GEM IN THE ROUGH**

## Testing Mobile Events with Simulator

Developing a mobile app on a desktop computer comes with a few tradeoffs. For example, your desktop is most likely clueless when you swipe your finger across the screen. It also probably doesn't respond much when you tilt it one way or the other. Those are mobile events that most computers don't recognize. Flash CS6 includes a new tool that can help out—the Simulator (see Figure 22-9). You see it pop up when you go to Control→Test Movie→"in Air Debug Launcher (Mobile)." The Simulator has three panels that you expand and collapse as needed. The accelerometer panel offers a way to simulate changes in orientation. So, for example, if you have an app that displays a map when held flat but activates a camera when held vertically, you can test it in the Simulator. The Touch and Gesture panel lets you test the usual touchscreen events. Turn on "Touch layer" in the upper-left corner and then choose one of the radio buttons: "Click and drag," "Press and tap," "Two-finger tap," Pan, Rotate, Zoom, or Swipe. At this point, when you move the mouse over your app in the test window (Figure 22-9, right), you see a special cursor, and you can tap, swipe, or perform other gestures using the mouse. If you're building an app that knows where it is in the world, use the Geolocation panel. Type information like latitude or longitude and then click Send.

Does the Simulator relieve you of the need to test your apps on real mobile devices? No. You still want to do real-world testing on the target device. However, the Simulator can be a great timesaver while you're in the early to mid stages of app development.

# Air for iOS App Settings

When you start a new document with the File→"AIR for iOS" command, Flash provides a bunch of new publishing settings for your document (Figure 22-10). These include *general settings* that identify folders and documents, *deployment settings* that record information about security certificates, and *icon settings* that are used to represent your app in iTunes, and on iPhones and iPads.

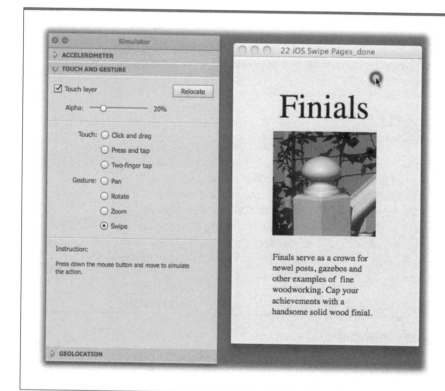

**FIGURE 22-9**

*When you test a mobile app in Flash, you see two panels.*

*Right: Your app appears in a window that's sized to match a phone or a tablet. Buttons respond to clicking, but you need help with other mobile events.*

*Left: The Simulator provides a way to test touchscreen gestures, and accelerometer and geolocation events.*

Tweaking the settings so that everything works isn't nearly as much fun as designing and testing your app. The good news is that with few exceptions, it's a "set and forget" operation. You don't have to go through these steps every time you build a new version of your app.

## General Settings

To see the settings for your iOS app, go to File→"Air 3.2 for iOS Settings." The window has three tabs: General, Deployment, and Icons.

Here's a rundown on the settings you find under the General tab:

- **Output file.** Choose a directory and provide a filename for your app. The extension for iOS apps is *.ipa*. Remember the name and location for your IPA file. You'll need to add the file to iTunes later in the app install process.

- **App name.** Give your application an official name. This is the name that appears under the apps icon on your iDevice and in the App store.

- **Version.** You can assign version numbers to your app. They usually take a form like *2.05*, where numbers to the left of the decimal indicate major version changes.

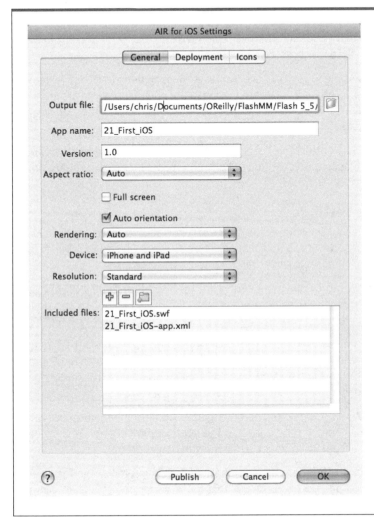

**FIGURE 22-10**

*The general "AIR for iOS Settings" window handles some of the basic housekeeping issues, such as filenames and locations. If you want your app to work in both portrait and landscape views, set the aspect ratio to Auto and check the "Auto orientation box."*

- **Aspect ratio.** Use this setting to specify whether your app is viewed in portrait or landscape orientation. Choose *Auto* if it works in both.

- **Full screen.** Check this box to force your app to fill the screen on an iPad or iPhone.

- **Auto orientation.** iDevices know which end is up. If you check this box, your app will automatically make adjustments when the iPad or iPhone's orientation changes.

- **Rendering.** It takes computing power to draw graphics on the screen. Devices have a special graphics processing unit (GPU) to handle these chores. In some cases, you may prefer to use the central processing unit (CPU). For the examples in this book, leave rendering set to Auto, which lets the device choose the unit.

- **Device.** You can designate whether your app is intended for iPhones (including iPod Touch), iPads, or both.

- **Resolution.** Apple's iDevices have increased in resolution in successive generations. The new Retina displays are high resolution. Older devices are standard resolution. If you want to be compatible with the widest range of devices, choose standard.

- **Included files.** For the projects covered in this book, Flash automatically adds the needed files to this list as you build your app. In other cases, you may need to manually add resources.

## Deployment Settings

To test, distribute, and sell your app, it needs official approval from Apple. In Flash, the Deployment tab is where you manage these issues. Go to File→"Air for iOS Settings" and click the Deployment tab (Figure 22-11).

You need to fill in the Deployment form with the following details (if you don't complete the form, the publishing process stops before it's complete and doesn't built the IPA file):

- **Certificate.** Follow the steps on page 727, and you receive a certificate from Apple that establishes your identity. The certificate takes the form of a small file with a .p12 extension that you store on your computer. Use the folder button to locate and identify the file for the deployment settings.

- **Password.** When you get your certificate from Apple, you provide a password. That password needs to be added to the deployment settings. This prevents someone else from using your certificate with his program.

- **Provisioning profile.** For each app that you build, you tell Apple the specific iPhones and iPads you're using for testing. A provisioning profile links and identifies you, your app, and your testing devices. Your provision profile is another document that's downloaded from Apple's Developer site. For details on creating and downloading a provisioning profile, see page 731

- **App ID.** Each app you develop has a unique ID. The common form used is to reverse your domain name and add the app name at the end. So a Missing Manuals app ID might be *com.missingmanuals.AngryAuthors*. For details on creating your own app ID, see page 729.

- **iOS deployment type.** Use these settings for different stages of the develop-ment process. Your choices are: "Quick publishing for device testing," "Quick publishing for device debugging," "Deployment – ad hoc," and "Deployment – Apple Store."

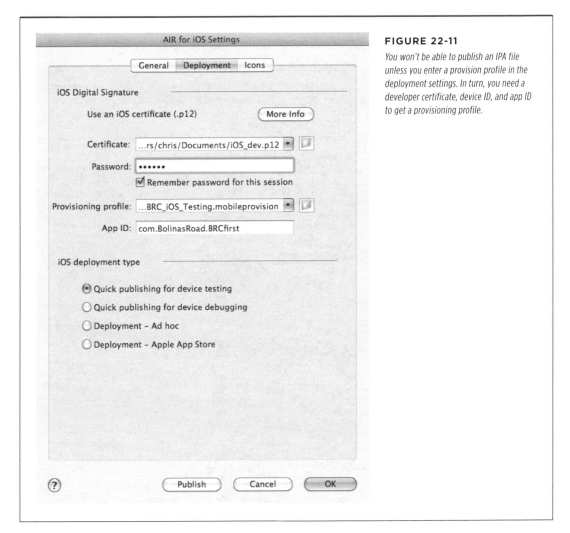

**FIGURE 22-11**
*You won't be able to publish an IPA file unless you enter a provision profile in the deployment settings. In turn, you need a developer certificate, device ID, and app ID to get a provisioning profile.*

## Icon Settings

iPads and iPhones are visual experiences. Each app is identified by a square icon that appears in the App Store and on the device. Icons need to be provided in a variety of sizes measured in pixels: 29x29, 57x57, 114x114, and 512x512. Apps that are also used on iPads need to include icons at 48x48 and 72x72.

You can produce icons in Flash and export the image files (File→Export→Export Image). But it's probably easier to create icons in Fireworks or Photoshop if they're available on your computer. Files should be saved in the PNG format, and it's helpful in the next step if you include the size in the filename. For example, use names like myAppIcon29.png and myAppIcon57.png. The process is easiest if you store the icons in the same folder as your FLA file.

Once you've created your icons in the necessary sizes, go to the Icons tab (Figure 22-12) and click an icon size, such as "icon 29x29," and then use the box at the bottom to locate the matching icon that you created.

> **TIP** Developing application icons is an art in itself. You can learn a lot by studying the icons used by your favorite apps. Icons need to have the impact of a company logo and be identifiable at very small sizes.

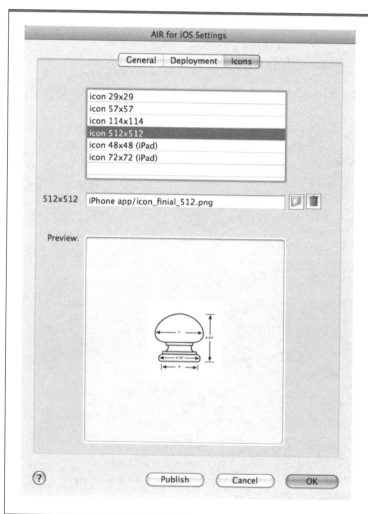

**FIGURE 22-12**

*Use the Icons tab to link your app to the icons that will identify it in the App Store, and on the iPhones and iPads of the world.*

Fill out the details in the General and Deployment tabs. Then, create and identify the icons for your project in the Icons tab. Once those chores are out of the way, you can publish, install, and test your app on an iPhone, iPodTouch, or iPad.

## ■ Publishing, Installing, and Testing Your App on an iDevice

When you publish an app that you've created with AIR for iOS, Flash creates both an SWF file and an IPA file. To install the app on your iDevice, you first add the app (IPA file) to iTunes, where it appears with the all the other apps you got from the App Store. Then, within iTunes, you move your app to the device.

These steps explain how to move your app from your computer onto a device that's plugged in to the USB port. If circumstances prevent you from plugging in, see the box on page 729.

1. **With your AIR for iOS Flash document open in Flash Professional, choose File→Publish.**

   You see two successive progress bars as Flash builds an SWF file and then translates it to an IPA file. If your AIR for iOS settings are incomplete, Flash stops in the middle of the process and displays an error message.

2. **In the Finder or Windows Explorer, double-click the IPA file; for example: *finials.ipa*.**

   This starts the process that copies your app to the Apps section in iTunes. If you're adding a new version of the same app, a dialog box asks if you want to replace the existing version.

3. **To locate your app in iTunes, in the upper-left corner, click Apps.**

   Your app appears in the main window identified by the name and icon you provided earlier. If, like a lot of people, you have a gazillion apps, you can search using the box in the upper-right corner.

4. **Connect one of your officially designated testing devices to the computer via USB.**

   The device appears in iTunes' left column under Devices. In many cases, iTunes goes through the "synchronizing" process. That means shuffling purchased apps and media back and forth between the computer and the device. This activity depends in part on the device's sync settings.

> **NOTE** Your iPhone or iPad must be registered with iTunes. Individual iPhones and iPads are registered with a specific copy of iTunes on a specific computer. That means, iTunes can add apps and purchased media to the device. In addition, your device must be registered as a test device on the Apple Developer site, as explained on page 729.

5. **If necessary, drag your app from the iTunes Apps window on to your device, as shown in Figure 22-13.**

There are different reasons why automatic syncing may not copy your app to the device. It might be your sync settings. Or you may already have a previous version of the same app on your device. The sure way to get the latest version on your device is to delete the previous version and then manually drag the app onto your device.

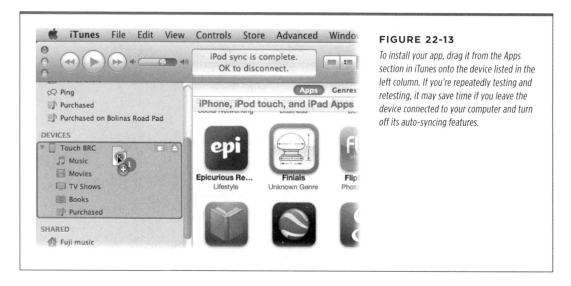

**FIGURE 22-13**

*To install your app, drag it from the Apps section in iTunes onto the device listed in the left column. If you're repeatedly testing and retesting, it may save time if you leave the device connected to your computer and turn off its auto-syncing features.*

6. **Test your app on the device.**

You don't have to disconnect your iDevice from the computer to test the app. Often it's best to stay connected, especially if you know you'll be making changes in Flash and reinstalling the app on your device. Staying connected eliminates some of the time spent while iTunes and the device synchronize.

## Removing Your Test App from the Device

Testing is a repetitive process. Build. Install. Test. Then, you do it all over again. Before you can install a new version of your app on a test device, you need to delete the old version. To do that, touch and hold the app's icon on the device. After a couple of seconds, all the app icons go wobbly and you see X buttons in their upper-left corners. Tap the X button on apps you want to remove.

**NOTE** If you want to examine a finished example of the project started on page 733, download *22-2_iOS_ Swipe_Pages_done.fla* from the Missing CD at *www.missingmanuals.com/cds/flashcs6mm*.

# ■ Building a Tap-Ready App

The previous example showed how to create an app that recognizes swipe gestures to move from one page to another. Often, you'll want to create buttons that respond to taps, just like buttons respond to mouse clicks in conventional programs. Since their function is virtually identical, Flash automatically recognizes MouseEvent clicks as single finger taps when it builds the IPA file. This makes life easier if you're repurposing a computer-based AIR app for iOS.

---

**DEVELOPERS' CORNER**

## Over-the-Air App Installation with Testflightapp.com

There's another unique way to move your test apps to iPhones and iPads. A website called TestFlight (*www.testflightapp.com*) is set up to deliver apps that are under development to testers. Currently, the service is free to developers and testers, though both need to sign up with their certificates and device UDIDs. Once that is done, developers upload their apps to the site using the site's tools (see Figure 22-14). Then, also through the site, developers notify testers via email that the app is ready to run through its paces. Testers can click links on the email to

download the app directly to their iDevice. There's no side trip through iTunes when you use TestFlight. The process is simple for both developers and testers.

In addition to bypassing the installation dance with iTunes, TestFlight gives developers an easy way to reach more testers scattered over a larger geographic area. If you don't already have a designated team of testers, you can use the volunteers who've signed up with TestFlight.

---

**FIGURE 22-14**

*Testflightapp.com is a website that distributes apps under development to testers. You can use it with a team of app testers or you can use it to easily install your apps on testing devices, bypassing the iTunes installation routine.*

Though it looks similar to the app in the previous exercise, it's constructed differently. Follow these steps to add tap-ability to the app:

1. **Open *22-3_iOS_Tap_Menu.fla* and then save it as *Finials Tap.fla*.**

    The main timeline for this app has a single frame. Two movie clips symbols are placed on the stage in that frame. mcMainContent, as the name suggests, holds the content for the app in several frames (pages). mcMenuBar holds buttons used to navigate through mcMainContent. Separating the content from the navigation tools has organizational benefits. By putting mcMenuBar on the one and only frame in the main timeline, the buttons are always available and ready to handle their chores.

2. **On the stage, double-click the mcMainContent movie clip.**

The content on the various frames will look familiar if you tackled the "swipe gesture" exercise earlier in this chapter. ActionScript code appears on the first two frames of the actions layer. In the first frame, a *stop()* method keeps the playhead from running through the entire movie clip on startup. The code on the second frame was added using the "Click to Go to a Frame and Stop" snippet. The result is when someone clicks on a finial profile in Frame 2, the playhead moves to the frame showing that finial's dimensions. Each *gotoAndStop()* method uses a frame label. For example, *gotoAndStop("nc3")* moves the frame labeled *nc3*.

3. **Click Scene 1 on the edit bar to close the mcMainContent movie clip.**

mcMainContent closes and you're back at the main timeline.

4. **On the stage, double-click the mcMenuBar movie clip.**

The movie clip opens on stage for editing. As shown in Figure 22-15, the movie clip holds three more movie clip symbols. By examining the properties, you see the instances are named btnBack, btnHome, and btnNext. You'll use these names to identify the navigation buttons in the following steps.

# Finials

Finals serve as a crown for newel posts, gazebos and other examples of fine woodworking. Cap your achievements with a handsome solid wood finial.

**FIGURE 22-15**

*The buttons for this app were placed at the bottom of the screen to make it easy for iPhone single-handed operation. It's common for iPhoners to hold their device in the left hand and use their thumb for simple navigation chores. Bottom buttons are easier to reach. The right hand is brought in for more complex gestures and operations.*

back    home    next

**Click Scene 1 on the edit bar to close the mcMenuBar movie clip.**

mcMenuBar closes and you're back at main timeline.

6. **Select mcMenuBar and then open Code Snippets→Timeline Navigation.**

The Timeline Navigation snippets include a number of predesigned chunks of code that move the playhead within a movie clip. Each has a descriptive name. You can use these snippets to handle mouse clicks or single finger taps.

7. **With mcMenuBar selected, double-click the snippet names "Click to Go to Previous Frame and Stop."**

The code is automatically added to the actions. An ActionScript symbol appears in Frame 1 of the actions layer.

8. **If necessary, press F9 (Option-F9) to open the Actions window.**

As usual, the comment at the beginning of snippet explains its purpose. Without the comment, the working code appears as follows:

```
mcMenuBar.addEventListener(MouseEvent.CLICK, fl_ClickToGoToPreviousFrame);

function fl_ClickToGoToPreviousFrame(event:MouseEvent):void
{
 prevFrame();
}
```

The *prevFrame()* method moves the playhead left one frame in the movie clip. That's fine, but in this case, you don't want to move the playhead in the main timeline; you want to control the playhead in mcMainContent.

9. **Change the method to read *mcMainContent.prevFrame()*;**

Now the code triggers the *prevFrame()* method in the mcMainContent movie clip.

You need to make a similar change to the event listener. As it is now, clicking any point in mcMenuBar triggers the *prevFrame()* method. Instead, you want ActionScript to listen for clicks on btnBack within the mcMenuBar movie clip.

10. **Change the event listener to read:**

```
mcMenuBar.btnBack.addEventListener
    (MouseEvent.CLICK, fl_ClickToGoToPrevious Frame);
```

The dot syntax identifies btnBack within mcMenuBar.

11. **Repeat steps 7–10 to add and modify a snippet for btnNext.**

Use the snippet named "Click to Go to Next Frame and Stop."

12. **Repeat the process to add and modify a snippet for btnHome.**

Use the snippet named "Click to Go to a Frame and Stop." As the instructions in the comment explain, you change the number 5 in the *gotoAndPlay(5)* method to customize this code. You can substitute the number 1 so the complete method reads as follows:

```
mcMainContent.gotoAndPlay(1);
```

Or you can use the "home" frame label in mcMainContent.

```
mcMainContent.gotoAndPlay("home");
```

13. **Go Control→Test Movie to check the buttons' operations.**

The buttons you created work with either mouse clicks or finger taps so you can quickly check their operation using the AIR Debug Launcher.

14. **In the main timeline, select Frame 1 in the actions layer.** Then, open Code Snippets→Mobile Actions and double-click "Swipe to Go to Next/Previous Frame and Stop."

As explained in the exercise on page 733, this code enables the "swipe" gesture so that users can move from page to page. As with the buttons, this gesture needs to identify the movie clip that holds the content: mcMainContent.

15. **In the Action window (Window→Actions), change the *prevFrame()* and *nextFrame()* methods in mcMainContent.**

After you've made changes, here's how the code for the snippet should read:

```
Multitouch.inputMode = MultitouchInputMode.GESTURE;

stage.addEventListener (TransformGestureEvent.GESTURE_SWIPE, fl_SwipeToGoTo
NextPreviousFrame);

function fl_SwipeToGoToNextPreviousFrame(event:TransformGestureEvent):void
{
 if(event.offsetX == 1)
 {
        // swiped right           mcMainContent.prevFrame();
 }
 else if(event.offsetX == -1)
 {
        // swiped left            mcMainContent.nextFrame();
 }
}
```

16. **Test your app.**

You can test the app again using AIR Debug Launcher to double-check for compiler errors and try out the buttons. However, you'll probably want to test it on an iDevice. That means you need to create a new app ID for this project and add details to the AIR for iOS settings.

When you test this app on an iPhone or iPad, you'll see that the mouse click events work as finger taps. The swipe gesture works as it did in the earlier exercise.

---

**NOTE** To see the finished example, download *22-4_iOS_Tap_Menu_done.fla* from the Missing CD at *www. missingmanuals.com/cds/flashcs6mm*. You'll need to provide your own AIR for iOS settings to test the app on a device.

---

# ■ Tips for iOS App Development

iPhones and iPads are remarkable devices that cram a lot of computing power into a tiny package. It's easy for users to think of them as desktop and laptop substitutes. As a developer, you need to consider the differences and limitations of the iDevice. You want your app to be quick and responsive. You don't want it to hog all the device resources. A well designed app will be used by many. A poorly designed app will remain undiscovered in some dusty corner of the App store.

Here are some things to consider as you design your winner:

- Make use of iOS behaviors like swipes, taps, and pinches. Avoid behaviors that won't work with iOS, like rollovers.

- Where possible, design for both portrait and landscape orientation and test your app both ways.

- Use tweens only when necessary—they hog iDevice brainpower.

- Use gradients and transparency sparingly—they also hog iDevice brainpower.

- Where possible, use bitmaps instead of vector artwork. iOS likes bitmaps, but the calculations necessary to draw vectors may use too much CPU power.

- If you use vector art, use the "cache as bitmap" option. This stores the vector art as a bitmap, making it easier for iDevices to display the image. In ActionScript, you can set the property for a movie clip: *mcMovieClip.cacheAsBitmap = true*. As always, test your app to make sure caching helps rather than hurts performance.

- Use system fonts: _san, _serif, and _typewriter.

- Remove event listeners when they are no longer needed.

- Remove objects from the display list and from memory when they are no longer needed.

# Building Android Apps

There are two ways to view Flash-developed content on Android devices like the HTC One smartphones or Motorola Xoom tablets. The old-fashioned way is to use the device's web browser to display Flash content that's embedded in the web page. The up-and-coming way is to develop an application using AIR for Android, and that's the focus of this chapter. (For a comparison of installed apps versus web-based animations, see the box on page 753.)

You can use all your animation and ActionScript skills to build apps for Android devices, but there are differences between mobile apps and web-based or desktop apps. For example, in an app you'll want to include touchscreen gestures. If your app is destined for smaller smartphone screens, you need to make your buttons large, and the text and images readable. Take a look back at Chapter 22—which explains how to create apps for Apple's iOS—even if you plan to focus on Android. That chapter's details on using code snippets to add touchscreen gestures, for example, also applies to Android.

This chapter explains how to create a new Android document in Flash. You'll also learn how to create an app that uses Android's accelerometer to move objects on the screen. The last section discusses how to convert an iOS app into an Android app to maximize your app-building efforts. It's not hard to convert an application so that it runs on AIR for desktops (Windows, Mac, and Linux), as well as Apple's iDevices and Android handsets.

# Meet AIR for Android

A philosophical argument is going on in the mobile computing world, and it's as hotly contested as the old Mac-vs.-Windows debate. For phones and tablets, the hot issue is open development (Android) versus controlled/moderated development (iOS). As covered in Chapter 22, Apple has a pretty firm thumb on application development for iPhones, iPads, and iPod Touch devices. Their argument is that Apple's oversight ensures a quality user experience and inhibits malware. For validation, they point to the Mac's track record. Android has a different pedigree, which comes from Linux, the mother of all open source projects. The philosophy behind open source is that transparency makes code better. Open source makes use of an army of coders ready to stress test and add to the existing code. This improves the source more quickly than a closed or proprietary system.

Today, the Android operating system is available under a free software/open source license. Google makes the entire source code available to developers and is a member of the Open Handset Alliance, which includes a number of phone manufactures including HTC, LG, Motorola, and Samsung.

**NOTE** The company that founded Android in 2003 included an ex-Apple engineer (Andy Rubin), a voice communication executive (Rich Miner), an ex-T-Mobile VP (Nick Sears), and an ex-WebTV developer (Chris White). Google acquired Android, Inc. in 2005.

If you're going to develop apps for Android devices, you want to visit the official developer's site: *http://developer.android.com.* The site is well-organized and easy to navigate. You'll find an SDK (software development kit) section where you can download the tools that Java programmers use to develop Android apps (see the box on page 755). The Dev Guide section provides documentation. Read through the guide and reference, and you'll have a renewed appreciation for Flash's ability to shield you from some of the nitty-gritty elements of Android programming. Other resources found on the website include sample code, tutorials, FAQs (frequently asked questions), and videos. For social interaction with other Android developers, visit the forums at *http://developer.android.com/community.*

**NOTE** At this writing, the most recent version of Android is 4.0, also known as Ice Cream Sandwich. It was developed specifically for tablets. Currently, the source code is not available, but there are promises that it will be in the future.

What does the difference between an open and a controlled market mean for you as an app developer? The process necessary to develop iPhone and iPad apps includes paying a developer subscription fee ($99) and registering each test device you use. With Android apps, by contrast, you don't need to pay anything or jump through as many hoops to build, test, and market apps. From the consumer end, the iPhone app store feels like a bricks-and-mortar Apple store—clean, vetted, and efficient. The

Android app stores (*https://play.google.com* and *www.amazon.com/appstore*) and the apps themselves have a little more Wild West feeling about them (Figure 23-1).

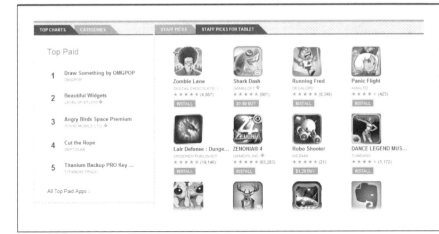

**FIGURE 23-1**
*Android users download apps directly to their phones and tablets. Apps are available at the Google app store shown here (http://play.google. com) or from other vendors such as Amazon.*

---

**UP TO SPEED**

## AIR for Android vs. Flash Player

The AIR for Android apps discussed in this chapter are different. They're standalone apps (.apk files) that are installed on Android devices along with the AIR runtime code. These apps appear as icons on the phone or tablet's touchscreen and behave like any other installed app.

As a developer, AIR apps are generally the best way to show off your Flash/ActionScript talents. On mobile devices, apps designed using AIR for Android simply perform better. AIR apps have use of the entire screen, and they aren't competing with HTML content. Since they're translated into Android-speak, AIR apps are more responsive. Also, a well-designed AIR for Android app makes use of all those touchscreen gestures like swipes and pinches.

If you do create a website that welcomes Android users, make sure you incorporate user interface elements that will work for handhelds. Avoid rollovers, for example, and scale the buttons and other widgets to accommodate big fingers on small screens.

When Android phones and tablets first hit the market, Adobe developed a Flash Player specifically for mobile browsers. They discontinued that effort with Flash Player 11.1 commenting in a blog that "HTML5 is now universally supported on major mobile devices, in some cases exclusively. This makes HTML5 the best solution for creating and deploying content in the browser across mobile platforms... Our future work with Flash on mobile devices will be focused on enabling Flash developers to package native apps with Adobe AIR for all the major app stores. "

If you're interested in dipping your toe in HTML5, CSS and JavaScript waters take a look at Adobe Edge a design/animation tool that has that familiar Adobe interface. Need missing manual guidance for Edge? Check out Adobe Edge Preview 5: The Missing Manual (O'Reilly Media).

## Your First "Hello Android" App

In Flash CS6 you start Android apps using a specially designed template that automatically sizes the stage and adjusts other settings. The process is nearly identical to creating a Flash document for AIR (desktop) or iOS. As you'll see on page 758, when you're ready to test your app on an Android smartphone or tablet, you fill in the deployment and security settings and then publish your AIR for Android app. At that point, Flash creates the APK file for the device. This exercise shows how to start an AIR or Android app and then how to test it in Flash's AIR Debug Launcher (Mobile). Why break with tradition? Here's how you build your first "Hello Android" app.

1. **Choose File→New.**

   The New Document window opens.

2. **Choose "AIR for Android" and click OK.**

   When you choose "AIR for Android," the width and height for the stage are automatically set to 480 x 800, as shown in Figure 23-2. You can change the stage color (background) and the frame rate, but for this first project, leave them as they are.

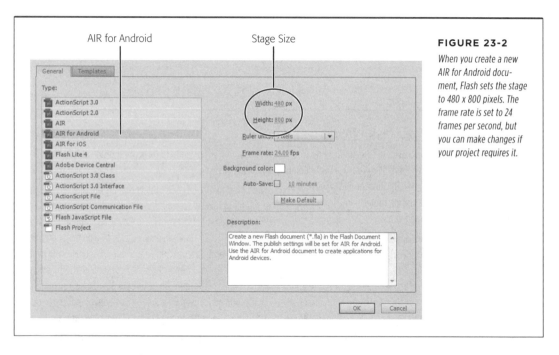

AIR for Android          Stage Size

**FIGURE 23-2**

*When you create a new AIR for Android document, Flash sets the stage to 480 x 800 pixels. The frame rate is set to 24 frames per second, but you can make changes if your project requires it.*

3. **Click the Text tool and then, in the Properties panel, set the Text engine to** *TLF* **and the text type to** *Read Only* **text.**

   Your "Hello Android" app doesn't need fancy text.

4. **In the Character settings, set the Family (font) to** *_serif* **and the size to** *72.*

   When you specify a device font like _serif, _sans, or _typewriter, your app uses a font already installed on the device. This practice keeps your app files small and is efficient for the device.

5. **Drag to create a text box on the stage and type** *Hello Android* **or a message of your choice.**

6. **Choose File→"AIR for Android Settings."** Set the aspect ratio to Auto and turn on auto-orientation. Click OK.

With these settings, Android devices will automatically orient the screen to portrait or landscape mode. The settings are covered in detail beginning on page 758. When you click OK, the settings window closes.

7. **Press Ctrl+S (⌘-S) to name and save your work.**

8. **Go to Control→Test Movie→"in AIR Debug Launcher."**

Your Hello Android app appears in a small window and displays the message.

The AIR Debug Launcher (ADL) is a special tool for viewing AIR animations on your desktop. It's useful for quick checks of graphics, animations, and simple buttons. If your app is set up to auto-orient (step 6 above), you can use the Device→Rotate Left and Device→Rotate Right commands to view it in different orientations. If you want to test out touch gestures or other mobile features, you can do a quick check with the Simulator described in the box on page 737. If you want to gauge app performance under real-world conditions, you need to move your Android app (.apk file) and the AIR runtime to a real device, as described in the next exercise.

**FREQUENTLY ASKED QUESTION**

### The Android-Java Connection

*If I didn't use Flash Professional, what tools would I use to create Android apps?*

Most Android development is done using Java, an object-oriented programming language that shares much with the C and C++ languages. Originally developed by Sun Microsystems, Java is now maintained by Oracle Corporation. Even though you're developing Android apps using AIR, at some point you may want some of the tools from the Java Development Kit (JDK). To download the JDK, head to *www.oracle.com/technetwork/java/javase/downloads.* Click the Download JDK

button on that page. Choose your platform, check the licensing agreement, and click Continue. On the next page, you'll see a link to download your version of the Java Developer kit.

You may be saying "Hey, I've already got Java on my computer." Chances are you have the Java Runtime Environment (JRE), the tools needed to run Java applications. You probably don't have the Java Developer Kit (JDK) unless you or your computer have already been involved in Java application development.

# ■ App Building with the Android Accelerometer Template

To truly get a feel for Android app development, you need to install your app on an Android device and test it. If you worked your way through the Apple iOS security process, you'll be pleased to learn that life is easier and less expensive in the Android world. Like the AIR applications described in Chapter 21, with AIR for Android, you can create a self-signed certificate. You don't need to get a certificate from an official certificate authority (CA) to install and test your app. With your self-signed certificate, you can move Android apps to devices connected to your computer by USB cables. This next exercise explains exactly how to do that. For testing purposes, you'll use a template that makes use of the Android accelerometer (the unit inside gadgets that knows which end is up).

---

**TIP** Flash Professional CS6 arrives on your computer with several prebuilt templates that provide examples of Android behaviors and techniques. These templates are easy to use, and they're great starting points for your own projects.

---

1. **Choose File→New.**

   The New Document window opens showing two tabs: General and Templates.

2. **Click the Templates tab.**

   Templates are grouped into categories such as Advertising, Media Playback, and Presentations.

3. **Click the AIR for Android category.**

   Shown in Figure 23-3, the Android templates include: "800 x 400 Blank," Accelerometer, Options Menu, and Swipe Gallery.

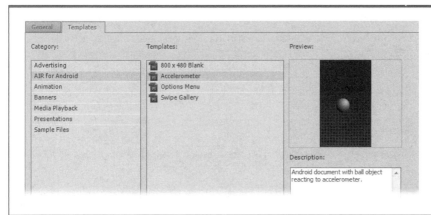

**FIGURE 23-3**

*Flash CS6 comes with templates that show how to use basic Android behaviors including the devices' built-in accelerometer. Choosing a template adds content and ActionScript code to your Flash document.*

4. **Click Accelerometer, and then click OK.**

   When you click a template, its image appears in the Preview panel, and a description provides some details on the template. The Accelerometer template's description explains that a ball reacts to the device's accelerometer. When you click OK, the template opens in Flash.

5. **Go to File→Save and then save the document with a name like**
   *TestAccelerometer.*

   It's a good practice to save your documents when you first create them. One
   benefit is that the name is used to fill in some of the blanks in the AIR for Android
   settings. Another benefit is that Flash's Auto-Save feature (Figure 23-2) can
   minimize disasters like unexpected power outages.

6. **Click the Library tab.**

   The Library shows that this animation has one movie clip symbol named "ball."
   The instance on the stage has the same name.

7. **Click the Timeline tab.**

   The template starts off with four layers: Instruction, Actions, Ball, and Background. Below the stage, you see the brief instructions included with the
   template.

8. **Click the first (and only) frame in the actions layer and then open the Actions window (Window→Actions).**

   The ActionScript code that manages Android accelerometer events appears in
   the Actions window as shown here:

```
import flash.events.Event;

var accelX:Number;
var accelY:Number;

var fl_Accelerometer:Accelerometer = new Accelerometer();
fl_Accelerometer.addEventListener(AccelerometerEvent.UPDATE, fl_Accelerom-
eter-
UpdateHandler);
function fl_AccelerometerUpdateHandler(event:AccelerometerEvent):void
{
    accelX = event.accelerationX;
    accelY = event.accelerationY;
}

ball.addEventListener(Event.ENTER_FRAME, moveBall);
function moveBall(evt:Event){
    ball.x -= accelX*30;
    ball.y += accelY*30;

    if(ball.x > (480-ball.width/2)){
            ball.x = 480-ball.width/2;
    }
    if(ball.x < (0+ball.width/2)){
            ball.x = 0+ball.width/2;
```

```
    }
    if(ball.y > (800-ball.width/2)){
        ball.y = 800-ball.width/2;
    }
    if(ball.y < (0+ball.width/2)){
            ball.y = 0+ball.width/2;
    }
}
```

The first line imports Flash events. Then number variables are created for tracking the X and Y properties of the ball. A new instance of the Accelerometer object is created and named *fl_Accelerometer.* Like all objects, *fl_Accelerometer* has an addEventListener method, which is put into action and triggers *fl_AccelerometerUpdateHandler().* The ball movie clip has an event listener that uses the ENTER_FRAME constant to trigger *moveBall().* The *moveBall()* function updates the position of the ball movie clip based on data provided by the accelerometer (accelX and accelY) and a series of *if* statements that keep the ball visible on the stage.

9. **Click File→"AIR for Android Settings."**

   When you start a document with an Android template, Flash automatically provides a group of settings specific to Android devices. The settings are grouped under four tabs: General, Deployment, Icons, and Permissions.

10. **Click the General tab.** Set the aspect ratio to Auto. Turn on Full Screen and Auto Orientation.

   With these settings, Android devices will automatically orient the screen to portrait or landscape mode. The output file, app name, and app ID are automatically filled in with the name you used when saving the Flash document. Note that the output file ends with the .apk extent used by Android apps.

11. **Click the Deployment tab.**

   The deployment tab, shown in Figure 23-4, is used to identify your developer's certificate and password, choose a deployment type, select a source for the AIR runtime, and set the behavior after publishing. The following steps describe each procedure.

12. **In the certificate box, identify your developer certificate.** If you don't have a certificate, click Create to create a self-signed certificate.

   If you've already created a certificate, you can choose it from the combo box. If you haven't created one, it's easy to create a self-signed certificate on the spot by clicking the Create button and filling in all the blanks on the form.

   You can put the same company/organization name in the "Publisher name," "Organization unit," and "Organization name" boxes. Provide and confirm your password. You can leave the type set to 1024-RSA and the validity period set to 25 years. Lastly, give your certificate a name and choose where to save it.

When you click OK, Flash automatically loads the new certificate in the deployment settings. There are more details about security certificates in Chapter 21 (page 710).

13. **Back in the Deployment tab of the "AIR for Android Settings" box, set Android development type to "Device release."**

Use this setting to test your app on an Android device that's connected to your computer by a USB cable.

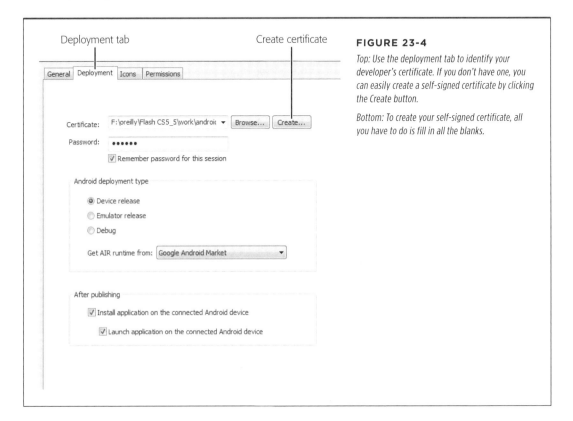

Deployment tab                              Create certificate

**FIGURE 23-4**

*Top: Use the deployment tab to identify your developer's certificate. If you don't have one, you can easily create a self-signed certificate by clicking the Create button.*

*Bottom: To create your self-signed certificate, all you have to do is fill in all the blanks.*

14. **Under "After publishing," turn on both "Install application on the connected Android device" and "Launch application on the connected Android device."**

As advertised, these options automatically install and launch the app on your Android gadget.

15. **Click the Icons tab.**

Each Android app is identified by an icon that users see on the touchscreen. Icons for Android are displayed in three different sizes measured in pixels: 36 x 36, 48 x 48, and 72 x 72. You will want to create distinctive icons for your app in each size. You can produce icons in Flash and export the image files (File→Export→Export Image). But it's easier to use Fireworks or Photoshop if they're available. Save files in the PNG format, and it's helpful if you include the size in the filename. For example: *TestAccelerometer_36.png* and *TestAccelerometer_48.png*.

16. **For each icon size, click the name/size in the top list and then, in the text box below, identify the icon's file.**

    Once you've selected the file, a preview appears in the box at the bottom.

17. **Click the Permissions tab and select Internet.**

    The Permission tab displays a list of Android abilities ranging from writing to storage to camera and audio recording access. You use this list to choose the abilities your app requires. When users install your app, they'll be notified about its capabilities and the resources it uses. Click on a permission, and a brief description appears at the bottom of the window. In this case, click Internet to allow device debugging.

18. **On your Android device, turn on USB debugging.**

    For example, on a Xoom tablet, go to Device Administration→Applications→Development and turn on the USB debugging box. If USB debugging isn't turned on, you'll see an error message when you publish.

19. **Click Publish to publish and test your Android app.**

    You can publish from the "AIR for Android Settings" window, or, if it is closed, you can publish by choosing File→Publish. A couple of progress bars appear as Flash creates an SWF file and then builds an APK file for Android devices. The APK file is installed on the attached device and then launched.

20. **Test your app.**

    You can test your Android accelerometer app while it's still connected by the USB cable, or you can disconnect it. Hold the device with the screen facing up. When you tilt it, the ball rolls to the low point on the screen.

---

**TIP** Templates aren't the only way to add prewritten code to your Android apps. As demonstrated in Chapter 22, there are many code snippets designed specifically for mobile devices. Page 733 explains how to add swipe gestures to your app to navigate between pages (movie clip frames).

---

# ■ Building Apps for Both iOS and Android

If you read through the iOS chapter before attacking Android, then you've probably noticed the many similarities. When you develop in Flash, you spend most of your time using your basic animation and ActionScript skills. The part of the process that's specific to a platform comes at the beginning, when you start your app, and at the end, when you publish. Flash handles the translation when you publish for iOS or Android. This system means you don't have to sweat many of the nitty-gritty details of writing low-level code for a specific environment. It's relatively easy to take an app that works for Apple's iDevices and convert it to work for Android, or vice versa. Here's an iOS-to-Android example:

1. **Open *23-1_iOS_to_Android.fla*.**

   This is an iOS project that was completed in Chapter 22. If you're not familiar with the project, go to Control→Test Movie to explore the app in the ADL (AIR Debug Launcher). Clickable buttons control the timeline of a movie clip (mcMainContent) placed on the stage.

2. **Go to File→New→"AIR for Android" to create a new Android document.** Save the new document with the name *AndroidConversion.fla*.

   An empty Android document is created.

3. **Go to the *23-1_iOS_to_Android.fla*.** Click the top layer; then, while holding the Shift key, click the bottom layer.

   All three layers are selected. The layers are named: named "actions," "content," and "menu."

4. **Right-click (Control-click) the layers and choose Copy Layers from the shortcut menu.**

   The layers and their content are copied to the Clipboard.

5. **Go to *AndroidConversion.fla*.** Right-click (Control-click) and then choose Paste Layers.

   The copied layers are pasted into the timeline. The stage content appears scrunched up in the upper-left corner of the stage. That's because the two documents have different dimensions. The iOS document is 360 x 480, but the Android document is 800 x 600.

6. **Examine the Android document's Library (Window→Library).**

   The movie clips and graphics that were in the iOS doc's library have been copied to the Android doc. The object and their instances on the stage have the same names that were used in the original iOS app.

7. **Right-click (Control-click) the first and only frame in the actions layer and then choose Actions.**

   The Actions window opens, displaying the ActionScript code that was copied from the original document and pasted into the new one. The code is unchanged, and because the objects and instance names are unchanged, the actions work in the new animation just as they did in the old one.

8. **Choose Control→Test Movie→"in AIR Debug Launcher (Mobile)" to test the movie as an Android app.**

   Everything works as it did in the iOS version. In ADL, you can click the Back, Home, and Next buttons to navigate. The second page shows five finial profiles, as shown in Figure 23-5. Click on a profile to jump to the page that shows the dimensions for the finial.

To test the app on an Android device, follow the steps from the previous exercise to complete the deployment settings. Go to File→"AIR for Android Settings" and fill in the blanks. You may want to reposition the two movie clips on the stage: mcMainContent and mcMenuBar. After you've made these changes, you can test the app with the Publish command (File→Publish). When you test the Finial app on an Android device, you can use swipe left and swipe right gestures to move from page to page. Instead of mouse clicks, single finger taps activate the buttons. For details on adding swipe gestures to your application, see the code snippets discussed on page 733.

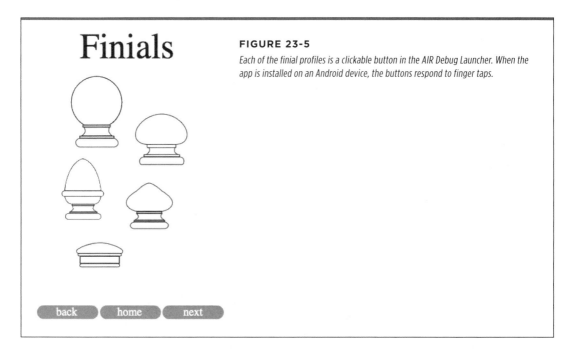

**FIGURE 23-5**

*Each of the finial profiles is a clickable button in the AIR Debug Launcher. When the app is installed on an Android device, the buttons respond to finger taps.*

## Resizing Graphics for Multiplatform Development

Even if you center the mcMainContent and mcMenuBar movie clips, the Finials app looks a little lost in its Android incarnation (Figure 23-6). It will look much better if you fill the screen with the content and make the navigation buttons bigger. The quick and easy way to do this is to simply scale the objects on the stage. There are two problems with that approach, which might not be a major issue with a simple app like this one, but could lead to trouble with bigger projects. First of all, the aesthetic issue: When you scale a bitmap up, the image is likely to become blocky and pixelated. The other issue has to do with Android resources. In general, it's best to place graphics on the stage at 100 percent scale. That way, the smartphone or tablet doesn't have to spend brainpower resizing the graphic. So, the best practice is to go back to the original artwork and resize it to fit Android's larger stage.

So, when you're planning to build an app that's destined for multiple devices such as iPhones, iPads, and Android phones and tablets, where do you start? Should you do your initial design for a small stage or a big stage? Many developers feel it's best to begin your development for the small screen, because that's likely to be the most challenging. Buttons and other widgets are proportionally bigger compared with the total stage, so every pixel makes a difference. In general, it's easier to scale your project up to a larger screen.

# Finials

Finals serve as a crown for newel posts, gazebos and other examples of fine woodworking. Cap your achievements with a handsome solid wood finial.

( back ) ( home ) ( next )

**FIGURE 23-6**

*The Android template's stage is bigger than the one for the original iPhone, so the iOS app looks a little lost in the extra space. Initially, the movie clips are positioned by the x/y coordinates for the smaller stage. Centering the movie clips helps some, but you'll probably want to resize the graphics for Android.*

**TIP** If you plan ahead, you can create your multiple-sized graphics in batches. Adobe Fireworks comes with most of the CS6 suites, and it's an excellent program for resizing graphics and outputting files in batches. In Fireworks, go to File→Batch Process. Fireworks also has a round-trip relationship with Flash. Right-click (Control-click) a bitmap in a Flash document and then choose "Edit with Fireworks."

# ■ Tips for Android App Development

Android devices are handheld computers, but they aren't quite as powerful as the computer that sits on your desktop. On top of that, Android apps use gestures like swipes and flicks for navigation and other functions. You need to build apps that work in the Android environment and that don't hog all the resources. When building

Android apps, you want to conserve the device's brainpower, battery power, and storage space. Your app has to share all those resources with the other installed apps.

Many of the tips for Android app building are the same as those for any handheld:

- Make use of behaviors like swipes, taps, and pinches. Avoid behaviors that won't work with a touchscreen, like rollovers, tiny buttons, and minuscule menus.

- Whenever possible, design for both portrait and landscape orientation. Make sure to test your app in both positions. If your app works only one way, you can lock in the orientation using the settings at File→"AIR for Android Settings"→General.

- Use tweens only when necessary. The calculations to execute a tween gobble up Android brainpower.

- Use gradients and transparency sparingly—they also hog Android brainpower.

- Where possible, use bitmaps instead of vector artwork. Mobile devices like bitmaps, but the calculations necessary to draw vectors may use too much CPU power.

- Pre-size your bitmaps for the application. There's no need to perform an extra "scale" calculation if your bitmaps are sized at 100% when they're on the stage.

- If you use vector art, use the Cache as Bitmap option (Properties→Display→ Render→"Cache as Bitmap.") This stores the vector art as a bitmap, making it easier for devices to display the image. In ActionScript, you can set the property for a movie clip: *mcMovieClip.cacheAsBitmap = true*. As always, test your app to make sure caching helps rather than hurts performance.

- Use device fonts: _san, _serif, and _typewriter. Using device fonts keeps your app smaller and increases its performance.

- Remove event listeners when they are no longer needed.

- Remove objects from the display list and from memory when they are no longer needed.

# Appendixes

APPENDIX A:

## Installation and Help

APPENDIX B:

## Flash Professional CS6, Menu by Menu

# Installation and Help

t's 2:00 a.m., you're *this close* to finishing your animation, and you run into a snag. If you can't find the answer to your question in the pages of this book, you have plenty of other possibilities. First of all, Flash has its own built-in help system, which may give you the answer you need on the spot. For more complex problems, you can seek technical support from Adobe or from fellow Flash fans via the Web. This appendix outlines all these options.

First, in case you need help getting Flash installed on your computer, some basic instructions follow.

## ■ Flash CS6 Minimum System Requirements

While the Flash box lists minimum requirements, *minimum* is the operative word. You'll want at least 20 GB free on your hard disk—not just for the program installation, but to give you room to create and store your Flash masterpieces and import additional files (like previously created images, sound files, and movies) from elsewhere.

Adobe lists the minimum amount of computer memory as 2 GB for both Macs and PCs, but as usual, you won't be sorry if you have two to four times that amount. The same is true of processor speed—faster multicore processors perform best. For Windows operating systems, Flash works with Windows XP with Service Pack 3, Vista, or Windows 7. It's best to have the most recent service packs (operating system upgrade) installed. For Macs, the requirement is an Intel multicore processor accompanied by Mac OS X version 10.6 or 10.7. Flash CS6 isn't compatible with PowerPC Macs. Last, and certainly not least, is screen size and video card. The minimum is listed as 1200 x 800 pixels with a 16-bit video card. Again, most of today's PCs and Macs, even laptops, meet this requirement. But Flash has so many windows and panels, it's great to have a system with more than one monitor or one very large display. That lets you display multiple panels, the Flash stage, and the Actions window without having to open, close, and then reopen them all the time. Adobe lists a DVD drive as one of the requirements. Installing Apple's QuickTime 7.6.6 or later (which is available for Windows as well as Macs) gives you access to additional file formats and multimedia features. To activate and to use some of the online services, such as Adobe TV help, you need a broadband Internet connection.

## Installing and Activating Flash Professional CS6

As with most programs, before you can use Flash, you need to install it on your computer and activate it. Flash Professional can arrive on your desktop via several routes. Your copy may come on a DVD, or it may arrive via a download from Adobe's online store. With Creative Suite 6, Adobe introduced a new way to acquire the various applications. You may subscribe to the suite by paying a monthly subscription fee. You may have purchased Flash Professional separately or as part of one of the Creative Suites. Also significant, your copy is for either a Windows PC or a Mac. These purchasing and system circumstances affect the installation. For example, if you got your copy of Flash CS6 through the subscription process, you will use the Adobe Application Manager to install and remove CS6 applications (Figure A-1). Depending on the settings, the Application Manager may automatically download and install updates to the applications when they're available. If you purchase a box version of Flash CS6, the process for installing and activating your application is more traditional. Insert the disc and follow instructions. In either case, the process is pretty straightforward with instructions on what is expected from you each step of the way.

Once the program is installed, you can start it up as you would any program on your system:

- **For Windows computers,** Flash is in the Adobe folder in your Program Files folder. That path and filename are usually *C:\Program Files\Adobe\Adobe Flash CS6\Flash.exe.* You can create a shortcut or drag the file to your Windows taskbar for quicker starting.

- **For Macs,** Flash is in the Adobe Flash CS6 folder in your Applications folder. That path and file name is usually *Macintosh HD\Applications\Adobe Flash CS6\ Adobe Flash CS6*. You can make an alias or drag the file to your Dock for quicker starting.

**FIGURE A-1**

*If you have a subscription to Adobe Creative Suite apps, you'll use the Adobe Application Manager to install and uninstall applications as you need them. The manager also notifies you when updates are available.*

# ◼ About Licenses and Activation

Your agreement with Adobe gives you a license to run the application on a limited number of computers. If you have the standard single license that gives you permission to install one copy on your computer. It also permits you to install a second copy on a laptop or home computer, providing both copies don't run at the same time. Adobe controls your account through the Application Manager or through the activation or deactivation process.

# Getting Help from Flash

In the olden days of computing, software companies provided nice, thick paperback manuals with their programs. They weren't always well-written, and sometimes they were downright wrong, but at least you could read them on the bus or train on the way to work or school. These days companies, including Adobe, provide book-length help files either in the program, online, or both. If you want printed pages, crank up your printer and load up a ream or two of paper. The online descriptions are more up to date and accurate than they were in those old printed volumes, but they're often a bit cryptic, as if they were written by the software engineers who designed the programs. Funny, that.

On the positive side, electronic help documents let you use your computer's search capabilities to hunt down an answer. Initially, Flash CS6 documents are presented as online documents. Go Help→Help and a web page appears with a number of links that lead to various references, videos and articles. A section at the top, serves somewhat like a table of contents. Click a link like Interactivity, Getting Started or ActionScript and the page scrolls to a spot with links related to that subject. At first it may be confusing the way official Adobe reference materials are mixed together with "community" content from the Adobe forums.

At the time this was written, the official help documents weren't available for download; however, there was a link on the help page that said CS6 Help PDF documents would be available in June 2012 (Figure A-2).

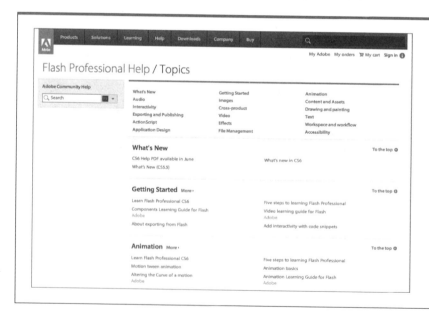

**FIGURE A-2**

*Adobe's online help files provide links to articles, videos and traditional reference materials. The Search box at the top searches the entire Adobe web site, so it may lead to pages that promote or sell Adobe products. The search box at the left lets you choose a product, but it searches for answers in the "community" also known as the Adobe Forums.*

## Flash Video Workshop Tutorials

Making good use of its own tools, Adobe serves up Adobe TV, where you can find video tutorials for Flash and other Creative Suite 6 programs. The company adds new programs, tutorials, and demonstrations all the time. Go to *http://tv.adobe.com*, and you'll see a page like Figure A-3. You can use the search box to hunt down videos on a particular topic, or you can select an index based on specific Adobe products. For beginners, the series "Flash in a Flash" is a good place to start.

# ■ Getting Help from Adobe

Adobe offers a variety of technical support options, from free to for-a-fee.

## Online Articles, FAQs, and Sample Code

Adobe maintains a website containing articles on Flash, as well as sample code and answers to frequently asked Flash-related questions. You can get there quickly through Help→Flash Support Center. You'll find lots of articles and tutorials. If you're looking for more advanced help, check out the Developer Centers listed in the column on the right side of the page. There are Developer Centers for Adobe AIR for Flash, Flash, Flash Lite, Flash Media Server, and Flash Player.

## Forums

Adobe hosts online forums, where anyone can ask a question about Flash, and anyone can answer. User-to-user means that Adobe employees don't officially monitor the forums or answer any questions, so the feedback you get has no official sanction or guarantee of accuracy. Still, the best and fastest answers and advice often come from other folks in the trenches, so if you've worked your way through Adobe's Tech Notes, Knowledgebase (online articles), FAQs, and documentation, these forums (Help→Adobe Online Forums) are definitely worth a look.

## Direct Person-to-Person Help

Sometimes, nothing will do but asking a real live technical support person for help. Adobe sells several different pay-to-play support plans. For example, single-incident support varies from $29 to $249. Other plans are available for workgroups and enterprises.

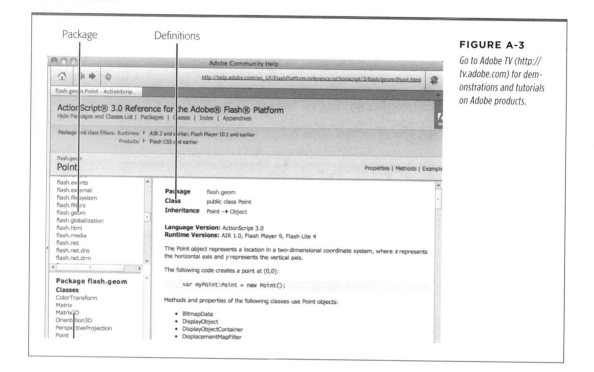

Package   Definitions

**FIGURE A-3**

*Go to Adobe TV (http://
tv.adobe.com) for dem-
onstrations and tutorials
on Adobe products.*

## ▪ More Flash Books

Flash and ActionScript are popular topics. Designers and developers who are serious about using these tools generally have a shelf full of books. Some of the books
mentioned here were written for Flash CS5, but by the time you read this they'll
probably be updated to cover CS6. You're very likely to find these among the titles:

- *Foundation Flash CS5 for Designers* by Tom Green and David Stiller. Good
  coverage of tools and techniques.

- *Flash CS5 Professional Digital Classroom* by Fred Gerantabee. A good beginner
  to intermediate Flash guide.

- *How to Cheat in Adobe Flash CS5* by Chris Georgenes. Great for drawing and
  animation tips and tricks.

- *Learning ActionScript 3.0* by Rich Shupe and Zevan Rosser. Very good introduction for those new to ActionScript.

- *Essential ActionScript 3.0* by Colin Moock. The bible when it comes to
  ActionScript 3.0.

# ◼ Finding Flash Gurus

Flash is one of those programs that people tend to get passionate about, so it's not surprising that there are hundreds of great resources on the Web offering everything from example code to free components, articles, tutorials, and more.

Here are a few that are definitely worth checking out:

- **Flashthusiast** (*http://flashthusiast.com*). A blog maintained by Team Tween of Flash at Adobe. You can read the new developments or search the archives.

- **Flash Kit** (*www.flashkit.com*). Surprisingly badly designed for a site that focuses on a design program, Flash Kit nevertheless offers a wealth of sound effects, fonts, components, and movie clips. It also hosts a well-attended online forum.

- **ActionScript.org** (*www.actionscript.org*). If you're interested in all things ActionScript, then check out this site offering tutorials, articles, and forums populated by ActionScript programmers. Once you've earned your stripes, there are even job listings where you can put your newfound skills to work.

- **FlashTuts+** (*http://active.tutsplus.com*). Tutorials on ActionScript, AIR, Flash, and other design tools.

- **Flashloaded** (*www.flashloaded.com*). A place to purchase predesigned Flash components. You'll find photo and media galleries, menu and navigation tools, and animated effects like book-style page flippers.

- **Keyframer** (*www.keyframer.com*). Chris Georgenes's website and blog is fun and has good info, especially for those interested in character animation.

- **Best Flash Animation Site** (*www.bestflashanimationsite.com*) and Webby Awards (*www.webbyawards.com*). There's nothing like watching a beautifully constructed Flash animation to get you thinking about good design. On these two sites, you can nominate the coolest Flash animation you've ever seen (including your own) or simply visit the sites others have nominated.

- **Boston Adobe Mobile and Devices User Group** (*www.flashmobilegroup.org*). If you're interested in creating Flash content for mobile devices (like mobile phones), you'll want to check out this site, which offers Flash Lite–specific articles, seminars, links, and live chats.

# Flash Professional CS6, Menu by Menu

*Flash CS6: The Missing Manual* is full of details, explanations, and examples. This appendix provides quick thumbnail descriptions of every command in every menu for quick reference.

## ■ File

The File menu commands work on your Flash document as a whole. Use the File menu for major events, like starting a new project, opening a file you created previously, and adjusting Flash's Publish and Preview settings.

### New

Windows: Ctrl+N

Mac: ⌘-N

The New command opens the New Document dialog box, where you can create many different types of Flash documents. For web pages, choose Flash File (ActionScript 2.0 or ActionScript 3.0). To create Flash files that will run on smartphones or tablets, use "AIR for iOS" or "AIR for Android." For other phones, organizers, or small handheld devices, use "Flash File (Mobile)."

### Open

Windows: Ctrl+O

Mac: ⌘-O

Opens the standard dialog box where you can navigate through your folders and open Flash files. Use the Open command to quickly find and then open files in Flash. Consider using the Browse command (described next) if you need to organize your files and perform other housekeeping chores.

## Browse in Bridge

Windows: Ctrl+Alt+O

Mac: Option-⌘-O

Opens Adobe Bridge, where you can organize, preview, import, and work with all different types of graphic files. Bridge shows thumbnail animations of SWF files and previews of JPEGs and other image files. Use Bridge to edit and search through the metadata and keywords attached to your graphic files.

## Open Recent

Leads to a submenu that shows a list of the last 10 Flash (.fla or .as) files that you opened and saved. Click a filename to open the Flash animation.

## Close

Windows: Ctrl+W

Mac: ⌘-W

Closes the active Flash document. If you made changes to the document, Flash asks if you want to save it before closing.

## Close All

Windows: Ctrl+Alt+W

Mac: Option-⌘-W

Closes all open Flash documents. If you made changes to the documents, Flash asks if you want to save them before closing.

## Save

Windows: Ctrl+S

Mac: ⌘-S

Saves the changes you've made to your Flash document. If you haven't made any changes since opening the document, the Save command is dimmed.

## Save As

Windows: Ctrl+Shift+ S

Mac: Shift-⌘-S

Use Save As to save the active Flash document with a new name or as a different file type. For example, you can save your CS6 file in the Flash CS4 file format or in the uncompressed (.xfl) format.

## Save as Template

Saves your document as a Flash template. Templates provide easy-to-use starting points for Flash projects. When you save a Flash file as a template, you provide a category and description of the template. You see templates listed when you use the File→New command and click the Templates button at the top of the New Document dialog box.

## Check In

Flash can use Adobe's Version Cue program to make it easier to track changes in your project and work collaboratively with others. After making changes to a file on your local computer, use Check In to post those changes on the Version Cue server.

## Save All

Saves all open Flash documents.

## Revert

Discards any changes you've made to your document and reverts to the last saved version.

## Import

Adds graphics, sound, video, and other media files to your Flash animation. Sub-commands on this menu let you import files to the stage or to the Library of your active Flash animation. You can also open files in an External Library, where they're available to all Flash animations. The last subcommand is used to import video files.

## Export

Lets you save images and movies in a variety of different file formats so you can use them in other programs. Some of the Image options include FXG, JPEG, GIF, and PNG. Some of the Movie options include SWF Movie, QuickTime, Animated GIF, and JPEG Sequence.

## Publish Settings

Windows: Shift+Ctrl+F12

Mac: Shift-Option-F12

Opens the extensive Publish Settings dialog box, where you can fine-tune the production of your Flash animations. Use Publish Settings to create web pages (HTML files) complete with commands to show your Flash animations and position them on the page. With Publish Settings, you can choose to create Flash *projectors* (standalone programs that run your animation for Windows or Mac).

## Publish Preview

Windows: F12

Mac: ⌘-F12

Publish Preview runs your Flash animation in the format of your choice. Using the factory setting for Publish Preview, you see your animation embedded in a web page. With the submenus, you can choose to see your animation in a projector file or other formats, like an animated GIF, JPEG, or PNG file.

## Publish

Windows: Alt+Shift+F12

Mac: Shift-⌘-F12

Produces the finished files that make up your Flash animation. Flash uses the Publish Settings dialog box (see page 685) to create the files of your choosing. These may include Flash movies (SWF), web pages (HTML), projector files (EXE for Windows, APP for Mac), and the whole spectrum of graphics files (JPEG, GIF, PICT, and PNG). If you're publishing for the iPhone, iPod Touch, or iPad, Flash produces both SWF and IPA files. If you publish for Android, Flash produces SWF and APK files.

## AIR Settings

AIR stands for Adobe Integrated Runtime, which is a system for creating desktop programs that run on PCs, Macs, and other systems using the AIR runtime and other web technologies, like HTML, JavaScript, and CSS. The benefits to programmers are that they can use familiar programming tools and don't have to rewrite programs for different computer systems. Once you create a new AIR file by selecting File→New→AIR, use this command to set up the AIR project files and to provide a code signing certificate. For more details on Adobe AIR, go to *www.adobe.com/products/air*.

## AIR for iOS Settings

Use these settings to publish apps for the iPhone, iPod Touch, and iPad. On the Deployment tab, you identify your developer's certificate, testing devices, and app IDs. For details see page 738.

## AIR for Android Settings

Use these settings to publish apps for Android smartphones and tablets. On the Deployment tab, you can create a self-signed certificate that permits testing apps on devices that are connected via USB cable. For details see page 758.

## File Info

Stores metadata for your Flash file. Metadata can include details like the date you created a file, the name of the file's author, and the copyright information. Programs like Adobe Bridge read the metadata stored in files and provide database-type features. For example, in Bridge you can search through all your media files for ones that were created or modified on certain dates.

## Share My Screen

Adobe ConnectNow lets you share your screen with up to three other people online. Click the Share My Screen option to open the ConnectNow panel and have live online meetings with others. Adobe IDs are required, but it's free to register for one.

## Page Setup

Flash documents are meant to be viewed on a computer or mobile device, but you can print frames of your document on paper. Page Setup opens the dialog box where you can choose a printer, page size, and orientation before you print from your Flash document.

## Print Margins (Mac only)

Opens the Print Margins dialog box, where you can position Flash frames on your page before printing. The settings include margin measurements and options for centering the document horizontally and vertically on the page. (To set margins for Windows computers, use the Page Setup command.)

## Print

Windows: Ctrl+P

Mac: ⌘-P

Prints a frame or a sequence of frames from your Flash document using the settings from Page Setup and Print Margins.

## Send (Windows only)

Opens your email program and attaches the current .fla file to a blank email message. All you need to do is type an address and message.

## Exit (Mac: Flash→Quit Flash)

Windows: Ctrl+Q

Mac: ⌘-Q

Stops the program, and then closes the Flash window. If there are open documents, Flash closes them. If there are unsaved documents, the program prompts you to save them before quitting.

# ▓ Edit

Use this menu to cut, copy, paste, and change items you've selected on Flash's stage.

## Undo

Windows: Ctrl+Z

Mac: ⌘-Z

This command undoes the last command you applied. So, if you accidentally deleted a drawing from your stage, the Undo command brings it back like magic. Remember the Undo command for those moments when you smack your forehead and say, "Oh no! Why'd I do that?" For extensive undoing, consider using the History panel: Window→Other Panels→History (Windows: Ctrl+F10; Mac: ⌘-F10).

## Redo

Windows: Ctrl+Y

Mac: ⌘-Y

Repeats the last command you used. So if the last thing you did was paste a circle on the stage, Redo pastes another circle on the stage. If you've just used the Undo command, Redo restores the change. Thus, you can use Undo to step backward through your recent commands and Redo to step forward again.

## Cut

Windows: Ctrl+X

Mac: ⌘-X

Removes the selected object from the stage and places a copy of it on your computer's Clipboard. Once it's on the Clipboard, you can paste it to a new location or a new document.

## Copy

Windows: Ctrl+C

Mac: ⌘-C

Makes a copy of any selected objects and places a copy on the Clipboard. The original objects remain on the stage. Once you've copied an object or group of objects to the Clipboard, you can paste them to a new location or a new document.

## Paste in Center

Windows: Ctrl+V

Mac: ⌘-V

Tells Flash to paste the cut (or copied) object right smack in the middle of the stage's visible area, on top of any other image that happens to be there.

## Paste in Place

Windows: Ctrl+Shift+V

Mac: Shift-⌘-V

Tells Flash to paste the cut or copied object in its original position on the stage. Useful for copying objects from one frame to another, this command ensures that the objects are positioned in exactly the same location in both frames.

## Clear

Windows: Backspace

Mac: Delete

Removes any selected objects from the stage. Flash doesn't store cleared objects on the Clipboard, so you can't use the Paste command to put them back on the stage.

## Duplicate

Windows: Ctrl+D

Mac: ⌘-D

Copies any selected objects, and then immediately pastes a duplicate on the stage. This one command combines the Copy and Paste commands.

## Select All

Windows: Ctrl+A

Mac: ⌘-A

Selects all the objects on the stage and work area.

## Deselect All

Windows: Ctrl+Shift+ A

Mac: Shift-⌘-A

Removes the selection from any currently selected objects.

## Find and Replace

Windows: Ctrl+F

Mac: ⌘-F

Opens the "Find and Replace" panel, where you search your document or scene for text, symbols, graphics, and media that you specify. You can then, if you wish, replace those items with something else.

## Find Next

Windows: F3

Mac: F3

Searches for the next occurrence of the items identified in the "Find and Replace" panel.

# Timeline

Leads to a submenu that shows Edit commands specific to Flash's timeline. The submenu commands include the following:

- **Remove Frames**

  Windows: Shift+F5

  Mac: Shift-F5

  Removes frames from the timeline, shortening the length of the timeline.

- **Cut Frames**

  Windows: Ctrl+Alt+X

  Mac: Option-⌘-X

  Cuts the contents of the frames, placing that content on the Clipboard, where you can paste it into other frames. Cut Frames doesn't reduce the number of frames in the timeline.

- **Copy Frames**

  Windows: Ctrl+Alt+C

  Mac: Option-⌘-C

  Copies the selected frames and places them on the Clipboard, so you can paste them to a different location in the timeline.

- **Paste Frames**

  Windows: Ctrl+Alt+V

  Mac: Option-⌘-V

  Pastes copied or cut frames into the timeline after the selected frame. Pasting frames increases the overall length of the timeline.

- **Clear Frames**

  Windows: Alt+Backspace

  Mac: Option-Delete

  Removes the contents of the selected frames, leaving empty frames in place. (Unlike Cut, Clear Frames *doesn't* place the frames on the Clipboard.)

- **Select All Frames**

  Windows: Ctrl+Alt+A

  Mac: Option-⌘-A

  Selects all the frames in all the layers in the visible timeline so you can make changes to the entire timeline at once.

- **Cut Layers**

  Remove one or more layer and all its content is added to the Clipboard so it can be pasted into a new timeline.

- **Copy Layers**

  Similar to Cut Layers (above) but the original layer and its content remain in place.

- **Paste Layers**

  Use this command to paste the layers and content that has been stored on the clipboard through a Cut Layers or Copy Layers command.

- **Duplicate Layers**

  A single command that copies and pastes layers.

- **Copy Motion**

  Copies the properties of a motion tween so you can paste them onto another object.

- **Copy Motion as ActionScript 3.0**

  Copies the properties of a motion tween and creates ActionScript 3.0 code, which you can then use in the Actions panel.

- **Paste Motion**

  Used after Copy Motion to paste the properties of a motion tween onto another object.

- **Paste Motion Special**

  Lets you choose specific tween properties you want to paste onto another object. For example, your choices include X and Y positions, horizontal and vertical scales, rotation, skew, colors, and filters.

## Edit Symbols/Document

Windows: Ctrl+E

Mac: ⌘-E

When you edit symbols, you change every instance of the symbol in your document. Edit Symbols opens the selected Flash symbol so you can edit it in its own timeline. (When you're in Edit Symbols mode, this command changes to Edit Document and brings you back to the document timeline.)

## Edit Selected

Lets you edit a selected group or object within a group. Other objects on the stage that aren't part of the group are dimmed and inaccessible. Use Edit All (below) to return to the normal stage.

### Edit in Place

Use "Edit in Place" to edit symbols within the context of the stage. Other objects on the stage are dimmed and inaccessible. When you edit a symbol, you change all instances of that symbol in your document.

### Edit All

Restores the normal stage after you use the Edit Selected command.

### Preferences (Mac: Flash→Preferences)

Windows: Ctrl+U

Opens the extensive Flash Preferences panel, where you can tweak dozens of settings to make Flash work the way you like to work. You can set Preferences in the following groups: General, ActionScript, AutoFormat, Clipboard, Drawing, Text, Warnings, PSD File Importer, AI File Importer, and Publish Cache. For example, General settings include Flash's startup options, how many levels of undo to save, and whether or not to display tooltips when the cursor is over a command or object.

### Customize Tools Panel (Mac: Flash→Customize Tools Panel)

Opens the Customize Tools panel, where you can set up the Tools panel with just the tools you want and arrange them any way you like.

### Font Mapping (Mac: Flash→Font Mapping)

Opens the Font Mapping panel, where you can choose substitute fonts for fonts that are missing on your system. For example, you can choose Times Roman to substitute for Times.

### Keyboard Shortcuts (Mac: Flash→Keyboard Shortcuts)

Use Keyboard Shortcuts to add or change the keys used to invoke specific commands.

# ■ View

Use this menu to alter the onscreen display, with features such as zoom, guides and rulers, preview mode, and snapping to a grid (or other objects).

### Go To

Lets you navigate Flash animations that are broken up into multiple scenes. The Go To command leads to a submenu where you can select scenes by name or choose First, Last, Previous, and Next options and specific scenes.

### Zoom In

Windows: Ctrl+=

Mac: ⌘-=

Changes the view of the stage by zooming in twice as much. So, if the view is at 500%, zooming in changes the view to 1,000%.

## Zoom Out

Windows: Ctrl+-

Mac: ⌘-hyphen (-)

Changes the view of the stage by adjusting the zoom to half as much. So, if the view is at 500%, zooming out changes the view to 250%.

## Magnification

Leads to a submenu where you can choose from several preset zoom levels that range from 25% to 800%. In addition, there are options to Show All (zoom to show all the contents of the current frame), Show Frame (shows the entire stage), and "Fit in Window" (scale the entire stage to fit in the program window).

## Preview Mode

Leads to a submenu with several options related to previewing your animation with the Control→Play command. The options include the following:

- **Outlines**

    Windows: Ctrl+Alt+Shift+O

    Mac: Shift-Option-⌘-O

    Displays shapes in the animation as outlines or wireframe representations. With older, slower computers, this mode can help speed up previews, although most of today's machines can keep pace with even the most complex Flash animations.

- **Fast**

    Windows: Ctrl+Alt+Shift+F

    Mac: Shift-Option-⌘-F

    Turns off antialiasing and other settings that slow down Flash previews.

- **Anti-Alias**

    Windows: Ctrl+Alt+Shift+A

    Mac: Shift-Option-⌘-A

    Turns on antialiasing, a computer graphics technique that makes shapes and lines appear smoother on computer screens.

- **Anti-Alias Text**

    Windows: Ctrl+Alt+Shift+T

    Mac: Shift-Option-⌘-T

Uses antialiasing on text to create a smoother appearance. These settings change the appearance of text while you're working inside Flash; to adjust anti-alias settings for your published files, use the Properties panel settings for the Text tool.

- **Full**

  Renders your Flash animation fully, providing a close approximation of the published animation.

## Pasteboard

Windows: Ctrl+Shift+W

Mac: Shift-⌘-W

Shows the workspace around the stage. Works in conjunction with the Magnification commands (page 785). A checkmark appears in the menu when this option is in force.

## Rulers

Windows: Ctrl+Alt+Shift+R

Mac: Shift-Option-⌘-R

Shows or hides the rulers that appear at the top and left of the program window. With rulers visible, you can drag guidelines to place on the stage. (Guides don't appear in your final animation; they're just visual aids to help you position items on the stage.) A checkmark appears in the menu when this option is turned on.

## Grid

The grid is another visual aid to help you position and align objects on your stage. The grid appears as horizontal and vertical lines, similar to graph paper. The Grid command leads to a submenu where you can show or hide the grid and change the color and spacing of the lines. You can turn the grid's "snapping" behavior on and off (see below).

## Guides

Show, hide, and lock guides using the submenu under the Guides command. Use the Edit Guides command to adjust the appearance and behavior of your guides. The Clear Guides command removes all guides from the stage.

## Snapping

When Snapping is turned on, objects automatically line up with other objects. So, for example, if you turn on Snapping for guides, then objects you drag snap into alignment with the nearest guide. You can turn Snapping on or off for the grid, guides, and objects. The Snapping submenu displays the following commands:

- **Snap Align**

  When Snap Align is turned on, dotted lines appear on the stage when you drag an object near another object or near the edge of the stage.

- **Snap to Grid**

  Windows: Ctrl+Shift+'

  Mac: Shift-⌘-'

  Toggles the snapping behavior of the grid on or off.

- **Snap to Guide**

  Windows: Ctrl+Shift+;

  Mac: Shift-⌘-;

  Toggles the snapping behavior of guides on or off.

- **Snap to Pixels**

  Use "Snap to Pixels" for super-accurate alignment. With "Snap to Pixels" on, a grid appears when the zoom level is 400% or greater. This grid represents individual pixels on your Flash stage.

- **Snap to Objects**

  Windows: Ctrl+Shift+/

  Mac: Shift-⌘-U

  Toggles the snapping behavior of objects on or off.

- **Edit Snapping**

  Windows: Ctrl+/

  Mac: ⌘-/

  Opens the Edit Snapping panel, where you can adjust the settings for snapping behaviors, including *tolerance* (how close objects need to be before snapping behavior kicks in).

## Hide Edges

Windows: Ctrl+H

Mac: Shift-⌘-E

Toggles the highlight that appears on objects when you select them. If you want to see the object without the highlight, click Hide Edges; a checkmark appears on the menu.

## Show Shape Hints

Windows: Ctrl+Alt+H

Mac: Option-⌘-H

Shows and hides shape hints on the stage. Shape hints are used to control shapes that are being tweened. By positioning shape hints, you control the appearance of an object as it changes shape during a tween. Turn Show Shape Hints on to make adjustments, and then turn the hints off to see your objects as they'll appear in your animation.

## Show Tab Order

Tab Order establishes keyboard navigation in forms and web pages. For example, if you create a form with the tab order Name = 1, Address = 2, and Phone number = 3, then your visitors can fill in their name, press the Tab key to move on to the Address field, and so on. Use Show tab order to see a visual representation of the Tab Order of items on your stage.

# ■ Insert

Use the Insert menu to add objects to your animation and to make changes to the timeline.

## New Symbol

Windows: Ctrl+F8

Mac: ⌘-F8

Opens the Create Symbol dialog box, where you name and select the symbol type (movie clip, button, or graphic).

## Motion Tween

Applies a motion tween to an object, which is great for animating movement and changing properties over time—like color, transparency, and dimensions. You can use the new Motion Editor to fine-tune every aspect of a motion tween.

## Shape Tween

Creates a shape tween between adjacent keyframes. Shape tweens work only on editable shapes (not text or symbols). They're great for morphing objects from one form to another—an acorn to an oak, for example.

## Classic Tween

Creates a motion tween between adjacent keyframes (represented by an arrow on a blue background). Use classic tweens to create nonlinear motions. Classic tweens work only on symbols, grouped objects, and text blocks. While Adobe still makes classic tweens available in CS6 for compatibility reasons, it's replaced them with the more versatile and powerful motion tween.

## Timeline

The Timeline command leads to a submenu with commands for adding layers and frames to your timeline:

- **Layer**

  Inserts a new layer in your timeline. You use layers to organize objects on the stage. For example, layers can hold elements like shapes and text. You can also create keyframes and tweens on individual layers.

- **Layer Folder**

  Creates a layer folder. Layer folders are used to organize and group layers. By opening and closing layer folders, you can simplify the appearance of your timeline.

- **Frame**

  Windows: F5

  Mac: F5

  Inserts frames into your timeline. If no frame is selected, then this command inserts one frame in every layer after the current position of the playhead. If one or more frames are selected, then an equal number of frames are inserted following the selection. If a position is selected on the right, outside the range of the current timeline, then Flash adds new frames up to the selected point.

- **Keyframe**

  Inserts new keyframes into the timeline (represented by a solid circle), similar to the Frame command. Keyframes are different from ordinary frames in that the changes and repositioning of objects in keyframes represent significant changes in the action of your animation. When you use the Insert Keyframe command, objects on the stage become part of the new keyframe.

- **Blank Keyframe**

  Inserts blank keyframes into your timeline (represented by a hollow circle). Similar to the Keyframe command, except there are no objects in a blank keyframe—you've got a clean slate where you can add new objects to the stage.

## Scene

Adds a new scene to your Flash animation. Scenes let you divide long animations into smaller, more manageable parts and create nonlinear animations or animations that repeat certain segments.

# ■ Modify

The commands in the Modify menu let you change the properties of your document, your timeline, and the objects in your animation. For example, you use commands in this menu to rotate, scale, and distort the shapes on the stage.

## Document

Windows: Ctrl+J

Mac: ⌘-J

Opens the Document window, where you set the width, height, and background color of the stage. Document settings also control the speed (frames per second) of your animation and the measurement units used by rulers.

## Convert to Symbol

Windows: F8

Mac: F8

Converts selected objects to a symbol, which can be a movie clip, a graphic, or a button. Symbols are key to many aspects of Flash animations. Among other things, symbols help to reduce the overall file size of Flash animations.

## Break Apart

Windows: Ctrl+B

Mac: ⌘-B

Used to break an imported bitmap into separate pixels that can be selected and edited. (When you first import a bitmap, Flash treats it as a single discrete element.) This command also separates grouped objects and symbols into their component parts.

## Bitmap

Flash has two Modify commands to help you work with imported bitmap (raster) images:

- **Swap Bitmap**

  Replace the selected instance of a bitmap with another bitmap.

- **Trace Bitmap**

  Converts the selected bitmap into a vector image, by converting areas of color into editable vector shapes. In some cases, this can reduce the Flash file size, but it's worth testing to see whether that's the case and that you're OK with the changes it makes to the image.

## Symbol

Flash has two Modify commands to help you work with symbols.

- **Swap Symbol**

  Replace the selected instance of a symbol with another symbol from the Library.

- **Duplicate Symbol**

  Creates a new instance of a symbol you've selected on the stage.

## Shape

Flash has several commands to help you modify shapes in your animation:

- **Advanced Smooth**

  Windows: Ctrl+Alt+Shift+N

  Mac: Shift-Option-⌘-N

  Removes the hard angles and bumps from shapes and lines. Applying this command repeatedly creates smoother and smoother shapes.

- **Advanced Straighten**

  Windows: Ctrl+Alt+Shift+N

  Mac: Shift-Option-⌘-M

  Removes the curves from lines and line segments. You can apply this command repeatedly, creating straighter lines each time.

- **Optimize**

  Windows: Shift+Ctrl+Alt+C

  Mac: Shift-Option-⌘-C

  Reduces the number of anchor points (control points) in a shape or line by removing unneeded anchor points. This doesn't change the shape, but it does reduce the file size and helps make shapes more manageable.

- **Convert Lines to Fills**

  Changes lines into fills, in effect giving them the properties of fills. For example, once a line is changed to a fill, you can change its shape.

- **Expand Fill**

  Opens the Expand Fill window, where you can expand (enlarge) or inset (shrink) the fill portion of a shape. This is similar to scaling a shape and works best on simple objects.

- **Soften Fill Edges**

  Softens the edges of the selected shape, giving it the appearance of fading away. In the Soften Fill Edges window, you can choose the distance and the steps (gradations) for the effect.

- **Add Shape Hint**

  Windows: Ctrl+Shift+H

  Mac: Shift-⌘-H

  When you're creating a shape tween, you can use hints to control the appearance of objects as they change from one shape to another. By adding hints, you can highlight important parts of the shape that should be defined during the transition.

- **Remove All Hints**

  If you've applied hints to a shape tween (see the previous command), this command removes them.

## Combine Objects

The Combine Objects submenu lets you create more complex objects by combining multiple objects created in object drawing mode and altering their grouped features:

- **Delete Envelope**

  Removes the Envelope modifier from the selected object.

- **Union**

  Combines two or more shapes to create a new object by deleting unseen overlapping sections. The new object consists of the visible portions of the joined shapes.

- **Intersect**

  Creates an object from the intersection of two or more objects. The new object shape consists of the overlapping portions of the combined shapes.

- **Punch**

  Removes portions of an object as defined by the overlapping portions of another object placed on top of it. Areas where the top object overlaps the lower object are removed, and the top object is deleted entirely.

- **Crop**

  Uses the shape of one object to crop another object. The front or topmost object defines the shape to be retained. Any part of an underlying shape that overlaps the top shape remains, while the visible portions of the underlying shapes are removed, and the topmost shape is deleted entirely.

# Timeline

The Timeline submenu's commands help you organize and manipulate the parts that comprise your animation, notably layers and frames:

- **Distribute to Layers**

  Windows: Shift+Ctrl+D

  Mac: Shift-⌘-D

  Distributes the selected objects so that each object is on its own layer. Useful for making sure different shapes are on separate layers before applying a tween.

- **Layer Properties**

  Opens the Layer Properties window, where you name layers and adjust settings like layer type, layer colors, layer height, layer visibility, and layer locking.

- **Reverse Frames**

  Rearranges the selected frames in reverse order. In effect, this arranges the frames so that the animation runs in reverse.

- **Synchronize Symbols**

  Synchronizes the animation of a graphic symbol instance to match the timeline. It also recalculates the number of frames in a tween to match the number of frames allotted to it in the timeline.

- **Convert to Keyframes**

  Windows: F6

  Mac: F6

  Converts the selected frames in the timeline into keyframes. This command retains the contents of the preceding keyframe. Keyframes are represented by a solid circle.

- **Clear Keyframe**

  Windows: Shift+F6

  Mac: Shift-F6

  Converts a keyframe to a standard frame.

- **Convert to Blank Keyframes**

  Windows: F7

  Mac: F7

  Converts the selected frame to a blank keyframe. Represented in the timeline by a hollow circle, blank keyframes have no content.

# Transform

Leads to a submenu with the following Transform commands:

- **Free Transform**

  Puts the selected object in Free Transform mode where you can perform scale, rotate, and skew transformations.

- **Distort**

  Puts the selected object in Distort mode. You can change the shape of the object using handles on the bounding box.

- **Envelope**

  The Envelope modifier lets you distort the shape of an object using handles on the bounding box.

- **Scale**

  Scale lets you change the height and width of an object by dragging the handles on the bounding box. Press Shift to resize the object proportionally.

- **Rotate and Skew**

  Places a bounding box around the selected object. Using the handles, you can freely rotate and skew the object.

- **Scale and Rotate**

  Windows: Ctrl+Alt+S

  Mac: Option-⌘-S

  Opens the Scale and Rotate window, where you can resize and rotate the selected object by typing numbers into text boxes.

- **Rotate 90 degrees CW**

  Windows: Ctrl+Shift+9

  Mac: Shift-⌘-9

  Rotates the selected object by 90 degrees in a clockwise direction.

- **Rotate 90 degrees CCW**

  Windows: Ctrl+Shift+7

  Mac: Shift-⌘-7

  Rotates the selected object by 90 degrees in a counterclockwise direction.

- **Flip Vertical**

  Flips the selected object vertically, putting the top of the object at the bottom.

- **Flip Horizontal**

  Flips the selected object horizontally, putting the left side of the object on the right.

- **Remove Transform**

  Windows: Ctrl+Shift+Z

  Mac: Shift-⌘-Z

  Removes the previously applied transformations from the selected object.

## Arrange

The Arrange submenu's commands act on the objects in your animation's layers:

- **Bring to Front**

  Windows: Ctrl+Shift+up arrow

  Mac: Shift-Option-up arrow

  Brings the selected object to the top level in the frame so that the object appears to be in front of all other objects in the same frame. This action pertains only to objects in the same layer in the timeline; it doesn't reposition layers or move objects from one layer to another.

- **Bring Forward**

  Windows: Ctrl+up arrow

  Mac: ⌘-up arrow

  Brings selected objects forward one step in front of other objects in the same frame. This action pertains only to objects in the same layer in the timeline; it doesn't reposition layers or move objects from the layer to another.

- **Send Backward**

  Windows: Ctrl+down arrow

  Mac: ⌘-down arrow

  Sends the selected object backward one step behind other objects in the same frame. This action pertains only to objects in the same layer in the timeline; it doesn't reposition layers or move objects from one layer to another.

- **Send to Back**

  Windows: Ctrl+Shift+down arrow

  Mac: Shift-Option-down arrow

  Sends the selected object to the bottom level in the frame so that the object appears to be behind every other object in the same frame. This action pertains only to objects in the same layer in the timeline; it doesn't reposition layers or move objects from one layer to another.

- **Lock**

  Windows: Ctrl+Alt+L

  Mac: Option-⌘-L

  Locks selected objects in their current position on the stage. Locked objects can't be selected to be moved or transformed in any other way.

- **Unlock All**

  Windows: Ctrl+Alt+Shift+L

  Mac: Shift-Option-⌘-L

  Unlocks objects that have been locked in position using the Lock command.

## Align

The Align submenu's commands help you position your animation's objects neatly in relation to the edges of the stage or to one another:

- **Left**

  Windows: Ctrl+Alt+1

  Mac: Option-⌘-1

  Aligns selected objects along the left edge.

- **Horizontal Center**

  Windows: Ctrl+Alt+2

  Mac: Option-⌘-2

  Aligns the center of the selected objects to the same horizontal position.

- **Right**

  Windows: Ctrl+Alt+3

  Mac: Option-⌘-3

  Aligns selected objects along the right edge.

- **Top**

  Windows: Ctrl+Alt+4

  Mac: Option-⌘-4

  Aligns selected objects along the top edge.

- **Vertical Center**

  Windows: Ctrl+Alt+5

  Mac: Option-⌘-5

  Aligns the center of the selected objects to the same vertical position.

- **Bottom**

  Windows: Ctrl+Alt+6

  Mac: Option-⌘-6

  Aligns selected objects along the bottom edge.

- **Distribute Widths**

  Windows: Ctrl+Alt+7

  Mac: Option-⌘-7

  Spaces selected objects evenly on the stage from left to right.

- **Distribute Heights**

  Windows: Ctrl+Alt+9

  Mac: Option-⌘-9

  Spaces selected objects evenly on the stage from top to bottom.

- **Make Same Width**

  Windows: Ctrl+Alt+Shift+7

  Mac: Shift-Option-⌘-7

  Makes the width property of selected objects equal.

- **Make Same Height**

  Windows: Ctrl+Alt+Shift+ 9

  Mac: Shift-Option-⌘-9

  Makes the height property of selected objects equal.

- **Align to Stage**

  Windows: Ctrl+Alt+8

  Mac: Option-⌘-8

  Toggles the To Stage behavior of alignment tools. For example, with To Stage selected, the Align Bottom command aligns selected objects with the bottom of the stage. A checkmark appears on the menu when this option is selected.

## Group

Windows: Ctrl+G

Mac: ⌘-G

Combines selected objects into a group. Grouped objects behave as if they're a single object. They can be selected with a single click and modified and transformed with a single command.

## Ungroup

Windows: Ctrl+Shift+G

Mac: Shift-⌘-G

Breaks grouped objects (see above) apart into their individual elements.

# ■ Text

Use the commands on the Text menu to modify the appearance of text on the stage:

## Font

Choose a typeface from a list of fonts available on your computer.

## Size

Apply a new size to the selected text. Sizes range from 8 point to 120 point.

## Style

Available type styles include Plain, Bold, Italic, Subscript, and Superscript.

## Align

Use this command to set the text alignment to Left, Centered, Right, or Justified.

## Letter Spacing

Letter spacing is a typographic effect sometimes used in headings and logos to increase or decrease the space between all letters by the same fixed amount.

## Scrollable

Use the Scrollable command to make dynamic text or input text fields scrollable, so the text can be longer than the available space in the text box.

## Check Spelling

Runs Flash's spell checker on the text in the Spelling Setup window (see below).

## Spelling Setup

Use the Spelling Setup command to identify the text that needs to be spell-checked, select your language, choose a personal dictionary, and set options for words you want the spell checker to ignore.

## Font Embedding

Opens the Font Embedding window, where you can manage all the fonts used in your animation and make sure the proper fonts are available for your audience. For the details, see page 582.

# ■ Commands

The Commands menu helps you automate tasks in Flash. You can create commands for tasks that you perform repeatedly and download prebuilt commands from the Adobe Exchange website.

## Manage Saved Commands

Opens the Manage Saved Commands panel, where you can rename and delete commands.

## Get More Commands

Opens your web browser to the Adobe Exchange page, where you can find commands others have created. Some are for sale and some are free.

## Run Command

Use Run Command to run a JavaScript command. An Open File dialog box opens, where you can navigate to the script you want to run.

## Convert Symbol to Flex Component

You can convert Flash content into a Flex component in the .swc file format. Your content in Flash must be a movie clip symbol and must use ActionScript 3.0 (as opposed to an earlier version).

## Convert Symbol to Flex Container

Similar to the option above that creates components for Flex, this option creates Flex containers.

## Copy Font Name for ActionScript

Font names are sometimes complicated, with odd combinations of upper- and lower-case letters. To make sure you use exactly the right name in your ActionScript code, select a text field and then use this command to copy the font name to the Clipboard. At that point, you can paste it into your code.

## Copy Motion as XML

Records an XML description of your animation that you can reuse in other projects.

## Export Motion XML

Exports a copied motion as an XML file so you can import and reuse it in other animations.

## Import Motion XML

Imports an XML file that defines a Flash motion so you can apply it to objects in your animation.

# ■ Control

Control menu commands provide playback controls to test your animation in the program window, the Flash Player, and HTML pages.

## Play

Windows: Enter

Mac: Return

Plays the timeline in the Flash window, showing the contents of each frame on the stage.

## Rewind

Windows: Shift+comma (,)

Mac: Shift-comma (,)

Moves the playhead in the timeline back to the first frame.

## Go To End

Windows: Shift+period (.)

Mac: Shift-period (.)

Moves the playhead in the timeline to the last frame.

## Step Forward One Frame

Windows: period (.)

Mac: period (.)

Moves the playhead in the timeline ahead one frame.

## Step Backward One Frame

Windows: comma (,)

Mac: comma (,)

Moves the playhead in the timeline back one frame.

## Test Movie

Windows: Ctrl+Enter

Mac: ⌘-Return

The Test Movie option leads to a submenu, where you can choose to test your movie in Flash Professional, Device Central, "AIR Debug Launcher (Desktop)," "AIR Debug Launcher (Mobile)," or "on Device via USB." These options may look similar, but in each case, they use the designated runtime environment. Once you've selected the environment for testing your movie, a checkmark appears next to its name. Then you can use the Ctrl+Enter (⌘-Return) command to test it. Flash compiles the animation and then runs it. If your movie has more than one scene, then this command plays all the scenes in order.

## Test Scene

Windows: Ctrl+Alt+Enter

Mac: Option-⌘-Return

Compiles and tests the scene in the timeline. If you want to test and view all the scenes in your movie, use Test Movie (above).

## Clear Publish Cache

Clears the publish cache of any previously stored files. Flash can create temporary files when you publish your animation. Doing so can speed up the process the next time you publish and test your animation. To adjust the publish cache settings, go to Edit→Preferences→Publish Cache (Flash→Preferences→Publish Cache).

## Clear Publish Cache and Test Movie

This command clears the cache of any previously stored files and then publishes and tests the animation.

## Loop Playback

Repeats the playback of your movie or scene when testing. When the movie reaches the end, it starts playing from the beginning again.

## Play All Scenes

Tells Flash to play all the scenes in your animation, not just the currently selected scene.

## Enable Simple Frame Actions

Windows: Ctrl+Alt+F

Mac: Option-⌘-F

Tells Flash to play the actions you've added to frames in the timeline. (These are basic actions like Play and Stop commands.) If you don't turn on Enable Simple Frame Actions, then Flash ignores frame actions.

## Enable Simple Buttons

Windows: Ctrl+Alt+B

Mac: Option-⌘-B

Makes your buttons work on the stage. If you turn off this menu item, mousing over and clicking buttons has no effect.

## Enable Live Preview

Displays components you've added to the stage as they'll appear in the Flash Player. If you turn this item off, then Flash displays components as outlines.

## Mute Sounds

Windows: Ctrl+Alt+M

Mac: Option-⌘-M

Prevents Flash from playing sound clips during playback.

# ■ Debug

Debug commands give you tools to play back your movie and, at the same time, examine the inner workings of the timeline, object properties, and ActionScript code. Similar to testing, you can debug your animation in different environments: Flash Professional, "AIR Debug Launcher (Desktop)," "AIR Debug Launcher (Mobile)," or "on Device via USB."

## Debug Movie

Windows: Ctrl+Shift+Enter

Mac: Shift-⌘-Return

Plays your animation while displaying information in the Debugger window, where you can monitor the list of objects and variables your animation and ActionScript are using.

## Continue

Windows: Alt+F5

Mac: Option-F5

Continues playback after being stopped by the debugger.

## End Debug Session

Windows: Alt+F12

Mac: Option-F12

Stops the debugging session and stops playback of the animation.

## Step In

Windows: Alt+F6

Mac: Option-F6

Used during debugging in combination with breakpoints, the Step In command runs ActionScript functions step by step.

## Step Over

Windows: Alt+F7

Mac: Option-F7

Use Step Over during debugging in combination with breakpoints to step through your ActionScript code a line at a time. Stepping over a line of code tells Flash to execute the code even if the line contains a function call.

## Step Out

Windows: Alt+F8

Mac: Option-F8

Use Step Out during debugging in combination with breakpoints. You use this command to return from examining a function in your ActionScript code (see Step In, above).

## Remove All Breakpoints

Windows: Ctrl+Shift+B

Mac: Shift-⌘-B

Breakpoints are used in debugging as a way to stop the animation and ActionScript program from running, which gives you the opportunity to examine the code, variables, and properties. This command removes all the breakpoints you previously placed in your ActionScript program.

## Begin Remote Debug Session

Remote debugging is the programmer's art of debugging an .swf file on a remote server. Use this command to begin remote debugging after you've done the necessary setup chores of choosing your ActionScript version, creating a remote debugging file (.swd), and uploading files to the server.

# ■ Window

This menu is Command Central for opening and closing the many windows you use when working in Flash. Checkmarks appear next to the names of currently open windows. Clicking next to the name opens or closes the window.

## Duplicate Window

Windows: Ctrl+Alt+K

Mac: Option-⌘-K

Creates a second program window. Use this command when you want more than one view of your animation or timeline. It's useful for side-by-side comparisons of two separate frames or other aspects of your Flash animation.

## Toolbars

Leads to a submenu with the following commands:

- **Main (Windows only)**

  Opens the Main toolbar, which includes buttons for frequently used commands including New, Open, "Go to Bridge," Save, Print, Cut, Copy, Paste, Undo, Redo, "Snap to Object," Smooth, Straighten, "Rotate and Skew," Scale, and Align. Like many toolbars, the Main toolbar can float or dock to the edge of the workspace.

- **Controller**

  Opens the Controller toolbar, which you use to play, pause, and navigate through the frames of your animation.

- **Edit Bar**

  Opens the Edit bar, which appears between the timeline and the stage in your program window.

## Timeline

Windows: Ctrl+Alt+T

Mac: Option-⌘-T

Displays the timeline in your program window, which you use to work with frames and layers in your animation.

## Motion Editor

Opens the Motion Editor panel, which you use to fine-tune motion tweens. The Motion Editor uses graphs to show how properties change over time. In particular, the Motion Editor gives you greater control over the easing applied to property changes.

## Tools

Windows: Ctrl+F2

Mac: ⌘-F2

Shows and hides the Tools palette, which holds tools for selection, drawing, shape creation, text, color application, and color picking.

## Properties

Windows: Ctrl+F3

Mac: ⌘-F3

Opens the Properties window, where you view—and edit—various aspects of objects in your animation.

## Library

Windows: Ctrl+L

Mac: ⌘-L

Opens the Library window, which stores objects used in your animation, like graphics, movie clips, buttons, and sound clips.

## Common Libraries

Opens the Common Library windows, which include Buttons, Classes, and Sounds.

## Motion Presets

Opens a panel with predesigned motion tweens like "Fly-in," "Fly-out," and Bounce. You can use Adobe-designed presets or store your own custom-designed presets using this panel.

## Project

Opens the Project window, where you can manage multiple files that are part of an application or large project.

## Actions

Windows: F9

Mac: Option-F9

Opens the Actions panel, where you define and edit ActionScript code used in your animation.

## Code Snippets

Opens a panel with dozens of chunks of code that you can use in your ActionScript programs. Snippets are organized in these groups: Actions, Timeline Navigation, Animation, "Load and Unload," "Audio and Video," Event Handlers, Mobile Touch Events, Mobile Gesture Events, Mobile Actions, "AIR for Mobile," and AIR.

## Behaviors

Windows: Shift+F3

Mac: Shift-F3

Opens the Behaviors panel, which automates the process of applying actions to objects in your animation. (Behaviors aren't available with ActionScript 3.0.)

## Compiler Errors

Windows: Alt+F2

Mac: Option-F2

Opens the Compiler Errors window, where Flash displays the problems that may happen during the compilation of your animation.

## Debug Panels

Opens the Debug panel, which you use to find errors in your ActionScript programs. The Debug panel displays the lines of your code, variables, values, and properties, while giving you the opportunity to execute code a line at a time. The Debug sub-panels are Debug Console, Variables, and ActionScript 2.0 Debugger.

## Movie Explorer

Windows: Alt+F3

Mac: Option-F3

Displays the Movie Explorer window, where you see a hierarchical representation of your Flash animation, breaking it down into scenes and objects.

## Output

Windows: F2

Mac: F2

Opens the Output window, which is used in combination with *trace()* statements to debug ActionScript code.

## Align

Windows: Ctrl+K

Mac: ⌘-K

Displays the Align window, which you use to align, distribute, and position objects on the stage. The Align commands are identical to those in the Modify→Align submenu, except that the window displays icons that visually indicate the alignment command.

## Color

Windows: Alt+Shift+F9

Mac: Shift-⌘-F9

Opens the Color window, from which you pick stroke, fill, and gradient colors. The Color window provides several tools to identify colors, including color pickers, swatches, and RBG color tools.

## Info

Windows: Ctrl+I

Mac: ⌘-I

Opens the Info panel, which provides details on the position of the mouse cursor and the colors at that location. The Info panel also provides height, width, and location information for selected objects on the stage.

## Swatches

Windows: Ctrl+F9

Mac: ⌘-F9

Opens the Swatches panel, where you can pick colors to apply them to objects in your animation. You use the Swatches panel to create and save custom colors for your animation.

## Transform

Windows: Ctrl+T

Mac: ⌘-T

Opens the Transform window, which you use to resize, rotate, and skew objects in your animation.

## Components

Windows: Ctrl+F7

Mac: ⌘-F7

Opens the Components window, where you choose components to add to your animation. Components are grouped in these categories: Flex, User Interface, and Video.

## Component Inspector

Windows: Shift+F7

Mac: Shift-F7

Displays the Component Inspector window, which you use to set parameters, bindings, and XML schema for components you add to your animation.

## Other Panels

Leads to a submenu with additional panels, including the following:

- **Accessibility**

    Windows: Alt+Shift+F11

    Mac: Shift-⌘-F11

    Opens the Accessibility window, which you use to provide accessibility information to screen readers and to set accessibility options for individual Flash objects.

- **History**

    Windows: Ctrl+F10

    Mac: ⌘-F10

    Displays the History panel, where you see a record of actions performed during the current Flash authoring session. Use the slider to the left of the list to backtrack and undo these actions. By selecting and saving multiple actions in the History panel, you can create *commands* (reusable actions, similar to macros) that you run from the Commands menu.

- **Scene**

    Windows: Shift+F2

    Mac: Shift-F2

    Opens the Scene window, which lists all the scenes in your animation. Reorganize the list of scenes to change the order in which scenes play in your animation.

- **Strings**

    Windows: Ctrl+F11

    Mac: ⌘-F11

    Opens the Strings panel, where you can create and update multilingual content for your animation. Using strings, you specify content for text fields that accommodate multiple languages. Flash can automatically determine which language to use based on the language used by the computer running Flash Player.

- **Web Services**

  Windows: Ctrl+Shift+F10

  Mac: Shift-⌘-F10

  This panel helps to connect your Flash application to web-based services, like those provided by the SOAP protocol or RESTful design architecture.

## Extensions

Leads to a submenu with additional Adobe services and community-based tools. Initially, there is only one item in the submenu::

- **Kuler**

  A community-based tool that lets Flash fans share, rate, and reuse color palettes. You can use this resource when you're looking for inspiration.

## Workspace

Leads to a submenu of commands that let you customize the Flash workspace and save your favorite workspace layouts for use with later projects. You can also use the Workspace menu on the main menu bar.

## Hide Panels

Windows: F4

Mac: F4

Hides all panels and toolbars, leaving only the main program window visible. This command works like a toggle.

# ■ Help

The Help menu provides access to Flash help files included with the product and links to the Adobe website. (Many of the Help and Support resources were still in the works at the time this book went to press.)

## Search Field (Mac Only)

The first help option on the Mac is a search field. Enter words to display and highlight the related menu command.

## Flash Help

Windows: F1

Mac: F1

Opens the Help window in Flash, where you can find and view the help information that's included with the Flash program. Use the panels on the left to select books and to type in search words and phrases. Help articles appear on the right side of the Help window.

### Flash Support Center

Opens your browser to the Flash Support pages, where you can find tech support.

### Get Latest Flash Player

Leads to Adobe's website, where you can find the latest version of Flash Player.

### Adobe Product Improvement Program

Opens a dialog box, where, if you wish, you can give Adobe permission to anonymously collect information about how you use its products. The company then uses this information to develop future products. If you choose to participate, you can always turn this feature off later through the same menu command.

### Flash Exchange

Opens Adobe's Extension manager and provides access to Flash Exchange, where you can download components and other extensions that add to Flash's features.

### Omniture

This command leads to a web page with information about Omniture SiteCatalyst, a product that provides tracking and analysis for Rich Internet Applications.

### Manage Extensions

Opens Adobe's Extension Manager, where you can add components and features to Flash.

### Manage AIR SDK

Use this tool to identify the location of the AIR SDK. AIR is the Adobe Intergrated Runtime that is used to develop standalone desktop and mobile apps. The SDK is the software development kit used to create AIR apps.

### Adobe Online Forums

Opens your browser to Adobe's forums, where you can interact with other designers and developers.

### Complete/Update Adobe ID Profile

To use some of the features provided with Flash CS6 Professional, you need an Adobe ID. This menu item provides a link to the online site where you can create or modify your Adobe ID.

### Product Registration

Many of Adobe's online services, such as CS Live, use your Adobe ID. Using this command, you can register your product and create or make changes to your ID profile.

## Deactivate

Opens a window where you can deactivate Flash. After deactivation, you can install Flash on another computer.

## Updates

Runs Adobe's product update tool. You have to have an activated product and Internet access to download updates from Adobe's website.

## About Adobe CS6 Professional (Mac: Flash→About Flash)

Opens the About Adobe CS6 Professional window, where you see the product name and version, as well as copyright information.

# Index